AF884372

Two Thousand Years of Economic Statistics

Volume 1: by Rank

2015

Two Thousand Years of Economic Statistics: Population, GDP at PPP, and GDP Per Capita

Years 1 to 2012

Volume 1: by Rank

2015

Alexander V. Avakov

Algora Publishing
New York

© 2010 by Algora Publishing.
All Rights Reserved
www.algora.com

No portion of this book (beyond what is permitted by Sections 107 or 108 of the United States Copyright Act of 1976) may be reproduced by any process, stored in a retrieval system, or transmitted in any form, or by any means, without the express written permission of the publisher.

Library of Congress Cataloging-in-Publication Data

Avakov, Aleksandr V. (Aleksandr Vladimirovich), 1954-
Two thousand years of economic statistics: world population, GDP, and PPP / Alexander V. Avakov.
p. cm.
Includes bibliographical references.
ISBN 978-1-62894-099-2 (soft cover: alk. paper) — ISBN 978-1-62894-100-5 (case laminate: alk. paper) — ISBN 978-1-62894-101-2 (eBook) 1. Economic history—Statistics. 2. Economic indicators. I. Title. II. Title: 2000 years of economic statistics.
HC21.A97 2010
339.3'1021—dc22

2009037757

Printed in the United States

Table of Contents

Introduction

Two Thousand Years of Economic Statistics presents historical data in two volumes, going far beyond the major powers and the BRICS countries. This is Volume 1, in which the data is arranged by rank, or size: (1) Population by rank, (2) GDP Per Capita by rank, (3) GDP by rank, (4) Growth Rates of Population by rank, (5) Growth Rates of GDP Per Capita by rank, and (6) Growth Rates of GDP by rank. [In Volume 2 — sold separately — the countries are listed alphabetically, presenting: (1) Population/Growth Rates of Population by country, (2) GDP Per Capita/Growth Rates of GDP Per Capita by country, and (3) GDP/Growth Rates of GDP by country.]

This work contains data generally not available elsewhere, presented in ways that help make it possible to draw useful comparisons. First, it provides statistical data for all countries of the world (236 countries, within their 2011 borders) since 1950 (by decade, with 2011 in addition), plus forecasts for 2020 and 2030. Second, it goes back to the year 1000 and provides data for 135 countries (with data for 1000, 1500, 1600, 1700, 1820, 1870, 1880, 1890, 1900, 1913, 1920, 1929, and 1938). Third, it goes back to the first year AD and provides data for 134 countries.

This handbook is based on the groundbreaking works of Angus Maddison, but it differs by giving data up to the most recent year available and calculating GDP (gross and per capita) in the prices of the most recent year. For recent years, I use the World Bank, CIA, and Encyclopedia Britannica as primary sources. But, despite my great debt to them, for the preponderance of the data I rely on original calculations. Among other computational techniques I use a new logarithmic interpolation which resolves cross-country statistical distortions when calculating in the prices of the most recent year. Another point that distinguishes this book is that for every line of data (for every country, each year) I note the technique used in obtaining my estimate (i.e., proxy, exponential interpolation, direct estimate with source citation, etc.).

This book has value with each new edition because every year, the data shown in the prices of the most recent year will be different; plus the logarithmic interpolation used requires recalculation based on the new data. This work is a complement to my annual *Quality of Life, Balance of Power, and Nuclear Weapons*. Where the current work gives the population and current price GDP data in a historical perspective, *Quality of Life* gives a current snapshot of a wide range of world statistics.

Alexander V. Avakov

SOURCES

The sources are shown in the form: XX(Source) or XX(Source A/SourceB), where XX is a year and (Source) (or Source A or Source B) is one of the following:

WB	The World Bank (1)
E	Encyclopedia Britannica
CIA	Central Intelligence Agency
WIKI	Wikipedia or other Internet source
EST	My estimate
REG	Regression is used
POP*GPC	Obtained by multiplication of Population by GDP Per Capita at Purchasing Power Parities
PROXY(X(Source))	Approximation based on data for country or group of countries X from source Source
PROXY(X(Source A/Source B))	Approximation based on data for country or group of countries X from sources Source A and Source B
INTERPOL(X(Source))	Exponential interpolation based on data for country or group of countries X from source Source
INTERPOL(X(Source A/ Source B))	Exponential interpolation based on data for country or group of countries X from sources Source A and Source B
YY(Source A) WEIGHT(Country X(Source B))	Data for year YY from Source A weighted to data for Country X from Source B
MIN	When estimated per capita GDP is less than minimum per capita GDP at purchasing power parities in 1990 international dollars (400 dollars) special algorithm described in the Appendix is used.
AVG(Region(Source))	Average for the region Region based on the source Source.

REGIONS

9 European cs	9 small European countries: Andorra, Channel Islands, Faeroe Islands, Gibraltar, Greenland, Isle of Man, Liechtenstein, Monaco, and San Marino, plus Svalbard
7 Caribbean cs	7 small Caribbean countries: Antigua & Barbuda, Bermuda, Guadeloupe, Guiana (Fr.), Martinique, former Netherlends Antilles (now Curacao and Sint Maarten), and Saint. Kitts & Nevis (also now Saint Martin)
8 Caribbean cs	8 small Caribbean countries: Anguilla, Aruba, Cayman Islands, Montserrat, Saint Pierre & Miquelon, Turks & Caicos Islands, Virgin Islands (U.S.), and British Virgin Islands
14 Pacific is	14 Pacific islands: American Samoa, French Polynesia, Guam, Kiribati, Marshall Islands, Micronesia, New Caledonia, Northern Mariana Islands, Palau, Solomon Islands, Tonga, Vanuatu, Wallis & Futuna, and (Western) Samoa
3 Afr. cs	3 small African countries: Mayotte, Saint Helena, and Western Sahara
E. Europe	Eastern Europe
Eur. Russia	European Russia
Eu. Rs./Sb.	European Russia & Siberia
Other W. offshots	Other Western offshots: Canada, Australia, and New Zealand

26 E. Asian cs	26 East Asian countries: Afghanistan, Cambodia, Laos, Mongolia, North Korea, Vietnam, Bhutan, Brunei, Fiji, Macao, Maldives, Papua New Guinea, American Samoa, French Polynesia, Guam, Kiribati, Marshall Islands, Micronesia, New Caledonia, Northern Mariana Islands, Palau, Solomon Islands, Tonga, Vanuatu, Wallis & Futuna, and (Western) Samoa
Other E. Asia	Other East Asia: East Asia other than Japan, China, and India
Pak./wh. India	Pakistan/whole India
Ban./wh. India	Bangladesh/whole India
Ind./wh. India	India/whole India
Other N. Africa	Other North Africa: Algeria, Tunisia, and Libya
Sahel & W. Africa	Sahel & Other West Africa
Sahel	Chad, Mauritania, Mali, and Niger
Other W. Africa	Other West Africa: Senegal, Gambia, Guinea-Bissau, Guinea, Sierra Leone, Liberia, Burkina Faso, Ivory Coast, Ghana, Togo, Benin, Nigeria, Cape Verde, and Western Sahara
Other E. Africa	Other East Africa: Burundi, Djibouti, Kenya, Rwanda, Tanzania, and Uganda
Rest of Africa	Africa other than North Africa, Sahel, and West Africa
Mal., Zam., Zim.	Malawi, Zambia, and Zimbabwe
S. Afr., Sw., Ls.	South Africa, Swaziland, and Lesotho
Ethiopia & Eritr.	Ethiopia & Eritrea
Namibia & Botsw.	Namibia & Botswana
Indian Ocean	Comoros, Mauritius, Mayotte, Reunion, and Seychelles
Gulf Coast	Bahrain, Kuwait, Qatar, and United Arab Emirates
Arabia	Bahrain, Kuwait, Oman, Qatar, Saudi Arabia, United Arab Emirates, and Yemen
W. Asia	West Asia
Other W. Asia	Other West Asia: West Asia other than Arabia, Iran, Iraq, and Turkey
Other L. Am.	Other Latin America: Latin America other than Mexico
8 L. American cs	8 Latin American countries: Argentina, Brazil, Chile, Colombia, Mexico, Peru, Uruguay, and Venezuela
15 L. American cs	15 Latin American countries: Bolivia, Costa Rica, Cuba, Dominican Republic, Ecuador, El Salvador, Guatemala, Haiti, Honduras, Jamaica, Nicaragua, Panama, Paraguay, Puerto Rico, and Trinidad and Tobago
Caribbean cs.	30 Caribbean countries: Cuba, Dominican Republic, Haiti, Jamaica, Puerto Rico, Trinidad and Tobago, Bahamas, Barbados, Belize, Dominica, Grenada, Guyana, former Netherlands Antilles (now Curacao and Sint Maarten), Saint Lucia, Saint Vincent, Suriname, Antigua & Barbuda, Bermuda, Guadeloupe, Guiana (Fr.), Martinique, Saint Kitts & Nevis, Anguilla, Aruba, Cayman Islands, Montserrat, Saint Pierre & Miquelon, Turks & Caicos Islands, Virgin Islands (U.S.), and British Virgin Islands (also now Saint Martin)
Other Sp. Am.	15 Other Spanish America (ex. Caribbean): Argentina, Chile, Colombia, Peru, Uruguay, Venezuela, Bolivia, Costa Rica, Ecuador, El Salvador, Guatemala, Honduras, Nicaragua, Panama, and Paraguay

ABBREVIATIONS

GPC	Gross Domestic Product at Purchasing Power Parities Per Capita
POP	Population
GDP	Gross Domestic Product at Purchasing Power Parities
GPCxxxx	Gross National Income Per Capita at Market Exchange Rates, Year xxxx
GPCxxxx	Gross Domestic Product Per Capita at Purchasing Power Parities, Year xxxx
GRPOP	Population Growth Rates
GRRL	GDP Real Growth Rates
GRPCRL	GDP Per Capita Real Growth Rates

1. Population by Rank

Table 1.1 Population, Thousands, Year 0001			
Rank	Country	POP	Source
1	India	62,924	PROXY(Undivided India(Maddison))
2	China	59,600	0001(Maddison)
3	Italy	8,000	0001(Maddison)
4	Bangladesh	7,177	PROXY(Undivided India(Maddison))
5	Turkey	6,866	PROXY(W. Asia(Maddison))
6	France	5,000	0001(Maddison)
7	Pakistan	4,899	PROXY(Undivided India(Maddison))
8	Iran	4,360	PROXY(W. Asia(Maddison))
9	Egypt	4,000	0001(Maddison)
10	Spain	3,750	0001(Maddison)
11	Indonesia	3,244	PROXY(Other E. Asia)
12.5	Germany	3,000	0001(Maddison)
12.5	Japan	3,000	0001(Maddison)
14	Yemen	2,445	PROXY(W. Asia(Maddison))
15	Mexico	2,200	0001(Maddison)
16.5	Algeria	2,000	0001(Maddison)
16.5	Greece	2,000	0001(Maddison)
18	Saudi Arabia	1,971	PROXY(W. Asia(Maddison))
19	Korea, South	1,658	PROXY(Other E. Asia(Maddison))
20	Sudan	1,654	PROXY(0001(Maddison))
21	Russia	1,409	PROXY(40(E)/Eu. Rs./Sb.(Maddison))
22	Syria	1,314	PROXY(W. Asia(Maddison))
23	Vietnam	1,163	PROXY(Other E. Asia(Maddison))
24	Iraq	1,090	PROXY(W. Asia(Maddison))
25	Morocco	1,000	0001(Maddison)
26.5	Romania	800	0001(Maddison)
26.5	Tunisia	800	0001(Maddison)

TABLE 1.1 POPULATION, THOUSANDS, YEAR 0001			
Rank	Country	POP	Source
28	Korea, North	767	PROXY(Other E. Asia(Maddison))
29	UK	747	PROXY(UK & Irealnd(Maddison))
30	Czechia	720	PROXY(Czechoslovakia(Maddison))
31	Nepal	689	PROXY(Other E. Asia(Maddison))
32	US	680	0001(Maddison)
33	Burma	622	PROXY(Other E. Asia(Maddison))
34	Thailand	606	PROXY(Other E. Asia(Maddison))
35	Afghanistan	582	PROXY(Other E. Asia(Maddison))
36	Serbia	540	PROXY(Yugoslavia(Maddison))
37	Ukraine	527	PROXY(40(E)/Eur. Russia(Maddison))
38	Peru	503	PROXY(Other L. Am.(Maddison))
39.5	Austria	500	0001(Maddison)
39.5	Bulgaria	500	0001(Maddison)
41	Uzbekistan	494	PROXY(40(E)/Turkestan(Maddison))
42	Ethiopia	468	PROXY(Ethiopia & Eritr.(Maddison))
43	Kazakhstan	464	PROXY(40(E)/Turkestan(Maddison))
44	Colombia	460	PROXY(Other L. Am.(Maddison))
45	Poland	450	0001(Maddison)
46	Bolivia	420	PROXY(Other L. Am.(Maddison))
47.5	Libya	400	0001(Maddison)
47.5	Portugal	400	0001(Maddison)
49	Cambodia	371	PROXY(Other E. Asia(Maddison))
50	Croatia	353	PROXY(Yugoslavia(Maddison))
51	South Sudan	346	PROXY(0001(Maddison))
52	Brazil	340	PROXY(Other L. Am.(Maddison))
53	Lebanon	326	PROXY(W. Asia(Maddison))
54	Sri Lanka	303	PROXY(Other E. Asia(Maddison))
56	Belgium	300	0001(Maddison)
56	Hungary	300	0001(Maddison)
56	Switzerland	300	0001(Maddison)
58	Oman	300	PROXY(W. Asia(Maddison))
59	Chile	291	PROXY(Other L. Am.(Maddison))
60	Slovakia	280	PROXY(Czechoslovakia(Maddison))
61	Venezuela	274	PROXY(Other L. Am.(Maddison))
62	Australia	248	PROXY(Other W. offshots(Maddison))
63	Bosnia	245	PROXY(Yugoslavia(Maddison))
64	Guatemala	227	PROXY(Other L. Am.(Maddison))
65	Jordan	213	PROXY(W. Asia(Maddison))
66	Argentina	204	PROXY(Other L. Am.(Maddison))
69	Albania	200	0001(Maddison)
69	Cyprus	200	0001(Maddison)
69	Netherlands	200	0001(Maddison)
69	Somalia	200	0001(Maddison)
69	Sweden	200	0001(Maddison)
72	Ghana	198	PROXY(Other W. Africa(Maddison))
73	Ecuador	191	PROXY(Other L. Am.(Maddison))
74	Israel	180	PROXY(W. Asia(Maddison))
75	Denmark	180	0001(Maddison)

TABLE 1.1 POPULATION, THOUSANDS, YEAR 0001

Rank	Country	POP	Source
76	Philippines	152	PROXY(Other E. Asia(Maddison))
77	Slovenia	135	PROXY(Yugoslavia(Maddison))
78	Guinea	135	PROXY(Other W. Africa(Maddison))
79	Ireland	116	PROXY(UK(Maddison))
80	Belarus	115	PROXY(40(E)/Eur. Russia(Maddison))
81	Kyrgyzstan	115	PROXY(40(E)/Turkestan(Maddison))
82	Tajikistan	115	PROXY(40(E)/Turkestan(Maddison))
83	Macedonia	113	PROXY(Yugoslavia(Maddison))
84	Mongolia	110	PROXY(Other E. Asia(Maddison))
85	Georgia	108	PROXY(40(E)/Caucasus(Maddison))
86	Sierra Leone	100	PROXY(Other W. Africa(Maddison))
87	Norway	100	0001(Maddison)
88	Turkmenistan	98	PROXY(40(E)/Turkestan(Maddison))
89	Azerbaijan	98	PROXY(40(E)/Caucasus(Maddison))
90	El Salvador	95	PROXY(Other L. Am.(Maddison))
91	South Africa	93	PROXY(S. Afr., Sw., Ls.(Maddison))
92	Laos	83	PROXY(Other E. Asia(Maddison))
93	Canada	80	0001(Maddison)
94	Kuwait	78	PROXY(W. Asia(Maddison))
95	Kosovo	77	PROXY(Yugoslavia(Maddison))
96	Nicaragua	71	PROXY(Other L. Am.(Maddison))
97	Taiwan	61	PROXY(Other E. Asia(Maddison))
98	Bahrain	59	PROXY(W. Asia(Maddison))
99	New Zealand	55	PROXY(Other W. offshots(Maddison))
100	Paraguay	55	PROXY(Other L. Am.(Maddison))
101	Honduras	52	PROXY(Other L. Am.(Maddison))
102	Malaysia	51	PROXY(Other E. Asia(Maddison))
103	Mozambique	50	0001(Maddison)
104	Haiti	42	PROXY(Other L. Am.(Maddison))
105	Namibia	40	PROXY(Namibia & Botsw. (Maddison))
106	Armenia	39	PROXY(40(E)/Caucasus(Maddison))
107	UAE	39	PROXY(W. Asia(Maddison))
108	Lithuania	37	PROXY(40(E)/Eur. Russia(Maddison))
109	Montenegro	37	PROXY(Yugoslavia(Maddison))
110	Panama	36	PROXY(Other L. Am.(Maddison))
111	Cuba	35	PROXY(Other L. Am.(Maddison))
112	Botswana	35	PROXY(Namibia & Botsw. (Maddison))
113	Eritrea	32	PROXY(Ethiopia & Eritr.(Maddison))
114	Moldova	31	PROXY(40(E)/Eur. Russia(Maddison))
115	Guinea-Biss	30	PROXY(Other W. Africa(Maddison))
116	Burundi	29	PROXY(Other E. Africa(Maddison))
117	Zimbabwe	26	PROXY(Mal., Zam., Zim.(Maddison))
118	Malawi	26	PROXY(Mal., Zam., Zim.(Maddison))
119	Costa Rica	24	PROXY(Other L. Am.(Maddison))
120	Latvia	24	PROXY(40(E)/Eur. Russia(Maddison))
121	Jamaica	23	PROXY(Other L. Am.(Maddison))
122	Zambia	23	PROXY(Mal., Zam., Zim.(Maddison))

TABLE 1.1 POPULATION, THOUSANDS, YEAR 0001			
Rank	Country	POP	Source
123	Uruguay	21	PROXY(Other L. Am.(Maddison))
124	Finland	20	0001(Maddison)
125	Puerto Rico	14	PROXY(Other L. Am.(Maddison))
126	Estonia	13	PROXY(40(E)/Eur. Russia(Maddison))
127	Qatar	13	PROXY(W. Asia(Maddison))
128	Dominican R	5	PROXY(Other L. Am.(Maddison))
129	Lesotho	5	PROXY(S. Afr., Sw., Ls.(Maddison))
130	Trinidad & T	3	PROXY(Other L. Am.(Maddison))
131	Hong Kong	3	PROXY(China(Maddison))
132	Swaziland	2	PROXY(S. Afr., Sw., Ls.(Maddison))
133	Madagascar	1	0001(EST)
134	Singapore	1	PROXY(Other E. Asia(Maddison))

TABLE 1.2 POPULATION, THOUSANDS, YEAR 1000

Rank	Country	POP	Source
1	India	62,924	PROXY(Undivided India(Maddison))
2	China	59,000	1000(Maddison)
3	Japan	7,500	1000(Maddison)
4	Bangladesh	7,177	PROXY(Undivided India(Maddison))
5	Turkey	7,079	PROXY(W. Asia(Maddison))
6	France	6,500	1000(Maddison)
7	Indonesia	6,005	PROXY(Other E. Asia)
8.5	Egypt	5,000	1000(Maddison)
8.5	Italy	5,000	1000(Maddison)
10	Pakistan	4,899	PROXY(Undivided India(Maddison))
11	Mexico	4,500	1000(Maddison)
12	Iran	4,494	PROXY(W. Asia(Maddison))
13	Spain	4,000	1000(Maddison)
14	Germany	3,500	1000(Maddison)
15	Korea, South	3,070	PROXY(Other E. Asia(Maddison))
16	Russia	2,750	PROXY(40(E)/Eu. Rs./ Sb.(Maddison))
17	Yemen	2,520	PROXY(W. Asia(Maddison))
18	Sudan	2,481	PROXY(1000(Maddison))
19	Vietnam	2,152	PROXY(Other E. Asia(Maddison))
20	Saudi Arabia	2,032	PROXY(W. Asia(Maddison))
21.5	Algeria	2,000	1000(Maddison)
21.5	Morocco	2,000	1000(Maddison)
23	UK	1,867	PROXY(UK & Ireland(Maddison))
24	Korea, North	1,420	PROXY(Other E. Asia(Maddison))
25	Syria	1,355	PROXY(W. Asia(Maddison))
26	US	1,300	1000(Maddison)
27	Nepal	1,275	PROXY(Other E. Asia(Maddison))
28	Poland	1,200	1000(Maddison)
29	Burma	1,152	PROXY(Other E. Asia(Maddison))
30	Iraq	1,124	PROXY(W. Asia(Maddison))
31	Thailand	1,122	PROXY(Other E. Asia(Maddison))
32	Greece	1,100	1000(Maddison)
33	Afghanistan	1,078	PROXY(Other E. Asia(Maddison))
34	Ukraine	1,053	PROXY(40(E)/Eur. Russia(Maddison))
35	Peru	1,020	PROXY(Other L. Am.(Maddison))
36	Tunisia	1,000	1000(Maddison)
37	Ethiopia	935	PROXY(Ethiopia & Eritr. (Maddison))
38	Colombia	934	PROXY(Other L. Am.(Maddison))
39	Czechia	900	PROXY(Czechoslovakia(Maddison))
40	Bolivia	852	PROXY(Other L. Am.(Maddison))
41	Uzbekistan	823	PROXY(40(E)/Turkestan(Maddison))
42.5	Bulgaria	800	1000(Maddison)
42.5	Romania	800	1000(Maddison)
44	Kazakhstan	773	PROXY(40(E)/Turkestan(Maddison))
45	Austria	700	1000(Maddison)
46	Brazil	690	PROXY(Other L. Am.(Maddison))

TABLE 1.2 POPULATION, THOUSANDS, YEAR 1000			
Rank	Country	POP	Source
47	Cambodia	687	PROXY(Other E. Asia(Maddison))
48	Serbia	630	PROXY(Yugoslavia(Maddison))
49	Portugal	600	1000(Maddison)
50	Chile	591	PROXY(Other L. Am.(Maddison))
51	Sri Lanka	561	PROXY(Other E. Asia(Maddison))
52	Venezuela	556	PROXY(Other L. Am.(Maddison))
53	South Sudan	519	PROXY(1000(Maddison))
54.5	Hungary	500	1000(Maddison)
54.5	Libya	500	1000(Maddison)
56	Ghana	463	PROXY(Other W. Africa(Maddison))
57	Guatemala	461	PROXY(Other L. Am.(Maddison))
58	Argentina	414	PROXY(Other L. Am.(Maddison))
59	Croatia	412	PROXY(Yugoslavia(Maddison))
61	Belgium	400	1000(Maddison)
61	Somalia	400	1000(Maddison)
61	Sweden	400	1000(Maddison)
63	Ecuador	387	PROXY(Other L. Am.(Maddison))
64	Denmark	360	1000(Maddison)
65	Slovakia	349	PROXY(Czechoslovakia(Maddison))
66	Lebanon	336	PROXY(W. Asia(Maddison))
67	Australia	321	PROXY(Other W. offshots(Maddison))
68	Guinea	315	PROXY(Other W. Africa(Maddison))
69	Oman	309	PROXY(W. Asia(Maddison))
71	Mozambique	300	1000(Maddison)
71	Netherlands	300	1000(Maddison)
71	Switzerland	300	1000(Maddison)
73	Burundi	293	PROXY(Other E. Africa(Maddison))
74	Ireland	289	PROXY(UK(Maddison))
75	Bosnia	286	PROXY(Yugoslavia(Maddison))
76	Philippines	281	PROXY(Other E. Asia(Maddison))
77	South Africa	279	PROXY(S. Afr., Sw., Ls.(Maddison))
78	Sierra Leone	234	PROXY(Other W. Africa(Maddison))
79	Belarus	230	PROXY(40(E)/Eur. Russia(Maddison))
80	Jordan	220	PROXY(W. Asia(Maddison))
81	Mongolia	203	PROXY(Other E. Asia(Maddison))
83	Albania	200	1000(Maddison)
83	Madagascar	200	1000(Maddison)
83	Norway	200	1000(Maddison)
85	El Salvador	192	PROXY(Other L. Am.(Maddison))
86	Kyrgyzstan	192	PROXY(40(E)/Turkestan(Maddison))
87	Tajikistan	192	PROXY(40(E)/Turkestan(Maddison))
88	Israel	186	PROXY(W. Asia(Maddison))
89	Georgia	180	PROXY(40(E)/Caucasus(Maddison))
90	Zimbabwe	173	PROXY(Mal., Zam., Zim.(Maddison))
91	Malawi	171	PROXY(Mal., Zam., Zim.(Maddison))
92	Turkmenistan	164	PROXY(40(E)/Turkestan(Maddison))
93	Azerbaijan	163	PROXY(40(E)/Caucasus(Maddison))

Table 1.2 Population, Thousands, Year 1000			
Rank	Country	POP	Source
94	Canada	160	1000(Maddison)
95	Slovenia	158	PROXY(Yugoslavia(Maddison))
96	Zambia	155	PROXY(Mal., Zam., Zim.(Maddison))
97	Laos	154	PROXY(Other E. Asia(Maddison))
98	Cyprus	150	1000(Maddison)
99	Nicaragua	144	PROXY(Other L. Am.(Maddison))
100	Macedonia	132	PROXY(Yugoslavia(Maddison))
101	Taiwan	112	PROXY(Other E. Asia(Maddison))
102	Paraguay	111	PROXY(Other L. Am.(Maddison))
103	Honduras	105	PROXY(Other L. Am.(Maddison))
104	Malaysia	94	PROXY(Other E. Asia(Maddison))
105	Haiti	85	PROXY(Other L. Am.(Maddison))
106	Kosovo	82	PROXY(Yugoslavia(Maddison))
107	Kuwait	80	PROXY(W. Asia(Maddison))
108	Lithuania	75	PROXY(40(E)/Eur. Russia(Maddison))
109	Panama	73	PROXY(Other L. Am.(Maddison))
110	Cuba	71	PROXY(Other L. Am.(Maddison))
111	New Zealand	71	PROXY(Other W. offshots(Maddison))
112	Guinea-Biss	69	PROXY(Other W. Africa(Maddison))
113	Armenia	66	PROXY(40(E)/Caucasus(Maddison))
114	Eritrea	65	PROXY(Ethiopia & Eritr. (Maddison))
115	Moldova	63	PROXY(40(E)/Eur. Russia(Maddison))
116	Bahrain	61	PROXY(W. Asia(Maddison))
117	Namibia	54	PROXY(Namibia & Botsw. (Maddison))
118	Costa Rica	49	PROXY(Other L. Am.(Maddison))
119	Latvia	48	PROXY(40(E)/Eur. Russia(Maddison))
120	Jamaica	47	PROXY(Other L. Am.(Maddison))
121	Botswana	46	PROXY(Namibia & Botsw. (Maddison))
122	Montenegro	43	PROXY(Yugoslavia(Maddison))
123	Uruguay	43	PROXY(Other L. Am.(Maddison))
124	Finland	40	1000(Maddison)
125	UAE	40	PROXY(W. Asia(Maddison))
126	Puerto Rico	29	PROXY(Other L. Am.(Maddison))
127	Estonia	27	PROXY(40(E)/Eur. Russia(Maddison))
128	Iceland	26	PROXY(Denmark)
129	Lesotho	15	PROXY(S. Afr., Sw., Ls.(Maddison))
130	Qatar	14	PROXY(W. Asia(Maddison))
131	Dominican R	10	PROXY(Other L. Am.(Maddison))
132	Trinidad & T	7	PROXY(Other L. Am.(Maddison))
133	Swaziland	6	PROXY(S. Afr., Sw., Ls.(Maddison))
134	Hong Kong	3	PROXY(China(Maddison))
135	Singapore	2	PROXY(Other E. Asia(Maddison))

Table 1.3 Population, Thousands, Year 1500			
Rank	Country	POP	Source
1	China	103,000	1500(Maddison)
2	India	92,289	PROXY(Undivided India(Maddison))
3	Japan	15,400	1500(Maddison)
4	France	15,000	1500(Maddison)
5	Germany	12,000	1500(Maddison)
6	Indonesia	10,700	1500(Maddison)
7	Bangladesh	10,526	PROXY(Undivided India(Maddison))
8	Italy	10,500	1500(Maddison)
9	Russia	8,183	PROXY(40(E)/Eu. Rs./Sb.(Maddison))
10	Mexico	7,500	1500(Maddison)
11	Pakistan	7,185	PROXY(Undivided India(Maddison))
12	Spain	6,800	1500(Maddison)
13	Turkey	6,300	1500(Maddison)
14	Korea, South	5,470	1500(Maddison)
16	Egypt	4,000	1500(Maddison)
16	Iran	4,000	1500(Maddison)
16	Poland	4,000	1500(Maddison)
18	Vietnam	3,835	PROXY(Other E. Asia(Maddison))
19	UK	3,681	PROXY(UK & Ireland(Maddison))
20	Sudan	3,308	PROXY(1500(Maddison))
21	Ukraine	3,160	PROXY(40(E)/Eur. Russia(Maddison))
22	Korea, North	2,530	1500(Maddison)
23	Nepal	2,272	PROXY(Other E. Asia(Maddison))
24	Yemen	2,243	PROXY(Arabia(Maddison))
25	Czechia	2,161	PROXY(Czechoslovakia(Maddison))
26	Burma	2,052	PROXY(Other E. Asia(Maddison))
28.5	Austria	2,000	1500(Maddison)
28.5	Romania	2,000	1500(Maddison)
28.5	Thailand	2,000	1500(Maddison)
28.5	US	2,000	1500(Maddison)
31	Afghanistan	1,920	PROXY(Other E. Asia(Maddison))
32	Ethiopia	1,870	PROXY(Ethiopia & Eritr.(Maddison))
33	Saudi Arabia	1,809	PROXY(Arabia(Maddison))
34.5	Algeria	1,500	1500(Maddison)
34.5	Morocco	1,500	1500(Maddison)
36	Peru	1,479	PROXY(Other Sp. Am.(Maddison))
37	Belgium	1,400	1500(Maddison)
38	Colombia	1,354	PROXY(Other Sp. Am.(Maddison))
39	Hungary	1,250	1500(Maddison)
40	Bolivia	1,235	PROXY(Other Sp. Am.(Maddison))
41	Cambodia	1,224	PROXY(Other E. Asia(Maddison))
42	Syria	1,206	PROXY(Other W. Asia(Maddison))
43	Uzbekistan	1,153	PROXY(40(E)/Turkestan(Maddison))
44	Kazakhstan	1,082	PROXY(40(E)/Turkestan(Maddison))
47.5	Brazil	1,000	1500(Maddison)
47.5	Greece	1,000	1500(Maddison)
47.5	Iraq	1,000	1500(Maddison)
47.5	Mozambique	1,000	1500(Maddison)

Table 1.3 Population, Thousands, Year 1500

Rank	Country	POP	Source
47.5	Portugal	1,000	1500(Maddison)
47.5	Sri Lanka	1,000	1500(Maddison)
51	Netherlands	950	1500(Maddison)
52	Chile	857	PROXY(Other Sp. Am.(Maddison))
53	Slovakia	839	PROXY(Czechoslovakia(Maddison))
54	Serbia	810	PROXY(Yugoslavia(Maddison))
55	Venezuela	806	PROXY(Other Sp. Am.(Maddison))
57	Bulgaria	800	1500(Maddison)
57	Somalia	800	1500(Maddison)
57	Tunisia	800	1500(Maddison)
59	Ghana	727	PROXY(Other W. Africa(Maddison))
60	Madagascar	700	1500(Maddison)
61	South Sudan	692	PROXY(1500(Maddison))
62	Belarus	691	PROXY(40(E)/Eur. Russia(Maddison))
63	Guatemala	668	PROXY(Other Sp. Am.(Maddison))
64	Switzerland	650	1500(Maddison)
65	Denmark	600	1500(Maddison)
66	Argentina	600	PROXY(Other Sp. Am.(Maddison))
67	Burundi	587	PROXY(Other E. Africa(Maddison))
68	Ireland	569	PROXY(whole Ireland(Maddison))
69	Ecuador	561	PROXY(Other Sp. Am.(Maddison))
70	South Africa	559	PROXY(S. Afr., Sw., Ls.(Maddison))
71	Sweden	550	1500(Maddison)
72	Croatia	530	PROXY(Yugoslavia(Maddison))
73.5	Libya	500	1500(Maddison)
73.5	Philippines	500	1500(Maddison)
75	Guinea	495	PROXY(Other W. Africa(Maddison))
76	Australia	450	1500(Maddison)
77	Georgia	450	PROXY(40(E)/Caucasus(Maddison))
78	Azerbaijan	408	PROXY(40(E)/Caucasus(Maddison))
79	Sierra Leone	367	PROXY(Other W. Africa(Maddison))
80	Bosnia	367	PROXY(Yugoslavia(Maddison))
81	Mongolia	362	PROXY(Other E. Asia(Maddison))
82	Zimbabwe	347	PROXY(Mal., Zam., Zim.(Maddison))
83	Malawi	343	PROXY(Mal., Zam., Zim.(Maddison))
84	Zambia	310	PROXY(Mal., Zam., Zim.(Maddison))
85.5	Finland	300	1500(Maddison)
85.5	Norway	300	1500(Maddison)
87	Lebanon	299	PROXY(Other W. Asia(Maddison))
88	El Salvador	278	PROXY(Other Sp. Am.(Maddison))
89	Laos	275	PROXY(Other E. Asia(Maddison))
90	Oman	275	PROXY(Arabia(Maddison))
91	Kyrgyzstan	269	PROXY(40(E)/Turkestan(Maddison))
92	Tajikistan	268	PROXY(40(E)/Turkestan(Maddison))
93	Canada	250	1500(Maddison)
94	Turkmenistan	229	PROXY(40(E)/Turkestan(Maddison))
95	Lithuania	224	PROXY(40(E)/Eur. Russia(Maddison))
96	Nicaragua	209	PROXY(Other Sp. Am.(Maddison))

TABLE 1.3 POPULATION, THOUSANDS, YEAR 1500

Rank	Country	POP	Source
97	Slovenia	203	PROXY(Yugoslavia(Maddison))
98.5	Albania	200	1500(Maddison)
98.5	Taiwan	200	1500(Maddison)
100	Jordan	196	PROXY(Other W. Asia(Maddison))
101	Moldova	189	PROXY(40(E)/Eur. Russia(Maddison))
102	Macedonia	170	PROXY(Yugoslavia(Maddison))
103	Malaysia	168	PROXY(Other E. Asia(Maddison))
104	Israel	166	PROXY(Other W. Asia(Maddison))
105	Armenia	164	PROXY(40(E)/Caucasus(Maddison))
106	Paraguay	161	PROXY(Other Sp. Am.(Maddison))
107	Honduras	152	PROXY(Other Sp. Am.(Maddison))
108	Latvia	144	PROXY(40(E)/Eur. Russia(Maddison))
109	Eritrea	130	PROXY(Ethiopia & Eritr.(Maddison))
110	Haiti	124	PROXY(Caribbean cs(Maddison))
111	Guinea-Biss	108	PROXY(Other W. Africa(Maddison))
112	Namibia	108	PROXY(Namibia & Botsw.(Maddison))
113	Panama	106	PROXY(Other Sp. Am.(Maddison))
114	Kosovo	105	PROXY(Yugoslavia(Maddison))
115	Cuba	103	PROXY(Caribbean cs(Maddison))
116	New Zealand	100	1500(Maddison)
117	Botswana	92	PROXY(Namibia & Botsw.(Maddison))
118	Estonia	81	PROXY(40(E)/Eur. Russia(Maddison))
119	Kuwait	71	PROXY(Arabia(Maddison))
120	Costa Rica	71	PROXY(Other Sp. Am.(Maddison))
121	Jamaica	69	PROXY(Caribbean cs(Maddison))
122	Cyprus	65	PROXY(Greece(Maddison))
123	Uruguay	62	PROXY(Other Sp. Am.(Maddison))
124	Montenegro	55	PROXY(Yugoslavia(Maddison))
125	Bahrain	54	PROXY(Arabia(Maddison))
126	Iceland	43	PROXY(Denmark)
127	Puerto Rico	42	PROXY(Caribbean cs(Maddison))
128	UAE	35	PROXY(Arabia(Maddison))
129	Lesotho	30	PROXY(S. Afr., Sw., Ls.(Maddison))
130	Dominican R	15	PROXY(Caribbean cs(Maddison))
131	Qatar	12	PROXY(Arabia(Maddison))
132	Swaziland	11	PROXY(S. Afr., Sw., Ls.(Maddison))
133	Trinidad & T	10	PROXY(Caribbean cs(Maddison))
134	Hong Kong	5	PROXY(China(Maddison))
135	Singapore	3	PROXY(Other E. Asia(Maddison))

Table 1.4 Population, Thousands, Year 1600			
Rank	Country	POP	Source
1	China	160,000	1600(Maddison)
2	India	113,264	PROXY(Undivided India(Maddison))
3.5	France	18,500	1600(Maddison)
3.5	Japan	18,500	1600(Maddison)
5	Germany	16,000	1600(Maddison)
6	Italy	13,100	1600(Maddison)
7	Bangladesh	12,919	PROXY(Undivided India(Maddison))
8	Indonesia	11,839	INTERPOL(Maddison)
9	Russia	10,195	PROXY(40(E)/Eu. Rs./ Sb.(Maddison))
10	Pakistan	8,818	PROXY(Undivided India(Maddison))
11	Spain	8,240	1600(Maddison)
12	Turkey	7,275	INTERPOL(Maddison)
13	Korea, South	6,755	INTERPOL(Maddison)
14	UK	5,761	PROXY(UK & Ireland(Maddison))
15.5	Egypt	5,000	1600(Maddison)
15.5	Poland	5,000	1600(Maddison)
17	Iran	4,472	INTERPOL(Maddison)
18	Vietnam	4,447	PROXY(Other E. Asia(Maddison))
19	Ukraine	3,950	PROXY(40(E)/Eur. Russia(Maddison))
20	Sudan	3,474	PROXY(1600(Maddison))
21	Czechia	3,242	PROXY(Czechoslovakia(Maddison))
22	Korea, North	3,124	INTERPOL(Maddison)
23	Nepal	2,635	PROXY(Other E. Asia(Maddison))
24.5	Austria	2,500	1600(Maddison)
24.5	Mexico	2,500	1600(Maddison)
26	Burma	2,380	PROXY(Other E. Asia(Maddison))
27.5	Algeria	2,250	1600(Maddison)
27.5	Morocco	2,250	1600(Maddison)
29	Yemen	2,243	INTERPOL(Maddison)
30	Thailand	2,236	INTERPOL(Maddison)
31	Afghanistan	2,227	PROXY(Other E. Asia(Maddison))
32	Ethiopia	2,104	PROXY(Ethiopia & Eritr.(Maddison))
33	Romania	2,000	1600(Maddison)
34	Saudi Arabia	1,809	INTERPOL(Maddison)
35	Belgium	1,600	1600(Maddison)
37	Greece	1,500	1600(Maddison)
37	Netherlands	1,500	1600(Maddison)
37	US	1,500	1600(Maddison)
39	Cambodia	1,419	PROXY(Other E. Asia(Maddison))
40	Uzbekistan	1,318	PROXY(40(E)/Turkestan(Maddison))
41	Slovakia	1,258	PROXY(Czechoslovakia(Maddison))
43	Bulgaria	1,250	1600(Maddison)
43	Hungary	1,250	1600(Maddison)
43	Mozambique	1,250	1600(Maddison)
45	Kazakhstan	1,236	PROXY(40(E)/Turkestan(Maddison))
46	Syria	1,175	INTERPOL(Maddison)

Rank	Country	POP	Source
47	Portugal	1,100	1600(Maddison)
48	Sri Lanka	1,095	INTERPOL(Maddison)
50	Iraq	1,000	INTERPOL(Maddison)
50	Switzerland	1,000	1600(Maddison)
50	Tunisia	1,000	1600(Maddison)
52	Serbia	990	PROXY(Yugoslavia(Maddison))
53	Ghana	926	PROXY(Other W. Africa(Maddison))
54	Peru	887	PROXY(Other Sp. Am.(Maddison))
55	Belarus	864	PROXY(40(E)/Eur. Russia(Maddison))
56	Colombia	812	PROXY(Other Sp. Am.(Maddison))
58	Brazil	800	1600(Maddison)
58	Madagascar	800	1600(Maddison)
58	Somalia	800	1600(Maddison)
60	Philippines	791	INTERPOL(Maddison)
61	Sweden	760	1600(Maddison)
62	Bolivia	741	PROXY(Other Sp. Am.(Maddison))
63	South Sudan	726	PROXY(1600(Maddison))
64	Ireland	712	PROXY(whole Ireland(Maddison))
65	Burundi	685	PROXY(Other E. Africa(Maddison))
66	South Africa	652	PROXY(S. Afr., Sw., Ls.(Maddison))
67	Denmark	650	1600(Maddison)
68	Croatia	647	PROXY(Yugoslavia(Maddison))
69	Guinea	630	PROXY(Other W. Africa(Maddison))
70	Georgia	540	PROXY(40(E)/Caucasus(Maddison))
71	Chile	519	PROXY(Other Sp. Am.(Maddison))
72	Libya	500	1600(Maddison)
73	Azerbaijan	498	PROXY(40(E)/Caucasus(Maddison))
74	Venezuela	484	PROXY(Other Sp. Am.(Maddison))
75	Sierra Leone	468	PROXY(Other W. Africa(Maddison))
76	Australia	450	1600(Maddison)
77	Bosnia	449	PROXY(Yugoslavia(Maddison))
78	Taiwan	447	INTERPOL(Maddison)
79	Mongolia	420	PROXY(Other E. Asia(Maddison))
80	Guatemala	401	PROXY(Other Sp. Am.(Maddison))
81.5	Finland	400	1600(Maddison)
81.5	Norway	400	1600(Maddison)
83	Zimbabwe	382	PROXY(Mal., Zam., Zim.(Maddison))
84	Malawi	377	PROXY(Mal., Zam., Zim.(Maddison))
85	Argentina	360	PROXY(Other Sp. Am.(Maddison))
86	Zambia	342	PROXY(Mal., Zam., Zim.(Maddison))
87	Ecuador	337	PROXY(Other Sp. Am.(Maddison))
88	Laos	319	PROXY(Other E. Asia(Maddison))
89	Kyrgyzstan	307	PROXY(40(E)/Turkestan(Maddison))
90	Tajikistan	307	PROXY(40(E)/Turkestan(Maddison))
91	Lebanon	292	INTERPOL(Maddison)
92	Lithuania	279	PROXY(40(E)/Eur. Russia(Maddison))
93	Oman	275	INTERPOL(Maddison)

Table 1.4 Population, Thousands, Year 1600			
Rank	Country	POP	Source
94	Turkmenistan	262	PROXY(40(E)/Turkestan(Maddison))
95	Canada	250	1600(Maddison)
96	Slovenia	248	PROXY(Yugoslavia(Maddison))
97	Moldova	236	PROXY(40(E)/Eur. Russia(Maddison))
98	Macedonia	208	PROXY(Yugoslavia(Maddison))
99	Albania	200	1600(Maddison)
100	Armenia	197	PROXY(40(E)/Caucasus(Maddison))
101	Malaysia	195	PROXY(Other E. Asia(Maddison))
102	Jordan	191	INTERPOL(Maddison)
103	Latvia	180	PROXY(40(E)/Eur. Russia(Maddison))
104	El Salvador	167	PROXY(Other Sp. Am.(Maddison))
105	Israel	161	INTERPOL(Maddison)
106	Eritrea	146	PROXY(Ethiopia & Eritr.(Maddison))
107	Guinea-Biss	138	PROXY(Other W. Africa(Maddison))
108	Kosovo	129	PROXY(Yugoslavia(Maddison))
109	Nicaragua	125	PROXY(Other Sp. Am.(Maddison))
110	Namibia	108	PROXY(Namibia & Botsw. (Maddison))
111	Estonia	101	PROXY(40(E)/Eur. Russia(Maddison))
112	New Zealand	100	1600(Maddison)
113	Cyprus	98	PROXY(Greece(Maddison))
114	Paraguay	96	PROXY(Other Sp. Am.(Maddison))
115	Botswana	92	PROXY(Namibia & Botsw. (Maddison))
116	Honduras	91	PROXY(Other Sp. Am.(Maddison))
117	Kuwait	71	INTERPOL(Maddison)
118	Montenegro	67	PROXY(Yugoslavia(Maddison))
119	Panama	64	PROXY(Other Sp. Am.(Maddison))
120	Bahrain	54	INTERPOL(Maddison)
121	Haiti	49	PROXY(Caribbean cs(Maddison))
122	Iceland	47	PROXY(Denmark)
123	Costa Rica	42	PROXY(Other Sp. Am.(Maddison))
124	Cuba	41	PROXY(Caribbean cs(Maddison))
125	Uruguay	37	PROXY(Other Sp. Am.(Maddison))
126	UAE	35	INTERPOL(Maddison)
127	Lesotho	35	PROXY(S. Afr., Sw., Ls.(Maddison))
128	Jamaica	27	PROXY(Caribbean cs(Maddison))
129	Puerto Rico	17	PROXY(Caribbean cs(Maddison))
130	Swaziland	13	PROXY(S. Afr., Sw., Ls.(Maddison))
131	Qatar	12	INTERPOL(Maddison)
132	Hong Kong	8	PROXY(China(Maddison))
133	Dominican R	6	PROXY(Caribbean cs(Maddison))
134	Trinidad & T	4	PROXY(Caribbean cs(Maddison))
135	Singapore	3	PROXY(Other E. Asia(Maddison))

Table 1.5 Population, Thousands, Year 1700

Rank	Country	POP	Source
1	India	138,433	PROXY(Undivided India(Maddison))
2	China	138,000	1700(Maddison)
3	Japan	27,000	1700(Maddison)
4	France	21,471	1700(Maddison)
5	Bangladesh	15,789	PROXY(Undivided India(Maddison))
6	Germany	15,000	1700(Maddison)
7	Russia	13,616	PROXY(40(E)/Eu. Rs./ Sb.(Maddison))
8	Italy	13,300	1700(Maddison)
9	Indonesia	13,100	1700(Maddison)
10	Pakistan	10,777	PROXY(Undivided India(Maddison))
11	Spain	8,770	1700(Maddison)
12	Turkey	8,400	1700(Maddison)
13	Korea, South	8,342	1700(Maddison)
14	UK	7,997	PROXY(UK & Ireland(Maddison))
15	Poland	6,000	1700(Maddison)
16	Ukraine	5,267	PROXY(40(E)/Eur. Russia(Maddison))
17	Vietnam	5,171	PROXY(Other E. Asia(Maddison))
18	Iran	5,000	1700(Maddison)
19.5	Egypt	4,500	1700(Maddison)
19.5	Mexico	4,500	1700(Maddison)
21	Korea, North	3,858	1700(Maddison)
22	Sudan	3,639	PROXY(1700(Maddison))
23	Czechia	3,242	PROXY(Czechoslovakia(Maddison))
24	Nepal	3,064	PROXY(Other E. Asia(Maddison))
25	Burma	2,768	PROXY(Other E. Asia(Maddison))
26	Afghanistan	2,589	PROXY(Other E. Asia(Maddison))
28	Austria	2,500	1700(Maddison)
28	Romania	2,500	1700(Maddison)
28	Thailand	2,500	1700(Maddison)
30	Ethiopia	2,338	PROXY(Ethiopia & Eritr.(Maddison))
31	Yemen	2,243	PROXY(Arabia(Maddison))
32.5	Belgium	2,000	1700(Maddison)
32.5	Portugal	2,000	1700(Maddison)
34	Netherlands	1,900	1700(Maddison)
35	Saudi Arabia	1,809	PROXY(Arabia(Maddison))
36.5	Algeria	1,750	1700(Maddison)
36.5	Morocco	1,750	1700(Maddison)
38	Cambodia	1,650	PROXY(Other E. Asia(Maddison))
40	Greece	1,500	1700(Maddison)
40	Hungary	1,500	1700(Maddison)
40	Mozambique	1,500	1700(Maddison)
42	Uzbekistan	1,482	PROXY(40(E)/Turkestan(Maddison))
43	Kazakhstan	1,391	PROXY(40(E)/Turkestan(Maddison))
44	Ireland	1,370	PROXY(whole Ireland(Maddison))
45	Sweden	1,260	1700(Maddison)
46	Slovakia	1,258	PROXY(Czechoslovakia(Maddison))

Table 1.5 Population, Thousands, Year 1700

Rank	Country	POP	Source
48	Brazil	1,250	1700(Maddison)
48	Bulgaria	1,250	1700(Maddison)
48	Philippines	1,250	1700(Maddison)
50.5	Sri Lanka	1,200	1700(Maddison)
50.5	Switzerland	1,200	1700(Maddison)
52	Ghana	1,190	PROXY(Other W. Africa(Maddison))
53	Belarus	1,152	PROXY(40(E)/Eur. Russia(Maddison))
54	Syria	1,145	PROXY(Other W. Asia(Maddison))
55	Peru	1,009	PROXY(Other Sp. Am.(Maddison))
57.5	Iraq	1,000	1700(Maddison)
57.5	Madagascar	1,000	1700(Maddison)
57.5	Taiwan	1,000	1700(Maddison)
57.5	US	1,000	1700(Maddison)
60	Serbia	990	PROXY(Yugoslavia(Maddison))
61	Somalia	950	1700(Maddison)
62	South Africa	931	PROXY(S. Afr., Sw., Ls.(Maddison))
63	Colombia	924	PROXY(Other Sp. Am.(Maddison))
64	Bolivia	843	PROXY(Other Sp. Am.(Maddison))
65	Guinea	810	PROXY(Other W. Africa(Maddison))
66	Tunisia	800	1700(Maddison)
67	Burundi	782	PROXY(Other E. Africa(Maddison))
68	South Sudan	761	PROXY(1700(Maddison))
69	Denmark	700	1700(Maddison)
70	Croatia	647	PROXY(Yugoslavia(Maddison))
71	Georgia	630	PROXY(40(E)/Caucasus(Maddison))
72	Sierra Leone	601	PROXY(Other W. Africa(Maddison))
73	Chile	591	PROXY(Other Sp. Am.(Maddison))
74	Azerbaijan	571	PROXY(40(E)/Caucasus(Maddison))
75	Venezuela	550	PROXY(Other Sp. Am.(Maddison))
76.5	Libya	500	1700(Maddison)
76.5	Norway	500	1700(Maddison)
78	Mongolia	489	PROXY(Other E. Asia(Maddison))
79	Guatemala	456	PROXY(Other Sp. Am.(Maddison))
80	Australia	450	1700(Maddison)
81	Bosnia	449	PROXY(YUgoslavia(Maddison))
82	Zimbabwe	416	PROXY(Mal., Zam., Zim.(Maddison))
83	Malawi	411	PROXY(Mal., Zam., Zim.(Maddison))
84	Argentina	409	PROXY(Other Sp. Am.(Maddison))
85	Finland	400	1700(Maddison)
86	Ecuador	383	PROXY(Other Sp. Am.(Maddison))
87	Lithuania	373	PROXY(40(E)/Eur. Russia(Maddison))
88	Zambia	373	PROXY(Mal., Zam., Zim.(Maddison))
89	Laos	371	PROXY(Other E. Asia(Maddison))
90	Kyrgyzstan	346	PROXY(40(E)/Turkestan(Maddison))
91	Tajikistan	345	PROXY(40(E)/Turkestan(Maddison))
92	Moldova	314	PROXY(40(E)/Eur. Russia(Maddison))

Table 1.5 Population, Thousands, Year 1700

Rank	Country	POP	Source
93	Albania	300	1700(Maddison)
94	Turkmenistan	295	PROXY(40(E)/Turkestan(Maddison))
95	Lebanon	284	PROXY(Other W. Asia(Maddison))
96	Oman	275	PROXY(Arabia(Maddison))
97	Slovenia	248	PROXY(Yugoslavia(Maddison))
98	Latvia	240	PROXY(40(E)/Eur. Russia(Maddison))
99	Armenia	230	PROXY(40(E)/Caucasus(Maddison))
100	Malaysia	227	PROXY(Other E. Asia(Maddison))
101	Macedonia	208	PROXY(Yugoslavia(Maddison))
102	Canada	200	1700(Maddison)
103	El Salvador	190	PROXY(Other Sp. Am.(Maddison))
104	Jordan	186	PROXY(Other W. Asia(Maddison))
105	Guinea-Biss	177	PROXY(Other W. Africa(Maddison))
106	Eritrea	162	PROXY(Ethiopia & Eritr.(Maddison))
107	Israel	157	PROXY(Other W. Asia(Maddison))
108	Nicaragua	142	PROXY(Other Sp. Am.(Maddison))
109	Estonia	134	PROXY(40(E)/Eur. Russia(Maddison))
110	Kosovo	129	PROXY(Yugoslavia(Maddison))
111	Haiti	124	PROXY(Caribbean cs(Maddison))
112	Paraguay	110	PROXY(Other Sp. Am.(Maddison))
113	Namibia	108	PROXY(Namibia & Botsw. (Maddison))
114	Honduras	103	PROXY(Other Sp. Am.(Maddison))
115	Cuba	103	PROXY(Caribbean cs(Maddison))
116	New Zealand	100	1700(Maddison)
117	Cyprus	98	PROXY(Greece(Maddison))
118	Botswana	92	PROXY(Namibia & Botsw. (Maddison))
119	Panama	72	PROXY(Other Sp. Am.(Maddison))
120	Kuwait	71	PROXY(Arabia(Maddison))
121	Jamaica	69	PROXY(Caribbean cs(Maddison))
122	Montenegro	67	PROXY(Yugoslavia(Maddison))
123	Bahrain	54	PROXY(Arabia(Maddison))
124	Iceland	50	1700(WIKI)
125	Lesotho	50	PROXY(S. Afr., Sw., Ls.(Maddison))
126	Costa Rica	48	PROXY(Other Sp. Am.(Maddison))
127	Puerto Rico	42	PROXY(Caribbean cs(Maddison))
128	Uruguay	42	PROXY(Other Sp. Am.(Maddison))
129	UAE	35	PROXY(Arabia(Maddison))
130	Swaziland	19	PROXY(S. Afr., Sw., Ls.(Maddison))
131	Dominican R	15	PROXY(Caribbean cs(Maddison))
132	Qatar	12	PROXY(Arabia(Maddison))
133	Trinidad & T	10	PROXY(Caribbean cs(Maddison))
134	Hong Kong	7	PROXY(China(Maddison))
135	Singapore	4	PROXY(Other E. Asia(Maddison))

TABLE 1.6 POPULATION, THOUSANDS, YEAR 1820			
Rank	Country	POP	Source
1	China	381,000	1820(Maddison)
2	India	175,349	1820(Maddison)
3	France	31,250	1820(Maddison)
4	Japan	31,000	1820(Maddison)
5	Russia	30,588	PROXY(40(E)/Eu. Rs./ Sb.(Maddison))
6	Germany	24,905	1820(Maddison)
7	Italy	20,176	1820(Maddison)
8	Bangladesh	20,000	1820(Maddison)
9	UK	19,831	PROXY(UK & Ireland(Maddison))
10	Indonesia	17,927	1820(Maddison)
11	Pakistan	13,651	1820(Maddison)
12	Spain	12,203	1820(Maddison)
13	Ukraine	11,629	PROXY(40(E)/Eur. Russia(Maddison))
14	Poland	10,426	1820(Maddison)
15	Turkey	10,074	1820(Maddison)
16	US	9,981	1820(Maddison)
17	Korea, South	9,395	1820(Maddison)
18	Mexico	6,587	1820(Maddison)
19	Iran	6,560	1820(Maddison)
20	Vietnam	6,551	1820(Maddison)
21	Romania	6,389	1820(Maddison)
22	Czechia	5,516	PROXY(Czechoslovakia(Maddison))
23	Ireland	5,053	PROXY(whole Ireland(Maddison))
24	Thailand	4,665	1820(Maddison)
25	Brazil	4,507	1820(Maddison)
26	Egypt	4,394	1820(Mitchell)
27	Korea, North	4,345	1820(Maddison)
28	Sudan	4,265	PROXY(1820(Maddison))
29	Hungary	4,146	1820(Maddison)
30	Nepal	3,881	1820(Maddison)
31	Burma	3,506	1820(Maddison)
32	Belgium	3,434	1820(Maddison)
33	Austria	3,369	1820(Maddison)
34	Portugal	3,297	1820(Maddison)
35	Afghanistan	3,280	1820(Maddison)
36	Ethiopia	2,949	PROXY(Ethiopia & Eritr. (Maddison))
37.5	Algeria	2,689	1820(Maddison)
37.5	Morocco	2,689	1820(Maddison)
39	Yemen	2,593	1820(Maddison)
40	Sweden	2,585	1820(Maddison)
41	Belarus	2,545	PROXY(40(E)/Eur. Russia(Maddison))
42	Netherlands	2,333	1820(Maddison)
43	Greece	2,312	1820(Maddison)
44	Uzbekistan	2,217	PROXY(40(E)/ Turkestan(Maddison))

TABLE 1.6 POPULATION, THOUSANDS, YEAR 1820			
Rank	Country	POP	Source
45	Bulgaria	2,187	1820(Maddison)
46	Philippines	2,176	1820(Maddison)
47	Slovakia	2,140	PROXY(Czechoslovakia(Maddison))
48	Mozambique	2,096	1820(Maddison)
49	Saudi Arabia	2,091	1820(Maddison)
50	Cambodia	2,090	1820(Maddison)
51	Kazakhstan	2,081	PROXY(40(E)/ Turkestan(Maddison))
52	Taiwan	2,000	1820(Maddison)
53	Switzerland	1,986	1820(Maddison)
54	Serbia	1,878	PROXY(Yugoslavia(Maddison))
55	Madagascar	1,683	1820(Maddison)
56	South Africa	1,444	PROXY(S. Afr., Sw., Ls.(Maddison))
57	Ghana	1,374	1820(Maddison)
58	Syria	1,337	1820(Maddison)
59	Peru	1,317	1820(Maddison)
60	Croatia	1,228	PROXY(Yugoslavia(Maddison))
61	Sri Lanka	1,213	1820(Maddison)
62	Colombia	1,206	1820(Maddison)
63	Finland	1,169	1820(Maddison)
64	Denmark	1,155	1820(Maddison)
65	Bolivia	1,100	1820(Maddison)
66	Iraq	1,093	1820(Maddison)
67	Burundi	1,016	PROXY(Other E. Africa(Maddison))
68	Somalia	1,000	1820(Maddison)
69	Norway	970	1820(Maddison)
70	Guinea	935	PROXY(Other W. Africa(Maddison))
71	South Sudan	891	PROXY(1820(Maddison))
72	Tunisia	875	1820(Maddison)
73	Georgia	874	PROXY(40(E)/Caucasus(Maddison))
74	Bosnia	851	PROXY(Yugoslavia(Maddison))
75	Lithuania	823	PROXY(40(E)/Eur. Russia(Maddison))
76	Canada	816	1820(Maddison)
77	Azerbaijan	792	PROXY(40(E)/Caucasus(Maddison))
78	Chile	771	1820(Maddison)
79	Haiti	723	1820(Maddison)
80	Venezuela	718	1820(Maddison)
81	Moldova	694	PROXY(40(E)/Eur. Russia(Maddison))
82	Sierra Leone	694	PROXY(Other W. Africa(Maddison))
83	Mongolia	619	1820(Maddison)
84	Cuba	605	1820(Maddison)
85	Guatemala	595	1820(Maddison)
86	Libya	538	1820(Maddison)
87	Argentina	534	1820(Maddison)
88	Latvia	531	PROXY(40(E)/Eur. Russia(Maddison))
89	Kyrgyzstan	517	PROXY(40(E)/ Turkestan(Maddison))

Table 1.6 Population, Thousands, Year 1820			
Rank	Country	POP	Source
90	Tajikistan	516	PROXY(40(E)/ Turkestan(Maddison))
91	Ecuador	500	1820(Maddison)
92	Laos	470	1820(Maddison)
93	Slovenia	469	PROXY(Yugoslavia(Maddison))
94	Zimbabwe	467	PROXY(Mal., Zam., Zim.(Maddison))
95	Malawi	461	PROXY(Mal., Zam., Zim.(Maddison))
96	Turkmenistan	441	PROXY(40(E)/ Turkestan(Maddison))
97	Albania	437	1820(Maddison)
98	Zambia	418	PROXY(Mal., Zam., Zim.(Maddison))
99	Jamaica	401	1820(Maddison)
100	Macedonia	394	PROXY(Yugoslavia(Maddison))
101	Australia	334	1820(Maddison)
102	Lebanon	332	1820(Maddison)
103	Armenia	319	PROXY(40(E)/Caucasus(Maddison))
104	Oman	318	1820(Maddison)
105	Estonia	296	PROXY(40(E)/Eur. Russia(Maddison))
106	Malaysia	287	1820(Maddison)
107.5	El Salvador	248	1820(Maddison)
107.5	Puerto Rico	248	1820(Maddison)
109	Kosovo	244	PROXY(Yugoslavia(Maddison))
110	Jordan	217	1820(Maddison)
111	Eritrea	205	PROXY(Ethiopia & Eritr. (Maddison))
112	Guinea-Biss	205	PROXY(Other W. Africa(Maddison))
113	Nicaragua	186	1820(Maddison)
114	Israel	184	PROXY(Palestine(Maddison))
115	Cyprus	151	PROXY(Greece(Maddison))
116	Paraguay	143	1820(Maddison)
117	Honduras	135	1820(Maddison)
118	Montenegro	127	PROXY(Yugoslavia(Maddison))
119	Namibia	118	PROXY(Namibia & Botsw. (Maddison))
120	Botswana	101	PROXY(Namibia & Botsw. (Maddison))
121	New Zealand	100	1820(Maddison)
122	Panama	94	PROXY(15 L. American cs(Maddison))
123	Dominican R	89	1820(Maddison)
124	Kuwait	82	PROXY(Gulf Coast(Maddison))
125	Lesotho	77	PROXY(S. Afr., Sw., Ls.(Maddison))
126	Costa Rica	63	1820(Maddison)
127	Bahrain	63	PROXY(Gulf Coast(Maddison))
128	Trinidad & T	60	1820(Maddison)
129	Uruguay	55	1820(Maddison)
130	Iceland	48	1820(WIKI)
131	UAE	41	PROXY(Gulf Coast(Maddison))
132	Swaziland	29	PROXY(S. Afr., Sw., Ls.(Maddison))

TABLE 1.6 POPULATION, THOUSANDS, YEAR 1820			
Rank	Country	POP	Source
133	Hong Kong	20	1820(Maddison)
134	Qatar	14	PROXY(Gulf Coast(Maddison))
135	Singapore	5	1820(Maddison)

Table 1.7 Population, Thousands, Year 1870			
Rank	Country	POP	Source
1	China	358,000	1870(Maddison)
2	India	212,189	1870(Maddison)
3	Russia	50,303	PROXY(40(E)/USSR(Maddison))
4	US	40,241	1870(Maddison)
5	Germany	39,231	1870(Maddison)
6	France	38,440	1870(Maddison)
7	Japan	34,437	1870(Maddison)
8	UK	29,319	PROXY(UK & Ireland(Maddison))
9	Indonesia	28,922	1870(Maddison)
10	Italy	27,888	1870(Maddison)
11	Bangladesh	24,721	1870(Maddison)
12	Ukraine	18,888	PROXY(40(E)/USSR(Maddison))
13	Poland	16,865	1870(Maddison)
14	Spain	16,201	1870(Maddison)
15	Pakistan	16,090	1870(Maddison)
16	Turkey	11,793	1870(Maddison)
17	Vietnam	10,528	1870(Maddison)
18	Brazil	9,797	1870(Maddison)
19	Korea, South	9,753	1870(Maddison)
20	Mexico	9,219	1870(Maddison)
21	Romania	9,179	1870(Maddison)
22	Iran	8,415	1870(Maddison)
23	Czechia	7,316	PROXY(Czechoslovakia(Maddison))
24	Egypt	6,394	1870(MItchell)
25	Ethiopia	6,179	INTERPOL(Maddison)
26	Hungary	5,917	1870(Maddison)
27	Thailand	5,775	1870(Maddison)
28	Belgium	5,096	1870(Maddison)
29	Philippines	5,063	1870(Maddison)
30	Sudan	5,062	INTERPOL(Maddison)
31	Nepal	4,698	1870(Maddison)
32	Austria	4,520	1870(Maddison)
33	Korea, North	4,511	1870(Maddison)
34	Portugal	4,327	1870(Maddison)
35	Burma	4,245	1870(Maddison)
36	Afghanistan	4,207	1870(Maddison)
37	Sweden	4,169	1870(Maddison)
38	Belarus	4,133	PROXY(40(E)/USSR(Maddison))
39	Ireland	3,856	PROXY(whole Ireland(Maddison))
40	Canada	3,781	1870(Maddison)
41.5	Algeria	3,776	1870(Maddison)
41.5	Morocco	3,776	1870(Maddison)
43	Greece	3,657	1870(Maddison)
44	Netherlands	3,610	1870(Maddison)
45	Mozambique	3,191	INTERPOL(Maddison)
46	Uzbekistan	2,993	PROXY(40(E)/USSR(Maddison))
47	Serbia	2,972	PROXY(Yugoslavia(Maddison))
48	Yemen	2,840	1870(Maddison)

TABLE 1.7 POPULATION, THOUSANDS, YEAR 1870			
Rank	Country	POP	Source
49	Slovakia	2,839	PROXY(Czechoslovakia(Maddison))
50	Kazakhstan	2,809	PROXY(40(E)/USSR(Maddison))
51	Sri Lanka	2,786	1870(Maddison)
52	Switzerland	2,655	1870(Maddison)
53	Peru	2,606	1870(Maddison)
54	Bulgaria	2,586	1870(Maddison)
55	South Africa	2,547	1870(Maddison)
56	Madagascar	2,400	INTERPOL(Maddison)
57	Colombia	2,392	1870(Maddison)
58	Taiwan	2,345	1870(Maddison)
59	Cambodia	2,340	1870(Maddison)
60	Saudi Arabia	2,338	1870(Maddison)
61	Chile	1,945	1870(Maddison)
62	Croatia	1,943	PROXY(Yugoslavia(Maddison))
63	Denmark	1,888	1870(Maddison)
64	Argentina	1,796	1870(Maddison)
65	Australia	1,775	1870(Maddison)
66	Finland	1,754	1870(Maddison)
67	Norway	1,735	1870(Maddison)
68	Venezuela	1,653	1870(Maddison)
69	Georgia	1,650	PROXY(40(E)/USSR(Maddison))
70	Syria	1,582	1870(Maddison)
71	Iraq	1,580	1870(Maddison)
72	Ghana	1,500	1870(Maddison)
73	Azerbaijan	1,496	PROXY(40(E)/USSR(Maddison))
74	Bolivia	1,495	1870(Maddison)
75	Burundi	1,406	INTERPOL(Maddison)
76	Guinea	1,389	INTERPOL(Maddison)
77	Somalia	1,369	INTERPOL(Maddison)
78	Bosnia	1,347	PROXY(Yugoslavia(Maddison))
79	Lithuania	1,336	PROXY(40(E)/USSR(Maddison))
80	Cuba	1,331	1870(Maddison)
81	Tunisia	1,176	1870(Maddison)
82	Haiti	1,150	1870(Maddison)
83	Moldova	1,128	PROXY(40(E)/USSR(Maddison))
84	Guatemala	1,080	1870(Maddison)
85	South Sudan	1,058	INTERPOL(Maddison)
86	Sierra Leone	1,031	INTERPOL(Maddison)
87	Ecuador	1,013	1870(Maddison)
88	Zimbabwe	936	INTERPOL(Maddison)
89	Malawi	924	INTERPOL(Maddison)
90	Latvia	862	PROXY(40(E)/USSR(Maddison))
91	Zambia	838	INTERPOL(Maddison)
92	Malaysia	800	1870(Maddison)
93	Laos	755	1870(Maddison)
94	Slovenia	743	PROXY(Yugoslavia(Maddison))
95	Kyrgyzstan	698	PROXY(40(E)/USSR(Maddison))
96	Tajikistan	697	PROXY(40(E)/USSR(Maddison))
97	Mongolia	668	1870(Maddison)

Table 1.7 Population, Thousands, Year 1870			
Rank	Country	POP	Source
98	Libya	660	INTERPOL(Maddison/Mitchell)
99	Puerto Rico	645	1870(Maddison)
100	Macedonia	623	PROXY(Yugoslavia(Maddison))
101	Armenia	603	PROXY(40(E)/USSR(Maddison))
102	Albania	603	1870(Maddison)
103	Turkmenistan	595	PROXY(40(E)/USSR(Maddison))
104	Jamaica	499	1870(Maddison)
105	El Salvador	492	1870(Maddison)
106	Estonia	482	PROXY(40(E)/USSR(Maddison))
107	Lebanon	476	1870(Maddison)
108	Eritrea	429	INTERPOL(Maddison)
109	Honduras	404	1870(Maddison)
110	Kosovo	387	PROXY(Yugoslavia(Maddison))
111	Paraguay	384	1870(Maddison)
112	Oman	367	1870(Maddison)
113	Uruguay	343	1870(Maddison)
114	Nicaragua	337	1870(Maddison)
115	Guinea-Biss	304	INTERPOL(Maddison)
116	New Zealand	291	1870(Maddison)
117	Jordan	266	1870(Maddison)
118	Dominican R	242	1870(Maddison)
119	Cyprus	239	PROXY(Greece(Maddison))
120	Israel	238	PROXY(Palestine(Maddison))
121	Namibia	203	INTERPOL(Maddison)
122	Montenegro	201	PROXY(Yugoslavia(Maddison))
123	Lesotho	184	INTERPOL(Maddison)
124	Panama	176	1870(Maddison)
125	Botswana	174	INTERPOL(Maddison)
126	Costa Rica	137	1870(Maddison)
127	Trinidad & T	124	1870(Maddison)
128	Hong Kong	123	1870(Maddison)
129	Singapore	84	1870(Maddison)
130	Kuwait	82	PROXY(Gulf Coast(Maddison))
131	Iceland	70	1870(WIKI)
132	Swaziland	68	INTERPOL(Maddison)
133	Bahrain	63	PROXY(Gulf Coast(Maddison))
134	UAE	41	PROXY(Gulf Coast(Maddison))
135	Qatar	14	PROXY(Gulf Coast(Maddison))

TABLE 1.8 POPULATION, THOUSANDS, YEAR 1880

Rank	Country	POP	Source
1	China	368,000	1880(Maddison)
2	India	215,157	INTERPOL(Ind./wh. India(Maddison))
3	Russia	56,196	40(E)/INTERPOL(Maddison)
4	US	50,458	1880(Maddison)
5	Germany	43,500	1880(Maddison)
6	France	39,045	1880(Maddison)
7	Japan	36,807	1880(Maddison)
8	Indonesia	32,876	1880(Maddison)
9	UK	32,328	PROXY(UK & Ireland(Maddison))
10	Italy	29,534	1880(Maddison)
11	Bangladesh	25,536	INTERPOL(Ban./wh. India(Maddison))
12	Ukraine	21,101	40(E)/INTERPOL(Maddison)
13	Poland	19,632	INTERPOL(Maddison)
14	Spain	16,859	1880(Maddison)
15	Pakistan	16,492	INTERPOL(Pak./wh. India(Maddison))
16	Turkey	12,472	INTERPOL(Maddison)
17	Vietnam	12,127	INTERPOL(Maddison)
18	Brazil	11,794	1880(Maddison)
19	Mexico	10,399	1880(Maddison)
20	Korea, South	9,800	INTERPOL(Maddison)
21	Romania	9,758	INTERPOL(Maddison)
22	Iran	8,955	INTERPOL(Maddison)
23	Czechia	7,701	INTERPOL(Maddison)
24	Egypt	7,578	1880(Mitchell)
25	Ethiopia	7,164	INTERPOL(Maddison)
26	Hungary	6,260	INTERPOL(Maddison)
27	Thailand	6,206	INTERPOL(Maddison)
28	Philippines	5,726	INTERPOL(Maddison)
29	Burma	5,638	INTERPOL(Maddison)
30	Belgium	5,541	1880(Maddison)
31	Sudan	5,238	INTERPOL(Maddison)
32	Austria	4,941	1880(Maddison)
33	Nepal	4,939	INTERPOL(Maddison)
34	Belarus	4,617	40(E)/INTERPOL(Maddison)
35	Portugal	4,610	1880(Maddison)
36	Korea, North	4,598	INTERPOL(Maddison)
37	Sweden	4,572	1880(Maddison)
38	Afghanistan	4,520	INTERPOL(Maddison)
39	Canada	4,384	1880(Maddison)
40	Algeria	4,183	1880(Maddison)
41	Morocco	4,051	INTERPOL(Maddison)
42	Greece	4,049	1880(Maddison)
43	Netherlands	4,043	1880(Maddison)
44	Ireland	3,702	PROXY(whole Ireland(Maddison))
45	Mozambique	3,470	INTERPOL(Maddison)
46	Uzbekistan	3,344	40(E)/INTERPOL(Maddison)
47	Serbia	3,220	INTERPOL(Maddison)
48	Kazakhstan	3,138	40(E)/INTERPOL(Maddison)

Table 1.8 Population, Thousands, Year 1880			
Rank	Country	POP	Source
49	South Africa	3,127	INTERPOL(Maddison)
50	Sri Lanka	3,021	1880(Maddison)
51	Slovakia	2,988	INTERPOL(Maddison)
52	Bulgaria	2,985	INTERPOL(Maddison)
53	Peru	2,953	INTERPOL(Maddison)
54	Yemen	2,938	INTERPOL(Maddison)
55	Switzerland	2,839	1880(Maddison)
56	Colombia	2,839	INTERPOL(Maddison)
57	Madagascar	2,576	INTERPOL(Maddison)
58	Cambodia	2,493	INTERPOL(Maddison)
59	Argentina	2,462	INTERPOL(Maddison)
60	Taiwan	2,421	INTERPOL(Maddison)
61	Saudi Arabia	2,413	INTERPOL(Maddison)
62	Chile	2,271	INTERPOL(Maddison)
63	Australia	2,197	1880(Maddison)
64	Croatia	2,105	INTERPOL(Maddison)
65	Denmark	2,081	1880(Maddison)
66	Finland	2,047	1880(Maddison)
67	Venezuela	1,952	1880(Maddison)
68	Norway	1,919	1880(Maddison)
69	Georgia	1,844	40(E)/INTERPOL(Maddison)
70	Iraq	1,776	INTERPOL(Maddison)
71	Azerbaijan	1,671	40(E)/INTERPOL(Maddison)
72	Syria	1,669	INTERPOL(Maddison)
73	Ghana	1,570	INTERPOL(Maddison)
74	Bolivia	1,559	INTERPOL(Maddison)
75	Guinea	1,504	INTERPOL(Maddison)
76	Burundi	1,500	INTERPOL(Maddison)
77	Lithuania	1,493	40(E)/INTERPOL(Maddison)
78	Bosnia	1,460	INTERPOL(Maddison)
79	Somalia	1,458	INTERPOL(Maddison)
80	Cuba	1,432	INTERPOL(Maddison)
81	Tunisia	1,310	INTERPOL(Maddison)
82	Haiti	1,273	INTERPOL(Maddison)
83	Moldova	1,260	40(E)/INTERPOL(Maddison)
84	Guatemala	1,149	INTERPOL(Maddison)
85	Ecuador	1,128	INTERPOL(Maddison)
86	Malaysia	1,126	INTERPOL(Maddison)
87	Sierra Leone	1,116	INTERPOL(Maddison)
88	South Sudan	1,095	INTERPOL(Maddison)
89	Zimbabwe	1,076	INTERPOL(Maddison)
90	Malawi	1,063	INTERPOL(Maddison)
91	Zambia	963	INTERPOL(Maddison)
92	Latvia	963	40(E)/INTERPOL(Maddison)
93	Laos	870	INTERPOL(Maddison)
94	Slovenia	805	INTERPOL(Maddison)
95	Kyrgyzstan	780	40(E)/INTERPOL(Maddison)
96	Tajikistan	778	40(E)/INTERPOL(Maddison)
97	Puerto Rico	736	INTERPOL(Maddison)

Table 1.8 Population, Thousands, Year 1880			
Rank	Country	POP	Source
98	Libya	688	INTERPOL(Maddison/Mitchell)
99	Mongolia	681	INTERPOL(Maddison)
100	Macedonia	675	INTERPOL(Maddison)
101	Armenia	674	40(E)/INTERPOL(Maddison)
102	Turkmenistan	665	40(E)/INTERPOL(Maddison)
103	Albania	662	INTERPOL(Maddison)
104	El Salvador	570	INTERPOL(Maddison)
105	Jamaica	564	INTERPOL(Maddison)
106	Estonia	538	40(E)/INTERPOL(Maddison)
107	New Zealand	520	1880(Maddison)
108	Lebanon	512	INTERPOL(Maddison)
109	Eritrea	498	INTERPOL(Maddison)
110	Uruguay	464	1880(Maddison)
111	Honduras	434	INTERPOL(Maddison)
112	Kosovo	419	INTERPOL(Maddison)
113	Paraguay	402	INTERPOL(Maddison)
114	Oman	384	INTERPOL(Maddison)
115	Nicaragua	379	INTERPOL(Maddison)
116	Guinea-Biss	329	INTERPOL(Maddison)
117	Dominican R	311	INTERPOL(Maddison)
118	Jordan	283	INTERPOL(Maddison)
119	Israel	266	INTERPOL(Maddison)
120	Cyprus	264	PROXY(Greece(Maddison))
121	Namibia	226	INTERPOL(Maddison)
122	Lesotho	219	INTERPOL(Maddison)
123	Montenegro	218	INTERPOL(Maddison)
124	Panama	201	INTERPOL(Maddison)
125	Botswana	194	INTERPOL(Maddison)
126	Costa Rica	177	INTERPOL(Maddison)
127	Hong Kong	162	INTERPOL(Maddison)
128	Trinidad & T	160	INTERPOL(Maddison)
129	Singapore	115	INTERPOL(Maddison)
130	Kuwait	87	INTERPOL(Maddison)
131	Swaziland	81	INTERPOL(Maddison)
132	Iceland	72	1880(WIKI)
133	Bahrain	66	INTERPOL(Maddison)
134	UAE	43	INTERPOL(Maddison)
135	Qatar	15	INTERPOL(Maddison)

Table 1.9 Population, Thousands, Year 1890			
Rank	Country	POP	Source
1	China	380,000	1890(Maddison)
2	India	233,315	INTERPOL(Ind./wh. India(Maddison))
3	US	63,302	1890(Maddison)
4	Russia	62,779	PROXY(40(E)/USSR(Maddison))
5	Germany	47,607	1890(Maddison)
6	Japan	40,077	1890(Maddison)
7	France	40,014	1890(Maddison)
8	Indonesia	37,579	1890(Maddison)
9	UK	35,001	PROXY(UK & Ireland(Maddison))
10	Italy	31,702	1890(Maddison)
11	Bangladesh	28,210	INTERPOL(Ban./wh. India(Maddison))
12	Ukraine	23,572	PROXY(40(E)/USSR(Maddison))
13	Poland	22,854	1890(Maddison)
14	Pakistan	18,078	INTERPOL(Pak./wh. India(Maddison))
15	Spain	17,757	1890(Maddison)
16	Brazil	14,199	1890(Maddison)
17	Vietnam	13,969	INTERPOL(Maddison)
18	Turkey	13,189	INTERPOL(Maddison)
19	Mexico	11,729	1890(Maddison)
20	Romania	10,373	1890(Maddison)
21	Korea, South	9,848	1890(Maddison)
22	Iran	9,529	INTERPOL(Maddison)
23	Egypt	8,777	1890(Mitchell)
24	Ethiopia	8,306	INTERPOL(Maddison)
25	Czechia	8,107	PROXY(Czechoslovakia(Maddison))
26	Burma	7,489	1890(Maddison)
27	Thailand	6,670	1890(Maddison)
28	Hungary	6,622	1890(Maddison)
29	Philippines	6,476	1890(Maddison)
30	Belgium	6,096	1890(Maddison)
31	Sudan	5,421	INTERPOL(Maddison)
32	Austria	5,394	1890(Maddison)
33	Nepal	5,192	1890(Maddison)
34	Belarus	5,158	PROXY(40(E)/USSR(Maddison))
35	Portugal	5,028	1890(Maddison)
36	Canada	4,918	1890(Maddison)
37	Afghanistan	4,857	INTERPOL(Maddison)
38	Sweden	4,780	1890(Maddison)
39	Korea, North	4,697	INTERPOL(Maddison)
40	Algeria	4,548	INTERPOL(Maddison)
41	Netherlands	4,535	1890(Maddison)
42	Greece	4,482	1890(Maddison)
43	Morocco	4,347	INTERPOL(Maddison)
44	South Africa	3,839	INTERPOL(Maddison)
45	Mozambique	3,775	INTERPOL(Maddison)
46	Uzbekistan	3,735	PROXY(40(E)/USSR(Maddison))

TABLE 1.9 POPULATION, THOUSANDS, YEAR 1890			
Rank	Country	POP	Source
47	Kazakhstan	3,506	PROXY(40(E)/USSR(Maddison))
48	Serbia	3,489	PROXY(Yugoslavia(Maddison))
49	Bulgaria	3,445	1890(Maddison)
50	Argentina	3,376	1890(Maddison)
51	Colombia	3,369	1890(Maddison)
52	Ireland	3,357	PROXY(whole Ireland(Maddison))
53	Peru	3,346	1890(Maddison)
54	Sri Lanka	3,343	1890(Maddison)
55	Slovakia	3,145	PROXY(Czechoslovakia(Maddison))
56	Australia	3,107	1890(Maddison)
57	Yemen	3,039	INTERPOL(Maddison)
58	Switzerland	2,951	1890(Maddison)
59	Madagascar	2,766	INTERPOL(Maddison)
60	Cambodia	2,655	INTERPOL(Maddison)
61	Chile	2,651	1890(Maddison)
62	Taiwan	2,500	1890(Maddison)
63	Saudi Arabia	2,490	INTERPOL(Maddison)
64	Finland	2,364	1890(Maddison)
65	Denmark	2,294	1890(Maddison)
66	Croatia	2,281	PROXY(Yugoslavia(Maddison))
67	Venezuela	2,224	1890(Maddison)
68	Georgia	2,060	PROXY(40(E)/USSR(Maddison))
69	Norway	1,997	1890(Maddison)
70	Iraq	1,997	INTERPOL(Maddison)
71	Azerbaijan	1,867	PROXY(40(E)/USSR(Maddison))
72	Syria	1,762	INTERPOL(Maddison)
73	Lithuania	1,668	PROXY(40(E)/USSR(Maddison))
74	Ghana	1,643	INTERPOL(Maddison)
75	Guinea	1,628	INTERPOL(Maddison)
76	Bolivia	1,626	INTERPOL(Maddison)
77	Burundi	1,601	INTERPOL(Maddison)
78	Malaysia	1,585	1890(Maddison)
79	Bosnia	1,582	PROXY(Yugoslavia(Maddison))
80	Somalia	1,553	INTERPOL(Maddison)
81	Cuba	1,541	INTERPOL(Maddison)
82	Tunisia	1,459	INTERPOL(Maddison)
83	Haiti	1,409	INTERPOL(Maddison)
84	Moldova	1,407	PROXY(40(E)/USSR(Maddison))
85	Ecuador	1,257	INTERPOL(Maddison)
86	Zimbabwe	1,237	INTERPOL(Maddison)
87	Guatemala	1,222	INTERPOL(Maddison)
88	Malawi	1,221	INTERPOL(Maddison)
89	Sierra Leone	1,208	INTERPOL(Maddison)
90	South Sudan	1,133	INTERPOL(Maddison)
91	Zambia	1,107	INTERPOL(Maddison)
92	Latvia	1,075	PROXY(40(E)/USSR(Maddison))
93	Laos	1,002	INTERPOL(Maddison)
94	Slovenia	872	PROXY(Yugoslavia(Maddison))
95	Kyrgyzstan	871	PROXY(40(E)/USSR(Maddison))

Table 1.9 Population, Thousands, Year 1890			
Rank	Country	POP	Source
96	Tajikistan	870	PROXY(40(E)/USSR(Maddison))
97	Puerto Rico	840	INTERPOL(Maddison)
98	Armenia	753	PROXY(40(E)/USSR(Maddison))
99	Turkmenistan	742	PROXY(40(E)/USSR(Maddison))
100	Macedonia	731	PROXY(Yugoslavia(Maddison))
101	Albania	726	1890(Maddison)
102	Libya	717	INTERPOL(Maddison/Mitchell)
103	Mongolia	694	INTERPOL(Maddison)
104	Uruguay	686	1890(Maddison)
105	New Zealand	665	1890(Maddison)
106	El Salvador	661	INTERPOL(Maddison)
107	Jamaica	637	INTERPOL(Maddison)
108	Estonia	601	PROXY(40(E)/USSR(Maddison))
109	Eritrea	577	INTERPOL(Maddison)
110	Lebanon	550	INTERPOL(Maddison)
111	Honduras	466	INTERPOL(Maddison)
112	Kosovo	454	PROXY(Yugoslavia(Maddison))
113	Nicaragua	425	INTERPOL(Maddison)
114	Paraguay	420	INTERPOL(Maddison)
115	Oman	401	INTERPOL(Maddison)
116	Dominican R	400	INTERPOL(Maddison)
117	Guinea-Biss	356	INTERPOL(Maddison)
118	Jordan	301	INTERPOL(Maddison)
119	Israel	298	INTERPOL(Maddison)
120	Cyprus	293	PROXY(Greece(Maddison))
121	Lesotho	260	INTERPOL(Maddison)
122	Namibia	252	INTERPOL(Maddison)
123	Montenegro	236	PROXY(Yugoslavia(Maddison))
124	Panama	230	INTERPOL(Maddison)
125	Costa Rica	229	INTERPOL(Maddison)
126	Botswana	217	INTERPOL(Maddison)
127	Hong Kong	214	1890(Maddison)
128	Trinidad & T	207	INTERPOL(Maddison)
129	Singapore	157	1890(Maddison)
130	Swaziland	97	INTERPOL(Maddison)
131	Kuwait	92	INTERPOL(Maddison)
132	Iceland	71	1890(WIKI)
133	Bahrain	70	INTERPOL(Maddison)
134	UAE	46	INTERPOL(Maddison)
135	Qatar	16	INTERPOL(Maddison)

TABLE 1.10 POPULATION, THOUSANDS, YEAR 1900			
Rank	Country	POP	Source
1	China	400,000	1900(Maddison)
2	India	236,772	INTERPOL(Ind./wh. India(Maddison))
3	US	76,391	1900(Maddison)
4	Russia	70,628	PROXY(40(E)/USSR(Maddison))
5	Germany	54,388	1900(Maddison)
6	Japan	44,103	1900(Maddison)
7	Indonesia	42,746	1900(Maddison)
8	France	40,598	1900(Maddison)
9	UK	38,428	PROXY(UK & Ireland(Maddison))
10	Italy	33,672	1900(Maddison)
11	Bangladesh	29,164	INTERPOL(Ban./wh. India(Maddison))
12	Ukraine	26,520	PROXY(40(E)/USSR(Maddison))
13	Poland	24,750	1900(Maddison)
14	Spain	18,566	1900(Maddison)
15	Pakistan	18,544	INTERPOL(Pak./wh. India(Maddison))
16	Brazil	17,984	1900(Maddison)
17	Vietnam	16,091	INTERPOL(Maddison)
18	Turkey	13,948	INTERPOL(Maddison)
19	Mexico	13,607	1900(Maddison)
20	Romania	11,000	1900(Maddison)
21	Egypt	10,186	1900(Mitchell)
22	Burma	10,174	1900(Maddison)
23	Iran	10,140	INTERPOL(Maddison)
24	Korea, South	9,896	1900(Maddison)
25	Ethiopia	9,630	INTERPOL(Maddison)
26	Czechia	8,747	PROXY(Czechoslovakia(Maddison))
27	Philippines	7,324	1900(Maddison)
28	Thailand	7,320	1900(Maddison)
29	Hungary	7,127	1900(Maddison)
30	Belgium	6,719	1900(Maddison)
31	Austria	5,973	1900(Maddison)
32	Belarus	5,803	PROXY(40(E)/USSR(Maddison))
33	Sudan	5,610	INTERPOL(Maddison)
34	Canada	5,457	1900(Maddison)
35	Portugal	5,404	1900(Maddison)
36	Nepal	5,283	1900(Maddison)
37	Afghanistan	5,219	INTERPOL(Maddison)
38	Netherlands	5,142	1900(Maddison)
39	Sweden	5,117	1900(Maddison)
40	Greece	4,962	1900(Maddison)
41	Algeria	4,946	INTERPOL(Maddison)
42	Korea, North	4,777	INTERPOL(Maddison)
43	South Africa	4,713	INTERPOL(Maddison)
44	Argentina	4,693	1900(Maddison)
45	Morocco	4,664	INTERPOL(Maddison)
46	Uzbekistan	4,202	PROXY(40(E)/USSR(Maddison))

Table 1.10 Population, Thousands, Year 1900			
Rank	Country	POP	Source
47	Mozambique	4,106	INTERPOL(Maddison)
48	Serbia	4,024	PROXY(Yugoslavia(Maddison))
49	Bulgaria	4,000	1900(Maddison)
50	Colombia	3,998	1900(Maddison)
51	Kazakhstan	3,944	PROXY(40(E)/USSR(Maddison))
52	Sri Lanka	3,912	1900(Maddison)
53	Peru	3,791	1900(Maddison)
54	Australia	3,741	1900(Maddison)
55	Slovakia	3,394	PROXY(Czechoslovakia(Maddison))
56	Switzerland	3,300	1900(Maddison)
57	Ireland	3,180	PROXY(whole Ireland(Maddison))
58	Yemen	3,143	INTERPOL(Maddison)
59	Chile	2,974	1900(Maddison)
60	Madagascar	2,969	INTERPOL(Maddison)
61	Taiwan	2,864	1900(Maddison)
62	Cambodia	2,828	INTERPOL(Maddison)
63	Finland	2,646	1900(Maddison)
64	Croatia	2,631	PROXY(Yugoslavia(Maddison))
65	Saudi Arabia	2,569	INTERPOL(Maddison)
66	Denmark	2,561	1900(Maddison)
67	Venezuela	2,542	1900(Maddison)
68	Georgia	2,317	PROXY(40(E)/USSR(Maddison))
69	Iraq	2,244	INTERPOL(Maddison)
70	Malaysia	2,232	1900(Maddison)
71	Norway	2,230	1900(Maddison)
72	Azerbaijan	2,100	PROXY(40(E)/USSR(Maddison))
73	Lithuania	1,876	PROXY(40(E)/USSR(Maddison))
74	Syria	1,859	INTERPOL(Maddison)
75	Bosnia	1,824	PROXY(Yugoslavia(Maddison))
76	Ghana	1,784	INTERPOL(Maddison)
77	Guinea	1,762	INTERPOL(Maddison)
78	Burundi	1,708	INTERPOL(Maddison)
79	Bolivia	1,696	1900(Maddison)
80	Cuba	1,658	1900(Maddison)
81	Somalia	1,653	INTERPOL(Maddison)
82	Tunisia	1,625	INTERPOL(Maddison)
83	Moldova	1,583	PROXY(40(E)/USSR(Maddison))
84	Haiti	1,560	1900(Maddison)
85	Zimbabwe	1,422	INTERPOL(Maddison)
86	Malawi	1,404	INTERPOL(Maddison)
87	Ecuador	1,400	1900(Maddison)
88	Sierra Leone	1,308	INTERPOL(Maddison)
89	Guatemala	1,300	1900(Maddison)
90	Zambia	1,272	INTERPOL(Maddison)
91	Latvia	1,210	PROXY(40(E)/USSR(Maddison))
92	South Sudan	1,173	INTERPOL(Maddison)
93	Laos	1,154	INTERPOL(Maddison)
94	Slovenia	1,006	PROXY(Yugoslavia(Maddison))

TABLE 1.10 POPULATION, THOUSANDS, YEAR 1900

Rank	Country	POP	Source
95	Kyrgyzstan	980	PROXY(40(E)/USSR(Maddison))
96	Tajikistan	978	PROXY(40(E)/USSR(Maddison))
97	Puerto Rico	959	1900(Maddison)
98	Uruguay	915	1900(Maddison)
99	Armenia	847	PROXY(40(E)/USSR(Maddison))
100	Macedonia	843	PROXY(Yugoslavia(Maddison))
101	Turkmenistan	835	PROXY(40(E)/USSR(Maddison))
102	New Zealand	807	1900(Maddison)
103	Albania	800	1900(Maddison)
104	El Salvador	766	1900(Maddison)
105	Libya	747	INTERPOL(Maddison/Mitchell)
106	Jamaica	720	1900(Maddison)
107	Mongolia	707	INTERPOL(Maddison)
108	Estonia	676	PROXY(40(E)/USSR(Maddison))
109	Eritrea	669	INTERPOL(Maddison)
110	Lebanon	591	INTERPOL(Maddison)
111	Kosovo	524	PROXY(Yugoslavia(Maddison))
112	Dominican R	515	1900(Maddison)
113	Honduras	500	1900(Maddison)
114	Nicaragua	478	1900(Maddison)
115	Paraguay	440	1900(Maddison)
116	Oman	419	INTERPOL(Maddison)
117	Guinea-Biss	386	INTERPOL(Maddison)
118	Israel	334	INTERPOL(Maddison)
119	Cyprus	324	PROXY(Greece(Maddison))
120	Jordan	321	INTERPOL(Maddison)
121	Lesotho	309	INTERPOL(Maddison)
122	Hong Kong	306	1900(Maddison)
123	Costa Rica	297	1900(Maddison)
124	Namibia	282	INTERPOL(Maddison)
125	Montenegro	272	PROXY(Yugoslavia(Maddison))
126	Trinidad & T	268	1900(Maddison)
127	Panama	263	1900(Maddison)
128	Botswana	241	INTERPOL(Maddison)
129	Singapore	215	1900(Maddison)
130	Swaziland	115	INTERPOL(Maddison)
131	Kuwait	97	INTERPOL(Maddison)
132	Iceland	78	1900(WIKI)
133	Bahrain	74	INTERPOL(Maddison)
134	UAE	48	INTERPOL(Maddison)
135	Qatar	17	INTERPOL(Maddison)

TABLE 1.11 POPULATION, THOUSANDS, YEAR 1913

Rank	Country	POP	Source
1	China	437,140	1913(Maddison)
2	India	251,906	1913(Maddison)
3	US	97,606	1913(Maddison)
4	Russia	88,606	PROXY(40(E)/USSR(Maddison))
5	Germany	65,058	1913(Maddison)
6	Japan	51,672	1913(Maddison)
7	Indonesia	49,934	1913(Maddison)
8	UK	42,624	PROXY(UK & Ireland(Maddison))
9	France	41,463	1913(Maddison)
10	Italy	37,248	1913(Maddison)
11	Ukraine	33,270	PROXY(40(E)/USSR(Maddison))
12	Bangladesh	31,786	1913(Maddison)
13	Poland	26,710	1913(Maddison)
14	Brazil	23,660	1913(Maddison)
15	Spain	20,263	1913(Maddison)
16	Pakistan	20,008	1913(Maddison)
17	Vietnam	19,339	1913(Maddison)
18	Turkey	15,000	1913(Maddison)
19	Mexico	14,970	1913(Maddison)
20	Romania	12,527	1913(Maddison)
21	Burma	12,326	1913(Maddison)
22	Egypt	12,186	1913(Mitchell)
23	Ethiopia	11,671	INTERPOL(Maddison)
24	Iran	10,994	1913(Maddison)
25	Korea, South	10,589	1913(Maddison)
26	Czechia	9,542	PROXY(Czechoslovakia(Maddison))
27	Philippines	9,384	1913(Maddison)
28	Thailand	8,689	1913(Maddison)
29	Canada	7,852	1913(Maddison)
30	Hungary	7,840	1913(Maddison)
31	Belgium	7,666	1913(Maddison)
32	Argentina	7,653	1913(Maddison)
33	Belarus	7,280	PROXY(40(E)/USSR(Maddison))
34	Austria	6,767	1913(Maddison)
35	Netherlands	6,164	1913(Maddison)
36	South Africa	6,153	1913(Maddison)
37	Portugal	5,972	1913(Maddison)
38	Sudan	5,866	INTERPOL(Maddison)
39	Afghanistan	5,730	1913(Maddison)
40	Nepal	5,639	1913(Maddison)
41	Sweden	5,621	1913(Maddison)
42	Algeria	5,497	1913(Maddison)
43	Greece	5,425	1913(Maddison)
44	Uzbekistan	5,272	PROXY(40(E)/USSR(Maddison))
45	Colombia	5,195	1913(Maddison)
46	Morocco	5,111	1913(Maddison)
47	Kazakhstan	4,948	PROXY(40(E)/USSR(Maddison))
48	Korea, North	4,897	1913(Maddison)

Table 1.11 Population, Thousands, Year 1913			
Rank	Country	POP	Source
49	Serbia	4,894	PROXY(Yugoslavia(Maddison))
50	Australia	4,821	1913(Maddison)
51	Sri Lanka	4,811	1913(Maddison)
52	Bulgaria	4,720	1913(Maddison)
53	Mozambique	4,580	INTERPOL(Maddison)
54	Peru	4,339	1913(Maddison)
55	Switzerland	3,864	1913(Maddison)
56	Slovakia	3,702	PROXY(Czechoslovakia(Maddison))
57	Taiwan	3,469	1913(Maddison)
58	Chile	3,431	1913(Maddison)
59	Yemen	3,284	1913(Maddison)
60	Madagascar	3,256	INTERPOL(Maddison)
61	Croatia	3,199	PROXY(Yugoslavia(Maddison))
62	Ireland	3,092	PROXY(whole Ireland(Maddison))
63	Malaysia	3,084	1913(Maddison)
64	Cambodia	3,070	1913(Maddison)
65	Finland	3,027	1913(Maddison)
66	Denmark	2,983	1913(Maddison)
67	Georgia	2,907	PROXY(40(E)/USSR(Maddison))
68	Venezuela	2,874	1913(Maddison)
69	Saudi Arabia	2,676	1913(Maddison)
70	Azerbaijan	2,635	PROXY(40(E)/USSR(Maddison))
71	Iraq	2,613	1913(Maddison)
72	Norway	2,447	1913(Maddison)
73	Cuba	2,431	1913(Maddison)
74	Lithuania	2,354	PROXY(40(E)/USSR(Maddison))
75	Bosnia	2,219	PROXY(Yugoslavia(Maddison))
76	Ghana	2,043	1913(Maddison)
77	Syria	1,994	1913(Maddison)
78	Moldova	1,986	PROXY(40(E)/USSR(Maddison))
79	Guinea	1,953	INTERPOL(Maddison)
80	Haiti	1,891	1913(Maddison)
81	Bolivia	1,881	1913(Maddison)
82	Tunisia	1,870	1913(Maddison)
83	Burundi	1,858	INTERPOL(Maddison)
84	Somalia	1,794	INTERPOL(Maddison)
85	Zimbabwe	1,704	INTERPOL(Maddison)
86	Ecuador	1,689	1913(Maddison)
87	Malawi	1,683	INTERPOL(Maddison)
88	Zambia	1,525	INTERPOL(Maddison)
89	Latvia	1,518	PROXY(40(E)/USSR(Maddison))
90	Guatemala	1,486	1913(Maddison)
91	Sierra Leone	1,450	INTERPOL(Maddison)
92	Laos	1,387	1913(Maddison)
93	Kyrgyzstan	1,230	PROXY(40(E)/USSR(Maddison))
94	Tajikistan	1,227	PROXY(40(E)/USSR(Maddison))
95	South Sudan	1,226	INTERPOL(Maddison)
96	Slovenia	1,223	PROXY(Yugoslavia(Maddison))
97	Puerto Rico	1,181	1913(Maddison)

Table 1.11 Population, Thousands, Year 1913			
Rank	Country	POP	Source
98	Uruguay	1,177	1913(Maddison)
99	New Zealand	1,122	1913(Maddison)
100	Armenia	1,062	PROXY(40(E)/USSR(Maddison))
101	Turkmenistan	1,048	PROXY(40(E)/USSR(Maddison))
102	Macedonia	1,026	PROXY(Yugoslavia(Maddison))
103	El Salvador	1,008	1913(Maddison)
104	Albania	898	1913(Maddison)
105	Estonia	848	PROXY(40(E)/USSR(Maddison))
106	Jamaica	837	1913(Maddison)
107	Eritrea	811	INTERPOL(Maddison)
108	Libya	788	INTERPOL(Maddison/Mitchell)
109	Dominican R	750	1913(Maddison)
110	Mongolia	725	1913(Maddison)
111	Honduras	660	1913(Maddison)
112	Lebanon	649	1913(Maddison)
113	Kosovo	637	PROXY(Yugoslavia(Maddison))
114	Paraguay	594	1913(Maddison)
115	Nicaragua	578	1913(Maddison)
116	Hong Kong	487	1913(Maddison)
117	Oman	444	1913(Maddison)
118	Guinea-Biss	427	INTERPOL(Maddison)
119	Israel	387	PROXY(Palestine(Maddison))
120	Lesotho	387	INTERPOL(Maddison)
121	Costa Rica	372	1913(Maddison)
122	Cyprus	354	PROXY(Greece(Maddison))
123	Trinidad & T	352	1913(Maddison)
124.5	Jordan	348	1913(Maddison)
124.5	Panama	348	1913(Maddison)
126	Montenegro	331	PROXY(Yugoslavia(Maddison))
127	Namibia	324	INTERPOL(Maddison)
128	Singapore	323	1913(Maddison)
129	Botswana	278	INTERPOL(Maddison)
130	Swaziland	144	INTERPOL(Maddison)
131	Kuwait	105	PROXY(Gulf Coast(Maddison))
132	Iceland	87	1913(WIKI)
133	Bahrain	79	PROXY(Gulf Coast(Maddison))
134	UAE	52	PROXY(Gulf Coast(Maddison))
135	Qatar	18	PROXY(Gulf Coast(Maddison))

TABLE 1.12 POPULATION, THOUSANDS, YEAR 1920			
Rank	Country	POP	Source
1	China	472,000	1920(Maddison)
2	India	253,309	INTERPOL(Ind./wh. India(Maddison))
3	US	106,881	1920(Maddison)
4	Russia	87,707	PROXY(40(E)/USSR(Maddison))
5	Germany	60,894	1920(Maddison)
6	Japan	55,818	1920(Maddison)
7	Indonesia	53,723	1920(Maddison)
8	UK	43,718	1920(Maddison)
9	France	39,000	1920(Maddison)
10	Italy	37,398	1920(Maddison)
11	Ukraine	32,933	PROXY(40(E)/USSR(Maddison))
12	Bangladesh	32,161	INTERPOL(Ban./wh. India(Maddison))
13	Brazil	27,404	1920(Maddison)
14	Poland	23,968	1920(Maddison)
15	Spain	21,232	1920(Maddison)
16	Vietnam	20,652	INTERPOL(Maddison)
17	Pakistan	20,477	INTERPOL(Pak./wh. India(Maddison))
18	Mexico	14,900	1920(Maddison)
19	Turkey	13,877	1923(Maddison)
20	Egypt	13,222	1920(Mitchell)
21	Burma	13,096	1920(Maddison)
22	Ethiopia	12,945	INTERPOL(Maddison)
23	Romania	12,340	1920(Maddison)
24	Iran	11,927	INTERPOL(Maddison)
25	Korea, South	11,804	1920(Maddison)
26	Philippines	10,725	1920(Maddison)
27	Thailand	9,802	1920(Maddison)
28	Czechia	9,350	PROXY(Czechoslovakia(Maddison))
29	Argentina	8,861	1920(Maddison)
30	Canada	8,798	1920(Maddison)
31	Hungary	7,950	1920(Maddison)
32	Belgium	7,552	1920(Maddison)
33	Belarus	7,206	PROXY(40(E)/USSR(Maddison))
34	South Africa	7,157	INTERPOL(Maddison)
35	Netherlands	6,848	1920(Maddison)
36	Austria	6,455	1920(Maddison)
37	Colombia	6,213	1920(Maddison)
38	Afghanistan	6,125	INTERPOL(Maddison)
39	Nepal	6,113	INTERPOL(Maddison)
40	Portugal	6,029	1920(Maddison)
41	Sudan	6,008	INTERPOL(Maddison)
42	Sweden	5,876	1920(Maddison)
43	Algeria	5,785	1920(Maddison)
44	Greece	5,700	1920(Maddison)
45	Morocco	5,683	INTERPOL(Maddison)
46	Korea, North	5,577	INTERPOL(Maddison)
47	Australia	5,358	1920(Maddison)

Table 1.12 Population, Thousands, Year 1920			
Rank	Country	POP	Source
48	Sri Lanka	5,250	1920(Maddison)
49	Uzbekistan	5,219	PROXY(40(E)/USSR(Maddison))
50	Bulgaria	5,072	1920(Maddison)
51	Kazakhstan	4,898	PROXY(40(E)/USSR(Maddison))
52	Mozambique	4,857	INTERPOL(Maddison)
53	Peru	4,667	1920(Maddison)
54	Serbia	4,473	PROXY(Yugoslavia(Maddison))
55	Switzerland	3,877	1920(Maddison)
56	Chile	3,827	1920(Maddison)
57	Taiwan	3,736	1920(Maddison)
58	Slovakia	3,628	PROXY(Czechoslovakia(Maddison))
59	Malaysia	3,545	1920(Maddison)
60	Yemen	3,525	INTERPOL(Maddison)
61	Madagascar	3,422	INTERPOL(Maddison)
62	Cambodia	3,296	INTERPOL(Maddison)
63	Denmark	3,242	1920(Maddison)
64	Finland	3,133	1920(Maddison)
65	Ireland	3,103	1920(Maddison)
66	Cuba	2,997	1920(Maddison)
67	Venezuela	2,992	1920(Maddison)
68	Iraq	2,991	INTERPOL(Maddison)
69	Croatia	2,924	PROXY(Yugoslavia(Maddison))
70	Georgia	2,877	PROXY(40(E)/USSR(Maddison))
71	Saudi Arabia	2,768	INTERPOL(Maddison)
72	Norway	2,625	1920(Maddison)
73	Azerbaijan	2,608	PROXY(40(E)/USSR(Maddison))
74	Ghana	2,447	INTERPOL(Maddison)
75	Lithuania	2,330	PROXY(40(E)/USSR(Maddison))
76	Syria	2,217	INTERPOL(Maddison)
77	Bolivia	2,136	1920(Maddison)
78	Haiti	2,124	1920(Maddison)
79	Tunisia	2,107	INTERPOL(Maddison)
80	Guinea	2,065	INTERPOL(Maddison)
81	Bosnia	2,028	PROXY(Yugoslavia(Maddison))
82	Moldova	1,966	PROXY(40(E)/USSR(Maddison))
83	Burundi	1,945	INTERPOL(Maddison)
84	Zimbabwe	1,879	INTERPOL(Maddison)
85	Somalia	1,875	INTERPOL(Maddison)
86	Malawi	1,855	INTERPOL(Maddison)
87	Ecuador	1,790	1920(Maddison)
88	Zambia	1,681	INTERPOL(Maddison)
89	Guatemala	1,597	1920(Maddison)
90	Sierra Leone	1,533	INTERPOL(Maddison)
91	Latvia	1,502	PROXY(40(E)/USSR(Maddison))
92	Laos	1,412	INTERPOL(Maddison)
93	Uruguay	1,371	1920(Maddison)
94	Puerto Rico	1,312	1920(Maddison)
95	South Sudan	1,256	INTERPOL(Maddison)
96	New Zealand	1,241	1920(Maddison)

TABLE 1.12 POPULATION, THOUSANDS, YEAR 1920			
Rank	Country	POP	Source
97	Kyrgyzstan	1,217	PROXY(40(E)/USSR(Maddison))
98	Tajikistan	1,215	PROXY(40(E)/USSR(Maddison))
99	El Salvador	1,170	1920(Maddison)
100	Slovenia	1,118	PROXY(Yugoslavia(Maddison))
101	Armenia	1,052	PROXY(40(E)/USSR(Maddison))
102	Turkmenistan	1,037	PROXY(40(E)/USSR(Maddison))
103	Macedonia	937	PROXY(Yugoslavia(Maddison))
104	Albania	932	1920(Maddison)
105	Eritrea	900	INTERPOL(Maddison)
106	Dominican R	879	1920(Maddison)
107	Jamaica	855	1920(Maddison)
108	Estonia	840	PROXY(40(E)/USSR(Maddison))
109	Libya	811	INTERPOL(Maddison/Mitchell)
110	Lebanon	755	INTERPOL(Maddison)
111	Mongolia	729	INTERPOL(Maddison)
112	Honduras	720	1920(Maddison)
113	Paraguay	699	1920(Maddison)
114	Hong Kong	648	1920(Maddison)
115	Nicaragua	640	1920(Maddison)
116	Kosovo	582	PROXY(Yugoslavia(Maddison))
117	Panama	487	1920(Maddison)
118	Israel	486	INTERPOL(Maddison)
119	Guinea-Biss	452	INTERPOL(Maddison)
120	Oman	446	INTERPOL(Maddison)
121	Lesotho	437	INTERPOL(Maddison)
122	Costa Rica	420	1920(Maddison)
123	Singapore	391	1920(Maddison)
124	Trinidad & T	389	1920(Maddison)
125	Cyprus	372	PROXY(Greece(Maddison))
126	Jordan	369	INTERPOL(Maddison)
127	Namibia	350	INTERPOL(Maddison)
128	Montenegro	303	PROXY(Yugoslavia(Maddison))
129	Botswana	300	INTERPOL(Maddison)
130	Swaziland	162	INTERPOL(Maddison)
131	Kuwait	111	INTERPOL(Maddison)
132	Iceland	94	1920(WIKI)
133	Bahrain	84	INTERPOL(Maddison)
134	UAE	55	INTERPOL(Maddison)
135	Qatar	19	INTERPOL(Maddison)

Table 1.13 Population, Thousands, Year 1929			
Rank	Country	POP	Source
1	China	487,273	1929(Maddison)
2	India	275,861	1929(Maddison)
3	US	122,245	1929(Maddison)
4	Russia	97,584	PROXY(40(E)/USSR(Maddison))
5	Germany	64,739	1929(Maddison)
6	Japan	63,244	1929(Maddison)
7	Indonesia	59,863	1929(Maddison)
8	UK	45,672	1929(Maddison)
9	France	41,230	1929(Maddison)
10	Italy	40,469	1929(Maddison)
11	Ukraine	36,641	PROXY(40(E)/USSR(Maddison))
12	Bangladesh	34,427	1929(Maddison)
13	Brazil	32,894	1929(Maddison)
14	Poland	27,856	1929(Maddison)
15	Spain	23,210	1929(Maddison)
16	Pakistan	22,812	1929(Maddison)
17	Vietnam	22,472	INTERPOL(Maddison)
18	Mexico	16,875	1929(Maddison)
19	Ethiopia	14,788	INTERPOL(Maddison)
20	Turkey	14,705	1929(Maddison)
21	Egypt	14,602	1929(Mitchell)
22	Burma	14,364	1929(Maddison)
23	Romania	13,952	1929(Maddison)
24	Korea, South	13,716	1929(Maddison)
25	Iran	13,245	INTERPOL(Maddison)
26	Philippines	12,890	1929(Maddison)
27	Thailand	12,058	1929(Maddison)
28	Argentina	11,592	1929(Maddison)
29	Canada	10,305	1929(Maddison)
30	Czechia	10,002	PROXY(Czechoslovakia(Maddison))
31	South Africa	8,693	INTERPOL(Maddison)
32	Hungary	8,583	1929(Maddison)
33	Belgium	8,032	1929(Maddison)
34	Belarus	8,018	PROXY(40(E)/USSR(Maddison))
35	Colombia	7,821	1929(Maddison)
36	Netherlands	7,782	1929(Maddison)
37	Nepal	6,783	INTERPOL(Maddison)
38	Portugal	6,701	1929(Maddison)
39	Afghanistan	6,673	INTERPOL(Maddison)
40	Austria	6,664	1929(Maddison)
41	Korea, North	6,592	INTERPOL(Maddison)
42	Morocco	6,513	INTERPOL(Maddison)
43	Algeria	6,431	INTERPOL(Maddison)
44	Australia	6,396	1929(Maddison)
45	Greece	6,275	1929(Maddison)
46	Sudan	6,197	INTERPOL(Maddison)
47	Sweden	6,113	1929(Maddison)
48	Bulgaria	5,950	1929(Maddison)

Table 1.13 Population, Thousands, Year 1929			
Rank	Country	POP	Source
49	Uzbekistan	5,806	PROXY(40(E)/USSR(Maddison))
50	Sri Lanka	5,669	1929(Maddison)
51	Kazakhstan	5,449	PROXY(40(E)/USSR(Maddison))
52	Peru	5,294	1929(Maddison)
53	Mozambique	5,239	INTERPOL(Maddison)
54	Serbia	5,111	PROXY(Yugoslavia(Maddison))
55	Taiwan	4,493	1929(Maddison)
56	Malaysia	4,316	1929(Maddison)
57	Chile	4,306	1929(Maddison)
58	Switzerland	4,022	1929(Maddison)
59	Slovakia	3,881	PROXY(Czechoslovakia(Maddison))
60	Yemen	3,862	INTERPOL(Maddison)
61	Cuba	3,742	1929(Maddison)
62	Madagascar	3,648	INTERPOL(Maddison)
63	Cambodia	3,612	INTERPOL(Maddison)
64	Iraq	3,559	INTERPOL(Maddison)
65	Denmark	3,518	1929(Maddison)
66	Finland	3,424	1929(Maddison)
67	Croatia	3,342	PROXY(Yugoslavia(Maddison))
68	Venezuela	3,259	1929(Maddison)
69	Georgia	3,201	PROXY(40(E)/USSR(Maddison))
70	Ghana	3,085	INTERPOL(Maddison)
71	Ireland	2,937	1929(Maddison)
72	Azerbaijan	2,902	PROXY(40(E)/USSR(Maddison))
73	Saudi Arabia	2,892	INTERPOL(Maddison)
74	Norway	2,795	1929(Maddison)
75	Lithuania	2,593	PROXY(40(E)/USSR(Maddison))
76	Syria	2,542	INTERPOL(Maddison)
77	Tunisia	2,457	INTERPOL(Maddison)
78	Haiti	2,390	1929(Maddison)
79	Bolivia	2,370	1929(Maddison)
80	Bosnia	2,317	PROXY(Yugoslavia(Maddison))
81	Guinea	2,217	INTERPOL(Maddison)
82	Moldova	2,187	PROXY(40(E)/USSR(Maddison))
83	Zimbabwe	2,130	INTERPOL(Maddison)
84	Malawi	2,103	INTERPOL(Maddison)
85	Burundi	2,062	INTERPOL(Maddison)
86	Somalia	1,984	INTERPOL(Maddison)
87	Ecuador	1,928	1929(Maddison)
88	Zambia	1,906	INTERPOL(Maddison)
89	Guatemala	1,753	1929(Maddison)
90	Uruguay	1,685	1929(Maddison)
91	Latvia	1,672	PROXY(40(E)/USSR(Maddison))
92	Sierra Leone	1,646	INTERPOL(Maddison)
93	Puerto Rico	1,526	1929(Maddison)
94	New Zealand	1,471	1929(Maddison)
95	Laos	1,445	INTERPOL(Maddison)
96	El Salvador	1,410	1929(Maddison)
97	Kyrgyzstan	1,354	PROXY(40(E)/USSR(Maddison))

Table 1.13 Population, Thousands, Year 1929			
Rank	Country	POP	Source
98	Tajikistan	1,352	PROXY(40(E)/USSR(Maddison))
99	South Sudan	1,295	INTERPOL(Maddison)
100	Slovenia	1,278	PROXY(Yugoslavia(Maddison))
101	Dominican R	1,213	1929(Maddison)
102	Armenia	1,170	PROXY(40(E)/USSR(Maddison))
103	Turkmenistan	1,154	PROXY(40(E)/USSR(Maddison))
104	Macedonia	1,071	PROXY(Yugoslavia(Maddison))
105	Eritrea	1,028	INTERPOL(Maddison)
106	Jamaica	985	1929(Maddison)
107	Albania	977	1929(Maddison)
108	Estonia	934	PROXY(40(E)/USSR(Maddison))
109	Honduras	930	1929(Maddison)
110	Lebanon	917	INTERPOL(Maddison)
111	Paraguay	860	1929(Maddison)
112	Libya	841	INTERPOL(Maddison/Mitchell)
113	Hong Kong	785	1929(Maddison)
114	Mongolia	734	INTERPOL(Maddison)
115	Nicaragua	680	1929(Maddison)
116	Kosovo	665	PROXY(Yugoslavia(Maddison))
117	Israel	650	INTERPOL(Maddison)
118	Singapore	575	1929(Maddison)
119	Lesotho	510	INTERPOL(Maddison)
120	Panama	506	1929(Maddison)
121	Costa Rica	490	1929(Maddison)
122	Guinea-Biss	485	INTERPOL(Maddison)
123	Oman	449	INTERPOL(Maddison)
124	Cyprus	410	PROXY(Greece(Maddison))
125	Trinidad & T	398	1929(Maddison)
126	Jordan	397	INTERPOL(Maddison)
127	Namibia	386	INTERPOL(Maddison)
128	Montenegro	346	PROXY(Yugoslavia(Maddison))
129	Botswana	331	INTERPOL(Maddison)
130	Swaziland	190	INTERPOL(Maddison)
131	Kuwait	120	INTERPOL(Maddison)
132	Iceland	106	1929(WIKI)
133	Bahrain	91	INTERPOL(Maddison)
134	UAE	60	INTERPOL(Maddison)
135	Qatar	21	INTERPOL(Maddison)

TABLE 1.14 POPULATION, THOUSANDS, YEAR 1938			
Rank	Country	POP	Source
1	China	513,336	1938(Maddison)
2	India	309,434	INTERPOL(Ind./wh. India(Maddison))
3	US	130,476	1938(Maddison)
4	Russia	106,933	PROXY(40(E)/USSR(Maddison))
5	Japan	71,879	1938(Maddison)
6	Germany	68,558	1938(Maddison)
7	Indonesia	68,131	1938(Maddison)
8	UK	47,494	1938(Maddison)
9	Italy	43,419	1938(Maddison)
10	France	41,960	1938(Maddison)
11	Ukraine	40,152	PROXY(40(E)/USSR(Maddison))
12	Bangladesh	39,934	INTERPOL(Ban./wh. India(Maddison))
13	Brazil	39,480	1938(Maddison)
14	Poland	31,062	1938(Maddison)
15	Pakistan	26,719	INTERPOL(Pak./wh. India(Maddison))
16	Spain	25,279	1938(Maddison)
17	Vietnam	24,452	INTERPOL(Maddison)
18	Mexico	19,705	1938(Maddison)
19	Turkey	17,016	1938(Maddison)
20	Ethiopia	16,894	INTERPOL(Maddison)
21	Egypt	16,295	1938(Mitchell)
22	Burma	16,145	1938(Maddison)
23	Philippines	15,934	1938(Maddison)
24	Romania	15,601	1938(Maddison)
25	Korea, South	15,381	1938(Maddison)
26	Thailand	14,980	1938(Maddison)
27	Iran	14,708	INTERPOL(Maddison)
28	Argentina	13,724	1938(Maddison)
29	Canada	11,452	1938(Maddison)
30	South Africa	10,559	INTERPOL(Maddison)
31	Czechia	10,520	PROXY(Czechoslovakia(Maddison))
32	Hungary	9,167	1938(Maddison)
33	Belarus	8,786	PROXY(40(E)/USSR(Maddison))
34	Colombia	8,702	1938(Maddison)
35	Netherlands	8,685	1938(Maddison)
36	Belgium	8,374	1938(Maddison)
37	Korea, North	7,791	INTERPOL(Maddison)
38	Nepal	7,525	INTERPOL(Maddison)
39	Portugal	7,488	1938(Maddison)
40	Morocco	7,465	INTERPOL(Maddison)
41	Algeria	7,326	INTERPOL(Maddison)
42	Afghanistan	7,271	INTERPOL(Maddison)
43	Greece	7,061	1938(Maddison)
44	Australia	6,904	1938(Maddison)
45	Austria	6,753	1938(Maddison)

Table 1.14 Population, Thousands, Year 1938			
Rank	Country	POP	Source
46	Bulgaria	6,564	1938(Maddison)
47	Sudan	6,391	INTERPOL(Maddison)
48	Uzbekistan	6,363	PROXY(40(E)/USSR(Maddison))
49	Sweden	6,298	1938(Maddison)
50	Peru	6,093	1938(Maddison)
51	Sri Lanka	6,045	1938(Maddison)
52	Kazakhstan	5,971	PROXY(40(E)/USSR(Maddison))
53	Serbia	5,792	PROXY(Yugoslavia(Maddison))
54	Taiwan	5,678	1938(Maddison)
55	Mozambique	5,650	INTERPOL(Maddison)
56	Malaysia	5,207	1938(Maddison)
57	Chile	4,915	1938(Maddison)
58	Cuba	4,428	1938(Maddison)
59	Iraq	4,235	INTERPOL(Maddison)
60	Yemen	4,230	INTERPOL(Maddison)
61	Switzerland	4,192	1938(Maddison)
62	Slovakia	4,082	PROXY(Czechoslovakia(Maddison))
63	Cambodia	3,958	INTERPOL(Maddison)
64	Ghana	3,889	INTERPOL(Maddison)
65	Madagascar	3,888	INTERPOL(Maddison)
66	Croatia	3,787	PROXY(Yugoslavia(Maddison))
67	Denmark	3,777	1938(Maddison)
68	Finland	3,656	1938(Maddison)
69	Venezuela	3,623	1938(Maddison)
70	Georgia	3,508	PROXY(40(E)/USSR(Maddison))
71	Azerbaijan	3,180	PROXY(40(E)/USSR(Maddison))
72	Saudi Arabia	3,020	INTERPOL(Maddison)
73	Ireland	2,937	1938(Maddison)
74	Norway	2,936	1938(Maddison)
75	Syria	2,913	INTERPOL(Maddison)
76	Tunisia	2,865	INTERPOL(Maddison)
77	Lithuania	2,841	PROXY(40(E)/USSR(Maddison))
78	Haiti	2,682	1938(Maddison)
79	Bolivia	2,629	1938(Maddison)
80	Bosnia	2,626	PROXY(Yugoslavia(Maddison))
81	Zimbabwe	2,414	INTERPOL(Maddison)
82	Moldova	2,397	PROXY(40(E)/USSR(Maddison))
83	Malawi	2,383	INTERPOL(Maddison)
84	Guinea	2,381	INTERPOL(Maddison)
85	Ecuador	2,355	1938(Maddison)
86	Burundi	2,186	INTERPOL(Maddison)
87	Zambia	2,160	INTERPOL(Maddison)
88	Guatemala	2,110	1938(Maddison)
89	Somalia	2,100	INTERPOL(Maddison)
90	Uruguay	1,952	1938(Maddison)
91	Latvia	1,832	PROXY(40(E)/USSR(Maddison))
92	Puerto Rico	1,810	1938(Maddison)
93	Sierra Leone	1,768	INTERPOL(Maddison)
94	New Zealand	1,604	1938(Maddison)

Table 1.14 Population, Thousands, Year 1938			
Rank	Country	POP	Source
95	Dominican R	1,596	1938(Maddison)
96	El Salvador	1,590	1938(Maddison)
97	Kyrgyzstan	1,484	PROXY(40(E)/USSR(Maddison))
98	Tajikistan	1,481	PROXY(40(E)/USSR(Maddison))
99	Hong Kong	1,479	1938(Maddison)
100	Laos	1,478	INTERPOL(Maddison)
101	Slovenia	1,448	PROXY(Yugoslavia(Maddison))
102	South Sudan	1,336	INTERPOL(Maddison)
103	Armenia	1,282	PROXY(40(E)/USSR(Maddison))
104	Turkmenistan	1,265	PROXY(40(E)/USSR(Maddison))
105	Macedonia	1,214	PROXY(Yugoslavia(Maddison))
106	Eritrea	1,174	INTERPOL(Maddison)
107	Jamaica	1,163	1938(Maddison)
108	Lebanon	1,114	INTERPOL(Maddison)
109	Honduras	1,100	1938(Maddison)
110	Paraguay	1,061	1938(Maddison)
111	Albania	1,040	1938(Maddison)
112	Estonia	1,024	PROXY(40(E)/USSR(Maddison))
113	Libya	873	INTERPOL(Mitchell/E)
114	Israel	871	INTERPOL(Maddison)
115	Nicaragua	780	1938(Maddison)
116	Kosovo	754	PROXY(Yugoslavia(Maddison))
117	Mongolia	740	INTERPOL(Maddison)
118	Singapore	710	1938(Maddison)
119	Panama	640	1938(Maddison)
120	Lesotho	596	INTERPOL(Maddison)
121	Costa Rica	590	1938(Maddison)
122	Guinea-Biss	521	INTERPOL(Maddison)
123	Cyprus	461	PROXY(Greece(Maddison))
124	Trinidad & T	458	1938(Maddison)
125	Oman	452	INTERPOL(Maddison)
126	Jordan	428	INTERPOL(Maddison)
127	Namibia	426	INTERPOL(Maddison)
128	Montenegro	392	PROXY(Yugoslavia(Maddison))
129	Botswana	365	INTERPOL(Maddison)
130	Swaziland	222	INTERPOL(Maddison)
131	Kuwait	130	INTERPOL(Maddison)
132	Iceland	118	1938(WIKI)
133	Bahrain	99	INTERPOL(Maddison)
134	UAE	65	INTERPOL(Maddison)
135	Qatar	22	INTERPOL(Maddison)

Table 1.15 Population, Thousands, Year 1950			
Rank	Country	POP	Source
1	China	562,580	50(E)
2	India	369,880	50(E)
3	US	152,271	50(E)
4	Russia	101,937	50(E)
5	Japan	83,625	50(E)
6	Indonesia	79,538	50(E)
7	Germany	68,377	50(E)
8	Brazil	53,975	50(E)
9	UK	50,290	50(E)
10	Italy	47,104	50(E)
11	Bangladesh	45,646	50(E)
12	France	41,736	50(E)
13	Pakistan	39,448	50(E)
14	Ukraine	36,906	50(E)
15	Nigeria	31,797	50(E)
16	Spain	27,868	50(E)
17	Mexico	27,741	50(E)
18	Vietnam	27,367	50(E)
19	Poland	24,824	50(E)
20	Turkey	21,484	50(E)
21	Korea, South	20,846	50(E)
22	Thailand	20,607	50(E)
23	Egypt	20,461	50(E)
24	Ethiopia	20,175	50(E)
25	Philippines	19,996	50(E)
26	Burma	19,488	50(E)
27	Argentina	17,150	50(E)
28	Iran	16,913	50(E)
29	Romania	16,311	50(E)
30	Canada	14,011	50(E)
31	South Africa	13,596	50(E)
32	Congo, Dem R	13,569	50(E)
33	Colombia	12,568	50(E)
34	Netherlands	10,090	50(E)
35	Korea, North	9,737	50(E)
36	Hungary	9,338	50(E)
37	Morocco	8,953	50(E)
38	Czechia	8,925	50(E)
39	Algeria	8,753	50(E)
40	Nepal	8,643	50(E)
41	Belgium	8,639	50(E)
42	Portugal	8,443	50(E)
43	Australia	8,219	50(E)
44	Afghanistan	8,151	50(E)
45	Tanzania	7,935	50(E)
46	Belarus	7,745	50(E)
47	Peru	7,632	50(E)
48	Taiwan	7,619	50(E)
49	Sudan	7,601	PROXY(Sudan+S.Sudan)

Table 1.15 Population, Thousands, Year 1950			
Rank	Country	POP	Source
50	Greece	7,566	50(E)
51	Sri Lanka	7,339	50(E)
52	Bulgaria	7,251	50(E)
53	Sweden	7,014	50(E)
54	Austria	6,935	50(E)
55	Kazakhstan	6,693	50(E)
56	Uzbekistan	6,293	50(E)
57	Mozambique	6,250	50(E)
58	Kenya	6,121	50(E)
59	Malaysia	6,110	50(E)
60	Chile	6,091	50(E)
61	Cuba	5,920	50(E)
62	Serbia	5,869	50(E)
63	Iraq	5,340	50(E)
64	Ghana	5,297	50(E)
65	Uganda	5,158	50(E)
66	Venezuela	5,094	50(E)
67	Cameroon	4,888	50(E)
68	Yemen	4,777	50(E)
69	Switzerland	4,694	50(E)
70	Cambodia	4,471	50(E)
71	Burkina Faso	4,376	50(E)
72	Denmark	4,271	50(E)
73	Madagascar	4,234	50(E)
74	Angola	4,118	50(E)
75	Finland	4,009	50(E)
76	Croatia	3,837	50(E)
77	Mali	3,688	50(E)
78	Georgia	3,527	50(E)
79	Tunisia	3,517	50(E)
80	Syria	3,495	50(E)
81	Slovakia	3,463	50(E)
82	Ecuador	3,387	50(E)
83	Norway	3,265	50(E)
84	Haiti	3,221	50(E)
85	Saudi Arabia	3,201	50(E)
86.5	Guatemala	2,969	50(E)
86.5	Ireland	2,969	50(E)
88	Azerbaijan	2,885	50(E)
89	Zimbabwe	2,853	50(E)
90	Malawi	2,817	50(E)
91	Bolivia	2,714	50(E)
92	Bosnia	2,661	50(E)
93	Guinea	2,619	50(E)
94	Chad	2,608	50(E)
95.5	Lithuania	2,553	50(E)
95.5	Zambia	2,553	50(E)
97	Senegal	2,543	50(E)
98	Ivory Coast	2,505	50(E)

TABLE 1.15 POPULATION, THOUSANDS, YEAR 1950			
Rank	Country	POP	Source
99	Burundi	2,363	50(E)
100	Dominican R	2,353	50(E)
101	Moldova	2,341	50(E)
102	Somalia	2,264	50(E)
103	Uruguay	2,239	50(E)
104	Hong Kong	2,237	50(E)
105	Puerto Rico	2,218	50(E)
106	Niger	2,208	50(E)
107	Rwanda	2,162	50(E)
108	El Salvador	1,951	50(E)
109	Latvia	1,949	50(E)
110	Sierra Leone	1,944	50(E)
111	New Zealand	1,909	50(E)
112	Kyrgyzstan	1,740	50(E)
113	Benin	1,673	50(E)
114	South Sudan	1,589	PROXY(Sudan+S.Sudan)
115	Tajikistan	1,532	50(E)
116	Laos	1,524	50(E)
117	Papua New G	1,485	50(EST)
118	Paraguay	1,473	50(E)
119	Slovenia	1,467	50(E)
120	Lebanon	1,443	50(E)
121	Honduras	1,431	50(E)
122	Jamaica	1,403	50(E)
123	Eritrea	1,402	50(E)
124	Armenia	1,354	50(E)
125	Togo	1,329	50(E)
126	CAR	1,314	50(E)
127	Nicaragua	1,295	50(E)
128	Israel	1,258	50(E)
129	Macedonia	1,230	50(E)
130	Albania	1,215	50(E)
131	Turkmenistan	1,204	50(E)
132	Estonia	1,096	50(E)
133	Libya	1,029	50(E)
134	Singapore	1,022	50(E)
135	Panama	893	50(E)
136	Costa Rica	862	50(E)
137	Liberia	824	50(E)
138	Congo, Rep	808	50(E)
139	West Bank	772	50(W Bank/(E)) Gaza(Maddison)-Gaza
140	Kosovo	764	50(E)
141	Mongolia	747	50(E)
142	Lesotho	734	50(E)
143	Mauritania	692	50(E)
144	Trinidad & T	668	50(E)
145	Guinea-Biss	573	50(E)
146	Cyprus	494	50(E)

Table 1.15 Population, Thousands, Year 1950			
Rank	Country	POP	Source
147	Mauritius	479	50(E)
148	Jordan	472	50(E)
149	Namibia	464	50(E)
150	Oman	456	50(E)
151	East Timor	435	50(E)
152	Botswana	430	50(E)
153	Guyana	423	50(E)
154	Gabon	416	50(E)
155	Montenegro	397	50(E)
156	Malta	312	50(E)
157	Luxembourg	296	50(E)
158	Gambia	294	50(E)
159	Fiji	289	50(E)
160	Swaziland	273	50(E)
161	Gaza Strip	245	50(E)
162	Reunion	244	50(E)
163	Martinique	222	50(E)
164	Suriname	215	50(E)
165.5	Barbados	211	50(E)
165.5	Equatorial G	211	50(E)
167	Guadeloupe	208	50(Maddison)
168	Macao	205	50(E)
169	Bhutan	168	50(E)
170	Comoros	148	50(E)
171	Cape Verde	146	50(E)
172	Kuwait	145	50(E)
173	Iceland	143	50(E)
174	Bahrain	110	50(E)
175	Curacao	102	00(WB)WEIGHT(Neth Antilles(50(E)))
176	Solomon Is	90	50(E)
177	St Lucia	83	50(E)
178	Samoa	82	50(E)
179.5	Bahamas	79	50(E)
179.5	Maldives	79	50(E)
181	Grenada	76	50(E)
182	UAE	72	50(E)
183	Belize	68	50(E)
184	St Vincent	67	50(E)
185	New Caledon	65	50(E)
186	Fr Polynesia	62	50(E)
188	Djibouti	60	50(E)
188	Guam	60	50(E)
188	Sao Tome & P	60	50(E)
190	Jersey	57	50(E)
191	Isle of Man	55	50(E)
192.5	Aruba	51	50(E)
192.5	Dominica	51	50(E)
194	Tonga	50	50(E)
195	St Kitts & N	49	50(E)

TABLE 1.15 POPULATION, THOUSANDS, YEAR 1950			
Rank	Country	POP	Source
196	Vanuatu	48	50(E)
197	Antigua & B	46	50(E)
198	Brunei	45	50(E)
199	Guernsey	44	50(E)
200	Bermuda	39	50(E)
201	Seychelles	34	50(E)
202	Kiribati	33	50(E)
203	Micronesia	32	50(E)
204	Faroe Is	31	50(E)
205.5	Guiana, Fr	27	50(E)
205.5	Virgin I, US	27	50(E)
207	Qatar	25	50(E)
208.5	Gibraltar	23	50(E)
208.5	Greenland	23	50(E)
210	Samoa, Amer	19	50(E)
211	Monaco	18	50(E)
212	Mayotte	17	50(E)
213.5	Liechtenstn	14	50(E)
213.5	W Sahara	14	50(E)
215	San Marino	13	50(E)
216	Marshall Is	11	50(E)
217	Palau	7	50(E)
218	Saint Helena	7	PROXY(Falkland Islands(E))
219	Cook Is	7	PROXY(14 Pacific is(Maddison))
221	Andorra	6	50(E)
221	Cayman Is	6	50(E)
221	N Mariana Is	6	50(E)
223	Montserrat	6	PROXY(8 Caribbean cs(Maddison))
224	Virgin I, Br	6	PROXY(8 Caribbean cs(Maddison))
225	Wallis & Fut	5	PROXY(14 Pacific is(Maddison))
226	Tuvalu	5	50(E)
227	Turks & C Is	5	PROXY(8 Caribbean cs(Maddison))
228	Saint Martin	4	60(WB)WEIGHT(Neth Antilles(50(E)))
229	Anguilla	3	PROXY(8 Caribbean cs(Maddison))
230	Svalbard	3	PROXY(Norway(E))
231	Nauru	3	50(E)
232	St Pierre&M	3	PROXY(8 Caribbean cs(Maddison))
233	Sint Maarten	2	60(E)WEIGHT(Neth Antilles(50(E)))
234	Falkland Is	2	50(E)
235	Niue	1	PROXY(14 Pacific is(Maddison))
236	Tokelau	1	PROXY(14 Pacific is(Maddison))

Table 1.16 Population, Thousands, Year 1960

Rank	Country	POP	Source
1	China	658,270	60(E)
2	India	447,844	60(E)
3	US	180,671	60(E)
4	Russia	119,906	60(E)
5	Japan	92,501	60(E)
6	Indonesia	91,947	60(E)
7	Germany	73,147	60(E)
8	Brazil	72,742	60(E)
9	Bangladesh	54,593	60(E)
10	UK	52,372	60(E)
11	Pakistan	51,719	60(E)
12	Italy	49,519	60(E)
13	Nigeria	45,926	60(E)
14	France	45,689	60(E)
15	Ukraine	42,783	60(E)
16	Mexico	38,419	60(E)
17	Vietnam	31,656	60(E)
18	Spain	30,641	60(E)
19	Poland	29,561	60(E)
20	Egypt	27,903	60(E)
21	Thailand	27,513	60(E)
22	Turkey	27,506	60(E)
23	Philippines	27,057	60(E)
24	Korea, South	25,074	60(E)
25	Burma	22,839	60(E)
26	Ethiopia	22,553	60(E)
27	Iran	21,999	60(E)
28	Argentina	20,685	60(E)
29	Romania	18,407	60(E)
30	Canada	17,909	60(E)
31	South Africa	17,396	60(E)
32	Colombia	15,953	60(E)
33	Congo, Dem R	15,368	60(E)
34	Morocco	12,423	60(E)
35	Netherlands	11,494	60(E)
36	Korea, North	10,946	60(E)
37	Algeria	10,800	60(E)
38	Taiwan	10,668	60(E)
39	Australia	10,315	60(E)
40	Tanzania	10,074	60(E)
41	Nepal	10,035	60(E)
42	Sri Lanka	10,020	60(E)
43	Kazakhstan	9,982	60(E)
44	Hungary	9,961	60(E)
45	Peru	9,931	60(E)
46	Afghanistan	9,829	60(E)
47	Czechia	9,539	60(E)

TABLE 1.16 POPULATION, THOUSANDS, YEAR 1960			
Rank	Country	POP	Source
48	Belgium	9,153	60(E)
49	Portugal	9,037	60(E)
50	Sudan	8,758	PROXY(Sudan+S.Sudan)
51	Uzbekistan	8,531	60(E)
52	Malaysia	8,428	60(E)
53	Greece	8,333	60(E)
54	Belarus	8,190	60(E)
55	Kenya	8,157	60(E)
56	Bulgaria	7,867	60(E)
57	Chile	7,652	60(E)
58	Venezuela	7,562	60(E)
59	Sweden	7,498	60(E)
60	Mozambique	7,472	60(E)
61	Iraq	7,380	60(E)
62	Uganda	7,262	60(E)
63	Cuba	7,077	60(E)
64	Austria	7,047	60(E)
65	Ghana	6,958	60(E)
66	Serbia	6,659	60(E)
67	Yemen	5,872	60(E)
68	Cambodia	5,761	60(E)
69	Cameroon	5,409	60(E)
70	Switzerland	5,328	60(E)
71	Madagascar	5,104	60(E)
72	Angola	5,012	60(E)
73	Burkina Faso	4,882	60(E)
74	Saudi Arabia	4,718	60(E)
75	Denmark	4,585	60(E)
76	Syria	4,567	60(E)
77	Mali	4,495	60(E)
78	Ecuador	4,439	60(E)
79	Finland	4,430	60(E)
80	Tunisia	4,221	60(E)
81.5	Georgia	4,159	60(E)
81.5	Guatemala	4,159	60(E)
83	Slovakia	4,145	60(E)
84	Croatia	4,036	60(E)
85	Zimbabwe	4,011	60(E)
86	Azerbaijan	3,894	60(E)
87	Haiti	3,697	60(E)
88	Norway	3,583	60(E)
89	Ivory Coast	3,576	60(E)
90	Guinea	3,541	60(E)
91	Malawi	3,525	60(E)
92	Bolivia	3,355	60(E)
93	Dominican R	3,294	60(E)
94	Senegal	3,270	60(E)
95	Zambia	3,254	60(E)

Table 1.16 Population, Thousands, Year 1960

Rank	Country	POP	Source
96	Niger	3,250	60(E)
97	Bosnia	3,180	60(E)
98	Hong Kong	3,076	60(E)
99	Moldova	3,004	60(E)
100	Somalia	2,956	60(E)
101	Chad	2,954	60(E)
102	Burundi	2,940	60(E)
103	Ireland	2,832	60(E)
104	Rwanda	2,771	60(E)
105	Lithuania	2,765	60(E)
106	El Salvador	2,582	60(E)
107	Uruguay	2,538	60(E)
108	Benin	2,420	60(E)
109	New Zealand	2,377	60(E)
110	Puerto Rico	2,358	60(E)
111	Sierra Leone	2,187	60(E)
112	Kyrgyzstan	2,173	60(E)
113	Latvia	2,132	60(E)
114	Laos	2,130	60(E)
115	Israel	2,090	60(E)
116	Tajikistan	2,082	60(E)
117	Honduras	2,000	60(E)
118	Paraguay	1,910	60(E)
119	Armenia	1,867	60(E)
120	South Sudan	1,831	PROXY(Sudan+S.Sudan)
121	Lebanon	1,786	60(E)
122	Nicaragua	1,773	60(E)
123	Papua New G	1,718	60(E)
124	Singapore	1,634	60(E)
125	Jamaica	1,629	60(E)
126	Albania	1,611	60(E)
127	Turkmenistan	1,585	60(E)
128	Slovenia	1,580	60(E)
129	Togo	1,578	60(E)
130	CAR	1,467	60(E)
131	Eritrea	1,424	60(E)
132	Macedonia	1,392	60(E)
133	Libya	1,349	60(E)
134	Costa Rica	1,277	60(E)
135	Estonia	1,216	60(E)
136	Panama	1,136	60(E)
137	Mauritania	1,117	60(E)
138	Liberia	1,116	60(E)
139	Congo, Rep	1,014	60(E)
140	Kosovo	947	60(E)
141	Mongolia	931	60(E)
142	Jordan	895	60(E)
143	Lesotho	859	60(E)

Table 1.16 Population, Thousands, Year 1960

Rank	Country	POP	Source
144	Trinidad & T	828	60(E)
145	West Bank	805	60(W Bank/Gaza(Maddison)-Gaza(E))
146	Mauritius	662	60(E)
147	Namibia	603	60(E)
148	Oman	601	60(E)
149	Guinea-Biss	593	60(E)
150	Cyprus	579	60(E)
151	Guyana	560	60(E)
152	Botswana	524	60(E)
153	East Timor	509	60(E)
154	Gabon	486	60(E)
155	Montenegro	467	60(E)
156	Fiji	393	60(E)
157	Gambia	352	60(E)
158	Swaziland	349	60(E)
159	Reunion	338	60(E)
160	Luxembourg	314	60(E)
161	Malta	313	60(E)
162	Gaza Strip	308	60(E)
163	Kuwait	292	60(E)
164	Suriname	290	60(E)
165	Martinique	282	60(E)
166	Guadeloupe	266	60(E)
167	Equatorial G	252	60(E)
168	Barbados	232	60(E)
169	Bhutan	212	60(E)
170	Cape Verde	211	60(E)
171	Comoros	193	60(E)
172	Iceland	176	60(E)
173	Macao	173	60(E)
174	Bahrain	149	60(E)
175	Curacao	124	60(E)
176	Solomon Is	118	60(E)
177.5	Bahamas	110	60(E)
177.5	Samoa	110	60(E)
179	Maldives	99	60(E)
181.5	Belize	90	60(E)
181.5	Grenada	90	60(E)
181.5	St Lucia	90	60(E)
181.5	UAE	90	60(E)
184	Djibouti	85	60(E)
185	Brunei	82	60(E)
186	St Vincent	81	60(E)
187.5	Fr Polynesia	79	60(E)
187.5	New Caledon	79	60(E)
189	Guam	67	60(E)
190	Tonga	65	60(E)
191.5	Sao Tome & P	64	60(E)

TABLE 1.16 POPULATION, THOUSANDS, YEAR 1960

Rank	Country	POP	Source
191.5	Vanuatu	64	60(E)
193	Jersey	63	60(E)
194	Dominica	60	60(E)
195	Aruba	57	60(E)
196	Antigua & B	55	60(E)
197	St Kitts & N	51	60(E)
198	Isle of Man	48	60(E)
200	Guernsey	45	60(E)
200	Micronesia	45	60(E)
200	Qatar	45	60(E)
202	Bermuda	44	60(E)
203.5	Kiribati	41	60(E)
203.5	Seychelles	41	60(E)
205	Faroe Is	34	60(E)
206.5	Greenland	33	60(E)
206.5	Virgin I, US	33	60(E)
208	Guiana, Fr	32	60(E)
209	W Sahara	28	60(E)
210	Mayotte	25	60(E)
211	Gibraltar	24	60(E)
212	Monaco	21	60(E)
213	Samoa, Amer	20	60(E)
214	Liechtenstn	16	60(E)
215.5	Marshall Is	15	60(E)
215.5	San Marino	15	60(E)
217.5	N Mariana Is	9	60(E)
217.5	Palau	9	60(E)
219	Cook Is	9	INTERPOL(14 Pacific is(Maddison))
220.5	Andorra	8	60(E)
220.5	Cayman Is	8	60(E)
222	Montserrat	7	INTERPOL(8 Caribbean cs(Maddison))
223	Virgin I, Br	7	INTERPOL(8 Caribbean is(Maddison))
224	Wallis & Fut	7	INTERPOL(14 Pacific is(Maddison))
225	Saint Helena	7	PROXY(Falkland Islands(E))
226	Turks & C Is	6	60(WB)
227	Tuvalu	5	60(E)
228	Saint Martin	4	60(WB)
229	Anguilla	4	INTERPOL(8 Caribbean cs(Maddison))
230	Nauru	4	60(E)
231	St Pierre&M	4	INTERPOL(8 Caribbean cs(Maddison))
232	Svalbard	3	PROXY(Norway(E))
233	Sint Maarten	3	60(E)
234	Falkland Is	2	60(E)
235	Niue	1	INTERPOL(14 Pacific is(Maddison))
236	Tokelau	1	INTERPOL(14 Pacific is(Maddison))

Table 1.17 Population, Thousands, Year 1970

Rank	Country	POP	Source
1	China	814,623	70(E)
2	India	553,874	70(E)
3	US	204,879	70(E)
4	Russia	130,392	70(E)
5	Indonesia	118,362	70(E)
6	Japan	103,710	70(E)
7	Brazil	95,989	70(E)
8	Germany	78,069	70(E)
9	Pakistan	67,491	70(E)
10	Bangladesh	67,331	70(E)
11	Nigeria	57,357	70(E)
12	UK	55,632	70(E)
13	Italy	53,325	70(E)
14	Mexico	51,868	70(E)
15	France	50,763	70(E)
16	Ukraine	47,317	70(E)
17	Vietnam	42,577	70(E)
18	Thailand	37,091	70(E)
19	Philippines	36,567	70(E)
20	Egypt	35,575	70(E)
21	Turkey	35,231	70(E)
22	Spain	33,876	70(E)
23	Poland	32,526	70(E)
24	Korea, South	31,443	70(E)
25	Ethiopia	28,959	70(E)
26	Iran	28,662	70(E)
27	Burma	27,393	70(E)
28	Argentina	24,003	70(E)
29	South Africa	22,502	70(E)
30	Canada	21,717	70(E)
31	Colombia	21,430	70(E)
32	Congo, Dem R	20,267	70(E)
33	Romania	20,253	70(E)
34	Morocco	15,909	70(E)
35	Taiwan	14,583	70(E)
36	Korea, North	14,247	70(E)
37	Algeria	13,746	70(E)
38	Tanzania	13,605	70(E)
39	Peru	13,193	70(E)
40	Kazakhstan	13,106	70(E)
41	Netherlands	13,020	70(E)
42	Sri Lanka	12,555	70(E)
43	Australia	12,552	70(E)
44	Afghanistan	12,431	70(E)
45	Uzbekistan	11,940	70(E)
46	Nepal	11,919	70(E)

TABLE 1.17 POPULATION, THOUSANDS, YEAR 1970

Rank	Country	POP	Source
47	Sudan	11,404	PROXY(Sudan+S.Sudan)
48	Kenya	11,247	70(E)
49	Malaysia	10,910	70(E)
50	Venezuela	10,681	70(E)
51	Hungary	10,301	70(E)
52	Iraq	10,022	70(E)
53	Czechia	9,805	70(E)
54	Uganda	9,715	70(E)
55	Belgium	9,690	70(E)
56	Chile	9,578	70(E)
57	Mozambique	9,304	70(E)
58	Portugal	9,044	70(E)
59	Belarus	9,040	70(E)
60	Greece	8,793	70(E)
61	Ghana	8,789	70(E)
62	Cuba	8,603	70(E)
63	Bulgaria	8,490	70(E)
64	Sweden	8,042	70(E)
65	Austria	7,467	70(E)
66	Cambodia	7,394	70(E)
67	Serbia	7,248	70(E)
68	Yemen	7,098	70(E)
69	Cameroon	6,842	70(E)
70	Madagascar	6,549	70(E)
71	Syria	6,368	70(E)
72	Switzerland	6,181	70(E)
73	Saudi Arabia	6,109	70(E)
74	Angola	6,083	70(E)
75	Ecuador	5,972	70(E)
76	Burkina Faso	5,807	70(E)
77	Ivory Coast	5,579	70(E)
78	Mali	5,546	70(E)
79	Zimbabwe	5,515	70(E)
80	Guatemala	5,448	70(E)
81	Azerbaijan	5,172	70(E)
82	Tunisia	5,127	70(E)
83	Denmark	4,938	70(E)
84	Georgia	4,707	70(E)
85	Finland	4,606	70(E)
86	Haiti	4,541	70(E)
87	Malawi	4,531	70(E)
88	Slovakia	4,528	70(E)
89	Dominican R	4,502	70(E)
90	Niger	4,373	70(E)
91	Senegal	4,318	70(E)
92	Zambia	4,248	70(E)
93	Bolivia	4,217	70(E)

Table 1.17 Population, Thousands, Year 1970

Rank	Country	POP	Source
94	Croatia	4,205	70(E)
95	Guinea	4,154	70(E)
96	Hong Kong	3,958	70(E)
97	Norway	3,877	70(E)
98	Rwanda	3,749	70(E)
99	Somalia	3,667	70(E)
100	Chad	3,656	70(E)
101	El Salvador	3,604	70(E)
102	Moldova	3,595	70(E)
103	Bosnia	3,564	70(E)
104	Burundi	3,513	70(E)
105	Lithuania	3,138	70(E)
106	Kyrgyzstan	2,964	70(E)
107	Ireland	2,950	70(E)
108	Tajikistan	2,942	70(E)
109.5	Benin	2,850	70(E)
109.5	Israel	2,850	70(E)
111	New Zealand	2,820	70(E)
112	Uruguay	2,809	70(E)
113	Puerto Rico	2,722	70(E)
114	Laos	2,691	70(E)
115	Honduras	2,688	70(E)
116	Sierra Leone	2,593	70(E)
117	Armenia	2,518	70(E)
118	Paraguay	2,477	70(E)
119	Nicaragua	2,398	70(E)
120	South Sudan	2,384	PROXY(Sudan+S.Sudan)
121	Lebanon	2,383	70(E)
122	Latvia	2,366	70(E)
123	Papua New G	2,214	70(E)
124	Turkmenistan	2,181	70(E)
125	Albania	2,136	70(E)
126	Togo	2,097	70(E)
127	Singapore	2,074	70(E)
128	Libya	1,994	70(E)
129	Jamaica	1,869	70(E)
130	Eritrea	1,847	70(E)
131	CAR	1,839	70(E)
132	Costa Rica	1,780	70(E)
133	Slovenia	1,670	70(E)
134	Jordan	1,667	70(E)
135	Macedonia	1,568	70(E)
136	Panama	1,524	70(E)
137	Liberia	1,440	70(E)
138	Estonia	1,365	70(E)
139	Congo, Rep	1,335	70(E)
140	Mauritania	1,289	70(E)

Table 1.17 Population, Thousands, Year 1970

Rank	Country	POP	Source
141	Mongolia	1,248	70(E)
142	Kosovo	1,219	70(E)
143	Lesotho	1,067	70(E)
144	Trinidad & T	941	70(E)
145	Mauritius	829	70(E)
146	Oman	783	70(E)
147	Namibia	780	70(E)
148	Kuwait	748	70(E)
149	Guyana	721	70(E)
150	Botswana	693	70(E)
151	Cyprus	627	70(E)
152	West Bank	608	70(E)
153	Guinea-Biss	603	70(E)
154	East Timor	598	70(E)
155	Gabon	530	70(E)
156	Fiji	521	70(E)
157	Montenegro	519	70(E)
158	Gambia	485	70(E)
159	Reunion	447	70(E)
160	Swaziland	446	70(E)
161	Suriname	372	70(E)
162	Gaza Strip	343	70(E)
163	Luxembourg	339	70(E)
164	Martinique	325	70(E)
165	Guadeloupe	310	70(E)
166	Bhutan	309	70(E)
167	Malta	304	70(E)
168	Equatorial G	291	70(E)
169	Cape Verde	274	70(E)
170	Macao	254	70(E)
171	Barbados	239	70(E)
172	Comoros	238	70(E)
173	UAE	232	70(E)
174	Bahrain	210	70(E)
175	Iceland	204	70(E)
176	Bahamas	170	70(E)
177	Djibouti	162	70(E)
178	Solomon Is	160	70(E)
179	Curacao	145	70(E)
180	Samoa	142	70(E)
181	Brunei	130	70(E)
182	Maldives	121	70(E)
183	Belize	120	70(E)
184	New Caledon	112	70(E)
185.5	Fr Polynesia	111	70(E)
185.5	Qatar	111	70(E)
187	St Lucia	104	70(E)

Table 1.17 Population, Thousands, Year 1970

Rank	Country	POP	Source
188	Grenada	95	70(E)
189	W Sahara	89	70(E)
190	St Vincent	88	70(E)
191	Vanuatu	86	70(E)
192	Guam	85	70(E)
193	Tonga	80	70(E)
194	Sao Tome & P	74	70(E)
195	Dominica	70	70(E)
196	Jersey	69	70(E)
197	Antigua & B	66	70(E)
198	Virgin I, US	63	70(E)
199.5	Aruba	61	70(E)
199.5	Micronesia	61	70(E)
201.5	Bermuda	53	70(E)
201.5	Isle of Man	53	70(E)
203	Seychelles	52	70(E)
204	Guernsey	51	70(E)
205.5	Guiana, Fr	49	70(E)
205.5	Kiribati	49	70(E)
207.5	Greenland	46	70(E)
207.5	St Kitts & N	46	70(E)
209	Faroe Is	39	70(E)
210	Mayotte	35	70(E)
211	Samoa, Amer	27	70(E)
212	Gibraltar	26	70(E)
213	Monaco	24	70(E)
214	Marshall Is	22	70(E)
215	Liechtenstn	21	70(E)
216	Andorra	20	70(E)
217	San Marino	19	70(E)
218.5	N Mariana Is	12	70(E)
218.5	Palau	12	70(E)
220	Cook Is	11	INTERPOL(14 Pacific is(Maddison))
221	Cayman Is	10	70(E)
222	Wallis & Fut	9	INTERPOL(14 Pacific is(Maddison))
223	Montserrat	9	INTERPOL(8 Caribbean cs(Maddison))
224	Virgin I, Br	9	INTERPOL(8 Caribbean cs(Maddison))
225	Nauru	7	70(E)
226	Saint Helena	7	PROXY(Falkland Islands(E))
227	Sint Maarten	6	70(E)
228	Tuvalu	6	70(E)
229	Turks & C Is	6	70(WB)
230	Saint Martin	5	70(WB)

Table 1.17 Population, Thousands, Year 1970

Rank	Country	POP	Source
231	Anguilla	5	INTERPOL(8 Caribbean cs(Maddison))
232	St Pierre&M	5	INTERPOL(8 Caribbean cs(Maddison))
233	Svalbard	4	PROXY(Norway(E))
234	Falkland Is	2	70(E)
235	Niue	1	INTERPOL(14 Pacific is(Maddison))
236	Tokelau	1	INTERPOL(14 Pacific is(Maddison))

Table 1.18 Population, Thousands, Year 1980			
Rank	Country	POP	Source
1	China	983,171	80(E)
2	India	700,059	80(E)
3	US	227,726	80(E)
4	Indonesia	150,820	80(E)
5	Russia	138,655	80(E)
6	Brazil	118,563	80(E)
7	Japan	115,915	80(E)
8	Bangladesh	87,937	80(E)
9	Pakistan	85,219	80(E)
10	Germany	78,397	80(E)
11	Nigeria	75,543	80(E)
12	Mexico	68,776	80(E)
13	UK	56,330	80(E)
14	Italy	56,221	80(E)
15	France	53,880	80(E)
16	Vietnam	53,715	80(E)
17	Ukraine	50,034	80(E)
18	Philippines	48,112	80(E)
19	Thailand	47,026	80(E)
20	Egypt	44,952	80(E)
21	Turkey	44,439	80(E)
22	Iran	38,577	80(E)
23	Spain	37,488	80(E)
24	Korea, South	37,460	80(E)
25	Poland	35,578	80(E)
26	Ethiopia	35,426	80(E)
27	Burma	33,336	80(E)
28	South Africa	29,075	80(E)
29	Argentina	28,154	80(E)
30	Congo, Dem R	27,019	80(E)
31	Colombia	26,631	80(E)
32	Canada	24,516	80(E)
33	Romania	22,201	80(E)
34	Morocco	19,487	80(E)
35	Algeria	18,811	80(E)
36	Tanzania	18,686	80(E)
37	Taiwan	17,642	80(E)
38	Peru	17,295	80(E)
39	Korea, North	17,239	80(E)
40	Kenya	16,331	80(E)
41	Sudan	16,114	PROXY(Sudan+S.Sudan)
42	Uzbekistan	15,994	80(E)
43	Sri Lanka	15,083	80(E)
44	Afghanistan	15,044	80(E)
45	Venezuela	15,036	80(E)

Table 1.18 Population, Thousands, Year 1980			
Rank	Country	POP	Source
46	Kazakhstan	15,000	80(E)
47	Nepal	14,665	80(E)
48	Australia	14,471	80(E)
49	Netherlands	14,150	80(E)
50	Iraq	13,744	80(E)
51	Malaysia	13,460	80(E)
52	Mozambique	12,103	80(E)
53	Uganda	12,020	80(E)
54	Chile	11,179	80(E)
55	Ghana	11,011	80(E)
56	Hungary	10,709	80(E)
57	Czechia	10,326	80(E)
58	Saudi Arabia	10,022	80(E)
59	Belgium	9,859	80(E)
60	Portugal	9,778	80(E)
61	Cuba	9,694	80(E)
62	Belarus	9,650	80(E)
63	Greece	9,643	80(E)
64	Yemen	9,133	80(E)
65	Cameroon	9,110	80(E)
66	Syria	8,907	80(E)
67	Bulgaria	8,862	80(E)
68	Madagascar	8,609	80(E)
69	Ivory Coast	8,593	80(E)
70	Sweden	8,310	80(E)
71	Ecuador	7,958	80(E)
72	Angola	7,854	80(E)
73	Serbia	7,588	80(E)
74	Austria	7,549	80(E)
75	Burkina Faso	7,212	80(E)
76	Zimbabwe	7,170	80(E)
77	Guatemala	7,036	80(E)
78	Cambodia	6,889	80(E)
79	Mali	6,822	80(E)
80	Tunisia	6,457	80(E)
81	Switzerland	6,319	80(E)
82	Malawi	6,240	80(E)
83	Azerbaijan	6,161	80(E)
84	Niger	5,871	80(E)
85	Dominican R	5,808	80(E)
86	Somalia	5,794	80(E)
87	Zambia	5,643	80(E)
88	Senegal	5,611	80(E)
89	Haiti	5,508	80(E)
90	Bolivia	5,353	80(E)
91	Rwanda	5,179	80(E)
92	Denmark	5,107	80(E)
93	Georgia	5,073	80(E)

Table 1.18 Population, Thousands, Year 1980			
Rank	Country	POP	Source
94	Hong Kong	5,054	80(E)
95	Slovakia	4,976	80(E)
96	Finland	4,799	80(E)
97	El Salvador	4,570	80(E)
98	Chad	4,554	80(E)
99	Guinea	4,407	80(E)
100	Croatia	4,383	80(E)
101	Burundi	4,130	80(E)
102	Norway	4,086	80(E)
103	Moldova	4,010	80(E)
104	Tajikistan	3,953	80(E)
105	Bosnia	3,914	80(E)
106	Israel	3,746	80(E)
107	Honduras	3,628	80(E)
108	Kyrgyzstan	3,627	80(E)
109	Benin	3,611	80(E)
110	Lithuania	3,436	80(E)
111	Ireland	3,401	80(E)
112	South Sudan	3,368	PROXY(Sudan+S.Sudan)
113	Nicaragua	3,242	80(E)
114	Laos	3,235	80(E)
115	Puerto Rico	3,210	80(E)
116	Paraguay	3,172	80(E)
117	Sierra Leone	3,162	80(E)
118	New Zealand	3,144	80(E)
119	Armenia	3,096	80(E)
120	Libya	3,063	80(E)
121	Uruguay	2,915	80(E)
122	Lebanon	2,899	80(E)
123	Turkmenistan	2,875	80(E)
124	Papua New G	2,846	80(E)
125	Albania	2,671	80(E)
126	Togo	2,667	80(E)
127	Latvia	2,513	80(E)
128	Eritrea	2,469	80(E)
129	Singapore	2,415	80(E)
130	CAR	2,349	80(E)
131	Costa Rica	2,316	80(E)
132	Jordan	2,299	80(E)
133	Jamaica	2,132	80(E)
134	Panama	1,982	80(E)
135	Liberia	1,923	80(E)
136	Slovenia	1,832	80(E)
137	Congo, Rep	1,798	80(E)
138	Macedonia	1,795	80(E)
139	Mongolia	1,663	80(E)
140	Mauritania	1,545	80(E)
141	Kosovo	1,521	80(E)

TABLE 1.18 POPULATION, THOUSANDS, YEAR 1980			
Rank	Country	POP	Source
142	Estonia	1,473	80(E)
143	Kuwait	1,370	80(E)
144	Lesotho	1,359	80(E)
145	Oman	1,185	80(E)
146	Trinidad & T	1,082	80(E)
147	UAE	1,016	80(E)
148	Namibia	1,013	80(E)
149	Botswana	996	80(E)
150	Mauritius	966	80(E)
151	Guinea-Biss	835	80(E)
152	Guyana	777	80(E)
153	West Bank	733	80(E)
154	Gabon	683	80(E)
155	Cyprus	658	80(E)
156	Gambia	652	80(E)
157	Fiji	635	80(E)
158	Swaziland	603	80(E)
159	Montenegro	576	80(E)
160	East Timor	557	80(E)
161	Reunion	507	80(E)
162	Gaza Strip	456	80(E)
163	Bhutan	446	80(E)
164	Suriname	366	80(E)
165	Luxembourg	364	80(E)
166	Djibouti	340	80(E)
167	Bahrain	334	80(E)
168	Comoros	329	80(E)
169	Malta	327	80(E)
170	Martinique	326	80(E)
171	Guadeloupe	318	80(E)
172	Cape Verde	300	80(E)
173.5	Barbados	252	80(E)
173.5	Macao	252	80(E)
175.5	Qatar	229	80(E)
175.5	Solomon Is	229	80(E)
177	Iceland	228	80(E)
178	Equatorial G	221	80(E)
179	Bahamas	210	80(E)
180	Brunei	193	80(E)
181	Maldives	158	80(E)
182	Samoa	155	80(E)
183	Fr Polynesia	151	80(E)
184	Curacao	148	80(E)
185	Belize	146	80(E)
186	New Caledon	139	80(E)
187	W Sahara	124	80(E)
188	St Lucia	118	80(E)
189	Vanuatu	117	80(E)

TABLE 1.18 POPULATION, THOUSANDS, YEAR 1980			
Rank	Country	POP	Source
190	Guam	107	80(E)
191	St Vincent	98	80(E)
192	Virgin I, US	97	80(E)
193	Sao Tome & P	95	80(E)
194	Tonga	92	80(E)
195	Grenada	90	80(E)
196	Jersey	76	80(E)
197	Dominica	74	80(E)
198	Micronesia	73	80(E)
199	Antigua & B	69	80(E)
200	Guiana, Fr	68	80(E)
201	Isle of Man	64	80(E)
202	Seychelles	63	80(E)
203	Aruba	60	80(E)
204	Kiribati	58	80(E)
205	Bermuda	55	80(E)
206	Guernsey	53	80(E)
207	Mayotte	52	80(E)
208	Greenland	50	80(E)
209	St Kitts & N	44	80(E)
210	Faroe Is	43	80(E)
211	Andorra	34	80(E)
212	Samoa, Amer	32	80(E)
213	Marshall Is	31	80(E)
214	Gibraltar	30	80(E)
215	Monaco	27	80(E)
216	Liechtenstn	25	80(E)
217	San Marino	21	80(E)
218.5	Cayman Is	17	80(E)
218.5	N Mariana Is	17	80(E)
220	Cook Is	14	INTERPOL(14 Pacific is(Maddison))
221	Palau	13	80(E)
222	Sint Maarten	12	80(E)
223	Wallis & Fut	12	INTERPOL(14 Pacific is(Maddison))
224	Montserrat	11	INTERPOL(8 Caribbean cs(Maddison))
225	Virgin I, Br	11	INTERPOL(8 Caribbean cs(Maddison))
226.5	Nauru	8	80(E)
226.5	Tuvalu	8	80(E)
228	Saint Martin	8	80(WB)
229	Turks & C Is	8	80(WB)
230	Saint Helena	7	PROXY(Falkland Islands(E))
231	Anguilla	6	INTERPOL(8 Caribbean cs(Maddison))
232	St Pierre&M	6	INTERPOL(8 Caribbean cs(Maddison))
233	Svalbard	4	PROXY(Norway(E))
234	Falkland Is	2	80(E)
235	Niue	2	INTERPOL(14 Pacific is(Maddison))
236	Tokelau	1	INTERPOL(14 Pacific is(Maddison))

TABLE 1.19 POPULATION, THOUSANDS, YEAR 1990			
Rank	Country	POP	Source
1	China	1,145,195	90(E)
2	India	873,785	90(E)
3	US	249,806	90(E)
4	Indonesia	184,346	90(E)
5	Russia	148,244	90(E)
6	Brazil	146,593	90(E)
7	Japan	122,251	90(E)
8	Pakistan	118,816	90(E)
9	Bangladesh	111,437	90(E)
10	Nigeria	97,552	90(E)
11	Mexico	84,307	90(E)
12	Germany	79,753	90(E)
13	Vietnam	67,258	90(E)
14	Philippines	60,939	90(E)
15	UK	57,237	90(E)
16	Egypt	56,843	90(E)
17	Italy	56,832	90(E)
18	France	56,708	90(E)
19	Thailand	55,197	90(E)
20	Turkey	55,120	90(E)
21	Iran	54,871	90(E)
22	Ukraine	51,892	90(E)
23	Ethiopia	48,333	90(E)
24	Korea, South	42,980	90(E)
25	Burma	40,464	90(E)
26	Spain	39,351	90(E)
27	Poland	38,031	90(E)
28	South Africa	36,745	90(E)
29	Congo, Dem R	36,406	90(E)
30	Colombia	33,147	90(E)
31	Argentina	32,498	90(E)
32	Canada	27,701	90(E)
33	Tanzania	25,479	90(E)
34	Algeria	25,299	90(E)
35	Morocco	24,000	90(E)
36	Kenya	23,361	90(E)
37	Romania	23,207	90(E)
38	Peru	21,565	90(E)
39	Sudan	21,412	PROXY(Sudan+S.Sudan)
40	Uzbekistan	20,530	90(E)
41	Taiwan	20,279	90(E)
42	Korea, North	20,143	90(E)
43	Venezuela	19,685	90(E)
44	Nepal	18,918	90(E)
45	Malaysia	17,882	90(E)
46	Iraq	17,374	90(E)
47	Sri Lanka	17,337	90(E)

Table 1.19 Population, Thousands, Year 1990			
Rank	Country	POP	Source
48	Australia	17,065	90(E)
49	Kazakhstan	16,775	90(E)
50	Uganda	16,549	90(E)
51	Saudi Arabia	16,061	90(E)
52	Ghana	15,408	90(E)
53	Netherlands	14,952	90(E)
54	Afghanistan	13,568	90(E)
55	Chile	13,188	90(E)
56	Mozambique	12,989	90(E)
57	Ivory Coast	12,491	90(E)
58	Yemen	12,416	90(E)
59	Syria	12,324	90(E)
60	Cameroon	12,181	90(E)
61	Madagascar	11,281	90(E)
62	Cuba	10,662	90(E)
63	Angola	10,661	90(E)
64	Hungary	10,374	90(E)
65	Czechia	10,363	90(E)
66	Ecuador	10,261	90(E)
67	Belarus	10,186	90(E)
68	Greece	10,161	90(E)
69	Zimbabwe	10,156	90(E)
70	Belgium	9,967	90(E)
71	Portugal	9,923	90(E)
72	Malawi	9,381	90(E)
73	Cambodia	9,368	90(E)
74	Burkina Faso	9,324	90(E)
75	Guatemala	8,923	90(E)
76	Bulgaria	8,718	90(E)
77	Sweden	8,559	90(E)
78	Mali	8,327	90(E)
79	Tunisia	8,215	90(E)
80	Zambia	7,858	90(E)
81	Niger	7,788	90(E)
82	Serbia	7,786	90(E)
83	Austria	7,678	90(E)
84	Senegal	7,348	90(E)
85	Azerbaijan	7,212	90(E)
86	Dominican R	7,179	90(E)
87	Rwanda	7,110	90(E)
88	Haiti	6,798	90(E)
89	Switzerland	6,712	90(E)
90	Somalia	6,692	90(E)
91	Bolivia	6,658	90(E)
92	Chad	6,011	90(E)
93	Hong Kong	5,794	90(E)
94	Guinea	5,759	90(E)
95	Burundi	5,602	90(E)

Table 1.19 Population, Thousands, Year 1990			
Rank	Country	POP	Source
96	Georgia	5,439	90(E)
97	Tajikistan	5,303	90(E)
98	Slovakia	5,256	90(E)
99	Denmark	5,135	90(E)
100	El Salvador	5,110	90(E)
101	Finland	4,986	90(E)
102	Honduras	4,889	90(E)
103	Benin	4,773	90(E)
104	Croatia	4,508	90(E)
105	Israel	4,500	90(E)
106	South Sudan	4,476	PROXY(Sudan+S.Sudan)
107	Kyrgyzstan	4,395	90(E)
108	Moldova	4,364	90(E)
109	Libya	4,334	90(E)
110	Bosnia	4,308	90(E)
111	Norway	4,241	90(E)
112	Paraguay	4,200	90(E)
113	Laos	4,192	90(E)
114	Nicaragua	4,121	90(E)
115	Sierra Leone	3,982	90(E)
116	Lithuania	3,698	90(E)
117	Papua New G	3,683	90(E)
118	Togo	3,666	90(E)
119	Turkmenistan	3,658	90(E)
120	Armenia	3,545	90(E)
121	Puerto Rico	3,537	90(E)
122	Ireland	3,506	90(E)
123	New Zealand	3,452	90(E)
124	Lebanon	3,440	90(E)
125	Jordan	3,416	90(E)
126	Albania	3,289	90(E)
127	Eritrea	3,158	90(E)
128	Uruguay	3,109	90(E)
129	CAR	3,085	90(E)
130	Costa Rica	3,057	90(E)
131	Singapore	3,017	90(E)
132	Latvia	2,664	90(E)
133	Panama	2,474	90(E)
134	Congo, Rep	2,389	90(E)
135	Jamaica	2,365	90(E)
136	Kuwait	2,131	90(E)
137	Liberia	2,127	90(E)
138	Mongolia	2,086	90(E)
139	Slovenia	1,927	90(E)
140	Mauritania	1,925	90(E)
141	Macedonia	1,909	90(E)
142	Kosovo	1,862	90(E)
143	UAE	1,809	90(E)

Table 1.19 Population, Thousands, Year 1990			
Rank	Country	POP	Source
144	Oman	1,794	90(E)
145	Lesotho	1,703	90(E)
146	Estonia	1,568	90(E)
147	Namibia	1,415	90(E)
148	Botswana	1,382	90(E)
149	Trinidad & T	1,235	90(E)
150	Mauritius	1,059	90(E)
151	Guinea-Biss	1,017	90(E)
152	West Bank	1,011	90(E)
153	Gambia	951	90(E)
154	Gabon	929	90(E)
155	Swaziland	863	90(E)
156	Cyprus	751	90(E)
157	East Timor	746	90(E)
158	Fiji	728	90(E)
159	Guyana	725	90(E)
160	Gaza Strip	646	90(E)
161	Bhutan	615	90(E)
162	Montenegro	609	90(E)
163	Reunion	601	90(E)
164	Djibouti	562	90(E)
165	Bahrain	503	90(E)
166	Qatar	467	90(E)
167	Comoros	438	90(E)
168	Suriname	407	90(E)
169	Luxembourg	381	90(E)
170	Equatorial G	374	90(E)
171	Macao	372	90(E)
172	Malta	368	90(E)
173	Martinique	360	90(E)
174	Guadeloupe	355	90(E)
175	Cape Verde	348	90(E)
176	Solomon Is	310	90(E)
177	Barbados	263	90(E)
178	Bahamas	256	90(E)
179	Iceland	255	90(E)
180	Brunei	253	90(E)
181	W Sahara	217	90(E)
182	Maldives	216	90(E)
183	Fr Polynesia	195	90(E)
184	Belize	189	90(E)
185	New Caledon	169	90(E)
186	Samoa	161	90(E)
187	Vanuatu	149	90(E)
188	Curacao	145	90(E)
189	St Lucia	138	90(E)
190	Guam	134	90(E)
191	Guiana, Fr	117	90(E)

Table 1.19 Population, Thousands, Year 1990			
Rank	Country	POP	Source
192	Sao Tome & P	116	90(E)
193	St Vincent	107	90(E)
194	Virgin I, US	102	90(E)
195.5	Micronesia	96	90(E)
195.5	Tonga	96	90(E)
197	Grenada	94	90(E)
198	Mayotte	89	90(E)
199	Jersey	84	90(E)
200.5	Kiribati	71	90(E)
200.5	Seychelles	71	90(E)
202	Dominica	70	90(E)
203	Isle of Man	69	90(E)
204	Antigua & B	64	90(E)
205	Aruba	63	90(E)
206	Guernsey	61	90(E)
207	Bermuda	58	90(E)
208	Greenland	56	90(E)
209	Andorra	53	90(E)
210	Faroe Is	48	90(E)
211	Samoa, Amer	47	90(E)
212.5	Marshall Is	44	90(E)
212.5	N Mariana Is	44	90(E)
214	St Kitts & N	42	90(E)
215	Gibraltar	31	90(E)
216	Saint Martin	30	90(WB)
217	Monaco	30	90(E)
218	Sint Maarten	29	90(E)
219	Liechtenstn	29	90(E)
220	Cayman Is	26	90(E)
221	San Marino	24	90(E)
222	Cook Is	18	90(CIA)
223	Palau	15	90(E)
224	Wallis & Fut	15	90(CIA)
225	Montserrat	12	90(CIA)
226	Virgin I, Br	12	90(CIA)
227	Turks & C Is	12	90(WB)
228.5	Nauru	9	90(E)
228.5	Tuvalu	9	90(E)
230	Anguilla	7	90(CIA)
231	Saint Helena	7	90(CIA)
232	St Pierre&M	6	90(CIA)
233	Svalbard	4	90(CIA)
234	Niue	2	90(CIA)
235	Falkland Is	2	90(E)
236	Tokelau	2	90(CIA)

Rank	Country	POP	Source
1	China	1,262,600	00(E)
2	India	1,053,898	00(E)
3	US	282,385	00(E)
4	Indonesia	206,265	00(E)
5	Brazil	169,421	00(E)
6	Pakistan	152,429	00(E)
7	Russia	146,670	00(E)
8	Bangladesh	129,592	00(E)
9	Japan	126,861	00(E)
10	Nigeria	124,208	00(E)
11	Mexico	98,439	00(E)
12	Germany	82,197	00(E)
13	Vietnam	77,631	00(E)
14	Philippines	76,748	00(E)
15	Iran	65,458	00(E)
16	Turkey	64,252	00(E)
17	Egypt	63,974	00(E)
18	Ethiopia	61,856	00(E)
19	Thailand	61,022	00(E)
20	France	59,045	00(E)
21	UK	58,887	00(E)
22	Italy	57,646	00(E)
23	Congo, Dem R	49,626	00(E)
24	Ukraine	49,177	00(E)
25	Burma	47,439	00(E)
26	Korea, South	46,059	00(E)
27	South Africa	44,872	00(E)
28	Spain	40,589	00(E)
29	Colombia	38,910	00(E)
30	Poland	38,230	00(E)
31	Argentina	36,120	00(E)
32	Tanzania	34,038	00(E)
33	Canada	30,667	00(E)
34	Kenya	30,606	00(E)
35	Algeria	30,129	00(E)
36	Morocco	28,113	00(E)
37	Sudan	27,067	00(E)
38	Peru	25,797	00(E)
39	Nepal	24,818	00(E)
40	Uzbekistan	24,488	00(E)
41	Venezuela	24,311	00(E)
42	Iraq	23,857	00(E)
43	Uganda	22,916	00(E)
44	Korea, North	22,785	00(E)
45	Romania	22,435	00(E)
46	Malaysia	22,198	00(E)
47	Taiwan	22,185	00(E)

TABLE 1.20 POPULATION, THOUSANDS, YEAR 2000			
Rank	Country	POP	Source
48	Saudi Arabia	21,312	00(E)
49	Afghanistan	20,016	00(E)
50	Ghana	19,043	00(E)
51	Sri Lanka	18,745	00(E)
52	Australia	18,572	00(E)
53	Mozambique	17,997	00(E)
54	Yemen	17,723	00(E)
55	Ivory Coast	16,885	00(E)
56	Syria	15,989	00(E)
57	Netherlands	15,926	00(E)
58	Madagascar	15,712	00(E)
59	Cameroon	15,678	00(E)
60	Chile	15,420	00(E)
61	Kazakhstan	14,884	00(E)
62	Angola	12,683	00(E)
63	Cambodia	12,351	00(E)
64	Ecuador	12,345	00(E)
65	Burkina Faso	12,294	00(E)
66	Zimbabwe	11,820	00(E)
67	Guatemala	11,237	00(E)
68	Malawi	11,229	00(E)
69	Cuba	11,146	00(E)
70	Greece	10,987	00(E)
71	Niger	10,922	00(E)
72	Mali	10,788	00(E)
73	Belgium	10,251	00(E)
74	Portugal	10,235	00(E)
75	Hungary	10,211	00(E)
76	Czechia	10,208	00(E)
77	Zambia	9,984	00(E)
78	Belarus	9,974	00(E)
79	Tunisia	9,553	00(E)
80	Senegal	9,469	00(E)
81	Sweden	8,872	00(E)
82	Haiti	8,413	00(E)
83	Guinea	8,344	00(E)
84	Dominican R	8,328	00(E)
85	Bolivia	8,307	00(E)
86	Chad	8,222	00(E)
87	Austria	8,187	00(E)
88	Rwanda	8,098	00(E)
89	Azerbaijan	8,074	00(E)
90	Bulgaria	7,973	00(E)
91	Serbia	7,516	00(E)
92	Somalia	7,501	00(E)
93	Switzerland	7,184	00(E)
94	Hong Kong	6,665	00(E)
95	Benin	6,518	00(E)
96	Burundi	6,374	00(E)

Table 1.20 Population, Thousands, Year 2000			
Rank	Country	POP	Source
97	South Sudan	6,296	00(E)
98	Honduras	6,218	00(E)
99	Tajikistan	6,181	00(E)
100	Israel	6,098	00(E)
101	El Salvador	5,850	00(E)
102	Paraguay	5,418	00(E)
103	Slovakia	5,401	00(E)
104	Denmark	5,330	00(E)
105	Laos	5,245	00(E)
106	Papua New G	5,191	00(E)
107	Finland	5,176	00(E)
108	Nicaragua	5,074	00(E)
109	Libya	5,025	00(E)
110	Kyrgyzstan	4,883	00(E)
111	Jordan	4,798	00(E)
112	Togo	4,629	00(E)
113	Norway	4,491	00(E)
114	Croatia	4,453	00(E)
115	Georgia	4,418	00(E)
116	Turkmenistan	4,385	00(E)
117	Moldova	4,223	00(E)
118	Sierra Leone	4,143	00(E)
119	Singapore	4,028	00(E)
120	CAR	3,980	00(E)
121	New Zealand	3,860	00(E)
122.5	Costa Rica	3,811	00(E)
122.5	Puerto Rico	3,811	00(E)
124	Ireland	3,801	00(E)
125	Lebanon	3,791	00(E)
126	Bosnia	3,781	00(E)
127	Eritrea	3,668	00(E)
128	Lithuania	3,500	00(E)
129	Uruguay	3,220	00(E)
130	Congo, Rep	3,136	00(E)
131	Armenia	3,076	00(E)
132	Albania	3,065	00(E)
133	Panama	3,041	00(E)
134	UAE	3,033	00(E)
135	Liberia	2,847	00(E)
136	Jamaica	2,582	00(E)
137	Mauritania	2,501	00(E)
138	Mongolia	2,385	00(E)
139	Latvia	2,370	00(E)
140	Oman	2,264	00(E)
141	Kuwait	2,236	00(E)
142	West Bank	2,175	00(E)
143	Macedonia	2,009	00(E)
144	Slovenia	1,985	00(E)
145	Lesotho	1,916	00(E)

Table 1.20 Population, Thousands, Year 2000			
Rank	**Country**	**POP**	**Source**
146	Namibia	1,896	00(E)
147	Botswana	1,758	00(E)
148	Kosovo	1,700	00(E)
149	Estonia	1,367	00(E)
150	Gambia	1,357	00(E)
151	Trinidad & T	1,263	00(E)
152	Guinea-Biss	1,241	00(E)
153	Gabon	1,235	00(E)
154	Mauritius	1,179	00(E)
155	Gaza Strip	1,110	00(E)
156	Swaziland	1,064	00(E)
157	Cyprus	906	00(E)
158	Fiji	812	00(E)
159	East Timor	767	00(E)
160	Guyana	733	00(E)
161	Djibouti	732	00(E)
162	Reunion	723	00(E)
163	Bahrain	638	00(E)
164	Montenegro	633	00(E)
165	Qatar	591	00(E)
166	Bhutan	571	00(E)
167	Comoros	545	00(E)
168	Equatorial G	520	00(E)
169	Suriname	467	00(E)
170.5	Cape Verde	435	00(E)
170.5	Luxembourg	435	00(E)
172	Macao	431	00(E)
173	Solomon Is	415	00(E)
174	Malta	390	00(E)
175	Guadeloupe	388	00(E)
176	Martinique	383	00(E)
177	W Sahara	336	00(E)
178	Brunei	325	00(E)
179	Bahamas	304	00(E)
180	Iceland	281	00(E)
181	Maldives	272	00(E)
182	Barbados	269	00(E)
183	Belize	241	00(E)
184	Fr Polynesia	238	00(E)
185	New Caledon	211	00(E)
186	Vanuatu	189	00(E)
187	Samoa	175	00(E)
188	Guiana, Fr	165	00(E)
189	St Lucia	157	00(E)
190	Guam	155	00(E)
191	Mayotte	147	00(E)
192	Sao Tome & P	141	00(E)
193	Curacao	134	00(E)
194	St Vincent	110	00(E)

Table 1.20 Population, Thousands, Year 2000			
Rank	Country	POP	Source
195	Virgin I, US	109	00(E)
196	Micronesia	107	00(E)
197	Grenada	103	00(E)
198	Tonga	99	00(E)
199	Aruba	96	00(E)
200	Jersey	87	00(E)
201	Kiribati	85	00(E)
202	Seychelles	80	00(E)
203.5	Antigua & B	76	00(E)
203.5	Isle of Man	76	00(E)
205	Dominica	70	00(E)
206	N Mariana Is	69	00(E)
207	Andorra	65	00(E)
208.5	Bermuda	62	00(E)
208.5	Guernsey	62	00(E)
210	Samoa, Amer	57	00(E)
211	Greenland	56	00(E)
212	Marshall Is	51	00(E)
213.5	Faroe Is	46	00(E)
213.5	St Kitts & N	46	00(E)
215	Cayman Is	40	00(E)
216	Monaco	35	00(E)
217	Liechtenstn	33	00(E)
218	Sint Maarten	31	00(E)
219	Gibraltar	29	00(CIA)
220	Saint Martin	28	00(WB)
221	San Marino	27	00(E)
222	Cook Is	20	00(CIA)
223	Virgin I, Br	20	00(CIA)
224	Palau	19	00(E)
225	Turks & C Is	19	00(WB)
226	Wallis & Fut	15	00(CIA)
227	Anguilla	12	00(CIA)
228	Nauru	10	00(E)
229	Tuvalu	9	00(E)
230	Saint Helena	7	00(CIA)
231	St Pierre&M	7	00(CIA)
232	Montserrat	6	00(CIA)
233	Falkland Is	3	00(CIA)
234	Svalbard	2	00(CIA)
235	Niue	2	00(CIA)
236	Tokelau	1	00(CIA)

Table 1.21 Population, Thousands, Year 2010			
Rank	Country	POP	Source
1	China	1,337,900	10(E)
2	India	1,195,520	10(E)
3	US	309,746	10(E)
4	Indonesia	237,920	10(E)
5	Brazil	190,571	10(E)
6	Pakistan	184,405	10(E)
7	Nigeria	161,605	10(E)
8	Bangladesh	148,569	10(E)
9	Russia	142,939	10(E)
10	Japan	128,070	10(E)
11	Mexico	112,437	10(E)
12	Philippines	92,628	10(E)
13	Vietnam	86,933	10(E)
14	Germany	81,777	10(E)
15	Ethiopia	79,456	10(E)
16	Egypt	78,685	10(E)
17	Iran	73,893	10(E)
18	Turkey	73,135	10(E)
19	Congo, Dem R	65,966	10(E)
20	Thailand	65,403	10(E)
21	France	62,913	10(E)
22	UK	62,843	10(E)
23	Italy	59,116	10(E)
24	Burma	53,414	10(E)
25	South Africa	50,824	10(E)
26	Korea, South	49,410	10(E)
27	Spain	45,968	10(E)
28	Ukraine	45,860	10(E)
29	Colombia	44,205	10(E)
30	Tanzania	42,446	10(E)
31	Kenya	40,843	10(E)
32	Argentina	39,968	10(E)
33	Poland	38,456	10(E)
34	Algeria	35,978	10(E)
35	Canada	33,147	10(E)
36	Sudan	32,997	10(E)
37	Iraq	31,672	10(E)
38	Morocco	31,627	10(E)
39	Uganda	31,507	10(E)
40	Peru	28,948	10(E)
41	Venezuela	28,369	10(E)
42	Malaysia	28,325	10(E)
43	Uzbekistan	28,001	10(E)
44	Saudi Arabia	27,287	10(E)
45	Nepal	26,147	10(E)
46	Afghanistan	25,873	10(E)
47	Ghana	24,830	10(E)

Table 1.21 Population, Thousands, Year 2010			
Rank	Country	POP	Source
48	Korea, North	24,326	10(E)
49	Yemen	23,939	10(E)
50	Taiwan	23,138	10(E)
51	Mozambique	22,417	10(E)
52	Australia	21,130	10(E)
53	Ivory Coast	21,059	10(E)
54	Madagascar	20,847	10(E)
55	Syria	20,411	10(E)
56	Romania	20,327	10(E)
57	Sri Lanka	20,032	10(E)
58	Cameroon	19,661	10(E)
59	Angola	17,043	10(E)
60	Netherlands	16,606	10(E)
61	Burkina Faso	16,469	10(E)
62	Kazakhstan	16,311	10(E)
63	Chile	16,290	10(E)
64	Niger	15,512	10(E)
65	Malawi	14,901	10(E)
66	Mali	14,583	10(E)
67	Cambodia	14,454	10(E)
68	Guatemala	14,389	10(E)
69	Ecuador	14,367	10(E)
70	Zambia	12,984	10(E)
71	Zimbabwe	12,675	10(E)
72	Senegal	12,323	10(E)
73	Chad	11,707	10(E)
74	Cuba	11,167	10(E)
75	Belgium	10,919	10(E)
76	Greece	10,782	10(E)
77.5	Portugal	10,547	10(E)
77.5	Tunisia	10,547	10(E)
79	Czechia	10,421	10(E)
80	Hungary	10,005	10(E)
81	Guinea	9,982	10(E)
82	Rwanda	9,971	10(E)
83	Bolivia	9,905	10(E)
84	Somalia	9,768	10(E)
85	Haiti	9,649	10(E)
86	South Sudan	9,584	10(E)
87	Belarus	9,499	10(E)
88	Dominican R	9,398	10(E)
89	Sweden	9,378	10(E)
90	Azerbaijan	9,054	10(E)
91	Benin	8,850	10(E)
92	Burundi	8,383	10(E)
93	Austria	8,379	10(E)
94	Switzerland	7,828	10(E)
95	Honduras	7,601	10(E)

Table 1.21 Population, Thousands, Year 2010			
Rank	Country	POP	Source
96	Tajikistan	7,531	10(E)
97	UAE	7,512	10(E)
98	Bulgaria	7,397	10(E)
99	Israel	7,306	10(E)
100	Serbia	7,227	10(E)
101	Hong Kong	7,030	10(E)
102	Papua New G	6,860	10(E)
103	Paraguay	6,376	10(E)
104	Laos	6,256	10(E)
105	Togo	6,127	10(E)
106	Libya	6,110	10(E)
107	El Salvador	6,052	10(E)
108	Jordan	6,047	10(E)
109	Sierra Leone	5,868	10(E)
110	Nicaragua	5,788	10(E)
111	Denmark	5,544	10(E)
112	Kyrgyzstan	5,448	10(E)
113	Slovakia	5,379	10(E)
114	Finland	5,362	10(E)
115	Eritrea	5,254	10(E)
116	Singapore	5,077	10(E)
117	Turkmenistan	4,941	10(E)
118	Norway	4,914	10(E)
119	CAR	4,845	10(E)
120	Ireland	4,537	10(E)
121	Georgia	4,453	10(E)
122	New Zealand	4,368	10(E)
123	Croatia	4,296	10(E)
124	Costa Rica	4,258	10(E)
125	Lebanon	4,125	10(E)
126	Congo, Rep	4,043	10(E)
127	Moldova	3,935	10(E)
128	Bosnia	3,843	10(E)
129	Liberia	3,823	10(E)
130	Puerto Rico	3,722	10(E)
131	Panama	3,662	10(E)
132	Kuwait	3,566	10(E)
133	Uruguay	3,279	10(E)
134	Mauritania	3,205	10(E)
135	Lithuania	3,100	10(E)
136	Albania	2,906	10(E)
137	Armenia	2,888	10(E)
138	West Bank	2,830	10(E)
139	Oman	2,743	10(E)
140	Jamaica	2,691	10(E)
141	Mongolia	2,637	10(E)
142	Latvia	2,098	10(E)
143	Namibia	2,071	10(E)

Table 1.21 Population, Thousands, Year 2010			
Rank	Country	POP	Source
144	Macedonia	2,055	10(E)
145	Slovenia	2,049	10(E)
146	Botswana	1,982	10(E)
147	Lesotho	1,920	10(E)
148	Kosovo	1,815	10(E)
149	Gambia	1,755	10(E)
150	Qatar	1,674	10(E)
151	Guinea-Biss	1,569	10(E)
152	Gaza Strip	1,535	10(E)
153	Gabon	1,505	10(E)
154	Trinidad & T	1,318	10(E)
155	Estonia	1,304	10(E)
156	Mauritius	1,232	10(E)
157	Bahrain	1,229	10(E)
158	Swaziland	1,186	10(E)
159	Cyprus	1,108	10(E)
160	East Timor	1,088	10(E)
161	Fiji	848	10(E)
162	Djibouti	829	10(E)
163	Reunion	825	10(E)
164	Guyana	754	10(E)
165	Bhutan	726	10(E)
166	Comoros	706	10(E)
167	Equatorial G	700	10(E)
168	Montenegro	620	10(E)
169	Macao	541	10(E)
170	Suriname	531	10(E)
171	Solomon Is	530	10(E)
172	Luxembourg	507	10(E)
173.5	Cape Verde	492	10(E)
173.5	W Sahara	492	10(E)
175	Malta	413	10(E)
176	Guadeloupe	403	10(E)
177	Martinique	393	10(E)
178	Brunei	387	10(E)
179	Bahamas	352	10(E)
180	Maldives	320	10(E)
181	Iceland	318	10(E)
182	Belize	314	10(E)
183	Barbados	276	10(E)
184	Fr Polynesia	268	10(E)
185	New Caledon	249	10(E)
186	Vanuatu	241	10(E)
187	Guiana, Fr	233	10(E)
188	Mayotte	204	10(E)
189	Samoa	186	10(E)
190	Sao Tome & P	178	10(E)
191	St Lucia	166	10(E)

TABLE 1.21 POPULATION, THOUSANDS, YEAR 2010

Rank	Country	POP	Source
192	Guam	159	10(E)
193	Curacao	149	10(E)
194	Virgin I, US	106	10(E)
196	Grenada	103	10(E)
196	Micronesia	103	10(E)
196	Tonga	103	10(E)
198	Kiribati	102	10(E)
199.5	Aruba	101	10(E)
199.5	St Vincent	101	10(E)
201	Jersey	97	10(E)
202	Seychelles	91	10(E)
203.5	Andorra	85	10(E)
203.5	Antigua & B	85	10(E)
205	Isle of Man	84	10(E)
206	Dominica	71	10(E)
207	Guernsey	65	10(E)
208	Bermuda	64	10(E)
209.5	Cayman Is	56	10(E)
209.5	Greenland	56	10(E)
211	Samoa, Amer	55	10(E)
212	N Mariana Is	54	10(E)
213	Marshall Is	53	10(E)
214	St Kitts & N	50	10(E)
215	Faroe Is	49	10(E)
216	Sint Maarten	38	10(E)
217.5	Liechtenstn	36	10(E)
217.5	Monaco	36	10(E)
219	San Marino	32	10(E)
220	Turks & C Is	31	10(WB)
221	Saint Martin	30	10(WB)
222	Gibraltar	29	10(CIA)
223	Virgin I, Br	25	10(CIA)
224	Palau	21	10(E)
225	Wallis & Fut	15	10(CIA)
226	Anguilla	15	10(CIA)
227	Cook Is	11	10(CIA)
228	Tuvalu	11	10(E)
229	Nauru	10	10(E)
230	Saint Helena	8	10(CIA)
231	St Pierre&M	6	10(CIA)
232	Montserrat	5	10(CIA)
233	Falkland Is	3	10(EST)
234	Svalbard	2	10(CIA)
235	Tokelau	1	10(CIA)
236	Niue	1	10(CIA)

Table 1.22 Population, Thousands, Year 2012			
Rank	Country	POP	Source
1	China	1,350,861	12(E)
2	India	1,235,002	12(E)
3	US	314,231	12(E)
4	Indonesia	244,814	12(E)
5	Brazil	194,158	12(E)
6	Pakistan	190,248	12(E)
7	Nigeria	170,096	12(E)
8	Bangladesh	152,638	12(E)
9	Russia	143,182	12(E)
10	Japan	127,529	12(E)
11	Mexico	116,585	12(E)
12	Philippines	94,191	12(E)
13	Vietnam	88,788	12(E)
14	Ethiopia	84,150	12(E)
15	Egypt	82,852	12(E)
16	Germany	81,035	12(E)
17	Iran	75,805	12(E)
18	Turkey	75,189	12(E)
19	Congo, Dem R	69,554	12(E)
20	Thailand	66,316	12(E)
21	UK	63,764	12(E)
22	France	63,538	12(E)
23	Italy	59,615	12(E)
24	Burma	54,576	12(E)
25	South Africa	52,311	12(E)
26	Korea, South	49,905	12(E)
27	Spain	47,239	12(E)
28	Ukraine	45,635	12(E)
29	Colombia	45,226	12(E)
30	Tanzania	44,745	12(E)
31	Kenya	42,946	12(E)
32	Argentina	40,883	12(E)
33	Poland	38,513	12(E)
34	Algeria	37,413	12(E)
35	Canada	34,304	12(E)
36	Sudan	34,220	12(E)
37	Iraq	33,709	12(E)
38	Uganda	33,639	12(E)
39	Morocco	32,305	12(E)
40	Malaysia	29,740	12(E)
41	Peru	29,546	12(E)
42	Venezuela	29,534	12(E)
43	Uzbekistan	29,314	12(E)
44	Saudi Arabia	29,088	12(E)
45	Afghanistan	26,961	12(E)
46	Nepal	26,862	12(E)
47	Ghana	26,183	12(E)

TABLE 1.22 POPULATION, THOUSANDS, YEAR 2012			
Rank	Country	POP	Source
48	Yemen	25,526	12(E)
49	Korea, North	24,588	12(E)
50	Mozambique	23,523	12(E)
51	Taiwan	23,286	12(E)
52	Australia	22,377	12(E)
53	Madagascar	21,999	12(E)
54	Ivory Coast	21,944	12(E)
55	Syria	21,110	12(E)
56	Cameroon	20,655	12(E)
57	Sri Lanka	20,318	12(E)
58	Romania	19,910	12(E)
59	Angola	18,043	12(E)
60	Burkina Faso	17,482	12(E)
61	Kazakhstan	16,809	12(E)
62	Netherlands	16,736	12(E)
63	Niger	16,644	12(E)
64	Chile	16,608	12(E)
65	Malawi	15,889	12(E)
66	Mali	15,493	12(E)
67	Ecuador	15,157	12(E)
68	Guatemala	15,139	12(E)
69	Cambodia	14,951	12(E)
70	Zambia	13,995	12(E)
71	Senegal	12,966	12(E)
72	Zimbabwe	12,955	12(E)
73	Chad	12,337	12(E)
74	Cuba	11,164	12(E)
75	Belgium	11,130	12(E)
76	Greece	10,856	12(E)
77	Tunisia	10,769	12(E)
78	Portugal	10,589	12(E)
79	South Sudan	10,563	12(E)
80	Rwanda	10,501	12(E)
81	Guinea	10,490	12(E)
82	Czechia	10,462	12(E)
83	Bolivia	10,308	12(E)
84	Somalia	10,088	12(E)
85	Hungary	9,877	12(E)
86	Haiti	9,812	12(E)
87	Dominican R	9,627	12(E)
88	Sweden	9,520	12(E)
89	Belarus	9,460	12(E)
90	Benin	9,348	12(E)
91	Azerbaijan	9,299	12(E)
92	Burundi	8,731	12(E)
93	Austria	8,457	12(E)
94	Switzerland	7,997	12(E)
95	UAE	7,969	12(E)

Table 1.22 Population, Thousands, Year 2012			
Rank	Country	POP	Source
96	Honduras	7,912	12(E)
97	Tajikistan	7,835	12(E)
98	Israel	7,557	12(E)
99	Bulgaria	7,311	12(E)
100	Serbia	7,163	12(E)
101	Papua New G	7,134	12(E)
102	Hong Kong	7,114	12(E)
103	Paraguay	6,540	12(E)
104	Laos	6,517	12(E)
105	Togo	6,481	12(E)
106	Jordan	6,318	12(E)
107	Sierra Leone	6,123	12(E)
108	El Salvador	6,090	12(E)
109	Libya	6,038	12(E)
110	Nicaragua	5,956	12(E)
111	Denmark	5,606	12(E)
112	Eritrea	5,578	12(E)
113	Kyrgyzstan	5,567	12(E)
114	Finland	5,413	12(E)
115	Slovakia	5,408	12(E)
116	Singapore	5,319	12(E)
117	CAR	5,057	12(E)
118	Turkmenistan	5,055	12(E)
119	Norway	5,027	12(E)
120	Ireland	4,575	12(E)
121	Georgia	4,499	12(E)
122	New Zealand	4,430	12(E)
123	Costa Rica	4,353	12(E)
124	Croatia	4,266	12(E)
125	Congo, Rep	4,228	12(E)
126	Lebanon	4,130	12(E)
127	Liberia	4,039	12(E)
128	Moldova	3,918	12(E)
129	Bosnia	3,843	12(E)
130	Kuwait	3,807	12(E)
131	Panama	3,787	12(E)
132	Puerto Rico	3,690	12(E)
133	Mauritania	3,359	12(E)
134	Uruguay	3,292	12(E)
135	Lithuania	3,009	12(E)
136	West Bank	2,994	12(E)
137	Oman	2,879	12(E)
138	Armenia	2,863	12(E)
139	Albania	2,817	12(E)
140	Jamaica	2,710	12(E)
141	Mongolia	2,691	12(E)
142	Namibia	2,130	12(E)
143	Macedonia	2,061	12(E)

Table 1.22 Population, Thousands, Year 2012			
Rank	Country	POP	Source
144	Botswana	2,057	12(E)
145	Slovenia	2,056	12(E)
146	Latvia	2,046	12(E)
147	Lesotho	1,931	12(E)
148	Qatar	1,879	12(E)
149	Gambia	1,839	12(E)
150	Kosovo	1,837	12(E)
151	Guinea-Biss	1,645	12(E)
152	Gaza Strip	1,644	12(E)
153	Gabon	1,564	12(E)
154	Trinidad & T	1,335	12(E)
155	Estonia	1,291	12(E)
156	Mauritius	1,243	12(E)
157	Swaziland	1,220	12(E)
158	Bahrain	1,218	12(E)
159	Cyprus	1,163	12(E)
160	East Timor	1,143	12(E)
161	Fiji	856	12(E)
162	Djibouti	850	12(E)
163	Reunion	842	12(E)
164	Guyana	757	12(E)
165	Bhutan	750	12(E)
166	Equatorial G	740	12(E)
167	Comoros	736	12(E)
168	Montenegro	620	12(E)
169	Solomon Is	578	12(E)
170	Macao	575	12(E)
171	Suriname	547	12(E)
172	Luxembourg	533	12(E)
173	W Sahara	523	12(E)
174	Cape Verde	505	12(E)
175	Malta	415	12(E)
176	Guadeloupe	404	12(E)
177	Brunei	400	12(E)
178	Martinique	389	12(E)
179	Bahamas	363	12(E)
180	Belize	331	12(E)
181	Maldives	331	12(E)
182	Iceland	321	12(E)
183	Barbados	277	12(E)
184	Fr Polynesia	275	12(E)
185	Vanuatu	257	12(E)
186	New Caledon	256	12(E)
187	Guiana, Fr	238	12(E)
188	Mayotte	216	12(E)
189	Samoa	189	12(E)
190	Sao Tome & P	189	12(E)
191	St Lucia	169	12(E)

Table 1.22 Population, Thousands, Year 2012			
Rank	Country	POP	Source
192	Guam	160	12(E)
193	Curacao	152	12(E)
194	Kiribati	107	12(E)
195	Virgin I, US	105	12(E)
196	Aruba	104	12(E)
197.5	Grenada	103	12(E)
197.5	Tonga	103	12(E)
199	St Vincent	103	12(E)
200	Micronesia	102	12(E)
201	Jersey	99	12(E)
202	Seychelles	88	12(E)
203	Antigua & B	87	12(E)
204	Isle of Man	86	12(E)
205	Andorra	78	12(E)
206	Dominica	71	12(E)
207	Guernsey	66	12(E)
208	Bermuda	65	12(E)
209	Greenland	56	12(E)
210	Cayman Is	56	12(E)
211	Samoa, Amer	55	12(E)
212	Marshall Is	53	12(E)
213	N Mariana Is	51	12(E)
214	St Kitts & N	51	12(E)
215	Faroe Is	48	12(E)
216	Sint Maarten	39	12(E)
217	Monaco	37	12(E)
218	Liechtenstn	37	12(E)
219	Turks & C Is	32	12(WB)
220	San Marino	32	12(E)
221	Virgin I, Br	31	12(CIA)
222	Saint Martin	31	12(WB)
223	Gibraltar	29	12(CIA)
224	Palau	21	12(E)
225	Wallis & Fut	15	12(CIA)
226	Anguilla	15	12(CIA)
227	Tuvalu	11	12(E)
228	Cook Is	11	12(CIA)
229	Nauru	10	12(E)
230	Saint Helena	8	12(CIA)
231	St Pierre&M	6	12(CIA)
232	Montserrat	5	12(CIA)
233	Falkland Is	3	12(EST)
234	Svalbard	2	12(CIA)
235	Tokelau	1	12(CIA)
236	Niue	1	12(CIA)

Table 1.23 Population, Thousands, Year 2020, Forecast			
Rank	Country	POP	Source
1	China	1,384,047	12(E)
2	India	1,364,293	12(E)
3	US	337,268	12(E)
4	Indonesia	264,023	12(E)
5	Pakistan	213,719	12(E)
6	Nigeria	207,699	12(E)
7	Brazil	206,414	12(E)
8	Bangladesh	167,603	12(E)
9	Russia	141,760	12(E)
10	Mexico	125,792	12(E)
11	Japan	125,707	12(E)
12	Philippines	106,173	12(E)
13	Ethiopia	99,038	12(E)
14	Vietnam	96,309	12(E)
15	Egypt	94,409	12(E)
16	Congo, Dem R	85,054	12(E)
17	Turkey	81,705	12(E)
18	Iran	81,440	12(E)
19	Germany	80,287	12(E)
20	UK	69,281	12(E)
21	Thailand	68,753	12(E)
22	France	65,689	12(E)
23	Italy	60,951	12(E)
24	Burma	59,126	12(E)
25	Tanzania	55,737	12(E)
26	South Africa	54,728	12(E)
27	Korea, South	51,435	12(E)
28	Kenya	49,858	12(E)
29	Spain	49,378	12(E)
30	Colombia	49,085	12(E)
31	Ukraine	43,843	12(E)
32	Argentina	43,648	12(E)
33	Uganda	43,518	12(E)
34	Iraq	42,684	12(E)
35	Algeria	41,375	12(E)
36	Sudan	39,161	12(E)
37	Poland	38,703	12(E)
38	Canada	36,305	12(E)
39	Morocco	34,956	12(E)
40	Malaysia	32,897	12(E)
41	Saudi Arabia	32,689	12(E)
42	Venezuela	32,612	12(E)
43	Uzbekistan	32,505	12(E)
44	Afghanistan	32,420	12(E)
45	Yemen	32,232	12(E)
46	Peru	31,915	12(E)
47	Ghana	31,305	12(E)

Table 1.23 Population, Thousands, Year 2020, Forecast			
Rank	Country	POP	Source
48	Nepal	30,359	12(E)
49	Mozambique	28,603	12(E)
50	Madagascar	26,956	12(E)
51	Korea, North	25,643	12(E)
52	Ivory Coast	25,504	12(E)
53	Australia	25,039	12(E)
54	Cameroon	24,383	12(E)
55	Syria	24,079	12(E)
56	Taiwan	23,594	12(E)
57	Angola	22,484	12(E)
58	Burkina Faso	22,150	12(E)
59	Niger	22,071	12(E)
60	Sri Lanka	21,699	12(E)
61	Malawi	20,677	12(E)
62	Mali	19,623	12(E)
63	Romania	19,502	12(E)
64	Kazakhstan	18,395	12(E)
65	Guatemala	18,382	12(E)
66	Zambia	17,804	12(E)
67	Chile	17,714	12(E)
68	Netherlands	17,166	12(E)
69	Cambodia	16,927	12(E)
70	Ecuador	16,443	12(E)
71	Senegal	15,736	12(E)
72	Zimbabwe	15,274	12(E)
73	Chad	15,087	12(E)
74	South Sudan	14,558	12(E)
75	Rwanda	13,037	12(E)
76	Guinea	12,765	12(E)
77	Somalia	11,757	12(E)
78	Bolivia	11,709	12(E)
79	Belgium	11,642	12(E)
80	Tunisia	11,543	12(E)
81	Benin	11,523	12(E)
82	Cuba	11,127	12(E)
83	Greece	11,042	12(E)
84	Czechia	10,699	12(E)
85	Haiti	10,693	12(E)
86	Portugal	10,672	12(E)
87	Dominican R	10,543	12(E)
88	Azerbaijan	10,160	12(E)
89	Sweden	10,137	12(E)
90	Burundi	10,057	12(E)
91	Hungary	9,648	12(E)
92	Belarus	9,225	12(E)
93	Honduras	9,179	12(E)
94	UAE	9,174	12(E)
95	Tajikistan	8,761	12(E)

TABLE 1.23 POPULATION, THOUSANDS, YEAR 2020, FORECAST			
Rank	Country	POP	Source
96	Austria	8,731	12(E)
97	Papua New G	8,584	12(E)
98	Israel	8,519	12(E)
99	Switzerland	8,472	12(E)
100	Hong Kong	7,648	12(E)
101	Togo	7,589	12(E)
102	Jordan	7,297	12(E)
103	Laos	7,272	12(E)
104	Paraguay	7,192	12(E)
105	Sierra Leone	7,178	12(E)
106	Bulgaria	6,976	12(E)
107	Libya	6,943	12(E)
108	Serbia	6,904	12(E)
109	Eritrea	6,848	12(E)
110	Nicaragua	6,603	12(E)
111	El Salvador	6,217	12(E)
112	Singapore	6,191	12(E)
113	Kyrgyzstan	6,126	12(E)
114	CAR	5,991	12(E)
115	Denmark	5,762	12(E)
116	Finland	5,617	12(E)
117	Norway	5,546	12(E)
118	Turkmenistan	5,529	12(E)
119	Slovakia	5,513	12(E)
120	Congo, Rep	5,003	12(E)
121	Ireland	4,963	12(E)
122	Liberia	4,945	12(E)
123	Costa Rica	4,806	12(E)
124	New Zealand	4,744	12(E)
125	Kuwait	4,511	12(E)
126	Georgia	4,322	12(E)
127	Panama	4,279	12(E)
128	Lebanon	4,243	12(E)
129	Croatia	4,185	12(E)
130	Mauritania	4,005	12(E)
131	Bosnia	3,739	12(E)
132	Moldova	3,713	12(E)
133	Puerto Rico	3,528	12(E)
134	West Bank	3,518	12(E)
135	Uruguay	3,362	12(E)
136	Oman	3,262	12(E)
137	Mongolia	3,022	12(E)
138	Lithuania	2,879	12(E)
139	Armenia	2,876	12(E)
140	Jamaica	2,775	12(E)
141	Albania	2,766	12(E)
142	Namibia	2,415	12(E)
143	Botswana	2,287	12(E)

Table 1.23 Population, Thousands, Year 2020, Forecast			
Rank	Country	POP	Source
144	Qatar	2,215	12(E)
145	Gambia	2,174	12(E)
146	Slovenia	2,110	12(E)
147	Macedonia	2,068	12(E)
148	Gaza Strip	2,047	12(E)
149	Latvia	1,970	12(E)
150	Lesotho	1,969	12(E)
151	Guinea-Biss	1,935	12(E)
152	Kosovo	1,933	12(E)
153	Gabon	1,818	12(E)
154	East Timor	1,384	12(E)
155	Bahrain	1,373	12(E)
156	Trinidad & T	1,362	12(E)
157	Swaziland	1,341	12(E)
158	Mauritius	1,290	12(E)
159.5	Cyprus	1,276	12(E)
159.5	Estonia	1,276	12(E)
161	Djibouti	994	12(E)
162	Reunion	910	12(E)
163	Equatorial G	905	12(E)
164	Fiji	890	12(E)
165	Comoros	846	12(E)
166	Bhutan	829	12(E)
167	Guyana	773	12(E)
168	Solomon Is	685	12(E)
169	Macao	680	12(E)
170	W Sahara	652	12(E)
171	Montenegro	624	12(E)
172	Luxembourg	594	12(E)
173	Suriname	584	12(E)
174	Cape Verde	543	12(E)
175	Brunei	452	12(E)
176	Malta	426	12(E)
177	Guadeloupe	415	12(E)
178	Bahamas	397	12(E)
179	Martinique	392	12(E)
180	Belize	385	12(E)
181	Maldives	364	12(E)
182	Iceland	346	12(E)
183	Vanuatu	309	12(E)
184	Guiana, Fr	298	12(E)
185	Fr Polynesia	296	12(E)
186.5	Barbados	282	12(E)
186.5	New Caledon	282	12(E)
188	Mayotte	265	12(E)
189	Sao Tome & P	221	12(E)
190	Samoa	194	12(E)
191	St Lucia	186	12(E)

TABLE 1.23 POPULATION, THOUSANDS, YEAR 2020, FORECAST

Rank	Country	POP	Source
192	Guam	169	12(E)
193	Curacao	158	12(E)
194	Kiribati	121	12(E)
195	Grenada	107	12(E)
196.5	Aruba	106	12(E)
196.5	Tonga	106	12(E)
198.5	Jersey	105	12(E)
198.5	St Vincent	105	12(E)
200.5	Micronesia	100	12(E)
200.5	Virgin I, US	100	12(E)
202	Seychelles	96	12(E)
203	Antigua & B	94	12(E)
204	Isle of Man	91	12(E)
205	Andorra	76	12(E)
206	Dominica	74	12(E)
207	Guernsey	69	12(E)
208	Bermuda	66	12(E)
209.5	Cayman Is	59	12(E)
209.5	Marshall Is	59	12(E)
211.5	Greenland	56	12(E)
211.5	N Mariana Is	56	12(E)
213.5	Samoa, Amer	54	12(E)
213.5	St Kitts & N	54	12(E)
215	Faroe Is	50	12(E)
216	Turks & C Is	47	12(EST)
217	Virgin I, Br	42	12(EST)
218	Sint Maarten	41	12(E)
219	Liechtenstn	39	12(E)
220	Monaco	38	12(E)
221	San Marino	33	12(E)
222	Saint Martin	33	12(EST)
223	Gibraltar	29	12(EST)
224	Palau	22	12(E)
225	Anguilla	18	12(EST)
226	Wallis & Fut	16	12(EST)
227	Tuvalu	12	12(E)
228	Nauru	10	12(E)
229	Saint Helena	8	12(EST)
230	Cook Is	7	12(EST)
231	St Pierre&M	5	12(EST)
232	Montserrat	4	12(EST)
233	Falkland Is	4	12(EST)
234	Svalbard	2	PROXY(Norway(E))
235	Tokelau	1	12(EST)
236	Niue	1	12(EST)

Table 1.24 Population, Thousands, Year 2030, Forecast			
Rank	Country	POP	Source
1	India	1,498,634	12(E)
2	China	1,389,315	12(E)
3	US	366,152	12(E)
4	Indonesia	281,941	12(E)
5	Nigeria	263,626	12(E)
6	Pakistan	242,862	12(E)
7	Brazil	218,284	12(E)
8	Bangladesh	182,240	12(E)
9	Russia	137,142	12(E)
10	Mexico	135,251	12(E)
11	Philippines	122,212	12(E)
12	Japan	121,088	12(E)
13	Ethiopia	116,160	12(E)
14	Egypt	106,047	12(E)
15	Congo, Dem R	105,956	12(E)
16	Vietnam	103,257	12(E)
17	Turkey	87,687	12(E)
18	Iran	84,850	12(E)
19	Germany	78,055	12(E)
20	UK	73,611	12(E)
21	Tanzania	72,411	12(E)
22	Thailand	70,465	12(E)
23	France	67,388	12(E)
24	Burma	64,103	12(E)
25	Italy	62,039	12(E)
26	Uganda	58,488	12(E)
27	South Africa	56,953	12(E)
28	Kenya	56,552	12(E)
29	Iraq	55,257	12(E)
30	Colombia	52,965	12(E)
31	Korea, South	52,160	12(E)
32	Spain	51,437	12(E)
33	Argentina	46,539	12(E)
34	Sudan	46,338	12(E)
35	Algeria	44,768	12(E)
36	Yemen	41,342	12(E)
37	Ukraine	41,264	12(E)
38	Afghanistan	40,401	12(E)
39	Canada	38,929	12(E)
40	Ghana	38,537	12(E)
41	Morocco	37,887	12(E)
42	Poland	37,866	12(E)
43	Malaysia	37,166	12(E)
44	Saudi Arabia	37,081	12(E)
45	Mozambique	36,622	12(E)
46	Venezuela	36,232	12(E)
47	Uzbekistan	35,250	12(E)

Table 1.24 Population, Thousands, Year 2030, Forecast

Rank	Country	POP	Source
48	Nepal	34,485	12(E)
49	Peru	34,444	12(E)
50	Madagascar	33,417	12(E)
51	Niger	30,841	12(E)
52	Ivory Coast	29,724	12(E)
53	Angola	29,155	12(E)
54	Cameroon	29,128	12(E)
55	Burkina Faso	29,112	12(E)
56	Malawi	28,174	12(E)
57	Syria	27,859	12(E)
58	Australia	27,549	12(E)
59	Korea, North	26,688	12(E)
60	Mali	25,619	12(E)
61	Zambia	23,637	12(E)
62	Taiwan	23,532	12(E)
63	Sri Lanka	22,865	12(E)
64	Guatemala	22,726	12(E)
65	Kazakhstan	19,634	12(E)
66	Senegal	19,485	12(E)
67	Chad	19,225	12(E)
68	Cambodia	19,031	12(E)
69	Chile	18,705	12(E)
70	South Sudan	18,682	12(E)
71	Romania	18,588	12(E)
72	Ecuador	17,989	12(E)
73	Netherlands	17,620	12(E)
74	Zimbabwe	17,322	12(E)
75	Rwanda	16,321	12(E)
76	Guinea	15,946	12(E)
77	Somalia	15,041	12(E)
78	Benin	14,630	12(E)
79	Bolivia	13,528	12(E)
80	Belgium	12,256	12(E)
81	Tunisia	12,138	12(E)
82	Haiti	11,784	12(E)
83	Burundi	11,441	12(E)
84	Dominican R	11,433	12(E)
85	Greece	11,091	12(E)
86	Cuba	11,017	12(E)
87	Azerbaijan	10,732	12(E)
88	Portugal	10,724	12(E)
89	Czechia	10,722	12(E)
90	Honduras	10,657	12(E)
91	Sweden	10,594	12(E)
92	UAE	10,489	12(E)
93	Papua New G	10,329	12(E)
94	Tajikistan	9,922	12(E)
95	Israel	9,650	12(E)

Table 1.24 Population, Thousands, Year 2030, Forecast			
Rank	Country	POP	Source
96	Hungary	9,306	12(E)
97	Austria	9,004	12(E)
98	Togo	8,975	12(E)
99	Belarus	8,828	12(E)
100	Switzerland	8,811	12(E)
101	Sierra Leone	8,532	12(E)
102	Eritrea	8,394	12(E)
103	Jordan	8,336	12(E)
104	Hong Kong	8,309	12(E)
105	Laos	8,004	12(E)
106	Paraguay	7,974	12(E)
107	Libya	7,773	12(E)
108	CAR	7,325	12(E)
109	Nicaragua	7,240	12(E)
110	Singapore	7,201	12(E)
111	Kyrgyzstan	6,793	12(E)
112	Serbia	6,569	12(E)
113	Bulgaria	6,543	12(E)
114	El Salvador	6,340	12(E)
115	Liberia	6,254	12(E)
116	Congo, Rep	6,169	12(E)
117	Norway	6,075	12(E)
118	Turkmenistan	6,027	12(E)
119	Denmark	5,958	12(E)
120	Finland	5,833	12(E)
121	Slovakia	5,516	12(E)
122	Ireland	5,347	12(E)
123	Kuwait	5,332	12(E)
124	Costa Rica	5,191	12(E)
125	New Zealand	5,145	12(E)
126	Mauritania	4,851	12(E)
127	Panama	4,835	12(E)
128	Lebanon	4,335	12(E)
129	West Bank	4,127	12(E)
130	Croatia	4,063	12(E)
131	Georgia	3,983	12(E)
132	Oman	3,572	12(E)
133	Bosnia	3,560	12(E)
134	Moldova	3,480	12(E)
135	Uruguay	3,441	12(E)
136	Mongolia	3,343	12(E)
137	Puerto Rico	3,220	12(E)
138	Armenia	2,838	12(E)
139	Albania	2,791	12(E)
140	Jamaica	2,789	12(E)
141	Lithuania	2,769	12(E)
142	Namibia	2,750	12(E)
143	Botswana	2,595	12(E)

TABLE 1.24 POPULATION, THOUSANDS, YEAR 2030, FORECAST			
Rank	Country	POP	Source
144	Gambia	2,554	12(E)
145	Gaza Strip	2,475	12(E)
146	Qatar	2,388	12(E)
147	Guinea-Biss	2,350	12(E)
148	Gabon	2,146	12(E)
149	Slovenia	2,122	12(E)
150	Kosovo	2,066	12(E)
151	Macedonia	2,038	12(E)
152	Lesotho	1,952	12(E)
153	Latvia	1,883	12(E)
154	East Timor	1,689	12(E)
155	Bahrain	1,506	12(E)
156	Swaziland	1,462	12(E)
157	Cyprus	1,387	12(E)
158	Trinidad & T	1,343	12(E)
159	Mauritius	1,321	12(E)
160	Estonia	1,244	12(E)
161	Djibouti	1,178	12(E)
162	Equatorial G	1,102	12(E)
163	Reunion	978	12(E)
164	Comoros	964	12(E)
165	Fiji	946	12(E)
166	Bhutan	899	12(E)
167	Solomon Is	846	12(E)
168	W Sahara	821	12(E)
169	Guyana	795	12(E)
170	Macao	745	12(E)
171	Luxembourg	657	12(E)
172	Montenegro	622	12(E)
173	Suriname	618	12(E)
174	Cape Verde	587	12(E)
175	Brunei	508	12(E)
176	Belize	448	12(E)
177	Bahamas	430	12(E)
178	Malta	429	12(E)
179	Guadeloupe	425	12(E)
180	Martinique	392	12(E)
181	Maldives	391	12(E)
182	Iceland	376	12(E)
183	Vanuatu	370	12(E)
184	Guiana, Fr	369	12(E)
185	Mayotte	324	12(E)
186	Fr Polynesia	316	12(E)
187	New Caledon	311	12(E)
188	Barbados	284	12(E)
189	Sao Tome & P	260	12(E)
190	Samoa	204	12(E)
191	St Lucia	196	12(E)

Table 1.24 Population, Thousands, Year 2030, Forecast			
Rank	Country	POP	Source
192	Guam	185	12(E)
193	Curacao	161	12(E)
194	Kiribati	138	12(E)
195	Tonga	111	12(E)
196	Jersey	110	12(E)
197.5	Aruba	107	12(E)
197.5	Grenada	107	12(E)
199	St Vincent	106	12(E)
200	Micronesia	103	12(E)
201	Antigua & B	102	12(E)
202	Seychelles	98	12(E)
203	Isle of Man	94	12(E)
204	Virgin I, US	91	12(E)
205	Dominica	77	12(E)
206	Andorra	74	12(E)
207	Turks & C Is	73	12(EST)
208	Guernsey	72	12(E)
209	Bermuda	67	12(E)
210.5	Marshall Is	64	12(E)
210.5	N Mariana Is	64	12(E)
212	Virgin I, Br	62	12(EST)
213	Cayman Is	62	12(E)
214	St Kitts & N	57	12(E)
215	Greenland	56	12(E)
216.5	Faroe Is	52	12(E)
216.5	Samoa, Amer	52	12(E)
218	Sint Maarten	43	12(E)
219	Liechtenstn	42	12(E)
220	Monaco	39	12(E)
221	Saint Martin	35	12(EST)
222	San Marino	34	12(E)
223	Gibraltar	28	12(EST)
224	Anguilla	23	12(EST)
225	Palau	23	12(E)
226	Wallis & Fut	16	12(EST)
227	Tuvalu	12	12(E)
228	Nauru	11	12(E)
229	Saint Helena	9	12(EST)
230	St Pierre&M	5	12(EST)
231	Falkland Is	4	12(EST)
232	Cook Is	4	12(EST)
233	Montserrat	4	12(EST)
234	Svalbard	2	PROXY(Norway(E))
235	Tokelau	1	12(EST)
236	Niue	1	12(EST)

2. GDP at Purchasing Power Parities Per Capita by Rank

Table 2.1 GDP at Purchasing Power Parities Per Capita, 2012 Dollars, Year 0001

Rank	Country	GPC	Source
1	Italy	1,266	0001(Maddison)
2	Syria	911	PROXY(W. Asia(Maddison))
3	Lebanon	911	PROXY(W. Asia(Maddison))
4	Cyprus	861	0001(Maddison)
5	Greece	861	0001(Maddison)
6	Israel	850	PROXY(W. Asia(Maddison))
7	Iran	831	PROXY(W. Asia(Maddison))
8	Turkey	831	PROXY(W. Asia(Maddison))
9	Jordan	814	PROXY(W. Asia(Maddison))
10	Iraq	791	PROXY(W. Asia(Maddison))
11	Egypt	782	0001(Maddison)
12	Spain	779	0001(Maddison)
13	Yemen	761	PROXY(W. Asia(Maddison))
14	Qatar	761	PROXY(W. Asia(Maddison))
16	Bahrain	761	PROXY(W. Asia(Maddison))
16	Saudi Arabia	761	PROXY(W. Asia(Maddison))
16	UAE	761	PROXY(W. Asia(Maddison))
18.5	Kuwait	761	PROXY(W. Asia(Maddison))
18.5	Oman	761	PROXY(W. Asia(Maddison))
20	Thailand	756	PROXY(Other E. Asia(Maddison))
21	France	740	0001(Maddison)
22	Malaysia	706	PROXY(Other E. Asia(Maddison))
23	Korea, North	704	PROXY(China(Maddison))
24	India	704	0001(Undivided India(Maddison))
26	Belgium	704	0001(Maddison)
26	China	704	0001(Maddison)
26	Korea, South	704	PROXY(China(Maddison))
28.5	Hong Kong	704	PROXY(China(Maddison))
28.5	Pakistan	704	0001(Undivided India(Maddison))
30	Bangladesh	704	0001(Undivided India(Maddison))
31	Portugal	704	0001(Maddison)
32	Philippines	684	PROXY(Other E. Asia(Maddison))
33	Indonesia	678	PROXY(Other E. Asia(Maddison))
34	Tunisia	673	PROXY(Other N. Africa(Maddison))
35	Libya	673	AVG(Other N. Africa(Maddison))
36	Algeria	673	PROXY(Other N. Africa(Maddison))
38	Austria	665	0001(Maddison)
38	Hungary	665	AVG(Danubian provinces(Maddison))
38	Switzerland	665	0001(Maddison)
40.5	Bulgaria	665	AVG(Danubian provinces(Maddison))
40.5	Romania	665	AVG(Danubian provinces(Maddison))
42.5	Netherlands	665	0001(Maddison)
42.5	Serbia	665	AVG(Danubian provinces(Maddison))

Table 2.1 GDP at Purchasing Power Parities Per Capita, 2012 Dollars, Year 0001			
Rank	Country	GPC	Source
44	Taiwan	644	PROXY(Other E. Asia(Maddison))
45	Sri Lanka	644	PROXY(Other E. Asia(Maddison))
46	Germany	638	0001(Maddison)
47	Slovenia	487	0001(MIN)
48	Denmark	485	0001(MIN)
49	UK	478	0001(MIN)
50	Estonia	474	0001(MIN)
51	Sweden	472	0001(MIN)
52	Poland	460	0001(MIN)
53	Latvia	458	0001(MIN)
54	Czechia	457	0001(MIN)
55	Norway	455	0001(MIN)
56	Kazakhstan	455	0001(MIN)
57	Lithuania	451	0001(MIN)
58	Morocco	438	0001(MIN)
59	Japan	434	0001(MIN)
60	Slovakia	428	0001(MIN)
61	Sudan	428	0001(MIN)
62	Russia	421	0001(MIN)
63	Croatia	415	0001(MIN)
64	Ireland	415	0001(MIN)
65	Vietnam	410	0001(MIN)
66	Armenia	406	0001(MIN)
67	Jamaica	405	0001(MIN)
68	Puerto Rico	405	0001(MIN)
69	Afghanistan	403	0001(MIN)
70	Trinidad & T	401	0001(MIN)
71	Burma	400	0001(MIN)
72	Georgia	400	0001(MIN)
73	Singapore	399	0001(MIN)
74	Cuba	396	0001(MIN)
75	Sierra Leone	395	0001(MIN)
76	Laos	393	0001(MIN)
77	US	389	0001(MIN)
78	Finland	383	0001(MIN)
79	Montenegro	381	0001(MIN)
80	Guatemala	381	0001(MIN)
81	Moldova	378	0001(MIN)
82	Belarus	373	0001(MIN)
83	Australia	372	0001(MIN)
84	Costa Rica	370	0001(MIN)
85	Mexico	370	0001(MIN)
86	Uzbekistan	368	0001(MIN)
87	Bolivia	367	0001(MIN)
88	Panama	366	0001(MIN)
89	Turkmenistan	366	0001(MIN)
90.5	Argentina	364	0001(MIN)
90.5	Uruguay	364	0001(MIN)

Table 2.1 GDP at Purchasing Power Parities Per Capita, 2012 Dollars, Year 0001			
Rank	Country	GPC	Source
92	Chile	364	0001(MIN)
93	Ecuador	361	0001(MIN)
94	Brazil	361	0001(MIN)
95	Ukraine	361	0001(MIN)
96	Peru	358	0001(MIN)
97	Cambodia	358	0001(MIN)
100.5	Madagascar	355	0001(MIN)
100.5	Mozambique	355	0001(MIN)
100.5	Namibia	355	0001(MIN)
100.5	Somalia	355	0001(MIN)
100.5	South Africa	355	0001(MIN)
100.5	Swaziland	355	0001(MIN)
104.5	Zambia	355	0001(MIN)
104.5	Zimbabwe	355	0001(MIN)
106	Venezuela	352	0001(MIN)
107	Canada	352	0001(MIN)
108	El Salvador	351	0001(MIN)
109	Azerbaijan	350	0001(MIN)
110	Haiti	350	0001(MIN)
111	Dominican R	347	0001(MIN)
112	Bosnia	346	0001(MIN)
113	Colombia	346	0001(MIN)
114	Tajikistan	344	0001(MIN)
115	Albania	338	0001(MIN)
116	Kyrgyzstan	338	0001(MIN)
117	Nicaragua	337	0001(MIN)
118	Ghana	334	0001(MIN)
119	Paraguay	334	0001(MIN)
120	Nepal	333	0001(MIN)
121	Honduras	330	0001(MIN)
122	Mongolia	329	0001(MIN)
123	New Zealand	328	0001(MIN)
124	Macedonia	326	0001(MIN)
125	South Sudan	324	0001(MIN)
126	Kosovo	324	0001(MIN)
127	Burundi	300	0001(MIN)
128	Lesotho	298	0001(MIN)
129	Botswana	295	0001(MIN)
130	Malawi	283	0001(MIN)
131	Guinea	273	0001(MIN)
132	Guinea-Biss	265	0001(MIN)
133	Eritrea	257	0001(MIN)l & W. Africa(Maddison))
134	Ethiopia	253	0001(MIN)

TABLE 2.2 GDP AT PURCHASING POWER PARITIES PER CAPITA, 2012 DOLLARS, YEAR 1000

Rank	Country	GPC	Source
1	Syria	1,084	PROXY(W. Asia(Maddison))
2	Lebanon	1,084	PROXY(W. Asia(Maddison))
3	Israel	1,011	PROXY(W. Asia(Maddison))
4	Iran	988	PROXY(W. Asia(Maddison))
5	Turkey	988	PROXY(W. Asia(Maddison))
6	Jordan	968	PROXY(W. Asia(Maddison))
7	Iraq	941	PROXY(W. Asia(Maddison))
8	Cyprus	939	1000(Maddison)
9	Yemen	906	PROXY(W. Asia(Maddison))
10.5	Bahrain	906	PROXY(W. Asia(Maddison))
10.5	Qatar	906	PROXY(W. Asia(Maddison))
13	Kuwait	906	PROXY(W. Asia(Maddison))
13	Saudi Arabia	906	PROXY(W. Asia(Maddison))
13	UAE	906	PROXY(W. Asia(Maddison))
15	Oman	906	PROXY(W. Asia(Maddison))
16	Slovenia	796	1000(MIN)
17	Denmark	790	1000(MIN)
18	Egypt	782	1000(Maddison)
19	UK	773	1000(MIN)
20	Estonia	764	1000(MIN)
21	Sweden	758	1000(MIN)
22	Thailand	756	PROXY(Other E. Asia(Maddison))
23	Poland	726	1000(MIN)
24	Latvia	722	1000(MIN)
25	Czechia	719	1000(MIN)
26	Norway	715	1000(MIN)
27	Kazakhstan	715	1000(MIN)
28	Malaysia	706	PROXY(Other E. Asia(Maddison))
29	Lithuania	705	1000(MIN)
30	Korea, North	704	PROXY(China(Maddison))
31	India	704	1000(Undivided India(Maddison))
33	China	704	1000(Maddison)
33	Italy	704	1000(Maddison)
33	Korea, South	704	PROXY(China(Maddison))
36	Hong Kong	704	PROXY(China(Maddison))
36	Pakistan	704	1000(Undivided India(Maddison))
36	Spain	704	1000(Maddison)
38	Bangladesh	704	1000(Undivided India(Maddison))
39	Philippines	684	PROXY(Other E. Asia(Maddison))
40	Indonesia	678	PROXY(Other E. Asia(Maddison))
41	Tunisia	673	PROXY(Other N. Africa(Maddison))
42	Morocco	673	1000(Maddison)
43	Libya	673	AVG(Other N. Africa(Maddison))
44	Algeria	673	PROXY(Other N. Africa(Maddison))
45	Austria	665	1000(Maddison)
46	France	665	1000(Maddison)

Table 2.2 GDP at Purchasing Power Parities Per Capita, 2012 Dollars, Year 1000			
Rank	Country	GPC	Source
47	Belgium	665	1000(Maddison)
49	Japan	665	1000(Maddison)
49	Netherlands	665	1000(Maddison)
49	Portugal	665	1000(Maddison)
51	Iceland	655	1000(MIN)
52	Slovakia	651	1000(MIN)
53	Sudan	649	1000(Sahel & W. Africa(Maddison))
54	Taiwan	644	PROXY(Other E. Asia(Maddison))
55	Sri Lanka	644	PROXY(Other E. Asia(Maddison))
56	Switzerland	642	1000(Maddison)
57	Germany	642	1000(Maddison)
58	Russia	634	1000(MIN)
59	Hungary	626	1000(Maddison)
60.5	Bulgaria	626	1000(Maddison)
60.5	Romania	626	1000(Maddison)
62	Greece	626	1000(Maddison)
63	Serbia	626	1000(Maddison)
64	Croatia	620	1000(MIN)
65	Ireland	619	1000(MIN)
66	Vietnam	609	1000(MIN)
67	Armenia	601	1000(MIN)
68	Jamaica	598	1000(MIN)
69	Puerto Rico	597	1000(MIN)
70	Afghanistan	595	1000(MIN)
71	Trinidad & T	590	1000(MIN)
72	Burma	588	1000(MIN)
73	Georgia	588	1000(MIN)
74	Singapore	585	1000(MIN)
75	Cuba	579	1000(MIN)
76	Sierra Leone	577	1000(MIN)
77	Laos	572	1000(MIN)
78	US	564	1000(MIN)
79	Finland	552	1000(MIN)
80	Montenegro	547	1000(MIN)
81	Guatemala	547	1000(MIN)
82	Moldova	542	1000(MIN)
83	Belarus	531	1000(MIN)
84	Australia	529	1000(MIN)
85	Costa Rica	526	1000(MIN)
86	Mexico	525	1000(MIN)
87	Uzbekistan	520	1000(MIN)
88	Bolivia	518	1000(MIN)
89	Panama	518	1000(MIN)
90	Turkmenistan	517	1000(MIN)
91.5	Argentina	513	1000(MIN)
91.5	Uruguay	513	1000(MIN)
93	Chile	513	1000(MIN)
94	Ecuador	508	1000(MIN)

Table 2.2 GDP at Purchasing Power Parities Per Capita, 2012 Dollars, Year 1000			
Rank	Country	GPC	Source
95	Brazil	507	1000(MIN)
96	Ukraine	507	1000(MIN)
97	Peru	501	1000(MIN)
98	Cambodia	501	1000(MIN)
99.5	Namibia	495	1000(MIN)
99.5	Somalia	495	1000(MIN)
101.5	South Africa	495	1000(MIN)
101.5	Swaziland	495	1000(MIN)
103.5	Madagascar	495	1000(MIN)
103.5	Mozambique	495	1000(MIN)
105.5	Zambia	495	1000(MIN)
105.5	Zimbabwe	495	1000(MIN)
107	Venezuela	489	1000(MIN)
108	Canada	489	1000(MIN)
109	El Salvador	488	1000(MIN)
110	Azerbaijan	485	1000(MIN)
111	Haiti	485	1000(MIN)
112	Dominican R	479	1000(MIN)
113	Bosnia	478	1000(MIN)
114	Colombia	477	1000(MIN)
115	Tajikistan	474	1000(MIN)
116	Albania	463	1000(MIN)
117	Kyrgyzstan	462	1000(MIN)
118	Nicaragua	461	1000(MIN)
119	Ghana	456	1000(MIN)
120	Paraguay	455	1000(MIN)
121	Nepal	454	1000(MIN)
122	Honduras	448	1000(MIN)
123	Mongolia	447	1000(MIN)
124	New Zealand	444	1000(MIN)
125	Macedonia	440	1000(MIN)
126	South Sudan	437	1000(MIN)
127	Kosovo	436	1000(MIN)
128	Burundi	395	1000(MIN)
129	Lesotho	391	1000(MIN)
130	Botswana	386	1000(MIN)
131	Malawi	366	1000(MIN)
132	Guinea	349	1000(MIN)
133	Guinea-Biss	337	1000(MIN)
134	Eritrea	324	1000(MIN)
135	Ethiopia	317	1000(MIN)

Table 2.3 GDP at Purchasing Power Parities Per Capita, 2012 Dollars, Year 1500			
Rank	Country	GPC	Source
1	Italy	1,721	1500(Maddison)
2	Belgium	1,369	1500(Maddison)
3	Netherlands	1,191	1500(Maddison)
4	Slovenia	1,167	INTERPOL (Maddison)
5	Denmark	1,155	1500(Maddison)
6	France	1,138	1500(Maddison)
7	UK	1,117	1500(Maddison)
8	Hungary	1,115	INTERPOL (Maddison)
9	Austria	1,106	1500(Maddison)
10	Estonia	1,099	INTERPOL (Maddison)
11	Sweden	1,088	1500(Maddison)
12	Germany	1,077	1500(Maddison)
13	Spain	1,034	1500(Maddison)
14	Syria	1,030	PROXY(Other W. Asia(Maddison))
15	Lebanon	1,030	PROXY(Other W. Asia(Maddison))
16	Poland	1,023	PROXY(E. Europe(Maddison))
17	Latvia	1,014	PROXY(USSR (Maddison))
18	Czechia	1,008	PROXY(E. Europe(Maddison))
19	Romania	1,006	PROXY(E. Europe(Maddison))
20	Norway	1,002	1500(Maddison)
21	Kazakhstan	1,001	PROXY(USSR (Maddison))
22	Switzerland	989	1500(Maddison)
23	Thailand	986	PROXY(Other E. Asia(Maddison))
24	Lithuania	980	PROXY(USSR (Maddison))
25	Israel	961	PROXY(Other W. Asia(Maddison))
26	Portugal	948	1500(Maddison)
27	Iran	939	1500(Maddison)
28	Korea, North	939	1500(Maddison)
29	China	939	1500(Maddison)
30	Turkey	939	1500(Maddison)
31.5	Hong Kong	939	PROXY(China (Maddison))
31.5	Korea, South	939	1500(Maddison)
33	Malaysia	920	PROXY(Other E. Asia(Maddison))
34	Jordan	920	PROXY(Other W. Asia(Maddison))
35	Bulgaria	908	PROXY(E. Europe (Maddison))
36	Iraq	894	PROXY(W. Asia (Maddison))
37	Philippines	891	PROXY(Other E. Asia (Maddison))
38	Iceland	886	PROXY(Denmark)
39	Indonesia	884	1500(Maddison)

TABLE 2.3 GDP AT PURCHASING POWER PARITIES PER CAPITA, 2012 DOLLARS, YEAR 1500

Rank	Country	GPC	Source
40	Slovakia	880	PROXY(E. Europe (Maddison))
41.5	Qatar	861	AVG(Arabia (Maddison))
41.5	Yemen	861	AVG(Arabia (Maddison))
43.5	Saudi Arabia	861	AVG(Arabia (Maddison))
43.5	UAE	861	AVG(Arabia (Maddison))
46	India	861	1500(Undivided India (Maddison))
46	Kuwait	861	AVG(Arabia (Maddison))
46	Pakistan	861	1500(Undivided India (Maddison))
48.5	Bahrain	861	AVG(Arabia (Maddison))
48.5	Oman	861	AVG(Arabia (Maddison))
50	Bangladesh	861	1500(Undivided India (Maddison))
51	Russia	849	PROXY(USSR (Maddison))
52	Taiwan	839	PROXY(Other E. Asia (Maddison))
53	Sri Lanka	839	PROXY(Other E. Asia (Maddison))
54	Croatia	824	PROXY(E. Europe (Maddison))
55	Ireland	823	1500(Maddison)
56	Vietnam	804	PROXY(Other E. Asia (Maddison))
57	Armenia	790	PROXY(USSR (Maddison))
58	Jamaica	785	1500(MIN)
59	Puerto Rico	784	1500(MIN)
60	Japan	782	1500(Maddison)
61	Afghanistan	780	PROXY(Other E. Asia (Maddison))
62	Trinidad & T	772	1500(MIN)
63	Burma	769	PROXY(Other E. Asia (Maddison))
64	Georgia	769	PROXY(USSR (Maddison))
65	Singapore	763	PROXY(Other E. Asia (Maddison))
66	Cuba	753	1500(MIN)
67	Sierra Leone	750	1500(MIN)
68	Egypt	743	1500(Maddison)
69	Laos	741	PROXY(Other E. Asia (Maddison))
70	US	729	1500(MIN)

Table 2.3 GDP at Purchasing Power Parities Per Capita, 2012 Dollars, Year 1500			
Rank	Country	GPC	Source
71	Serbia	712	PROXY(E. Europe (Maddison))
72	Finland	709	1500(Maddison)
73	Montenegro	700	PROXY(E. Europe (Maddison))
74	Guatemala	700	1500(MIN)
75	Moldova	691	PROXY(USSR (Maddison))
76	Greece	678	1500(Maddison)
77	Belarus	674	PROXY(USSR (Maddison))
78	Tunisia	673	PROXY(Other N. Africa(Maddison))
79	Morocco	673	1500(Maddison)
80	Libya	673	AVG(Other N. Africa (Maddison))
81	Algeria	673	PROXY(Other N. Africa(Maddison))
82	Australia	671	1500(MIN)
83	Cyprus	666	PROXY(Greece (Maddison))
84	Costa Rica	666	1500(MIN)
85	Mexico	665	1500(Maddison)
86	Uzbekistan	657	PROXY(USSR (Maddison))
87	Bolivia	653	1500(MIN)
88	Panama	652	1500(MIN)
89	Turkmenistan	652	1500(MIN)
90	Sudan	649	1500(Sahel & W. Africa(Maddison))
91.5	Argentina	645	AVG(Other Sp. Am. (Maddison))
91.5	Uruguay	645	AVG(Other Sp. Am. (Maddison))
93	Chile	645	AVG(Other Sp. Am. (Maddison))
94	Ecuador	637	1500(MIN)
95	Brazil	636	1500(MIN)
96	Ukraine	635	PROXY(USSR (Maddison))
97	Peru	626	1500(MIN)
98	Cambodia	626	PROXY(Other E. Asia (Maddison))
99.5	Namibia	617	1500(MIN)
99.5	Somalia	617	1500(MIN)
101.5	South Africa	617	1500(MIN)
101.5	Swaziland	617	1500(MIN)
103.5	Madagascar	617	1500(MIN)
103.5	Mozambique	617	1500(MIN)
105.5	Zambia	617	1500(MIN)
105.5	Zimbabwe	617	1500(MIN)
107	Venezuela	608	1500(MIN)
108	Canada	608	1500(MIN)
109	El Salvador	606	1500(MIN)

TABLE 2.3 GDP AT PURCHASING POWER PARITIES PER CAPITA, 2012 DOLLARS, YEAR 1500			
Rank	Country	GPC	Source
110	Azerbaijan	602	1500(MIN)
111	Haiti	601	1500(MIN)
112	Dominican R	593	1500(MIN)
113	Bosnia	590	1500(MIN)
114	Colombia	590	1500(MIN)
115	Tajikistan	585	1500(MIN)
116	Albania	568	1500(MIN)
117	Kyrgyzstan	567	1500(MIN)
118	Nicaragua	565	1500(MIN)
119	Ghana	557	1500(MIN)
120	Paraguay	555	1500(MIN)
121	Nepal	555	1500(MIN)
122	Honduras	546	1500(MIN)
123	Mongolia	544	1500(MIN)
124	New Zealand	540	1500(MIN)
125	Macedonia	534	1500(MIN)
126	South Sudan	529	1500(MIN)
127	Kosovo	528	1500(MIN)
128	Burundi	468	1500(MIN)
129	Lesotho	463	1500(MIN)
130	Botswana	457	1500(MIN)
131	Malawi	429	1500(MIN)
132	Guinea	405	1500(MIN)
133	Guinea-Biss	389	1500(MIN)
134	Eritrea	372	1500(MIN)
135	Ethiopia	363	1500(MIN)

TABLE 2.4 GDP AT PURCHASING POWER PARITIES PER CAPITA, 2012 DOLLARS, YEAR 1600

Rank	Country	GPC	Source
1	Netherlands	2,161	1600(Maddison)
2	Italy	1,721	1600(Maddison)
3	Belgium	1,527	1600(Maddison)
4	UK	1,524	1600(Maddison)
5	Denmark	1,369	1600(Maddison)
6	Spain	1,335	1600(Maddison)
7	Slovenia	1,321	INTERPOL(Maddison)
8	France	1,316	1600(Maddison)
9	Austria	1,310	1600(Maddison)
10	Sweden	1,289	1600(Maddison)
11	Hungary	1,251	INTERPOL(Maddison)
12	Germany	1,238	1600(Maddison)
13	Estonia	1,229	INTERPOL(Maddison)
14	Norway	1,189	1600(Maddison)
15	Switzerland	1,174	1600(Maddison)
16	Portugal	1,158	1600(Maddison)
17	Poland	1,130	PROXY(E. Europe(Maddison))
18	Latvia	1,122	PROXY(USSR(Maddison))
19	Czechia	1,114	PROXY(E. Europe(Maddison))
20	Romania	1,112	PROXY(E. Europe(Maddison))
21	Kazakhstan	1,108	PROXY(USSR(Maddison))
22	Lithuania	1,085	PROXY(USSR(Maddison))
23	Uruguay	1,077	INTERPOL(Maddison)
24	Iceland	1,051	PROXY(Denmark)
25	Syria	1,030	INTERPOL(Maddison)
26	Lebanon	1,030	INTERPOL(Maddison)
27	Thailand	1,004	PROXY(Other E. Asia(Maddison))
28	Bulgaria	1,003	PROXY(E. Europe(Maddison))
29	Slovakia	972	PROXY(E. Europe(Maddison))
30	Ireland	962	1600(Maddison)
31	Israel	961	INTERPOL(Maddison)
32	Russia	939	PROXY(USSR(Maddison))
33	Iran	939	INTERPOL(Maddison)
34	Korea, North	939	INTERPOL(Maddison)
35	China	939	1600(Maddison)
36	Turkey	939	INTERPOL(Maddison)
37.5	Hong Kong	939	PROXY(China(Maddison))
37.5	Korea, South	939	INTERPOL(Maddison)
39	Malaysia	937	PROXY(Other E. Asia(Maddison))
40	Jordan	920	INTERPOL(Maddison)
41	Argentina	919	INTERPOL(Maddison)
42	Croatia	910	PROXY(E. Europe(Maddison))
43	Philippines	907	PROXY(Other E. Asia(Maddison))
44	Iraq	896	PROXY(W. Asia(Maddison))
45	Indonesia	896	INTERPOL(Maddison)
46	Armenia	874	PROXY(USSR(Maddison))
47.5	Qatar	861	INTERPOL(Maddison)

TABLE 2.4 GDP AT PURCHASING POWER PARITIES PER CAPITA, 2012 DOLLARS, YEAR 1600			
Rank	Country	GPC	Source
47.5	Yemen	861	INTERPOL(Maddison)
49.5	Saudi Arabia	861	INTERPOL(Maddison)
49.5	UAE	861	INTERPOL(Maddison)
52	India	861	1600(Undivided India(Maddison))
52	Kuwait	861	INTERPOL(Maddison)
52	Pakistan	861	1600(Undivided India(Maddison))
54.5	Bahrain	861	INTERPOL(Maddison)
54.5	Oman	861	INTERPOL(Maddison)
56	Bangladesh	861	1600(Undivided India(Maddison))
57	Taiwan	855	PROXY(Other E. Asia(Maddison))
58	Sri Lanka	855	PROXY(Other E. Asia(Maddison))
59	Georgia	850	PROXY(USSR(Maddison))
60	Finland	842	1600(Maddison)
61	Jamaica	838	INTERPOL(Maddison)
62	Puerto Rico	837	1600(MIN)
63	Trinidad & T	823	INTERPOL(Maddison)
64	Vietnam	819	PROXY(Other E. Asia(Maddison))
65	Japan	814	1600(Maddison)
66	Cuba	801	1600(MIN)
67	Sierra Leone	798	1600(MIN)
68	Afghanistan	794	PROXY(Other E. Asia(Maddison))
69	Serbia	786	PROXY(E. Europe(Maddison))
70	Burma	783	PROXY(Other E. Asia(Maddison))
71	Singapore	777	PROXY(Other E. Asia(Maddison))
72	US	774	1600(MIN)
73	Montenegro	773	PROXY(E. Europe(Maddison))
74	Moldova	765	PROXY(USSR(Maddison))
75	Chile	759	INTERPOL(Maddison)
76	Greece	756	1600(Maddison)
77	Laos	754	PROXY(Other E. Asia(Maddison))
78	Belarus	746	PROXY(USSR(Maddison))
79	Egypt	743	1600(Maddison)
80	Cyprus	743	PROXY(Greece(Maddison))
81	Guatemala	741	1600(MIN)
82	Uzbekistan	727	PROXY(USSR(Maddison))
83	Mexico	710	1600(Maddison)
84	Australia	710	1600(MIN)
85	Costa Rica	703	1600(MIN)
86	Ukraine	702	PROXY(USSR(Maddison))
87	Bolivia	689	1600(MIN)
88	Panama	688	1600(MIN)
89	Turkmenistan	688	PROXY(USSR(Maddison))
90	Tunisia	673	PROXY(Other N. Africa(Maddison))
91	Morocco	673	1600(Maddison)
92	Libya	673	AVG(Other N. Africa(Maddison))
93	Algeria	673	PROXY(Other N. Africa(Maddison))
94	Ecuador	672	1600(MIN)
95	Brazil	670	1600(Maddison)

Table 2.4 GDP at Purchasing Power Parities Per Capita, 2012 Dollars, Year 1600

Rank	Country	GPC	Source
96	Peru	659	1600(MIN)
97.5	Namibia	649	1600(Rest of Africa(Maddison))
97.5	Somalia	649	1600(Rest of Africa(Maddison))
100	South Africa	649	1600(Rest of Africa(Maddison))
100	Sudan	649	1600(Sahel & W. Africa(Maddison))
100	Swaziland	649	1600(Rest of Africa(Maddison))
102.5	Madagascar	649	1600(Rest of Africa(Maddison))
102.5	Mozambique	649	1600(Rest of Africa(Maddison))
104	Zambia	649	1600(Rest of Africa(Maddison))
105	Zimbabwe	649	1600(Rest of Africa(Maddison))
106	Venezuela	639	1600(MIN)
107	Canada	639	1600(MIN)
108	Cambodia	637	PROXY(Other E. Asia(Maddison))
109	El Salvador	637	1600(MIN)
110	Azerbaijan	632	PROXY(USSR(Maddison))
111	Haiti	631	1600(MIN)
112	Dominican R	622	1600(MIN)
113	Bosnia	619	1600(MIN)
114	Colombia	619	1600(MIN)
115	Tajikistan	614	1600(MIN)
116	Albania	595	1600(MIN)
117	Kyrgyzstan	594	1600(MIN)
118	Nicaragua	592	1600(MIN)
119	Ghana	583	1600(MIN)
120	Paraguay	581	1600(MIN)
121	Nepal	580	1600(MIN)
122	Honduras	571	1600(MIN)
123	Mongolia	568	1600(MIN)
124	New Zealand	564	1600(MIN)
125	Macedonia	557	1600(MIN)
126	South Sudan	553	1600(MIN)
127	Kosovo	552	1600(MIN)
128	Burundi	487	1600(MIN)
129	Lesotho	481	1600(MIN)
130	Botswana	474	1600(MIN)
131	Malawi	444	1600(MIN)
132	Guinea	419	1600(MIN)
133	Guinea-Biss	401	1600(MIN)
134	Eritrea	383	1600(MIN)
135	Ethiopia	373	1600(MIN)

TABLE 2.5 GDP AT PURCHASING POWER PARITIES PER CAPITA, 2012 DOLLARS, YEAR 1700			
Rank	Country	GPC	Source
1	Netherlands	3,333	1700(Maddison)
2	UK	1,956	1700(Maddison)
3	Uruguay	1,800	INTERPOL(Maddison)
4	Belgium	1,790	1700(Maddison)
5	Italy	1,721	1700(Maddison)
6	Denmark	1,626	1700(Maddison)
7	Austria	1,554	1700(Maddison)
8	Sweden	1,529	1700(Maddison)
9	Slovenia	1,497	INTERPOL(Maddison)
10.5	France	1,424	1700(Maddison)
10.5	Germany	1,424	1700(Maddison)
12	Norway	1,408	1700(Maddison)
13	Hungary	1,404	INTERPOL(Maddison)
14	Switzerland	1,393	1700(Maddison)
15	Estonia	1,376	INTERPOL(Maddison)
16	Spain	1,335	1700(Maddison)
17	Argentina	1,309	INTERPOL(Maddison)
18	Portugal	1,282	1700(Maddison)
19	Poland	1,249	PROXY(E. Europe(Maddison))
20	Iceland	1,248	PROXY(Denmark)
21	Latvia	1,240	PROXY(USSR(Maddison))
22	Czechia	1,232	PROXY(E. Europe(Maddison))
23	Romania	1,230	PROXY(E. Europe(Maddison))
24	Kazakhstan	1,224	PROXY(USSR(Maddison))
25	Lithuania	1,199	PROXY(USSR(Maddison))
26	Jamaica	1,121	PROXY(Caribbean cs(Maddison))
27	Ireland	1,119	1700(Maddison)
28	Bulgaria	1,109	PROXY(E. Europe(Maddison))
29	Trinidad & T	1,081	INTERPOL(Maddison)
30	Slovakia	1,075	PROXY(E. Europe(Maddison))
31	Russia	1,038	PROXY(USSR(Maddison))
32	Syria	1,030	PROXY(Other W. Asia(Maddison))
33	Lebanon	1,030	PROXY(Other W. Asia(Maddison))
34	Croatia	1,006	PROXY(E. Europe(Maddison))
35	Thailand	998	PROXY(Other E. Asia(Maddison))
36	Finland	998	1700(Maddison)
37	Armenia	966	PROXY(USSR(Maddison))
38	Israel	961	PROXY(Other W. Asia(Maddison))
39	Georgia	940	PROXY(USSR(Maddison))
40	Iran	939	1700(Maddison)
41	Korea, North	939	1700(Maddison)
42	China	939	1700(Maddison)
43	Turkey	939	1700(Maddison)
44.5	Hong Kong	939	PROXY(China(Maddison))
44.5	Korea, South	939	1700(Maddison)
46	Malaysia	932	PROXY(Other E. Asia(Maddison))
47	Jordan	920	PROXY(Other W. Asia(Maddison))

Table 2.5 GDP at Purchasing Power Parities Per Capita, 2012 Dollars, Year 1700			
Rank	Country	GPC	Source
48	Indonesia	908	1700(Maddison)
49	Philippines	903	PROXY(Other E. Asia(Maddison))
50	Puerto Rico	897	PROXY(Caribbean cs(Maddison))
51	Iraq	896	PROXY(W. Asia(Maddison))
52	Chile	893	INTERPOL(Maddison)
53	Japan	892	1700(Maddison)
54	Mexico	889	1700(Maddison)
55	Serbia	869	PROXY(E. Europe(Maddison))
56.5	Qatar	861	AVG(Arabia(Maddison))
56.5	Yemen	861	AVG(Arabia(Maddison))
58.5	Saudi Arabia	861	AVG(Arabia(Maddison))
58.5	UAE	861	AVG(Arabia(Maddison))
61	India	861	1700(Undivided India(Maddison))
61	Kuwait	861	AVG(Arabia(Maddison))
61	Pakistan	861	1700(Undivided India(Maddison))
63.5	Bahrain	861	AVG(Arabia(Maddison))
63.5	Oman	861	AVG(Arabia(Maddison))
65	Bangladesh	861	1700(Undivided India(Maddison))
66	Cuba	856	PROXY(Caribean cs(Maddison))
67	Montenegro	855	PROXY(E. Europe(Maddison))
68	Sierra Leone	852	1700(MIN)
69	Taiwan	850	PROXY(Other E. Asia(Maddison))
70	Sri Lanka	850	PROXY(Other E. Asia(Maddison))
71	Moldova	845	PROXY(USSR(Maddison))
72	Greece	829	1700(Maddison)
73	US	825	1700(Maddison)
74	Belarus	824	PROXY(USSR(Maddison))
75	Cyprus	815	PROXY(Greece(Maddison))
76	Vietnam	815	PROXY(Other E. Asia(Maddison))
77	Uzbekistan	803	PROXY(USSR(Maddison))
78	Afghanistan	790	PROXY(Other E. Asia(Maddison))
79	Guatemala	788	1700(MIN)
80	Burma	779	PROXY(Other E. Asia(Maddison))
81	Ukraine	776	PROXY(USSR(Maddison))
82	Singapore	773	PROXY(Other E. Asia(Maddison))
83	Turkmenistan	760	PROXY(USSR(Maddison))
84	Australia	752	1700(MIN)
85	Laos	750	PROXY(Other E. Asia(Maddison))
86	Costa Rica	745	1700(MIN)
87	Egypt	743	1700(Maddison)
88	Bolivia	729	1700(MIN)
89	Panama	728	1700(MIN)
90	Brazil	718	1700(Maddison)
91	Ecuador	710	1700(MIN)
92	Azerbaijan	699	PROXY(USSR(Maddison))
93	Peru	696	1700(MIN)
94	Venezuela	673	1700(MIN)
95	Tunisia	673	PROXY(Other N. Africa(Maddison))

TABLE 2.5 GDP AT PURCHASING POWER PARITIES PER CAPITA, 2012 DOLLARS, YEAR 1700			
Rank	Country	GPC	Source
96.5	Canada	673	1700(Maddison)
96.5	Morocco	673	1700(Maddison)
98	Libya	673	AVG(Other N. Africa(Maddison))
99	Algeria	673	PROXY(Other N. Africa(Maddison))
100	El Salvador	671	1700(MIN)
101	Haiti	665	1700(MIN)
102	Dominican R	655	1700(MIN)
103	Bosnia	652	1700(MIN)
104	Colombia	651	PROXY(Other Sp. Am.(Maddison))
105.5	Namibia	649	1700(Rest of Africa(Maddison))
105.5	Somalia	649	1700(Rest of Africa(Maddison))
108	South Africa	649	1700(Rest of Africa(Maddison))
108	Sudan	649	1700(Sahel & W. Africa(Maddison))
108	Swaziland	649	1700(Rest of Africa(Maddison))
110.5	Madagascar	649	1700(Rest of Africa(Maddison))
110.5	Mozambique	649	1700(Rest of Africa(Maddison))
112	Zambia	649	1700(Rest of Africa(Maddison))
113	Zimbabwe	649	1700(Rest of Africa(Maddison))
114	Tajikistan	645	PROXY(USSR(Maddison))
115	Cambodia	634	PROXY(Other E. Asia(Maddison))
116	Albania	624	1700(MIN)
117	Kyrgyzstan	624	1700(MIN)
118	Nicaragua	621	1700(MIN)
119	Ghana	611	1700(MIN)
120	Paraguay	610	1700(MIN)
121	Nepal	609	1700(MIN)
122	Honduras	598	1700(MIN)
123	Mongolia	595	1700(MIN)
124	New Zealand	591	1700(MIN)
125	Macedonia	583	1700(MIN)
126	South Sudan	578	1700(MIN)
127	Kosovo	577	1700(MIN)
128	Burundi	506	1700(MIN)
129	Lesotho	500	1700(MIN)
130	Botswana	492	1700(MIN)
131	Malawi	460	1700(MIN)
132	Guinea	433	1700(MIN)
133	Guinea-Biss	415	1700(MIN)
134	Eritrea	395	1700(MIN)
135	Ethiopia	385	1700(MIN)

Table 2.6 GDP at Purchasing Power Parities Per Capita, 2012 Dollars, Year 1820			
Rank	Country	GPC	Source
1	Uruguay	3,332	PROXY(Other L. Am.(Maddison))
2	Netherlands	2,876	1820(Maddison)
3	UK	2,670	1820(Maddison)
4	Belgium	2,064	1820(Maddison)
5	Argentina	2,003	PROXY(Other L. Am.(Maddison))
6	Denmark	1,994	1820(Maddison)
7	US	1,967	1820(Maddison)
8	Austria	1,906	1820(Maddison)
9	Sweden	1,875	1820(Maddison)
10	France	1,776	1820(Maddison)
11	Italy	1,748	1820(Maddison)
12	Slovenia	1,738	INTERPOL(Maddison)
13	Norway	1,728	1820(Maddison)
14	Switzerland	1,706	1820(Maddison)
15	Germany	1,685	1820(Maddison)
16	Hungary	1,613	INTERPOL(Maddison)
17	Spain	1,577	1820(Maddison)
18	Estonia	1,575	PROXY(USSR(Maddison))
19	Iceland	1,530	PROXY(Denmark)
20	Trinidad & T	1,501	PROXY(Other L. Am.(Maddison))
21	Portugal	1,444	1820(Maddison)
22	Canada	1,415	1820(Maddison)
23	Poland	1,408	PROXY(E. Europe(Maddison))
24	Latvia	1,398	PROXY(USSR(Maddison))
25	Czechia	1,388	PROXY(Czechoslovakia(Maddison))
26	Romania	1,386	PROXY(E. Europe(Maddison))
27	Kazakhstan	1,381	PROXY(USSR(Maddison))
28	Ireland	1,372	1820(Maddison)
29	Lithuania	1,352	PROXY(USSR(Maddison))
30	Bulgaria	1,250	PROXY(E. Europe(Maddison))
31	Finland	1,222	1820(Maddison)
32	Slovakia	1,212	PROXY(Czechoslovakia(Maddison))
33	Mexico	1,188	1820(Maddison)
34	Russia	1,170	PROXY(USSR(Maddison))
35	Croatia	1,134	PROXY(E. Europe(Maddison))
36	Jamaica	1,095	1820(Maddison)
37	Armenia	1,090	PROXY(USSR(Maddison))
38	Chile	1,086	1820(Maddison)
39	Georgia	1,060	PROXY(USSR(Maddison))
40	Japan	1,047	1820(Maddison)
41	Syria	1,030	1820(Maddison)
42	Lebanon	1,030	1820(Maddison)
43	Brazil	1,011	1820(Maddison)
44	Thailand	1,011	1820(Maddison)
45	Turkey	1,006	1820(Maddison)
46	Greece	1,003	1820(Maddison)
47	Cyprus	986	PROXY(Greece(Maddison))

Table 2.6 GDP at Purchasing Power Parities Per Capita, 2012 Dollars, Year 1820

Rank	Country	GPC	Source
48	Serbia	980	PROXY(E. Europe(Maddison))
49	Montenegro	964	PROXY(E. Europe(Maddison))
50	Israel	961	1820(Palestine(Maddison))
51	Indonesia	958	1820(Maddison)
52	Moldova	953	PROXY(USSR(Maddison))
53	Malaysia	944	1820(Maddison)
54	Korea, North	939	1820(Maddison)
55	China	939	1820(Maddison)
56.5	Hong Kong	939	1820(Maddison)
56.5	Korea, South	939	1820(Maddison)
58	Belarus	930	PROXY(USSR(Maddison))
59	Sierra Leone	928	1820(MIN)
60	Jordan	920	1820(Maddison)
61.5	Iran	920	1820(Maddison)
61.5	Iraq	920	1820(Maddison)
63	Philippines	914	1820(Maddison)
64	Uzbekistan	909	PROXY(USSR(Maddison))
65	Colombia	889	PROXY(Other L. Am.(Maddison))
66	Puerto Rico	876	PROXY(Other L. Am.(Maddison))
67	Ukraine	876	PROXY(USSR(Maddison))
68	Taiwan	861	1820(Maddison)
69.5	Qatar	861	AVG(Arabia(Maddison))
69.5	Yemen	861	AVG(Arabia(Maddison))
71.5	Saudi Arabia	861	AVG(Arabia(Maddison))
71.5	UAE	861	AVG(Arabia(Maddison))
73	Kuwait	861	AVG(Arabia(Maddison))
75	Bahrain	861	AVG(Arabia(Maddison))
75	Oman	861	AVG(Arabia(Maddison))
75	Sri Lanka	861	1820(Maddison)
77	Turkmenistan	858	PROXY(USSR(Maddison))
78	Guatemala	852	PROXY(Other L. Am.(Maddison))
79	Cuba	836	PROXY(Other L. Am.(Maddison))
80	Pakistan	831	1820(Maddison)
81	India	831	1820(Maddison)
82	Bangladesh	831	1820(Maddison)
83	Vietnam	825	1820(Maddison)
84	Australia	811	1820(Maddison)
85	Costa Rica	802	PROXY(Other L. Am.(Maddison))
86	Afghanistan	799	PROXY(26 E. Asian cs(Maddison))
87	Burma	789	1820(Maddison)
88	Azerbaijan	788	PROXY(USSR(Maddison))
89	Bolivia	784	PROXY(Other L. Am.(Maddison))
90	Panama	783	PROXY(Other L. Am.(Maddison))
91	Singapore	782	1820(Maddison)
92	Ecuador	761	PROXY(Other L. Am.(Maddison))
93	Laos	760	PROXY(26 E. Asian cs(Maddison))
94	Peru	746	PROXY(Other L. Am.(Maddison))
95	Egypt	743	1820(Maddison)

Table 2.6 GDP at Purchasing Power Parities Per Capita, 2012 Dollars, Year 1820			
Rank	Country	GPC	Source
96	Tajikistan	728	PROXY(USSR(Maddison))
97	Venezuela	720	1820(Maddison)
98	El Salvador	717	1820(MIN)
99	Haiti	710	1820(MIN)
100	Dominican R	699	1820(MIN)
101	Bosnia	695	1820(MIN)
102	Tunisia	673	1820(Maddison)
103	Morocco	673	1820(Maddison)
104	Libya	673	AVG(Other N. Africa(Maddison))
105	Algeria	673	1820(Maddison)
106	Albania	664	PROXY(E. Europe(Maddison))
107	Kyrgyzstan	663	PROXY(USSR(Maddison))
108	Nicaragua	660	PROXY(Other L. Am.(Maddison))
109	Ghana	649	1820(Maddison)
110.5	Namibia	649	1820(Rest of Africa(Maddison))
110.5	Somalia	649	1820(Rest of Africa(Maddison))
113	South Africa	649	1820(Maddison)
113	Sudan	649	1820(Sahel & W. Africa(Maddison))
113	Swaziland	649	1820(Rest of Africa(Maddison))
115.5	Madagascar	649	1820(Rest of Africa(Maddison))
115.5	Mozambique	649	1820(Rest of Africa(Maddison))
117	Zambia	649	1820(Rest of Africa(Maddison))
118	Zimbabwe	649	1820(Rest of Africa(Maddison))
119	Paraguay	647	PROXY(Other L. Am.(Maddison))
120	Nepal	646	1820(MIN)
121	Cambodia	642	PROXY(26 E. Asian cs(Maddison))
122	Honduras	635	1820(MIN)
123	Mongolia	631	1820(MIN)
124	New Zealand	626	1820(Maddison)
125	Macedonia	618	1820(MIN)
126	South Sudan	612	1820(MIN)
127	Kosovo	611	1820(MIN)
128	Burundi	532	1820(MIN)
129	Lesotho	525	1820(MIN)
130	Botswana	517	1820(MIN)
131	Malawi	482	1820(MIN)
132	Guinea	452	1820(MIN)
133	Guinea-Biss	432	1820(MIN)
134	Eritrea	411	1820(MIN)
135	Ethiopia	400	1820(MIN)

Table 2.7 GDP at Purchasing Power Parities Per Capita, 2012 Dollars, Year 1870

Rank	Country	GPC	Source
1	Australia	5,122	1870(Maddison)
2	UK	4,992	1870(Maddison)
3	New Zealand	4,851	1870(Maddison)
4	Netherlands	4,314	1870(Maddison)
5	Belgium	4,213	1870(Maddison)
6	US	3,826	1870(Maddison)
7	Uruguay	3,413	1870(Maddison)
8	Switzerland	3,289	1870(Maddison)
9	Denmark	3,134	1870(Maddison)
10	France	2,936	1870(Maddison)
11	Austria	2,915	1870(Maddison)
12	Germany	2,878	1870(Maddison)
13	Ireland	2,778	1870(Maddison)
14	Canada	2,652	1870(Maddison)
15	Sweden	2,601	1870(Maddison)
16	Iceland	2,406	PROXY(Denmark)
17	Italy	2,346	1870(Maddison)
18	Norway	2,241	1870(Maddison)
19	Estonia	2,158	PROXY(USSR(Maddison))
20	Argentina	2,052	1870(Maddison)
21	Chile	2,019	1870(Maddison)
22	Latvia	1,917	PROXY(USSR(Maddison))
23	Czechia	1,903	PROXY(Czechoslovakia(Maddison))
24	Kazakhstan	1,892	PROXY(USSR(Maddison))
25	Spain	1,889	1870(Maddison)
26	Lithuania	1,853	PROXY(USSR(Maddison))
27	Slovenia	1,850	PROXY(Yugoslavia(Maddison))
28	Finland	1,784	1870(Maddison)
29	Hungary	1,709	1870(Maddison)
30	Slovakia	1,661	PROXY(Czechoslovakia(Maddison))
31	Russia	1,604	PROXY(USSR(Maddison))
32	Trinidad & T	1,538	PROXY(Other L. Am.(Maddison))
33	Portugal	1,526	1870(Maddison)
34	Armenia	1,493	PROXY(USSR(Maddison))
35	Poland	1,480	1870(Maddison)
36	Romania	1,457	1870(Maddison)
37	Georgia	1,453	PROXY(USSR(Maddison))
38	Greece	1,377	1870(Maddison)
39	Cyprus	1,354	PROXY(Greece(Maddison))
40	South Africa	1,343	1870(Maddison)
41	Sri Lanka	1,332	1870(Maddison)
42	Syria	1,321	1870(Maddison)
43	Lebanon	1,321	1870(Maddison)
44	Bulgaria	1,314	1870(Maddison)
45	Moldova	1,307	PROXY(USSR(Maddison))
46	Turkey	1,291	1870(Maddison)
47	Belarus	1,274	PROXY(USSR(Maddison))

Table 2.7 GDP at Purchasing Power Parities Per Capita, 2012 Dollars, Year 1870			
Rank	Country	GPC	Source
48	Uzbekistan	1,241	PROXY(USSR(Maddison))
49	Namibia	1,225	INTERPOL(Maddison)
50	Ukraine	1,200	PROXY(USSR(Maddison))
51	Croatia	1,192	PROXY(Yugoslavia(Maddison))
52	Turkmenistan	1,175	PROXY(USSR(Maddison))
53	Israel	1,175	1870(Palestine(Maddison))
54	Japan	1,153	1870(Maddison)
55	Jordan	1,125	1870(Maddison)
56.5	Iran	1,125	1870(Maddison)
56.5	Iraq	1,125	1870(Maddison)
58	Algeria	1,119	1870(Maddison)
59	Brazil	1,116	1870(Maddison)
60	Thailand	1,114	1870(Maddison)
61	Azerbaijan	1,080	PROXY(USSR(Maddison))
62	Hong Kong	1,069	1870(Maddison)
63	Singapore	1,067	1870(Maddison)
64	Mexico	1,055	1870(Maddison)
65	Malaysia	1,037	1870(Maddison)
66	Serbia	1,030	PROXY(Yugoslavia(Maddison))
67	Indonesia	1,023	1870(Maddison)
68	Egypt	1,016	1870(Maddison)
69	Montenegro	1,013	PROXY(Yugoslavia(Maddison))
70	Tajikistan	997	PROXY(USSR(Maddison))
71	Tunisia	991	1870(Maddison)
72	Philippines	976	1870(Maddison)
73	Pakistan	976	INTERPOL(Maddison)
74	Sierra Leone	963	1870(MIN)
75	Mozambique	956	INTERPOL(Maddison)
76	Korea, North	945	1870(Maddison)
77	Korea, South	945	1870(Maddison)
78	Somalia	930	INTERPOL(Maddison)
79	Colombia	911	PROXY(Other L. Am.(Maddison))
80	Kyrgyzstan	909	PROXY(USSR(Maddison))
81	Yemen	900	AVG(Arabia(Maddison))
82.5	Qatar	900	AVG(Arabia(Maddison))
82.5	UAE	900	AVG(Arabia(Maddison))
85	Bahrain	900	AVG(Arabia(Maddison))
85	Kuwait	900	AVG(Arabia(Maddison))
85	Saudi Arabia	900	AVG(Arabia(Maddison))
87	Oman	900	AVG(Arabia(Maddison))
88	Puerto Rico	897	PROXY(Other L. Am.(Maddison))
89	Madagascar	893	INTERPOL(Maddison)
90	Venezuela	890	1870(Maddison)
91	Morocco	881	1870(Maddison)
92	Bangladesh	879	INTERPOL(Maddison)
93	Libya	877	INTERPOL(Maddison)
94	India	873	1870(Maddison)
95	Guatemala	873	PROXY(Other L. Am.(Maddison))

Table 2.7 GDP at Purchasing Power Parities Per Capita, 2012 Dollars, Year 1870			
Rank	Country	GPC	Source
96	Taiwan	861	1870(Maddison)
97	Cuba	856	PROXY(Other L. Am.(Maddison))
98	Sudan	844	INTERPOL(Maddison)
99	Jamaica	837	1870(Maddison)
100	China	829	1870(Maddison)
101	Costa Rica	822	PROXY(Other L. Am.(Maddison))
102	Bolivia	803	PROXY(Other L. Am.(Maddison))
103	Swaziland	803	INTERPOL(Maddison)
104	Panama	802	PROXY(Other L. Am.(Maddison))
105	Zimbabwe	794	INTERPOL(Maddison)
106	Vietnam	790	1870(Maddison)
107	Burma	789	1870(Maddison)
108	Ecuador	780	PROXY(Other L. Am.(Maddison))
109	Zambia	777	INTERPOL(Maddison)
110	Afghanistan	769	PROXY(26 E. Asian cs(Maddison))
111	Peru	764	PROXY(Other L. Am.(Maddison))
112	El Salvador	738	1870(MIN)
113	Laos	731	PROXY(26 E. Asian cs(Maddison))
114	Haiti	731	1870(MIN)
115	Ghana	723	1870(Maddison)
116	Dominican R	719	1870(MIN)
117	Bosnia	715	1870(MIN)
118	Albania	698	1870(Maddison)
119	Nicaragua	676	PROXY(Other L. Am.(Maddison))
120	Nepal	663	1870(MIN)
121	Paraguay	663	PROXY(Other L. Am.(Maddison))
122	Honduras	651	1870(MIN)
123	Mongolia	648	1870(MIN)
124	Macedonia	633	PROXY(Yugoslavia(Maddison))
125	South Sudan	627	1870(MIN)
126	Kosovo	626	PROXY(Yugoslavia(Maddison))
127	Cambodia	626	MIN(PROXY(26 E. Asian cs(Maddison)))
128	Burundi	544	1870(MIN)
129	Lesotho	536	1870(MIN)
130	Botswana	528	1870(MIN)
131	Malawi	491	1870(MIN)
132	Guinea	460	1870(MIN)
133	Guinea-Biss	440	1870(MIN)
134	Eritrea	417	1870(MIN)
135	Ethiopia	406	1870(MIN)

TABLE 2.8 GDP AT PURCHASING POWER PARITIES PER CAPITA, 2012 DOLLARS, YEAR 1880			
Rank	Country	GPC	Source
1	Australia	6,705	1880(Maddison)
2	New Zealand	5,863	1880(Maddison)
3	UK	5,441	1880(Maddison)
4	Belgium	4,796	1880(Maddison)
5	Netherlands	4,767	1880(Maddison)
6	US	4,507	1880(Maddison)
7	Switzerland	3,834	1880(Maddison)
8	Denmark	3,413	1880(Maddison)
9	France	3,317	1880(Maddison)
10	Uruguay	3,258	1880(Maddison)
11	Austria	3,253	1880(Maddison)
12	Germany	3,116	1880(Maddison)
13	Ireland	3,072	INTERPOL(Maddison)
14	Sweden	2,889	1880(Maddison)
15	Canada	2,842	1880(Maddison)
16	Argentina	2,628	INTERPOL(Maddison)
17	Iceland	2,619	PROXY(Denmark)
18	Spain	2,576	1880(Maddison)
19	Norway	2,485	1880(Maddison)
20	Italy	2,474	1880(Maddison)
21	Chile	2,410	INTERPOL(Maddison)
22	Estonia	2,363	INTERPOL(Maddison)
23	Slovenia	2,194	INTERPOL(Maddison)
24	Czechia	2,164	INTERPOL(Maddison)
25	Latvia	2,098	INTERPOL(Maddison)
26	Kazakhstan	2,071	INTERPOL(Maddison)
27	Lithuania	2,028	INTERPOL(Maddison)
28	Hungary	1,985	INTERPOL(Maddison)
29	Slovakia	1,889	INTERPOL(Maddison)
30	Trinidad & T	1,832	INTERPOL(Maddison)
31	Finland	1,807	1880(Maddison)
32	Russia	1,756	INTERPOL(Maddison)
33	Poland	1,725	INTERPOL(Maddison)
34	Romania	1,685	INTERPOL(Maddison)
35	Armenia	1,635	INTERPOL(Maddison)
36	Greece	1,593	INTERPOL(Maddison)
37	Georgia	1,590	INTERPOL(Maddison)
38	Cyprus	1,566	PROXY(Greece(Maddison))
39	South Africa	1,552	INTERPOL(Maddison)
40	Bulgaria	1,525	INTERPOL(Maddison)
41	Portugal	1,482	1880(Maddison)
42.5	Lebanon	1,473	INTERPOL(Maddison)
42.5	Syria	1,473	INTERPOL(Maddison)
44	Moldova	1,430	INTERPOL(Maddison)
45	Croatia	1,414	INTERPOL(Maddison)
46	Turkey	1,412	INTERPOL(Maddison)
47	Belarus	1,395	INTERPOL(Maddison)

TABLE 2.8 GDP AT PURCHASING POWER PARITIES PER CAPITA, 2012 DOLLARS, YEAR 1880

Rank	Country	GPC	Source
48	Namibia	1,390	INTERPOL(Maddison)
49	Uzbekistan	1,359	INTERPOL(Maddison)
50	Japan	1,350	1880(Maddison)
51	Israel	1,323	INTERPOL(Maddison)
52	Ukraine	1,314	INTERPOL(Maddison)
53	Sri Lanka	1,300	1880(Maddison)
54	Mexico	1,292	INTERPOL(Maddison)
55	Turkmenistan	1,287	INTERPOL(Maddison)
56	Algeria	1,239	1880(Maddison)
57	Hong Kong	1,237	INTERPOL(Maddison)
58	Singapore	1,235	INTERPOL(Maddison)
59	Serbia	1,222	INTERPOL(Maddison)
61	Iran	1,215	INTERPOL(Maddison)
61	Iraq	1,215	INTERPOL(Maddison)
61	Jordan	1,215	INTERPOL(Maddison)
63	Montenegro	1,202	INTERPOL(Maddison)
64	Azerbaijan	1,182	INTERPOL(Maddison)
65	Brazil	1,177	1880(Maddison)
66	Thailand	1,169	INTERPOL(Maddison)
67	Tajikistan	1,092	INTERPOL(Maddison)
68	Malaysia	1,086	INTERPOL(Maddison)
69	Colombia	1,081	INTERPOL(Maddison)
70	Egypt	1,079	INTERPOL(Maddison)
71	Tunisia	1,070	INTERPOL(Maddison)
72	Puerto Rico	1,069	INTERPOL(Maddison)
73	Guatemala	1,040	INTERPOL(Maddison)
74	Indonesia	1,036	1880(Maddison)
75	Mozambique	1,032	INTERPOL(Maddison)
76	Cuba	1,020	INTERPOL(Maddison)
77	Korea, North	1,015	INTERPOL(Maddison)
78	Korea, South	1,015	INTERPOL(Maddison)
79	Philippines	1,012	INTERPOL(Maddison)
80	Pakistan	1,008	INTERPOL(Maddison)
81	Venezuela	1,006	INTERPOL(Maddison)
82	Somalia	1,000	INTERPOL(Maddison)
83	Kyrgyzstan	995	INTERPOL(Maddison)
84	Costa Rica	979	INTERPOL(Maddison)
85	Sierra Leone	971	1880(MIN)
86	Bolivia	957	INTERPOL(Maddison)
87	Panama	956	INTERPOL(Maddison)
88	Madagascar	952	INTERPOL(Maddison)
89	Morocco	930	INTERPOL(Maddison)
90	Ecuador	929	INTERPOL(Maddison)
91	Libya	925	INTERPOL(Maddison)
92	Taiwan	918	INTERPOL(Maddison)
93	India	911	INTERPOL(Maddison)
94.5	Qatar	909	INTERPOL(Maddison)
94.5	Yemen	909	INTERPOL(Maddison)

TABLE 2.8 GDP AT PURCHASING POWER PARITIES PER CAPITA, 2012 DOLLARS, YEAR 1880			
Rank	Country	GPC	Source
97	Kuwait	909	INTERPOL(Maddison)
97	Saudi Arabia	909	INTERPOL(Maddison)
97	UAE	909	INTERPOL(Maddison)
99	Bahrain	909	INTERPOL(Maddison)
100	Oman	909	INTERPOL(Maddison)
101	Peru	907	INTERPOL(Maddison)
102	Sudan	890	INTERPOL(Maddison)
103	Bangladesh	889	INTERPOL(Maddison)
104	Jamaica	866	INTERPOL(Maddison)
105	Vietnam	860	INTERPOL(Maddison)
106	Burma	847	INTERPOL(Maddison)
107	Swaziland	838	INTERPOL(Maddison)
108	China	837	INTERPOL(Maddison)
109	Afghanistan	833	INTERPOL(Maddison)
110	Zimbabwe	827	INTERPOL(Maddison)
111	Albania	808	INTERPOL(Maddison)
112	Nicaragua	806	INTERPOL(Maddison)
113	Zambia	805	INTERPOL(Maddison)
114	Laos	791	INTERPOL(Maddison)
115	Paraguay	790	INTERPOL(Maddison)
116	Macedonia	751	INTERPOL(Maddison)
117	Kosovo	743	PROXY(Yugoslavia(Maddison))
118	El Salvador	743	INTERPOL(Maddison)
119	Ghana	739	INTERPOL(Maddison)
120	Haiti	735	1880(MIN)
121	Dominican R	723	1880(MIN)
122	Bosnia	719	PROXY(Yugoslavia(Maddison))
123	Cambodia	669	INTERPOL(Maddison)
124	Nepal	667	INTERPOL(Maddison)
125	Honduras	655	INTERPOL(Maddison)
126	Mongolia	651	1880(MIN)
127	South Sudan	631	1880(MIN)
128	Burundi	546	1880(MIN)
129	Lesotho	539	1880(MIN)
130	Botswana	530	1880(MIN)
131	Malawi	493	1880(MIN)
132	Guinea	462	1880(MIN)
133	Guinea-Biss	441	1880(MIN)
134	Eritrea	419	1880(MIN)
135	Ethiopia	408	1880(MIN)

Table 2.9 GDP at Purchasing Power Parities Per Capita, 2012 Dollars, Year 1890

Rank	Country	GPC	Source
1	Australia	6,976	1890(Maddison)
2	UK	6,273	1890(Maddison)
3	New Zealand	5,876	1890(Maddison)
4	Belgium	5,364	1890(Maddison)
5	US	5,308	1890(Maddison)
6	Netherlands	5,200	1890(Maddison)
7	Switzerland	4,979	1890(Maddison)
8	Denmark	3,948	1890(Maddison)
9	Austria	3,823	1890(Maddison)
10	Germany	3,799	1890(Maddison)
11	Canada	3,721	1890(Maddison)
12	France	3,718	1890(Maddison)
13	Ireland	3,397	INTERPOL(Maddison)
14	Argentina	3,368	1890(Maddison)
15	Uruguay	3,360	1890(Maddison)
16	Sweden	3,264	1890(Maddison)
17	Iceland	3,030	PROXY(Denmark)
18	Chile	2,877	INTERPOL(Maddison)
19	Norway	2,781	1890(Maddison)
20	Italy	2,609	1890(Maddison)
21	Slovenia	2,603	PROXY(Yugoslavia(Maddison))
22	Estonia	2,587	INTERPOL(Maddison)
23	Spain	2,541	1890(Maddison)
24	Czechia	2,461	PROXY(Czechoslovakia(Maddison))
25	Hungary	2,305	1890(Maddison)
26	Latvia	2,297	INTERPOL(Maddison)
27	Kazakhstan	2,268	INTERPOL(Maddison)
28	Lithuania	2,220	INTERPOL(Maddison)
29	Trinidad & T	2,183	INTERPOL(Maddison)
30	Finland	2,161	1890(Maddison)
31	Slovakia	2,148	PROXY(Czechoslovakia(Maddison))
32	Poland	2,009	1890(Maddison)
33	Romania	1,950	1890(Maddison)
34	Russia	1,922	INTERPOL(Maddison)
35	Greece	1,843	1890(Maddison)
36	Cyprus	1,812	PROXY(Greece(Maddison))
37	South Africa	1,795	INTERPOL(Maddison)
38	Armenia	1,790	INTERPOL(Maddison)
39	Bulgaria	1,770	1890(Maddison)
40	Portugal	1,765	1890(Maddison)
41	Georgia	1,741	INTERPOL(Maddison)
42	Croatia	1,678	PROXY(Yugoslavia(Maddison))
43	Syria	1,643	INTERPOL(Maddison)
44	Lebanon	1,643	INTERPOL(Maddison)
45	Sri Lanka	1,635	1890(Maddison)
46	Japan	1,584	1890(Maddison)
47	Mexico	1,582	1890(Maddison)

Table 2.9 GDP at Purchasing Power Parities Per Capita, 2012 Dollars, Year 1890			
Rank	Country	GPC	Source
48	Namibia	1,579	INTERPOL(Maddison)
49	Moldova	1,566	INTERPOL(Maddison)
50	Turkey	1,545	INTERPOL(Maddison)
51	Belarus	1,527	INTERPOL(Maddison)
52	Israel	1,489	INTERPOL(Maddison)
53	Uzbekistan	1,488	INTERPOL(Maddison)
54	Serbia	1,450	PROXY(Yugoslavia(Maddison))
55	Ukraine	1,438	INTERPOL(Maddison)
56	Hong Kong	1,431	INTERPOL(Maddison)
57	Singapore	1,430	INTERPOL(Maddison)
58	Montenegro	1,426	PROXY(Yugoslavia(Maddison))
59	Turkmenistan	1,408	INTERPOL(Maddison)
60	Algeria	1,392	INTERPOL(Maddison)
61	Jordan	1,312	INTERPOL(Maddison)
62	Iran	1,312	INTERPOL(Maddison)
63	Iraq	1,312	INTERPOL(Maddison)
64	Azerbaijan	1,294	INTERPOL(Maddison)
65	Colombia	1,283	INTERPOL(Maddison)
66	Puerto Rico	1,274	INTERPOL(Maddison)
67	Brazil	1,242	1890(Maddison)
68	Guatemala	1,239	INTERPOL(Maddison)
69	Thailand	1,227	1890(Maddison)
70	Cuba	1,216	INTERPOL(Maddison)
71	Tajikistan	1,195	INTERPOL(Maddison)
72	Costa Rica	1,166	INTERPOL(Maddison)
73	Tunisia	1,156	INTERPOL(Maddison)
74	Egypt	1,155	INTERPOL(Maddison)
75	Bolivia	1,140	INTERPOL(Maddison)
76	Panama	1,139	INTERPOL(Maddison)
77	Malaysia	1,138	INTERPOL(Maddison)
78	Venezuela	1,137	INTERPOL(Maddison)
79	Mozambique	1,115	INTERPOL(Maddison)
80	Ecuador	1,107	INTERPOL(Maddison)
81	Korea, North	1,090	INTERPOL(Maddison)
82	Korea, South	1,090	INTERPOL(Maddison)
83	Kyrgyzstan	1,090	INTERPOL(Maddison)
84	Peru	1,077	INTERPOL(Maddison)
85	Somalia	1,074	INTERPOL(Maddison)
86	Philippines	1,048	INTERPOL(Maddison)
87	Pakistan	1,041	INTERPOL(Maddison)
88	Indonesia	1,033	1890(Maddison)
89	Madagascar	1,015	INTERPOL(Maddison)
90	Morocco	981	INTERPOL(Maddison)
91	Taiwan	980	INTERPOL(Maddison)
92	Sierra Leone	978	1890(MIN)
93	Libya	975	INTERPOL(Maddison)
94	Nicaragua	960	INTERPOL(Maddison)
95	India	951	1890(Maddison)

Table 2.9 GDP at Purchasing Power Parities Per Capita, 2012 Dollars, Year 1890

Rank	Country	GPC	Source
96	Paraguay	941	INTERPOL(Maddison)
97	Sudan	938	INTERPOL(Maddison)
98	Vietnam	936	INTERPOL(Maddison)
99	Albania	936	1890(Maddison)
100.5	Qatar	918	INTERPOL(Maddison)
100.5	Yemen	918	INTERPOL(Maddison)
103	Bahrain	918	INTERPOL(Maddison)
103	Kuwait	918	INTERPOL(Maddison)
103	UAE	918	INTERPOL(Maddison)
105	Oman	918	INTERPOL(Maddison)
106	Saudi Arabia	918	INTERPOL(Maddison)
107	Burma	910	INTERPOL(Maddison)
108	Afghanistan	901	INTERPOL(Maddison)
109	Bangladesh	899	INTERPOL(Maddison)
110	Jamaica	897	INTERPOL(Maddison)
111	Macedonia	891	PROXY(Yugoslavia(Maddison))
112	El Salvador	885	INTERPOL(Maddison)
113	Kosovo	881	PROXY(Yugoslavia(Maddison))
114	Swaziland	874	INTERPOL(Maddison)
115	Zimbabwe	861	INTERPOL(Maddison)
116	Laos	856	INTERPOL(Maddison)
117	Bosnia	853	PROXY(Yugoslavia(Maddison))
118	China	845	1890(Maddison)
119	Zambia	834	INTERPOL(Maddison)
120	Honduras	780	INTERPOL(Maddison)
121	Ghana	756	INTERPOL(Maddison)
122	Haiti	740	1890(MIN)
123	Dominican R	727	INTERPOL(Maddison)
124	Cambodia	724	INTERPOL(Maddison)
125	Nepal	716	INTERPOL(Maddison)
126	Mongolia	654	1890(MIN)
127	South Sudan	634	1890(MIN)
128	Burundi	549	1890(MIN)
129	Lesotho	541	1890(MIN)
130	Botswana	532	1890(MIN)
131	Malawi	495	1890(MIN)
132	Guinea	464	1890(MIN)
133	Guinea-Biss	443	1890(MIN)
134	Eritrea	420	1890(MIN)
135	Ethiopia	409	1890(MIN)

Table 2.10 GDP at Purchasing Power Parities Per Capita, 2012 Dollars, Year 1900			
Rank	Country	GPC	Source
1	UK	7,029	1900(Maddison)
2	New Zealand	6,726	1900(Maddison)
3	US	6,402	1900(Maddison)
4	Australia	6,280	1900(Maddison)
5	Switzerland	5,998	1900(Maddison)
6	Belgium	5,838	1900(Maddison)
7	Netherlands	5,358	1900(Maddison)
8	Denmark	4,721	1900(Maddison)
9	Germany	4,671	1900(Maddison)
10	Canada	4,555	1900(Maddison)
11	Austria	4,510	1900(Maddison)
12	France	4,500	1900(Maddison)
13	Argentina	4,313	1900(Maddison)
14	Sweden	4,008	1900(Maddison)
15	Ireland	3,756	INTERPOL(Maddison)
16	Iceland	3,623	PROXY(Denmark)
17	Uruguay	3,472	1900(Maddison)
18	Chile	3,435	1900(Maddison)
19	Norway	3,031	1900(Maddison)
20	Estonia	2,831	PROXY(USSR(Maddison))
21	Czechia	2,827	PROXY(Czechoslovakia(Maddison))
22	Spain	2,795	1900(Maddison)
23	Italy	2,793	1900(Maddison)
24	Slovenia	2,785	PROXY(Yugoslavia(Maddison))
25	Hungary	2,632	1900(Maddison)
26	Finland	2,610	1900(Maddison)
27	Trinidad & T	2,601	INTERPOL(Maddison)
28	Latvia	2,514	PROXY(USSR(Maddison))
29	Kazakhstan	2,482	PROXY(USSR(Maddison))
30	Slovakia	2,467	PROXY(Czechoslovakia(Maddison))
31	Lithuania	2,431	PROXY(USSR(Maddison))
32	Poland	2,404	1900(Maddison)
33	Romania	2,214	1900(Maddison)
34	Mexico	2,138	1900(Maddison)
35	Greece	2,114	1900(Maddison)
36	Russia	2,104	PROXY(USSR(Maddison))
37	Cyprus	2,078	PROXY(Greece(Maddison))
38	South Africa	2,076	INTERPOL(Maddison)
39	Portugal	2,037	1900(Maddison)
40	Sri Lanka	2,019	1900(Maddison)
41	Armenia	1,959	PROXY(USSR(Maddison))
42	Bulgaria	1,914	1900(Maddison)
43	Georgia	1,906	PROXY(USSR(Maddison))
44	Japan	1,847	1900(Maddison)
45.5	Lebanon	1,833	INTERPOL(Maddison)
45.5	Syria	1,833	INTERPOL(Maddison)
47	Croatia	1,795	PROXY(Yugoslavia(Maddison))

Table 2.10 GDP at Purchasing Power Parities Per Capita, 2012 Dollars, Year 1900			
Rank	Country	GPC	Source
48	Namibia	1,792	INTERPOL(Maddison)
49	Moldova	1,714	PROXY(USSR(Maddison))
50	Turkey	1,689	INTERPOL(Maddison)
51	Israel	1,677	INTERPOL(Maddison)
52	Belarus	1,672	PROXY(USSR(Maddison))
53	Hong Kong	1,656	INTERPOL(Maddison)
54	Singapore	1,655	INTERPOL(Maddison)
55	Uzbekistan	1,628	PROXY(USSR(Maddison))
56	Ukraine	1,574	PROXY(USSR(Maddison))
57	Algeria	1,564	INTERPOL(Maddison)
58	Serbia	1,551	PROXY(Yugoslavia(Maddison))
59	Turkmenistan	1,542	PROXY(USSR(Maddison))
60	Montenegro	1,525	PROXY(Yugoslavia(Maddison))
61	Colombia	1,523	1900(Maddison)
62	Puerto Rico	1,518	INTERPOL(Maddison)
63	Guatemala	1,476	INTERPOL(Maddison)
64	Cuba	1,449	INTERPOL(Maddison)
65	Azerbaijan	1,417	PROXY(USSR(Maddison))
66	Jordan	1,416	INTERPOL(Maddison)
67	Iran	1,416	INTERPOL(Maddison)
68	Iraq	1,416	INTERPOL(Maddison)
69	Costa Rica	1,390	INTERPOL(Maddison)
70	Bolivia	1,359	INTERPOL(Maddison)
71	Panama	1,357	INTERPOL(Maddison)
72	Ecuador	1,319	INTERPOL(Maddison)
73	Tajikistan	1,308	PROXY(USSR(Maddison))
74	Venezuela	1,285	1900(Maddison)
75	Peru	1,278	1900(Maddison)
76	Thailand	1,265	INTERPOL(Maddison)
77	Egypt	1,260	INTERPOL(Maddison)
78	Tunisia	1,249	INTERPOL(Maddison)
79	Mozambique	1,205	INTERPOL(Maddison)
80	Kyrgyzstan	1,193	PROXY(USSR(Maddison))
81	Malaysia	1,191	INTERPOL(Maddison)
82	Korea, North	1,170	INTERPOL(Maddison)
83	Korea, South	1,170	INTERPOL(Maddison)
84	Indonesia	1,163	1900(Maddison)
85	Somalia	1,154	INTERPOL(Maddison)
86	Nicaragua	1,144	INTERPOL(Maddison)
87	Paraguay	1,121	INTERPOL(Maddison)
88	Philippines	1,086	INTERPOL(Maddison)
89	Madagascar	1,082	INTERPOL(Maddison)
90	Pakistan	1,075	1900(Maddison)
91	Albania	1,072	1900(Maddison)
92	Brazil	1,061	1900(Maddison)
93	El Salvador	1,054	INTERPOL(Maddison)
94	Taiwan	1,045	INTERPOL(Maddison)
95	Morocco	1,036	INTERPOL(Maddison)

Table 2.10 GDP at Purchasing Power Parities Per Capita, 2012 Dollars, Year 1900

Rank	Country	GPC	Source
96	Libya	1,029	INTERPOL(Maddison)
97	Vietnam	1,019	INTERPOL(Maddison)
98	Sudan	988	INTERPOL(Maddison)
99	Sierra Leone	986	1900(MIN)
100	India	978	1900(Maddison)
101	Burma	977	INTERPOL(Maddison)
102	Afghanistan	975	INTERPOL(Maddison)
103	Macedonia	954	PROXY(Yugoslavia(Maddison))
104	Kosovo	943	PROXY(Yugoslavia(Maddison))
105	Honduras	930	INTERPOL(Maddison)
106	Jamaica	928	INTERPOL(Maddison)
107	Laos	927	INTERPOL(Maddison)
108	Yemen	927	INTERPOL(Maddison)
110	Bahrain	927	INTERPOL(Maddison)
110	Qatar	927	INTERPOL(Maddison)
110	UAE	927	INTERPOL(Maddison)
112.5	Kuwait	927	INTERPOL(Maddison)
112.5	Saudi Arabia	927	INTERPOL(Maddison)
114	Oman	927	INTERPOL(Maddison)
115	Bosnia	913	PROXY(Yugoslavia(Maddison))
116	Swaziland	912	INTERPOL(Maddison)
117	Bangladesh	909	1900(Maddison)
118	Dominican R	903	INTERPOL(Maddison)
119	Zimbabwe	897	INTERPOL(Maddison)
120	Zambia	865	INTERPOL(Maddison)
121	China	853	1900(Maddison)
122	Ghana	826	INTERPOL(Maddison)
123	Cambodia	783	INTERPOL(Maddison)
124	Nepal	769	INTERPOL(Maddison)
125	Haiti	744	INTERPOL(Maddison)
126	Mongolia	658	INTERPOL(Maddison)
127	South Sudan	637	1900(MIN)
128	Burundi	551	1900(MIN)
129	Lesotho	543	1900(MIN)
130	Botswana	534	1900(MIN)
131	Malawi	497	1900(MIN)
132	Guinea	465	1900(MIN)
133	Guinea-Biss	444	1900(MIN)
134	Eritrea	422	1900(MIN)
135	Ethiopia	410	1900(MIN)

TABLE 2.11 GDP AT PURCHASING POWER PARITIES PER CAPITA, 2012 DOLLARS, YEAR 1913

Rank	Country	GPC	Source
1	US	8,295	1913(Maddison)
2	Australia	8,070	1913(Maddison)
3	New Zealand	8,062	1913(Maddison)
4	UK	7,701	1913(Maddison)
5	Canada	6,959	1913(Maddison)
6	Switzerland	6,676	1913(Maddison)
7	Belgium	6,604	1913(Maddison)
8	Netherlands	6,336	1913(Maddison)
9	Denmark	6,122	1913(Maddison)
10	Argentina	5,942	1913(Maddison)
11	Germany	5,709	1913(Maddison)
12	France	5,453	1913(Maddison)
13	Austria	5,422	1913(Maddison)
14	Uruguay	5,180	1913(Maddison)
15	Sweden	4,845	1913(Maddison)
16	Iceland	4,698	PROXY(Denmark)
17	Chile	4,676	1913(Maddison)
18	Ireland	4,281	1913(Maddison)
19	Italy	4,012	1913(Maddison)
20	Norway	3,914	1913(Maddison)
21	Czechia	3,427	PROXY(Czechoslovakia(Maddison))
22	Estonia	3,406	PROXY(USSR(Maddison))
23	Finland	3,303	1913(Maddison)
24	Hungary	3,283	1913(Maddison)
25	Trinidad & T	3,266	PROXY(Other L. Am.(Maddison))
26	Slovenia	3,264	PROXY(Yugoslavia(Maddison))
27	Spain	3,217	1913(Maddison)
28	Latvia	3,024	PROXY(USSR(Maddison))
29	Slovakia	2,991	PROXY(Czechoslovakia(Maddison))
30	Kazakhstan	2,986	PROXY(USSR(Maddison))
31	Lithuania	2,924	PROXY(USSR(Maddison))
32	Romania	2,724	1913(Maddison)
33	Poland	2,721	1913(Maddison)
34	Mexico	2,710	1913(Maddison)
35	Russia	2,531	PROXY(USSR(Maddison))
36	South Africa	2,507	1913(Maddison)
37	Greece	2,491	1913(Maddison)
38	Cyprus	2,449	PROXY(Greece(Maddison))
39	Bulgaria	2,400	1913(Maddison)
40	Armenia	2,356	PROXY(USSR(Maddison))
41	Georgia	2,293	PROXY(USSR(Maddison))
42	Japan	2,170	1913(Maddison)
43	Namibia	2,114	INTERPOL(Maddison)
44	Syria	2,113	1913(Maddison)
45	Lebanon	2,113	1913(Maddison)
46	Croatia	2,104	PROXY(Yugoslavia(Maddison))
47	Moldova	2,062	PROXY(USSR(Maddison))

Table 2.11 GDP at Purchasing Power Parities Per Capita, 2012 Dollars, Year 1913			
Rank	Country	GPC	Source
48	Belarus	2,011	PROXY(USSR(Maddison))
49	Singapore	2,001	1913(Maddison)
50	Hong Kong	2,001	1913(Maddison)
51	Uzbekistan	1,959	PROXY(USSR(Maddison))
52.5	Israel	1,956	1913(Palestine(Maddison))
52.5	Portugal	1,956	1913(Maddison)
54	Colombia	1,934	1913(Maddison)
55	Sri Lanka	1,931	1913(Maddison)
56	Puerto Rico	1,906	PROXY(Other L. Am.(Maddison))
57	Turkey	1,898	1913(Maddison)
58	Ukraine	1,894	PROXY(USSR(Maddison))
59	Turkmenistan	1,855	PROXY(USSR(Maddison))
60	Guatemala	1,854	PROXY(Other L. Am.(Maddison))
61	Algeria	1,820	1913(Maddison)
62	Cuba	1,819	PROXY(Other L. Am.(Maddison))
63	Serbia	1,817	PROXY(Yugoslavia(Maddison))
64	Montenegro	1,787	PROXY(Yugoslavia(Maddison))
65	Costa Rica	1,745	PROXY(Other L. Am.(Maddison))
66	Venezuela	1,728	1913(Maddison)
67	Bolivia	1,706	PROXY(Other L. Am.(Maddison))
68	Azerbaijan	1,704	PROXY(USSR(Maddison))
69	Panama	1,703	PROXY(Other L. Am.(Maddison))
70	Ecuador	1,656	PROXY(Other L. Am.(Maddison))
71	Philippines	1,648	1913(Maddison)
72	Peru	1,623	1913(Maddison)
73	Tajikistan	1,574	PROXY(USSR(Maddison))
74	Iran	1,565	1913(Maddison)
75	Jordan	1,565	1913(Maddison)
76	Iraq	1,565	1913(Maddison)
77	Nicaragua	1,437	PROXY(Other L. Am.(Maddison))
78	Kyrgyzstan	1,435	PROXY(USSR(Maddison))
79	Indonesia	1,415	1913(Maddison)
80	Egypt	1,411	1913(Maddison)
81	Malaysia	1,408	1913(Maddison)
82	Paraguay	1,408	PROXY(Other L. Am.(Maddison))
83	Tunisia	1,382	1913(Maddison)
84	Mozambique	1,332	INTERPOL(Maddison)
85	El Salvador	1,324	PROXY(Other L. Am.(Maddison))
86	Thailand	1,316	1913(Maddison)
87	Korea, North	1,283	1913(Maddison)
88	Korea, South	1,283	1913(Maddison)
89	Brazil	1,269	1913(Maddison)
90	Albania	1,269	1913(Maddison)
91	Somalia	1,268	INTERPOL(Maddison)
92	Ghana	1,222	1913(Maddison)
93	Madagascar	1,175	INTERPOL(Maddison)
94	Taiwan	1,169	1913(Maddison)
95	Honduras	1,167	PROXY(Other L. Am.(Maddison))

Table 2.11 GDP at Purchasing Power Parities Per Capita, 2012 Dollars, Year 1913

Rank	Country	GPC	Source
96	Pakistan	1,141	1913(Maddison)
97	Vietnam	1,138	1913(Maddison)
98	Macedonia	1,118	PROXY(Yugoslavia(Maddison))
99	Morocco	1,111	1913(Maddison)
100	Kosovo	1,105	PROXY(Yugoslavia(Maddison))
101	Libya	1,102	INTERPOL(Maddison)
102	Afghanistan	1,081	PROXY(26 E. Asian cs(Maddison))
103	Burma	1,072	1913(Maddison)
104	Bosnia	1,070	PROXY(Yugoslavia(Maddison))
105	Sudan	1,058	INTERPOL(Maddison)
106	India	1,037	1913(Maddison)
107	Laos	1,028	PROXY(26 E. Asian cs(Maddison))
108	Sierra Leone	996	1913(MIN)
109	Jamaica	970	1913(Maddison)
110	Bangladesh	966	1913(Maddison)
111	Swaziland	964	INTERPOL(Maddison)
112	Zimbabwe	945	INTERPOL(Maddison)
113.5	Qatar	939	AVG(Arabia(Maddison))
113.5	Yemen	939	AVG(Arabia(Maddison))
115	Bahrain	939	AVG(Arabia(Maddison))
117.5	Kuwait	939	AVG(Arabia(Maddison))
117.5	Oman	939	AVG(Arabia(Maddison))
117.5	Saudi Arabia	939	AVG(Arabia(Maddison))
117.5	UAE	939	AVG(Arabia(Maddison))
120	Haiti	934	PROXY(Other L. Am.(Maddison))
121	Dominican R	913	PROXY(Other L. Am.(Maddison))
122	Zambia	906	INTERPOL(Maddison)
123	Cambodia	868	PROXY(26 E. Asian cs(Maddison))
124	China	864	1913(Maddison)
125	Nepal	843	1913(Maddison)
126	Mongolia	729	PROXY(26 E. Asian cs(Maddison))
127	South Sudan	641	1913(MIN)
128	Burundi	554	1913(MIN)
129	Lesotho	547	1913(MIN)
130	Botswana	537	1913(MIN)
131	Malawi	500	1913(MIN)
132	Guinea	468	1913(MIN)
133	Guinea-Biss	446	1913(MIN)
134	Eritrea	424	1913(MIN)
135	Ethiopia	412	1913(MIN)

Table 2.12 GDP at Purchasing Power Parities Per Capita, 2012 Dollars, Year 1920			
Rank	Country	GPC	Source
1	New Zealand	8,827	1920(Maddison)
2	US	8,688	1920(Maddison)
3	Australia	7,458	1920(Maddison)
4	UK	7,117	1920(Maddison)
5	Switzerland	6,751	1920(Maddison)
6	Netherlands	6,604	1920(Maddison)
7	Denmark	6,247	1920(Maddison)
8	Belgium	6,200	1920(Maddison)
9	Canada	6,042	1920(Maddison)
10	Argentina	5,435	1920(Maddison)
11	France	5,050	1920(Maddison)
12	Iceland	4,794	PROXY(Denmark)
13	Sweden	4,385	1920(Maddison)
14	Germany	4,375	1920(Maddison)
15	Norway	4,350	1920(Maddison)
16	Chile	4,283	1920(Maddison)
17	Uruguay	4,184	1920(Maddison)
18	Italy	4,048	1920(Maddison)
19	Ireland	4,002	INTERPOL(Maddison)
20	Austria	3,774	1920(Maddison)
21	Trinidad & T	3,635	INTERPOL(Maddison)
22	Spain	3,407	1920(Maddison)
23	Slovenia	3,184	PROXY(Yugoslavia(Maddison))
24	Czechia	3,161	PROXY(Czechoslovakia(Maddison))
25	Estonia	2,978	PROXY(Finland(Maddison))
26	Poland	2,966	INTERPOL(Maddison)
27	Greece	2,932	INTERPOL(Maddison)
28	Finland	2,889	1920(Maddison)
29	Cyprus	2,883	PROXY(Greece(Maddison))
30	Mexico	2,853	1920(Maddison)
31	Slovakia	2,758	PROXY(Czechoslovakia(Maddison))
32	South Africa	2,734	INTERPOL(Maddison)
33	Hungary	2,674	1920(Maddison)
34	Japan	2,654	1920(Maddison)
35	Latvia	2,645	PROXY(Finland(Maddison))
36	Lithuania	2,557	PROXY(Finland(Maddison))
37	Costa Rica	2,541	1920(Maddison)
38	Lebanon	2,361	INTERPOL(Maddison)
39	Syria	2,357	INTERPOL(Maddison)
40	Namibia	2,310	INTERPOL(Maddison)
41	Israel	2,281	INTERPOL(Maddison)
42	Singapore	2,221	INTERPOL(Maddison)
43	Hong Kong	2,221	INTERPOL(Maddison)
44	Puerto Rico	2,121	INTERPOL(Maddison)
45	Peru	2,083	1920(Maddison)
46	Croatia	2,052	PROXY(Yugoslavia(Maddison))
47	Cuba	2,024	INTERPOL(Maddison)

Table 2.12 GDP at Purchasing Power Parities Per Capita, 2012 Dollars, Year 1920

Rank	Country	GPC	Source
48	Philippines	2,017	1920(Maddison)
49	Honduras	1,994	1920(Maddison)
50	Guatemala	1,990	1920(Maddison)
51	Nicaragua	1,978	1920(Maddison)
52	Algeria	1,976	1920(Maddison)
53	Qatar	1,973	INTERPOL(Maddison)
54	Colombia	1,964	1920(Maddison)
55	Kuwait	1,954	INTERPOL(Maddison)
56	Portugal	1,923	1920(Maddison)
57	Bolivia	1,899	INTERPOL(Maddison)
58	Panama	1,896	INTERPOL(Maddison)
59	Ecuador	1,843	INTERPOL(Maddison)
60	Venezuela	1,836	1920(Maddison)
61	Serbia	1,773	PROXY(Yugoslavia(Maddison))
62	Montenegro	1,743	PROXY(Yugoslavia(Maddison))
63	UAE	1,743	INTERPOL(Maddison)
64	Malaysia	1,737	1920(Maddison)
65	Iran	1,734	INTERPOL(Maddison)
66	Jordan	1,723	INTERPOL(Maddison)
67	Sri Lanka	1,709	1920(Maddison)
68	Iraq	1,660	INTERPOL(Maddison)
69	Romania	1,614	PROXY(Bulgaria(Maddison))
70	Korea, North	1,579	1920(Maddison)
71	Korea, South	1,579	1920(Maddison)
72	Paraguay	1,567	INTERPOL(Maddison)
73	Brazil	1,507	1920(Maddison)
74	Taiwan	1,501	1920(Maddison)
75	Indonesia	1,479	1920(Maddison)
76	El Salvador	1,458	1920(Maddison)
77	Tunisia	1,444	INTERPOL(Maddison)
78	Bulgaria	1,422	1924(Maddison)
79	Mozambique	1,406	INTERPOL(Maddison)
80	Egypt	1,391	INTERPOL(Maddison)
81	Georgia	1,359	PROXY(Bulgaria(Maddison))
82	Albania	1,345	INTERPOL(Maddison)
83	Somalia	1,333	INTERPOL(Maddison)
84	Ghana	1,309	INTERPOL(Maddison)
85	Thailand	1,283	INTERPOL(Maddison)
86	Morocco	1,273	INTERPOL(Maddison)
87	Madagascar	1,229	INTERPOL(Maddison)
88	Moldova	1,222	PROXY(Romania(Maddison))
89	Saudi Arabia	1,204	INTERPOL(Maddison)
90	Bahrain	1,190	INTERPOL(Maddison)
91	Kazakhstan	1,157	PROXY(USSR(Davies))
92	Burma	1,146	INTERPOL(Maddison)
93	Pakistan	1,145	INTERPOL(Maddison)
94	Libya	1,144	INTERPOL(Maddison)
95	Vietnam	1,116	INTERPOL(Maddison)

Table 2.12 GDP at Purchasing Power Parities Per Capita, 2012 Dollars, Year 1920			
Rank	Country	GPC	Source
96	Turkey	1,114	1923(Maddison)
97	Jamaica	1,100	INTERPOL(Maddison)
98	Sudan	1,098	INTERPOL(Maddison)
99	Macedonia	1,090	PROXY(Yugoslavia(Maddison))
100	Kosovo	1,077	PROXY(Yugoslavia(Maddison))
101	Afghanistan	1,067	INTERPOL(Maddison)
102	Bosnia	1,043	PROXY(Yugoslavia(Maddison))
103	Haiti	1,040	INTERPOL(Maddison)
104	Dominican R	1,016	INTERPOL(Maddison)
105	Yemen	1,016	INTERPOL(Maddison)
106	Laos	1,014	INTERPOL(Maddison)
107	Sierra Leone	1,002	1920(MIN)
108	Swaziland	993	INTERPOL(Maddison)
109	India	984	1920(Maddison)
110	Russia	981	PROXY(USSR(Davies))
111	Zimbabwe	972	INTERPOL(Maddison)
112	Bangladesh	967	INTERPOL(Maddison)
113	Oman	946	INTERPOL(Maddison)
114	Zambia	929	INTERPOL(Maddison)
115	Armenia	913	PROXY(USSR(Davies))
116	China	871	INTERPOL(Maddison)
117	Cambodia	857	INTERPOL(Maddison)
118	Nepal	831	INTERPOL(Maddison)
119	Belarus	779	PROXY(USSR(Davies))
120	Uzbekistan	759	PROXY(USSR(Davies))
121	Ukraine	734	PROXY(USSR(Davies))
122	Mongolia	720	INTERPOL(Maddison)
123	Turkmenistan	719	PROXY(USSR(Davies))
124	Azerbaijan	660	PROXY(USSR(Davies))
125	South Sudan	644	1920(MIN)
126	Tajikistan	610	PROXY(USSR(Davies))
127	Kyrgyzstan	556	PROXY(USSR(Davies))
128	Burundi	556	1920(MIN)
129	Lesotho	548	1920(MIN)
130	Botswana	539	1920(MIN)
131	Malawi	501	1920(MIN)
132	Guinea	469	1920(MIN)
133	Guinea-Biss	447	1920(MIN)
134	Eritrea	425	1920(MIN)
135	Ethiopia	413	1920(MIN)

Table 2.13 GDP at Purchasing Power Parities Per Capita, 2012 Dollars, Year 1929			
Rank	Country	GPC	Source
1	US	10,796	1929(Maddison)
2	Switzerland	9,909	1929(Maddison)
3	Netherlands	8,902	1929(Maddison)
4	UK	8,611	1929(Maddison)
5	Australia	8,236	1929(Maddison)
6	New Zealand	8,234	1929(Maddison)
7	Denmark	7,942	1929(Maddison)
8	Canada	7,926	1929(Maddison)
9	Belgium	7,909	1929(Maddison)
10	France	7,370	1929(Maddison)
11	Argentina	6,834	1929(Maddison)
12	Germany	6,339	1929(Maddison)
13	Iceland	6,095	PROXY(Denmark)
14	Sweden	6,054	1929(Maddison)
15	Uruguay	6,020	1929(Maddison)
16	Chile	5,985	1929(Maddison)
17	Austria	5,788	1929(Maddison)
18	Norway	5,433	1929(Maddison)
19	Venezuela	5,361	1929(Maddison)
20	Qatar	5,125	INTERPOL(Maddison)
21	Kuwait	5,014	INTERPOL(Maddison)
22	Czechia	4,974	PROXY(Czechoslovakia (Maddison))
23	Italy	4,840	1929(Maddison)
24	Ireland	4,419	1929(Maddison)
25	Estonia	4,384	PROXY(Finland (Maddison))
26	Slovakia	4,341	PROXY(Czechoslovakia (Maddison))
27	Spain	4,286	1929(Maddison)
28	Finland	4,252	1929(Maddison)
29	Slovenia	4,212	PROXY(Yugoslavia (Maddison))
30	Trinidad & T	4,171	INTERPOL(Maddison)
31	Latvia	3,893	PROXY(Finland (Maddison))
32	Hungary	3,875	1929(Maddison)
33	UAE	3,863	INTERPOL(Maddison)
34	Lithuania	3,763	PROXY(Finland (Maddison))
35	Greece	3,665	1929(Maddison)
36	Cyprus	3,603	PROXY(Greece (Maddison))
37	Poland	3,313	1929(Maddison)
38	Japan	3,170	1929(Maddison)
39	South Africa	3,057	INTERPOL(Maddison)
40	Kazakhstan	2,856	PROXY(USSR(Maddison))
41	Israel	2,780	INTERPOL(Maddison)
42	Mexico	2,749	1929(Maddison)

Table 2.13 GDP at Purchasing Power Parities Per Capita, 2012 Dollars, Year 1929

Rank	Country	GPC	Source
43	Nicaragua	2,738	1929(Maddison)
44	Lebanon	2,723	INTERPOL(Maddison)
45	Croatia	2,715	PROXY(Yugoslavia(Maddison))
46	Syria	2,714	INTERPOL(Maddison)
47	Guatemala	2,692	1929(Maddison)
48	Malaysia	2,632	1929(Maddison)
49	Namibia	2,589	INTERPOL(Maddison)
50	Cuba	2,565	1929(Maddison)
51	Singapore	2,540	INTERPOL(Maddison)
52	Hong Kong	2,539	INTERPOL(Maddison)
53	Peru	2,533	1929(Maddison)
54	Portugal	2,519	1929(Maddison)
55	Costa Rica	2,476	1929(Maddison)
56	Puerto Rico	2,434	INTERPOL(Maddison)
57	Russia	2,421	PROXY(USSR(Maddison))
58	Colombia	2,355	1929(Maddison)
59	Philippines	2,350	1929(Maddison)
60	Honduras	2,346	1929(Maddison)
61	Serbia	2,345	PROXY(Yugoslavia(Maddison))
62	Montenegro	2,307	PROXY(Yugoslavia(Maddison))
63	Armenia	2,254	PROXY(USSR(Maddison))
64	Georgia	2,193	PROXY(USSR(Maddison))
65	Bolivia	2,179	INTERPOL(Maddison)
66	Panama	2,175	INTERPOL(Maddison)
67	Algeria	2,136	INTERPOL(Maddison)
68	Ecuador	2,115	INTERPOL(Maddison)
69	Sri Lanka	2,091	1929(Maddison)
70	Iran	1,978	INTERPOL(Maddison)
71	Jordan	1,950	INTERPOL(Maddison)
72	Belarus	1,923	PROXY(USSR(Maddison))
73	Turkey	1,898	1929(Maddison)
74	Uzbekistan	1,873	PROXY(USSR(Maddison))
75	Bulgaria	1,847	1929(Maddison)
76	Indonesia	1,831	1929(Maddison)
77	Ukraine	1,811	PROXY(USSR(Maddison))
78	Romania	1,803	1929(Maddison)
79	Paraguay	1,798	INTERPOL(Maddison)
80	Taiwan	1,793	1929(Maddison)
81	Iraq	1,790	INTERPOL(Maddison)
82	Brazil	1,779	1929(Maddison)
83	Turkmenistan	1,774	PROXY(USSR(Maddison))
84	Saudi Arabia	1,657	INTERPOL(Maddison)
85	Azerbaijan	1,630	PROXY(USSR(Maddison))
86	El Salvador	1,629	1929(Maddison)
87	Bahrain	1,615	INTERPOL(Maddison)
88	Korea, North	1,587	1929(Maddison)
89	Korea, South	1,587	1929(Maddison)
90	Tunisia	1,528	INTERPOL(Maddison)

Table 2.13 GDP at Purchasing Power Parities Per Capita, 2012 Dollars, Year 1929			
Rank	Country	GPC	Source
91	Morocco	1,515	INTERPOL(Maddison)
92	Mozambique	1,507	INTERPOL(Maddison)
93	Tajikistan	1,505	PROXY(USSR(Maddison))
94	Albania	1,449	1920(Maddison)
95	Macedonia	1,442	PROXY(Yugoslavia(Maddison))
96	Ghana	1,429	INTERPOL(Maddison)
97	Kosovo	1,425	PROXY(Yugoslavia(Maddison))
98	Somalia	1,422	INTERPOL(Maddison)
99	Bosnia	1,380	PROXY(Yugoslavia(Maddison))
100	Kyrgyzstan	1,372	PROXY(USSR(Maddison))
101	Egypt	1,366	1929(Maddison)
102	Moldova	1,364	PROXY(Romania(Maddison))
103	Burma	1,355	INTERPOL(Maddison)
104	Madagascar	1,302	INTERPOL(Maddison)
105	Jamaica	1,294	INTERPOL(Maddison)
106	Thailand	1,241	1929(Maddison)
107	Libya	1,200	INTERPOL(Maddison)
108	Haiti	1,193	INTERPOL(Maddison)
109	Dominican R	1,166	INTERPOL(Maddison)
110	Sudan	1,151	INTERPOL(Maddison)
111	Pakistan	1,150	1929(Maddison)
112	Yemen	1,125	INTERPOL(Maddison)
113	Vietnam	1,090	INTERPOL(Maddison)
114	Afghanistan	1,050	INTERPOL(Maddison)
115	India	1,041	1929(Maddison)
116	Swaziland	1,032	INTERPOL(Maddison)
117	Sierra Leone	1,009	1929(MIN)
118	Zimbabwe	1,008	INTERPOL(Maddison)
119	Laos	997	INTERPOL(Maddison)
120	Bangladesh	969	1929(Maddison)
121	Zambia	959	INTERPOL(Maddison)
122	Oman	954	INTERPOL(Maddison)
123	China	879	1929(Maddison)
124	Cambodia	843	INTERPOL(Maddison)
125	Nepal	814	INTERPOL(Maddison)
126	Mongolia	708	INTERPOL(Maddison)
127	South Sudan	647	1929(MIN)
128	Burundi	558	1929(MIN)
129	Lesotho	550	1929(MIN)
130	Botswana	541	1929(MIN)
131	Malawi	503	1929(MIN)
132	Guinea	470	1929(MIN)
133	Guinea-Biss	449	1929(MIN)
134	Eritrea	426	1929(MIN)
135	Ethiopia	414	1929(MIN)

Table 2.14 GDP at Purchasing Power Parities Per Capita, 2012 Dollars, Year 1938			
Rank	Country	GPC	Source
1	Qatar	13,315	INTERPOL(Maddison)
2	Kuwait	12,864	INTERPOL(Maddison)
3	New Zealand	10,112	1938(Maddison)
4	Switzerland	9,999	1938(Maddison)
5	UK	9,805	1938(Maddison)
6	US	9,586	1938(Maddison)
7	Australia	9,211	1938(Maddison)
8	Denmark	9,017	1938(Maddison)
9	UAE	8,558	INTERPOL(Maddison)
10	Netherlands	8,215	1938(Maddison)
11	Germany	7,815	1938(Maddison)
12	Belgium	7,561	1938(Maddison)
13	Sweden	7,394	1938(Maddison)
14	Canada	7,114	1938(Maddison)
15	France	6,989	1938(Maddison)
16	Iceland	6,920	PROXY(Denmark)
17	Norway	6,787	1938(Maddison)
18	Venezuela	6,485	1938(Maddison)
19	Argentina	6,372	1938(Maddison)
20	Estonia	5,791	PROXY(Finland(Maddison))
21	Uruguay	5,752	1938(Maddison)
22	Finland	5,616	1938(Maddison)
23	Austria	5,569	1938(Maddison)
24	Chile	5,532	1938(Maddison)
25	Italy	5,189	1938(Maddison)
26	Latvia	5,142	PROXY(Finland(Maddison))
27	Lithuania	4,971	PROXY(Finland(Maddison))
28	Trinidad & T	4,786	INTERPOL(Maddison)
29	Ireland	4,776	1938(Maddison)
30	Czechia	4,712	PROXY(37Czechoslovakia(Maddison))
31	Kazakhstan	4,430	PROXY(USSR(Maddison))
32	Greece	4,189	1938(Maddison)
33	Slovenia	4,187	PROXY(Yugoslavia(Maddison))
34	Hungary	4,155	1938(Maddison)
35	Cyprus	4,118	PROXY(Greece(Maddison))
36	Slovakia	4,113	PROXY(37Czechoslovakia(Maddison))
37	Japan	3,832	1938(Maddison)
38	Russia	3,756	PROXY(USSR(Maddison))
39	Armenia	3,496	PROXY(USSR(Maddison))
40	Guatemala	3,480	1938(Maddison)
41	South Africa	3,418	INTERPOL(Maddison)
42	Poland	3,414	1938(Maddison)
43	Georgia	3,401	PROXY(USSR(Maddison))
44	Israel	3,387	INTERPOL(Maddison)
45	Lebanon	3,142	INTERPOL(Maddison)

Table 2.14 GDP at Purchasing Power Parities Per Capita, 2012 Dollars, Year 1938			
Rank	Country	GPC	Source
46	Syria	3,124	INTERPOL(Maddison)
47	Belarus	2,984	PROXY(USSR(Maddison))
48	Costa Rica	2,936	1938(Maddison)
49	Uzbekistan	2,906	PROXY(USSR(Maddison))
50	Singapore	2,904	INTERPOL(Maddison)
51	Hong Kong	2,903	INTERPOL(Maddison)
52	Namibia	2,903	INTERPOL(Maddison)
53	Colombia	2,884	1938(Maddison)
54	Ukraine	2,809	PROXY(USSR(Maddison))
55	Mexico	2,807	1938(Maddison)
56	Spain	2,801	1938(Maddison)
57	Puerto Rico	2,793	INTERPOL(Maddison)
58	Turkmenistan	2,752	PROXY(USSR(Maddison))
59	Peru	2,749	1938(Maddison)
60	Portugal	2,734	1938(Maddison)
61	Croatia	2,699	PROXY(Yugoslavia(Maddison))
62	Turkey	2,698	1938(Maddison)
63	Azerbaijan	2,528	PROXY(USSR(Maddison))
64	Bolivia	2,500	INTERPOL(Maddison)
65	Panama	2,496	INTERPOL(Maddison)
66	Bulgaria	2,496	1938(Maddison)
67	Ecuador	2,427	INTERPOL(Maddison)
68	Philippines	2,382	1938(Maddison)
69	Tajikistan	2,335	PROXY(USSR(Maddison))
70	Serbia	2,332	PROXY(Yugoslavia(Maddison))
71	Montenegro	2,293	PROXY(Yugoslavia(Maddison))
72	Korea, North	2,283	1938(Maddison)
73	Korea, South	2,283	1938(Maddison)
74	Saudi Arabia	2,280	INTERPOL(Maddison)
75	Iran	2,257	INTERPOL(Maddison)
76	Jordan	2,207	INTERPOL(Maddison)
77	Bahrain	2,192	INTERPOL(Maddison)
78	Algeria	2,147	INTERPOL(Maddison)
79	Malaysia	2,130	1938(Maddison)
80	Kyrgyzstan	2,129	PROXY(USSR(Maddison))
81	Cuba	2,125	1938(Maddison)
82	Paraguay	2,063	INTERPOL(Maddison)
83	Taiwan	2,037	1938(Maddison)
84	Brazil	1,997	1938(Maddison)
85	Romania	1,944	1938(Maddison)
86	Iraq	1,930	INTERPOL(Maddison)
87	Sri Lanka	1,917	1938(Maddison)
88	Indonesia	1,839	1938(Maddison)
89	Morocco	1,804	INTERPOL(Maddison)
90	Honduras	1,729	1938(Maddison)
91	Nicaragua	1,684	1938(Maddison)
92	Tunisia	1,618	INTERPOL(Maddison)
93	Mozambique	1,616	INTERPOL(Maddison)

Table 2.14 GDP at Purchasing Power Parities Per Capita, 2012 Dollars, Year 1938			
Rank	Country	GPC	Source
94	Ghana	1,561	INTERPOL(Maddison)
95	El Salvador	1,529	1938(Maddison)
96	Jamaica	1,521	1938(Maddison)
97	Somalia	1,517	INTERPOL(Maddison)
98	Albania	1,498	INTERPOL(Maddison)
99	Moldova	1,471	PROXY(Romania(Maddison))
100	Macedonia	1,434	PROXY(Yugoslavia(Maddison))
101	Kosovo	1,417	PROXY(Yugoslavia(Maddison))
102	Egypt	1,393	INTERPOL(Maddison)
103	Madagascar	1,379	INTERPOL(Maddison)
104	Bosnia	1,372	PROXY(Yugoslavia(Maddison))
105	Haiti	1,369	INTERPOL(Maddison)
106	Dominican R	1,338	INTERPOL(Maddison)
107	Thailand	1,293	1938(Maddison)
108	Libya	1,258	INTERPOL(Maddison)
109	Yemen	1,245	INTERPOL(Maddison)
110	Sudan	1,206	INTERPOL(Maddison)
111	Burma	1,158	1938(Maddison)
112	Swaziland	1,072	INTERPOL(Maddison)
113	Pakistan	1,064	1938(Maddison)
114	Vietnam	1,064	INTERPOL(Maddison)
115	Zimbabwe	1,045	INTERPOL(Maddison)
116	Afghanistan	1,032	INTERPOL(Maddison)
117	Sierra Leone	1,017	1938(MIN)
118	Zambia	991	INTERPOL(Maddison)
119	Laos	981	INTERPOL(Maddison)
120	India	969	1938(Maddison)
121	Oman	963	INTERPOL(Maddison)
122	Bangladesh	895	1938(Maddison)
123	China	879	1938(Maddison)
124	Cambodia	829	INTERPOL(Maddison)
125	Nepal	797	INTERPOL(Maddison)
126	Mongolia	696	INTERPOL(Maddison)
127	South Sudan	650	1938(MIN)
128	Burundi	560	1938(MIN)
129	Lesotho	553	1938(MIN)
130	Botswana	543	1938(MIN)
131	Malawi	505	1938(MIN)
132	Guinea	472	1938(MIN)
133	Guinea-Biss	450	1938(MIN)
134	Eritrea	427	1938(MIN)
135	Ethiopia	415	1938(MIN)

Table 2.15 GDP at Purchasing Power Parities Per Capita, 2012 Dollars, Year 1950			
Rank	Country	GPC	Source
1	Qatar	47,551	50(Maddison)
2	Kuwait	45,190	50(Maddison)
3	UAE	24,721	50(Maddison)
4	Cayman Is	15,717	PROXY(8 Caribbean cs(Maddison))
5	Bahamas	14,975	50(Maddison)
6	US	14,962	50(Maddison)
7	Guam	14,860	PROXY(14 Pacific is(Maddison))
8	Switzerland	14,184	50(Maddison)
9	New Zealand	13,232	50(Maddison)
10	Luxembourg	13,116	50(Maddison)
11	Svalbard	12,986	PROXY(Norway(Maddison))
12	Falkland Is	12,450	PROXY(8 Caribbean cs(Maddison))
13	N Mariana Is	11,707	PROXY(14 Pacific is(Maddison))
14	Venezuela	11,677	50(Maddison)
15	Aruba	11,617	PROXY(8 Caribbean cs(Maddison))
16	Australia	11,599	50(Maddison)
17	Palau	11,490	PROXY(14 Pacific is(Maddison))
18	Canada	11,409	50(Maddison)
19	Denmark	10,865	50(Maddison)
20	UK	10,858	50(Maddison)
21	Sweden	10,546	50(Maddison)
22	Liechtenstn	10,343	PROXY(9 European cs(Maddison))
23	Nauru	9,820	PROXY(14 Pacific is(Maddison))
24	Jersey	9,742	PROXY(9 European cs(Maddison))
25	Netherlands	9,383	50(Maddison)
26	Virgin I, US	9,204	PROXY(8 Caribbean cs(Maddison))
27	Norway	8,549	50(Maddison)
28	Belgium	8,547	50(Maddison)
29	Iceland	8,339	50(Maddison)
30	Monaco	8,251	PROXY(9 European cs(Maddison))
31	France	8,248	50(Maddison)
32	Guiana, Fr	7,998	50(Maddison)
33	Argentina	7,804	50(Maddison)
34	Brunei	7,789	50(Maddison)
35	Guernsey	7,544	PROXY(9 European cs(Maddison))
36	Virgin I, Br	7,463	PROXY(8 Caribbean cs(Maddison))
37	San Marino	7,431	PROXY(9 European cs(Maddison))
38	Uruguay	7,291	50(Maddison)
39	St Pierre&M	6,924	PROXY(8 Caribbean cs(Maddison))
40	Fr Polynesia	6,874	PROXY(14 Pacific is(Maddison))
41	Greenland	6,812	PROXY(9 European cs(Maddison))
42	Finland	6,655	50(Maddison)
43	Faroe Is	6,533	PROXY(9 European cs(Maddison))
44	Estonia	6,503	PROXY(USSR(Maddison))
45	Andorra	6,502	PROXY(9 European cs(Maddison))
46	New Caledon	6,368	PROXY(14 Pacific is(Maddison))
47	Germany	6,073	50(Maddison)

Table 2.15 GDP at Purchasing Power Parities Per Capita, 2012 Dollars, Year 1950			
Rank	Country	GPC	Source
48	Chile	5,979	50(Maddison)
49	Austria	5,799	50(Maddison)
50	Latvia	5,774	PROXY(USSR(Maddison))
51	Trinidad & T	5,749	50(Maddison)
52	Czechia	5,724	PROXY(Czechoslovakia(Maddison))
53	Kazakhstan	5,701	PROXY(USSR(Maddison))
54	Lithuania	5,582	PROXY(USSR(Maddison))
55	Italy	5,480	50(Maddison)
56	Ireland	5,403	50(Maddison)
57	Sint Maarten	5,304	06(CIA)WEIGHT(Curacao)
58	Curacao	5,148	50(Maddison)WEIGHT(Neth Antilles)
59	Slovakia	4,996	PROXY(Czechoslovakia(Maddison))
60	Saint Martin	4,921	05(CIA)WEIGHT(Curacao)
61	Gabon	4,864	50(Maddison)
62	Russia	4,833	PROXY(USSR(Maddison))
63	Isle of Man	4,816	PROXY(9 European cs(Maddison))
64	Slovenia	4,789	PROXY(Yugoslavia(Maddison))
65	Anguilla	4,783	PROXY(8 Caribbean cs(Maddison))
66	Fiji	4,608	50(Maddison)
67	Armenia	4,499	PROXY(USSR(Maddison))
68	Israel	4,408	50(Maddison)
69	Georgia	4,377	PROXY(USSR(Maddison))
70	Turks & C Is	4,155	PROXY(8 Caribbean cs(Maddison))
71	South Africa	3,967	50(Maddison)
72	Moldova	3,936	PROXY(USSR(Maddison))
73	Mauritius	3,896	50(Maddison)
74	Hungary	3,881	50(Maddison)
75	Belarus	3,840	PROXY(USSR(Maddison))
76	Poland	3,829	50(Maddison)
77	Lebanon	3,801	50(Maddison)
78	Syria	3,770	50(Maddison)
79	Uzbekistan	3,740	PROXY(USSR(Maddison))
80	Mexico	3,701	50(Maddison)
81	Ukraine	3,615	PROXY(USSR(Maddison))
82	Peru	3,541	50(Maddison)
83	Turkmenistan	3,541	PROXY(USSR(Maddison))
84	Saudi Arabia	3,491	50(Maddison)
85	Singapore	3,472	50(Maddison)
86	Hong Kong	3,471	50(Maddison)
87	Spain	3,425	50(Maddison)
88	Namibia	3,380	50(Maddison)
89	Colombia	3,369	50(Maddison)
90	Puerto Rico	3,355	50(Maddison)
91	Barbados	3,323	50(Maddison)
92	Bahrain	3,292	50(Maddison)
93	Portugal	3,264	50(Maddison)
94	Guatemala	3,263	50(Maddison)
95	Azerbaijan	3,253	PROXY(USSR(Maddison))

Table 2.15 GDP at Purchasing Power Parities Per Capita, 2012 Dollars, Year 1950

Rank	Country	GPC	Source
96	Cuba	3,202	50(Maddison)
97	Reunion	3,112	50(Maddison)
98	Croatia	3,087	PROXY(Yugoslavia(Maddison))
99	Costa Rica	3,072	50(Maddison)
100	Gibraltar	3,025	PROXY(9 European cs(Maddison))
101	Japan	3,006	50(Maddison)
102	Tajikistan	3,005	PROXY(USSR(Maddison))
103	Bolivia	3,003	50(Maddison)
104	Panama	2,998	50(Maddison)
105	Greece	2,997	50(Maddison)
106	Seychelles	2,992	50(Maddison)
107	Montserrat	2,977	PROXY(8 Caribbean cs(Maddison))
108	Cyprus	2,946	50(Maddison)
109	Cook Is	2,946	PROXY(14 Pacific is(Maddison))
110	Ecuador	2,915	50(Maddison)
111	Antigua & B	2,790	50(Maddison)
112	Samoa, Amer	2,760	PROXY(14 Pacific is(Maddison))
113	Kyrgyzstan	2,739	PROXY(USSR(Maddison))
114	Guadeloupe	2,701	50(Maddison)
115	Iran	2,692	50(Maddison)
116	Serbia	2,667	PROXY(Yugoslavia(Maddison))
117	Montenegro	2,623	PROXY(Yugoslavia(Maddison))
118	Brazil	2,616	50(Maddison)
119	Bermuda	2,608	50(Maddison)
120	Jordan	2,602	50(Maddison)
121	Bulgaria	2,584	50(Maddison)
122	Turkey	2,540	50(Maddison)
123	Belize	2,531	50(Maddison)
124	Nicaragua	2,529	50(Maddison)
125	Dominica	2,516	50(Maddison)
126	Paraguay	2,479	50(Maddison)
127	Malaysia	2,440	50(Maddison)
128	Djibouti	2,347	50(Maddison)
129	El Salvador	2,330	50(Maddison)
130	Suriname	2,293	50(Maddison)
131	Morocco	2,277	50(Maddison)
132	Vanuatu	2,191	PROXY(14 Pacific is(Maddison))
133	Micronesia	2,162	PROXY(14 Pacific is(Maddison))
134	Algeria	2,136	50(Maddison)
135	Iraq	2,134	50(Maddison)
136	Jamaica	2,077	50(Maddison)
137	Martinique	2,065	50(Maddison)
138	Samoa	2,065	PROXY(14 Pacific is(Maddison))
139	Honduras	2,055	50(Maddison)
140	Congo, Rep	2,017	50(Maddison)
141	Saint Helena	1,991	PROXY(3 Afr. cs(Maddison))
142	Senegal	1,970	50(Maddison)
143	Sri Lanka	1,961	50(Maddison)

TABLE 2.15 GDP AT PURCHASING POWER PARITIES PER CAPITA, 2012 DOLLARS, YEAR 1950			
Rank	Country	GPC	Source
144	St Kitts & N	1,948	50(Maddison)
145	Tonga	1,948	PROXY(14 Pacific is(Maddison))
146	Wallis & Fut	1,871	PROXY(14 Pacific is(Maddison))
147	Romania	1,850	50(Maddison)
148	St Vincent	1,845	50(Maddison)
149	Mozambique	1,773	50(Maddison)
150	Ghana	1,756	50(Maddison)
151	Tunisia	1,745	50(Maddison)
152	Guyana	1,709	50(Maddison)
153	Benin	1,696	50(Maddison)
154	West Bank	1,681	PROXY(West Bank & Gaza(Maddison))
155	Philippines	1,674	50(Maddison)
156	Somalia	1,654	50(Maddison)
157	Liberia	1,651	50(Maddison)
158	Angola	1,646	50(Maddison)
159	Haiti	1,645	50(Maddison)
160	Macedonia	1,640	PROXY(Yugoslavia(Maddison))
161	Ivory Coast	1,629	50(Maddison)
162	Kosovo	1,621	PROXY(Yugoslavia(Maddison))
163	Macao	1,618	PROXY(Maddison)
164	Dominican R	1,607	50(Maddison)
165	Bosnia	1,569	PROXY(Yugoslavia(Maddison))
166	Albania	1,566	50(Maddison)
167	Marshall Is	1,527	PROXY(14 Pacific is(Maddison))
168	Madagascar	1,488	50(Maddison)
169	Grenada	1,462	50(Maddison)
170	Taiwan	1,446	50(Maddison)
171	Yemen	1,426	50(Maddison)
172	Egypt	1,424	50(Maddison)
173	Malta	1,394	50(Maddison)
174	Libya	1,341	50(Maddison)
175	Indonesia	1,314	50(Maddison)
176	Sudan	1,285	50(Maddison)
177	Sao Tome & P	1,283	50(Maddison)
178	Thailand	1,278	50(Maddison)
179	Niger	1,272	50(Maddison)
180	CAR	1,208	50(Maddison)
181	Korea, North	1,205	50(Maddison)
182	Korea, South	1,205	50(Maddison)
183	Papua New G	1,180	50(Maddison)
184	Niue	1,178	PROXY(14 Pacific is(Maddison))
185	Nigeria	1,178	50(Maddison)
186	St Lucia	1,150	50(Maddison)
187	Swaziland	1,128	50(Maddison)
188	Gaza Strip	1,120	PROXY(West Bank & Gaza(Maddison))
189	Zimbabwe	1,097	50(Maddison)
190	Uganda	1,075	50(Maddison)
191	Cameroon	1,050	50(Maddison)

Table 2.15 GDP at Purchasing Power Parities Per Capita, 2012 Dollars, Year 1950

Rank	Country	GPC	Source
192	Zambia	1,034	50(Maddison)
193	Vietnam	1,030	50(Maddison)
194	Sierra Leone	1,027	50(Maddison)
195	Kenya	1,019	50(Maddison)
196	Afghanistan	1,009	50(Maddison)
197	Pakistan	1,006	50(Maddison)
198	Tokelau	982	PROXY(14 Pacific is(Maddison))
199	Oman	975	50(Maddison)
200	India	969	50(Maddison)
201	Laos	959	50(Maddison)
202	Gambia	950	50(Maddison)
203	Solomon Is	928	PROXY(14 Pacific is(Maddison))
204	Kiribati	915	PROXY(14 Pacific is(Maddison))
205	Togo	898	50(Maddison)
206	Congo, Dem R	892	50(Maddison)
207	Comoros	876	50(Maddison)
208	Rwanda	856	50(Maddison)
209	Maldives	852	50(Maddison)
210	Equatorial G	845	50(Maddison)
211	Bangladesh	845	50(Maddison)
212	Cambodia	811	50(Maddison)
213	Bhutan	787	50(Maddison)
214	Tuvalu	786	PROXY(14 Pacific is(Maddison))
215	Nepal	776	50(Maddison)
216	Chad	745	50(Maddison)
217	Burkina Faso	742	50(Maddison)
218	Mauritania	726	50(Maddison)
219	Mali	715	50(Maddison)
220	Cape Verde	704	50(Maddison)
221	China	687	50(Maddison)
222	Mongolia	681	50(Maddison)
223	Tanzania	663	50(Maddison)
224	East Timor	655	PROXY(14 Pacific is(Maddison))
225	South Sudan	654	PROXY(Sudan(Maddison))
226	Burma	620	50(Maddison)
227	Burundi	563	50(Maddison)
228	Lesotho	556	50(Maddison)
229	Botswana	546	50(Maddison)
230	Malawi	507	50(Maddison)
231	Mayotte	493	PROXY(3 Afr. cs(Maddison))
232	Guinea	474	50(Maddison)
233	Guinea-Biss	452	50(Maddison)
234	Eritrea	429	PROXY(Ethiopia & Eritr.(Maddison))
235	Ethiopia	417	PROXY(Ethiopia & Eritr.(Maddison))
236	W Sahara	360	PROXY(3 Afr. cs(Maddison))

Table 2.16 GDP at Purchasing Power Parities Per Capita, 2012 Dollars, Year 1960			
Rank	Country	GPC	Source
1	UAE	54,855	60(Maddison)
2	Qatar	52,978	60(Maddison)
3	Kuwait	45,197	60(Maddison)
4	Switzerland	21,453	60(Maddison)
5	Cayman Is	20,718	INTERPOL(8 Caribbean cs(Maddison))
6	Bahamas	20,531	INTERPOL(Maddison)
7	Luxembourg	19,554	INTERPOL(Maddison)
8	Svalbard	17,890	PROXY(Norway(Maddison))
9	US	17,869	60(Maddison)
10	Guam	17,343	INTERPOL(14 Pacific is(Maddison))
11	Falkland Is	16,302	INTERPOL(8 Caribbean cs(Maddison))
12	Aruba	15,560	INTERPOL(8 Caribbean cs(Maddison))
13	New Zealand	15,209	60(Maddison)
14	Liechtenstn	14,954	INTERPOL(9 European cs(Maddison))
15	Denmark	14,190	60(Maddison)
16	Jersey	14,116	INTERPOL(9 European cs(Maddison))
17	Brunei	14,084	INTERPOL(Maddison)
18	Sweden	13,999	60(Maddison)
19	Australia	13,952	60(Maddison)
20	Venezuela	13,928	60(Maddison)
21	Canada	13,840	60(Maddison)
22	UK	13,362	60(Maddison)
23	Netherlands	13,281	60(Maddison)
24	Palau	13,196	INTERPOL(14 Pacific is(Maddison))
25	Iceland	12,962	INTERPOL(Maddison)
26	N Mariana Is	12,913	INTERPOL(14 Pacific is(Maddison))
27	Germany	12,687	60(Maddison)
28	Monaco	12,161	INTERPOL(9 European cs(Maddison))
29	France	11,902	60(Maddison)
30	Virgin I, US	11,892	INTERPOL(8 Caribbean cs(Maddison))
31	Norway	11,777	60(Maddison)
32	San Marino	11,304	INTERPOL(9 European cs(Maddison))
33	Nauru	11,300	INTERPOL(14 Pacific is(Maddison))
34	Belgium	11,260	60(Maddison)
35	Guernsey	10,974	INTERPOL(9 European cs(Maddison))
36	Austria	10,737	60(Maddison)
37	Finland	10,012	60(Maddison)
38	Greenland	9,953	INTERPOL(9 European cs(Maddison))
39	Virgin I, Br	9,853	INTERPOL(8 Caribbean cs(Maddison))
40	Italy	9,804	60(Maddison)
41	Faroe Is	9,588	INTERPOL(9 European cs(Maddison))
42	Andorra	9,495	INTERPOL(9 European cs(Maddison))
43	Trinidad & T	9,402	60(Maddison)
44	St Pierre&M	9,056	INTERPOL(8 Caribbean cs(Maddison))
45	Czechia	9,034	PROXY(Czechoslovakia(Maddison))
46	Estonia	8,991	PROXY(USSR(Maddison))
47	Argentina	8,340	60(Maddison)

Table 2.16 GDP at Purchasing Power Parities Per Capita, 2012 Dollars, Year 1960

Rank	Country	GPC	Source
48	Fr Polynesia	8,139	INTERPOL(14 Pacific is(Maddison))
49	Lithuania	8,135	PROXY(USSR(Maddison))
50	Gabon	7,901	60(Maddison)
51	Latvia	7,729	PROXY(USSR(Maddison))
52	Slovenia	7,622	PROXY(Yugoslavia(Maddison))
53	Slovakia	7,569	PROXY(Czechoslovakia(Maddison))
54	Guiana, Fr	7,549	INTERPOL(Maddison)
55	Russia	7,514	PROXY(USSR(Maddison))
56	Sint Maarten	7,402	06(CIA)WEIGHT(Curacao)
57	New Caledon	7,391	INTERPOL(14 Pacific is(Maddison))
58	Uruguay	7,385	60(Maddison)
59	Israel	7,304	60(Maddison)
60	Isle of Man	7,266	INTERPOL(9 European cs(Maddison))
61	Kazakhstan	7,255	PROXY(USSR(Maddison))
62	Curacao	7,201	INTERPOL(Maddison)
63	Ireland	6,931	60(Maddison)
64	Bahrain	6,869	60(Maddison)
65	Saint Martin	6,847	05(CIA)WEIGHT(Curacao)
66	Saudi Arabia	6,745	60(Maddison)
67	Hungary	6,496	60(Maddison)
68	Barbados	6,487	INTERPOL(Maddison)
69	Anguilla	6,224	INTERPOL(8 Caribbean cs(Maddison))
70	Japan	6,216	60(Maddison)
71	Chile	6,173	60(Maddison)
72	Georgia	5,609	PROXY(USSR(Maddison))
73	Turks & C Is	5,508	INTERPOL(8 Caribbean cs(Maddison))
74	Greece	5,436	60(Maddison)
75	Poland	5,314	60(Maddison)
76	South Africa	5,300	60(Maddison)
77	Croatia	5,261	PROXY(Yugoslavia(Maddison))
78	Moldova	5,183	PROXY(USSR(Maddison))
79	Turkmenistan	5,177	PROXY(USSR(Maddison))
80	Armenia	5,161	PROXY(USSR(Maddison))
81	Mexico	5,120	60(Maddison)
82	Spain	5,046	60(Maddison)
83	Cyprus	5,037	INTERPOL(Maddison)
84	Puerto Rico	5,011	60(Maddison)
85	Ukraine	4,992	PROXY(USSR(Maddison))
86	Hong Kong	4,893	60(Maddison)
87	Gibraltar	4,883	INTERPOL(9 European cs(Maddison))
88	Peru	4,829	60(Maddison)
89	Belarus	4,790	PROXY(USSR(Maddison))
90	Portugal	4,742	60(Maddison)
91	Lebanon	4,636	60(Maddison)
92	Uzbekistan	4,634	PROXY(USSR(Maddison))
93	Fiji	4,597	INTERPOL(14 Pacific is(Maddison))
94	Iraq	4,568	60(Maddison)
95	Montenegro	4,566	PROXY(Yugoslavia(Maddison))

Table 2.16 GDP at Purchasing Power Parities Per Capita, 2012 Dollars, Year 1960			
Rank	Country	GPC	Source
96	Serbia	4,512	PROXY(Yugoslavia(Maddison))
97	Bermuda	4,502	INTERPOL(Maddison)
98	Bulgaria	4,490	60(Maddison)
99	Seychelles	4,450	60(Maddison)
100	Guadeloupe	4,357	INTERPOL(Maddison)
101	Azerbaijan	4,198	PROXY(USSR(Maddison))
102	Costa Rica	4,188	60(Maddison)
103	Jamaica	4,009	60(Maddison)
104	Namibia	3,955	60(Maddison)
105	Mauritius	3,861	60(Maddison)
106	Tajikistan	3,856	PROXY(USSR(Maddison))
107	Antigua & B	3,845	INTERPOL
108	Singapore	3,843	60(Maddison)
109	St Kitts & N	3,819	INTERPOL(Maddison)
110	Colombia	3,812	60(Maddison)
111	Martinique	3,739	INTERPOL(Maddison)
112	Syria	3,725	60(Maddison)
113	Brazil	3,714	60(Maddison)
114	Ecuador	3,713	60(Maddison)
115	Panama	3,690	60(Maddison)
116	Montserrat	3,634	INTERPOL(8 Caribbean cs(Maddison))
117	Algeria	3,626	60(Maddison)
118	Iran	3,607	60(Maddison)
119	Turkey	3,499	60(Maddison)
120	Reunion	3,494	60(Maddison)
121	Cook Is	3,483	INTERPOL(14 Pacific is(Maddison))
122	Samoa, Amer	3,457	INTERPOL(14 Pacific is(Maddison))
123	Romania	3,433	60(Maddison)
124	Guatemala	3,346	60(Maddison)
125	Suriname	3,316	INTERPOL(Maddison)
126	Dominica	3,301	INTERPOL(Maddison)
127	Nicaragua	3,295	60(Maddison)
128	Malta	3,274	INTERPOL(Maddison)
129	Macao	3,225	INTERPOL(Maddison)
130	Cuba	3,209	60(Maddison)
131	Jordan	3,209	60(Maddison)
132	Kyrgyzstan	3,208	PROXY(USSR(Maddison))
133	Saint Helena	3,023	PROXY(3 Afr. cs(Maddison))
134	Libya	2,999	60(Maddison)
135	Djibouti	2,974	60(Maddison)
136	El Salvador	2,965	60(Maddison)
137	Belize	2,932	INTERPOL(Maddison)
138	Macedonia	2,913	PROXY(Yugoslavia(Maddison))
139	Kosovo	2,769	PROXY(Yugoslavia(Maddison))
140	Bosnia	2,642	PROXY(Yugoslavia(Maddison))
141	Vanuatu	2,557	INTERPOL(14 Pacific is(Maddison))
142	Bolivia	2,481	60(Maddison)
143	Micronesia	2,478	INTERPOL(14 Pacific is(Maddison))

Table 2.16 GDP at Purchasing Power Parities Per Capita, 2012 Dollars, Year 1960			
Rank	Country	GPC	Source
144	Angola	2,457	60(Maddison)
145	Paraguay	2,438	60(Maddison)
146	Congo, Rep	2,386	60(Maddison)
147	Tonga	2,386	INTERPOL(14 Pacific is(Maddison))
148	Samoa	2,385	INTERPOL(14 Pacific is(Maddison))
149	Albania	2,378	60(Maddison)
150	Malaysia	2,378	60(Maddison)
151	St Vincent	2,348	INTERPOL(Maddison)
152	Taiwan	2,309	60(Maddison)
153	Honduras	2,208	60(Maddison)
154	Philippines	2,201	60(Maddison)
155	Grenada	2,170	INTERPOL(Maddison)
156	Somalia	2,165	60(Maddison)
157	Wallis & Fut	2,136	INTERPOL(14 Pacific is(Maddison))
158	Dominican R	2,104	60(Maddison)
159	Mozambique	2,093	60(Maddison)
160	Tunisia	2,089	60(Maddison)
161	Senegal	2,070	60(Maddison)
162	St Lucia	1,981	INTERPOL(Maddison)
163	West Bank	1,964	PROXY(West Bank & Gaza(Maddison))
164	Morocco	1,955	60(Maddison)
165	Ivory Coast	1,906	60(Maddison)
166	Guyana	1,906	INTERPOL(Maddison)
167	Ghana	1,871	60(Maddison)
168	Benin	1,856	60(Maddison)
169	Sri Lanka	1,800	60(Maddison)
170	Marshall Is	1,753	INTERPOL(14 Pacific is(Maddison))
171	Madagascar	1,747	60(Maddison)
172	Korea, North	1,734	60(Maddison)
173	Oman	1,697	60(Maddison)
174	Korea, South	1,685	60(Maddison)
175	Haiti	1,651	60(Maddison)
176	Papua New G	1,641	INTERPOL(Maddison)
177	Zambia	1,625	60(Maddison)
178	Sudan	1,543	60(Maddison)
179	Egypt	1,523	60(Maddison)
180	Thailand	1,493	60(Maddison)
181	Niger	1,473	60(Maddison)
182	Swaziland	1,460	60(Maddison)
183	Liberia	1,448	60(Maddison)
184	Niue	1,426	INTERPOL(14 Pacific is(Maddison))
185	Indonesia	1,395	60(Maddison)
186	Cameroon	1,389	60(Maddison)
187	CAR	1,359	60(Maddison)
188	Zimbabwe	1,353	60(Maddison)
189	Sao Tome & P	1,330	60(Maddison)
190	Yemen	1,320	60(Maddison)
191	Comoros	1,304	60(Maddison)

Table 2.16 GDP at Purchasing Power Parities Per Capita, 2012 Dollars, Year 1960			
Rank	Country	GPC	Source
192	Afghanistan	1,299	60(Maddison)
193	Nigeria	1,299	60(Maddison)
194	Kiribati	1,261	INTERPOL(14 Pacific is(Maddison))
195	Gaza Strip	1,233	PROXY(West Bank & Gaza(Maddison))
196	Sierra Leone	1,216	60(Maddison)
197	Gambia	1,208	60(Maddison)
198	Solomon Is	1,179	INTERPOL(14 Pacific is(Maddison))
199	Congo, Dem R	1,152	60(Maddison)
200	Vietnam	1,147	60(Maddison)
201	Equatorial G	1,146	60(Maddison)
202	Tokelau	1,146	INTERPOL(14 Pacific is(Maddison))
203	Kenya	1,122	60(Maddison)
204	Mauritania	1,076	60(Maddison)
205	India	1,065	60(Maddison)
206	Cambodia	1,063	60(Maddison)
207	Chad	1,053	60(Maddison)
208	Maldives	1,031	INTERPOL(Maddison)
209	Uganda	1,019	60(Maddison)
210	Togo	1,010	60(Maddison)
211	Mongolia	984	60(Maddison)
212	Laos	981	60(Maddison)
213	Pakistan	941	60(Maddison)
214	Tuvalu	914	INTERPOL(14 Pacific is(Maddison))
215	Rwanda	894	60(Maddison)
216	Burkina Faso	864	60(Maddison)
217	Nepal	854	60(Maddison)
218	Burma	852	60(Maddison)
219	China	840	60(Maddison)
220	Bhutan	838	INTERPOL(Maddison)
221	Bangladesh	813	60(Maddison)
222	South Sudan	785	PROXY(Sudan(Maddison))
223	Mali	772	60(Maddison)
224	East Timor	765	INTERPOL(14 Pacific is(Maddison))
225	Guinea-Biss	761	60(Maddison)
226	Tanzania	745	60(Maddison)
227	Botswana	732	60(Maddison)
228	Cape Verde	700	60(Maddison)
229	Mayotte	654	PROXY(3 Afr. cs(Maddison))
230	Guinea	640	60(Maddison)
231	Lesotho	617	60(Maddison)
232	Malawi	570	60(Maddison)
233	W Sahara	550	PROXY(3 Afr. cs(Maddison))
234	Burundi	548	60(Maddison)
235	Eritrea	482	PROXY(Ethiopia & Eritr.(Maddison))
236	Ethiopia	469	PROXY(Ethiopia & Eritr.(Maddison))

TABLE 2.17 GDP AT PURCHASING POWER PARITIES PER CAPITA, 2012 DOLLARS, YEAR 1970			
Rank	Country	GPC	Source
1	UAE	90,599	70(Maddison)
2	Qatar	53,091	70(Maddison)
3	Kuwait	44,995	70(Maddison)
4	Switzerland	31,975	70(Maddison)
5	Luxembourg	29,153	INTERPOL(Maddison)
6	Bahamas	28,149	INTERPOL(Maddison)
7	Cayman Is	27,309	INTERPOL(8 Caribbean cs(Maddison))
8	Svalbard	26,268	PROXY(Norway(Maddison))
9	Brunei	25,465	INTERPOL(Maddison)
10	US	23,899	70(Maddison)
11	Liechtenstn	21,621	INTERPOL(9 European cs(Maddison))
12	Falkland Is	21,347	INTERPOL(8 Caribbean cs(Maddison))
13	Denmark	21,341	70(Maddison)
14	Sweden	21,169	70(Maddison)
15	Aruba	20,840	INTERPOL(8 Caribbean cs(Maddison))
16	Jersey	20,454	INTERPOL(9 European cs(Maddison))
17	Guam	20,242	INTERPOL(14 Pacific is(Maddison))
18	Iceland	20,150	INTERPOL(Maddison)
19	Netherlands	19,690	70(Maddison)
20	Australia	19,507	70(Maddison)
21	Canada	19,271	70(Maddison)
22	Germany	18,662	70(Maddison)
23	France	18,631	70(Maddison)
24	New Zealand	18,547	70(Maddison)
25	Belgium	17,956	70(Maddison)
26	Monaco	17,926	INTERPOL(9 European cs(Maddison))
27	Norway	17,292	70(Maddison)
28	San Marino	17,194	INTERPOL(9 European cs(Maddison))
29	Italy	17,025	70(Maddison)
30	Austria	16,814	70(Maddison)
31	Libya	16,463	70(Maddison)
32	UK	16,438	70(Maddison)
33	Saudi Arabia	16,267	70(Maddison)
34	Guernsey	15,963	INTERPOL(9 European cs(Maddison))
35	Finland	15,837	70(Maddison)
36	Virgin I, US	15,366	INTERPOL(8 Caribbean cs(Maddison))
37	Palau	15,155	INTERPOL(14 Pacific is(Maddison))
38	Japan	15,067	70(Maddison)
39	Venezuela	14,599	70(Maddison)
40	Greenland	14,540	INTERPOL(9 European cs(Maddison))
41	N Mariana Is	14,244	INTERPOL(14 Pacific is(Maddison))
42	Bahrain	14,103	70(Maddison)
43	Faroe Is	14,072	INTERPOL(9 European cs(Maddison))
44	Andorra	13,865	INTERPOL(9 European cs(Maddison))
45	Gabon	13,361	70(Maddison)
46	Virgin I, Br	13,008	INTERPOL(8 Caribbean cs(Maddison))
47	Nauru	13,004	INTERPOL(14 Pacific is(Maddison))

Table 2.17 GDP at Purchasing Power Parities Per Capita, 2012 Dollars, Year 1970			
Rank	Country	GPC	Source
48	Israel	12,694	70(Maddison)
49	Barbados	12,664	INTERPOL(Maddison)
50	Estonia	12,649	PROXY(USSR(Maddison))
51	Czechia	12,422	PROXY(Czechoslovakia(Maddison))
52	Lithuania	12,084	PROXY(USSR(Maddison))
53	Greece	12,006	70(Maddison)
54	Russia	11,955	PROXY(USSR(Maddison))
55	Trinidad & T	11,901	70(Maddison)
56	Slovenia	11,889	PROXY(Yugoslavia(Maddison))
57	St Pierre&M	11,844	INTERPOL(8 Caribbean cs(Maddison))
58	Spain	11,172	70(Maddison)
59	Isle of Man	10,962	INTERPOL(9 European cs(Maddison))
60	Latvia	10,543	PROXY(USSR(Maddison))
61	Argentina	10,523	70(Maddison)
62	Ireland	10,431	70(Maddison)
63	Sint Maarten	10,332	06(CIA)WEIGHT(Curacao)
64	Hungary	10,115	70(Maddison)
65	Curacao	10,073	INTERPOL(Maddison)
66	Slovakia	9,798	PROXY(Czechoslovakia(Maddison))
67	Fr Polynesia	9,636	INTERPOL(14 Pacific is(Maddison))
68	Saint Martin	9,526	05(CIA)WEIGHT(Curacao)
69	Kazakhstan	9,396	PROXY(USSR(Maddison))
70	Portugal	9,141	70(Maddison)
71	Hong Kong	8,865	70(Maddison)
72	Croatia	8,760	PROXY(Yugoslavia(Maddison))
73	Cyprus	8,614	INTERPOL(Maddison)
74	New Caledon	8,578	INTERPOL(14 Pacific is(Maddison))
75	Puerto Rico	8,521	70(Maddison)
76	Oman	8,239	70(Maddison)
77	Anguilla	8,098	INTERPOL(8 Caribbean cs(Maddison))
78	South Africa	7,890	70(Maddison)
79	Gibraltar	7,882	INTERPOL(9 European cs(Maddison))
80	Singapore	7,863	70(Maddison)
81	Bermuda	7,773	INTERPOL(Maddison)
82	Montenegro	7,761	PROXY(Yugoslavia(Maddison))
83	Poland	7,749	70(Maddison)
84	Turkmenistan	7,703	PROXY(USSR(Maddison))
85	Malta	7,689	INTERPOL(Maddison)
86	Iran	7,594	70(Maddison)
87	St Kitts & N	7,487	INTERPOL(Maddison)
88	Serbia	7,462	PROXY(Yugoslavia(Maddison))
89	Georgia	7,349	PROXY(USSR(Maddison))
90	Uruguay	7,343	70(Maddison)
91	Turks & C Is	7,301	INTERPOL(8 Caribbean cs(Maddison))
92	Mexico	7,298	70(Maddison)
93	Bulgaria	7,257	70(Maddison)
94	Guiana, Fr	7,126	INTERPOL(Maddison)
95	Guadeloupe	7,029	INTERPOL(Maddison)

TABLE 2.17 GDP AT PURCHASING POWER PARITIES PER CAPITA, 2012 DOLLARS, YEAR 1970

Rank	Country	GPC	Source
96	Ukraine	7,010	PROXY(USSR(Maddison))
97	Lebanon	6,998	70(Maddison)
98	Chile	6,980	70(Maddison)
99	Moldova	6,924	PROXY(USSR(Maddison))
100	Martinique	6,768	INTERPOL(Maddison)
101	Macao	6,430	INTERPOL(Maddison)
102	Romania	6,312	70(Maddison)
103	Peru	6,210	70(Maddison)
104	Belarus	6,082	PROXY(USSR(Maddison))
105	Armenia	5,963	PROXY(USSR(Maddison))
106	Iraq	5,933	70(Maddison)
107	Uzbekistan	5,816	PROXY(USSR(Maddison))
108	Seychelles	5,792	70(Maddison)
109	Panama	5,786	70(Maddison)
110	Costa Rica	5,708	70(Maddison)
111	Jamaica	5,705	70(Maddison)
112	Azerbaijan	5,514	PROXY(USSR(Maddison))
113	Reunion	5,349	70(Maddison)
114	Antigua & B	5,300	INTERPOL
115	Macedonia	5,066	PROXY(Yugoslavia(Maddison))
116	Tajikistan	5,035	PROXY(USSR(Maddison))
117	Nicaragua	4,993	70(Maddison)
118	Brazil	4,940	70(Maddison)
119	Namibia	4,845	70(Maddison)
120	Suriname	4,796	INTERPOL(Maddison)
121	Ecuador	4,784	70(Maddison)
122	Turkey	4,760	70(Maddison)
123	Kosovo	4,622	PROXY(Yugoslavia(Maddison))
124	Colombia	4,604	70(Maddison)
125	Fiji	4,586	INTERPOL(14 Pacific is(Maddison))
126	Taiwan	4,540	70(Maddison)
127	Montserrat	4,436	INTERPOL(8 Caribbean cs(Maddison))
128	Bosnia	4,348	PROXY(Yugoslavia(Maddison))
129	Angola	4,347	70(Maddison)
130	Dominica	4,331	INTERPOL(Maddison)
131	Samoa, Amer	4,330	INTERPOL(14 Pacific is(Maddison))
132	Algeria	4,306	70(Maddison)
133	Cook Is	4,119	INTERPOL(14 Pacific is(Maddison))
134	Guatemala	3,991	70(Maddison)
135	El Salvador	3,960	70(Maddison)
136	Kyrgyzstan	3,822	PROXY(USSR(Maddison))
137	Djibouti	3,727	70(Maddison)
138	Mauritius	3,646	70(Maddison)
139	Syria	3,520	70(Maddison)
140	Albania	3,430	70(Maddison)
141	Bolivia	3,427	70(Maddison)
142	St Lucia	3,411	INTERPOL(Maddison)
143	Belize	3,395	INTERPOL(Maddison)

Table 2.17 GDP at Purchasing Power Parities Per Capita, 2012 Dollars, Year 1970			
Rank	Country	GPC	Source
144	Grenada	3,221	INTERPOL(Maddison)
145	Malaysia	3,216	70(Maddison)
146	Saint Helena	3,148	PROXY(3 Afr. cs(Maddison))
147	Korea, North	3,078	70(Maddison)
148	Cuba	3,036	70(Maddison)
149	St Vincent	2,988	INTERPOL(Maddison)
150	Vanuatu	2,985	INTERPOL(14 Pacific is(Maddison))
151	Swaziland	2,959	70(Maddison)
152	Jordan	2,954	70(Maddison)
153	Tonga	2,922	INTERPOL(14 Pacific is(Maddison))
154	Paraguay	2,904	70(Maddison)
155	Korea, South	2,898	70(Maddison)
156	Congo, Rep	2,859	70(Maddison)
157	Micronesia	2,841	INTERPOL(14 Pacific is(Maddison))
158	Tunisia	2,827	70(Maddison)
159	Mozambique	2,771	70(Maddison)
160	Samoa	2,754	INTERPOL(14 Pacific is(Maddison))
161	Dominican R	2,603	70(Maddison)
162	Ivory Coast	2,593	70(Maddison)
163	Honduras	2,557	70(Maddison)
164	Philippines	2,509	70(Maddison)
165	Wallis & Fut	2,439	INTERPOL(14 Pacific is(Maddison))
166	West Bank	2,285	PROXY(West Bank & Gaza(Maddison))
167	Papua New G	2,281	INTERPOL(Maddison)
168	Comoros	2,222	70(Maddison)
169	Morocco	2,202	70(Maddison)
170	Guyana	2,125	INTERPOL(Maddison)
171	Thailand	2,068	70(Maddison)
172	Mauritania	2,028	70(Maddison)
173	Marshall Is	2,013	INTERPOL(14 Pacific is(Maddison))
174	Equatorial G	1,975	70(Maddison)
175	Senegal	1,962	70(Maddison)
176	Zambia	1,899	70(Maddison)
177	Egypt	1,883	70(Maddison)
178	Madagascar	1,875	70(Maddison)
179	Sao Tome & P	1,841	70(Maddison)
180	Sri Lanka	1,838	70(Maddison)
181	Somalia	1,837	70(Maddison)
182	Benin	1,778	70(Maddison)
183	Ghana	1,762	70(Maddison)
184	Nigeria	1,747	70(Maddison)
185	Cameroon	1,745	70(Maddison)
186	Kiribati	1,739	INTERPOL(14 Pacific is(Maddison))
187	Niue	1,727	INTERPOL(14 Pacific is(Maddison))
188	Zimbabwe	1,694	70(Maddison)
189	Gambia	1,572	70(Maddison)
190	Solomon Is	1,499	INTERPOL(14 Pacific is(Maddison))

TABLE 2.17 GDP AT PURCHASING POWER PARITIES PER CAPITA, 2012 DOLLARS, YEAR 1970			
Rank	Country	GPC	Source
191	Niger	1,489	70(Maddison)
192	Yemen	1,475	70(Maddison)
193	Sierra Leone	1,455	70(Maddison)
194	Indonesia	1,434	70(Maddison)
195	Haiti	1,428	70(Maddison)
196	Mongolia	1,423	70(Maddison)
197	Kenya	1,397	70(Maddison)
198	Botswana	1,367	70(Maddison)
199	Sudan	1,357	70(Maddison)
200	Gaza Strip	1,354	PROXY(West Bank & Gaza(Maddison))
201	Togo	1,338	70(Maddison)
202	Tokelau	1,336	INTERPOL(14 Pacific is(Maddison))
203	Liberia	1,306	70(Maddison)
204	Guinea-Biss	1,285	70(Maddison)
205	Pakistan	1,278	70(Maddison)
206	Maldives	1,247	INTERPOL(Maddison)
207	CAR	1,234	70(Maddison)
208	Afghanistan	1,203	70(Maddison)
209	Congo, Dem R	1,165	70(Maddison)
210	Uganda	1,136	70(Maddison)
211	India	1,112	70(Maddison)
212	Chad	1,101	70(Maddison)
213	Tuvalu	1,062	INTERPOL(14 Pacific is(Maddison))
214	Cambodia	1,019	70(Maddison)
215	Laos	998	70(Maddison)
216	Vietnam	968	70(Maddison)
217	Burma	958	70(Maddison)
218	Tanzania	954	70(Maddison)
219	Burkina Faso	907	70(Maddison)
220	Bangladesh	898	70(Maddison)
221	East Timor	892	INTERPOL(14 Pacific is(Maddison))
222	Bhutan	892	INTERPOL(Maddison)
223	Rwanda	857	70(Maddison)
224	Nepal	833	70(Maddison)
225	China	795	70(Maddison)
226	Guinea	788	70(Maddison)
227	Mali	781	70(Maddison)
228	Cape Verde	750	70(Maddison)
229	Lesotho	700	70(Maddison)
230	South Sudan	691	PROXY(Sudan(Maddison))
231	Mayotte	672	PROXY(3 Afr. cs(Maddison))
232	Eritrea	647	PROXY(Ethiopia & Eritr.(Maddison))
233	Ethiopia	631	PROXY(Ethiopia & Eritr.(Maddison))
234	Malawi	602	70(Maddison)
235	W Sahara	573	PROXY(3 Afr. cs(Maddison))
236	Burundi	533	70(Maddison)

Table 2.18 GDP at Purchasing Power Parities Per Capita, 2012 Dollars, Year 1980

Rank	Country	GPC	Source
1	UAE	154,935	80(WB)
2	Brunei	53,816	80(WB)
3	Kuwait	47,742	80(WB)
4	Qatar	45,908	80(Maddison)
5	Svalbard	42,424	PROXY(Norway(WB))
6	Switzerland	37,846	80(WB)
7	Saudi Arabia	32,956	80(WB)
8	Cayman Is	32,368	INTERPOL(8 Caribbean cs(Maddison))
9	Luxembourg	31,768	80(WB)
10	Bahamas	31,132	80(WB)
11	US	29,775	80(WB)
12	Norway	27,928	80(WB)
13	Liechtenstn	27,540	INTERPOL(9 European cs(Maddison))
14	Iceland	26,614	80(WB)
15	Denmark	26,183	80(WB)
16	Canada	26,160	80(WB)
17	Jersey	26,092	INTERPOL(9 European cs(Maddison))
18	Sweden	25,540	80(WB)
19	Belgium	25,430	80(WB)
20	Germany	25,376	80(WB)
21	Falkland Is	25,199	INTERPOL(8 Caribbean cs(Maddison))
22	Aruba	24,945	INTERPOL(8 Caribbean cs(Maddison))
23	Austria	24,819	80(WB)
24	Bahrain	24,663	80(WB)
25	Netherlands	24,614	80(WB)
26	France	24,172	80(WB)
27	Italy	24,021	80(WB)
28	Australia	23,728	80(WB)
29	Monaco	23,124	INTERPOL(9 European cs(Maddison))
30	San Marino	22,644	INTERPOL(9 European cs(Maddison))
31	Finland	21,919	80(WB)
32	Guam	21,507	INTERPOL(14 Pacific is(Maddison))
33	New Zealand	20,990	80(WB)
34	Japan	20,866	80(WB)
35	Guernsey	20,414	INTERPOL(9 European cs(Maddison))
36	UK	19,522	80(WB)
37	Slovenia	19,454	PROXY(Yugoslavia(Maddison))
38	Greece	18,974	80(WB)
39	Barbados	18,735	80(WB)
40	Gabon	18,691	80(WB)
41	Greenland	18,648	INTERPOL(9 European cs(Maddison))
42	Macao	18,585	82(WB)
43	Faroe Is	18,101	INTERPOL(9 European cs(Maddison))
44	Virgin I, US	17,990	INTERPOL(8 Caribbean cs(Maddison))
45	Andorra	17,777	INTERPOL(9 European cs(Maddison))
46	Israel	17,278	80(WB)

Table 2.18 GDP at Purchasing Power Parities Per Capita, 2012 Dollars, Year 1980

Rank	Country	GPC	Source
47	Trinidad & T	17,165	80(WB)
48	Spain	17,122	80(WB)
49	Singapore	17,086	80(WB)
50	Czechia	16,626	PROXY(Czechoslovakia(Maddison))
51	Hong Kong	16,299	80(WB)
52	Palau	16,001	INTERPOL(14 Pacific is(Maddison))
53	Virgin I, Br	15,432	INTERPOL(8 Caribbean cs(Maddison))
54	Croatia	15,416	PROXY(Yugoslavia(Maddison))
55	Estonia	15,020	INTERPOL(Estonia(Maddison))
56	Ireland	14,916	80(WB)
57	N Mariana Is	14,802	INTERPOL(14 Pacific is(Maddison))
58	Russia	14,742	INTERPOL(Russia(Maddison))
59	Cyprus	14,729	80(WB)
60	Isle of Man	14,358	INTERPOL(9 European cs(Maddison))
61	Lithuania	14,302	INTERPOL(Lithuanua(Maddison))
62	Hungary	14,199	80(WB)
63	Montenegro	13,971	PROXY(Yugoslavia(Maddison))
64	St Pierre&M	13,971	INTERPOL(8 Caribbean cs(Maddison))
65	Portugal	13,803	80(WB)
66	Nauru	13,740	INTERPOL(14 Pacific is(Maddison))
67	Venezuela	13,485	80(WB)
68	Serbia	13,030	PROXY(Yugoslavia(Maddison))
69	Libya	12,955	80(Maddison)
70	Slovakia	12,335	PROXY(Czechoslovakia(Maddison))
71	Latvia	12,000	80(WB)
72	Malta	11,900	80(WB)
73	Seychelles	11,627	80(WB)
74	Iraq	11,532	80(Maddison)
75	Argentina	11,339	80(WB)
76	Mexico	11,160	80(WB)
77	Gibraltar	10,793	INTERPOL(9 European cs(Maddison))
78	Romania	10,772	80(WB)
79	Poland	10,604	80(Maddison)
80	Puerto Rico	10,595	80(Maddison)
81	Lebanon	10,475	80(Maddison)
82	Fr Polynesia	10,297	INTERPOL(14 Pacific is(Maddison))
83	Oman	10,140	80(WB)
84	Sint Maarten	10,126	06(CIA)WEIGHT(Curacao)
85	Bermuda	9,938	INTERPOL(Maddison)
86	Curacao	9,870	INTERPOL(Maddison)
87	Anguilla	9,522	INTERPOL(8 Caribbean cs(Maddison))
88	South Africa	9,492	80(WB)
89	Saint Martin	9,337	05(CIA)WEIGHT(Curacao)
90	Macedonia	9,271	PROXY(Yugoslavia(Maddison))
91	Kazakhstan	9,196	INTERPOL(Kazakhstan(Maddison))
92	New Caledon	9,094	INTERPOL(14 Pacific is(Maddison))
93	Bulgaria	9,085	80(WB)
94	Uruguay	8,869	80(WB)

TABLE 2.18 GDP AT PURCHASING POWER PARITIES PER CAPITA, 2012 DOLLARS, YEAR 1980			
Rank	Country	GPC	Source
95	Taiwan	8,803	80(Maddison)
96	Turks & C Is	8,684	INTERPOL(8 Caribbean cs(Maddison))
97	Brazil	8,548	80(WB)
98	Guadeloupe	8,507	INTERPOL(Maddison)
99	Martinique	8,408	INTERPOL(Maddison)
100	Ukraine	8,224	INTERPOL(Ukraine(Maddison))
101	Kosovo	8,155	PROXY(Yugoslavia(Maddison))
102	Georgia	7,844	80(WB)
103	Turkmenistan	7,830	INTERPOL(Turkmenistan(Maddison))
104	Moldova	7,789	INTERPOL(Moldova(Maddison))
105	Iran	7,637	80(WB)
106	Panama	7,611	80(WB)
107	Bosnia	7,552	PROXY(Yugoslavia(Maddison))
108	Costa Rica	7,364	80(WB)
109	Antigua & B	7,306	80(WB)
110	Suriname	7,217	80(WB)
111	Ecuador	7,187	80(WB)
112	Peru	7,013	80(WB)
113	Guiana, Fr	6,976	INTERPOL(Maddison)
114	Chile	6,872	80(WB)
115	Belarus	6,766	INTERPOL(Belarus(Maddison))
116	Algeria	6,666	80(WB)
117	St Kitts & N	6,413	80(WB)
118	Colombia	6,177	80(WB)
119	Armenia	6,163	INTERPOL(Armenia(Maddison))
120	Turkey	6,116	80(WB)
121	Korea, South	5,919	80(WB)
122	Uzbekistan	5,837	INTERPOL(Uzbekistan(Maddison))
123	Namibia	5,761	80(WB)
124	Reunion	5,685	80(Maddison)
125	Azerbaijan	5,672	INTERPOL(Azerbaijan(Maddison))
126	Malaysia	5,644	80(WB)
127	Montserrat	5,014	INTERPOL(8 Caribbean cs(Maddison))
128	Paraguay	4,951	80(WB)
129	Jordan	4,784	80(WB)
130	Mauritius	4,747	80(WB)
131	Samoa, Amer	4,730	INTERPOL(14 Pacific is(Maddison))
132	Guatemala	4,704	80(WB)
133	Jamaica	4,676	80(Maddison)
134	St Lucia	4,617	80(WB)
135	El Salvador	4,550	80(WB)
136	Dominica	4,538	80(WB)
137	Tunisia	4,534	80(WB)
138	Korea, North	4,488	80(Maddison)
139	Syria	4,449	80(WB)
140	Tajikistan	4,446	INTERPOL(Tajikistan(Maddison))
141	Fiji	4,420	80(WB)
142	Cook Is	4,399	INTERPOL(14 Pacific is(Maddison))

Table 2.18 GDP at Purchasing Power Parities Per Capita, 2012 Dollars, Year 1980			
Rank	Country	GPC	Source
143	Botswana	4,288	80(WB)
144	Albania	4,150	80(WB)
145	Grenada	4,118	80(WB)
146	Dominican R	4,096	80(WB)
147	Bolivia	4,093	80(WB)
148	Belize	4,021	80(WB)
149	Nicaragua	3,983	80(WB)
150	Cuba	3,948	80(Maddison)
151	Saint Helena	3,871	PROXY(3 Afr. cs(Maddison))
152	Congo, Rep	3,710	80(WB)
153	St Vincent	3,665	80(WB)
154	Swaziland	3,522	80(WB)
155	Kyrgyzstan	3,463	INTERPOL(Kyrgyzstan(Maddison))
156	Philippines	3,222	80(WB)
157	Djibouti	3,193	80(Maddison)
158	Vanuatu	3,183	80(WB)
159	Honduras	3,123	80(WB)
160	Egypt	3,005	80(WB)
161	Micronesia	2,974	INTERPOL(14 Pacific is(Maddison))
162	Angola	2,961	80(Maddison)
163	Ivory Coast	2,938	80(WB)
164	Morocco	2,846	80(WB)
165	Samoa	2,802	82(WB)
166	Thailand	2,750	80(WB)
167	Tonga	2,748	81(WB)
168	West Bank	2,619	PROXY(West Bank & Gaza(Maddison))
169	Wallis & Fut	2,569	INTERPOL(14 Pacific is(Maddison))
170	Guyana	2,536	80(WB)
171	Yemen	2,409	80(Maddison)
172	Sao Tome & P	2,279	80(Maddison)
173	Cameroon	2,262	80(WB)
174	Papua New G	2,244	80(WB)
175	Equatorial G	2,188	80(Maddison)
176	Kiribati	2,171	80(WB)
177	Marshall Is	2,125	INTERPOL(14 Pacific is(Maddison))
178	Mauritania	2,088	80(WB)
179	Mongolia	2,055	80(Maddison)
180	Haiti	2,019	80(Maddison)
181	Nigeria	1,998	80(WB)
182	Gambia	1,987	80(WB)
183	Maldives	1,983	INTERPOL(Maddison)
184	Sri Lanka	1,977	80(WB)
185	Indonesia	1,923	80(WB)
186	Niue	1,861	INTERPOL(14 Pacific is(Maddison))
187	Senegal	1,744	80(WB)
188	Solomon Is	1,740	80(WB)
189	Zimbabwe	1,706	80(Maddison)
190	Benin	1,632	80(WB)

Table 2.18 GDP at Purchasing Power Parities Per Capita, 2012 Dollars, Year 1980			
Rank	Country	GPC	Source
191	Zambia	1,627	80(WB)
192	Somalia	1,610	80(Maddison)
193	Madagascar	1,558	80(WB)
194	Kenya	1,554	80(WB)
195	Gaza Strip	1,472	PROXY(West Bank & Gaza(Maddison))
196	Pakistan	1,444	80(WB)
197	Tokelau	1,420	INTERPOL(14 Pacific is(Maddison))
198	Sudan	1,405	80(WB)
199	Ghana	1,396	80(WB)
200	Comoros	1,391	80(WB)
201	Sierra Leone	1,323	80(WB)
202	Togo	1,290	80(WB)
203	Niger	1,282	80(WB)
204	Cambodia	1,252	80(Maddison)
205	Burma	1,199	80(Maddison)
206	Afghanistan	1,162	80(Maddison)
207	Guinea-Biss	1,151	80(WB)
208	Tuvalu	1,127	INTERPOL(14 Pacific is(Maddison))
209	India	1,090	80(WB)
210	Laos	1,079	80(Maddison)
211	Bhutan	1,036	80(WB)
212	Tanzania	1,035	80(Maddison)
213	CAR	995	80(WB)
214	Lesotho	991	80(WB)
215	Rwanda	984	80(WB)
216	Guinea	978	80(Maddison)
217	East Timor	948	INTERPOL(14 Pacific is(Maddison))
218	Vietnam	916	80(Maddison)
219	Mali	903	80(WB)
220	Congo, Dem R	900	80(WB)
221	Cape Verde	893	80(WB)
222	China	871	80(WB)
223	Liberia	852	80(WB)
224	Chad	827	80(WB)
225	Malawi	795	80(WB)
226	Burkina Faso	790	80(WB)
227	Mayotte	773	PROXY(3 Afr. cs(Maddison))
228	Bangladesh	746	80(WB)
229	Nepal	742	80(WB)
230	South Sudan	715	PROXY(Sudan(WB))
231	W Sahara	707	PROXY(3 Afr. cs(Maddison))
232	Eritrea	703	PROXY(Ethiopia & Eritr.(Maddison))
233	Uganda	686	80(Maddison)
234	Ethiopia	684	PROXY(Ethiopia & Eritr.(Maddison))
235	Burundi	522	80(WB)
236	Mozambique	496	80(WB)

TABLE 2.19 GDP AT PURCHASING POWER PARITIES PER CAPITA, 2012 DOLLARS, YEAR 1990

Rank	Country	GPC	Source
1	UAE	86,187	90(WB)
2	Svalbard	54,541	PROXY(Norway(WB))
3	Luxembourg	52,011	90(WB)
4	Kuwait	50,425	90(Maddison)WEIGHT(80(WB))
5	Switzerland	45,449	90(WB)
6	US	37,628	90(WB)
7	Cayman Is	36,656	93(CIA)WEIGHT(US(Maddison))
8	Norway	35,906	90(WB)
9	Bahamas	34,391	90(WB)
10	Liechtenstn	33,226	90(CIA)
11	Denmark	32,827	90(WB)
12	Germany	31,606	90(WB)
13	Jersey	31,515	99(CIA)WEIGHT(US(Maddison))
14	Iceland	31,122	90(WB)
15	Belgium	30,990	90(WB)
16	Sweden	30,970	90(WB)
17	Japan	30,873	90(WB)
18	Italy	30,789	90(WB)
19	Austria	30,665	90(WB)
20	Canada	30,585	90(WB)
21	Netherlands	29,314	90(WB)
22	France	29,229	90(WB)
23	Australia	28,914	90(WB)
24	Finland	28,708	90(WB)
25	Singapore	28,558	90(WB)
26	Aruba	28,453	93(CIA)WEIGHT(US(Maddison))
27	Falkland Is	28,452	95(CIA)WEIGHT(US(Maddison))
28	Brunei	28,208	90(WB)
29	Monaco	28,174	93(CIA)WEIGHT(US(Maddison))
30	San Marino	28,034	92(CIA)WEIGHT(US(Maddison))
31	Hong Kong	27,687	90(WB)
32	UK	24,913	90(WB)
33	Guernsey	24,706	97(CIA)WEIGHT(US(Maddison))
34	Cyprus	24,220	90(WB)
35	Macao	24,201	90(WB)
36	New Zealand	24,100	90(WB)
37	Greenland	22,617	95(CIA)WEIGHT(US(Maddison))
38	Spain	22,399	90(WB)
39	Faroe Is	22,005	89(CIA)WEIGHT(US(Maddison))
40	Guam	21,951	91(CIA)WEIGHT(US(Maddison))
41	Andorra	21,556	92(CIA)WEIGHT(US(Maddison))
42	Ireland	20,893	90(WB)
43	Israel	20,487	90(WB)
44	Bahrain	20,378	90(Maddison)
45	Barbados	20,271	90(WB)
46	Virgin I, US	20,191	87(CIA)WEIGHT(US(Maddison))

Table 2.19 GDP at Purchasing Power Parities Per Capita, 2012 Dollars, Year 1990			
Rank	Country	GPC	Source
47	Qatar	19,510	90(CIA)
48	Greece	19,310	90(WB)
49	Czechia	19,234	90(WB)
50	Portugal	18,916	90(WB)
51	Slovenia	18,574	90(WB)
52	Saudi Arabia	18,023	90(WB)
53	Isle of Man	17,701	94(CIA)WEIGHT(US(Maddison))
54	Virgin I, Br	17,488	91(CIA)WEIGHT(US(Maddison))
55	Gabon	17,187	90(WB)
56	Russia	16,919	90(WB)
57	Estonia	16,682	90(Maddison)
58	Hungary	16,664	90(WB)
59	Palau	16,296	91(WB)WEIGHT(US(Maddison))
60	Lithuania	15,819	90(WB)
61	Malta	15,810	90(WB)
62	St Pierre&M	15,766	92(CIA)WEIGHT(US(Maddison))
63	Oman	15,459	90(WB)
64	Antigua & B	15,424	90(WB)
65	Seychelles	15,227	90(WB)
66	N Mariana Is	14,995	92(CIA)WEIGHT(US(Maddison))
67	Latvia	14,907	90(WB)
68	Taiwan	14,651	90(Maddison)
69	Croatia	14,568	90(Maddison)
70	Nauru	13,997	93(CIA)WEIGHT(US(Maddison))
71	Gibraltar	13,772	93(CIA)WEIGHT(US(Maddison))
72	Slovakia	13,207	90(WB)
73	Montenegro	13,173	PROXY(Serbia(WB))
74	Puerto Rico	13,166	90(Maddison)
75	Serbia	12,323	90(WB)
76	Trinidad & T	12,127	90(WB)
77	Korea, South	12,050	90(WB)
78	Bulgaria	11,700	90(WB)
79	St Kitts & N	11,564	90(Maddison)
80	Venezuela	11,545	90(WB)
81	Bermuda	11,172	90(Maddison)
82	Romania	11,140	90(WB)
83	Mexico	10,874	90(WB)
84	Anguilla	10,720	93(CIA)WEIGHT(US(Maddison))
85	Fr Polynesia	10,529	93(CIA)WEIGHT(US(Maddison))
86	Turks & C Is	9,860	92(CIA)WEIGHT(US(Maddison))
87	Poland	9,783	90(WB)
88	Macedonia	9,556	90(WB)
89	New Caledon	9,274	91(CIA)WEIGHT(US(Maddison))
90	Ukraine	9,191	90(WB)
91	Martinique	8,888	90(Maddison)
92	Botswana	8,727	90(WB)
93	Turkey	8,720	90(WB)
94	Guadeloupe	8,681	90(Maddison)

Table 2.19 GDP at Purchasing Power Parities Per Capita, 2012 Dollars, Year 1990			
Rank	Country	GPC	Source
95	Chile	8,650	90(WB)
96	South Africa	8,601	90(WB)
97	Sint Maarten	8,528	06(CIA)WEIGHT(Curacao)
98	Argentina	8,367	90(WB)
99	Moldova	8,341	90(Maddison)
100	Curacao	8,303	90(Maddison)WEIGHT(Neth Antilles)
101	Uruguay	8,292	90(WB)
102	Dominica	8,156	90(WB)
103	Brazil	8,105	90(WB)
104	Kazakhstan	8,067	90(WB)
105	St Lucia	7,944	90(WB)
106	Saint Martin	7,877	05(CIA)WEIGHT(Curacao)
107	Kosovo	7,704	PROXY(Serbia & Montenegro(Maddison))
108	Malaysia	7,681	90(WB)
109	Mauritius	7,611	90(WB)
110	Belarus	7,323	90(WB)
111	Ecuador	7,258	90(WB)
112	Costa Rica	7,201	90(WB)
113	Bosnia	7,146	90(Maddison)
114	Lebanon	7,122	90(WB)
115	Colombia	7,090	90(WB)
116	Panama	6,984	90(WB)
117	Turkmenistan	6,962	90(WB)
118	Guiana, Fr	6,937	90(Maddison)
119	Reunion	6,924	90(Maddison)
120	Georgia	6,816	90(WB)
121	Iraq	6,622	90(Maddison)WEIGHT(00(WB))
122	Grenada	6,620	90(WB)
123	Algeria	6,498	90(WB)
124	Iran	6,430	90(WB)
125	St Vincent	6,159	90(WB)
126	Armenia	6,155	90(WB)
127	Suriname	5,757	90(WB)
128	Swaziland	5,561	90(WB)
129	Paraguay	5,526	90(WB)
130	Montserrat	5,485	92(CIA)WEIGHT(US(Maddison))
131	Uzbekistan	5,439	90(Maddison)
132	Azerbaijan	5,410	90(WB)
133	Jamaica	5,367	90(Maddison)
134	Libya	5,221	90(Maddison)
135	Peru	5,165	90(WB)
136	Tunisia	5,041	90(WB)
137	Belize	4,981	90(WB)
138	Samoa, Amer	4,873	91(CIA)WEIGHT(US(Maddison))
139	Thailand	4,836	90(WB)
140	Namibia	4,680	90(WB)
141	Saint Helena	4,523	PROXY(3 Afr. cs(Maddison))

TABLE 2.19 GDP AT PURCHASING POWER PARITIES PER CAPITA, 2012 DOLLARS, YEAR 1990

Rank	Country	GPC	Source
142	Cook Is	4,497	93(CIA)WEIGHT(US(Maddison))
143	Korea, North	4,488	90(Maddison)
144	Fiji	4,419	90(WB)
145	Congo, Rep	4,399	90(WB)
146	Cuba	4,315	90(Maddison)
147	Dominican R	4,164	90(WB)
148	Syria	4,136	90(WB)
149	Guatemala	4,105	90(WB)
150	Jordan	4,047	90(WB)
151	Egypt	4,035	90(WB)
152	Vanuatu	3,945	90(WB)
153	El Salvador	3,775	90(WB)
154	Albania	3,712	90(WB)
155	Maldives	3,546	90(Maddison)
156	Angola	3,451	90(WB)
157	Tajikistan	3,418	90(WB)
158	Morocco	3,302	90(WB)
159	Bolivia	3,224	90(WB)
160	Tonga	3,193	90(WB)
161	West Bank	3,003	PROXY(West Bank & Gaza(Maddison))
162	Micronesia	2,996	90(WB)
163	Djibouti	2,975	90(WB)
164	Samoa	2,965	90(WB)
165	Honduras	2,937	90(WB)
166	Philippines	2,915	90(WB)
167	Kyrgyzstan	2,868	90(WB)
168	Indonesia	2,807	90(WB)
169	Mongolia	2,783	90(WB)
170	Nicaragua	2,686	90(WB)
171	Solomon Is	2,645	90(WB)
172	Wallis & Fut	2,614	94(CIA)WEIGHT(US(Maddison))
173	Sri Lanka	2,552	90(WB)
174	Cameroon	2,325	90(WB)
175	Ivory Coast	2,297	90(WB)
176	Equatorial G	2,275	90(WB)
177	Marshall Is	2,164	92(CIA)WEIGHT(US(Maddison))
178	Yemen	2,091	90(WB)
179	Bhutan	2,051	90(WB)
180	Papua New G	1,971	90(WB)
181	Guyana	1,966	90(WB)
182	Niue	1,909	93(CIA)WEIGHT(US(Maddison))
183	Pakistan	1,904	90(WB)
184	Kiribati	1,893	90(WB)
185	Gambia	1,872	90(WB)
186	Mauritania	1,855	90(WB)
187	Sao Tome & P	1,800	90(Maddison)
188	Zimbabwe	1,764	90(Maddison)
189	China	1,737	90(WB)

TABLE 2.19 GDP AT PURCHASING POWER PARITIES PER CAPITA, 2012 DOLLARS, YEAR 1990

Rank	Country	GPC	Source
190	Nigeria	1,722	90(WB)
191	Somalia	1,712	90(Maddison)
192	Senegal	1,690	90(WB)
193	Haiti	1,630	90(Maddison)
194	Kenya	1,608	90(WB)
195	Gaza Strip	1,601	PROXY(West Bank & Gaza(Maddison))
196	Benin	1,601	90(WB)
197	India	1,491	90(WB)
198	Guinea-Biss	1,467	90(WB)
199	Tokelau	1,449	93(CIA)WEIGHT(US(Maddison))
200	Comoros	1,414	90(WB)
201	Sudan	1,342	90(WB)
202	Cambodia	1,330	90(Maddison)
203	Zambia	1,312	90(WB)
204	Ghana	1,308	90(WB)
205	Cape Verde	1,264	90(WB)
206	Madagascar	1,220	90(WB)
207	Burma	1,168	90(Maddison)
208	Lesotho	1,167	90(WB)
209	Vietnam	1,153	90(WB)
210	Tuvalu	1,150	93(CIA)WEIGHT(US(Maddison))
211	Sierra Leone	1,143	90(WB)
212	Togo	1,102	90(WB)
213	Laos	1,061	90(WB)
214	Chad	1,059	90(WB)
215	Tanzania	977	90(WB)
216	Guinea	973	90(WB)
217	East Timor	968	00(WB)WEIGHT(US(Maddison))
218	Nepal	922	90(WB)
219	Niger	899	90(WB)
220	Afghanistan	883	90(Maddison)
221	Rwanda	866	90(WB)
222	Burkina Faso	860	90(WB)
223	CAR	860	90(WB)
224	Mayotte	858	93(CIA)WEIGHT(US(Maddison))
225	W Sahara	828	PROXY(3 Afr. cs(Maddison))
226	Bangladesh	827	90(WB)
227	Mali	808	90(WB)
228	Congo, Dem R	743	90(WB)
229	South Sudan	683	PROXY(Sudan(WB))
230	Malawi	656	90(WB)
231	Uganda	643	90(WB)
232	Eritrea	637	90(WB)
233	Ethiopia	618	90(WB)
234	Burundi	514	90(WB)
235	Mozambique	451	90(WB)
236	Liberia	352	90(WB)

TABLE 2.20 GDP AT PURCHASING POWER PARITIES PER CAPITA, 2012 DOLLARS, YEAR 2000

Rank	Country	GPC	Source
1	Svalbard	91,620	PROXY(Norway(WB))
2	UAE	86,187	00(WB)
3	Luxembourg	82,301	00(WB)
4	Qatar	79,512	00(WB)
5	Norway	60,315	00(WB)
6	Brunei	55,340	00(WB)
7	Switzerland	47,870	00(WB)
8	US	46,759	00(WB)
9	Kuwait	46,516	00(WB)
10	Singapore	43,412	00(WB)
11	Denmark	41,828	00(WB)
12	Ireland	40,445	00(WB)
13	Cayman Is	40,176	99(CIA)WEIGHT(US(WB))
14	San Marino	39,942	00(CIA)WEIGHT(US(WB))
15	Netherlands	39,860	00(WB)
16	Austria	38,427	00(WB)
17	Belgium	37,594	00(WB)
18	Canada	37,123	00(WB)
19	Germany	36,388	00(WB)
20	Italy	36,034	00(WB)
21	Australia	35,937	00(WB)
22	Sweden	35,596	00(WB)
23	Liechtenstn	35,236	99(CIA)WEIGHT(US(WB))
24	Bahamas	34,929	00(WB)
25	France	34,682	00(WB)
26	Bermuda	34,666	00(CIA)WEIGHT(US(WB))
27	Aruba	34,640	00(CIA)WEIGHT(US(WB))
28	Iceland	34,615	00(WB)
29	Hong Kong	34,615	00(WB)
30	Jersey	34,282	99(CIA)WEIGHT(US(WB))
31	Monaco	34,031	00(CIA)WEIGHT(US(WB))
32	Finland	33,691	00(WB)
33	Gibraltar	33,161	00(CIA)WEIGHT(US(WB))
34	Japan	32,775	00(WB)
35	UK	32,450	00(WB)
36	Bahrain	32,202	00(WB)
37	Spain	30,900	00(WB)
38	St Pierre&M	30,550	96(CIA)WEIGHT(US(WB))
39	Falkland Is	30,393	02(CIA)WEIGHT(US(WB))
40	Cyprus	29,779	00(WB)
41	New Zealand	27,741	00(WB)
42	Guernsey	27,436	99(CIA)WEIGHT(US(WB))
43	Macao	27,033	00(WB)
44	Guam	26,785	00(CIA)WEIGHT(US(WB))
45	Malta	26,528	00(WB)
46	Israel	26,166	00(WB)

TABLE 2.20 GDP AT PURCHASING POWER PARITIES PER CAPITA, 2012 DOLLARS, YEAR 2000

Rank	Country	GPC	Source
47	Portugal	25,915	00(WB)
48	Greenland	25,782	00(CIA)WEIGHT(US(WB))
49	Faroe Is	25,653	00(CIA)WEIGHT(US(WB))
50	Barbados	25,428	00(WB)
51	Isle of Man	24,915	01(CIA)WEIGHT(US(WB))
52	Greece	24,786	00(WB)
53	Andorra	24,511	00(CIA)WEIGHT(US(WB))
54	Slovenia	22,870	00(WB)
55	Taiwan	22,597	00(CIA)WEIGHT(US(WB))
56	Oman	22,284	00(WB)
57	Saudi Arabia	22,270	00(WB)
58	Seychelles	21,274	00(WB)
59	Korea, South	20,179	00(WB)
60	Czechia	20,085	00(WB)
61	Virgin I, US	19,877	00(CIA)WEIGHT(US(WB))
62	Virgin I, Br	19,835	00(CIA)WEIGHT(US(WB))
63	New Caledon	19,203	00(CIA)WEIGHT(US(WB))
64	Antigua & B	18,923	00(WB)
65	Palau	18,353	00(WB)
66	Hungary	17,720	00(WB)
67	Trinidad & T	16,129	00(WB)
68	St Kitts & N	15,930	00(WB)
69	N Mariana Is	15,510	00(CIA)WEIGHT(US(WB))
70	Croatia	15,472	00(WB)
71	Gabon	15,258	00(WB)
72	Fr Polynesia	15,087	97(CIA)WEIGHT(US(WB))
73	Estonia	14,753	00(WB)
74	Libya	14,726	00(WB)
75	Slovakia	14,693	00(WB)
76	Mexico	14,627	00(WB)
77	Poland	14,303	00(WB)
78	Chile	14,199	00(WB)
79	Puerto Rico	13,393	00(CIA)WEIGHT(US(WB))
80	Sint Maarten	12,911	06(CIA)WEIGHT(Curacao)
81	Turkey	12,648	00(WB)
82	Martinique	12,637	01(CIA)WEIGHT(US(WB))
83	Curacao	12,606	00(CIA)WEIGHT(US(WB))/(Neth Antilles
84	Guadeloupe	12,459	97(CIA)WEIGHT(US(WB))
85	Malaysia	12,089	00(WB)
86	Saint Martin	11,879	05(CIA)WEIGHT(Curacao)
87	Argentina	11,689	00(WB)
88	Turks & C Is	11,658	00(CIA)WEIGHT(US(WB))
89	Lithuania	11,636	00(WB)
90	Lebanon	11,387	00(WB)
91	Botswana	11,381	00(WB)
92	Latvia	11,255	00(WB)
93	Venezuela	11,247	00(WB)

TABLE 2.20 GDP AT PURCHASING POWER PARITIES PER CAPITA, 2012 DOLLARS, YEAR 2000			
Rank	Country	GPC	Source
94	Samoa, Amer	11,226	00(CIA)WEIGHT(US(WB))
95	Russia	11,212	00(WB)
96	Anguilla	11,094	99(CIA)WEIGHT(US(WB))
97	Uruguay	10,888	00(WB)
98	Mauritius	10,606	00(WB)
99	St Lucia	10,377	00(WB)
100	Equatorial G	9,856	00(WB)
101	Dominica	9,534	00(WB)
102	Romania	9,516	00(WB)
103	Bulgaria	9,422	00(WB)
104	Costa Rica	9,284	00(WB)
105	Grenada	9,252	00(WB)
106	Montenegro	9,165	00(WB)
107	Saint Helena	9,133	98(CIA)WEIGHT(US(WB))
108	Panama	9,059	00(WB)
109	Brazil	9,011	00(WB)
110	Macedonia	8,977	00(WB)
111	South Africa	8,627	00(WB)
112	Iran	8,387	00(WB)
113	Guiana, Fr	8,302	98(CIA)WEIGHT(US(WB))
114	St Vincent	8,206	00(WB)
115	Colombia	7,564	00(WB)
116	Serbia	7,423	00(WB)
117	Ecuador	7,080	00(WB)
118	Tunisia	6,898	00(WB)
119	Belize	6,734	00(WB)
120	Reunion	6,696	99(CIA)WEIGHT(US(WB))
121	Belarus	6,624	00(WB)
122	Algeria	6,510	00(WB)
123	Dominican R	6,504	00(WB)
124	Thailand	6,419	00(WB)
125	Nauru	6,378	00(CIA)WEIGHT(US(WB))
126	Cook Is	6,369	99(CIA)WEIGHT(US(WB))
127	Peru	6,320	00(WB)
128	Kazakhstan	6,160	00(WB)
129	Iraq	6,047	00(WB)
130	Bosnia	5,893	00(WB)
131	El Salvador	5,820	00(WB)
132	Suriname	5,589	00(WB)
133	Paraguay	5,266	00(WB)
134	Namibia	5,161	00(WB)
135	Maldives	5,109	00(WB)
136	Albania	4,967	00(WB)
137	Jamaica	4,901	00(CIA)WEIGHT(US(WB))
138	Egypt	4,892	00(WB)
139	Swaziland	4,868	00(WB)
140	Fiji	4,623	00(WB)
141	Guatemala	4,581	00(WB)

Table 2.20 GDP at Purchasing Power Parities Per Capita, 2012 Dollars, Year 2000			
Rank	Country	GPC	Source
142	Turkmenistan	4,464	00(WB)
143	Armenia	4,464	00(WB)
144	Syria	4,387	00(WB)
145	Vanuatu	4,377	00(WB)
146	Tonga	4,363	00(WB)
147	Montserrat	4,245	99(CIA)WEIGHT(US(WB))
148	Ukraine	4,213	00(WB)
149	Jordan	4,187	00(WB)
150	Niue	4,008	00(CIA)WEIGHT(US(WB))
151	Kosovo	3,955	PROXY(Serbia)
152	Bolivia	3,911	00(WB)
153	Mayotte	3,679	98(CIA)WEIGHT(US(WB))
154	Congo, Rep	3,640	00(WB)
155	Samoa	3,531	00(WB)
156	Sri Lanka	3,523	00(WB)
157	Micronesia	3,442	00(WB)
158	Morocco	3,415	00(WB)
159	China	3,290	00(WB)
160	Honduras	3,265	00(WB)
161	Indonesia	3,180	00(WB)
162	Bhutan	3,169	00(WB)
163	Nicaragua	3,117	00(WB)
164	Philippines	3,070	00(WB)
165	Cuba	2,928	00(CIA)WEIGHT(US(WB))
166	West Bank	2,900	00(WB)
167	Guyana	2,839	00(WB)
168	Azerbaijan	2,836	00(WB)
169	Angola	2,766	00(WB)
170	Cape Verde	2,763	00(WB)
171	Wallis & Fut	2,738	00(CIA)WEIGHT(US(WB))
172	Kiribati	2,672	00(WB)
173	Solomon Is	2,558	00(WB)
174	Korea, North	2,546	00(EST)WEIGHT(US(WB))
175	Mongolia	2,533	00(WB)
176	Yemen	2,448	00(WB)
177	Georgia	2,363	00(WB)
178	Uzbekistan	2,326	00(WB)
179	W Sahara	2,311	07(CIA)WEIGHT(US(WB))
180	Papua New G	2,236	00(WB)
181	Marshall Is	2,226	01(CIA)WEIGHT(US(WB))
182	Pakistan	2,125	00(WB)
183	Ivory Coast	2,099	00(WB)
184	Moldova	2,077	00(WB)
185	Cameroon	2,073	00(WB)
186	Vietnam	2,041	00(WB)
187	India	2,031	00(WB)
188	Djibouti	2,020	00(WB)
189	Zimbabwe	2,004	00(CIA)WEIGHT(US(WB))

Table 2.20 GDP at Purchasing Power Parities Per Capita, 2012 Dollars, Year 2000			
Rank	Country	GPC	Source
190	Mauritania	1,950	00(WB)
191	Gambia	1,889	00(WB)
192	Tokelau	1,760	93(CIA)WEIGHT(US(WB))
193	Senegal	1,745	00(WB)
194	Kyrgyzstan	1,727	00(WB)
195	Nigeria	1,713	00(WB)
196	Burma	1,709	00(CIA)WEIGHT(US(WB))
197	Benin	1,702	00(WB)
198	Sudan	1,546	00(WB)
199	Gaza Strip	1,543	00(WB)
200	Laos	1,525	00(WB)
201	Sao Tome & P	1,464	00(WB)
202	Kenya	1,460	00(WB)
203	Ghana	1,421	00(WB)
204	Tuvalu	1,390	00(CIA)WEIGHT(US(WB))
205	Cambodia	1,365	00(WB)
206	Lesotho	1,356	00(WB)
207	Haiti	1,303	00(WB)
208	Comoros	1,293	00(WB)
209	East Timor	1,188	00(WB)
210	Guinea-Biss	1,147	00(WB)
211	Zambia	1,133	00(WB)
212	Tajikistan	1,124	00(WB)
213	Nepal	1,106	00(WB)
214	Bangladesh	1,080	00(WB)
215	Burkina Faso	1,049	00(WB)
216	Afghanistan	1,033	00(CIA)WEIGHT(US(WB))
217	Togo	1,031	00(WB)
218	Chad	1,014	00(WB)
219	Madagascar	1,010	00(WB)
220	Tanzania	990	00(WB)
221	Guinea	985	00(WB)
222	Mali	948	00(WB)
223	Uganda	877	00(WB)
224	Sierra Leone	863	00(WB)
225	Somalia	830	00(CIA)WEIGHT(US(WB))
226	South Sudan	787	PROXY(Sudan(WB))
227	CAR	772	00(WB)
228	Malawi	758	00(WB)
229	Rwanda	755	00(WB)
230	Eritrea	682	00(WB)
231	Niger	660	00(WB)
232	Ethiopia	591	00(WB)
233	Mozambique	569	00(WB)
234	Burundi	553	00(WB)
235	Liberia	450	00(WB)
236	Congo, Dem R	315	00(WB)

Table 2.21 GDP at Purchasing Power Parities Per Capita, 2012 Dollars, Year 2010

Rank	Country	GPC	Source
1	Monaco	161,841	10(CIA)WEIGHT(US(WB))
2	Svalbard	98,601	PROXY(Norway(WB))
3	Liechtenstn	95,550	09(CIA)WEIGHT(US(WB))
4	Luxembourg	92,510	10(WB)
5	Qatar	88,491	10(WB)
6	Bermuda	85,831	11(CIA)WEIGHT(US(WB))
7	Macao	67,012	10(WB)
8	Norway	64,911	10(WB)
9	Jersey	64,601	05(CIA)WEIGHT(US(WB))
10	Singapore	59,711	10(WB)
11	Isle of Man	56,027	07(CIA)WEIGHT(US(WB))
12	Falkland Is	55,272	07(CIA)WEIGHT(US(WB))
13	Switzerland	52,798	10(WB)
14	Brunei	51,448	10(WB)
15	Guernsey	50,532	05(CIA)WEIGHT(US(WB))
16	US	50,169	10(WB)
17	Hong Kong	48,915	10(WB)
18	Cayman Is	48,666	08(CIA)WEIGHT(US(WB))
19	Gibraltar	46,831	08(CIA)WEIGHT(US(WB))
20	Kuwait	46,510	10(WB)
21	Netherlands	43,870	10(WB)
22	Virgin I, Br	43,827	10(CIA)WEIGHT(US(WB))
23	Virgin I, US	43,796	10(REG)WEIGHT(US(WB))
24	Ireland	43,064	10(WB)
25	Denmark	42,814	10(WB)
26	Austria	42,699	10(WB)
27	Australia	42,606	10(WB)
28	Sweden	41,857	10(WB)
29	UAE	41,673	10(WB)
30	Belgium	40,777	10(WB)
31	Canada	40,469	10(WB)
32	Germany	40,321	10(WB)
33	Andorra	39,084	10(CIA)WEIGHT(US(WB))
34	New Caledon	39,070	08(CIA)WEIGHT(US(WB))
35	Finland	38,825	10(WB)
36	Iceland	37,891	10(WB)
37	Greenland	37,704	10(CIA)WEIGHT(US(WB))
38	St Pierre&M	37,691	06(CIA)WEIGHT(US(WB))
39	Taiwan	37,688	10(CIA)WEIGHT(US(WB))
40	France	36,396	10(WB)
41	UK	35,725	10(WB)
42	San Marino	35,192	10(CIA)WEIGHT(US(WB))
43	Japan	35,171	10(WB)
44	Italy	35,120	10(WB)
45	Cyprus	33,174	10(WB)
46	Spain	32,826	10(WB)

Table 2.21 GDP at Purchasing Power Parities Per Capita, 2012 Dollars, Year 2010			
Rank	Country	GPC	Source
47	Martinique	32,318	10(REG)WEIGHT(US(WB))
48	New Zealand	31,586	10(WB)
49	Guadeloupe	31,214	10(REG)WEIGHT(US(WB))
50	Faroe Is	31,146	10(CIA)WEIGHT(US(WB))
51	Bahamas	31,019	10(WB)
52	Turks & C Is	30,316	07(CIA)WEIGHT(US(WB))
53	Reunion	30,118	10(REG)WEIGHT(US(WB))
54	Israel	30,111	10(WB)
55	Guam	29,738	10(CIA)WEIGHT(US(WB))
56	Greece	29,625	10(WB)
57	Equatorial G	29,243	10(WB)
58	Slovenia	29,139	10(WB)
59	Bahrain	28,839	10(WB)
60	Korea, South	28,721	10(WB)
61	Malta	28,475	10(WB)
62	Oman	28,317	10(WB)
63	Saudi Arabia	28,188	10(WB)
64	Czechia	27,405	10(WB)
65	Portugal	27,075	10(WB)
66	Trinidad & T	26,766	10(WB)
67	Barbados	26,554	10(WB)
68	Guiana, Fr	25,706	10(REG)WEIGHT(US(WB))
69	Slovakia	24,601	10(WB)
70	Fr Polynesia	23,664	06(CIA)WEIGHT(US(WB))
71	Seychelles	23,514	10(WB)
72	Aruba	22,993	09(CIA)WEIGHT(US(WB))
73	Hungary	22,468	10(WB)
74	Sint Maarten	21,746	10(CIA)WEIGHT(US(WB))
75	Saint Martin	21,723	05(CIA)WEIGHT(US(WB))
76	Russia	21,579	10(WB)
77	Poland	21,562	10(WB)
78	Estonia	21,387	10(WB)
79	Lithuania	21,134	10(WB)
80	Croatia	20,829	10(WB)
81	Curacao	20,159	08(CIA)WEIGHT(US(WB))
82	Antigua & B	20,120	10(WB)
83	Chile	19,332	10(WB)
84	Latvia	18,927	10(WB)
85	Libya	17,590	09(WB)WEIGHT(US(WB))
86	Romania	17,360	10(WB)
87	St Kitts & N	17,206	10(WB)
88	Palau	17,046	10(WB)
89	Puerto Rico	16,985	10(CIA)WEIGHT(US(WB))
90	Turkey	16,880	10(WB)
91	Argentina	16,792	10(CIA)WEIGHT(US(WB))
92	Malaysia	15,745	10(WB)
93	Mexico	15,486	10(WB)
94	Bulgaria	15,449	10(WB)

TABLE 2.21 GDP AT PURCHASING POWER PARITIES PER CAPITA, 2012 DOLLARS, YEAR 2010			
Rank	Country	GPC	Source
95	Botswana	14,816	10(WB)
96	Gabon	14,649	10(WB)
97	Uruguay	14,342	10(WB)
98	Belarus	14,272	10(WB)
99	N Mariana Is	14,259	10(CIA)WEIGHT(US(WB))
100	Mauritius	14,052	10(WB)
101	Lebanon	14,027	10(WB)
102	Montenegro	13,929	10(WB)
103	Panama	13,807	10(WB)
104	Mayotte	13,238	09(CIA)WEIGHT(US(WB))
105	Anguilla	12,975	09(CIA)WEIGHT(US(WB))
106	Dominica	12,778	10(WB)
107	Venezuela	12,572	10(WB)
108	Iran	12,475	10(WB)
109	Kazakhstan	12,458	10(WB)
110	Costa Rica	11,940	10(WB)
111	Serbia	11,687	10(WB)
112	Macedonia	11,532	10(WB)
113	Brazil	11,504	10(WB)
114	St Lucia	11,452	10(WB)
115	Grenada	10,837	10(WB)
116	St Vincent	10,789	10(WB)
117	South Africa	10,653	10(WB)
118	Cuba	10,601	10(CIA)WEIGHT(US(WB))
119	Cook Is	10,262	05(CIA)WEIGHT(US(WB))
120	Azerbaijan	10,167	10(WB)
121	Peru	9,713	10(WB)
122	Tunisia	9,696	10(WB)
123	Colombia	9,656	10(WB)
124	Dominican R	9,479	10(WB)
125	Bosnia	9,295	10(WB)
126	Montserrat	9,254	06(CIA)WEIGHT(US(WB))
127	Jamaica	9,221	10(CIA)WEIGHT(US(WB))
128	Thailand	9,129	10(WB)
129	Albania	8,996	10(WB)
130	Ecuador	8,788	10(WB)
131	Marshall Is	8,453	12(CIA)WEIGHT(US(WB))
132	Maldives	8,384	10(WB)
133	Turkmenistan	8,379	10(WB)
134	Algeria	8,272	10(WB)
135	Samoa, Amer	8,217	07(CIA)WEIGHT(US(WB))
136	Suriname	8,101	10(WB)
137	Saint Helena	7,972	10(CIA)WEIGHT(US(WB))
138	China	7,870	10(WB)
139	Belize	7,739	10(WB)
140	Niue	7,268	03(CIA)WEIGHT(US(WB))
141	Namibia	6,964	10(WB)
142	Ukraine	6,881	10(WB)

Table 2.21 GDP at Purchasing Power Parities Per Capita, 2012 Dollars, Year 2010			
Rank	Country	GPC	Source
143	El Salvador	6,783	10(WB)
144	Egypt	6,576	10(WB)
145	Kosovo	6,492	10(CIA)WEIGHT(US(WB))
146	Iraq	6,455	10(WB)
147	Armenia	6,241	10(WB)
148	Paraguay	6,063	10(WB)
149	Jordan	5,994	10(WB)
150	Angola	5,762	10(WB)
151	Bhutan	5,742	10(WB)
152	Nauru	5,670	05(CIA)WEIGHT(US(WB))
153	Swaziland	5,359	10(WB)
154	Sri Lanka	5,290	10(WB)
155	Georgia	5,030	10(WB)
156	Syria	5,006	10(WB)
157	Guatemala	4,929	10(WB)
158	Morocco	4,889	10(WB)
159	Bolivia	4,832	10(WB)
160	Fiji	4,809	10(WB)
161	Tonga	4,736	10(WB)
162	Cape Verde	4,594	10(WB)
163	Vanuatu	4,571	10(WB)
164	Wallis & Fut	4,562	04(CIA)WEIGHT(US(WB))
165	Indonesia	4,458	10(WB)
166	Samoa	4,371	10(WB)
167	Congo, Rep	4,285	10(WB)
168	Mongolia	4,197	10(WB)
169	Philippines	4,057	10(WB)
170	Honduras	4,026	10(WB)
171	Nicaragua	3,704	10(WB)
172	Micronesia	3,627	10(WB)
173	India	3,563	10(WB)
174	Tuvalu	3,528	10(CIA)WEIGHT(US(WB))
175	Vietnam	3,458	10(WB)
176	Uzbekistan	3,273	10(WB)
177	Moldova	3,217	10(WB)
178	Guyana	3,082	10(WB)
179	Yemen	2,864	10(WB)
180	Solomon Is	2,835	10(WB)
181	Djibouti	2,680	10(CIA)WEIGHT(US(WB))
182	Pakistan	2,655	10(WB)
183	W Sahara	2,569	07(CIA)WEIGHT(US(WB))
184	Laos	2,559	10(WB)
185	Kiribati	2,550	10(WB)
186	Papua New G	2,536	10(WB)
187	Nigeria	2,441	10(WB)
188	Mauritania	2,402	10(WB)
189	Korea, North	2,377	10(EST)WEIGHT(US(WB))
190	Kyrgyzstan	2,314	10(WB)

Table 2.21 GDP at Purchasing Power Parities Per Capita, 2012 Dollars, Year 2010			
Rank	Country	GPC	Source
191	West Bank	2,265	10(CIA)WEIGHT(US(WB))
192	Cambodia	2,252	10(WB)
193	Cameroon	2,231	10(WB)
194	Chad	2,077	10(WB)
195	Sudan	2,048	10(WB)
196	Gambia	2,010	10(WB)
197	Ivory Coast	2,010	10(WB)
198	Tajikistan	1,995	10(WB)
199	Senegal	1,913	10(WB)
200	Tokelau	1,894	93(CIA)WEIGHT(US(WB))
201	Lesotho	1,834	10(WB)
202	Sao Tome & P	1,783	10(WB)
203	Ghana	1,780	10(WB)
204	Kenya	1,678	10(WB)
205	Bangladesh	1,670	10(WB)
206	Benin	1,601	10(WB)
207	East Timor	1,557	10(WB)
208	Zambia	1,550	10(WB)
209	Burma	1,529	10(CIA)WEIGHT(US(WB))
210	Tanzania	1,471	10(WB)
211	Nepal	1,380	10(WB)
212	Burkina Faso	1,380	10(WB)
213	Gaza Strip	1,325	10(CIA)WEIGHT(US(WB))
214	Uganda	1,289	10(WB)
215	Mali	1,251	10(WB)
216	Rwanda	1,214	10(WB)
217	Comoros	1,207	10(WB)
218	Afghanistan	1,206	10(WB)
219	Guinea-Biss	1,174	10(WB)
220	Haiti	1,147	10(WB)
221	Sierra Leone	1,145	10(WB)
222	South Sudan	1,042	PROXY(Sudan(WB))
223	Guinea	1,025	10(WB)
224	Ethiopia	1,003	10(WB)
225	Togo	999	10(WB)
226	CAR	994	10(WB)
227	Madagascar	970	10(WB)
228	Mozambique	919	10(WB)
229	Malawi	751	10(WB)
230	Niger	725	10(WB)
231	Somalia	614	10(CIA)WEIGHT(US(WB))
232	Liberia	585	10(WB)
233	Burundi	552	10(WB)
234	Eritrea	512	10(WB)
235	Zimbabwe	460	10(CIA)WEIGHT(US(WB))
236	Congo, Dem R	383	10(WB)

TABLE 2.22 GDP AT PURCHASING POWER PARITIES PER CAPITA, 2012 DOLLARS, YEAR 2012

Rank	Country	GPC	Source
1	Monaco	195,372	11(CIA)WEIGHT(US(WB))
2	Svalbard	100,469	(REG)
3	Liechtenstn	98,435	09(CIA)WEIGHT(US(WB))
4	Qatar	91,189	12(WB)
5	Luxembourg	89,510	12(WB)
6	Bermuda	89,269	11(CIA)WEIGHT(US(WB))
7	Macao	86,341	12(WB)
8	Jersey	66,564	05(CIA)WEIGHT(US(WB))
9	Norway	66,141	12(WB)
10	Singapore	60,800	12(WB)
11	Isle of Man	57,917	07(CIA)WEIGHT(US(WB))
12	Falkland Is	57,033	07(CIA)WEIGHT(US(WB))
13	San Marino	55,000	12(CIA)
14	Switzerland	53,191	12(WB)
15	Brunei	52,482	12(WB)
16	Guernsey	52,083	05(CIA)WEIGHT(US(WB))
17	US	51,749	12(WB)
18	Hong Kong	51,103	12(WB)
19	Cayman Is	50,255	08(CIA)WEIGHT(US(WB))
20	Gibraltar	48,676	08(CIA)WEIGHT(US(WB))
21	Kuwait	46,385	12(WB)
22	Virgin I, US	45,617	12(REG)
23	Virgin I, Br	45,266	10(CIA)WEIGHT(US(WB))
24	Austria	44,122	12(WB)
25	Ireland	43,834	12(WB)
26	Australia	43,818	12(WB)
27	Netherlands	43,339	12(WB)
28	Sweden	42,866	12(WB)
29	Denmark	42,775	12(WB)
30	Germany	42,700	12(WB)
31	UAE	41,397	12(WB)
32	Canada	41,298	12(WB)
33	Belgium	40,566	12(WB)
34	New Caledon	40,302	08(CIA)WEIGHT(US(WB))
35	Finland	39,199	12(WB)
36	Iceland	39,097	12(WB)
37	Taiwan	38,900	12(CIA)
38	St Pierre&M	38,886	06(CIA)WEIGHT(US(WB))
39	Greenland	38,392	11(CIA)WEIGHT(US(WB))
40	Andorra	37,176	12(CIA)
41	France	36,785	12(WB)
42	UK	35,722	12(WB)
43	Japan	35,618	12(WB)
44	Italy	34,926	12(WB)
45	New Zealand	32,926	12(WB)
46	Spain	32,134	12(WB)

Table 2.22 GDP at Purchasing Power Parities Per Capita, 2012 Dollars, Year 2012

Rank	Country	GPC	Source
47	Faroe Is	32,088	10(CIA)WEIGHT(US(WB))
48	Martinique	31,370	12(REG)
49	Israel	31,345	12(WB)
50	Turks & C Is	31,327	07(CIA)WEIGHT(US(WB))
51	Saudi Arabia	31,214	12(WB)
52	Bahamas	31,116	12(WB)
53	Cyprus	30,768	12(WB)
54	Guam	30,712	10(CIA)WEIGHT(US(WB))
55	Guadeloupe	30,074	12(REG)
56	Korea, South	30,011	12(WB)
57	Equatorial G	29,742	12(WB)
58	Malta	28,955	12(WB)
59	Bahrain	28,924	12(WB)
60	Slovenia	28,476	12(WB)
61	Czechia	27,523	12(WB)
62	Seychelles	26,572	12(WB)
63	Trinidad & T	26,550	12(WB)
64	Barbados	26,488	12(WB)
65	Reunion	26,467	12(REG)
66	Oman	26,223	12(WB)
67	Greece	26,041	12(WB)
68	Portugal	25,958	12(WB)
69	Slovakia	25,842	12(WB)
70	Aruba	24,582	11(CIA)WEIGHT(US(WB))
71	Fr Polynesia	24,513	06(CIA)WEIGHT(US(WB))
72	Estonia	24,450	12(WB)
73	Lithuania	24,356	12(WB)
74	Russia	23,589	12(WB)
75	Guiana, Fr	23,356	12(REG)
76	Poland	22,783	12(WB)
77	Hungary	22,635	12(WB)
78	Sint Maarten	22,570	10(CIA)WEIGHT(US(WB))
79	Saint Martin	22,538	05(CIA)WEIGHT(US(WB))
80	Latvia	21,810	12(WB)
81	Chile	21,468	12(WB)
82	Croatia	20,961	12(WB)
83	Curacao	20,928	08(CIA)WEIGHT(US(WB))
84	Antigua & B	19,640	12(WB)
85	Palau	18,722	12(WB)
86	Turkey	18,551	12(WB)
87	St Kitts & N	18,384	12(WB)
88	Argentina	18,200	12(CIA)
89	Romania	18,063	12(WB)
90	Puerto Rico	17,443	10(CIA)WEIGHT(US(WB))
91	Malaysia	16,919	12(WB)
92	Mexico	16,426	12(WB)
93	Panama	16,346	12(WB)
94	Botswana	16,105	12(WB)

Table 2.22 GDP at Purchasing Power Parities Per Capita, 2012 Dollars, Year 2012			
Rank	Country	GPC	Source
95	Bulgaria	16,041	12(WB)
96	Uruguay	15,777	12(WB)
97	Gabon	15,765	12(WB)
98	Belarus	15,327	12(WB)
99	Mauritius	14,902	12(WB)
100	N Mariana Is	14,554	10(CIA)WEIGHT(US(WB))
101	Lebanon	14,373	12(WB)
102	Montenegro	14,358	12(WB)
103	Kazakhstan	13,672	12(WB)
104	Anguilla	13,378	09(CIA)WEIGHT(US(WB))
105	Venezuela	13,267	12(WB)
106	Costa Rica	12,733	12(WB)
107	Mayotte	12,530	12(REG)
108	Dominica	12,426	12(WB)
109	Iran	12,275	12(WB)
110	Libya	12,100	12(CIA)
111	Macedonia	11,834	12(WB)
112	Serbia	11,801	12(WB)
113	Brazil	11,716	12(WB)
114	St Lucia	11,427	12(WB)
115	St Vincent	11,047	12(WB)
116	South Africa	11,021	12(WB)
117	Grenada	10,928	12(WB)
118	Cuba	10,925	12(CIA)
119	Peru	10,765	12(WB)
120	Cook Is	10,627	05(CIA)WEIGHT(US(WB))
121	Colombia	10,436	12(WB)
122	Turkmenistan	10,411	12(WB)
123	Azerbaijan	10,127	12(WB)
124	Dominican R	10,038	12(WB)
125	Thailand	9,660	12(WB)
126	Ecuador	9,637	12(WB)
127	Tunisia	9,636	12(WB)
128	Montserrat	9,471	06(CIA)WEIGHT(US(WB))
129	Albania	9,403	12(WB)
130	Bosnia	9,392	12(WB)
131	China	9,083	12(WB)
132	Jamaica	9,000	12(CIA)
133	Maldives	8,925	12(WB)
134	Suriname	8,722	12(WB)
135	Marshall Is	8,700	12(CIA)
136	Samoa, Amer	8,612	07(CIA)WEIGHT(US(WB))
137	Algeria	8,447	12(WB)
138	Saint Helena	8,347	10(CIA)WEIGHT(US(WB))
139	Belize	7,937	12(WB)
140	Niue	7,564	03(CIA)WEIGHT(US(WB))
141	Kosovo	7,500	12(CIA)
142	Namibia	7,442	12(WB)

TABLE 2.22 GDP AT PURCHASING POWER PARITIES PER CAPITA, 2012 DOLLARS, YEAR 2012			
Rank	Country	GPC	Source
143	Iraq	7,435	12(WB)
144	Ukraine	7,298	12(WB)
145	El Salvador	6,991	12(WB)
146	Egypt	6,614	12(WB)
147	Bhutan	6,591	12(WB)
148	Armenia	6,544	12(WB)
149	Sri Lanka	6,146	12(WB)
150	Paraguay	6,038	12(WB)
151	Jordan	6,037	12(WB)
152	Angola	6,006	12(WB)
153	Nauru	5,839	05(CIA)WEIGHT(US(WB))
154	Georgia	5,833	12(WB)
155	Mongolia	5,374	12(WB)
156	Morocco	5,220	12(WB)
157	Bolivia	5,196	12(WB)
158	Swaziland	5,161	12(WB)
159	Guatemala	5,019	12(WB)
160	Tonga	4,881	12(WB)
161	Fiji	4,877	12(WB)
162	Indonesia	4,876	12(WB)
163	Cape Verde	4,846	12(WB)
164	Syria	4,776	12(CIA)
165	Wallis & Fut	4,690	04(CIA)WEIGHT(US(WB))
166	Vanuatu	4,531	12(WB)
167	Samoa	4,493	12(WB)
168	Congo, Rep	4,354	12(WB)
169	Philippines	4,339	12(WB)
170	Honduras	4,174	12(WB)
171	Nicaragua	4,006	12(WB)
172	India	3,870	12(WB)
173	Vietnam	3,787	12(WB)
174	Micronesia	3,726	12(WB)
175	Uzbekistan	3,533	12(WB)
176	Tuvalu	3,500	12(CIA)
177	Moldova	3,368	12(WB)
178	Guyana	3,344	12(WB)
179	Solomon Is	3,076	12(WB)
180	Laos	2,879	12(WB)
181	Papua New G	2,851	12(WB)
182	Pakistan	2,741	12(WB)
183	Djibouti	2,700	12(CIA)
184	W Sahara	2,691	07(CIA)WEIGHT(US(WB))
185	Nigeria	2,620	12(WB)
186	Kiribati	2,618	12(WB)
187	Mauritania	2,561	12(WB)
188	Cambodia	2,454	12(WB)
189	Yemen	2,448	12(WB)
190	Korea, North	2,402	12(EST)

Table 2.22 GDP at Purchasing Power Parities Per Capita, 2012 Dollars, Year 2012			
Rank	Country	GPC	Source
191	Kyrgyzstan	2,360	12(WB)
192	Cameroon	2,312	12(WB)
193	West Bank	2,210	11(CIA)WEIGHT(US(WB))
194	Tajikistan	2,192	12(WB)
195	Sudan	2,162	12(WB)
196	Chad	2,135	12(WB)
197	Ghana	2,014	12(WB)
198	Ivory Coast	2,006	12(WB)
199	Tokelau	1,955	93(CIA)WEIGHT(US(WB))
200	Lesotho	1,931	12(WB)
201	Senegal	1,908	12(WB)
202	Gambia	1,903	12(WB)
203	Bangladesh	1,851	12(WB)
204	Sao Tome & P	1,822	12(WB)
205	Kenya	1,737	12(WB)
206	Zambia	1,683	12(WB)
207	East Timor	1,660	12(WB)
208	Burma	1,600	12(CIA)
209	Tanzania	1,575	12(WB)
210	Afghanistan	1,561	12(WB)
211	Benin	1,557	12(WB)
212	Burkina Faso	1,482	12(WB)
213	Nepal	1,457	12(WB)
214	Sierra Leone	1,337	12(WB)
215	Rwanda	1,332	12(WB)
216	Uganda	1,330	12(WB)
217	Gaza Strip	1,306	11(CIA)WEIGHT(US(WB))
218	Comoros	1,210	12(WB)
219	Haiti	1,208	12(WB)
220	Mali	1,204	12(WB)
221	Ethiopia	1,109	12(WB)
222	Guinea-Biss	1,101	12(WB)
223	South Sudan	1,100	12(CIA)
224	CAR	1,077	12(WB)
225	Guinea	1,051	12(WB)
226	Togo	1,034	12(WB)
227	Mozambique	1,007	12(WB)
228	Madagascar	962	12(WB)
229	Niger	769	12(WB)
230	Malawi	753	12(WB)
231	Somalia	642	10(CIA)WEIGHT(US(WB))
232	Liberia	639	12(WB)
233	Zimbabwe	600	12(CIA)
234	Eritrea	557	12(WB)
235	Burundi	551	12(WB)
236	Congo, Dem R	415	12(WB)

Table 2.23 GDP at Purchasing Power Parities Per Capita, 2012 Dollars, Year 2020, Forecast

Rank	Country	GPC	Source
1	Monaco	430,572	FORECAST
2	Bermuda	166,705	FORECAST
3	Macao	159,422	FORECAST
4	Liechtenstn	154,941	FORECAST
5	Qatar	127,682	FORECAST
6	Svalbard	122,324	FORECAST
7	Luxembourg	108,966	FORECAST
8	Jersey	91,356	FORECAST
9	Isle of Man	89,808	FORECAST
10	Singapore	83,191	FORECAST
11	San Marino	81,475	FORECAST
12	Norway	80,528	FORECAST
13	Falkland Is	75,989	FORECAST
14	Guernsey	71,166	FORECAST
15	Gibraltar	70,812	FORECAST
16	Hong Kong	68,614	FORECAST
17	Virgin I, Br	65,853	FORECAST
18	Virgin I, US	64,953	FORECAST
19	Brunei	64,018	FORECAST
20	New Caledon	62,321	FORECAST
21	Equatorial G	61,840	FORECAST
22	US	58,746	FORECAST
23	Switzerland	58,243	FORECAST
24	Taiwan	57,667	FORECAST
25	Cayman Is	57,665	FORECAST
26	Ireland	54,727	FORECAST
27	Austria	51,652	FORECAST
28	Australia	51,380	FORECAST
29	St Pierre&M	50,033	FORECAST
30	Martinique	49,822	FORECAST
31	Germany	49,683	FORECAST
32	Netherlands	49,602	FORECAST
33	Sweden	49,365	FORECAST
34	Reunion	49,236	FORECAST
35	Turks & C Is	48,976	FORECAST
36	Greenland	47,947	FORECAST
37	Andorra	47,482	FORECAST
38	Denmark	47,217	FORECAST
39	Guadeloupe	47,065	FORECAST
40	Kuwait	46,756	FORECAST
41	Canada	46,567	FORECAST
42	Belgium	45,593	FORECAST
43	Finland	45,354	FORECAST
44	Iceland	43,896	FORECAST
45	Korea, South	43,599	FORECAST
46	UAE	43,423	FORECAST

TABLE 2.23 GDP AT PURCHASING POWER PARITIES PER CAPITA, 2012 DOLLARS, YEAR 2020, FORECAST			
Rank	Country	GPC	Source
47	France	40,734	FORECAST
48	Japan	40,492	FORECAST
49	UK	40,473	FORECAST
50	Saudi Arabia	40,096	FORECAST
51	Italy	38,218	FORECAST
52	Faroe Is	37,771	FORECAST
53	Spain	37,466	FORECAST
54	Guiana, Fr	37,426	FORECAST
55	New Zealand	37,289	FORECAST
56	Israel	37,224	FORECAST
57	Cyprus	36,545	FORECAST
58	Malta	35,847	FORECAST
59	Trinidad & T	34,953	FORECAST
60	Lithuania	34,231	FORECAST
61	Guam	34,139	FORECAST
62	Slovakia	33,926	FORECAST
63	Oman	33,847	FORECAST
64	Seychelles	33,828	FORECAST
65	Slovenia	33,769	FORECAST
66	Bahrain	33,352	FORECAST
67	Russia	33,131	FORECAST
68	Czechia	32,586	FORECAST
69	Fr Polynesia	32,105	FORECAST
70	Bahamas	32,070	FORECAST
71	Saint Martin	31,655	FORECAST
72	Estonia	31,337	FORECAST
73	Sint Maarten	30,748	FORECAST
74	Greece	30,691	FORECAST
75	Poland	30,323	FORECAST
76	Portugal	30,041	FORECAST
77	Latvia	29,937	FORECAST
78	Barbados	29,557	FORECAST
79	Chile	28,844	FORECAST
80	Curacao	27,973	FORECAST
81	Mayotte	27,640	FORECAST
82	Aruba	27,363	FORECAST
83	Hungary	26,389	FORECAST
84	Croatia	24,924	FORECAST
85	Turkey	24,773	FORECAST
86	Romania	24,441	FORECAST
87	Argentina	23,511	FORECAST
88	Antigua & B	23,063	FORECAST
89	Panama	22,788	FORECAST
90	St Kitts & N	22,640	FORECAST
91	Malaysia	22,591	FORECAST
92	Botswana	22,589	FORECAST
93	Belarus	21,867	FORECAST
94	Bulgaria	20,842	FORECAST

Table 2.23 GDP at Purchasing Power Parities Per Capita, 2012 Dollars, Year 2020, Forecast			
Rank	Country	GPC	Source
95	Palau	20,408	FORECAST
96	Puerto Rico	20,398	FORECAST
97	Uruguay	19,647	FORECAST
98	Mauritius	19,315	FORECAST
99	Kazakhstan	19,052	FORECAST
100	Mexico	18,973	FORECAST
101	Cuba	18,710	FORECAST
102	Montenegro	17,957	FORECAST
103	Lebanon	17,785	FORECAST
104	Gabon	17,028	FORECAST
105	Azerbaijan	16,834	FORECAST
106	Libya	16,678	FORECAST
107	China	16,617	FORECAST
108	Costa Rica	15,596	FORECAST
109	Iran	15,333	FORECAST
110	Dominica	15,299	FORECAST
111	Turkmenistan	15,255	FORECAST
112	Marshall Is	15,084	FORECAST
113	Anguilla	14,953	FORECAST
114	N Mariana Is	14,917	FORECAST
115	Serbia	14,752	FORECAST
116	Venezuela	14,318	FORECAST
117	Peru	14,176	FORECAST
118	Cook Is	14,027	FORECAST
119	St Vincent	14,018	FORECAST
120	Macedonia	13,910	FORECAST
121	Brazil	13,747	FORECAST
122	St Lucia	13,591	FORECAST
123	Dominican R	13,422	FORECAST
124	Grenada	13,328	FORECAST
125	Montserrat	13,220	FORECAST
126	Albania	13,058	FORECAST
127	Maldives	12,982	FORECAST
128	Thailand	12,973	FORECAST
129	Colombia	12,517	FORECAST
130	South Africa	12,445	FORECAST
131	Tunisia	12,124	FORECAST
132	Jamaica	11,803	FORECAST
133	Bosnia	11,749	FORECAST
134	Ecuador	11,356	FORECAST
135	Niue	11,308	FORECAST
136	Suriname	10,822	FORECAST
137	Samoa, Amer	10,559	FORECAST
138	Bhutan	10,431	FORECAST
139	Kosovo	10,301	FORECAST
140	Saint Helena	10,116	FORECAST
141	Algeria	9,660	FORECAST
142	Ukraine	9,372	FORECAST

Table 2.23 GDP at Purchasing Power Parities Per Capita, 2012 Dollars, Year 2020, Forecast

Rank	Country	GPC	Source
143	Belize	9,288	FORECAST
144	Namibia	8,952	FORECAST
145	Iraq	8,681	FORECAST
146	Georgia	8,589	FORECAST
147	Sri Lanka	8,539	FORECAST
148	Angola	8,415	FORECAST
149	El Salvador	8,316	FORECAST
150	Egypt	8,137	FORECAST
151	Mongolia	7,983	FORECAST
152	Armenia	7,688	FORECAST
153	Cape Verde	7,328	FORECAST
154	Jordan	7,172	FORECAST
155	Paraguay	6,629	FORECAST
156	Morocco	6,431	FORECAST
157	Indonesia	6,282	FORECAST
158	Bolivia	6,183	FORECAST
159	Nauru	5,994	FORECAST
160	Wallis & Fut	5,890	FORECAST
161	Swaziland	5,752	FORECAST
162	Tonga	5,552	FORECAST
163	Vietnam	5,551	FORECAST
164	India	5,491	FORECAST
165	Guatemala	5,389	FORECAST
166	Tuvalu	5,243	FORECAST
167	Samoa	5,170	FORECAST
168	Philippines	5,153	FORECAST
169	Syria	5,133	FORECAST
170	Fiji	5,033	FORECAST
171	Congo, Rep	4,839	FORECAST
172	Vanuatu	4,835	FORECAST
173	Honduras	4,771	FORECAST
174	Nicaragua	4,661	FORECAST
175	Uzbekistan	4,237	FORECAST
176	Moldova	4,175	FORECAST
177	Laos	4,032	FORECAST
178	Micronesia	3,993	FORECAST
179	Guyana	3,925	FORECAST
180	W Sahara	3,621	FORECAST
181	Solomon Is	3,543	FORECAST
182	Papua New G	3,316	FORECAST
183	Pakistan	3,224	FORECAST
184	Cambodia	3,193	FORECAST
185	Nigeria	3,167	FORECAST
186	Djibouti	3,043	FORECAST
187	Mauritania	2,965	FORECAST
188	Chad	2,936	FORECAST
189	Tajikistan	2,906	FORECAST
190	Kiribati	2,902	FORECAST

TABLE 2.23 GDP AT PURCHASING POWER PARITIES PER CAPITA, 2012 DOLLARS, YEAR 2020, FORECAST			
Rank	Country	GPC	Source
191	Yemen	2,747	FORECAST
192	Kyrgyzstan	2,683	FORECAST
193	Sudan	2,557	FORECAST
194	Korea, North	2,505	FORECAST
195	Cameroon	2,484	FORECAST
196	Bangladesh	2,465	FORECAST
197	Ghana	2,395	FORECAST
198	Lesotho	2,378	FORECAST
199	West Bank	2,266	FORECAST
200	Tokelau	2,146	FORECAST
201	Ivory Coast	2,037	FORECAST
202	Sao Tome & P	2,024	FORECAST
203	Zambia	2,006	FORECAST
204	East Timor	2,004	FORECAST
205	Afghanistan	1,995	FORECAST
206	Gambia	1,991	FORECAST
207	Senegal	1,988	FORECAST
208	Tanzania	1,929	FORECAST
209	Kenya	1,895	FORECAST
210	Burkina Faso	1,797	FORECAST
211	Burma	1,797	FORECAST
212	Nepal	1,728	FORECAST
213	Rwanda	1,696	FORECAST
214	Uganda	1,665	FORECAST
215	Sierra Leone	1,640	FORECAST
216	Benin	1,577	FORECAST
217	Ethiopia	1,454	FORECAST
218	Mali	1,390	FORECAST
219	Mozambique	1,342	FORECAST
220	Gaza Strip	1,326	FORECAST
221	South Sudan	1,301	FORECAST
222	Haiti	1,266	FORECAST
223	CAR	1,242	FORECAST
224	Comoros	1,235	FORECAST
225	Guinea-Biss	1,159	FORECAST
226	Guinea	1,106	FORECAST
227	Togo	1,063	FORECAST
228	Madagascar	966	FORECAST
229	Niger	826	FORECAST
230	Malawi	788	FORECAST
231	Liberia	778	FORECAST
232	Zimbabwe	729	FORECAST
233	Somalia	665	FORECAST
234	Eritrea	600	FORECAST
235	Burundi	559	FORECAST
236	Congo, Dem R	470	FORECAST

Table 2.24 GDP at Purchasing Power Parities Per Capita, 2012 Dollars, Year 2030, Forecast			
Rank	Country	GPC	Source
1	Monaco	542,295	FORECAST
2	Bermuda	215,348	FORECAST
3	Macao	206,213	FORECAST
4	Liechtenstn	202,199	FORECAST
5	Qatar	164,779	FORECAST
6	Svalbard	150,775	FORECAST
7	Luxembourg	134,301	FORECAST
8	Jersey	117,421	FORECAST
9	Isle of Man	117,153	FORECAST
10	Singapore	106,854	FORECAST
11	San Marino	105,970	FORECAST
12	Norway	99,258	FORECAST
13	Falkland Is	96,951	FORECAST
14	Gibraltar	91,921	FORECAST
15	Guernsey	91,380	FORECAST
16	Hong Kong	87,724	FORECAST
17	Virgin I, Br	85,484	FORECAST
18	Virgin I, US	84,064	FORECAST
19	New Caledon	81,289	FORECAST
20	Brunei	78,981	FORECAST
21	Equatorial G	78,661	FORECAST
22	Taiwan	75,009	FORECAST
23	US	69,425	FORECAST
24	Cayman Is	68,658	FORECAST
25	Ireland	68,245	FORECAST
26	Switzerland	66,923	FORECAST
27	Martinique	65,026	FORECAST
28	Turks & C Is	63,904	FORECAST
29	Reunion	63,632	FORECAST
30	St Pierre&M	63,132	FORECAST
31	Austria	62,298	FORECAST
32	Australia	62,032	FORECAST
33	Guadeloupe	61,413	FORECAST
34	Greenland	59,798	FORECAST
35	Andorra	59,753	FORECAST
36	Germany	59,695	FORECAST
37	Netherlands	58,954	FORECAST
38	Sweden	58,919	FORECAST
39	Korea, South	56,586	FORECAST
40	Canada	54,763	FORECAST
41	Denmark	54,618	FORECAST
42	Finland	54,298	FORECAST
43	Belgium	53,488	FORECAST
44	Iceland	51,458	FORECAST
45	Saudi Arabia	50,565	FORECAST
46	Kuwait	49,383	FORECAST

Table 2.24 GDP at Purchasing Power Parities Per Capita, 2012 Dollars, Year 2030, Forecast

Rank	Country	GPC	Source
47	Guiana, Fr	48,849	FORECAST
48	UAE	47,937	FORECAST
49	Japan	47,901	FORECAST
50	UK	47,763	FORECAST
51	France	47,240	FORECAST
52	Faroe Is	45,706	FORECAST
53	Israel	45,277	FORECAST
54	Spain	45,074	FORECAST
55	Malta	44,535	FORECAST
56	Cyprus	44,456	FORECAST
57	Trinidad & T	44,439	FORECAST
58	Lithuania	44,206	FORECAST
59	New Zealand	43,991	FORECAST
60	Italy	43,889	FORECAST
61	Slovakia	43,097	FORECAST
62	Russia	42,781	FORECAST
63	Oman	42,757	FORECAST
64	Seychelles	42,517	FORECAST
65	Slovenia	41,042	FORECAST
66	Saint Martin	40,875	FORECAST
67	Fr Polynesia	40,752	FORECAST
68	Bahrain	39,841	FORECAST
69	Guam	39,712	FORECAST
70	Czechia	39,568	FORECAST
71	Estonia	39,487	FORECAST
72	Sint Maarten	39,455	FORECAST
73	Poland	38,675	FORECAST
74	Latvia	38,480	FORECAST
75	Greece	37,167	FORECAST
76	Chile	36,885	FORECAST
77	Portugal	35,971	FORECAST
78	Curacao	35,720	FORECAST
79	Mayotte	34,807	FORECAST
80	Bahamas	34,751	FORECAST
81	Barbados	34,486	FORECAST
82	Aruba	31,864	FORECAST
83	Hungary	31,746	FORECAST
84	Turkey	31,626	FORECAST
85	Romania	31,309	FORECAST
86	Croatia	30,339	FORECAST
87	Argentina	29,708	FORECAST
88	Panama	29,384	FORECAST
89	Botswana	29,161	FORECAST
90	Malaysia	28,841	FORECAST
91	Belarus	28,309	FORECAST
92	St Kitts & N	28,060	FORECAST
93	Antigua & B	27,869	FORECAST
94	Bulgaria	26,388	FORECAST

Table 2.24 GDP at Purchasing Power Parities Per Capita, 2012 Dollars, Year 2030, Forecast

Rank	Country	GPC	Source
95	Puerto Rico	24,586	FORECAST
96	Kazakhstan	24,565	FORECAST
97	Uruguay	24,474	FORECAST
98	Mauritius	24,434	FORECAST
99	Cuba	24,366	FORECAST
100	Palau	23,360	FORECAST
101	Mexico	22,688	FORECAST
102	Montenegro	22,410	FORECAST
103	Lebanon	22,090	FORECAST
104	Azerbaijan	21,956	FORECAST
105	China	21,516	FORECAST
106	Libya	21,457	FORECAST
107	Turkmenistan	19,819	FORECAST
108	Marshall Is	19,627	FORECAST
109	Gabon	19,334	FORECAST
110	Costa Rica	19,279	FORECAST
111	Iran	19,125	FORECAST
112	Dominica	18,958	FORECAST
113	Serbia	18,406	FORECAST
114	Peru	18,024	FORECAST
115	Cook Is	17,848	FORECAST
116	St Vincent	17,597	FORECAST
117	Anguilla	17,468	FORECAST
118	Dominican R	17,141	FORECAST
119	Montserrat	17,051	FORECAST
120	Maldives	16,852	FORECAST
121	Albania	16,825	FORECAST
122	Macedonia	16,818	FORECAST
123	Brazil	16,603	FORECAST
124	Thailand	16,587	FORECAST
125	St Lucia	16,545	FORECAST
126	Grenada	16,441	FORECAST
127	Venezuela	16,245	FORECAST
128	N Mariana Is	16,063	FORECAST
129	Colombia	15,309	FORECAST
130	Tunisia	15,168	FORECAST
131	Jamaica	14,988	FORECAST
132	Niue	14,719	FORECAST
133	Bosnia	14,663	FORECAST
134	South Africa	14,651	FORECAST
135	Ecuador	13,752	FORECAST
136	Bhutan	13,614	FORECAST
137	Suriname	13,458	FORECAST
138	Kosovo	13,243	FORECAST
139	Samoa, Amer	13,059	FORECAST
140	Saint Helena	12,440	FORECAST
141	Ukraine	11,817	FORECAST
142	Algeria	11,476	FORECAST

Table 2.24 GDP at Purchasing Power Parities Per Capita, 2012 Dollars, Year 2030, Forecast

Rank	Country	GPC	Source
143	Belize	11,201	FORECAST
144	Georgia	11,165	FORECAST
145	Sri Lanka	11,004	FORECAST
146	Namibia	10,966	FORECAST
147	Angola	10,862	FORECAST
148	Iraq	10,453	FORECAST
149	Mongolia	10,385	FORECAST
150	El Salvador	10,125	FORECAST
151	Egypt	10,080	FORECAST
152	Cape Verde	9,548	FORECAST
153	Armenia	9,292	FORECAST
154	Jordan	8,726	FORECAST
155	Morocco	7,973	FORECAST
156	Indonesia	7,930	FORECAST
157	Paraguay	7,634	FORECAST
158	Bolivia	7,529	FORECAST
159	Wallis & Fut	7,364	FORECAST
160	Vietnam	7,212	FORECAST
161	India	7,103	FORECAST
162	Tuvalu	6,825	FORECAST
163	Swaziland	6,704	FORECAST
164	Tonga	6,570	FORECAST
165	Nauru	6,466	FORECAST
166	Philippines	6,268	FORECAST
167	Samoa	6,167	FORECAST
168	Guatemala	6,084	FORECAST
169	Syria	5,802	FORECAST
170	Honduras	5,665	FORECAST
171	Congo, Rep	5,627	FORECAST
172	Nicaragua	5,600	FORECAST
173	Fiji	5,461	FORECAST
174	Vanuatu	5,428	FORECAST
175	Laos	5,204	FORECAST
176	Moldova	5,189	FORECAST
177	Uzbekistan	5,182	FORECAST
178	Guyana	4,741	FORECAST
179	W Sahara	4,632	FORECAST
180	Micronesia	4,501	FORECAST
181	Solomon Is	4,229	FORECAST
182	Cambodia	4,044	FORECAST
183	Papua New G	3,984	FORECAST
184	Pakistan	3,899	FORECAST
185	Nigeria	3,889	FORECAST
186	Chad	3,775	FORECAST
187	Tajikistan	3,703	FORECAST
188	Djibouti	3,578	FORECAST
189	Mauritania	3,550	FORECAST
190	Kiribati	3,368	FORECAST

Table 2.24 GDP at Purchasing Power Parities Per Capita, 2012 Dollars, Year 2030, Forecast

Rank	Country	GPC	Source
191	Yemen	3,219	FORECAST
192	Kyrgyzstan	3,174	FORECAST
193	Bangladesh	3,145	FORECAST
194	Sudan	3,104	FORECAST
195	Lesotho	2,946	FORECAST
196	Ghana	2,915	FORECAST
197	Cameroon	2,806	FORECAST
198	Korea, North	2,750	FORECAST
199	Afghanistan	2,511	FORECAST
200	Tokelau	2,470	FORECAST
201	East Timor	2,459	FORECAST
202	Zambia	2,445	FORECAST
203	West Bank	2,441	FORECAST
204	Tanzania	2,385	FORECAST
205	Sao Tome & P	2,354	FORECAST
206	Burkina Faso	2,210	FORECAST
207	Gambia	2,193	FORECAST
208	Senegal	2,181	FORECAST
209	Kenya	2,170	FORECAST
210	Ivory Coast	2,170	FORECAST
211	Rwanda	2,132	FORECAST
212	Burma	2,106	FORECAST
213	Nepal	2,100	FORECAST
214	Uganda	2,078	FORECAST
215	Sierra Leone	2,028	FORECAST
216	Ethiopia	1,847	FORECAST
217	Mozambique	1,712	FORECAST
218	Benin	1,675	FORECAST
219	Mali	1,661	FORECAST
220	South Sudan	1,579	FORECAST
221	CAR	1,485	FORECAST
222	Gaza Strip	1,412	FORECAST
223	Haiti	1,396	FORECAST
224	Comoros	1,324	FORECAST
225	Guinea-Biss	1,283	FORECAST
226	Guinea	1,225	FORECAST
227	Togo	1,149	FORECAST
228	Madagascar	1,015	FORECAST
229	Liberia	958	FORECAST
230	Niger	933	FORECAST
231	Zimbabwe	899	FORECAST
232	Malawi	868	FORECAST
233	Somalia	724	FORECAST
234	Eritrea	680	FORECAST
235	Burundi	595	FORECAST
236	Congo, Dem R	555	FORECAST

3. Gross Domestic Product at Purchasing Power Parities by Rank

Table 3.1 Gross Domestic Product at Purchasing Power Parities, Millions of 2012 Dollars, Year 0001			
Rank	Country	GDP	Source
1	India	44,310	POP*GPC
2	China	41,969	POP*GPC
3	Italy	10,128	POP*GPC
4	Turkey	5,704	POP*GPC
5	Bangladesh	5,054	POP*GPC
6	France	3,701	POP*GPC
7	Iran	3,621	POP*GPC
8	Pakistan	3,450	POP*GPC
9	Egypt	3,130	POP*GPC
10	Spain	2,922	POP*GPC
11	Indonesia	2,200	POP*GPC
12	Germany	1,915	POP*GPC
13	Yemen	1,862	POP*GPC
14	Greece	1,721	POP*GPC
15	Saudi Arabia	1,501	POP*GPC
16	Algeria	1,346	POP*GPC
17	Japan	1,303	POP*GPC
18	Syria	1,197	POP*GPC
19	Korea, South	1,168	POP*GPC
20	Iraq	862	POP*GPC
21	Mexico	815	POP*GPC
22	Sudan	708	POP*GPC
23	Russia	593	POP*GPC
24	Korea, North	540	POP*GPC
25	Tunisia	538	POP*GPC
26	Romania	532	POP*GPC
27	Vietnam	476	POP*GPC
28	Thailand	459	POP*GPC
29	Morocco	438	POP*GPC
30	Serbia	359	POP*GPC
31	UK	357	POP*GPC
32	Austria	333	POP*GPC
33	Bulgaria	333	POP*GPC
34	Czechia	329	POP*GPC
35	Lebanon	297	POP*GPC
36	Portugal	282	POP*GPC
37	Libya	269	POP*GPC
38	US	265	POP*GPC
39	Burma	249	POP*GPC
40	Afghanistan	235	POP*GPC
41	Nepal	230	POP*GPC
42	Oman	228	POP*GPC

Table 3.1 Gross Domestic Product at Purchasing Power Parities, Millions of 2012 Dollars, Year 0001			
Rank	Country	GDP	Source
43	Belgium	211	POP*GPC
44	Kazakhstan	211	POP*GPC
45	Poland	207	POP*GPC
46.5	Hungary	200	POP*GPC
46.5	Switzerland	200	POP*GPC
48	Sri Lanka	195	POP*GPC
49	Ukraine	190	POP*GPC
50	Uzbekistan	182	POP*GPC
51	Peru	180	POP*GPC
52	Jordan	174	POP*GPC
53	Cyprus	172	POP*GPC
54	Colombia	159	POP*GPC
55	Bolivia	154	POP*GPC
56	Israel	153	POP*GPC
57	Croatia	146	POP*GPC
58	Netherlands	133	POP*GPC
59	Cambodia	133	POP*GPC
60	Brazil	123	POP*GPC
61	Slovakia	120	POP*GPC
62	Ethiopia	118	POP*GPC
63	South Sudan	112	POP*GPC
64	Chile	106	POP*GPC
65	Philippines	104	POP*GPC
66	Venezuela	96	POP*GPC
67	Sweden	94	POP*GPC
68	Australia	92	POP*GPC
69	Denmark	87	POP*GPC
70	Guatemala	86	POP*GPC
71	Bosnia	85	POP*GPC
72	Argentina	74	POP*GPC
73	Somalia	71	POP*GPC
74	Ecuador	69	POP*GPC
75	Albania	68	POP*GPC
76	Ghana	66	POP*GPC
77	Slovenia	66	POP*GPC
78	Kuwait	59	POP*GPC
79	Ireland	48	POP*GPC
80	Norway	46	POP*GPC
81	Bahrain	45	POP*GPC
82	Georgia	43	POP*GPC
83	Belarus	43	POP*GPC
84	Sierra Leone	40	POP*GPC
85	Tajikistan	40	POP*GPC
86	Taiwan	39	POP*GPC
87	Kyrgyzstan	39	POP*GPC
88	Macedonia	37	POP*GPC
89	Guinea	37	POP*GPC
90	Mongolia	36	POP*GPC

TABLE 3.1 GROSS DOMESTIC PRODUCT AT PURCHASING POWER PARITIES, MILLIONS OF 2012 DOLLARS, YEAR 0001

Rank	Country	GDP	Source
91	Malaysia	36	POP*GPC
92	Turkmenistan	36	POP*GPC
93	Azerbaijan	34	POP*GPC
94	El Salvador	33	POP*GPC
95	South Africa	33	POP*GPC
96	Laos	33	POP*GPC
97	UAE	29	POP*GPC
98	Canada	28	POP*GPC
99	Kosovo	25	POP*GPC
100	Nicaragua	24	POP*GPC
101	Paraguay	18	POP*GPC
102	New Zealand	18	POP*GPC
103	Mozambique	18	POP*GPC
104	Honduras	17	POP*GPC
105	Lithuania	17	POP*GPC
106	Armenia	16	POP*GPC
107	Haiti	15	POP*GPC
108	Namibia	14	POP*GPC
109	Cuba	14	POP*GPC
110	Montenegro	14	POP*GPC
111	Panama	13	POP*GPC
112	Moldova	12	POP*GPC
113	Latvia	11	POP*GPC
114	Botswana	10	POP*GPC
115	Qatar	10	POP*GPC
116	Jamaica	9	POP*GPC
117	Zimbabwe	9	POP*GPC
118	Costa Rica	9	POP*GPC
119	Burundi	9	POP*GPC
120	Eritrea	8	POP*GPC
121	Zambia	8	POP*GPC
122	Guinea-Biss	8	POP*GPC
123	Finland	8	POP*GPC
124	Uruguay	8	POP*GPC
125	Malawi	7	POP*GPC
126	Estonia	6	POP*GPC
127	Puerto Rico	6	POP*GPC
128	Hong Kong	2	POP*GPC
129	Dominican R	2	POP*GPC
130	Lesotho	1	POP*GPC
131	Trinidad & T	1	POP*GPC
132	Swaziland	1	POP*GPC
133	Madagascar	0	POP*GPC
134	Singapore	0	POP*GPC

Table 3.2 Gross Domestic Product at Purchasing Power Parities, Millions of 2012 Dollars, Year 1000

Rank	Country	GDP	Source
1	India	44,310	POP*GPC
2	China	41,547	POP*GPC
3	Turkey	6,995	POP*GPC
4	Bangladesh	5,054	POP*GPC
5	Japan	4,988	POP*GPC
6	Iran	4,442	POP*GPC
7	France	4,323	POP*GPC
8	Indonesia	4,073	POP*GPC
9	Egypt	3,912	POP*GPC
10	Italy	3,521	POP*GPC
11	Pakistan	3,450	POP*GPC
12	Spain	2,817	POP*GPC
13	Mexico	2,365	POP*GPC
14	Yemen	2,283	POP*GPC
15	Germany	2,246	POP*GPC
16	Korea, South	2,162	POP*GPC
17	Saudi Arabia	1,841	POP*GPC
18	Russia	1,743	POP*GPC
19	Sudan	1,611	POP*GPC
20	Syria	1,468	POP*GPC
21	UK	1,443	POP*GPC
22	Morocco	1,346	POP*GPC
23	Algeria	1,346	POP*GPC
24	Vietnam	1,310	POP*GPC
25	Iraq	1,058	POP*GPC
26	Korea, North	1,000	POP*GPC
27	Poland	871	POP*GPC
28	Thailand	849	POP*GPC
29	US	734	POP*GPC
30	Greece	689	POP*GPC
31	Burma	678	POP*GPC
32	Tunisia	673	POP*GPC
33	Czechia	647	POP*GPC
34	Afghanistan	641	POP*GPC
35	Nepal	579	POP*GPC
36	Kazakhstan	553	POP*GPC
37	Ukraine	534	POP*GPC
38	Peru	511	POP*GPC
39.5	Bulgaria	501	POP*GPC
39.5	Romania	501	POP*GPC
41	Austria	466	POP*GPC
42	Colombia	446	POP*GPC
43	Bolivia	441	POP*GPC
44	Uzbekistan	428	POP*GPC
45	Portugal	399	POP*GPC
46	Serbia	394	POP*GPC
47	Lebanon	365	POP*GPC

TABLE 3.2 GROSS DOMESTIC PRODUCT AT PURCHASING POWER PARITIES, MILLIONS OF 2012 DOLLARS, YEAR 1000

Rank	Country	GDP	Source
48	Sri Lanka	361	POP*GPC
49	Brazil	350	POP*GPC
50	Cambodia	344	POP*GPC
51	Libya	336	POP*GPC
52	Hungary	313	POP*GPC
53	Sweden	303	POP*GPC
54	Chile	303	POP*GPC
55	Ethiopia	296	POP*GPC
56	Denmark	285	POP*GPC
57	Oman	280	POP*GPC
58	Venezuela	272	POP*GPC
59	Belgium	266	POP*GPC
60	Croatia	255	POP*GPC
61	Guatemala	252	POP*GPC
62	Slovakia	227	POP*GPC
63	South Sudan	227	POP*GPC
64	Jordan	213	POP*GPC
65	Argentina	212	POP*GPC
66	Ghana	211	POP*GPC
67	Netherlands	200	POP*GPC
68	Somalia	198	POP*GPC
69	Ecuador	197	POP*GPC
70	Switzerland	192	POP*GPC
71	Philippines	192	POP*GPC
72	Israel	188	POP*GPC
73	Ireland	179	POP*GPC
74	Australia	170	POP*GPC
75	Mozambique	149	POP*GPC
76	Norway	143	POP*GPC
77	Cyprus	141	POP*GPC
78	South Africa	138	POP*GPC
79	Bosnia	136	POP*GPC
80	Sierra Leone	135	POP*GPC
81	Slovenia	125	POP*GPC
82	Belarus	122	POP*GPC
83	Burundi	116	POP*GPC
84	Guinea	110	POP*GPC
85	Georgia	106	POP*GPC
86	Madagascar	99	POP*GPC
87	El Salvador	94	POP*GPC
88	Albania	93	POP*GPC
89	Tajikistan	91	POP*GPC
90	Mongolia	91	POP*GPC
91	Kyrgyzstan	89	POP*GPC
92	Laos	88	POP*GPC
93	Zimbabwe	86	POP*GPC
94	Turkmenistan	85	POP*GPC
95	Azerbaijan	79	POP*GPC

TABLE 3.2 GROSS DOMESTIC PRODUCT AT PURCHASING POWER PARITIES, MILLIONS OF 2012 DOLLARS, YEAR 1000

Rank	Country	GDP	Source
96	Canada	78	POP*GPC
97	Zambia	77	POP*GPC
98	Kuwait	73	POP*GPC
99	Taiwan	72	POP*GPC
100	Malaysia	67	POP*GPC
101	Nicaragua	66	POP*GPC
102	Malawi	63	POP*GPC
103	Macedonia	58	POP*GPC
104	Bahrain	55	POP*GPC
105	Lithuania	53	POP*GPC
106	Paraguay	50	POP*GPC
107	Honduras	47	POP*GPC
108	Haiti	41	POP*GPC
109	Cuba	41	POP*GPC
110	Armenia	39	POP*GPC
111	Panama	38	POP*GPC
112	UAE	36	POP*GPC
113	Kosovo	36	POP*GPC
114	Latvia	35	POP*GPC
115	Moldova	34	POP*GPC
116	New Zealand	32	POP*GPC
117	Jamaica	28	POP*GPC
118	Namibia	27	POP*GPC
119	Costa Rica	26	POP*GPC
120	Montenegro	23	POP*GPC
121	Guinea-Biss	23	POP*GPC
122	Finland	22	POP*GPC
123	Uruguay	22	POP*GPC
124	Eritrea	21	POP*GPC
125	Estonia	21	POP*GPC
126	Botswana	18	POP*GPC
127	Puerto Rico	17	POP*GPC
128	Iceland	17	POP*GPC
129	Qatar	13	POP*GPC
130	Lesotho	6	POP*GPC
131	Dominican R	5	POP*GPC
132	Trinidad & T	4	POP*GPC
133	Swaziland	3	POP*GPC
134	Hong Kong	2	POP*GPC
135	Singapore	1	POP*GPC

TABLE 3.3 GROSS DOMESTIC PRODUCT AT PURCHASING POWER PARITIES, MILLIONS OF 2012 DOLLARS, YEAR 1500

Rank	Country	GDP	Source
1	China	96,708	POP*GPC
2	India	79,430	POP*GPC
3	Italy	18,074	POP*GPC
4	France	17,065	POP*GPC
5	Germany	12,919	POP*GPC
6	Japan	12,049	POP*GPC
7	Indonesia	9,460	POP*GPC
8	Bangladesh	9,060	POP*GPC
9	Spain	7,034	POP*GPC
10	Russia	6,946	POP*GPC
11	Pakistan	6,184	POP*GPC
12	Turkey	5,915	POP*GPC
13	Korea, South	5,136	POP*GPC
14	Mexico	4,988	POP*GPC
15	UK	4,113	POP*GPC
16	Poland	4,091	POP*GPC
17	Iran	3,756	POP*GPC
18	Vietnam	3,085	POP*GPC
19	Egypt	2,973	POP*GPC
20	Korea, North	2,375	POP*GPC
21	Austria	2,213	POP*GPC
22	Czechia	2,179	POP*GPC
23	Sudan	2,149	POP*GPC
24	Romania	2,013	POP*GPC
25	Ukraine	2,007	POP*GPC
26	Thailand	1,972	POP*GPC
27	Yemen	1,931	POP*GPC
28	Belgium	1,917	POP*GPC
29	Burma	1,579	POP*GPC
30	Saudi Arabia	1,557	POP*GPC
31	Afghanistan	1,497	POP*GPC
32	US	1,457	POP*GPC
33	Hungary	1,394	POP*GPC
34	Nepal	1,260	POP*GPC
35	Syria	1,241	POP*GPC
36	Netherlands	1,131	POP*GPC
37	Kazakhstan	1,083	POP*GPC
38	Morocco	1,009	POP*GPC
39	Algeria	1,009	POP*GPC
40	Portugal	948	POP*GPC
41	Peru	926	POP*GPC
42	Iraq	894	POP*GPC
43	Sri Lanka	839	POP*GPC
44	Bolivia	807	POP*GPC
45	Colombia	799	POP*GPC
46	Cambodia	766	POP*GPC

Table 3.3 Gross Domestic Product at Purchasing Power Parities, Millions of 2012 Dollars, Year 1500

Rank	Country	GDP	Source
47	Uzbekistan	757	POP*GPC
48	Slovakia	738	POP*GPC
49	Bulgaria	726	POP*GPC
50	Denmark	693	POP*GPC
51	Ethiopia	678	POP*GPC
52	Greece	678	POP*GPC
53	Switzerland	643	POP*GPC
54	Brazil	636	POP*GPC
55	Mozambique	617	POP*GPC
56	Sweden	598	POP*GPC
57	Serbia	577	POP*GPC
58	Chile	552	POP*GPC
59	Tunisia	538	POP*GPC
60	Somalia	494	POP*GPC
61	Venezuela	490	POP*GPC
62	Ireland	469	POP*GPC
63	Guatemala	467	POP*GPC
64	Belarus	466	POP*GPC
65	Philippines	446	POP*GPC
66	Croatia	436	POP*GPC
67	Madagascar	432	POP*GPC
68	Ghana	405	POP*GPC
69	Argentina	387	POP*GPC
70	South Sudan	366	POP*GPC
71	Ecuador	358	POP*GPC
72	Georgia	346	POP*GPC
73	South Africa	345	POP*GPC
74	Libya	336	POP*GPC
75	Lebanon	308	POP*GPC
76	Australia	302	POP*GPC
77	Norway	300	POP*GPC
78	Sierra Leone	275	POP*GPC
79	Burundi	275	POP*GPC
80	Azerbaijan	245	POP*GPC
81	Oman	237	POP*GPC
82	Slovenia	236	POP*GPC
83	Lithuania	219	POP*GPC
84	Bosnia	217	POP*GPC
85	Zimbabwe	214	POP*GPC
86	Finland	213	POP*GPC
87	Laos	204	POP*GPC
88	Guinea	200	POP*GPC
89	Mongolia	197	POP*GPC
90	Zambia	192	POP*GPC
91	Jordan	180	POP*GPC
92	El Salvador	169	POP*GPC
93	Taiwan	168	POP*GPC
94	Israel	159	POP*GPC

Table 3.3 Gross Domestic Product at Purchasing Power Parities, Millions of 2012 Dollars, Year 1500

Rank	Country	GDP	Source
95	Tajikistan	157	POP*GPC
96	Malaysia	155	POP*GPC
97	Kyrgyzstan	153	POP*GPC
98	Canada	152	POP*GPC
99	Turkmenistan	149	POP*GPC
100	Malawi	147	POP*GPC
101	Latvia	146	POP*GPC
102	Moldova	130	POP*GPC
103	Armenia	130	POP*GPC
104	Nicaragua	118	POP*GPC
105	Albania	114	POP*GPC
106	Macedonia	91	POP*GPC
107	Paraguay	89	POP*GPC
108	Estonia	89	POP*GPC
109	Honduras	83	POP*GPC
110	Cuba	78	POP*GPC
111	Haiti	74	POP*GPC
112	Panama	69	POP*GPC
113	Namibia	66	POP*GPC
114	Kuwait	61	POP*GPC
115	Kosovo	56	POP*GPC
116	New Zealand	54	POP*GPC
117	Jamaica	54	POP*GPC
118	Eritrea	48	POP*GPC
119	Costa Rica	47	POP*GPC
120	Bahrain	47	POP*GPC
121	Cyprus	43	POP*GPC
122	Botswana	42	POP*GPC
123	Guinea-Biss	42	POP*GPC
124	Uruguay	40	POP*GPC
125	Montenegro	38	POP*GPC
126	Iceland	38	POP*GPC
127	Puerto Rico	33	POP*GPC
128	UAE	30	POP*GPC
129	Lesotho	14	POP*GPC
130	Qatar	11	POP*GPC
131	Dominican R	9	POP*GPC
132	Trinidad & T	8	POP*GPC
133	Swaziland	7	POP*GPC
134	Hong Kong	5	POP*GPC
135	Singapore	2	POP*GPC

Table 3.4 Gross Domestic Product at Purchasing Power Parities, Millions of 2012 Dollars, Year 1600

Rank	Country	GDP	Source
1	China	150,225	POP*GPC
2	India	97,482	POP*GPC
3	France	24,347	POP*GPC
4	Italy	22,549	POP*GPC
5	Germany	19,805	POP*GPC
6	Japan	15,054	POP*GPC
7	Bangladesh	11,119	POP*GPC
8	Spain	10,999	POP*GPC
9	Indonesia	10,606	POP*GPC
10	Russia	9,574	POP*GPC
11	UK	8,781	POP*GPC
12	Pakistan	7,589	POP*GPC
13	Turkey	6,830	POP*GPC
14	Korea, South	6,342	POP*GPC
15	Poland	5,649	POP*GPC
16	Iran	4,199	POP*GPC
17	Egypt	3,717	POP*GPC
18	Vietnam	3,642	POP*GPC
19	Czechia	3,611	POP*GPC
20	Austria	3,274	POP*GPC
21	Netherlands	3,242	POP*GPC
22	Korea, North	2,933	POP*GPC
23	Ukraine	2,775	POP*GPC
24	Belgium	2,444	POP*GPC
25	Sudan	2,256	POP*GPC
26	Thailand	2,245	POP*GPC
27	Romania	2,224	POP*GPC
28	Yemen	1,931	POP*GPC
29	Burma	1,864	POP*GPC
30	Mexico	1,776	POP*GPC
31	Afghanistan	1,767	POP*GPC
32	Hungary	1,564	POP*GPC
33	Saudi Arabia	1,557	POP*GPC
34	Nepal	1,529	POP*GPC
35	Morocco	1,514	POP*GPC
36	Algeria	1,514	POP*GPC
37	Kazakhstan	1,370	POP*GPC
38	Portugal	1,274	POP*GPC
39	Bulgaria	1,254	POP*GPC
40	Slovakia	1,223	POP*GPC
41	Syria	1,210	POP*GPC
42	Switzerland	1,174	POP*GPC
43	US	1,161	POP*GPC
44	Greece	1,134	POP*GPC
45	Sweden	980	POP*GPC
46	Uzbekistan	957	POP*GPC
47	Sri Lanka	936	POP*GPC

Table 3.4 Gross Domestic Product at Purchasing Power Parities, Millions of 2012 Dollars, Year 1600

Rank	Country	GDP	Source
48	Cambodia	904	POP*GPC
49	Iraq	896	POP*GPC
50	Denmark	890	POP*GPC
51	Mozambique	812	POP*GPC
52	Ethiopia	786	POP*GPC
53	Serbia	778	POP*GPC
54	Philippines	717	POP*GPC
55	Ireland	685	POP*GPC
56	Tunisia	673	POP*GPC
57	Belarus	645	POP*GPC
58	Croatia	589	POP*GPC
59	Peru	585	POP*GPC
60	Ghana	540	POP*GPC
61	Brazil	536	POP*GPC
62	Somalia	520	POP*GPC
63	Madagascar	520	POP*GPC
64	Bolivia	511	POP*GPC
65	Colombia	503	POP*GPC
66	Norway	476	POP*GPC
67	Georgia	459	POP*GPC
68	South Africa	423	POP*GPC
69	South Sudan	401	POP*GPC
70	Chile	394	POP*GPC
71	Taiwan	382	POP*GPC
72	Sierra Leone	373	POP*GPC
73	Finland	337	POP*GPC
74	Libya	336	POP*GPC
75	Burundi	333	POP*GPC
76	Argentina	331	POP*GPC
77	Slovenia	327	POP*GPC
78	Australia	319	POP*GPC
79	Azerbaijan	315	POP*GPC
80	Venezuela	309	POP*GPC
81	Lithuania	303	POP*GPC
82	Lebanon	300	POP*GPC
83	Guatemala	297	POP*GPC
84	Bosnia	278	POP*GPC
85	Guinea	264	POP*GPC
86	Zimbabwe	248	POP*GPC
87	Laos	241	POP*GPC
88	Mongolia	239	POP*GPC
89	Oman	237	POP*GPC
90	Ecuador	226	POP*GPC
91	Zambia	222	POP*GPC
92	Latvia	202	POP*GPC
93	Tajikistan	188	POP*GPC
94	Kyrgyzstan	183	POP*GPC
95	Malaysia	183	POP*GPC

Table 3.4 Gross Domestic Product at Purchasing Power Parities, Millions of 2012 Dollars, Year 1600

Rank	Country	GDP	Source
96	Moldova	180	POP*GPC
97	Turkmenistan	180	POP*GPC
98	Jordan	175	POP*GPC
99	Armenia	172	POP*GPC
100	Malawi	167	POP*GPC
101	Canada	160	POP*GPC
102	Israel	155	POP*GPC
103	Estonia	124	POP*GPC
104	Albania	119	POP*GPC
105	Macedonia	116	POP*GPC
106	El Salvador	106	POP*GPC
107	Nicaragua	74	POP*GPC
108	Cyprus	73	POP*GPC
109	Kosovo	71	POP*GPC
110	Namibia	70	POP*GPC
111	Kuwait	61	POP*GPC
112	New Zealand	56	POP*GPC
113	Eritrea	56	POP*GPC
114	Paraguay	56	POP*GPC
115	Guinea-Biss	55	POP*GPC
116	Honduras	52	POP*GPC
117	Montenegro	52	POP*GPC
118	Iceland	49	POP*GPC
119	Bahrain	47	POP*GPC
120	Botswana	44	POP*GPC
121	Panama	44	POP*GPC
122	Uruguay	40	POP*GPC
123	Cuba	33	POP*GPC
124	Haiti	31	POP*GPC
125	UAE	30	POP*GPC
126	Costa Rica	30	POP*GPC
127	Jamaica	23	POP*GPC
128	Lesotho	17	POP*GPC
129	Puerto Rico	14	POP*GPC
130	Qatar	11	POP*GPC
131	Swaziland	8	POP*GPC
132	Hong Kong	8	POP*GPC
133	Dominican R	4	POP*GPC
134	Trinidad & T	3	POP*GPC
135	Singapore	3	POP*GPC

Table 3.5 Gross Domestic Product at Purchasing Power Parities, Millions of 2012 Dollars, Year 1700

Rank	Country	GDP	Source
1	China	129,569	POP*GPC
2	India	119,145	POP*GPC
3	France	30,575	POP*GPC
4	Japan	24,083	POP*GPC
5	Italy	22,894	POP*GPC
6	Germany	21,360	POP*GPC
7	UK	15,643	POP*GPC
8	Russia	14,130	POP*GPC
9	Bangladesh	13,589	POP*GPC
10	Indonesia	11,890	POP*GPC
11	Spain	11,706	POP*GPC
12	Pakistan	9,275	POP*GPC
13	Turkey	7,887	POP*GPC
14	Korea, South	7,832	POP*GPC
15	Poland	7,497	POP*GPC
16	Netherlands	6,333	POP*GPC
17	Iran	4,695	POP*GPC
18	Vietnam	4,212	POP*GPC
19	Ukraine	4,088	POP*GPC
20	Mexico	4,000	POP*GPC
21	Czechia	3,993	POP*GPC
22	Austria	3,885	POP*GPC
23	Korea, North	3,622	POP*GPC
24	Belgium	3,580	POP*GPC
25	Egypt	3,345	POP*GPC
26	Romania	3,074	POP*GPC
27	Portugal	2,563	POP*GPC
28	Thailand	2,496	POP*GPC
29	Sudan	2,363	POP*GPC
30	Burma	2,156	POP*GPC
31	Hungary	2,106	POP*GPC
32	Afghanistan	2,044	POP*GPC
33	Yemen	1,931	POP*GPC
34	Sweden	1,926	POP*GPC
35	Nepal	1,865	POP*GPC
36	Kazakhstan	1,703	POP*GPC
37	Switzerland	1,671	POP*GPC
38	Saudi Arabia	1,557	POP*GPC
39	Ireland	1,533	POP*GPC
40	Bulgaria	1,387	POP*GPC
41	Slovakia	1,352	POP*GPC
42	Greece	1,244	POP*GPC
43	Uzbekistan	1,190	POP*GPC
44	Syria	1,179	POP*GPC
45	Morocco	1,178	POP*GPC
46	Algeria	1,178	POP*GPC

Table 3.5 Gross Domestic Product at Purchasing Power Parities, Millions of 2012 Dollars, Year 1700

Rank	Country	GDP	Source
47	Denmark	1,138	POP*GPC
48	Philippines	1,128	POP*GPC
49	Cambodia	1,046	POP*GPC
50	Sri Lanka	1,020	POP*GPC
51	Mozambique	974	POP*GPC
52	Belarus	950	POP*GPC
53	Ethiopia	900	POP*GPC
54	Brazil	898	POP*GPC
55	Iraq	896	POP*GPC
56	Serbia	861	POP*GPC
57	Taiwan	850	POP*GPC
58	US	825	POP*GPC
59	Ghana	728	POP*GPC
60	Norway	704	POP*GPC
61	Peru	702	POP*GPC
62	Croatia	652	POP*GPC
63	Madagascar	649	POP*GPC
64	Somalia	617	POP*GPC
65	Bolivia	615	POP*GPC
66	South Africa	605	POP*GPC
67	Colombia	602	POP*GPC
68	Georgia	592	POP*GPC
69	Tunisia	538	POP*GPC
70	Argentina	536	POP*GPC
71	Chile	528	POP*GPC
72	Sierra Leone	512	POP*GPC
73	Lithuania	447	POP*GPC
74	South Sudan	440	POP*GPC
75	Finland	399	POP*GPC
76	Azerbaijan	399	POP*GPC
77	Burundi	396	POP*GPC
78	Slovenia	370	POP*GPC
79	Venezuela	370	POP*GPC
80	Guatemala	359	POP*GPC
81	Guinea	351	POP*GPC
82	Australia	338	POP*GPC
83	Libya	336	POP*GPC
84	Latvia	298	POP*GPC
85	Lebanon	293	POP*GPC
86	Bosnia	293	POP*GPC
87	Mongolia	291	POP*GPC
88	Laos	278	POP*GPC
89	Ecuador	272	POP*GPC
90	Zimbabwe	270	POP*GPC
91	Moldova	266	POP*GPC
92	Zambia	242	POP*GPC
93	Oman	237	POP*GPC
94	Turkmenistan	224	POP*GPC

Table 3.5 Gross Domestic Product at Purchasing Power Parities, Millions of 2012 Dollars, Year 1700

Rank	Country	GDP	Source
95	Tajikistan	223	POP*GPC
96	Armenia	222	POP*GPC
97	Kyrgyzstan	216	POP*GPC
98	Malaysia	211	POP*GPC
99	Malawi	189	POP*GPC
100	Albania	187	POP*GPC
101	Estonia	185	POP*GPC
102	Jordan	171	POP*GPC
103	Israel	151	POP*GPC
104	Canada	135	POP*GPC
105	El Salvador	127	POP*GPC
106	Macedonia	121	POP*GPC
107	Nicaragua	89	POP*GPC
108	Cuba	88	POP*GPC
109	Haiti	82	POP*GPC
110	Cyprus	80	POP*GPC
111	Jamaica	77	POP*GPC
112	Uruguay	76	POP*GPC
113	Kosovo	74	POP*GPC
114	Guinea-Biss	73	POP*GPC
115	Namibia	70	POP*GPC
116	Paraguay	67	POP*GPC
117	Eritrea	64	POP*GPC
118	Iceland	63	POP*GPC
119	Honduras	62	POP*GPC
120	Kuwait	61	POP*GPC
121	New Zealand	59	POP*GPC
122	Montenegro	57	POP*GPC
123	Panama	53	POP*GPC
124	Bahrain	47	POP*GPC
125	Botswana	45	POP*GPC
126	Puerto Rico	38	POP*GPC
127	Costa Rica	36	POP*GPC
128	UAE	30	POP*GPC
129	Lesotho	25	POP*GPC
130	Swaziland	12	POP*GPC
131	Trinidad & T	11	POP*GPC
132	Qatar	11	POP*GPC
133	Dominican R	10	POP*GPC
134	Hong Kong	7	POP*GPC
135	Singapore	3	POP*GPC

Table 3.6 Gross Domestic Product at Purchasing Power Parities, Millions of 2012 Dollars, Year 1820

Rank	Country	GDP	Source
1	China	357,724	POP*GPC
2	India	145,703	POP*GPC
3	France	55,503	POP*GPC
4	UK	52,943	POP*GPC
5	Germany	41,973	POP*GPC
6	Russia	35,801	POP*GPC
7	Italy	35,266	POP*GPC
8	Japan	32,453	POP*GPC
9	US	19,633	POP*GPC
10	Spain	19,249	POP*GPC
11	Indonesia	17,168	POP*GPC
12	Bangladesh	16,619	POP*GPC
13	Poland	14,682	POP*GPC
14	Pakistan	11,343	POP*GPC
15	Ukraine	10,181	POP*GPC
16	Turkey	10,136	POP*GPC
17	Romania	8,854	POP*GPC
18	Korea, South	8,821	POP*GPC
19	Mexico	7,824	POP*GPC
20	Czechia	7,657	POP*GPC
21	Belgium	7,088	POP*GPC
22	Ireland	6,934	POP*GPC
23	Netherlands	6,710	POP*GPC
24	Hungary	6,687	POP*GPC
25	Austria	6,421	POP*GPC
26	Iran	6,036	POP*GPC
27	Vietnam	5,402	POP*GPC
28	Sweden	4,846	POP*GPC
29	Portugal	4,762	POP*GPC
30	Thailand	4,716	POP*GPC
31	Brazil	4,556	POP*GPC
32	Korea, North	4,080	POP*GPC
33	Switzerland	3,387	POP*GPC
34	Egypt	3,266	POP*GPC
35	Kazakhstan	2,873	POP*GPC
36	Sudan	2,769	POP*GPC
37	Burma	2,765	POP*GPC
38	Bulgaria	2,735	POP*GPC
39	Afghanistan	2,622	POP*GPC
40	Slovakia	2,593	POP*GPC
41	Nepal	2,509	POP*GPC
42	Belarus	2,366	POP*GPC
43	Greece	2,319	POP*GPC
44	Denmark	2,303	POP*GPC
45	Yemen	2,232	POP*GPC
46	Uzbekistan	2,015	POP*GPC

Table 3.6 Gross Domestic Product at Purchasing Power Parities, Millions of 2012 Dollars, Year 1820

Rank	Country	GDP	Source
47	Philippines	1,989	POP*GPC
48	Serbia	1,840	POP*GPC
49	Morocco	1,809	POP*GPC
50	Algeria	1,809	POP*GPC
51	Saudi Arabia	1,800	POP*GPC
52	Taiwan	1,721	POP*GPC
53	Norway	1,676	POP*GPC
54	Finland	1,429	POP*GPC
55	Croatia	1,393	POP*GPC
56	Syria	1,377	POP*GPC
57	Mozambique	1,361	POP*GPC
58	Cambodia	1,342	POP*GPC
59	Ethiopia	1,179	POP*GPC
60	Canada	1,154	POP*GPC
61	Lithuania	1,112	POP*GPC
62	Madagascar	1,093	POP*GPC
63	Colombia	1,072	POP*GPC
64	Argentina	1,070	POP*GPC
65	Sri Lanka	1,044	POP*GPC
66	Iraq	1,006	POP*GPC
67	Peru	982	POP*GPC
68	South Africa	938	POP*GPC
69	Georgia	926	POP*GPC
70	Ghana	892	POP*GPC
71	Bolivia	863	POP*GPC
72	Chile	837	POP*GPC
73	Slovenia	816	POP*GPC
74	Latvia	742	POP*GPC
75	Moldova	662	POP*GPC
76	Somalia	649	POP*GPC
77	Sierra Leone	644	POP*GPC
78	Azerbaijan	624	POP*GPC
79	Bosnia	592	POP*GPC
80	Tunisia	589	POP*GPC
81	South Sudan	546	POP*GPC
82	Burundi	541	POP*GPC
83	Venezuela	517	POP*GPC
84	Haiti	514	POP*GPC
85	Guatemala	507	POP*GPC
86	Cuba	506	POP*GPC
87	Estonia	467	POP*GPC
88	Jamaica	439	POP*GPC
89	Guinea	422	POP*GPC
90	Mongolia	391	POP*GPC
91	Ecuador	381	POP*GPC
92	Turkmenistan	378	POP*GPC
93	Tajikistan	376	POP*GPC
94	Libya	362	POP*GPC

Table 3.6 Gross Domestic Product at Purchasing Power Parities, Millions of 2012 Dollars, Year 1820

Rank	Country	GDP	Source
95	Laos	357	POP*GPC
96	Armenia	348	POP*GPC
97	Kyrgyzstan	343	POP*GPC
98	Lebanon	342	POP*GPC
99	Zimbabwe	303	POP*GPC
100	Albania	290	POP*GPC
101	Oman	274	POP*GPC
102	Zambia	271	POP*GPC
103	Malaysia	271	POP*GPC
104	Australia	271	POP*GPC
105	Macedonia	243	POP*GPC
106	Malawi	222	POP*GPC
107	Puerto Rico	217	POP*GPC
108	Jordan	200	POP*GPC
109	Uruguay	183	POP*GPC
110	El Salvador	178	POP*GPC
111	Israel	176	POP*GPC
112	Kosovo	149	POP*GPC
113	Cyprus	149	POP*GPC
114	Nicaragua	123	POP*GPC
115	Montenegro	122	POP*GPC
116	Paraguay	93	POP*GPC
117	Trinidad & T	90	POP*GPC
118	Guinea-Biss	88	POP*GPC
119	Honduras	86	POP*GPC
120	Eritrea	84	POP*GPC
121	Namibia	77	POP*GPC
122	Panama	74	POP*GPC
123	Iceland	73	POP*GPC
124	Kuwait	71	POP*GPC
125	New Zealand	63	POP*GPC
126	Dominican R	62	POP*GPC
127	Bahrain	54	POP*GPC
128	Botswana	52	POP*GPC
129	Costa Rica	51	POP*GPC
130	Lesotho	41	POP*GPC
131	UAE	35	POP*GPC
132	Hong Kong	19	POP*GPC
133	Swaziland	19	POP*GPC
134	Qatar	12	POP*GPC
135	Singapore	4	POP*GPC

TABLE 3.7 GROSS DOMESTIC PRODUCT AT PURCHASING POWER PARITIES, MILLIONS OF 2012 DOLLARS, YEAR 1870

Rank	Country	GDP	Source
1	China	296,914	POP*GPC
2	India	185,280	POP*GPC
3	US	153,964	POP*GPC
4	UK	146,356	POP*GPC
5	Germany	112,897	POP*GPC
6	France	112,846	POP*GPC
7	Russia	80,699	POP*GPC
8	Italy	65,417	POP*GPC
9	Japan	39,716	POP*GPC
10	Spain	30,600	POP*GPC
11	Indonesia	29,599	POP*GPC
12	Poland	24,966	POP*GPC
13	Ukraine	22,666	POP*GPC
14	Bangladesh	21,730	POP*GPC
15	Belgium	21,467	POP*GPC
16	Pakistan	15,705	POP*GPC
17	Netherlands	15,575	POP*GPC
18	Turkey	15,225	POP*GPC
19	Czechia	13,923	POP*GPC
20	Romania	13,373	POP*GPC
21	Austria	13,177	POP*GPC
22	Brazil	10,931	POP*GPC
23	Sweden	10,843	POP*GPC
24	Ireland	10,710	POP*GPC
25	Hungary	10,111	POP*GPC
26	Canada	10,029	POP*GPC
27	Mexico	9,723	POP*GPC
28	Iran	9,468	POP*GPC
29	Korea, South	9,218	POP*GPC
30	Australia	9,091	POP*GPC
31	Switzerland	8,733	POP*GPC
32	Vietnam	8,320	POP*GPC
33	Portugal	6,602	POP*GPC
34	Egypt	6,494	POP*GPC
35	Thailand	6,434	POP*GPC
36	Denmark	5,918	POP*GPC
37	Kazakhstan	5,315	POP*GPC
38	Belarus	5,268	POP*GPC
39	Greece	5,036	POP*GPC
40	Philippines	4,944	POP*GPC
41	Slovakia	4,715	POP*GPC
42	Sudan	4,274	POP*GPC
43	Korea, North	4,264	POP*GPC
44	Algeria	4,225	POP*GPC
45	Chile	3,926	POP*GPC
46	Norway	3,888	POP*GPC

Table 3.7 Gross Domestic Product at Purchasing Power Parities, Millions of 2012 Dollars, Year 1870

Rank	Country	GDP	Source
47	Uzbekistan	3,716	POP*GPC
48	Sri Lanka	3,710	POP*GPC
49	Argentina	3,685	POP*GPC
50	South Africa	3,420	POP*GPC
51	Bulgaria	3,399	POP*GPC
52	Burma	3,348	POP*GPC
53	Morocco	3,327	POP*GPC
54	Afghanistan	3,236	POP*GPC
55	Finland	3,129	POP*GPC
56	Nepal	3,117	POP*GPC
57	Serbia	3,061	POP*GPC
58	Mozambique	3,049	POP*GPC
59	Yemen	2,555	POP*GPC
60	Ethiopia	2,510	POP*GPC
61	Lithuania	2,476	POP*GPC
62	Georgia	2,398	POP*GPC
63	Croatia	2,316	POP*GPC
64	Colombia	2,178	POP*GPC
65	Madagascar	2,144	POP*GPC
66	Saudi Arabia	2,104	POP*GPC
67	Syria	2,089	POP*GPC
68	Taiwan	2,018	POP*GPC
69	Peru	1,991	POP*GPC
70	Iraq	1,778	POP*GPC
71	Latvia	1,652	POP*GPC
72	Azerbaijan	1,615	POP*GPC
73	Moldova	1,473	POP*GPC
74	Venezuela	1,472	POP*GPC
75	Cambodia	1,465	POP*GPC
76	New Zealand	1,412	POP*GPC
77	Slovenia	1,374	POP*GPC
78	Somalia	1,274	POP*GPC
79	Bolivia	1,201	POP*GPC
80	Uruguay	1,171	POP*GPC
81	Tunisia	1,165	POP*GPC
82	Cuba	1,140	POP*GPC
83	Ghana	1,084	POP*GPC
84	Estonia	1,039	POP*GPC
85	Sierra Leone	993	POP*GPC
86	Bosnia	963	POP*GPC
87	Guatemala	943	POP*GPC
88	Armenia	901	POP*GPC
89	Haiti	841	POP*GPC
90	Malaysia	830	POP*GPC
91	Ecuador	790	POP*GPC
92	Burundi	764	POP*GPC
93	Zimbabwe	744	POP*GPC
94	Turkmenistan	699	POP*GPC

Table 3.7 Gross Domestic Product at Purchasing Power Parities, Millions of 2012 Dollars, Year 1870

Rank	Country	GDP	Source
95	Tajikistan	695	POP*GPC
96	South Sudan	664	POP*GPC
97	Zambia	651	POP*GPC
98	Guinea	639	POP*GPC
99	Kyrgyzstan	635	POP*GPC
100	Lebanon	629	POP*GPC
101	Libya	579	POP*GPC
102	Puerto Rico	579	POP*GPC
103	Laos	552	POP*GPC
104	Malawi	454	POP*GPC
105	Mongolia	433	POP*GPC
106	Albania	421	POP*GPC
107	Jamaica	418	POP*GPC
108	Macedonia	394	POP*GPC
109	El Salvador	363	POP*GPC
110	Oman	330	POP*GPC
111	Cyprus	323	POP*GPC
112	Jordan	299	POP*GPC
113	Israel	279	POP*GPC
114	Honduras	263	POP*GPC
115	Paraguay	255	POP*GPC
116	Namibia	249	POP*GPC
117	Kosovo	242	POP*GPC
118	Nicaragua	228	POP*GPC
119	Montenegro	204	POP*GPC
120	Trinidad & T	191	POP*GPC
121	Eritrea	179	POP*GPC
122	Dominican R	174	POP*GPC
123	Iceland	168	POP*GPC
124	Panama	141	POP*GPC
125	Guinea-Biss	134	POP*GPC
126	Hong Kong	131	POP*GPC
127	Costa Rica	113	POP*GPC
128	Lesotho	99	POP*GPC
129	Botswana	92	POP*GPC
130	Singapore	90	POP*GPC
131	Kuwait	74	POP*GPC
132	Bahrain	56	POP*GPC
133	Swaziland	55	POP*GPC
134	UAE	37	POP*GPC
135	Qatar	13	POP*GPC

Table 3.8 Gross Domestic Product at Purchasing Power Parities, Millions of 2012 Dollars, Year 1880

Rank	Country	GDP	Source
1	China	308,076	POP*GPC
2	US	227,402	POP*GPC
3	India	196,107	POP*GPC
4	UK	175,898	POP*GPC
5	Germany	135,529	POP*GPC
6	France	129,531	POP*GPC
7	Russia	98,688	POP*GPC
8	Italy	73,068	POP*GPC
9	Japan	49,706	POP*GPC
10	Spain	43,424	POP*GPC
11	Indonesia	34,057	POP*GPC
12	Poland	33,859	POP*GPC
13	Ukraine	27,719	POP*GPC
14	Belgium	26,576	POP*GPC
15	Bangladesh	22,701	POP*GPC
16	Netherlands	19,271	POP*GPC
17	Turkey	17,611	POP*GPC
18	Czechia	16,666	POP*GPC
19	Pakistan	16,624	POP*GPC
20	Romania	16,446	POP*GPC
21	Austria	16,075	POP*GPC
22	Australia	14,732	POP*GPC
23	Brazil	13,879	POP*GPC
24	Mexico	13,433	POP*GPC
25	Sweden	13,207	POP*GPC
26	Canada	12,458	POP*GPC
27	Hungary	12,423	POP*GPC
28	Ireland	11,372	POP*GPC
29	Switzerland	10,884	POP*GPC
30	Iran	10,879	POP*GPC
31	Vietnam	10,431	POP*GPC
32	Korea, South	9,946	POP*GPC
33	Egypt	8,174	POP*GPC
34	Thailand	7,256	POP*GPC
35	Denmark	7,102	POP*GPC
36	Portugal	6,832	POP*GPC
37	Kazakhstan	6,500	POP*GPC
38	Argentina	6,472	POP*GPC
39	Greece	6,451	POP*GPC
40	Belarus	6,442	POP*GPC
41	Philippines	5,793	POP*GPC
42	Slovakia	5,644	POP*GPC
43	Chile	5,472	POP*GPC
44	Algeria	5,184	POP*GPC
45	South Africa	4,854	POP*GPC
46	Burma	4,776	POP*GPC

TABLE 3.8 GROSS DOMESTIC PRODUCT AT PURCHASING POWER PARITIES, MILLIONS OF 2012 DOLLARS, YEAR 1880

Rank	Country	GDP	Source
47	Norway	4,769	POP*GPC
48	Korea, North	4,666	POP*GPC
49	Sudan	4,661	POP*GPC
50	Bulgaria	4,553	POP*GPC
51	Uzbekistan	4,544	POP*GPC
52	Serbia	3,935	POP*GPC
53	Sri Lanka	3,928	POP*GPC
54	Morocco	3,767	POP*GPC
55	Afghanistan	3,764	POP*GPC
56	Finland	3,700	POP*GPC
57	Mozambique	3,583	POP*GPC
58	Nepal	3,294	POP*GPC
59	Colombia	3,068	POP*GPC
60	New Zealand	3,049	POP*GPC
61	Lithuania	3,028	POP*GPC
62	Croatia	2,978	POP*GPC
63	Georgia	2,932	POP*GPC
64	Ethiopia	2,919	POP*GPC
65	Peru	2,678	POP*GPC
66	Yemen	2,669	POP*GPC
67	Syria	2,459	POP*GPC
68	Madagascar	2,453	POP*GPC
69	Taiwan	2,223	POP*GPC
70	Saudi Arabia	2,192	POP*GPC
71	Iraq	2,158	POP*GPC
72	Latvia	2,020	POP*GPC
73	Azerbaijan	1,975	POP*GPC
74	Venezuela	1,964	POP*GPC
75	Moldova	1,802	POP*GPC
76	Slovenia	1,766	POP*GPC
77	Cambodia	1,667	POP*GPC
78	Uruguay	1,512	POP*GPC
79	Bolivia	1,492	POP*GPC
80	Cuba	1,461	POP*GPC
81	Somalia	1,458	POP*GPC
82	Tunisia	1,402	POP*GPC
83	Estonia	1,271	POP*GPC
84	Malaysia	1,223	POP*GPC
85	Guatemala	1,195	POP*GPC
86	Ghana	1,160	POP*GPC
87	Armenia	1,101	POP*GPC
88	Sierra Leone	1,084	POP*GPC
89	Bosnia	1,050	POP*GPC
90	Ecuador	1,048	POP*GPC
91	Haiti	936	POP*GPC
92	Zimbabwe	890	POP*GPC
93	Turkmenistan	855	POP*GPC
94	Tajikistan	850	POP*GPC

Table 3.8 Gross Domestic Product at Purchasing Power Parities, Millions of 2012 Dollars, Year 1880

Rank	Country	GDP	Source
95	Burundi	819	POP*GPC
96	Puerto Rico	787	POP*GPC
97	Kyrgyzstan	776	POP*GPC
98	Zambia	775	POP*GPC
99	Lebanon	754	POP*GPC
100	Guinea	695	POP*GPC
101	South Sudan	690	POP*GPC
102	Laos	688	POP*GPC
103	Libya	636	POP*GPC
104	Albania	535	POP*GPC
105	Malawi	524	POP*GPC
106	Macedonia	507	POP*GPC
107	Jamaica	489	POP*GPC
108	Mongolia	443	POP*GPC
109	El Salvador	423	POP*GPC
110	Cyprus	414	POP*GPC
111	Israel	352	POP*GPC
112	Oman	349	POP*GPC
113	Jordan	344	POP*GPC
114	Paraguay	317	POP*GPC
115	Namibia	315	POP*GPC
116	Kosovo	311	POP*GPC
117	Nicaragua	305	POP*GPC
118	Trinidad & T	294	POP*GPC
119	Honduras	284	POP*GPC
120	Montenegro	262	POP*GPC
121	Dominican R	225	POP*GPC
122	Eritrea	209	POP*GPC
123	Hong Kong	201	POP*GPC
124	Panama	192	POP*GPC
125	Iceland	189	POP*GPC
126	Costa Rica	174	POP*GPC
127	Guinea-Biss	145	POP*GPC
128	Singapore	142	POP*GPC
129	Lesotho	118	POP*GPC
130	Botswana	103	POP*GPC
131	Kuwait	79	POP*GPC
132	Swaziland	68	POP*GPC
133	Bahrain	60	POP*GPC
134	UAE	39	POP*GPC
135	Qatar	14	POP*GPC

TABLE 3.9 GROSS DOMESTIC PRODUCT AT PURCHASING POWER PARITIES, MILLIONS OF 2012 DOLLARS, YEAR 1890

Rank	Country	GDP	Source
1	US	336,005	POP*GPC
2	China	321,107	POP*GPC
3	India	221,983	POP*GPC
4	UK	219,576	POP*GPC
5	Germany	180,880	POP*GPC
6	France	148,775	POP*GPC
7	Russia	120,687	POP*GPC
8	Italy	82,698	POP*GPC
9	Japan	63,467	POP*GPC
10	Poland	45,920	POP*GPC
11	Spain	45,126	POP*GPC
12	Indonesia	38,812	POP*GPC
13	Ukraine	33,897	POP*GPC
14	Belgium	32,701	POP*GPC
15	Bangladesh	25,361	POP*GPC
16	Netherlands	23,582	POP*GPC
17	Australia	21,675	POP*GPC
18	Austria	20,621	POP*GPC
19	Turkey	20,371	POP*GPC
20	Romania	20,225	POP*GPC
21	Czechia	19,949	POP*GPC
22	Pakistan	18,818	POP*GPC
23	Mexico	18,556	POP*GPC
24	Canada	18,301	POP*GPC
25	Brazil	17,642	POP*GPC
26	Sweden	15,603	POP*GPC
27	Hungary	15,264	POP*GPC
28	Switzerland	14,694	POP*GPC
29	Vietnam	13,078	POP*GPC
30	Iran	12,500	POP*GPC
31	Ireland	11,403	POP*GPC
32	Argentina	11,369	POP*GPC
33	Korea, South	10,730	POP*GPC
34	Egypt	10,137	POP*GPC
35	Denmark	9,057	POP*GPC
36	Portugal	8,875	POP*GPC
37	Greece	8,262	POP*GPC
38	Thailand	8,183	POP*GPC
39	Kazakhstan	7,949	POP*GPC
40	Belarus	7,878	POP*GPC
41	Chile	7,627	POP*GPC
42	South Africa	6,891	POP*GPC
43	Burma	6,813	POP*GPC
44	Philippines	6,788	POP*GPC
45	Slovakia	6,755	POP*GPC
46	Algeria	6,333	POP*GPC
47	Bulgaria	6,097	POP*GPC

Table 3.9 Gross Domestic Product at Purchasing Power Parities, Millions of 2012 Dollars, Year 1890			
Rank	Country	GDP	Source
48	Uzbekistan	5,557	POP*GPC
49	Norway	5,553	POP*GPC
50	Sri Lanka	5,467	POP*GPC
51	Korea, North	5,117	POP*GPC
52	Finland	5,109	POP*GPC
53	Sudan	5,083	POP*GPC
54	Serbia	5,058	POP*GPC
55	Afghanistan	4,377	POP*GPC
56	Colombia	4,322	POP*GPC
57	Morocco	4,266	POP*GPC
58	Mozambique	4,210	POP*GPC
59	New Zealand	3,908	POP*GPC
60	Croatia	3,828	POP*GPC
61	Nepal	3,718	POP*GPC
62	Lithuania	3,703	POP*GPC
63	Peru	3,603	POP*GPC
64	Georgia	3,586	POP*GPC
65	Ethiopia	3,396	POP*GPC
66	Syria	2,895	POP*GPC
67	Madagascar	2,807	POP*GPC
68	Yemen	2,789	POP*GPC
69	Iraq	2,619	POP*GPC
70	Venezuela	2,529	POP*GPC
71	Latvia	2,470	POP*GPC
72	Taiwan	2,449	POP*GPC
73	Azerbaijan	2,416	POP*GPC
74	Uruguay	2,305	POP*GPC
75	Saudi Arabia	2,285	POP*GPC
76	Slovenia	2,271	POP*GPC
77	Moldova	2,203	POP*GPC
78	Cambodia	1,922	POP*GPC
79	Cuba	1,873	POP*GPC
80	Bolivia	1,854	POP*GPC
81	Malaysia	1,803	POP*GPC
82	Tunisia	1,687	POP*GPC
83	Somalia	1,668	POP*GPC
84	Estonia	1,554	POP*GPC
85	Guatemala	1,514	POP*GPC
86	Ecuador	1,391	POP*GPC
87	Bosnia	1,350	POP*GPC
88	Armenia	1,347	POP*GPC
89	Ghana	1,241	POP*GPC
90	Sierra Leone	1,182	POP*GPC
91	Puerto Rico	1,070	POP*GPC
92	Zimbabwe	1,065	POP*GPC
93	Turkmenistan	1,046	POP*GPC
94	Haiti	1,042	POP*GPC
95	Tajikistan	1,039	POP*GPC

Table 3.9 Gross Domestic Product at Purchasing Power Parities, Millions of 2012 Dollars, Year 1890

Rank	Country	GDP	Source
96	Kyrgyzstan	949	POP*GPC
97	Zambia	924	POP*GPC
98	Lebanon	903	POP*GPC
99	Burundi	878	POP*GPC
100	Laos	858	POP*GPC
101	Guinea	755	POP*GPC
102	South Sudan	718	POP*GPC
103	Libya	699	POP*GPC
104	Albania	679	POP*GPC
105	Macedonia	652	POP*GPC
106	Malawi	605	POP*GPC
107	El Salvador	585	POP*GPC
108	Jamaica	571	POP*GPC
109	Cyprus	530	POP*GPC
110	Mongolia	454	POP*GPC
111	Trinidad & T	453	POP*GPC
112	Israel	444	POP*GPC
113	Nicaragua	409	POP*GPC
114	Kosovo	400	POP*GPC
115	Namibia	399	POP*GPC
116	Paraguay	396	POP*GPC
117	Jordan	395	POP*GPC
118	Oman	368	POP*GPC
119	Honduras	363	POP*GPC
120	Montenegro	336	POP*GPC
121	Hong Kong	306	POP*GPC
122	Dominican R	291	POP*GPC
123	Costa Rica	268	POP*GPC
124	Panama	262	POP*GPC
125	Eritrea	243	POP*GPC
126	Singapore	224	POP*GPC
127	Iceland	214	POP*GPC
128	Guinea-Biss	158	POP*GPC
129	Lesotho	141	POP*GPC
130	Botswana	115	POP*GPC
131	Swaziland	85	POP*GPC
132	Kuwait	85	POP*GPC
133	Bahrain	64	POP*GPC
134	UAE	42	POP*GPC
135	Qatar	15	POP*GPC

Table 3.10 Gross Domestic Product at Purchasing Power Parities, Millions of 2012 Dollars, Year 1900

Rank	Country	GDP	Source
1	US	489,039	POP*GPC
2	China	341,137	POP*GPC
3	UK	270,118	POP*GPC
4	Germany	254,050	POP*GPC
5	India	231,570	POP*GPC
6	France	182,711	POP*GPC
7	Russia	148,630	POP*GPC
8	Italy	94,054	POP*GPC
9	Japan	81,437	POP*GPC
10	Poland	59,489	POP*GPC
11	Spain	51,889	POP*GPC
12	Indonesia	49,700	POP*GPC
13	Ukraine	41,746	POP*GPC
14	Belgium	39,229	POP*GPC
15	Mexico	29,086	POP*GPC
16	Netherlands	27,551	POP*GPC
17	Austria	26,938	POP*GPC
18	Bangladesh	26,515	POP*GPC
19	Canada	24,858	POP*GPC
20	Czechia	24,728	POP*GPC
21	Romania	24,357	POP*GPC
22	Turkey	23,563	POP*GPC
23	Australia	23,492	POP*GPC
24	Sweden	20,507	POP*GPC
25	Argentina	20,240	POP*GPC
26	Pakistan	19,936	POP*GPC
27	Switzerland	19,794	POP*GPC
28	Brazil	19,080	POP*GPC
29	Hungary	18,759	POP*GPC
30	Vietnam	16,397	POP*GPC
31	Iran	14,362	POP*GPC
32	Egypt	12,836	POP*GPC
33	Denmark	12,091	POP*GPC
34	Ireland	11,945	POP*GPC
35	Korea, South	11,577	POP*GPC
36	Portugal	11,010	POP*GPC
37	Greece	10,490	POP*GPC
38	Chile	10,216	POP*GPC
39	Burma	9,939	POP*GPC
40	Kazakhstan	9,790	POP*GPC
41	South Africa	9,782	POP*GPC
42	Belarus	9,702	POP*GPC
43	Thailand	9,259	POP*GPC
44	Slovakia	8,374	POP*GPC
45	Philippines	7,955	POP*GPC
46	Sri Lanka	7,897	POP*GPC

Table 3.10 Gross Domestic Product at Purchasing Power Parities, Millions of 2012 Dollars, Year 1900

Rank	Country	GDP	Source
47	Algeria	7,736	POP*GPC
48	Bulgaria	7,655	POP*GPC
49	Finland	6,906	POP*GPC
50	Uzbekistan	6,843	POP*GPC
51	Norway	6,759	POP*GPC
52	Serbia	6,241	POP*GPC
53	Colombia	6,087	POP*GPC
54	Korea, North	5,588	POP*GPC
55	Sudan	5,544	POP*GPC
56	New Zealand	5,428	POP*GPC
57	Afghanistan	5,091	POP*GPC
58	Mozambique	4,947	POP*GPC
59	Peru	4,847	POP*GPC
60	Morocco	4,831	POP*GPC
61	Croatia	4,723	POP*GPC
62	Lithuania	4,561	POP*GPC
63	Georgia	4,416	POP*GPC
64	Nepal	4,063	POP*GPC
65	Ethiopia	3,950	POP*GPC
66	Syria	3,408	POP*GPC
67	Venezuela	3,266	POP*GPC
68	Madagascar	3,212	POP*GPC
69	Iraq	3,179	POP*GPC
70	Uruguay	3,177	POP*GPC
71	Latvia	3,042	POP*GPC
72	Taiwan	2,994	POP*GPC
73	Azerbaijan	2,975	POP*GPC
74	Yemen	2,913	POP*GPC
75	Slovenia	2,801	POP*GPC
76	Moldova	2,714	POP*GPC
77	Malaysia	2,659	POP*GPC
78	Cuba	2,402	POP*GPC
79	Saudi Arabia	2,381	POP*GPC
80	Bolivia	2,304	POP*GPC
81	Cambodia	2,215	POP*GPC
82	Tunisia	2,031	POP*GPC
83	Guatemala	1,919	POP*GPC
84	Estonia	1,914	POP*GPC
85	Somalia	1,909	POP*GPC
86	Ecuador	1,847	POP*GPC
87	Bosnia	1,665	POP*GPC
88	Armenia	1,659	POP*GPC
89	Ghana	1,474	POP*GPC
90	Puerto Rico	1,456	POP*GPC
91	Sierra Leone	1,290	POP*GPC
92	Turkmenistan	1,288	POP*GPC
93	Tajikistan	1,280	POP*GPC
94	Zimbabwe	1,275	POP*GPC

Table 3.10 Gross Domestic Product at Purchasing Power Parities, Millions of 2012 Dollars, Year 1900

Rank	Country	GDP	Source
95	Kyrgyzstan	1,169	POP*GPC
96	Haiti	1,161	POP*GPC
97	Zambia	1,100	POP*GPC
98	Lebanon	1,083	POP*GPC
99	Laos	1,070	POP*GPC
100	Burundi	941	POP*GPC
101	Albania	858	POP*GPC
102	Guinea	820	POP*GPC
103	El Salvador	808	POP*GPC
104	Macedonia	804	POP*GPC
105	Libya	768	POP*GPC
106	South Sudan	747	POP*GPC
107	Malawi	698	POP*GPC
108	Trinidad & T	697	POP*GPC
109	Cyprus	673	POP*GPC
110	Jamaica	668	POP*GPC
111	Israel	560	POP*GPC
112	Nicaragua	547	POP*GPC
113	Hong Kong	507	POP*GPC
114	Namibia	505	POP*GPC
115	Kosovo	494	POP*GPC
116	Paraguay	493	POP*GPC
117	Mongolia	465	POP*GPC
118	Dominican R	465	POP*GPC
119	Honduras	465	POP*GPC
120	Jordan	454	POP*GPC
121	Montenegro	415	POP*GPC
122	Costa Rica	413	POP*GPC
123	Oman	389	POP*GPC
124	Panama	357	POP*GPC
125	Singapore	356	POP*GPC
126	Iceland	283	POP*GPC
127	Eritrea	282	POP*GPC
128	Guinea-Biss	171	POP*GPC
129	Lesotho	168	POP*GPC
130	Botswana	129	POP*GPC
131	Swaziland	105	POP*GPC
132	Kuwait	90	POP*GPC
133	Bahrain	68	POP*GPC
134	UAE	45	POP*GPC
135	Qatar	16	POP*GPC

Rank	Country	GDP	Source
1	US	809,667	POP*GPC
2	China	377,600	POP*GPC
3	Germany	371,388	POP*GPC
4	UK	328,228	POP*GPC
5	India	261,351	POP*GPC
6	France	226,118	POP*GPC
7	Russia	224,301	POP*GPC
8	Italy	149,449	POP*GPC
9	Japan	112,151	POP*GPC
10	Poland	72,685	POP*GPC
11	Indonesia	70,638	POP*GPC
12	Spain	65,193	POP*GPC
13	Ukraine	62,999	POP*GPC
14	Canada	54,641	POP*GPC
15	Belgium	50,624	POP*GPC
16	Argentina	45,472	POP*GPC
17	Mexico	40,573	POP*GPC
18	Netherlands	39,056	POP*GPC
19	Australia	38,905	POP*GPC
20	Austria	36,692	POP*GPC
21	Romania	34,129	POP*GPC
22	Czechia	32,700	POP*GPC
23	Bangladesh	30,690	POP*GPC
24	Brazil	30,027	POP*GPC
25	Turkey	28,472	POP*GPC
26	Sweden	27,232	POP*GPC
27	Switzerland	25,795	POP*GPC
28	Hungary	25,739	POP*GPC
29	Pakistan	22,825	POP*GPC
30	Vietnam	22,001	POP*GPC
31	Denmark	18,261	POP*GPC
32	Iran	17,204	POP*GPC
33	Egypt	17,200	POP*GPC
34	Chile	16,043	POP*GPC
35	Philippines	15,463	POP*GPC
36	South Africa	15,425	POP*GPC
37	Kazakhstan	14,774	POP*GPC
38	Belarus	14,641	POP*GPC
39	Korea, South	13,588	POP*GPC
40	Greece	13,515	POP*GPC
41	Ireland	13,240	POP*GPC
42	Burma	13,212	POP*GPC
43	Portugal	11,682	POP*GPC
44	Thailand	11,435	POP*GPC
45	Bulgaria	11,330	POP*GPC
46	Slovakia	11,073	POP*GPC
47	Uzbekistan	10,327	POP*GPC

Table 3.11 Gross Domestic Product at Purchasing Power Parities, Millions of 2012 Dollars, Year 1913

Rank	Country	GDP	Source
48	Colombia	10,048	POP*GPC
49	Algeria	10,004	POP*GPC
50	Finland	9,999	POP*GPC
51	Norway	9,577	POP*GPC
52	Sri Lanka	9,290	POP*GPC
53	New Zealand	9,046	POP*GPC
54	Serbia	8,895	POP*GPC
55	Peru	7,041	POP*GPC
56	Lithuania	6,883	POP*GPC
57	Croatia	6,732	POP*GPC
58	Georgia	6,664	POP*GPC
59	Korea, North	6,284	POP*GPC
60	Sudan	6,206	POP*GPC
61	Afghanistan	6,195	POP*GPC
62	Mozambique	6,101	POP*GPC
63	Uruguay	6,096	POP*GPC
64	Morocco	5,679	POP*GPC
65	Venezuela	4,965	POP*GPC
66	Ethiopia	4,808	POP*GPC
67	Nepal	4,756	POP*GPC
68	Latvia	4,591	POP*GPC
69	Azerbaijan	4,490	POP*GPC
70	Cuba	4,422	POP*GPC
71	Malaysia	4,343	POP*GPC
72	Syria	4,212	POP*GPC
73	Moldova	4,095	POP*GPC
74	Iraq	4,089	POP*GPC
75	Taiwan	4,055	POP*GPC
76	Slovenia	3,993	POP*GPC
77	Madagascar	3,827	POP*GPC
78	Bolivia	3,209	POP*GPC
79	Yemen	3,083	POP*GPC
80	Estonia	2,889	POP*GPC
81	Ecuador	2,798	POP*GPC
82	Guatemala	2,755	POP*GPC
83	Cambodia	2,666	POP*GPC
84	Tunisia	2,584	POP*GPC
85	Saudi Arabia	2,513	POP*GPC
86	Armenia	2,503	POP*GPC
87	Ghana	2,497	POP*GPC
88	Bosnia	2,373	POP*GPC
89	Somalia	2,274	POP*GPC
90	Puerto Rico	2,251	POP*GPC
91	Turkmenistan	1,943	POP*GPC
92	Tajikistan	1,931	POP*GPC
93	Haiti	1,767	POP*GPC
94	Kyrgyzstan	1,764	POP*GPC
95	Zimbabwe	1,610	POP*GPC

Table 3.11 Gross Domestic Product at Purchasing Power Parities, Millions of 2012 Dollars, Year 1913

Rank	Country	GDP	Source
96	Sierra Leone	1,445	POP*GPC
97	Laos	1,425	POP*GPC
98	Zambia	1,382	POP*GPC
99	Lebanon	1,371	POP*GPC
100	El Salvador	1,334	POP*GPC
101	Trinidad & T	1,150	POP*GPC
102	Macedonia	1,146	POP*GPC
103	Albania	1,140	POP*GPC
104	Burundi	1,030	POP*GPC
105	Hong Kong	975	POP*GPC
106	Guinea	913	POP*GPC
107	Libya	868	POP*GPC
108	Cyprus	867	POP*GPC
109	Malawi	841	POP*GPC
110	Paraguay	837	POP*GPC
111	Nicaragua	830	POP*GPC
112	Jamaica	812	POP*GPC
113	South Sudan	786	POP*GPC
114	Honduras	770	POP*GPC
115	Israel	757	POP*GPC
116	Kosovo	704	POP*GPC
117	Namibia	685	POP*GPC
118	Dominican R	685	POP*GPC
119	Costa Rica	649	POP*GPC
120	Singapore	646	POP*GPC
121	Panama	593	POP*GPC
122	Montenegro	592	POP*GPC
123	Jordan	545	POP*GPC
124	Mongolia	529	POP*GPC
125	Oman	417	POP*GPC
126	Iceland	409	POP*GPC
127	Eritrea	344	POP*GPC
128	Lesotho	212	POP*GPC
129	Guinea-Biss	191	POP*GPC
130	Botswana	149	POP*GPC
131	Swaziland	139	POP*GPC
132	Kuwait	98	POP*GPC
133	Bahrain	75	POP*GPC
134	UAE	49	POP*GPC
135	Qatar	17	POP*GPC

Table 3.12 Gross Domestic Product at Purchasing Power Parities, Millions of 2012 Dollars, Year 1920

Rank	Country	GDP	Source
1	US	928,585	POP*GPC
2	China	410,924	POP*GPC
3	UK	311,138	POP*GPC
4	Germany	266,430	POP*GPC
5	India	249,329	POP*GPC
6	France	196,941	POP*GPC
7	Italy	151,397	POP*GPC
8	Japan	148,140	POP*GPC
9	Russia	86,028	POP*GPC
10	Indonesia	79,445	POP*GPC
11	Spain	72,330	POP*GPC
12	Poland	71,084	POP*GPC
13	Canada	53,156	POP*GPC
14	Argentina	48,157	POP*GPC
15	Belgium	46,822	POP*GPC
16	Netherlands	45,222	POP*GPC
17	Mexico	42,505	POP*GPC
18	Brazil	41,296	POP*GPC
19	Australia	39,960	POP*GPC
20	Bangladesh	31,096	POP*GPC
21	Czechia	29,552	POP*GPC
22	Switzerland	26,173	POP*GPC
23	Sweden	25,765	POP*GPC
24	Austria	24,364	POP*GPC
25	Ukraine	24,163	POP*GPC
26	Pakistan	23,444	POP*GPC
27	Vietnam	23,055	POP*GPC
28	Philippines	21,633	POP*GPC
29	Hungary	21,261	POP*GPC
30	Iran	20,681	POP*GPC
31	Denmark	20,252	POP*GPC
32	Romania	19,922	POP*GPC
33	South Africa	19,570	POP*GPC
34	Korea, South	18,638	POP*GPC
35	Egypt	18,398	POP*GPC
36	Greece	16,714	POP*GPC
37	Chile	16,390	POP*GPC
38	Turkey	15,461	POP*GPC
39	Burma	15,003	POP*GPC
40	Thailand	12,572	POP*GPC
41	Ireland	12,419	POP*GPC
42	Colombia	12,202	POP*GPC
43	Portugal	11,595	POP*GPC
44	Algeria	11,433	POP*GPC
45	Norway	11,419	POP*GPC
46	New Zealand	10,955	POP*GPC
47	Slovakia	10,007	POP*GPC

Table 3.12 Gross Domestic Product at Purchasing Power Parities, Millions of 2012 Dollars, Year 1920

Rank	Country	GDP	Source
48	Peru	9,720	POP*GPC
49	Finland	9,050	POP*GPC
50	Sri Lanka	8,971	POP*GPC
51	Korea, North	8,806	POP*GPC
52	Serbia	7,930	POP*GPC
53	Morocco	7,232	POP*GPC
54	Bulgaria	7,215	POP*GPC
55	Mozambique	6,830	POP*GPC
56	Sudan	6,595	POP*GPC
57	Afghanistan	6,537	POP*GPC
58	Malaysia	6,158	POP*GPC
59	Cuba	6,067	POP*GPC
60	Croatia	6,002	POP*GPC
61	Lithuania	5,958	POP*GPC
62	Uruguay	5,737	POP*GPC
63	Kazakhstan	5,667	POP*GPC
64	Belarus	5,615	POP*GPC
65	Taiwan	5,607	POP*GPC
66	Venezuela	5,492	POP*GPC
67	Ethiopia	5,345	POP*GPC
68	Syria	5,227	POP*GPC
69	Nepal	5,079	POP*GPC
70	Iraq	4,964	POP*GPC
71	Madagascar	4,206	POP*GPC
72	Bolivia	4,056	POP*GPC
73	Latvia	3,974	POP*GPC
74	Uzbekistan	3,961	POP*GPC
75	Georgia	3,909	POP*GPC
76	Yemen	3,582	POP*GPC
77	Slovenia	3,560	POP*GPC
78	Saudi Arabia	3,332	POP*GPC
79	Ecuador	3,300	POP*GPC
80	Ghana	3,202	POP*GPC
81	Guatemala	3,179	POP*GPC
82	Tunisia	3,043	POP*GPC
83	Cambodia	2,825	POP*GPC
84	Puerto Rico	2,783	POP*GPC
85	Estonia	2,501	POP*GPC
86	Somalia	2,499	POP*GPC
87	Moldova	2,402	POP*GPC
88	Haiti	2,209	POP*GPC
89	Bosnia	2,116	POP*GPC
90	Zimbabwe	1,826	POP*GPC
91	Lebanon	1,782	POP*GPC
92	Azerbaijan	1,722	POP*GPC
93	El Salvador	1,706	POP*GPC
94	Zambia	1,562	POP*GPC
95	Sierra Leone	1,536	POP*GPC

Table 3.12 Gross Domestic Product at Purchasing Power Parities, Millions of 2012 Dollars, Year 1920			
Rank	Country	GDP	Source
96	Hong Kong	1,439	POP*GPC
97	Honduras	1,435	POP*GPC
98	Laos	1,432	POP*GPC
99	Trinidad & T	1,414	POP*GPC
100	Nicaragua	1,266	POP*GPC
101	Albania	1,253	POP*GPC
102	Israel	1,108	POP*GPC
103	Paraguay	1,096	POP*GPC
104	Burundi	1,081	POP*GPC
105	Cyprus	1,073	POP*GPC
106	Costa Rica	1,067	POP*GPC
107	Macedonia	1,022	POP*GPC
108	Guinea	968	POP*GPC
109	Armenia	960	POP*GPC
110	Jamaica	941	POP*GPC
111	Malawi	929	POP*GPC
112	Libya	927	POP*GPC
113	Panama	923	POP*GPC
114	Dominican R	893	POP*GPC
115	Singapore	869	POP*GPC
116	Namibia	808	POP*GPC
117	South Sudan	808	POP*GPC
118	Turkmenistan	745	POP*GPC
119	Tajikistan	741	POP*GPC
120	Kyrgyzstan	677	POP*GPC
121	Jordan	635	POP*GPC
122	Kosovo	627	POP*GPC
123	Montenegro	528	POP*GPC
124	Mongolia	525	POP*GPC
125	Iceland	451	POP*GPC
126	Oman	422	POP*GPC
127	Eritrea	382	POP*GPC
128	Lesotho	239	POP*GPC
129	Kuwait	217	POP*GPC
130	Guinea-Biss	202	POP*GPC
131	Botswana	162	POP*GPC
132	Swaziland	161	POP*GPC
133	Bahrain	101	POP*GPC
134	UAE	96	POP*GPC
135	Qatar	38	POP*GPC

Table 3.13 Gross Domestic Product at Purchasing Power Parities, Millions of 2012 Dollars, Year 1929

Rank	Country	GDP	Source
1	US	1,319,742	POP*GPC
2	China	428,529	POP*GPC
3	Germany	410,393	POP*GPC
4	UK	393,298	POP*GPC
5	France	303,883	POP*GPC
6	India	287,067	POP*GPC
7	Russia	236,264	POP*GPC
8	Japan	200,508	POP*GPC
9	Italy	195,873	POP*GPC
10	Indonesia	109,601	POP*GPC
11	Spain	99,481	POP*GPC
12	Poland	92,281	POP*GPC
13	Canada	81,677	POP*GPC
14	Argentina	79,216	POP*GPC
15	Netherlands	69,279	POP*GPC
16	Ukraine	66,359	POP*GPC
17	Belgium	63,523	POP*GPC
18	Brazil	58,526	POP*GPC
19	Australia	52,676	POP*GPC
20	Czechia	49,749	POP*GPC
21	Mexico	46,397	POP*GPC
22	Switzerland	39,852	POP*GPC
23	Austria	38,574	POP*GPC
24	Sweden	37,011	POP*GPC
25	Bangladesh	33,347	POP*GPC
26	Hungary	33,255	POP*GPC
27	Philippines	30,297	POP*GPC
28	Denmark	27,939	POP*GPC
29	Turkey	27,912	POP*GPC
30	South Africa	26,577	POP*GPC
31	Pakistan	26,238	POP*GPC
32	Iran	26,204	POP*GPC
33	Chile	25,773	POP*GPC
34	Romania	25,151	POP*GPC
35	Vietnam	24,486	POP*GPC
36	Greece	22,997	POP*GPC
37	Korea, South	21,764	POP*GPC
38	Egypt	19,948	POP*GPC
39	Burma	19,459	POP*GPC
40	Colombia	18,419	POP*GPC
41	Venezuela	17,472	POP*GPC
42	Portugal	16,883	POP*GPC
43	Slovakia	16,846	POP*GPC
44	Kazakhstan	15,562	POP*GPC
45	Belarus	15,422	POP*GPC
46	Norway	15,186	POP*GPC
47	Thailand	14,963	POP*GPC

Table 3.13 Gross Domestic Product at Purchasing Power Parities, Millions of 2012 Dollars, Year 1929

Rank	Country	GDP	Source
48	Finland	14,558	POP*GPC
49	Algeria	13,738	POP*GPC
50	Peru	13,412	POP*GPC
51	Ireland	12,979	POP*GPC
52	New Zealand	12,113	POP*GPC
53	Serbia	11,988	POP*GPC
54	Sri Lanka	11,852	POP*GPC
55	Malaysia	11,360	POP*GPC
56	Bulgaria	10,987	POP*GPC
57	Uzbekistan	10,878	POP*GPC
58	Korea, North	10,460	POP*GPC
59	Uruguay	10,144	POP*GPC
60	Morocco	9,869	POP*GPC
61	Lithuania	9,756	POP*GPC
62	Cuba	9,597	POP*GPC
63	Croatia	9,073	POP*GPC
64	Taiwan	8,057	POP*GPC
65	Mozambique	7,897	POP*GPC
66	Sudan	7,130	POP*GPC
67	Georgia	7,020	POP*GPC
68	Afghanistan	7,004	POP*GPC
69	Syria	6,897	POP*GPC
70	Latvia	6,507	POP*GPC
71	Iraq	6,370	POP*GPC
72	Ethiopia	6,124	POP*GPC
73	Nepal	5,519	POP*GPC
74	Slovenia	5,381	POP*GPC
75	Bolivia	5,163	POP*GPC
76	Saudi Arabia	4,791	POP*GPC
77	Madagascar	4,748	POP*GPC
78	Azerbaijan	4,729	POP*GPC
79	Guatemala	4,718	POP*GPC
80	Ghana	4,409	POP*GPC
81	Yemen	4,343	POP*GPC
82	Estonia	4,095	POP*GPC
83	Ecuador	4,078	POP*GPC
84	Tunisia	3,756	POP*GPC
85	Puerto Rico	3,714	POP*GPC
86	Bosnia	3,199	POP*GPC
87	Cambodia	3,044	POP*GPC
88	Moldova	2,984	POP*GPC
89	Haiti	2,852	POP*GPC
90	Somalia	2,822	POP*GPC
91	Armenia	2,637	POP*GPC
92	Lebanon	2,497	POP*GPC
93	El Salvador	2,297	POP*GPC
94	Honduras	2,182	POP*GPC
95	Zimbabwe	2,146	POP*GPC

TABLE 3.13 GROSS DOMESTIC PRODUCT AT PURCHASING POWER PARITIES, MILLIONS OF 2012 DOLLARS, YEAR 1929

Rank	Country	GDP	Source
96	Turkmenistan	2,047	POP*GPC
97	Tajikistan	2,034	POP*GPC
98	Hong Kong	1,993	POP*GPC
99	Nicaragua	1,862	POP*GPC
100	Kyrgyzstan	1,858	POP*GPC
101	Zambia	1,828	POP*GPC
102	Israel	1,808	POP*GPC
103	Sierra Leone	1,661	POP*GPC
104	Trinidad & T	1,660	POP*GPC
105	Paraguay	1,547	POP*GPC
106	Macedonia	1,545	POP*GPC
107	Cyprus	1,476	POP*GPC
108	Singapore	1,460	POP*GPC
109	Laos	1,441	POP*GPC
110	Albania	1,416	POP*GPC
111	Dominican R	1,414	POP*GPC
112	Jamaica	1,274	POP*GPC
113	Costa Rica	1,213	POP*GPC
114	Burundi	1,151	POP*GPC
115	Panama	1,101	POP*GPC
116	Malawi	1,057	POP*GPC
117	Guinea	1,043	POP*GPC
118	Libya	1,009	POP*GPC
119	Namibia	999	POP*GPC
120	Kosovo	948	POP*GPC
121	South Sudan	837	POP*GPC
122	Montenegro	797	POP*GPC
123	Jordan	774	POP*GPC
124	Iceland	646	POP*GPC
125	Kuwait	604	POP*GPC
126	Mongolia	520	POP*GPC
127	Eritrea	438	POP*GPC
128	Oman	429	POP*GPC
129	Lesotho	281	POP*GPC
130	UAE	231	POP*GPC
131	Guinea-Biss	218	POP*GPC
132	Swaziland	196	POP*GPC
133	Botswana	179	POP*GPC
134	Bahrain	148	POP*GPC
135	Qatar	106	POP*GPC

Table 3.14 Gross Domestic Product at Purchasing Power Parities, Millions of 2012 Dollars, Year 1938			
Rank	Country	GDP	Source
1	US	1,250,776	POP*GPC
2	Germany	535,770	POP*GPC
3	UK	465,694	POP*GPC
4	China	451,450	POP*GPC
5	Russia	401,613	POP*GPC
6	India	299,731	POP*GPC
7	France	293,242	POP*GPC
8	Japan	275,463	POP*GPC
9	Italy	225,303	POP*GPC
10	Indonesia	125,272	POP*GPC
11	Ukraine	112,801	POP*GPC
12	Poland	106,061	POP*GPC
13	Argentina	87,450	POP*GPC
14	Canada	81,467	POP*GPC
15	Brazil	78,831	POP*GPC
16	Netherlands	71,351	POP*GPC
17	Spain	70,808	POP*GPC
18	Australia	63,591	POP*GPC
19	Belgium	63,319	POP*GPC
20	Mexico	55,319	POP*GPC
21	Czechia	49,573	POP*GPC
22	Sweden	46,567	POP*GPC
23	Turkey	45,906	POP*GPC
24	Switzerland	41,917	POP*GPC
25	Hungary	38,086	POP*GPC
26	Philippines	37,950	POP*GPC
27	Austria	37,609	POP*GPC
28	South Africa	36,092	POP*GPC
29	Bangladesh	35,745	POP*GPC
30	Korea, South	35,117	POP*GPC
31	Denmark	34,056	POP*GPC
32	Iran	33,202	POP*GPC
33	Romania	30,321	POP*GPC
34	Greece	29,579	POP*GPC
35	Pakistan	28,431	POP*GPC
36	Chile	27,191	POP*GPC
37	Kazakhstan	26,453	POP*GPC
38	Belarus	26,215	POP*GPC
39	Vietnam	26,006	POP*GPC
40	Colombia	25,097	POP*GPC
41	Venezuela	23,494	POP*GPC
42	Egypt	22,696	POP*GPC
43	Finland	20,533	POP*GPC
44	Portugal	20,471	POP*GPC
45	Norway	19,926	POP*GPC
46	Thailand	19,363	POP*GPC
47	Burma	18,696	POP*GPC

TABLE 3.14 GROSS DOMESTIC PRODUCT AT PURCHASING POWER PARITIES, MILLIONS OF 2012 DOLLARS, YEAR 1938

Rank	Country	GDP	Source
48	Uzbekistan	18,491	POP*GPC
49	Korea, North	17,789	POP*GPC
50	Slovakia	16,787	POP*GPC
51	Peru	16,752	POP*GPC
52	Bulgaria	16,383	POP*GPC
53	New Zealand	16,220	POP*GPC
54	Algeria	15,732	POP*GPC
55	Lithuania	14,122	POP*GPC
56	Ireland	14,027	POP*GPC
57	Serbia	13,505	POP*GPC
58	Morocco	13,467	POP*GPC
59	Georgia	11,933	POP*GPC
60	Sri Lanka	11,588	POP*GPC
61	Taiwan	11,569	POP*GPC
62	Uruguay	11,229	POP*GPC
63	Malaysia	11,090	POP*GPC
64	Croatia	10,221	POP*GPC
65	Latvia	9,419	POP*GPC
66	Cuba	9,410	POP*GPC
67	Mozambique	9,131	POP*GPC
68	Syria	9,102	POP*GPC
69	Iraq	8,174	POP*GPC
70	Azerbaijan	8,039	POP*GPC
71	Sudan	7,709	POP*GPC
72	Afghanistan	7,504	POP*GPC
73	Guatemala	7,343	POP*GPC
74	Ethiopia	7,017	POP*GPC
75	Saudi Arabia	6,887	POP*GPC
76	Bolivia	6,572	POP*GPC
77	Ghana	6,071	POP*GPC
78	Slovenia	6,062	POP*GPC
79	Nepal	6,000	POP*GPC
80	Estonia	5,928	POP*GPC
81	Ecuador	5,715	POP*GPC
82	Madagascar	5,360	POP*GPC
83	Yemen	5,267	POP*GPC
84	Puerto Rico	5,055	POP*GPC
85	Tunisia	4,635	POP*GPC
86	Armenia	4,482	POP*GPC
87	Hong Kong	4,294	POP*GPC
88	Haiti	3,672	POP*GPC
89	Bosnia	3,603	POP*GPC
90	Moldova	3,526	POP*GPC
91	Lebanon	3,499	POP*GPC
92	Turkmenistan	3,480	POP*GPC
93	Tajikistan	3,458	POP*GPC
94	Cambodia	3,280	POP*GPC
95	Somalia	3,186	POP*GPC

TABLE 3.14 GROSS DOMESTIC PRODUCT AT PURCHASING POWER PARITIES, MILLIONS OF 2012 DOLLARS, YEAR 1938

Rank	Country	GDP	Source
96	Kyrgyzstan	3,159	POP*GPC
97	Israel	2,949	POP*GPC
98	Zimbabwe	2,523	POP*GPC
99	El Salvador	2,431	POP*GPC
100	Trinidad & T	2,192	POP*GPC
101	Paraguay	2,189	POP*GPC
102	Zambia	2,140	POP*GPC
103	Dominican R	2,135	POP*GPC
104	Singapore	2,062	POP*GPC
105	Honduras	1,902	POP*GPC
106	Cyprus	1,899	POP*GPC
107	Sierra Leone	1,797	POP*GPC
108	Jamaica	1,769	POP*GPC
109	Macedonia	1,740	POP*GPC
110	Costa Rica	1,732	POP*GPC
111	Kuwait	1,678	POP*GPC
112	Panama	1,597	POP*GPC
113	Albania	1,558	POP*GPC
114	Laos	1,450	POP*GPC
115	Nicaragua	1,313	POP*GPC
116	Namibia	1,235	POP*GPC
117	Burundi	1,225	POP*GPC
118	Malawi	1,203	POP*GPC
119	Guinea	1,124	POP*GPC
120	Libya	1,098	POP*GPC
121	Kosovo	1,068	POP*GPC
122	Jordan	943	POP*GPC
123	Montenegro	898	POP*GPC
124	South Sudan	868	POP*GPC
125	Iceland	817	POP*GPC
126	UAE	554	POP*GPC
127	Mongolia	515	POP*GPC
128	Eritrea	501	POP*GPC
129	Oman	435	POP*GPC
130	Lesotho	330	POP*GPC
131	Qatar	299	POP*GPC
132	Swaziland	238	POP*GPC
133	Guinea-Biss	235	POP*GPC
134	Bahrain	217	POP*GPC
135	Botswana	198	POP*GPC

Table 3.15 Gross Domestic Product at Purchasing Power Parities, Millions of 2012 Dollars, Year 1950

Rank	Country	GDP	Source
1	US	2,278,203	POP*GPC
2	UK	546,073	POP*GPC
3	Russia	492,682	POP*GPC
4	Germany	415,265	POP*GPC
5	China	386,474	POP*GPC
6	India	358,281	POP*GPC
7	France	344,251	POP*GPC
8	Italy	258,134	POP*GPC
9	Japan	251,383	POP*GPC
10	Canada	159,856	POP*GPC
11	Brazil	141,221	POP*GPC
12	Argentina	133,837	POP*GPC
13	Ukraine	133,427	POP*GPC
14	Indonesia	104,550	POP*GPC
15	Mexico	102,666	POP*GPC
16	Spain	95,460	POP*GPC
17	Australia	95,329	POP*GPC
18	Poland	95,056	POP*GPC
19	Netherlands	94,673	POP*GPC
20	Sweden	73,966	POP*GPC
21	Belgium	73,839	POP*GPC
22	Switzerland	66,579	POP*GPC
23	Venezuela	59,482	POP*GPC
24	Turkey	54,564	POP*GPC
25	South Africa	53,934	POP*GPC
26	Czechia	51,090	POP*GPC
27	Denmark	46,403	POP*GPC
28	Iran	45,522	POP*GPC
29	Colombia	42,343	POP*GPC
30	Austria	40,218	POP*GPC
31	Pakistan	39,692	POP*GPC
32	Bangladesh	38,572	POP*GPC
33	Kazakhstan	38,157	POP*GPC
34	Nigeria	37,467	POP*GPC
35	Chile	36,420	POP*GPC
36	Hungary	36,239	POP*GPC
37	Philippines	33,481	POP*GPC
38	Romania	30,170	POP*GPC
39	Belarus	29,738	POP*GPC
40	Egypt	29,137	POP*GPC
41	Vietnam	28,179	POP*GPC
42	Norway	27,912	POP*GPC
43	Portugal	27,560	POP*GPC
44	Peru	27,027	POP*GPC
45	Finland	26,681	POP*GPC
46	Thailand	26,346	POP*GPC
47	New Zealand	25,261	POP*GPC

TABLE 3.15 GROSS DOMESTIC PRODUCT AT PURCHASING POWER PARITIES, MILLIONS OF 2012 DOLLARS, YEAR 1950

Rank	Country	GDP	Source
48	Korea, South	25,118	POP*GPC
49	Uzbekistan	23,535	POP*GPC
50	Greece	22,673	POP*GPC
51	Morocco	20,385	POP*GPC
52	Cuba	18,954	POP*GPC
53	Bulgaria	18,733	POP*GPC
54	Algeria	18,697	POP*GPC
55	Slovakia	17,301	POP*GPC
56	Uruguay	16,324	POP*GPC
57	Ireland	16,043	POP*GPC
58	Serbia	15,652	POP*GPC
59	Georgia	15,439	POP*GPC
60	Malaysia	14,906	POP*GPC
61	Sri Lanka	14,390	POP*GPC
62	Lithuania	14,251	POP*GPC
63	Syria	13,175	POP*GPC
64	Congo, Dem R	12,103	POP*GPC
65	Burma	12,076	POP*GPC
66	Croatia	11,846	POP*GPC
67	Korea, North	11,732	POP*GPC
68	Iraq	11,398	POP*GPC
69	Latvia	11,254	POP*GPC
70	Saudi Arabia	11,175	POP*GPC
71	Mozambique	11,081	POP*GPC
72	Taiwan	11,016	POP*GPC
73	Ecuador	9,874	POP*GPC
74	Sudan	9,766	POP*GPC
75	Guatemala	9,687	POP*GPC
76	Azerbaijan	9,386	POP*GPC
77	Ghana	9,300	POP*GPC
78	Moldova	9,215	POP*GPC
79	Ethiopia	8,413	POP*GPC
80	Afghanistan	8,227	POP*GPC
81	Bolivia	8,150	POP*GPC
82	Hong Kong	7,764	POP*GPC
83	Puerto Rico	7,441	POP*GPC
84	Estonia	7,127	POP*GPC
85	Slovenia	7,026	POP*GPC
86	Yemen	6,810	POP*GPC
87	Angola	6,779	POP*GPC
88	Nepal	6,708	POP*GPC
89	Kuwait	6,552	POP*GPC
90	Madagascar	6,301	POP*GPC
91	Kenya	6,236	POP*GPC
92	Tunisia	6,136	POP*GPC
93	Armenia	6,092	POP*GPC
94	Israel	5,545	POP*GPC
95	Uganda	5,545	POP*GPC

TABLE 3.15 GROSS DOMESTIC PRODUCT AT PURCHASING POWER PARITIES, MILLIONS OF 2012 DOLLARS, YEAR 1950

Rank	Country	GDP	Source
96	Lebanon	5,485	POP*GPC
97	Haiti	5,297	POP*GPC
98	Tanzania	5,265	POP*GPC
99	Cameroon	5,132	POP*GPC
100	Senegal	5,010	POP*GPC
101	Kyrgyzstan	4,766	POP*GPC
102	Tajikistan	4,603	POP*GPC
103	El Salvador	4,546	POP*GPC
104	Turkmenistan	4,263	POP*GPC
105	Bosnia	4,176	POP*GPC
106	Ivory Coast	4,081	POP*GPC
107	Luxembourg	3,882	POP*GPC
108	Trinidad & T	3,840	POP*GPC
109	Dominican R	3,782	POP*GPC
110	Somalia	3,745	POP*GPC
111	Paraguay	3,651	POP*GPC
112	Cambodia	3,624	POP*GPC
113	Singapore	3,549	POP*GPC
114	Nicaragua	3,275	POP*GPC
115	Burkina Faso	3,246	POP*GPC
116	Zimbabwe	3,130	POP*GPC
117	Honduras	2,940	POP*GPC
118	Jamaica	2,913	POP*GPC
119	Benin	2,838	POP*GPC
120	Niger	2,809	POP*GPC
121	Panama	2,677	POP*GPC
122	Costa Rica	2,648	POP*GPC
123	Zambia	2,641	POP*GPC
124	Mali	2,637	POP*GPC
125	Gabon	2,023	POP*GPC
126	Macedonia	2,017	POP*GPC
127	Sierra Leone	1,996	POP*GPC
128	Chad	1,943	POP*GPC
129	Albania	1,903	POP*GPC
130	Mauritius	1,866	POP*GPC
131	Rwanda	1,851	POP*GPC
132	UAE	1,780	POP*GPC
133	Papua New G	1,753	POP*GPC
134	Congo, Rep	1,630	POP*GPC
135	CAR	1,587	POP*GPC
136	Namibia	1,568	POP*GPC
137	Laos	1,462	POP*GPC
138	Cyprus	1,455	POP*GPC
139	Malawi	1,428	POP*GPC
140	Libya	1,380	POP*GPC
141	Liberia	1,360	POP*GPC
142	Fiji	1,332	POP*GPC
143	Burundi	1,331	POP*GPC

Table 3.15 Gross Domestic Product at Purchasing Power Parities, Millions of 2012 Dollars, Year 1950

Rank	Country	GDP	Source
144	West Bank	1,297	POP*GPC
145	Guinea	1,242	POP*GPC
146	Kosovo	1,238	POP*GPC
147	Jordan	1,228	POP*GPC
148	Togo	1,194	POP*GPC
149	Iceland	1,192	POP*GPC
150	Qatar	1,189	POP*GPC
151	Bahamas	1,183	POP*GPC
152	Montenegro	1,041	POP*GPC
153	South Sudan	1,038	POP*GPC
154	Guam	892	POP*GPC
155	Reunion	759	POP*GPC
156	Guyana	723	POP*GPC
157	Barbados	701	POP*GPC
158	Eritrea	601	POP*GPC
159	Aruba	592	POP*GPC
160	Guadeloupe	562	POP*GPC
161	Jersey	555	POP*GPC
162	Curacao	526	POP*GPC
163	Mongolia	508	POP*GPC
164	Mauritania	502	POP*GPC
165	Suriname	493	POP*GPC
166	Martinique	459	POP*GPC
167	Oman	445	POP*GPC
168	Malta	435	POP*GPC
169	Fr Polynesia	426	POP*GPC
170	New Caledon	414	POP*GPC
171	Lesotho	408	POP*GPC
172	Bahrain	362	POP*GPC
173	Brunei	351	POP*GPC
174	Guernsey	332	POP*GPC
175	Macao	332	POP*GPC
176	Swaziland	308	POP*GPC
177	East Timor	285	POP*GPC
178	Gambia	279	POP*GPC
179	Gaza Strip	275	POP*GPC
180	Isle of Man	265	POP*GPC
181	Guinea-Biss	259	POP*GPC
182	Virgin I, US	249	POP*GPC
183	Botswana	235	POP*GPC
184	Guiana, Fr	216	POP*GPC
185	Faroe Is	203	POP*GPC
186	Equatorial G	178	POP*GPC
187	Belize	172	POP*GPC
188	Samoa	169	POP*GPC
189	Greenland	157	POP*GPC
190	Monaco	149	POP*GPC
191	Liechtenstn	145	POP*GPC

Table 3.15 Gross Domestic Product at Purchasing Power Parities, Millions of 2012 Dollars, Year 1950

Rank	Country	GDP	Source
192	Djibouti	141	POP*GPC
193	Bhutan	132	POP*GPC
194	Comoros	130	POP*GPC
195	Antigua & B	128	POP*GPC
196	Dominica	128	POP*GPC
197	St Vincent	124	POP*GPC
198	Grenada	111	POP*GPC
199	Vanuatu	105	POP*GPC
200	Cape Verde	103	POP*GPC
201	Seychelles	102	POP*GPC
202	Bermuda	102	POP*GPC
203	Tonga	97	POP*GPC
204	San Marino	97	POP*GPC
205	St Kitts & N	95	POP*GPC
206	St Lucia	95	POP*GPC
207	Cayman Is	94	POP*GPC
208	Solomon Is	84	POP*GPC
209	Palau	80	POP*GPC
210	Sao Tome & P	77	POP*GPC
211	N Mariana Is	70	POP*GPC
212	Gibraltar	70	POP*GPC
213	Micronesia	69	POP*GPC
214	Maldives	67	POP*GPC
215	Samoa, Amer	52	POP*GPC
216	Virgin I, Br	43	POP*GPC
217	Svalbard	39	POP*GPC
218	Andorra	39	POP*GPC
219	Kiribati	30	POP*GPC
220	Nauru	29	POP*GPC
221	Falkland Is	25	POP*GPC
222	St Pierre&M	21	POP*GPC
223	Cook Is	20	POP*GPC
224	Turks & C Is	19	POP*GPC
225	Montserrat	17	POP*GPC
226	Saint Martin	17	POP*GPC
227	Marshall Is	17	POP*GPC
228	Anguilla	15	POP*GPC
229	Saint Helena	13	POP*GPC
230	Sint Maarten	12	POP*GPC
231	Wallis & Fut	10	POP*GPC
232	Mayotte	8	POP*GPC
233	W Sahara	5	POP*GPC
234	Tuvalu	4	POP*GPC
235	Niue	1	POP*GPC
236	Tokelau	1	POP*GPC

Table 3.16 Gross Domestic Product at Purchasing Power Parities, Millions of 2012 Dollars, Year 1960			
Rank	Country	GDP	Source
1	US	3,228,373	POP*GPC
2	Germany	927,989	POP*GPC
3	Russia	901,020	POP*GPC
4	UK	699,807	POP*GPC
5	Japan	575,024	POP*GPC
6	China	552,968	POP*GPC
7	France	543,800	POP*GPC
8	Italy	485,496	POP*GPC
9	India	477,013	POP*GPC
10	Brazil	270,161	POP*GPC
11	Canada	247,856	POP*GPC
12	Ukraine	213,554	POP*GPC
13	Mexico	196,704	POP*GPC
14	Argentina	172,520	POP*GPC
15	Poland	157,091	POP*GPC
16	Spain	154,621	POP*GPC
17	Netherlands	152,650	POP*GPC
18	Australia	143,919	POP*GPC
19	Indonesia	128,261	POP*GPC
20	Switzerland	114,299	POP*GPC
21	Venezuela	105,324	POP*GPC
22	Sweden	104,962	POP*GPC
23	Belgium	103,067	POP*GPC
24	Turkey	96,233	POP*GPC
25	South Africa	92,200	POP*GPC
26	Czechia	86,179	POP*GPC
27	Iran	79,354	POP*GPC
28	Austria	75,661	POP*GPC
29	Kazakhstan	72,417	POP*GPC
30	Denmark	65,059	POP*GPC
31	Hungary	64,710	POP*GPC
32	Romania	63,192	POP*GPC
33	Colombia	60,816	POP*GPC
34	Nigeria	59,656	POP*GPC
35	Philippines	59,566	POP*GPC
36	Pakistan	48,655	POP*GPC
37	Peru	47,955	POP*GPC
38	Chile	47,239	POP*GPC
39	Greece	45,298	POP*GPC
40	Bangladesh	44,367	POP*GPC
41	Finland	44,353	POP*GPC
42	Portugal	42,856	POP*GPC
43	Egypt	42,508	POP*GPC
44	Korea, South	42,260	POP*GPC
45	Norway	42,198	POP*GPC
46	Thailand	41,076	POP*GPC
47	Uzbekistan	39,533	POP*GPC

TABLE 3.16 GROSS DOMESTIC PRODUCT AT PURCHASING POWER PARITIES, MILLIONS OF 2012 DOLLARS, YEAR 1960			
Rank	Country	GDP	Source
48	Belarus	39,233	POP*GPC
49	Algeria	39,157	POP*GPC
50	Vietnam	36,318	POP*GPC
51	New Zealand	36,151	POP*GPC
52	Bulgaria	35,322	POP*GPC
53	Iraq	33,715	POP*GPC
54	Saudi Arabia	31,824	POP*GPC
55	Slovakia	31,373	POP*GPC
56	Serbia	30,045	POP*GPC
57	Taiwan	24,635	POP*GPC
58	Morocco	24,285	POP*GPC
59	Georgia	23,328	POP*GPC
60	Cuba	22,713	POP*GPC
61	Lithuania	22,494	POP*GPC
62	Croatia	21,233	POP*GPC
63	Malaysia	20,038	POP*GPC
64	Ireland	19,629	POP*GPC
65	Burma	19,469	POP*GPC
66	Korea, North	18,977	POP*GPC
67	Uruguay	18,742	POP*GPC
68	Sri Lanka	18,032	POP*GPC
69	Congo, Dem R	17,701	POP*GPC
70	Syria	17,011	POP*GPC
71	Ecuador	16,484	POP*GPC
72	Latvia	16,478	POP*GPC
73	Azerbaijan	16,349	POP*GPC
74	Mozambique	15,641	POP*GPC
75	Moldova	15,568	POP*GPC
76	Israel	15,266	POP*GPC
77	Hong Kong	15,051	POP*GPC
78	Guatemala	13,915	POP*GPC
79	Sudan	13,511	POP*GPC
80	Kuwait	13,197	POP*GPC
81	Ghana	13,022	POP*GPC
82	Afghanistan	12,770	POP*GPC
83	Angola	12,316	POP*GPC
84	Slovenia	12,042	POP*GPC
85	Puerto Rico	11,816	POP*GPC
86	Estonia	10,933	POP*GPC
87	Ethiopia	10,573	POP*GPC
88	Armenia	9,635	POP*GPC
89	Kenya	9,156	POP*GPC
90	Madagascar	8,916	POP*GPC
91	Tunisia	8,818	POP*GPC
92	Nepal	8,572	POP*GPC
93	Bosnia	8,401	POP*GPC
94	Bolivia	8,324	POP*GPC
95	Lebanon	8,280	POP*GPC

Table 3.16 Gross Domestic Product at Purchasing Power Parities, Millions of 2012 Dollars, Year 1960			
Rank	Country	GDP	Source
96	Turkmenistan	8,205	POP*GPC
97	Tajikistan	8,028	POP*GPC
98	Trinidad & T	7,785	POP*GPC
99	Yemen	7,753	POP*GPC
100	El Salvador	7,656	POP*GPC
101	Cameroon	7,513	POP*GPC
102	Tanzania	7,503	POP*GPC
103	Uganda	7,400	POP*GPC
104	Kyrgyzstan	6,970	POP*GPC
105	Dominican R	6,931	POP*GPC
106	Ivory Coast	6,817	POP*GPC
107	Senegal	6,768	POP*GPC
108	Jamaica	6,531	POP*GPC
109	Somalia	6,399	POP*GPC
110	Singapore	6,280	POP*GPC
111	Luxembourg	6,140	POP*GPC
112	Cambodia	6,124	POP*GPC
113	Haiti	6,102	POP*GPC
114	Nicaragua	5,843	POP*GPC
115	Zimbabwe	5,426	POP*GPC
116	Costa Rica	5,348	POP*GPC
117	Zambia	5,288	POP*GPC
118	UAE	4,937	POP*GPC
119	Niger	4,787	POP*GPC
120	Paraguay	4,656	POP*GPC
121	Benin	4,492	POP*GPC
122	Honduras	4,416	POP*GPC
123	Burkina Faso	4,216	POP*GPC
124	Panama	4,192	POP*GPC
125	Macedonia	4,055	POP*GPC
126	Libya	4,045	POP*GPC
127	Gabon	3,840	POP*GPC
128	Albania	3,831	POP*GPC
129	Mali	3,469	POP*GPC
130	Chad	3,111	POP*GPC
131	Cyprus	2,917	POP*GPC
132	Jordan	2,872	POP*GPC
133	Papua New G	2,819	POP*GPC
134	Sierra Leone	2,659	POP*GPC
135	Kosovo	2,622	POP*GPC
136	Mauritius	2,556	POP*GPC
137	Rwanda	2,478	POP*GPC
138	Congo, Rep	2,419	POP*GPC
139	Namibia	2,385	POP*GPC
140	Qatar	2,384	POP*GPC
141	Iceland	2,281	POP*GPC
142	Guinea	2,266	POP*GPC
143	Bahamas	2,258	POP*GPC

Table 3.16 Gross Domestic Product at Purchasing Power Parities, Millions of 2012 Dollars, Year 1960

Rank	Country	GDP	Source
144	Montenegro	2,132	POP*GPC
145	Laos	2,089	POP*GPC
146	Malawi	2,010	POP*GPC
147	CAR	1,994	POP*GPC
148	Fiji	1,807	POP*GPC
149	Liberia	1,616	POP*GPC
150	Burundi	1,610	POP*GPC
151	Togo	1,594	POP*GPC
152	West Bank	1,581	POP*GPC
153	Barbados	1,505	POP*GPC
154	South Sudan	1,437	POP*GPC
155	Mauritania	1,202	POP*GPC
156	Reunion	1,181	POP*GPC
157	Guam	1,162	POP*GPC
158	Guadeloupe	1,159	POP*GPC
159	Brunei	1,155	POP*GPC
160	Guyana	1,067	POP*GPC
161	Martinique	1,054	POP*GPC
162	Malta	1,025	POP*GPC
163	Bahrain	1,024	POP*GPC
164	Oman	1,020	POP*GPC
165	Suriname	962	POP*GPC
166	Mongolia	916	POP*GPC
167	Curacao	893	POP*GPC
168	Jersey	889	POP*GPC
169	Aruba	887	POP*GPC
170	Eritrea	687	POP*GPC
171	Fr Polynesia	643	POP*GPC
172	New Caledon	584	POP*GPC
173	Macao	558	POP*GPC
174	Lesotho	530	POP*GPC
175	Swaziland	510	POP*GPC
176	Guernsey	494	POP*GPC
177	Guinea-Biss	451	POP*GPC
178	Gambia	425	POP*GPC
179	Virgin I, US	392	POP*GPC
180	East Timor	389	POP*GPC
181	Botswana	383	POP*GPC
182	Gaza Strip	380	POP*GPC
183	Isle of Man	349	POP*GPC
184	Greenland	328	POP*GPC
185	Faroe Is	326	POP*GPC
186	Equatorial G	289	POP*GPC
187	Belize	264	POP*GPC
188	Samoa	262	POP*GPC
189	Monaco	255	POP*GPC
190	Djibouti	253	POP*GPC
191	Comoros	252	POP*GPC

Table 3.16 Gross Domestic Product at Purchasing Power Parities, Millions of 2012 Dollars, Year 1960

Rank	Country	GDP	Source
192	Guiana, Fr	242	POP*GPC
193	Liechtenstn	239	POP*GPC
194	Antigua & B	211	POP*GPC
195	Bermuda	198	POP*GPC
196	Dominica	198	POP*GPC
197	Grenada	195	POP*GPC
198	St Kitts & N	195	POP*GPC
199	St Vincent	190	POP*GPC
200	Seychelles	182	POP*GPC
201	St Lucia	178	POP*GPC
202	Bhutan	178	POP*GPC
203	San Marino	170	POP*GPC
204	Cayman Is	166	POP*GPC
205	Vanuatu	164	POP*GPC
206	Tonga	155	POP*GPC
207	Cape Verde	148	POP*GPC
208	Solomon Is	139	POP*GPC
209	Palau	119	POP*GPC
210	Gibraltar	117	POP*GPC
211	N Mariana Is	116	POP*GPC
212	Micronesia	112	POP*GPC
213	Maldives	102	POP*GPC
214	Sao Tome & P	85	POP*GPC
215	Andorra	76	POP*GPC
216	Virgin I, Br	71	POP*GPC
217	Samoa, Amer	69	POP*GPC
218	Svalbard	60	POP*GPC
219	Kiribati	52	POP*GPC
220	Nauru	45	POP*GPC
221	St Pierre&M	34	POP*GPC
222	Falkland Is	33	POP*GPC
223	Turks & C Is	32	POP*GPC
224	Cook Is	30	POP*GPC
225	Saint Martin	29	POP*GPC
226	Montserrat	27	POP*GPC
227	Marshall Is	26	POP*GPC
228	Anguilla	25	POP*GPC
229	Saint Helena	20	POP*GPC
230	Sint Maarten	20	POP*GPC
231	Mayotte	16	POP*GPC
232	W Sahara	15	POP*GPC
233	Wallis & Fut	15	POP*GPC
234	Tuvalu	5	POP*GPC
235	Niue	1	POP*GPC
236	Tokelau	1	POP*GPC

Table 3.17 Gross Domestic Product at Purchasing Power Parities, Millions of 2012 Dollars, Year 1970

Rank	Country	GDP	Source
1	US	4,896,307	POP*GPC
2	Japan	1,562,630	POP*GPC
3	Russia	1,558,873	POP*GPC
4	Germany	1,456,958	POP*GPC
5	France	945,753	POP*GPC
6	UK	914,492	POP*GPC
7	Italy	907,847	POP*GPC
8	China	647,609	POP*GPC
9	India	615,692	POP*GPC
10	Brazil	474,229	POP*GPC
11	Canada	418,504	POP*GPC
12	Mexico	378,538	POP*GPC
13	Spain	378,467	POP*GPC
14	Ukraine	331,677	POP*GPC
15	Netherlands	256,370	POP*GPC
16	Argentina	252,581	POP*GPC
17	Poland	252,060	POP*GPC
18	Australia	244,854	POP*GPC
19	Iran	217,673	POP*GPC
20	Switzerland	197,637	POP*GPC
21	South Africa	177,539	POP*GPC
22	Belgium	173,998	POP*GPC
23	Sweden	170,244	POP*GPC
24	Indonesia	169,739	POP*GPC
25	Turkey	167,698	POP*GPC
26	Venezuela	155,934	POP*GPC
27	Romania	127,835	POP*GPC
28	Austria	125,553	POP*GPC
29	Kazakhstan	123,142	POP*GPC
30	Czechia	121,797	POP*GPC
31	Greece	105,570	POP*GPC
32	Denmark	105,380	POP*GPC
33	Hungary	104,199	POP*GPC
34	Nigeria	100,215	POP*GPC
35	Saudi Arabia	99,375	POP*GPC
36	Colombia	98,670	POP*GPC
37	Philippines	91,760	POP*GPC
38	Korea, South	91,111	POP*GPC
39	Pakistan	86,281	POP*GPC
40	Portugal	82,671	POP*GPC
41	Peru	81,933	POP*GPC
42	Thailand	76,697	POP*GPC
43	Finland	72,947	POP*GPC
44	Uzbekistan	69,437	POP*GPC
45	Norway	67,042	POP*GPC
46	Egypt	66,991	POP*GPC
47	Chile	66,850	POP*GPC

Table 3.17 Gross Domestic Product at Purchasing Power Parities, Millions of 2012 Dollars, Year 1970

Rank	Country	GDP	Source
48	Taiwan	66,201	POP*GPC
49	Bulgaria	61,609	POP*GPC
50	Bangladesh	60,459	POP*GPC
51	Iraq	59,456	POP*GPC
52	Algeria	59,188	POP*GPC
53	Belarus	54,984	POP*GPC
54	Serbia	54,082	POP*GPC
55	New Zealand	52,302	POP*GPC
56	Slovakia	44,365	POP*GPC
57	Korea, North	43,858	POP*GPC
58	Vietnam	41,215	POP*GPC
59	Lithuania	37,921	POP*GPC
60	Croatia	36,838	POP*GPC
61	Israel	36,177	POP*GPC
62	Malaysia	35,092	POP*GPC
63	Hong Kong	35,087	POP*GPC
64	Morocco	35,029	POP*GPC
65	Georgia	34,592	POP*GPC
66	Kuwait	33,656	POP*GPC
67	Libya	32,827	POP*GPC
68	Ireland	30,770	POP*GPC
69	Ecuador	28,572	POP*GPC
70	Azerbaijan	28,519	POP*GPC
71	Angola	26,440	POP*GPC
72	Burma	26,244	POP*GPC
73	Cuba	26,117	POP*GPC
74	Mozambique	25,786	POP*GPC
75	Latvia	24,946	POP*GPC
76	Moldova	24,892	POP*GPC
77	Congo, Dem R	23,617	POP*GPC
78	Puerto Rico	23,194	POP*GPC
79	Sri Lanka	23,080	POP*GPC
80	Syria	22,416	POP*GPC
81	Guatemala	21,744	POP*GPC
82	UAE	21,019	POP*GPC
83	Uruguay	20,627	POP*GPC
84	Slovenia	19,854	POP*GPC
85	Ethiopia	18,260	POP*GPC
86	Estonia	17,266	POP*GPC
87	Turkmenistan	16,800	POP*GPC
88	Lebanon	16,676	POP*GPC
89	Singapore	16,308	POP*GPC
90	Kenya	15,714	POP*GPC
91	Bosnia	15,496	POP*GPC
92	Ghana	15,487	POP*GPC
93	Sudan	15,479	POP*GPC
94	Armenia	15,015	POP*GPC
95	Afghanistan	14,955	POP*GPC

Table 3.17 Gross Domestic Product at Purchasing Power Parities, Millions of 2012 Dollars, Year 1970			
Rank	Country	GDP	Source
96	Tajikistan	14,814	POP*GPC
97	Tunisia	14,492	POP*GPC
98	Ivory Coast	14,465	POP*GPC
99	Bolivia	14,454	POP*GPC
100	El Salvador	14,271	POP*GPC
101	Tanzania	12,984	POP*GPC
102	Madagascar	12,282	POP*GPC
103	Nicaragua	11,974	POP*GPC
104	Cameroon	11,942	POP*GPC
105	Dominican R	11,717	POP*GPC
106	Kyrgyzstan	11,329	POP*GPC
107	Trinidad & T	11,199	POP*GPC
108	Uganda	11,036	POP*GPC
109	Jamaica	10,663	POP*GPC
110	Yemen	10,472	POP*GPC
111	Costa Rica	10,161	POP*GPC
112	Nepal	9,934	POP*GPC
113	Luxembourg	9,883	POP*GPC
114	Zimbabwe	9,341	POP*GPC
115	Panama	8,818	POP*GPC
116	Senegal	8,473	POP*GPC
117	Zambia	8,069	POP*GPC
118	Macedonia	7,944	POP*GPC
119	Cambodia	7,535	POP*GPC
120	Albania	7,326	POP*GPC
121	Paraguay	7,192	POP*GPC
122	Gabon	7,081	POP*GPC
123	Honduras	6,874	POP*GPC
124	Somalia	6,737	POP*GPC
125	Niger	6,513	POP*GPC
126	Haiti	6,485	POP*GPC
127	Oman	6,451	POP*GPC
128	Qatar	5,893	POP*GPC
129	Kosovo	5,634	POP*GPC
130	Cyprus	5,401	POP*GPC
131	Burkina Faso	5,265	POP*GPC
132	Benin	5,068	POP*GPC
133	Papua New G	5,051	POP*GPC
134	Jordan	4,924	POP*GPC
135	Bahamas	4,785	POP*GPC
136	Mali	4,331	POP*GPC
137	Iceland	4,111	POP*GPC
138	Montenegro	4,028	POP*GPC
139	Chad	4,027	POP*GPC
140	Congo, Rep	3,816	POP*GPC
141	Namibia	3,779	POP*GPC
142	Sierra Leone	3,772	POP*GPC
143	Brunei	3,310	POP*GPC

Table 3.17 Gross Domestic Product at Purchasing Power Parities, Millions of 2012 Dollars, Year 1970

Rank	Country	GDP	Source
144	Guinea	3,274	POP*GPC
145	Rwanda	3,214	POP*GPC
146	Barbados	3,027	POP*GPC
147	Mauritius	3,023	POP*GPC
148	Bahrain	2,962	POP*GPC
149	Togo	2,807	POP*GPC
150	Malawi	2,727	POP*GPC
151	Laos	2,685	POP*GPC
152	Mauritania	2,614	POP*GPC
153	Reunion	2,391	POP*GPC
154	Fiji	2,389	POP*GPC
155	Malta	2,337	POP*GPC
156	CAR	2,270	POP*GPC
157	Martinique	2,200	POP*GPC
158	Guadeloupe	2,179	POP*GPC
159	Liberia	1,881	POP*GPC
160	Burundi	1,872	POP*GPC
161	Suriname	1,784	POP*GPC
162	Mongolia	1,775	POP*GPC
163	Guam	1,721	POP*GPC
164	South Sudan	1,646	POP*GPC
165	Macao	1,633	POP*GPC
166	Guyana	1,532	POP*GPC
167	Curacao	1,461	POP*GPC
168	Jersey	1,411	POP*GPC
169	West Bank	1,390	POP*GPC
170	Swaziland	1,320	POP*GPC
171	Aruba	1,271	POP*GPC
172	Eritrea	1,196	POP*GPC
173	Fr Polynesia	1,070	POP*GPC
174	Virgin I, US	968	POP*GPC
175	New Caledon	961	POP*GPC
176	Botswana	947	POP*GPC
177	Guernsey	814	POP*GPC
178	Guinea-Biss	775	POP*GPC
179	Gambia	762	POP*GPC
180	Lesotho	747	POP*GPC
181	Greenland	669	POP*GPC
182	Djibouti	604	POP*GPC
183	Isle of Man	581	POP*GPC
184	Equatorial G	575	POP*GPC
185	Faroe Is	549	POP*GPC
186	East Timor	534	POP*GPC
187	Comoros	529	POP*GPC
188	Gaza Strip	464	POP*GPC
189	Liechtenstn	454	POP*GPC
190	Monaco	430	POP*GPC
191	Bermuda	412	POP*GPC

TABLE 3.17 GROSS DOMESTIC PRODUCT AT PURCHASING POWER PARITIES, MILLIONS OF 2012 DOLLARS, YEAR 1970

Rank	Country	GDP	Source
192	Belize	407	POP*GPC
193	Samoa	391	POP*GPC
194	St Lucia	355	POP*GPC
195	Antigua & B	350	POP*GPC
196	Guiana, Fr	349	POP*GPC
197	St Kitts & N	344	POP*GPC
198	San Marino	327	POP*GPC
199	Grenada	306	POP*GPC
200	Dominica	303	POP*GPC
201	Seychelles	301	POP*GPC
202	Andorra	277	POP*GPC
203	Bhutan	276	POP*GPC
204	Cayman Is	273	POP*GPC
205	St Vincent	263	POP*GPC
206	Vanuatu	257	POP*GPC
207	Solomon Is	240	POP*GPC
208	Tonga	234	POP*GPC
209	Cape Verde	205	POP*GPC
210	Gibraltar	205	POP*GPC
211	Palau	182	POP*GPC
212	Micronesia	173	POP*GPC
213	N Mariana Is	171	POP*GPC
214	Maldives	151	POP*GPC
215	Sao Tome & P	136	POP*GPC
216	Virgin I, Br	117	POP*GPC
217	Samoa, Amer	117	POP*GPC
218	Svalbard	95	POP*GPC
219	Nauru	91	POP*GPC
220	Kiribati	85	POP*GPC
221	Sint Maarten	67	POP*GPC
222	St Pierre&M	55	POP*GPC
223	Saint Martin	52	POP*GPC
224	W Sahara	51	POP*GPC
225	Cook Is	47	POP*GPC
226	Marshall Is	44	POP*GPC
227	Falkland Is	43	POP*GPC
228	Turks & C Is	41	POP*GPC
229	Anguilla	41	POP*GPC
230	Montserrat	41	POP*GPC
231	Mayotte	24	POP*GPC
232	Wallis & Fut	23	POP*GPC
233	Saint Helena	21	POP*GPC
234	Tuvalu	6	POP*GPC
235	Niue	2	POP*GPC
236	Tokelau	1	POP*GPC

Table 3.18 Gross Domestic Product at Purchasing Power Parities, Millions of 2012 Dollars, Year 1980

Rank	Country	GDP	Source
1	US	6,780,639	POP*GPC
2	Japan	2,418,685	POP*GPC
3	Russia	2,044,021	POP*GPC
4	Germany	1,989,435	POP*GPC
5	Italy	1,350,480	POP*GPC
6	France	1,302,394	POP*GPC
7	UK	1,099,683	POP*GPC
8	Brazil	1,013,479	POP*GPC
9	China	856,698	POP*GPC
10	Mexico	767,564	POP*GPC
11	India	762,819	POP*GPC
12	Spain	641,853	POP*GPC
13	Canada	641,347	POP*GPC
14	Ukraine	411,465	POP*GPC
15	Poland	377,262	POP*GPC
16	Netherlands	348,288	POP*GPC
17	Australia	343,367	POP*GPC
18	Saudi Arabia	330,284	POP*GPC
19	Argentina	319,241	POP*GPC
20	Iran	294,598	POP*GPC
21	Indonesia	290,032	POP*GPC
22	South Africa	275,992	POP*GPC
23	Turkey	271,797	POP*GPC
24	Belgium	250,714	POP*GPC
25	Switzerland	239,152	POP*GPC
26	Romania	239,140	POP*GPC
27	Korea, South	221,736	POP*GPC
28	Sweden	212,236	POP*GPC
29	Venezuela	202,756	POP*GPC
30	Austria	187,356	POP*GPC
31	Greece	182,963	POP*GPC
32	Czechia	171,682	POP*GPC
33	Colombia	164,505	POP*GPC
34	Iraq	158,496	POP*GPC
35	UAE	157,414	POP*GPC
36	Taiwan	155,296	POP*GPC
37	Philippines	155,014	POP*GPC
38	Hungary	152,053	POP*GPC
39	Nigeria	150,957	POP*GPC
40	Kazakhstan	137,944	POP*GPC
41	Egypt	135,081	POP*GPC
42	Portugal	134,961	POP*GPC
43	Denmark	133,715	POP*GPC
44	Thailand	129,343	POP*GPC
45	Algeria	125,399	POP*GPC
46	Pakistan	123,074	POP*GPC
47	Peru	121,284	POP*GPC

Table 3.18 Gross Domestic Product at Purchasing Power Parities, Millions of 2012 Dollars, Year 1980

Rank	Country	GDP	Source
48	Norway	114,115	POP*GPC
49	Finland	105,188	POP*GPC
50	Serbia	98,875	POP*GPC
51	Uzbekistan	93,356	POP*GPC
52	Hong Kong	82,376	POP*GPC
53	Bulgaria	80,511	POP*GPC
54	Korea, North	77,369	POP*GPC
55	Chile	76,823	POP*GPC
56	Malaysia	75,973	POP*GPC
57	Croatia	67,568	POP*GPC
58	New Zealand	65,994	POP*GPC
59	Bangladesh	65,608	POP*GPC
60	Kuwait	65,406	POP*GPC
61	Belarus	65,289	POP*GPC
62	Israel	64,725	POP*GPC
63	Slovakia	61,380	POP*GPC
64	Ecuador	57,192	POP*GPC
65	Morocco	55,465	POP*GPC
66	Ireland	50,728	POP*GPC
67	Vietnam	49,193	POP*GPC
68	Lithuania	49,142	POP*GPC
69	Singapore	41,263	POP*GPC
70	Burma	39,954	POP*GPC
71	Georgia	39,791	POP*GPC
72	Libya	39,682	POP*GPC
73	Syria	39,625	POP*GPC
74	Cuba	38,270	POP*GPC
75	Slovenia	35,639	POP*GPC
76	Azerbaijan	34,944	POP*GPC
77	Puerto Rico	34,010	POP*GPC
78	Guatemala	33,099	POP*GPC
79	Moldova	31,232	POP*GPC
80	Lebanon	30,368	POP*GPC
81	Latvia	30,155	POP*GPC
82	Sri Lanka	29,827	POP*GPC
83	Bosnia	29,560	POP*GPC
84	Tunisia	29,276	POP*GPC
85	Uruguay	25,853	POP*GPC
86	Kenya	25,386	POP*GPC
87	Ivory Coast	25,244	POP*GPC
88	Congo, Dem R	24,317	POP*GPC
89	Ethiopia	24,234	POP*GPC
90	Dominican R	23,788	POP*GPC
91	Angola	23,252	POP*GPC
92	Sudan	22,636	POP*GPC
93	Turkmenistan	22,511	POP*GPC
94	Estonia	22,125	POP*GPC
95	Yemen	22,001	POP*GPC

Table 3.18 Gross Domestic Product at Purchasing Power Parities, Millions of 2012 Dollars, Year 1980

Rank	Country	GDP	Source
96	Bolivia	21,910	POP*GPC
97	El Salvador	20,794	POP*GPC
98	Cameroon	20,608	POP*GPC
99	Tanzania	19,340	POP*GPC
100	Armenia	19,080	POP*GPC
101	Trinidad & T	18,573	POP*GPC
102	Tajikistan	17,576	POP*GPC
103	Afghanistan	17,488	POP*GPC
104	Costa Rica	17,056	POP*GPC
105	Macedonia	16,641	POP*GPC
106	Paraguay	15,704	POP*GPC
107	Ghana	15,369	POP*GPC
108	Panama	15,084	POP*GPC
109	Madagascar	13,411	POP*GPC
110	Nicaragua	12,913	POP*GPC
111	Gabon	12,766	POP*GPC
112	Kyrgyzstan	12,561	POP*GPC
113	Kosovo	12,403	POP*GPC
114	Zimbabwe	12,233	POP*GPC
115	Oman	12,016	POP*GPC
116	Luxembourg	11,563	POP*GPC
117	Honduras	11,329	POP*GPC
118	Haiti	11,122	POP*GPC
119	Albania	11,083	POP*GPC
120	Jordan	10,999	POP*GPC
121	Nepal	10,885	POP*GPC
122	Qatar	10,513	POP*GPC
123	Brunei	10,387	POP*GPC
124	Jamaica	9,969	POP*GPC
125	Senegal	9,784	POP*GPC
126	Cyprus	9,692	POP*GPC
127	Somalia	9,327	POP*GPC
128	Zambia	9,181	POP*GPC
129	Cambodia	8,623	POP*GPC
130	Uganda	8,247	POP*GPC
131	Bahrain	8,237	POP*GPC
132	Montenegro	8,048	POP*GPC
133	Niger	7,524	POP*GPC
134	Congo, Rep	6,670	POP*GPC
135	Bahamas	6,538	POP*GPC
136	Papua New G	6,386	POP*GPC
137	Mali	6,158	POP*GPC
138	Iceland	6,068	POP*GPC
139	Mozambique	6,008	POP*GPC
140	Benin	5,893	POP*GPC
141	Namibia	5,836	POP*GPC
142	Burkina Faso	5,694	POP*GPC
143	Rwanda	5,096	POP*GPC

TABLE 3.18 GROSS DOMESTIC PRODUCT AT PURCHASING POWER PARITIES, MILLIONS OF 2012 DOLLARS, YEAR 1980

Rank	Country	GDP	Source
144	Malawi	4,963	POP*GPC
145	Barbados	4,721	POP*GPC
146	Macao	4,684	POP*GPC
147	Mauritius	4,585	POP*GPC
148	Guinea	4,310	POP*GPC
149	Botswana	4,271	POP*GPC
150	Sierra Leone	4,182	POP*GPC
151	Malta	3,891	POP*GPC
152	Chad	3,765	POP*GPC
153	Laos	3,490	POP*GPC
154	Togo	3,441	POP*GPC
155	Mongolia	3,418	POP*GPC
156	Mauritania	3,226	POP*GPC
157	Reunion	2,882	POP*GPC
158	Fiji	2,806	POP*GPC
159	Martinique	2,741	POP*GPC
160	Guadeloupe	2,705	POP*GPC
161	Suriname	2,641	POP*GPC
162	South Sudan	2,407	POP*GPC
163	CAR	2,338	POP*GPC
164	Guam	2,301	POP*GPC
165	Burundi	2,157	POP*GPC
166	Swaziland	2,124	POP*GPC
167	Jersey	1,983	POP*GPC
168	Guyana	1,970	POP*GPC
169	West Bank	1,920	POP*GPC
170	Virgin I, US	1,745	POP*GPC
171	Eritrea	1,735	POP*GPC
172	Liberia	1,638	POP*GPC
173	Fr Polynesia	1,555	POP*GPC
174	Aruba	1,497	POP*GPC
175	Curacao	1,461	POP*GPC
176	Lesotho	1,347	POP*GPC
177	Gambia	1,296	POP*GPC
178	New Caledon	1,264	POP*GPC
179	Djibouti	1,086	POP*GPC
180	Guernsey	1,082	POP*GPC
181	Guinea-Biss	961	POP*GPC
182	Greenland	932	POP*GPC
183	Isle of Man	919	POP*GPC
184	Faroe Is	778	POP*GPC
185	Seychelles	733	POP*GPC
186	Liechtenstn	689	POP*GPC
187	Gaza Strip	671	POP*GPC
188	Monaco	624	POP*GPC
189	Andorra	604	POP*GPC
190	Belize	587	POP*GPC
191	Cayman Is	550	POP*GPC

Table 3.18 Gross Domestic Product at Purchasing Power Parities, Millions of 2012 Dollars, Year 1980			
Rank	Country	GDP	Source
192	Bermuda	547	POP*GPC
193	St Lucia	545	POP*GPC
194	East Timor	528	POP*GPC
195	Antigua & B	504	POP*GPC
196	Equatorial G	484	POP*GPC
197	San Marino	476	POP*GPC
198	Guiana, Fr	474	POP*GPC
199	Bhutan	462	POP*GPC
200	Comoros	458	POP*GPC
201	Samoa	434	POP*GPC
202	Solomon Is	398	POP*GPC
203	Vanuatu	372	POP*GPC
204	Grenada	371	POP*GPC
205	St Vincent	359	POP*GPC
206	Dominica	336	POP*GPC
207	Gibraltar	324	POP*GPC
208	Maldives	313	POP*GPC
209	St Kitts & N	282	POP*GPC
210	Cape Verde	268	POP*GPC
211	Tonga	253	POP*GPC
212	N Mariana Is	252	POP*GPC
213	Micronesia	217	POP*GPC
214	Sao Tome & P	217	POP*GPC
215	Palau	208	POP*GPC
216	Virgin I, Br	164	POP*GPC
217	Svalbard	161	POP*GPC
218	Samoa, Amer	151	POP*GPC
219	Kiribati	126	POP*GPC
220	Sint Maarten	126	POP*GPC
221	Nauru	110	POP*GPC
222	W Sahara	88	POP*GPC
223	St Pierre&M	77	POP*GPC
224	Saint Martin	71	POP*GPC
225	Marshall Is	66	POP*GPC
226	Turks & C Is	65	POP*GPC
227	Cook Is	64	POP*GPC
228	Anguilla	57	POP*GPC
229	Montserrat	54	POP*GPC
230	Falkland Is	50	POP*GPC
231	Mayotte	40	POP*GPC
232	Wallis & Fut	31	POP*GPC
233	Saint Helena	26	POP*GPC
234	Tuvalu	9	POP*GPC
235	Niue	3	POP*GPC
236	Tokelau	2	POP*GPC

TABLE 3.19 GROSS DOMESTIC PRODUCT AT PURCHASING POWER PARITIES, MILLIONS OF 2012 DOLLARS, YEAR 1990			
Rank	Country	GDP	Source
1	US	9,399,767	POP*GPC
2	Japan	3,774,309	POP*GPC
3	Germany	2,520,685	POP*GPC
4	Russia	2,508,098	POP*GPC
5	China	1,988,657	POP*GPC
6	Italy	1,749,789	POP*GPC
7	France	1,657,535	POP*GPC
8	UK	1,425,969	POP*GPC
9	India	1,302,715	POP*GPC
10	Brazil	1,188,141	POP*GPC
11	Mexico	916,759	POP*GPC
12	Spain	881,441	POP*GPC
13	Canada	847,230	POP*GPC
14	Korea, South	517,905	POP*GPC
15	Indonesia	517,496	POP*GPC
16	Australia	493,419	POP*GPC
17	Turkey	480,628	POP*GPC
18	Ukraine	476,954	POP*GPC
19	Netherlands	438,310	POP*GPC
20	Poland	372,061	POP*GPC
21	Iran	352,833	POP*GPC
22	South Africa	316,041	POP*GPC
23	Belgium	308,880	POP*GPC
24	Switzerland	305,054	POP*GPC
25	Taiwan	297,110	POP*GPC
26	Saudi Arabia	289,472	POP*GPC
27	Argentina	271,910	POP*GPC
28	Thailand	266,925	POP*GPC
29	Sweden	265,069	POP*GPC
30	Romania	258,532	POP*GPC
31	Austria	235,443	POP*GPC
32	Colombia	234,999	POP*GPC
33	Egypt	229,371	POP*GPC
34	Venezuela	227,272	POP*GPC
35	Pakistan	226,204	POP*GPC
36	Czechia	199,321	POP*GPC
37	Greece	196,213	POP*GPC
38	Portugal	187,700	POP*GPC
39	Philippines	177,633	POP*GPC
40	Hungary	172,871	POP*GPC
41	Denmark	168,569	POP*GPC
42	Nigeria	167,964	POP*GPC
43	Algeria	164,380	POP*GPC
44	Hong Kong	160,419	POP*GPC
45	UAE	155,911	POP*GPC
46	Norway	152,276	POP*GPC
47	Finland	143,139	POP*GPC

Table 3.19 Gross Domestic Product at Purchasing Power Parities, Millions of 2012 Dollars, Year 1990

Rank	Country	GDP	Source
48	Malaysia	137,348	POP*GPC
49	Kazakhstan	135,327	POP*GPC
50	Iraq	115,057	POP*GPC
51	Chile	114,080	POP*GPC
52	Uzbekistan	111,661	POP*GPC
53	Peru	111,392	POP*GPC
54	Kuwait	107,456	POP*GPC
55	Bulgaria	102,003	POP*GPC
56	Serbia	95,946	POP*GPC
57	Israel	92,192	POP*GPC
58	Bangladesh	92,124	POP*GPC
59	Korea, North	90,402	POP*GPC
60	Singapore	86,159	POP*GPC
61	New Zealand	83,192	POP*GPC
62	Morocco	79,255	POP*GPC
63	Vietnam	77,560	POP*GPC
64	Belarus	74,589	POP*GPC
65	Ecuador	74,470	POP*GPC
66	Ireland	73,250	POP*GPC
67	Slovakia	69,416	POP*GPC
68	Croatia	65,672	POP*GPC
69	Lithuania	58,500	POP*GPC
70	Syria	50,970	POP*GPC
71	Burma	47,273	POP*GPC
72	Puerto Rico	46,567	POP*GPC
73	Cuba	46,006	POP*GPC
74	Sri Lanka	44,250	POP*GPC
75	Tunisia	41,408	POP*GPC
76	Latvia	39,713	POP*GPC
77	Azerbaijan	39,019	POP*GPC
78	Kenya	37,553	POP*GPC
79	Georgia	37,072	POP*GPC
80	Angola	36,788	POP*GPC
81	Guatemala	36,630	POP*GPC
82	Moldova	36,399	POP*GPC
83	Slovenia	35,791	POP*GPC
84	Bosnia	30,786	POP*GPC
85	Dominican R	29,892	POP*GPC
86	Ethiopia	29,871	POP*GPC
87	Sudan	28,742	POP*GPC
88	Ivory Coast	28,692	POP*GPC
89	Cameroon	28,315	POP*GPC
90	Oman	27,734	POP*GPC
91	Congo, Dem R	27,049	POP*GPC
92	Estonia	26,157	POP*GPC
93	Yemen	25,967	POP*GPC
94	Uruguay	25,780	POP*GPC
95	Turkmenistan	25,466	POP*GPC

Table 3.19 Gross Domestic Product at Purchasing Power Parities, Millions of 2012 Dollars, Year 1990			
Rank	Country	GDP	Source
96	Tanzania	24,892	POP*GPC
97	Lebanon	24,499	POP*GPC
98	Paraguay	23,209	POP*GPC
99	Libya	22,628	POP*GPC
100	Costa Rica	22,014	POP*GPC
101	Armenia	21,819	POP*GPC
102	Bolivia	21,467	POP*GPC
103	Ghana	20,158	POP*GPC
104	Luxembourg	19,816	POP*GPC
105	El Salvador	19,289	POP*GPC
106	Macedonia	18,242	POP*GPC
107	Cyprus	18,189	POP*GPC
108	Tajikistan	18,127	POP*GPC
109	Zimbabwe	17,910	POP*GPC
110	Nepal	17,436	POP*GPC
111	Panama	17,280	POP*GPC
112	Gabon	15,967	POP*GPC
113	Trinidad & T	14,977	POP*GPC
114	Honduras	14,357	POP*GPC
115	Kosovo	14,345	POP*GPC
116	Jordan	13,825	POP*GPC
117	Madagascar	13,759	POP*GPC
118	Jamaica	12,693	POP*GPC
119	Kyrgyzstan	12,604	POP*GPC
120	Cambodia	12,458	POP*GPC
121	Senegal	12,417	POP*GPC
122	Albania	12,209	POP*GPC
123	Botswana	12,061	POP*GPC
124	Afghanistan	11,974	POP*GPC
125	Somalia	11,458	POP*GPC
126	Haiti	11,079	POP*GPC
127	Nicaragua	11,068	POP*GPC
128	Uganda	10,639	POP*GPC
129	Congo, Rep	10,508	POP*GPC
130	Zambia	10,311	POP*GPC
131	Bahrain	10,250	POP*GPC
132	Qatar	9,111	POP*GPC
133	Macao	9,003	POP*GPC
134	Bahamas	8,804	POP*GPC
135	Mauritius	8,060	POP*GPC
136	Burkina Faso	8,023	POP*GPC
137	Montenegro	8,022	POP*GPC
138	Iceland	7,936	POP*GPC
139	Benin	7,642	POP*GPC
140	Papua New G	7,260	POP*GPC
141	Brunei	7,137	POP*GPC
142	Niger	6,998	POP*GPC
143	Mali	6,728	POP*GPC

Table 3.19 Gross Domestic Product at Purchasing Power Parities, Millions of 2012 Dollars, Year 1990

Rank	Country	GDP	Source
144	Namibia	6,622	POP*GPC
145	Chad	6,366	POP*GPC
146	Rwanda	6,158	POP*GPC
147	Malawi	6,151	POP*GPC
148	Mozambique	5,857	POP*GPC
149	Malta	5,818	POP*GPC
150	Mongolia	5,805	POP*GPC
151	Guinea	5,604	POP*GPC
152	Barbados	5,331	POP*GPC
153	Swaziland	4,799	POP*GPC
154	Sierra Leone	4,553	POP*GPC
155	Laos	4,446	POP*GPC
156	Reunion	4,161	POP*GPC
157	Togo	4,041	POP*GPC
158	Mauritania	3,571	POP*GPC
159	Fiji	3,217	POP*GPC
160	Martinique	3,200	POP*GPC
161	Guadeloupe	3,082	POP*GPC
162	South Sudan	3,056	POP*GPC
163	West Bank	3,036	POP*GPC
164	Guam	2,941	POP*GPC
165	Burundi	2,877	POP*GPC
166	CAR	2,653	POP*GPC
167	Jersey	2,647	POP*GPC
168	Suriname	2,343	POP*GPC
169	Virgin I, US	2,059	POP*GPC
170	Fr Polynesia	2,053	POP*GPC
171	Eritrea	2,010	POP*GPC
172	Lesotho	1,987	POP*GPC
173	Aruba	1,793	POP*GPC
174	Gambia	1,780	POP*GPC
175	Djibouti	1,672	POP*GPC
176	New Caledon	1,567	POP*GPC
177	Guernsey	1,507	POP*GPC
178	Guinea-Biss	1,492	POP*GPC
179	Guyana	1,425	POP*GPC
180	Greenland	1,267	POP*GPC
181	Bhutan	1,261	POP*GPC
182	Isle of Man	1,221	POP*GPC
183	Curacao	1,204	POP*GPC
184	Andorra	1,142	POP*GPC
185	St Lucia	1,096	POP*GPC
186	Seychelles	1,081	POP*GPC
187	Faroe Is	1,056	POP*GPC
188	Gaza Strip	1,034	POP*GPC
189	Antigua & B	987	POP*GPC
190	Liechtenstn	964	POP*GPC
191	Cayman Is	953	POP*GPC

Table 3.19 Gross Domestic Product at Purchasing Power Parities, Millions of 2012 Dollars, Year 1990

Rank	Country	GDP	Source
192	Belize	941	POP*GPC
193	Equatorial G	851	POP*GPC
194	Monaco	845	POP*GPC
195	Solomon Is	820	POP*GPC
196	Guiana, Fr	812	POP*GPC
197	Maldives	766	POP*GPC
198	Liberia	748	POP*GPC
199	East Timor	722	POP*GPC
200	San Marino	673	POP*GPC
201	N Mariana Is	660	POP*GPC
202	St Vincent	659	POP*GPC
203	Bermuda	648	POP*GPC
204	Grenada	622	POP*GPC
205	Comoros	620	POP*GPC
206	Vanuatu	588	POP*GPC
207	Dominica	571	POP*GPC
208	St Kitts & N	486	POP*GPC
209	Samoa	477	POP*GPC
210	Cape Verde	440	POP*GPC
211	Gibraltar	427	POP*GPC
212	Tonga	307	POP*GPC
213	Micronesia	288	POP*GPC
214	Sint Maarten	250	POP*GPC
215	Palau	244	POP*GPC
216	Saint Martin	237	POP*GPC
217	Samoa, Amer	229	POP*GPC
218	Svalbard	215	POP*GPC
219	Virgin I, Br	214	POP*GPC
220	Sao Tome & P	209	POP*GPC
221	W Sahara	180	POP*GPC
222	Kiribati	134	POP*GPC
223	Nauru	126	POP*GPC
224	Turks & C Is	114	POP*GPC
225	St Pierre&M	100	POP*GPC
226	Marshall Is	95	POP*GPC
227	Cook Is	82	POP*GPC
228	Mayotte	76	POP*GPC
229	Anguilla	74	POP*GPC
230	Montserrat	68	POP*GPC
231	Falkland Is	57	POP*GPC
232	Wallis & Fut	39	POP*GPC
233	Saint Helena	30	POP*GPC
234	Tuvalu	10	POP*GPC
235	Niue	4	POP*GPC
236	Tokelau	2	POP*GPC

Table 3.20 Gross Domestic Product at Purchasing Power Parities, Millions of 2012 Dollars, Year 2000

Rank	Country	GDP	Source
1	US	13,204,165	POP*GPC
2	Japan	4,157,896	POP*GPC
3	China	4,154,457	POP*GPC
4	Germany	2,990,962	POP*GPC
5	India	2,140,903	POP*GPC
6	Italy	2,077,191	POP*GPC
7	France	2,047,810	POP*GPC
8	UK	1,910,854	POP*GPC
9	Russia	1,644,432	POP*GPC
10	Brazil	1,526,600	POP*GPC
11	Mexico	1,439,873	POP*GPC
12	Spain	1,254,201	POP*GPC
13	Canada	1,138,465	POP*GPC
14	Korea, South	929,410	POP*GPC
15	Turkey	812,662	POP*GPC
16	Australia	667,424	POP*GPC
17	Indonesia	655,987	POP*GPC
18	Netherlands	634,816	POP*GPC
19	Iran	549,022	POP*GPC
20	Poland	546,802	POP*GPC
21	Taiwan	501,320	POP*GPC
22	Saudi Arabia	474,609	POP*GPC
23	Argentina	422,190	POP*GPC
24	Thailand	391,712	POP*GPC
25	South Africa	387,108	POP*GPC
26	Belgium	385,381	POP*GPC
27	Switzerland	343,900	POP*GPC
28	Pakistan	323,938	POP*GPC
29	Sweden	315,805	POP*GPC
30	Austria	314,605	POP*GPC
31	Egypt	312,978	POP*GPC
32	Colombia	294,334	POP*GPC
33	Venezuela	273,434	POP*GPC
34	Greece	272,321	POP*GPC
35	Norway	270,873	POP*GPC
36	Malaysia	268,357	POP*GPC
37	Portugal	265,244	POP*GPC
38	UAE	261,404	POP*GPC
39	Philippines	235,628	POP*GPC
40	Hong Kong	230,708	POP*GPC
41	Denmark	222,946	POP*GPC
42	Chile	218,952	POP*GPC
43	Romania	213,482	POP*GPC
44	Nigeria	212,809	POP*GPC
45	Ukraine	207,183	POP*GPC
46	Czechia	205,023	POP*GPC
47	Algeria	196,144	POP*GPC

Table 3.20 Gross Domestic Product at Purchasing Power Parities, Millions of 2012 Dollars, Year 2000

Rank	Country	GDP	Source
48	Hungary	180,941	POP*GPC
49	Singapore	174,865	POP*GPC
50	Finland	174,385	POP*GPC
51	Peru	163,044	POP*GPC
52	Israel	159,558	POP*GPC
53	Vietnam	158,452	POP*GPC
54	Ireland	153,733	POP*GPC
55	Iraq	144,261	POP*GPC
56	Bangladesh	139,899	POP*GPC
57	New Zealand	107,081	POP*GPC
58	Kuwait	104,010	POP*GPC
59	Morocco	96,005	POP*GPC
60	Kazakhstan	91,681	POP*GPC
61	Ecuador	87,403	POP*GPC
62	Burma	81,091	POP*GPC
63	Slovakia	79,359	POP*GPC
64	Bulgaria	75,118	POP*GPC
65	Libya	73,997	POP*GPC
66	Syria	70,148	POP*GPC
67	Croatia	68,895	POP*GPC
68	Belarus	66,070	POP*GPC
69	Sri Lanka	66,046	POP*GPC
70	Tunisia	65,900	POP*GPC
71	Korea, North	58,015	POP*GPC
72	Uzbekistan	56,969	POP*GPC
73	Serbia	55,795	POP*GPC
74	Dominican R	54,169	POP*GPC
75	Guatemala	51,479	POP*GPC
76	Puerto Rico	51,040	POP*GPC
77	Oman	50,452	POP*GPC
78	Qatar	46,992	POP*GPC
79	Slovenia	45,397	POP*GPC
80	Kenya	44,671	POP*GPC
81	Yemen	43,378	POP*GPC
82	Lebanon	43,170	POP*GPC
83	Sudan	41,848	POP*GPC
84	Lithuania	40,727	POP*GPC
85	Ethiopia	36,567	POP*GPC
86	Luxembourg	35,801	POP*GPC
87	Ivory Coast	35,444	POP*GPC
88	Costa Rica	35,381	POP*GPC
89	Angola	35,087	POP*GPC
90	Uruguay	35,061	POP*GPC
91	El Salvador	34,047	POP*GPC
92	Tanzania	33,709	POP*GPC
93	Cuba	32,631	POP*GPC
94	Cameroon	32,505	POP*GPC
95	Bolivia	32,489	POP*GPC

Table 3.20 Gross Domestic Product at Purchasing Power Parities, Millions of 2012 Dollars, Year 2000

Rank	Country	GDP	Source
96	Paraguay	28,533	POP*GPC
97	Panama	27,547	POP*GPC
98	Nepal	27,446	POP*GPC
99	Ghana	27,063	POP*GPC
100	Cyprus	26,979	POP*GPC
101	Latvia	26,674	POP*GPC
102	Zimbabwe	23,684	POP*GPC
103	Azerbaijan	22,899	POP*GPC
104	Bosnia	22,282	POP*GPC
105	Afghanistan	20,667	POP*GPC
106	Bahrain	20,545	POP*GPC
107	Trinidad & T	20,371	POP*GPC
108	Honduras	20,299	POP*GPC
109	Estonia	20,167	POP*GPC
110	Uganda	20,107	POP*GPC
111	Jordan	20,090	POP*GPC
112	Botswana	20,008	POP*GPC
113	Turkmenistan	19,576	POP*GPC
114	Gabon	18,844	POP*GPC
115	Macedonia	18,034	POP*GPC
116	Brunei	17,985	POP*GPC
117	Cambodia	16,859	POP*GPC
118	Senegal	16,519	POP*GPC
119	Madagascar	15,876	POP*GPC
120	Nicaragua	15,816	POP*GPC
121	Congo, Dem R	15,612	POP*GPC
122	Albania	15,225	POP*GPC
123	Armenia	13,731	POP*GPC
124	Burkina Faso	12,901	POP*GPC
125	Jamaica	12,655	POP*GPC
126	Mauritius	12,504	POP*GPC
127	Macao	11,651	POP*GPC
128	Papua New G	11,607	POP*GPC
129	Congo, Rep	11,417	POP*GPC
130	Zambia	11,307	POP*GPC
131	Benin	11,095	POP*GPC
132	Haiti	10,963	POP*GPC
133	Bahamas	10,619	POP*GPC
134	Georgia	10,440	POP*GPC
135	Malta	10,346	POP*GPC
136	Mozambique	10,243	POP*GPC
137	Mali	10,226	POP*GPC
138	Namibia	9,785	POP*GPC
139	Iceland	9,727	POP*GPC
140	Moldova	8,773	POP*GPC
141	Malawi	8,513	POP*GPC
142	Kyrgyzstan	8,431	POP*GPC
143	Chad	8,340	POP*GPC

Table 3.20 Gross Domestic Product at Purchasing Power Parities, Millions of 2012 Dollars, Year 2000

Rank	Country	GDP	Source
144	Guinea	8,215	POP*GPC
145	Laos	7,999	POP*GPC
146	Niger	7,210	POP*GPC
147	Tajikistan	6,950	POP*GPC
148	Barbados	6,840	POP*GPC
149	Kosovo	6,723	POP*GPC
150	West Bank	6,307	POP*GPC
151	Somalia	6,230	POP*GPC
152	Rwanda	6,110	POP*GPC
153	Mongolia	6,042	POP*GPC
154	Montenegro	5,802	POP*GPC
155	Swaziland	5,180	POP*GPC
156	Equatorial G	5,125	POP*GPC
157	South Sudan	4,952	POP*GPC
158	Mauritania	4,876	POP*GPC
159	Reunion	4,842	POP*GPC
160	Martinique	4,840	POP*GPC
161	Guadeloupe	4,834	POP*GPC
162	Togo	4,774	POP*GPC
163	Guam	4,152	POP*GPC
164	New Caledon	4,052	POP*GPC
165	Fiji	3,754	POP*GPC
166	Fr Polynesia	3,591	POP*GPC
167	Sierra Leone	3,576	POP*GPC
168	Burundi	3,522	POP*GPC
169	Aruba	3,325	POP*GPC
170	CAR	3,072	POP*GPC
171	Jersey	2,983	POP*GPC
172	Suriname	2,610	POP*GPC
173	Lesotho	2,598	POP*GPC
174	Gambia	2,564	POP*GPC
175	Eritrea	2,500	POP*GPC
176	Virgin I, US	2,167	POP*GPC
177	Bermuda	2,149	POP*GPC
178	Guyana	2,081	POP*GPC
179	Isle of Man	1,894	POP*GPC
180	Bhutan	1,810	POP*GPC
181	Gaza Strip	1,713	POP*GPC
182	Seychelles	1,702	POP*GPC
183	Guernsey	1,701	POP*GPC
184	Curacao	1,689	POP*GPC
185	St Lucia	1,629	POP*GPC
186	Belize	1,623	POP*GPC
187	Cayman Is	1,607	POP*GPC
188	Andorra	1,593	POP*GPC
189	Djibouti	1,479	POP*GPC
190	Greenland	1,444	POP*GPC
191	Antigua & B	1,438	POP*GPC

Table 3.20 Gross Domestic Product at Purchasing Power Parities, Millions of 2012 Dollars, Year 2000			
Rank	Country	GDP	Source
192	Guinea-Biss	1,423	POP*GPC
193	Maldives	1,390	POP*GPC
194	Guiana, Fr	1,370	POP*GPC
195	Liberia	1,282	POP*GPC
196	Cape Verde	1,202	POP*GPC
197	Monaco	1,191	POP*GPC
198	Faroe Is	1,180	POP*GPC
199	Liechtenstn	1,163	POP*GPC
200	San Marino	1,078	POP*GPC
201	N Mariana Is	1,070	POP*GPC
202	Solomon Is	1,062	POP*GPC
203	Gibraltar	978	POP*GPC
204	Grenada	953	POP*GPC
205	East Timor	911	POP*GPC
206	St Vincent	903	POP*GPC
207	Vanuatu	827	POP*GPC
208	W Sahara	776	POP*GPC
209	St Kitts & N	733	POP*GPC
210	Comoros	704	POP*GPC
211	Dominica	667	POP*GPC
212	Samoa, Amer	640	POP*GPC
213	Samoa	618	POP*GPC
214	Mayotte	541	POP*GPC
215	Tonga	432	POP*GPC
216	Sint Maarten	394	POP*GPC
217	Virgin I, Br	389	POP*GPC
218	Micronesia	368	POP*GPC
219	Palau	349	POP*GPC
220	Saint Martin	337	POP*GPC
221	Kiribati	227	POP*GPC
222	Svalbard	221	POP*GPC
223	Turks & C Is	220	POP*GPC
224	St Pierre&M	211	POP*GPC
225	Sao Tome & P	206	POP*GPC
226	Anguilla	131	POP*GPC
227	Cook Is	130	POP*GPC
228	Marshall Is	114	POP*GPC
229	Falkland Is	86	POP*GPC
230	Saint Helena	66	POP*GPC
231	Nauru	64	POP*GPC
232	Wallis & Fut	42	POP*GPC
233	Montserrat	27	POP*GPC
234	Tuvalu	13	POP*GPC
235	Niue	8	POP*GPC
236	Tokelau	3	POP*GPC

TABLE 3.21 GROSS DOMESTIC PRODUCT AT PURCHASING POWER PARITIES, MILLIONS OF 2012 DOLLARS, YEAR 2010

Rank	Country	GDP	Source
1	US	15,539,778	POP*GPC
2	China	10,528,805	POP*GPC
3	Japan	4,504,409	POP*GPC
4	India	4,259,456	POP*GPC
5	Germany	3,297,337	POP*GPC
6	Russia	3,084,444	POP*GPC
7	France	2,289,757	POP*GPC
8	UK	2,245,040	POP*GPC
9	Brazil	2,192,294	POP*GPC
10	Italy	2,076,136	POP*GPC
11	Mexico	1,741,186	POP*GPC
12	Spain	1,508,964	POP*GPC
13	Korea, South	1,419,117	POP*GPC
14	Canada	1,341,418	POP*GPC
15	Turkey	1,234,522	POP*GPC
16	Indonesia	1,060,535	POP*GPC
17	Iran	921,800	POP*GPC
18	Australia	900,256	POP*GPC
19	Taiwan	872,025	POP*GPC
20	Poland	829,200	POP*GPC
21	Saudi Arabia	769,166	POP*GPC
22	Netherlands	728,499	POP*GPC
23	Argentina	671,145	POP*GPC
24	Thailand	597,092	POP*GPC
25	South Africa	541,446	POP*GPC
26	Egypt	517,428	POP*GPC
27	Pakistan	489,504	POP*GPC
28	Malaysia	445,969	POP*GPC
29	Belgium	445,249	POP*GPC
30	Colombia	426,821	POP*GPC
31	Switzerland	413,301	POP*GPC
32	Nigeria	394,400	POP*GPC
33	Sweden	392,532	POP*GPC
34	Philippines	375,824	POP*GPC
35	Austria	357,777	POP*GPC
36	Venezuela	356,663	POP*GPC
37	Romania	352,884	POP*GPC
38	Hong Kong	343,873	POP*GPC
39	Greece	319,417	POP*GPC
40	Norway	318,971	POP*GPC
41	Ukraine	315,542	POP*GPC
42	Chile	314,923	POP*GPC
43	UAE	313,049	POP*GPC
44	Singapore	303,153	POP*GPC
45	Vietnam	300,655	POP*GPC
46	Algeria	297,593	POP*GPC
47	Czechia	285,592	POP*GPC

Table 3.21 Gross Domestic Product at Purchasing Power Parities, Millions of 2012 Dollars, Year 2010

Rank	Country	GDP	Source
48	Portugal	285,564	POP*GPC
49	Peru	281,179	POP*GPC
50	Bangladesh	248,146	POP*GPC
51	Denmark	237,363	POP*GPC
52	Hungary	224,792	POP*GPC
53	Israel	219,990	POP*GPC
54	Finland	208,179	POP*GPC
55	Iraq	204,452	POP*GPC
56	Kazakhstan	203,210	POP*GPC
57	Ireland	195,380	POP*GPC
58	Kuwait	165,854	POP*GPC
59	Morocco	154,624	POP*GPC
60	Qatar	148,133	POP*GPC
61	New Zealand	137,968	POP*GPC
62	Belarus	135,571	POP*GPC
63	Slovakia	132,330	POP*GPC
64	Ecuador	126,255	POP*GPC
65	Cuba	118,381	POP*GPC
66	Bulgaria	114,273	POP*GPC
67	Libya	107,475	POP*GPC
68	Sri Lanka	105,962	POP*GPC
69	Tunisia	102,268	POP*GPC
70	Syria	102,187	POP*GPC
71	Angola	98,198	POP*GPC
72	Azerbaijan	92,049	POP*GPC
73	Uzbekistan	91,655	POP*GPC
74	Croatia	89,482	POP*GPC
75	Dominican R	89,085	POP*GPC
76	Serbia	84,461	POP*GPC
77	Burma	81,673	POP*GPC
78	Ethiopia	79,709	POP*GPC
79	Oman	77,675	POP*GPC
80	Guatemala	70,922	POP*GPC
81	Yemen	68,553	POP*GPC
82	Kenya	68,547	POP*GPC
83	Sudan	67,565	POP*GPC
84	Lithuania	65,515	POP*GPC
85	Puerto Rico	63,218	POP*GPC
86	Tanzania	62,418	POP*GPC
87	Slovenia	59,705	POP*GPC
88	Lebanon	57,860	POP*GPC
89	Korea, North	57,828	POP*GPC
90	Costa Rica	50,841	POP*GPC
91	Panama	50,562	POP*GPC
92	Bolivia	47,859	POP*GPC
93	Uruguay	47,028	POP*GPC
94	Luxembourg	46,902	POP*GPC
95	Ghana	44,209	POP*GPC

TABLE 3.21 GROSS DOMESTIC PRODUCT AT PURCHASING POWER PARITIES, MILLIONS OF 2012 DOLLARS, YEAR 2010

Rank	Country	GDP	Source
96	Cameroon	43,862	POP*GPC
97	Ivory Coast	42,320	POP*GPC
98	Turkmenistan	41,402	POP*GPC
99	El Salvador	41,052	POP*GPC
100	Uganda	40,620	POP*GPC
101	Latvia	39,709	POP*GPC
102	Paraguay	38,655	POP*GPC
103	Cyprus	36,756	POP*GPC
104	Macao	36,254	POP*GPC
105	Jordan	36,243	POP*GPC
106	Nepal	36,088	POP*GPC
107	Bosnia	35,722	POP*GPC
108	Bahrain	35,443	POP*GPC
109	Trinidad & T	35,277	POP*GPC
110	Cambodia	32,552	POP*GPC
111	Afghanistan	31,200	POP*GPC
112	Honduras	30,604	POP*GPC
113	Botswana	29,366	POP*GPC
114	Estonia	27,889	POP*GPC
115	Albania	26,141	POP*GPC
116	Congo, Dem R	25,292	POP*GPC
117	Reunion	24,847	POP*GPC
118	Jamaica	24,815	POP*GPC
119	Chad	24,316	POP*GPC
120	Macedonia	23,699	POP*GPC
121	Senegal	23,572	POP*GPC
122	Burkina Faso	22,722	POP*GPC
123	Georgia	22,399	POP*GPC
124	Gabon	22,046	POP*GPC
125	Nicaragua	21,440	POP*GPC
126	Mozambique	20,599	POP*GPC
127	Equatorial G	20,470	POP*GPC
128	Madagascar	20,218	POP*GPC
129	Zambia	20,119	POP*GPC
130	Brunei	19,910	POP*GPC
131	Mali	18,246	POP*GPC
132	Armenia	18,024	POP*GPC
133	Papua New G	17,397	POP*GPC
134	Congo, Rep	17,326	POP*GPC
135	Mauritius	17,312	POP*GPC
136	Laos	16,007	POP*GPC
137	Tajikistan	15,021	POP*GPC
138	Namibia	14,423	POP*GPC
139	Benin	14,172	POP*GPC
140	Martinique	12,701	POP*GPC
141	Moldova	12,659	POP*GPC
142	Kyrgyzstan	12,604	POP*GPC
143	Guadeloupe	12,579	POP*GPC

Table 3.21 Gross Domestic Product at Purchasing Power Parities, Millions of 2012 Dollars, Year 2010

Rank	Country	GDP	Source
144	Rwanda	12,108	POP*GPC
145	Iceland	12,049	POP*GPC
146	Kosovo	11,782	POP*GPC
147	Malta	11,760	POP*GPC
148	Niger	11,247	POP*GPC
149	Malawi	11,188	POP*GPC
150	Mongolia	11,068	POP*GPC
151	Haiti	11,067	POP*GPC
152	Bahamas	10,919	POP*GPC
153	Guinea	10,231	POP*GPC
154	South Sudan	9,984	POP*GPC
155	New Caledon	9,728	POP*GPC
156	Montenegro	8,636	POP*GPC
157	Mauritania	7,699	POP*GPC
158	Barbados	7,329	POP*GPC
159	Sierra Leone	6,717	POP*GPC
160	West Bank	6,409	POP*GPC
161	Swaziland	6,355	POP*GPC
162	Fr Polynesia	6,342	POP*GPC
163	Jersey	6,266	POP*GPC
164	Togo	6,120	POP*GPC
165	Somalia	6,001	POP*GPC
166	Guiana, Fr	5,990	POP*GPC
167	Zimbabwe	5,833	POP*GPC
168	Monaco	5,826	POP*GPC
169	Bermuda	5,493	POP*GPC
170	CAR	4,817	POP*GPC
171	Guam	4,728	POP*GPC
172	Isle of Man	4,706	POP*GPC
173	Virgin I, US	4,642	POP*GPC
174	Burundi	4,631	POP*GPC
175	Suriname	4,302	POP*GPC
176	Bhutan	4,169	POP*GPC
177	Fiji	4,078	POP*GPC
178	Gambia	3,527	POP*GPC
179	Lesotho	3,521	POP*GPC
180	Liechtenstn	3,440	POP*GPC
181	Andorra	3,322	POP*GPC
182	Guernsey	3,285	POP*GPC
183	Curacao	3,004	POP*GPC
184	Cayman Is	2,725	POP*GPC
185	Mayotte	2,701	POP*GPC
186	Eritrea	2,689	POP*GPC
187	Maldives	2,683	POP*GPC
188	Belize	2,430	POP*GPC
189	Guyana	2,324	POP*GPC
190	Aruba	2,322	POP*GPC
191	Cape Verde	2,260	POP*GPC

Table 3.21 Gross Domestic Product at Purchasing Power Parities, Millions of 2012 Dollars, Year 2010

Rank	Country	GDP	Source
192	Liberia	2,235	POP*GPC
193	Djibouti	2,222	POP*GPC
194	Seychelles	2,140	POP*GPC
195	Greenland	2,111	POP*GPC
196	Gaza Strip	2,034	POP*GPC
197	St Lucia	1,901	POP*GPC
198	Guinea-Biss	1,841	POP*GPC
199	Antigua & B	1,710	POP*GPC
200	East Timor	1,694	POP*GPC
201	Faroe Is	1,526	POP*GPC
202	Solomon Is	1,503	POP*GPC
203	Gibraltar	1,352	POP*GPC
204	W Sahara	1,264	POP*GPC
205	San Marino	1,126	POP*GPC
206	Grenada	1,116	POP*GPC
207	Vanuatu	1,102	POP*GPC
208	Virgin I, Br	1,093	POP*GPC
209	St Vincent	1,090	POP*GPC
210	Turks & C Is	940	POP*GPC
211	Dominica	907	POP*GPC
212	St Kitts & N	860	POP*GPC
213	Comoros	852	POP*GPC
214	Sint Maarten	826	POP*GPC
215	Samoa	813	POP*GPC
216	N Mariana Is	770	POP*GPC
217	Saint Martin	657	POP*GPC
218	Tonga	488	POP*GPC
219	Samoa, Amer	452	POP*GPC
220	Marshall Is	448	POP*GPC
221	Micronesia	374	POP*GPC
222	Palau	349	POP*GPC
223	Sao Tome & P	317	POP*GPC
224	Kiribati	260	POP*GPC
225	St Pierre&M	227	POP*GPC
226	Svalbard	204	POP*GPC
227	Anguilla	192	POP*GPC
228	Falkland Is	178	POP*GPC
229	Cook Is	118	POP*GPC
230	Wallis & Fut	70	POP*GPC
231	Saint Helena	61	POP*GPC
232	Nauru	57	POP*GPC
233	Montserrat	47	POP*GPC
234	Tuvalu	39	POP*GPC
235	Niue	10	POP*GPC
236	Tokelau	3	POP*GPC

Table 3.22 Gross Domestic Product at Purchasing Power Parities, Millions of 2012 Dollars, Year 2012

Rank	Country	GDP	Source
1	US	16,261,009	POP*GPC
2	China	12,270,138	POP*GPC
3	India	4,779,027	POP*GPC
4	Japan	4,542,373	POP*GPC
5	Germany	3,460,217	POP*GPC
6	Russia	3,377,570	POP*GPC
7	France	2,337,236	POP*GPC
8	UK	2,277,784	POP*GPC
9	Brazil	2,274,691	POP*GPC
10	Italy	2,082,113	POP*GPC
11	Mexico	1,915,028	POP*GPC
12	Spain	1,518,003	POP*GPC
13	Korea, South	1,497,670	POP*GPC
14	Canada	1,416,659	POP*GPC
15	Turkey	1,394,855	POP*GPC
16	Indonesia	1,193,641	POP*GPC
17	Australia	980,527	POP*GPC
18	Iran	930,499	POP*GPC
19	Saudi Arabia	907,968	POP*GPC
20	Taiwan	905,842	POP*GPC
21	Poland	877,433	POP*GPC
22	Argentina	744,067	POP*GPC
23	Netherlands	725,339	POP*GPC
24	Thailand	640,643	POP*GPC
25	South Africa	576,522	POP*GPC
26	Egypt	548,000	POP*GPC
27	Pakistan	521,541	POP*GPC
28	Malaysia	503,159	POP*GPC
29	Colombia	471,983	POP*GPC
30	Belgium	451,494	POP*GPC
31	Nigeria	445,639	POP*GPC
32	Switzerland	425,375	POP*GPC
33	Philippines	408,666	POP*GPC
34	Sweden	408,088	POP*GPC
35	Venezuela	391,824	POP*GPC
36	Austria	373,132	POP*GPC
37	Hong Kong	363,566	POP*GPC
38	Romania	359,633	POP*GPC
39	Chile	356,552	POP*GPC
40	Vietnam	336,277	POP*GPC
41	Ukraine	333,049	POP*GPC
42	Norway	332,469	POP*GPC
43	UAE	329,898	POP*GPC
44	Singapore	323,386	POP*GPC
45	Peru	318,070	POP*GPC
46	Algeria	316,012	POP*GPC
47	Czechia	287,954	POP*GPC

TABLE 3.22 GROSS DOMESTIC PRODUCT AT PURCHASING POWER PARITIES, MILLIONS OF 2012 DOLLARS, YEAR 2012

Rank	Country	GDP	Source
48	Greece	282,695	POP*GPC
49	Bangladesh	282,537	POP*GPC
50	Portugal	274,872	POP*GPC
51	Iraq	250,620	POP*GPC
52	Denmark	239,819	POP*GPC
53	Israel	236,877	POP*GPC
54	Kazakhstan	229,811	POP*GPC
55	Hungary	223,558	POP*GPC
56	Finland	212,192	POP*GPC
57	Ireland	200,536	POP*GPC
58	Kuwait	176,570	POP*GPC
59	Qatar	171,360	POP*GPC
60	Morocco	168,627	POP*GPC
61	Ecuador	146,068	POP*GPC
62	New Zealand	145,855	POP*GPC
63	Belarus	144,993	POP*GPC
64	Slovakia	139,742	POP*GPC
65	Sri Lanka	124,873	POP*GPC
66	Cuba	121,973	POP*GPC
67	Bulgaria	117,270	POP*GPC
68	Angola	108,373	POP*GPC
69	Tunisia	103,768	POP*GPC
70	Uzbekistan	103,571	POP*GPC
71	Syria	100,817	POP*GPC
72	Dominican R	96,639	POP*GPC
73	Azerbaijan	94,172	POP*GPC
74	Ethiopia	93,303	POP*GPC
75	Croatia	89,417	POP*GPC
76	Burma	87,322	POP*GPC
77	Serbia	84,531	POP*GPC
78	Guatemala	75,987	POP*GPC
79	Oman	75,503	POP*GPC
80	Kenya	74,593	POP*GPC
81	Sudan	73,988	POP*GPC
82	Lithuania	73,278	POP*GPC
83	Libya	73,057	POP*GPC
84	Tanzania	70,464	POP*GPC
85	Puerto Rico	64,363	POP*GPC
86	Yemen	62,499	POP*GPC
87	Panama	61,900	POP*GPC
88	Lebanon	59,355	POP*GPC
89	Korea, North	59,051	POP*GPC
90	Slovenia	58,555	POP*GPC
91	Costa Rica	55,435	POP*GPC
92	Bolivia	53,557	POP*GPC
93	Ghana	52,732	POP*GPC
94	Turkmenistan	52,630	POP*GPC
95	Uruguay	51,931	POP*GPC

Table 3.22 Gross Domestic Product at Purchasing Power Parities, Millions of 2012 Dollars, Year 2012

Rank	Country	GDP	Source
96	Macao	49,658	POP*GPC
97	Cameroon	47,747	POP*GPC
98	Luxembourg	47,680	POP*GPC
99	Uganda	44,727	POP*GPC
100	Latvia	44,630	POP*GPC
101	Ivory Coast	44,022	POP*GPC
102	El Salvador	42,575	POP*GPC
103	Afghanistan	42,077	POP*GPC
104	Paraguay	39,486	POP*GPC
105	Nepal	39,134	POP*GPC
106	Jordan	38,142	POP*GPC
107	Cambodia	36,689	POP*GPC
108	Bosnia	36,095	POP*GPC
109	Cyprus	35,793	POP*GPC
110	Trinidad & T	35,451	POP*GPC
111	Bahrain	35,219	POP*GPC
112	Botswana	33,132	POP*GPC
113	Honduras	33,027	POP*GPC
114	Estonia	31,572	POP*GPC
115	Congo, Dem R	28,888	POP*GPC
116	Albania	26,492	POP*GPC
117	Chad	26,338	POP*GPC
118	Georgia	26,242	POP*GPC
119	Burkina Faso	25,904	POP*GPC
120	Senegal	24,736	POP*GPC
121	Gabon	24,652	POP*GPC
122	Jamaica	24,393	POP*GPC
123	Macedonia	24,391	POP*GPC
124	Nicaragua	23,860	POP*GPC
125	Mozambique	23,694	POP*GPC
126	Zambia	23,552	POP*GPC
127	Reunion	22,292	POP*GPC
128	Equatorial G	22,012	POP*GPC
129	Madagascar	21,174	POP*GPC
130	Brunei	21,005	POP*GPC
131	Papua New G	20,340	POP*GPC
132	Laos	18,762	POP*GPC
133	Armenia	18,734	POP*GPC
134	Mali	18,657	POP*GPC
135	Mauritius	18,518	POP*GPC
136	Congo, Rep	18,411	POP*GPC
137	Tajikistan	17,172	POP*GPC
138	Namibia	15,852	POP*GPC
139	Benin	14,556	POP*GPC
140	Mongolia	14,462	POP*GPC
141	Rwanda	13,991	POP*GPC
142	Kosovo	13,777	POP*GPC
143	Moldova	13,198	POP*GPC

TABLE 3.22 GROSS DOMESTIC PRODUCT AT PURCHASING POWER PARITIES, MILLIONS OF 2012 DOLLARS, YEAR 2012

Rank	Country	GDP	Source
144	Kyrgyzstan	13,137	POP*GPC
145	Niger	12,802	POP*GPC
146	Iceland	12,563	POP*GPC
147	Martinique	12,203	POP*GPC
148	Guadeloupe	12,160	POP*GPC
149	Malta	12,016	POP*GPC
150	Malawi	11,970	POP*GPC
151	Haiti	11,853	POP*GPC
152	South Sudan	11,620	POP*GPC
153	Bahamas	11,282	POP*GPC
154	Guinea	11,030	POP*GPC
155	New Caledon	10,329	POP*GPC
156	Montenegro	8,902	POP*GPC
157	Mauritania	8,601	POP*GPC
158	Sierra Leone	8,187	POP*GPC
159	Zimbabwe	7,773	POP*GPC
160	Barbados	7,346	POP*GPC
161	Monaco	7,176	POP*GPC
162	Fr Polynesia	6,732	POP*GPC
163	Togo	6,700	POP*GPC
164	West Bank	6,617	POP*GPC
165	Jersey	6,563	POP*GPC
166	Somalia	6,477	POP*GPC
167	Swaziland	6,295	POP*GPC
168	Bermuda	5,773	POP*GPC
169	Guiana, Fr	5,566	POP*GPC
170	CAR	5,445	POP*GPC
171	Isle of Man	4,965	POP*GPC
172	Bhutan	4,942	POP*GPC
173	Guam	4,924	POP*GPC
174	Burundi	4,813	POP*GPC
175	Virgin I, US	4,805	POP*GPC
176	Suriname	4,770	POP*GPC
177	Fiji	4,175	POP*GPC
178	Lesotho	3,728	POP*GPC
179	Liechtenstn	3,609	POP*GPC
180	Gambia	3,501	POP*GPC
181	Guernsey	3,420	POP*GPC
182	Curacao	3,174	POP*GPC
183	Eritrea	3,108	POP*GPC
184	Maldives	2,950	POP*GPC
185	Andorra	2,915	POP*GPC
186	Cayman Is	2,814	POP*GPC
187	Mayotte	2,712	POP*GPC
188	Belize	2,628	POP*GPC
189	Liberia	2,581	POP*GPC
190	Aruba	2,548	POP*GPC
191	Guyana	2,533	POP*GPC

Table 3.22 Gross Domestic Product at Purchasing Power Parities, Millions of 2012 Dollars, Year 2012

Rank	Country	GDP	Source
192	Cape Verde	2,445	POP*GPC
193	Seychelles	2,345	POP*GPC
194	Djibouti	2,296	POP*GPC
195	Greenland	2,155	POP*GPC
196	Gaza Strip	2,146	POP*GPC
197	St Lucia	1,935	POP*GPC
198	East Timor	1,898	POP*GPC
199	Guinea-Biss	1,811	POP*GPC
200	San Marino	1,782	POP*GPC
201	Solomon Is	1,779	POP*GPC
202	Antigua & B	1,714	POP*GPC
203	Faroe Is	1,555	POP*GPC
204	Gibraltar	1,413	POP*GPC
205	Virgin I, Br	1,410	POP*GPC
206	W Sahara	1,407	POP*GPC
207	Vanuatu	1,163	POP*GPC
208	St Vincent	1,138	POP*GPC
209	Grenada	1,126	POP*GPC
210	Turks & C Is	1,016	POP*GPC
211	St Kitts & N	933	POP*GPC
212	Comoros	891	POP*GPC
213	Dominica	888	POP*GPC
214	Sint Maarten	870	POP*GPC
215	Samoa	848	POP*GPC
216	N Mariana Is	744	POP*GPC
217	Saint Martin	698	POP*GPC
218	Tonga	503	POP*GPC
219	Samoa, Amer	472	POP*GPC
220	Marshall Is	465	POP*GPC
221	Palau	389	POP*GPC
222	Micronesia	381	POP*GPC
223	Sao Tome & P	344	POP*GPC
224	Kiribati	279	POP*GPC
225	St Pierre&M	227	POP*GPC
226	Anguilla	206	POP*GPC
227	Svalbard	198	POP*GPC
228	Falkland Is	189	POP*GPC
229	Cook Is	115	POP*GPC
230	Wallis & Fut	72	POP*GPC
231	Saint Helena	65	POP*GPC
232	Nauru	58	POP*GPC
233	Montserrat	49	POP*GPC
234	Tuvalu	39	POP*GPC
235	Niue	10	POP*GPC
236	Tokelau	3	POP*GPC

TABLE 3.23 GROSS DOMESTIC PRODUCT AT PURCHASING POWER PARITIES, MILLIONS OF 2012 DOLLARS, YEAR 2020, FORECAST

Rank	Country	GDP	Source
1	China	22,998,958	POP*GPC
2	US	19,813,222	POP*GPC
3	India	7,491,408	POP*GPC
4	Japan	5,090,130	POP*GPC
5	Russia	4,696,674	POP*GPC
6	Germany	3,988,877	POP*GPC
7	Brazil	2,837,518	POP*GPC
8	UK	2,804,032	POP*GPC
9	France	2,675,765	POP*GPC
10	Mexico	2,386,590	POP*GPC
11	Italy	2,329,409	POP*GPC
12	Korea, South	2,242,518	POP*GPC
13	Turkey	2,024,053	POP*GPC
14	Spain	1,849,995	POP*GPC
15	Canada	1,690,602	POP*GPC
16	Indonesia	1,658,554	POP*GPC
17	Taiwan	1,360,589	POP*GPC
18	Saudi Arabia	1,310,712	POP*GPC
19	Australia	1,286,515	POP*GPC
20	Iran	1,248,740	POP*GPC
21	Poland	1,173,573	POP*GPC
22	Argentina	1,026,210	POP*GPC
23	Thailand	891,914	POP*GPC
24	Netherlands	851,465	POP*GPC
25	Egypt	768,205	POP*GPC
26	Malaysia	743,185	POP*GPC
27	Pakistan	689,042	POP*GPC
28	South Africa	681,082	POP*GPC
29	Nigeria	657,707	POP*GPC
30	Colombia	614,409	POP*GPC
31	Philippines	547,072	POP*GPC
32	Vietnam	534,618	POP*GPC
33	Belgium	530,792	POP*GPC
34	Hong Kong	524,760	POP*GPC
35	Singapore	515,034	POP*GPC
36	Chile	510,950	POP*GPC
37	Sweden	500,415	POP*GPC
38	Switzerland	493,434	POP*GPC
39	Romania	476,640	POP*GPC
40	Venezuela	466,937	POP*GPC
41	Peru	452,412	POP*GPC
42	Austria	450,975	POP*GPC
43	Norway	446,607	POP*GPC
44	Bangladesh	413,181	POP*GPC
45	Ukraine	410,886	POP*GPC
46	Algeria	399,700	POP*GPC
47	UAE	398,359	POP*GPC
48	Iraq	370,525	POP*GPC

TABLE 3.23 GROSS DOMESTIC PRODUCT AT PURCHASING POWER PARITIES, MILLIONS OF 2012 DOLLARS, YEAR 2020, FORECAST

Rank	Country	GDP	Source
49	Kazakhstan	350,455	POP*GPC
50	Czechia	348,641	POP*GPC
51	Greece	338,890	POP*GPC
52	Portugal	320,600	POP*GPC
53	Israel	317,109	POP*GPC
54	Qatar	282,816	POP*GPC
55	Denmark	272,063	POP*GPC
56	Ireland	271,610	POP*GPC
57	Finland	254,752	POP*GPC
58	Hungary	254,599	POP*GPC
59	Morocco	224,815	POP*GPC
60	Kuwait	210,916	POP*GPC
61	Cuba	208,186	POP*GPC
62	Belarus	201,719	POP*GPC
63	Angola	189,214	POP*GPC
64	Slovakia	187,036	POP*GPC
65	Ecuador	186,734	POP*GPC
66	Sri Lanka	185,287	POP*GPC
67	New Zealand	176,898	POP*GPC
68	Azerbaijan	171,037	POP*GPC
69	Bulgaria	145,395	POP*GPC
70	Ethiopia	144,031	POP*GPC
71	Dominican R	141,503	POP*GPC
72	Tunisia	139,948	POP*GPC
73	Uzbekistan	137,721	POP*GPC
74	Syria	123,598	POP*GPC
75	Libya	115,798	POP*GPC
76	Oman	110,410	POP*GPC
77	Macao	108,407	POP*GPC
78	Tanzania	107,539	POP*GPC
79	Burma	106,221	POP*GPC
80	Croatia	104,308	POP*GPC
81	Serbia	101,849	POP*GPC
82	Sudan	100,154	POP*GPC
83	Guatemala	99,053	POP*GPC
84	Lithuania	98,550	POP*GPC
85	Panama	97,509	POP*GPC
86	Kenya	94,468	POP*GPC
87	Yemen	88,547	POP*GPC
88	Turkmenistan	84,346	POP*GPC
89	Lebanon	75,460	POP*GPC
90	Ghana	74,973	POP*GPC
91	Costa Rica	74,953	POP*GPC
92	Uganda	72,446	POP*GPC
93	Bolivia	72,394	POP*GPC
94	Puerto Rico	71,965	POP*GPC
95	Slovenia	71,252	POP*GPC
96	Uruguay	66,055	POP*GPC

Table 3.23 Gross Domestic Product at Purchasing Power Parities, Millions of 2012 Dollars, Year 2020, Forecast

Rank	Country	GDP	Source
97	Luxembourg	64,726	POP*GPC
98	Afghanistan	64,675	POP*GPC
99	Korea, North	64,238	POP*GPC
100	Cameroon	60,556	POP*GPC
101	Latvia	58,976	POP*GPC
102	Equatorial G	55,965	POP*GPC
103	Cambodia	54,044	POP*GPC
104	Nepal	52,451	POP*GPC
105	Jordan	52,335	POP*GPC
106	Ivory Coast	51,944	POP*GPC
107	El Salvador	51,703	POP*GPC
108	Botswana	51,661	POP*GPC
109	Paraguay	47,676	POP*GPC
110	Trinidad & T	47,605	POP*GPC
111	Cyprus	46,631	POP*GPC
112	Bahrain	45,793	POP*GPC
113	Reunion	44,805	POP*GPC
114	Chad	44,294	POP*GPC
115	Bosnia	43,929	POP*GPC
116	Honduras	43,793	POP*GPC
117	Congo, Dem R	40,006	POP*GPC
118	Estonia	39,987	POP*GPC
119	Burkina Faso	39,799	POP*GPC
120	Mozambique	38,378	POP*GPC
121	Georgia	37,124	POP*GPC
122	Albania	36,118	POP*GPC
123	Zambia	35,712	POP*GPC
124	Jamaica	32,752	POP*GPC
125	Senegal	31,289	POP*GPC
126	Gabon	30,956	POP*GPC
127	Nicaragua	30,774	POP*GPC
128	Laos	29,322	POP*GPC
129	Brunei	28,936	POP*GPC
130	Macedonia	28,766	POP*GPC
131	Papua New G	28,466	POP*GPC
132	Mali	27,273	POP*GPC
133	Madagascar	26,038	POP*GPC
134	Tajikistan	25,461	POP*GPC
135	Mauritius	24,916	POP*GPC
136	Congo, Rep	24,207	POP*GPC
137	Mongolia	24,124	POP*GPC
138	Rwanda	22,114	POP*GPC
139	Armenia	22,110	POP*GPC
140	Namibia	21,620	POP*GPC
141	Kosovo	19,912	POP*GPC
142	Guadeloupe	19,532	POP*GPC
143	Martinique	19,530	POP*GPC
144	South Sudan	18,942	POP*GPC

Table 3.23 Gross Domestic Product at Purchasing Power Parities, Millions of 2012 Dollars, Year 2020, Forecast

Rank	Country	GDP	Source
145	Niger	18,236	POP*GPC
146	Benin	18,171	POP*GPC
147	New Caledon	17,575	POP*GPC
148	Kyrgyzstan	16,436	POP*GPC
149	Monaco	16,362	POP*GPC
150	Malawi	16,302	POP*GPC
151	Moldova	15,500	POP*GPC
152	Malta	15,271	POP*GPC
153	Iceland	15,188	POP*GPC
154	Guinea	14,120	POP*GPC
155	Haiti	13,534	POP*GPC
156	Bahamas	12,732	POP*GPC
157	Mauritania	11,873	POP*GPC
158	Sierra Leone	11,769	POP*GPC
159	Montenegro	11,205	POP*GPC
160	Guiana, Fr	11,153	POP*GPC
161	Zimbabwe	11,142	POP*GPC
162	Bermuda	11,003	POP*GPC
163	Jersey	9,592	POP*GPC
164	Fr Polynesia	9,503	POP*GPC
165	Bhutan	8,648	POP*GPC
166	Barbados	8,335	POP*GPC
167	Isle of Man	8,172	POP*GPC
168	Togo	8,069	POP*GPC
169	West Bank	7,971	POP*GPC
170	Somalia	7,814	POP*GPC
171	Swaziland	7,713	POP*GPC
172	CAR	7,443	POP*GPC
173	Mayotte	7,325	POP*GPC
174	Virgin I, US	6,495	POP*GPC
175	Suriname	6,320	POP*GPC
176	Liechtenstn	6,043	POP*GPC
177	Guam	5,770	POP*GPC
178	Burundi	5,621	POP*GPC
179	Guernsey	4,910	POP*GPC
180	Maldives	4,726	POP*GPC
181	Lesotho	4,681	POP*GPC
182	Fiji	4,479	POP*GPC
183	Curacao	4,420	POP*GPC
184	Gambia	4,329	POP*GPC
185	Eritrea	4,109	POP*GPC
186	Cape Verde	3,979	POP*GPC
187	Liberia	3,845	POP*GPC
188	Andorra	3,609	POP*GPC
189	Belize	3,576	POP*GPC
190	Cayman Is	3,402	POP*GPC
191	Seychelles	3,247	POP*GPC
192	Guyana	3,034	POP*GPC

Table 3.23 Gross Domestic Product at Purchasing Power Parities, Millions of 2012 Dollars, Year 2020, Forecast

Rank	Country	GDP	Source
193	Djibouti	3,025	POP*GPC
194	Aruba	2,900	POP*GPC
195	Virgin I, Br	2,792	POP*GPC
196	East Timor	2,773	POP*GPC
197	Gaza Strip	2,714	POP*GPC
198	San Marino	2,689	POP*GPC
199	Greenland	2,685	POP*GPC
200	St Lucia	2,528	POP*GPC
201	Solomon Is	2,427	POP*GPC
202	W Sahara	2,361	POP*GPC
203	Turks & C Is	2,278	POP*GPC
204	Guinea-Biss	2,242	POP*GPC
205	Antigua & B	2,168	POP*GPC
206	Gibraltar	2,035	POP*GPC
207	Faroe Is	1,889	POP*GPC
208	Vanuatu	1,494	POP*GPC
209	St Vincent	1,472	POP*GPC
210	Grenada	1,426	POP*GPC
211	Sint Maarten	1,254	POP*GPC
212	St Kitts & N	1,223	POP*GPC
213	Dominica	1,132	POP*GPC
214	Comoros	1,045	POP*GPC
215	Saint Martin	1,038	POP*GPC
216	Samoa	1,003	POP*GPC
217	Marshall Is	890	POP*GPC
218	N Mariana Is	835	POP*GPC
219	Tonga	588	POP*GPC
220	Samoa, Amer	570	POP*GPC
221	Palau	449	POP*GPC
222	Sao Tome & P	447	POP*GPC
223	Micronesia	399	POP*GPC
224	Kiribati	351	POP*GPC
225	Falkland Is	279	POP*GPC
226	Anguilla	276	POP*GPC
227	Svalbard	267	POP*GPC
228	St Pierre&M	261	POP*GPC
229	Cook Is	99	POP*GPC
230	Wallis & Fut	92	POP*GPC
231	Saint Helena	82	POP*GPC
232	Tuvalu	63	POP*GPC
233	Nauru	60	POP*GPC
234	Montserrat	59	POP*GPC
235	Niue	10	POP*GPC
236	Tokelau	3	POP*GPC

Table 3.24 Gross Domestic Product at Purchasing Power Parities, Millions of 2012 Dollars, Year 2030, Forecast

Rank	Country	GDP	Source
1	China	29,893,111	POP*GPC
2	US	25,420,199	POP*GPC
3	India	10,644,522	POP*GPC
4	Russia	5,867,069	POP*GPC
5	Japan	5,800,240	POP*GPC
6	Germany	4,659,470	POP*GPC
7	Brazil	3,624,210	POP*GPC
8	UK	3,515,909	POP*GPC
9	France	3,183,418	POP*GPC
10	Mexico	3,068,634	POP*GPC
11	Korea, South	2,951,535	POP*GPC
12	Turkey	2,773,176	POP*GPC
13	Italy	2,722,809	POP*GPC
14	Spain	2,318,480	POP*GPC
15	Indonesia	2,235,884	POP*GPC
16	Canada	2,131,855	POP*GPC
17	Saudi Arabia	1,874,985	POP*GPC
18	Taiwan	1,765,120	POP*GPC
19	Australia	1,708,915	POP*GPC
20	Iran	1,622,745	POP*GPC
21	Poland	1,464,484	POP*GPC
22	Argentina	1,382,594	POP*GPC
23	Thailand	1,168,769	POP*GPC
24	Malaysia	1,071,890	POP*GPC
25	Egypt	1,068,945	POP*GPC
26	Netherlands	1,038,766	POP*GPC
27	Nigeria	1,025,177	POP*GPC
28	Pakistan	947,018	POP*GPC
29	South Africa	834,392	POP*GPC
30	Colombia	810,866	POP*GPC
31	Singapore	769,453	POP*GPC
32	Philippines	765,970	POP*GPC
33	Vietnam	744,696	POP*GPC
34	Hong Kong	728,901	POP*GPC
35	Chile	689,931	POP*GPC
36	Belgium	655,550	POP*GPC
37	Sweden	624,185	POP*GPC
38	Peru	620,812	POP*GPC
39	Norway	602,990	POP*GPC
40	Switzerland	589,656	POP*GPC
41	Venezuela	588,590	POP*GPC
42	Romania	581,977	POP*GPC
43	Iraq	577,582	POP*GPC
44	Bangladesh	573,128	POP*GPC
45	Austria	560,929	POP*GPC
46	Algeria	513,771	POP*GPC
47	UAE	502,806	POP*GPC
48	Ukraine	487,621	POP*GPC

Table 3.24 Gross Domestic Product at Purchasing Power Parities, Millions of 2012 Dollars, Year 2030, Forecast			
Rank	Country	GDP	Source
49	Kazakhstan	482,303	POP*GPC
50	Israel	436,924	POP*GPC
51	Czechia	424,243	POP*GPC
52	Greece	412,218	POP*GPC
53	Qatar	393,493	POP*GPC
54	Portugal	385,752	POP*GPC
55	Ireland	364,906	POP*GPC
56	Denmark	325,413	POP*GPC
57	Finland	316,718	POP*GPC
58	Angola	316,676	POP*GPC
59	Morocco	302,061	POP*GPC
60	Hungary	295,430	POP*GPC
61	Cuba	268,436	POP*GPC
62	Kuwait	263,310	POP*GPC
63	Sri Lanka	251,596	POP*GPC
64	Belarus	249,912	POP*GPC
65	Ecuador	247,376	POP*GPC
66	Slovakia	237,724	POP*GPC
67	Azerbaijan	235,631	POP*GPC
68	New Zealand	226,336	POP*GPC
69	Ethiopia	214,535	POP*GPC
70	Dominican R	195,967	POP*GPC
71	Tunisia	184,111	POP*GPC
72	Uzbekistan	182,649	POP*GPC
73	Tanzania	172,733	POP*GPC
74	Bulgaria	172,655	POP*GPC
75	Libya	166,786	POP*GPC
76	Syria	161,643	POP*GPC
77	Macao	153,628	POP*GPC
78	Oman	152,729	POP*GPC
79	Sudan	143,820	POP*GPC
80	Panama	142,073	POP*GPC
81	Guatemala	138,273	POP*GPC
82	Burma	135,005	POP*GPC
83	Yemen	133,070	POP*GPC
84	Croatia	123,267	POP*GPC
85	Kenya	122,726	POP*GPC
86	Lithuania	122,407	POP*GPC
87	Uganda	121,563	POP*GPC
88	Serbia	120,908	POP*GPC
89	Turkmenistan	119,450	POP*GPC
90	Ghana	112,347	POP*GPC
91	Bolivia	101,854	POP*GPC
92	Afghanistan	101,456	POP*GPC
93	Costa Rica	100,078	POP*GPC
94	Lebanon	95,760	POP*GPC
95	Luxembourg	88,236	POP*GPC
96	Slovenia	87,090	POP*GPC

Table 3.24 Gross Domestic Product at Purchasing Power Parities, Millions of 2012 Dollars, Year 2030, Forecast

Rank	Country	GDP	Source
97	Equatorial G	86,684	POP*GPC
98	Uruguay	84,214	POP*GPC
99	Cameroon	81,736	POP*GPC
100	Puerto Rico	79,168	POP*GPC
101	Cambodia	76,963	POP*GPC
102	Botswana	75,674	POP*GPC
103	Korea, North	73,380	POP*GPC
104	Jordan	72,736	POP*GPC
105	Chad	72,578	POP*GPC
106	Latvia	72,457	POP*GPC
107	Nepal	72,411	POP*GPC
108	Ivory Coast	64,487	POP*GPC
109	Burkina Faso	64,344	POP*GPC
110	El Salvador	64,194	POP*GPC
111	Mozambique	62,689	POP*GPC
112	Reunion	62,232	POP*GPC
113	Cyprus	61,660	POP*GPC
114	Paraguay	60,874	POP*GPC
115	Honduras	60,373	POP*GPC
116	Bahrain	60,000	POP*GPC
117	Trinidad & T	59,681	POP*GPC
118	Congo, Dem R	58,795	POP*GPC
119	Zambia	57,788	POP*GPC
120	Bosnia	52,199	POP*GPC
121	Estonia	49,122	POP*GPC
122	Albania	46,958	POP*GPC
123	Georgia	44,471	POP*GPC
124	Mali	42,559	POP*GPC
125	Senegal	42,490	POP*GPC
126	Jamaica	41,801	POP*GPC
127	Laos	41,651	POP*GPC
128	Gabon	41,490	POP*GPC
129	Papua New G	41,147	POP*GPC
130	Nicaragua	40,541	POP*GPC
131	Brunei	40,123	POP*GPC
132	Tajikistan	36,739	POP*GPC
133	Rwanda	34,798	POP*GPC
134	Mongolia	34,719	POP*GPC
135	Congo, Rep	34,713	POP*GPC
136	Macedonia	34,274	POP*GPC
137	Madagascar	33,911	POP*GPC
138	Mauritius	32,278	POP*GPC
139	Namibia	30,157	POP*GPC
140	South Sudan	29,500	POP*GPC
141	Niger	28,788	POP*GPC
142	Kosovo	27,359	POP*GPC
143	Armenia	26,371	POP*GPC
144	Guadeloupe	26,101	POP*GPC

Table 3.24 Gross Domestic Product at Purchasing Power Parities, Millions of 2012 Dollars, Year 2030, Forecast

Rank	Country	GDP	Source
145	Martinique	25,490	POP*GPC
146	New Caledon	25,281	POP*GPC
147	Benin	24,503	POP*GPC
148	Malawi	24,463	POP*GPC
149	Kyrgyzstan	21,563	POP*GPC
150	Monaco	21,150	POP*GPC
151	Guinea	19,532	POP*GPC
152	Iceland	19,348	POP*GPC
153	Malta	19,106	POP*GPC
154	Moldova	18,058	POP*GPC
155	Guiana, Fr	18,025	POP*GPC
156	Sierra Leone	17,304	POP*GPC
157	Mauritania	17,223	POP*GPC
158	Haiti	16,446	POP*GPC
159	Zimbabwe	15,564	POP*GPC
160	Bahamas	14,943	POP*GPC
161	Bermuda	14,428	POP*GPC
162	Montenegro	13,939	POP*GPC
163	Jersey	12,916	POP*GPC
164	Fr Polynesia	12,878	POP*GPC
165	Bhutan	12,239	POP*GPC
166	Mayotte	11,277	POP*GPC
167	Isle of Man	11,012	POP*GPC
168	Somalia	10,883	POP*GPC
169	CAR	10,877	POP*GPC
170	Togo	10,315	POP*GPC
171	West Bank	10,073	POP*GPC
172	Swaziland	9,801	POP*GPC
173	Barbados	9,794	POP*GPC
174	Liechtenstn	8,492	POP*GPC
175	Suriname	8,317	POP*GPC
176	Virgin I, US	7,650	POP*GPC
177	Guam	7,347	POP*GPC
178	Burundi	6,802	POP*GPC
179	Maldives	6,589	POP*GPC
180	Guernsey	6,579	POP*GPC
181	Liberia	5,993	POP*GPC
182	Lesotho	5,751	POP*GPC
183	Curacao	5,751	POP*GPC
184	Eritrea	5,705	POP*GPC
185	Cape Verde	5,604	POP*GPC
186	Gambia	5,601	POP*GPC
187	Virgin I, Br	5,328	POP*GPC
188	Fiji	5,166	POP*GPC
189	Belize	5,018	POP*GPC
190	Turks & C Is	4,666	POP*GPC
191	Andorra	4,422	POP*GPC
192	Cayman Is	4,257	POP*GPC

Table 3.24 Gross Domestic Product at Purchasing Power Parities, Millions of 2012 Dollars, Year 2030, Forecast			
Rank	Country	GDP	Source
193	Djibouti	4,214	POP*GPC
194	Seychelles	4,167	POP*GPC
195	East Timor	4,153	POP*GPC
196	W Sahara	3,803	POP*GPC
197	Guyana	3,769	POP*GPC
198	San Marino	3,603	POP*GPC
199	Solomon Is	3,578	POP*GPC
200	Gaza Strip	3,495	POP*GPC
201	Aruba	3,409	POP*GPC
202	Greenland	3,349	POP*GPC
203	St Lucia	3,243	POP*GPC
204	Guinea-Biss	3,015	POP*GPC
205	Antigua & B	2,843	POP*GPC
206	Gibraltar	2,608	POP*GPC
207	Faroe Is	2,377	POP*GPC
208	Vanuatu	2,008	POP*GPC
209	St Vincent	1,865	POP*GPC
210	Grenada	1,759	POP*GPC
211	Sint Maarten	1,679	POP*GPC
212	St Kitts & N	1,599	POP*GPC
213	Dominica	1,460	POP*GPC
214	Saint Martin	1,442	POP*GPC
215	Comoros	1,277	POP*GPC
216	Samoa	1,258	POP*GPC
217	Marshall Is	1,256	POP*GPC
218	N Mariana Is	1,028	POP*GPC
219	Tonga	729	POP*GPC
220	Samoa, Amer	679	POP*GPC
221	Sao Tome & P	612	POP*GPC
222	Palau	537	POP*GPC
223	Kiribati	465	POP*GPC
224	Micronesia	464	POP*GPC
225	Falkland Is	407	POP*GPC
226	Anguilla	403	POP*GPC
227	Svalbard	361	POP*GPC
228	St Pierre&M	286	POP*GPC
229	Wallis & Fut	116	POP*GPC
230	Saint Helena	107	POP*GPC
231	Tuvalu	82	POP*GPC
232	Cook Is	74	POP*GPC
233	Nauru	71	POP*GPC
234	Montserrat	64	POP*GPC
235	Niue	9	POP*GPC
236	Tokelau	3	POP*GPC

4. Population Growth Rates by Rank

Table 4.1 Population Growth Rates, 0001-1000

Rank	Country	GRPOP	Source
1	Madagascar	0.53	(POP1000/POP0001)**(1/999)-1
2	Burundi	0.23	(POP1000/POP0001)**(1/999)-1
3	Zambia	0.19	(POP1000/POP0001)**(1/999)-1
4	Malawi	0.19	(POP1000/POP0001)**(1/999)-1
5	Zimbabwe	0.19	(POP1000/POP0001)**(1/999)-1
6	Mozambique	0.18	(POP1000/POP0001)**(1/999)-1
7	Swaziland	0.11	(POP1000/POP0001)**(1/999)-1
8	South Africa	0.11	(POP1000/POP0001)**(1/999)-1
9	Lesotho	0.11	(POP1000/POP0001)**(1/999)-1
10	Poland	0.10	(POP1000/POP0001)**(1/999)-1
11	Ireland	0.09	(POP1000/POP0001)**(1/999)-1
12	UK	0.09	(POP1000/POP0001)**(1/999)-1
13	Japan	0.09	(POP1000/POP0001)**(1/999)-1
14	Guinea	0.08	(POP1000/POP0001)**(1/999)-1
15	Ghana	0.08	(POP1000/POP0001)**(1/999)-1
16	Sierra Leone	0.08	(POP1000/POP0001)**(1/999)-1
17	Guinea-Biss	0.08	(POP1000/POP0001)**(1/999)-1
18	Mexico	0.07	(POP1000/POP0001)**(1/999)-1
19	Trinidad & T	0.07	(POP1000/POP0001)**(1/999)-1
20	Jamaica	0.07	(POP1000/POP0001)**(1/999)-1
21	Panama	0.07	(POP1000/POP0001)**(1/999)-1
22	Costa Rica	0.07	(POP1000/POP0001)**(1/999)-1
23	Puerto Rico	0.07	(POP1000/POP0001)**(1/999)-1
24	Haiti	0.07	(POP1000/POP0001)**(1/999)-1
25	Honduras	0.07	(POP1000/POP0001)**(1/999)-1
26	Cuba	0.07	(POP1000/POP0001)**(1/999)-1
27	Guatemala	0.07	(POP1000/POP0001)**(1/999)-1
28	Ecuador	0.07	(POP1000/POP0001)**(1/999)-1
29	Colombia	0.07	(POP1000/POP0001)**(1/999)-1
30	Brazil	0.07	(POP1000/POP0001)**(1/999)-1
31	Peru	0.07	(POP1000/POP0001)**(1/999)-1
32	Chile	0.07	(POP1000/POP0001)**(1/999)-1
33	Bolivia	0.07	(POP1000/POP0001)**(1/999)-1
34	Nicaragua	0.07	(POP1000/POP0001)**(1/999)-1
35	Venezuela	0.07	(POP1000/POP0001)**(1/999)-1
36	Argentina	0.07	(POP1000/POP0001)**(1/999)-1
37	Paraguay	0.07	(POP1000/POP0001)**(1/999)-1
38	El Salvador	0.07	(POP1000/POP0001)**(1/999)-1
39	Dominican R	0.07	(POP1000/POP0001)**(1/999)-1
40	Uruguay	0.07	(POP1000/POP0001)**(1/999)-1
41	Latvia	0.07	(POP1000/POP0001)**(1/999)-1
42	Eritrea	0.07	(POP1000/POP0001)**(1/999)-1
48.5	Belarus	0.07	(POP1000/POP0001)**(1/999)-1
48.5	Canada	0.07	(POP1000/POP0001)**(1/999)-1
48.5	Denmark	0.07	(POP1000/POP0001)**(1/999)-1

TABLE 4.1 POPULATION GROWTH RATES, 0001-1000

Rank	Country	GRPOP	Source
48.5	Estonia	0.07	(POP1000/POP0001)**(1/999)-1
48.5	Finland	0.07	(POP1000/POP0001)**(1/999)-1
48.5	Lithuania	0.07	(POP1000/POP0001)**(1/999)-1
48.5	Moldova	0.07	(POP1000/POP0001)**(1/999)-1
48.5	Morocco	0.07	(POP1000/POP0001)**(1/999)-1
48.5	Norway	0.07	(POP1000/POP0001)**(1/999)-1
48.5	Somalia	0.07	(POP1000/POP0001)**(1/999)-1
48.5	Sweden	0.07	(POP1000/POP0001)**(1/999)-1
48.5	Ukraine	0.07	(POP1000/POP0001)**(1/999)-1
55	Ethiopia	0.07	(POP1000/POP0001)**(1/999)-1
56	Russia	0.07	(POP1000/POP0001)**(1/999)-1
57	US	0.06	(POP1000/POP0001)**(1/999)-1
58	Singapore	0.06	(POP1000/POP0001)**(1/999)-1
59	Taiwan	0.06	(POP1000/POP0001)**(1/999)-1
60	Malaysia	0.06	(POP1000/POP0001)**(1/999)-1
61	Sri Lanka	0.06	(POP1000/POP0001)**(1/999)-1
62	Korea, North	0.06	(POP1000/POP0001)**(1/999)-1
63	Burma	0.06	(POP1000/POP0001)**(1/999)-1
64	Korea, South	0.06	(POP1000/POP0001)**(1/999)-1
65	Nepal	0.06	(POP1000/POP0001)**(1/999)-1
66	Indonesia	0.06	(POP1000/POP0001)**(1/999)-1
67	Afghanistan	0.06	(POP1000/POP0001)**(1/999)-1
68	Vietnam	0.06	(POP1000/POP0001)**(1/999)-1
69	Thailand	0.06	(POP1000/POP0001)**(1/999)-1
70	Cambodia	0.06	(POP1000/POP0001)**(1/999)-1
71	Mongolia	0.06	(POP1000/POP0001)**(1/999)-1
72	Philippines	0.06	(POP1000/POP0001)**(1/999)-1
73	Laos	0.06	(POP1000/POP0001)**(1/999)-1
74	Kazakhstan	0.05	(POP1000/POP0001)**(1/999)-1
76	Armenia	0.05	(POP1000/POP0001)**(1/999)-1
76	Hungary	0.05	(POP1000/POP0001)**(1/999)-1
76	Turkmenistan	0.05	(POP1000/POP0001)**(1/999)-1
78	Uzbekistan	0.05	(POP1000/POP0001)**(1/999)-1
79	Kyrgyzstan	0.05	(POP1000/POP0001)**(1/999)-1
80	Georgia	0.05	(POP1000/POP0001)**(1/999)-1
81	Tajikistan	0.05	(POP1000/POP0001)**(1/999)-1
82	Azerbaijan	0.05	(POP1000/POP0001)**(1/999)-1
83	Bulgaria	0.05	(POP1000/POP0001)**(1/999)-1
84	Sudan	0.04	(POP1000/POP0001)**(1/999)-1
85.5	Netherlands	0.04	(POP1000/POP0001)**(1/999)-1
85.5	Portugal	0.04	(POP1000/POP0001)**(1/999)-1
87	South Sudan	0.04	(POP1000/POP0001)**(1/999)-1
88	Austria	0.03	(POP1000/POP0001)**(1/999)-1
89	Botswana	0.03	(POP1000/POP0001)**(1/999)-1
90	Belgium	0.03	(POP1000/POP0001)**(1/999)-1
91	Namibia	0.03	(POP1000/POP0001)**(1/999)-1
92	France	0.03	(POP1000/POP0001)**(1/999)-1
93.5	Australia	0.03	(POP1000/POP0001)**(1/999)-1

TABLE 4.1 POPULATION GROWTH RATES, 0001-1000			
Rank	Country	GRPOP	Source
93.5	New Zealand	0.03	(POP1000/POP0001)**(1/999)-1
95	Slovakia	0.02	(POP1000/POP0001)**(1/999)-1
97	Egypt	0.02	(POP1000/POP0001)**(1/999)-1
97	Libya	0.02	(POP1000/POP0001)**(1/999)-1
97	Tunisia	0.02	(POP1000/POP0001)**(1/999)-1
99	Czechia	0.02	(POP1000/POP0001)**(1/999)-1
100	Montenegro	0.02	(POP1000/POP0001)**(1/999)-1
101	Bosnia	0.02	(POP1000/POP0001)**(1/999)-1
102	Croatia	0.02	(POP1000/POP0001)**(1/999)-1
103	Germany	0.02	(POP1000/POP0001)**(1/999)-1
104	Serbia	0.02	(POP1000/POP0001)**(1/999)-1
105	Macedonia	0.02	(POP1000/POP0001)**(1/999)-1
106	Slovenia	0.02	(POP1000/POP0001)**(1/999)-1
107	Spain	0.01	(POP1000/POP0001)**(1/999)-1
108	Kosovo	0.01	(POP1000/POP0001)**(1/999)-1
109	Hong Kong	0.00	(POP1000/POP0001)**(1/999)-1
110	UAE	0.00	(POP1000/POP0001)**(1/999)-1
111	Jordan	0.00	(POP1000/POP0001)**(1/999)-1
112	Oman	0.00	(POP1000/POP0001)**(1/999)-1
113	Yemen	0.00	(POP1000/POP0001)**(1/999)-1
114	Saudi Arabia	0.00	(POP1000/POP0001)**(1/999)-1
115	Iraq	0.00	(POP1000/POP0001)**(1/999)-1
116	Syria	0.00	(POP1000/POP0001)**(1/999)-1
117	Turkey	0.00	(POP1000/POP0001)**(1/999)-1
118	Iran	0.00	(POP1000/POP0001)**(1/999)-1
119	Israel	0.00	(POP1000/POP0001)**(1/999)-1
120	Lebanon	0.00	(POP1000/POP0001)**(1/999)-1
121	Kuwait	0.00	(POP1000/POP0001)**(1/999)-1
122	Bahrain	0.00	(POP1000/POP0001)**(1/999)-1
123	Qatar	0.00	(POP1000/POP0001)**(1/999)-1
127	Albania	0.00	(POP1000/POP0001)**(1/999)-1
127	Algeria	0.00	(POP1000/POP0001)**(1/999)-1
127	Bangladesh	0.00	(POP1000/POP0001)**(1/999)-1
127	India	0.00	(POP1000/POP0001)**(1/999)-1
127	Pakistan	0.00	(POP1000/POP0001)**(1/999)-1
127	Romania	0.00	(POP1000/POP0001)**(1/999)-1
127	Switzerland	0.00	(POP1000/POP0001)**(1/999)-1
131	China	0.00	(POP1000/POP0001)**(1/999)-1
132	Cyprus	-0.03	(POP1000/POP0001)**(1/999)-1
133	Italy	-0.05	(POP1000/POP0001)**(1/999)-1
134	Greece	-0.06	(POP1000/POP0001)**(1/999)-1

Table 4.2 Population Growth Rates, 1000-1500

Rank	Country	GRPOP	Source
1	Finland	0.40	(POP1500/POP1000)**(1/500)-1
2.5	Belgium	0.25	(POP1500/POP1000)**(1/500)-1
2.5	Madagascar	0.25	(POP1500/POP1000)**(1/500)-1
4	Germany	0.25	(POP1500/POP1000)**(1/500)-1
5.5	Mozambique	0.24	(POP1500/POP1000)**(1/500)-1
5.5	Poland	0.24	(POP1500/POP1000)**(1/500)-1
7	Netherlands	0.23	(POP1500/POP1000)**(1/500)-1
8	Lithuania	0.22	(POP1500/POP1000)**(1/500)-1
9	Ukraine	0.22	(POP1500/POP1000)**(1/500)-1
11	Belarus	0.22	(POP1500/POP1000)**(1/500)-1
11	Latvia	0.22	(POP1500/POP1000)**(1/500)-1
11	Moldova	0.22	(POP1500/POP1000)**(1/500)-1
13	Estonia	0.22	(POP1500/POP1000)**(1/500)-1
14	Russia	0.22	(POP1500/POP1000)**(1/500)-1
15	Austria	0.21	(POP1500/POP1000)**(1/500)-1
16	Azerbaijan	0.18	(POP1500/POP1000)**(1/500)-1
17.5	Hungary	0.18	(POP1500/POP1000)**(1/500)-1
17.5	Romania	0.18	(POP1500/POP1000)**(1/500)-1
19	Georgia	0.18	(POP1500/POP1000)**(1/500)-1
20	Armenia	0.18	(POP1500/POP1000)**(1/500)-1
21	Czechia	0.18	(POP1500/POP1000)**(1/500)-1
22	Slovakia	0.18	(POP1500/POP1000)**(1/500)-1
23	France	0.17	(POP1500/POP1000)**(1/500)-1
24	Switzerland	0.15	(POP1500/POP1000)**(1/500)-1
25	Italy	0.15	(POP1500/POP1000)**(1/500)-1
26	Japan	0.14	(POP1500/POP1000)**(1/500)-1
27	Zambia	0.14	(POP1500/POP1000)**(1/500)-1
28	Burundi	0.14	(POP1500/POP1000)**(1/500)-1
29	Ethiopia	0.14	(POP1500/POP1000)**(1/500)-1
33.5	Botswana	0.14	(POP1500/POP1000)**(1/500)-1
33.5	Lesotho	0.14	(POP1500/POP1000)**(1/500)-1
33.5	Malawi	0.14	(POP1500/POP1000)**(1/500)-1
33.5	Namibia	0.14	(POP1500/POP1000)**(1/500)-1
33.5	Somalia	0.14	(POP1500/POP1000)**(1/500)-1
33.5	South Africa	0.14	(POP1500/POP1000)**(1/500)-1
33.5	Swaziland	0.14	(POP1500/POP1000)**(1/500)-1
33.5	Zimbabwe	0.14	(POP1500/POP1000)**(1/500)-1
38	Eritrea	0.14	(POP1500/POP1000)**(1/500)-1
39	Ireland	0.14	(POP1500/POP1000)**(1/500)-1
40	UK	0.14	(POP1500/POP1000)**(1/500)-1
41	Malaysia	0.12	(POP1500/POP1000)**(1/500)-1
42	Mongolia	0.12	(POP1500/POP1000)**(1/500)-1
43	Laos	0.12	(POP1500/POP1000)**(1/500)-1
45.5	Philippines	0.12	(POP1500/POP1000)**(1/500)-1
45.5	Sri Lanka	0.12	(POP1500/POP1000)**(1/500)-1
45.5	Taiwan	0.12	(POP1500/POP1000)**(1/500)-1
45.5	Thailand	0.12	(POP1500/POP1000)**(1/500)-1
48	Nepal	0.12	(POP1500/POP1000)**(1/500)-1
49	Burma	0.12	(POP1500/POP1000)**(1/500)-1

Table 4.2 Population Growth Rates, 1000-1500			
Rank	Country	GRPOP	Source
50	Indonesia	0.12	(POP1500/POP1000)**(1/500)-1
51	Afghanistan	0.12	(POP1500/POP1000)**(1/500)-1
52	Korea, South	0.12	(POP1500/POP1000)**(1/500)-1
53	Vietnam	0.12	(POP1500/POP1000)**(1/500)-1
54	Korea, North	0.12	(POP1500/POP1000)**(1/500)-1
55	Cambodia	0.12	(POP1500/POP1000)**(1/500)-1
56	Singapore	0.12	(POP1500/POP1000)**(1/500)-1
57	Hong Kong	0.11	(POP1500/POP1000)**(1/500)-1
58	China	0.11	(POP1500/POP1000)**(1/500)-1
59	Spain	0.11	(POP1500/POP1000)**(1/500)-1
60	Iceland	0.10	(POP1500/POP1000)**(1/500)-1
62	Denmark	0.10	(POP1500/POP1000)**(1/500)-1
62	Mexico	0.10	(POP1500/POP1000)**(1/500)-1
62	Portugal	0.10	(POP1500/POP1000)**(1/500)-1
64	Sierra Leone	0.09	(POP1500/POP1000)**(1/500)-1
65	Guinea-Biss	0.09	(POP1500/POP1000)**(1/500)-1
66	Ghana	0.09	(POP1500/POP1000)**(1/500)-1
67	Guinea	0.09	(POP1500/POP1000)**(1/500)-1
68	Canada	0.09	(POP1500/POP1000)**(1/500)-1
69	US	0.09	(POP1500/POP1000)**(1/500)-1
70	Norway	0.08	(POP1500/POP1000)**(1/500)-1
71	Bangladesh	0.08	(POP1500/POP1000)**(1/500)-1
72	Pakistan	0.08	(POP1500/POP1000)**(1/500)-1
73	India	0.08	(POP1500/POP1000)**(1/500)-1
74	Paraguay	0.07	(POP1500/POP1000)**(1/500)-1
75	Cuba	0.07	(POP1500/POP1000)**(1/500)-1
76	El Salvador	0.07	(POP1500/POP1000)**(1/500)-1
77	Haiti	0.07	(POP1500/POP1000)**(1/500)-1
78	Venezuela	0.07	(POP1500/POP1000)**(1/500)-1
79	Argentina	0.07	(POP1500/POP1000)**(1/500)-1
80	Bolivia	0.07	(POP1500/POP1000)**(1/500)-1
81	Chile	0.07	(POP1500/POP1000)**(1/500)-1
82	Peru	0.07	(POP1500/POP1000)**(1/500)-1
83	Brazil	0.07	(POP1500/POP1000)**(1/500)-1
84	Guatemala	0.07	(POP1500/POP1000)**(1/500)-1
85	Colombia	0.07	(POP1500/POP1000)**(1/500)-1
86	Nicaragua	0.07	(POP1500/POP1000)**(1/500)-1
87	Ecuador	0.07	(POP1500/POP1000)**(1/500)-1
88	Honduras	0.07	(POP1500/POP1000)**(1/500)-1
89	Uruguay	0.07	(POP1500/POP1000)**(1/500)-1
90	Costa Rica	0.07	(POP1500/POP1000)**(1/500)-1
91	Panama	0.07	(POP1500/POP1000)**(1/500)-1
92	Jamaica	0.07	(POP1500/POP1000)**(1/500)-1
93	Puerto Rico	0.07	(POP1500/POP1000)**(1/500)-1
94	Dominican R	0.07	(POP1500/POP1000)**(1/500)-1
95	Trinidad & T	0.07	(POP1500/POP1000)**(1/500)-1
96.5	Australia	0.07	(POP1500/POP1000)**(1/500)-1
96.5	New Zealand	0.07	(POP1500/POP1000)**(1/500)-1
98	Uzbekistan	0.07	(POP1500/POP1000)**(1/500)-1

Table 4.2 Population Growth Rates, 1000-1500			
Rank	Country	GRPOP	Source
99	Kazakhstan	0.07	(POP1500/POP1000)**(1/500)-1
100	Turkmenistan	0.07	(POP1500/POP1000)**(1/500)-1
101	Kyrgyzstan	0.07	(POP1500/POP1000)**(1/500)-1
102	Tajikistan	0.07	(POP1500/POP1000)**(1/500)-1
103	Sweden	0.06	(POP1500/POP1000)**(1/500)-1
104	South Sudan	0.06	(POP1500/POP1000)**(1/500)-1
105	Sudan	0.06	(POP1500/POP1000)**(1/500)-1
106	Slovenia	0.05	(POP1500/POP1000)**(1/500)-1
107	Macedonia	0.05	(POP1500/POP1000)**(1/500)-1
108	Bosnia	0.05	(POP1500/POP1000)**(1/500)-1
109	Croatia	0.05	(POP1500/POP1000)**(1/500)-1
110	Serbia	0.05	(POP1500/POP1000)**(1/500)-1
111	Kosovo	0.05	(POP1500/POP1000)**(1/500)-1
112	Montenegro	0.05	(POP1500/POP1000)**(1/500)-1
114	Albania	0.00	(POP1500/POP1000)**(1/500)-1
114	Bulgaria	0.00	(POP1500/POP1000)**(1/500)-1
114	Libya	0.00	(POP1500/POP1000)**(1/500)-1
116	Greece	-0.02	(POP1500/POP1000)**(1/500)-1
117	Bahrain	-0.02	(POP1500/POP1000)**(1/500)-1
118	Kuwait	-0.02	(POP1500/POP1000)**(1/500)-1
119	Jordan	-0.02	(POP1500/POP1000)**(1/500)-1
120	Israel	-0.02	(POP1500/POP1000)**(1/500)-1
121	Iran	-0.02	(POP1500/POP1000)**(1/500)-1
122	Turkey	-0.02	(POP1500/POP1000)**(1/500)-1
123	Yemen	-0.02	(POP1500/POP1000)**(1/500)-1
124	Saudi Arabia	-0.02	(POP1500/POP1000)**(1/500)-1
125	Syria	-0.02	(POP1500/POP1000)**(1/500)-1
126	Iraq	-0.02	(POP1500/POP1000)**(1/500)-1
127	Lebanon	-0.02	(POP1500/POP1000)**(1/500)-1
128	Oman	-0.02	(POP1500/POP1000)**(1/500)-1
129	UAE	-0.02	(POP1500/POP1000)**(1/500)-1
130	Qatar	-0.02	(POP1500/POP1000)**(1/500)-1
131.5	Egypt	-0.04	(POP1500/POP1000)**(1/500)-1
131.5	Tunisia	-0.04	(POP1500/POP1000)**(1/500)-1
133.5	Algeria	-0.06	(POP1500/POP1000)**(1/500)-1
133.5	Morocco	-0.06	(POP1500/POP1000)**(1/500)-1
135	Cyprus	-0.17	(POP1500/POP1000)**(1/500)-1

TABLE 4.3 POPULATION GROWTH RATES, 1500-1600			
Rank	Country	GRPOP	Source
1	Taiwan	0.81	(POP1600/POP1500)**(1/100)-1
2	Philippines	0.46	(POP1600/POP1500)**(1/100)-1
3	Netherlands	0.46	(POP1600/POP1500)**(1/100)-1
4	UK	0.45	(POP1600/POP1500)**(1/100)-1
5	Bulgaria	0.45	(POP1600/POP1500)**(1/100)-1
6	China	0.44	(POP1600/POP1500)**(1/100)-1
7	Hong Kong	0.44	(POP1600/POP1500)**(1/100)-1
8	Switzerland	0.43	(POP1600/POP1500)**(1/100)-1
9	Slovakia	0.41	(POP1600/POP1500)**(1/100)-1
10	Czechia	0.41	(POP1600/POP1500)**(1/100)-1
12.5	Algeria	0.41	(POP1600/POP1500)**(1/100)-1
12.5	Cyprus	0.41	(POP1600/POP1500)**(1/100)-1
12.5	Greece	0.41	(POP1600/POP1500)**(1/100)-1
12.5	Morocco	0.41	(POP1600/POP1500)**(1/100)-1
15	Sweden	0.32	(POP1600/POP1500)**(1/100)-1
17	Finland	0.29	(POP1600/POP1500)**(1/100)-1
17	Germany	0.29	(POP1600/POP1500)**(1/100)-1
17	Norway	0.29	(POP1600/POP1500)**(1/100)-1
19	Sierra Leone	0.24	(POP1600/POP1500)**(1/100)-1
20	Guinea-Biss	0.24	(POP1600/POP1500)**(1/100)-1
21	Ghana	0.24	(POP1600/POP1500)**(1/100)-1
22	Guinea	0.24	(POP1600/POP1500)**(1/100)-1
23	Moldova	0.22	(POP1600/POP1500)**(1/100)-1
24	Estonia	0.22	(POP1600/POP1500)**(1/100)-1
25	Belarus	0.22	(POP1600/POP1500)**(1/100)-1
26	Ireland	0.22	(POP1600/POP1500)**(1/100)-1
27	Ukraine	0.22	(POP1600/POP1500)**(1/100)-1
30	Austria	0.22	(POP1600/POP1500)**(1/100)-1
30	Egypt	0.22	(POP1600/POP1500)**(1/100)-1
30	Mozambique	0.22	(POP1600/POP1500)**(1/100)-1
30	Poland	0.22	(POP1600/POP1500)**(1/100)-1
30	Tunisia	0.22	(POP1600/POP1500)**(1/100)-1
33	Lithuania	0.22	(POP1600/POP1500)**(1/100)-1
34	Latvia	0.22	(POP1600/POP1500)**(1/100)-1
35	Italy	0.22	(POP1600/POP1500)**(1/100)-1
36	Russia	0.22	(POP1600/POP1500)**(1/100)-1
37	Korea, South	0.21	(POP1600/POP1500)**(1/100)-1
38	Korea, North	0.21	(POP1600/POP1500)**(1/100)-1
39	France	0.21	(POP1600/POP1500)**(1/100)-1
40	Pakistan	0.21	(POP1600/POP1500)**(1/100)-1
41	India	0.21	(POP1600/POP1500)**(1/100)-1
42	Bangladesh	0.21	(POP1600/POP1500)**(1/100)-1
43	Montenegro	0.20	(POP1600/POP1500)**(1/100)-1
44	Slovenia	0.20	(POP1600/POP1500)**(1/100)-1
45	Macedonia	0.20	(POP1600/POP1500)**(1/100)-1
46	Bosnia	0.20	(POP1600/POP1500)**(1/100)-1
47	Croatia	0.20	(POP1600/POP1500)**(1/100)-1
48	Serbia	0.20	(POP1600/POP1500)**(1/100)-1

Table 4.3 Population Growth Rates, 1500-1600			
Rank	Country	GRPOP	Source
49	Kosovo	0.20	(POP1600/POP1500)**(1/100)-1
50	Azerbaijan	0.20	(POP1600/POP1500)**(1/100)-1
51	Spain	0.19	(POP1600/POP1500)**(1/100)-1
52	Japan	0.18	(POP1600/POP1500)**(1/100)-1
53	Armenia	0.18	(POP1600/POP1500)**(1/100)-1
54	Georgia	0.18	(POP1600/POP1500)**(1/100)-1
55	Swaziland	0.15	(POP1600/POP1500)**(1/100)-1
56	South Africa	0.15	(POP1600/POP1500)**(1/100)-1
57	Burundi	0.15	(POP1600/POP1500)**(1/100)-1
58	Lesotho	0.15	(POP1600/POP1500)**(1/100)-1
59	Malaysia	0.15	(POP1600/POP1500)**(1/100)-1
60	Afghanistan	0.15	(POP1600/POP1500)**(1/100)-1
61	Burma	0.15	(POP1600/POP1500)**(1/100)-1
62	Cambodia	0.15	(POP1600/POP1500)**(1/100)-1
63	Vietnam	0.15	(POP1600/POP1500)**(1/100)-1
64	Nepal	0.15	(POP1600/POP1500)**(1/100)-1
65	Laos	0.15	(POP1600/POP1500)**(1/100)-1
66	Mongolia	0.15	(POP1600/POP1500)**(1/100)-1
67	Singapore	0.15	(POP1600/POP1500)**(1/100)-1
68	Turkey	0.14	(POP1600/POP1500)**(1/100)-1
69	Kyrgyzstan	0.13	(POP1600/POP1500)**(1/100)-1
70	Kazakhstan	0.13	(POP1600/POP1500)**(1/100)-1
71	Uzbekistan	0.13	(POP1600/POP1500)**(1/100)-1
73	Belgium	0.13	(POP1600/POP1500)**(1/100)-1
73	Madagascar	0.13	(POP1600/POP1500)**(1/100)-1
73	Turkmenistan	0.13	(POP1600/POP1500)**(1/100)-1
75	Tajikistan	0.13	(POP1600/POP1500)**(1/100)-1
76	Ethiopia	0.12	(POP1600/POP1500)**(1/100)-1
77	Eritrea	0.12	(POP1600/POP1500)**(1/100)-1
78.5	Iran	0.11	(POP1600/POP1500)**(1/100)-1
78.5	Thailand	0.11	(POP1600/POP1500)**(1/100)-1
80	Indonesia	0.10	(POP1600/POP1500)**(1/100)-1
81	Portugal	0.10	(POP1600/POP1500)**(1/100)-1
82	Zambia	0.10	(POP1600/POP1500)**(1/100)-1
83	Zimbabwe	0.10	(POP1600/POP1500)**(1/100)-1
84	Malawi	0.10	(POP1600/POP1500)**(1/100)-1
85	Sri Lanka	0.09	(POP1600/POP1500)**(1/100)-1
86	Denmark	0.08	(POP1600/POP1500)**(1/100)-1
87	Iceland	0.08	(POP1600/POP1500)**(1/100)-1
88	Sudan	0.05	(POP1600/POP1500)**(1/100)-1
89	South Sudan	0.05	(POP1600/POP1500)**(1/100)-1
98.5	Albania	0.00	(POP1600/POP1500)**(1/100)-1
98.5	Australia	0.00	(POP1600/POP1500)**(1/100)-1
98.5	Bahrain	0.00	(POP1600/POP1500)**(1/100)-1
98.5	Botswana	0.00	(POP1600/POP1500)**(1/100)-1
98.5	Canada	0.00	(POP1600/POP1500)**(1/100)-1
98.5	Hungary	0.00	(POP1600/POP1500)**(1/100)-1
98.5	Iraq	0.00	(POP1600/POP1500)**(1/100)-1

Table 4.3 Population Growth Rates, 1500-1600

Rank	Country	GRPOP	Source
98.5	Kuwait	0.00	(POP1600/POP1500)**(1/100)-1
98.5	Libya	0.00	(POP1600/POP1500)**(1/100)-1
98.5	Namibia	0.00	(POP1600/POP1500)**(1/100)-1
98.5	New Zealand	0.00	(POP1600/POP1500)**(1/100)-1
98.5	Oman	0.00	(POP1600/POP1500)**(1/100)-1
98.5	Qatar	0.00	(POP1600/POP1500)**(1/100)-1
98.5	Romania	0.00	(POP1600/POP1500)**(1/100)-1
98.5	Saudi Arabia	0.00	(POP1600/POP1500)**(1/100)-1
98.5	Somalia	0.00	(POP1600/POP1500)**(1/100)-1
98.5	UAE	0.00	(POP1600/POP1500)**(1/100)-1
98.5	Yemen	0.00	(POP1600/POP1500)**(1/100)-1
108	Lebanon	-0.03	(POP1600/POP1500)**(1/100)-1
109	Syria	-0.03	(POP1600/POP1500)**(1/100)-1
110	Jordan	-0.03	(POP1600/POP1500)**(1/100)-1
111	Israel	-0.03	(POP1600/POP1500)**(1/100)-1
112	Brazil	-0.22	(POP1600/POP1500)**(1/100)-1
113	US	-0.29	(POP1600/POP1500)**(1/100)-1
114	Chile	-0.50	(POP1600/POP1500)**(1/100)-1
115	El Salvador	-0.51	(POP1600/POP1500)**(1/100)-1
116	Nicaragua	-0.51	(POP1600/POP1500)**(1/100)-1
117	Ecuador	-0.51	(POP1600/POP1500)**(1/100)-1
118	Peru	-0.51	(POP1600/POP1500)**(1/100)-1
121	Argentina	-0.51	(POP1600/POP1500)**(1/100)-1
121	Costa Rica	-0.51	(POP1600/POP1500)**(1/100)-1
121	Guatemala	-0.51	(POP1600/POP1500)**(1/100)-1
121	Honduras	-0.51	(POP1600/POP1500)**(1/100)-1
121	Panama	-0.51	(POP1600/POP1500)**(1/100)-1
124	Colombia	-0.51	(POP1600/POP1500)**(1/100)-1
125	Venezuela	-0.51	(POP1600/POP1500)**(1/100)-1
126	Bolivia	-0.51	(POP1600/POP1500)**(1/100)-1
127	Paraguay	-0.51	(POP1600/POP1500)**(1/100)-1
128	Uruguay	-0.51	(POP1600/POP1500)**(1/100)-1
129	Haiti	-0.91	(POP1600/POP1500)**(1/100)-1
130	Cuba	-0.91	(POP1600/POP1500)**(1/100)-1
131	Jamaica	-0.91	(POP1600/POP1500)**(1/100)-1
132	Dominican R	-0.91	(POP1600/POP1500)**(1/100)-1
133	Puerto Rico	-0.91	(POP1600/POP1500)**(1/100)-1
134	Trinidad & T	-0.91	(POP1600/POP1500)**(1/100)-1
135	Mexico	-1.09	(POP1600/POP1500)**(1/100)-1

Table 4.4 Population Growth Rates, 1600-1700

Rank	Country	GRPOP	Source
1	Trinidad & T	0.92	(POP1700/POP1600)**(1/100)-1
2	Puerto Rico	0.92	(POP1700/POP1600)**(1/100)-1
3	Dominican R	0.92	(POP1700/POP1600)**(1/100)-1
4	Jamaica	0.92	(POP1700/POP1600)**(1/100)-1
5	Cuba	0.92	(POP1700/POP1600)**(1/100)-1
6	Haiti	0.92	(POP1700/POP1600)**(1/100)-1
7	Taiwan	0.81	(POP1700/POP1600)**(1/100)-1
8	Ireland	0.66	(POP1700/POP1600)**(1/100)-1
9	Portugal	0.60	(POP1700/POP1600)**(1/100)-1
10	Mexico	0.59	(POP1700/POP1600)**(1/100)-1
11	Sweden	0.51	(POP1700/POP1600)**(1/100)-1
12	Philippines	0.46	(POP1700/POP1600)**(1/100)-1
13	Brazil	0.45	(POP1700/POP1600)**(1/100)-1
14	Albania	0.41	(POP1700/POP1600)**(1/100)-1
15	Japan	0.38	(POP1700/POP1600)**(1/100)-1
16	Lesotho	0.36	(POP1700/POP1600)**(1/100)-1
17	South Africa	0.36	(POP1700/POP1600)**(1/100)-1
18	Swaziland	0.36	(POP1700/POP1600)**(1/100)-1
19	UK	0.33	(POP1700/POP1600)**(1/100)-1
20	Russia	0.29	(POP1700/POP1600)**(1/100)-1
21	Estonia	0.29	(POP1700/POP1600)**(1/100)-1
22	Lithuania	0.29	(POP1700/POP1600)**(1/100)-1
23	Belarus	0.29	(POP1700/POP1600)**(1/100)-1
24	Ukraine	0.29	(POP1700/POP1600)**(1/100)-1
25	Moldova	0.29	(POP1700/POP1600)**(1/100)-1
26	Latvia	0.29	(POP1700/POP1600)**(1/100)-1
27	Guinea	0.25	(POP1700/POP1600)**(1/100)-1
28	Ghana	0.25	(POP1700/POP1600)**(1/100)-1
29	Guinea-Biss	0.25	(POP1700/POP1600)**(1/100)-1
30	Sierra Leone	0.25	(POP1700/POP1600)**(1/100)-1
31	Netherlands	0.24	(POP1700/POP1600)**(1/100)-1
33.5	Belgium	0.22	(POP1700/POP1600)**(1/100)-1
33.5	Madagascar	0.22	(POP1700/POP1600)**(1/100)-1
33.5	Norway	0.22	(POP1700/POP1600)**(1/100)-1
33.5	Romania	0.22	(POP1700/POP1600)**(1/100)-1
36	Korea, South	0.21	(POP1700/POP1600)**(1/100)-1
37	Korea, North	0.21	(POP1700/POP1600)**(1/100)-1
38	Bangladesh	0.20	(POP1700/POP1600)**(1/100)-1
39	India	0.20	(POP1700/POP1600)**(1/100)-1
40	Pakistan	0.20	(POP1700/POP1600)**(1/100)-1
42.5	Hungary	0.18	(POP1700/POP1600)**(1/100)-1
42.5	Mozambique	0.18	(POP1700/POP1600)**(1/100)-1
42.5	Poland	0.18	(POP1700/POP1600)**(1/100)-1
42.5	Switzerland	0.18	(POP1700/POP1600)**(1/100)-1
45	Somalia	0.17	(POP1700/POP1600)**(1/100)-1
46	Armenia	0.15	(POP1700/POP1600)**(1/100)-1
47	Georgia	0.15	(POP1700/POP1600)**(1/100)-1
48	Singapore	0.15	(POP1700/POP1600)**(1/100)-1

Table 4.4 Population Growth Rates, 1600-1700

Rank	Country	GRPOP	Source
49	Vietnam	0.15	(POP1700/POP1600)**(1/100)-1
50	Nepal	0.15	(POP1700/POP1600)**(1/100)-1
51	Burma	0.15	(POP1700/POP1600)**(1/100)-1
52	Afghanistan	0.15	(POP1700/POP1600)**(1/100)-1
53	Cambodia	0.15	(POP1700/POP1600)**(1/100)-1
54	Malaysia	0.15	(POP1700/POP1600)**(1/100)-1
55	Mongolia	0.15	(POP1700/POP1600)**(1/100)-1
56	Laos	0.15	(POP1700/POP1600)**(1/100)-1
57	France	0.15	(POP1700/POP1600)**(1/100)-1
58	Turkey	0.14	(POP1700/POP1600)**(1/100)-1
59	Azerbaijan	0.14	(POP1700/POP1600)**(1/100)-1
60	Burundi	0.13	(POP1700/POP1600)**(1/100)-1
61	Paraguay	0.13	(POP1700/POP1600)**(1/100)-1
62	Costa Rica	0.13	(POP1700/POP1600)**(1/100)-1
63	Panama	0.13	(POP1700/POP1600)**(1/100)-1
64	Honduras	0.13	(POP1700/POP1600)**(1/100)-1
65	Chile	0.13	(POP1700/POP1600)**(1/100)-1
66	Colombia	0.13	(POP1700/POP1600)**(1/100)-1
67	Venezuela	0.13	(POP1700/POP1600)**(1/100)-1
68	Bolivia	0.13	(POP1700/POP1600)**(1/100)-1
69	Ecuador	0.13	(POP1700/POP1600)**(1/100)-1
70	Peru	0.13	(POP1700/POP1600)**(1/100)-1
71	Guatemala	0.13	(POP1700/POP1600)**(1/100)-1
72	Nicaragua	0.13	(POP1700/POP1600)**(1/100)-1
73	Argentina	0.13	(POP1700/POP1600)**(1/100)-1
74	El Salvador	0.13	(POP1700/POP1600)**(1/100)-1
75	Uruguay	0.13	(POP1700/POP1600)**(1/100)-1
76	Tajikistan	0.12	(POP1700/POP1600)**(1/100)-1
77	Kyrgyzstan	0.12	(POP1700/POP1600)**(1/100)-1
78	Uzbekistan	0.12	(POP1700/POP1600)**(1/100)-1
79	Turkmenistan	0.12	(POP1700/POP1600)**(1/100)-1
80	Kazakhstan	0.12	(POP1700/POP1600)**(1/100)-1
81.5	Iran	0.11	(POP1700/POP1600)**(1/100)-1
81.5	Thailand	0.11	(POP1700/POP1600)**(1/100)-1
83	Ethiopia	0.11	(POP1700/POP1600)**(1/100)-1
84	Eritrea	0.11	(POP1700/POP1600)**(1/100)-1
85	Indonesia	0.10	(POP1700/POP1600)**(1/100)-1
86	Sri Lanka	0.09	(POP1700/POP1600)**(1/100)-1
87	Malawi	0.09	(POP1700/POP1600)**(1/100)-1
88	Zambia	0.09	(POP1700/POP1600)**(1/100)-1
89	Zimbabwe	0.09	(POP1700/POP1600)**(1/100)-1
90	Iceland	0.07	(POP1700/POP1600)**(1/100)-1
91	Denmark	0.07	(POP1700/POP1600)**(1/100)-1
92	Spain	0.06	(POP1700/POP1600)**(1/100)-1
93	South Sudan	0.05	(POP1700/POP1600)**(1/100)-1
94	Sudan	0.05	(POP1700/POP1600)**(1/100)-1
95	Italy	0.02	(POP1700/POP1600)**(1/100)-1
109	Australia	0.00	(POP1700/POP1600)**(1/100)-1

TABLE 4.4 POPULATION GROWTH RATES, 1600-1700

Rank	Country	GRPOP	Source
109	Austria	0.00	(POP1700/POP1600)**(1/100)-1
109	Bahrain	0.00	(POP1700/POP1600)**(1/100)-1
109	Bosnia	0.00	(POP1700/POP1600)**(1/100)-1
109	Botswana	0.00	(POP1700/POP1600)**(1/100)-1
109	Bulgaria	0.00	(POP1700/POP1600)**(1/100)-1
109	Croatia	0.00	(POP1700/POP1600)**(1/100)-1
109	Cyprus	0.00	(POP1700/POP1600)**(1/100)-1
109	Czechia	0.00	(POP1700/POP1600)**(1/100)-1
109	Finland	0.00	(POP1700/POP1600)**(1/100)-1
109	Greece	0.00	(POP1700/POP1600)**(1/100)-1
109	Iraq	0.00	(POP1700/POP1600)**(1/100)-1
109	Kosovo	0.00	(POP1700/POP1600)**(1/100)-1
109	Kuwait	0.00	(POP1700/POP1600)**(1/100)-1
109	Libya	0.00	(POP1700/POP1600)**(1/100)-1
109	Macedonia	0.00	(POP1700/POP1600)**(1/100)-1
109	Montenegro	0.00	(POP1700/POP1600)**(1/100)-1
109	Namibia	0.00	(POP1700/POP1600)**(1/100)-1
109	New Zealand	0.00	(POP1700/POP1600)**(1/100)-1
109	Oman	0.00	(POP1700/POP1600)**(1/100)-1
109	Qatar	0.00	(POP1700/POP1600)**(1/100)-1
109	Saudi Arabia	0.00	(POP1700/POP1600)**(1/100)-1
109	Serbia	0.00	(POP1700/POP1600)**(1/100)-1
109	Slovakia	0.00	(POP1700/POP1600)**(1/100)-1
109	Slovenia	0.00	(POP1700/POP1600)**(1/100)-1
109	UAE	0.00	(POP1700/POP1600)**(1/100)-1
109	Yemen	0.00	(POP1700/POP1600)**(1/100)-1
123	Israel	-0.03	(POP1700/POP1600)**(1/100)-1
124	Jordan	-0.03	(POP1700/POP1600)**(1/100)-1
125	Syria	-0.03	(POP1700/POP1600)**(1/100)-1
126	Lebanon	-0.03	(POP1700/POP1600)**(1/100)-1
127	Germany	-0.06	(POP1700/POP1600)**(1/100)-1
128	Egypt	-0.11	(POP1700/POP1600)**(1/100)-1
129	China	-0.15	(POP1700/POP1600)**(1/100)-1
130	Hong Kong	-0.15	(POP1700/POP1600)**(1/100)-1
131.5	Canada	-0.22	(POP1700/POP1600)**(1/100)-1
131.5	Tunisia	-0.22	(POP1700/POP1600)**(1/100)-1
133.5	Algeria	-0.25	(POP1700/POP1600)**(1/100)-1
133.5	Morocco	-0.25	(POP1700/POP1600)**(1/100)-1
135	US	-0.40	(POP1700/POP1600)**(1/100)-1

Table 4.5 Population Growth Rates, 1700-1820

Rank	Country	GRPOP	Source
1	US	1.94	(POP1820/POP1700)**(1/120)-1
2	Dominican R	1.48	(POP1820/POP1700)**(1/120)-1
3	Cuba	1.48	(POP1820/POP1700)**(1/120)-1
4	Haiti	1.48	(POP1820/POP1700)**(1/120)-1
5	Jamaica	1.48	(POP1820/POP1700)**(1/120)-1
6	Puerto Rico	1.48	(POP1820/POP1700)**(1/120)-1
7	Trinidad & T	1.48	(POP1820/POP1700)**(1/120)-1
8	Canada	1.18	(POP1820/POP1700)**(1/120)-1
9	Ireland	1.09	(POP1820/POP1700)**(1/120)-1
10	Brazil	1.07	(POP1820/POP1700)**(1/120)-1
11	Finland	0.90	(POP1820/POP1700)**(1/120)-1
12	Hungary	0.85	(POP1820/POP1700)**(1/120)-1
13	Hong Kong	0.85	(POP1820/POP1700)**(1/120)-1
14	China	0.85	(POP1820/POP1700)**(1/120)-1
15	Romania	0.78	(POP1820/POP1700)**(1/120)-1
16	UK	0.76	(POP1820/POP1700)**(1/120)-1
17	Russia	0.68	(POP1820/POP1700)**(1/120)-1
18	Latvia	0.66	(POP1820/POP1700)**(1/120)-1
19	Ukraine	0.66	(POP1820/POP1700)**(1/120)-1
20	Belarus	0.66	(POP1820/POP1700)**(1/120)-1
21	Lithuania	0.66	(POP1820/POP1700)**(1/120)-1
22	Moldova	0.66	(POP1820/POP1700)**(1/120)-1
23	Estonia	0.66	(POP1820/POP1700)**(1/120)-1
24	Sweden	0.60	(POP1820/POP1700)**(1/120)-1
25	Taiwan	0.58	(POP1820/POP1700)**(1/120)-1
26	Norway	0.55	(POP1820/POP1700)**(1/120)-1
27	Kosovo	0.53	(POP1820/POP1700)**(1/120)-1
28	Serbia	0.53	(POP1820/POP1700)**(1/120)-1
29	Croatia	0.53	(POP1820/POP1700)**(1/120)-1
30	Macedonia	0.53	(POP1820/POP1700)**(1/120)-1
31	Bosnia	0.53	(POP1820/POP1700)**(1/120)-1
32	Slovenia	0.53	(POP1820/POP1700)**(1/120)-1
33	Montenegro	0.53	(POP1820/POP1700)**(1/120)-1
34	Thailand	0.52	(POP1820/POP1700)**(1/120)-1
35	Bulgaria	0.47	(POP1820/POP1700)**(1/120)-1
36	Philippines	0.46	(POP1820/POP1700)**(1/120)-1
37	Poland	0.46	(POP1820/POP1700)**(1/120)-1
38	Belgium	0.45	(POP1820/POP1700)**(1/120)-1
39	Czechia	0.44	(POP1820/POP1700)**(1/120)-1
40	Slovakia	0.44	(POP1820/POP1700)**(1/120)-1
41	Madagascar	0.43	(POP1820/POP1700)**(1/120)-1
42	Germany	0.42	(POP1820/POP1700)**(1/120)-1
43	Switzerland	0.42	(POP1820/POP1700)**(1/120)-1
44	Denmark	0.42	(POP1820/POP1700)**(1/120)-1
45	Portugal	0.42	(POP1820/POP1700)**(1/120)-1
46	South Africa	0.37	(POP1820/POP1700)**(1/120)-1
47	Lesotho	0.37	(POP1820/POP1700)**(1/120)-1
48	Swaziland	0.37	(POP1820/POP1700)**(1/120)-1

Table 4.5 Population Growth Rates, 1700-1820			
Rank	Country	GRPOP	Source
49	Greece	0.36	(POP1820/POP1700)**(1/120)-1
50	Cyprus	0.36	(POP1820/POP1700)**(1/120)-1
51.5	Algeria	0.36	(POP1820/POP1700)**(1/120)-1
51.5	Morocco	0.36	(POP1820/POP1700)**(1/120)-1
53	Italy	0.35	(POP1820/POP1700)**(1/120)-1
54	Turkmenistan	0.34	(POP1820/POP1700)**(1/120)-1
55	Kazakhstan	0.34	(POP1820/POP1700)**(1/120)-1
56	Uzbekistan	0.34	(POP1820/POP1700)**(1/120)-1
57	Kyrgyzstan	0.34	(POP1820/POP1700)**(1/120)-1
58	Tajikistan	0.34	(POP1820/POP1700)**(1/120)-1
59	Mexico	0.32	(POP1820/POP1700)**(1/120)-1
60	Albania	0.31	(POP1820/POP1700)**(1/120)-1
61	France	0.31	(POP1820/POP1700)**(1/120)-1
62	Mozambique	0.28	(POP1820/POP1700)**(1/120)-1
63	Spain	0.28	(POP1820/POP1700)**(1/120)-1
64	Azerbaijan	0.27	(POP1820/POP1700)**(1/120)-1
65	Georgia	0.27	(POP1820/POP1700)**(1/120)-1
66	Armenia	0.27	(POP1820/POP1700)**(1/120)-1
67	Indonesia	0.26	(POP1820/POP1700)**(1/120)-1
68	Austria	0.25	(POP1820/POP1700)**(1/120)-1
69	Iran	0.23	(POP1820/POP1700)**(1/120)-1
70	Uruguay	0.22	(POP1820/POP1700)**(1/120)-1
71	Costa Rica	0.22	(POP1820/POP1700)**(1/120)-1
72	Argentina	0.22	(POP1820/POP1700)**(1/120)-1
73.5	El Salvador	0.22	(POP1820/POP1700)**(1/120)-1
73.5	Nicaragua	0.22	(POP1820/POP1700)**(1/120)-1
75	Guatemala	0.22	(POP1820/POP1700)**(1/120)-1
76	Venezuela	0.22	(POP1820/POP1700)**(1/120)-1
77	Bolivia	0.22	(POP1820/POP1700)**(1/120)-1
78	Peru	0.22	(POP1820/POP1700)**(1/120)-1
79	Colombia	0.22	(POP1820/POP1700)**(1/120)-1
80	Honduras	0.22	(POP1820/POP1700)**(1/120)-1
81	Chile	0.22	(POP1820/POP1700)**(1/120)-1
82	Ecuador	0.22	(POP1820/POP1700)**(1/120)-1
83	Paraguay	0.22	(POP1820/POP1700)**(1/120)-1
84	Panama	0.22	(POP1820/POP1700)**(1/120)-1
85	Burundi	0.22	(POP1820/POP1700)**(1/120)-1
86	Laos	0.20	(POP1820/POP1700)**(1/120)-1
87	Mongolia	0.20	(POP1820/POP1700)**(1/120)-1
88	Cambodia	0.20	(POP1820/POP1700)**(1/120)-1
89	Afghanistan	0.20	(POP1820/POP1700)**(1/120)-1
90	Burma	0.20	(POP1820/POP1700)**(1/120)-1
91	Vietnam	0.20	(POP1820/POP1700)**(1/120)-1
92	Nepal	0.20	(POP1820/POP1700)**(1/120)-1
93	Malaysia	0.20	(POP1820/POP1700)**(1/120)-1
94	Singapore	0.20	(POP1820/POP1700)**(1/120)-1
95	Pakistan	0.20	(POP1820/POP1700)**(1/120)-1
96	India	0.20	(POP1820/POP1700)**(1/120)-1

Table 4.5 Population Growth Rates, 1700-1820

Rank	Country	GRPOP	Source
97	Bangladesh	0.20	(POP1820/POP1700)**(1/120)-1
98	Eritrea	0.19	(POP1820/POP1700)**(1/120)-1
99	Ethiopia	0.19	(POP1820/POP1700)**(1/120)-1
100	Netherlands	0.17	(POP1820/POP1700)**(1/120)-1
101	Turkey	0.15	(POP1820/POP1700)**(1/120)-1
102	Sudan	0.13	(POP1820/POP1700)**(1/120)-1
103	South Sudan	0.13	(POP1820/POP1700)**(1/120)-1
104	Lebanon	0.13	(POP1820/POP1700)**(1/120)-1
105	Jordan	0.13	(POP1820/POP1700)**(1/120)-1
106	Syria	0.13	(POP1820/POP1700)**(1/120)-1
107	Israel	0.13	(POP1820/POP1700)**(1/120)-1
108	UAE	0.12	(POP1820/POP1700)**(1/120)-1
109	Qatar	0.12	(POP1820/POP1700)**(1/120)-1
110	Kuwait	0.12	(POP1820/POP1700)**(1/120)-1
111	Yemen	0.12	(POP1820/POP1700)**(1/120)-1
112	Saudi Arabia	0.12	(POP1820/POP1700)**(1/120)-1
113	Oman	0.12	(POP1820/POP1700)**(1/120)-1
114	Bahrain	0.12	(POP1820/POP1700)**(1/120)-1
115	Guinea-Biss	0.12	(POP1820/POP1700)**(1/120)-1
116	Sierra Leone	0.12	(POP1820/POP1700)**(1/120)-1
117	Guinea	0.12	(POP1820/POP1700)**(1/120)-1
118	Ghana	0.12	(POP1820/POP1700)**(1/120)-1
119	Japan	0.12	(POP1820/POP1700)**(1/120)-1
120	Korea, North	0.10	(POP1820/POP1700)**(1/120)-1
121	Korea, South	0.10	(POP1820/POP1700)**(1/120)-1
122	Zimbabwe	0.10	(POP1820/POP1700)**(1/120)-1
123	Zambia	0.10	(POP1820/POP1700)**(1/120)-1
124	Malawi	0.10	(POP1820/POP1700)**(1/120)-1
125	Namibia	0.08	(POP1820/POP1700)**(1/120)-1
126	Botswana	0.08	(POP1820/POP1700)**(1/120)-1
127	Tunisia	0.07	(POP1820/POP1700)**(1/120)-1
128	Iraq	0.07	(POP1820/POP1700)**(1/120)-1
129	Libya	0.06	(POP1820/POP1700)**(1/120)-1
130	Somalia	0.04	(POP1820/POP1700)**(1/120)-1
131	Sri Lanka	0.01	(POP1820/POP1700)**(1/120)-1
132	New Zealand	0.00	(POP1820/POP1700)**(1/120)-1
133	Egypt	-0.02	(POP1820/POP1700)**(1/120)-1
134	Iceland	-0.04	(POP1820/POP1700)**(1/120)-1
135	Australia	-0.25	(POP1820/POP1700)**(1/120)-1

Table 4.6 Population Growth Rates, 1820-1870			
Rank	Country	GRPOP	Source
1	Singapore	5.80	(POP1870/POP1820)**(1/50)-1
2	Uruguay	3.73	(POP1870/POP1820)**(1/50)-1
3	Hong Kong	3.70	(POP1870/POP1820)**(1/50)-1
4	Australia	3.40	(POP1870/POP1820)**(1/50)-1
5	Canada	3.11	(POP1870/POP1820)**(1/50)-1
6	US	2.83	(POP1870/POP1820)**(1/50)-1
7	Argentina	2.46	(POP1870/POP1820)**(1/50)-1
8	Honduras	2.22	(POP1870/POP1820)**(1/50)-1
9	New Zealand	2.16	(POP1870/POP1820)**(1/50)-1
10	Malaysia	2.07	(POP1870/POP1820)**(1/50)-1
11	Dominican R	2.02	(POP1870/POP1820)**(1/50)-1
12	Paraguay	2.00	(POP1870/POP1820)**(1/50)-1
13	Puerto Rico	1.93	(POP1870/POP1820)**(1/50)-1
14	Chile	1.87	(POP1870/POP1820)**(1/50)-1
15	Swaziland	1.74	(POP1870/POP1820)**(1/50)-1
16	Lesotho	1.74	(POP1870/POP1820)**(1/50)-1
17	Philippines	1.70	(POP1870/POP1820)**(1/50)-1
18	Venezuela	1.68	(POP1870/POP1820)**(1/50)-1
19	Sri Lanka	1.68	(POP1870/POP1820)**(1/50)-1
20	Cuba	1.59	(POP1870/POP1820)**(1/50)-1
21	Costa Rica	1.57	(POP1870/POP1820)**(1/50)-1
22	Brazil	1.57	(POP1870/POP1820)**(1/50)-1
23	Ethiopia	1.49	(POP1870/POP1820)**(1/50)-1
24	Eritrea	1.49	(POP1870/POP1820)**(1/50)-1
25	Trinidad & T	1.46	(POP1870/POP1820)**(1/50)-1
26	Ecuador	1.42	(POP1870/POP1820)**(1/50)-1
27	Malawi	1.40	(POP1870/POP1820)**(1/50)-1
28	Zimbabwe	1.40	(POP1870/POP1820)**(1/50)-1
29	Zambia	1.40	(POP1870/POP1820)**(1/50)-1
30	El Salvador	1.38	(POP1870/POP1820)**(1/50)-1
31	Colombia	1.38	(POP1870/POP1820)**(1/50)-1
32	Peru	1.37	(POP1870/POP1820)**(1/50)-1
33	Armenia	1.28	(POP1870/POP1820)**(1/50)-1
34	Georgia	1.28	(POP1870/POP1820)**(1/50)-1
35	Azerbaijan	1.28	(POP1870/POP1820)**(1/50)-1
36	Panama	1.26	(POP1870/POP1820)**(1/50)-1
37	Guatemala	1.20	(POP1870/POP1820)**(1/50)-1
38	Nicaragua	1.20	(POP1870/POP1820)**(1/50)-1
39	Norway	1.17	(POP1870/POP1820)**(1/50)-1
40	South Africa	1.14	(POP1870/POP1820)**(1/50)-1
41	Botswana	1.09	(POP1870/POP1820)**(1/50)-1
42	Namibia	1.09	(POP1870/POP1820)**(1/50)-1
43	Russia	1.00	(POP1870/POP1820)**(1/50)-1
44	Denmark	0.99	(POP1870/POP1820)**(1/50)-1
45	Lithuania	0.97	(POP1870/POP1820)**(1/50)-1
46	Ukraine	0.97	(POP1870/POP1820)**(1/50)-1
47	Belarus	0.97	(POP1870/POP1820)**(1/50)-1
48	Latvia	0.97	(POP1870/POP1820)**(1/50)-1

Table 4.6 Population Growth Rates, 1820-1870

Rank	Country	GRPOP	Source
49	Moldova	0.97	(POP1870/POP1820)**(1/50)-1
50	Estonia	0.97	(POP1870/POP1820)**(1/50)-1
51	Poland	0.97	(POP1870/POP1820)**(1/50)-1
52	Indonesia	0.96	(POP1870/POP1820)**(1/50)-1
53	Sweden	0.96	(POP1870/POP1820)**(1/50)-1
54	Vietnam	0.95	(POP1870/POP1820)**(1/50)-1
55	Laos	0.95	(POP1870/POP1820)**(1/50)-1
56	Haiti	0.93	(POP1870/POP1820)**(1/50)-1
57	Kosovo	0.92	(POP1870/POP1820)**(1/50)-1
58	Montenegro	0.92	(POP1870/POP1820)**(1/50)-1
59	Bosnia	0.92	(POP1870/POP1820)**(1/50)-1
60	Serbia	0.92	(POP1870/POP1820)**(1/50)-1
61	Croatia	0.92	(POP1870/POP1820)**(1/50)-1
62	Macedonia	0.92	(POP1870/POP1820)**(1/50)-1
63	Slovenia	0.92	(POP1870/POP1820)**(1/50)-1
64	Cyprus	0.92	(POP1870/POP1820)**(1/50)-1
65	Greece	0.92	(POP1870/POP1820)**(1/50)-1
66	Germany	0.91	(POP1870/POP1820)**(1/50)-1
67	Netherlands	0.88	(POP1870/POP1820)**(1/50)-1
68	Mozambique	0.84	(POP1870/POP1820)**(1/50)-1
69	Finland	0.81	(POP1870/POP1820)**(1/50)-1
70	Guinea-Biss	0.80	(POP1870/POP1820)**(1/50)-1
71	Sierra Leone	0.80	(POP1870/POP1820)**(1/50)-1
72	Guinea	0.80	(POP1870/POP1820)**(1/50)-1
73	Belgium	0.79	(POP1870/POP1820)**(1/50)-1
74	UK	0.79	(POP1870/POP1820)**(1/50)-1
75	Egypt	0.75	(POP1870/POP1820)**(1/50)-1
76	Iceland	0.75	(POP1870/POP1820)**(1/50)-1
77	Iraq	0.74	(POP1870/POP1820)**(1/50)-1
78	Romania	0.73	(POP1870/POP1820)**(1/50)-1
79	Lebanon	0.72	(POP1870/POP1820)**(1/50)-1
80	Hungary	0.71	(POP1870/POP1820)**(1/50)-1
81	Madagascar	0.71	(POP1870/POP1820)**(1/50)-1
82.5	Algeria	0.68	(POP1870/POP1820)**(1/50)-1
82.5	Morocco	0.68	(POP1870/POP1820)**(1/50)-1
84	Mexico	0.67	(POP1870/POP1820)**(1/50)-1
85	Burundi	0.65	(POP1870/POP1820)**(1/50)-1
86	Italy	0.65	(POP1870/POP1820)**(1/50)-1
87	Albania	0.65	(POP1870/POP1820)**(1/50)-1
88	Somalia	0.63	(POP1870/POP1820)**(1/50)-1
89	Bolivia	0.62	(POP1870/POP1820)**(1/50)-1
90	Tajikistan	0.60	(POP1870/POP1820)**(1/50)-1
91	Turkmenistan	0.60	(POP1870/POP1820)**(1/50)-1
92	Uzbekistan	0.60	(POP1870/POP1820)**(1/50)-1
93	Kazakhstan	0.60	(POP1870/POP1820)**(1/50)-1
94	Kyrgyzstan	0.60	(POP1870/POP1820)**(1/50)-1
95	Tunisia	0.59	(POP1870/POP1820)**(1/50)-1
96	Austria	0.59	(POP1870/POP1820)**(1/50)-1

Table 4.6 Population Growth Rates, 1820-1870			
Rank	Country	GRPOP	Source
97	Switzerland	0.58	(POP1870/POP1820)**(1/50)-1
98	Spain	0.57	(POP1870/POP1820)**(1/50)-1
99	Slovakia	0.57	(POP1870/POP1820)**(1/50)-1
100	Czechia	0.57	(POP1870/POP1820)**(1/50)-1
101	Portugal	0.55	(POP1870/POP1820)**(1/50)-1
102	Israel	0.52	(POP1870/POP1820)**(1/50)-1
103	Iran	0.50	(POP1870/POP1820)**(1/50)-1
104	Afghanistan	0.50	(POP1870/POP1820)**(1/50)-1
105	Jamaica	0.44	(POP1870/POP1820)**(1/50)-1
106	Thailand	0.43	(POP1870/POP1820)**(1/50)-1
107	Bangladesh	0.42	(POP1870/POP1820)**(1/50)-1
108	France	0.42	(POP1870/POP1820)**(1/50)-1
109	Libya	0.41	(POP1870/POP1820)**(1/50)-1
110	Jordan	0.41	(POP1870/POP1820)**(1/50)-1
111	Burma	0.38	(POP1870/POP1820)**(1/50)-1
112	Nepal	0.38	(POP1870/POP1820)**(1/50)-1
113	India	0.38	(POP1870/POP1820)**(1/50)-1
114	Sudan	0.34	(POP1870/POP1820)**(1/50)-1
115	South Sudan	0.34	(POP1870/POP1820)**(1/50)-1
116	Syria	0.34	(POP1870/POP1820)**(1/50)-1
117	Bulgaria	0.34	(POP1870/POP1820)**(1/50)-1
118	Pakistan	0.33	(POP1870/POP1820)**(1/50)-1
119	Taiwan	0.32	(POP1870/POP1820)**(1/50)-1
120	Turkey	0.32	(POP1870/POP1820)**(1/50)-1
121	Oman	0.29	(POP1870/POP1820)**(1/50)-1
122	Cambodia	0.23	(POP1870/POP1820)**(1/50)-1
123	Saudi Arabia	0.22	(POP1870/POP1820)**(1/50)-1
124	Japan	0.21	(POP1870/POP1820)**(1/50)-1
125	Yemen	0.18	(POP1870/POP1820)**(1/50)-1
126	Ghana	0.18	(POP1870/POP1820)**(1/50)-1
127	Mongolia	0.15	(POP1870/POP1820)**(1/50)-1
128	Korea, North	0.08	(POP1870/POP1820)**(1/50)-1
129	Korea, South	0.07	(POP1870/POP1820)**(1/50)-1
131.5	Bahrain	0.00	(POP1870/POP1820)**(1/50)-1
131.5	Kuwait	0.00	(POP1870/POP1820)**(1/50)-1
131.5	Qatar	0.00	(POP1870/POP1820)**(1/50)-1
131.5	UAE	0.00	(POP1870/POP1820)**(1/50)-1
134	China	-0.12	(POP1870/POP1820)**(1/50)-1
135	Ireland	-0.54	(POP1870/POP1820)**(1/50)-1

Table 4.7 Population Growth Rates, 1870-1880			
Rank	Country	GRPOP	Source
1	New Zealand	5.98	(POP1880/POP1870)**(1/10)-1
2	Malaysia	3.48	(POP1880/POP1870)**(1/10)-1
3	Argentina	3.21	(POP1880/POP1870)**(1/10)-1
4	Singapore	3.18	(POP1880/POP1870)**(1/10)-1
5	Uruguay	3.07	(POP1880/POP1870)**(1/10)-1
6	Burma	2.88	(POP1880/POP1870)**(1/10)-1
7	Hong Kong	2.81	(POP1880/POP1870)**(1/10)-1
8	Costa Rica	2.61	(POP1880/POP1870)**(1/10)-1
9	Trinidad & T	2.60	(POP1880/POP1870)**(1/10)-1
10	Dominican R	2.55	(POP1880/POP1870)**(1/10)-1
11	US	2.29	(POP1880/POP1870)**(1/10)-1
12	Australia	2.16	(POP1880/POP1870)**(1/10)-1
13	South Africa	2.07	(POP1880/POP1870)**(1/10)-1
14	Brazil	1.87	(POP1880/POP1870)**(1/10)-1
15	Swaziland	1.75	(POP1880/POP1870)**(1/10)-1
16	Lesotho	1.74	(POP1880/POP1870)**(1/10)-1
17	Colombia	1.73	(POP1880/POP1870)**(1/10)-1
18	Egypt	1.71	(POP1880/POP1870)**(1/10)-1
19	Venezuela	1.68	(POP1880/POP1870)**(1/10)-1
20	Chile	1.56	(POP1880/POP1870)**(1/10)-1
21	Finland	1.56	(POP1880/POP1870)**(1/10)-1
22	Poland	1.53	(POP1880/POP1870)**(1/10)-1
23	Canada	1.49	(POP1880/POP1870)**(1/10)-1
24	Eritrea	1.49	(POP1880/POP1870)**(1/10)-1
25	Ethiopia	1.49	(POP1880/POP1870)**(1/10)-1
26	El Salvador	1.49	(POP1880/POP1870)**(1/10)-1
27	Bulgaria	1.44	(POP1880/POP1870)**(1/10)-1
28	Laos	1.42	(POP1880/POP1870)**(1/10)-1
29	Vietnam	1.42	(POP1880/POP1870)**(1/10)-1
30	Zambia	1.40	(POP1880/POP1870)**(1/10)-1
31	Zimbabwe	1.40	(POP1880/POP1870)**(1/10)-1
32	Malawi	1.40	(POP1880/POP1870)**(1/10)-1
33	Panama	1.35	(POP1880/POP1870)**(1/10)-1
34	Puerto Rico	1.33	(POP1880/POP1870)**(1/10)-1
35	Indonesia	1.29	(POP1880/POP1870)**(1/10)-1
36	Peru	1.26	(POP1880/POP1870)**(1/10)-1
37	Philippines	1.24	(POP1880/POP1870)**(1/10)-1
38	Jamaica	1.23	(POP1880/POP1870)**(1/10)-1
39	Mexico	1.21	(POP1880/POP1870)**(1/10)-1
40	Iraq	1.18	(POP1880/POP1870)**(1/10)-1
41	Nicaragua	1.17	(POP1880/POP1870)**(1/10)-1
42	Netherlands	1.14	(POP1880/POP1870)**(1/10)-1
43	Israel	1.12	(POP1880/POP1870)**(1/10)-1
44	Ukraine	1.11	(POP1880/POP1870)**(1/10)-1
45	Estonia	1.11	(POP1880/POP1870)**(1/10)-1
46	Kyrgyzstan	1.11	(POP1880/POP1870)**(1/10)-1
47	Tajikistan	1.11	(POP1880/POP1870)**(1/10)-1
48	Azerbaijan	1.11	(POP1880/POP1870)**(1/10)-1

Table 4.7 Population Growth Rates, 1870-1880			
Rank	Country	GRPOP	Source
49	Kazakhstan	1.11	(POP1880/POP1870)**(1/10)-1
50	Moldova	1.11	(POP1880/POP1870)**(1/10)-1
51	Georgia	1.11	(POP1880/POP1870)**(1/10)-1
52	Belarus	1.11	(POP1880/POP1870)**(1/10)-1
53	Uzbekistan	1.11	(POP1880/POP1870)**(1/10)-1
54	Russia	1.11	(POP1880/POP1870)**(1/10)-1
55	Latvia	1.11	(POP1880/POP1870)**(1/10)-1
56	Lithuania	1.11	(POP1880/POP1870)**(1/10)-1
57	Armenia	1.11	(POP1880/POP1870)**(1/10)-1
58	Turkmenistan	1.11	(POP1880/POP1870)**(1/10)-1
59	Namibia	1.09	(POP1880/POP1870)**(1/10)-1
60	Botswana	1.09	(POP1880/POP1870)**(1/10)-1
61	Tunisia	1.08	(POP1880/POP1870)**(1/10)-1
62	Ecuador	1.08	(POP1880/POP1870)**(1/10)-1
63	Germany	1.04	(POP1880/POP1870)**(1/10)-1
64	Algeria	1.03	(POP1880/POP1870)**(1/10)-1
65	Cyprus	1.02	(POP1880/POP1870)**(1/10)-1
66	Greece	1.02	(POP1880/POP1870)**(1/10)-1
67	Haiti	1.02	(POP1880/POP1870)**(1/10)-1
68	Norway	1.01	(POP1880/POP1870)**(1/10)-1
69	UK	0.98	(POP1880/POP1870)**(1/10)-1
70	Denmark	0.98	(POP1880/POP1870)**(1/10)-1
71	Albania	0.93	(POP1880/POP1870)**(1/10)-1
72	Sweden	0.93	(POP1880/POP1870)**(1/10)-1
73	Austria	0.89	(POP1880/POP1870)**(1/10)-1
74	Mozambique	0.84	(POP1880/POP1870)**(1/10)-1
75	Belgium	0.84	(POP1880/POP1870)**(1/10)-1
76	Sri Lanka	0.81	(POP1880/POP1870)**(1/10)-1
77	Slovenia	0.81	(POP1880/POP1870)**(1/10)-1
78	Macedonia	0.81	(POP1880/POP1870)**(1/10)-1
79	Bosnia	0.81	(POP1880/POP1870)**(1/10)-1
80	Croatia	0.81	(POP1880/POP1870)**(1/10)-1
81	Serbia	0.81	(POP1880/POP1870)**(1/10)-1
82	Montenegro	0.81	(POP1880/POP1870)**(1/10)-1
83	Kosovo	0.81	(POP1880/POP1870)**(1/10)-1
84	Sierra Leone	0.80	(POP1880/POP1870)**(1/10)-1
85	Guinea	0.80	(POP1880/POP1870)**(1/10)-1
86	Guinea-Biss	0.80	(POP1880/POP1870)**(1/10)-1
87	Cuba	0.73	(POP1880/POP1870)**(1/10)-1
88	Lebanon	0.72	(POP1880/POP1870)**(1/10)-1
89	Thailand	0.72	(POP1880/POP1870)**(1/10)-1
90	Afghanistan	0.72	(POP1880/POP1870)**(1/10)-1
91	Honduras	0.71	(POP1880/POP1870)**(1/10)-1
92	Madagascar	0.71	(POP1880/POP1870)**(1/10)-1
93	Morocco	0.71	(POP1880/POP1870)**(1/10)-1
94	Switzerland	0.67	(POP1880/POP1870)**(1/10)-1
95	Japan	0.67	(POP1880/POP1870)**(1/10)-1
96	Burundi	0.65	(POP1880/POP1870)**(1/10)-1

TABLE 4.7 POPULATION GROWTH RATES, 1870-1880			
Rank	Country	GRPOP	Source
97	Portugal	0.64	(POP1880/POP1870)**(1/10)-1
98	Cambodia	0.63	(POP1880/POP1870)**(1/10)-1
99	Somalia	0.63	(POP1880/POP1870)**(1/10)-1
100	Jordan	0.63	(POP1880/POP1870)**(1/10)-1
101	Iran	0.62	(POP1880/POP1870)**(1/10)-1
102	Guatemala	0.62	(POP1880/POP1870)**(1/10)-1
103	Romania	0.61	(POP1880/POP1870)**(1/10)-1
104	Italy	0.58	(POP1880/POP1870)**(1/10)-1
105	Hungary	0.56	(POP1880/POP1870)**(1/10)-1
106	Turkey	0.56	(POP1880/POP1870)**(1/10)-1
107	Qatar	0.56	(POP1880/POP1870)**(1/10)-1
108	Kuwait	0.56	(POP1880/POP1870)**(1/10)-1
109	Bahrain	0.56	(POP1880/POP1870)**(1/10)-1
110	UAE	0.56	(POP1880/POP1870)**(1/10)-1
111	Syria	0.54	(POP1880/POP1870)**(1/10)-1
112	Czechia	0.51	(POP1880/POP1870)**(1/10)-1
113	Slovakia	0.51	(POP1880/POP1870)**(1/10)-1
114	Nepal	0.50	(POP1880/POP1870)**(1/10)-1
115	Ghana	0.45	(POP1880/POP1870)**(1/10)-1
116	Paraguay	0.45	(POP1880/POP1870)**(1/10)-1
117	Oman	0.44	(POP1880/POP1870)**(1/10)-1
118	Bolivia	0.42	(POP1880/POP1870)**(1/10)-1
119	Libya	0.41	(POP1880/POP1870)**(1/10)-1
120	Spain	0.40	(POP1880/POP1870)**(1/10)-1
121	Iceland	0.36	(POP1880/POP1870)**(1/10)-1
122	Sudan	0.34	(POP1880/POP1870)**(1/10)-1
123	South Sudan	0.34	(POP1880/POP1870)**(1/10)-1
124	Yemen	0.34	(POP1880/POP1870)**(1/10)-1
125	Bangladesh	0.32	(POP1880/POP1870)**(1/10)-1
126	Taiwan	0.32	(POP1880/POP1870)**(1/10)-1
127	Saudi Arabia	0.31	(POP1880/POP1870)**(1/10)-1
128	China	0.28	(POP1880/POP1870)**(1/10)-1
129	Pakistan	0.25	(POP1880/POP1870)**(1/10)-1
130	Korea, North	0.19	(POP1880/POP1870)**(1/10)-1
131	Mongolia	0.19	(POP1880/POP1870)**(1/10)-1
132	France	0.16	(POP1880/POP1870)**(1/10)-1
133	India	0.14	(POP1880/POP1870)**(1/10)-1
134	Korea, South	0.05	(POP1880/POP1870)**(1/10)-1
135	Ireland	-0.41	(POP1880/POP1870)**(1/10)-1

Table 4.8 Population Growth Rates, 1880-1890

Rank	Country	GRPOP	Source
1	Uruguay	3.99	(POP1890/POP1880)**(1/10)-1
2	Australia	3.53	(POP1890/POP1880)**(1/10)-1
3	Malaysia	3.48	(POP1890/POP1880)**(1/10)-1
4	Argentina	3.21	(POP1890/POP1880)**(1/10)-1
5	Singapore	3.18	(POP1890/POP1880)**(1/10)-1
6	Burma	2.88	(POP1890/POP1880)**(1/10)-1
7	Hong Kong	2.81	(POP1890/POP1880)**(1/10)-1
8	Costa Rica	2.61	(POP1890/POP1880)**(1/10)-1
9	Trinidad & T	2.60	(POP1890/POP1880)**(1/10)-1
10	Dominican R	2.55	(POP1890/POP1880)**(1/10)-1
11	New Zealand	2.49	(POP1890/POP1880)**(1/10)-1
12	US	2.29	(POP1890/POP1880)**(1/10)-1
13	South Africa	2.07	(POP1890/POP1880)**(1/10)-1
14	Brazil	1.87	(POP1890/POP1880)**(1/10)-1
15	Swaziland	1.75	(POP1890/POP1880)**(1/10)-1
16	Lesotho	1.74	(POP1890/POP1880)**(1/10)-1
17	Colombia	1.73	(POP1890/POP1880)**(1/10)-1
18	Chile	1.56	(POP1890/POP1880)**(1/10)-1
19	Poland	1.53	(POP1890/POP1880)**(1/10)-1
20	Eritrea	1.49	(POP1890/POP1880)**(1/10)-1
21	Ethiopia	1.49	(POP1890/POP1880)**(1/10)-1
22	El Salvador	1.49	(POP1890/POP1880)**(1/10)-1
23	Egypt	1.48	(POP1890/POP1880)**(1/10)-1
24	Finland	1.45	(POP1890/POP1880)**(1/10)-1
25	Bulgaria	1.44	(POP1890/POP1880)**(1/10)-1
26	Laos	1.42	(POP1890/POP1880)**(1/10)-1
27	Vietnam	1.42	(POP1890/POP1880)**(1/10)-1
28	Zambia	1.40	(POP1890/POP1880)**(1/10)-1
29	Malawi	1.40	(POP1890/POP1880)**(1/10)-1
30	Zimbabwe	1.40	(POP1890/POP1880)**(1/10)-1
31	Panama	1.35	(POP1890/POP1880)**(1/10)-1
32	Indonesia	1.35	(POP1890/POP1880)**(1/10)-1
33	Puerto Rico	1.33	(POP1890/POP1880)**(1/10)-1
34	Venezuela	1.31	(POP1890/POP1880)**(1/10)-1
35	Peru	1.26	(POP1890/POP1880)**(1/10)-1
36	Philippines	1.24	(POP1890/POP1880)**(1/10)-1
37	Jamaica	1.23	(POP1890/POP1880)**(1/10)-1
38	Mexico	1.21	(POP1890/POP1880)**(1/10)-1
39	Iraq	1.18	(POP1890/POP1880)**(1/10)-1
40	Nicaragua	1.17	(POP1890/POP1880)**(1/10)-1
41	Canada	1.16	(POP1890/POP1880)**(1/10)-1
42	Netherlands	1.16	(POP1890/POP1880)**(1/10)-1
43	Israel	1.15	(POP1890/POP1880)**(1/10)-1
44	Turkmenistan	1.11	(POP1890/POP1880)**(1/10)-1
45	Tajikistan	1.11	(POP1890/POP1880)**(1/10)-1
46	Latvia	1.11	(POP1890/POP1880)**(1/10)-1
47	Georgia	1.11	(POP1890/POP1880)**(1/10)-1
48	Armenia	1.11	(POP1890/POP1880)**(1/10)-1

TABLE 4.8 POPULATION GROWTH RATES, 1880-1890

Rank	Country	GRPOP	Source
49	Belarus	1.11	(POP1890/POP1880)**(1/10)-1
50	Kazakhstan	1.11	(POP1890/POP1880)**(1/10)-1
51	Russia	1.11	(POP1890/POP1880)**(1/10)-1
52	Uzbekistan	1.11	(POP1890/POP1880)**(1/10)-1
53	Lithuania	1.11	(POP1890/POP1880)**(1/10)-1
54	Azerbaijan	1.11	(POP1890/POP1880)**(1/10)-1
55	Moldova	1.11	(POP1890/POP1880)**(1/10)-1
56	Kyrgyzstan	1.11	(POP1890/POP1880)**(1/10)-1
57	Estonia	1.11	(POP1890/POP1880)**(1/10)-1
58	Ukraine	1.11	(POP1890/POP1880)**(1/10)-1
59	Botswana	1.09	(POP1890/POP1880)**(1/10)-1
60	Namibia	1.09	(POP1890/POP1880)**(1/10)-1
61	Tunisia	1.08	(POP1890/POP1880)**(1/10)-1
62	Ecuador	1.08	(POP1890/POP1880)**(1/10)-1
63	Haiti	1.02	(POP1890/POP1880)**(1/10)-1
64	Greece	1.02	(POP1890/POP1880)**(1/10)-1
65	Cyprus	1.02	(POP1890/POP1880)**(1/10)-1
66	Sri Lanka	1.02	(POP1890/POP1880)**(1/10)-1
67	Bangladesh	1.00	(POP1890/POP1880)**(1/10)-1
68	Denmark	0.98	(POP1890/POP1880)**(1/10)-1
69	Belgium	0.96	(POP1890/POP1880)**(1/10)-1
70	Albania	0.93	(POP1890/POP1880)**(1/10)-1
71	Pakistan	0.92	(POP1890/POP1880)**(1/10)-1
72	Germany	0.91	(POP1890/POP1880)**(1/10)-1
73	Austria	0.88	(POP1890/POP1880)**(1/10)-1
74	Portugal	0.87	(POP1890/POP1880)**(1/10)-1
75	Japan	0.85	(POP1890/POP1880)**(1/10)-1
76	Mozambique	0.84	(POP1890/POP1880)**(1/10)-1
77	Algeria	0.84	(POP1890/POP1880)**(1/10)-1
78	India	0.81	(POP1890/POP1880)**(1/10)-1
79	Montenegro	0.81	(POP1890/POP1880)**(1/10)-1
80	Serbia	0.81	(POP1890/POP1880)**(1/10)-1
81	Bosnia	0.81	(POP1890/POP1880)**(1/10)-1
82	Croatia	0.81	(POP1890/POP1880)**(1/10)-1
83	Macedonia	0.81	(POP1890/POP1880)**(1/10)-1
84	Slovenia	0.81	(POP1890/POP1880)**(1/10)-1
85	Kosovo	0.81	(POP1890/POP1880)**(1/10)-1
86	UK	0.80	(POP1890/POP1880)**(1/10)-1
87	Guinea	0.80	(POP1890/POP1880)**(1/10)-1
88	Sierra Leone	0.80	(POP1890/POP1880)**(1/10)-1
89	Guinea-Biss	0.80	(POP1890/POP1880)**(1/10)-1
90	Cuba	0.73	(POP1890/POP1880)**(1/10)-1
91	Lebanon	0.72	(POP1890/POP1880)**(1/10)-1
92	Thailand	0.72	(POP1890/POP1880)**(1/10)-1
93	Afghanistan	0.72	(POP1890/POP1880)**(1/10)-1
94	Honduras	0.71	(POP1890/POP1880)**(1/10)-1
95	Madagascar	0.71	(POP1890/POP1880)**(1/10)-1
96	Italy	0.71	(POP1890/POP1880)**(1/10)-1

Table 4.8 Population Growth Rates, 1880-1890			
Rank	Country	GRPOP	Source
97	Morocco	0.71	(POP1890/POP1880)**(1/10)-1
98	Burundi	0.65	(POP1890/POP1880)**(1/10)-1
99	Cambodia	0.63	(POP1890/POP1880)**(1/10)-1
100	Somalia	0.63	(POP1890/POP1880)**(1/10)-1
101	Jordan	0.63	(POP1890/POP1880)**(1/10)-1
102	Iran	0.62	(POP1890/POP1880)**(1/10)-1
103	Guatemala	0.62	(POP1890/POP1880)**(1/10)-1
104	Romania	0.61	(POP1890/POP1880)**(1/10)-1
105	Hungary	0.56	(POP1890/POP1880)**(1/10)-1
106	Turkey	0.56	(POP1890/POP1880)**(1/10)-1
107	UAE	0.56	(POP1890/POP1880)**(1/10)-1
108	Kuwait	0.56	(POP1890/POP1880)**(1/10)-1
109	Bahrain	0.56	(POP1890/POP1880)**(1/10)-1
110	Qatar	0.56	(POP1890/POP1880)**(1/10)-1
111	Syria	0.54	(POP1890/POP1880)**(1/10)-1
112	Spain	0.52	(POP1890/POP1880)**(1/10)-1
113	Slovakia	0.51	(POP1890/POP1880)**(1/10)-1
114	Czechia	0.51	(POP1890/POP1880)**(1/10)-1
115	Nepal	0.50	(POP1890/POP1880)**(1/10)-1
116	Ghana	0.45	(POP1890/POP1880)**(1/10)-1
117	Paraguay	0.45	(POP1890/POP1880)**(1/10)-1
118	Sweden	0.45	(POP1890/POP1880)**(1/10)-1
119	Oman	0.44	(POP1890/POP1880)**(1/10)-1
120	Bolivia	0.42	(POP1890/POP1880)**(1/10)-1
121	Libya	0.41	(POP1890/POP1880)**(1/10)-1
122	Norway	0.40	(POP1890/POP1880)**(1/10)-1
123	Switzerland	0.39	(POP1890/POP1880)**(1/10)-1
124	South Sudan	0.34	(POP1890/POP1880)**(1/10)-1
125	Sudan	0.34	(POP1890/POP1880)**(1/10)-1
126	Yemen	0.34	(POP1890/POP1880)**(1/10)-1
127	China	0.32	(POP1890/POP1880)**(1/10)-1
128	Taiwan	0.32	(POP1890/POP1880)**(1/10)-1
129	Saudi Arabia	0.31	(POP1890/POP1880)**(1/10)-1
130	France	0.25	(POP1890/POP1880)**(1/10)-1
131	Korea, North	0.21	(POP1890/POP1880)**(1/10)-1
132	Mongolia	0.19	(POP1890/POP1880)**(1/10)-1
133	Korea, South	0.05	(POP1890/POP1880)**(1/10)-1
134	Iceland	-0.24	(POP1890/POP1880)**(1/10)-1
135	Ireland	-0.97	(POP1890/POP1880)**(1/10)-1

TABLE 4.9 POPULATION GROWTH RATES, 1890-1900

Rank	Country	GRPOP	Source
1	Hong Kong	3.64	(POP1900/POP1890)**(1/10)-1
2	Malaysia	3.48	(POP1900/POP1890)**(1/10)-1
3	Argentina	3.35	(POP1900/POP1890)**(1/10)-1
4	Singapore	3.19	(POP1900/POP1890)**(1/10)-1
5	Burma	3.11	(POP1900/POP1890)**(1/10)-1
6	Uruguay	2.92	(POP1900/POP1890)**(1/10)-1
7	Costa Rica	2.61	(POP1900/POP1890)**(1/10)-1
8	Trinidad & T	2.60	(POP1900/POP1890)**(1/10)-1
9	Dominican R	2.55	(POP1900/POP1890)**(1/10)-1
10	Brazil	2.39	(POP1900/POP1890)**(1/10)-1
11	South Africa	2.07	(POP1900/POP1890)**(1/10)-1
12	New Zealand	1.95	(POP1900/POP1890)**(1/10)-1
13	US	1.90	(POP1900/POP1890)**(1/10)-1
14	Australia	1.87	(POP1900/POP1890)**(1/10)-1
15	Lesotho	1.74	(POP1900/POP1890)**(1/10)-1
16	Swaziland	1.74	(POP1900/POP1890)**(1/10)-1
17	Colombia	1.73	(POP1900/POP1890)**(1/10)-1
18	Sri Lanka	1.58	(POP1900/POP1890)**(1/10)-1
19	Bulgaria	1.50	(POP1900/POP1890)**(1/10)-1
20	Egypt	1.50	(POP1900/POP1890)**(1/10)-1
21	Mexico	1.50	(POP1900/POP1890)**(1/10)-1
22	Ethiopia	1.49	(POP1900/POP1890)**(1/10)-1
23	Eritrea	1.49	(POP1900/POP1890)**(1/10)-1
24	El Salvador	1.49	(POP1900/POP1890)**(1/10)-1
25	Kosovo	1.44	(POP1900/POP1890)**(1/10)-1
26	Macedonia	1.44	(POP1900/POP1890)**(1/10)-1
27	Croatia	1.44	(POP1900/POP1890)**(1/10)-1
28	Serbia	1.44	(POP1900/POP1890)**(1/10)-1
29	Slovenia	1.44	(POP1900/POP1890)**(1/10)-1
30	Bosnia	1.44	(POP1900/POP1890)**(1/10)-1
31	Montenegro	1.44	(POP1900/POP1890)**(1/10)-1
32	Laos	1.42	(POP1900/POP1890)**(1/10)-1
33	Vietnam	1.42	(POP1900/POP1890)**(1/10)-1
34	Zimbabwe	1.40	(POP1900/POP1890)**(1/10)-1
35	Zambia	1.40	(POP1900/POP1890)**(1/10)-1
36	Malawi	1.40	(POP1900/POP1890)**(1/10)-1
37	Taiwan	1.37	(POP1900/POP1890)**(1/10)-1
38	Panama	1.35	(POP1900/POP1890)**(1/10)-1
39	Venezuela	1.35	(POP1900/POP1890)**(1/10)-1
40	Germany	1.34	(POP1900/POP1890)**(1/10)-1
41	Puerto Rico	1.33	(POP1900/POP1890)**(1/10)-1
42	Indonesia	1.30	(POP1900/POP1890)**(1/10)-1
43	Netherlands	1.26	(POP1900/POP1890)**(1/10)-1
44	Peru	1.26	(POP1900/POP1890)**(1/10)-1
45	Philippines	1.24	(POP1900/POP1890)**(1/10)-1
46	Jamaica	1.23	(POP1900/POP1890)**(1/10)-1
47	Azerbaijan	1.19	(POP1900/POP1890)**(1/10)-1
48	Lithuania	1.19	(POP1900/POP1890)**(1/10)-1

Table 4.9 Population Growth Rates, 1890-1900			
Rank	Country	GRPOP	Source
49	Latvia	1.19	(POP1900/POP1890)**(1/10)-1
50	Uzbekistan	1.19	(POP1900/POP1890)**(1/10)-1
51	Moldova	1.19	(POP1900/POP1890)**(1/10)-1
52	Kazakhstan	1.19	(POP1900/POP1890)**(1/10)-1
53	Russia	1.19	(POP1900/POP1890)**(1/10)-1
54	Ukraine	1.19	(POP1900/POP1890)**(1/10)-1
55	Estonia	1.19	(POP1900/POP1890)**(1/10)-1
56	Georgia	1.19	(POP1900/POP1890)**(1/10)-1
57	Kyrgyzstan	1.19	(POP1900/POP1890)**(1/10)-1
58	Belarus	1.19	(POP1900/POP1890)**(1/10)-1
59	Tajikistan	1.19	(POP1900/POP1890)**(1/10)-1
60	Armenia	1.19	(POP1900/POP1890)**(1/10)-1
61	Turkmenistan	1.19	(POP1900/POP1890)**(1/10)-1
62	Iraq	1.18	(POP1900/POP1890)**(1/10)-1
63	Nicaragua	1.17	(POP1900/POP1890)**(1/10)-1
64	Chile	1.16	(POP1900/POP1890)**(1/10)-1
65	Israel	1.15	(POP1900/POP1890)**(1/10)-1
66	Finland	1.13	(POP1900/POP1890)**(1/10)-1
67	Switzerland	1.12	(POP1900/POP1890)**(1/10)-1
68	Norway	1.11	(POP1900/POP1890)**(1/10)-1
69	Denmark	1.11	(POP1900/POP1890)**(1/10)-1
70	Botswana	1.09	(POP1900/POP1890)**(1/10)-1
71	Namibia	1.09	(POP1900/POP1890)**(1/10)-1
72	Tunisia	1.08	(POP1900/POP1890)**(1/10)-1
73	Ecuador	1.08	(POP1900/POP1890)**(1/10)-1
74	Canada	1.05	(POP1900/POP1890)**(1/10)-1
75	Austria	1.02	(POP1900/POP1890)**(1/10)-1
76	Greece	1.02	(POP1900/POP1890)**(1/10)-1
77	Cyprus	1.02	(POP1900/POP1890)**(1/10)-1
78	Haiti	1.02	(POP1900/POP1890)**(1/10)-1
79	Iceland	1.00	(POP1900/POP1890)**(1/10)-1
80	Belgium	0.98	(POP1900/POP1890)**(1/10)-1
81	Albania	0.98	(POP1900/POP1890)**(1/10)-1
82	Japan	0.96	(POP1900/POP1890)**(1/10)-1
83	UK	0.94	(POP1900/POP1890)**(1/10)-1
84	Thailand	0.93	(POP1900/POP1890)**(1/10)-1
85	Mozambique	0.84	(POP1900/POP1890)**(1/10)-1
86	Algeria	0.84	(POP1900/POP1890)**(1/10)-1
87	Ghana	0.83	(POP1900/POP1890)**(1/10)-1
88	Poland	0.80	(POP1900/POP1890)**(1/10)-1
89	Sierra Leone	0.80	(POP1900/POP1890)**(1/10)-1
90	Guinea	0.80	(POP1900/POP1890)**(1/10)-1
91	Guinea-Biss	0.80	(POP1900/POP1890)**(1/10)-1
92	Czechia	0.76	(POP1900/POP1890)**(1/10)-1
93	Slovakia	0.76	(POP1900/POP1890)**(1/10)-1
94	Hungary	0.74	(POP1900/POP1890)**(1/10)-1
95	Cuba	0.73	(POP1900/POP1890)**(1/10)-1
96	Portugal	0.72	(POP1900/POP1890)**(1/10)-1

Table 4.9 Population Growth Rates, 1890-1900			
Rank	Country	GRPOP	Source
97	Lebanon	0.72	(POP1900/POP1890)**(1/10)-1
98	Afghanistan	0.72	(POP1900/POP1890)**(1/10)-1
99	Honduras	0.71	(POP1900/POP1890)**(1/10)-1
100	Madagascar	0.71	(POP1900/POP1890)**(1/10)-1
101	Morocco	0.71	(POP1900/POP1890)**(1/10)-1
102	Sweden	0.68	(POP1900/POP1890)**(1/10)-1
103	Burundi	0.65	(POP1900/POP1890)**(1/10)-1
104	Cambodia	0.63	(POP1900/POP1890)**(1/10)-1
105	Somalia	0.63	(POP1900/POP1890)**(1/10)-1
106	Jordan	0.63	(POP1900/POP1890)**(1/10)-1
107	Iran	0.62	(POP1900/POP1890)**(1/10)-1
108	Guatemala	0.62	(POP1900/POP1890)**(1/10)-1
109	Italy	0.60	(POP1900/POP1890)**(1/10)-1
110	Romania	0.59	(POP1900/POP1890)**(1/10)-1
111	Turkey	0.56	(POP1900/POP1890)**(1/10)-1
112	Bahrain	0.56	(POP1900/POP1890)**(1/10)-1
113	Kuwait	0.56	(POP1900/POP1890)**(1/10)-1
114	UAE	0.56	(POP1900/POP1890)**(1/10)-1
115	Qatar	0.56	(POP1900/POP1890)**(1/10)-1
116	Syria	0.54	(POP1900/POP1890)**(1/10)-1
117	China	0.51	(POP1900/POP1890)**(1/10)-1
118	Paraguay	0.45	(POP1900/POP1890)**(1/10)-1
119	Spain	0.45	(POP1900/POP1890)**(1/10)-1
120	Oman	0.44	(POP1900/POP1890)**(1/10)-1
121	Bolivia	0.42	(POP1900/POP1890)**(1/10)-1
122	Libya	0.41	(POP1900/POP1890)**(1/10)-1
123	Sudan	0.34	(POP1900/POP1890)**(1/10)-1
124	South Sudan	0.34	(POP1900/POP1890)**(1/10)-1
125	Yemen	0.34	(POP1900/POP1890)**(1/10)-1
126	Bangladesh	0.33	(POP1900/POP1890)**(1/10)-1
127	Saudi Arabia	0.31	(POP1900/POP1890)**(1/10)-1
128	Pakistan	0.26	(POP1900/POP1890)**(1/10)-1
129	Mongolia	0.19	(POP1900/POP1890)**(1/10)-1
130	Nepal	0.17	(POP1900/POP1890)**(1/10)-1
131	Korea, North	0.17	(POP1900/POP1890)**(1/10)-1
132	India	0.15	(POP1900/POP1890)**(1/10)-1
133	France	0.14	(POP1900/POP1890)**(1/10)-1
134	Korea, South	0.05	(POP1900/POP1890)**(1/10)-1
135	Ireland	-0.54	(POP1900/POP1890)**(1/10)-1

Table 4.10 Population Growth Rates, 1900-1913

Rank	Country	GRPOP	Source
1	Argentina	3.83	(POP1913/POP1900)**(1/13)-1
2	Hong Kong	3.64	(POP1913/POP1900)**(1/13)-1
3	Singapore	3.18	(POP1913/POP1900)**(1/13)-1
4	Cuba	2.99	(POP1913/POP1900)**(1/13)-1
5	Dominican R	2.93	(POP1913/POP1900)**(1/13)-1
6	Canada	2.84	(POP1913/POP1900)**(1/13)-1
7	New Zealand	2.57	(POP1913/POP1900)**(1/13)-1
8	Malaysia	2.52	(POP1913/POP1900)**(1/13)-1
9	Paraguay	2.34	(POP1913/POP1900)**(1/13)-1
10	Panama	2.18	(POP1913/POP1900)**(1/13)-1
11	Honduras	2.16	(POP1913/POP1900)**(1/13)-1
12	El Salvador	2.13	(POP1913/POP1900)**(1/13)-1
13	Brazil	2.13	(POP1913/POP1900)**(1/13)-1
14	Trinidad & T	2.12	(POP1913/POP1900)**(1/13)-1
15	South Africa	2.07	(POP1913/POP1900)**(1/13)-1
16	Colombia	2.04	(POP1913/POP1900)**(1/13)-1
17	Australia	1.97	(POP1913/POP1900)**(1/13)-1
18	Uruguay	1.96	(POP1913/POP1900)**(1/13)-1
19	Philippines	1.92	(POP1913/POP1900)**(1/13)-1
20	US	1.90	(POP1913/POP1900)**(1/13)-1
21	Turkmenistan	1.76	(POP1913/POP1900)**(1/13)-1
22	Armenia	1.76	(POP1913/POP1900)**(1/13)-1
23	Moldova	1.76	(POP1913/POP1900)**(1/13)-1
24	Belarus	1.76	(POP1913/POP1900)**(1/13)-1
25	Lithuania	1.76	(POP1913/POP1900)**(1/13)-1
26	Ukraine	1.76	(POP1913/POP1900)**(1/13)-1
27	Russia	1.76	(POP1913/POP1900)**(1/13)-1
28	Estonia	1.76	(POP1913/POP1900)**(1/13)-1
29	Georgia	1.76	(POP1913/POP1900)**(1/13)-1
30	Kazakhstan	1.76	(POP1913/POP1900)**(1/13)-1
31	Uzbekistan	1.76	(POP1913/POP1900)**(1/13)-1
32	Kyrgyzstan	1.76	(POP1913/POP1900)**(1/13)-1
33	Latvia	1.76	(POP1913/POP1900)**(1/13)-1
34	Tajikistan	1.76	(POP1913/POP1900)**(1/13)-1
35	Azerbaijan	1.76	(POP1913/POP1900)**(1/13)-1
36	Costa Rica	1.75	(POP1913/POP1900)**(1/13)-1
37	Swaziland	1.75	(POP1913/POP1900)**(1/13)-1
38	Lesotho	1.74	(POP1913/POP1900)**(1/13)-1
39	Puerto Rico	1.61	(POP1913/POP1900)**(1/13)-1
40	Sri Lanka	1.60	(POP1913/POP1900)**(1/13)-1
41	Montenegro	1.52	(POP1913/POP1900)**(1/13)-1
42	Bosnia	1.52	(POP1913/POP1900)**(1/13)-1
43	Slovenia	1.52	(POP1913/POP1900)**(1/13)-1
44	Serbia	1.52	(POP1913/POP1900)**(1/13)-1
45	Macedonia	1.52	(POP1913/POP1900)**(1/13)-1
46	Croatia	1.52	(POP1913/POP1900)**(1/13)-1
47	Kosovo	1.52	(POP1913/POP1900)**(1/13)-1
48	Haiti	1.49	(POP1913/POP1900)**(1/13)-1

TABLE 4.10 POPULATION GROWTH RATES, 1900-1913			
Rank	Country	GRPOP	Source
49	Eritrea	1.49	(POP1913/POP1900)**(1/13)-1
50	Ethiopia	1.49	(POP1913/POP1900)**(1/13)-1
51	Burma	1.49	(POP1913/POP1900)**(1/13)-1
52	Taiwan	1.49	(POP1913/POP1900)**(1/13)-1
53	Nicaragua	1.47	(POP1913/POP1900)**(1/13)-1
54	Ecuador	1.45	(POP1913/POP1900)**(1/13)-1
55	Laos	1.42	(POP1913/POP1900)**(1/13)-1
56	Vietnam	1.42	(POP1913/POP1900)**(1/13)-1
57	Netherlands	1.40	(POP1913/POP1900)**(1/13)-1
58	Malawi	1.40	(POP1913/POP1900)**(1/13)-1
59	Zimbabwe	1.40	(POP1913/POP1900)**(1/13)-1
60	Zambia	1.40	(POP1913/POP1900)**(1/13)-1
61	Egypt	1.39	(POP1913/POP1900)**(1/13)-1
62	Germany	1.39	(POP1913/POP1900)**(1/13)-1
63	Thailand	1.33	(POP1913/POP1900)**(1/13)-1
64	Bulgaria	1.28	(POP1913/POP1900)**(1/13)-1
65	Japan	1.23	(POP1913/POP1900)**(1/13)-1
66	Switzerland	1.22	(POP1913/POP1900)**(1/13)-1
67	Indonesia	1.20	(POP1913/POP1900)**(1/13)-1
68	Denmark	1.18	(POP1913/POP1900)**(1/13)-1
69	Iraq	1.18	(POP1913/POP1900)**(1/13)-1
70	Jamaica	1.16	(POP1913/POP1900)**(1/13)-1
71	Israel	1.15	(POP1913/POP1900)**(1/13)-1
72	Chile	1.11	(POP1913/POP1900)**(1/13)-1
73	Namibia	1.09	(POP1913/POP1900)**(1/13)-1
74	Botswana	1.09	(POP1913/POP1900)**(1/13)-1
75	Tunisia	1.08	(POP1913/POP1900)**(1/13)-1
76	Ghana	1.05	(POP1913/POP1900)**(1/13)-1
77	Peru	1.04	(POP1913/POP1900)**(1/13)-1
78	Finland	1.04	(POP1913/POP1900)**(1/13)-1
79	Guatemala	1.03	(POP1913/POP1900)**(1/13)-1
80	Belgium	1.02	(POP1913/POP1900)**(1/13)-1
81	Romania	1.00	(POP1913/POP1900)**(1/13)-1
82	Austria	0.96	(POP1913/POP1900)**(1/13)-1
83	Venezuela	0.95	(POP1913/POP1900)**(1/13)-1
84	Albania	0.89	(POP1913/POP1900)**(1/13)-1
85	Mozambique	0.84	(POP1913/POP1900)**(1/13)-1
86	Iceland	0.84	(POP1913/POP1900)**(1/13)-1
87	Algeria	0.82	(POP1913/POP1900)**(1/13)-1
88	UK	0.80	(POP1913/POP1900)**(1/13)-1
89	Bolivia	0.80	(POP1913/POP1900)**(1/13)-1
90	Guinea-Biss	0.80	(POP1913/POP1900)**(1/13)-1
91	Guinea	0.80	(POP1913/POP1900)**(1/13)-1
92	Sierra Leone	0.80	(POP1913/POP1900)**(1/13)-1
93	Italy	0.78	(POP1913/POP1900)**(1/13)-1
94	Portugal	0.77	(POP1913/POP1900)**(1/13)-1
95	Mexico	0.74	(POP1913/POP1900)**(1/13)-1
96	Hungary	0.74	(POP1913/POP1900)**(1/13)-1

Table 4.10 Population Growth Rates, 1900-1913			
Rank	Country	GRPOP	Source
97	Sweden	0.73	(POP1913/POP1900)**(1/13)-1
98	Lebanon	0.72	(POP1913/POP1900)**(1/13)-1
99	Afghanistan	0.72	(POP1913/POP1900)**(1/13)-1
100	Norway	0.72	(POP1913/POP1900)**(1/13)-1
101	Madagascar	0.71	(POP1913/POP1900)**(1/13)-1
102	Morocco	0.71	(POP1913/POP1900)**(1/13)-1
103	Cyprus	0.69	(POP1913/POP1900)**(1/13)-1
104	Greece	0.69	(POP1913/POP1900)**(1/13)-1
105	China	0.69	(POP1913/POP1900)**(1/13)-1
106	Spain	0.68	(POP1913/POP1900)**(1/13)-1
107	Slovakia	0.67	(POP1913/POP1900)**(1/13)-1
108	Czechia	0.67	(POP1913/POP1900)**(1/13)-1
109	Bangladesh	0.66	(POP1913/POP1900)**(1/13)-1
110	Burundi	0.65	(POP1913/POP1900)**(1/13)-1
111	Cambodia	0.63	(POP1913/POP1900)**(1/13)-1
112	Somalia	0.63	(POP1913/POP1900)**(1/13)-1
113	Jordan	0.63	(POP1913/POP1900)**(1/13)-1
114	Iran	0.62	(POP1913/POP1900)**(1/13)-1
115	Poland	0.59	(POP1913/POP1900)**(1/13)-1
116	Pakistan	0.59	(POP1913/POP1900)**(1/13)-1
117	Turkey	0.56	(POP1913/POP1900)**(1/13)-1
118	Qatar	0.56	(POP1913/POP1900)**(1/13)-1
119	UAE	0.56	(POP1913/POP1900)**(1/13)-1
120	Kuwait	0.56	(POP1913/POP1900)**(1/13)-1
121	Bahrain	0.56	(POP1913/POP1900)**(1/13)-1
122	Syria	0.54	(POP1913/POP1900)**(1/13)-1
123	Korea, South	0.52	(POP1913/POP1900)**(1/13)-1
124	Nepal	0.50	(POP1913/POP1900)**(1/13)-1
125	India	0.48	(POP1913/POP1900)**(1/13)-1
126	Oman	0.44	(POP1913/POP1900)**(1/13)-1
127	Libya	0.41	(POP1913/POP1900)**(1/13)-1
128	Sudan	0.34	(POP1913/POP1900)**(1/13)-1
129	South Sudan	0.34	(POP1913/POP1900)**(1/13)-1
130	Yemen	0.34	(POP1913/POP1900)**(1/13)-1
131	Saudi Arabia	0.31	(POP1913/POP1900)**(1/13)-1
132	Korea, North	0.19	(POP1913/POP1900)**(1/13)-1
133	Mongolia	0.19	(POP1913/POP1900)**(1/13)-1
134	France	0.16	(POP1913/POP1900)**(1/13)-1
135	Ireland	-0.21	(POP1913/POP1900)**(1/13)-1

Table 4.11 Population Growth Rates, 1913-1920			
Rank	Country	GRPOP	Source
1	Panama	4.92	(POP1920/POP1913)**(1/7)-1
2	Hong Kong	4.16	(POP1920/POP1913)**(1/7)-1
3	Israel	3.30	(POP1920/POP1913)**(1/7)-1
4	Cuba	3.04	(POP1920/POP1913)**(1/7)-1
5	Singapore	2.77	(POP1920/POP1913)**(1/7)-1
6	Ghana	2.61	(POP1920/POP1913)**(1/7)-1
7	Colombia	2.59	(POP1920/POP1913)**(1/7)-1
8	Paraguay	2.35	(POP1920/POP1913)**(1/7)-1
9	Dominican R	2.29	(POP1920/POP1913)**(1/7)-1
10	Uruguay	2.20	(POP1920/POP1913)**(1/7)-1
11	South Africa	2.18	(POP1920/POP1913)**(1/7)-1
12	Lebanon	2.18	(POP1920/POP1913)**(1/7)-1
13	El Salvador	2.15	(POP1920/POP1913)**(1/7)-1
14	Brazil	2.12	(POP1920/POP1913)**(1/7)-1
15	Argentina	2.12	(POP1920/POP1913)**(1/7)-1
16	Malaysia	2.01	(POP1920/POP1913)**(1/7)-1
17	Iraq	1.95	(POP1920/POP1913)**(1/7)-1
18	Philippines	1.93	(POP1920/POP1913)**(1/7)-1
19	Korea, North	1.87	(POP1920/POP1913)**(1/7)-1
20	Bolivia	1.83	(POP1920/POP1913)**(1/7)-1
21	Costa Rica	1.75	(POP1920/POP1913)**(1/7)-1
22	Lesotho	1.74	(POP1920/POP1913)**(1/7)-1
23	Swaziland	1.74	(POP1920/POP1913)**(1/7)-1
24	Thailand	1.74	(POP1920/POP1913)**(1/7)-1
25	Tunisia	1.72	(POP1920/POP1913)**(1/7)-1
26	Haiti	1.67	(POP1920/POP1913)**(1/7)-1
27	Canada	1.64	(POP1920/POP1913)**(1/7)-1
28	Chile	1.57	(POP1920/POP1913)**(1/7)-1
29	Korea, South	1.56	(POP1920/POP1913)**(1/7)-1
30	Syria	1.53	(POP1920/POP1913)**(1/7)-1
31	Morocco	1.53	(POP1920/POP1913)**(1/7)-1
32	Australia	1.52	(POP1920/POP1913)**(1/7)-1
33	Netherlands	1.51	(POP1920/POP1913)**(1/7)-1
34	Puerto Rico	1.51	(POP1920/POP1913)**(1/7)-1
35	Eritrea	1.49	(POP1920/POP1913)**(1/7)-1
36	Ethiopia	1.49	(POP1920/POP1913)**(1/7)-1
37	Nicaragua	1.47	(POP1920/POP1913)**(1/7)-1
38	New Zealand	1.45	(POP1920/POP1913)**(1/7)-1
39	Trinidad & T	1.44	(POP1920/POP1913)**(1/7)-1
40	Zambia	1.40	(POP1920/POP1913)**(1/7)-1
41	Malawi	1.40	(POP1920/POP1913)**(1/7)-1
42	Zimbabwe	1.40	(POP1920/POP1913)**(1/7)-1
43	US	1.31	(POP1920/POP1913)**(1/7)-1
44	Sri Lanka	1.26	(POP1920/POP1913)**(1/7)-1
45	Honduras	1.25	(POP1920/POP1913)**(1/7)-1
46	Denmark	1.20	(POP1920/POP1913)**(1/7)-1
47	Egypt	1.17	(POP1920/POP1913)**(1/7)-1
48	Iran	1.17	(POP1920/POP1913)**(1/7)-1

Table 4.11 Population Growth Rates, 1913-1920

Rank	Country	GRPOP	Source
49	Nepal	1.16	(POP1920/POP1913)**(1/7)-1
50	Iceland	1.11	(POP1920/POP1913)**(1/7)-1
51	Japan	1.11	(POP1920/POP1913)**(1/7)-1
52	China	1.10	(POP1920/POP1913)**(1/7)-1
53	Namibia	1.09	(POP1920/POP1913)**(1/7)-1
54	Botswana	1.09	(POP1920/POP1913)**(1/7)-1
55	Taiwan	1.06	(POP1920/POP1913)**(1/7)-1
56	Indonesia	1.05	(POP1920/POP1913)**(1/7)-1
57	Peru	1.05	(POP1920/POP1913)**(1/7)-1
58	Guatemala	1.03	(POP1920/POP1913)**(1/7)-1
59	Bulgaria	1.03	(POP1920/POP1913)**(1/7)-1
60	Cambodia	1.02	(POP1920/POP1913)**(1/7)-1
61	Yemen	1.02	(POP1920/POP1913)**(1/7)-1
62	Norway	1.01	(POP1920/POP1913)**(1/7)-1
63	Afghanistan	0.96	(POP1920/POP1913)**(1/7)-1
64	Vietnam	0.94	(POP1920/POP1913)**(1/7)-1
65	Qatar	0.89	(POP1920/POP1913)**(1/7)-1
66	Kuwait	0.89	(POP1920/POP1913)**(1/7)-1
67	Bahrain	0.89	(POP1920/POP1913)**(1/7)-1
68	UAE	0.89	(POP1920/POP1913)**(1/7)-1
69	Burma	0.87	(POP1920/POP1913)**(1/7)-1
70	Mozambique	0.84	(POP1920/POP1913)**(1/7)-1
71	Ecuador	0.83	(POP1920/POP1913)**(1/7)-1
72	Jordan	0.83	(POP1920/POP1913)**(1/7)-1
73	Sierra Leone	0.80	(POP1920/POP1913)**(1/7)-1
74	Guinea	0.80	(POP1920/POP1913)**(1/7)-1
75	Guinea-Biss	0.80	(POP1920/POP1913)**(1/7)-1
76	Algeria	0.73	(POP1920/POP1913)**(1/7)-1
77	Madagascar	0.71	(POP1920/POP1913)**(1/7)-1
78	Greece	0.71	(POP1920/POP1913)**(1/7)-1
79	Cyprus	0.71	(POP1920/POP1913)**(1/7)-1
80	Spain	0.67	(POP1920/POP1913)**(1/7)-1
81	Burundi	0.65	(POP1920/POP1913)**(1/7)-1
82	Sweden	0.64	(POP1920/POP1913)**(1/7)-1
83	Somalia	0.63	(POP1920/POP1913)**(1/7)-1
84	Venezuela	0.58	(POP1920/POP1913)**(1/7)-1
85	Albania	0.53	(POP1920/POP1913)**(1/7)-1
86	Finland	0.49	(POP1920/POP1913)**(1/7)-1
87	Saudi Arabia	0.49	(POP1920/POP1913)**(1/7)-1
88	Libya	0.41	(POP1920/POP1913)**(1/7)-1
89	UK	0.36	(POP1920/POP1913)**(1/7)-1
90	South Sudan	0.34	(POP1920/POP1913)**(1/7)-1
91	Sudan	0.34	(POP1920/POP1913)**(1/7)-1
92	Pakistan	0.33	(POP1920/POP1913)**(1/7)-1
93	Jamaica	0.30	(POP1920/POP1913)**(1/7)-1
94	Laos	0.25	(POP1920/POP1913)**(1/7)-1
95	Hungary	0.20	(POP1920/POP1913)**(1/7)-1
96	Bangladesh	0.17	(POP1920/POP1913)**(1/7)-1

TABLE 4.11 POPULATION GROWTH RATES, 1913-1920

Rank	Country	GRPOP	Source
97	Portugal	0.14	(POP1920/POP1913)**(1/7)-1
98	Mongolia	0.08	(POP1920/POP1913)**(1/7)-1
99	India	0.08	(POP1920/POP1913)**(1/7)-1
100	Oman	0.07	(POP1920/POP1913)**(1/7)-1
101	Italy	0.06	(POP1920/POP1913)**(1/7)-1
102	Ireland	0.05	(POP1920/POP1913)**(1/7)-1
103	Switzerland	0.05	(POP1920/POP1913)**(1/7)-1
104	Mexico	-0.07	(POP1920/POP1913)**(1/7)-1
105	Turkmenistan	-0.15	(POP1920/POP1913)**(1/7)-1
106	Kyrgyzstan	-0.15	(POP1920/POP1913)**(1/7)-1
107	Georgia	-0.15	(POP1920/POP1913)**(1/7)-1
108	Armenia	-0.15	(POP1920/POP1913)**(1/7)-1
109	Kazakhstan	-0.15	(POP1920/POP1913)**(1/7)-1
110	Azerbaijan	-0.15	(POP1920/POP1913)**(1/7)-1
111	Uzbekistan	-0.15	(POP1920/POP1913)**(1/7)-1
112	Russia	-0.15	(POP1920/POP1913)**(1/7)-1
113	Ukraine	-0.15	(POP1920/POP1913)**(1/7)-1
114	Belarus	-0.15	(POP1920/POP1913)**(1/7)-1
115	Moldova	-0.15	(POP1920/POP1913)**(1/7)-1
116	Estonia	-0.15	(POP1920/POP1913)**(1/7)-1
117	Latvia	-0.15	(POP1920/POP1913)**(1/7)-1
118	Lithuania	-0.15	(POP1920/POP1913)**(1/7)-1
119	Tajikistan	-0.15	(POP1920/POP1913)**(1/7)-1
120	Belgium	-0.21	(POP1920/POP1913)**(1/7)-1
121	Romania	-0.21	(POP1920/POP1913)**(1/7)-1
122	Slovakia	-0.29	(POP1920/POP1913)**(1/7)-1
123	Czechia	-0.29	(POP1920/POP1913)**(1/7)-1
124	Austria	-0.67	(POP1920/POP1913)**(1/7)-1
125	France	-0.87	(POP1920/POP1913)**(1/7)-1
126	Germany	-0.94	(POP1920/POP1913)**(1/7)-1
127	Turkey	-1.11	(POP1920/POP1913)**(1/7)-1
128	Kosovo	-1.28	(POP1920/POP1913)**(1/7)-1
129	Macedonia	-1.28	(POP1920/POP1913)**(1/7)-1
130	Montenegro	-1.28	(POP1920/POP1913)**(1/7)-1
131	Serbia	-1.28	(POP1920/POP1913)**(1/7)-1
132	Slovenia	-1.28	(POP1920/POP1913)**(1/7)-1
133	Croatia	-1.28	(POP1920/POP1913)**(1/7)-1
134	Bosnia	-1.28	(POP1920/POP1913)**(1/7)-1
135	Poland	-1.54	(POP1920/POP1913)**(1/7)-1

Table 4.12 Population Growth Rates, 1920-1929			
Rank	Country	GRPOP	Source
1	Singapore	4.38	(POP1929/POP1920)**(1/9)-1
2	Dominican R	3.64	(POP1929/POP1920)**(1/9)-1
3	Israel	3.30	(POP1929/POP1920)**(1/9)-1
4	Argentina	3.03	(POP1929/POP1920)**(1/9)-1
5	Honduras	2.88	(POP1929/POP1920)**(1/9)-1
6	Ghana	2.61	(POP1929/POP1920)**(1/9)-1
7	Colombia	2.59	(POP1929/POP1920)**(1/9)-1
8	Cuba	2.50	(POP1929/POP1920)**(1/9)-1
9	Paraguay	2.33	(POP1929/POP1920)**(1/9)-1
10	Thailand	2.33	(POP1929/POP1920)**(1/9)-1
11	Uruguay	2.32	(POP1929/POP1920)**(1/9)-1
12	Malaysia	2.21	(POP1929/POP1920)**(1/9)-1
13	South Africa	2.18	(POP1929/POP1920)**(1/9)-1
14	Lebanon	2.18	(POP1929/POP1920)**(1/9)-1
15	Hong Kong	2.15	(POP1929/POP1920)**(1/9)-1
16	El Salvador	2.09	(POP1929/POP1920)**(1/9)-1
17	Taiwan	2.07	(POP1929/POP1920)**(1/9)-1
18	Philippines	2.06	(POP1929/POP1920)**(1/9)-1
19	Brazil	2.05	(POP1929/POP1920)**(1/9)-1
20	Australia	1.99	(POP1929/POP1920)**(1/9)-1
21	Iraq	1.95	(POP1929/POP1920)**(1/9)-1
22	New Zealand	1.91	(POP1929/POP1920)**(1/9)-1
23	Korea, North	1.87	(POP1929/POP1920)**(1/9)-1
24	Bulgaria	1.79	(POP1929/POP1920)**(1/9)-1
25	Canada	1.77	(POP1929/POP1920)**(1/9)-1
26	Swaziland	1.75	(POP1929/POP1920)**(1/9)-1
27	Lesotho	1.74	(POP1929/POP1920)**(1/9)-1
28	Costa Rica	1.73	(POP1929/POP1920)**(1/9)-1
29	Tunisia	1.72	(POP1929/POP1920)**(1/9)-1
30	Puerto Rico	1.69	(POP1929/POP1920)**(1/9)-1
31	Poland	1.68	(POP1929/POP1920)**(1/9)-1
32	Korea, South	1.68	(POP1929/POP1920)**(1/9)-1
33	Jamaica	1.59	(POP1929/POP1920)**(1/9)-1
34	Syria	1.53	(POP1929/POP1920)**(1/9)-1
35	Morocco	1.53	(POP1929/POP1920)**(1/9)-1
36	US	1.50	(POP1929/POP1920)**(1/9)-1
37	Montenegro	1.49	(POP1929/POP1920)**(1/9)-1
38	Bosnia	1.49	(POP1929/POP1920)**(1/9)-1
39	Slovenia	1.49	(POP1929/POP1920)**(1/9)-1
40	Kosovo	1.49	(POP1929/POP1920)**(1/9)-1
41	Croatia	1.49	(POP1929/POP1920)**(1/9)-1
42	Serbia	1.49	(POP1929/POP1920)**(1/9)-1
43	Macedonia	1.49	(POP1929/POP1920)**(1/9)-1
44	Ethiopia	1.49	(POP1929/POP1920)**(1/9)-1
45	Eritrea	1.49	(POP1929/POP1920)**(1/9)-1
46	Netherlands	1.43	(POP1929/POP1920)**(1/9)-1
47	Peru	1.41	(POP1929/POP1920)**(1/9)-1
48	Malawi	1.40	(POP1929/POP1920)**(1/9)-1

TABLE 4.12 POPULATION GROWTH RATES, 1920-1929

Rank	Country	GRPOP	Source
49	Zambia	1.40	(POP1929/POP1920)**(1/9)-1
50	Zimbabwe	1.40	(POP1929/POP1920)**(1/9)-1
51	Japan	1.40	(POP1929/POP1920)**(1/9)-1
52	Mexico	1.39	(POP1929/POP1920)**(1/9)-1
53	Romania	1.37	(POP1929/POP1920)**(1/9)-1
54	Iceland	1.34	(POP1929/POP1920)**(1/9)-1
55	Haiti	1.32	(POP1929/POP1920)**(1/9)-1
56	Chile	1.32	(POP1929/POP1920)**(1/9)-1
57	Indonesia	1.21	(POP1929/POP1920)**(1/9)-1
58	Pakistan	1.21	(POP1929/POP1920)**(1/9)-1
59	Tajikistan	1.19	(POP1929/POP1920)**(1/9)-1
60	Estonia	1.19	(POP1929/POP1920)**(1/9)-1
61	Azerbaijan	1.19	(POP1929/POP1920)**(1/9)-1
62	Latvia	1.19	(POP1929/POP1920)**(1/9)-1
63	Uzbekistan	1.19	(POP1929/POP1920)**(1/9)-1
64	Kyrgyzstan	1.19	(POP1929/POP1920)**(1/9)-1
65	Belarus	1.19	(POP1929/POP1920)**(1/9)-1
66	Lithuania	1.19	(POP1929/POP1920)**(1/9)-1
67	Russia	1.19	(POP1929/POP1920)**(1/9)-1
68	Ukraine	1.19	(POP1929/POP1920)**(1/9)-1
69	Kazakhstan	1.19	(POP1929/POP1920)**(1/9)-1
70	Georgia	1.19	(POP1929/POP1920)**(1/9)-1
71	Moldova	1.19	(POP1929/POP1920)**(1/9)-1
72	Armenia	1.19	(POP1929/POP1920)**(1/9)-1
73	Turkmenistan	1.19	(POP1929/POP1920)**(1/9)-1
74	Algeria	1.18	(POP1929/POP1920)**(1/9)-1
75	Portugal	1.18	(POP1929/POP1920)**(1/9)-1
76	Iran	1.17	(POP1929/POP1920)**(1/9)-1
77	Bolivia	1.16	(POP1929/POP1920)**(1/9)-1
78	Nepal	1.16	(POP1929/POP1920)**(1/9)-1
79	Egypt	1.11	(POP1929/POP1920)**(1/9)-1
80	Botswana	1.09	(POP1929/POP1920)**(1/9)-1
81	Namibia	1.09	(POP1929/POP1920)**(1/9)-1
82	Cyprus	1.07	(POP1929/POP1920)**(1/9)-1
83	Greece	1.07	(POP1929/POP1920)**(1/9)-1
84	Guatemala	1.04	(POP1929/POP1920)**(1/9)-1
85	Burma	1.03	(POP1929/POP1920)**(1/9)-1
86	Cambodia	1.02	(POP1929/POP1920)**(1/9)-1
87	Yemen	1.02	(POP1929/POP1920)**(1/9)-1
88	Spain	0.99	(POP1929/POP1920)**(1/9)-1
89	Finland	0.99	(POP1929/POP1920)**(1/9)-1
90	Afghanistan	0.96	(POP1929/POP1920)**(1/9)-1
91	Venezuela	0.95	(POP1929/POP1920)**(1/9)-1
92	India	0.95	(POP1929/POP1920)**(1/9)-1
93	Vietnam	0.94	(POP1929/POP1920)**(1/9)-1
94	Denmark	0.91	(POP1929/POP1920)**(1/9)-1
95	Bahrain	0.89	(POP1929/POP1920)**(1/9)-1
96	UAE	0.89	(POP1929/POP1920)**(1/9)-1

Table 4.12 Population Growth Rates, 1920-1929

Rank	Country	GRPOP	Source
97	Kuwait	0.89	(POP1929/POP1920)**(1/9)-1
98	Qatar	0.89	(POP1929/POP1920)**(1/9)-1
99	Italy	0.88	(POP1929/POP1920)**(1/9)-1
100	Sri Lanka	0.86	(POP1929/POP1920)**(1/9)-1
101	Hungary	0.85	(POP1929/POP1920)**(1/9)-1
102	Mozambique	0.84	(POP1929/POP1920)**(1/9)-1
103	Ecuador	0.83	(POP1929/POP1920)**(1/9)-1
104	Jordan	0.83	(POP1929/POP1920)**(1/9)-1
105	Sierra Leone	0.80	(POP1929/POP1920)**(1/9)-1
106	Guinea	0.80	(POP1929/POP1920)**(1/9)-1
107	Guinea-Biss	0.80	(POP1929/POP1920)**(1/9)-1
108	Bangladesh	0.76	(POP1929/POP1920)**(1/9)-1
109	Slovakia	0.75	(POP1929/POP1920)**(1/9)-1
110	Czechia	0.75	(POP1929/POP1920)**(1/9)-1
111	Madagascar	0.71	(POP1929/POP1920)**(1/9)-1
112	Norway	0.70	(POP1929/POP1920)**(1/9)-1
113	Belgium	0.69	(POP1929/POP1920)**(1/9)-1
114	Germany	0.68	(POP1929/POP1920)**(1/9)-1
115	Nicaragua	0.68	(POP1929/POP1920)**(1/9)-1
116	Burundi	0.65	(POP1929/POP1920)**(1/9)-1
117	Turkey	0.65	(POP1929/POP1920)**(1/9)-1
118	Somalia	0.63	(POP1929/POP1920)**(1/9)-1
119	France	0.62	(POP1929/POP1920)**(1/9)-1
120	Albania	0.53	(POP1929/POP1920)**(1/9)-1
121	UK	0.49	(POP1929/POP1920)**(1/9)-1
122	Saudi Arabia	0.49	(POP1929/POP1920)**(1/9)-1
123	Sweden	0.44	(POP1929/POP1920)**(1/9)-1
124	Panama	0.43	(POP1929/POP1920)**(1/9)-1
125	Libya	0.41	(POP1929/POP1920)**(1/9)-1
126	Switzerland	0.41	(POP1929/POP1920)**(1/9)-1
127	Austria	0.35	(POP1929/POP1920)**(1/9)-1
128	China	0.35	(POP1929/POP1920)**(1/9)-1
129	Sudan	0.34	(POP1929/POP1920)**(1/9)-1
130	South Sudan	0.34	(POP1929/POP1920)**(1/9)-1
131	Laos	0.25	(POP1929/POP1920)**(1/9)-1
132	Trinidad & T	0.25	(POP1929/POP1920)**(1/9)-1
133	Mongolia	0.08	(POP1929/POP1920)**(1/9)-1
134	Oman	0.07	(POP1929/POP1920)**(1/9)-1
135	Ireland	-0.61	(POP1929/POP1920)**(1/9)-1

TABLE 4.13 POPULATION GROWTH RATES, 1929-1938			
Rank	Country	GRPOP	Source
1	Hong Kong	7.29	(POP1938/POP1929)**(1/9)-1
2	Israel	3.30	(POP1938/POP1929)**(1/9)-1
3	Dominican R	3.10	(POP1938/POP1929)**(1/9)-1
4	Panama	2.64	(POP1938/POP1929)**(1/9)-1
5	Taiwan	2.63	(POP1938/POP1929)**(1/9)-1
6	Ghana	2.61	(POP1938/POP1929)**(1/9)-1
7	Thailand	2.44	(POP1938/POP1929)**(1/9)-1
8	Philippines	2.38	(POP1938/POP1929)**(1/9)-1
9	Singapore	2.37	(POP1938/POP1929)**(1/9)-1
10	Paraguay	2.36	(POP1938/POP1929)**(1/9)-1
11	Ecuador	2.25	(POP1938/POP1929)**(1/9)-1
12	South Africa	2.18	(POP1938/POP1929)**(1/9)-1
13	Lebanon	2.18	(POP1938/POP1929)**(1/9)-1
14	Malaysia	2.11	(POP1938/POP1929)**(1/9)-1
15	Costa Rica	2.08	(POP1938/POP1929)**(1/9)-1
16	Guatemala	2.08	(POP1938/POP1929)**(1/9)-1
17	Brazil	2.05	(POP1938/POP1929)**(1/9)-1
18	Iraq	1.95	(POP1938/POP1929)**(1/9)-1
19	Puerto Rico	1.91	(POP1938/POP1929)**(1/9)-1
20	Argentina	1.89	(POP1938/POP1929)**(1/9)-1
21	Cuba	1.89	(POP1938/POP1929)**(1/9)-1
22	Honduras	1.88	(POP1938/POP1929)**(1/9)-1
23	Korea, North	1.87	(POP1938/POP1929)**(1/9)-1
24	Jamaica	1.86	(POP1938/POP1929)**(1/9)-1
25	Pakistan	1.77	(POP1938/POP1929)**(1/9)-1
26	Lesotho	1.74	(POP1938/POP1929)**(1/9)-1
27	Swaziland	1.74	(POP1938/POP1929)**(1/9)-1
28	Mexico	1.74	(POP1938/POP1929)**(1/9)-1
29	Tunisia	1.72	(POP1938/POP1929)**(1/9)-1
30	Bangladesh	1.66	(POP1938/POP1929)**(1/9)-1
31	Uruguay	1.65	(POP1938/POP1929)**(1/9)-1
32	Turkey	1.64	(POP1938/POP1929)**(1/9)-1
33	Peru	1.57	(POP1938/POP1929)**(1/9)-1
34	Trinidad & T	1.57	(POP1938/POP1929)**(1/9)-1
35	Nicaragua	1.54	(POP1938/POP1929)**(1/9)-1
36	Syria	1.53	(POP1938/POP1929)**(1/9)-1
37	Morocco	1.53	(POP1938/POP1929)**(1/9)-1
38	Eritrea	1.49	(POP1938/POP1929)**(1/9)-1
39	Ethiopia	1.49	(POP1938/POP1929)**(1/9)-1
40	Chile	1.48	(POP1938/POP1929)**(1/9)-1
41	Algeria	1.46	(POP1938/POP1929)**(1/9)-1
42	Indonesia	1.45	(POP1938/POP1929)**(1/9)-1
43	Japan	1.43	(POP1938/POP1929)**(1/9)-1
44	Zambia	1.40	(POP1938/POP1929)**(1/9)-1
45	Malawi	1.40	(POP1938/POP1929)**(1/9)-1
46	Zimbabwe	1.40	(POP1938/POP1929)**(1/9)-1
47	Slovenia	1.40	(POP1938/POP1929)**(1/9)-1
48	Macedonia	1.40	(POP1938/POP1929)**(1/9)-1
49	Croatia	1.40	(POP1938/POP1929)**(1/9)-1

Table 4.13 Population Growth Rates, 1929-1938			
Rank	Country	GRPOP	Source
50	Serbia	1.40	(POP1938/POP1929)**(1/9)-1
51	Bosnia	1.40	(POP1938/POP1929)**(1/9)-1
52	Montenegro	1.40	(POP1938/POP1929)**(1/9)-1
53	Kosovo	1.40	(POP1938/POP1929)**(1/9)-1
54	El Salvador	1.34	(POP1938/POP1929)**(1/9)-1
55	Greece	1.32	(POP1938/POP1929)**(1/9)-1
56	Cyprus	1.32	(POP1938/POP1929)**(1/9)-1
57	Burma	1.31	(POP1938/POP1929)**(1/9)-1
58	Haiti	1.29	(POP1938/POP1929)**(1/9)-1
59	India	1.28	(POP1938/POP1929)**(1/9)-1
60	Korea, South	1.28	(POP1938/POP1929)**(1/9)-1
61	Romania	1.25	(POP1938/POP1929)**(1/9)-1
62	Portugal	1.24	(POP1938/POP1929)**(1/9)-1
63	Netherlands	1.23	(POP1938/POP1929)**(1/9)-1
64	Egypt	1.23	(POP1938/POP1929)**(1/9)-1
65	Poland	1.22	(POP1938/POP1929)**(1/9)-1
66	Iceland	1.20	(POP1938/POP1929)**(1/9)-1
67	Colombia	1.19	(POP1938/POP1929)**(1/9)-1
68	Venezuela	1.18	(POP1938/POP1929)**(1/9)-1
69	Canada	1.18	(POP1938/POP1929)**(1/9)-1
70	Iran	1.17	(POP1938/POP1929)**(1/9)-1
71	Nepal	1.16	(POP1938/POP1929)**(1/9)-1
72	Bolivia	1.16	(POP1938/POP1929)**(1/9)-1
73	Bulgaria	1.10	(POP1938/POP1929)**(1/9)-1
74	Namibia	1.09	(POP1938/POP1929)**(1/9)-1
75	Botswana	1.09	(POP1938/POP1929)**(1/9)-1
76	Armenia	1.02	(POP1938/POP1929)**(1/9)-1
77	Moldova	1.02	(POP1938/POP1929)**(1/9)-1
78	Turkmenistan	1.02	(POP1938/POP1929)**(1/9)-1
79	Lithuania	1.02	(POP1938/POP1929)**(1/9)-1
80	Tajikistan	1.02	(POP1938/POP1929)**(1/9)-1
81	Kazakhstan	1.02	(POP1938/POP1929)**(1/9)-1
82	Azerbaijan	1.02	(POP1938/POP1929)**(1/9)-1
83	Belarus	1.02	(POP1938/POP1929)**(1/9)-1
84	Ukraine	1.02	(POP1938/POP1929)**(1/9)-1
85	Russia	1.02	(POP1938/POP1929)**(1/9)-1
86	Uzbekistan	1.02	(POP1938/POP1929)**(1/9)-1
87	Georgia	1.02	(POP1938/POP1929)**(1/9)-1
88	Kyrgyzstan	1.02	(POP1938/POP1929)**(1/9)-1
89	Latvia	1.02	(POP1938/POP1929)**(1/9)-1
90	Estonia	1.02	(POP1938/POP1929)**(1/9)-1
91	Cambodia	1.02	(POP1938/POP1929)**(1/9)-1
92	Yemen	1.02	(POP1938/POP1929)**(1/9)-1
93	New Zealand	0.97	(POP1938/POP1929)**(1/9)-1
94	Afghanistan	0.96	(POP1938/POP1929)**(1/9)-1
95	Spain	0.95	(POP1938/POP1929)**(1/9)-1
96	Vietnam	0.94	(POP1938/POP1929)**(1/9)-1
97	UAE	0.89	(POP1938/POP1929)**(1/9)-1
98	Qatar	0.89	(POP1938/POP1929)**(1/9)-1

Table 4.13 Population Growth Rates, 1929-1938			
Rank	Country	GRPOP	Source
99	Bahrain	0.89	(POP1938/POP1929)**(1/9)-1
100	Kuwait	0.89	(POP1938/POP1929)**(1/9)-1
101	Australia	0.85	(POP1938/POP1929)**(1/9)-1
102	Mozambique	0.84	(POP1938/POP1929)**(1/9)-1
103	Jordan	0.83	(POP1938/POP1929)**(1/9)-1
104	Guinea	0.80	(POP1938/POP1929)**(1/9)-1
105	Guinea-Biss	0.80	(POP1938/POP1929)**(1/9)-1
106	Sierra Leone	0.80	(POP1938/POP1929)**(1/9)-1
107	Denmark	0.79	(POP1938/POP1929)**(1/9)-1
108	Italy	0.78	(POP1938/POP1929)**(1/9)-1
109	Hungary	0.73	(POP1938/POP1929)**(1/9)-1
110	Finland	0.73	(POP1938/POP1929)**(1/9)-1
111	US	0.73	(POP1938/POP1929)**(1/9)-1
112	Sri Lanka	0.72	(POP1938/POP1929)**(1/9)-1
113	Madagascar	0.71	(POP1938/POP1929)**(1/9)-1
114	Albania	0.70	(POP1938/POP1929)**(1/9)-1
115	Burundi	0.65	(POP1938/POP1929)**(1/9)-1
116	Germany	0.64	(POP1938/POP1929)**(1/9)-1
117	Somalia	0.63	(POP1938/POP1929)**(1/9)-1
118	China	0.58	(POP1938/POP1929)**(1/9)-1
119	Czechia	0.56	(POP1938/POP1929)**(1/9)-1
120	Slovakia	0.56	(POP1938/POP1929)**(1/9)-1
121	Norway	0.55	(POP1938/POP1929)**(1/9)-1
122	Saudi Arabia	0.49	(POP1938/POP1929)**(1/9)-1
123	Belgium	0.46	(POP1938/POP1929)**(1/9)-1
124	Switzerland	0.46	(POP1938/POP1929)**(1/9)-1
125	UK	0.44	(POP1938/POP1929)**(1/9)-1
126	Libya	0.41	(POP1938/POP1929)**(1/9)-1
127	South Sudan	0.34	(POP1938/POP1929)**(1/9)-1
128	Sudan	0.34	(POP1938/POP1929)**(1/9)-1
129	Sweden	0.33	(POP1938/POP1929)**(1/9)-1
130	Laos	0.25	(POP1938/POP1929)**(1/9)-1
131	France	0.20	(POP1938/POP1929)**(1/9)-1
132	Austria	0.15	(POP1938/POP1929)**(1/9)-1
133	Mongolia	0.08	(POP1938/POP1929)**(1/9)-1
134	Oman	0.07	(POP1938/POP1929)**(1/9)-1
135	Ireland	0.00	(POP1938/POP1929)**(1/9)-1

Table 4.14 Population Growth Rates, 1938-1950			
Rank	Country	GRPOP	Source
1	Nicaragua	4.32	(POP1950/POP1938)**(1/12)-1
2	Hong Kong	3.51	(POP1950/POP1938)**(1/12)-1
3	Pakistan	3.30	(POP1950/POP1938)**(1/12)-1
4	Dominican R	3.29	(POP1950/POP1938)**(1/12)-1
5	Costa Rica	3.21	(POP1950/POP1938)**(1/12)-1
6	Trinidad & T	3.20	(POP1950/POP1938)**(1/12)-1
7	Israel	3.11	(POP1950/POP1938)**(1/12)-1
8	Colombia	3.11	(POP1950/POP1938)**(1/12)-1
9	Singapore	3.08	(POP1950/POP1938)**(1/12)-1
10	Ecuador	3.07	(POP1950/POP1938)**(1/12)-1
11	Mexico	2.89	(POP1950/POP1938)**(1/12)-1
12	Guatemala	2.89	(POP1950/POP1938)**(1/12)-1
13	Venezuela	2.88	(POP1950/POP1938)**(1/12)-1
14	Panama	2.81	(POP1950/POP1938)**(1/12)-1
15	Paraguay	2.77	(POP1950/POP1938)**(1/12)-1
16	Thailand	2.69	(POP1950/POP1938)**(1/12)-1
17	Brazil	2.64	(POP1950/POP1938)**(1/12)-1
18	Ghana	2.61	(POP1950/POP1938)**(1/12)-1
19	Korea, South	2.57	(POP1950/POP1938)**(1/12)-1
20	Taiwan	2.48	(POP1950/POP1938)**(1/12)-1
21	Cuba	2.45	(POP1950/POP1938)**(1/12)-1
22	Honduras	2.22	(POP1950/POP1938)**(1/12)-1
23	Lebanon	2.18	(POP1950/POP1938)**(1/12)-1
24	South Africa	2.13	(POP1950/POP1938)**(1/12)-1
25	Turkey	1.96	(POP1950/POP1938)**(1/12)-1
26	Iraq	1.95	(POP1950/POP1938)**(1/12)-1
27	Egypt	1.92	(POP1950/POP1938)**(1/12)-1
28	Philippines	1.91	(POP1950/POP1938)**(1/12)-1
29	Peru	1.89	(POP1950/POP1938)**(1/12)-1
30	Korea, North	1.87	(POP1950/POP1938)**(1/12)-1
31	Argentina	1.87	(POP1950/POP1938)**(1/12)-1
32	Chile	1.80	(POP1950/POP1938)**(1/12)-1
33	Lesotho	1.74	(POP1950/POP1938)**(1/12)-1
34	Swaziland	1.74	(POP1950/POP1938)**(1/12)-1
35	Tunisia	1.72	(POP1950/POP1938)**(1/12)-1
36	El Salvador	1.72	(POP1950/POP1938)**(1/12)-1
37	Puerto Rico	1.71	(POP1950/POP1938)**(1/12)-1
38	Canada	1.69	(POP1950/POP1938)**(1/12)-1
39	Sri Lanka	1.63	(POP1950/POP1938)**(1/12)-1
40	Iceland	1.61	(POP1950/POP1938)**(1/12)-1
41	Burma	1.58	(POP1950/POP1938)**(1/12)-1
42	Jamaica	1.58	(POP1950/POP1938)**(1/12)-1
43	Haiti	1.54	(POP1950/POP1938)**(1/12)-1
44	Syria	1.53	(POP1950/POP1938)**(1/12)-1
45	Morocco	1.53	(POP1950/POP1938)**(1/12)-1
46	India	1.50	(POP1950/POP1938)**(1/12)-1
47	Algeria	1.49	(POP1950/POP1938)**(1/12)-1
48	Ethiopia	1.49	(POP1950/POP1938)**(1/12)-1

Table 4.14 Population Growth Rates, 1938-1950

Rank	Country	GRPOP	Source
49	Eritrea	1.49	(POP1950/POP1938)**(1/12)-1
50	Australia	1.46	(POP1950/POP1938)**(1/12)-1
51	New Zealand	1.46	(POP1950/POP1938)**(1/12)-1
52	South Sudan	1.46	(POP1950/POP1938)**(1/12)-1
53	Sudan	1.46	(POP1950/POP1938)**(1/12)-1
54	Zimbabwe	1.40	(POP1950/POP1938)**(1/12)-1
55	Malawi	1.40	(POP1950/POP1938)**(1/12)-1
56	Zambia	1.40	(POP1950/POP1938)**(1/12)-1
57	Libya	1.38	(POP1950/POP1938)**(1/12)-1
58	Botswana	1.37	(POP1950/POP1938)**(1/12)-1
59	Malaysia	1.34	(POP1950/POP1938)**(1/12)-1
60	Kyrgyzstan	1.33	(POP1950/POP1938)**(1/12)-1
61	Albania	1.30	(POP1950/POP1938)**(1/12)-1
62	Indonesia	1.30	(POP1950/POP1938)**(1/12)-1
63	US	1.30	(POP1950/POP1938)**(1/12)-1
64	Japan	1.27	(POP1950/POP1938)**(1/12)-1
65	Netherlands	1.26	(POP1950/POP1938)**(1/12)-1
66	Iran	1.17	(POP1950/POP1938)**(1/12)-1
67	Nepal	1.16	(POP1950/POP1938)**(1/12)-1
68	Uruguay	1.15	(POP1950/POP1938)**(1/12)-1
69	Bangladesh	1.12	(POP1950/POP1938)**(1/12)-1
70	Denmark	1.03	(POP1950/POP1938)**(1/12)-1
71	Cambodia	1.02	(POP1950/POP1938)**(1/12)-1
72	Yemen	1.02	(POP1950/POP1938)**(1/12)-1
73	Portugal	1.01	(POP1950/POP1938)**(1/12)-1
74	Afghanistan	0.96	(POP1950/POP1938)**(1/12)-1
75	Kazakhstan	0.96	(POP1950/POP1938)**(1/12)-1
76	Switzerland	0.95	(POP1950/POP1938)**(1/12)-1
77	Vietnam	0.94	(POP1950/POP1938)**(1/12)-1
78	Sweden	0.90	(POP1950/POP1938)**(1/12)-1
79	Norway	0.89	(POP1950/POP1938)**(1/12)-1
80	Kuwait	0.89	(POP1950/POP1938)**(1/12)-1
81	Bahrain	0.89	(POP1950/POP1938)**(1/12)-1
82	UAE	0.89	(POP1950/POP1938)**(1/12)-1
83	Qatar	0.89	(POP1950/POP1938)**(1/12)-1
84	Mozambique	0.84	(POP1950/POP1938)**(1/12)-1
85	Bulgaria	0.83	(POP1950/POP1938)**(1/12)-1
86	Jordan	0.83	(POP1950/POP1938)**(1/12)-1
87	Spain	0.82	(POP1950/POP1938)**(1/12)-1
88	Guinea-Biss	0.80	(POP1950/POP1938)**(1/12)-1
89	Sierra Leone	0.80	(POP1950/POP1938)**(1/12)-1
90	Guinea	0.80	(POP1950/POP1938)**(1/12)-1
91	Finland	0.77	(POP1950/POP1938)**(1/12)-1
92	China	0.77	(POP1950/POP1938)**(1/12)-1
93	Namibia	0.72	(POP1950/POP1938)**(1/12)-1
94	Madagascar	0.71	(POP1950/POP1938)**(1/12)-1
95	Italy	0.68	(POP1950/POP1938)**(1/12)-1
96	Burundi	0.65	(POP1950/POP1938)**(1/12)-1

Table 4.14 Population Growth Rates, 1938-1950			
Rank	Country	GRPOP	Source
97	Somalia	0.63	(POP1950/POP1938)**(1/12)-1
98	Cyprus	0.58	(POP1950/POP1938)**(1/12)-1
99	Greece	0.58	(POP1950/POP1938)**(1/12)-1
100	Estonia	0.57	(POP1950/POP1938)**(1/12)-1
101	Latvia	0.52	(POP1950/POP1938)**(1/12)-1
102	Saudi Arabia	0.49	(POP1950/POP1938)**(1/12)-1
103	UK	0.48	(POP1950/POP1938)**(1/12)-1
104	Armenia	0.46	(POP1950/POP1938)**(1/12)-1
105	Romania	0.37	(POP1950/POP1938)**(1/12)-1
106	Tajikistan	0.28	(POP1950/POP1938)**(1/12)-1
107	Bolivia	0.27	(POP1950/POP1938)**(1/12)-1
108	Belgium	0.26	(POP1950/POP1938)**(1/12)-1
109	Laos	0.25	(POP1950/POP1938)**(1/12)-1
110	Austria	0.22	(POP1950/POP1938)**(1/12)-1
111	Hungary	0.15	(POP1950/POP1938)**(1/12)-1
112	Montenegro	0.11	(POP1950/POP1938)**(1/12)-1
113	Macedonia	0.11	(POP1950/POP1938)**(1/12)-1
114	Kosovo	0.11	(POP1950/POP1938)**(1/12)-1
115	Croatia	0.11	(POP1950/POP1938)**(1/12)-1
116	Serbia	0.11	(POP1950/POP1938)**(1/12)-1
117	Bosnia	0.11	(POP1950/POP1938)**(1/12)-1
118	Slovenia	0.11	(POP1950/POP1938)**(1/12)-1
119	Ireland	0.09	(POP1950/POP1938)**(1/12)-1
120	Mongolia	0.08	(POP1950/POP1938)**(1/12)-1
121	Oman	0.07	(POP1950/POP1938)**(1/12)-1
122	Georgia	0.04	(POP1950/POP1938)**(1/12)-1
123	Germany	-0.02	(POP1950/POP1938)**(1/12)-1
124	France	-0.04	(POP1950/POP1938)**(1/12)-1
125	Uzbekistan	-0.09	(POP1950/POP1938)**(1/12)-1
126	Moldova	-0.20	(POP1950/POP1938)**(1/12)-1
127	Russia	-0.40	(POP1950/POP1938)**(1/12)-1
128	Turkmenistan	-0.41	(POP1950/POP1938)**(1/12)-1
129	Ukraine	-0.70	(POP1950/POP1938)**(1/12)-1
130	Azerbaijan	-0.81	(POP1950/POP1938)**(1/12)-1
131	Lithuania	-0.89	(POP1950/POP1938)**(1/12)-1
132	Belarus	-1.05	(POP1950/POP1938)**(1/12)-1
133	Czechia	-1.36	(POP1950/POP1938)**(1/12)-1
134	Slovakia	-1.36	(POP1950/POP1938)**(1/12)-1
135	Poland	-1.85	(POP1950/POP1938)**(1/12)-1

Table 4.15 Population Growth Rates, 1950-1960

Rank	Country	GRPOP	Source
1	Kuwait	7.25	(POP1960/POP1950)**(1/10)-1
2	W Sahara	7.18	(POP1960/POP1950)**(1/10)-1
3	Jordan	6.61	(POP1960/POP1950)**(1/10)-1
4	Brunei	6.18	(POP1960/POP1950)**(1/10)-1
5	Qatar	6.05	(POP1960/POP1950)**(1/10)-1
6	Israel	5.21	(POP1960/POP1950)**(1/10)-1
7	Mauritania	4.90	(POP1960/POP1950)**(1/10)-1
8	Singapore	4.80	(POP1960/POP1950)**(1/10)-1
9	N Mariana Is	4.14	(POP1960/POP1950)**(1/10)-1
10	Kazakhstan	4.08	(POP1960/POP1950)**(1/10)-1
11	Venezuela	4.03	(POP1960/POP1950)**(1/10)-1
12	Costa Rica	4.01	(POP1960/POP1950)**(1/10)-1
13	Saudi Arabia	3.96	(POP1960/POP1950)**(1/10)-1
14	Niger	3.94	(POP1960/POP1950)**(1/10)-1
15	Mayotte	3.93	(POP1960/POP1950)**(1/10)-1
16	Benin	3.76	(POP1960/POP1950)**(1/10)-1
17	Cape Verde	3.75	(POP1960/POP1950)**(1/10)-1
18	Nigeria	3.75	(POP1960/POP1950)**(1/10)-1
19	Greenland	3.68	(POP1960/POP1950)**(1/10)-1
20	Ivory Coast	3.62	(POP1960/POP1950)**(1/10)-1
21	Djibouti	3.54	(POP1960/POP1950)**(1/10)-1
22	Uganda	3.48	(POP1960/POP1950)**(1/10)-1
23	Micronesia	3.47	(POP1960/POP1950)**(1/10)-1
24	Zimbabwe	3.47	(POP1960/POP1950)**(1/10)-1
25	Guatemala	3.43	(POP1960/POP1950)**(1/10)-1
26	Taiwan	3.42	(POP1960/POP1950)**(1/10)-1
27	Dominican R	3.42	(POP1960/POP1950)**(1/10)-1
28	Laos	3.40	(POP1960/POP1950)**(1/10)-1
29	Honduras	3.40	(POP1960/POP1950)**(1/10)-1
30	Bahamas	3.37	(POP1960/POP1950)**(1/10)-1
31	Morocco	3.33	(POP1960/POP1950)**(1/10)-1
32	Reunion	3.31	(POP1960/POP1950)**(1/10)-1
33	Mexico	3.31	(POP1960/POP1950)**(1/10)-1
34	Mauritius	3.29	(POP1960/POP1950)**(1/10)-1
35	Iraq	3.29	(POP1960/POP1950)**(1/10)-1
36	Malaysia	3.27	(POP1960/POP1950)**(1/10)-1
37	Armenia	3.26	(POP1960/POP1950)**(1/10)-1
38	Hong Kong	3.24	(POP1960/POP1950)**(1/10)-1
39	Nicaragua	3.19	(POP1960/POP1950)**(1/10)-1
40	Sri Lanka	3.16	(POP1960/POP1950)**(1/10)-1
41	Egypt	3.15	(POP1960/POP1950)**(1/10)-1
42	Marshall Is	3.15	(POP1960/POP1950)**(1/10)-1
43	Fiji	3.12	(POP1960/POP1950)**(1/10)-1
44	Tajikistan	3.12	(POP1960/POP1950)**(1/10)-1
45	Uzbekistan	3.09	(POP1960/POP1950)**(1/10)-1
46	Bahrain	3.08	(POP1960/POP1950)**(1/10)-1
47	Liberia	3.08	(POP1960/POP1950)**(1/10)-1
48	Philippines	3.07	(POP1960/POP1950)**(1/10)-1

Table 4.15 Population Growth Rates, 1950-1960

Rank	Country	GRPOP	Source
49	Guinea	3.06	(POP1960/POP1950)**(1/10)-1
50	Azerbaijan	3.04	(POP1960/POP1950)**(1/10)-1
51	Suriname	3.04	(POP1960/POP1950)**(1/10)-1
52	Brazil	3.03	(POP1960/POP1950)**(1/10)-1
53	Samoa	2.98	(POP1960/POP1950)**(1/10)-1
54	Thailand	2.93	(POP1960/POP1950)**(1/10)-1
56.5	Andorra	2.92	(POP1960/POP1950)**(1/10)-1
56.5	Cayman Is	2.92	(POP1960/POP1950)**(1/10)-1
56.5	Nauru	2.92	(POP1960/POP1950)**(1/10)-1
56.5	Vanuatu	2.92	(POP1960/POP1950)**(1/10)-1
59	Kenya	2.91	(POP1960/POP1950)**(1/10)-1
60	Albania	2.86	(POP1960/POP1950)**(1/10)-1
61	Guyana	2.85	(POP1960/POP1950)**(1/10)-1
62	Belize	2.84	(POP1960/POP1950)**(1/10)-1
63	El Salvador	2.84	(POP1960/POP1950)**(1/10)-1
64	Oman	2.80	(POP1960/POP1950)**(1/10)-1
65	Turkmenistan	2.79	(POP1960/POP1950)**(1/10)-1
66	Ghana	2.77	(POP1960/POP1950)**(1/10)-1
67	Tokelau	2.75	(POP1960/POP1950)**(1/10)-1
68	Niue	2.75	(POP1960/POP1950)**(1/10)-1
69	Solomon Is	2.75	(POP1960/POP1950)**(1/10)-1
70	Pakistan	2.75	(POP1960/POP1950)**(1/10)-1
71	Wallis & Fut	2.75	(POP1960/POP1950)**(1/10)-1
72	Cook Is	2.74	(POP1960/POP1950)**(1/10)-1
73	Libya	2.74	(POP1960/POP1950)**(1/10)-1
74	Ecuador	2.74	(POP1960/POP1950)**(1/10)-1
75	Syria	2.71	(POP1960/POP1950)**(1/10)-1
76	Somalia	2.70	(POP1960/POP1950)**(1/10)-1
77	Comoros	2.69	(POP1960/POP1950)**(1/10)-1
78	Peru	2.67	(POP1960/POP1950)**(1/10)-1
79	Iran	2.66	(POP1960/POP1950)**(1/10)-1
80	Tonga	2.66	(POP1960/POP1950)**(1/10)-1
81	Namibia	2.65	(POP1960/POP1950)**(1/10)-1
82	Paraguay	2.63	(POP1960/POP1950)**(1/10)-1
83	Cambodia	2.57	(POP1960/POP1950)**(1/10)-1
84	Senegal	2.55	(POP1960/POP1950)**(1/10)-1
85	Palau	2.54	(POP1960/POP1950)**(1/10)-1
86	Moldova	2.53	(POP1960/POP1950)**(1/10)-1
87	Rwanda	2.51	(POP1960/POP1950)**(1/10)-1
88	Turkey	2.50	(POP1960/POP1950)**(1/10)-1
89	South Africa	2.50	(POP1960/POP1950)**(1/10)-1
90	Guadeloupe	2.49	(POP1960/POP1950)**(1/10)-1
91	Swaziland	2.49	(POP1960/POP1950)**(1/10)-1
92	Canada	2.48	(POP1960/POP1950)**(1/10)-1
93	Zambia	2.46	(POP1960/POP1950)**(1/10)-1
94	Fr Polynesia	2.45	(POP1960/POP1950)**(1/10)-1
95	Panama	2.44	(POP1960/POP1950)**(1/10)-1
96	Martinique	2.42	(POP1960/POP1950)**(1/10)-1

TABLE 4.15 POPULATION GROWTH RATES, 1950-1960

Rank	Country	GRPOP	Source
97	Tanzania	2.42	(POP1960/POP1950)**(1/10)-1
98	Colombia	2.41	(POP1960/POP1950)**(1/10)-1
99	Bhutan	2.35	(POP1960/POP1950)**(1/10)-1
100	Gaza Strip	2.31	(POP1960/POP1950)**(1/10)-1
101	Chile	2.31	(POP1960/POP1950)**(1/10)-1
102	Australia	2.30	(POP1960/POP1950)**(1/10)-1
103	Congo, Rep	2.30	(POP1960/POP1950)**(1/10)-1
104	St Pierre&M	2.29	(POP1960/POP1950)**(1/10)-1
105	Turks & C Is	2.29	(POP1960/POP1950)**(1/10)-1
106	Anguilla	2.29	(POP1960/POP1950)**(1/10)-1
107	Montserrat	2.29	(POP1960/POP1950)**(1/10)-1
108	Virgin I, Br	2.29	(POP1960/POP1950)**(1/10)-1
109	Maldives	2.28	(POP1960/POP1950)**(1/10)-1
110	Malawi	2.27	(POP1960/POP1950)**(1/10)-1
111	UAE	2.26	(POP1960/POP1950)**(1/10)-1
112	Kyrgyzstan	2.25	(POP1960/POP1950)**(1/10)-1
113	Mongolia	2.23	(POP1960/POP1950)**(1/10)-1
114	New Zealand	2.22	(POP1960/POP1950)**(1/10)-1
115	Burundi	2.21	(POP1960/POP1950)**(1/10)-1
116	Kiribati	2.19	(POP1960/POP1950)**(1/10)-1
117	Kosovo	2.17	(POP1960/POP1950)**(1/10)-1
118	Trinidad & T	2.17	(POP1960/POP1950)**(1/10)-1
119	Lebanon	2.16	(POP1960/POP1950)**(1/10)-1
120	Bolivia	2.14	(POP1960/POP1950)**(1/10)-1
121	Algeria	2.12	(POP1960/POP1950)**(1/10)-1
122	Iceland	2.10	(POP1960/POP1950)**(1/10)-1
123	Yemen	2.09	(POP1960/POP1950)**(1/10)-1
124	Virgin I, US	2.03	(POP1960/POP1950)**(1/10)-1
125	Mali	2.00	(POP1960/POP1950)**(1/10)-1
126	Botswana	2.00	(POP1960/POP1950)**(1/10)-1
127	Angola	1.98	(POP1960/POP1950)**(1/10)-1
128	New Caledon	1.97	(POP1960/POP1950)**(1/10)-1
129	Curacao	1.96	(POP1960/POP1950)**(1/10)-1
130	Saint Martin	1.96	(POP1960/POP1950)**(1/10)-1
131	Sint Maarten	1.96	(POP1960/POP1950)**(1/10)-1
132	India	1.93	(POP1960/POP1950)**(1/10)-1
133	St Vincent	1.92	(POP1960/POP1950)**(1/10)-1
134	Argentina	1.89	(POP1960/POP1950)**(1/10)-1
135	Seychelles	1.89	(POP1960/POP1950)**(1/10)-1
136	Afghanistan	1.89	(POP1960/POP1950)**(1/10)-1
137	Madagascar	1.89	(POP1960/POP1950)**(1/10)-1
138	Korea, South	1.86	(POP1960/POP1950)**(1/10)-1
139	Tunisia	1.84	(POP1960/POP1950)**(1/10)-1
140	Gambia	1.82	(POP1960/POP1950)**(1/10)-1
141	Slovakia	1.81	(POP1960/POP1950)**(1/10)-1
142	Bangladesh	1.81	(POP1960/POP1950)**(1/10)-1
143	Antigua & B	1.80	(POP1960/POP1950)**(1/10)-1
144	Mozambique	1.80	(POP1960/POP1950)**(1/10)-1

Table 4.15 Population Growth Rates, 1950-1960

Rank	Country	GRPOP	Source
145	Cuba	1.80	(POP1960/POP1950)**(1/10)-1
146	Bosnia	1.80	(POP1960/POP1950)**(1/10)-1
147	Equatorial G	1.79	(POP1960/POP1950)**(1/10)-1
148	Poland	1.76	(POP1960/POP1950)**(1/10)-1
149	Togo	1.73	(POP1960/POP1950)**(1/10)-1
150	US	1.72	(POP1960/POP1950)**(1/10)-1
151	Guiana, Fr	1.71	(POP1960/POP1950)**(1/10)-1
152	Grenada	1.71	(POP1960/POP1950)**(1/10)-1
153	Georgia	1.66	(POP1960/POP1950)**(1/10)-1
154	Dominica	1.64	(POP1960/POP1950)**(1/10)-1
155	Montenegro	1.64	(POP1960/POP1950)**(1/10)-1
156	Russia	1.64	(POP1960/POP1950)**(1/10)-1
157	Cyprus	1.60	(POP1960/POP1950)**(1/10)-1
158	Burma	1.60	(POP1960/POP1950)**(1/10)-1
159	Lesotho	1.59	(POP1960/POP1950)**(1/10)-1
160	East Timor	1.58	(POP1960/POP1950)**(1/10)-1
161	China	1.58	(POP1960/POP1950)**(1/10)-1
162	Gabon	1.57	(POP1960/POP1950)**(1/10)-1
163	Monaco	1.55	(POP1960/POP1950)**(1/10)-1
164	Jamaica	1.50	(POP1960/POP1950)**(1/10)-1
165	Nepal	1.50	(POP1960/POP1950)**(1/10)-1
166	Ukraine	1.49	(POP1960/POP1950)**(1/10)-1
167	Papua New G	1.47	(POP1960/POP1950)**(1/10)-1
168	Vietnam	1.47	(POP1960/POP1950)**(1/10)-1
169	Indonesia	1.46	(POP1960/POP1950)**(1/10)-1
170	San Marino	1.44	(POP1960/POP1950)**(1/10)-1
171	South Sudan	1.43	(POP1960/POP1950)**(1/10)-1
172	Sudan	1.43	(POP1960/POP1950)**(1/10)-1
173	Haiti	1.39	(POP1960/POP1950)**(1/10)-1
174	Liechtenstn	1.34	(POP1960/POP1950)**(1/10)-1
175	Netherlands	1.31	(POP1960/POP1950)**(1/10)-1
176	Switzerland	1.27	(POP1960/POP1950)**(1/10)-1
177	Serbia	1.27	(POP1960/POP1950)**(1/10)-1
178	Uruguay	1.26	(POP1960/POP1950)**(1/10)-1
179	Chad	1.25	(POP1960/POP1950)**(1/10)-1
180	Congo, Dem R	1.25	(POP1960/POP1950)**(1/10)-1
181	Macedonia	1.24	(POP1960/POP1950)**(1/10)-1
182	Romania	1.22	(POP1960/POP1950)**(1/10)-1
183	Bermuda	1.21	(POP1960/POP1950)**(1/10)-1
184	Sierra Leone	1.18	(POP1960/POP1950)**(1/10)-1
185	Korea, North	1.18	(POP1960/POP1950)**(1/10)-1
186	Ethiopia	1.12	(POP1960/POP1950)**(1/10)-1
187	Aruba	1.12	(POP1960/POP1950)**(1/10)-1
188	Guam	1.11	(POP1960/POP1950)**(1/10)-1
189	CAR	1.11	(POP1960/POP1950)**(1/10)-1
190	Burkina Faso	1.10	(POP1960/POP1950)**(1/10)-1
191	Estonia	1.04	(POP1960/POP1950)**(1/10)-1
192	Cameroon	1.02	(POP1960/POP1950)**(1/10)-1

Table 4.15 Population Growth Rates, 1950-1960

Rank	Country	GRPOP	Source
193	Japan	1.01	(POP1960/POP1950)**(1/10)-1
194	Jersey	1.01	(POP1960/POP1950)**(1/10)-1
195	Finland	1.00	(POP1960/POP1950)**(1/10)-1
196	Greece	0.97	(POP1960/POP1950)**(1/10)-1
197	Barbados	0.95	(POP1960/POP1950)**(1/10)-1
198	Spain	0.95	(POP1960/POP1950)**(1/10)-1
199	Norway	0.93	(POP1960/POP1950)**(1/10)-1
200	Svalbard	0.93	(POP1960/POP1950)**(1/10)-1
201	Faroe Is	0.93	(POP1960/POP1950)**(1/10)-1
202	France	0.91	(POP1960/POP1950)**(1/10)-1
203	Latvia	0.90	(POP1960/POP1950)**(1/10)-1
204	Bulgaria	0.82	(POP1960/POP1950)**(1/10)-1
205	St Lucia	0.81	(POP1960/POP1950)**(1/10)-1
206	Lithuania	0.80	(POP1960/POP1950)**(1/10)-1
207	Slovenia	0.74	(POP1960/POP1950)**(1/10)-1
208	Denmark	0.71	(POP1960/POP1950)**(1/10)-1
209	Portugal	0.68	(POP1960/POP1950)**(1/10)-1
210	Germany	0.68	(POP1960/POP1950)**(1/10)-1
211	Sweden	0.67	(POP1960/POP1950)**(1/10)-1
212	Czechia	0.67	(POP1960/POP1950)**(1/10)-1
213	Hungary	0.65	(POP1960/POP1950)**(1/10)-1
214	Sao Tome & P	0.65	(POP1960/POP1950)**(1/10)-1
215	Puerto Rico	0.61	(POP1960/POP1950)**(1/10)-1
216	Luxembourg	0.59	(POP1960/POP1950)**(1/10)-1
217	Belgium	0.58	(POP1960/POP1950)**(1/10)-1
218	Belarus	0.56	(POP1960/POP1950)**(1/10)-1
219	Samoa, Amer	0.51	(POP1960/POP1950)**(1/10)-1
220	Croatia	0.51	(POP1960/POP1950)**(1/10)-1
221	Italy	0.50	(POP1960/POP1950)**(1/10)-1
222	Gibraltar	0.43	(POP1960/POP1950)**(1/10)-1
223	West Bank	0.42	(POP1960/POP1950)**(1/10)-1
224	UK	0.41	(POP1960/POP1950)**(1/10)-1
225	St Kitts & N	0.40	(POP1960/POP1950)**(1/10)-1
226	Guinea-Biss	0.34	(POP1960/POP1950)**(1/10)-1
227	Guernsey	0.22	(POP1960/POP1950)**(1/10)-1
228	Austria	0.16	(POP1960/POP1950)**(1/10)-1
229	Eritrea	0.16	(POP1960/POP1950)**(1/10)-1
230	Malta	0.03	(POP1960/POP1950)**(1/10)-1
232	Falkland Is	0.00	(POP1960/POP1950)**(1/10)-1
232	Saint Helena	0.00	(POP1960/POP1950)**(1/10)-1
232	Tuvalu	0.00	(POP1960/POP1950)**(1/10)-1
234	Ireland	-0.47	(POP1960/POP1950)**(1/10)-1
235	Isle of Man	-1.35	(POP1960/POP1950)**(1/10)-1
236	Macao	-1.68	(POP1960/POP1950)**(1/10)-1

Table 4.16 Population Growth Rates, 1960-1970

Rank	Country	GRPOP	Source
1	W Sahara	12.26	(POP1970/POP1960)**(1/10)-1
2	UAE	9.93	(POP1970/POP1960)**(1/10)-1
3	Kuwait	9.86	(POP1970/POP1960)**(1/10)-1
4	Andorra	9.60	(POP1970/POP1960)**(1/10)-1
5	Qatar	9.45	(POP1970/POP1960)**(1/10)-1
6	Sint Maarten	9.13	(POP1970/POP1960)**(1/10)-1
7	Virgin I, US	6.68	(POP1970/POP1960)**(1/10)-1
8	Djibouti	6.66	(POP1970/POP1960)**(1/10)-1
9	Jordan	6.42	(POP1970/POP1960)**(1/10)-1
10	Nauru	5.76	(POP1970/POP1960)**(1/10)-1
11	Brunei	4.72	(POP1970/POP1960)**(1/10)-1
12	Ivory Coast	4.55	(POP1970/POP1960)**(1/10)-1
13	Bahamas	4.45	(POP1970/POP1960)**(1/10)-1
14	Guiana, Fr	4.35	(POP1970/POP1960)**(1/10)-1
15	Libya	3.99	(POP1970/POP1960)**(1/10)-1
16	Macao	3.92	(POP1970/POP1960)**(1/10)-1
17	Marshall Is	3.90	(POP1970/POP1960)**(1/10)-1
18	Bhutan	3.84	(POP1970/POP1960)**(1/10)-1
19	New Caledon	3.55	(POP1970/POP1960)**(1/10)-1
20	Tajikistan	3.52	(POP1970/POP1960)**(1/10)-1
21	Venezuela	3.51	(POP1970/POP1960)**(1/10)-1
22	Bahrain	3.49	(POP1970/POP1960)**(1/10)-1
23	Fr Polynesia	3.46	(POP1970/POP1960)**(1/10)-1
24	Mayotte	3.42	(POP1970/POP1960)**(1/10)-1
25	Uzbekistan	3.42	(POP1970/POP1960)**(1/10)-1
26	El Salvador	3.39	(POP1970/POP1960)**(1/10)-1
27	Syria	3.38	(POP1970/POP1960)**(1/10)-1
28	Greenland	3.38	(POP1970/POP1960)**(1/10)-1
29	Costa Rica	3.38	(POP1970/POP1960)**(1/10)-1
30	Kenya	3.26	(POP1970/POP1960)**(1/10)-1
31	Gambia	3.26	(POP1970/POP1960)**(1/10)-1
32	Turkmenistan	3.24	(POP1970/POP1960)**(1/10)-1
33	Zimbabwe	3.24	(POP1970/POP1960)**(1/10)-1
34	Taiwan	3.18	(POP1970/POP1960)**(1/10)-1
35	Dominican R	3.17	(POP1970/POP1960)**(1/10)-1
36	Kyrgyzstan	3.15	(POP1970/POP1960)**(1/10)-1
37	Israel	3.15	(POP1970/POP1960)**(1/10)-1
38	Iraq	3.11	(POP1970/POP1960)**(1/10)-1
39	Solomon Is	3.09	(POP1970/POP1960)**(1/10)-1
40	Micronesia	3.09	(POP1970/POP1960)**(1/10)-1
41	Rwanda	3.07	(POP1970/POP1960)**(1/10)-1
42	Nicaragua	3.07	(POP1970/POP1960)**(1/10)-1
43	Philippines	3.06	(POP1970/POP1960)**(1/10)-1
44	Tanzania	3.05	(POP1970/POP1960)**(1/10)-1
45	Mexico	3.05	(POP1970/POP1960)**(1/10)-1
46	Samoa, Amer	3.05	(POP1970/POP1960)**(1/10)-1
47	Armenia	3.04	(POP1970/POP1960)**(1/10)-1
48	Thailand	3.03	(POP1970/POP1960)**(1/10)-1

TABLE 4.16 POPULATION GROWTH RATES, 1960-1970			
Rank	Country	GRPOP	Source
49	Niger	3.01	(POP1970/POP1960)**(1/10)-1
50	Ecuador	3.01	(POP1970/POP1960)**(1/10)-1
51	Vietnam	3.01	(POP1970/POP1960)**(1/10)-1
52	Honduras	3.00	(POP1970/POP1960)**(1/10)-1
53	Vanuatu	3.00	(POP1970/POP1960)**(1/10)-1
54	Colombia	3.00	(POP1970/POP1960)**(1/10)-1
55	Panama	2.98	(POP1970/POP1960)**(1/10)-1
56	Mongolia	2.97	(POP1970/POP1960)**(1/10)-1
57	Uganda	2.95	(POP1970/POP1960)**(1/10)-1
58	Lebanon	2.93	(POP1970/POP1960)**(1/10)-1
60	Belize	2.92	(POP1970/POP1960)**(1/10)-1
60	N Mariana Is	2.92	(POP1970/POP1960)**(1/10)-1
60	Palau	2.92	(POP1970/POP1960)**(1/10)-1
62	Togo	2.88	(POP1970/POP1960)**(1/10)-1
63	Peru	2.88	(POP1970/POP1960)**(1/10)-1
64	Azerbaijan	2.88	(POP1970/POP1960)**(1/10)-1
65	Albania	2.86	(POP1970/POP1960)**(1/10)-1
66	Fiji	2.86	(POP1970/POP1960)**(1/10)-1
67	Botswana	2.83	(POP1970/POP1960)**(1/10)-1
68	Reunion	2.83	(POP1970/POP1960)**(1/10)-1
69	Senegal	2.82	(POP1970/POP1960)**(1/10)-1
70	Brazil	2.81	(POP1970/POP1960)**(1/10)-1
71	Congo, Dem R	2.81	(POP1970/POP1960)**(1/10)-1
72	Congo, Rep	2.79	(POP1970/POP1960)**(1/10)-1
73	Kazakhstan	2.76	(POP1970/POP1960)**(1/10)-1
74	Liechtenstn	2.76	(POP1970/POP1960)**(1/10)-1
75	Niue	2.75	(POP1970/POP1960)**(1/10)-1
76	Wallis & Fut	2.75	(POP1970/POP1960)**(1/10)-1
77	Cook Is	2.75	(POP1970/POP1960)**(1/10)-1
78	Tokelau	2.74	(POP1970/POP1960)**(1/10)-1
79	Guatemala	2.74	(POP1970/POP1960)**(1/10)-1
80	Zambia	2.70	(POP1970/POP1960)**(1/10)-1
81	Pakistan	2.70	(POP1970/POP1960)**(1/10)-1
82	Iran	2.68	(POP1970/POP1960)**(1/10)-1
83	Oman	2.68	(POP1970/POP1960)**(1/10)-1
84	Sudan	2.67	(POP1970/POP1960)**(1/10)-1
85	South Sudan	2.67	(POP1970/POP1960)**(1/10)-1
86	Korea, North	2.67	(POP1970/POP1960)**(1/10)-1
87	Cape Verde	2.65	(POP1970/POP1960)**(1/10)-1
88	Eritrea	2.64	(POP1970/POP1960)**(1/10)-1
89	Paraguay	2.63	(POP1970/POP1960)**(1/10)-1
90	Saudi Arabia	2.62	(POP1970/POP1960)**(1/10)-1
91	Malaysia	2.61	(POP1970/POP1960)**(1/10)-1
92	Namibia	2.61	(POP1970/POP1960)**(1/10)-1
93	South Africa	2.61	(POP1970/POP1960)**(1/10)-1
94	Samoa	2.59	(POP1970/POP1960)**(1/10)-1
95	Liberia	2.58	(POP1970/POP1960)**(1/10)-1
96	Papua New G	2.57	(POP1970/POP1960)**(1/10)-1

TABLE 4.16 POPULATION GROWTH RATES, 1960-1970			
Rank	Country	GRPOP	Source
97	Guyana	2.56	(POP1970/POP1960)**(1/10)-1
98	Indonesia	2.56	(POP1970/POP1960)**(1/10)-1
99	Kosovo	2.56	(POP1970/POP1960)**(1/10)-1
100	Hong Kong	2.55	(POP1970/POP1960)**(1/10)-1
101	Malawi	2.54	(POP1970/POP1960)**(1/10)-1
102	Ethiopia	2.53	(POP1970/POP1960)**(1/10)-1
103	Cambodia	2.53	(POP1970/POP1960)**(1/10)-1
104	Madagascar	2.52	(POP1970/POP1960)**(1/10)-1
105	Suriname	2.52	(POP1970/POP1960)**(1/10)-1
106	Turkey	2.51	(POP1970/POP1960)**(1/10)-1
107	Morocco	2.50	(POP1970/POP1960)**(1/10)-1
108	Swaziland	2.48	(POP1970/POP1960)**(1/10)-1
109	Egypt	2.46	(POP1970/POP1960)**(1/10)-1
110	Saint Martin	2.45	(POP1970/POP1960)**(1/10)-1
111	Algeria	2.44	(POP1970/POP1960)**(1/10)-1
112	Singapore	2.41	(POP1970/POP1960)**(1/10)-1
113	Guam	2.41	(POP1970/POP1960)**(1/10)-1
114	Seychelles	2.41	(POP1970/POP1960)**(1/10)-1
115	San Marino	2.39	(POP1970/POP1960)**(1/10)-1
116	Cameroon	2.38	(POP1970/POP1960)**(1/10)-1
117	Afghanistan	2.38	(POP1970/POP1960)**(1/10)-1
118	Laos	2.37	(POP1970/POP1960)**(1/10)-1
119	Ghana	2.36	(POP1970/POP1960)**(1/10)-1
120	Bolivia	2.31	(POP1970/POP1960)**(1/10)-1
121	Virgin I, Br	2.29	(POP1970/POP1960)**(1/10)-1
122	Montserrat	2.29	(POP1970/POP1960)**(1/10)-1
123	Anguilla	2.29	(POP1970/POP1960)**(1/10)-1
124	St Pierre&M	2.29	(POP1970/POP1960)**(1/10)-1
125	Korea, South	2.29	(POP1970/POP1960)**(1/10)-1
126	CAR	2.29	(POP1970/POP1960)**(1/10)-1
127	Sri Lanka	2.28	(POP1970/POP1960)**(1/10)-1
128	Mauritius	2.28	(POP1970/POP1960)**(1/10)-1
129	Chile	2.27	(POP1970/POP1960)**(1/10)-1
130	Cayman Is	2.26	(POP1970/POP1960)**(1/10)-1
131	Nigeria	2.25	(POP1970/POP1960)**(1/10)-1
132	Mozambique	2.22	(POP1970/POP1960)**(1/10)-1
133	Lesotho	2.19	(POP1970/POP1960)**(1/10)-1
134	Somalia	2.18	(POP1970/POP1960)**(1/10)-1
135	Chad	2.15	(POP1970/POP1960)**(1/10)-1
136	China	2.15	(POP1970/POP1960)**(1/10)-1
137	India	2.15	(POP1970/POP1960)**(1/10)-1
138	Mali	2.12	(POP1970/POP1960)**(1/10)-1
139	Bangladesh	2.12	(POP1970/POP1960)**(1/10)-1
140	Comoros	2.12	(POP1970/POP1960)**(1/10)-1
141	Tonga	2.10	(POP1970/POP1960)**(1/10)-1
142	Haiti	2.08	(POP1970/POP1960)**(1/10)-1
143	Maldives	2.03	(POP1970/POP1960)**(1/10)-1
144	Australia	1.98	(POP1970/POP1960)**(1/10)-1

TABLE 4.16 POPULATION GROWTH RATES, 1960-1970

Rank	Country	GRPOP	Source
145	Cuba	1.97	(POP1970/POP1960)**(1/10)-1
146	Tunisia	1.96	(POP1970/POP1960)**(1/10)-1
147	Angola	1.96	(POP1970/POP1960)**(1/10)-1
148	Canada	1.95	(POP1970/POP1960)**(1/10)-1
149	Yemen	1.91	(POP1970/POP1960)**(1/10)-1
150	Bermuda	1.88	(POP1970/POP1960)**(1/10)-1
151.5	Antigua & B	1.84	(POP1970/POP1960)**(1/10)-1
151.5	Tuvalu	1.84	(POP1970/POP1960)**(1/10)-1
153	Burma	1.83	(POP1970/POP1960)**(1/10)-1
154	Moldova	1.81	(POP1970/POP1960)**(1/10)-1
155	Kiribati	1.80	(POP1970/POP1960)**(1/10)-1
156	Burundi	1.80	(POP1970/POP1960)**(1/10)-1
157	Burkina Faso	1.75	(POP1970/POP1960)**(1/10)-1
158	Nepal	1.74	(POP1970/POP1960)**(1/10)-1
159	New Zealand	1.72	(POP1970/POP1960)**(1/10)-1
160	Sierra Leone	1.72	(POP1970/POP1960)**(1/10)-1
161	Benin	1.65	(POP1970/POP1960)**(1/10)-1
162	East Timor	1.62	(POP1970/POP1960)**(1/10)-1
163	Guinea	1.61	(POP1970/POP1960)**(1/10)-1
164	Curacao	1.58	(POP1970/POP1960)**(1/10)-1
165	Dominica	1.55	(POP1970/POP1960)**(1/10)-1
166	Guadeloupe	1.54	(POP1970/POP1960)**(1/10)-1
167	Argentina	1.50	(POP1970/POP1960)**(1/10)-1
168	Switzerland	1.50	(POP1970/POP1960)**(1/10)-1
169	Iceland	1.49	(POP1970/POP1960)**(1/10)-1
170	Sao Tome & P	1.46	(POP1970/POP1960)**(1/10)-1
171	St Lucia	1.46	(POP1970/POP1960)**(1/10)-1
172	Equatorial G	1.45	(POP1970/POP1960)**(1/10)-1
173	Puerto Rico	1.45	(POP1970/POP1960)**(1/10)-1
174	Mauritania	1.44	(POP1970/POP1960)**(1/10)-1
175	Martinique	1.43	(POP1970/POP1960)**(1/10)-1
176	Jamaica	1.38	(POP1970/POP1960)**(1/10)-1
177	Faroe Is	1.38	(POP1970/POP1960)**(1/10)-1
178	Monaco	1.34	(POP1970/POP1960)**(1/10)-1
179	Trinidad & T	1.29	(POP1970/POP1960)**(1/10)-1
180	Lithuania	1.27	(POP1970/POP1960)**(1/10)-1
181	US	1.27	(POP1970/POP1960)**(1/10)-1
182	Guernsey	1.26	(POP1970/POP1960)**(1/10)-1
183	Netherlands	1.25	(POP1970/POP1960)**(1/10)-1
184	Georgia	1.25	(POP1970/POP1960)**(1/10)-1
185	Macedonia	1.20	(POP1970/POP1960)**(1/10)-1
186	Estonia	1.16	(POP1970/POP1960)**(1/10)-1
187	Japan	1.15	(POP1970/POP1960)**(1/10)-1
188	Bosnia	1.15	(POP1970/POP1960)**(1/10)-1
189	Gaza Strip	1.08	(POP1970/POP1960)**(1/10)-1
190	Montenegro	1.06	(POP1970/POP1960)**(1/10)-1
191	France	1.06	(POP1970/POP1960)**(1/10)-1
192	Latvia	1.05	(POP1970/POP1960)**(1/10)-1

Table 4.16 Population Growth Rates, 1960-1970			
Rank	Country	GRPOP	Source
193	Uruguay	1.02	(POP1970/POP1960)**(1/10)-1
194	Ukraine	1.01	(POP1970/POP1960)**(1/10)-1
195	Spain	1.01	(POP1970/POP1960)**(1/10)-1
196	Isle of Man	1.00	(POP1970/POP1960)**(1/10)-1
197	Belarus	0.99	(POP1970/POP1960)**(1/10)-1
198	Poland	0.96	(POP1970/POP1960)**(1/10)-1
199	Romania	0.96	(POP1970/POP1960)**(1/10)-1
200	Jersey	0.91	(POP1970/POP1960)**(1/10)-1
201	Slovakia	0.89	(POP1970/POP1960)**(1/10)-1
202	Gabon	0.87	(POP1970/POP1960)**(1/10)-1
203	Serbia	0.85	(POP1970/POP1960)**(1/10)-1
204	Russia	0.84	(POP1970/POP1960)**(1/10)-1
205	St Vincent	0.83	(POP1970/POP1960)**(1/10)-1
206	Gibraltar	0.80	(POP1970/POP1960)**(1/10)-1
207	Cyprus	0.80	(POP1970/POP1960)**(1/10)-1
208	Svalbard	0.79	(POP1970/POP1960)**(1/10)-1
209	Norway	0.79	(POP1970/POP1960)**(1/10)-1
210	Luxembourg	0.77	(POP1970/POP1960)**(1/10)-1
211	Bulgaria	0.77	(POP1970/POP1960)**(1/10)-1
212	Denmark	0.74	(POP1970/POP1960)**(1/10)-1
213	Italy	0.74	(POP1970/POP1960)**(1/10)-1
214	Sweden	0.70	(POP1970/POP1960)**(1/10)-1
215	Aruba	0.68	(POP1970/POP1960)**(1/10)-1
216	Germany	0.65	(POP1970/POP1960)**(1/10)-1
217	UK	0.61	(POP1970/POP1960)**(1/10)-1
218	Austria	0.58	(POP1970/POP1960)**(1/10)-1
219	Belgium	0.57	(POP1970/POP1960)**(1/10)-1
220	Slovenia	0.56	(POP1970/POP1960)**(1/10)-1
221	Grenada	0.54	(POP1970/POP1960)**(1/10)-1
222	Greece	0.54	(POP1970/POP1960)**(1/10)-1
223	Croatia	0.41	(POP1970/POP1960)**(1/10)-1
224	Ireland	0.41	(POP1970/POP1960)**(1/10)-1
225	Finland	0.39	(POP1970/POP1960)**(1/10)-1
226	Hungary	0.34	(POP1970/POP1960)**(1/10)-1
227	Barbados	0.30	(POP1970/POP1960)**(1/10)-1
228	Czechia	0.28	(POP1970/POP1960)**(1/10)-1
229	Guinea-Biss	0.17	(POP1970/POP1960)**(1/10)-1
230	Portugal	0.01	(POP1970/POP1960)**(1/10)-1
231.5	Falkland Is	0.00	(POP1970/POP1960)**(1/10)-1
231.5	Saint Helena	0.00	(POP1970/POP1960)**(1/10)-1
233	Turks & C Is	-0.16	(POP1970/POP1960)**(1/10)-1
234	Malta	-0.29	(POP1970/POP1960)**(1/10)-1
235	St Kitts & N	-1.03	(POP1970/POP1960)**(1/10)-1
236	West Bank	-2.77	(POP1970/POP1960)**(1/10)-1

Table 4.17 Population Growth Rates, 1970-1980			
Rank	Country	GRPOP	Source
1	UAE	15.92	(POP1980/POP1970)**(1/10)-1
2	Djibouti	7.70	(POP1980/POP1970)**(1/10)-1
3	Qatar	7.51	(POP1980/POP1970)**(1/10)-1
4	Sint Maarten	6.72	(POP1980/POP1970)**(1/10)-1
5	Kuwait	6.24	(POP1980/POP1970)**(1/10)-1
6.5	Andorra	5.45	(POP1980/POP1970)**(1/10)-1
6.5	Cayman Is	5.45	(POP1980/POP1970)**(1/10)-1
8	Saudi Arabia	5.07	(POP1980/POP1970)**(1/10)-1
9	Bahrain	4.75	(POP1980/POP1970)**(1/10)-1
10	Somalia	4.68	(POP1980/POP1970)**(1/10)-1
11	Ivory Coast	4.41	(POP1980/POP1970)**(1/10)-1
12	Virgin I, US	4.41	(POP1980/POP1970)**(1/10)-1
13	Libya	4.39	(POP1980/POP1970)**(1/10)-1
14	Oman	4.23	(POP1980/POP1970)**(1/10)-1
15	Mayotte	4.04	(POP1980/POP1970)**(1/10)-1
16	Brunei	4.03	(POP1980/POP1970)**(1/10)-1
17	Kenya	3.80	(POP1980/POP1970)**(1/10)-1
18	Bhutan	3.74	(POP1980/POP1970)**(1/10)-1
19	Botswana	3.69	(POP1980/POP1970)**(1/10)-1
20	Solomon Is	3.65	(POP1980/POP1970)**(1/10)-1
21	N Mariana Is	3.54	(POP1980/POP1970)**(1/10)-1
22	Sudan	3.52	(POP1980/POP1970)**(1/10)-1
23	South Sudan	3.52	(POP1980/POP1970)**(1/10)-1
24	Marshall Is	3.49	(POP1980/POP1970)**(1/10)-1
25	Venezuela	3.48	(POP1980/POP1970)**(1/10)-1
26	Syria	3.41	(POP1980/POP1970)**(1/10)-1
27	W Sahara	3.37	(POP1980/POP1970)**(1/10)-1
28	Saint Martin	3.35	(POP1980/POP1970)**(1/10)-1
29	Guiana, Fr	3.33	(POP1980/POP1970)**(1/10)-1
30	Guinea-Biss	3.31	(POP1980/POP1970)**(1/10)-1
31	Comoros	3.29	(POP1980/POP1970)**(1/10)-1
32	Rwanda	3.28	(POP1980/POP1970)**(1/10)-1
33	Jordan	3.27	(POP1980/POP1970)**(1/10)-1
34	Malawi	3.25	(POP1980/POP1970)**(1/10)-1
35	Tanzania	3.22	(POP1980/POP1970)**(1/10)-1
36	Iraq	3.21	(POP1980/POP1970)**(1/10)-1
37	Algeria	3.19	(POP1980/POP1970)**(1/10)-1
38	Vanuatu	3.13	(POP1980/POP1970)**(1/10)-1
39	Fr Polynesia	3.13	(POP1980/POP1970)**(1/10)-1
40	Swaziland	3.06	(POP1980/POP1970)**(1/10)-1
41	Nicaragua	3.06	(POP1980/POP1970)**(1/10)-1
42	Honduras	3.04	(POP1980/POP1970)**(1/10)-1
43	Congo, Rep	3.02	(POP1980/POP1970)**(1/10)-1
44	Iran	3.02	(POP1980/POP1970)**(1/10)-1
45	Gambia	3.00	(POP1980/POP1970)**(1/10)-1
46	Tajikistan	3.00	(POP1980/POP1970)**(1/10)-1
47	Niger	2.99	(POP1980/POP1970)**(1/10)-1
48	Uzbekistan	2.97	(POP1980/POP1970)**(1/10)-1

Table 4.17 Population Growth Rates, 1970-1980

Rank	Country	GRPOP	Source
49	Eritrea	2.95	(POP1980/POP1970)**(1/10)-1
50	Turks & C Is	2.94	(POP1980/POP1970)**(1/10)-1
51	Liberia	2.93	(POP1980/POP1970)**(1/10)-1
52	Tuvalu	2.92	(POP1980/POP1970)**(1/10)-1
53	Congo, Dem R	2.92	(POP1980/POP1970)**(1/10)-1
54	Ecuador	2.91	(POP1980/POP1970)**(1/10)-1
55	Mongolia	2.91	(POP1980/POP1970)**(1/10)-1
56	Cameroon	2.90	(POP1980/POP1970)**(1/10)-1
57	Gaza Strip	2.89	(POP1980/POP1970)**(1/10)-1
58	Zambia	2.88	(POP1980/POP1970)**(1/10)-1
59	Mexico	2.86	(POP1980/POP1970)**(1/10)-1
60	Turkmenistan	2.80	(POP1980/POP1970)**(1/10)-1
61	Nigeria	2.79	(POP1980/POP1970)**(1/10)-1
62	Philippines	2.78	(POP1980/POP1970)**(1/10)-1
63	Madagascar	2.77	(POP1980/POP1970)**(1/10)-1
64	Israel	2.77	(POP1980/POP1970)**(1/10)-1
65	Peru	2.74	(POP1980/POP1970)**(1/10)-1
66	Bangladesh	2.71	(POP1980/POP1970)**(1/10)-1
67	Maldives	2.70	(POP1980/POP1970)**(1/10)-1
68	Costa Rica	2.67	(POP1980/POP1970)**(1/10)-1
69	Mozambique	2.66	(POP1980/POP1970)**(1/10)-1
70	Panama	2.66	(POP1980/POP1970)**(1/10)-1
71	Zimbabwe	2.66	(POP1980/POP1970)**(1/10)-1
72	Senegal	2.65	(POP1980/POP1970)**(1/10)-1
73	Namibia	2.65	(POP1980/POP1970)**(1/10)-1
74	South Africa	2.60	(POP1980/POP1970)**(1/10)-1
75	Guatemala	2.59	(POP1980/POP1970)**(1/10)-1
76	Angola	2.59	(POP1980/POP1970)**(1/10)-1
77	Dominican R	2.58	(POP1980/POP1970)**(1/10)-1
78	Gabon	2.57	(POP1980/POP1970)**(1/10)-1
79	Yemen	2.55	(POP1980/POP1970)**(1/10)-1
80	Papua New G	2.54	(POP1980/POP1970)**(1/10)-1
81	Sao Tome & P	2.53	(POP1980/POP1970)**(1/10)-1
82	Paraguay	2.50	(POP1980/POP1970)**(1/10)-1
83	CAR	2.48	(POP1980/POP1970)**(1/10)-1
84	Hong Kong	2.47	(POP1980/POP1970)**(1/10)-1
85	Indonesia	2.45	(POP1980/POP1970)**(1/10)-1
86	Lesotho	2.45	(POP1980/POP1970)**(1/10)-1
87	Tokelau	2.44	(POP1980/POP1970)**(1/10)-1
88	Niue	2.44	(POP1980/POP1970)**(1/10)-1
89	Wallis & Fut	2.44	(POP1980/POP1970)**(1/10)-1
90	Cook Is	2.44	(POP1980/POP1970)**(1/10)-1
91	Togo	2.43	(POP1980/POP1970)**(1/10)-1
92	Bolivia	2.41	(POP1980/POP1970)**(1/10)-1
93	El Salvador	2.40	(POP1980/POP1970)**(1/10)-1
94	Thailand	2.40	(POP1980/POP1970)**(1/10)-1
95	Benin	2.39	(POP1980/POP1970)**(1/10)-1
96	India	2.37	(POP1980/POP1970)**(1/10)-1

TABLE 4.17 POPULATION GROWTH RATES, 1970-1980

Rank	Country	GRPOP	Source
97	Egypt	2.37	(POP1980/POP1970)**(1/10)-1
98	Pakistan	2.36	(POP1980/POP1970)**(1/10)-1
99	Vietnam	2.35	(POP1980/POP1970)**(1/10)-1
100	Turkey	2.35	(POP1980/POP1970)**(1/10)-1
101	Tunisia	2.33	(POP1980/POP1970)**(1/10)-1
102	Guam	2.33	(POP1980/POP1970)**(1/10)-1
103	Ghana	2.28	(POP1980/POP1970)**(1/10)-1
104	Albania	2.26	(POP1980/POP1970)**(1/10)-1
105	Kosovo	2.24	(POP1980/POP1970)**(1/10)-1
106	Chad	2.22	(POP1980/POP1970)**(1/10)-1
107	Colombia	2.20	(POP1980/POP1970)**(1/10)-1
108	Burkina Faso	2.19	(POP1980/POP1970)**(1/10)-1
109	New Caledon	2.18	(POP1980/POP1970)**(1/10)-1
110	Uganda	2.15	(POP1980/POP1970)**(1/10)-1
111	Bahamas	2.14	(POP1980/POP1970)**(1/10)-1
112	Brazil	2.13	(POP1980/POP1970)**(1/10)-1
113	Malaysia	2.12	(POP1980/POP1970)**(1/10)-1
114	Nepal	2.09	(POP1980/POP1970)**(1/10)-1
115	Mali	2.09	(POP1980/POP1970)**(1/10)-1
116	Armenia	2.09	(POP1980/POP1970)**(1/10)-1
117	Morocco	2.05	(POP1980/POP1970)**(1/10)-1
118	Kyrgyzstan	2.04	(POP1980/POP1970)**(1/10)-1
119	Ethiopia	2.04	(POP1980/POP1970)**(1/10)-1
120	Sierra Leone	2.00	(POP1980/POP1970)**(1/10)-1
121	Fiji	2.00	(POP1980/POP1970)**(1/10)-1
122	Burma	1.98	(POP1980/POP1970)**(1/10)-1
123	Belize	1.98	(POP1980/POP1970)**(1/10)-1
124	Lebanon	1.98	(POP1980/POP1970)**(1/10)-1
125	Haiti	1.95	(POP1980/POP1970)**(1/10)-1
126	Seychelles	1.94	(POP1980/POP1970)**(1/10)-1
127	Afghanistan	1.93	(POP1980/POP1970)**(1/10)-1
128	Korea, North	1.92	(POP1980/POP1970)**(1/10)-1
129	Taiwan	1.92	(POP1980/POP1970)**(1/10)-1
130	Isle of Man	1.90	(POP1980/POP1970)**(1/10)-1
131	China	1.90	(POP1980/POP1970)**(1/10)-1
132	West Bank	1.89	(POP1980/POP1970)**(1/10)-1
133	Laos	1.86	(POP1980/POP1970)**(1/10)-1
134	Sri Lanka	1.85	(POP1980/POP1970)**(1/10)-1
135	Mauritania	1.83	(POP1980/POP1970)**(1/10)-1
136	Micronesia	1.81	(POP1980/POP1970)**(1/10)-1
137	Korea, South	1.77	(POP1980/POP1970)**(1/10)-1
138	Azerbaijan	1.77	(POP1980/POP1970)**(1/10)-1
139	Liechtenstn	1.76	(POP1980/POP1970)**(1/10)-1
140	Samoa, Amer	1.71	(POP1980/POP1970)**(1/10)-1
141	Kiribati	1.70	(POP1980/POP1970)**(1/10)-1
142	Anguilla	1.68	(POP1980/POP1970)**(1/10)-1
143	St Pierre&M	1.67	(POP1980/POP1970)**(1/10)-1
144	Montserrat	1.67	(POP1980/POP1970)**(1/10)-1

Table 4.17 Population Growth Rates, 1970-1980

Rank	Country	GRPOP	Source
145	Virgin I, Br	1.67	(POP1980/POP1970)**(1/10)-1
146	Puerto Rico	1.66	(POP1980/POP1970)**(1/10)-1
147	Burundi	1.63	(POP1980/POP1970)**(1/10)-1
148	Argentina	1.61	(POP1980/POP1970)**(1/10)-1
149	Chile	1.56	(POP1980/POP1970)**(1/10)-1
150	Mauritius	1.54	(POP1980/POP1970)**(1/10)-1
151	Singapore	1.53	(POP1980/POP1970)**(1/10)-1
152	Gibraltar	1.44	(POP1980/POP1970)**(1/10)-1
153	Australia	1.43	(POP1980/POP1970)**(1/10)-1
154	Ireland	1.43	(POP1980/POP1970)**(1/10)-1
155	Tonga	1.41	(POP1980/POP1970)**(1/10)-1
156	Trinidad & T	1.41	(POP1980/POP1970)**(1/10)-1
157	Macedonia	1.36	(POP1980/POP1970)**(1/10)-1
158	Kazakhstan	1.36	(POP1980/POP1970)**(1/10)-1
159	Nauru	1.34	(POP1980/POP1970)**(1/10)-1
160	Jamaica	1.33	(POP1980/POP1970)**(1/10)-1
161	St Lucia	1.27	(POP1980/POP1970)**(1/10)-1
162	Reunion	1.27	(POP1980/POP1970)**(1/10)-1
163	Canada	1.22	(POP1980/POP1970)**(1/10)-1
164	Cuba	1.20	(POP1980/POP1970)**(1/10)-1
165	Monaco	1.18	(POP1980/POP1970)**(1/10)-1
166	Japan	1.12	(POP1980/POP1970)**(1/10)-1
167	Iceland	1.12	(POP1980/POP1970)**(1/10)-1
168	Moldova	1.10	(POP1980/POP1970)**(1/10)-1
169	New Zealand	1.09	(POP1980/POP1970)**(1/10)-1
170	St Vincent	1.08	(POP1980/POP1970)**(1/10)-1
171	US	1.06	(POP1980/POP1970)**(1/10)-1
172	Montenegro	1.05	(POP1980/POP1970)**(1/10)-1
173	Spain	1.02	(POP1980/POP1970)**(1/10)-1
174	San Marino	1.01	(POP1980/POP1970)**(1/10)-1
175	Faroe Is	0.98	(POP1980/POP1970)**(1/10)-1
176	Jersey	0.97	(POP1980/POP1970)**(1/10)-1
177	Slovakia	0.95	(POP1980/POP1970)**(1/10)-1
178	Bosnia	0.94	(POP1980/POP1970)**(1/10)-1
179	Slovenia	0.93	(POP1980/POP1970)**(1/10)-1
180	Greece	0.93	(POP1980/POP1970)**(1/10)-1
181	Romania	0.92	(POP1980/POP1970)**(1/10)-1
182	Lithuania	0.91	(POP1980/POP1970)**(1/10)-1
183	Cape Verde	0.91	(POP1980/POP1970)**(1/10)-1
184	Poland	0.90	(POP1980/POP1970)**(1/10)-1
185	Samoa	0.88	(POP1980/POP1970)**(1/10)-1
186	Greenland	0.84	(POP1980/POP1970)**(1/10)-1
187	Netherlands	0.84	(POP1980/POP1970)**(1/10)-1
188	Palau	0.80	(POP1980/POP1970)**(1/10)-1
189	Portugal	0.78	(POP1980/POP1970)**(1/10)-1
190	Estonia	0.76	(POP1980/POP1970)**(1/10)-1
191	Georgia	0.75	(POP1980/POP1970)**(1/10)-1
192	Guyana	0.75	(POP1980/POP1970)**(1/10)-1

Table 4.17 Population Growth Rates, 1970-1980			
Rank	Country	GRPOP	Source
193	Malta	0.73	(POP1980/POP1970)**(1/10)-1
194	Luxembourg	0.71	(POP1980/POP1970)**(1/10)-1
195	Belarus	0.66	(POP1980/POP1970)**(1/10)-1
196	Russia	0.62	(POP1980/POP1970)**(1/10)-1
197	Latvia	0.60	(POP1980/POP1970)**(1/10)-1
198	France	0.60	(POP1980/POP1970)**(1/10)-1
199	Guinea	0.59	(POP1980/POP1970)**(1/10)-1
200	Ukraine	0.56	(POP1980/POP1970)**(1/10)-1
201	Dominica	0.56	(POP1980/POP1970)**(1/10)-1
202	Barbados	0.53	(POP1980/POP1970)**(1/10)-1
203	Italy	0.53	(POP1980/POP1970)**(1/10)-1
204	Norway	0.53	(POP1980/POP1970)**(1/10)-1
205	Svalbard	0.53	(POP1980/POP1970)**(1/10)-1
206	Czechia	0.52	(POP1980/POP1970)**(1/10)-1
207	Cyprus	0.48	(POP1980/POP1970)**(1/10)-1
208	Serbia	0.46	(POP1980/POP1970)**(1/10)-1
209	Antigua & B	0.45	(POP1980/POP1970)**(1/10)-1
210	Bulgaria	0.43	(POP1980/POP1970)**(1/10)-1
211	Croatia	0.42	(POP1980/POP1970)**(1/10)-1
212	Finland	0.41	(POP1980/POP1970)**(1/10)-1
213	Hungary	0.39	(POP1980/POP1970)**(1/10)-1
214	Guernsey	0.39	(POP1980/POP1970)**(1/10)-1
215.5	Bermuda	0.37	(POP1980/POP1970)**(1/10)-1
215.5	Uruguay	0.37	(POP1980/POP1970)**(1/10)-1
217	Denmark	0.34	(POP1980/POP1970)**(1/10)-1
218	Sweden	0.33	(POP1980/POP1970)**(1/10)-1
219	Guadeloupe	0.26	(POP1980/POP1970)**(1/10)-1
220	Switzerland	0.22	(POP1980/POP1970)**(1/10)-1
221	Curacao	0.20	(POP1980/POP1970)**(1/10)-1
222	Belgium	0.17	(POP1980/POP1970)**(1/10)-1
223	UK	0.12	(POP1980/POP1970)**(1/10)-1
224	Austria	0.11	(POP1980/POP1970)**(1/10)-1
225	Germany	0.04	(POP1980/POP1970)**(1/10)-1
226	Martinique	0.03	(POP1980/POP1970)**(1/10)-1
227.5	Falkland Is	0.00	(POP1980/POP1970)**(1/10)-1
227.5	Saint Helena	0.00	(POP1980/POP1970)**(1/10)-1
229	Macao	-0.08	(POP1980/POP1970)**(1/10)-1
230	Suriname	-0.16	(POP1980/POP1970)**(1/10)-1
231	Aruba	-0.17	(POP1980/POP1970)**(1/10)-1
232	St Kitts & N	-0.44	(POP1980/POP1970)**(1/10)-1
233	Grenada	-0.54	(POP1980/POP1970)**(1/10)-1
234	Cambodia	-0.70	(POP1980/POP1970)**(1/10)-1
235	East Timor	-0.71	(POP1980/POP1970)**(1/10)-1
236	Equatorial G	-2.71	(POP1980/POP1970)**(1/10)-1

Table 4.18 Population Growth Rates, 1980-1990

Rank	Country	GRPOP	Source
1	Saint Martin	14.76	(POP1990/POP1980)**(1/10)-1
2	N Mariana Is	9.98	(POP1990/POP1980)**(1/10)-1
3	Sint Maarten	8.96	(POP1990/POP1980)**(1/10)-1
4	Qatar	7.39	(POP1990/POP1980)**(1/10)-1
5	UAE	5.94	(POP1990/POP1980)**(1/10)-1
6	W Sahara	5.76	(POP1990/POP1980)**(1/10)-1
7	Guiana, Fr	5.58	(POP1990/POP1980)**(1/10)-1
8	Mayotte	5.52	(POP1990/POP1980)**(1/10)-1
9	Equatorial G	5.40	(POP1990/POP1980)**(1/10)-1
10	Djibouti	5.15	(POP1990/POP1980)**(1/10)-1
11	Saudi Arabia	4.83	(POP1990/POP1980)**(1/10)-1
12	Andorra	4.54	(POP1990/POP1980)**(1/10)-1
13	Kuwait	4.52	(POP1990/POP1980)**(1/10)-1
14	Turks & C Is	4.38	(POP1990/POP1980)**(1/10)-1
15	Cayman Is	4.34	(POP1990/POP1980)**(1/10)-1
16	Oman	4.23	(POP1990/POP1980)**(1/10)-1
17	Bahrain	4.18	(POP1990/POP1980)**(1/10)-1
18	Malawi	4.16	(POP1990/POP1980)**(1/10)-1
19	Jordan	4.04	(POP1990/POP1980)**(1/10)-1
20	Macao	3.97	(POP1990/POP1980)**(1/10)-1
21	Samoa, Amer	3.92	(POP1990/POP1980)**(1/10)-1
22	Gambia	3.85	(POP1990/POP1980)**(1/10)-1
23	Ivory Coast	3.81	(POP1990/POP1980)**(1/10)-1
24	Swaziland	3.65	(POP1990/POP1980)**(1/10)-1
25	Kenya	3.64	(POP1990/POP1980)**(1/10)-1
26	Iran	3.59	(POP1990/POP1980)**(1/10)-1
27	Marshall Is	3.56	(POP1990/POP1980)**(1/10)-1
28	Gaza Strip	3.54	(POP1990/POP1980)**(1/10)-1
29	Zimbabwe	3.54	(POP1990/POP1980)**(1/10)-1
30	Libya	3.53	(POP1990/POP1980)**(1/10)-1
31	Ghana	3.42	(POP1990/POP1980)**(1/10)-1
32	Namibia	3.40	(POP1990/POP1980)**(1/10)-1
33	Pakistan	3.38	(POP1990/POP1980)**(1/10)-1
34	Zambia	3.37	(POP1990/POP1980)**(1/10)-1
35	Botswana	3.33	(POP1990/POP1980)**(1/10)-1
36	Syria	3.30	(POP1990/POP1980)**(1/10)-1
37	West Bank	3.27	(POP1990/POP1980)**(1/10)-1
38	Bhutan	3.27	(POP1990/POP1980)**(1/10)-1
39	Uganda	3.25	(POP1990/POP1980)**(1/10)-1
40	Togo	3.23	(POP1990/POP1980)**(1/10)-1
41	Rwanda	3.22	(POP1990/POP1980)**(1/10)-1
42	Maldives	3.18	(POP1990/POP1980)**(1/10)-1
43	Ethiopia	3.16	(POP1990/POP1980)**(1/10)-1
44	Tanzania	3.15	(POP1990/POP1980)**(1/10)-1
45	Gabon	3.12	(POP1990/POP1980)**(1/10)-1
46	Cambodia	3.12	(POP1990/POP1980)**(1/10)-1
47	Yemen	3.12	(POP1990/POP1980)**(1/10)-1
48	Angola	3.10	(POP1990/POP1980)**(1/10)-1

Table 4.18 Population Growth Rates, 1980-1990

Rank	Country	GRPOP	Source
49	Burundi	3.10	(POP1990/POP1980)**(1/10)-1
50	Solomon Is	3.07	(POP1990/POP1980)**(1/10)-1
51	Honduras	3.03	(POP1990/POP1980)**(1/10)-1
52	Congo, Dem R	3.03	(POP1990/POP1980)**(1/10)-1
53	Algeria	3.01	(POP1990/POP1980)**(1/10)-1
54	Tajikistan	2.98	(POP1990/POP1980)**(1/10)-1
55	East Timor	2.96	(POP1990/POP1980)**(1/10)-1
56	Cameroon	2.95	(POP1990/POP1980)**(1/10)-1
57	Comoros	2.90	(POP1990/POP1980)**(1/10)-1
58	South Sudan	2.88	(POP1990/POP1980)**(1/10)-1
59	Sudan	2.88	(POP1990/POP1980)**(1/10)-1
60	Congo, Rep	2.88	(POP1990/POP1980)**(1/10)-1
61	Malaysia	2.88	(POP1990/POP1980)**(1/10)-1
62	Niger	2.87	(POP1990/POP1980)**(1/10)-1
63	Paraguay	2.85	(POP1990/POP1980)**(1/10)-1
64	Benin	2.83	(POP1990/POP1980)**(1/10)-1
65	Costa Rica	2.81	(POP1990/POP1980)**(1/10)-1
66	Chad	2.81	(POP1990/POP1980)**(1/10)-1
67	Micronesia	2.78	(POP1990/POP1980)**(1/10)-1
68	CAR	2.76	(POP1990/POP1980)**(1/10)-1
69	Brunei	2.74	(POP1990/POP1980)**(1/10)-1
70	Madagascar	2.74	(POP1990/POP1980)**(1/10)-1
71	Senegal	2.73	(POP1990/POP1980)**(1/10)-1
72	Venezuela	2.73	(POP1990/POP1980)**(1/10)-1
73	Guinea	2.71	(POP1990/POP1980)**(1/10)-1
74	Laos	2.63	(POP1990/POP1980)**(1/10)-1
75	Belize	2.62	(POP1990/POP1980)**(1/10)-1
76	Papua New G	2.61	(POP1990/POP1980)**(1/10)-1
77	Burkina Faso	2.60	(POP1990/POP1980)**(1/10)-1
78	Fr Polynesia	2.59	(POP1990/POP1980)**(1/10)-1
79	Nigeria	2.59	(POP1990/POP1980)**(1/10)-1
80	Nepal	2.58	(POP1990/POP1980)**(1/10)-1
81	Ecuador	2.57	(POP1990/POP1980)**(1/10)-1
82	Uzbekistan	2.53	(POP1990/POP1980)**(1/10)-1
83	Eritrea	2.49	(POP1990/POP1980)**(1/10)-1
84	Vanuatu	2.45	(POP1990/POP1980)**(1/10)-1
85	Turkmenistan	2.44	(POP1990/POP1980)**(1/10)-1
86	Tunisia	2.44	(POP1990/POP1980)**(1/10)-1
87	Nicaragua	2.43	(POP1990/POP1980)**(1/10)-1
88	Guatemala	2.40	(POP1990/POP1980)**(1/10)-1
89	Bangladesh	2.40	(POP1990/POP1980)**(1/10)-1
90	Philippines	2.39	(POP1990/POP1980)**(1/10)-1
91	Egypt	2.37	(POP1990/POP1980)**(1/10)-1
92	Iraq	2.37	(POP1990/POP1980)**(1/10)-1
93	South Africa	2.37	(POP1990/POP1980)**(1/10)-1
94	Sierra Leone	2.33	(POP1990/POP1980)**(1/10)-1
95	Cook Is	2.30	(POP1990/POP1980)**(1/10)-1
96	Wallis & Fut	2.30	(POP1990/POP1980)**(1/10)-1

Table 4.18 Population Growth Rates, 1980-1990

Rank	Country	GRPOP	Source
97	Niue	2.30	(POP1990/POP1980)**(1/10)-1
98	Tokelau	2.30	(POP1990/POP1980)**(1/10)-1
99	Mongolia	2.29	(POP1990/POP1980)**(1/10)-1
100	Lesotho	2.28	(POP1990/POP1980)**(1/10)-1
101	Guam	2.28	(POP1990/POP1980)**(1/10)-1
102	Vietnam	2.27	(POP1990/POP1980)**(1/10)-1
103	Singapore	2.25	(POP1990/POP1980)**(1/10)-1
104	Panama	2.24	(POP1990/POP1980)**(1/10)-1
105	India	2.24	(POP1990/POP1980)**(1/10)-1
106	Peru	2.23	(POP1990/POP1980)**(1/10)-1
107	Mauritania	2.22	(POP1990/POP1980)**(1/10)-1
108	Colombia	2.21	(POP1990/POP1980)**(1/10)-1
109	Bolivia	2.21	(POP1990/POP1980)**(1/10)-1
110	Turkey	2.18	(POP1990/POP1980)**(1/10)-1
111	Brazil	2.14	(POP1990/POP1980)**(1/10)-1
112	Dominican R	2.14	(POP1990/POP1980)**(1/10)-1
113	Haiti	2.13	(POP1990/POP1980)**(1/10)-1
114	Morocco	2.10	(POP1990/POP1980)**(1/10)-1
115	Albania	2.10	(POP1990/POP1980)**(1/10)-1
116	Mexico	2.06	(POP1990/POP1980)**(1/10)-1
117	Kosovo	2.04	(POP1990/POP1980)**(1/10)-1
118	Kiribati	2.04	(POP1990/POP1980)**(1/10)-1
119	Indonesia	2.03	(POP1990/POP1980)**(1/10)-1
120	Sao Tome & P	2.02	(POP1990/POP1980)**(1/10)-1
121	Mali	2.01	(POP1990/POP1980)**(1/10)-1
122	Bahamas	2.00	(POP1990/POP1980)**(1/10)-1
123	Guinea-Biss	1.99	(POP1990/POP1980)**(1/10)-1
124	New Caledon	1.97	(POP1990/POP1980)**(1/10)-1
125	Burma	1.96	(POP1990/POP1980)**(1/10)-1
126	Kyrgyzstan	1.94	(POP1990/POP1980)**(1/10)-1
127	Israel	1.85	(POP1990/POP1980)**(1/10)-1
128	Lebanon	1.73	(POP1990/POP1980)**(1/10)-1
129	Reunion	1.72	(POP1990/POP1980)**(1/10)-1
130	Chile	1.67	(POP1990/POP1980)**(1/10)-1
131	Australia	1.66	(POP1990/POP1980)**(1/10)-1
132	Thailand	1.61	(POP1990/POP1980)**(1/10)-1
133	Azerbaijan	1.59	(POP1990/POP1980)**(1/10)-1
134	St Lucia	1.58	(POP1990/POP1980)**(1/10)-1
135	Korea, North	1.57	(POP1990/POP1980)**(1/10)-1
136	China	1.54	(POP1990/POP1980)**(1/10)-1
137.5	Cape Verde	1.50	(POP1990/POP1980)**(1/10)-1
137.5	Liechtenstn	1.50	(POP1990/POP1980)**(1/10)-1
139	Somalia	1.45	(POP1990/POP1980)**(1/10)-1
140	Argentina	1.45	(POP1990/POP1980)**(1/10)-1
141	Palau	1.44	(POP1990/POP1980)**(1/10)-1
142	Guernsey	1.42	(POP1990/POP1980)**(1/10)-1
143	St Pierre&M	1.41	(POP1990/POP1980)**(1/10)-1
144	Virgin I, Br	1.41	(POP1990/POP1980)**(1/10)-1

TABLE 4.18 POPULATION GROWTH RATES, 1980-1990

Rank	Country	GRPOP	Source
145	Anguilla	1.41	(POP1990/POP1980)**(1/10)-1
146	Montserrat	1.41	(POP1990/POP1980)**(1/10)-1
147	Taiwan	1.40	(POP1990/POP1980)**(1/10)-1
148	Sri Lanka	1.40	(POP1990/POP1980)**(1/10)-1
149	Korea, South	1.38	(POP1990/POP1980)**(1/10)-1
150	Fiji	1.38	(POP1990/POP1980)**(1/10)-1
151	Hong Kong	1.38	(POP1990/POP1980)**(1/10)-1
152	Armenia	1.36	(POP1990/POP1980)**(1/10)-1
153	San Marino	1.34	(POP1990/POP1980)**(1/10)-1
154	Trinidad & T	1.33	(POP1990/POP1980)**(1/10)-1
155	Cyprus	1.33	(POP1990/POP1980)**(1/10)-1
156	Canada	1.23	(POP1990/POP1980)**(1/10)-1
157	Seychelles	1.20	(POP1990/POP1980)**(1/10)-1
158	Malta	1.19	(POP1990/POP1980)**(1/10)-1
159.5	Nauru	1.18	(POP1990/POP1980)**(1/10)-1
159.5	Tuvalu	1.18	(POP1990/POP1980)**(1/10)-1
161	Greenland	1.14	(POP1990/POP1980)**(1/10)-1
162	Iceland	1.13	(POP1990/POP1980)**(1/10)-1
163	Kazakhstan	1.12	(POP1990/POP1980)**(1/10)-1
164	El Salvador	1.12	(POP1990/POP1980)**(1/10)-1
165	Guadeloupe	1.11	(POP1990/POP1980)**(1/10)-1
166	Faroe Is	1.11	(POP1990/POP1980)**(1/10)-1
167	Suriname	1.07	(POP1990/POP1980)**(1/10)-1
168	Monaco	1.06	(POP1990/POP1980)**(1/10)-1
169	Jamaica	1.04	(POP1990/POP1980)**(1/10)-1
170	Liberia	1.01	(POP1990/POP1980)**(1/10)-1
171	Jersey	1.01	(POP1990/POP1980)**(1/10)-1
172	Martinique	1.00	(POP1990/POP1980)**(1/10)-1
173	Puerto Rico	0.97	(POP1990/POP1980)**(1/10)-1
174	Bosnia	0.96	(POP1990/POP1980)**(1/10)-1
175	Cuba	0.96	(POP1990/POP1980)**(1/10)-1
176	New Zealand	0.94	(POP1990/POP1980)**(1/10)-1
177	US	0.93	(POP1990/POP1980)**(1/10)-1
178	Mauritius	0.92	(POP1990/POP1980)**(1/10)-1
179	St Vincent	0.88	(POP1990/POP1980)**(1/10)-1
180	Moldova	0.85	(POP1990/POP1980)**(1/10)-1
181	Isle of Man	0.76	(POP1990/POP1980)**(1/10)-1
182	Lithuania	0.74	(POP1990/POP1980)**(1/10)-1
183	Mozambique	0.71	(POP1990/POP1980)**(1/10)-1
184	Georgia	0.70	(POP1990/POP1980)**(1/10)-1
185	Russia	0.67	(POP1990/POP1980)**(1/10)-1
186	Poland	0.67	(POP1990/POP1980)**(1/10)-1
187	Uruguay	0.65	(POP1990/POP1980)**(1/10)-1
188	Estonia	0.63	(POP1990/POP1980)**(1/10)-1
189	Macedonia	0.62	(POP1990/POP1980)**(1/10)-1
190	Switzerland	0.61	(POP1990/POP1980)**(1/10)-1
191	Latvia	0.59	(POP1990/POP1980)**(1/10)-1
192	Montenegro	0.56	(POP1990/POP1980)**(1/10)-1

Table 4.18 Population Growth Rates, 1980-1990

Rank	Country	GRPOP	Source
193	Netherlands	0.55	(POP1990/POP1980)**(1/10)-1
194	Slovakia	0.55	(POP1990/POP1980)**(1/10)-1
195	Belarus	0.54	(POP1990/POP1980)**(1/10)-1
196	Japan	0.53	(POP1990/POP1980)**(1/10)-1
197	Bermuda	0.53	(POP1990/POP1980)**(1/10)-1
198	Greece	0.52	(POP1990/POP1980)**(1/10)-1
199	France	0.51	(POP1990/POP1980)**(1/10)-1
200	Slovenia	0.51	(POP1990/POP1980)**(1/10)-1
201	Virgin I, US	0.50	(POP1990/POP1980)**(1/10)-1
202	Aruba	0.49	(POP1990/POP1980)**(1/10)-1
203	Spain	0.49	(POP1990/POP1980)**(1/10)-1
204	Luxembourg	0.46	(POP1990/POP1980)**(1/10)-1
205	Romania	0.44	(POP1990/POP1980)**(1/10)-1
206	Grenada	0.44	(POP1990/POP1980)**(1/10)-1
207	Barbados	0.43	(POP1990/POP1980)**(1/10)-1
208	Tonga	0.43	(POP1990/POP1980)**(1/10)-1
209	Finland	0.38	(POP1990/POP1980)**(1/10)-1
210	Samoa	0.38	(POP1990/POP1980)**(1/10)-1
211	Norway	0.37	(POP1990/POP1980)**(1/10)-1
212	Svalbard	0.37	(POP1990/POP1980)**(1/10)-1
213	Ukraine	0.37	(POP1990/POP1980)**(1/10)-1
214	Gibraltar	0.33	(POP1990/POP1980)**(1/10)-1
215	Ireland	0.30	(POP1990/POP1980)**(1/10)-1
216	Sweden	0.30	(POP1990/POP1980)**(1/10)-1
217	Croatia	0.28	(POP1990/POP1980)**(1/10)-1
218	Serbia	0.26	(POP1990/POP1980)**(1/10)-1
219	Germany	0.17	(POP1990/POP1980)**(1/10)-1
220	Austria	0.17	(POP1990/POP1980)**(1/10)-1
221	UK	0.16	(POP1990/POP1980)**(1/10)-1
222	Portugal	0.15	(POP1990/POP1980)**(1/10)-1
223	Belgium	0.11	(POP1990/POP1980)**(1/10)-1
224	Italy	0.11	(POP1990/POP1980)**(1/10)-1
225	Denmark	0.05	(POP1990/POP1980)**(1/10)-1
226	Czechia	0.04	(POP1990/POP1980)**(1/10)-1
227.5	Falkland Is	0.00	(POP1990/POP1980)**(1/10)-1
227.5	Saint Helena	0.00	(POP1990/POP1980)**(1/10)-1
229	Bulgaria	-0.16	(POP1990/POP1980)**(1/10)-1
230	Curacao	-0.20	(POP1990/POP1980)**(1/10)-1
231	Hungary	-0.32	(POP1990/POP1980)**(1/10)-1
232	St Kitts & N	-0.46	(POP1990/POP1980)**(1/10)-1
233	Dominica	-0.55	(POP1990/POP1980)**(1/10)-1
234	Guyana	-0.69	(POP1990/POP1980)**(1/10)-1
235	Antigua & B	-0.75	(POP1990/POP1980)**(1/10)-1
236	Afghanistan	-1.03	(POP1990/POP1980)**(1/10)-1

TABLE 4.19 POPULATION GROWTH RATES, 1990-2000			
Rank	Country	GRPOP	Source
1	West Bank	7.96	(POP2000/POP1990)**(1/10)-1
2	Gaza Strip	5.56	(POP2000/POP1990)**(1/10)-1
3	Anguilla	5.54	(POP2000/POP1990)**(1/10)-1
4	UAE	5.30	(POP2000/POP1990)**(1/10)-1
5	Mayotte	5.15	(POP2000/POP1990)**(1/10)-1
6	Turks & C Is	5.03	(POP2000/POP1990)**(1/10)-1
7	Virgin I, Br	4.81	(POP2000/POP1990)**(1/10)-1
8	N Mariana Is	4.60	(POP2000/POP1990)**(1/10)-1
9	W Sahara	4.47	(POP2000/POP1990)**(1/10)-1
10	Cayman Is	4.40	(POP2000/POP1990)**(1/10)-1
11	Aruba	4.30	(POP2000/POP1990)**(1/10)-1
12	Afghanistan	3.96	(POP2000/POP1990)**(1/10)-1
13	Guinea	3.78	(POP2000/POP1990)**(1/10)-1
14	Yemen	3.62	(POP2000/POP1990)**(1/10)-1
15	Gambia	3.62	(POP2000/POP1990)**(1/10)-1
16	Falkland Is	3.52	(POP2000/POP1990)**(1/10)-1
17	Guiana, Fr	3.50	(POP2000/POP1990)**(1/10)-1
18	Papua New G	3.49	(POP2000/POP1990)**(1/10)-1
19	South Sudan	3.47	(POP2000/POP1990)**(1/10)-1
20	Jordan	3.46	(POP2000/POP1990)**(1/10)-1
21	Niger	3.44	(POP2000/POP1990)**(1/10)-1
22	Madagascar	3.37	(POP2000/POP1990)**(1/10)-1
23	Equatorial G	3.35	(POP2000/POP1990)**(1/10)-1
24	Mozambique	3.31	(POP2000/POP1990)**(1/10)-1
25	Uganda	3.31	(POP2000/POP1990)**(1/10)-1
26	Iraq	3.22	(POP2000/POP1990)**(1/10)-1
27	Chad	3.18	(POP2000/POP1990)**(1/10)-1
28	Benin	3.16	(POP2000/POP1990)**(1/10)-1
29	Congo, Dem R	3.15	(POP2000/POP1990)**(1/10)-1
30	Israel	3.09	(POP2000/POP1990)**(1/10)-1
31	Ivory Coast	3.06	(POP2000/POP1990)**(1/10)-1
32	Namibia	2.97	(POP2000/POP1990)**(1/10)-1
33	Solomon Is	2.96	(POP2000/POP1990)**(1/10)-1
34	Liberia	2.96	(POP2000/POP1990)**(1/10)-1
35	Tanzania	2.94	(POP2000/POP1990)**(1/10)-1
36	Singapore	2.93	(POP2000/POP1990)**(1/10)-1
37	Gabon	2.89	(POP2000/POP1990)**(1/10)-1
38	Saudi Arabia	2.87	(POP2000/POP1990)**(1/10)-1
39	Burkina Faso	2.80	(POP2000/POP1990)**(1/10)-1
40	Cambodia	2.80	(POP2000/POP1990)**(1/10)-1
41	Congo, Rep	2.76	(POP2000/POP1990)**(1/10)-1
42	Nepal	2.75	(POP2000/POP1990)**(1/10)-1
43	Kenya	2.74	(POP2000/POP1990)**(1/10)-1
44	Djibouti	2.68	(POP2000/POP1990)**(1/10)-1
45	Mauritania	2.65	(POP2000/POP1990)**(1/10)-1
46	Syria	2.64	(POP2000/POP1990)**(1/10)-1
47	Mali	2.62	(POP2000/POP1990)**(1/10)-1
48	CAR	2.58	(POP2000/POP1990)**(1/10)-1

Table 4.19 Population Growth Rates, 1990-2000

Rank	Country	GRPOP	Source
49	Paraguay	2.58	(POP2000/POP1990)**(1/10)-1
50	Senegal	2.57	(POP2000/POP1990)**(1/10)-1
51	Cameroon	2.56	(POP2000/POP1990)**(1/10)-1
52	Brunei	2.54	(POP2000/POP1990)**(1/10)-1
53	Pakistan	2.52	(POP2000/POP1990)**(1/10)-1
54	Ethiopia	2.50	(POP2000/POP1990)**(1/10)-1
55	Belize	2.46	(POP2000/POP1990)**(1/10)-1
56	Nigeria	2.45	(POP2000/POP1990)**(1/10)-1
57	Botswana	2.44	(POP2000/POP1990)**(1/10)-1
58	Honduras	2.43	(POP2000/POP1990)**(1/10)-1
59	Zambia	2.42	(POP2000/POP1990)**(1/10)-1
60	Vanuatu	2.41	(POP2000/POP1990)**(1/10)-1
61	Bahrain	2.41	(POP2000/POP1990)**(1/10)-1
62	Palau	2.39	(POP2000/POP1990)**(1/10)-1
63	Qatar	2.38	(POP2000/POP1990)**(1/10)-1
64	Sudan	2.37	(POP2000/POP1990)**(1/10)-1
65	Togo	2.36	(POP2000/POP1990)**(1/10)-1
66	Oman	2.35	(POP2000/POP1990)**(1/10)-1
67	Philippines	2.33	(POP2000/POP1990)**(1/10)-1
68	Guatemala	2.33	(POP2000/POP1990)**(1/10)-1
69	Maldives	2.33	(POP2000/POP1990)**(1/10)-1
70	Laos	2.27	(POP2000/POP1990)**(1/10)-1
71	Cape Verde	2.26	(POP2000/POP1990)**(1/10)-1
72	New Caledon	2.24	(POP2000/POP1990)**(1/10)-1
73	Bolivia	2.24	(POP2000/POP1990)**(1/10)-1
74	Costa Rica	2.23	(POP2000/POP1990)**(1/10)-1
75	Comoros	2.21	(POP2000/POP1990)**(1/10)-1
76	Malaysia	2.19	(POP2000/POP1990)**(1/10)-1
77	Haiti	2.15	(POP2000/POP1990)**(1/10)-1
78	Ghana	2.14	(POP2000/POP1990)**(1/10)-1
79	Venezuela	2.13	(POP2000/POP1990)**(1/10)-1
80	Swaziland	2.12	(POP2000/POP1990)**(1/10)-1
81	Nicaragua	2.10	(POP2000/POP1990)**(1/10)-1
82	Panama	2.08	(POP2000/POP1990)**(1/10)-1
83	Andorra	2.06	(POP2000/POP1990)**(1/10)-1
84	South Africa	2.02	(POP2000/POP1990)**(1/10)-1
85	Fr Polynesia	2.01	(POP2000/POP1990)**(1/10)-1
86	Guinea-Biss	2.01	(POP2000/POP1990)**(1/10)-1
87	Sao Tome & P	1.97	(POP2000/POP1990)**(1/10)-1
88	Samoa, Amer	1.95	(POP2000/POP1990)**(1/10)-1
89	Cyprus	1.89	(POP2000/POP1990)**(1/10)-1
90	India	1.89	(POP2000/POP1990)**(1/10)-1
91	Ecuador	1.87	(POP2000/POP1990)**(1/10)-1
92	Reunion	1.87	(POP2000/POP1990)**(1/10)-1
93	Turkmenistan	1.83	(POP2000/POP1990)**(1/10)-1
94	Kiribati	1.82	(POP2000/POP1990)**(1/10)-1
95	Malawi	1.81	(POP2000/POP1990)**(1/10)-1
96	Peru	1.81	(POP2000/POP1990)**(1/10)-1

TABLE 4.19 POPULATION GROWTH RATES, 1990-2000

Rank	Country	GRPOP	Source
97	Iran	1.78	(POP2000/POP1990)**(1/10)-1
98	Uzbekistan	1.78	(POP2000/POP1990)**(1/10)-1
99	Algeria	1.76	(POP2000/POP1990)**(1/10)-1
100	Angola	1.75	(POP2000/POP1990)**(1/10)-1
101.5	Antigua & B	1.73	(POP2000/POP1990)**(1/10)-1
101.5	Bahamas	1.73	(POP2000/POP1990)**(1/10)-1
103	Colombia	1.62	(POP2000/POP1990)**(1/10)-1
104	Burma	1.60	(POP2000/POP1990)**(1/10)-1
105	Morocco	1.59	(POP2000/POP1990)**(1/10)-1
106	Chile	1.58	(POP2000/POP1990)**(1/10)-1
107	Mexico	1.56	(POP2000/POP1990)**(1/10)-1
108	Monaco	1.55	(POP2000/POP1990)**(1/10)-1
109	Turkey	1.54	(POP2000/POP1990)**(1/10)-1
110	Tajikistan	1.54	(POP2000/POP1990)**(1/10)-1
111	Zimbabwe	1.53	(POP2000/POP1990)**(1/10)-1
112	Bangladesh	1.52	(POP2000/POP1990)**(1/10)-1
113	Tunisia	1.52	(POP2000/POP1990)**(1/10)-1
114	Eritrea	1.51	(POP2000/POP1990)**(1/10)-1
115	Dominican R	1.50	(POP2000/POP1990)**(1/10)-1
116	Libya	1.49	(POP2000/POP1990)**(1/10)-1
117	Marshall Is	1.49	(POP2000/POP1990)**(1/10)-1
118	Macao	1.48	(POP2000/POP1990)**(1/10)-1
119	Guam	1.47	(POP2000/POP1990)**(1/10)-1
120	Brazil	1.46	(POP2000/POP1990)**(1/10)-1
121	Vietnam	1.44	(POP2000/POP1990)**(1/10)-1
122	Hong Kong	1.41	(POP2000/POP1990)**(1/10)-1
123	Suriname	1.38	(POP2000/POP1990)**(1/10)-1
124	El Salvador	1.36	(POP2000/POP1990)**(1/10)-1
125	Mongolia	1.35	(POP2000/POP1990)**(1/10)-1
126	Luxembourg	1.33	(POP2000/POP1990)**(1/10)-1
127	Rwanda	1.31	(POP2000/POP1990)**(1/10)-1
128	Liechtenstn	1.30	(POP2000/POP1990)**(1/10)-1
129	Burundi	1.30	(POP2000/POP1990)**(1/10)-1
130	St Lucia	1.30	(POP2000/POP1990)**(1/10)-1
131	Korea, North	1.24	(POP2000/POP1990)**(1/10)-1
132	US	1.23	(POP2000/POP1990)**(1/10)-1
133	Seychelles	1.20	(POP2000/POP1990)**(1/10)-1
134	Egypt	1.19	(POP2000/POP1990)**(1/10)-1
135	Lesotho	1.19	(POP2000/POP1990)**(1/10)-1
136	San Marino	1.18	(POP2000/POP1990)**(1/10)-1
137	Cook Is	1.16	(POP2000/POP1990)**(1/10)-1
138	Somalia	1.15	(POP2000/POP1990)**(1/10)-1
139	Azerbaijan	1.14	(POP2000/POP1990)**(1/10)-1
140	Indonesia	1.13	(POP2000/POP1990)**(1/10)-1
141	New Zealand	1.12	(POP2000/POP1990)**(1/10)-1
142	Fiji	1.10	(POP2000/POP1990)**(1/10)-1
143	Micronesia	1.09	(POP2000/POP1990)**(1/10)-1
144	Mauritius	1.08	(POP2000/POP1990)**(1/10)-1

TABLE 4.19 POPULATION GROWTH RATES, 1990-2000

Rank	Country	GRPOP	Source
145	Argentina	1.06	(POP2000/POP1990)**(1/10)-1
146	Nauru	1.06	(POP2000/POP1990)**(1/10)-1
147	Kyrgyzstan	1.06	(POP2000/POP1990)**(1/10)-1
148	Canada	1.02	(POP2000/POP1990)**(1/10)-1
149	Thailand	1.01	(POP2000/POP1990)**(1/10)-1
150	China	0.98	(POP2000/POP1990)**(1/10)-1
151	Lebanon	0.98	(POP2000/POP1990)**(1/10)-1
152	Iceland	0.98	(POP2000/POP1990)**(1/10)-1
153	Isle of Man	0.97	(POP2000/POP1990)**(1/10)-1
154	Grenada	0.92	(POP2000/POP1990)**(1/10)-1
155	St Kitts & N	0.91	(POP2000/POP1990)**(1/10)-1
156	Taiwan	0.90	(POP2000/POP1990)**(1/10)-1
157	Guadeloupe	0.89	(POP2000/POP1990)**(1/10)-1
158	Jamaica	0.88	(POP2000/POP1990)**(1/10)-1
159	St Pierre&M	0.86	(POP2000/POP1990)**(1/10)-1
160	Australia	0.85	(POP2000/POP1990)**(1/10)-1
161	Samoa	0.84	(POP2000/POP1990)**(1/10)-1
162	Ireland	0.81	(POP2000/POP1990)**(1/10)-1
163	Saint Helena	0.80	(POP2000/POP1990)**(1/10)-1
164	Greece	0.78	(POP2000/POP1990)**(1/10)-1
165	Sri Lanka	0.78	(POP2000/POP1990)**(1/10)-1
166	Puerto Rico	0.75	(POP2000/POP1990)**(1/10)-1
167	Korea, South	0.69	(POP2000/POP1990)**(1/10)-1
168	Switzerland	0.68	(POP2000/POP1990)**(1/10)-1
169	Bermuda	0.67	(POP2000/POP1990)**(1/10)-1
170	Virgin I, US	0.67	(POP2000/POP1990)**(1/10)-1
171	Austria	0.64	(POP2000/POP1990)**(1/10)-1
172	Netherlands	0.63	(POP2000/POP1990)**(1/10)-1
173	Martinique	0.62	(POP2000/POP1990)**(1/10)-1
174	Malta	0.58	(POP2000/POP1990)**(1/10)-1
175	Norway	0.57	(POP2000/POP1990)**(1/10)-1
176	Macedonia	0.51	(POP2000/POP1990)**(1/10)-1
177	Kuwait	0.48	(POP2000/POP1990)**(1/10)-1
178	Niue	0.46	(POP2000/POP1990)**(1/10)-1
179	Cuba	0.44	(POP2000/POP1990)**(1/10)-1
180	Sint Maarten	0.41	(POP2000/POP1990)**(1/10)-1
181	France	0.40	(POP2000/POP1990)**(1/10)-1
182	Sierra Leone	0.40	(POP2000/POP1990)**(1/10)-1
183	Montenegro	0.39	(POP2000/POP1990)**(1/10)-1
184	Finland	0.37	(POP2000/POP1990)**(1/10)-1
185	Denmark	0.37	(POP2000/POP1990)**(1/10)-1
186	Japan	0.37	(POP2000/POP1990)**(1/10)-1
187	Sweden	0.36	(POP2000/POP1990)**(1/10)-1
188	Jersey	0.35	(POP2000/POP1990)**(1/10)-1
189	Uruguay	0.35	(POP2000/POP1990)**(1/10)-1
190	Spain	0.31	(POP2000/POP1990)**(1/10)-1
191	Portugal	0.31	(POP2000/POP1990)**(1/10)-1
192	Tonga	0.31	(POP2000/POP1990)**(1/10)-1

Table 4.19 Population Growth Rates, 1990-2000			
Rank	Country	GRPOP	Source
193	Germany	0.30	(POP2000/POP1990)**(1/10)-1
194	Slovenia	0.30	(POP2000/POP1990)**(1/10)-1
195	UK	0.28	(POP2000/POP1990)**(1/10)-1
196	Belgium	0.28	(POP2000/POP1990)**(1/10)-1
197	East Timor	0.28	(POP2000/POP1990)**(1/10)-1
198	St Vincent	0.28	(POP2000/POP1990)**(1/10)-1
199	Slovakia	0.27	(POP2000/POP1990)**(1/10)-1
200	Wallis & Fut	0.25	(POP2000/POP1990)**(1/10)-1
201	Barbados	0.23	(POP2000/POP1990)**(1/10)-1
202	Trinidad & T	0.22	(POP2000/POP1990)**(1/10)-1
203	Guernsey	0.16	(POP2000/POP1990)**(1/10)-1
204	Italy	0.14	(POP2000/POP1990)**(1/10)-1
205	Guyana	0.11	(POP2000/POP1990)**(1/10)-1
206	Poland	0.05	(POP2000/POP1990)**(1/10)-1
208	Dominica	0.00	(POP2000/POP1990)**(1/10)-1
208	Greenland	0.00	(POP2000/POP1990)**(1/10)-1
208	Tuvalu	0.00	(POP2000/POP1990)**(1/10)-1
210	Russia	-0.11	(POP2000/POP1990)**(1/10)-1
211	Croatia	-0.12	(POP2000/POP1990)**(1/10)-1
212	Czechia	-0.15	(POP2000/POP1990)**(1/10)-1
213	Hungary	-0.16	(POP2000/POP1990)**(1/10)-1
214	Belarus	-0.21	(POP2000/POP1990)**(1/10)-1
215	Moldova	-0.33	(POP2000/POP1990)**(1/10)-1
216	Romania	-0.34	(POP2000/POP1990)**(1/10)-1
217	Serbia	-0.35	(POP2000/POP1990)**(1/10)-1
218	Faroe Is	-0.42	(POP2000/POP1990)**(1/10)-1
219	Gibraltar	-0.50	(POP2000/POP1990)**(1/10)-1
220	Ukraine	-0.54	(POP2000/POP1990)**(1/10)-1
221	Lithuania	-0.55	(POP2000/POP1990)**(1/10)-1
222	Saint Martin	-0.56	(POP2000/POP1990)**(1/10)-1
223	Albania	-0.70	(POP2000/POP1990)**(1/10)-1
224	Bhutan	-0.74	(POP2000/POP1990)**(1/10)-1
225	Curacao	-0.79	(POP2000/POP1990)**(1/10)-1
226	Bulgaria	-0.89	(POP2000/POP1990)**(1/10)-1
227	Kosovo	-0.91	(POP2000/POP1990)**(1/10)-1
228	Latvia	-1.16	(POP2000/POP1990)**(1/10)-1
229	Kazakhstan	-1.19	(POP2000/POP1990)**(1/10)-1
230	Bosnia	-1.30	(POP2000/POP1990)**(1/10)-1
231	Estonia	-1.36	(POP2000/POP1990)**(1/10)-1
232	Armenia	-1.41	(POP2000/POP1990)**(1/10)-1
233	Tokelau	-1.52	(POP2000/POP1990)**(1/10)-1
234	Georgia	-2.06	(POP2000/POP1990)**(1/10)-1
235	Svalbard	-4.78	(POP2000/POP1990)**(1/10)-1
236	Montserrat	-6.44	(POP2000/POP1990)**(1/10)-1

TABLE 4.20 POPULATION GROWTH RATES, 2000-2010

Rank	Country	GRPOP	Source
1	Qatar	10.97	(POP2010/POP2000)**(1/10)-1
2	UAE	9.49	(POP2010/POP2000)**(1/10)-1
3	Bahrain	6.78	(POP2010/POP2000)**(1/10)-1
4	Turks & C Is	5.08	(POP2010/POP2000)**(1/10)-1
5	Kuwait	4.78	(POP2010/POP2000)**(1/10)-1
6	South Sudan	4.29	(POP2010/POP2000)**(1/10)-1
7	W Sahara	3.89	(POP2010/POP2000)**(1/10)-1
8	Eritrea	3.66	(POP2010/POP2000)**(1/10)-1
9	Chad	3.60	(POP2010/POP2000)**(1/10)-1
10	Niger	3.57	(POP2010/POP2000)**(1/10)-1
11	East Timor	3.56	(POP2010/POP2000)**(1/10)-1
12	Sierra Leone	3.54	(POP2010/POP2000)**(1/10)-1
13	Guiana, Fr	3.51	(POP2010/POP2000)**(1/10)-1
14	Cayman Is	3.42	(POP2010/POP2000)**(1/10)-1
15	Mayotte	3.33	(POP2010/POP2000)**(1/10)-1
16	Gaza Strip	3.29	(POP2010/POP2000)**(1/10)-1
17	Uganda	3.23	(POP2010/POP2000)**(1/10)-1
18	Benin	3.11	(POP2010/POP2000)**(1/10)-1
19	Mali	3.06	(POP2010/POP2000)**(1/10)-1
20	Yemen	3.05	(POP2010/POP2000)**(1/10)-1
21	Equatorial G	3.02	(POP2010/POP2000)**(1/10)-1
22	Angola	3.00	(POP2010/POP2000)**(1/10)-1
23	Liberia	2.99	(POP2010/POP2000)**(1/10)-1
24	Burkina Faso	2.97	(POP2010/POP2000)**(1/10)-1
25	Kenya	2.93	(POP2010/POP2000)**(1/10)-1
26	Congo, Dem R	2.89	(POP2010/POP2000)**(1/10)-1
27	Iraq	2.87	(POP2010/POP2000)**(1/10)-1
28	Malawi	2.87	(POP2010/POP2000)**(1/10)-1
29	Madagascar	2.87	(POP2010/POP2000)**(1/10)-1
30	Togo	2.84	(POP2010/POP2000)**(1/10)-1
31	Papua New G	2.83	(POP2010/POP2000)**(1/10)-1
32	Burundi	2.78	(POP2010/POP2000)**(1/10)-1
33	Andorra	2.72	(POP2010/POP2000)**(1/10)-1
34	Ghana	2.69	(POP2010/POP2000)**(1/10)-1
35	Belize	2.68	(POP2010/POP2000)**(1/10)-1
36	Somalia	2.68	(POP2010/POP2000)**(1/10)-1
37	Senegal	2.67	(POP2010/POP2000)**(1/10)-1
38	West Bank	2.67	(POP2010/POP2000)**(1/10)-1
39	Nigeria	2.67	(POP2010/POP2000)**(1/10)-1
40	Zambia	2.66	(POP2010/POP2000)**(1/10)-1
41	Comoros	2.62	(POP2010/POP2000)**(1/10)-1
42	Gambia	2.61	(POP2010/POP2000)**(1/10)-1
43	Afghanistan	2.60	(POP2010/POP2000)**(1/10)-1
44	Congo, Rep	2.57	(POP2010/POP2000)**(1/10)-1
45	Ethiopia	2.54	(POP2010/POP2000)**(1/10)-1
46	Mauritania	2.51	(POP2010/POP2000)**(1/10)-1
47	Guatemala	2.50	(POP2010/POP2000)**(1/10)-1
48	Saudi Arabia	2.50	(POP2010/POP2000)**(1/10)-1

Table 4.20 Population Growth Rates, 2000-2010

Rank	Country	GRPOP	Source
49	Solomon Is	2.48	(POP2010/POP2000)**(1/10)-1
50	Syria	2.47	(POP2010/POP2000)**(1/10)-1
51	Malaysia	2.47	(POP2010/POP2000)**(1/10)-1
52	Vanuatu	2.46	(POP2010/POP2000)**(1/10)-1
53	Bhutan	2.43	(POP2010/POP2000)**(1/10)-1
54	Virgin I, Br	2.43	(POP2010/POP2000)**(1/10)-1
55	Guinea-Biss	2.37	(POP2010/POP2000)**(1/10)-1
56	Sao Tome & P	2.36	(POP2010/POP2000)**(1/10)-1
57	Singapore	2.34	(POP2010/POP2000)**(1/10)-1
58	Jordan	2.34	(POP2010/POP2000)**(1/10)-1
59	Macao	2.30	(POP2010/POP2000)**(1/10)-1
60	Cameroon	2.29	(POP2010/POP2000)**(1/10)-1
61	Anguilla	2.27	(POP2010/POP2000)**(1/10)-1
62	Ivory Coast	2.23	(POP2010/POP2000)**(1/10)-1
63	Tanzania	2.23	(POP2010/POP2000)**(1/10)-1
64	Mozambique	2.22	(POP2010/POP2000)**(1/10)-1
65	Sint Maarten	2.21	(POP2010/POP2000)**(1/10)-1
66	Rwanda	2.10	(POP2010/POP2000)**(1/10)-1
67	Egypt	2.09	(POP2010/POP2000)**(1/10)-1
68	Cyprus	2.03	(POP2010/POP2000)**(1/10)-1
69	Honduras	2.03	(POP2010/POP2000)**(1/10)-1
70	Tuvalu	2.03	(POP2010/POP2000)**(1/10)-1
71	Sudan	2.00	(POP2010/POP2000)**(1/10)-1
72	Gabon	2.00	(POP2010/POP2000)**(1/10)-1
73	Tajikistan	2.00	(POP2010/POP2000)**(1/10)-1
74	CAR	1.99	(POP2010/POP2000)**(1/10)-1
75	Libya	1.97	(POP2010/POP2000)**(1/10)-1
76	Oman	1.94	(POP2010/POP2000)**(1/10)-1
77	Pakistan	1.92	(POP2010/POP2000)**(1/10)-1
78	Philippines	1.90	(POP2010/POP2000)**(1/10)-1
79	Panama	1.88	(POP2010/POP2000)**(1/10)-1
80	Kiribati	1.84	(POP2010/POP2000)**(1/10)-1
81	Israel	1.82	(POP2010/POP2000)**(1/10)-1
82	Guinea	1.81	(POP2010/POP2000)**(1/10)-1
83	Algeria	1.79	(POP2010/POP2000)**(1/10)-1
84	Ireland	1.79	(POP2010/POP2000)**(1/10)-1
85	Laos	1.78	(POP2010/POP2000)**(1/10)-1
86	Bolivia	1.77	(POP2010/POP2000)**(1/10)-1
87	Brunei	1.76	(POP2010/POP2000)**(1/10)-1
88	San Marino	1.71	(POP2010/POP2000)**(1/10)-1
89	New Caledon	1.67	(POP2010/POP2000)**(1/10)-1
90	Paraguay	1.64	(POP2010/POP2000)**(1/10)-1
91	Maldives	1.64	(POP2010/POP2000)**(1/10)-1
92	Cambodia	1.58	(POP2010/POP2000)**(1/10)-1
93	Venezuela	1.56	(POP2010/POP2000)**(1/10)-1
94	Luxembourg	1.54	(POP2010/POP2000)**(1/10)-1
95	Ecuador	1.53	(POP2010/POP2000)**(1/10)-1
96	Bahamas	1.48	(POP2010/POP2000)**(1/10)-1

Table 4.20 Population Growth Rates, 2000-2010

Rank	Country	GRPOP	Source
97	Indonesia	1.44	(POP2010/POP2000)**(1/10)-1
98	Haiti	1.38	(POP2010/POP2000)**(1/10)-1
99	Bangladesh	1.38	(POP2010/POP2000)**(1/10)-1
100	Uzbekistan	1.35	(POP2010/POP2000)**(1/10)-1
101	Mexico	1.34	(POP2010/POP2000)**(1/10)-1
102	Reunion	1.33	(POP2010/POP2000)**(1/10)-1
103	Falkland Is	1.33	(POP2010/POP2000)**(1/10)-1
104	Nicaragua	1.33	(POP2010/POP2000)**(1/10)-1
105	Turkey	1.30	(POP2010/POP2000)**(1/10)-1
106	Australia	1.30	(POP2010/POP2000)**(1/10)-1
107	Seychelles	1.30	(POP2010/POP2000)**(1/10)-1
108	Suriname	1.29	(POP2010/POP2000)**(1/10)-1
109	Colombia	1.28	(POP2010/POP2000)**(1/10)-1
110	India	1.27	(POP2010/POP2000)**(1/10)-1
111	South Africa	1.25	(POP2010/POP2000)**(1/10)-1
112	Spain	1.25	(POP2010/POP2000)**(1/10)-1
113	Djibouti	1.25	(POP2010/POP2000)**(1/10)-1
114	Iceland	1.24	(POP2010/POP2000)**(1/10)-1
115	New Zealand	1.24	(POP2010/POP2000)**(1/10)-1
116	Cape Verde	1.24	(POP2010/POP2000)**(1/10)-1
117	Iran	1.22	(POP2010/POP2000)**(1/10)-1
118	Dominican R	1.22	(POP2010/POP2000)**(1/10)-1
119	Botswana	1.21	(POP2010/POP2000)**(1/10)-1
120	Turkmenistan	1.20	(POP2010/POP2000)**(1/10)-1
121	Fr Polynesia	1.19	(POP2010/POP2000)**(1/10)-1
122	Burma	1.19	(POP2010/POP2000)**(1/10)-1
123	Morocco	1.18	(POP2010/POP2000)**(1/10)-1
124	Brazil	1.18	(POP2010/POP2000)**(1/10)-1
125	Peru	1.16	(POP2010/POP2000)**(1/10)-1
126	Azerbaijan	1.15	(POP2010/POP2000)**(1/10)-1
127	Vietnam	1.14	(POP2010/POP2000)**(1/10)-1
128	Antigua & B	1.13	(POP2010/POP2000)**(1/10)-1
129	Costa Rica	1.12	(POP2010/POP2000)**(1/10)-1
130	Kyrgyzstan	1.10	(POP2010/POP2000)**(1/10)-1
131	Jersey	1.09	(POP2010/POP2000)**(1/10)-1
132	Swaziland	1.09	(POP2010/POP2000)**(1/10)-1
133	Curacao	1.07	(POP2010/POP2000)**(1/10)-1
134	Argentina	1.02	(POP2010/POP2000)**(1/10)-1
135	Mongolia	1.01	(POP2010/POP2000)**(1/10)-1
136	Isle of Man	1.01	(POP2010/POP2000)**(1/10)-1
137	Tunisia	0.99	(POP2010/POP2000)**(1/10)-1
138	US	0.93	(POP2010/POP2000)**(1/10)-1
139	Kazakhstan	0.92	(POP2010/POP2000)**(1/10)-1
140	Norway	0.90	(POP2010/POP2000)**(1/10)-1
141	Namibia	0.89	(POP2010/POP2000)**(1/10)-1
142	Liechtenstn	0.87	(POP2010/POP2000)**(1/10)-1
143	Switzerland	0.86	(POP2010/POP2000)**(1/10)-1
144	Lebanon	0.85	(POP2010/POP2000)**(1/10)-1

Table 4.20 Population Growth Rates, 2000-2010

Rank	Country	GRPOP	Source
145	St Kitts & N	0.84	(POP2010/POP2000)**(1/10)-1
146	Canada	0.78	(POP2010/POP2000)**(1/10)-1
147	Palau	0.76	(POP2010/POP2000)**(1/10)-1
148	Korea, South	0.70	(POP2010/POP2000)**(1/10)-1
149	Zimbabwe	0.70	(POP2010/POP2000)**(1/10)-1
150	Thailand	0.70	(POP2010/POP2000)**(1/10)-1
151	Sri Lanka	0.67	(POP2010/POP2000)**(1/10)-1
152	Kosovo	0.66	(POP2010/POP2000)**(1/10)-1
153	Korea, North	0.66	(POP2010/POP2000)**(1/10)-1
154	UK	0.65	(POP2010/POP2000)**(1/10)-1
155	France	0.64	(POP2010/POP2000)**(1/10)-1
156	Faroe Is	0.63	(POP2010/POP2000)**(1/10)-1
157	Saint Martin	0.63	(POP2010/POP2000)**(1/10)-1
158	Belgium	0.63	(POP2010/POP2000)**(1/10)-1
159	Saint Helena	0.62	(POP2010/POP2000)**(1/10)-1
160	Samoa	0.61	(POP2010/POP2000)**(1/10)-1
161	China	0.58	(POP2010/POP2000)**(1/10)-1
162	Malta	0.57	(POP2010/POP2000)**(1/10)-1
163	St Lucia	0.56	(POP2010/POP2000)**(1/10)-1
164	Sweden	0.56	(POP2010/POP2000)**(1/10)-1
165	Chile	0.55	(POP2010/POP2000)**(1/10)-1
166	Hong Kong	0.53	(POP2010/POP2000)**(1/10)-1
167	Nepal	0.52	(POP2010/POP2000)**(1/10)-1
168	Aruba	0.51	(POP2010/POP2000)**(1/10)-1
169	Guernsey	0.47	(POP2010/POP2000)**(1/10)-1
170	Mauritius	0.44	(POP2010/POP2000)**(1/10)-1
171	Fiji	0.43	(POP2010/POP2000)**(1/10)-1
172	Trinidad & T	0.43	(POP2010/POP2000)**(1/10)-1
173	Taiwan	0.42	(POP2010/POP2000)**(1/10)-1
174	Netherlands	0.42	(POP2010/POP2000)**(1/10)-1
175	Jamaica	0.41	(POP2010/POP2000)**(1/10)-1
176	Tonga	0.40	(POP2010/POP2000)**(1/10)-1
177	Denmark	0.39	(POP2010/POP2000)**(1/10)-1
178	Marshall Is	0.39	(POP2010/POP2000)**(1/10)-1
179	Guadeloupe	0.38	(POP2010/POP2000)**(1/10)-1
180	Finland	0.35	(POP2010/POP2000)**(1/10)-1
181	El Salvador	0.34	(POP2010/POP2000)**(1/10)-1
182	Bermuda	0.32	(POP2010/POP2000)**(1/10)-1
183	Slovenia	0.32	(POP2010/POP2000)**(1/10)-1
184	Portugal	0.30	(POP2010/POP2000)**(1/10)-1
185	Guyana	0.28	(POP2010/POP2000)**(1/10)-1
186	Monaco	0.28	(POP2010/POP2000)**(1/10)-1
187	Martinique	0.26	(POP2010/POP2000)**(1/10)-1
188	Barbados	0.26	(POP2010/POP2000)**(1/10)-1
189	Guam	0.26	(POP2010/POP2000)**(1/10)-1
190	Italy	0.25	(POP2010/POP2000)**(1/10)-1
191	Austria	0.23	(POP2010/POP2000)**(1/10)-1
192	Macedonia	0.23	(POP2010/POP2000)**(1/10)-1

Table 4.20 Population Growth Rates, 2000-2010

Rank	Country	GRPOP	Source
193	Czechia	0.21	(POP2010/POP2000)**(1/10)-1
194	Uruguay	0.18	(POP2010/POP2000)**(1/10)-1
195	Bosnia	0.16	(POP2010/POP2000)**(1/10)-1
196	Dominica	0.14	(POP2010/POP2000)**(1/10)-1
197	Japan	0.09	(POP2010/POP2000)**(1/10)-1
198	Georgia	0.08	(POP2010/POP2000)**(1/10)-1
199	Poland	0.06	(POP2010/POP2000)**(1/10)-1
200	Wallis & Fut	0.04	(POP2010/POP2000)**(1/10)-1
201	Lesotho	0.02	(POP2010/POP2000)**(1/10)-1
202	Cuba	0.02	(POP2010/POP2000)**(1/10)-1
204	Greenland	0.00	(POP2010/POP2000)**(1/10)-1
204	Grenada	0.00	(POP2010/POP2000)**(1/10)-1
204	Nauru	0.00	(POP2010/POP2000)**(1/10)-1
206	Slovakia	-0.04	(POP2010/POP2000)**(1/10)-1
207	Germany	-0.05	(POP2010/POP2000)**(1/10)-1
208	Greece	-0.19	(POP2010/POP2000)**(1/10)-1
209	Hungary	-0.20	(POP2010/POP2000)**(1/10)-1
210	Gibraltar	-0.21	(POP2010/POP2000)**(1/10)-1
211	Montenegro	-0.21	(POP2010/POP2000)**(1/10)-1
212	Puerto Rico	-0.24	(POP2010/POP2000)**(1/10)-1
213	Russia	-0.26	(POP2010/POP2000)**(1/10)-1
214	Virgin I, US	-0.28	(POP2010/POP2000)**(1/10)-1
215	Samoa, Amer	-0.36	(POP2010/POP2000)**(1/10)-1
216	Croatia	-0.36	(POP2010/POP2000)**(1/10)-1
217	Micronesia	-0.38	(POP2010/POP2000)**(1/10)-1
218	Serbia	-0.39	(POP2010/POP2000)**(1/10)-1
219	Tokelau	-0.41	(POP2010/POP2000)**(1/10)-1
220	Estonia	-0.47	(POP2010/POP2000)**(1/10)-1
221	Belarus	-0.49	(POP2010/POP2000)**(1/10)-1
222	Albania	-0.53	(POP2010/POP2000)**(1/10)-1
223	Armenia	-0.63	(POP2010/POP2000)**(1/10)-1
224	Ukraine	-0.70	(POP2010/POP2000)**(1/10)-1
225	Moldova	-0.70	(POP2010/POP2000)**(1/10)-1
226	Bulgaria	-0.75	(POP2010/POP2000)**(1/10)-1
227	St Vincent	-0.85	(POP2010/POP2000)**(1/10)-1
228	Romania	-0.98	(POP2010/POP2000)**(1/10)-1
229	Lithuania	-1.21	(POP2010/POP2000)**(1/10)-1
230	Latvia	-1.21	(POP2010/POP2000)**(1/10)-1
231	St Pierre&M	-1.37	(POP2010/POP2000)**(1/10)-1
232	Svalbard	-1.55	(POP2010/POP2000)**(1/10)-1
233	Montserrat	-2.22	(POP2010/POP2000)**(1/10)-1
234	N Mariana Is	-2.42	(POP2010/POP2000)**(1/10)-1
235	Niue	-4.35	(POP2010/POP2000)**(1/10)-1
236	Cook Is	-5.58	(POP2010/POP2000)**(1/10)-1

TABLE 4.21 POPULATION GROWTH RATES, 2010-2012			
Rank	Country	GRPOP	Source
1	Virgin I, Br	11.76	(POP2012/POP2010)**(1/2)-1
2	Qatar	5.95	(POP2012/POP2010)**(1/2)-1
3	South Sudan	4.99	(POP2012/POP2010)**(1/2)-1
4	Solomon Is	4.45	(POP2012/POP2010)**(1/2)-1
5	Zambia	3.82	(POP2012/POP2010)**(1/2)-1
6	Niger	3.58	(POP2012/POP2010)**(1/2)-1
7	Gaza Strip	3.48	(POP2012/POP2010)**(1/2)-1
8	Uganda	3.33	(POP2012/POP2010)**(1/2)-1
9	Kuwait	3.32	(POP2012/POP2010)**(1/2)-1
10	Malawi	3.26	(POP2012/POP2010)**(1/2)-1
11	Yemen	3.26	(POP2012/POP2010)**(1/2)-1
12	Saudi Arabia	3.25	(POP2012/POP2010)**(1/2)-1
13	Vanuatu	3.22	(POP2012/POP2010)**(1/2)-1
14	Iraq	3.17	(POP2012/POP2010)**(1/2)-1
15	Macao	3.11	(POP2012/POP2010)**(1/2)-1
16	W Sahara	3.09	(POP2012/POP2010)**(1/2)-1
17	Mali	3.07	(POP2012/POP2010)**(1/2)-1
18	Eritrea	3.04	(POP2012/POP2010)**(1/2)-1
19	Burkina Faso	3.03	(POP2012/POP2010)**(1/2)-1
20	Mayotte	3.01	(POP2012/POP2010)**(1/2)-1
21	UAE	3.00	(POP2012/POP2010)**(1/2)-1
22	Ethiopia	2.91	(POP2012/POP2010)**(1/2)-1
23	Sao Tome & P	2.91	(POP2012/POP2010)**(1/2)-1
24	Australia	2.91	(POP2012/POP2010)**(1/2)-1
25	Angola	2.89	(POP2012/POP2010)**(1/2)-1
26	West Bank	2.85	(POP2012/POP2010)**(1/2)-1
27	Togo	2.85	(POP2012/POP2010)**(1/2)-1
28	Equatorial G	2.82	(POP2012/POP2010)**(1/2)-1
29	Liberia	2.79	(POP2012/POP2010)**(1/2)-1
30	Benin	2.77	(POP2012/POP2010)**(1/2)-1
31	Madagascar	2.73	(POP2012/POP2010)**(1/2)-1
32	Ecuador	2.71	(POP2012/POP2010)**(1/2)-1
33	Ghana	2.69	(POP2012/POP2010)**(1/2)-1
34	Belize	2.69	(POP2012/POP2010)**(1/2)-1
35	Congo, Dem R	2.68	(POP2012/POP2010)**(1/2)-1
36	Tanzania	2.67	(POP2012/POP2010)**(1/2)-1
37	Chad	2.65	(POP2012/POP2010)**(1/2)-1
38	Rwanda	2.62	(POP2012/POP2010)**(1/2)-1
39	Egypt	2.61	(POP2012/POP2010)**(1/2)-1
40	Nigeria	2.59	(POP2012/POP2010)**(1/2)-1
41	Senegal	2.58	(POP2012/POP2010)**(1/2)-1
42	Guatemala	2.57	(POP2012/POP2010)**(1/2)-1
43	Kenya	2.54	(POP2012/POP2010)**(1/2)-1
44	Guinea	2.51	(POP2012/POP2010)**(1/2)-1
45	East Timor	2.51	(POP2012/POP2010)**(1/2)-1
46	Luxembourg	2.50	(POP2012/POP2010)**(1/2)-1
47	Cameroon	2.50	(POP2012/POP2010)**(1/2)-1
48	Malaysia	2.47	(POP2012/POP2010)**(1/2)-1

Table 4.21 Population Growth Rates, 2010-2012

Rank	Country	GRPOP	Source
49	Cyprus	2.47	(POP2012/POP2010)**(1/2)-1
50	Oman	2.45	(POP2012/POP2010)**(1/2)-1
51	Mozambique	2.44	(POP2012/POP2010)**(1/2)-1
52	Guinea-Biss	2.39	(POP2012/POP2010)**(1/2)-1
53	Gambia	2.37	(POP2012/POP2010)**(1/2)-1
54	Mauritania	2.37	(POP2012/POP2010)**(1/2)-1
55	Singapore	2.35	(POP2012/POP2010)**(1/2)-1
56	Uzbekistan	2.32	(POP2012/POP2010)**(1/2)-1
57	Turks & C Is	2.29	(POP2012/POP2010)**(1/2)-1
58	Congo, Rep	2.27	(POP2012/POP2010)**(1/2)-1
59	Kiribati	2.24	(POP2012/POP2010)**(1/2)-1
60	Jordan	2.22	(POP2012/POP2010)**(1/2)-1
61	Anguilla	2.21	(POP2012/POP2010)**(1/2)-1
62	CAR	2.17	(POP2012/POP2010)**(1/2)-1
63	Sierra Leone	2.15	(POP2012/POP2010)**(1/2)-1
64	Comoros	2.13	(POP2012/POP2010)**(1/2)-1
65	Afghanistan	2.08	(POP2012/POP2010)**(1/2)-1
66	Ivory Coast	2.08	(POP2012/POP2010)**(1/2)-1
67	Laos	2.06	(POP2012/POP2010)**(1/2)-1
68	Burundi	2.06	(POP2012/POP2010)**(1/2)-1
69	Venezuela	2.03	(POP2012/POP2010)**(1/2)-1
70	Honduras	2.02	(POP2012/POP2010)**(1/2)-1
71	Bolivia	2.02	(POP2012/POP2010)**(1/2)-1
72	Tajikistan	2.00	(POP2012/POP2010)**(1/2)-1
73	Papua New G	1.98	(POP2012/POP2010)**(1/2)-1
74	Algeria	1.97	(POP2012/POP2010)**(1/2)-1
75	Gabon	1.93	(POP2012/POP2010)**(1/2)-1
76	Botswana	1.88	(POP2012/POP2010)**(1/2)-1
77	Sudan	1.84	(POP2012/POP2010)**(1/2)-1
78	Mexico	1.83	(POP2012/POP2010)**(1/2)-1
79	Canada	1.73	(POP2012/POP2010)**(1/2)-1
80	Cambodia	1.71	(POP2012/POP2010)**(1/2)-1
81	Israel	1.70	(POP2012/POP2010)**(1/2)-1
82	Syria	1.70	(POP2012/POP2010)**(1/2)-1
83	Brunei	1.69	(POP2012/POP2010)**(1/2)-1
84	Panama	1.69	(POP2012/POP2010)**(1/2)-1
85	Maldives	1.64	(POP2012/POP2010)**(1/2)-1
86	India	1.64	(POP2012/POP2010)**(1/2)-1
87	Bhutan	1.63	(POP2012/POP2010)**(1/2)-1
88	Somalia	1.63	(POP2012/POP2010)**(1/2)-1
89	Pakistan	1.57	(POP2012/POP2010)**(1/2)-1
90	Kazakhstan	1.52	(POP2012/POP2010)**(1/2)-1
91	Bahamas	1.49	(POP2012/POP2010)**(1/2)-1
92	Suriname	1.48	(POP2012/POP2010)**(1/2)-1
93	South Africa	1.45	(POP2012/POP2010)**(1/2)-1
94	New Caledon	1.45	(POP2012/POP2010)**(1/2)-1
95	Nicaragua	1.44	(POP2012/POP2010)**(1/2)-1
96	Indonesia	1.44	(POP2012/POP2010)**(1/2)-1

Table 4.21 Population Growth Rates, 2010-2012

Rank	Country	GRPOP	Source
97	Swaziland	1.41	(POP2012/POP2010)**(1/2)-1
98	Namibia	1.41	(POP2012/POP2010)**(1/2)-1
99	Turkey	1.39	(POP2012/POP2010)**(1/2)-1
100	Spain	1.37	(POP2012/POP2010)**(1/2)-1
101	Bangladesh	1.36	(POP2012/POP2010)**(1/2)-1
102	Nepal	1.36	(POP2012/POP2010)**(1/2)-1
103	Azerbaijan	1.34	(POP2012/POP2010)**(1/2)-1
104	Falkland Is	1.32	(POP2012/POP2010)**(1/2)-1
105	Antigua & B	1.32	(POP2012/POP2010)**(1/2)-1
106	Aruba	1.30	(POP2012/POP2010)**(1/2)-1
107	Iran	1.29	(POP2012/POP2010)**(1/2)-1
108	Paraguay	1.27	(POP2012/POP2010)**(1/2)-1
109	Cape Verde	1.27	(POP2012/POP2010)**(1/2)-1
110	Djibouti	1.27	(POP2012/POP2010)**(1/2)-1
111	Fr Polynesia	1.23	(POP2012/POP2010)**(1/2)-1
112	Dominican R	1.21	(POP2012/POP2010)**(1/2)-1
113	Saint Martin	1.19	(POP2012/POP2010)**(1/2)-1
114	Colombia	1.15	(POP2012/POP2010)**(1/2)-1
115	Turkmenistan	1.15	(POP2012/POP2010)**(1/2)-1
116	Norway	1.14	(POP2012/POP2010)**(1/2)-1
117	Argentina	1.14	(POP2012/POP2010)**(1/2)-1
118	Guiana, Fr	1.13	(POP2012/POP2010)**(1/2)-1
119	Costa Rica	1.11	(POP2012/POP2010)**(1/2)-1
120	Zimbabwe	1.10	(POP2012/POP2010)**(1/2)-1
121	Kyrgyzstan	1.09	(POP2012/POP2010)**(1/2)-1
122	Burma	1.08	(POP2012/POP2010)**(1/2)-1
123	Switzerland	1.07	(POP2012/POP2010)**(1/2)-1
124	Morocco	1.07	(POP2012/POP2010)**(1/2)-1
125	Vietnam	1.06	(POP2012/POP2010)**(1/2)-1
126	Tunisia	1.05	(POP2012/POP2010)**(1/2)-1
127	Reunion	1.04	(POP2012/POP2010)**(1/2)-1
128	Peru	1.03	(POP2012/POP2010)**(1/2)-1
129	Mongolia	1.03	(POP2012/POP2010)**(1/2)-1
130	Isle of Man	1.02	(POP2012/POP2010)**(1/2)-1
131	Monaco	1.01	(POP2012/POP2010)**(1/2)-1
132	St Lucia	0.99	(POP2012/POP2010)**(1/2)-1
133	St Vincent	0.98	(POP2012/POP2010)**(1/2)-1
134	Chile	0.97	(POP2012/POP2010)**(1/2)-1
135	Belgium	0.96	(POP2012/POP2010)**(1/2)-1
136	Brazil	0.94	(POP2012/POP2010)**(1/2)-1
137	Liechtenstn	0.92	(POP2012/POP2010)**(1/2)-1
138	Tuvalu	0.90	(POP2012/POP2010)**(1/2)-1
139	Curacao	0.89	(POP2012/POP2010)**(1/2)-1
140	Philippines	0.84	(POP2012/POP2010)**(1/2)-1
141	Haiti	0.84	(POP2012/POP2010)**(1/2)-1
142	Jersey	0.82	(POP2012/POP2010)**(1/2)-1
143	Sweden	0.75	(POP2012/POP2010)**(1/2)-1
144	UK	0.73	(POP2012/POP2010)**(1/2)-1

TABLE 4.21 POPULATION GROWTH RATES, 2010-2012			
Rank	Country	GRPOP	Source
145	St Kitts & N	0.73	(POP2012/POP2010)**(1/2)-1
146	US	0.72	(POP2012/POP2010)**(1/2)-1
147	Sri Lanka	0.71	(POP2012/POP2010)**(1/2)-1
148	Samoa	0.71	(POP2012/POP2010)**(1/2)-1
149	New Zealand	0.70	(POP2012/POP2010)**(1/2)-1
150	Sint Maarten	0.70	(POP2012/POP2010)**(1/2)-1
151	Thailand	0.70	(POP2012/POP2010)**(1/2)-1
152	Trinidad & T	0.65	(POP2012/POP2010)**(1/2)-1
153	Palau	0.65	(POP2012/POP2010)**(1/2)-1
154	San Marino	0.62	(POP2012/POP2010)**(1/2)-1
155	Kosovo	0.60	(POP2012/POP2010)**(1/2)-1
156	Hong Kong	0.60	(POP2012/POP2010)**(1/2)-1
157	Denmark	0.56	(POP2012/POP2010)**(1/2)-1
158	Korea, North	0.54	(POP2012/POP2010)**(1/2)-1
159	Iceland	0.52	(POP2012/POP2010)**(1/2)-1
160	Bermuda	0.52	(POP2012/POP2010)**(1/2)-1
161	Georgia	0.51	(POP2012/POP2010)**(1/2)-1
162	Guernsey	0.51	(POP2012/POP2010)**(1/2)-1
163	Korea, South	0.50	(POP2012/POP2010)**(1/2)-1
164	France	0.50	(POP2012/POP2010)**(1/2)-1
165	China	0.48	(POP2012/POP2010)**(1/2)-1
166	Finland	0.48	(POP2012/POP2010)**(1/2)-1
167	Fiji	0.47	(POP2012/POP2010)**(1/2)-1
168	Austria	0.46	(POP2012/POP2010)**(1/2)-1
169	Montserrat	0.45	(POP2012/POP2010)**(1/2)-1
170	Mauritius	0.43	(POP2012/POP2010)**(1/2)-1
171	Italy	0.42	(POP2012/POP2010)**(1/2)-1
172	Guam	0.42	(POP2012/POP2010)**(1/2)-1
173	Ireland	0.42	(POP2012/POP2010)**(1/2)-1
174	Netherlands	0.39	(POP2012/POP2010)**(1/2)-1
175	Saint Helena	0.38	(POP2012/POP2010)**(1/2)-1
176	Marshall Is	0.38	(POP2012/POP2010)**(1/2)-1
177	Jamaica	0.36	(POP2012/POP2010)**(1/2)-1
178	Wallis & Fut	0.36	(POP2012/POP2010)**(1/2)-1
179	Greece	0.34	(POP2012/POP2010)**(1/2)-1
180	Dominica	0.33	(POP2012/POP2010)**(1/2)-1
181	Taiwan	0.32	(POP2012/POP2010)**(1/2)-1
182	El Salvador	0.31	(POP2012/POP2010)**(1/2)-1
183	Lesotho	0.28	(POP2012/POP2010)**(1/2)-1
184	Gibraltar	0.27	(POP2012/POP2010)**(1/2)-1
185	Slovakia	0.27	(POP2012/POP2010)**(1/2)-1
186	Barbados	0.24	(POP2012/POP2010)**(1/2)-1
187	Malta	0.24	(POP2012/POP2010)**(1/2)-1
188	Guyana	0.22	(POP2012/POP2010)**(1/2)-1
189	Portugal	0.20	(POP2012/POP2010)**(1/2)-1
190	Czechia	0.20	(POP2012/POP2010)**(1/2)-1
191	Uruguay	0.19	(POP2012/POP2010)**(1/2)-1
192	Slovenia	0.18	(POP2012/POP2010)**(1/2)-1

Table 4.21 Population Growth Rates, 2010-2012

Rank	Country	GRPOP	Source
193	Guadeloupe	0.17	(POP2012/POP2010)**(1/2)-1
194	Macedonia	0.15	(POP2012/POP2010)**(1/2)-1
195	Greenland	0.12	(POP2012/POP2010)**(1/2)-1
196	Russia	0.09	(POP2012/POP2010)**(1/2)-1
197	Poland	0.07	(POP2012/POP2010)**(1/2)-1
198	Lebanon	0.06	(POP2012/POP2010)**(1/2)-1
201	Bosnia	0.00	(POP2012/POP2010)**(1/2)-1
201	Cayman Is	0.00	(POP2012/POP2010)**(1/2)-1
201	Grenada	0.00	(POP2012/POP2010)**(1/2)-1
201	Montenegro	0.00	(POP2012/POP2010)**(1/2)-1
201	Tonga	0.00	(POP2012/POP2010)**(1/2)-1
204	Cuba	-0.01	(POP2012/POP2010)**(1/2)-1
205	Samoa, Amer	-0.18	(POP2012/POP2010)**(1/2)-1
206	Belarus	-0.20	(POP2012/POP2010)**(1/2)-1
207	Japan	-0.21	(POP2012/POP2010)**(1/2)-1
208	Moldova	-0.21	(POP2012/POP2010)**(1/2)-1
209	Ukraine	-0.25	(POP2012/POP2010)**(1/2)-1
210	Virgin I, US	-0.32	(POP2012/POP2010)**(1/2)-1
211	Micronesia	-0.33	(POP2012/POP2010)**(1/2)-1
212	Nauru	-0.34	(POP2012/POP2010)**(1/2)-1
213	Croatia	-0.35	(POP2012/POP2010)**(1/2)-1
214	Puerto Rico	-0.43	(POP2012/POP2010)**(1/2)-1
215	Armenia	-0.44	(POP2012/POP2010)**(1/2)-1
216	Serbia	-0.44	(POP2012/POP2010)**(1/2)-1
217	Germany	-0.45	(POP2012/POP2010)**(1/2)-1
218	Bahrain	-0.46	(POP2012/POP2010)**(1/2)-1
219	Estonia	-0.49	(POP2012/POP2010)**(1/2)-1
220	Martinique	-0.51	(POP2012/POP2010)**(1/2)-1
221	Faroe Is	-0.55	(POP2012/POP2010)**(1/2)-1
222	Bulgaria	-0.58	(POP2012/POP2010)**(1/2)-1
223	Libya	-0.59	(POP2012/POP2010)**(1/2)-1
224	Hungary	-0.64	(POP2012/POP2010)**(1/2)-1
225	Romania	-1.03	(POP2012/POP2010)**(1/2)-1
226	Tokelau	-1.15	(POP2012/POP2010)**(1/2)-1
227	Latvia	-1.24	(POP2012/POP2010)**(1/2)-1
228	Lithuania	-1.48	(POP2012/POP2010)**(1/2)-1
229	St Pierre&M	-1.50	(POP2012/POP2010)**(1/2)-1
230	Seychelles	-1.52	(POP2012/POP2010)**(1/2)-1
231	Albania	-1.54	(POP2012/POP2010)**(1/2)-1
232	Svalbard	-2.37	(POP2012/POP2010)**(1/2)-1
233	N Mariana Is	-2.73	(POP2012/POP2010)**(1/2)-1
234	Cook Is	-3.14	(POP2012/POP2010)**(1/2)-1
235	Niue	-3.19	(POP2012/POP2010)**(1/2)-1
236	Andorra	-3.96	(POP2012/POP2010)**(1/2)-1

Table 4.22 Population Growth Rates, 2012-2020, Forecast			
Rank	Country	GRPOP	Source
1	Turks & C Is	4.61	(POP2020/POP2012)**(1/8)-1
2	South Sudan	4.09	(POP2020/POP2012)**(1/8)-1
3	Virgin I, Br	3.93	(POP2020/POP2012)**(1/8)-1
4	Niger	3.59	(POP2020/POP2012)**(1/8)-1
5	Malawi	3.35	(POP2020/POP2012)**(1/8)-1
6	Uganda	3.27	(POP2020/POP2012)**(1/8)-1
7	Zambia	3.05	(POP2020/POP2012)**(1/8)-1
8	Burkina Faso	3.00	(POP2020/POP2012)**(1/8)-1
9	Mali	3.00	(POP2020/POP2012)**(1/8)-1
10	Iraq	2.99	(POP2020/POP2012)**(1/8)-1
11	Yemen	2.96	(POP2020/POP2012)**(1/8)-1
12	Guiana, Fr	2.83	(POP2020/POP2012)**(1/8)-1
13	W Sahara	2.80	(POP2020/POP2012)**(1/8)-1
14	Angola	2.79	(POP2020/POP2012)**(1/8)-1
15	Tanzania	2.78	(POP2020/POP2012)**(1/8)-1
16	Gaza Strip	2.78	(POP2020/POP2012)**(1/8)-1
17	Rwanda	2.74	(POP2020/POP2012)**(1/8)-1
18	Benin	2.65	(POP2020/POP2012)**(1/8)-1
19	Eritrea	2.60	(POP2020/POP2012)**(1/8)-1
20	Madagascar	2.57	(POP2020/POP2012)**(1/8)-1
21	Liberia	2.56	(POP2020/POP2012)**(1/8)-1
22	Mayotte	2.56	(POP2020/POP2012)**(1/8)-1
23	Chad	2.55	(POP2020/POP2012)**(1/8)-1
24	Congo, Dem R	2.55	(POP2020/POP2012)**(1/8)-1
25	Equatorial G	2.55	(POP2020/POP2012)**(1/8)-1
26	Nigeria	2.53	(POP2020/POP2012)**(1/8)-1
27	Guinea	2.48	(POP2020/POP2012)**(1/8)-1
28	Mozambique	2.47	(POP2020/POP2012)**(1/8)-1
29	Guatemala	2.46	(POP2020/POP2012)**(1/8)-1
30	Senegal	2.45	(POP2020/POP2012)**(1/8)-1
31	East Timor	2.42	(POP2020/POP2012)**(1/8)-1
32	Vanuatu	2.34	(POP2020/POP2012)**(1/8)-1
33	Papua New G	2.34	(POP2020/POP2012)**(1/8)-1
34	Afghanistan	2.33	(POP2020/POP2012)**(1/8)-1
35	Ghana	2.26	(POP2020/POP2012)**(1/8)-1
36	Anguilla	2.26	(POP2020/POP2012)**(1/8)-1
37	Mauritania	2.22	(POP2020/POP2012)**(1/8)-1
38	Kuwait	2.14	(POP2020/POP2012)**(1/8)-1
39	CAR	2.14	(POP2020/POP2012)**(1/8)-1
40	Solomon Is	2.14	(POP2020/POP2012)**(1/8)-1
41	Congo, Rep	2.13	(POP2020/POP2012)**(1/8)-1
42	Macao	2.12	(POP2020/POP2012)**(1/8)-1
43	Gambia	2.11	(POP2020/POP2012)**(1/8)-1
44	Cameroon	2.10	(POP2020/POP2012)**(1/8)-1
45	Zimbabwe	2.08	(POP2020/POP2012)**(1/8)-1
46	Qatar	2.08	(POP2020/POP2012)**(1/8)-1
47	Ethiopia	2.06	(POP2020/POP2012)**(1/8)-1

Table 4.22 Population Growth Rates, 2012-2020, Forecast

Rank	Country	GRPOP	Source
48	Guinea-Biss	2.05	(POP2020/POP2012)**(1/8)-1
49	West Bank	2.04	(POP2020/POP2012)**(1/8)-1
50	Sao Tome & P	2.01	(POP2020/POP2012)**(1/8)-1
51	Sierra Leone	2.01	(POP2020/POP2012)**(1/8)-1
52	Togo	1.99	(POP2020/POP2012)**(1/8)-1
53	Djibouti	1.97	(POP2020/POP2012)**(1/8)-1
54	Somalia	1.93	(POP2020/POP2012)**(1/8)-1
55	Singapore	1.92	(POP2020/POP2012)**(1/8)-1
56	Belize	1.90	(POP2020/POP2012)**(1/8)-1
57	Gabon	1.90	(POP2020/POP2012)**(1/8)-1
58	Ivory Coast	1.90	(POP2020/POP2012)**(1/8)-1
59	Kenya	1.88	(POP2020/POP2012)**(1/8)-1
60	Honduras	1.87	(POP2020/POP2012)**(1/8)-1
61	Jordan	1.82	(POP2020/POP2012)**(1/8)-1
62	Burundi	1.78	(POP2020/POP2012)**(1/8)-1
63	UAE	1.78	(POP2020/POP2012)**(1/8)-1
64	Libya	1.76	(POP2020/POP2012)**(1/8)-1
65	Comoros	1.75	(POP2020/POP2012)**(1/8)-1
66	Sudan	1.70	(POP2020/POP2012)**(1/8)-1
67	Syria	1.66	(POP2020/POP2012)**(1/8)-1
68	Egypt	1.65	(POP2020/POP2012)**(1/8)-1
69	Bolivia	1.61	(POP2020/POP2012)**(1/8)-1
70	Kiribati	1.59	(POP2020/POP2012)**(1/8)-1
71	Namibia	1.58	(POP2020/POP2012)**(1/8)-1
72	Oman	1.57	(POP2020/POP2012)**(1/8)-1
73	Cambodia	1.56	(POP2020/POP2012)**(1/8)-1
74	Nepal	1.54	(POP2020/POP2012)**(1/8)-1
75	Panama	1.54	(POP2020/POP2012)**(1/8)-1
76	Brunei	1.53	(POP2020/POP2012)**(1/8)-1
77	Bahrain	1.51	(POP2020/POP2012)**(1/8)-1
78	Israel	1.51	(POP2020/POP2012)**(1/8)-1
79	Philippines	1.51	(POP2020/POP2012)**(1/8)-1
80	Saudi Arabia	1.47	(POP2020/POP2012)**(1/8)-1
81	Pakistan	1.46	(POP2020/POP2012)**(1/8)-1
82	Mongolia	1.46	(POP2020/POP2012)**(1/8)-1
83	Australia	1.41	(POP2020/POP2012)**(1/8)-1
84	Tajikistan	1.41	(POP2020/POP2012)**(1/8)-1
85	Laos	1.38	(POP2020/POP2012)**(1/8)-1
86	Luxembourg	1.37	(POP2020/POP2012)**(1/8)-1
87	Botswana	1.33	(POP2020/POP2012)**(1/8)-1
88	Falkland Is	1.33	(POP2020/POP2012)**(1/8)-1
89	Svalbard	1.30	(POP2020/POP2012)**(1/8)-1
90	Uzbekistan	1.30	(POP2020/POP2012)**(1/8)-1
91	Nicaragua	1.30	(POP2020/POP2012)**(1/8)-1
92	Malaysia	1.27	(POP2020/POP2012)**(1/8)-1
93	Algeria	1.27	(POP2020/POP2012)**(1/8)-1
94	Bhutan	1.26	(POP2020/POP2012)**(1/8)-1
95	Marshall Is	1.25	(POP2020/POP2012)**(1/8)-1

Table 4.22 Population Growth Rates, 2012-2020, Forecast

Rank	Country	GRPOP	Source
96	India	1.25	(POP2020/POP2012)**(1/8)-1
97	Venezuela	1.25	(POP2020/POP2012)**(1/8)-1
98	Costa Rica	1.24	(POP2020/POP2012)**(1/8)-1
99	Norway	1.24	(POP2020/POP2012)**(1/8)-1
100	Maldives	1.21	(POP2020/POP2012)**(1/8)-1
101	New Caledon	1.20	(POP2020/POP2012)**(1/8)-1
102	Kyrgyzstan	1.20	(POP2020/POP2012)**(1/8)-1
103	Paraguay	1.20	(POP2020/POP2012)**(1/8)-1
104	Swaziland	1.19	(POP2020/POP2012)**(1/8)-1
105	St Lucia	1.18	(POP2020/POP2012)**(1/8)-1
106	Bangladesh	1.18	(POP2020/POP2012)**(1/8)-1
107	Cyprus	1.16	(POP2020/POP2012)**(1/8)-1
108	N Mariana Is	1.15	(POP2020/POP2012)**(1/8)-1
109	Dominican R	1.14	(POP2020/POP2012)**(1/8)-1
110	Bahamas	1.14	(POP2020/POP2012)**(1/8)-1
111	Kazakhstan	1.13	(POP2020/POP2012)**(1/8)-1
112	Turkmenistan	1.13	(POP2020/POP2012)**(1/8)-1
113	Azerbaijan	1.11	(POP2020/POP2012)**(1/8)-1
114	Haiti	1.08	(POP2020/POP2012)**(1/8)-1
115	Seychelles	1.06	(POP2020/POP2012)**(1/8)-1
116	Turkey	1.04	(POP2020/POP2012)**(1/8)-1
117	UK	1.04	(POP2020/POP2012)**(1/8)-1
118	Colombia	1.03	(POP2020/POP2012)**(1/8)-1
119	Ecuador	1.02	(POP2020/POP2012)**(1/8)-1
120	Ireland	1.02	(POP2020/POP2012)**(1/8)-1
121	Vietnam	1.02	(POP2020/POP2012)**(1/8)-1
122	Burma	1.01	(POP2020/POP2012)**(1/8)-1
123	Morocco	0.99	(POP2020/POP2012)**(1/8)-1
124	Reunion	0.97	(POP2020/POP2012)**(1/8)-1
125	Peru	0.97	(POP2020/POP2012)**(1/8)-1
126	Mexico	0.95	(POP2020/POP2012)**(1/8)-1
127	Indonesia	0.95	(POP2020/POP2012)**(1/8)-1
128	Fr Polynesia	0.94	(POP2020/POP2012)**(1/8)-1
129	Antigua & B	0.94	(POP2020/POP2012)**(1/8)-1
130	Iceland	0.93	(POP2020/POP2012)**(1/8)-1
131	Cape Verde	0.92	(POP2020/POP2012)**(1/8)-1
132	Hong Kong	0.91	(POP2020/POP2012)**(1/8)-1
133	Iran	0.90	(POP2020/POP2012)**(1/8)-1
134	US	0.89	(POP2020/POP2012)**(1/8)-1
135	Tunisia	0.87	(POP2020/POP2012)**(1/8)-1
136	Tuvalu	0.87	(POP2020/POP2012)**(1/8)-1
137	New Zealand	0.86	(POP2020/POP2012)**(1/8)-1
138	Sri Lanka	0.83	(POP2020/POP2012)**(1/8)-1
139	Suriname	0.82	(POP2020/POP2012)**(1/8)-1
140	Argentina	0.82	(POP2020/POP2012)**(1/8)-1
141	Chile	0.81	(POP2020/POP2012)**(1/8)-1
142	Jersey	0.79	(POP2020/POP2012)**(1/8)-1
143	Sweden	0.79	(POP2020/POP2012)**(1/8)-1

Table 4.22 Population Growth Rates, 2012-2020, Forecast			
Rank	Country	GRPOP	Source
144	St Kitts & N	0.78	(POP2020/POP2012)**(1/8)-1
145	Liechtenstn	0.78	(POP2020/POP2012)**(1/8)-1
146	Brazil	0.77	(POP2020/POP2012)**(1/8)-1
147	Isle of Man	0.75	(POP2020/POP2012)**(1/8)-1
148	Saint Martin	0.73	(POP2020/POP2012)**(1/8)-1
149	Palau	0.72	(POP2020/POP2012)**(1/8)-1
150	Switzerland	0.72	(POP2020/POP2012)**(1/8)-1
151	Sint Maarten	0.71	(POP2020/POP2012)**(1/8)-1
152	Canada	0.71	(POP2020/POP2012)**(1/8)-1
153	Guam	0.66	(POP2020/POP2012)**(1/8)-1
154	Cayman Is	0.65	(POP2020/POP2012)**(1/8)-1
155	Kosovo	0.64	(POP2020/POP2012)**(1/8)-1
156	Guernsey	0.62	(POP2020/POP2012)**(1/8)-1
157	Saint Helena	0.58	(POP2020/POP2012)**(1/8)-1
158	South Africa	0.57	(POP2020/POP2012)**(1/8)-1
159	Belgium	0.56	(POP2020/POP2012)**(1/8)-1
160	Spain	0.56	(POP2020/POP2012)**(1/8)-1
161	Korea, North	0.53	(POP2020/POP2012)**(1/8)-1
162	Curacao	0.51	(POP2020/POP2012)**(1/8)-1
163	Fiji	0.49	(POP2020/POP2012)**(1/8)-1
164	Grenada	0.48	(POP2020/POP2012)**(1/8)-1
165	Mauritius	0.47	(POP2020/POP2012)**(1/8)-1
166	Finland	0.46	(POP2020/POP2012)**(1/8)-1
167	Thailand	0.45	(POP2020/POP2012)**(1/8)-1
168	Dominica	0.44	(POP2020/POP2012)**(1/8)-1
169	Monaco	0.43	(POP2020/POP2012)**(1/8)-1
170	France	0.42	(POP2020/POP2012)**(1/8)-1
171	Austria	0.40	(POP2020/POP2012)**(1/8)-1
172	Faroe Is	0.39	(POP2020/POP2012)**(1/8)-1
173	Korea, South	0.38	(POP2020/POP2012)**(1/8)-1
174	Tonga	0.36	(POP2020/POP2012)**(1/8)-1
175	Samoa	0.35	(POP2020/POP2012)**(1/8)-1
176	Denmark	0.34	(POP2020/POP2012)**(1/8)-1
177	Lebanon	0.34	(POP2020/POP2012)**(1/8)-1
178	Malta	0.33	(POP2020/POP2012)**(1/8)-1
179	Guadeloupe	0.33	(POP2020/POP2012)**(1/8)-1
180	Slovenia	0.32	(POP2020/POP2012)**(1/8)-1
181	Netherlands	0.32	(POP2020/POP2012)**(1/8)-1
182	China	0.30	(POP2020/POP2012)**(1/8)-1
183	Jamaica	0.30	(POP2020/POP2012)**(1/8)-1
184	Aruba	0.28	(POP2020/POP2012)**(1/8)-1
185	Czechia	0.28	(POP2020/POP2012)**(1/8)-1
186	Italy	0.28	(POP2020/POP2012)**(1/8)-1
187	Uruguay	0.26	(POP2020/POP2012)**(1/8)-1
188	El Salvador	0.26	(POP2020/POP2012)**(1/8)-1
189	Guyana	0.26	(POP2020/POP2012)**(1/8)-1
190	Bermuda	0.26	(POP2020/POP2012)**(1/8)-1
191	Trinidad & T	0.25	(POP2020/POP2012)**(1/8)-1

Table 4.22 Population Growth Rates, 2012-2020, Forecast			
Rank	Country	GRPOP	Source
192	Lesotho	0.25	(POP2020/POP2012)**(1/8)-1
193	St Vincent	0.24	(POP2020/POP2012)**(1/8)-1
194	Slovakia	0.24	(POP2020/POP2012)**(1/8)-1
195	San Marino	0.23	(POP2020/POP2012)**(1/8)-1
196	Greece	0.21	(POP2020/POP2012)**(1/8)-1
197	Barbados	0.21	(POP2020/POP2012)**(1/8)-1
198	Taiwan	0.16	(POP2020/POP2012)**(1/8)-1
199	Portugal	0.10	(POP2020/POP2012)**(1/8)-1
200	Martinique	0.10	(POP2020/POP2012)**(1/8)-1
201	Wallis & Fut	0.09	(POP2020/POP2012)**(1/8)-1
202	Nauru	0.08	(POP2020/POP2012)**(1/8)-1
203	Montenegro	0.08	(POP2020/POP2012)**(1/8)-1
204	Poland	0.06	(POP2020/POP2012)**(1/8)-1
205	Armenia	0.06	(POP2020/POP2012)**(1/8)-1
206	Macedonia	0.04	(POP2020/POP2012)**(1/8)-1
207	Greenland	-0.03	(POP2020/POP2012)**(1/8)-1
208	Cuba	-0.04	(POP2020/POP2012)**(1/8)-1
209	Germany	-0.12	(POP2020/POP2012)**(1/8)-1
210	Russia	-0.12	(POP2020/POP2012)**(1/8)-1
211	Gibraltar	-0.13	(POP2020/POP2012)**(1/8)-1
212	Estonia	-0.15	(POP2020/POP2012)**(1/8)-1
213	Japan	-0.18	(POP2020/POP2012)**(1/8)-1
214	Samoa, Amer	-0.18	(POP2020/POP2012)**(1/8)-1
215	Albania	-0.23	(POP2020/POP2012)**(1/8)-1
216	Croatia	-0.24	(POP2020/POP2012)**(1/8)-1
217	Romania	-0.26	(POP2020/POP2012)**(1/8)-1
218	Micronesia	-0.29	(POP2020/POP2012)**(1/8)-1
219	Hungary	-0.29	(POP2020/POP2012)**(1/8)-1
220	Belarus	-0.31	(POP2020/POP2012)**(1/8)-1
221	Bosnia	-0.34	(POP2020/POP2012)**(1/8)-1
222	Andorra	-0.39	(POP2020/POP2012)**(1/8)-1
223	Serbia	-0.46	(POP2020/POP2012)**(1/8)-1
224	Latvia	-0.47	(POP2020/POP2012)**(1/8)-1
225	Ukraine	-0.50	(POP2020/POP2012)**(1/8)-1
226	Georgia	-0.50	(POP2020/POP2012)**(1/8)-1
227	Tokelau	-0.53	(POP2020/POP2012)**(1/8)-1
228	Lithuania	-0.55	(POP2020/POP2012)**(1/8)-1
229	Puerto Rico	-0.56	(POP2020/POP2012)**(1/8)-1
230	Bulgaria	-0.58	(POP2020/POP2012)**(1/8)-1
231	Virgin I, US	-0.65	(POP2020/POP2012)**(1/8)-1
232	Moldova	-0.67	(POP2020/POP2012)**(1/8)-1
233	St Pierre&M	-1.39	(POP2020/POP2012)**(1/8)-1
234	Montserrat	-1.79	(POP2020/POP2012)**(1/8)-1
235	Niue	-4.16	(POP2020/POP2012)**(1/8)-1
236	Cook Is	-5.18	(POP2020/POP2012)**(1/8)-1

Table 4.23 Population Growth Rates, 2020-2030, Forecast			
Rank	Country	GRPOP	Source
1	Turks & C Is	4.61	(POP2030/POP2020)**(1/10)-1
2	Virgin I, Br	3.93	(POP2030/POP2020)**(1/10)-1
3	Niger	3.40	(POP2030/POP2020)**(1/10)-1
4	Malawi	3.14	(POP2030/POP2020)**(1/10)-1
5	Uganda	3.00	(POP2030/POP2020)**(1/10)-1
6	Zambia	2.87	(POP2030/POP2020)**(1/10)-1
7	Burkina Faso	2.77	(POP2030/POP2020)**(1/10)-1
8	Mali	2.70	(POP2030/POP2020)**(1/10)-1
9	Tanzania	2.65	(POP2030/POP2020)**(1/10)-1
10	Angola	2.63	(POP2030/POP2020)**(1/10)-1
11	Iraq	2.62	(POP2030/POP2020)**(1/10)-1
12	South Sudan	2.53	(POP2030/POP2020)**(1/10)-1
13	Yemen	2.52	(POP2030/POP2020)**(1/10)-1
14	Mozambique	2.50	(POP2030/POP2020)**(1/10)-1
15	Somalia	2.49	(POP2030/POP2020)**(1/10)-1
16	Chad	2.45	(POP2030/POP2020)**(1/10)-1
17	Benin	2.42	(POP2030/POP2020)**(1/10)-1
18	Nigeria	2.41	(POP2030/POP2020)**(1/10)-1
19	Liberia	2.38	(POP2030/POP2020)**(1/10)-1
20	W Sahara	2.33	(POP2030/POP2020)**(1/10)-1
21	Rwanda	2.27	(POP2030/POP2020)**(1/10)-1
22	Anguilla	2.26	(POP2030/POP2020)**(1/10)-1
23	Guinea	2.25	(POP2030/POP2020)**(1/10)-1
24	Afghanistan	2.23	(POP2030/POP2020)**(1/10)-1
25	Congo, Dem R	2.22	(POP2030/POP2020)**(1/10)-1
26	Madagascar	2.17	(POP2030/POP2020)**(1/10)-1
27	Guiana, Fr	2.16	(POP2030/POP2020)**(1/10)-1
28	Senegal	2.16	(POP2030/POP2020)**(1/10)-1
29	Guatemala	2.14	(POP2030/POP2020)**(1/10)-1
30	Solomon Is	2.13	(POP2030/POP2020)**(1/10)-1
31	Congo, Rep	2.12	(POP2030/POP2020)**(1/10)-1
32	Ghana	2.10	(POP2030/POP2020)**(1/10)-1
33	Eritrea	2.06	(POP2030/POP2020)**(1/10)-1
34	CAR	2.03	(POP2030/POP2020)**(1/10)-1
35	Mayotte	2.03	(POP2030/POP2020)**(1/10)-1
36	East Timor	2.01	(POP2030/POP2020)**(1/10)-1
37	Equatorial G	1.99	(POP2030/POP2020)**(1/10)-1
38	Guinea-Biss	1.96	(POP2030/POP2020)**(1/10)-1
39	Mauritania	1.93	(POP2030/POP2020)**(1/10)-1
40	Gaza Strip	1.92	(POP2030/POP2020)**(1/10)-1
41	Papua New G	1.87	(POP2030/POP2020)**(1/10)-1
42	Vanuatu	1.82	(POP2030/POP2020)**(1/10)-1
43	Cameroon	1.79	(POP2030/POP2020)**(1/10)-1
44	Sierra Leone	1.74	(POP2030/POP2020)**(1/10)-1
45	Djibouti	1.71	(POP2030/POP2020)**(1/10)-1
46	Sudan	1.70	(POP2030/POP2020)**(1/10)-1
47	Togo	1.69	(POP2030/POP2020)**(1/10)-1

TABLE 4.23 POPULATION GROWTH RATES, 2020-2030, FORECAST			
Rank	Country	GRPOP	Source
48	Kuwait	1.69	(POP2030/POP2020)**(1/10)-1
49	Gabon	1.67	(POP2030/POP2020)**(1/10)-1
50	Sao Tome & P	1.64	(POP2030/POP2020)**(1/10)-1
51	Gambia	1.62	(POP2030/POP2020)**(1/10)-1
52	West Bank	1.61	(POP2030/POP2020)**(1/10)-1
53	Ethiopia	1.61	(POP2030/POP2020)**(1/10)-1
54	Ivory Coast	1.54	(POP2030/POP2020)**(1/10)-1
55	Belize	1.53	(POP2030/POP2020)**(1/10)-1
56	Singapore	1.52	(POP2030/POP2020)**(1/10)-1
57	Honduras	1.50	(POP2030/POP2020)**(1/10)-1
58	Syria	1.47	(POP2030/POP2020)**(1/10)-1
59	Bolivia	1.45	(POP2030/POP2020)**(1/10)-1
60	Philippines	1.42	(POP2030/POP2020)**(1/10)-1
61	UAE	1.35	(POP2030/POP2020)**(1/10)-1
62	N Mariana Is	1.34	(POP2030/POP2020)**(1/10)-1
63	Jordan	1.34	(POP2030/POP2020)**(1/10)-1
64	Falkland Is	1.32	(POP2030/POP2020)**(1/10)-1
65	Kiribati	1.32	(POP2030/POP2020)**(1/10)-1
66	Comoros	1.31	(POP2030/POP2020)**(1/10)-1
67	Namibia	1.31	(POP2030/POP2020)**(1/10)-1
68	Burundi	1.30	(POP2030/POP2020)**(1/10)-1
69	Pakistan	1.29	(POP2030/POP2020)**(1/10)-1
70	Nepal	1.28	(POP2030/POP2020)**(1/10)-1
71	Botswana	1.27	(POP2030/POP2020)**(1/10)-1
72	Saudi Arabia	1.27	(POP2030/POP2020)**(1/10)-1
73	Kenya	1.27	(POP2030/POP2020)**(1/10)-1
74	Zimbabwe	1.27	(POP2030/POP2020)**(1/10)-1
75	Israel	1.25	(POP2030/POP2020)**(1/10)-1
76	Tajikistan	1.25	(POP2030/POP2020)**(1/10)-1
77	Panama	1.23	(POP2030/POP2020)**(1/10)-1
78	Malaysia	1.23	(POP2030/POP2020)**(1/10)-1
79	Cambodia	1.18	(POP2030/POP2020)**(1/10)-1
80	Brunei	1.17	(POP2030/POP2020)**(1/10)-1
81	Egypt	1.17	(POP2030/POP2020)**(1/10)-1
82	Libya	1.14	(POP2030/POP2020)**(1/10)-1
83	Venezuela	1.06	(POP2030/POP2020)**(1/10)-1
84	Kyrgyzstan	1.04	(POP2030/POP2020)**(1/10)-1
85	Paraguay	1.04	(POP2030/POP2020)**(1/10)-1
86	Mongolia	1.01	(POP2030/POP2020)**(1/10)-1
87	Luxembourg	1.01	(POP2030/POP2020)**(1/10)-1
88	New Caledon	0.98	(POP2030/POP2020)**(1/10)-1
89	Haiti	0.98	(POP2030/POP2020)**(1/10)-1
90	Laos	0.96	(POP2030/POP2020)**(1/10)-1
91	Australia	0.96	(POP2030/POP2020)**(1/10)-1
92	Nauru	0.96	(POP2030/POP2020)**(1/10)-1
93	India	0.94	(POP2030/POP2020)**(1/10)-1
94	Bahrain	0.93	(POP2030/POP2020)**(1/10)-1
95	Nicaragua	0.93	(POP2030/POP2020)**(1/10)-1

Table 4.23 Population Growth Rates, 2020-2030, Forecast			
Rank	Country	GRPOP	Source
96	Svalbard	0.92	(POP2030/POP2020)**(1/10)-1
97	Macao	0.92	(POP2030/POP2020)**(1/10)-1
98	Norway	0.92	(POP2030/POP2020)**(1/10)-1
99	Oman	0.91	(POP2030/POP2020)**(1/10)-1
100	Guam	0.91	(POP2030/POP2020)**(1/10)-1
101	Ecuador	0.90	(POP2030/POP2020)**(1/10)-1
102	Swaziland	0.87	(POP2030/POP2020)**(1/10)-1
103	Turkmenistan	0.87	(POP2030/POP2020)**(1/10)-1
104	Bangladesh	0.84	(POP2030/POP2020)**(1/10)-1
105	Cyprus	0.84	(POP2030/POP2020)**(1/10)-1
106	Iceland	0.83	(POP2030/POP2020)**(1/10)-1
107	Hong Kong	0.83	(POP2030/POP2020)**(1/10)-1
108	US	0.83	(POP2030/POP2020)**(1/10)-1
109	Antigua & B	0.82	(POP2030/POP2020)**(1/10)-1
110	Marshall Is	0.82	(POP2030/POP2020)**(1/10)-1
111	New Zealand	0.81	(POP2030/POP2020)**(1/10)-1
112	Uzbekistan	0.81	(POP2030/POP2020)**(1/10)-1
113	Bhutan	0.81	(POP2030/POP2020)**(1/10)-1
114	Dominican R	0.81	(POP2030/POP2020)**(1/10)-1
115	Burma	0.81	(POP2030/POP2020)**(1/10)-1
116	Morocco	0.81	(POP2030/POP2020)**(1/10)-1
117	Bahamas	0.80	(POP2030/POP2020)**(1/10)-1
118	Algeria	0.79	(POP2030/POP2020)**(1/10)-1
119	Cape Verde	0.78	(POP2030/POP2020)**(1/10)-1
120	Costa Rica	0.77	(POP2030/POP2020)**(1/10)-1
121	Peru	0.77	(POP2030/POP2020)**(1/10)-1
122	Colombia	0.76	(POP2030/POP2020)**(1/10)-1
123	Qatar	0.75	(POP2030/POP2020)**(1/10)-1
124	Ireland	0.75	(POP2030/POP2020)**(1/10)-1
125	Liechtenstn	0.74	(POP2030/POP2020)**(1/10)-1
126	Mexico	0.73	(POP2030/POP2020)**(1/10)-1
127	Saint Martin	0.73	(POP2030/POP2020)**(1/10)-1
128	Reunion	0.72	(POP2030/POP2020)**(1/10)-1
129	Maldives	0.72	(POP2030/POP2020)**(1/10)-1
130	Turkey	0.71	(POP2030/POP2020)**(1/10)-1
131	Canada	0.70	(POP2030/POP2020)**(1/10)-1
132	Vietnam	0.70	(POP2030/POP2020)**(1/10)-1
133	Kosovo	0.67	(POP2030/POP2020)**(1/10)-1
134	Indonesia	0.66	(POP2030/POP2020)**(1/10)-1
135	Fr Polynesia	0.66	(POP2030/POP2020)**(1/10)-1
136	Kazakhstan	0.65	(POP2030/POP2020)**(1/10)-1
137	Argentina	0.64	(POP2030/POP2020)**(1/10)-1
138	Fiji	0.61	(POP2030/POP2020)**(1/10)-1
139	UK	0.61	(POP2030/POP2020)**(1/10)-1
140	Saint Helena	0.58	(POP2030/POP2020)**(1/10)-1
141	Suriname	0.57	(POP2030/POP2020)**(1/10)-1
142	Brazil	0.56	(POP2030/POP2020)**(1/10)-1
143	Azerbaijan	0.55	(POP2030/POP2020)**(1/10)-1

Table 4.23 Population Growth Rates, 2020-2030, Forecast

Rank	Country	GRPOP	Source
144	Chile	0.55	(POP2030/POP2020)**(1/10)-1
145	St Kitts & N	0.54	(POP2030/POP2020)**(1/10)-1
146	St Lucia	0.53	(POP2030/POP2020)**(1/10)-1
147	Sri Lanka	0.52	(POP2030/POP2020)**(1/10)-1
148	Belgium	0.52	(POP2030/POP2020)**(1/10)-1
149.5	Samoa	0.50	(POP2030/POP2020)**(1/10)-1
149.5	Tunisia	0.50	(POP2030/POP2020)**(1/10)-1
151	Cayman Is	0.50	(POP2030/POP2020)**(1/10)-1
152	Jersey	0.47	(POP2030/POP2020)**(1/10)-1
153	Tonga	0.46	(POP2030/POP2020)**(1/10)-1
154	Palau	0.45	(POP2030/POP2020)**(1/10)-1
155	Sweden	0.44	(POP2030/POP2020)**(1/10)-1
156	Guernsey	0.43	(POP2030/POP2020)**(1/10)-1
157	Sint Maarten	0.43	(POP2030/POP2020)**(1/10)-1
158	Iran	0.41	(POP2030/POP2020)**(1/10)-1
159	Spain	0.41	(POP2030/POP2020)**(1/10)-1
160	Korea, North	0.40	(POP2030/POP2020)**(1/10)-1
161	South Africa	0.40	(POP2030/POP2020)**(1/10)-1
162	Dominica	0.40	(POP2030/POP2020)**(1/10)-1
163	Switzerland	0.39	(POP2030/POP2020)**(1/10)-1
164	Faroe Is	0.39	(POP2030/POP2020)**(1/10)-1
165	Finland	0.38	(POP2030/POP2020)**(1/10)-1
166	Denmark	0.34	(POP2030/POP2020)**(1/10)-1
167	Isle of Man	0.32	(POP2030/POP2020)**(1/10)-1
168	Austria	0.31	(POP2030/POP2020)**(1/10)-1
169	San Marino	0.30	(POP2030/POP2020)**(1/10)-1
170	Micronesia	0.30	(POP2030/POP2020)**(1/10)-1
171	Guyana	0.28	(POP2030/POP2020)**(1/10)-1
172	Netherlands	0.26	(POP2030/POP2020)**(1/10)-1
173	Monaco	0.26	(POP2030/POP2020)**(1/10)-1
174	France	0.26	(POP2030/POP2020)**(1/10)-1
175	Thailand	0.25	(POP2030/POP2020)**(1/10)-1
176	Guadeloupe	0.24	(POP2030/POP2020)**(1/10)-1
177	Mauritius	0.24	(POP2030/POP2020)**(1/10)-1
178	Uruguay	0.23	(POP2030/POP2020)**(1/10)-1
179	Lebanon	0.21	(POP2030/POP2020)**(1/10)-1
180	Seychelles	0.21	(POP2030/POP2020)**(1/10)-1
181	El Salvador	0.20	(POP2030/POP2020)**(1/10)-1
182	Curacao	0.19	(POP2030/POP2020)**(1/10)-1
183	Italy	0.18	(POP2030/POP2020)**(1/10)-1
184	Bermuda	0.15	(POP2030/POP2020)**(1/10)-1
185	Korea, South	0.14	(POP2030/POP2020)**(1/10)-1
186	St Vincent	0.09	(POP2030/POP2020)**(1/10)-1
187	Aruba	0.09	(POP2030/POP2020)**(1/10)-1
188	Wallis & Fut	0.09	(POP2030/POP2020)**(1/10)-1
189	Albania	0.09	(POP2030/POP2020)**(1/10)-1
190	Barbados	0.07	(POP2030/POP2020)**(1/10)-1
191	Malta	0.07	(POP2030/POP2020)**(1/10)-1

Table 4.23 Population Growth Rates, 2020-2030, Forecast			
Rank	Country	GRPOP	Source
192	Slovenia	0.06	(POP2030/POP2020)**(1/10)-1
193	Jamaica	0.05	(POP2030/POP2020)**(1/10)-1
194	Portugal	0.05	(POP2030/POP2020)**(1/10)-1
195	Greece	0.04	(POP2030/POP2020)**(1/10)-1
196	China	0.04	(POP2030/POP2020)**(1/10)-1
197	Czechia	0.02	(POP2030/POP2020)**(1/10)-1
198	Slovakia	0.01	(POP2030/POP2020)**(1/10)-1
200.5	Greenland	0.00	(POP2030/POP2020)**(1/10)-1
200.5	Grenada	0.00	(POP2030/POP2020)**(1/10)-1
200.5	Martinique	0.00	(POP2030/POP2020)**(1/10)-1
200.5	Tuvalu	0.00	(POP2030/POP2020)**(1/10)-1
203	Taiwan	-0.03	(POP2030/POP2020)**(1/10)-1
204	Montenegro	-0.03	(POP2030/POP2020)**(1/10)-1
205	Lesotho	-0.09	(POP2030/POP2020)**(1/10)-1
206	Cuba	-0.10	(POP2030/POP2020)**(1/10)-1
207	Gibraltar	-0.13	(POP2030/POP2020)**(1/10)-1
208	Armenia	-0.13	(POP2030/POP2020)**(1/10)-1
209	Trinidad & T	-0.14	(POP2030/POP2020)**(1/10)-1
210	Macedonia	-0.15	(POP2030/POP2020)**(1/10)-1
211	Poland	-0.22	(POP2030/POP2020)**(1/10)-1
212	Estonia	-0.25	(POP2030/POP2020)**(1/10)-1
213	Andorra	-0.27	(POP2030/POP2020)**(1/10)-1
214	Germany	-0.28	(POP2030/POP2020)**(1/10)-1
215	Croatia	-0.30	(POP2030/POP2020)**(1/10)-1
216	Russia	-0.33	(POP2030/POP2020)**(1/10)-1
217	Hungary	-0.36	(POP2030/POP2020)**(1/10)-1
218	Japan	-0.37	(POP2030/POP2020)**(1/10)-1
219	Samoa, Amer	-0.38	(POP2030/POP2020)**(1/10)-1
220	Lithuania	-0.39	(POP2030/POP2020)**(1/10)-1
221	Belarus	-0.44	(POP2030/POP2020)**(1/10)-1
222	Latvia	-0.45	(POP2030/POP2020)**(1/10)-1
223	Romania	-0.48	(POP2030/POP2020)**(1/10)-1
224	Bosnia	-0.49	(POP2030/POP2020)**(1/10)-1
225	Serbia	-0.50	(POP2030/POP2020)**(1/10)-1
226	Tokelau	-0.53	(POP2030/POP2020)**(1/10)-1
227	Ukraine	-0.60	(POP2030/POP2020)**(1/10)-1
228	Bulgaria	-0.64	(POP2030/POP2020)**(1/10)-1
229	Moldova	-0.65	(POP2030/POP2020)**(1/10)-1
230	Georgia	-0.81	(POP2030/POP2020)**(1/10)-1
231	Puerto Rico	-0.91	(POP2030/POP2020)**(1/10)-1
232	Virgin I, US	-0.94	(POP2030/POP2020)**(1/10)-1
233	St Pierre&M	-1.39	(POP2030/POP2020)**(1/10)-1
234	Montserrat	-1.78	(POP2030/POP2020)**(1/10)-1
235	Niue	-4.15	(POP2030/POP2020)**(1/10)-1
236	Cook Is	-5.18	(POP2030/POP2020)**(1/10)-1

5. Gross Domestic Product Per Capita Growth Rates by Rank

Table 5.1 GDP Per Capita Growth Rates, 0001-1000			
Rank	Country	GRPCRL	Source
1	Slovenia	0.05	(GPC1000/GPC0001)**(1/999)-1
2	Denmark	0.05	(GPC1000/GPC0001)**(1/999)-1
3	UK	0.05	(GPC1000/GPC0001)**(1/999)-1
4	Estonia	0.05	(GPC1000/GPC0001)**(1/999)-1
5	Sweden	0.05	(GPC1000/GPC0001)**(1/999)-1
6	Poland	0.05	(GPC1000/GPC0001)**(1/999)-1
7	Latvia	0.05	(GPC1000/GPC0001)**(1/999)-1
8	Czechia	0.05	(GPC1000/GPC0001)**(1/999)-1
9	Norway	0.05	(GPC1000/GPC0001)**(1/999)-1
10	Kazakhstan	0.05	(GPC1000/GPC0001)**(1/999)-1
11	Lithuania	0.04	(GPC1000/GPC0001)**(1/999)-1
12	Morocco	0.04	(GPC1000/GPC0001)**(1/999)-1
13	Japan	0.04	(GPC1000/GPC0001)**(1/999)-1
14	Slovakia	0.04	(GPC1000/GPC0001)**(1/999)-1
15	Sudan	0.04	(GPC1000/GPC0001)**(1/999)-1
16	Russia	0.04	(GPC1000/GPC0001)**(1/999)-1
17	Croatia	0.04	(GPC1000/GPC0001)**(1/999)-1
18	Ireland	0.04	(GPC1000/GPC0001)**(1/999)-1
19	Vietnam	0.04	(GPC1000/GPC0001)**(1/999)-1
20	Armenia	0.04	(GPC1000/GPC0001)**(1/999)-1
21	Jamaica	0.04	(GPC1000/GPC0001)**(1/999)-1
22	Puerto Rico	0.04	(GPC1000/GPC0001)**(1/999)-1
23	Afghanistan	0.04	(GPC1000/GPC0001)**(1/999)-1
24	Trinidad & T	0.04	(GPC1000/GPC0001)**(1/999)-1
25	Burma	0.04	(GPC1000/GPC0001)**(1/999)-1
26	Georgia	0.04	(GPC1000/GPC0001)**(1/999)-1
27	Singapore	0.04	(GPC1000/GPC0001)**(1/999)-1
28	Cuba	0.04	(GPC1000/GPC0001)**(1/999)-1
29	Sierra Leone	0.04	(GPC1000/GPC0001)**(1/999)-1
30	Laos	0.04	(GPC1000/GPC0001)**(1/999)-1
31	US	0.04	(GPC1000/GPC0001)**(1/999)-1
32	Finland	0.04	(GPC1000/GPC0001)**(1/999)-1
33	Montenegro	0.04	(GPC1000/GPC0001)**(1/999)-1
34	Guatemala	0.04	(GPC1000/GPC0001)**(1/999)-1
35	Moldova	0.04	(GPC1000/GPC0001)**(1/999)-1
36	Belarus	0.04	(GPC1000/GPC0001)**(1/999)-1
37	Australia	0.04	(GPC1000/GPC0001)**(1/999)-1
38	Costa Rica	0.04	(GPC1000/GPC0001)**(1/999)-1
39	Mexico	0.04	(GPC1000/GPC0001)**(1/999)-1
40	Uzbekistan	0.03	(GPC1000/GPC0001)**(1/999)-1
41	Bolivia	0.03	(GPC1000/GPC0001)**(1/999)-1
42	Panama	0.03	(GPC1000/GPC0001)**(1/999)-1
43	Turkmenistan	0.03	(GPC1000/GPC0001)**(1/999)-1

Table 5.1 GDP Per Capita Growth Rates, 0001-1000			
Rank	Country	GRPCRL	Source
45	Argentina	0.03	(GPC1000/GPC0001)**(1/999)-1
45	Chile	0.03	(GPC1000/GPC0001)**(1/999)-1
45	Uruguay	0.03	(GPC1000/GPC0001)**(1/999)-1
47	Ecuador	0.03	(GPC1000/GPC0001)**(1/999)-1
48	Brazil	0.03	(GPC1000/GPC0001)**(1/999)-1
49	Ukraine	0.03	(GPC1000/GPC0001)**(1/999)-1
50	Peru	0.03	(GPC1000/GPC0001)**(1/999)-1
51	Cambodia	0.03	(GPC1000/GPC0001)**(1/999)-1
55.5	Madagascar	0.03	(GPC1000/GPC0001)**(1/999)-1
55.5	Mozambique	0.03	(GPC1000/GPC0001)**(1/999)-1
55.5	Namibia	0.03	(GPC1000/GPC0001)**(1/999)-1
55.5	Somalia	0.03	(GPC1000/GPC0001)**(1/999)-1
55.5	South Africa	0.03	(GPC1000/GPC0001)**(1/999)-1
55.5	Swaziland	0.03	(GPC1000/GPC0001)**(1/999)-1
55.5	Zambia	0.03	(GPC1000/GPC0001)**(1/999)-1
55.5	Zimbabwe	0.03	(GPC1000/GPC0001)**(1/999)-1
60	Venezuela	0.03	(GPC1000/GPC0001)**(1/999)-1
61	Canada	0.03	(GPC1000/GPC0001)**(1/999)-1
62	El Salvador	0.03	(GPC1000/GPC0001)**(1/999)-1
63	Azerbaijan	0.03	(GPC1000/GPC0001)**(1/999)-1
64	Haiti	0.03	(GPC1000/GPC0001)**(1/999)-1
65	Dominican R	0.03	(GPC1000/GPC0001)**(1/999)-1
66	Bosnia	0.03	(GPC1000/GPC0001)**(1/999)-1
67	Colombia	0.03	(GPC1000/GPC0001)**(1/999)-1
68	Tajikistan	0.03	(GPC1000/GPC0001)**(1/999)-1
69	Albania	0.03	(GPC1000/GPC0001)**(1/999)-1
70	Kyrgyzstan	0.03	(GPC1000/GPC0001)**(1/999)-1
71	Nicaragua	0.03	(GPC1000/GPC0001)**(1/999)-1
72	Ghana	0.03	(GPC1000/GPC0001)**(1/999)-1
73	Paraguay	0.03	(GPC1000/GPC0001)**(1/999)-1
74	Nepal	0.03	(GPC1000/GPC0001)**(1/999)-1
75	Honduras	0.03	(GPC1000/GPC0001)**(1/999)-1
76	Mongolia	0.03	(GPC1000/GPC0001)**(1/999)-1
77	New Zealand	0.03	(GPC1000/GPC0001)**(1/999)-1
78	Macedonia	0.03	(GPC1000/GPC0001)**(1/999)-1
79	South Sudan	0.03	(GPC1000/GPC0001)**(1/999)-1
80	Kosovo	0.03	(GPC1000/GPC0001)**(1/999)-1
81	Burundi	0.03	(GPC1000/GPC0001)**(1/999)-1
82	Lesotho	0.03	(GPC1000/GPC0001)**(1/999)-1
83	Botswana	0.03	(GPC1000/GPC0001)**(1/999)-1
84	Malawi	0.03	(GPC1000/GPC0001)**(1/999)-1
85	Guinea	0.02	(GPC1000/GPC0001)**(1/999)-1
86	Guinea-Biss	0.02	(GPC1000/GPC0001)**(1/999)-1
87	Eritrea	0.02	(GPC1000/GPC0001)**(1/999)-1
88	Ethiopia	0.02	(GPC1000/GPC0001)**(1/999)-1
89	Israel	0.02	(GPC1000/GPC0001)**(1/999)-1
93	Bahrain	0.02	(GPC1000/GPC0001)**(1/999)-1
93	Kuwait	0.02	(GPC1000/GPC0001)**(1/999)-1

Table 5.1 GDP Per Capita Growth Rates, 0001-1000			
Rank	Country	GRPCRL	Source
93	Oman	0.02	(GPC1000/GPC0001)**(1/999)-1
93	Qatar	0.02	(GPC1000/GPC0001)**(1/999)-1
93	Saudi Arabia	0.02	(GPC1000/GPC0001)**(1/999)-1
93	UAE	0.02	(GPC1000/GPC0001)**(1/999)-1
93	Yemen	0.02	(GPC1000/GPC0001)**(1/999)-1
97.5	Iran	0.02	(GPC1000/GPC0001)**(1/999)-1
97.5	Turkey	0.02	(GPC1000/GPC0001)**(1/999)-1
99.5	Lebanon	0.02	(GPC1000/GPC0001)**(1/999)-1
99.5	Syria	0.02	(GPC1000/GPC0001)**(1/999)-1
101	Iraq	0.02	(GPC1000/GPC0001)**(1/999)-1
102	Jordan	0.02	(GPC1000/GPC0001)**(1/999)-1
103	Cyprus	0.01	(GPC1000/GPC0001)**(1/999)-1
104	Germany	0.00	(GPC1000/GPC0001)**(1/999)-1
114	Algeria	0.00	(GPC1000/GPC0001)**(1/999)-1
114	Austria	0.00	(GPC1000/GPC0001)**(1/999)-1
114	Bangladesh	0.00	(GPC1000/GPC0001)**(1/999)-1
114	China	0.00	(GPC1000/GPC0001)**(1/999)-1
114	Egypt	0.00	(GPC1000/GPC0001)**(1/999)-1
114	Hong Kong	0.00	(GPC1000/GPC0001)**(1/999)-1
114	India	0.00	(GPC1000/GPC0001)**(1/999)-1
114	Indonesia	0.00	(GPC1000/GPC0001)**(1/999)-1
114	Korea, North	0.00	(GPC1000/GPC0001)**(1/999)-1
114	Korea, South	0.00	(GPC1000/GPC0001)**(1/999)-1
114	Libya	0.00	(GPC1000/GPC0001)**(1/999)-1
114	Malaysia	0.00	(GPC1000/GPC0001)**(1/999)-1
114	Netherlands	0.00	(GPC1000/GPC0001)**(1/999)-1
114	Pakistan	0.00	(GPC1000/GPC0001)**(1/999)-1
114	Philippines	0.00	(GPC1000/GPC0001)**(1/999)-1
114	Sri Lanka	0.00	(GPC1000/GPC0001)**(1/999)-1
114	Taiwan	0.00	(GPC1000/GPC0001)**(1/999)-1
114	Thailand	0.00	(GPC1000/GPC0001)**(1/999)-1
114	Tunisia	0.00	(GPC1000/GPC0001)**(1/999)-1
124	Switzerland	0.00	(GPC1000/GPC0001)**(1/999)-1
125.5	Belgium	-0.01	(GPC1000/GPC0001)**(1/999)-1
125.5	Portugal	-0.01	(GPC1000/GPC0001)**(1/999)-1
128.5	Bulgaria	-0.01	(GPC1000/GPC0001)**(1/999)-1
128.5	Hungary	-0.01	(GPC1000/GPC0001)**(1/999)-1
128.5	Romania	-0.01	(GPC1000/GPC0001)**(1/999)-1
128.5	Serbia	-0.01	(GPC1000/GPC0001)**(1/999)-1
131	Spain	-0.01	(GPC1000/GPC0001)**(1/999)-1
132	France	-0.01	(GPC1000/GPC0001)**(1/999)-1
133	Greece	-0.03	(GPC1000/GPC0001)**(1/999)-1
134	Italy	-0.06	(GPC1000/GPC0001)**(1/999)-1

TABLE 5.2 GDP PER CAPITA GROWTH RATES, 1000-1500			
Rank	Country	GRPCRL	Source
1	Italy	0.18	(GPC1500/GPC1000)**(1/500)-1
2	Belgium	0.14	(GPC1500/GPC1000)**(1/500)-1
3	Netherlands	0.12	(GPC1500/GPC1000)**(1/500)-1
4	Hungary	0.12	(GPC1500/GPC1000)**(1/500)-1
5	France	0.11	(GPC1500/GPC1000)**(1/500)-1
6	Germany	0.10	(GPC1500/GPC1000)**(1/500)-1
7	Austria	0.10	(GPC1500/GPC1000)**(1/500)-1
8	Romania	0.10	(GPC1500/GPC1000)**(1/500)-1
9	Switzerland	0.09	(GPC1500/GPC1000)**(1/500)-1
10	Spain	0.08	(GPC1500/GPC1000)**(1/500)-1
11	Slovenia	0.08	(GPC1500/GPC1000)**(1/500)-1
12	Denmark	0.08	(GPC1500/GPC1000)**(1/500)-1
13	Bulgaria	0.07	(GPC1500/GPC1000)**(1/500)-1
14	UK	0.07	(GPC1500/GPC1000)**(1/500)-1
15	Estonia	0.07	(GPC1500/GPC1000)**(1/500)-1
16	Sweden	0.07	(GPC1500/GPC1000)**(1/500)-1
17	Portugal	0.07	(GPC1500/GPC1000)**(1/500)-1
18	Poland	0.07	(GPC1500/GPC1000)**(1/500)-1
19	Latvia	0.07	(GPC1500/GPC1000)**(1/500)-1
20	Czechia	0.07	(GPC1500/GPC1000)**(1/500)-1
21	Norway	0.07	(GPC1500/GPC1000)**(1/500)-1
22	Kazakhstan	0.07	(GPC1500/GPC1000)**(1/500)-1
23	Lithuania	0.07	(GPC1500/GPC1000)**(1/500)-1
24	Iceland	0.06	(GPC1500/GPC1000)**(1/500)-1
25	Slovakia	0.06	(GPC1500/GPC1000)**(1/500)-1
26	Russia	0.06	(GPC1500/GPC1000)**(1/500)-1
28.5	China	0.06	(GPC1500/GPC1000)**(1/500)-1
28.5	Hong Kong	0.06	(GPC1500/GPC1000)**(1/500)-1
28.5	Korea, North	0.06	(GPC1500/GPC1000)**(1/500)-1
28.5	Korea, South	0.06	(GPC1500/GPC1000)**(1/500)-1
31	Croatia	0.06	(GPC1500/GPC1000)**(1/500)-1
32	Ireland	0.06	(GPC1500/GPC1000)**(1/500)-1
33	Vietnam	0.06	(GPC1500/GPC1000)**(1/500)-1
34	Armenia	0.05	(GPC1500/GPC1000)**(1/500)-1
35	Jamaica	0.05	(GPC1500/GPC1000)**(1/500)-1
36	Puerto Rico	0.05	(GPC1500/GPC1000)**(1/500)-1
37	Afghanistan	0.05	(GPC1500/GPC1000)**(1/500)-1
38	Trinidad & T	0.05	(GPC1500/GPC1000)**(1/500)-1
39	Burma	0.05	(GPC1500/GPC1000)**(1/500)-1
40	Georgia	0.05	(GPC1500/GPC1000)**(1/500)-1
41	Singapore	0.05	(GPC1500/GPC1000)**(1/500)-1
42	Philippines	0.05	(GPC1500/GPC1000)**(1/500)-1
43	Thailand	0.05	(GPC1500/GPC1000)**(1/500)-1
44	Malaysia	0.05	(GPC1500/GPC1000)**(1/500)-1
45.5	Sri Lanka	0.05	(GPC1500/GPC1000)**(1/500)-1
45.5	Taiwan	0.05	(GPC1500/GPC1000)**(1/500)-1
47	Indonesia	0.05	(GPC1500/GPC1000)**(1/500)-1
48	Cuba	0.05	(GPC1500/GPC1000)**(1/500)-1

Table 5.2 GDP Per Capita Growth Rates, 1000-1500

Rank	Country	GRPCRL	Source
49	Sierra Leone	0.05	(GPC1500/GPC1000)**(1/500)-1
50	Laos	0.05	(GPC1500/GPC1000)**(1/500)-1
51	US	0.05	(GPC1500/GPC1000)**(1/500)-1
52	Finland	0.05	(GPC1500/GPC1000)**(1/500)-1
53	Montenegro	0.05	(GPC1500/GPC1000)**(1/500)-1
54	Guatemala	0.05	(GPC1500/GPC1000)**(1/500)-1
55	Moldova	0.05	(GPC1500/GPC1000)**(1/500)-1
56	Belarus	0.05	(GPC1500/GPC1000)**(1/500)-1
57	Australia	0.05	(GPC1500/GPC1000)**(1/500)-1
58	Costa Rica	0.05	(GPC1500/GPC1000)**(1/500)-1
59	Mexico	0.05	(GPC1500/GPC1000)**(1/500)-1
60	Uzbekistan	0.05	(GPC1500/GPC1000)**(1/500)-1
61	Bolivia	0.05	(GPC1500/GPC1000)**(1/500)-1
62	Panama	0.05	(GPC1500/GPC1000)**(1/500)-1
63	Turkmenistan	0.05	(GPC1500/GPC1000)**(1/500)-1
65	Argentina	0.05	(GPC1500/GPC1000)**(1/500)-1
65	Chile	0.05	(GPC1500/GPC1000)**(1/500)-1
65	Uruguay	0.05	(GPC1500/GPC1000)**(1/500)-1
67	Ecuador	0.05	(GPC1500/GPC1000)**(1/500)-1
68	Brazil	0.05	(GPC1500/GPC1000)**(1/500)-1
69	Ukraine	0.05	(GPC1500/GPC1000)**(1/500)-1
70	Peru	0.04	(GPC1500/GPC1000)**(1/500)-1
71	Cambodia	0.04	(GPC1500/GPC1000)**(1/500)-1
75.5	Madagascar	0.04	(GPC1500/GPC1000)**(1/500)-1
75.5	Mozambique	0.04	(GPC1500/GPC1000)**(1/500)-1
75.5	Namibia	0.04	(GPC1500/GPC1000)**(1/500)-1
75.5	Somalia	0.04	(GPC1500/GPC1000)**(1/500)-1
75.5	South Africa	0.04	(GPC1500/GPC1000)**(1/500)-1
75.5	Swaziland	0.04	(GPC1500/GPC1000)**(1/500)-1
75.5	Zambia	0.04	(GPC1500/GPC1000)**(1/500)-1
75.5	Zimbabwe	0.04	(GPC1500/GPC1000)**(1/500)-1
80	Venezuela	0.04	(GPC1500/GPC1000)**(1/500)-1
81	Canada	0.04	(GPC1500/GPC1000)**(1/500)-1
82	El Salvador	0.04	(GPC1500/GPC1000)**(1/500)-1
83	Azerbaijan	0.04	(GPC1500/GPC1000)**(1/500)-1
84	Haiti	0.04	(GPC1500/GPC1000)**(1/500)-1
85	Dominican R	0.04	(GPC1500/GPC1000)**(1/500)-1
86	Bosnia	0.04	(GPC1500/GPC1000)**(1/500)-1
87	Colombia	0.04	(GPC1500/GPC1000)**(1/500)-1
88	Tajikistan	0.04	(GPC1500/GPC1000)**(1/500)-1
89	Albania	0.04	(GPC1500/GPC1000)**(1/500)-1
90	Kyrgyzstan	0.04	(GPC1500/GPC1000)**(1/500)-1
91	Nicaragua	0.04	(GPC1500/GPC1000)**(1/500)-1
92	Ghana	0.04	(GPC1500/GPC1000)**(1/500)-1
94	Bangladesh	0.04	(GPC1500/GPC1000)**(1/500)-1
94	India	0.04	(GPC1500/GPC1000)**(1/500)-1
94	Pakistan	0.04	(GPC1500/GPC1000)**(1/500)-1
96	Paraguay	0.04	(GPC1500/GPC1000)**(1/500)-1

TABLE 5.2 GDP PER CAPITA GROWTH RATES, 1000-1500			
Rank	Country	GRPCRL	Source
97	Nepal	0.04	(GPC1500/GPC1000)**(1/500)-1
98	Honduras	0.04	(GPC1500/GPC1000)**(1/500)-1
99	Mongolia	0.04	(GPC1500/GPC1000)**(1/500)-1
100	New Zealand	0.04	(GPC1500/GPC1000)**(1/500)-1
101	Macedonia	0.04	(GPC1500/GPC1000)**(1/500)-1
102	South Sudan	0.04	(GPC1500/GPC1000)**(1/500)-1
103	Kosovo	0.04	(GPC1500/GPC1000)**(1/500)-1
104	Burundi	0.03	(GPC1500/GPC1000)**(1/500)-1
105	Lesotho	0.03	(GPC1500/GPC1000)**(1/500)-1
106	Botswana	0.03	(GPC1500/GPC1000)**(1/500)-1
107	Japan	0.03	(GPC1500/GPC1000)**(1/500)-1
108	Malawi	0.03	(GPC1500/GPC1000)**(1/500)-1
109	Guinea	0.03	(GPC1500/GPC1000)**(1/500)-1
110	Guinea-Biss	0.03	(GPC1500/GPC1000)**(1/500)-1
111	Eritrea	0.03	(GPC1500/GPC1000)**(1/500)-1
112	Ethiopia	0.03	(GPC1500/GPC1000)**(1/500)-1
113	Serbia	0.03	(GPC1500/GPC1000)**(1/500)-1
114	Greece	0.02	(GPC1500/GPC1000)**(1/500)-1
117	Algeria	0.00	(GPC1500/GPC1000)**(1/500)-1
117	Libya	0.00	(GPC1500/GPC1000)**(1/500)-1
117	Morocco	0.00	(GPC1500/GPC1000)**(1/500)-1
117	Sudan	0.00	(GPC1500/GPC1000)**(1/500)-1
117	Tunisia	0.00	(GPC1500/GPC1000)**(1/500)-1
120	Jordan	-0.01	(GPC1500/GPC1000)**(1/500)-1
121.5	Lebanon	-0.01	(GPC1500/GPC1000)**(1/500)-1
121.5	Syria	-0.01	(GPC1500/GPC1000)**(1/500)-1
123	Israel	-0.01	(GPC1500/GPC1000)**(1/500)-1
124	Iraq	-0.01	(GPC1500/GPC1000)**(1/500)-1
128	Bahrain	-0.01	(GPC1500/GPC1000)**(1/500)-1
128	Kuwait	-0.01	(GPC1500/GPC1000)**(1/500)-1
128	Oman	-0.01	(GPC1500/GPC1000)**(1/500)-1
128	Qatar	-0.01	(GPC1500/GPC1000)**(1/500)-1
128	Saudi Arabia	-0.01	(GPC1500/GPC1000)**(1/500)-1
128	UAE	-0.01	(GPC1500/GPC1000)**(1/500)-1
128	Yemen	-0.01	(GPC1500/GPC1000)**(1/500)-1
132.5	Iran	-0.01	(GPC1500/GPC1000)**(1/500)-1
132.5	Turkey	-0.01	(GPC1500/GPC1000)**(1/500)-1
134	Egypt	-0.01	(GPC1500/GPC1000)**(1/500)-1
135	Cyprus	-0.07	(GPC1500/GPC1000)**(1/500)-1

Table 5.3 GDP Per Capita Growth Rates, 1500-1600			
Rank	Country	GRPCRL	Source
1	Netherlands	0.60	(GPC1600/GPC1500)**(1/100)-1
2	Uruguay	0.51	(GPC1600/GPC1500)**(1/100)-1
3	Argentina	0.35	(GPC1600/GPC1500)**(1/100)-1
4	UK	0.31	(GPC1600/GPC1500)**(1/100)-1
5	Spain	0.26	(GPC1600/GPC1500)**(1/100)-1
6	Portugal	0.20	(GPC1600/GPC1500)**(1/100)-1
7	Finland	0.17	(GPC1600/GPC1500)**(1/100)-1
8	Norway	0.17	(GPC1600/GPC1500)**(1/100)-1
9	Switzerland	0.17	(GPC1600/GPC1500)**(1/100)-1
10	Denmark	0.17	(GPC1600/GPC1500)**(1/100)-1
11	Iceland	0.17	(GPC1600/GPC1500)**(1/100)-1
12	Sweden	0.17	(GPC1600/GPC1500)**(1/100)-1
13	Austria	0.17	(GPC1600/GPC1500)**(1/100)-1
14	Chile	0.16	(GPC1600/GPC1500)**(1/100)-1
15	Ireland	0.16	(GPC1600/GPC1500)**(1/100)-1
16	France	0.15	(GPC1600/GPC1500)**(1/100)-1
17	Germany	0.14	(GPC1600/GPC1500)**(1/100)-1
18	Slovenia	0.12	(GPC1600/GPC1500)**(1/100)-1
19	Hungary	0.12	(GPC1600/GPC1500)**(1/100)-1
20	Estonia	0.11	(GPC1600/GPC1500)**(1/100)-1
21	Cyprus	0.11	(GPC1600/GPC1500)**(1/100)-1
22	Greece	0.11	(GPC1600/GPC1500)**(1/100)-1
23	Belgium	0.11	(GPC1600/GPC1500)**(1/100)-1
24	Georgia	0.10	(GPC1600/GPC1500)**(1/100)-1
25	Belarus	0.10	(GPC1600/GPC1500)**(1/100)-1
26	Kazakhstan	0.10	(GPC1600/GPC1500)**(1/100)-1
27	Armenia	0.10	(GPC1600/GPC1500)**(1/100)-1
28	Moldova	0.10	(GPC1600/GPC1500)**(1/100)-1
29	Lithuania	0.10	(GPC1600/GPC1500)**(1/100)-1
30	Russia	0.10	(GPC1600/GPC1500)**(1/100)-1
31	Latvia	0.10	(GPC1600/GPC1500)**(1/100)-1
32	Ukraine	0.10	(GPC1600/GPC1500)**(1/100)-1
33	Uzbekistan	0.10	(GPC1600/GPC1500)**(1/100)-1
34	Romania	0.10	(GPC1600/GPC1500)**(1/100)-1
35	Czechia	0.10	(GPC1600/GPC1500)**(1/100)-1
36	Montenegro	0.10	(GPC1600/GPC1500)**(1/100)-1
37	Poland	0.10	(GPC1600/GPC1500)**(1/100)-1
38	Croatia	0.10	(GPC1600/GPC1500)**(1/100)-1
39	Slovakia	0.10	(GPC1600/GPC1500)**(1/100)-1
40	Bulgaria	0.10	(GPC1600/GPC1500)**(1/100)-1
41	Serbia	0.10	(GPC1600/GPC1500)**(1/100)-1
42	Mexico	0.07	(GPC1600/GPC1500)**(1/100)-1
43	Jamaica	0.06	(GPC1600/GPC1500)**(1/100)-1
44	Puerto Rico	0.06	(GPC1600/GPC1500)**(1/100)-1
45	Trinidad & T	0.06	(GPC1600/GPC1500)**(1/100)-1
46	Cuba	0.06	(GPC1600/GPC1500)**(1/100)-1
47	Sierra Leone	0.06	(GPC1600/GPC1500)**(1/100)-1
48	US	0.06	(GPC1600/GPC1500)**(1/100)-1

Table 5.3 GDP Per Capita Growth Rates, 1500-1600

Rank	Country	GRPCRL	Source
49	Guatemala	0.06	(GPC1600/GPC1500)**(1/100)-1
50	Australia	0.06	(GPC1600/GPC1500)**(1/100)-1
51	Costa Rica	0.05	(GPC1600/GPC1500)**(1/100)-1
52	Bolivia	0.05	(GPC1600/GPC1500)**(1/100)-1
53	Panama	0.05	(GPC1600/GPC1500)**(1/100)-1
54	Turkmenistan	0.05	(GPC1600/GPC1500)**(1/100)-1
55	Ecuador	0.05	(GPC1600/GPC1500)**(1/100)-1
56	Brazil	0.05	(GPC1600/GPC1500)**(1/100)-1
57	Peru	0.05	(GPC1600/GPC1500)**(1/100)-1
61.5	Madagascar	0.05	(GPC1600/GPC1500)**(1/100)-1
61.5	Mozambique	0.05	(GPC1600/GPC1500)**(1/100)-1
61.5	Namibia	0.05	(GPC1600/GPC1500)**(1/100)-1
61.5	Somalia	0.05	(GPC1600/GPC1500)**(1/100)-1
61.5	South Africa	0.05	(GPC1600/GPC1500)**(1/100)-1
61.5	Swaziland	0.05	(GPC1600/GPC1500)**(1/100)-1
61.5	Zambia	0.05	(GPC1600/GPC1500)**(1/100)-1
61.5	Zimbabwe	0.05	(GPC1600/GPC1500)**(1/100)-1
66	Venezuela	0.05	(GPC1600/GPC1500)**(1/100)-1
67	Canada	0.05	(GPC1600/GPC1500)**(1/100)-1
68	El Salvador	0.05	(GPC1600/GPC1500)**(1/100)-1
69	Azerbaijan	0.05	(GPC1600/GPC1500)**(1/100)-1
70	Haiti	0.05	(GPC1600/GPC1500)**(1/100)-1
71	Dominican R	0.05	(GPC1600/GPC1500)**(1/100)-1
72	Bosnia	0.05	(GPC1600/GPC1500)**(1/100)-1
73	Colombia	0.05	(GPC1600/GPC1500)**(1/100)-1
74	Tajikistan	0.05	(GPC1600/GPC1500)**(1/100)-1
75	Albania	0.05	(GPC1600/GPC1500)**(1/100)-1
76	Kyrgyzstan	0.05	(GPC1600/GPC1500)**(1/100)-1
77	Nicaragua	0.05	(GPC1600/GPC1500)**(1/100)-1
78	Ghana	0.05	(GPC1600/GPC1500)**(1/100)-1
79	Paraguay	0.05	(GPC1600/GPC1500)**(1/100)-1
80	Nepal	0.05	(GPC1600/GPC1500)**(1/100)-1
81	Honduras	0.04	(GPC1600/GPC1500)**(1/100)-1
82	Mongolia	0.04	(GPC1600/GPC1500)**(1/100)-1
83	New Zealand	0.04	(GPC1600/GPC1500)**(1/100)-1
84	Macedonia	0.04	(GPC1600/GPC1500)**(1/100)-1
85	South Sudan	0.04	(GPC1600/GPC1500)**(1/100)-1
86	Kosovo	0.04	(GPC1600/GPC1500)**(1/100)-1
87	Japan	0.04	(GPC1600/GPC1500)**(1/100)-1
88	Burundi	0.04	(GPC1600/GPC1500)**(1/100)-1
89	Lesotho	0.04	(GPC1600/GPC1500)**(1/100)-1
90	Botswana	0.04	(GPC1600/GPC1500)**(1/100)-1
91	Malawi	0.03	(GPC1600/GPC1500)**(1/100)-1
92	Guinea	0.03	(GPC1600/GPC1500)**(1/100)-1
93	Guinea-Biss	0.03	(GPC1600/GPC1500)**(1/100)-1
94	Eritrea	0.03	(GPC1600/GPC1500)**(1/100)-1
95	Ethiopia	0.03	(GPC1600/GPC1500)**(1/100)-1
96.5	Sri Lanka	0.02	(GPC1600/GPC1500)**(1/100)-1

Table 5.3 GDP Per Capita Growth Rates, 1500-1600			
Rank	Country	GRPCRL	Source
96.5	Taiwan	0.02	(GPC1600/GPC1500)**(1/100)-1
98	Laos	0.02	(GPC1600/GPC1500)**(1/100)-1
99	Vietnam	0.02	(GPC1600/GPC1500)**(1/100)-1
100	Philippines	0.02	(GPC1600/GPC1500)**(1/100)-1
101	Thailand	0.02	(GPC1600/GPC1500)**(1/100)-1
102	Singapore	0.02	(GPC1600/GPC1500)**(1/100)-1
103	Burma	0.02	(GPC1600/GPC1500)**(1/100)-1
104	Afghanistan	0.02	(GPC1600/GPC1500)**(1/100)-1
105	Cambodia	0.02	(GPC1600/GPC1500)**(1/100)-1
106	Malaysia	0.02	(GPC1600/GPC1500)**(1/100)-1
107	Indonesia	0.01	(GPC1600/GPC1500)**(1/100)-1
108	Iraq	0.00	(GPC1600/GPC1500)**(1/100)-1
122	Algeria	0.00	(GPC1600/GPC1500)**(1/100)-1
122	Bahrain	0.00	(GPC1600/GPC1500)**(1/100)-1
122	Bangladesh	0.00	(GPC1600/GPC1500)**(1/100)-1
122	China	0.00	(GPC1600/GPC1500)**(1/100)-1
122	Egypt	0.00	(GPC1600/GPC1500)**(1/100)-1
122	Hong Kong	0.00	(GPC1600/GPC1500)**(1/100)-1
122	India	0.00	(GPC1600/GPC1500)**(1/100)-1
122	Iran	0.00	(GPC1600/GPC1500)**(1/100)-1
122	Israel	0.00	(GPC1600/GPC1500)**(1/100)-1
122	Italy	0.00	(GPC1600/GPC1500)**(1/100)-1
122	Jordan	0.00	(GPC1600/GPC1500)**(1/100)-1
122	Korea, North	0.00	(GPC1600/GPC1500)**(1/100)-1
122	Korea, South	0.00	(GPC1600/GPC1500)**(1/100)-1
122	Kuwait	0.00	(GPC1600/GPC1500)**(1/100)-1
122	Lebanon	0.00	(GPC1600/GPC1500)**(1/100)-1
122	Libya	0.00	(GPC1600/GPC1500)**(1/100)-1
122	Morocco	0.00	(GPC1600/GPC1500)**(1/100)-1
122	Oman	0.00	(GPC1600/GPC1500)**(1/100)-1
122	Pakistan	0.00	(GPC1600/GPC1500)**(1/100)-1
122	Qatar	0.00	(GPC1600/GPC1500)**(1/100)-1
122	Saudi Arabia	0.00	(GPC1600/GPC1500)**(1/100)-1
122	Sudan	0.00	(GPC1600/GPC1500)**(1/100)-1
122	Syria	0.00	(GPC1600/GPC1500)**(1/100)-1
122	Tunisia	0.00	(GPC1600/GPC1500)**(1/100)-1
122	Turkey	0.00	(GPC1600/GPC1500)**(1/100)-1
122	UAE	0.00	(GPC1600/GPC1500)**(1/100)-1
122	Yemen	0.00	(GPC1600/GPC1500)**(1/100)-1

TABLE 5.4 GDP PER CAPITA GROWTH RATES, 1600-1700

Rank	Country	GRPCRL	Source
1	Uruguay	0.51	(GPC1700/GPC1600)**(1/100)-1
2	Netherlands	0.43	(GPC1700/GPC1600)**(1/100)-1
3	Argentina	0.35	(GPC1700/GPC1600)**(1/100)-1
4	Jamaica	0.29	(GPC1700/GPC1600)**(1/100)-1
5	Trinidad & T	0.27	(GPC1700/GPC1600)**(1/100)-1
6	UK	0.25	(GPC1700/GPC1600)**(1/100)-1
7	Mexico	0.22	(GPC1700/GPC1600)**(1/100)-1
8	Iceland	0.17	(GPC1700/GPC1600)**(1/100)-1
9	Denmark	0.17	(GPC1700/GPC1600)**(1/100)-1
10	Switzerland	0.17	(GPC1700/GPC1600)**(1/100)-1
11	Austria	0.17	(GPC1700/GPC1600)**(1/100)-1
12	Finland	0.17	(GPC1700/GPC1600)**(1/100)-1
13	Sweden	0.17	(GPC1700/GPC1600)**(1/100)-1
14	Norway	0.17	(GPC1700/GPC1600)**(1/100)-1
15	Chile	0.16	(GPC1700/GPC1600)**(1/100)-1
16	Belgium	0.16	(GPC1700/GPC1600)**(1/100)-1
17	Ireland	0.15	(GPC1700/GPC1600)**(1/100)-1
18	Germany	0.14	(GPC1700/GPC1600)**(1/100)-1
19	Slovenia	0.12	(GPC1700/GPC1600)**(1/100)-1
20	Hungary	0.12	(GPC1700/GPC1600)**(1/100)-1
21	Estonia	0.11	(GPC1700/GPC1600)**(1/100)-1
22	Portugal	0.10	(GPC1700/GPC1600)**(1/100)-1
23	Bulgaria	0.10	(GPC1700/GPC1600)**(1/100)-1
24	Slovakia	0.10	(GPC1700/GPC1600)**(1/100)-1
25	Romania	0.10	(GPC1700/GPC1600)**(1/100)-1
26	Serbia	0.10	(GPC1700/GPC1600)**(1/100)-1
27	Poland	0.10	(GPC1700/GPC1600)**(1/100)-1
28	Montenegro	0.10	(GPC1700/GPC1600)**(1/100)-1
29	Croatia	0.10	(GPC1700/GPC1600)**(1/100)-1
30	Czechia	0.10	(GPC1700/GPC1600)**(1/100)-1
31	Uzbekistan	0.10	(GPC1700/GPC1600)**(1/100)-1
32	Ukraine	0.10	(GPC1700/GPC1600)**(1/100)-1
33	Latvia	0.10	(GPC1700/GPC1600)**(1/100)-1
34	Russia	0.10	(GPC1700/GPC1600)**(1/100)-1
35	Moldova	0.10	(GPC1700/GPC1600)**(1/100)-1
36	Turkmenistan	0.10	(GPC1700/GPC1600)**(1/100)-1
37	Armenia	0.10	(GPC1700/GPC1600)**(1/100)-1
38	Georgia	0.10	(GPC1700/GPC1600)**(1/100)-1
39	Kazakhstan	0.10	(GPC1700/GPC1600)**(1/100)-1
40	Lithuania	0.10	(GPC1700/GPC1600)**(1/100)-1
41	Belarus	0.10	(GPC1700/GPC1600)**(1/100)-1
42	Azerbaijan	0.10	(GPC1700/GPC1600)**(1/100)-1
43	Greece	0.09	(GPC1700/GPC1600)**(1/100)-1
44	Cyprus	0.09	(GPC1700/GPC1600)**(1/100)-1
45	Japan	0.09	(GPC1700/GPC1600)**(1/100)-1
46	France	0.08	(GPC1700/GPC1600)**(1/100)-1
47	Brazil	0.07	(GPC1700/GPC1600)**(1/100)-1
48	Puerto Rico	0.07	(GPC1700/GPC1600)**(1/100)-1

Table 5.4 GDP Per Capita Growth Rates, 1600-1700

Rank	Country	GRPCRL	Source
49	Cuba	0.07	(GPC1700/GPC1600)**(1/100)-1
50	Sierra Leone	0.07	(GPC1700/GPC1600)**(1/100)-1
51	US	0.06	(GPC1700/GPC1600)**(1/100)-1
52	Guatemala	0.06	(GPC1700/GPC1600)**(1/100)-1
53	Australia	0.06	(GPC1700/GPC1600)**(1/100)-1
54	Costa Rica	0.06	(GPC1700/GPC1600)**(1/100)-1
55	Bolivia	0.06	(GPC1700/GPC1600)**(1/100)-1
56	Panama	0.06	(GPC1700/GPC1600)**(1/100)-1
57	Ecuador	0.06	(GPC1700/GPC1600)**(1/100)-1
58	Peru	0.05	(GPC1700/GPC1600)**(1/100)-1
59	Venezuela	0.05	(GPC1700/GPC1600)**(1/100)-1
60	Canada	0.05	(GPC1700/GPC1600)**(1/100)-1
61	El Salvador	0.05	(GPC1700/GPC1600)**(1/100)-1
62	Haiti	0.05	(GPC1700/GPC1600)**(1/100)-1
63	Dominican R	0.05	(GPC1700/GPC1600)**(1/100)-1
64	Bosnia	0.05	(GPC1700/GPC1600)**(1/100)-1
65	Colombia	0.05	(GPC1700/GPC1600)**(1/100)-1
66	Tajikistan	0.05	(GPC1700/GPC1600)**(1/100)-1
67	Albania	0.05	(GPC1700/GPC1600)**(1/100)-1
68	Kyrgyzstan	0.05	(GPC1700/GPC1600)**(1/100)-1
69	Nicaragua	0.05	(GPC1700/GPC1600)**(1/100)-1
70	Ghana	0.05	(GPC1700/GPC1600)**(1/100)-1
71	Paraguay	0.05	(GPC1700/GPC1600)**(1/100)-1
72	Nepal	0.05	(GPC1700/GPC1600)**(1/100)-1
73	Honduras	0.05	(GPC1700/GPC1600)**(1/100)-1
74	Mongolia	0.05	(GPC1700/GPC1600)**(1/100)-1
75	New Zealand	0.05	(GPC1700/GPC1600)**(1/100)-1
76	Macedonia	0.05	(GPC1700/GPC1600)**(1/100)-1
77	South Sudan	0.05	(GPC1700/GPC1600)**(1/100)-1
78	Kosovo	0.05	(GPC1700/GPC1600)**(1/100)-1
79	Burundi	0.04	(GPC1700/GPC1600)**(1/100)-1
80	Lesotho	0.04	(GPC1700/GPC1600)**(1/100)-1
81	Botswana	0.04	(GPC1700/GPC1600)**(1/100)-1
82	Malawi	0.04	(GPC1700/GPC1600)**(1/100)-1
83	Guinea	0.03	(GPC1700/GPC1600)**(1/100)-1
84	Guinea-Biss	0.03	(GPC1700/GPC1600)**(1/100)-1
85	Eritrea	0.03	(GPC1700/GPC1600)**(1/100)-1
86	Ethiopia	0.03	(GPC1700/GPC1600)**(1/100)-1
87	Indonesia	0.01	(GPC1700/GPC1600)**(1/100)-1
106	Algeria	0.00	(GPC1700/GPC1600)**(1/100)-1
106	Bahrain	0.00	(GPC1700/GPC1600)**(1/100)-1
106	Bangladesh	0.00	(GPC1700/GPC1600)**(1/100)-1
106	China	0.00	(GPC1700/GPC1600)**(1/100)-1
106	Egypt	0.00	(GPC1700/GPC1600)**(1/100)-1
106	Hong Kong	0.00	(GPC1700/GPC1600)**(1/100)-1
106	India	0.00	(GPC1700/GPC1600)**(1/100)-1
106	Iran	0.00	(GPC1700/GPC1600)**(1/100)-1
106	Iraq	0.00	(GPC1700/GPC1600)**(1/100)-1

Table 5.4 GDP Per Capita Growth Rates, 1600-1700			
Rank	Country	GRPCRL	Source
106	Israel	0.00	(GPC1700/GPC1600)**(1/100)-1
106	Italy	0.00	(GPC1700/GPC1600)**(1/100)-1
106	Jordan	0.00	(GPC1700/GPC1600)**(1/100)-1
106	Korea, North	0.00	(GPC1700/GPC1600)**(1/100)-1
106	Korea, South	0.00	(GPC1700/GPC1600)**(1/100)-1
106	Kuwait	0.00	(GPC1700/GPC1600)**(1/100)-1
106	Lebanon	0.00	(GPC1700/GPC1600)**(1/100)-1
106	Libya	0.00	(GPC1700/GPC1600)**(1/100)-1
106	Madagascar	0.00	(GPC1700/GPC1600)**(1/100)-1
106	Morocco	0.00	(GPC1700/GPC1600)**(1/100)-1
106	Mozambique	0.00	(GPC1700/GPC1600)**(1/100)-1
106	Namibia	0.00	(GPC1700/GPC1600)**(1/100)-1
106	Oman	0.00	(GPC1700/GPC1600)**(1/100)-1
106	Pakistan	0.00	(GPC1700/GPC1600)**(1/100)-1
106	Qatar	0.00	(GPC1700/GPC1600)**(1/100)-1
106	Saudi Arabia	0.00	(GPC1700/GPC1600)**(1/100)-1
106	Somalia	0.00	(GPC1700/GPC1600)**(1/100)-1
106	South Africa	0.00	(GPC1700/GPC1600)**(1/100)-1
106	Spain	0.00	(GPC1700/GPC1600)**(1/100)-1
106	Sudan	0.00	(GPC1700/GPC1600)**(1/100)-1
106	Swaziland	0.00	(GPC1700/GPC1600)**(1/100)-1
106	Syria	0.00	(GPC1700/GPC1600)**(1/100)-1
106	Tunisia	0.00	(GPC1700/GPC1600)**(1/100)-1
106	Turkey	0.00	(GPC1700/GPC1600)**(1/100)-1
106	UAE	0.00	(GPC1700/GPC1600)**(1/100)-1
106	Yemen	0.00	(GPC1700/GPC1600)**(1/100)-1
106	Zambia	0.00	(GPC1700/GPC1600)**(1/100)-1
106	Zimbabwe	0.00	(GPC1700/GPC1600)**(1/100)-1
125	Laos	-0.01	(GPC1700/GPC1600)**(1/100)-1
126	Malaysia	-0.01	(GPC1700/GPC1600)**(1/100)-1
127	Vietnam	-0.01	(GPC1700/GPC1600)**(1/100)-1
128	Burma	-0.01	(GPC1700/GPC1600)**(1/100)-1
129	Thailand	-0.01	(GPC1700/GPC1600)**(1/100)-1
130	Singapore	-0.01	(GPC1700/GPC1600)**(1/100)-1
131	Afghanistan	-0.01	(GPC1700/GPC1600)**(1/100)-1
132	Cambodia	-0.01	(GPC1700/GPC1600)**(1/100)-1
133.5	Sri Lanka	-0.01	(GPC1700/GPC1600)**(1/100)-1
133.5	Taiwan	-0.01	(GPC1700/GPC1600)**(1/100)-1
135	Philippines	-0.01	(GPC1700/GPC1600)**(1/100)-1

Table 5.5 GDP Per Capita Growth Rates, 1700-1820			
Rank	Country	GRPCRL	Source
1	US	0.73	(GPC1820/GPC1700)**(1/120)-1
2	Canada	0.62	(GPC1820/GPC1700)**(1/120)-1
3	Uruguay	0.51	(GPC1820/GPC1700)**(1/120)-1
4	Argentina	0.35	(GPC1820/GPC1700)**(1/120)-1
5	Brazil	0.29	(GPC1820/GPC1700)**(1/120)-1
6	Trinidad & T	0.27	(GPC1820/GPC1700)**(1/120)-1
7	Colombia	0.26	(GPC1820/GPC1700)**(1/120)-1
8	UK	0.26	(GPC1820/GPC1700)**(1/120)-1
9	Mexico	0.24	(GPC1820/GPC1700)**(1/120)-1
10	France	0.18	(GPC1820/GPC1700)**(1/120)-1
11	Norway	0.17	(GPC1820/GPC1700)**(1/120)-1
12	Austria	0.17	(GPC1820/GPC1700)**(1/120)-1
13	Ireland	0.17	(GPC1820/GPC1700)**(1/120)-1
14	Sweden	0.17	(GPC1820/GPC1700)**(1/120)-1
15	Iceland	0.17	(GPC1820/GPC1700)**(1/120)-1
16	Denmark	0.17	(GPC1820/GPC1700)**(1/120)-1
17	Switzerland	0.17	(GPC1820/GPC1700)**(1/120)-1
18	Finland	0.17	(GPC1820/GPC1700)**(1/120)-1
19	Chile	0.16	(GPC1820/GPC1700)**(1/120)-1
20	Greece	0.16	(GPC1820/GPC1700)**(1/120)-1
21	Cyprus	0.16	(GPC1820/GPC1700)**(1/120)-1
22	Germany	0.14	(GPC1820/GPC1700)**(1/120)-1
23	Spain	0.14	(GPC1820/GPC1700)**(1/120)-1
24	Japan	0.13	(GPC1820/GPC1700)**(1/120)-1
25	Slovenia	0.12	(GPC1820/GPC1700)**(1/120)-1
26	Belgium	0.12	(GPC1820/GPC1700)**(1/120)-1
27	Hungary	0.12	(GPC1820/GPC1700)**(1/120)-1
28	Estonia	0.11	(GPC1820/GPC1700)**(1/120)-1
29	Uzbekistan	0.10	(GPC1820/GPC1700)**(1/120)-1
30	Tajikistan	0.10	(GPC1820/GPC1700)**(1/120)-1
31	Belarus	0.10	(GPC1820/GPC1700)**(1/120)-1
32	Armenia	0.10	(GPC1820/GPC1700)**(1/120)-1
33	Lithuania	0.10	(GPC1820/GPC1700)**(1/120)-1
34	Ukraine	0.10	(GPC1820/GPC1700)**(1/120)-1
35	Azerbaijan	0.10	(GPC1820/GPC1700)**(1/120)-1
36	Kazakhstan	0.10	(GPC1820/GPC1700)**(1/120)-1
37	Moldova	0.10	(GPC1820/GPC1700)**(1/120)-1
38	Russia	0.10	(GPC1820/GPC1700)**(1/120)-1
39	Latvia	0.10	(GPC1820/GPC1700)**(1/120)-1
40	Georgia	0.10	(GPC1820/GPC1700)**(1/120)-1
41	Turkmenistan	0.10	(GPC1820/GPC1700)**(1/120)-1
42	Serbia	0.10	(GPC1820/GPC1700)**(1/120)-1
43	Montenegro	0.10	(GPC1820/GPC1700)**(1/120)-1
44	Czechia	0.10	(GPC1820/GPC1700)**(1/120)-1
45	Poland	0.10	(GPC1820/GPC1700)**(1/120)-1
46	Romania	0.10	(GPC1820/GPC1700)**(1/120)-1
47	Croatia	0.10	(GPC1820/GPC1700)**(1/120)-1
48	Slovakia	0.10	(GPC1820/GPC1700)**(1/120)-1

TABLE 5.5 GDP PER CAPITA GROWTH RATES, 1700-1820

Rank	Country	GRPCRL	Source
49	Bulgaria	0.10	(GPC1820/GPC1700)**(1/120)-1
50	Portugal	0.10	(GPC1820/GPC1700)**(1/120)-1
51	Sierra Leone	0.07	(GPC1820/GPC1700)**(1/120)-1
52	Guatemala	0.07	(GPC1820/GPC1700)**(1/120)-1
53	Australia	0.06	(GPC1820/GPC1700)**(1/120)-1
54	Costa Rica	0.06	(GPC1820/GPC1700)**(1/120)-1
55	Bolivia	0.06	(GPC1820/GPC1700)**(1/120)-1
56	Panama	0.06	(GPC1820/GPC1700)**(1/120)-1
57	Ecuador	0.06	(GPC1820/GPC1700)**(1/120)-1
58	Turkey	0.06	(GPC1820/GPC1700)**(1/120)-1
59	Peru	0.06	(GPC1820/GPC1700)**(1/120)-1
60	Venezuela	0.06	(GPC1820/GPC1700)**(1/120)-1
61	El Salvador	0.06	(GPC1820/GPC1700)**(1/120)-1
62	Haiti	0.05	(GPC1820/GPC1700)**(1/120)-1
63	Dominican R	0.05	(GPC1820/GPC1700)**(1/120)-1
64	Bosnia	0.05	(GPC1820/GPC1700)**(1/120)-1
65	Albania	0.05	(GPC1820/GPC1700)**(1/120)-1
66	Kyrgyzstan	0.05	(GPC1820/GPC1700)**(1/120)-1
67	Nicaragua	0.05	(GPC1820/GPC1700)**(1/120)-1
68	Ghana	0.05	(GPC1820/GPC1700)**(1/120)-1
69	Paraguay	0.05	(GPC1820/GPC1700)**(1/120)-1
70	Nepal	0.05	(GPC1820/GPC1700)**(1/120)-1
71	Honduras	0.05	(GPC1820/GPC1700)**(1/120)-1
72	Mongolia	0.05	(GPC1820/GPC1700)**(1/120)-1
73	New Zealand	0.05	(GPC1820/GPC1700)**(1/120)-1
74	Macedonia	0.05	(GPC1820/GPC1700)**(1/120)-1
75	South Sudan	0.05	(GPC1820/GPC1700)**(1/120)-1
76	Kosovo	0.05	(GPC1820/GPC1700)**(1/120)-1
77	Indonesia	0.04	(GPC1820/GPC1700)**(1/120)-1
78	Burundi	0.04	(GPC1820/GPC1700)**(1/120)-1
79	Lesotho	0.04	(GPC1820/GPC1700)**(1/120)-1
80	Botswana	0.04	(GPC1820/GPC1700)**(1/120)-1
81	Malawi	0.04	(GPC1820/GPC1700)**(1/120)-1
82	Guinea	0.04	(GPC1820/GPC1700)**(1/120)-1
83	Guinea-Biss	0.03	(GPC1820/GPC1700)**(1/120)-1
84	Eritrea	0.03	(GPC1820/GPC1700)**(1/120)-1
85	Ethiopia	0.03	(GPC1820/GPC1700)**(1/120)-1
86	Iraq	0.02	(GPC1820/GPC1700)**(1/120)-1
87	Italy	0.01	(GPC1820/GPC1700)**(1/120)-1
88	Cambodia	0.01	(GPC1820/GPC1700)**(1/120)-1
89	Afghanistan	0.01	(GPC1820/GPC1700)**(1/120)-1
90	Philippines	0.01	(GPC1820/GPC1700)**(1/120)-1
91.5	Sri Lanka	0.01	(GPC1820/GPC1700)**(1/120)-1
91.5	Taiwan	0.01	(GPC1820/GPC1700)**(1/120)-1
93	Thailand	0.01	(GPC1820/GPC1700)**(1/120)-1
94	Malaysia	0.01	(GPC1820/GPC1700)**(1/120)-1
95	Burma	0.01	(GPC1820/GPC1700)**(1/120)-1
96	Singapore	0.01	(GPC1820/GPC1700)**(1/120)-1

Table 5.5 GDP Per Capita Growth Rates, 1700-1820			
Rank	Country	GRPCRL	Source
97	Laos	0.01	(GPC1820/GPC1700)**(1/120)-1
98	Vietnam	0.01	(GPC1820/GPC1700)**(1/120)-1
113	Algeria	0.00	(GPC1820/GPC1700)**(1/120)-1
113	Bahrain	0.00	(GPC1820/GPC1700)**(1/120)-1
113	China	0.00	(GPC1820/GPC1700)**(1/120)-1
113	Egypt	0.00	(GPC1820/GPC1700)**(1/120)-1
113	Hong Kong	0.00	(GPC1820/GPC1700)**(1/120)-1
113	Israel	0.00	(GPC1820/GPC1700)**(1/120)-1
113	Jordan	0.00	(GPC1820/GPC1700)**(1/120)-1
113	Korea, North	0.00	(GPC1820/GPC1700)**(1/120)-1
113	Korea, South	0.00	(GPC1820/GPC1700)**(1/120)-1
113	Kuwait	0.00	(GPC1820/GPC1700)**(1/120)-1
113	Lebanon	0.00	(GPC1820/GPC1700)**(1/120)-1
113	Libya	0.00	(GPC1820/GPC1700)**(1/120)-1
113	Madagascar	0.00	(GPC1820/GPC1700)**(1/120)-1
113	Morocco	0.00	(GPC1820/GPC1700)**(1/120)-1
113	Mozambique	0.00	(GPC1820/GPC1700)**(1/120)-1
113	Namibia	0.00	(GPC1820/GPC1700)**(1/120)-1
113	Oman	0.00	(GPC1820/GPC1700)**(1/120)-1
113	Qatar	0.00	(GPC1820/GPC1700)**(1/120)-1
113	Saudi Arabia	0.00	(GPC1820/GPC1700)**(1/120)-1
113	Somalia	0.00	(GPC1820/GPC1700)**(1/120)-1
113	South Africa	0.00	(GPC1820/GPC1700)**(1/120)-1
113	Sudan	0.00	(GPC1820/GPC1700)**(1/120)-1
113	Swaziland	0.00	(GPC1820/GPC1700)**(1/120)-1
113	Syria	0.00	(GPC1820/GPC1700)**(1/120)-1
113	Tunisia	0.00	(GPC1820/GPC1700)**(1/120)-1
113	UAE	0.00	(GPC1820/GPC1700)**(1/120)-1
113	Yemen	0.00	(GPC1820/GPC1700)**(1/120)-1
113	Zambia	0.00	(GPC1820/GPC1700)**(1/120)-1
113	Zimbabwe	0.00	(GPC1820/GPC1700)**(1/120)-1
128	Iran	-0.02	(GPC1820/GPC1700)**(1/120)-1
129	Cuba	-0.02	(GPC1820/GPC1700)**(1/120)-1
130	Puerto Rico	-0.02	(GPC1820/GPC1700)**(1/120)-1
131	Jamaica	-0.02	(GPC1820/GPC1700)**(1/120)-1
133	Bangladesh	-0.03	(GPC1820/GPC1700)**(1/120)-1
133	India	-0.03	(GPC1820/GPC1700)**(1/120)-1
133	Pakistan	-0.03	(GPC1820/GPC1700)**(1/120)-1
135	Netherlands	-0.12	(GPC1820/GPC1700)**(1/120)-1

TABLE 5.6 GDP PER CAPITA GROWTH RATES, 1820-1870			
Rank	Country	GRPCRL	Source
1	New Zealand	4.18	(GPC1870/GPC1820)**(1/50)-1
2	Australia	3.76	(GPC1870/GPC1820)**(1/50)-1
3	South Africa	1.46	(GPC1870/GPC1820)**(1/50)-1
4	Belgium	1.44	(GPC1870/GPC1820)**(1/50)-1
5	Ireland	1.42	(GPC1870/GPC1820)**(1/50)-1
6	US	1.34	(GPC1870/GPC1820)**(1/50)-1
7	Switzerland	1.32	(GPC1870/GPC1820)**(1/50)-1
8	Namibia	1.28	(GPC1870/GPC1820)**(1/50)-1
9	Canada	1.27	(GPC1870/GPC1820)**(1/50)-1
10	UK	1.26	(GPC1870/GPC1820)**(1/50)-1
11	Chile	1.25	(GPC1870/GPC1820)**(1/50)-1
12	Germany	1.08	(GPC1870/GPC1820)**(1/50)-1
13	Algeria	1.02	(GPC1870/GPC1820)**(1/50)-1
14	France	1.01	(GPC1870/GPC1820)**(1/50)-1
15	Iceland	0.91	(GPC1870/GPC1820)**(1/50)-1
16	Denmark	0.91	(GPC1870/GPC1820)**(1/50)-1
17	Sri Lanka	0.88	(GPC1870/GPC1820)**(1/50)-1
18	Austria	0.85	(GPC1870/GPC1820)**(1/50)-1
19	Netherlands	0.81	(GPC1870/GPC1820)**(1/50)-1
20	Tunisia	0.78	(GPC1870/GPC1820)**(1/50)-1
21	Mozambique	0.78	(GPC1870/GPC1820)**(1/50)-1
22	Finland	0.76	(GPC1870/GPC1820)**(1/50)-1
23	Somalia	0.72	(GPC1870/GPC1820)**(1/50)-1
24	Sweden	0.66	(GPC1870/GPC1820)**(1/50)-1
25	Madagascar	0.64	(GPC1870/GPC1820)**(1/50)-1
26	Cyprus	0.64	(GPC1870/GPC1820)**(1/50)-1
27	Greece	0.64	(GPC1870/GPC1820)**(1/50)-1
28	Czechia	0.63	(GPC1870/GPC1820)**(1/50)-1
29	Slovakia	0.63	(GPC1870/GPC1820)**(1/50)-1
30	Moldova	0.63	(GPC1870/GPC1820)**(1/50)-1
31	Latvia	0.63	(GPC1870/GPC1820)**(1/50)-1
32	Kyrgyzstan	0.63	(GPC1870/GPC1820)**(1/50)-1
33	Georgia	0.63	(GPC1870/GPC1820)**(1/50)-1
34	Kazakhstan	0.63	(GPC1870/GPC1820)**(1/50)-1
35	Estonia	0.63	(GPC1870/GPC1820)**(1/50)-1
36	Russia	0.63	(GPC1870/GPC1820)**(1/50)-1
37	Turkmenistan	0.63	(GPC1870/GPC1820)**(1/50)-1
38	Belarus	0.63	(GPC1870/GPC1820)**(1/50)-1
39	Lithuania	0.63	(GPC1870/GPC1820)**(1/50)-1
40	Ukraine	0.63	(GPC1870/GPC1820)**(1/50)-1
41	Azerbaijan	0.63	(GPC1870/GPC1820)**(1/50)-1
42	Armenia	0.63	(GPC1870/GPC1820)**(1/50)-1
43	Tajikistan	0.63	(GPC1870/GPC1820)**(1/50)-1
44	Egypt	0.63	(GPC1870/GPC1820)**(1/50)-1
45	Uzbekistan	0.63	(GPC1870/GPC1820)**(1/50)-1
46	Singapore	0.62	(GPC1870/GPC1820)**(1/50)-1
47	Italy	0.59	(GPC1870/GPC1820)**(1/50)-1
48	Morocco	0.54	(GPC1870/GPC1820)**(1/50)-1

TABLE 5.6 GDP PER CAPITA GROWTH RATES, 1820-1870

Rank	Country	GRPCRL	Source
49	Libya	0.53	(GPC1870/GPC1820)**(1/50)-1
50	Sudan	0.53	(GPC1870/GPC1820)**(1/50)-1
51	Norway	0.52	(GPC1870/GPC1820)**(1/50)-1
52	Turkey	0.50	(GPC1870/GPC1820)**(1/50)-1
53.5	Lebanon	0.50	(GPC1870/GPC1820)**(1/50)-1
53.5	Syria	0.50	(GPC1870/GPC1820)**(1/50)-1
55	Venezuela	0.43	(GPC1870/GPC1820)**(1/50)-1
56	Swaziland	0.43	(GPC1870/GPC1820)**(1/50)-1
57	Zimbabwe	0.40	(GPC1870/GPC1820)**(1/50)-1
58	Israel	0.40	(GPC1870/GPC1820)**(1/50)-1
60	Iran	0.40	(GPC1870/GPC1820)**(1/50)-1
60	Iraq	0.40	(GPC1870/GPC1820)**(1/50)-1
60	Jordan	0.40	(GPC1870/GPC1820)**(1/50)-1
62	Spain	0.36	(GPC1870/GPC1820)**(1/50)-1
63	Zambia	0.36	(GPC1870/GPC1820)**(1/50)-1
64	Pakistan	0.32	(GPC1870/GPC1820)**(1/50)-1
65	Hong Kong	0.26	(GPC1870/GPC1820)**(1/50)-1
66	Ghana	0.21	(GPC1870/GPC1820)**(1/50)-1
67	Brazil	0.20	(GPC1870/GPC1820)**(1/50)-1
68	Thailand	0.19	(GPC1870/GPC1820)**(1/50)-1
69	Japan	0.19	(GPC1870/GPC1820)**(1/50)-1
70	Malaysia	0.19	(GPC1870/GPC1820)**(1/50)-1
71	Indonesia	0.13	(GPC1870/GPC1820)**(1/50)-1
72	Philippines	0.13	(GPC1870/GPC1820)**(1/50)-1
73	Slovenia	0.12	(GPC1870/GPC1820)**(1/50)-1
74	Hungary	0.12	(GPC1870/GPC1820)**(1/50)-1
75	Bangladesh	0.11	(GPC1870/GPC1820)**(1/50)-1
76	Portugal	0.11	(GPC1870/GPC1820)**(1/50)-1
77	Bulgaria	0.10	(GPC1870/GPC1820)**(1/50)-1
78	Albania	0.10	(GPC1870/GPC1820)**(1/50)-1
79	Croatia	0.10	(GPC1870/GPC1820)**(1/50)-1
80	Romania	0.10	(GPC1870/GPC1820)**(1/50)-1
81	Poland	0.10	(GPC1870/GPC1820)**(1/50)-1
82	Montenegro	0.10	(GPC1870/GPC1820)**(1/50)-1
83	Serbia	0.10	(GPC1870/GPC1820)**(1/50)-1
84	India	0.10	(GPC1870/GPC1820)**(1/50)-1
88	Bahrain	0.09	(GPC1870/GPC1820)**(1/50)-1
88	Kuwait	0.09	(GPC1870/GPC1820)**(1/50)-1
88	Oman	0.09	(GPC1870/GPC1820)**(1/50)-1
88	Qatar	0.09	(GPC1870/GPC1820)**(1/50)-1
88	Saudi Arabia	0.09	(GPC1870/GPC1820)**(1/50)-1
88	UAE	0.09	(GPC1870/GPC1820)**(1/50)-1
88	Yemen	0.09	(GPC1870/GPC1820)**(1/50)-1
92	Sierra Leone	0.08	(GPC1870/GPC1820)**(1/50)-1
93	El Salvador	0.06	(GPC1870/GPC1820)**(1/50)-1
94	Haiti	0.06	(GPC1870/GPC1820)**(1/50)-1
95	Dominican R	0.06	(GPC1870/GPC1820)**(1/50)-1
96	Bosnia	0.06	(GPC1870/GPC1820)**(1/50)-1

Table 5.6 GDP Per Capita Growth Rates, 1820-1870

Rank	Country	GRPCRL	Source
97	Nepal	0.05	(GPC1870/GPC1820)**(1/50)-1
98	Honduras	0.05	(GPC1870/GPC1820)**(1/50)-1
99	Mongolia	0.05	(GPC1870/GPC1820)**(1/50)-1
100	Macedonia	0.05	(GPC1870/GPC1820)**(1/50)-1
101	South Sudan	0.05	(GPC1870/GPC1820)**(1/50)-1
102	Kosovo	0.05	(GPC1870/GPC1820)**(1/50)-1
103	Ecuador	0.05	(GPC1870/GPC1820)**(1/50)-1
104	Peru	0.05	(GPC1870/GPC1820)**(1/50)-1
105	Uruguay	0.05	(GPC1870/GPC1820)**(1/50)-1
106	Costa Rica	0.05	(GPC1870/GPC1820)**(1/50)-1
107	Guatemala	0.05	(GPC1870/GPC1820)**(1/50)-1
108	Bolivia	0.05	(GPC1870/GPC1820)**(1/50)-1
109	Argentina	0.05	(GPC1870/GPC1820)**(1/50)-1
110	Colombia	0.05	(GPC1870/GPC1820)**(1/50)-1
111	Panama	0.05	(GPC1870/GPC1820)**(1/50)-1
112	Trinidad & T	0.05	(GPC1870/GPC1820)**(1/50)-1
113	Puerto Rico	0.05	(GPC1870/GPC1820)**(1/50)-1
114	Cuba	0.05	(GPC1870/GPC1820)**(1/50)-1
115	Paraguay	0.05	(GPC1870/GPC1820)**(1/50)-1
116	Nicaragua	0.05	(GPC1870/GPC1820)**(1/50)-1
117	Burundi	0.04	(GPC1870/GPC1820)**(1/50)-1
118	Lesotho	0.04	(GPC1870/GPC1820)**(1/50)-1
119	Botswana	0.04	(GPC1870/GPC1820)**(1/50)-1
120	Malawi	0.04	(GPC1870/GPC1820)**(1/50)-1
121	Guinea	0.04	(GPC1870/GPC1820)**(1/50)-1
122	Guinea-Biss	0.03	(GPC1870/GPC1820)**(1/50)-1
123	Eritrea	0.03	(GPC1870/GPC1820)**(1/50)-1
124	Ethiopia	0.03	(GPC1870/GPC1820)**(1/50)-1
125.5	Korea, North	0.01	(GPC1870/GPC1820)**(1/50)-1
125.5	Korea, South	0.01	(GPC1870/GPC1820)**(1/50)-1
127.5	Burma	0.00	(GPC1870/GPC1820)**(1/50)-1
127.5	Taiwan	0.00	(GPC1870/GPC1820)**(1/50)-1
129	Cambodia	-0.05	(GPC1870/GPC1820)**(1/50)-1
130	Afghanistan	-0.08	(GPC1870/GPC1820)**(1/50)-1
131	Laos	-0.08	(GPC1870/GPC1820)**(1/50)-1
132	Vietnam	-0.09	(GPC1870/GPC1820)**(1/50)-1
133	Mexico	-0.24	(GPC1870/GPC1820)**(1/50)-1
134	China	-0.25	(GPC1870/GPC1820)**(1/50)-1
135	Jamaica	-0.54	(GPC1870/GPC1820)**(1/50)-1

Table 5.7 GDP Per Capita Growth Rates, 1870-1880

Rank	Country	GRPCRL	Source
1	Spain	3.15	(GPC1880/GPC1870)**(1/10)-1
2	Australia	2.73	(GPC1880/GPC1870)**(1/10)-1
3	Argentina	2.51	(GPC1880/GPC1870)**(1/10)-1
4	Mexico	2.05	(GPC1880/GPC1870)**(1/10)-1
5	New Zealand	1.91	(GPC1880/GPC1870)**(1/10)-1
6	Chile	1.79	(GPC1880/GPC1870)**(1/10)-1
7	Bolivia	1.77	(GPC1880/GPC1870)**(1/10)-1
8	Nicaragua	1.77	(GPC1880/GPC1870)**(1/10)-1
9	Paraguay	1.77	(GPC1880/GPC1870)**(1/10)-1
10	Ecuador	1.77	(GPC1880/GPC1870)**(1/10)-1
11	Guatemala	1.77	(GPC1880/GPC1870)**(1/10)-1
12	Puerto Rico	1.77	(GPC1880/GPC1870)**(1/10)-1
13	Costa Rica	1.77	(GPC1880/GPC1870)**(1/10)-1
14	Cuba	1.77	(GPC1880/GPC1870)**(1/10)-1
15	Trinidad & T	1.77	(GPC1880/GPC1870)**(1/10)-1
16	Panama	1.77	(GPC1880/GPC1870)**(1/10)-1
17	Peru	1.73	(GPC1880/GPC1870)**(1/10)-1
18	Colombia	1.73	(GPC1880/GPC1870)**(1/10)-1
19	Serbia	1.72	(GPC1880/GPC1870)**(1/10)-1
20	Croatia	1.72	(GPC1880/GPC1870)**(1/10)-1
21	Slovenia	1.72	(GPC1880/GPC1870)**(1/10)-1
22	Montenegro	1.72	(GPC1880/GPC1870)**(1/10)-1
23	Kosovo	1.72	(GPC1880/GPC1870)**(1/10)-1
24	Macedonia	1.72	(GPC1880/GPC1870)**(1/10)-1
25	US	1.65	(GPC1880/GPC1870)**(1/10)-1
26	Japan	1.59	(GPC1880/GPC1870)**(1/10)-1
27	Switzerland	1.54	(GPC1880/GPC1870)**(1/10)-1
28	Poland	1.54	(GPC1880/GPC1870)**(1/10)-1
29	Hungary	1.51	(GPC1880/GPC1870)**(1/10)-1
30	Bulgaria	1.50	(GPC1880/GPC1870)**(1/10)-1
31	Albania	1.48	(GPC1880/GPC1870)**(1/10)-1
32	Singapore	1.47	(GPC1880/GPC1870)**(1/10)-1
33	Hong Kong	1.47	(GPC1880/GPC1870)**(1/10)-1
34	Greece	1.47	(GPC1880/GPC1870)**(1/10)-1
35	Cyprus	1.47	(GPC1880/GPC1870)**(1/10)-1
36	Romania	1.47	(GPC1880/GPC1870)**(1/10)-1
37	South Africa	1.46	(GPC1880/GPC1870)**(1/10)-1
38	Belgium	1.31	(GPC1880/GPC1870)**(1/10)-1
39	Czechia	1.29	(GPC1880/GPC1870)**(1/10)-1
40	Slovakia	1.29	(GPC1880/GPC1870)**(1/10)-1
41	Namibia	1.28	(GPC1880/GPC1870)**(1/10)-1
42	France	1.23	(GPC1880/GPC1870)**(1/10)-1
43	Venezuela	1.23	(GPC1880/GPC1870)**(1/10)-1
44	Israel	1.19	(GPC1880/GPC1870)**(1/10)-1
45	Austria	1.10	(GPC1880/GPC1870)**(1/10)-1
46.5	Lebanon	1.10	(GPC1880/GPC1870)**(1/10)-1
46.5	Syria	1.10	(GPC1880/GPC1870)**(1/10)-1
48	Sweden	1.06	(GPC1880/GPC1870)**(1/10)-1

TABLE 5.7 GDP PER CAPITA GROWTH RATES, 1870-1880

Rank	Country	GRPCRL	Source
49	Norway	1.04	(GPC1880/GPC1870)**(1/10)-1
50	Algeria	1.03	(GPC1880/GPC1870)**(1/10)-1
51	Ireland	1.01	(GPC1880/GPC1870)**(1/10)-1
52	Netherlands	1.00	(GPC1880/GPC1870)**(1/10)-1
53	Azerbaijan	0.91	(GPC1880/GPC1870)**(1/10)-1
54	Kyrgyzstan	0.91	(GPC1880/GPC1870)**(1/10)-1
55	Tajikistan	0.91	(GPC1880/GPC1870)**(1/10)-1
56	Russia	0.91	(GPC1880/GPC1870)**(1/10)-1
57	Turkmenistan	0.91	(GPC1880/GPC1870)**(1/10)-1
58	Latvia	0.91	(GPC1880/GPC1870)**(1/10)-1
59	Armenia	0.91	(GPC1880/GPC1870)**(1/10)-1
60	Lithuania	0.91	(GPC1880/GPC1870)**(1/10)-1
61	Moldova	0.91	(GPC1880/GPC1870)**(1/10)-1
62	Ukraine	0.91	(GPC1880/GPC1870)**(1/10)-1
63	Georgia	0.91	(GPC1880/GPC1870)**(1/10)-1
64	Uzbekistan	0.91	(GPC1880/GPC1870)**(1/10)-1
65	Kazakhstan	0.91	(GPC1880/GPC1870)**(1/10)-1
66	Estonia	0.91	(GPC1880/GPC1870)**(1/10)-1
67	Belarus	0.91	(GPC1880/GPC1870)**(1/10)-1
68	Turkey	0.90	(GPC1880/GPC1870)**(1/10)-1
69	UK	0.87	(GPC1880/GPC1870)**(1/10)-1
70	Denmark	0.86	(GPC1880/GPC1870)**(1/10)-1
71	Iceland	0.85	(GPC1880/GPC1870)**(1/10)-1
72	Vietnam	0.85	(GPC1880/GPC1870)**(1/10)-1
73	Germany	0.80	(GPC1880/GPC1870)**(1/10)-1
74	Laos	0.80	(GPC1880/GPC1870)**(1/10)-1
75	Afghanistan	0.79	(GPC1880/GPC1870)**(1/10)-1
76	Tunisia	0.78	(GPC1880/GPC1870)**(1/10)-1
77	Mozambique	0.78	(GPC1880/GPC1870)**(1/10)-1
79	Iran	0.77	(GPC1880/GPC1870)**(1/10)-1
79	Iraq	0.77	(GPC1880/GPC1870)**(1/10)-1
79	Jordan	0.77	(GPC1880/GPC1870)**(1/10)-1
81	Somalia	0.72	(GPC1880/GPC1870)**(1/10)-1
82	Burma	0.72	(GPC1880/GPC1870)**(1/10)-1
83.5	Korea, North	0.71	(GPC1880/GPC1870)**(1/10)-1
83.5	Korea, South	0.71	(GPC1880/GPC1870)**(1/10)-1
85	Canada	0.69	(GPC1880/GPC1870)**(1/10)-1
86	Cambodia	0.66	(GPC1880/GPC1870)**(1/10)-1
87	Taiwan	0.65	(GPC1880/GPC1870)**(1/10)-1
88	Madagascar	0.64	(GPC1880/GPC1870)**(1/10)-1
89	Egypt	0.60	(GPC1880/GPC1870)**(1/10)-1
90	Morocco	0.54	(GPC1880/GPC1870)**(1/10)-1
91	Italy	0.53	(GPC1880/GPC1870)**(1/10)-1
92	Brazil	0.53	(GPC1880/GPC1870)**(1/10)-1
93	Libya	0.53	(GPC1880/GPC1870)**(1/10)-1
94	Sudan	0.53	(GPC1880/GPC1870)**(1/10)-1
95	Thailand	0.48	(GPC1880/GPC1870)**(1/10)-1
96	Malaysia	0.46	(GPC1880/GPC1870)**(1/10)-1

Table 5.7 GDP Per Capita Growth Rates, 1870-1880			
Rank	Country	GRPCRL	Source
97	India	0.43	(GPC1880/GPC1870)**(1/10)-1
98	Swaziland	0.43	(GPC1880/GPC1870)**(1/10)-1
99	Zimbabwe	0.40	(GPC1880/GPC1870)**(1/10)-1
100	Zambia	0.36	(GPC1880/GPC1870)**(1/10)-1
101	Philippines	0.36	(GPC1880/GPC1870)**(1/10)-1
102	Jamaica	0.34	(GPC1880/GPC1870)**(1/10)-1
103	Pakistan	0.32	(GPC1880/GPC1870)**(1/10)-1
104	Ghana	0.22	(GPC1880/GPC1870)**(1/10)-1
105	Finland	0.13	(GPC1880/GPC1870)**(1/10)-1
106	Indonesia	0.12	(GPC1880/GPC1870)**(1/10)-1
107	Bangladesh	0.11	(GPC1880/GPC1870)**(1/10)-1
111	Bahrain	0.10	(GPC1880/GPC1870)**(1/10)-1
111	Kuwait	0.10	(GPC1880/GPC1870)**(1/10)-1
111	Oman	0.10	(GPC1880/GPC1870)**(1/10)-1
111	Qatar	0.10	(GPC1880/GPC1870)**(1/10)-1
111	Saudi Arabia	0.10	(GPC1880/GPC1870)**(1/10)-1
111	UAE	0.10	(GPC1880/GPC1870)**(1/10)-1
111	Yemen	0.10	(GPC1880/GPC1870)**(1/10)-1
115	China	0.09	(GPC1880/GPC1870)**(1/10)-1
116	Sierra Leone	0.08	(GPC1880/GPC1870)**(1/10)-1
117	El Salvador	0.06	(GPC1880/GPC1870)**(1/10)-1
118	Haiti	0.06	(GPC1880/GPC1870)**(1/10)-1
119	Dominican R	0.06	(GPC1880/GPC1870)**(1/10)-1
120	Bosnia	0.06	(GPC1880/GPC1870)**(1/10)-1
121	Nepal	0.05	(GPC1880/GPC1870)**(1/10)-1
122	Honduras	0.05	(GPC1880/GPC1870)**(1/10)-1
123	Mongolia	0.05	(GPC1880/GPC1870)**(1/10)-1
124	South Sudan	0.05	(GPC1880/GPC1870)**(1/10)-1
125	Burundi	0.04	(GPC1880/GPC1870)**(1/10)-1
126	Lesotho	0.04	(GPC1880/GPC1870)**(1/10)-1
127	Botswana	0.04	(GPC1880/GPC1870)**(1/10)-1
128	Malawi	0.04	(GPC1880/GPC1870)**(1/10)-1
129	Guinea	0.04	(GPC1880/GPC1870)**(1/10)-1
130	Guinea-Biss	0.04	(GPC1880/GPC1870)**(1/10)-1
131	Eritrea	0.03	(GPC1880/GPC1870)**(1/10)-1
132	Ethiopia	0.03	(GPC1880/GPC1870)**(1/10)-1
133	Sri Lanka	-0.24	(GPC1880/GPC1870)**(1/10)-1
134	Portugal	-0.29	(GPC1880/GPC1870)**(1/10)-1
135	Uruguay	-0.46	(GPC1880/GPC1870)**(1/10)-1

TABLE 5.8 GDP PER CAPITA GROWTH RATES, 1880-1890			
Rank	Country	GRPCRL	Source
1	Canada	2.73	(GPC1890/GPC1880)**(1/10)-1
2	Switzerland	2.65	(GPC1890/GPC1880)**(1/10)-1
3	Argentina	2.51	(GPC1890/GPC1880)**(1/10)-1
4	Sri Lanka	2.32	(GPC1890/GPC1880)**(1/10)-1
5	Mexico	2.05	(GPC1890/GPC1880)**(1/10)-1
6	Germany	2.00	(GPC1890/GPC1880)**(1/10)-1
7	Finland	1.80	(GPC1890/GPC1880)**(1/10)-1
8	Chile	1.79	(GPC1890/GPC1880)**(1/10)-1
9	El Salvador	1.77	(GPC1890/GPC1880)**(1/10)-1
10	Puerto Rico	1.77	(GPC1890/GPC1880)**(1/10)-1
11	Trinidad & T	1.77	(GPC1890/GPC1880)**(1/10)-1
12	Ecuador	1.77	(GPC1890/GPC1880)**(1/10)-1
13	Costa Rica	1.77	(GPC1890/GPC1880)**(1/10)-1
14	Panama	1.77	(GPC1890/GPC1880)**(1/10)-1
15	Paraguay	1.77	(GPC1890/GPC1880)**(1/10)-1
16	Guatemala	1.77	(GPC1890/GPC1880)**(1/10)-1
17	Cuba	1.77	(GPC1890/GPC1880)**(1/10)-1
18	Nicaragua	1.77	(GPC1890/GPC1880)**(1/10)-1
19	Bolivia	1.77	(GPC1890/GPC1880)**(1/10)-1
20	Honduras	1.77	(GPC1890/GPC1880)**(1/10)-1
21	Portugal	1.76	(GPC1890/GPC1880)**(1/10)-1
22	Peru	1.73	(GPC1890/GPC1880)**(1/10)-1
23	Colombia	1.73	(GPC1890/GPC1880)**(1/10)-1
24	Macedonia	1.72	(GPC1890/GPC1880)**(1/10)-1
25	Bosnia	1.72	(GPC1890/GPC1880)**(1/10)-1
26	Slovenia	1.72	(GPC1890/GPC1880)**(1/10)-1
27	Serbia	1.72	(GPC1890/GPC1880)**(1/10)-1
28	Croatia	1.72	(GPC1890/GPC1880)**(1/10)-1
29	Montenegro	1.72	(GPC1890/GPC1880)**(1/10)-1
30	Kosovo	1.72	(GPC1890/GPC1880)**(1/10)-1
31	US	1.65	(GPC1890/GPC1880)**(1/10)-1
32	Austria	1.63	(GPC1890/GPC1880)**(1/10)-1
33	Japan	1.61	(GPC1890/GPC1880)**(1/10)-1
34	Poland	1.54	(GPC1890/GPC1880)**(1/10)-1
35	Hungary	1.51	(GPC1890/GPC1880)**(1/10)-1
36	Bulgaria	1.50	(GPC1890/GPC1880)**(1/10)-1
37	Albania	1.48	(GPC1890/GPC1880)**(1/10)-1
38	Singapore	1.47	(GPC1890/GPC1880)**(1/10)-1
39	Hong Kong	1.47	(GPC1890/GPC1880)**(1/10)-1
40	Greece	1.47	(GPC1890/GPC1880)**(1/10)-1
41	Cyprus	1.47	(GPC1890/GPC1880)**(1/10)-1
42	Romania	1.47	(GPC1890/GPC1880)**(1/10)-1
43	Denmark	1.47	(GPC1890/GPC1880)**(1/10)-1
44	Iceland	1.47	(GPC1890/GPC1880)**(1/10)-1
45	South Africa	1.46	(GPC1890/GPC1880)**(1/10)-1
46	UK	1.43	(GPC1890/GPC1880)**(1/10)-1
47	Slovakia	1.29	(GPC1890/GPC1880)**(1/10)-1
48	Czechia	1.29	(GPC1890/GPC1880)**(1/10)-1

Table 5.8 GDP Per Capita Growth Rates, 1880-1890

Rank	Country	GRPCRL	Source
49	Namibia	1.28	(GPC1890/GPC1880)**(1/10)-1
50	Sweden	1.23	(GPC1890/GPC1880)**(1/10)-1
51	Venezuela	1.23	(GPC1890/GPC1880)**(1/10)-1
52	Israel	1.19	(GPC1890/GPC1880)**(1/10)-1
53	Algeria	1.17	(GPC1890/GPC1880)**(1/10)-1
54	France	1.15	(GPC1890/GPC1880)**(1/10)-1
55	Norway	1.13	(GPC1890/GPC1880)**(1/10)-1
56	Belgium	1.13	(GPC1890/GPC1880)**(1/10)-1
57.5	Lebanon	1.10	(GPC1890/GPC1880)**(1/10)-1
57.5	Syria	1.10	(GPC1890/GPC1880)**(1/10)-1
59	Ireland	1.01	(GPC1890/GPC1880)**(1/10)-1
60	Belarus	0.91	(GPC1890/GPC1880)**(1/10)-1
61	Lithuania	0.91	(GPC1890/GPC1880)**(1/10)-1
62	Tajikistan	0.91	(GPC1890/GPC1880)**(1/10)-1
63	Kazakhstan	0.91	(GPC1890/GPC1880)**(1/10)-1
64	Russia	0.91	(GPC1890/GPC1880)**(1/10)-1
65	Turkmenistan	0.91	(GPC1890/GPC1880)**(1/10)-1
66	Latvia	0.91	(GPC1890/GPC1880)**(1/10)-1
67	Uzbekistan	0.91	(GPC1890/GPC1880)**(1/10)-1
68	Kyrgyzstan	0.91	(GPC1890/GPC1880)**(1/10)-1
69	Estonia	0.91	(GPC1890/GPC1880)**(1/10)-1
70	Ukraine	0.91	(GPC1890/GPC1880)**(1/10)-1
71	Armenia	0.91	(GPC1890/GPC1880)**(1/10)-1
72	Georgia	0.91	(GPC1890/GPC1880)**(1/10)-1
73	Moldova	0.91	(GPC1890/GPC1880)**(1/10)-1
74	Azerbaijan	0.91	(GPC1890/GPC1880)**(1/10)-1
75	Turkey	0.90	(GPC1890/GPC1880)**(1/10)-1
76	Netherlands	0.87	(GPC1890/GPC1880)**(1/10)-1
77	Vietnam	0.85	(GPC1890/GPC1880)**(1/10)-1
78	Cambodia	0.79	(GPC1890/GPC1880)**(1/10)-1
79	Afghanistan	0.79	(GPC1890/GPC1880)**(1/10)-1
80	Laos	0.79	(GPC1890/GPC1880)**(1/10)-1
81	Tunisia	0.78	(GPC1890/GPC1880)**(1/10)-1
82	Mozambique	0.78	(GPC1890/GPC1880)**(1/10)-1
84	Iran	0.77	(GPC1890/GPC1880)**(1/10)-1
84	Iraq	0.77	(GPC1890/GPC1880)**(1/10)-1
84	Jordan	0.77	(GPC1890/GPC1880)**(1/10)-1
86	Somalia	0.72	(GPC1890/GPC1880)**(1/10)-1
87	Burma	0.72	(GPC1890/GPC1880)**(1/10)-1
88.5	Korea, North	0.71	(GPC1890/GPC1880)**(1/10)-1
88.5	Korea, South	0.71	(GPC1890/GPC1880)**(1/10)-1
90	Nepal	0.71	(GPC1890/GPC1880)**(1/10)-1
91	Egypt	0.69	(GPC1890/GPC1880)**(1/10)-1
92	Taiwan	0.65	(GPC1890/GPC1880)**(1/10)-1
93	Madagascar	0.64	(GPC1890/GPC1880)**(1/10)-1
94	Brazil	0.54	(GPC1890/GPC1880)**(1/10)-1
95	Morocco	0.54	(GPC1890/GPC1880)**(1/10)-1
96	Libya	0.53	(GPC1890/GPC1880)**(1/10)-1

Table 5.8 GDP Per Capita Growth Rates, 1880-1890

Rank	Country	GRPCRL	Source
97	Italy	0.53	(GPC1890/GPC1880)**(1/10)-1
98	Sudan	0.53	(GPC1890/GPC1880)**(1/10)-1
99	Thailand	0.48	(GPC1890/GPC1880)**(1/10)-1
100	Malaysia	0.46	(GPC1890/GPC1880)**(1/10)-1
101	India	0.43	(GPC1890/GPC1880)**(1/10)-1
102	Swaziland	0.43	(GPC1890/GPC1880)**(1/10)-1
103	Zimbabwe	0.40	(GPC1890/GPC1880)**(1/10)-1
104	Australia	0.40	(GPC1890/GPC1880)**(1/10)-1
105	Zambia	0.36	(GPC1890/GPC1880)**(1/10)-1
106	Philippines	0.36	(GPC1890/GPC1880)**(1/10)-1
107	Jamaica	0.34	(GPC1890/GPC1880)**(1/10)-1
108	Pakistan	0.32	(GPC1890/GPC1880)**(1/10)-1
109	Uruguay	0.31	(GPC1890/GPC1880)**(1/10)-1
110	Ghana	0.22	(GPC1890/GPC1880)**(1/10)-1
111	Bangladesh	0.11	(GPC1890/GPC1880)**(1/10)-1
115	Bahrain	0.10	(GPC1890/GPC1880)**(1/10)-1
115	Kuwait	0.10	(GPC1890/GPC1880)**(1/10)-1
115	Oman	0.10	(GPC1890/GPC1880)**(1/10)-1
115	Qatar	0.10	(GPC1890/GPC1880)**(1/10)-1
115	Saudi Arabia	0.10	(GPC1890/GPC1880)**(1/10)-1
115	UAE	0.10	(GPC1890/GPC1880)**(1/10)-1
115	Yemen	0.10	(GPC1890/GPC1880)**(1/10)-1
119	China	0.09	(GPC1890/GPC1880)**(1/10)-1
120	Sierra Leone	0.08	(GPC1890/GPC1880)**(1/10)-1
121	Haiti	0.06	(GPC1890/GPC1880)**(1/10)-1
122	Dominican R	0.06	(GPC1890/GPC1880)**(1/10)-1
123	Mongolia	0.05	(GPC1890/GPC1880)**(1/10)-1
124	South Sudan	0.05	(GPC1890/GPC1880)**(1/10)-1
125	Burundi	0.04	(GPC1890/GPC1880)**(1/10)-1
126	Lesotho	0.04	(GPC1890/GPC1880)**(1/10)-1
127	Botswana	0.04	(GPC1890/GPC1880)**(1/10)-1
128	Malawi	0.04	(GPC1890/GPC1880)**(1/10)-1
129	Guinea	0.04	(GPC1890/GPC1880)**(1/10)-1
130	Guinea-Biss	0.04	(GPC1890/GPC1880)**(1/10)-1
131	Eritrea	0.03	(GPC1890/GPC1880)**(1/10)-1
132	Ethiopia	0.03	(GPC1890/GPC1880)**(1/10)-1
133	New Zealand	0.02	(GPC1890/GPC1880)**(1/10)-1
134	Indonesia	-0.03	(GPC1890/GPC1880)**(1/10)-1
135	Spain	-0.13	(GPC1890/GPC1880)**(1/10)-1

Table 5.9 GDP Per Capita Growth Rates, 1890-1900			
Rank	Country	GRPCRL	Source
1	Mexico	3.06	(GPC1900/GPC1890)**(1/10)-1
2	Argentina	2.50	(GPC1900/GPC1890)**(1/10)-1
3	Dominican R	2.19	(GPC1900/GPC1890)**(1/10)-1
4	Sri Lanka	2.13	(GPC1900/GPC1890)**(1/10)-1
5	Germany	2.09	(GPC1900/GPC1890)**(1/10)-1
6	Sweden	2.07	(GPC1900/GPC1890)**(1/10)-1
7	Canada	2.04	(GPC1900/GPC1890)**(1/10)-1
8	France	1.93	(GPC1900/GPC1890)**(1/10)-1
9	Finland	1.91	(GPC1900/GPC1890)**(1/10)-1
10	US	1.89	(GPC1900/GPC1890)**(1/10)-1
11	Switzerland	1.88	(GPC1900/GPC1890)**(1/10)-1
12	Poland	1.81	(GPC1900/GPC1890)**(1/10)-1
13	Iceland	1.80	(GPC1900/GPC1890)**(1/10)-1
14	Denmark	1.80	(GPC1900/GPC1890)**(1/10)-1
15	Chile	1.79	(GPC1900/GPC1890)**(1/10)-1
16	Cuba	1.77	(GPC1900/GPC1890)**(1/10)-1
17	Honduras	1.77	(GPC1900/GPC1890)**(1/10)-1
18	Nicaragua	1.77	(GPC1900/GPC1890)**(1/10)-1
19	Guatemala	1.77	(GPC1900/GPC1890)**(1/10)-1
20	Costa Rica	1.77	(GPC1900/GPC1890)**(1/10)-1
21	Bolivia	1.77	(GPC1900/GPC1890)**(1/10)-1
22	Panama	1.77	(GPC1900/GPC1890)**(1/10)-1
23	Paraguay	1.77	(GPC1900/GPC1890)**(1/10)-1
24	Trinidad & T	1.77	(GPC1900/GPC1890)**(1/10)-1
25	El Salvador	1.77	(GPC1900/GPC1890)**(1/10)-1
26	Puerto Rico	1.77	(GPC1900/GPC1890)**(1/10)-1
27	Ecuador	1.77	(GPC1900/GPC1890)**(1/10)-1
28	Peru	1.73	(GPC1900/GPC1890)**(1/10)-1
29	Colombia	1.73	(GPC1900/GPC1890)**(1/10)-1
30	Austria	1.67	(GPC1900/GPC1890)**(1/10)-1
31	Japan	1.55	(GPC1900/GPC1890)**(1/10)-1
32	Singapore	1.47	(GPC1900/GPC1890)**(1/10)-1
33	Hong Kong	1.47	(GPC1900/GPC1890)**(1/10)-1
34	South Africa	1.46	(GPC1900/GPC1890)**(1/10)-1
35	Portugal	1.44	(GPC1900/GPC1890)**(1/10)-1
36	Czechia	1.40	(GPC1900/GPC1890)**(1/10)-1
37	Slovakia	1.40	(GPC1900/GPC1890)**(1/10)-1
38	Cyprus	1.38	(GPC1900/GPC1890)**(1/10)-1
39	Greece	1.38	(GPC1900/GPC1890)**(1/10)-1
40	Albania	1.37	(GPC1900/GPC1890)**(1/10)-1
41	New Zealand	1.36	(GPC1900/GPC1890)**(1/10)-1
42	Hungary	1.34	(GPC1900/GPC1890)**(1/10)-1
43	Romania	1.28	(GPC1900/GPC1890)**(1/10)-1
44	Namibia	1.28	(GPC1900/GPC1890)**(1/10)-1
45	Venezuela	1.23	(GPC1900/GPC1890)**(1/10)-1
46	Israel	1.19	(GPC1900/GPC1890)**(1/10)-1
47	Indonesia	1.19	(GPC1900/GPC1890)**(1/10)-1
48	Algeria	1.17	(GPC1900/GPC1890)**(1/10)-1

TABLE 5.9 GDP PER CAPITA GROWTH RATES, 1890-1900			
Rank	Country	GRPCRL	Source
49	UK	1.14	(GPC1900/GPC1890)**(1/10)-1
50.5	Lebanon	1.10	(GPC1900/GPC1890)**(1/10)-1
50.5	Syria	1.10	(GPC1900/GPC1890)**(1/10)-1
52	Ireland	1.01	(GPC1900/GPC1890)**(1/10)-1
53	Spain	0.96	(GPC1900/GPC1890)**(1/10)-1
54	Kyrgyzstan	0.91	(GPC1900/GPC1890)**(1/10)-1
55	Armenia	0.91	(GPC1900/GPC1890)**(1/10)-1
56	Moldova	0.91	(GPC1900/GPC1890)**(1/10)-1
57	Ukraine	0.91	(GPC1900/GPC1890)**(1/10)-1
58	Azerbaijan	0.91	(GPC1900/GPC1890)**(1/10)-1
59	Lithuania	0.91	(GPC1900/GPC1890)**(1/10)-1
60	Turkmenistan	0.91	(GPC1900/GPC1890)**(1/10)-1
61	Estonia	0.91	(GPC1900/GPC1890)**(1/10)-1
62	Latvia	0.91	(GPC1900/GPC1890)**(1/10)-1
63	Georgia	0.91	(GPC1900/GPC1890)**(1/10)-1
64	Russia	0.91	(GPC1900/GPC1890)**(1/10)-1
65	Tajikistan	0.91	(GPC1900/GPC1890)**(1/10)-1
66	Uzbekistan	0.91	(GPC1900/GPC1890)**(1/10)-1
67	Kazakhstan	0.91	(GPC1900/GPC1890)**(1/10)-1
68	Belarus	0.91	(GPC1900/GPC1890)**(1/10)-1
69	Turkey	0.90	(GPC1900/GPC1890)**(1/10)-1
70	Ghana	0.89	(GPC1900/GPC1890)**(1/10)-1
71	Egypt	0.88	(GPC1900/GPC1890)**(1/10)-1
72	Norway	0.87	(GPC1900/GPC1890)**(1/10)-1
73	Vietnam	0.85	(GPC1900/GPC1890)**(1/10)-1
74	Belgium	0.85	(GPC1900/GPC1890)**(1/10)-1
75	Afghanistan	0.80	(GPC1900/GPC1890)**(1/10)-1
76	Laos	0.79	(GPC1900/GPC1890)**(1/10)-1
77	Cambodia	0.79	(GPC1900/GPC1890)**(1/10)-1
78	Bulgaria	0.79	(GPC1900/GPC1890)**(1/10)-1
79	Tunisia	0.78	(GPC1900/GPC1890)**(1/10)-1
80	Mozambique	0.78	(GPC1900/GPC1890)**(1/10)-1
82	Iran	0.77	(GPC1900/GPC1890)**(1/10)-1
82	Iraq	0.77	(GPC1900/GPC1890)**(1/10)-1
82	Jordan	0.77	(GPC1900/GPC1890)**(1/10)-1
84	Somalia	0.72	(GPC1900/GPC1890)**(1/10)-1
85	Burma	0.72	(GPC1900/GPC1890)**(1/10)-1
86	Nepal	0.71	(GPC1900/GPC1890)**(1/10)-1
87.5	Korea, North	0.71	(GPC1900/GPC1890)**(1/10)-1
87.5	Korea, South	0.71	(GPC1900/GPC1890)**(1/10)-1
89	Italy	0.69	(GPC1900/GPC1890)**(1/10)-1
90	Montenegro	0.68	(GPC1900/GPC1890)**(1/10)-1
91	Croatia	0.68	(GPC1900/GPC1890)**(1/10)-1
92	Serbia	0.68	(GPC1900/GPC1890)**(1/10)-1
93	Kosovo	0.68	(GPC1900/GPC1890)**(1/10)-1
94	Bosnia	0.68	(GPC1900/GPC1890)**(1/10)-1
95	Slovenia	0.68	(GPC1900/GPC1890)**(1/10)-1
96	Macedonia	0.68	(GPC1900/GPC1890)**(1/10)-1

Table 5.9 GDP Per Capita Growth Rates, 1890-1900

Rank	Country	GRPCRL	Source
97	Taiwan	0.65	(GPC1900/GPC1890)**(1/10)-1
98	Madagascar	0.64	(GPC1900/GPC1890)**(1/10)-1
99	Morocco	0.54	(GPC1900/GPC1890)**(1/10)-1
100	Libya	0.53	(GPC1900/GPC1890)**(1/10)-1
101	Sudan	0.53	(GPC1900/GPC1890)**(1/10)-1
102	Malaysia	0.46	(GPC1900/GPC1890)**(1/10)-1
103	Swaziland	0.43	(GPC1900/GPC1890)**(1/10)-1
104	Zimbabwe	0.40	(GPC1900/GPC1890)**(1/10)-1
105	Zambia	0.36	(GPC1900/GPC1890)**(1/10)-1
106	Philippines	0.36	(GPC1900/GPC1890)**(1/10)-1
107	Jamaica	0.34	(GPC1900/GPC1890)**(1/10)-1
108	Uruguay	0.33	(GPC1900/GPC1890)**(1/10)-1
109	Pakistan	0.32	(GPC1900/GPC1890)**(1/10)-1
110	Thailand	0.31	(GPC1900/GPC1890)**(1/10)-1
111	Netherlands	0.30	(GPC1900/GPC1890)**(1/10)-1
112	India	0.28	(GPC1900/GPC1890)**(1/10)-1
113	Bangladesh	0.11	(GPC1900/GPC1890)**(1/10)-1
117	Bahrain	0.10	(GPC1900/GPC1890)**(1/10)-1
117	Kuwait	0.10	(GPC1900/GPC1890)**(1/10)-1
117	Oman	0.10	(GPC1900/GPC1890)**(1/10)-1
117	Qatar	0.10	(GPC1900/GPC1890)**(1/10)-1
117	Saudi Arabia	0.10	(GPC1900/GPC1890)**(1/10)-1
117	UAE	0.10	(GPC1900/GPC1890)**(1/10)-1
117	Yemen	0.10	(GPC1900/GPC1890)**(1/10)-1
121	China	0.09	(GPC1900/GPC1890)**(1/10)-1
122	Sierra Leone	0.08	(GPC1900/GPC1890)**(1/10)-1
123	Haiti	0.06	(GPC1900/GPC1890)**(1/10)-1
124	Mongolia	0.05	(GPC1900/GPC1890)**(1/10)-1
125	South Sudan	0.05	(GPC1900/GPC1890)**(1/10)-1
126	Burundi	0.04	(GPC1900/GPC1890)**(1/10)-1
127	Lesotho	0.04	(GPC1900/GPC1890)**(1/10)-1
128	Botswana	0.04	(GPC1900/GPC1890)**(1/10)-1
129	Malawi	0.04	(GPC1900/GPC1890)**(1/10)-1
130	Guinea	0.04	(GPC1900/GPC1890)**(1/10)-1
131	Guinea-Biss	0.04	(GPC1900/GPC1890)**(1/10)-1
132	Eritrea	0.03	(GPC1900/GPC1890)**(1/10)-1
133	Ethiopia	0.03	(GPC1900/GPC1890)**(1/10)-1
134	Australia	-1.05	(GPC1900/GPC1890)**(1/10)-1
135	Brazil	-1.57	(GPC1900/GPC1890)**(1/10)-1

Table 5.10 GDP Per Capita Growth Rates, 1900-1913

Rank	Country	GRPCRL	Source
1	Canada	3.31	(GPC1913/GPC1900)**(1/13)-1
2	Philippines	3.26	(GPC1913/GPC1900)**(1/13)-1
3	Uruguay	3.12	(GPC1913/GPC1900)**(1/13)-1
4	Ghana	3.06	(GPC1913/GPC1900)**(1/13)-1
5	Italy	2.82	(GPC1913/GPC1900)**(1/13)-1
6	Argentina	2.50	(GPC1913/GPC1900)**(1/13)-1
7	Chile	2.40	(GPC1913/GPC1900)**(1/13)-1
8	Venezuela	2.30	(GPC1913/GPC1900)**(1/13)-1
9	Denmark	2.02	(GPC1913/GPC1900)**(1/13)-1
10	Iceland	2.02	(GPC1913/GPC1900)**(1/13)-1
11	US	2.01	(GPC1913/GPC1900)**(1/13)-1
12	Norway	1.99	(GPC1913/GPC1900)**(1/13)-1
13	Australia	1.95	(GPC1913/GPC1900)**(1/13)-1
14	Colombia	1.86	(GPC1913/GPC1900)**(1/13)-1
15	Peru	1.85	(GPC1913/GPC1900)**(1/13)-1
16	Mexico	1.84	(GPC1913/GPC1900)**(1/13)-1
17	Finland	1.83	(GPC1913/GPC1900)**(1/13)-1
18	Haiti	1.77	(GPC1913/GPC1900)**(1/13)-1
19	Paraguay	1.77	(GPC1913/GPC1900)**(1/13)-1
20	Nicaragua	1.77	(GPC1913/GPC1900)**(1/13)-1
21	Puerto Rico	1.77	(GPC1913/GPC1900)**(1/13)-1
22	El Salvador	1.77	(GPC1913/GPC1900)**(1/13)-1
23	Ecuador	1.77	(GPC1913/GPC1900)**(1/13)-1
24	Guatemala	1.77	(GPC1913/GPC1900)**(1/13)-1
25	Bolivia	1.77	(GPC1913/GPC1900)**(1/13)-1
26	Trinidad & T	1.77	(GPC1913/GPC1900)**(1/13)-1
27	Panama	1.77	(GPC1913/GPC1900)**(1/13)-1
28	Costa Rica	1.77	(GPC1913/GPC1900)**(1/13)-1
29	Honduras	1.77	(GPC1913/GPC1900)**(1/13)-1
30	Cuba	1.77	(GPC1913/GPC1900)**(1/13)-1
31	Bulgaria	1.76	(GPC1913/GPC1900)**(1/13)-1
32	Hungary	1.71	(GPC1913/GPC1900)**(1/13)-1
33	Romania	1.61	(GPC1913/GPC1900)**(1/13)-1
34	Germany	1.55	(GPC1913/GPC1900)**(1/13)-1
35	Indonesia	1.52	(GPC1913/GPC1900)**(1/13)-1
36	Slovakia	1.49	(GPC1913/GPC1900)**(1/13)-1
37	Czechia	1.49	(GPC1913/GPC1900)**(1/13)-1
38	France	1.49	(GPC1913/GPC1900)**(1/13)-1
39	Singapore	1.47	(GPC1913/GPC1900)**(1/13)-1
40	Sweden	1.47	(GPC1913/GPC1900)**(1/13)-1
41	Hong Kong	1.47	(GPC1913/GPC1900)**(1/13)-1
42	South Africa	1.46	(GPC1913/GPC1900)**(1/13)-1
43	Turkmenistan	1.43	(GPC1913/GPC1900)**(1/13)-1
44	Azerbaijan	1.43	(GPC1913/GPC1900)**(1/13)-1
45	Belarus	1.43	(GPC1913/GPC1900)**(1/13)-1
46	Estonia	1.43	(GPC1913/GPC1900)**(1/13)-1
47	Georgia	1.43	(GPC1913/GPC1900)**(1/13)-1
48	Kazakhstan	1.43	(GPC1913/GPC1900)**(1/13)-1

Table 5.10 GDP Per Capita Growth Rates, 1900-1913			
Rank	Country	GRPCRL	Source
49	Ukraine	1.43	(GPC1913/GPC1900)**(1/13)-1
50	Latvia	1.43	(GPC1913/GPC1900)**(1/13)-1
51	Armenia	1.43	(GPC1913/GPC1900)**(1/13)-1
52	Uzbekistan	1.43	(GPC1913/GPC1900)**(1/13)-1
53	Russia	1.43	(GPC1913/GPC1900)**(1/13)-1
54	Lithuania	1.43	(GPC1913/GPC1900)**(1/13)-1
55	Tajikistan	1.43	(GPC1913/GPC1900)**(1/13)-1
56	Moldova	1.43	(GPC1913/GPC1900)**(1/13)-1
57	Kyrgyzstan	1.43	(GPC1913/GPC1900)**(1/13)-1
58	Austria	1.43	(GPC1913/GPC1900)**(1/13)-1
59	New Zealand	1.40	(GPC1913/GPC1900)**(1/13)-1
60	Brazil	1.39	(GPC1913/GPC1900)**(1/13)-1
61	Albania	1.31	(GPC1913/GPC1900)**(1/13)-1
62	Netherlands	1.30	(GPC1913/GPC1900)**(1/13)-1
63	Malaysia	1.29	(GPC1913/GPC1900)**(1/13)-1
64	Namibia	1.28	(GPC1913/GPC1900)**(1/13)-1
65	Greece	1.27	(GPC1913/GPC1900)**(1/13)-1
66	Cyprus	1.27	(GPC1913/GPC1900)**(1/13)-1
67	Japan	1.25	(GPC1913/GPC1900)**(1/13)-1
68	Bosnia	1.23	(GPC1913/GPC1900)**(1/13)-1
69	Kosovo	1.23	(GPC1913/GPC1900)**(1/13)-1
70	Croatia	1.23	(GPC1913/GPC1900)**(1/13)-1
71	Slovenia	1.23	(GPC1913/GPC1900)**(1/13)-1
72	Macedonia	1.23	(GPC1913/GPC1900)**(1/13)-1
73	Serbia	1.23	(GPC1913/GPC1900)**(1/13)-1
74	Montenegro	1.23	(GPC1913/GPC1900)**(1/13)-1
75	Israel	1.19	(GPC1913/GPC1900)**(1/13)-1
76	Algeria	1.17	(GPC1913/GPC1900)**(1/13)-1
77.5	Lebanon	1.10	(GPC1913/GPC1900)**(1/13)-1
77.5	Syria	1.10	(GPC1913/GPC1900)**(1/13)-1
79	Spain	1.09	(GPC1913/GPC1900)**(1/13)-1
80	Ireland	1.01	(GPC1913/GPC1900)**(1/13)-1
81	Poland	0.96	(GPC1913/GPC1900)**(1/13)-1
82	Belgium	0.95	(GPC1913/GPC1900)**(1/13)-1
83	Turkey	0.90	(GPC1913/GPC1900)**(1/13)-1
84	Egypt	0.88	(GPC1913/GPC1900)**(1/13)-1
85	Taiwan	0.86	(GPC1913/GPC1900)**(1/13)-1
86	Vietnam	0.85	(GPC1913/GPC1900)**(1/13)-1
87	Switzerland	0.83	(GPC1913/GPC1900)**(1/13)-1
88	Cambodia	0.80	(GPC1913/GPC1900)**(1/13)-1
89	Mongolia	0.79	(GPC1913/GPC1900)**(1/13)-1
90	Laos	0.79	(GPC1913/GPC1900)**(1/13)-1
91	Afghanistan	0.79	(GPC1913/GPC1900)**(1/13)-1
92	Tunisia	0.78	(GPC1913/GPC1900)**(1/13)-1
93	Mozambique	0.78	(GPC1913/GPC1900)**(1/13)-1
95	Iran	0.77	(GPC1913/GPC1900)**(1/13)-1
95	Iraq	0.77	(GPC1913/GPC1900)**(1/13)-1
95	Jordan	0.77	(GPC1913/GPC1900)**(1/13)-1

Table 5.10 GDP Per Capita Growth Rates, 1900-1913			
Rank	Country	GRPCRL	Source
97	Somalia	0.72	(GPC1913/GPC1900)**(1/13)-1
98	Burma	0.72	(GPC1913/GPC1900)**(1/13)-1
99	Nepal	0.71	(GPC1913/GPC1900)**(1/13)-1
100.5	Korea, North	0.71	(GPC1913/GPC1900)**(1/13)-1
100.5	Korea, South	0.71	(GPC1913/GPC1900)**(1/13)-1
102	UK	0.70	(GPC1913/GPC1900)**(1/13)-1
103	Madagascar	0.64	(GPC1913/GPC1900)**(1/13)-1
104	Morocco	0.54	(GPC1913/GPC1900)**(1/13)-1
105	Libya	0.53	(GPC1913/GPC1900)**(1/13)-1
106	Sudan	0.53	(GPC1913/GPC1900)**(1/13)-1
107	Bangladesh	0.46	(GPC1913/GPC1900)**(1/13)-1
108	Pakistan	0.46	(GPC1913/GPC1900)**(1/13)-1
109	India	0.46	(GPC1913/GPC1900)**(1/13)-1
110	Swaziland	0.43	(GPC1913/GPC1900)**(1/13)-1
111	Zimbabwe	0.40	(GPC1913/GPC1900)**(1/13)-1
112	Zambia	0.36	(GPC1913/GPC1900)**(1/13)-1
113	Jamaica	0.34	(GPC1913/GPC1900)**(1/13)-1
114	Thailand	0.31	(GPC1913/GPC1900)**(1/13)-1
118	Bahrain	0.10	(GPC1913/GPC1900)**(1/13)-1
118	Kuwait	0.10	(GPC1913/GPC1900)**(1/13)-1
118	Oman	0.10	(GPC1913/GPC1900)**(1/13)-1
118	Qatar	0.10	(GPC1913/GPC1900)**(1/13)-1
118	Saudi Arabia	0.10	(GPC1913/GPC1900)**(1/13)-1
118	UAE	0.10	(GPC1913/GPC1900)**(1/13)-1
118	Yemen	0.10	(GPC1913/GPC1900)**(1/13)-1
122	China	0.10	(GPC1913/GPC1900)**(1/13)-1
123	Dominican R	0.09	(GPC1913/GPC1900)**(1/13)-1
124	Sierra Leone	0.08	(GPC1913/GPC1900)**(1/13)-1
125	South Sudan	0.05	(GPC1913/GPC1900)**(1/13)-1
126	Burundi	0.04	(GPC1913/GPC1900)**(1/13)-1
127	Lesotho	0.04	(GPC1913/GPC1900)**(1/13)-1
128	Botswana	0.04	(GPC1913/GPC1900)**(1/13)-1
129	Malawi	0.04	(GPC1913/GPC1900)**(1/13)-1
130	Guinea	0.04	(GPC1913/GPC1900)**(1/13)-1
131	Guinea-Biss	0.04	(GPC1913/GPC1900)**(1/13)-1
132	Eritrea	0.03	(GPC1913/GPC1900)**(1/13)-1
133	Ethiopia	0.03	(GPC1913/GPC1900)**(1/13)-1
134	Portugal	-0.31	(GPC1913/GPC1900)**(1/13)-1
135	Sri Lanka	-0.34	(GPC1913/GPC1900)**(1/13)-1

Table 5.11 GDP Per Capita Growth Rates, 1913-1920			
Rank	Country	GRPCRL	Source
1	Qatar	11.19	(GPC1920/GPC1913)**(1/7)-1
2	Kuwait	11.04	(GPC1920/GPC1913)**(1/7)-1
3	UAE	9.24	(GPC1920/GPC1913)**(1/7)-1
4	Honduras	7.95	(GPC1920/GPC1913)**(1/7)-1
5	Costa Rica	5.51	(GPC1920/GPC1913)**(1/7)-1
6	Nicaragua	4.67	(GPC1920/GPC1913)**(1/7)-1
7	Taiwan	3.63	(GPC1920/GPC1913)**(1/7)-1
8	Peru	3.63	(GPC1920/GPC1913)**(1/7)-1
9	Saudi Arabia	3.61	(GPC1920/GPC1913)**(1/7)-1
10	Bahrain	3.45	(GPC1920/GPC1913)**(1/7)-1
11	Malaysia	3.04	(GPC1920/GPC1913)**(1/7)-1
12.5	Korea, North	3.01	(GPC1920/GPC1913)**(1/7)-1
12.5	Korea, South	3.01	(GPC1920/GPC1913)**(1/7)-1
14	Philippines	2.93	(GPC1920/GPC1913)**(1/7)-1
15	Japan	2.91	(GPC1920/GPC1913)**(1/7)-1
16	Brazil	2.48	(GPC1920/GPC1913)**(1/7)-1
17	Greece	2.36	(GPC1920/GPC1913)**(1/7)-1
18	Cyprus	2.36	(GPC1920/GPC1913)**(1/7)-1
19	Israel	2.22	(GPC1920/GPC1913)**(1/7)-1
20	Morocco	1.96	(GPC1920/GPC1913)**(1/7)-1
21	Jamaica	1.81	(GPC1920/GPC1913)**(1/7)-1
22	Lebanon	1.60	(GPC1920/GPC1913)**(1/7)-1
23	Syria	1.58	(GPC1920/GPC1913)**(1/7)-1
24	Paraguay	1.54	(GPC1920/GPC1913)**(1/7)-1
25	Cuba	1.54	(GPC1920/GPC1913)**(1/7)-1
26	Trinidad & T	1.54	(GPC1920/GPC1913)**(1/7)-1
27	Panama	1.54	(GPC1920/GPC1913)**(1/7)-1
28	Haiti	1.54	(GPC1920/GPC1913)**(1/7)-1
29	Ecuador	1.54	(GPC1920/GPC1913)**(1/7)-1
30	Dominican R	1.54	(GPC1920/GPC1913)**(1/7)-1
31	Bolivia	1.54	(GPC1920/GPC1913)**(1/7)-1
32	Puerto Rico	1.54	(GPC1920/GPC1913)**(1/7)-1
33	Norway	1.52	(GPC1920/GPC1913)**(1/7)-1
34	Singapore	1.50	(GPC1920/GPC1913)**(1/7)-1
35	Hong Kong	1.50	(GPC1920/GPC1913)**(1/7)-1
36	Iran	1.48	(GPC1920/GPC1913)**(1/7)-1
37	El Salvador	1.39	(GPC1920/GPC1913)**(1/7)-1
38	Jordan	1.38	(GPC1920/GPC1913)**(1/7)-1
39	New Zealand	1.30	(GPC1920/GPC1913)**(1/7)-1
40	Namibia	1.28	(GPC1920/GPC1913)**(1/7)-1
41	South Africa	1.25	(GPC1920/GPC1913)**(1/7)-1
42	Poland	1.24	(GPC1920/GPC1913)**(1/7)-1
43	Algeria	1.19	(GPC1920/GPC1913)**(1/7)-1
44	Yemen	1.14	(GPC1920/GPC1913)**(1/7)-1
45	Guatemala	1.02	(GPC1920/GPC1913)**(1/7)-1
46	Ghana	0.98	(GPC1920/GPC1913)**(1/7)-1
47	Burma	0.95	(GPC1920/GPC1913)**(1/7)-1
48	Venezuela	0.87	(GPC1920/GPC1913)**(1/7)-1

Table 5.11 GDP Per Capita Growth Rates, 1913-1920

Rank	Country	GRPCRL	Source
49	Iraq	0.84	(GPC1920/GPC1913)**(1/7)-1
50	Albania	0.83	(GPC1920/GPC1913)**(1/7)-1
51	Spain	0.82	(GPC1920/GPC1913)**(1/7)-1
52	Mozambique	0.78	(GPC1920/GPC1913)**(1/7)-1
53	Mexico	0.73	(GPC1920/GPC1913)**(1/7)-1
54	Somalia	0.72	(GPC1920/GPC1913)**(1/7)-1
55	US	0.66	(GPC1920/GPC1913)**(1/7)-1
56	Madagascar	0.64	(GPC1920/GPC1913)**(1/7)-1
57	Indonesia	0.64	(GPC1920/GPC1913)**(1/7)-1
58	Tunisia	0.63	(GPC1920/GPC1913)**(1/7)-1
59	Netherlands	0.59	(GPC1920/GPC1913)**(1/7)-1
60	Libya	0.53	(GPC1920/GPC1913)**(1/7)-1
61	Sudan	0.53	(GPC1920/GPC1913)**(1/7)-1
62	Swaziland	0.43	(GPC1920/GPC1913)**(1/7)-1
63	Zimbabwe	0.40	(GPC1920/GPC1913)**(1/7)-1
64	Zambia	0.36	(GPC1920/GPC1913)**(1/7)-1
65	Iceland	0.29	(GPC1920/GPC1913)**(1/7)-1
66	Denmark	0.29	(GPC1920/GPC1913)**(1/7)-1
67	Colombia	0.22	(GPC1920/GPC1913)**(1/7)-1
68	Switzerland	0.16	(GPC1920/GPC1913)**(1/7)-1
69	Italy	0.13	(GPC1920/GPC1913)**(1/7)-1
70	China	0.11	(GPC1920/GPC1913)**(1/7)-1
71	Oman	0.10	(GPC1920/GPC1913)**(1/7)-1
72	Sierra Leone	0.08	(GPC1920/GPC1913)**(1/7)-1
73	South Sudan	0.05	(GPC1920/GPC1913)**(1/7)-1
74	Pakistan	0.05	(GPC1920/GPC1913)**(1/7)-1
75	Burundi	0.04	(GPC1920/GPC1913)**(1/7)-1
76	Lesotho	0.04	(GPC1920/GPC1913)**(1/7)-1
77	Botswana	0.04	(GPC1920/GPC1913)**(1/7)-1
78	Malawi	0.04	(GPC1920/GPC1913)**(1/7)-1
79	Guinea	0.04	(GPC1920/GPC1913)**(1/7)-1
80	Guinea-Biss	0.04	(GPC1920/GPC1913)**(1/7)-1
81	Eritrea	0.03	(GPC1920/GPC1913)**(1/7)-1
82	Ethiopia	0.03	(GPC1920/GPC1913)**(1/7)-1
83	Bangladesh	0.02	(GPC1920/GPC1913)**(1/7)-1
84	Laos	-0.19	(GPC1920/GPC1913)**(1/7)-1
85	Afghanistan	-0.19	(GPC1920/GPC1913)**(1/7)-1
86	Cambodia	-0.19	(GPC1920/GPC1913)**(1/7)-1
87	Mongolia	-0.19	(GPC1920/GPC1913)**(1/7)-1
88	Egypt	-0.20	(GPC1920/GPC1913)**(1/7)-1
89	Nepal	-0.22	(GPC1920/GPC1913)**(1/7)-1
90	Portugal	-0.24	(GPC1920/GPC1913)**(1/7)-1
91	Vietnam	-0.27	(GPC1920/GPC1913)**(1/7)-1
92	Kosovo	-0.36	(GPC1920/GPC1913)**(1/7)-1
93	Serbia	-0.36	(GPC1920/GPC1913)**(1/7)-1
94	Slovenia	-0.36	(GPC1920/GPC1913)**(1/7)-1
95	Macedonia	-0.36	(GPC1920/GPC1913)**(1/7)-1
96	Montenegro	-0.36	(GPC1920/GPC1913)**(1/7)-1

Table 5.11 GDP Per Capita Growth Rates, 1913-1920			
Rank	Country	GRPCRL	Source
97	Croatia	-0.36	(GPC1920/GPC1913)**(1/7)-1
98	Bosnia	-0.36	(GPC1920/GPC1913)**(1/7)-1
99	Thailand	-0.37	(GPC1920/GPC1913)**(1/7)-1
100	India	-0.75	(GPC1920/GPC1913)**(1/7)-1
101	Belgium	-0.90	(GPC1920/GPC1913)**(1/7)-1
102	Ireland	-0.96	(GPC1920/GPC1913)**(1/7)-1
103	France	-1.09	(GPC1920/GPC1913)**(1/7)-1
104	UK	-1.12	(GPC1920/GPC1913)**(1/7)-1
105	Australia	-1.12	(GPC1920/GPC1913)**(1/7)-1
106	Czechia	-1.15	(GPC1920/GPC1913)**(1/7)-1
107	Slovakia	-1.15	(GPC1920/GPC1913)**(1/7)-1
108	Chile	-1.25	(GPC1920/GPC1913)**(1/7)-1
109	Argentina	-1.27	(GPC1920/GPC1913)**(1/7)-1
110	Sweden	-1.42	(GPC1920/GPC1913)**(1/7)-1
111	Sri Lanka	-1.73	(GPC1920/GPC1913)**(1/7)-1
112	Estonia	-1.90	(GPC1920/GPC1913)**(1/7)-1
113	Finland	-1.90	(GPC1920/GPC1913)**(1/7)-1
114	Latvia	-1.90	(GPC1920/GPC1913)**(1/7)-1
115	Lithuania	-1.90	(GPC1920/GPC1913)**(1/7)-1
116	Canada	-2.00	(GPC1920/GPC1913)**(1/7)-1
117	Hungary	-2.89	(GPC1920/GPC1913)**(1/7)-1
118	Uruguay	-3.00	(GPC1920/GPC1913)**(1/7)-1
119	Germany	-3.73	(GPC1920/GPC1913)**(1/7)-1
120	Austria	-5.04	(GPC1920/GPC1913)**(1/7)-1
121	Bulgaria	-7.20	(GPC1920/GPC1913)**(1/7)-1
122	Georgia	-7.20	(GPC1920/GPC1913)**(1/7)-1
123	Romania	-7.20	(GPC1920/GPC1913)**(1/7)-1
124	Moldova	-7.20	(GPC1920/GPC1913)**(1/7)-1
125	Turkey	-7.33	(GPC1920/GPC1913)**(1/7)-1
126	Ukraine	-12.67	(GPC1920/GPC1913)**(1/7)-1
127	Uzbekistan	-12.67	(GPC1920/GPC1913)**(1/7)-1
128	Kazakhstan	-12.67	(GPC1920/GPC1913)**(1/7)-1
129	Armenia	-12.67	(GPC1920/GPC1913)**(1/7)-1
130	Tajikistan	-12.67	(GPC1920/GPC1913)**(1/7)-1
131	Belarus	-12.67	(GPC1920/GPC1913)**(1/7)-1
132	Russia	-12.67	(GPC1920/GPC1913)**(1/7)-1
133	Azerbaijan	-12.67	(GPC1920/GPC1913)**(1/7)-1
134	Turkmenistan	-12.67	(GPC1920/GPC1913)**(1/7)-1
135	Kyrgyzstan	-12.67	(GPC1920/GPC1913)**(1/7)-1

Table 5.12 GDP Per Capita Growth Rates, 1920-1929

Rank	Country	GRPCRL	Source
1	Venezuela	12.65	(GPC1929/GPC1920)**(1/9)-1
2	Qatar	11.19	(GPC1929/GPC1920)**(1/9)-1
3	Kuwait	11.04	(GPC1929/GPC1920)**(1/9)-1
4	Kyrgyzstan	10.56	(GPC1929/GPC1920)**(1/9)-1
5	Tajikistan	10.56	(GPC1929/GPC1920)**(1/9)-1
6	Azerbaijan	10.56	(GPC1929/GPC1920)**(1/9)-1
7	Turkmenistan	10.56	(GPC1929/GPC1920)**(1/9)-1
8	Belarus	10.56	(GPC1929/GPC1920)**(1/9)-1
9	Armenia	10.56	(GPC1929/GPC1920)**(1/9)-1
10	Russia	10.56	(GPC1929/GPC1920)**(1/9)-1
11	Kazakhstan	10.56	(GPC1929/GPC1920)**(1/9)-1
12	Uzbekistan	10.56	(GPC1929/GPC1920)**(1/9)-1
13	Ukraine	10.56	(GPC1929/GPC1920)**(1/9)-1
14	UAE	9.24	(GPC1929/GPC1920)**(1/9)-1
15	Turkey	6.10	(GPC1929/GPC1920)**(1/9)-1
16	Georgia	5.46	(GPC1929/GPC1920)**(1/9)-1
17	Slovakia	5.17	(GPC1929/GPC1920)**(1/9)-1
18	Czechia	5.17	(GPC1929/GPC1920)**(1/9)-1
19	Austria	4.87	(GPC1929/GPC1920)**(1/9)-1
20	Malaysia	4.73	(GPC1929/GPC1920)**(1/9)-1
21	Lithuania	4.39	(GPC1929/GPC1920)**(1/9)-1
22	Latvia	4.39	(GPC1929/GPC1920)**(1/9)-1
23	Finland	4.39	(GPC1929/GPC1920)**(1/9)-1
24	Estonia	4.39	(GPC1929/GPC1920)**(1/9)-1
25	Switzerland	4.36	(GPC1929/GPC1920)**(1/9)-1
26	France	4.29	(GPC1929/GPC1920)**(1/9)-1
27	Germany	4.21	(GPC1929/GPC1920)**(1/9)-1
28	Hungary	4.21	(GPC1929/GPC1920)**(1/9)-1
29	Uruguay	4.12	(GPC1929/GPC1920)**(1/9)-1
30	Chile	3.79	(GPC1929/GPC1920)**(1/9)-1
31	Nicaragua	3.68	(GPC1929/GPC1920)**(1/9)-1
32	Sweden	3.65	(GPC1929/GPC1920)**(1/9)-1
33	Saudi Arabia	3.61	(GPC1929/GPC1920)**(1/9)-1
34	Bahrain	3.45	(GPC1929/GPC1920)**(1/9)-1
35	Guatemala	3.41	(GPC1929/GPC1920)**(1/9)-1
36	Netherlands	3.37	(GPC1929/GPC1920)**(1/9)-1
37	Macedonia	3.16	(GPC1929/GPC1920)**(1/9)-1
38	Montenegro	3.16	(GPC1929/GPC1920)**(1/9)-1
39	Croatia	3.16	(GPC1929/GPC1920)**(1/9)-1
40	Slovenia	3.16	(GPC1929/GPC1920)**(1/9)-1
41	Serbia	3.16	(GPC1929/GPC1920)**(1/9)-1
42	Bosnia	3.16	(GPC1929/GPC1920)**(1/9)-1
43	Kosovo	3.16	(GPC1929/GPC1920)**(1/9)-1
44	Canada	3.06	(GPC1929/GPC1920)**(1/9)-1
45	Portugal	3.05	(GPC1929/GPC1920)**(1/9)-1
46	Bulgaria	2.94	(GPC1929/GPC1920)**(1/9)-1
47	Belgium	2.74	(GPC1929/GPC1920)**(1/9)-1
48	Iceland	2.70	(GPC1929/GPC1920)**(1/9)-1

Table 5.12 GDP Per Capita Growth Rates, 1920-1929

Rank	Country	GRPCRL	Source
49	Denmark	2.70	(GPC1929/GPC1920)**(1/9)-1
50	Cuba	2.66	(GPC1929/GPC1920)**(1/9)-1
51	Spain	2.58	(GPC1929/GPC1920)**(1/9)-1
52	Argentina	2.58	(GPC1929/GPC1920)**(1/9)-1
53	Greece	2.51	(GPC1929/GPC1920)**(1/9)-1
54	Cyprus	2.51	(GPC1929/GPC1920)**(1/9)-1
55	Norway	2.50	(GPC1929/GPC1920)**(1/9)-1
56	US	2.44	(GPC1929/GPC1920)**(1/9)-1
57	Indonesia	2.40	(GPC1929/GPC1920)**(1/9)-1
58	Sri Lanka	2.27	(GPC1929/GPC1920)**(1/9)-1
59	Israel	2.22	(GPC1929/GPC1920)**(1/9)-1
60	Peru	2.20	(GPC1929/GPC1920)**(1/9)-1
61	UK	2.14	(GPC1929/GPC1920)**(1/9)-1
62	Colombia	2.04	(GPC1929/GPC1920)**(1/9)-1
63	Italy	2.00	(GPC1929/GPC1920)**(1/9)-1
64	Taiwan	2.00	(GPC1929/GPC1920)**(1/9)-1
65	Japan	2.00	(GPC1929/GPC1920)**(1/9)-1
66	Morocco	1.96	(GPC1929/GPC1920)**(1/9)-1
67	Burma	1.88	(GPC1929/GPC1920)**(1/9)-1
68	Brazil	1.86	(GPC1929/GPC1920)**(1/9)-1
69	Honduras	1.82	(GPC1929/GPC1920)**(1/9)-1
70	Jamaica	1.81	(GPC1929/GPC1920)**(1/9)-1
71	Philippines	1.71	(GPC1929/GPC1920)**(1/9)-1
72	Lebanon	1.60	(GPC1929/GPC1920)**(1/9)-1
73	Syria	1.58	(GPC1929/GPC1920)**(1/9)-1
74	Puerto Rico	1.54	(GPC1929/GPC1920)**(1/9)-1
75	Haiti	1.54	(GPC1929/GPC1920)**(1/9)-1
76	Ecuador	1.54	(GPC1929/GPC1920)**(1/9)-1
77	Panama	1.54	(GPC1929/GPC1920)**(1/9)-1
78	Bolivia	1.54	(GPC1929/GPC1920)**(1/9)-1
79	Trinidad & T	1.54	(GPC1929/GPC1920)**(1/9)-1
80	Paraguay	1.54	(GPC1929/GPC1920)**(1/9)-1
81	Dominican R	1.54	(GPC1929/GPC1920)**(1/9)-1
82	Singapore	1.50	(GPC1929/GPC1920)**(1/9)-1
83	Hong Kong	1.50	(GPC1929/GPC1920)**(1/9)-1
84	Iran	1.48	(GPC1929/GPC1920)**(1/9)-1
85	Jordan	1.38	(GPC1929/GPC1920)**(1/9)-1
86	Namibia	1.28	(GPC1929/GPC1920)**(1/9)-1
87	South Africa	1.25	(GPC1929/GPC1920)**(1/9)-1
88	Poland	1.24	(GPC1929/GPC1920)**(1/9)-1
89	El Salvador	1.24	(GPC1929/GPC1920)**(1/9)-1
90	Romania	1.23	(GPC1929/GPC1920)**(1/9)-1
91	Moldova	1.23	(GPC1929/GPC1920)**(1/9)-1
92	Yemen	1.13	(GPC1929/GPC1920)**(1/9)-1
93	Australia	1.11	(GPC1929/GPC1920)**(1/9)-1
94	Ireland	1.11	(GPC1929/GPC1920)**(1/9)-1
95	Ghana	0.98	(GPC1929/GPC1920)**(1/9)-1
96	Algeria	0.87	(GPC1929/GPC1920)**(1/9)-1

TABLE 5.12 GDP PER CAPITA GROWTH RATES, 1920-1929

Rank	Country	GRPCRL	Source
97	Iraq	0.84	(GPC1929/GPC1920)**(1/9)-1
98	Albania	0.83	(GPC1929/GPC1920)**(1/9)-1
99	Mozambique	0.78	(GPC1929/GPC1920)**(1/9)-1
100	Somalia	0.72	(GPC1929/GPC1920)**(1/9)-1
101	Madagascar	0.64	(GPC1929/GPC1920)**(1/9)-1
102	Tunisia	0.63	(GPC1929/GPC1920)**(1/9)-1
103	India	0.62	(GPC1929/GPC1920)**(1/9)-1
104	Libya	0.53	(GPC1929/GPC1920)**(1/9)-1
105	Sudan	0.53	(GPC1929/GPC1920)**(1/9)-1
106	Swaziland	0.43	(GPC1929/GPC1920)**(1/9)-1
107	Zimbabwe	0.40	(GPC1929/GPC1920)**(1/9)-1
108	Zambia	0.36	(GPC1929/GPC1920)**(1/9)-1
109	China	0.11	(GPC1929/GPC1920)**(1/9)-1
110	Oman	0.10	(GPC1929/GPC1920)**(1/9)-1
111	Sierra Leone	0.08	(GPC1929/GPC1920)**(1/9)-1
112.5	Korea, North	0.05	(GPC1929/GPC1920)**(1/9)-1
112.5	Korea, South	0.05	(GPC1929/GPC1920)**(1/9)-1
114	South Sudan	0.05	(GPC1929/GPC1920)**(1/9)-1
115	Pakistan	0.05	(GPC1929/GPC1920)**(1/9)-1
116	Burundi	0.04	(GPC1929/GPC1920)**(1/9)-1
117	Lesotho	0.04	(GPC1929/GPC1920)**(1/9)-1
118	Botswana	0.04	(GPC1929/GPC1920)**(1/9)-1
119	Malawi	0.04	(GPC1929/GPC1920)**(1/9)-1
120	Guinea	0.04	(GPC1929/GPC1920)**(1/9)-1
121	Guinea-Biss	0.04	(GPC1929/GPC1920)**(1/9)-1
122	Eritrea	0.03	(GPC1929/GPC1920)**(1/9)-1
123	Ethiopia	0.03	(GPC1929/GPC1920)**(1/9)-1
124	Bangladesh	0.02	(GPC1929/GPC1920)**(1/9)-1
125	Afghanistan	-0.19	(GPC1929/GPC1920)**(1/9)-1
126	Mongolia	-0.19	(GPC1929/GPC1920)**(1/9)-1
127	Cambodia	-0.19	(GPC1929/GPC1920)**(1/9)-1
128	Laos	-0.19	(GPC1929/GPC1920)**(1/9)-1
129	Egypt	-0.20	(GPC1929/GPC1920)**(1/9)-1
130	Nepal	-0.23	(GPC1929/GPC1920)**(1/9)-1
131	Vietnam	-0.27	(GPC1929/GPC1920)**(1/9)-1
132	Costa Rica	-0.29	(GPC1929/GPC1920)**(1/9)-1
133	Thailand	-0.37	(GPC1929/GPC1920)**(1/9)-1
134	Mexico	-0.41	(GPC1929/GPC1920)**(1/9)-1
135	New Zealand	-0.77	(GPC1929/GPC1920)**(1/9)-1

Table 5.13 GDP Per Capita Growth Rates, 1929-1938

Rank	Country	GRPCRL	Source
1	Qatar	11.19	(GPC1938/GPC1929)**(1/9)-1
2	Kuwait	11.04	(GPC1938/GPC1929)**(1/9)-1
3	UAE	9.24	(GPC1938/GPC1929)**(1/9)-1
4	Ukraine	5.00	(GPC1938/GPC1929)**(1/9)-1
5	Russia	5.00	(GPC1938/GPC1929)**(1/9)-1
6	Uzbekistan	5.00	(GPC1938/GPC1929)**(1/9)-1
7	Georgia	5.00	(GPC1938/GPC1929)**(1/9)-1
8	Belarus	5.00	(GPC1938/GPC1929)**(1/9)-1
9	Kazakhstan	5.00	(GPC1938/GPC1929)**(1/9)-1
10	Azerbaijan	5.00	(GPC1938/GPC1929)**(1/9)-1
11	Turkmenistan	5.00	(GPC1938/GPC1929)**(1/9)-1
12	Kyrgyzstan	5.00	(GPC1938/GPC1929)**(1/9)-1
13	Tajikistan	5.00	(GPC1938/GPC1929)**(1/9)-1
14	Armenia	5.00	(GPC1938/GPC1929)**(1/9)-1
15.5	Korea, North	4.13	(GPC1938/GPC1929)**(1/9)-1
15.5	Korea, South	4.13	(GPC1938/GPC1929)**(1/9)-1
17	Turkey	3.98	(GPC1938/GPC1929)**(1/9)-1
18	Saudi Arabia	3.61	(GPC1938/GPC1929)**(1/9)-1
19	Bahrain	3.45	(GPC1938/GPC1929)**(1/9)-1
20	Bulgaria	3.41	(GPC1938/GPC1929)**(1/9)-1
21	Lithuania	3.14	(GPC1938/GPC1929)**(1/9)-1
22	Finland	3.14	(GPC1938/GPC1929)**(1/9)-1
23	Estonia	3.14	(GPC1938/GPC1929)**(1/9)-1
24	Latvia	3.14	(GPC1938/GPC1929)**(1/9)-1
25	Guatemala	2.90	(GPC1938/GPC1929)**(1/9)-1
26	Norway	2.50	(GPC1938/GPC1929)**(1/9)-1
27	Germany	2.35	(GPC1938/GPC1929)**(1/9)-1
28	New Zealand	2.31	(GPC1938/GPC1929)**(1/9)-1
29	Colombia	2.28	(GPC1938/GPC1929)**(1/9)-1
30	Sweden	2.25	(GPC1938/GPC1929)**(1/9)-1
31	Israel	2.22	(GPC1938/GPC1929)**(1/9)-1
32	Venezuela	2.14	(GPC1938/GPC1929)**(1/9)-1
33	Japan	2.13	(GPC1938/GPC1929)**(1/9)-1
34	Morocco	1.96	(GPC1938/GPC1929)**(1/9)-1
35	Costa Rica	1.91	(GPC1938/GPC1929)**(1/9)-1
36	Jamaica	1.81	(GPC1938/GPC1929)**(1/9)-1
37	Lebanon	1.60	(GPC1938/GPC1929)**(1/9)-1
38	Syria	1.58	(GPC1938/GPC1929)**(1/9)-1
39	Panama	1.54	(GPC1938/GPC1929)**(1/9)-1
40	Ecuador	1.54	(GPC1938/GPC1929)**(1/9)-1
41	Bolivia	1.54	(GPC1938/GPC1929)**(1/9)-1
42	Dominican R	1.54	(GPC1938/GPC1929)**(1/9)-1
43	Trinidad & T	1.54	(GPC1938/GPC1929)**(1/9)-1
44	Puerto Rico	1.54	(GPC1938/GPC1929)**(1/9)-1
45	Paraguay	1.54	(GPC1938/GPC1929)**(1/9)-1
46	Haiti	1.54	(GPC1938/GPC1929)**(1/9)-1
47	Singapore	1.50	(GPC1938/GPC1929)**(1/9)-1
48	Hong Kong	1.50	(GPC1938/GPC1929)**(1/9)-1

Table 5.13 GDP Per Capita Growth Rates, 1929-1938			
Rank	Country	GRPCRL	Source
49	Cyprus	1.50	(GPC1938/GPC1929)**(1/9)-1
50	Greece	1.50	(GPC1938/GPC1929)**(1/9)-1
51	Iran	1.48	(GPC1938/GPC1929)**(1/9)-1
52	UK	1.45	(GPC1938/GPC1929)**(1/9)-1
53	Taiwan	1.43	(GPC1938/GPC1929)**(1/9)-1
54	Iceland	1.42	(GPC1938/GPC1929)**(1/9)-1
55	Denmark	1.42	(GPC1938/GPC1929)**(1/9)-1
56	Jordan	1.38	(GPC1938/GPC1929)**(1/9)-1
57	Brazil	1.29	(GPC1938/GPC1929)**(1/9)-1
58	Namibia	1.28	(GPC1938/GPC1929)**(1/9)-1
59	Australia	1.25	(GPC1938/GPC1929)**(1/9)-1
60	South Africa	1.25	(GPC1938/GPC1929)**(1/9)-1
61	Yemen	1.14	(GPC1938/GPC1929)**(1/9)-1
62	Ghana	0.98	(GPC1938/GPC1929)**(1/9)-1
63	Peru	0.91	(GPC1938/GPC1929)**(1/9)-1
64	Portugal	0.91	(GPC1938/GPC1929)**(1/9)-1
65	Ireland	0.87	(GPC1938/GPC1929)**(1/9)-1
66	Iraq	0.84	(GPC1938/GPC1929)**(1/9)-1
67	Moldova	0.84	(GPC1938/GPC1929)**(1/9)-1
68	Romania	0.84	(GPC1938/GPC1929)**(1/9)-1
69	Hungary	0.78	(GPC1938/GPC1929)**(1/9)-1
70	Italy	0.78	(GPC1938/GPC1929)**(1/9)-1
71	Mozambique	0.78	(GPC1938/GPC1929)**(1/9)-1
72	Somalia	0.72	(GPC1938/GPC1929)**(1/9)-1
73	Madagascar	0.64	(GPC1938/GPC1929)**(1/9)-1
74	Tunisia	0.63	(GPC1938/GPC1929)**(1/9)-1
75	Libya	0.53	(GPC1938/GPC1929)**(1/9)-1
76	Sudan	0.53	(GPC1938/GPC1929)**(1/9)-1
77	Thailand	0.45	(GPC1938/GPC1929)**(1/9)-1
78	Swaziland	0.43	(GPC1938/GPC1929)**(1/9)-1
79	Zimbabwe	0.40	(GPC1938/GPC1929)**(1/9)-1
80	Albania	0.37	(GPC1938/GPC1929)**(1/9)-1
81	Zambia	0.36	(GPC1938/GPC1929)**(1/9)-1
82	Poland	0.34	(GPC1938/GPC1929)**(1/9)-1
83	Mexico	0.23	(GPC1938/GPC1929)**(1/9)-1
84	Egypt	0.22	(GPC1938/GPC1929)**(1/9)-1
85	Philippines	0.15	(GPC1938/GPC1929)**(1/9)-1
86	Oman	0.10	(GPC1938/GPC1929)**(1/9)-1
87	Switzerland	0.10	(GPC1938/GPC1929)**(1/9)-1
88	Sierra Leone	0.08	(GPC1938/GPC1929)**(1/9)-1
89	Algeria	0.06	(GPC1938/GPC1929)**(1/9)-1
90	South Sudan	0.05	(GPC1938/GPC1929)**(1/9)-1
91	Indonesia	0.05	(GPC1938/GPC1929)**(1/9)-1
92	Burundi	0.04	(GPC1938/GPC1929)**(1/9)-1
93	Lesotho	0.04	(GPC1938/GPC1929)**(1/9)-1
94	Botswana	0.04	(GPC1938/GPC1929)**(1/9)-1
95	Malawi	0.04	(GPC1938/GPC1929)**(1/9)-1
96	Guinea	0.04	(GPC1938/GPC1929)**(1/9)-1

Table 5.13 GDP Per Capita Growth Rates, 1929-1938			
Rank	Country	GRPCRL	Source
97	Guinea-Biss	0.04	(GPC1938/GPC1929)**(1/9)-1
98	Eritrea	0.03	(GPC1938/GPC1929)**(1/9)-1
99	Ethiopia	0.03	(GPC1938/GPC1929)**(1/9)-1
100	China	0.00	(GPC1938/GPC1929)**(1/9)-1
101	Bosnia	-0.07	(GPC1938/GPC1929)**(1/9)-1
102	Croatia	-0.07	(GPC1938/GPC1929)**(1/9)-1
103	Montenegro	-0.07	(GPC1938/GPC1929)**(1/9)-1
104	Slovenia	-0.07	(GPC1938/GPC1929)**(1/9)-1
105	Serbia	-0.07	(GPC1938/GPC1929)**(1/9)-1
106	Macedonia	-0.07	(GPC1938/GPC1929)**(1/9)-1
107	Kosovo	-0.07	(GPC1938/GPC1929)**(1/9)-1
108	Cambodia	-0.19	(GPC1938/GPC1929)**(1/9)-1
109	Laos	-0.19	(GPC1938/GPC1929)**(1/9)-1
110	Mongolia	-0.19	(GPC1938/GPC1929)**(1/9)-1
111	Afghanistan	-0.19	(GPC1938/GPC1929)**(1/9)-1
112	Nepal	-0.22	(GPC1938/GPC1929)**(1/9)-1
113	Vietnam	-0.27	(GPC1938/GPC1929)**(1/9)-1
114	Austria	-0.43	(GPC1938/GPC1929)**(1/9)-1
115	Belgium	-0.50	(GPC1938/GPC1929)**(1/9)-1
116	Uruguay	-0.50	(GPC1938/GPC1929)**(1/9)-1
117	France	-0.59	(GPC1938/GPC1929)**(1/9)-1
118	Czechia	-0.60	(GPC1938/GPC1929)**(1/9)-1
119	Slovakia	-0.60	(GPC1938/GPC1929)**(1/9)-1
120	El Salvador	-0.70	(GPC1938/GPC1929)**(1/9)-1
121	Argentina	-0.77	(GPC1938/GPC1929)**(1/9)-1
122	India	-0.79	(GPC1938/GPC1929)**(1/9)-1
123	Pakistan	-0.86	(GPC1938/GPC1929)**(1/9)-1
124	Chile	-0.87	(GPC1938/GPC1929)**(1/9)-1
125	Bangladesh	-0.87	(GPC1938/GPC1929)**(1/9)-1
126	Netherlands	-0.89	(GPC1938/GPC1929)**(1/9)-1
127	Sri Lanka	-0.96	(GPC1938/GPC1929)**(1/9)-1
128	Canada	-1.19	(GPC1938/GPC1929)**(1/9)-1
129	US	-1.31	(GPC1938/GPC1929)**(1/9)-1
130	Burma	-1.73	(GPC1938/GPC1929)**(1/9)-1
131	Cuba	-2.07	(GPC1938/GPC1929)**(1/9)-1
132	Malaysia	-2.33	(GPC1938/GPC1929)**(1/9)-1
133	Honduras	-3.33	(GPC1938/GPC1929)**(1/9)-1
134	Spain	-4.62	(GPC1938/GPC1929)**(1/9)-1
135	Nicaragua	-5.26	(GPC1938/GPC1929)**(1/9)-1

TABLE 5.14 GDP PER CAPITA GROWTH RATES, 1938-1950

Rank	Country	GRPCRL	Source
1	Qatar	11.19	(GPC1950/GPC1938)**(1/12)-1
2	Kuwait	11.04	(GPC1950/GPC1938)**(1/12)-1
3	UAE	9.24	(GPC1950/GPC1938)**(1/12)-1
4	Moldova	8.55	(GPC1950/GPC1938)**(1/12)-1
5	Venezuela	5.02	(GPC1950/GPC1938)**(1/12)-1
6	Canada	4.02	(GPC1950/GPC1938)**(1/12)-1
7	US	3.78	(GPC1950/GPC1938)**(1/12)-1
8	Saudi Arabia	3.61	(GPC1950/GPC1938)**(1/12)-1
9	El Salvador	3.57	(GPC1950/GPC1938)**(1/12)-1
10	Cuba	3.47	(GPC1950/GPC1938)**(1/12)-1
11	Bahrain	3.45	(GPC1950/GPC1938)**(1/12)-1
12	Nicaragua	3.45	(GPC1950/GPC1938)**(1/12)-1
13	Sweden	3.00	(GPC1950/GPC1938)**(1/12)-1
14	Switzerland	2.96	(GPC1950/GPC1938)**(1/12)-1
15	Jamaica	2.63	(GPC1950/GPC1938)**(1/12)-1
16	Mexico	2.33	(GPC1950/GPC1938)**(1/12)-1
17	Brazil	2.28	(GPC1950/GPC1938)**(1/12)-1
18	New Zealand	2.27	(GPC1950/GPC1938)**(1/12)-1
19	Israel	2.22	(GPC1950/GPC1938)**(1/12)-1
20	Peru	2.13	(GPC1950/GPC1938)**(1/12)-1
21	Armenia	2.12	(GPC1950/GPC1938)**(1/12)-1
22	Tajikistan	2.12	(GPC1950/GPC1938)**(1/12)-1
23	Georgia	2.12	(GPC1950/GPC1938)**(1/12)-1
24	Turkmenistan	2.12	(GPC1950/GPC1938)**(1/12)-1
25	Kyrgyzstan	2.12	(GPC1950/GPC1938)**(1/12)-1
26	Kazakhstan	2.12	(GPC1950/GPC1938)**(1/12)-1
27	Russia	2.12	(GPC1950/GPC1938)**(1/12)-1
28	Belarus	2.12	(GPC1950/GPC1938)**(1/12)-1
29	Ukraine	2.12	(GPC1950/GPC1938)**(1/12)-1
30	Uzbekistan	2.12	(GPC1950/GPC1938)**(1/12)-1
31	Azerbaijan	2.12	(GPC1950/GPC1938)**(1/12)-1
32	Uruguay	1.99	(GPC1950/GPC1938)**(1/12)-1
33	Morocco	1.96	(GPC1950/GPC1938)**(1/12)-1
34	Norway	1.94	(GPC1950/GPC1938)**(1/12)-1
35	Australia	1.94	(GPC1950/GPC1938)**(1/12)-1
36	Argentina	1.70	(GPC1950/GPC1938)**(1/12)-1
37	Spain	1.69	(GPC1950/GPC1938)**(1/12)-1
38	Slovakia	1.63	(GPC1950/GPC1938)**(1/12)-1
39	Czechia	1.63	(GPC1950/GPC1938)**(1/12)-1
40	Lebanon	1.60	(GPC1950/GPC1938)**(1/12)-1
41	Syria	1.58	(GPC1950/GPC1938)**(1/12)-1
42	Denmark	1.57	(GPC1950/GPC1938)**(1/12)-1
43	Iceland	1.57	(GPC1950/GPC1938)**(1/12)-1
44	Haiti	1.54	(GPC1950/GPC1938)**(1/12)-1
45	Puerto Rico	1.54	(GPC1950/GPC1938)**(1/12)-1
46	Paraguay	1.54	(GPC1950/GPC1938)**(1/12)-1
47	Panama	1.54	(GPC1950/GPC1938)**(1/12)-1
48	Trinidad & T	1.54	(GPC1950/GPC1938)**(1/12)-1

TABLE 5.14 GDP PER CAPITA GROWTH RATES, 1938-1950			
Rank	Country	GRPCRL	Source
49	Ecuador	1.54	(GPC1950/GPC1938)**(1/12)-1
50	Bolivia	1.54	(GPC1950/GPC1938)**(1/12)-1
51	Dominican R	1.54	(GPC1950/GPC1938)**(1/12)-1
52	Singapore	1.50	(GPC1950/GPC1938)**(1/12)-1
53	Hong Kong	1.50	(GPC1950/GPC1938)**(1/12)-1
54	Portugal	1.49	(GPC1950/GPC1938)**(1/12)-1
55	Iran	1.48	(GPC1950/GPC1938)**(1/12)-1
56	Honduras	1.45	(GPC1950/GPC1938)**(1/12)-1
57	Finland	1.42	(GPC1950/GPC1938)**(1/12)-1
58	France	1.39	(GPC1950/GPC1938)**(1/12)-1
59	Jordan	1.38	(GPC1950/GPC1938)**(1/12)-1
60	Colombia	1.30	(GPC1950/GPC1938)**(1/12)-1
61	Namibia	1.28	(GPC1950/GPC1938)**(1/12)-1
62	South Africa	1.25	(GPC1950/GPC1938)**(1/12)-1
63	Malaysia	1.14	(GPC1950/GPC1938)**(1/12)-1
64	Yemen	1.14	(GPC1950/GPC1938)**(1/12)-1
65	Kosovo	1.13	(GPC1950/GPC1938)**(1/12)-1
66	Macedonia	1.13	(GPC1950/GPC1938)**(1/12)-1
67	Bosnia	1.13	(GPC1950/GPC1938)**(1/12)-1
68	Serbia	1.13	(GPC1950/GPC1938)**(1/12)-1
69	Slovenia	1.13	(GPC1950/GPC1938)**(1/12)-1
70	Croatia	1.13	(GPC1950/GPC1938)**(1/12)-1
71	Montenegro	1.13	(GPC1950/GPC1938)**(1/12)-1
72	Netherlands	1.11	(GPC1950/GPC1938)**(1/12)-1
73	Ireland	1.03	(GPC1950/GPC1938)**(1/12)-1
74	Belgium	1.03	(GPC1950/GPC1938)**(1/12)-1
75	Ghana	0.98	(GPC1950/GPC1938)**(1/12)-1
76	Latvia	0.97	(GPC1950/GPC1938)**(1/12)-1
77	Estonia	0.97	(GPC1950/GPC1938)**(1/12)-1
78	Lithuania	0.97	(GPC1950/GPC1938)**(1/12)-1
79	Poland	0.96	(GPC1950/GPC1938)**(1/12)-1
80	UK	0.85	(GPC1950/GPC1938)**(1/12)-1
81	Iraq	0.84	(GPC1950/GPC1938)**(1/12)-1
82	Mozambique	0.78	(GPC1950/GPC1938)**(1/12)-1
83	Somalia	0.72	(GPC1950/GPC1938)**(1/12)-1
84	Chile	0.65	(GPC1950/GPC1938)**(1/12)-1
85	Madagascar	0.64	(GPC1950/GPC1938)**(1/12)-1
86	Tunisia	0.63	(GPC1950/GPC1938)**(1/12)-1
87	Libya	0.53	(GPC1950/GPC1938)**(1/12)-1
88	Sudan	0.53	(GPC1950/GPC1938)**(1/12)-1
89	Italy	0.46	(GPC1950/GPC1938)**(1/12)-1
90	Swaziland	0.43	(GPC1950/GPC1938)**(1/12)-1
91	Zimbabwe	0.40	(GPC1950/GPC1938)**(1/12)-1
92	Costa Rica	0.38	(GPC1950/GPC1938)**(1/12)-1
93	Albania	0.37	(GPC1950/GPC1938)**(1/12)-1
94	Zambia	0.36	(GPC1950/GPC1938)**(1/12)-1
95	Austria	0.34	(GPC1950/GPC1938)**(1/12)-1
96	Bulgaria	0.29	(GPC1950/GPC1938)**(1/12)-1

Table 5.14 GDP Per Capita Growth Rates, 1938-1950

Rank	Country	GRPCRL	Source
97	Sri Lanka	0.19	(GPC1950/GPC1938)**(1/12)-1
98	Egypt	0.18	(GPC1950/GPC1938)**(1/12)-1
99	Oman	0.10	(GPC1950/GPC1938)**(1/12)-1
100	Sierra Leone	0.08	(GPC1950/GPC1938)**(1/12)-1
101	South Sudan	0.05	(GPC1950/GPC1938)**(1/12)-1
102	Burundi	0.04	(GPC1950/GPC1938)**(1/12)-1
103	Lesotho	0.04	(GPC1950/GPC1938)**(1/12)-1
104	Botswana	0.04	(GPC1950/GPC1938)**(1/12)-1
105	Malawi	0.04	(GPC1950/GPC1938)**(1/12)-1
106	Guinea	0.04	(GPC1950/GPC1938)**(1/12)-1
107	Guinea-Biss	0.04	(GPC1950/GPC1938)**(1/12)-1
108	Eritrea	0.03	(GPC1950/GPC1938)**(1/12)-1
109	Ethiopia	0.03	(GPC1950/GPC1938)**(1/12)-1
110	India	0.00	(GPC1950/GPC1938)**(1/12)-1
111	Algeria	-0.04	(GPC1950/GPC1938)**(1/12)-1
112	Thailand	-0.09	(GPC1950/GPC1938)**(1/12)-1
113	Cambodia	-0.19	(GPC1950/GPC1938)**(1/12)-1
114	Mongolia	-0.19	(GPC1950/GPC1938)**(1/12)-1
115	Afghanistan	-0.19	(GPC1950/GPC1938)**(1/12)-1
116	Laos	-0.19	(GPC1950/GPC1938)**(1/12)-1
117	Nepal	-0.22	(GPC1950/GPC1938)**(1/12)-1
118	Vietnam	-0.27	(GPC1950/GPC1938)**(1/12)-1
119	Romania	-0.41	(GPC1950/GPC1938)**(1/12)-1
120	Pakistan	-0.47	(GPC1950/GPC1938)**(1/12)-1
121	Bangladesh	-0.48	(GPC1950/GPC1938)**(1/12)-1
122	Turkey	-0.50	(GPC1950/GPC1938)**(1/12)-1
123	Guatemala	-0.54	(GPC1950/GPC1938)**(1/12)-1
124	Hungary	-0.57	(GPC1950/GPC1938)**(1/12)-1
125	Japan	-2.00	(GPC1950/GPC1938)**(1/12)-1
126	China	-2.04	(GPC1950/GPC1938)**(1/12)-1
127	Germany	-2.08	(GPC1950/GPC1938)**(1/12)-1
128	Cyprus	-2.75	(GPC1950/GPC1938)**(1/12)-1
129	Greece	-2.75	(GPC1950/GPC1938)**(1/12)-1
130	Indonesia	-2.76	(GPC1950/GPC1938)**(1/12)-1
131	Taiwan	-2.82	(GPC1950/GPC1938)**(1/12)-1
132	Philippines	-2.89	(GPC1950/GPC1938)**(1/12)-1
133	Burma	-5.08	(GPC1950/GPC1938)**(1/12)-1
134	Korea, South	-5.19	(GPC1950/GPC1938)**(1/12)-1
135	Korea, North	-5.19	(GPC1950/GPC1938)**(1/12)-1

Table 5.15 GDP Per Capita Growth Rates, 1950-1960			
Rank	Country	GRPCRL	Source
1	Malta	8.91	(GPC1960/GPC1950)**(1/10)-1
2	Libya	8.38	(GPC1960/GPC1950)**(1/10)-1
3	UAE	8.30	(GPC1960/GPC1950)**(1/10)-1
4	Iraq	7.91	(GPC1960/GPC1950)**(1/10)-1
5	Germany	7.64	(GPC1960/GPC1950)**(1/10)-1
6	Bahrain	7.63	(GPC1960/GPC1950)**(1/10)-1
7	Japan	7.54	(GPC1960/GPC1950)**(1/10)-1
8	Macao	7.14	(GPC1960/GPC1950)**(1/10)-1
9	St Kitts & N	6.96	(GPC1960/GPC1950)**(1/10)-1
10	Barbados	6.92	(GPC1960/GPC1950)**(1/10)-1
11	Saudi Arabia	6.81	(GPC1960/GPC1950)**(1/10)-1
12	Jamaica	6.80	(GPC1960/GPC1950)**(1/10)-1
13	Romania	6.38	(GPC1960/GPC1950)**(1/10)-1
14	Austria	6.35	(GPC1960/GPC1950)**(1/10)-1
15	Greece	6.14	(GPC1960/GPC1950)**(1/10)-1
16	Martinique	6.11	(GPC1960/GPC1950)**(1/10)-1
17	Brunei	6.10	(GPC1960/GPC1950)**(1/10)-1
18	Italy	5.99	(GPC1960/GPC1950)**(1/10)-1
19	Macedonia	5.91	(GPC1960/GPC1950)**(1/10)-1
20	Montenegro	5.70	(GPC1960/GPC1950)**(1/10)-1
21	Oman	5.70	(GPC1960/GPC1950)**(1/10)-1
22	Bulgaria	5.68	(GPC1960/GPC1950)**(1/10)-1
23	Bermuda	5.61	(GPC1960/GPC1950)**(1/10)-1
24	St Lucia	5.59	(GPC1960/GPC1950)**(1/10)-1
25	Cyprus	5.51	(GPC1960/GPC1950)**(1/10)-1
26	Kosovo	5.50	(GPC1960/GPC1950)**(1/10)-1
27	Croatia	5.47	(GPC1960/GPC1950)**(1/10)-1
28	Algeria	5.43	(GPC1960/GPC1950)**(1/10)-1
29	Serbia	5.40	(GPC1960/GPC1950)**(1/10)-1
30	Bosnia	5.35	(GPC1960/GPC1950)**(1/10)-1
31	Guinea-Biss	5.34	(GPC1960/GPC1950)**(1/10)-1
32	Hungary	5.29	(GPC1960/GPC1950)**(1/10)-1
33	Israel	5.18	(GPC1960/GPC1950)**(1/10)-1
34	Trinidad & T	5.04	(GPC1960/GPC1950)**(1/10)-1
35	Gabon	4.97	(GPC1960/GPC1950)**(1/10)-1
36	Gibraltar	4.90	(GPC1960/GPC1950)**(1/10)-1
37	Guadeloupe	4.90	(GPC1960/GPC1950)**(1/10)-1
38	Taiwan	4.79	(GPC1960/GPC1950)**(1/10)-1
39	Slovenia	4.76	(GPC1960/GPC1950)**(1/10)-1
40	Czechia	4.67	(GPC1960/GPC1950)**(1/10)-1
41	Zambia	4.62	(GPC1960/GPC1950)**(1/10)-1
42	Russia	4.51	(GPC1960/GPC1950)**(1/10)-1
43	Iceland	4.51	(GPC1960/GPC1950)**(1/10)-1
44	W Sahara	4.33	(GPC1960/GPC1950)**(1/10)-1
45	San Marino	4.28	(GPC1960/GPC1950)**(1/10)-1
46	Albania	4.26	(GPC1960/GPC1950)**(1/10)-1
47	Saint Helena	4.26	(GPC1960/GPC1950)**(1/10)-1
48	Slovakia	4.24	(GPC1960/GPC1950)**(1/10)-1

TABLE 5.15 GDP PER CAPITA GROWTH RATES, 1950-1960			
Rank	Country	GRPCRL	Source
49	Switzerland	4.22	(GPC1960/GPC1950)**(1/10)-1
50	Isle of Man	4.20	(GPC1960/GPC1950)**(1/10)-1
51	Finland	4.17	(GPC1960/GPC1950)**(1/10)-1
52	Puerto Rico	4.09	(GPC1960/GPC1950)**(1/10)-1
53	Angola	4.09	(GPC1960/GPC1950)**(1/10)-1
54	Luxembourg	4.07	(GPC1960/GPC1950)**(1/10)-1
55	Comoros	4.05	(GPC1960/GPC1950)**(1/10)-1
56	Seychelles	4.05	(GPC1960/GPC1950)**(1/10)-1
57	Grenada	4.03	(GPC1960/GPC1950)**(1/10)-1
58	Mauritania	4.02	(GPC1960/GPC1950)**(1/10)-1
59	Monaco	3.96	(GPC1960/GPC1950)**(1/10)-1
60	Spain	3.95	(GPC1960/GPC1950)**(1/10)-1
61	Faroe Is	3.91	(GPC1960/GPC1950)**(1/10)-1
62	Turkmenistan	3.87	(GPC1960/GPC1950)**(1/10)-1
63	Greenland	3.86	(GPC1960/GPC1950)**(1/10)-1
64	Andorra	3.86	(GPC1960/GPC1950)**(1/10)-1
65	Lithuania	3.84	(GPC1960/GPC1950)**(1/10)-1
66	Guernsey	3.82	(GPC1960/GPC1950)**(1/10)-1
67	Portugal	3.81	(GPC1960/GPC1950)**(1/10)-1
68	Jersey	3.78	(GPC1960/GPC1950)**(1/10)-1
69	Suriname	3.76	(GPC1960/GPC1950)**(1/10)-1
70	Liechtenstn	3.76	(GPC1960/GPC1950)**(1/10)-1
71	Mongolia	3.75	(GPC1960/GPC1950)**(1/10)-1
72	France	3.74	(GPC1960/GPC1950)**(1/10)-1
73	Korea, North	3.71	(GPC1960/GPC1950)**(1/10)-1
74	Brazil	3.56	(GPC1960/GPC1950)**(1/10)-1
75	Netherlands	3.54	(GPC1960/GPC1950)**(1/10)-1
76	Chad	3.52	(GPC1960/GPC1950)**(1/10)-1
77	Hong Kong	3.49	(GPC1960/GPC1950)**(1/10)-1
78	Curacao	3.41	(GPC1960/GPC1950)**(1/10)-1
79	Korea, South	3.41	(GPC1960/GPC1950)**(1/10)-1
80	Sint Maarten	3.39	(GPC1960/GPC1950)**(1/10)-1
81	Saint Martin	3.36	(GPC1960/GPC1950)**(1/10)-1
82	Papua New G	3.35	(GPC1960/GPC1950)**(1/10)-1
83	Poland	3.33	(GPC1960/GPC1950)**(1/10)-1
84	Mexico	3.30	(GPC1960/GPC1950)**(1/10)-1
85	Estonia	3.29	(GPC1960/GPC1950)**(1/10)-1
86	Ukraine	3.28	(GPC1960/GPC1950)**(1/10)-1
87	Kiribati	3.26	(GPC1960/GPC1950)**(1/10)-1
88	Antigua & B	3.26	(GPC1960/GPC1950)**(1/10)-1
89	Svalbard	3.26	(GPC1960/GPC1950)**(1/10)-1
90	Norway	3.26	(GPC1960/GPC1950)**(1/10)-1
91	Turkey	3.25	(GPC1960/GPC1950)**(1/10)-1
92	Burma	3.24	(GPC1960/GPC1950)**(1/10)-1
93	Bahamas	3.21	(GPC1960/GPC1950)**(1/10)-1
94	Peru	3.15	(GPC1960/GPC1950)**(1/10)-1
95	Costa Rica	3.15	(GPC1960/GPC1950)**(1/10)-1
96	Equatorial G	3.10	(GPC1960/GPC1950)**(1/10)-1

Table 5.15 GDP Per Capita Growth Rates, 1950-1960

Rank	Country	GRPCRL	Source
97	Guinea	3.04	(GPC1960/GPC1950)**(1/10)-1
98	Iran	2.97	(GPC1960/GPC1950)**(1/10)-1
99	Botswana	2.97	(GPC1960/GPC1950)**(1/10)-1
100	Aruba	2.97	(GPC1960/GPC1950)**(1/10)-1
101	Latvia	2.96	(GPC1960/GPC1950)**(1/10)-1
102	South Africa	2.94	(GPC1960/GPC1950)**(1/10)-1
103	Sweden	2.87	(GPC1960/GPC1950)**(1/10)-1
104	Mayotte	2.86	(GPC1960/GPC1950)**(1/10)-1
105	Turks & C Is	2.86	(GPC1960/GPC1950)**(1/10)-1
106	Cameroon	2.84	(GPC1960/GPC1950)**(1/10)-1
107	Virgin I, Br	2.82	(GPC1960/GPC1950)**(1/10)-1
108	Cayman Is	2.80	(GPC1960/GPC1950)**(1/10)-1
109	Belgium	2.80	(GPC1960/GPC1950)**(1/10)-1
110	Moldova	2.79	(GPC1960/GPC1950)**(1/10)-1
111	Philippines	2.77	(GPC1960/GPC1950)**(1/10)-1
112	Dominica	2.75	(GPC1960/GPC1950)**(1/10)-1
113	Cambodia	2.75	(GPC1960/GPC1950)**(1/10)-1
114	Falkland Is	2.73	(GPC1960/GPC1950)**(1/10)-1
115	Dominican R	2.73	(GPC1960/GPC1950)**(1/10)-1
116	Somalia	2.73	(GPC1960/GPC1950)**(1/10)-1
117	St Pierre&M	2.72	(GPC1960/GPC1950)**(1/10)-1
118	Denmark	2.71	(GPC1960/GPC1950)**(1/10)-1
119	Nicaragua	2.68	(GPC1960/GPC1950)**(1/10)-1
120	Anguilla	2.67	(GPC1960/GPC1950)**(1/10)-1
121	Swaziland	2.61	(GPC1960/GPC1950)**(1/10)-1
122	Virgin I, US	2.60	(GPC1960/GPC1950)**(1/10)-1
123	Congo, Dem R	2.59	(GPC1960/GPC1950)**(1/10)-1
124	Azerbaijan	2.58	(GPC1960/GPC1950)**(1/10)-1
125	Afghanistan	2.56	(GPC1960/GPC1950)**(1/10)-1
126	Tajikistan	2.53	(GPC1960/GPC1950)**(1/10)-1
127	Ireland	2.52	(GPC1960/GPC1950)**(1/10)-1
128	Georgia	2.51	(GPC1960/GPC1950)**(1/10)-1
129	Ecuador	2.45	(GPC1960/GPC1950)**(1/10)-1
130	St Vincent	2.44	(GPC1960/GPC1950)**(1/10)-1
131	Kazakhstan	2.44	(GPC1960/GPC1950)**(1/10)-1
132	El Salvador	2.44	(GPC1960/GPC1950)**(1/10)-1
133	Gambia	2.43	(GPC1960/GPC1950)**(1/10)-1
134	Solomon Is	2.43	(GPC1960/GPC1950)**(1/10)-1
135	Djibouti	2.39	(GPC1960/GPC1950)**(1/10)-1
136	Samoa, Amer	2.28	(GPC1960/GPC1950)**(1/10)-1
137	Belarus	2.24	(GPC1960/GPC1950)**(1/10)-1
138	Uzbekistan	2.17	(GPC1960/GPC1950)**(1/10)-1
139	Zimbabwe	2.12	(GPC1960/GPC1950)**(1/10)-1
140	Jordan	2.12	(GPC1960/GPC1950)**(1/10)-1
141	Panama	2.10	(GPC1960/GPC1950)**(1/10)-1
142	UK	2.10	(GPC1960/GPC1950)**(1/10)-1
143	Tonga	2.05	(GPC1960/GPC1950)**(1/10)-1
144	China	2.03	(GPC1960/GPC1950)**(1/10)-1

TABLE 5.15 GDP PER CAPITA GROWTH RATES, 1950-1960			
Rank	Country	GRPCRL	Source
145	Montserrat	2.01	(GPC1960/GPC1950)**(1/10)-1
146	Lebanon	2.01	(GPC1960/GPC1950)**(1/10)-1
147	Canada	1.95	(GPC1960/GPC1950)**(1/10)-1
148	Niue	1.93	(GPC1960/GPC1950)**(1/10)-1
149	Maldives	1.93	(GPC1960/GPC1950)**(1/10)-1
150	Australia	1.86	(GPC1960/GPC1950)**(1/10)-1
151	South Sudan	1.85	(GPC1960/GPC1950)**(1/10)-1
152	Sudan	1.85	(GPC1960/GPC1950)**(1/10)-1
153	Tunisia	1.82	(GPC1960/GPC1950)**(1/10)-1
154	US	1.79	(GPC1960/GPC1950)**(1/10)-1
155	Venezuela	1.78	(GPC1960/GPC1950)**(1/10)-1
156	Sierra Leone	1.71	(GPC1960/GPC1950)**(1/10)-1
157	Fr Polynesia	1.70	(GPC1960/GPC1950)**(1/10)-1
158	Congo, Rep	1.69	(GPC1960/GPC1950)**(1/10)-1
159	Cook Is	1.69	(GPC1960/GPC1950)**(1/10)-1
160	Mozambique	1.67	(GPC1960/GPC1950)**(1/10)-1
161	Madagascar	1.62	(GPC1960/GPC1950)**(1/10)-1
162	Kyrgyzstan	1.59	(GPC1960/GPC1950)**(1/10)-1
163	Ivory Coast	1.58	(GPC1960/GPC1950)**(1/10)-1
164	Namibia	1.58	(GPC1960/GPC1950)**(1/10)-1
165	West Bank	1.57	(GPC1960/GPC1950)**(1/10)-1
166	Thailand	1.56	(GPC1960/GPC1950)**(1/10)-1
167	Vanuatu	1.56	(GPC1960/GPC1950)**(1/10)-1
168	Guam	1.56	(GPC1960/GPC1950)**(1/10)-1
169	East Timor	1.55	(GPC1960/GPC1950)**(1/10)-1
170	Tokelau	1.55	(GPC1960/GPC1950)**(1/10)-1
171	Burkina Faso	1.53	(GPC1960/GPC1950)**(1/10)-1
172	Tuvalu	1.52	(GPC1960/GPC1950)**(1/10)-1
173	New Caledon	1.50	(GPC1960/GPC1950)**(1/10)-1
174	Belize	1.48	(GPC1960/GPC1950)**(1/10)-1
175	Niger	1.48	(GPC1960/GPC1950)**(1/10)-1
176	Samoa	1.45	(GPC1960/GPC1950)**(1/10)-1
177	Nauru	1.41	(GPC1960/GPC1950)**(1/10)-1
178	New Zealand	1.40	(GPC1960/GPC1950)**(1/10)-1
179	Palau	1.39	(GPC1960/GPC1950)**(1/10)-1
180	Marshall Is	1.39	(GPC1960/GPC1950)**(1/10)-1
181	Armenia	1.38	(GPC1960/GPC1950)**(1/10)-1
182	Micronesia	1.38	(GPC1960/GPC1950)**(1/10)-1
183	Wallis & Fut	1.33	(GPC1960/GPC1950)**(1/10)-1
184	Colombia	1.24	(GPC1960/GPC1950)**(1/10)-1
185	CAR	1.19	(GPC1960/GPC1950)**(1/10)-1
186	Malawi	1.18	(GPC1960/GPC1950)**(1/10)-1
187	Eritrea	1.18	(GPC1960/GPC1950)**(1/10)-1
188	Togo	1.18	(GPC1960/GPC1950)**(1/10)-1
189	Ethiopia	1.18	(GPC1960/GPC1950)**(1/10)-1
190	Tanzania	1.16	(GPC1960/GPC1950)**(1/10)-1
191	Reunion	1.16	(GPC1960/GPC1950)**(1/10)-1
192	Guyana	1.09	(GPC1960/GPC1950)**(1/10)-1

Table 5.15 GDP Per Capita Growth Rates, 1950-1960

Rank	Country	GRPCRL	Source
193	Vietnam	1.09	(GPC1960/GPC1950)**(1/10)-1
194	Qatar	1.09	(GPC1960/GPC1950)**(1/10)-1
195	Lesotho	1.06	(GPC1960/GPC1950)**(1/10)-1
196	Singapore	1.02	(GPC1960/GPC1950)**(1/10)-1
197	N Mariana Is	0.99	(GPC1960/GPC1950)**(1/10)-1
198	Nigeria	0.98	(GPC1960/GPC1950)**(1/10)-1
199	Kenya	0.97	(GPC1960/GPC1950)**(1/10)-1
200	Gaza Strip	0.96	(GPC1960/GPC1950)**(1/10)-1
201	Nepal	0.96	(GPC1960/GPC1950)**(1/10)-1
202	India	0.95	(GPC1960/GPC1950)**(1/10)-1
203	Benin	0.90	(GPC1960/GPC1950)**(1/10)-1
204	Mali	0.77	(GPC1960/GPC1950)**(1/10)-1
205	Honduras	0.72	(GPC1960/GPC1950)**(1/10)-1
206	Egypt	0.68	(GPC1960/GPC1950)**(1/10)-1
207	Argentina	0.67	(GPC1960/GPC1950)**(1/10)-1
208	Ghana	0.64	(GPC1960/GPC1950)**(1/10)-1
209	Bhutan	0.63	(GPC1960/GPC1950)**(1/10)-1
210	Indonesia	0.60	(GPC1960/GPC1950)**(1/10)-1
211	Senegal	0.49	(GPC1960/GPC1950)**(1/10)-1
212	Rwanda	0.44	(GPC1960/GPC1950)**(1/10)-1
213	Sao Tome & P	0.36	(GPC1960/GPC1950)**(1/10)-1
214	Chile	0.32	(GPC1960/GPC1950)**(1/10)-1
215	Guatemala	0.25	(GPC1960/GPC1950)**(1/10)-1
216	Laos	0.22	(GPC1960/GPC1950)**(1/10)-1
217	Uruguay	0.13	(GPC1960/GPC1950)**(1/10)-1
218	Haiti	0.04	(GPC1960/GPC1950)**(1/10)-1
219	Cuba	0.02	(GPC1960/GPC1950)**(1/10)-1
220	Kuwait	0.00	(GPC1960/GPC1950)**(1/10)-1
221	Fiji	-0.02	(GPC1960/GPC1950)**(1/10)-1
222	Cape Verde	-0.06	(GPC1960/GPC1950)**(1/10)-1
223	Mauritius	-0.09	(GPC1960/GPC1950)**(1/10)-1
224	Syria	-0.12	(GPC1960/GPC1950)**(1/10)-1
225	Paraguay	-0.17	(GPC1960/GPC1950)**(1/10)-1
226	Malaysia	-0.26	(GPC1960/GPC1950)**(1/10)-1
227	Burundi	-0.28	(GPC1960/GPC1950)**(1/10)-1
228	Bangladesh	-0.39	(GPC1960/GPC1950)**(1/10)-1
229	Uganda	-0.53	(GPC1960/GPC1950)**(1/10)-1
230	Guiana, Fr	-0.58	(GPC1960/GPC1950)**(1/10)-1
231	Pakistan	-0.67	(GPC1960/GPC1950)**(1/10)-1
232	Yemen	-0.76	(GPC1960/GPC1950)**(1/10)-1
233	Sri Lanka	-0.85	(GPC1960/GPC1950)**(1/10)-1
234	Liberia	-1.30	(GPC1960/GPC1950)**(1/10)-1
235	Morocco	-1.51	(GPC1960/GPC1950)**(1/10)-1
236	Bolivia	-1.89	(GPC1960/GPC1950)**(1/10)-1

Table 5.16 GDP Per Capita Growth Rates, 1960-1970

Rank	Country	GRPCRL	Source
1	Libya	18.57	(GPC1970/GPC1960)**(1/10)-1
2	Oman	17.12	(GPC1970/GPC1960)**(1/10)-1
3	Japan	9.26	(GPC1970/GPC1960)**(1/10)-1
4	Saudi Arabia	9.20	(GPC1970/GPC1960)**(1/10)-1
5	Malta	8.91	(GPC1970/GPC1960)**(1/10)-1
6	Spain	8.27	(GPC1970/GPC1960)**(1/10)-1
7	Greece	8.25	(GPC1970/GPC1960)**(1/10)-1
8	Iran	7.73	(GPC1970/GPC1960)**(1/10)-1
9	Bahrain	7.46	(GPC1970/GPC1960)**(1/10)-1
10	Singapore	7.42	(GPC1970/GPC1960)**(1/10)-1
11	Swaziland	7.32	(GPC1970/GPC1960)**(1/10)-1
12	Macao	7.14	(GPC1970/GPC1960)**(1/10)-1
13	Taiwan	6.99	(GPC1970/GPC1960)**(1/10)-1
14	St Kitts & N	6.96	(GPC1970/GPC1960)**(1/10)-1
15	Barbados	6.92	(GPC1970/GPC1960)**(1/10)-1
16	Portugal	6.78	(GPC1970/GPC1960)**(1/10)-1
17	Mauritania	6.54	(GPC1970/GPC1960)**(1/10)-1
18	Botswana	6.45	(GPC1970/GPC1960)**(1/10)-1
19	Romania	6.28	(GPC1970/GPC1960)**(1/10)-1
20	Hong Kong	6.12	(GPC1970/GPC1960)**(1/10)-1
21	Martinique	6.11	(GPC1970/GPC1960)**(1/10)-1
22	Brunei	6.10	(GPC1970/GPC1960)**(1/10)-1
23	Korea, North	5.91	(GPC1970/GPC1960)**(1/10)-1
24	Angola	5.87	(GPC1970/GPC1960)**(1/10)-1
25	Macedonia	5.69	(GPC1970/GPC1960)**(1/10)-1
26	Israel	5.68	(GPC1970/GPC1960)**(1/10)-1
27	Italy	5.67	(GPC1970/GPC1960)**(1/10)-1
28	Bermuda	5.61	(GPC1970/GPC1960)**(1/10)-1
29	Equatorial G	5.59	(GPC1970/GPC1960)**(1/10)-1
30	St Lucia	5.59	(GPC1970/GPC1960)**(1/10)-1
31	Korea, South	5.57	(GPC1970/GPC1960)**(1/10)-1
32	Cyprus	5.51	(GPC1970/GPC1960)**(1/10)-1
33	Comoros	5.48	(GPC1970/GPC1960)**(1/10)-1
34	Puerto Rico	5.45	(GPC1970/GPC1960)**(1/10)-1
35	Montenegro	5.45	(GPC1970/GPC1960)**(1/10)-1
36	Gabon	5.39	(GPC1970/GPC1960)**(1/10)-1
37	Guinea-Biss	5.38	(GPC1970/GPC1960)**(1/10)-1
38	Kosovo	5.26	(GPC1970/GPC1960)**(1/10)-1
39	Croatia	5.23	(GPC1970/GPC1960)**(1/10)-1
40	Serbia	5.16	(GPC1970/GPC1960)**(1/10)-1
41	UAE	5.15	(GPC1970/GPC1960)**(1/10)-1
42	Bosnia	5.11	(GPC1970/GPC1960)**(1/10)-1
43	Bulgaria	4.92	(GPC1970/GPC1960)**(1/10)-1
44	Gibraltar	4.90	(GPC1970/GPC1960)**(1/10)-1
45	Guadeloupe	4.90	(GPC1970/GPC1960)**(1/10)-1
46	Belgium	4.78	(GPC1970/GPC1960)**(1/10)-1
47	Russia	4.75	(GPC1970/GPC1960)**(1/10)-1
48	Finland	4.69	(GPC1970/GPC1960)**(1/10)-1

TABLE 5.16 GDP PER CAPITA GROWTH RATES, 1960-1970			
Rank	Country	GRPCRL	Source
49	Panama	4.60	(GPC1970/GPC1960)**(1/10)-1
50	Austria	4.59	(GPC1970/GPC1960)**(1/10)-1
51	France	4.58	(GPC1970/GPC1960)**(1/10)-1
52	Slovenia	4.55	(GPC1970/GPC1960)**(1/10)-1
53	Hungary	4.53	(GPC1970/GPC1960)**(1/10)-1
54	Iceland	4.51	(GPC1970/GPC1960)**(1/10)-1
55	Reunion	4.35	(GPC1970/GPC1960)**(1/10)-1
56	San Marino	4.28	(GPC1970/GPC1960)**(1/10)-1
57	Nicaragua	4.24	(GPC1970/GPC1960)**(1/10)-1
58	Sweden	4.22	(GPC1970/GPC1960)**(1/10)-1
59	Lebanon	4.20	(GPC1970/GPC1960)**(1/10)-1
60	Isle of Man	4.20	(GPC1970/GPC1960)**(1/10)-1
61	Ireland	4.17	(GPC1970/GPC1960)**(1/10)-1
62	Denmark	4.17	(GPC1970/GPC1960)**(1/10)-1
63	Luxembourg	4.07	(GPC1970/GPC1960)**(1/10)-1
64	Switzerland	4.07	(GPC1970/GPC1960)**(1/10)-1
65	South Africa	4.06	(GPC1970/GPC1960)**(1/10)-1
66	Turkmenistan	4.05	(GPC1970/GPC1960)**(1/10)-1
67	Lithuania	4.04	(GPC1970/GPC1960)**(1/10)-1
68	Grenada	4.03	(GPC1970/GPC1960)**(1/10)-1
69	Netherlands	4.02	(GPC1970/GPC1960)**(1/10)-1
70	Monaco	3.96	(GPC1970/GPC1960)**(1/10)-1
71	Germany	3.94	(GPC1970/GPC1960)**(1/10)-1
72	Svalbard	3.92	(GPC1970/GPC1960)**(1/10)-1
73	Norway	3.92	(GPC1970/GPC1960)**(1/10)-1
74	Faroe Is	3.91	(GPC1970/GPC1960)**(1/10)-1
75	Greenland	3.86	(GPC1970/GPC1960)**(1/10)-1
76	Andorra	3.86	(GPC1970/GPC1960)**(1/10)-1
77	Poland	3.84	(GPC1970/GPC1960)**(1/10)-1
78	Guernsey	3.82	(GPC1970/GPC1960)**(1/10)-1
79	Jersey	3.78	(GPC1970/GPC1960)**(1/10)-1
80	Suriname	3.76	(GPC1970/GPC1960)**(1/10)-1
81	Mongolia	3.76	(GPC1970/GPC1960)**(1/10)-1
82	Liechtenstn	3.76	(GPC1970/GPC1960)**(1/10)-1
83	Albania	3.73	(GPC1970/GPC1960)**(1/10)-1
84	Mexico	3.61	(GPC1970/GPC1960)**(1/10)-1
85	Jamaica	3.59	(GPC1970/GPC1960)**(1/10)-1
86	Estonia	3.47	(GPC1970/GPC1960)**(1/10)-1
87	Ukraine	3.45	(GPC1970/GPC1960)**(1/10)-1
88	Curacao	3.41	(GPC1970/GPC1960)**(1/10)-1
89	Australia	3.41	(GPC1970/GPC1960)**(1/10)-1
90	Sint Maarten	3.39	(GPC1970/GPC1960)**(1/10)-1
91	Canada	3.37	(GPC1970/GPC1960)**(1/10)-1
92	Saint Martin	3.36	(GPC1970/GPC1960)**(1/10)-1
93	Papua New G	3.35	(GPC1970/GPC1960)**(1/10)-1
94	Thailand	3.31	(GPC1970/GPC1960)**(1/10)-1
95	Sao Tome & P	3.31	(GPC1970/GPC1960)**(1/10)-1
96	Bolivia	3.28	(GPC1970/GPC1960)**(1/10)-1

TABLE 5.16 GDP PER CAPITA GROWTH RATES, 1960-1970

Rank	Country	GRPCRL	Source
97	Kiribati	3.26	(GPC1970/GPC1960)**(1/10)-1
98	Antigua & B	3.26	(GPC1970/GPC1960)**(1/10)-1
99	Czechia	3.24	(GPC1970/GPC1960)**(1/10)-1
100	Bahamas	3.21	(GPC1970/GPC1960)**(1/10)-1
101	Latvia	3.15	(GPC1970/GPC1960)**(1/10)-1
102	Costa Rica	3.15	(GPC1970/GPC1960)**(1/10)-1
103	Turkey	3.13	(GPC1970/GPC1960)**(1/10)-1
104	Ivory Coast	3.12	(GPC1970/GPC1960)**(1/10)-1
105	Pakistan	3.11	(GPC1970/GPC1960)**(1/10)-1
106	Tunisia	3.07	(GPC1970/GPC1960)**(1/10)-1
107	Malaysia	3.07	(GPC1970/GPC1960)**(1/10)-1
108	Nigeria	3.01	(GPC1970/GPC1960)**(1/10)-1
109	Ethiopia	3.01	(GPC1970/GPC1960)**(1/10)-1
110	Eritrea	2.99	(GPC1970/GPC1960)**(1/10)-1
111	Aruba	2.97	(GPC1970/GPC1960)**(1/10)-1
112	US	2.95	(GPC1970/GPC1960)**(1/10)-1
113	Moldova	2.94	(GPC1970/GPC1960)**(1/10)-1
114	El Salvador	2.94	(GPC1970/GPC1960)**(1/10)-1
115	Brazil	2.89	(GPC1970/GPC1960)**(1/10)-1
116	Turks & C Is	2.86	(GPC1970/GPC1960)**(1/10)-1
117	Togo	2.86	(GPC1970/GPC1960)**(1/10)-1
118	Mozambique	2.85	(GPC1970/GPC1960)**(1/10)-1
119	Virgin I, Br	2.82	(GPC1970/GPC1960)**(1/10)-1
120	Cayman Is	2.80	(GPC1970/GPC1960)**(1/10)-1
121	Azerbaijan	2.76	(GPC1970/GPC1960)**(1/10)-1
122	Dominica	2.75	(GPC1970/GPC1960)**(1/10)-1
123	Georgia	2.74	(GPC1970/GPC1960)**(1/10)-1
124	Falkland Is	2.73	(GPC1970/GPC1960)**(1/10)-1
125	St Pierre&M	2.72	(GPC1970/GPC1960)**(1/10)-1
126	Tajikistan	2.70	(GPC1970/GPC1960)**(1/10)-1
127	Seychelles	2.67	(GPC1970/GPC1960)**(1/10)-1
128	Anguilla	2.67	(GPC1970/GPC1960)**(1/10)-1
129	Gambia	2.67	(GPC1970/GPC1960)**(1/10)-1
130	Iraq	2.65	(GPC1970/GPC1960)**(1/10)-1
131	Kazakhstan	2.62	(GPC1970/GPC1960)**(1/10)-1
132	Slovakia	2.61	(GPC1970/GPC1960)**(1/10)-1
133	Virgin I, US	2.60	(GPC1970/GPC1960)**(1/10)-1
134	Ecuador	2.57	(GPC1970/GPC1960)**(1/10)-1
135	Peru	2.55	(GPC1970/GPC1960)**(1/10)-1
136	Tanzania	2.51	(GPC1970/GPC1960)**(1/10)-1
137	St Vincent	2.44	(GPC1970/GPC1960)**(1/10)-1
138	Solomon Is	2.43	(GPC1970/GPC1960)**(1/10)-1
139	Belarus	2.42	(GPC1970/GPC1960)**(1/10)-1
140	Trinidad & T	2.38	(GPC1970/GPC1960)**(1/10)-1
141	Argentina	2.35	(GPC1970/GPC1960)**(1/10)-1
142	Cameroon	2.31	(GPC1970/GPC1960)**(1/10)-1
143	Uzbekistan	2.30	(GPC1970/GPC1960)**(1/10)-1
144	Djibouti	2.28	(GPC1970/GPC1960)**(1/10)-1

Table 5.16 GDP Per Capita Growth Rates, 1960-1970

Rank	Country	GRPCRL	Source
145	Samoa, Amer	2.28	(GPC1970/GPC1960)**(1/10)-1
146	Zimbabwe	2.27	(GPC1970/GPC1960)**(1/10)-1
147	Kenya	2.21	(GPC1970/GPC1960)**(1/10)-1
148	Dominican R	2.15	(GPC1970/GPC1960)**(1/10)-1
149	Egypt	2.14	(GPC1970/GPC1960)**(1/10)-1
150	Guinea	2.11	(GPC1970/GPC1960)**(1/10)-1
151	UK	2.09	(GPC1970/GPC1960)**(1/10)-1
152	Namibia	2.05	(GPC1970/GPC1960)**(1/10)-1
153	Tonga	2.05	(GPC1970/GPC1960)**(1/10)-1
154	Montserrat	2.01	(GPC1970/GPC1960)**(1/10)-1
155	New Zealand	2.00	(GPC1970/GPC1960)**(1/10)-1
156	Niue	1.93	(GPC1970/GPC1960)**(1/10)-1
157	Maldives	1.93	(GPC1970/GPC1960)**(1/10)-1
158	Colombia	1.91	(GPC1970/GPC1960)**(1/10)-1
159	Congo, Rep	1.82	(GPC1970/GPC1960)**(1/10)-1
160	Sierra Leone	1.81	(GPC1970/GPC1960)**(1/10)-1
161	Guatemala	1.78	(GPC1970/GPC1960)**(1/10)-1
162	Kyrgyzstan	1.77	(GPC1970/GPC1960)**(1/10)-1
163	Paraguay	1.76	(GPC1970/GPC1960)**(1/10)-1
164	Algeria	1.73	(GPC1970/GPC1960)**(1/10)-1
165	Fr Polynesia	1.70	(GPC1970/GPC1960)**(1/10)-1
166	Cook Is	1.69	(GPC1970/GPC1960)**(1/10)-1
167	Zambia	1.57	(GPC1970/GPC1960)**(1/10)-1
168	Vanuatu	1.56	(GPC1970/GPC1960)**(1/10)-1
169	Guam	1.56	(GPC1970/GPC1960)**(1/10)-1
170	East Timor	1.55	(GPC1970/GPC1960)**(1/10)-1
171	Tokelau	1.55	(GPC1970/GPC1960)**(1/10)-1
172	West Bank	1.53	(GPC1970/GPC1960)**(1/10)-1
173	Tuvalu	1.52	(GPC1970/GPC1960)**(1/10)-1
174	New Caledon	1.50	(GPC1970/GPC1960)**(1/10)-1
175	Honduras	1.48	(GPC1970/GPC1960)**(1/10)-1
176	Belize	1.48	(GPC1970/GPC1960)**(1/10)-1
177	Armenia	1.46	(GPC1970/GPC1960)**(1/10)-1
178	Samoa	1.45	(GPC1970/GPC1960)**(1/10)-1
179	Nauru	1.41	(GPC1970/GPC1960)**(1/10)-1
180	Palau	1.39	(GPC1970/GPC1960)**(1/10)-1
181	Marshall Is	1.39	(GPC1970/GPC1960)**(1/10)-1
182	Micronesia	1.38	(GPC1970/GPC1960)**(1/10)-1
183	Wallis & Fut	1.33	(GPC1970/GPC1960)**(1/10)-1
184	Philippines	1.32	(GPC1970/GPC1960)**(1/10)-1
185	Lesotho	1.27	(GPC1970/GPC1960)**(1/10)-1
186	Chile	1.23	(GPC1970/GPC1960)**(1/10)-1
187	Morocco	1.20	(GPC1970/GPC1960)**(1/10)-1
188	Burma	1.17	(GPC1970/GPC1960)**(1/10)-1
189	Yemen	1.12	(GPC1970/GPC1960)**(1/10)-1
190	Guyana	1.09	(GPC1970/GPC1960)**(1/10)-1
191	Uganda	1.09	(GPC1970/GPC1960)**(1/10)-1
192	Bangladesh	1.00	(GPC1970/GPC1960)**(1/10)-1

TABLE 5.16 GDP PER CAPITA GROWTH RATES, 1960-1970

Rank	Country	GRPCRL	Source
193	N Mariana Is	0.99	(GPC1970/GPC1960)**(1/10)-1
194	Gaza Strip	0.94	(GPC1970/GPC1960)**(1/10)-1
195	Madagascar	0.71	(GPC1970/GPC1960)**(1/10)-1
196	Cape Verde	0.69	(GPC1970/GPC1960)**(1/10)-1
197	Bhutan	0.63	(GPC1970/GPC1960)**(1/10)-1
198	Malawi	0.54	(GPC1970/GPC1960)**(1/10)-1
199	Burkina Faso	0.49	(GPC1970/GPC1960)**(1/10)-1
200	Venezuela	0.47	(GPC1970/GPC1960)**(1/10)-1
201	Chad	0.45	(GPC1970/GPC1960)**(1/10)-1
202	India	0.43	(GPC1970/GPC1960)**(1/10)-1
203	W Sahara	0.41	(GPC1970/GPC1960)**(1/10)-1
204	Saint Helena	0.41	(GPC1970/GPC1960)**(1/10)-1
205	Indonesia	0.28	(GPC1970/GPC1960)**(1/10)-1
206	Mayotte	0.27	(GPC1970/GPC1960)**(1/10)-1
207	Sri Lanka	0.21	(GPC1970/GPC1960)**(1/10)-1
208	Laos	0.17	(GPC1970/GPC1960)**(1/10)-1
209	Congo, Dem R	0.12	(GPC1970/GPC1960)**(1/10)-1
210	Mali	0.12	(GPC1970/GPC1960)**(1/10)-1
211	Niger	0.11	(GPC1970/GPC1960)**(1/10)-1
212	Qatar	0.02	(GPC1970/GPC1960)**(1/10)-1
213	Fiji	-0.02	(GPC1970/GPC1960)**(1/10)-1
214	Kuwait	-0.04	(GPC1970/GPC1960)**(1/10)-1
215	Uruguay	-0.06	(GPC1970/GPC1960)**(1/10)-1
216	Nepal	-0.25	(GPC1970/GPC1960)**(1/10)-1
217	Burundi	-0.27	(GPC1970/GPC1960)**(1/10)-1
218	Rwanda	-0.42	(GPC1970/GPC1960)**(1/10)-1
219	Cambodia	-0.42	(GPC1970/GPC1960)**(1/10)-1
220	Benin	-0.43	(GPC1970/GPC1960)**(1/10)-1
221	Senegal	-0.53	(GPC1970/GPC1960)**(1/10)-1
222	China	-0.55	(GPC1970/GPC1960)**(1/10)-1
223	Cuba	-0.55	(GPC1970/GPC1960)**(1/10)-1
224	Syria	-0.56	(GPC1970/GPC1960)**(1/10)-1
225	Mauritius	-0.57	(GPC1970/GPC1960)**(1/10)-1
226	Guiana, Fr	-0.58	(GPC1970/GPC1960)**(1/10)-1
227	Ghana	-0.60	(GPC1970/GPC1960)**(1/10)-1
228	Afghanistan	-0.77	(GPC1970/GPC1960)**(1/10)-1
229	Jordan	-0.82	(GPC1970/GPC1960)**(1/10)-1
230	CAR	-0.96	(GPC1970/GPC1960)**(1/10)-1
231	Liberia	-1.03	(GPC1970/GPC1960)**(1/10)-1
232	South Sudan	-1.27	(GPC1970/GPC1960)**(1/10)-1
233	Sudan	-1.27	(GPC1970/GPC1960)**(1/10)-1
234	Haiti	-1.44	(GPC1970/GPC1960)**(1/10)-1
235	Somalia	-1.63	(GPC1970/GPC1960)**(1/10)-1
236	Vietnam	-1.68	(GPC1970/GPC1960)**(1/10)-1

Table 5.17 GDP Per Capita Growth Rates, 1970-1980

Rank	Country	GRPCRL	Source
1	Botswana	12.11	(GPC1980/GPC1970)**(1/10)-1
2	Macao	11.20	(GPC1980/GPC1970)**(1/10)-1
3	Singapore	8.07	(GPC1980/GPC1970)**(1/10)-1
4	Brunei	7.77	(GPC1980/GPC1970)**(1/10)-1
5	Korea, South	7.40	(GPC1980/GPC1970)**(1/10)-1
6	Saudi Arabia	7.32	(GPC1980/GPC1970)**(1/10)-1
7	Seychelles	7.22	(GPC1980/GPC1970)**(1/10)-1
8	Iraq	6.87	(GPC1980/GPC1970)**(1/10)-1
9	Taiwan	6.85	(GPC1980/GPC1970)**(1/10)-1
10	Hong Kong	6.28	(GPC1980/GPC1970)**(1/10)-1
11	Macedonia	6.23	(GPC1980/GPC1970)**(1/10)-1
12	Montenegro	6.06	(GPC1980/GPC1970)**(1/10)-1
13	Kosovo	5.84	(GPC1980/GPC1970)**(1/10)-1
14	Croatia	5.81	(GPC1980/GPC1970)**(1/10)-1
15	Malaysia	5.78	(GPC1980/GPC1970)**(1/10)-1
16	Bahrain	5.75	(GPC1980/GPC1970)**(1/10)-1
17	Serbia	5.73	(GPC1980/GPC1970)**(1/10)-1
18	Bosnia	5.68	(GPC1980/GPC1970)**(1/10)-1
19	Brazil	5.64	(GPC1980/GPC1970)**(1/10)-1
20	UAE	5.51	(GPC1980/GPC1970)**(1/10)-1
21	Cyprus	5.51	(GPC1980/GPC1970)**(1/10)-1
22	Romania	5.49	(GPC1980/GPC1970)**(1/10)-1
23	Paraguay	5.48	(GPC1980/GPC1970)**(1/10)-1
24	Slovenia	5.05	(GPC1980/GPC1970)**(1/10)-1
25	Yemen	5.02	(GPC1980/GPC1970)**(1/10)-1
26	Jordan	4.94	(GPC1980/GPC1970)**(1/10)-1
27	Norway	4.91	(GPC1980/GPC1970)**(1/10)-1
28	Svalbard	4.91	(GPC1980/GPC1970)**(1/10)-1
29	Tunisia	4.84	(GPC1980/GPC1970)**(1/10)-1
30	Egypt	4.78	(GPC1980/GPC1970)**(1/10)-1
31	Maldives	4.75	(GPC1980/GPC1970)**(1/10)-1
32	Greece	4.68	(GPC1980/GPC1970)**(1/10)-1
33	Dominican R	4.64	(GPC1980/GPC1970)**(1/10)-1
34	Algeria	4.47	(GPC1980/GPC1970)**(1/10)-1
35	Malta	4.47	(GPC1980/GPC1970)**(1/10)-1
36	Spain	4.36	(GPC1980/GPC1970)**(1/10)-1
37	Mexico	4.34	(GPC1980/GPC1970)**(1/10)-1
38	Portugal	4.21	(GPC1980/GPC1970)**(1/10)-1
39	Suriname	4.17	(GPC1980/GPC1970)**(1/10)-1
40	Ecuador	4.15	(GPC1980/GPC1970)**(1/10)-1
41	Lebanon	4.12	(GPC1980/GPC1970)**(1/10)-1
42	Barbados	3.99	(GPC1980/GPC1970)**(1/10)-1
43	Austria	3.97	(GPC1980/GPC1970)**(1/10)-1
44	Korea, North	3.84	(GPC1980/GPC1970)**(1/10)-1
45	Mongolia	3.75	(GPC1980/GPC1970)**(1/10)-1
46	Trinidad & T	3.73	(GPC1980/GPC1970)**(1/10)-1
47	Ireland	3.64	(GPC1980/GPC1970)**(1/10)-1
48	Belgium	3.54	(GPC1980/GPC1970)**(1/10)-1

Table 5.17 GDP Per Capita Growth Rates, 1970-1980

Rank	Country	GRPCRL	Source
49	Lesotho	3.53	(GPC1980/GPC1970)**(1/10)-1
50	Haiti	3.53	(GPC1980/GPC1970)**(1/10)-1
51	Italy	3.50	(GPC1980/GPC1970)**(1/10)-1
52	Hungary	3.45	(GPC1980/GPC1970)**(1/10)-1
53	Gabon	3.41	(GPC1980/GPC1970)**(1/10)-1
54	Japan	3.31	(GPC1980/GPC1970)**(1/10)-1
55	Finland	3.30	(GPC1980/GPC1970)**(1/10)-1
56	Antigua & B	3.26	(GPC1980/GPC1970)**(1/10)-1
57	Gibraltar	3.19	(GPC1980/GPC1970)**(1/10)-1
58	Poland	3.19	(GPC1980/GPC1970)**(1/10)-1
59	Israel	3.13	(GPC1980/GPC1970)**(1/10)-1
60	Germany	3.12	(GPC1980/GPC1970)**(1/10)-1
61	Canada	3.10	(GPC1980/GPC1970)**(1/10)-1
62	St Lucia	3.07	(GPC1980/GPC1970)**(1/10)-1
63	Colombia	2.98	(GPC1980/GPC1970)**(1/10)-1
64	Indonesia	2.98	(GPC1980/GPC1970)**(1/10)-1
65	Czechia	2.96	(GPC1980/GPC1970)**(1/10)-1
66	Thailand	2.89	(GPC1980/GPC1970)**(1/10)-1
67	Malawi	2.83	(GPC1980/GPC1970)**(1/10)-1
68	Iceland	2.82	(GPC1980/GPC1970)**(1/10)-1
69	San Marino	2.79	(GPC1980/GPC1970)**(1/10)-1
70	Panama	2.78	(GPC1980/GPC1970)**(1/10)-1
71	Isle of Man	2.74	(GPC1980/GPC1970)**(1/10)-1
72	Mauritius	2.67	(GPC1980/GPC1970)**(1/10)-1
73	Cuba	2.66	(GPC1980/GPC1970)**(1/10)-1
74	Congo, Rep	2.64	(GPC1980/GPC1970)**(1/10)-1
75	France	2.64	(GPC1980/GPC1970)**(1/10)-1
76	Cameroon	2.63	(GPC1980/GPC1970)**(1/10)-1
77	Morocco	2.60	(GPC1980/GPC1970)**(1/10)-1
78	Costa Rica	2.58	(GPC1980/GPC1970)**(1/10)-1
79	Monaco	2.58	(GPC1980/GPC1970)**(1/10)-1
80	Faroe Is	2.55	(GPC1980/GPC1970)**(1/10)-1
81	Turkey	2.54	(GPC1980/GPC1970)**(1/10)-1
82	Philippines	2.53	(GPC1980/GPC1970)**(1/10)-1
83	Greenland	2.52	(GPC1980/GPC1970)**(1/10)-1
84	Andorra	2.52	(GPC1980/GPC1970)**(1/10)-1
85	Guernsey	2.49	(GPC1980/GPC1970)**(1/10)-1
86	Bermuda	2.49	(GPC1980/GPC1970)**(1/10)-1
87	Grenada	2.49	(GPC1980/GPC1970)**(1/10)-1
88	Jersey	2.46	(GPC1980/GPC1970)**(1/10)-1
89	Liechtenstn	2.45	(GPC1980/GPC1970)**(1/10)-1
90	Gambia	2.37	(GPC1980/GPC1970)**(1/10)-1
91	Syria	2.37	(GPC1980/GPC1970)**(1/10)-1
92	Slovakia	2.33	(GPC1980/GPC1970)**(1/10)-1
93	Bulgaria	2.27	(GPC1980/GPC1970)**(1/10)-1
94	Burma	2.26	(GPC1980/GPC1970)**(1/10)-1
95	Netherlands	2.26	(GPC1980/GPC1970)**(1/10)-1
96	Kiribati	2.24	(GPC1980/GPC1970)**(1/10)-1

TABLE 5.17 GDP PER CAPITA GROWTH RATES, 1970-1980			
Rank	Country	GRPCRL	Source
97	US	2.22	(GPC1980/GPC1970)**(1/10)-1
98	Puerto Rico	2.20	(GPC1980/GPC1970)**(1/10)-1
99	Martinique	2.19	(GPC1980/GPC1970)**(1/10)-1
100	Guinea	2.18	(GPC1980/GPC1970)**(1/10)-1
101	Sao Tome & P	2.16	(GPC1980/GPC1970)**(1/10)-1
102	W Sahara	2.12	(GPC1980/GPC1970)**(1/10)-1
103	Russia	2.12	(GPC1980/GPC1970)**(1/10)-1
104	Oman	2.10	(GPC1980/GPC1970)**(1/10)-1
105	Saint Helena	2.09	(GPC1980/GPC1970)**(1/10)-1
106	Cambodia	2.08	(GPC1980/GPC1970)**(1/10)-1
107	Denmark	2.07	(GPC1980/GPC1970)**(1/10)-1
108	St Vincent	2.06	(GPC1980/GPC1970)**(1/10)-1
109	Honduras	2.02	(GPC1980/GPC1970)**(1/10)-1
110	Australia	1.98	(GPC1980/GPC1970)**(1/10)-1
111	Guadeloupe	1.93	(GPC1980/GPC1970)**(1/10)-1
112	Albania	1.92	(GPC1980/GPC1970)**(1/10)-1
113	Uruguay	1.91	(GPC1980/GPC1970)**(1/10)-1
114	Sweden	1.89	(GPC1980/GPC1970)**(1/10)-1
115	South Africa	1.87	(GPC1980/GPC1970)**(1/10)-1
116	Aruba	1.81	(GPC1980/GPC1970)**(1/10)-1
117	Bolivia	1.79	(GPC1980/GPC1970)**(1/10)-1
118	Guyana	1.78	(GPC1980/GPC1970)**(1/10)-1
119	Cape Verde	1.76	(GPC1980/GPC1970)**(1/10)-1
120	Swaziland	1.76	(GPC1980/GPC1970)**(1/10)-1
121	Turks & C Is	1.75	(GPC1980/GPC1970)**(1/10)-1
122	Namibia	1.75	(GPC1980/GPC1970)**(1/10)-1
123	UK	1.73	(GPC1980/GPC1970)**(1/10)-1
124	Estonia	1.73	(GPC1980/GPC1970)**(1/10)-1
125	Virgin I, Br	1.72	(GPC1980/GPC1970)**(1/10)-1
126	Cayman Is	1.71	(GPC1980/GPC1970)**(1/10)-1
127	Belize	1.71	(GPC1980/GPC1970)**(1/10)-1
128	Switzerland	1.70	(GPC1980/GPC1970)**(1/10)-1
129	Lithuania	1.70	(GPC1980/GPC1970)**(1/10)-1
130	Falkland Is	1.67	(GPC1980/GPC1970)**(1/10)-1
131	St Pierre&M	1.67	(GPC1980/GPC1970)**(1/10)-1
132	Guatemala	1.66	(GPC1980/GPC1970)**(1/10)-1
133	Anguilla	1.63	(GPC1980/GPC1970)**(1/10)-1
134	Ukraine	1.61	(GPC1980/GPC1970)**(1/10)-1
135	Virgin I, US	1.59	(GPC1980/GPC1970)**(1/10)-1
136	Bhutan	1.51	(GPC1980/GPC1970)**(1/10)-1
137	Solomon Is	1.50	(GPC1980/GPC1970)**(1/10)-1
138	Mali	1.46	(GPC1980/GPC1970)**(1/10)-1
139	Mayotte	1.41	(GPC1980/GPC1970)**(1/10)-1
140	El Salvador	1.40	(GPC1980/GPC1970)**(1/10)-1
141	Rwanda	1.39	(GPC1980/GPC1970)**(1/10)-1
142	West Bank	1.37	(GPC1980/GPC1970)**(1/10)-1
143	Nigeria	1.35	(GPC1980/GPC1970)**(1/10)-1
144	Latvia	1.30	(GPC1980/GPC1970)**(1/10)-1

Table 5.17 GDP Per Capita Growth Rates, 1970-1980

Rank	Country	GRPCRL	Source
145	Ivory Coast	1.26	(GPC1980/GPC1970)**(1/10)-1
146	New Zealand	1.25	(GPC1980/GPC1970)**(1/10)-1
147	Montserrat	1.23	(GPC1980/GPC1970)**(1/10)-1
148	Pakistan	1.23	(GPC1980/GPC1970)**(1/10)-1
149	Peru	1.22	(GPC1980/GPC1970)**(1/10)-1
150	Moldova	1.18	(GPC1980/GPC1970)**(1/10)-1
151	Kenya	1.07	(GPC1980/GPC1970)**(1/10)-1
152	Belarus	1.07	(GPC1980/GPC1970)**(1/10)-1
153	Equatorial G	1.03	(GPC1980/GPC1970)**(1/10)-1
154	Bahamas	1.01	(GPC1980/GPC1970)**(1/10)-1
155	China	0.92	(GPC1980/GPC1970)**(1/10)-1
156	Samoa, Amer	0.89	(GPC1980/GPC1970)**(1/10)-1
157	Luxembourg	0.86	(GPC1980/GPC1970)**(1/10)-1
158	Gaza Strip	0.84	(GPC1980/GPC1970)**(1/10)-1
159	Eritrea	0.82	(GPC1980/GPC1970)**(1/10)-1
160	Ethiopia	0.82	(GPC1980/GPC1970)**(1/10)-1
161	Tanzania	0.81	(GPC1980/GPC1970)**(1/10)-1
162	Laos	0.78	(GPC1980/GPC1970)**(1/10)-1
163	Niue	0.75	(GPC1980/GPC1970)**(1/10)-1
164	Argentina	0.75	(GPC1980/GPC1970)**(1/10)-1
165	Sri Lanka	0.73	(GPC1980/GPC1970)**(1/10)-1
166	Fr Polynesia	0.67	(GPC1980/GPC1970)**(1/10)-1
167	Cook Is	0.66	(GPC1980/GPC1970)**(1/10)-1
168	Georgia	0.65	(GPC1980/GPC1970)**(1/10)-1
169	Vanuatu	0.64	(GPC1980/GPC1970)**(1/10)-1
170	Reunion	0.61	(GPC1980/GPC1970)**(1/10)-1
171	Guam	0.61	(GPC1980/GPC1970)**(1/10)-1
172	East Timor	0.61	(GPC1980/GPC1970)**(1/10)-1
173	Tokelau	0.61	(GPC1980/GPC1970)**(1/10)-1
174	Kuwait	0.59	(GPC1980/GPC1970)**(1/10)-1
175	Tuvalu	0.59	(GPC1980/GPC1970)**(1/10)-1
176	New Caledon	0.59	(GPC1980/GPC1970)**(1/10)-1
177	Nauru	0.55	(GPC1980/GPC1970)**(1/10)-1
178	Palau	0.54	(GPC1980/GPC1970)**(1/10)-1
179	Marshall Is	0.54	(GPC1980/GPC1970)**(1/10)-1
180	Wallis & Fut	0.52	(GPC1980/GPC1970)**(1/10)-1
181	Dominica	0.47	(GPC1980/GPC1970)**(1/10)-1
182	Micronesia	0.46	(GPC1980/GPC1970)**(1/10)-1
183	N Mariana Is	0.39	(GPC1980/GPC1970)**(1/10)-1
184	Sudan	0.34	(GPC1980/GPC1970)**(1/10)-1
185	South Sudan	0.34	(GPC1980/GPC1970)**(1/10)-1
186	Armenia	0.33	(GPC1980/GPC1970)**(1/10)-1
187	Mauritania	0.29	(GPC1980/GPC1970)**(1/10)-1
188	Azerbaijan	0.28	(GPC1980/GPC1970)**(1/10)-1
189	Samoa	0.17	(GPC1980/GPC1970)**(1/10)-1
190	Turkmenistan	0.16	(GPC1980/GPC1970)**(1/10)-1
191	Zimbabwe	0.07	(GPC1980/GPC1970)**(1/10)-1
192	Iran	0.06	(GPC1980/GPC1970)**(1/10)-1

TABLE 5.17 GDP PER CAPITA GROWTH RATES, 1970-1980			
Rank	Country	GRPCRL	Source
193	Uzbekistan	0.04	(GPC1980/GPC1970)**(1/10)-1
194	Chile	-0.16	(GPC1980/GPC1970)**(1/10)-1
195	Papua New G	-0.16	(GPC1980/GPC1970)**(1/10)-1
196	India	-0.20	(GPC1980/GPC1970)**(1/10)-1
197	Saint Martin	-0.20	(GPC1980/GPC1970)**(1/10)-1
198	Burundi	-0.20	(GPC1980/GPC1970)**(1/10)-1
199	Sint Maarten	-0.20	(GPC1980/GPC1970)**(1/10)-1
200	Curacao	-0.20	(GPC1980/GPC1970)**(1/10)-1
201	Guiana, Fr	-0.21	(GPC1980/GPC1970)**(1/10)-1
202	Kazakhstan	-0.21	(GPC1980/GPC1970)**(1/10)-1
203	Afghanistan	-0.34	(GPC1980/GPC1970)**(1/10)-1
204	Togo	-0.37	(GPC1980/GPC1970)**(1/10)-1
205	Fiji	-0.37	(GPC1980/GPC1970)**(1/10)-1
206	Vietnam	-0.55	(GPC1980/GPC1970)**(1/10)-1
207	Tonga	-0.61	(GPC1980/GPC1970)**(1/10)-1
208	Venezuela	-0.79	(GPC1980/GPC1970)**(1/10)-1
209	Benin	-0.86	(GPC1980/GPC1970)**(1/10)-1
210	Sierra Leone	-0.95	(GPC1980/GPC1970)**(1/10)-1
211	Kyrgyzstan	-0.98	(GPC1980/GPC1970)**(1/10)-1
212	Guinea-Biss	-1.09	(GPC1980/GPC1970)**(1/10)-1
213	Nepal	-1.15	(GPC1980/GPC1970)**(1/10)-1
214	Senegal	-1.17	(GPC1980/GPC1970)**(1/10)-1
215	Tajikistan	-1.24	(GPC1980/GPC1970)**(1/10)-1
216	Somalia	-1.31	(GPC1980/GPC1970)**(1/10)-1
217	Burkina Faso	-1.37	(GPC1980/GPC1970)**(1/10)-1
218	Qatar	-1.44	(GPC1980/GPC1970)**(1/10)-1
219	Niger	-1.49	(GPC1980/GPC1970)**(1/10)-1
220	Djibouti	-1.53	(GPC1980/GPC1970)**(1/10)-1
221	Zambia	-1.54	(GPC1980/GPC1970)**(1/10)-1
222	St Kitts & N	-1.54	(GPC1980/GPC1970)**(1/10)-1
223	Bangladesh	-1.84	(GPC1980/GPC1970)**(1/10)-1
224	Madagascar	-1.84	(GPC1980/GPC1970)**(1/10)-1
225	Jamaica	-1.97	(GPC1980/GPC1970)**(1/10)-1
226	CAR	-2.13	(GPC1980/GPC1970)**(1/10)-1
227	Nicaragua	-2.24	(GPC1980/GPC1970)**(1/10)-1
228	Ghana	-2.30	(GPC1980/GPC1970)**(1/10)-1
229	Libya	-2.37	(GPC1980/GPC1970)**(1/10)-1
230	Congo, Dem R	-2.55	(GPC1980/GPC1970)**(1/10)-1
231	Chad	-2.83	(GPC1980/GPC1970)**(1/10)-1
232	Angola	-3.77	(GPC1980/GPC1970)**(1/10)-1
233	Liberia	-4.18	(GPC1980/GPC1970)**(1/10)-1
234	Comoros	-4.58	(GPC1980/GPC1970)**(1/10)-1
235	Uganda	-4.92	(GPC1980/GPC1970)**(1/10)-1
236	Mozambique	-15.80	(GPC1980/GPC1970)**(1/10)-1

TABLE 5.18 GDP PER CAPITA GROWTH RATES, 1980-1990

Rank	Country	GRPCRL	Source
1	Antigua & B	7.76	(GPC1990/GPC1980)**(1/10)-1
2	Korea, South	7.37	(GPC1990/GPC1980)**(1/10)-1
3	Botswana	7.37	(GPC1990/GPC1980)**(1/10)-1
4	China	7.14	(GPC1990/GPC1980)**(1/10)-1
5	Bhutan	7.06	(GPC1990/GPC1980)**(1/10)-1
6	St Kitts & N	6.07	(GPC1990/GPC1980)**(1/10)-1
7	Dominica	6.04	(GPC1990/GPC1980)**(1/10)-1
8	Maldives	5.98	(GPC1990/GPC1980)**(1/10)-1
9	Thailand	5.81	(GPC1990/GPC1980)**(1/10)-1
10	St Lucia	5.58	(GPC1990/GPC1980)**(1/10)-1
11	Hong Kong	5.44	(GPC1990/GPC1980)**(1/10)-1
12	St Vincent	5.33	(GPC1990/GPC1980)**(1/10)-1
13	Singapore	5.27	(GPC1990/GPC1980)**(1/10)-1
14	Taiwan	5.23	(GPC1990/GPC1980)**(1/10)-1
15	Cyprus	5.10	(GPC1990/GPC1980)**(1/10)-1
16	Luxembourg	5.05	(GPC1990/GPC1980)**(1/10)-1
17	Grenada	4.86	(GPC1990/GPC1980)**(1/10)-1
18	Mauritius	4.83	(GPC1990/GPC1980)**(1/10)-1
19	Swaziland	4.67	(GPC1990/GPC1980)**(1/10)-1
20	Oman	4.31	(GPC1990/GPC1980)**(1/10)-1
21	Solomon Is	4.28	(GPC1990/GPC1980)**(1/10)-1
22	Japan	4.00	(GPC1990/GPC1980)**(1/10)-1
23	Indonesia	3.86	(GPC1990/GPC1980)**(1/10)-1
24	Turkey	3.61	(GPC1990/GPC1980)**(1/10)-1
25	Cape Verde	3.54	(GPC1990/GPC1980)**(1/10)-1
26	Ireland	3.43	(GPC1990/GPC1980)**(1/10)-1
27	Portugal	3.20	(GPC1990/GPC1980)**(1/10)-1
28	India	3.18	(GPC1990/GPC1980)**(1/10)-1
29	Malaysia	3.13	(GPC1990/GPC1980)**(1/10)-1
30	Mongolia	3.08	(GPC1990/GPC1980)**(1/10)-1
31	Egypt	2.99	(GPC1990/GPC1980)**(1/10)-1
32	Malta	2.88	(GPC1990/GPC1980)**(1/10)-1
33	Pakistan	2.80	(GPC1990/GPC1980)**(1/10)-1
34	Finland	2.74	(GPC1990/GPC1980)**(1/10)-1
35	Seychelles	2.73	(GPC1990/GPC1980)**(1/10)-1
36	Spain	2.72	(GPC1990/GPC1980)**(1/10)-1
37	Macao	2.68	(GPC1990/GPC1980)**(1/10)-1
38	Sri Lanka	2.58	(GPC1990/GPC1980)**(1/10)-1
39	Bulgaria	2.56	(GPC1990/GPC1980)**(1/10)-1
40	Svalbard	2.54	(GPC1990/GPC1980)**(1/10)-1
41	Norway	2.54	(GPC1990/GPC1980)**(1/10)-1
42	Italy	2.51	(GPC1990/GPC1980)**(1/10)-1
43	Chad	2.51	(GPC1990/GPC1980)**(1/10)-1
44	UK	2.47	(GPC1990/GPC1980)**(1/10)-1
45	Gibraltar	2.47	(GPC1990/GPC1980)**(1/10)-1
46	Guinea-Biss	2.46	(GPC1990/GPC1980)**(1/10)-1
47	US	2.37	(GPC1990/GPC1980)**(1/10)-1
48	Vietnam	2.33	(GPC1990/GPC1980)**(1/10)-1

TABLE 5.18 GDP PER CAPITA GROWTH RATES, 1980-1990

Rank	Country	GRPCRL	Source
49	Chile	2.33	(GPC1990/GPC1980)**(1/10)-1
50	Denmark	2.29	(GPC1990/GPC1980)**(1/10)-1
51	Germany	2.22	(GPC1990/GPC1980)**(1/10)-1
52	Puerto Rico	2.20	(GPC1990/GPC1980)**(1/10)-1
53	Latvia	2.19	(GPC1990/GPC1980)**(1/10)-1
54	Nepal	2.19	(GPC1990/GPC1980)**(1/10)-1
55	Vanuatu	2.17	(GPC1990/GPC1980)**(1/10)-1
56	Belize	2.16	(GPC1990/GPC1980)**(1/10)-1
57	San Marino	2.16	(GPC1990/GPC1980)**(1/10)-1
58	Austria	2.14	(GPC1990/GPC1980)**(1/10)-1
59	Isle of Man	2.12	(GPC1990/GPC1980)**(1/10)-1
60	Belgium	2.00	(GPC1990/GPC1980)**(1/10)-1
61	Australia	2.00	(GPC1990/GPC1980)**(1/10)-1
62	Monaco	1.99	(GPC1990/GPC1980)**(1/10)-1
63	Reunion	1.99	(GPC1990/GPC1980)**(1/10)-1
64	Faroe Is	1.97	(GPC1990/GPC1980)**(1/10)-1
65	Greenland	1.95	(GPC1990/GPC1980)**(1/10)-1
66	Sweden	1.95	(GPC1990/GPC1980)**(1/10)-1
67	Andorra	1.95	(GPC1990/GPC1980)**(1/10)-1
68	Guernsey	1.93	(GPC1990/GPC1980)**(1/10)-1
69	France	1.92	(GPC1990/GPC1980)**(1/10)-1
70	Jersey	1.91	(GPC1990/GPC1980)**(1/10)-1
71	Liechtenstn	1.89	(GPC1990/GPC1980)**(1/10)-1
72	Switzerland	1.85	(GPC1990/GPC1980)**(1/10)-1
73	Netherlands	1.76	(GPC1990/GPC1980)**(1/10)-1
74	Congo, Rep	1.72	(GPC1990/GPC1980)**(1/10)-1
75	Israel	1.72	(GPC1990/GPC1980)**(1/10)-1
76	Lesotho	1.65	(GPC1990/GPC1980)**(1/10)-1
77	Hungary	1.61	(GPC1990/GPC1980)**(1/10)-1
78	W Sahara	1.59	(GPC1990/GPC1980)**(1/10)-1
79	Iceland	1.58	(GPC1990/GPC1980)**(1/10)-1
80	Canada	1.57	(GPC1990/GPC1980)**(1/10)-1
81	Saint Helena	1.57	(GPC1990/GPC1980)**(1/10)-1
82	Angola	1.54	(GPC1990/GPC1980)**(1/10)-1
83	Tonga	1.51	(GPC1990/GPC1980)**(1/10)-1
84	Morocco	1.50	(GPC1990/GPC1980)**(1/10)-1
85	Czechia	1.47	(GPC1990/GPC1980)**(1/10)-1
86	New Zealand	1.39	(GPC1990/GPC1980)**(1/10)-1
87	Jamaica	1.39	(GPC1990/GPC1980)**(1/10)-1
88	Colombia	1.39	(GPC1990/GPC1980)**(1/10)-1
89	Russia	1.39	(GPC1990/GPC1980)**(1/10)-1
90	West Bank	1.38	(GPC1990/GPC1980)**(1/10)-1
91	Aruba	1.32	(GPC1990/GPC1980)**(1/10)-1
92	Turks & C Is	1.28	(GPC1990/GPC1980)**(1/10)-1
93	Virgin I, Br	1.26	(GPC1990/GPC1980)**(1/10)-1
94	Cayman Is	1.25	(GPC1990/GPC1980)**(1/10)-1
95	Falkland Is	1.22	(GPC1990/GPC1980)**(1/10)-1
96	St Pierre&M	1.22	(GPC1990/GPC1980)**(1/10)-1

TABLE 5.18 GDP PER CAPITA GROWTH RATES, 1980-1990

Rank	Country	GRPCRL	Source
97	Anguilla	1.19	(GPC1990/GPC1980)**(1/10)-1
98	Bermuda	1.18	(GPC1990/GPC1980)**(1/10)-1
99	Virgin I, US	1.16	(GPC1990/GPC1980)**(1/10)-1
100	Ukraine	1.12	(GPC1990/GPC1980)**(1/10)-1
101	Paraguay	1.11	(GPC1990/GPC1980)**(1/10)-1
102	Tunisia	1.06	(GPC1990/GPC1980)**(1/10)-1
103	Mayotte	1.06	(GPC1990/GPC1980)**(1/10)-1
104	Estonia	1.05	(GPC1990/GPC1980)**(1/10)-1
105	Bangladesh	1.03	(GPC1990/GPC1980)**(1/10)-1
106	Lithuania	1.01	(GPC1990/GPC1980)**(1/10)-1
107	Bahamas	1.00	(GPC1990/GPC1980)**(1/10)-1
108	Montserrat	0.90	(GPC1990/GPC1980)**(1/10)-1
109	Cuba	0.89	(GPC1990/GPC1980)**(1/10)-1
110	Burkina Faso	0.86	(GPC1990/GPC1980)**(1/10)-1
111	Gaza Strip	0.84	(GPC1990/GPC1980)**(1/10)-1
112	Belarus	0.79	(GPC1990/GPC1980)**(1/10)-1
113	Barbados	0.79	(GPC1990/GPC1980)**(1/10)-1
114	Moldova	0.69	(GPC1990/GPC1980)**(1/10)-1
115	Slovakia	0.69	(GPC1990/GPC1980)**(1/10)-1
116	Somalia	0.62	(GPC1990/GPC1980)**(1/10)-1
117	Cambodia	0.61	(GPC1990/GPC1980)**(1/10)-1
118	Samoa	0.57	(GPC1990/GPC1980)**(1/10)-1
119	Martinique	0.56	(GPC1990/GPC1980)**(1/10)-1
120	Kuwait	0.55	(GPC1990/GPC1980)**(1/10)-1
121	Equatorial G	0.39	(GPC1990/GPC1980)**(1/10)-1
122	Romania	0.34	(GPC1990/GPC1980)**(1/10)-1
123	Kenya	0.34	(GPC1990/GPC1980)**(1/10)-1
124	Zimbabwe	0.33	(GPC1990/GPC1980)**(1/10)-1
125	Macedonia	0.30	(GPC1990/GPC1980)**(1/10)-1
126	Samoa, Amer	0.30	(GPC1990/GPC1980)**(1/10)-1
127	Cameroon	0.27	(GPC1990/GPC1980)**(1/10)-1
128	Niue	0.25	(GPC1990/GPC1980)**(1/10)-1
129	Fr Polynesia	0.22	(GPC1990/GPC1980)**(1/10)-1
130	Cook Is	0.22	(GPC1990/GPC1980)**(1/10)-1
131	Guam	0.20	(GPC1990/GPC1980)**(1/10)-1
132	East Timor	0.20	(GPC1990/GPC1980)**(1/10)-1
133	Tokelau	0.20	(GPC1990/GPC1980)**(1/10)-1
134	Guadeloupe	0.20	(GPC1990/GPC1980)**(1/10)-1
135	Tuvalu	0.20	(GPC1990/GPC1980)**(1/10)-1
136	New Caledon	0.20	(GPC1990/GPC1980)**(1/10)-1
137	Nauru	0.19	(GPC1990/GPC1980)**(1/10)-1
138	Palau	0.18	(GPC1990/GPC1980)**(1/10)-1
139	Marshall Is	0.18	(GPC1990/GPC1980)**(1/10)-1
140	Greece	0.18	(GPC1990/GPC1980)**(1/10)-1
141	Wallis & Fut	0.17	(GPC1990/GPC1980)**(1/10)-1
142	Comoros	0.17	(GPC1990/GPC1980)**(1/10)-1
143	Dominican R	0.17	(GPC1990/GPC1980)**(1/10)-1
144	N Mariana Is	0.13	(GPC1990/GPC1980)**(1/10)-1

Table 5.18 GDP Per Capita Growth Rates, 1980-1990

Rank	Country	GRPCRL	Source
145	Ecuador	0.10	(GPC1990/GPC1980)**(1/10)-1
146	Micronesia	0.07	(GPC1990/GPC1980)**(1/10)-1
147	Korea, North	0.00	(GPC1990/GPC1980)**(1/10)-1
148	Fiji	0.00	(GPC1990/GPC1980)**(1/10)-1
149	Armenia	-0.01	(GPC1990/GPC1980)**(1/10)-1
150	Guinea	-0.05	(GPC1990/GPC1980)**(1/10)-1
151	Guiana, Fr	-0.06	(GPC1990/GPC1980)**(1/10)-1
152	Burundi	-0.17	(GPC1990/GPC1980)**(1/10)-1
153	Laos	-0.17	(GPC1990/GPC1980)**(1/10)-1
154	Benin	-0.19	(GPC1990/GPC1980)**(1/10)-1
155	Costa Rica	-0.22	(GPC1990/GPC1980)**(1/10)-1
156	Burma	-0.26	(GPC1990/GPC1980)**(1/10)-1
157	Algeria	-0.26	(GPC1990/GPC1980)**(1/10)-1
158	Mexico	-0.26	(GPC1990/GPC1980)**(1/10)-1
159	Senegal	-0.31	(GPC1990/GPC1980)**(1/10)-1
160	South Sudan	-0.45	(GPC1990/GPC1980)**(1/10)-1
161	Sudan	-0.45	(GPC1990/GPC1980)**(1/10)-1
162	Slovenia	-0.46	(GPC1990/GPC1980)**(1/10)-1
163	Azerbaijan	-0.47	(GPC1990/GPC1980)**(1/10)-1
164	Brazil	-0.53	(GPC1990/GPC1980)**(1/10)-1
165	Bosnia	-0.55	(GPC1990/GPC1980)**(1/10)-1
166	Serbia	-0.56	(GPC1990/GPC1980)**(1/10)-1
167	Croatia	-0.56	(GPC1990/GPC1980)**(1/10)-1
168	Kosovo	-0.57	(GPC1990/GPC1980)**(1/10)-1
169	Tanzania	-0.58	(GPC1990/GPC1980)**(1/10)-1
170	Montenegro	-0.59	(GPC1990/GPC1980)**(1/10)-1
171	Gambia	-0.59	(GPC1990/GPC1980)**(1/10)-1
172	Honduras	-0.61	(GPC1990/GPC1980)**(1/10)-1
173	Ghana	-0.65	(GPC1990/GPC1980)**(1/10)-1
174	Uganda	-0.65	(GPC1990/GPC1980)**(1/10)-1
175	Uruguay	-0.67	(GPC1990/GPC1980)**(1/10)-1
176	Uzbekistan	-0.70	(GPC1990/GPC1980)**(1/10)-1
177	Djibouti	-0.71	(GPC1990/GPC1980)**(1/10)-1
178	Syria	-0.73	(GPC1990/GPC1980)**(1/10)-1
179	Poland	-0.80	(GPC1990/GPC1980)**(1/10)-1
180	Gabon	-0.84	(GPC1990/GPC1980)**(1/10)-1
181	Panama	-0.85	(GPC1990/GPC1980)**(1/10)-1
182	Mozambique	-0.96	(GPC1990/GPC1980)**(1/10)-1
183	South Africa	-0.98	(GPC1990/GPC1980)**(1/10)-1
184	Eritrea	-0.98	(GPC1990/GPC1980)**(1/10)-1
185	Philippines	-1.00	(GPC1990/GPC1980)**(1/10)-1
186	Ethiopia	-1.01	(GPC1990/GPC1980)**(1/10)-1
187	Mali	-1.10	(GPC1990/GPC1980)**(1/10)-1
188	Albania	-1.11	(GPC1990/GPC1980)**(1/10)-1
189	Turkmenistan	-1.17	(GPC1990/GPC1980)**(1/10)-1
190	Mauritania	-1.18	(GPC1990/GPC1980)**(1/10)-1
191	Rwanda	-1.27	(GPC1990/GPC1980)**(1/10)-1
192	Papua New G	-1.29	(GPC1990/GPC1980)**(1/10)-1

Table 5.18 GDP Per Capita Growth Rates, 1980-1990

Rank	Country	GRPCRL	Source
193	Kazakhstan	-1.30	(GPC1990/GPC1980)**(1/10)-1
194	Guatemala	-1.35	(GPC1990/GPC1980)**(1/10)-1
195	Kiribati	-1.36	(GPC1990/GPC1980)**(1/10)-1
196	Georgia	-1.39	(GPC1990/GPC1980)**(1/10)-1
197	Yemen	-1.40	(GPC1990/GPC1980)**(1/10)-1
198	Sierra Leone	-1.45	(GPC1990/GPC1980)**(1/10)-1
199	CAR	-1.45	(GPC1990/GPC1980)**(1/10)-1
200	Nigeria	-1.48	(GPC1990/GPC1980)**(1/10)-1
201	Venezuela	-1.54	(GPC1990/GPC1980)**(1/10)-1
202	Togo	-1.56	(GPC1990/GPC1980)**(1/10)-1
203	Jordan	-1.66	(GPC1990/GPC1980)**(1/10)-1
204	Saint Martin	-1.69	(GPC1990/GPC1980)**(1/10)-1
205	Sint Maarten	-1.70	(GPC1990/GPC1980)**(1/10)-1
206	Iran	-1.70	(GPC1990/GPC1980)**(1/10)-1
207	Curacao	-1.71	(GPC1990/GPC1980)**(1/10)-1
208	El Salvador	-1.85	(GPC1990/GPC1980)**(1/10)-1
209	Kyrgyzstan	-1.87	(GPC1990/GPC1980)**(1/10)-1
210	Bahrain	-1.89	(GPC1990/GPC1980)**(1/10)-1
211	Congo, Dem R	-1.90	(GPC1990/GPC1980)**(1/10)-1
212	Malawi	-1.91	(GPC1990/GPC1980)**(1/10)-1
213	Namibia	-2.06	(GPC1990/GPC1980)**(1/10)-1
214	Haiti	-2.12	(GPC1990/GPC1980)**(1/10)-1
215	Zambia	-2.13	(GPC1990/GPC1980)**(1/10)-1
216	Suriname	-2.24	(GPC1990/GPC1980)**(1/10)-1
217	Sao Tome & P	-2.33	(GPC1990/GPC1980)**(1/10)-1
218	Bolivia	-2.36	(GPC1990/GPC1980)**(1/10)-1
219	Madagascar	-2.42	(GPC1990/GPC1980)**(1/10)-1
220	Ivory Coast	-2.43	(GPC1990/GPC1980)**(1/10)-1
221	Guyana	-2.51	(GPC1990/GPC1980)**(1/10)-1
222	Tajikistan	-2.60	(GPC1990/GPC1980)**(1/10)-1
223	Afghanistan	-2.72	(GPC1990/GPC1980)**(1/10)-1
224	Argentina	-2.99	(GPC1990/GPC1980)**(1/10)-1
225	Peru	-3.01	(GPC1990/GPC1980)**(1/10)-1
226	Trinidad & T	-3.41	(GPC1990/GPC1980)**(1/10)-1
227	Niger	-3.49	(GPC1990/GPC1980)**(1/10)-1
228	Lebanon	-3.79	(GPC1990/GPC1980)**(1/10)-1
229	Nicaragua	-3.86	(GPC1990/GPC1980)**(1/10)-1
230	Iraq	-5.40	(GPC1990/GPC1980)**(1/10)-1
231	UAE	-5.70	(GPC1990/GPC1980)**(1/10)-1
232	Saudi Arabia	-5.86	(GPC1990/GPC1980)**(1/10)-1
233	Brunei	-6.26	(GPC1990/GPC1980)**(1/10)-1
234	Qatar	-8.20	(GPC1990/GPC1980)**(1/10)-1
235	Liberia	-8.47	(GPC1990/GPC1980)**(1/10)-1
236	Libya	-8.69	(GPC1990/GPC1980)**(1/10)-1

TABLE 5.19 GDP PER CAPITA GROWTH RATES, 1990-2000

Rank	Country	GRPCRL	Source
1	Equatorial G	15.79	(GPC2000/GPC1990)**(1/10)-1
2	Mayotte	15.66	(GPC2000/GPC1990)**(1/10)-1
3	Qatar	15.08	(GPC2000/GPC1990)**(1/10)-1
4	Bermuda	11.99	(GPC2000/GPC1990)**(1/10)-1
5	Libya	10.93	(GPC2000/GPC1990)**(1/10)-1
6	W Sahara	10.81	(GPC2000/GPC1990)**(1/10)-1
7	Gibraltar	9.19	(GPC2000/GPC1990)**(1/10)-1
8	Samoa, Amer	8.70	(GPC2000/GPC1990)**(1/10)-1
9	Cape Verde	8.13	(GPC2000/GPC1990)**(1/10)-1
10	Niue	7.70	(GPC2000/GPC1990)**(1/10)-1
11	New Caledon	7.55	(GPC2000/GPC1990)**(1/10)-1
12	Saint Helena	7.28	(GPC2000/GPC1990)**(1/10)-1
13	Brunei	6.97	(GPC2000/GPC1990)**(1/10)-1
14	St Pierre&M	6.84	(GPC2000/GPC1990)**(1/10)-1
15	Ireland	6.83	(GPC2000/GPC1990)**(1/10)-1
16	China	6.60	(GPC2000/GPC1990)**(1/10)-1
17	Vietnam	5.88	(GPC2000/GPC1990)**(1/10)-1
18	Norway	5.32	(GPC2000/GPC1990)**(1/10)-1
19	Svalbard	5.32	(GPC2000/GPC1990)**(1/10)-1
20	Malta	5.31	(GPC2000/GPC1990)**(1/10)-1
21	Korea, South	5.29	(GPC2000/GPC1990)**(1/10)-1
22	Chile	5.08	(GPC2000/GPC1990)**(1/10)-1
23	Lebanon	4.81	(GPC2000/GPC1990)**(1/10)-1
24	Luxembourg	4.70	(GPC2000/GPC1990)**(1/10)-1
25	Bahrain	4.68	(GPC2000/GPC1990)**(1/10)-1
26	Malaysia	4.64	(GPC2000/GPC1990)**(1/10)-1
27	Dominican R	4.56	(GPC2000/GPC1990)**(1/10)-1
28	Bhutan	4.45	(GPC2000/GPC1990)**(1/10)-1
29	Taiwan	4.43	(GPC2000/GPC1990)**(1/10)-1
30	El Salvador	4.42	(GPC2000/GPC1990)**(1/10)-1
31	Singapore	4.28	(GPC2000/GPC1990)**(1/10)-1
32	Curacao	4.26	(GPC2000/GPC1990)**(1/10)-1
33	Sint Maarten	4.23	(GPC2000/GPC1990)**(1/10)-1
34	Saint Martin	4.19	(GPC2000/GPC1990)**(1/10)-1
35	Burma	3.88	(GPC2000/GPC1990)**(1/10)-1
36	Poland	3.87	(GPC2000/GPC1990)**(1/10)-1
37	Turkey	3.79	(GPC2000/GPC1990)**(1/10)-1
38	Guyana	3.74	(GPC2000/GPC1990)**(1/10)-1
39	Oman	3.72	(GPC2000/GPC1990)**(1/10)-1
40	Maldives	3.72	(GPC2000/GPC1990)**(1/10)-1
41	Laos	3.70	(GPC2000/GPC1990)**(1/10)-1
42	Guadeloupe	3.68	(GPC2000/GPC1990)**(1/10)-1
43	Fr Polynesia	3.66	(GPC2000/GPC1990)**(1/10)-1
44	San Marino	3.60	(GPC2000/GPC1990)**(1/10)-1
45	Martinique	3.58	(GPC2000/GPC1990)**(1/10)-1
46	Cook Is	3.54	(GPC2000/GPC1990)**(1/10)-1
47	Kiribati	3.51	(GPC2000/GPC1990)**(1/10)-1
48	Isle of Man	3.48	(GPC2000/GPC1990)**(1/10)-1

TABLE 5.19 GDP PER CAPITA GROWTH RATES, 1990-2000

Rank	Country	GRPCRL	Source
49	Grenada	3.40	(GPC2000/GPC1990)**(1/10)-1
50	Seychelles	3.40	(GPC2000/GPC1990)**(1/10)-1
51	Argentina	3.40	(GPC2000/GPC1990)**(1/10)-1
52	Mauritius	3.37	(GPC2000/GPC1990)**(1/10)-1
53	Sri Lanka	3.28	(GPC2000/GPC1990)**(1/10)-1
54	Spain	3.27	(GPC2000/GPC1990)**(1/10)-1
55	St Kitts & N	3.25	(GPC2000/GPC1990)**(1/10)-1
56	Portugal	3.20	(GPC2000/GPC1990)**(1/10)-1
57	Tunisia	3.19	(GPC2000/GPC1990)**(1/10)-1
58	Tonga	3.17	(GPC2000/GPC1990)**(1/10)-1
59	Uganda	3.16	(GPC2000/GPC1990)**(1/10)-1
60	India	3.14	(GPC2000/GPC1990)**(1/10)-1
61	Netherlands	3.12	(GPC2000/GPC1990)**(1/10)-1
62	Belize	3.06	(GPC2000/GPC1990)**(1/10)-1
63	Mexico	3.01	(GPC2000/GPC1990)**(1/10)-1
64	Albania	2.96	(GPC2000/GPC1990)**(1/10)-1
65	St Vincent	2.91	(GPC2000/GPC1990)**(1/10)-1
66	Trinidad & T	2.89	(GPC2000/GPC1990)**(1/10)-1
67	Thailand	2.87	(GPC2000/GPC1990)**(1/10)-1
68	Uruguay	2.76	(GPC2000/GPC1990)**(1/10)-1
69	St Lucia	2.71	(GPC2000/GPC1990)**(1/10)-1
70	Bangladesh	2.70	(GPC2000/GPC1990)**(1/10)-1
71	Iran	2.69	(GPC2000/GPC1990)**(1/10)-1
72	Botswana	2.69	(GPC2000/GPC1990)**(1/10)-1
73	UK	2.68	(GPC2000/GPC1990)**(1/10)-1
74	Panama	2.63	(GPC2000/GPC1990)**(1/10)-1
75	Costa Rica	2.57	(GPC2000/GPC1990)**(1/10)-1
76	Greece	2.53	(GPC2000/GPC1990)**(1/10)-1
77	Liberia	2.51	(GPC2000/GPC1990)**(1/10)-1
78	Israel	2.48	(GPC2000/GPC1990)**(1/10)-1
79	Denmark	2.45	(GPC2000/GPC1990)**(1/10)-1
80	Mozambique	2.36	(GPC2000/GPC1990)**(1/10)-1
81	Barbados	2.29	(GPC2000/GPC1990)**(1/10)-1
82	Austria	2.28	(GPC2000/GPC1990)**(1/10)-1
83	Hong Kong	2.26	(GPC2000/GPC1990)**(1/10)-1
84	Australia	2.20	(GPC2000/GPC1990)**(1/10)-1
85	US	2.20	(GPC2000/GPC1990)**(1/10)-1
86	Saudi Arabia	2.14	(GPC2000/GPC1990)**(1/10)-1
87	Slovenia	2.10	(GPC2000/GPC1990)**(1/10)-1
88	Cyprus	2.09	(GPC2000/GPC1990)**(1/10)-1
89	East Timor	2.07	(GPC2000/GPC1990)**(1/10)-1
90	Antigua & B	2.07	(GPC2000/GPC1990)**(1/10)-1
91	Peru	2.04	(GPC2000/GPC1990)**(1/10)-1
92	Guam	2.01	(GPC2000/GPC1990)**(1/10)-1
93	Burkina Faso	2.00	(GPC2000/GPC1990)**(1/10)-1
94	Aruba	1.99	(GPC2000/GPC1990)**(1/10)-1
95	Tokelau	1.97	(GPC2000/GPC1990)**(1/10)-1
96	Canada	1.96	(GPC2000/GPC1990)**(1/10)-1

Table 5.19 GDP Per Capita Growth Rates, 1990-2000

Rank	Country	GRPCRL	Source
97	Belgium	1.95	(GPC2000/GPC1990)**(1/10)-1
98	Bolivia	1.95	(GPC2000/GPC1990)**(1/10)-1
99	Egypt	1.94	(GPC2000/GPC1990)**(1/10)-1
100	Tuvalu	1.92	(GPC2000/GPC1990)**(1/10)-1
101	Monaco	1.91	(GPC2000/GPC1990)**(1/10)-1
102	Nepal	1.84	(GPC2000/GPC1990)**(1/10)-1
103	Guiana, Fr	1.81	(GPC2000/GPC1990)**(1/10)-1
104	Samoa	1.76	(GPC2000/GPC1990)**(1/10)-1
105	France	1.73	(GPC2000/GPC1990)**(1/10)-1
106	Turks & C Is	1.69	(GPC2000/GPC1990)**(1/10)-1
107	Finland	1.61	(GPC2000/GPC1990)**(1/10)-1
108	Mali	1.61	(GPC2000/GPC1990)**(1/10)-1
109	Italy	1.59	(GPC2000/GPC1990)**(1/10)-1
110	Yemen	1.59	(GPC2000/GPC1990)**(1/10)-1
111	Afghanistan	1.58	(GPC2000/GPC1990)**(1/10)-1
112	Dominica	1.57	(GPC2000/GPC1990)**(1/10)-1
113	Faroe Is	1.55	(GPC2000/GPC1990)**(1/10)-1
114	Lesotho	1.51	(GPC2000/GPC1990)**(1/10)-1
115	Nicaragua	1.50	(GPC2000/GPC1990)**(1/10)-1
116	Malawi	1.46	(GPC2000/GPC1990)**(1/10)-1
117	South Sudan	1.42	(GPC2000/GPC1990)**(1/10)-1
118	Sudan	1.42	(GPC2000/GPC1990)**(1/10)-1
119	Germany	1.42	(GPC2000/GPC1990)**(1/10)-1
120	New Zealand	1.42	(GPC2000/GPC1990)**(1/10)-1
121	Sweden	1.40	(GPC2000/GPC1990)**(1/10)-1
122	Micronesia	1.40	(GPC2000/GPC1990)**(1/10)-1
123	Greenland	1.32	(GPC2000/GPC1990)**(1/10)-1
124	Andorra	1.29	(GPC2000/GPC1990)**(1/10)-1
125	Zimbabwe	1.29	(GPC2000/GPC1990)**(1/10)-1
126	Papua New G	1.27	(GPC2000/GPC1990)**(1/10)-1
127	Virgin I, Br	1.27	(GPC2000/GPC1990)**(1/10)-1
128	Indonesia	1.26	(GPC2000/GPC1990)**(1/10)-1
129	Palau	1.20	(GPC2000/GPC1990)**(1/10)-1
130	Macao	1.11	(GPC2000/GPC1990)**(1/10)-1
131	Pakistan	1.11	(GPC2000/GPC1990)**(1/10)-1
132	Guatemala	1.10	(GPC2000/GPC1990)**(1/10)-1
133	Slovakia	1.07	(GPC2000/GPC1990)**(1/10)-1
134	Iceland	1.07	(GPC2000/GPC1990)**(1/10)-1
135	Brazil	1.06	(GPC2000/GPC1990)**(1/10)-1
136	Honduras	1.06	(GPC2000/GPC1990)**(1/10)-1
137	Guernsey	1.05	(GPC2000/GPC1990)**(1/10)-1
138	Vanuatu	1.05	(GPC2000/GPC1990)**(1/10)-1
139	Namibia	0.98	(GPC2000/GPC1990)**(1/10)-1
140	Cayman Is	0.92	(GPC2000/GPC1990)**(1/10)-1
141	Jersey	0.85	(GPC2000/GPC1990)**(1/10)-1
142	Ghana	0.83	(GPC2000/GPC1990)**(1/10)-1
143	Burundi	0.73	(GPC2000/GPC1990)**(1/10)-1
144	Eritrea	0.69	(GPC2000/GPC1990)**(1/10)-1

Table 5.19 GDP Per Capita Growth Rates, 1990-2000

Rank	Country	GRPCRL	Source
145	Falkland Is	0.66	(GPC2000/GPC1990)**(1/10)-1
146	Colombia	0.65	(GPC2000/GPC1990)**(1/10)-1
147	Hungary	0.62	(GPC2000/GPC1990)**(1/10)-1
148	Benin	0.61	(GPC2000/GPC1990)**(1/10)-1
149	Croatia	0.60	(GPC2000/GPC1990)**(1/10)-1
150	Japan	0.60	(GPC2000/GPC1990)**(1/10)-1
151	Syria	0.59	(GPC2000/GPC1990)**(1/10)-1
152	Liechtenstn	0.59	(GPC2000/GPC1990)**(1/10)-1
153	Switzerland	0.52	(GPC2000/GPC1990)**(1/10)-1
154	Philippines	0.52	(GPC2000/GPC1990)**(1/10)-1
155	Mauritania	0.50	(GPC2000/GPC1990)**(1/10)-1
156	Wallis & Fut	0.46	(GPC2000/GPC1990)**(1/10)-1
157	Fiji	0.45	(GPC2000/GPC1990)**(1/10)-1
158	Czechia	0.43	(GPC2000/GPC1990)**(1/10)-1
159	Anguilla	0.34	(GPC2000/GPC1990)**(1/10)-1
160	Jordan	0.34	(GPC2000/GPC1990)**(1/10)-1
161	N Mariana Is	0.34	(GPC2000/GPC1990)**(1/10)-1
162	Morocco	0.34	(GPC2000/GPC1990)**(1/10)-1
163	Senegal	0.32	(GPC2000/GPC1990)**(1/10)-1
164	Marshall Is	0.29	(GPC2000/GPC1990)**(1/10)-1
165	Cambodia	0.26	(GPC2000/GPC1990)**(1/10)-1
166	Puerto Rico	0.17	(GPC2000/GPC1990)**(1/10)-1
167	Bahamas	0.16	(GPC2000/GPC1990)**(1/10)-1
168	Tanzania	0.14	(GPC2000/GPC1990)**(1/10)-1
169	Guinea	0.12	(GPC2000/GPC1990)**(1/10)-1
170	Gambia	0.09	(GPC2000/GPC1990)**(1/10)-1
171	South Africa	0.03	(GPC2000/GPC1990)**(1/10)-1
172	Algeria	0.02	(GPC2000/GPC1990)**(1/10)-1
173	UAE	0.00	(GPC2000/GPC1990)**(1/10)-1
174	Nigeria	-0.05	(GPC2000/GPC1990)**(1/10)-1
175	Virgin I, US	-0.16	(GPC2000/GPC1990)**(1/10)-1
176	Ecuador	-0.25	(GPC2000/GPC1990)**(1/10)-1
177	Venezuela	-0.26	(GPC2000/GPC1990)**(1/10)-1
178	Suriname	-0.29	(GPC2000/GPC1990)**(1/10)-1
179	Reunion	-0.33	(GPC2000/GPC1990)**(1/10)-1
180	Solomon Is	-0.33	(GPC2000/GPC1990)**(1/10)-1
181	West Bank	-0.35	(GPC2000/GPC1990)**(1/10)-1
182	Gaza Strip	-0.37	(GPC2000/GPC1990)**(1/10)-1
183	Chad	-0.43	(GPC2000/GPC1990)**(1/10)-1
184	Ethiopia	-0.44	(GPC2000/GPC1990)**(1/10)-1
185	Paraguay	-0.48	(GPC2000/GPC1990)**(1/10)-1
186	Macedonia	-0.62	(GPC2000/GPC1990)**(1/10)-1
187	Togo	-0.66	(GPC2000/GPC1990)**(1/10)-1
188	Kuwait	-0.80	(GPC2000/GPC1990)**(1/10)-1
189	Ivory Coast	-0.90	(GPC2000/GPC1990)**(1/10)-1
190	Comoros	-0.90	(GPC2000/GPC1990)**(1/10)-1
191	Jamaica	-0.90	(GPC2000/GPC1990)**(1/10)-1
192	Iraq	-0.90	(GPC2000/GPC1990)**(1/10)-1

Table 5.19 GDP Per Capita Growth Rates, 1990-2000

Rank	Country	GRPCRL	Source
193	Mongolia	-0.93	(GPC2000/GPC1990)**(1/10)-1
194	Kenya	-0.96	(GPC2000/GPC1990)**(1/10)-1
195	Belarus	-1.00	(GPC2000/GPC1990)**(1/10)-1
196	CAR	-1.08	(GPC2000/GPC1990)**(1/10)-1
197	Cameroon	-1.14	(GPC2000/GPC1990)**(1/10)-1
198	Gabon	-1.18	(GPC2000/GPC1990)**(1/10)-1
199	Estonia	-1.22	(GPC2000/GPC1990)**(1/10)-1
200	Swaziland	-1.32	(GPC2000/GPC1990)**(1/10)-1
201	Rwanda	-1.37	(GPC2000/GPC1990)**(1/10)-1
202	Zambia	-1.46	(GPC2000/GPC1990)**(1/10)-1
203	Romania	-1.56	(GPC2000/GPC1990)**(1/10)-1
204	Madagascar	-1.86	(GPC2000/GPC1990)**(1/10)-1
205	Congo, Rep	-1.87	(GPC2000/GPC1990)**(1/10)-1
206	Bosnia	-1.91	(GPC2000/GPC1990)**(1/10)-1
207	Sao Tome & P	-2.04	(GPC2000/GPC1990)**(1/10)-1
208	Bulgaria	-2.14	(GPC2000/GPC1990)**(1/10)-1
209	Angola	-2.19	(GPC2000/GPC1990)**(1/10)-1
210	Haiti	-2.21	(GPC2000/GPC1990)**(1/10)-1
211	Guinea-Biss	-2.43	(GPC2000/GPC1990)**(1/10)-1
212	Montserrat	-2.53	(GPC2000/GPC1990)**(1/10)-1
213	Kazakhstan	-2.66	(GPC2000/GPC1990)**(1/10)-1
214	Latvia	-2.77	(GPC2000/GPC1990)**(1/10)-1
215	Sierra Leone	-2.77	(GPC2000/GPC1990)**(1/10)-1
216	Lithuania	-3.02	(GPC2000/GPC1990)**(1/10)-1
217	Niger	-3.04	(GPC2000/GPC1990)**(1/10)-1
218	Armenia	-3.16	(GPC2000/GPC1990)**(1/10)-1
219	Montenegro	-3.56	(GPC2000/GPC1990)**(1/10)-1
220	Djibouti	-3.79	(GPC2000/GPC1990)**(1/10)-1
221	Cuba	-3.80	(GPC2000/GPC1990)**(1/10)-1
222	Russia	-4.03	(GPC2000/GPC1990)**(1/10)-1
223	Turkmenistan	-4.35	(GPC2000/GPC1990)**(1/10)-1
224	Serbia	-4.94	(GPC2000/GPC1990)**(1/10)-1
225	Kyrgyzstan	-4.95	(GPC2000/GPC1990)**(1/10)-1
226	Korea, North	-5.51	(GPC2000/GPC1990)**(1/10)-1
227	Azerbaijan	-6.25	(GPC2000/GPC1990)**(1/10)-1
228	Kosovo	-6.45	(GPC2000/GPC1990)**(1/10)-1
229	Somalia	-6.98	(GPC2000/GPC1990)**(1/10)-1
230	Ukraine	-7.50	(GPC2000/GPC1990)**(1/10)-1
231	Nauru	-7.56	(GPC2000/GPC1990)**(1/10)-1
232	Uzbekistan	-8.14	(GPC2000/GPC1990)**(1/10)-1
233	Congo, Dem R	-8.23	(GPC2000/GPC1990)**(1/10)-1
234	Georgia	-10.05	(GPC2000/GPC1990)**(1/10)-1
235	Tajikistan	-10.52	(GPC2000/GPC1990)**(1/10)-1
236	Moldova	-12.98	(GPC2000/GPC1990)**(1/10)-1

TABLE 5.20 GDP PER CAPITA GROWTH RATES, 2000-2010			
Rank	Country	GRPCRL	Source
1	Monaco	16.88	(GPC2010/GPC2000)**(1/10)-1
2	Reunion	16.22	(GPC2010/GPC2000)**(1/10)-1
3	Marshall Is	14.27	(GPC2010/GPC2000)**(1/10)-1
4	Cuba	13.73	(GPC2010/GPC2000)**(1/10)-1
5	Mayotte	13.66	(GPC2010/GPC2000)**(1/10)-1
6	Azerbaijan	13.62	(GPC2010/GPC2000)**(1/10)-1
7	Guiana, Fr	11.97	(GPC2010/GPC2000)**(1/10)-1
8	Equatorial G	11.49	(GPC2010/GPC2000)**(1/10)-1
9	Liechtenstn	10.49	(GPC2010/GPC2000)**(1/10)-1
10	Turks & C Is	10.03	(GPC2010/GPC2000)**(1/10)-1
11	Martinique	9.85	(GPC2010/GPC2000)**(1/10)-1
12	Tuvalu	9.76	(GPC2010/GPC2000)**(1/10)-1
13	Guadeloupe	9.62	(GPC2010/GPC2000)**(1/10)-1
14	Macao	9.50	(GPC2010/GPC2000)**(1/10)-1
15	Bermuda	9.49	(GPC2010/GPC2000)**(1/10)-1
16	China	9.11	(GPC2010/GPC2000)**(1/10)-1
17	Isle of Man	8.44	(GPC2010/GPC2000)**(1/10)-1
18	Virgin I, Br	8.25	(GPC2010/GPC2000)**(1/10)-1
19	Virgin I, US	8.22	(GPC2010/GPC2000)**(1/10)-1
20	Montserrat	8.10	(GPC2010/GPC2000)**(1/10)-1
21	Belarus	7.98	(GPC2010/GPC2000)**(1/10)-1
22	Georgia	7.85	(GPC2010/GPC2000)**(1/10)-1
23	Angola	7.61	(GPC2010/GPC2000)**(1/10)-1
24	Chad	7.43	(GPC2010/GPC2000)**(1/10)-1
25	New Caledon	7.36	(GPC2010/GPC2000)**(1/10)-1
26	Kazakhstan	7.30	(GPC2010/GPC2000)**(1/10)-1
27	Russia	6.77	(GPC2010/GPC2000)**(1/10)-1
28	Jersey	6.54	(GPC2010/GPC2000)**(1/10)-1
29	Jamaica	6.52	(GPC2010/GPC2000)**(1/10)-1
30	Turkmenistan	6.50	(GPC2010/GPC2000)**(1/10)-1
31	Guernsey	6.30	(GPC2010/GPC2000)**(1/10)-1
32	Saint Martin	6.22	(GPC2010/GPC2000)**(1/10)-1
33	Romania	6.20	(GPC2010/GPC2000)**(1/10)-1
34	Falkland Is	6.16	(GPC2010/GPC2000)**(1/10)-1
35	Lithuania	6.15	(GPC2010/GPC2000)**(1/10)-1
36	Niue	6.13	(GPC2010/GPC2000)**(1/10)-1
37	Bhutan	6.12	(GPC2010/GPC2000)**(1/10)-1
38	Albania	6.12	(GPC2010/GPC2000)**(1/10)-1
39	Tajikistan	5.90	(GPC2010/GPC2000)**(1/10)-1
40	India	5.78	(GPC2010/GPC2000)**(1/10)-1
41	Ethiopia	5.43	(GPC2010/GPC2000)**(1/10)-1
42	Vietnam	5.41	(GPC2010/GPC2000)**(1/10)-1
43	Sint Maarten	5.35	(GPC2010/GPC2000)**(1/10)-1
44	Latvia	5.34	(GPC2010/GPC2000)**(1/10)-1
45	Laos	5.31	(GPC2010/GPC2000)**(1/10)-1
46	Slovakia	5.29	(GPC2010/GPC2000)**(1/10)-1
47	Taiwan	5.25	(GPC2010/GPC2000)**(1/10)-1
48	Wallis & Fut	5.24	(GPC2010/GPC2000)**(1/10)-1

Table 5.20 GDP Per Capita Growth Rates, 2000-2010

Rank	Country	GRPCRL	Source
49	Cape Verde	5.22	(GPC2010/GPC2000)**(1/10)-1
50	Trinidad & T	5.20	(GPC2010/GPC2000)**(1/10)-1
51	Mongolia	5.18	(GPC2010/GPC2000)**(1/10)-1
52	Cambodia	5.13	(GPC2010/GPC2000)**(1/10)-1
53	Kosovo	5.08	(GPC2010/GPC2000)**(1/10)-1
54	Maldives	5.08	(GPC2010/GPC2000)**(1/10)-1
55	Bulgaria	5.07	(GPC2010/GPC2000)**(1/10)-1
56	Ukraine	5.03	(GPC2010/GPC2000)**(1/10)-1
57	Mozambique	4.91	(GPC2010/GPC2000)**(1/10)-1
58	Cook Is	4.88	(GPC2010/GPC2000)**(1/10)-1
59	Rwanda	4.87	(GPC2010/GPC2000)**(1/10)-1
60	Curacao	4.81	(GPC2010/GPC2000)**(1/10)-1
61	Andorra	4.78	(GPC2010/GPC2000)**(1/10)-1
62	Bosnia	4.66	(GPC2010/GPC2000)**(1/10)-1
63	Serbia	4.64	(GPC2010/GPC2000)**(1/10)-1
64	Fr Polynesia	4.60	(GPC2010/GPC2000)**(1/10)-1
65	Moldova	4.47	(GPC2010/GPC2000)**(1/10)-1
66	Bangladesh	4.46	(GPC2010/GPC2000)**(1/10)-1
67	Peru	4.39	(GPC2010/GPC2000)**(1/10)-1
68	Panama	4.30	(GPC2010/GPC2000)**(1/10)-1
69	Montenegro	4.27	(GPC2010/GPC2000)**(1/10)-1
70	Poland	4.19	(GPC2010/GPC2000)**(1/10)-1
71	Sri Lanka	4.15	(GPC2010/GPC2000)**(1/10)-1
72	Iran	4.05	(GPC2010/GPC2000)**(1/10)-1
73	Tanzania	4.03	(GPC2010/GPC2000)**(1/10)-1
74	Uganda	3.92	(GPC2010/GPC2000)**(1/10)-1
75	Greenland	3.87	(GPC2010/GPC2000)**(1/10)-1
76	Dominican R	3.84	(GPC2010/GPC2000)**(1/10)-1
77	Estonia	3.78	(GPC2010/GPC2000)**(1/10)-1
78	Suriname	3.78	(GPC2010/GPC2000)**(1/10)-1
79	Argentina	3.69	(GPC2010/GPC2000)**(1/10)-1
80	Morocco	3.65	(GPC2010/GPC2000)**(1/10)-1
81	Jordan	3.65	(GPC2010/GPC2000)**(1/10)-1
82	Nigeria	3.60	(GPC2010/GPC2000)**(1/10)-1
83	Korea, South	3.59	(GPC2010/GPC2000)**(1/10)-1
84	Thailand	3.58	(GPC2010/GPC2000)**(1/10)-1
85	Hong Kong	3.52	(GPC2010/GPC2000)**(1/10)-1
86	Gibraltar	3.51	(GPC2010/GPC2000)**(1/10)-1
87	Uzbekistan	3.47	(GPC2010/GPC2000)**(1/10)-1
88	Tunisia	3.46	(GPC2010/GPC2000)**(1/10)-1
89	Indonesia	3.43	(GPC2010/GPC2000)**(1/10)-1
90	Armenia	3.41	(GPC2010/GPC2000)**(1/10)-1
91	Singapore	3.24	(GPC2010/GPC2000)**(1/10)-1
92	Zambia	3.18	(GPC2010/GPC2000)**(1/10)-1
93	Czechia	3.16	(GPC2010/GPC2000)**(1/10)-1
94	Chile	3.13	(GPC2010/GPC2000)**(1/10)-1
95	Lesotho	3.07	(GPC2010/GPC2000)**(1/10)-1
96	Namibia	3.04	(GPC2010/GPC2000)**(1/10)-1

TABLE 5.20 GDP PER CAPITA GROWTH RATES, 2000-2010			
Rank	Country	GRPCRL	Source
97	Croatia	3.02	(GPC2010/GPC2000)**(1/10)-1
98	Egypt	3.00	(GPC2010/GPC2000)**(1/10)-1
99	Dominica	2.97	(GPC2010/GPC2000)**(1/10)-1
100	Kyrgyzstan	2.97	(GPC2010/GPC2000)**(1/10)-1
101	Turkey	2.93	(GPC2010/GPC2000)**(1/10)-1
102	Djibouti	2.87	(GPC2010/GPC2000)**(1/10)-1
103	Sierra Leone	2.86	(GPC2010/GPC2000)**(1/10)-1
104	Mauritius	2.85	(GPC2010/GPC2000)**(1/10)-1
105	Sudan	2.85	(GPC2010/GPC2000)**(1/10)-1
106	South Sudan	2.85	(GPC2010/GPC2000)**(1/10)-1
107	Philippines	2.83	(GPC2010/GPC2000)**(1/10)-1
108	Mali	2.82	(GPC2010/GPC2000)**(1/10)-1
109	Uruguay	2.79	(GPC2010/GPC2000)**(1/10)-1
110	St Vincent	2.77	(GPC2010/GPC2000)**(1/10)-1
111	Burkina Faso	2.77	(GPC2010/GPC2000)**(1/10)-1
112	East Timor	2.74	(GPC2010/GPC2000)**(1/10)-1
113	Malaysia	2.68	(GPC2010/GPC2000)**(1/10)-1
114	Botswana	2.67	(GPC2010/GPC2000)**(1/10)-1
115	Liberia	2.64	(GPC2010/GPC2000)**(1/10)-1
116	CAR	2.56	(GPC2010/GPC2000)**(1/10)-1
117	Costa Rica	2.55	(GPC2010/GPC2000)**(1/10)-1
118	Macedonia	2.54	(GPC2010/GPC2000)**(1/10)-1
119	Brazil	2.47	(GPC2010/GPC2000)**(1/10)-1
120	Colombia	2.47	(GPC2010/GPC2000)**(1/10)-1
121	Slovenia	2.45	(GPC2010/GPC2000)**(1/10)-1
122	Oman	2.42	(GPC2010/GPC2000)**(1/10)-1
123	Algeria	2.42	(GPC2010/GPC2000)**(1/10)-1
124	Puerto Rico	2.40	(GPC2010/GPC2000)**(1/10)-1
125	Hungary	2.40	(GPC2010/GPC2000)**(1/10)-1
126	Saudi Arabia	2.38	(GPC2010/GPC2000)**(1/10)-1
127	Ghana	2.28	(GPC2010/GPC2000)**(1/10)-1
128	Pakistan	2.25	(GPC2010/GPC2000)**(1/10)-1
129	Nepal	2.24	(GPC2010/GPC2000)**(1/10)-1
130	Ecuador	2.18	(GPC2010/GPC2000)**(1/10)-1
131	Samoa	2.16	(GPC2010/GPC2000)**(1/10)-1
132	Bolivia	2.14	(GPC2010/GPC2000)**(1/10)-1
133	South Africa	2.13	(GPC2010/GPC2000)**(1/10)-1
134	St Pierre&M	2.12	(GPC2010/GPC2000)**(1/10)-1
135	Honduras	2.12	(GPC2010/GPC2000)**(1/10)-1
136	Mauritania	2.11	(GPC2010/GPC2000)**(1/10)-1
137	Lebanon	2.11	(GPC2010/GPC2000)**(1/10)-1
138	Congo, Dem R	2.00	(GPC2010/GPC2000)**(1/10)-1
139	Sao Tome & P	1.99	(GPC2010/GPC2000)**(1/10)-1
140	Faroe Is	1.96	(GPC2010/GPC2000)**(1/10)-1
141	Cayman Is	1.94	(GPC2010/GPC2000)**(1/10)-1
142	Greece	1.80	(GPC2010/GPC2000)**(1/10)-1
143	Libya	1.79	(GPC2010/GPC2000)**(1/10)-1
144	Nicaragua	1.74	(GPC2010/GPC2000)**(1/10)-1

Table 5.20 GDP Per Capita Growth Rates, 2000-2010

Rank	Country	GRPCRL	Source
145	Australia	1.72	(GPC2010/GPC2000)**(1/10)-1
146	Congo, Rep	1.64	(GPC2010/GPC2000)**(1/10)-1
147	Sweden	1.63	(GPC2010/GPC2000)**(1/10)-1
148	Grenada	1.59	(GPC2010/GPC2000)**(1/10)-1
149	Yemen	1.58	(GPC2010/GPC2000)**(1/10)-1
150	Anguilla	1.58	(GPC2010/GPC2000)**(1/10)-1
151	Afghanistan	1.56	(GPC2010/GPC2000)**(1/10)-1
152	El Salvador	1.54	(GPC2010/GPC2000)**(1/10)-1
153	Finland	1.43	(GPC2010/GPC2000)**(1/10)-1
154	Paraguay	1.42	(GPC2010/GPC2000)**(1/10)-1
155	Israel	1.41	(GPC2010/GPC2000)**(1/10)-1
156	Kenya	1.41	(GPC2010/GPC2000)**(1/10)-1
157	Belize	1.40	(GPC2010/GPC2000)**(1/10)-1
158	Syria	1.33	(GPC2010/GPC2000)**(1/10)-1
159	New Zealand	1.31	(GPC2010/GPC2000)**(1/10)-1
160	Papua New G	1.27	(GPC2010/GPC2000)**(1/10)-1
161	Luxembourg	1.18	(GPC2010/GPC2000)**(1/10)-1
162	Venezuela	1.12	(GPC2010/GPC2000)**(1/10)-1
163	Cyprus	1.09	(GPC2010/GPC2000)**(1/10)-1
164	Qatar	1.08	(GPC2010/GPC2000)**(1/10)-1
165	W Sahara	1.06	(GPC2010/GPC2000)**(1/10)-1
166	Austria	1.06	(GPC2010/GPC2000)**(1/10)-1
167	Guam	1.05	(GPC2010/GPC2000)**(1/10)-1
168	Solomon Is	1.03	(GPC2010/GPC2000)**(1/10)-1
169	Germany	1.03	(GPC2010/GPC2000)**(1/10)-1
170	Seychelles	1.01	(GPC2010/GPC2000)**(1/10)-1
171	St Lucia	0.99	(GPC2010/GPC2000)**(1/10)-1
172	Switzerland	0.98	(GPC2010/GPC2000)**(1/10)-1
173	UK	0.97	(GPC2010/GPC2000)**(1/10)-1
174	Swaziland	0.96	(GPC2010/GPC2000)**(1/10)-1
175	Netherlands	0.96	(GPC2010/GPC2000)**(1/10)-1
176	Niger	0.94	(GPC2010/GPC2000)**(1/10)-1
177	Senegal	0.93	(GPC2010/GPC2000)**(1/10)-1
178	Iceland	0.91	(GPC2010/GPC2000)**(1/10)-1
179	Canada	0.87	(GPC2010/GPC2000)**(1/10)-1
180	Guyana	0.82	(GPC2010/GPC2000)**(1/10)-1
181	Tonga	0.82	(GPC2010/GPC2000)**(1/10)-1
182	Belgium	0.82	(GPC2010/GPC2000)**(1/10)-1
183	St Kitts & N	0.77	(GPC2010/GPC2000)**(1/10)-1
184	Norway	0.74	(GPC2010/GPC2000)**(1/10)-1
185	Svalbard	0.74	(GPC2010/GPC2000)**(1/10)-1
186	Cameroon	0.74	(GPC2010/GPC2000)**(1/10)-1
187	Guatemala	0.73	(GPC2010/GPC2000)**(1/10)-1
188	Tokelau	0.73	(GPC2010/GPC2000)**(1/10)-1
189	Malta	0.71	(GPC2010/GPC2000)**(1/10)-1
190	Japan	0.71	(GPC2010/GPC2000)**(1/10)-1
191	US	0.71	(GPC2010/GPC2000)**(1/10)-1
192	Iraq	0.66	(GPC2010/GPC2000)**(1/10)-1

TABLE 5.20 GDP PER CAPITA GROWTH RATES, 2000-2010

Rank	Country	GRPCRL	Source
193	Ireland	0.63	(GPC2010/GPC2000)**(1/10)-1
194	Gambia	0.62	(GPC2010/GPC2000)**(1/10)-1
195	Antigua & B	0.62	(GPC2010/GPC2000)**(1/10)-1
196	Spain	0.61	(GPC2010/GPC2000)**(1/10)-1
197	Mexico	0.57	(GPC2010/GPC2000)**(1/10)-1
198	Micronesia	0.53	(GPC2010/GPC2000)**(1/10)-1
199	France	0.48	(GPC2010/GPC2000)**(1/10)-1
200	Portugal	0.44	(GPC2010/GPC2000)**(1/10)-1
201	Vanuatu	0.44	(GPC2010/GPC2000)**(1/10)-1
202	Barbados	0.43	(GPC2010/GPC2000)**(1/10)-1
203	Guinea	0.40	(GPC2010/GPC2000)**(1/10)-1
204	Fiji	0.39	(GPC2010/GPC2000)**(1/10)-1
205	Guinea-Biss	0.23	(GPC2010/GPC2000)**(1/10)-1
206	Denmark	0.23	(GPC2010/GPC2000)**(1/10)-1
207	Kuwait	0.00	(GPC2010/GPC2000)**(1/10)-1
208	Burundi	0.00	(GPC2010/GPC2000)**(1/10)-1
209	Malawi	-0.10	(GPC2010/GPC2000)**(1/10)-1
210	Italy	-0.26	(GPC2010/GPC2000)**(1/10)-1
211	Togo	-0.32	(GPC2010/GPC2000)**(1/10)-1
212	Gabon	-0.41	(GPC2010/GPC2000)**(1/10)-1
213	Madagascar	-0.41	(GPC2010/GPC2000)**(1/10)-1
214	Ivory Coast	-0.44	(GPC2010/GPC2000)**(1/10)-1
215	Kiribati	-0.47	(GPC2010/GPC2000)**(1/10)-1
216	Benin	-0.61	(GPC2010/GPC2000)**(1/10)-1
217	Korea, North	-0.68	(GPC2010/GPC2000)**(1/10)-1
218	Comoros	-0.69	(GPC2010/GPC2000)**(1/10)-1
219	Brunei	-0.73	(GPC2010/GPC2000)**(1/10)-1
220	Palau	-0.74	(GPC2010/GPC2000)**(1/10)-1
221	N Mariana Is	-0.84	(GPC2010/GPC2000)**(1/10)-1
222	Bahrain	-1.10	(GPC2010/GPC2000)**(1/10)-1
223	Burma	-1.11	(GPC2010/GPC2000)**(1/10)-1
224	Nauru	-1.17	(GPC2010/GPC2000)**(1/10)-1
225	Bahamas	-1.18	(GPC2010/GPC2000)**(1/10)-1
226	San Marino	-1.26	(GPC2010/GPC2000)**(1/10)-1
227	Haiti	-1.27	(GPC2010/GPC2000)**(1/10)-1
228	Saint Helena	-1.35	(GPC2010/GPC2000)**(1/10)-1
229	Gaza Strip	-1.51	(GPC2010/GPC2000)**(1/10)-1
230	West Bank	-2.44	(GPC2010/GPC2000)**(1/10)-1
231	Eritrea	-2.82	(GPC2010/GPC2000)**(1/10)-1
232	Somalia	-2.97	(GPC2010/GPC2000)**(1/10)-1
233	Samoa, Amer	-3.07	(GPC2010/GPC2000)**(1/10)-1
234	Aruba	-4.02	(GPC2010/GPC2000)**(1/10)-1
235	UAE	-7.01	(GPC2010/GPC2000)**(1/10)-1
236	Zimbabwe	-13.68	(GPC2010/GPC2000)**(1/10)-1

Table 5.21 GDP Per Capita Growth Rates, 2010-2012

Rank	Country	GRPCRL	Source
1	San Marino	25.02	(GPC2012/GPC2010)**(1/2)-1
2	Zimbabwe	14.19	(GPC2012/GPC2010)**(1/2)-1
3	Afghanistan	13.76	(GPC2012/GPC2010)**(1/2)-1
4	Macao	13.51	(GPC2012/GPC2010)**(1/2)-1
5	Mongolia	13.15	(GPC2012/GPC2010)**(1/2)-1
6	Turkmenistan	11.47	(GPC2012/GPC2010)**(1/2)-1
7	Monaco	9.87	(GPC2012/GPC2010)**(1/2)-1
8	Panama	8.80	(GPC2012/GPC2010)**(1/2)-1
9	Sierra Leone	8.07	(GPC2012/GPC2010)**(1/2)-1
10	Sri Lanka	7.79	(GPC2012/GPC2010)**(1/2)-1
11	Georgia	7.69	(GPC2012/GPC2010)**(1/2)-1
12	Kosovo	7.49	(GPC2012/GPC2010)**(1/2)-1
13	China	7.43	(GPC2012/GPC2010)**(1/2)-1
14	Lithuania	7.35	(GPC2012/GPC2010)**(1/2)-1
15	Latvia	7.35	(GPC2012/GPC2010)**(1/2)-1
16	Iraq	7.32	(GPC2012/GPC2010)**(1/2)-1
17	Bhutan	7.14	(GPC2012/GPC2010)**(1/2)-1
18	Estonia	6.92	(GPC2012/GPC2010)**(1/2)-1
19	Ghana	6.36	(GPC2012/GPC2010)**(1/2)-1
20	Seychelles	6.30	(GPC2012/GPC2010)**(1/2)-1
21	Laos	6.07	(GPC2012/GPC2010)**(1/2)-1
22	Papua New G	6.03	(GPC2012/GPC2010)**(1/2)-1
23	Chile	5.38	(GPC2012/GPC2010)**(1/2)-1
24	Peru	5.28	(GPC2012/GPC2010)**(1/2)-1
25	Bangladesh	5.27	(GPC2012/GPC2010)**(1/2)-1
26	Saudi Arabia	5.23	(GPC2012/GPC2010)**(1/2)-1
27	Ethiopia	5.13	(GPC2012/GPC2010)**(1/2)-1
28	Uruguay	4.88	(GPC2012/GPC2010)**(1/2)-1
29	Turkey	4.83	(GPC2012/GPC2010)**(1/2)-1
30	Tajikistan	4.83	(GPC2012/GPC2010)**(1/2)-1
31	Palau	4.80	(GPC2012/GPC2010)**(1/2)-1
32	Kazakhstan	4.76	(GPC2012/GPC2010)**(1/2)-1
33	Rwanda	4.75	(GPC2012/GPC2010)**(1/2)-1
34	Ecuador	4.72	(GPC2012/GPC2010)**(1/2)-1
35	Mozambique	4.70	(GPC2012/GPC2010)**(1/2)-1
36	Vietnam	4.65	(GPC2012/GPC2010)**(1/2)-1
37	Indonesia	4.59	(GPC2012/GPC2010)**(1/2)-1
38	Russia	4.55	(GPC2012/GPC2010)**(1/2)-1
39	Liberia	4.54	(GPC2012/GPC2010)**(1/2)-1
40	Cambodia	4.38	(GPC2012/GPC2010)**(1/2)-1
41	Eritrea	4.32	(GPC2012/GPC2010)**(1/2)-1
42	Botswana	4.26	(GPC2012/GPC2010)**(1/2)-1
43	India	4.22	(GPC2012/GPC2010)**(1/2)-1
44	Zambia	4.21	(GPC2012/GPC2010)**(1/2)-1
45	Guyana	4.17	(GPC2012/GPC2010)**(1/2)-1
46	Solomon Is	4.16	(GPC2012/GPC2010)**(1/2)-1
47	Argentina	4.11	(GPC2012/GPC2010)**(1/2)-1
48	Congo, Dem R	4.08	(GPC2012/GPC2010)**(1/2)-1

Table 5.21 GDP Per Capita Growth Rates, 2010-2012

Rank	Country	GRPCRL	Source
49	CAR	4.06	(GPC2012/GPC2010)**(1/2)-1
50	Nicaragua	3.99	(GPC2012/GPC2010)**(1/2)-1
51	Colombia	3.96	(GPC2012/GPC2010)**(1/2)-1
52	Uzbekistan	3.89	(GPC2012/GPC2010)**(1/2)-1
53	Suriname	3.76	(GPC2012/GPC2010)**(1/2)-1
54	Gabon	3.74	(GPC2012/GPC2010)**(1/2)-1
55	Bolivia	3.70	(GPC2012/GPC2010)**(1/2)-1
56	Malaysia	3.66	(GPC2012/GPC2010)**(1/2)-1
57	Burkina Faso	3.63	(GPC2012/GPC2010)**(1/2)-1
58	Belarus	3.63	(GPC2012/GPC2010)**(1/2)-1
59	Nigeria	3.61	(GPC2012/GPC2010)**(1/2)-1
60	Tanzania	3.48	(GPC2012/GPC2010)**(1/2)-1
61	Philippines	3.41	(GPC2012/GPC2010)**(1/2)-1
62	Aruba	3.40	(GPC2012/GPC2010)**(1/2)-1
63	Namibia	3.38	(GPC2012/GPC2010)**(1/2)-1
64	St Kitts & N	3.37	(GPC2012/GPC2010)**(1/2)-1
65	Morocco	3.33	(GPC2012/GPC2010)**(1/2)-1
66	Costa Rica	3.27	(GPC2012/GPC2010)**(1/2)-1
67	East Timor	3.27	(GPC2012/GPC2010)**(1/2)-1
68	Mauritania	3.25	(GPC2012/GPC2010)**(1/2)-1
69	Maldives	3.17	(GPC2012/GPC2010)**(1/2)-1
70	Niger	3.00	(GPC2012/GPC2010)**(1/2)-1
71	Mexico	2.99	(GPC2012/GPC2010)**(1/2)-1
72	Ukraine	2.99	(GPC2012/GPC2010)**(1/2)-1
73	Mauritius	2.98	(GPC2012/GPC2010)**(1/2)-1
74	Germany	2.91	(GPC2012/GPC2010)**(1/2)-1
75	Dominican R	2.91	(GPC2012/GPC2010)**(1/2)-1
76	Thailand	2.87	(GPC2012/GPC2010)**(1/2)-1
77	Poland	2.79	(GPC2012/GPC2010)**(1/2)-1
78	Sudan	2.76	(GPC2012/GPC2010)**(1/2)-1
79	South Sudan	2.76	(GPC2012/GPC2010)**(1/2)-1
80	Nepal	2.74	(GPC2012/GPC2010)**(1/2)-1
81	Venezuela	2.72	(GPC2012/GPC2010)**(1/2)-1
82	Cape Verde	2.71	(GPC2012/GPC2010)**(1/2)-1
83	Haiti	2.63	(GPC2012/GPC2010)**(1/2)-1
84	Lesotho	2.62	(GPC2012/GPC2010)**(1/2)-1
85	Slovakia	2.49	(GPC2012/GPC2010)**(1/2)-1
86	Armenia	2.40	(GPC2012/GPC2010)**(1/2)-1
87	Samoa, Amer	2.38	(GPC2012/GPC2010)**(1/2)-1
88	W Sahara	2.36	(GPC2012/GPC2010)**(1/2)-1
89	Moldova	2.32	(GPC2012/GPC2010)**(1/2)-1
90	Saint Helena	2.32	(GPC2012/GPC2010)**(1/2)-1
91	Burma	2.29	(GPC2012/GPC2010)**(1/2)-1
92	Albania	2.24	(GPC2012/GPC2010)**(1/2)-1
93	Somalia	2.23	(GPC2012/GPC2010)**(1/2)-1
94	Korea, South	2.22	(GPC2012/GPC2010)**(1/2)-1
95	Hong Kong	2.21	(GPC2012/GPC2010)**(1/2)-1
96	Angola	2.10	(GPC2012/GPC2010)**(1/2)-1

Table 5.21 GDP Per Capita Growth Rates, 2010-2012

Rank	Country	GRPCRL	Source
97	New Zealand	2.10	(GPC2012/GPC2010)**(1/2)-1
98	Virgin I, US	2.06	(GPC2012/GPC2010)**(1/2)-1
99	Israel	2.03	(GPC2012/GPC2010)**(1/2)-1
100	Niue	2.01	(GPC2012/GPC2010)**(1/2)-1
101	Romania	2.00	(GPC2012/GPC2010)**(1/2)-1
102	Bermuda	1.98	(GPC2012/GPC2010)**(1/2)-1
103	Gibraltar	1.95	(GPC2012/GPC2010)**(1/2)-1
104	Bulgaria	1.90	(GPC2012/GPC2010)**(1/2)-1
105	Curacao	1.89	(GPC2012/GPC2010)**(1/2)-1
106	Sint Maarten	1.88	(GPC2012/GPC2010)**(1/2)-1
107	Saint Martin	1.86	(GPC2012/GPC2010)**(1/2)-1
108	Honduras	1.82	(GPC2012/GPC2010)**(1/2)-1
109	Cameroon	1.79	(GPC2012/GPC2010)**(1/2)-1
110	Fr Polynesia	1.78	(GPC2012/GPC2010)**(1/2)-1
111	Cook Is	1.76	(GPC2012/GPC2010)**(1/2)-1
112	Togo	1.74	(GPC2012/GPC2010)**(1/2)-1
113	Kenya	1.73	(GPC2012/GPC2010)**(1/2)-1
114	South Africa	1.71	(GPC2012/GPC2010)**(1/2)-1
115	Isle of Man	1.67	(GPC2012/GPC2010)**(1/2)-1
116	Turks & C Is	1.65	(GPC2012/GPC2010)**(1/2)-1
117	Austria	1.65	(GPC2012/GPC2010)**(1/2)-1
118	Virgin I, Br	1.63	(GPC2012/GPC2010)**(1/2)-1
119	Guam	1.62	(GPC2012/GPC2010)**(1/2)-1
120	Pakistan	1.62	(GPC2012/GPC2010)**(1/2)-1
121	Tokelau	1.62	(GPC2012/GPC2010)**(1/2)-1
122	Cayman Is	1.62	(GPC2012/GPC2010)**(1/2)-1
123	Taiwan	1.60	(GPC2012/GPC2010)**(1/2)-1
124	Falkland Is	1.58	(GPC2012/GPC2010)**(1/2)-1
125	Iceland	1.58	(GPC2012/GPC2010)**(1/2)-1
126	St Pierre&M	1.57	(GPC2012/GPC2010)**(1/2)-1
127	New Caledon	1.56	(GPC2012/GPC2010)**(1/2)-1
128	US	1.56	(GPC2012/GPC2010)**(1/2)-1
129	Uganda	1.55	(GPC2012/GPC2010)**(1/2)-1
130	Anguilla	1.54	(GPC2012/GPC2010)**(1/2)-1
131	Montenegro	1.53	(GPC2012/GPC2010)**(1/2)-1
132	Guernsey	1.52	(GPC2012/GPC2010)**(1/2)-1
133	Tonga	1.52	(GPC2012/GPC2010)**(1/2)-1
134	El Salvador	1.52	(GPC2012/GPC2010)**(1/2)-1
135	Cuba	1.52	(GPC2012/GPC2010)**(1/2)-1
136	Qatar	1.51	(GPC2012/GPC2010)**(1/2)-1
137	Jersey	1.51	(GPC2012/GPC2010)**(1/2)-1
138	Faroe Is	1.50	(GPC2012/GPC2010)**(1/2)-1
139	Liechtenstn	1.50	(GPC2012/GPC2010)**(1/2)-1
140	Nauru	1.48	(GPC2012/GPC2010)**(1/2)-1
141	Marshall Is	1.45	(GPC2012/GPC2010)**(1/2)-1
142	Australia	1.41	(GPC2012/GPC2010)**(1/2)-1
143	Wallis & Fut	1.39	(GPC2012/GPC2010)**(1/2)-1
144	Chad	1.38	(GPC2012/GPC2010)**(1/2)-1

TABLE 5.21 GDP PER CAPITA GROWTH RATES, 2010-2012

Rank	Country	GRPCRL	Source
145	Samoa	1.37	(GPC2012/GPC2010)**(1/2)-1
146	Micronesia	1.35	(GPC2012/GPC2010)**(1/2)-1
147	Puerto Rico	1.34	(GPC2012/GPC2010)**(1/2)-1
148	Kiribati	1.33	(GPC2012/GPC2010)**(1/2)-1
149	Macedonia	1.30	(GPC2012/GPC2010)**(1/2)-1
150	Guinea	1.29	(GPC2012/GPC2010)**(1/2)-1
151	Belize	1.27	(GPC2012/GPC2010)**(1/2)-1
152	Lebanon	1.23	(GPC2012/GPC2010)**(1/2)-1
153	Sweden	1.20	(GPC2012/GPC2010)**(1/2)-1
154	St Vincent	1.19	(GPC2012/GPC2010)**(1/2)-1
155	Montserrat	1.17	(GPC2012/GPC2010)**(1/2)-1
156	Sao Tome & P	1.08	(GPC2012/GPC2010)**(1/2)-1
157	Algeria	1.05	(GPC2012/GPC2010)**(1/2)-1
158	N Mariana Is	1.03	(GPC2012/GPC2010)**(1/2)-1
159	Canada	1.02	(GPC2012/GPC2010)**(1/2)-1
160	Brunei	1.00	(GPC2012/GPC2010)**(1/2)-1
161	Kyrgyzstan	0.99	(GPC2012/GPC2010)**(1/2)-1
162	Svalbard	0.94	(GPC2012/GPC2010)**(1/2)-1
163	Norway	0.94	(GPC2012/GPC2010)**(1/2)-1
164	Brazil	0.92	(GPC2012/GPC2010)**(1/2)-1
165	Guatemala	0.91	(GPC2012/GPC2010)**(1/2)-1
166	Greenland	0.91	(GPC2012/GPC2010)**(1/2)-1
167	Singapore	0.91	(GPC2012/GPC2010)**(1/2)-1
168	Ireland	0.89	(GPC2012/GPC2010)**(1/2)-1
169	Equatorial G	0.85	(GPC2012/GPC2010)**(1/2)-1
170	Malta	0.84	(GPC2012/GPC2010)**(1/2)-1
171	Congo, Rep	0.80	(GPC2012/GPC2010)**(1/2)-1
172	Fiji	0.71	(GPC2012/GPC2010)**(1/2)-1
173	Japan	0.63	(GPC2012/GPC2010)**(1/2)-1
174	France	0.53	(GPC2012/GPC2010)**(1/2)-1
175	Bosnia	0.52	(GPC2012/GPC2010)**(1/2)-1
176	Korea, North	0.51	(GPC2012/GPC2010)**(1/2)-1
177	Serbia	0.49	(GPC2012/GPC2010)**(1/2)-1
178	Finland	0.48	(GPC2012/GPC2010)**(1/2)-1
179	Grenada	0.42	(GPC2012/GPC2010)**(1/2)-1
180	Switzerland	0.37	(GPC2012/GPC2010)**(1/2)-1
181	Hungary	0.37	(GPC2012/GPC2010)**(1/2)-1
182	Djibouti	0.37	(GPC2012/GPC2010)**(1/2)-1
183	Jordan	0.36	(GPC2012/GPC2010)**(1/2)-1
184	Croatia	0.32	(GPC2012/GPC2010)**(1/2)-1
185	Egypt	0.29	(GPC2012/GPC2010)**(1/2)-1
186	Czechia	0.21	(GPC2012/GPC2010)**(1/2)-1
187	Malawi	0.17	(GPC2012/GPC2010)**(1/2)-1
188	Bahamas	0.16	(GPC2012/GPC2010)**(1/2)-1
189	Bahrain	0.15	(GPC2012/GPC2010)**(1/2)-1
190	Comoros	0.13	(GPC2012/GPC2010)**(1/2)-1
191	UK	0.00	(GPC2012/GPC2010)**(1/2)-1
192	Denmark	-0.05	(GPC2012/GPC2010)**(1/2)-1

Table 5.21 GDP Per Capita Growth Rates, 2010-2012			
Rank	Country	GRPCRL	Source
193	Ivory Coast	-0.09	(GPC2012/GPC2010)**(1/2)-1
194	Burundi	-0.10	(GPC2012/GPC2010)**(1/2)-1
195	St Lucia	-0.11	(GPC2012/GPC2010)**(1/2)-1
196	Barbados	-0.12	(GPC2012/GPC2010)**(1/2)-1
197	Senegal	-0.13	(GPC2012/GPC2010)**(1/2)-1
198	Kuwait	-0.13	(GPC2012/GPC2010)**(1/2)-1
199	Azerbaijan	-0.19	(GPC2012/GPC2010)**(1/2)-1
200	Paraguay	-0.20	(GPC2012/GPC2010)**(1/2)-1
201	Belgium	-0.26	(GPC2012/GPC2010)**(1/2)-1
202	Italy	-0.28	(GPC2012/GPC2010)**(1/2)-1
203	Tunisia	-0.31	(GPC2012/GPC2010)**(1/2)-1
204	UAE	-0.33	(GPC2012/GPC2010)**(1/2)-1
205	Madagascar	-0.38	(GPC2012/GPC2010)**(1/2)-1
206	Tuvalu	-0.40	(GPC2012/GPC2010)**(1/2)-1
207	Trinidad & T	-0.40	(GPC2012/GPC2010)**(1/2)-1
208	Vanuatu	-0.45	(GPC2012/GPC2010)**(1/2)-1
209	Netherlands	-0.61	(GPC2012/GPC2010)**(1/2)-1
210	Gaza Strip	-0.75	(GPC2012/GPC2010)**(1/2)-1
211	Iran	-0.80	(GPC2012/GPC2010)**(1/2)-1
212	Spain	-1.06	(GPC2012/GPC2010)**(1/2)-1
213	Slovenia	-1.14	(GPC2012/GPC2010)**(1/2)-1
214	Antigua & B	-1.20	(GPC2012/GPC2010)**(1/2)-1
215	Jamaica	-1.21	(GPC2012/GPC2010)**(1/2)-1
216	West Bank	-1.21	(GPC2012/GPC2010)**(1/2)-1
217	Dominica	-1.39	(GPC2012/GPC2010)**(1/2)-1
218	Benin	-1.39	(GPC2012/GPC2010)**(1/2)-1
219	Martinique	-1.48	(GPC2012/GPC2010)**(1/2)-1
220	Luxembourg	-1.63	(GPC2012/GPC2010)**(1/2)-1
221	Guadeloupe	-1.84	(GPC2012/GPC2010)**(1/2)-1
222	Swaziland	-1.86	(GPC2012/GPC2010)**(1/2)-1
223	Mali	-1.90	(GPC2012/GPC2010)**(1/2)-1
224	Portugal	-2.08	(GPC2012/GPC2010)**(1/2)-1
225	Syria	-2.33	(GPC2012/GPC2010)**(1/2)-1
226	Andorra	-2.47	(GPC2012/GPC2010)**(1/2)-1
227	Gambia	-2.69	(GPC2012/GPC2010)**(1/2)-1
228	Mayotte	-2.71	(GPC2012/GPC2010)**(1/2)-1
229	Guinea-Biss	-3.13	(GPC2012/GPC2010)**(1/2)-1
230	Cyprus	-3.69	(GPC2012/GPC2010)**(1/2)-1
231	Oman	-3.77	(GPC2012/GPC2010)**(1/2)-1
232	Guiana, Fr	-4.68	(GPC2012/GPC2010)**(1/2)-1
233	Greece	-6.24	(GPC2012/GPC2010)**(1/2)-1
234	Reunion	-6.26	(GPC2012/GPC2010)**(1/2)-1
235	Yemen	-7.53	(GPC2012/GPC2010)**(1/2)-1
236	Libya	-17.06	(GPC2012/GPC2010)**(1/2)-1

Table 5.22 GDP Per Capita Growth Rates, 2012-2020, Forecast

Rank	Country	GRPCRL	Source
1	Mayotte	10.39	(GPC2020/GPC2012)**(1/8)-1
2	Monaco	10.38	(GPC2020/GPC2012)**(1/8)-1
3	Equatorial G	9.58	(GPC2020/GPC2012)**(1/8)-1
4	Bermuda	8.12	(GPC2020/GPC2012)**(1/8)-1
5	Reunion	8.07	(GPC2020/GPC2012)**(1/8)-1
6	Macao	7.97	(GPC2020/GPC2012)**(1/8)-1
7	China	7.84	(GPC2020/GPC2012)**(1/8)-1
8	Marshall Is	7.12	(GPC2020/GPC2012)**(1/8)-1
9	Cuba	6.96	(GPC2020/GPC2012)**(1/8)-1
10	Azerbaijan	6.56	(GPC2020/GPC2012)**(1/8)-1
11	Guiana, Fr	6.07	(GPC2020/GPC2012)**(1/8)-1
12	Martinique	5.95	(GPC2020/GPC2012)**(1/8)-1
13	Bhutan	5.91	(GPC2020/GPC2012)**(1/8)-1
14	Liechtenstn	5.83	(GPC2020/GPC2012)**(1/8)-1
15	Guadeloupe	5.76	(GPC2020/GPC2012)**(1/8)-1
16	Turks & C Is	5.74	(GPC2020/GPC2012)**(1/8)-1
17	Isle of Man	5.64	(GPC2020/GPC2012)**(1/8)-1
18	New Caledon	5.60	(GPC2020/GPC2012)**(1/8)-1
19	Cape Verde	5.31	(GPC2020/GPC2012)**(1/8)-1
20	Tuvalu	5.18	(GPC2020/GPC2012)**(1/8)-1
21	Niue	5.16	(GPC2020/GPC2012)**(1/8)-1
22	Mongolia	5.07	(GPC2020/GPC2012)**(1/8)-1
23	Taiwan	5.04	(GPC2020/GPC2012)**(1/8)-1
24	San Marino	5.03	(GPC2020/GPC2012)**(1/8)-1
25	Georgia	4.96	(GPC2020/GPC2012)**(1/8)-1
26	Vietnam	4.89	(GPC2020/GPC2012)**(1/8)-1
27	Turkmenistan	4.89	(GPC2020/GPC2012)**(1/8)-1
28	Virgin I, Br	4.80	(GPC2020/GPC2012)**(1/8)-1
29	Gibraltar	4.80	(GPC2020/GPC2012)**(1/8)-1
30	Maldives	4.80	(GPC2020/GPC2012)**(1/8)-1
31	Korea, South	4.78	(GPC2020/GPC2012)**(1/8)-1
32	Belarus	4.54	(GPC2020/GPC2012)**(1/8)-1
33	Virgin I, US	4.52	(GPC2020/GPC2012)**(1/8)-1
34	India	4.47	(GPC2020/GPC2012)**(1/8)-1
35	Lithuania	4.35	(GPC2020/GPC2012)**(1/8)-1
36	Saint Martin	4.34	(GPC2020/GPC2012)**(1/8)-1
37	Russia	4.34	(GPC2020/GPC2012)**(1/8)-1
38	Botswana	4.32	(GPC2020/GPC2012)**(1/8)-1
39	Angola	4.31	(GPC2020/GPC2012)**(1/8)-1
40	Laos	4.30	(GPC2020/GPC2012)**(1/8)-1
41	Qatar	4.30	(GPC2020/GPC2012)**(1/8)-1
42	Montserrat	4.26	(GPC2020/GPC2012)**(1/8)-1
43	Panama	4.24	(GPC2020/GPC2012)**(1/8)-1
44	Kazakhstan	4.23	(GPC2020/GPC2012)**(1/8)-1
45	Sri Lanka	4.20	(GPC2020/GPC2012)**(1/8)-1
46	Albania	4.19	(GPC2020/GPC2012)**(1/8)-1
47	Libya	4.09	(GPC2020/GPC2012)**(1/8)-1
48	Chad	4.06	(GPC2020/GPC2012)**(1/8)-1

Table 5.22 GDP Per Capita Growth Rates, 2012-2020, Forecast			
Rank	Country	GRPCRL	Source
49	Kosovo	4.05	(GPC2020/GPC2012)**(1/8)-1
50	Latvia	4.04	(GPC2020/GPC2012)**(1/8)-1
51	Jersey	4.04	(GPC2020/GPC2012)**(1/8)-1
52	Singapore	4.00	(GPC2020/GPC2012)**(1/8)-1
53	Guernsey	3.98	(GPC2020/GPC2012)**(1/8)-1
54	Sint Maarten	3.94	(GPC2020/GPC2012)**(1/8)-1
55	Romania	3.85	(GPC2020/GPC2012)**(1/8)-1
56	W Sahara	3.78	(GPC2020/GPC2012)**(1/8)-1
57	Chile	3.76	(GPC2020/GPC2012)**(1/8)-1
58	Thailand	3.75	(GPC2020/GPC2012)**(1/8)-1
59	Hong Kong	3.75	(GPC2020/GPC2012)**(1/8)-1
60	Dominican R	3.70	(GPC2020/GPC2012)**(1/8)-1
61	Curacao	3.69	(GPC2020/GPC2012)**(1/8)-1
62	Turkey	3.68	(GPC2020/GPC2012)**(1/8)-1
63	Malaysia	3.68	(GPC2020/GPC2012)**(1/8)-1
64	Falkland Is	3.65	(GPC2020/GPC2012)**(1/8)-1
65	Mozambique	3.65	(GPC2020/GPC2012)**(1/8)-1
66	Bangladesh	3.65	(GPC2020/GPC2012)**(1/8)-1
67	Poland	3.64	(GPC2020/GPC2012)**(1/8)-1
68	Tajikistan	3.59	(GPC2020/GPC2012)**(1/8)-1
69	Cook Is	3.53	(GPC2020/GPC2012)**(1/8)-1
70	Peru	3.50	(GPC2020/GPC2012)**(1/8)-1
71	Trinidad & T	3.50	(GPC2020/GPC2012)**(1/8)-1
72	Slovakia	3.46	(GPC2020/GPC2012)**(1/8)-1
73	Ethiopia	3.45	(GPC2020/GPC2012)**(1/8)-1
74	Jamaica	3.45	(GPC2020/GPC2012)**(1/8)-1
75	Fr Polynesia	3.43	(GPC2020/GPC2012)**(1/8)-1
76	Cambodia	3.34	(GPC2020/GPC2012)**(1/8)-1
77	Bulgaria	3.33	(GPC2020/GPC2012)**(1/8)-1
78	Mauritius	3.30	(GPC2020/GPC2012)**(1/8)-1
79	Argentina	3.25	(GPC2020/GPC2012)**(1/8)-1
80	Oman	3.24	(GPC2020/GPC2012)**(1/8)-1
81	Indonesia	3.22	(GPC2020/GPC2012)**(1/8)-1
82	St Pierre&M	3.20	(GPC2020/GPC2012)**(1/8)-1
83	Saudi Arabia	3.18	(GPC2020/GPC2012)**(1/8)-1
84	Ukraine	3.18	(GPC2020/GPC2012)**(1/8)-1
85	Estonia	3.15	(GPC2020/GPC2012)**(1/8)-1
86	Afghanistan	3.12	(GPC2020/GPC2012)**(1/8)-1
87	Andorra	3.11	(GPC2020/GPC2012)**(1/8)-1
88	Rwanda	3.07	(GPC2020/GPC2012)**(1/8)-1
89	Seychelles	3.06	(GPC2020/GPC2012)**(1/8)-1
90	St Vincent	3.02	(GPC2020/GPC2012)**(1/8)-1
91	Tunisia	2.91	(GPC2020/GPC2012)**(1/8)-1
92	Wallis & Fut	2.89	(GPC2020/GPC2012)**(1/8)-1
93	Uganda	2.85	(GPC2020/GPC2012)**(1/8)-1
94	Bosnia	2.84	(GPC2020/GPC2012)**(1/8)-1
95	Montenegro	2.84	(GPC2020/GPC2012)**(1/8)-1
96	Serbia	2.83	(GPC2020/GPC2012)**(1/8)-1

Table 5.22 GDP Per Capita Growth Rates, 2012-2020, Forecast			
Rank	Country	GRPCRL	Source
97	Iran	2.82	(GPC2020/GPC2012)**(1/8)-1
98	Greenland	2.82	(GPC2020/GPC2012)**(1/8)-1
99	Ireland	2.81	(GPC2020/GPC2012)**(1/8)-1
100	Uruguay	2.78	(GPC2020/GPC2012)**(1/8)-1
101	Suriname	2.73	(GPC2020/GPC2012)**(1/8)-1
102	Moldova	2.72	(GPC2020/GPC2012)**(1/8)-1
103	Malta	2.70	(GPC2020/GPC2012)**(1/8)-1
104	Lebanon	2.70	(GPC2020/GPC2012)**(1/8)-1
105	Morocco	2.64	(GPC2020/GPC2012)**(1/8)-1
106	St Kitts & N	2.64	(GPC2020/GPC2012)**(1/8)-1
107	Dominica	2.63	(GPC2020/GPC2012)**(1/8)-1
108	Lesotho	2.63	(GPC2020/GPC2012)**(1/8)-1
109	Egypt	2.62	(GPC2020/GPC2012)**(1/8)-1
110	Sierra Leone	2.58	(GPC2020/GPC2012)**(1/8)-1
111	Samoa, Amer	2.58	(GPC2020/GPC2012)**(1/8)-1
112	Tanzania	2.57	(GPC2020/GPC2012)**(1/8)-1
113	Costa Rica	2.57	(GPC2020/GPC2012)**(1/8)-1
114	Brunei	2.51	(GPC2020/GPC2012)**(1/8)-1
115	Grenada	2.51	(GPC2020/GPC2012)**(1/8)-1
116	Svalbard	2.49	(GPC2020/GPC2012)**(1/8)-1
117	Norway	2.49	(GPC2020/GPC2012)**(1/8)-1
118	Luxembourg	2.49	(GPC2020/GPC2012)**(1/8)-1
119	Liberia	2.49	(GPC2020/GPC2012)**(1/8)-1
120	Zimbabwe	2.47	(GPC2020/GPC2012)**(1/8)-1
121	Burkina Faso	2.44	(GPC2020/GPC2012)**(1/8)-1
122	Saint Helena	2.43	(GPC2020/GPC2012)**(1/8)-1
123	Nigeria	2.40	(GPC2020/GPC2012)**(1/8)-1
124	East Timor	2.38	(GPC2020/GPC2012)**(1/8)-1
125	Namibia	2.34	(GPC2020/GPC2012)**(1/8)-1
126	Colombia	2.30	(GPC2020/GPC2012)**(1/8)-1
127	Uzbekistan	2.30	(GPC2020/GPC2012)**(1/8)-1
128	Zambia	2.22	(GPC2020/GPC2012)**(1/8)-1
129	Bolivia	2.20	(GPC2020/GPC2012)**(1/8)-1
130	El Salvador	2.19	(GPC2020/GPC2012)**(1/8)-1
131	St Lucia	2.19	(GPC2020/GPC2012)**(1/8)-1
132	Ghana	2.19	(GPC2020/GPC2012)**(1/8)-1
133	Croatia	2.19	(GPC2020/GPC2012)**(1/8)-1
134	Jordan	2.18	(GPC2020/GPC2012)**(1/8)-1
135	Cyprus	2.17	(GPC2020/GPC2012)**(1/8)-1
136	Philippines	2.17	(GPC2020/GPC2012)**(1/8)-1
137	Israel	2.17	(GPC2020/GPC2012)**(1/8)-1
138	Nepal	2.15	(GPC2020/GPC2012)**(1/8)-1
139	Slovenia	2.15	(GPC2020/GPC2012)**(1/8)-1
140	Czechia	2.13	(GPC2020/GPC2012)**(1/8)-1
141	Sudan	2.12	(GPC2020/GPC2012)**(1/8)-1
142	South Sudan	2.12	(GPC2020/GPC2012)**(1/8)-1
143	Greece	2.08	(GPC2020/GPC2012)**(1/8)-1
144	Ecuador	2.07	(GPC2020/GPC2012)**(1/8)-1

Table 5.22 GDP Per Capita Growth Rates, 2012-2020, Forecast

Rank	Country	GRPCRL	Source
145	Faroe Is	2.06	(GPC2020/GPC2012)**(1/8)-1
146	Pakistan	2.05	(GPC2020/GPC2012)**(1/8)-1
147	Macedonia	2.04	(GPC2020/GPC2012)**(1/8)-1
148	Armenia	2.03	(GPC2020/GPC2012)**(1/8)-1
149	Antigua & B	2.03	(GPC2020/GPC2012)**(1/8)-1
150	Guyana	2.02	(GPC2020/GPC2012)**(1/8)-1
151	Brazil	2.02	(GPC2020/GPC2012)**(1/8)-1
152	Australia	2.01	(GPC2020/GPC2012)**(1/8)-1
153	Austria	1.99	(GPC2020/GPC2012)**(1/8)-1
154	Belize	1.99	(GPC2020/GPC2012)**(1/8)-1
155	Puerto Rico	1.98	(GPC2020/GPC2012)**(1/8)-1
156	Iraq	1.96	(GPC2020/GPC2012)**(1/8)-1
157	Spain	1.94	(GPC2020/GPC2012)**(1/8)-1
158	Hungary	1.94	(GPC2020/GPC2012)**(1/8)-1
159	Germany	1.91	(GPC2020/GPC2012)**(1/8)-1
160	Nicaragua	1.91	(GPC2020/GPC2012)**(1/8)-1
161	Papua New G	1.91	(GPC2020/GPC2012)**(1/8)-1
162	Mauritania	1.85	(GPC2020/GPC2012)**(1/8)-1
163	Portugal	1.84	(GPC2020/GPC2012)**(1/8)-1
164	Finland	1.84	(GPC2020/GPC2012)**(1/8)-1
165	Mexico	1.82	(GPC2020/GPC2012)**(1/8)-1
166	Mali	1.81	(GPC2020/GPC2012)**(1/8)-1
167	CAR	1.81	(GPC2020/GPC2012)**(1/8)-1
168	Bahrain	1.80	(GPC2020/GPC2012)**(1/8)-1
169	Solomon Is	1.78	(GPC2020/GPC2012)**(1/8)-1
170	Sweden	1.78	(GPC2020/GPC2012)**(1/8)-1
171	Samoa	1.77	(GPC2020/GPC2012)**(1/8)-1
172	Cayman Is	1.73	(GPC2020/GPC2012)**(1/8)-1
173	Netherlands	1.70	(GPC2020/GPC2012)**(1/8)-1
174	Algeria	1.69	(GPC2020/GPC2012)**(1/8)-1
175	Honduras	1.68	(GPC2020/GPC2012)**(1/8)-1
176	Tonga	1.62	(GPC2020/GPC2012)**(1/8)-1
177	Kyrgyzstan	1.62	(GPC2020/GPC2012)**(1/8)-1
178	Japan	1.62	(GPC2020/GPC2012)**(1/8)-1
179	US	1.60	(GPC2020/GPC2012)**(1/8)-1
180	UK	1.57	(GPC2020/GPC2012)**(1/8)-1
181	New Zealand	1.57	(GPC2020/GPC2012)**(1/8)-1
182	Congo, Dem R	1.57	(GPC2020/GPC2012)**(1/8)-1
183	South Africa	1.53	(GPC2020/GPC2012)**(1/8)-1
184	Canada	1.51	(GPC2020/GPC2012)**(1/8)-1
185	Djibouti	1.51	(GPC2020/GPC2012)**(1/8)-1
186	Belgium	1.47	(GPC2020/GPC2012)**(1/8)-1
187	Burma	1.46	(GPC2020/GPC2012)**(1/8)-1
188	Iceland	1.46	(GPC2020/GPC2012)**(1/8)-1
189	Yemen	1.45	(GPC2020/GPC2012)**(1/8)-1
190	Anguilla	1.40	(GPC2020/GPC2012)**(1/8)-1
191	Barbados	1.38	(GPC2020/GPC2012)**(1/8)-1
192	Swaziland	1.36	(GPC2020/GPC2012)**(1/8)-1

TABLE 5.22 GDP PER CAPITA GROWTH RATES, 2012-2020, FORECAST			
Rank	Country	GRPCRL	Source
193	Aruba	1.35	(GPC2020/GPC2012)**(1/8)-1
194	Guam	1.33	(GPC2020/GPC2012)**(1/8)-1
195	Congo, Rep	1.33	(GPC2020/GPC2012)**(1/8)-1
196	Sao Tome & P	1.32	(GPC2020/GPC2012)**(1/8)-1
197	Kiribati	1.29	(GPC2020/GPC2012)**(1/8)-1
198	France	1.28	(GPC2020/GPC2012)**(1/8)-1
199	Denmark	1.24	(GPC2020/GPC2012)**(1/8)-1
200	Paraguay	1.17	(GPC2020/GPC2012)**(1/8)-1
201	Tokelau	1.17	(GPC2020/GPC2012)**(1/8)-1
202	Switzerland	1.14	(GPC2020/GPC2012)**(1/8)-1
203	Italy	1.13	(GPC2020/GPC2012)**(1/8)-1
204	Kenya	1.09	(GPC2020/GPC2012)**(1/8)-1
205	Palau	1.08	(GPC2020/GPC2012)**(1/8)-1
206	Gabon	0.97	(GPC2020/GPC2012)**(1/8)-1
207	Venezuela	0.96	(GPC2020/GPC2012)**(1/8)-1
208	Eritrea	0.93	(GPC2020/GPC2012)**(1/8)-1
209	Syria	0.91	(GPC2020/GPC2012)**(1/8)-1
210	Cameroon	0.90	(GPC2020/GPC2012)**(1/8)-1
211	Niger	0.90	(GPC2020/GPC2012)**(1/8)-1
212	Guatemala	0.89	(GPC2020/GPC2012)**(1/8)-1
213	Micronesia	0.87	(GPC2020/GPC2012)**(1/8)-1
214	Vanuatu	0.81	(GPC2020/GPC2012)**(1/8)-1
215	Guinea-Biss	0.64	(GPC2020/GPC2012)**(1/8)-1
216	Guinea	0.64	(GPC2020/GPC2012)**(1/8)-1
217	UAE	0.60	(GPC2020/GPC2012)**(1/8)-1
218	Haiti	0.58	(GPC2020/GPC2012)**(1/8)-1
219	Malawi	0.57	(GPC2020/GPC2012)**(1/8)-1
220	Gambia	0.57	(GPC2020/GPC2012)**(1/8)-1
221	Korea, North	0.53	(GPC2020/GPC2012)**(1/8)-1
222	Senegal	0.52	(GPC2020/GPC2012)**(1/8)-1
223	Somalia	0.43	(GPC2020/GPC2012)**(1/8)-1
224	Fiji	0.39	(GPC2020/GPC2012)**(1/8)-1
225	Bahamas	0.38	(GPC2020/GPC2012)**(1/8)-1
226	Togo	0.35	(GPC2020/GPC2012)**(1/8)-1
227	Nauru	0.33	(GPC2020/GPC2012)**(1/8)-1
228	West Bank	0.31	(GPC2020/GPC2012)**(1/8)-1
229	N Mariana Is	0.31	(GPC2020/GPC2012)**(1/8)-1
230	Comoros	0.26	(GPC2020/GPC2012)**(1/8)-1
231	Gaza Strip	0.19	(GPC2020/GPC2012)**(1/8)-1
232	Ivory Coast	0.19	(GPC2020/GPC2012)**(1/8)-1
233	Burundi	0.17	(GPC2020/GPC2012)**(1/8)-1
234	Benin	0.16	(GPC2020/GPC2012)**(1/8)-1
235	Kuwait	0.10	(GPC2020/GPC2012)**(1/8)-1
236	Madagascar	0.04	(GPC2020/GPC2012)**(1/8)-1

Table 5.23 GDP Per Capita Growth Rates, 2020-2030, Forecast

Rank	Country	GRPCRL	Source
1	Guiana, Fr	2.70	(GPC2030/GPC2020)**(1/10)-1
2	Martinique	2.70	(GPC2030/GPC2020)**(1/10)-1
3	Bhutan	2.70	(GPC2030/GPC2020)**(1/10)-1
4	Liechtenstn	2.70	(GPC2030/GPC2020)**(1/10)-1
5	Guadeloupe	2.70	(GPC2030/GPC2020)**(1/10)-1
6	Turks & C Is	2.70	(GPC2030/GPC2020)**(1/10)-1
7	Isle of Man	2.69	(GPC2030/GPC2020)**(1/10)-1
8	New Caledon	2.69	(GPC2030/GPC2020)**(1/10)-1
9	Azerbaijan	2.69	(GPC2030/GPC2020)**(1/10)-1
10	Cape Verde	2.68	(GPC2030/GPC2020)**(1/10)-1
11	Cuba	2.68	(GPC2030/GPC2020)**(1/10)-1
12	Tuvalu	2.67	(GPC2030/GPC2020)**(1/10)-1
13	Niue	2.67	(GPC2030/GPC2020)**(1/10)-1
14	Marshall Is	2.67	(GPC2030/GPC2020)**(1/10)-1
15	Mongolia	2.67	(GPC2030/GPC2020)**(1/10)-1
16	Taiwan	2.66	(GPC2030/GPC2020)**(1/10)-1
17	San Marino	2.66	(GPC2030/GPC2020)**(1/10)-1
18	Georgia	2.66	(GPC2030/GPC2020)**(1/10)-1
19	Vietnam	2.65	(GPC2030/GPC2020)**(1/10)-1
20	Turkmenistan	2.65	(GPC2030/GPC2020)**(1/10)-1
21	Virgin I, Br	2.64	(GPC2030/GPC2020)**(1/10)-1
22	Gibraltar	2.64	(GPC2030/GPC2020)**(1/10)-1
23	Maldives	2.64	(GPC2030/GPC2020)**(1/10)-1
24	Korea, South	2.64	(GPC2030/GPC2020)**(1/10)-1
25	China	2.62	(GPC2030/GPC2020)**(1/10)-1
26	Belarus	2.62	(GPC2030/GPC2020)**(1/10)-1
27	Virgin I, US	2.61	(GPC2030/GPC2020)**(1/10)-1
28	India	2.61	(GPC2030/GPC2020)**(1/10)-1
29	Macao	2.61	(GPC2030/GPC2020)**(1/10)-1
30	Reunion	2.60	(GPC2030/GPC2020)**(1/10)-1
31	Bermuda	2.59	(GPC2030/GPC2020)**(1/10)-1
32	Lithuania	2.59	(GPC2030/GPC2020)**(1/10)-1
33	Saint Martin	2.59	(GPC2030/GPC2020)**(1/10)-1
34	Russia	2.59	(GPC2030/GPC2020)**(1/10)-1
35	Botswana	2.59	(GPC2030/GPC2020)**(1/10)-1
36	Angola	2.58	(GPC2030/GPC2020)**(1/10)-1
37	Laos	2.58	(GPC2030/GPC2020)**(1/10)-1
38	Qatar	2.58	(GPC2030/GPC2020)**(1/10)-1
39	Montserrat	2.58	(GPC2030/GPC2020)**(1/10)-1
40	Panama	2.58	(GPC2030/GPC2020)**(1/10)-1
41	Kazakhstan	2.57	(GPC2030/GPC2020)**(1/10)-1
42	Sri Lanka	2.57	(GPC2030/GPC2020)**(1/10)-1
43	Albania	2.57	(GPC2030/GPC2020)**(1/10)-1
44	Libya	2.55	(GPC2030/GPC2020)**(1/10)-1
45	Chad	2.55	(GPC2030/GPC2020)**(1/10)-1
46	Kosovo	2.54	(GPC2030/GPC2020)**(1/10)-1
47	Latvia	2.54	(GPC2030/GPC2020)**(1/10)-1
48	Jersey	2.54	(GPC2030/GPC2020)**(1/10)-1

Table 5.23 GDP Per Capita Growth Rates, 2020-2030, Forecast

Rank	Country	GRPCRL	Source
49	Singapore	2.53	(GPC2030/GPC2020)**(1/10)-1
50	Guernsey	2.53	(GPC2030/GPC2020)**(1/10)-1
51	Sint Maarten	2.52	(GPC2030/GPC2020)**(1/10)-1
52	Romania	2.51	(GPC2030/GPC2020)**(1/10)-1
53	W Sahara	2.49	(GPC2030/GPC2020)**(1/10)-1
54	Chile	2.49	(GPC2030/GPC2020)**(1/10)-1
55	Thailand	2.49	(GPC2030/GPC2020)**(1/10)-1
56	Hong Kong	2.49	(GPC2030/GPC2020)**(1/10)-1
57	Dominican R	2.48	(GPC2030/GPC2020)**(1/10)-1
58	Curacao	2.48	(GPC2030/GPC2020)**(1/10)-1
59	Turkey	2.47	(GPC2030/GPC2020)**(1/10)-1
60	Malaysia	2.47	(GPC2030/GPC2020)**(1/10)-1
61	Falkland Is	2.47	(GPC2030/GPC2020)**(1/10)-1
62	Mozambique	2.47	(GPC2030/GPC2020)**(1/10)-1
63	Bangladesh	2.46	(GPC2030/GPC2020)**(1/10)-1
64	Poland	2.46	(GPC2030/GPC2020)**(1/10)-1
65	Tajikistan	2.45	(GPC2030/GPC2020)**(1/10)-1
66	Cook Is	2.44	(GPC2030/GPC2020)**(1/10)-1
67	Equatorial G	2.44	(GPC2030/GPC2020)**(1/10)-1
68	Peru	2.43	(GPC2030/GPC2020)**(1/10)-1
69	Trinidad & T	2.43	(GPC2030/GPC2020)**(1/10)-1
70	Slovakia	2.42	(GPC2030/GPC2020)**(1/10)-1
71	Ethiopia	2.42	(GPC2030/GPC2020)**(1/10)-1
72	Jamaica	2.42	(GPC2030/GPC2020)**(1/10)-1
73	Fr Polynesia	2.41	(GPC2030/GPC2020)**(1/10)-1
74	Cambodia	2.39	(GPC2030/GPC2020)**(1/10)-1
75	Bulgaria	2.39	(GPC2030/GPC2020)**(1/10)-1
76	Mauritius	2.38	(GPC2030/GPC2020)**(1/10)-1
77	Argentina	2.37	(GPC2030/GPC2020)**(1/10)-1
78	Oman	2.36	(GPC2030/GPC2020)**(1/10)-1
79	Indonesia	2.36	(GPC2030/GPC2020)**(1/10)-1
80	St Pierre&M	2.35	(GPC2030/GPC2020)**(1/10)-1
81	Saudi Arabia	2.35	(GPC2030/GPC2020)**(1/10)-1
82	Ukraine	2.35	(GPC2030/GPC2020)**(1/10)-1
83	Estonia	2.34	(GPC2030/GPC2020)**(1/10)-1
84	Monaco	2.33	(GPC2030/GPC2020)**(1/10)-1
85	Mayotte	2.33	(GPC2030/GPC2020)**(1/10)-1
86	Afghanistan	2.33	(GPC2030/GPC2020)**(1/10)-1
87	Andorra	2.33	(GPC2030/GPC2020)**(1/10)-1
88	Rwanda	2.31	(GPC2030/GPC2020)**(1/10)-1
89	Seychelles	2.31	(GPC2030/GPC2020)**(1/10)-1
90	St Vincent	2.30	(GPC2030/GPC2020)**(1/10)-1
91	Tunisia	2.27	(GPC2030/GPC2020)**(1/10)-1
92	Wallis & Fut	2.26	(GPC2030/GPC2020)**(1/10)-1
93	Uganda	2.24	(GPC2030/GPC2020)**(1/10)-1
94	Bosnia	2.24	(GPC2030/GPC2020)**(1/10)-1
95	Montenegro	2.24	(GPC2030/GPC2020)**(1/10)-1
96	Serbia	2.24	(GPC2030/GPC2020)**(1/10)-1

Table 5.23 GDP Per Capita Growth Rates, 2020-2030, Forecast

Rank	Country	GRPCRL	Source
97	Iran	2.23	(GPC2030/GPC2020)**(1/10)-1
98	Greenland	2.23	(GPC2030/GPC2020)**(1/10)-1
99	Ireland	2.23	(GPC2030/GPC2020)**(1/10)-1
100	Uruguay	2.22	(GPC2030/GPC2020)**(1/10)-1
101	Suriname	2.20	(GPC2030/GPC2020)**(1/10)-1
102	Moldova	2.20	(GPC2030/GPC2020)**(1/10)-1
103	Malta	2.19	(GPC2030/GPC2020)**(1/10)-1
104	Lebanon	2.19	(GPC2030/GPC2020)**(1/10)-1
105	Morocco	2.17	(GPC2030/GPC2020)**(1/10)-1
106	St Kitts & N	2.17	(GPC2030/GPC2020)**(1/10)-1
107	Dominica	2.17	(GPC2030/GPC2020)**(1/10)-1
108	Lesotho	2.17	(GPC2030/GPC2020)**(1/10)-1
109	Egypt	2.16	(GPC2030/GPC2020)**(1/10)-1
110	Sierra Leone	2.15	(GPC2030/GPC2020)**(1/10)-1
111	Samoa, Amer	2.15	(GPC2030/GPC2020)**(1/10)-1
112	Tanzania	2.14	(GPC2030/GPC2020)**(1/10)-1
113	Costa Rica	2.14	(GPC2030/GPC2020)**(1/10)-1
114	Brunei	2.12	(GPC2030/GPC2020)**(1/10)-1
115	Grenada	2.12	(GPC2030/GPC2020)**(1/10)-1
116	Svalbard	2.11	(GPC2030/GPC2020)**(1/10)-1
117	Norway	2.11	(GPC2030/GPC2020)**(1/10)-1
118	Luxembourg	2.11	(GPC2030/GPC2020)**(1/10)-1
119	Liberia	2.11	(GPC2030/GPC2020)**(1/10)-1
120	Zimbabwe	2.11	(GPC2030/GPC2020)**(1/10)-1
121	Burkina Faso	2.09	(GPC2030/GPC2020)**(1/10)-1
122	Saint Helena	2.09	(GPC2030/GPC2020)**(1/10)-1
123	Nigeria	2.08	(GPC2030/GPC2020)**(1/10)-1
124	East Timor	2.07	(GPC2030/GPC2020)**(1/10)-1
125	Namibia	2.05	(GPC2030/GPC2020)**(1/10)-1
126	Colombia	2.03	(GPC2030/GPC2020)**(1/10)-1
127	Uzbekistan	2.03	(GPC2030/GPC2020)**(1/10)-1
128	Zambia	2.00	(GPC2030/GPC2020)**(1/10)-1
129	Bolivia	1.99	(GPC2030/GPC2020)**(1/10)-1
130	El Salvador	1.99	(GPC2030/GPC2020)**(1/10)-1
131	St Lucia	1.99	(GPC2030/GPC2020)**(1/10)-1
132	Ghana	1.99	(GPC2030/GPC2020)**(1/10)-1
133	Croatia	1.99	(GPC2030/GPC2020)**(1/10)-1
134	Jordan	1.98	(GPC2030/GPC2020)**(1/10)-1
135	Cyprus	1.98	(GPC2030/GPC2020)**(1/10)-1
136	Philippines	1.98	(GPC2030/GPC2020)**(1/10)-1
137	Israel	1.98	(GPC2030/GPC2020)**(1/10)-1
138	Nepal	1.97	(GPC2030/GPC2020)**(1/10)-1
139	Slovenia	1.97	(GPC2030/GPC2020)**(1/10)-1
140	Czechia	1.96	(GPC2030/GPC2020)**(1/10)-1
141	Sudan	1.95	(GPC2030/GPC2020)**(1/10)-1
142	South Sudan	1.95	(GPC2030/GPC2020)**(1/10)-1
143	Greece	1.93	(GPC2030/GPC2020)**(1/10)-1
144	Ecuador	1.93	(GPC2030/GPC2020)**(1/10)-1

TABLE 5.23 GDP PER CAPITA GROWTH RATES, 2020-2030, FORECAST

Rank	Country	GRPCRL	Source
145	Faroe Is	1.93	(GPC2030/GPC2020)**(1/10)-1
146	Pakistan	1.92	(GPC2030/GPC2020)**(1/10)-1
147	Macedonia	1.92	(GPC2030/GPC2020)**(1/10)-1
148	Armenia	1.91	(GPC2030/GPC2020)**(1/10)-1
149	Antigua & B	1.91	(GPC2030/GPC2020)**(1/10)-1
150	Guyana	1.91	(GPC2030/GPC2020)**(1/10)-1
151	Brazil	1.91	(GPC2030/GPC2020)**(1/10)-1
152	Australia	1.90	(GPC2030/GPC2020)**(1/10)-1
153	Austria	1.89	(GPC2030/GPC2020)**(1/10)-1
154	Belize	1.89	(GPC2030/GPC2020)**(1/10)-1
155	Puerto Rico	1.88	(GPC2030/GPC2020)**(1/10)-1
156	Iraq	1.87	(GPC2030/GPC2020)**(1/10)-1
157	Spain	1.87	(GPC2030/GPC2020)**(1/10)-1
158	Hungary	1.87	(GPC2030/GPC2020)**(1/10)-1
159	Germany	1.85	(GPC2030/GPC2020)**(1/10)-1
160	Nicaragua	1.85	(GPC2030/GPC2020)**(1/10)-1
161	Papua New G	1.85	(GPC2030/GPC2020)**(1/10)-1
162	Mauritania	1.82	(GPC2030/GPC2020)**(1/10)-1
163	Portugal	1.82	(GPC2030/GPC2020)**(1/10)-1
164	Finland	1.82	(GPC2030/GPC2020)**(1/10)-1
165	Mexico	1.80	(GPC2030/GPC2020)**(1/10)-1
166	Mali	1.80	(GPC2030/GPC2020)**(1/10)-1
167	CAR	1.80	(GPC2030/GPC2020)**(1/10)-1
168	Bahrain	1.79	(GPC2030/GPC2020)**(1/10)-1
169	Solomon Is	1.79	(GPC2030/GPC2020)**(1/10)-1
170	Sweden	1.78	(GPC2030/GPC2020)**(1/10)-1
171	Samoa	1.78	(GPC2030/GPC2020)**(1/10)-1
172	Cayman Is	1.76	(GPC2030/GPC2020)**(1/10)-1
173	Netherlands	1.74	(GPC2030/GPC2020)**(1/10)-1
174	Algeria	1.74	(GPC2030/GPC2020)**(1/10)-1
175	Honduras	1.73	(GPC2030/GPC2020)**(1/10)-1
176	Tonga	1.70	(GPC2030/GPC2020)**(1/10)-1
177	Kyrgyzstan	1.70	(GPC2030/GPC2020)**(1/10)-1
178	Japan	1.69	(GPC2030/GPC2020)**(1/10)-1
179	US	1.68	(GPC2030/GPC2020)**(1/10)-1
180	UK	1.67	(GPC2030/GPC2020)**(1/10)-1
181	New Zealand	1.67	(GPC2030/GPC2020)**(1/10)-1
182	Congo, Dem R	1.67	(GPC2030/GPC2020)**(1/10)-1
183	South Africa	1.65	(GPC2030/GPC2020)**(1/10)-1
184	Canada	1.63	(GPC2030/GPC2020)**(1/10)-1
185	Djibouti	1.63	(GPC2030/GPC2020)**(1/10)-1
186	Belgium	1.61	(GPC2030/GPC2020)**(1/10)-1
187	Burma	1.60	(GPC2030/GPC2020)**(1/10)-1
188	Iceland	1.60	(GPC2030/GPC2020)**(1/10)-1
189	Yemen	1.60	(GPC2030/GPC2020)**(1/10)-1
190	Anguilla	1.57	(GPC2030/GPC2020)**(1/10)-1
191	Barbados	1.55	(GPC2030/GPC2020)**(1/10)-1
192	Swaziland	1.54	(GPC2030/GPC2020)**(1/10)-1

Table 5.23 GDP Per Capita Growth Rates, 2020-2030, Forecast

Rank	Country	GRPCRL	Source
193	Aruba	1.53	(GPC2030/GPC2020)**(1/10)-1
194	Guam	1.52	(GPC2030/GPC2020)**(1/10)-1
195	Congo, Rep	1.52	(GPC2030/GPC2020)**(1/10)-1
196	Sao Tome & P	1.52	(GPC2030/GPC2020)**(1/10)-1
197	Kiribati	1.50	(GPC2030/GPC2020)**(1/10)-1
198	France	1.49	(GPC2030/GPC2020)**(1/10)-1
199	Denmark	1.47	(GPC2030/GPC2020)**(1/10)-1
200	Paraguay	1.42	(GPC2030/GPC2020)**(1/10)-1
201	Tokelau	1.42	(GPC2030/GPC2020)**(1/10)-1
202	Switzerland	1.40	(GPC2030/GPC2020)**(1/10)-1
203	Italy	1.39	(GPC2030/GPC2020)**(1/10)-1
204	Kenya	1.37	(GPC2030/GPC2020)**(1/10)-1
205	Palau	1.36	(GPC2030/GPC2020)**(1/10)-1
206	Gabon	1.28	(GPC2030/GPC2020)**(1/10)-1
207	Venezuela	1.27	(GPC2030/GPC2020)**(1/10)-1
208	Eritrea	1.25	(GPC2030/GPC2020)**(1/10)-1
209	Syria	1.23	(GPC2030/GPC2020)**(1/10)-1
210	Cameroon	1.23	(GPC2030/GPC2020)**(1/10)-1
211	Niger	1.23	(GPC2030/GPC2020)**(1/10)-1
212	Guatemala	1.22	(GPC2030/GPC2020)**(1/10)-1
213	Micronesia	1.20	(GPC2030/GPC2020)**(1/10)-1
214	Vanuatu	1.16	(GPC2030/GPC2020)**(1/10)-1
215	Guinea-Biss	1.02	(GPC2030/GPC2020)**(1/10)-1
216	Guinea	1.02	(GPC2030/GPC2020)**(1/10)-1
217	UAE	0.99	(GPC2030/GPC2020)**(1/10)-1
218	Haiti	0.98	(GPC2030/GPC2020)**(1/10)-1
219	Malawi	0.97	(GPC2030/GPC2020)**(1/10)-1
220	Gambia	0.97	(GPC2030/GPC2020)**(1/10)-1
221	Korea, North	0.94	(GPC2030/GPC2020)**(1/10)-1
222	Senegal	0.93	(GPC2030/GPC2020)**(1/10)-1
223	Somalia	0.85	(GPC2030/GPC2020)**(1/10)-1
224	Fiji	0.82	(GPC2030/GPC2020)**(1/10)-1
225	Bahamas	0.81	(GPC2030/GPC2020)**(1/10)-1
226	Togo	0.78	(GPC2030/GPC2020)**(1/10)-1
227	Nauru	0.76	(GPC2030/GPC2020)**(1/10)-1
228	West Bank	0.75	(GPC2030/GPC2020)**(1/10)-1
229	N Mariana Is	0.74	(GPC2030/GPC2020)**(1/10)-1
230	Comoros	0.70	(GPC2030/GPC2020)**(1/10)-1
231	Gaza Strip	0.64	(GPC2030/GPC2020)**(1/10)-1
232	Ivory Coast	0.63	(GPC2030/GPC2020)**(1/10)-1
233	Burundi	0.62	(GPC2030/GPC2020)**(1/10)-1
234	Benin	0.60	(GPC2030/GPC2020)**(1/10)-1
235	Kuwait	0.55	(GPC2030/GPC2020)**(1/10)-1
236	Madagascar	0.49	(GPC2030/GPC2020)**(1/10)-1

6. Gross Domestic Product Growth Rates by Rank

Table 6.1 GDP Growth Rates, 0001-1000

Rank	Country	GRRL	Source
1	Madagascar	0.57	(GDP1000/GDP0001)**(1/999)-1
2	Burundi	0.26	(GDP1000/GDP0001)**(1/999)-1
3	Zambia	0.22	(GDP1000/GDP0001)**(1/999)-1
4	Zimbabwe	0.22	(GDP1000/GDP0001)**(1/999)-1
5	Malawi	0.22	(GDP1000/GDP0001)**(1/999)-1
6	Mozambique	0.21	(GDP1000/GDP0001)**(1/999)-1
7	Poland	0.14	(GDP1000/GDP0001)**(1/999)-1
8	Swaziland	0.14	(GDP1000/GDP0001)**(1/999)-1
9	South Africa	0.14	(GDP1000/GDP0001)**(1/999)-1
10	UK	0.14	(GDP1000/GDP0001)**(1/999)-1
11	Lesotho	0.14	(GDP1000/GDP0001)**(1/999)-1
12	Japan	0.13	(GDP1000/GDP0001)**(1/999)-1
13	Ireland	0.13	(GDP1000/GDP0001)**(1/999)-1
14	Sierra Leone	0.12	(GDP1000/GDP0001)**(1/999)-1
15	Denmark	0.12	(GDP1000/GDP0001)**(1/999)-1
16	Estonia	0.12	(GDP1000/GDP0001)**(1/999)-1
17	Sweden	0.12	(GDP1000/GDP0001)**(1/999)-1
18	Ghana	0.12	(GDP1000/GDP0001)**(1/999)-1
19	Latvia	0.11	(GDP1000/GDP0001)**(1/999)-1
20	Norway	0.11	(GDP1000/GDP0001)**(1/999)-1
21	Lithuania	0.11	(GDP1000/GDP0001)**(1/999)-1
22	Morocco	0.11	(GDP1000/GDP0001)**(1/999)-1
23	Jamaica	0.11	(GDP1000/GDP0001)**(1/999)-1
24	Puerto Rico	0.11	(GDP1000/GDP0001)**(1/999)-1
25	Trinidad & T	0.11	(GDP1000/GDP0001)**(1/999)-1
26	Guinea	0.11	(GDP1000/GDP0001)**(1/999)-1
27	Cuba	0.11	(GDP1000/GDP0001)**(1/999)-1
28	Guinea-Biss	0.11	(GDP1000/GDP0001)**(1/999)-1
29	Russia	0.11	(GDP1000/GDP0001)**(1/999)-1
30	Guatemala	0.11	(GDP1000/GDP0001)**(1/999)-1
31	Mexico	0.11	(GDP1000/GDP0001)**(1/999)-1
32	Finland	0.11	(GDP1000/GDP0001)**(1/999)-1
33	Costa Rica	0.11	(GDP1000/GDP0001)**(1/999)-1
34	Bolivia	0.11	(GDP1000/GDP0001)**(1/999)-1
35	Panama	0.11	(GDP1000/GDP0001)**(1/999)-1
36	Moldova	0.11	(GDP1000/GDP0001)**(1/999)-1
37	Chile	0.11	(GDP1000/GDP0001)**(1/999)-1
38	Argentina	0.11	(GDP1000/GDP0001)**(1/999)-1
39	Uruguay	0.11	(GDP1000/GDP0001)**(1/999)-1
40	Ecuador	0.10	(GDP1000/GDP0001)**(1/999)-1
41	Brazil	0.10	(GDP1000/GDP0001)**(1/999)-1
42	Belarus	0.10	(GDP1000/GDP0001)**(1/999)-1
43	Peru	0.10	(GDP1000/GDP0001)**(1/999)-1
44	Venezuela	0.10	(GDP1000/GDP0001)**(1/999)-1
45	El Salvador	0.10	(GDP1000/GDP0001)**(1/999)-1

Table 6.1 GDP Growth Rates, 0001-1000			
Rank	Country	GRRL	Source
46	Haiti	0.10	(GDP1000/GDP0001)**(1/999)-1
47	Ukraine	0.10	(GDP1000/GDP0001)**(1/999)-1
48	Dominican R	0.10	(GDP1000/GDP0001)**(1/999)-1
49	Colombia	0.10	(GDP1000/GDP0001)**(1/999)-1
50	Somalia	0.10	(GDP1000/GDP0001)**(1/999)-1
51	Canada	0.10	(GDP1000/GDP0001)**(1/999)-1
52	Nicaragua	0.10	(GDP1000/GDP0001)**(1/999)-1
53	US	0.10	(GDP1000/GDP0001)**(1/999)-1
54	Paraguay	0.10	(GDP1000/GDP0001)**(1/999)-1
55	Honduras	0.10	(GDP1000/GDP0001)**(1/999)-1
56	Vietnam	0.10	(GDP1000/GDP0001)**(1/999)-1
57	Afghanistan	0.10	(GDP1000/GDP0001)**(1/999)-1
58	Burma	0.10	(GDP1000/GDP0001)**(1/999)-1
59	Singapore	0.10	(GDP1000/GDP0001)**(1/999)-1
60	Laos	0.10	(GDP1000/GDP0001)**(1/999)-1
61	Kazakhstan	0.10	(GDP1000/GDP0001)**(1/999)-1
62	Cambodia	0.10	(GDP1000/GDP0001)**(1/999)-1
63	Nepal	0.09	(GDP1000/GDP0001)**(1/999)-1
64	Eritrea	0.09	(GDP1000/GDP0001)**(1/999)-1
65	Mongolia	0.09	(GDP1000/GDP0001)**(1/999)-1
66	Ethiopia	0.09	(GDP1000/GDP0001)**(1/999)-1
67	Armenia	0.09	(GDP1000/GDP0001)**(1/999)-1
68	Georgia	0.09	(GDP1000/GDP0001)**(1/999)-1
69	Uzbekistan	0.09	(GDP1000/GDP0001)**(1/999)-1
70	Turkmenistan	0.09	(GDP1000/GDP0001)**(1/999)-1
71	Azerbaijan	0.08	(GDP1000/GDP0001)**(1/999)-1
72	Tajikistan	0.08	(GDP1000/GDP0001)**(1/999)-1
73	Kyrgyzstan	0.08	(GDP1000/GDP0001)**(1/999)-1
74	Sudan	0.08	(GDP1000/GDP0001)**(1/999)-1
75	South Sudan	0.07	(GDP1000/GDP0001)**(1/999)-1
76	Czechia	0.07	(GDP1000/GDP0001)**(1/999)-1
77	Slovenia	0.06	(GDP1000/GDP0001)**(1/999)-1
78	Slovakia	0.06	(GDP1000/GDP0001)**(1/999)-1
79	Namibia	0.06	(GDP1000/GDP0001)**(1/999)-1
80	Taiwan	0.06	(GDP1000/GDP0001)**(1/999)-1
81	Malaysia	0.06	(GDP1000/GDP0001)**(1/999)-1
82	Sri Lanka	0.06	(GDP1000/GDP0001)**(1/999)-1
83	Korea, North	0.06	(GDP1000/GDP0001)**(1/999)-1
84	Korea, South	0.06	(GDP1000/GDP0001)**(1/999)-1
85	Indonesia	0.06	(GDP1000/GDP0001)**(1/999)-1
86	Thailand	0.06	(GDP1000/GDP0001)**(1/999)-1
87	Philippines	0.06	(GDP1000/GDP0001)**(1/999)-1
88	Australia	0.06	(GDP1000/GDP0001)**(1/999)-1
89	New Zealand	0.06	(GDP1000/GDP0001)**(1/999)-1
90	Botswana	0.06	(GDP1000/GDP0001)**(1/999)-1
91	Croatia	0.06	(GDP1000/GDP0001)**(1/999)-1
92	Montenegro	0.05	(GDP1000/GDP0001)**(1/999)-1
93	Bosnia	0.05	(GDP1000/GDP0001)**(1/999)-1

TABLE 6.1 GDP GROWTH RATES, 0001-1000			
Rank	Country	GRRL	Source
94	Macedonia	0.05	(GDP1000/GDP0001)**(1/999)-1
95	Hungary	0.05	(GDP1000/GDP0001)**(1/999)-1
96	Bulgaria	0.04	(GDP1000/GDP0001)**(1/999)-1
97	Netherlands	0.04	(GDP1000/GDP0001)**(1/999)-1
98	Kosovo	0.04	(GDP1000/GDP0001)**(1/999)-1
99	Portugal	0.03	(GDP1000/GDP0001)**(1/999)-1
100	Austria	0.03	(GDP1000/GDP0001)**(1/999)-1
101	Albania	0.03	(GDP1000/GDP0001)**(1/999)-1
102	Belgium	0.02	(GDP1000/GDP0001)**(1/999)-1
104	Egypt	0.02	(GDP1000/GDP0001)**(1/999)-1
104	Libya	0.02	(GDP1000/GDP0001)**(1/999)-1
104	Tunisia	0.02	(GDP1000/GDP0001)**(1/999)-1
106	UAE	0.02	(GDP1000/GDP0001)**(1/999)-1
107	Israel	0.02	(GDP1000/GDP0001)**(1/999)-1
108	Oman	0.02	(GDP1000/GDP0001)**(1/999)-1
109	Yemen	0.02	(GDP1000/GDP0001)**(1/999)-1
110	Saudi Arabia	0.02	(GDP1000/GDP0001)**(1/999)-1
111	Turkey	0.02	(GDP1000/GDP0001)**(1/999)-1
112	Iran	0.02	(GDP1000/GDP0001)**(1/999)-1
113	Syria	0.02	(GDP1000/GDP0001)**(1/999)-1
114	Lebanon	0.02	(GDP1000/GDP0001)**(1/999)-1
115	Kuwait	0.02	(GDP1000/GDP0001)**(1/999)-1
116	Iraq	0.02	(GDP1000/GDP0001)**(1/999)-1
117	Bahrain	0.02	(GDP1000/GDP0001)**(1/999)-1
118	Jordan	0.02	(GDP1000/GDP0001)**(1/999)-1
119	Qatar	0.02	(GDP1000/GDP0001)**(1/999)-1
120	Germany	0.02	(GDP1000/GDP0001)**(1/999)-1
121	France	0.02	(GDP1000/GDP0001)**(1/999)-1
122	Serbia	0.01	(GDP1000/GDP0001)**(1/999)-1
123	Hong Kong	0.00	(GDP1000/GDP0001)**(1/999)-1
125.5	Algeria	0.00	(GDP1000/GDP0001)**(1/999)-1
125.5	Bangladesh	0.00	(GDP1000/GDP0001)**(1/999)-1
125.5	India	0.00	(GDP1000/GDP0001)**(1/999)-1
125.5	Pakistan	0.00	(GDP1000/GDP0001)**(1/999)-1
128	China	0.00	(GDP1000/GDP0001)**(1/999)-1
129	Switzerland	0.00	(GDP1000/GDP0001)**(1/999)-1
130	Spain	0.00	(GDP1000/GDP0001)**(1/999)-1
131	Romania	-0.01	(GDP1000/GDP0001)**(1/999)-1
132	Cyprus	-0.02	(GDP1000/GDP0001)**(1/999)-1
133	Greece	-0.09	(GDP1000/GDP0001)**(1/999)-1
134	Italy	-0.11	(GDP1000/GDP0001)**(1/999)-1

TABLE 6.2 GDP GROWTH RATES, 1000-1500			
Rank	Country	GRRL	Source
1	Finland	0.45	(GDP1500/GDP1000)**(1/500)-1
2	Belgium	0.40	(GDP1500/GDP1000)**(1/500)-1
3	Germany	0.35	(GDP1500/GDP1000)**(1/500)-1
4	Netherlands	0.35	(GDP1500/GDP1000)**(1/500)-1
5	Italy	0.33	(GDP1500/GDP1000)**(1/500)-1
6	Austria	0.31	(GDP1500/GDP1000)**(1/500)-1
7	Poland	0.31	(GDP1500/GDP1000)**(1/500)-1
8	Hungary	0.30	(GDP1500/GDP1000)**(1/500)-1
9	Madagascar	0.30	(GDP1500/GDP1000)**(1/500)-1
10	Estonia	0.29	(GDP1500/GDP1000)**(1/500)-1
11	Latvia	0.29	(GDP1500/GDP1000)**(1/500)-1
12	Lithuania	0.29	(GDP1500/GDP1000)**(1/500)-1
13	Mozambique	0.29	(GDP1500/GDP1000)**(1/500)-1
14	Romania	0.28	(GDP1500/GDP1000)**(1/500)-1
15	Russia	0.28	(GDP1500/GDP1000)**(1/500)-1
16	France	0.27	(GDP1500/GDP1000)**(1/500)-1
17	Moldova	0.27	(GDP1500/GDP1000)**(1/500)-1
18	Belarus	0.27	(GDP1500/GDP1000)**(1/500)-1
19	Ukraine	0.27	(GDP1500/GDP1000)**(1/500)-1
20	Czechia	0.24	(GDP1500/GDP1000)**(1/500)-1
21	Switzerland	0.24	(GDP1500/GDP1000)**(1/500)-1
22	Armenia	0.24	(GDP1500/GDP1000)**(1/500)-1
23	Georgia	0.24	(GDP1500/GDP1000)**(1/500)-1
24	Slovakia	0.24	(GDP1500/GDP1000)**(1/500)-1
25	Azerbaijan	0.23	(GDP1500/GDP1000)**(1/500)-1
26	UK	0.21	(GDP1500/GDP1000)**(1/500)-1
27	Ireland	0.19	(GDP1500/GDP1000)**(1/500)-1
28	Spain	0.18	(GDP1500/GDP1000)**(1/500)-1
29	Zambia	0.18	(GDP1500/GDP1000)**(1/500)-1
32	Namibia	0.18	(GDP1500/GDP1000)**(1/500)-1
32	Somalia	0.18	(GDP1500/GDP1000)**(1/500)-1
32	South Africa	0.18	(GDP1500/GDP1000)**(1/500)-1
32	Swaziland	0.18	(GDP1500/GDP1000)**(1/500)-1
32	Zimbabwe	0.18	(GDP1500/GDP1000)**(1/500)-1
35	Denmark	0.18	(GDP1500/GDP1000)**(1/500)-1
36	Japan	0.18	(GDP1500/GDP1000)**(1/500)-1
37	Portugal	0.17	(GDP1500/GDP1000)**(1/500)-1
38	Korea, South	0.17	(GDP1500/GDP1000)**(1/500)-1
39	Korea, North	0.17	(GDP1500/GDP1000)**(1/500)-1
40	Burundi	0.17	(GDP1500/GDP1000)**(1/500)-1
41	Lesotho	0.17	(GDP1500/GDP1000)**(1/500)-1
42	Botswana	0.17	(GDP1500/GDP1000)**(1/500)-1
43	Vietnam	0.17	(GDP1500/GDP1000)**(1/500)-1
44	Malawi	0.17	(GDP1500/GDP1000)**(1/500)-1
45	Afghanistan	0.17	(GDP1500/GDP1000)**(1/500)-1
46	Burma	0.17	(GDP1500/GDP1000)**(1/500)-1
47	Hong Kong	0.17	(GDP1500/GDP1000)**(1/500)-1

TABLE 6.2 GDP GROWTH RATES, 1000-1500			
Rank	Country	GRRL	Source
48	China	0.17	(GDP1500/GDP1000)**(1/500)-1
49	Singapore	0.17	(GDP1500/GDP1000)**(1/500)-1
50	Philippines	0.17	(GDP1500/GDP1000)**(1/500)-1
51	Thailand	0.17	(GDP1500/GDP1000)**(1/500)-1
52	Malaysia	0.17	(GDP1500/GDP1000)**(1/500)-1
53.5	Sri Lanka	0.17	(GDP1500/GDP1000)**(1/500)-1
53.5	Taiwan	0.17	(GDP1500/GDP1000)**(1/500)-1
55	Indonesia	0.17	(GDP1500/GDP1000)**(1/500)-1
56	Laos	0.17	(GDP1500/GDP1000)**(1/500)-1
57	Eritrea	0.17	(GDP1500/GDP1000)**(1/500)-1
58	Ethiopia	0.17	(GDP1500/GDP1000)**(1/500)-1
59	Iceland	0.16	(GDP1500/GDP1000)**(1/500)-1
60	Cambodia	0.16	(GDP1500/GDP1000)**(1/500)-1
61	Nepal	0.16	(GDP1500/GDP1000)**(1/500)-1
62	Mongolia	0.15	(GDP1500/GDP1000)**(1/500)-1
63	Mexico	0.15	(GDP1500/GDP1000)**(1/500)-1
64	Norway	0.15	(GDP1500/GDP1000)**(1/500)-1
65	Sierra Leone	0.14	(GDP1500/GDP1000)**(1/500)-1
66	US	0.14	(GDP1500/GDP1000)**(1/500)-1
67	Sweden	0.14	(GDP1500/GDP1000)**(1/500)-1
68	Kazakhstan	0.13	(GDP1500/GDP1000)**(1/500)-1
69	Canada	0.13	(GDP1500/GDP1000)**(1/500)-1
70	Ghana	0.13	(GDP1500/GDP1000)**(1/500)-1
71	Jamaica	0.13	(GDP1500/GDP1000)**(1/500)-1
72	Puerto Rico	0.13	(GDP1500/GDP1000)**(1/500)-1
73	Trinidad & T	0.13	(GDP1500/GDP1000)**(1/500)-1
74	Cuba	0.13	(GDP1500/GDP1000)**(1/500)-1
75	Slovenia	0.13	(GDP1500/GDP1000)**(1/500)-1
76	Guatemala	0.12	(GDP1500/GDP1000)**(1/500)-1
77	Costa Rica	0.12	(GDP1500/GDP1000)**(1/500)-1
78	Bolivia	0.12	(GDP1500/GDP1000)**(1/500)-1
79	Panama	0.12	(GDP1500/GDP1000)**(1/500)-1
80	Guinea	0.12	(GDP1500/GDP1000)**(1/500)-1
81	Argentina	0.12	(GDP1500/GDP1000)**(1/500)-1
82	Chile	0.12	(GDP1500/GDP1000)**(1/500)-1
83	Uruguay	0.12	(GDP1500/GDP1000)**(1/500)-1
84	Ecuador	0.12	(GDP1500/GDP1000)**(1/500)-1
85	Brazil	0.12	(GDP1500/GDP1000)**(1/500)-1
86	Guinea-Biss	0.12	(GDP1500/GDP1000)**(1/500)-1
87	Peru	0.12	(GDP1500/GDP1000)**(1/500)-1
88	Venezuela	0.12	(GDP1500/GDP1000)**(1/500)-1
89	El Salvador	0.12	(GDP1500/GDP1000)**(1/500)-1
90	Haiti	0.12	(GDP1500/GDP1000)**(1/500)-1
91	Bangladesh	0.12	(GDP1500/GDP1000)**(1/500)-1
92	Pakistan	0.12	(GDP1500/GDP1000)**(1/500)-1
93	India	0.12	(GDP1500/GDP1000)**(1/500)-1
94	Dominican R	0.12	(GDP1500/GDP1000)**(1/500)-1
95	Colombia	0.12	(GDP1500/GDP1000)**(1/500)-1

Table 6.2 GDP Growth Rates, 1000-1500

Rank	Country	GRRL	Source
96	Australia	0.12	(GDP1500/GDP1000)**(1/500)-1
97	Nicaragua	0.11	(GDP1500/GDP1000)**(1/500)-1
98	Paraguay	0.11	(GDP1500/GDP1000)**(1/500)-1
99	Uzbekistan	0.11	(GDP1500/GDP1000)**(1/500)-1
100	Honduras	0.11	(GDP1500/GDP1000)**(1/500)-1
101	Turkmenistan	0.11	(GDP1500/GDP1000)**(1/500)-1
102	Tajikistan	0.11	(GDP1500/GDP1000)**(1/500)-1
103	Kyrgyzstan	0.11	(GDP1500/GDP1000)**(1/500)-1
104	Croatia	0.11	(GDP1500/GDP1000)**(1/500)-1
105	New Zealand	0.11	(GDP1500/GDP1000)**(1/500)-1
106	Montenegro	0.10	(GDP1500/GDP1000)**(1/500)-1
107	South Sudan	0.10	(GDP1500/GDP1000)**(1/500)-1
108	Bosnia	0.09	(GDP1500/GDP1000)**(1/500)-1
109	Macedonia	0.09	(GDP1500/GDP1000)**(1/500)-1
110	Kosovo	0.09	(GDP1500/GDP1000)**(1/500)-1
111	Serbia	0.08	(GDP1500/GDP1000)**(1/500)-1
112	Bulgaria	0.07	(GDP1500/GDP1000)**(1/500)-1
113	Sudan	0.06	(GDP1500/GDP1000)**(1/500)-1
114	Albania	0.04	(GDP1500/GDP1000)**(1/500)-1
115	Libya	0.00	(GDP1500/GDP1000)**(1/500)-1
116	Greece	0.00	(GDP1500/GDP1000)**(1/500)-1
117	Jordan	-0.03	(GDP1500/GDP1000)**(1/500)-1
118	Syria	-0.03	(GDP1500/GDP1000)**(1/500)-1
119	Lebanon	-0.03	(GDP1500/GDP1000)**(1/500)-1
120	Bahrain	-0.03	(GDP1500/GDP1000)**(1/500)-1
121	Israel	-0.03	(GDP1500/GDP1000)**(1/500)-1
122	Kuwait	-0.03	(GDP1500/GDP1000)**(1/500)-1
123	Iraq	-0.03	(GDP1500/GDP1000)**(1/500)-1
124	Yemen	-0.03	(GDP1500/GDP1000)**(1/500)-1
125	Saudi Arabia	-0.03	(GDP1500/GDP1000)**(1/500)-1
126	Oman	-0.03	(GDP1500/GDP1000)**(1/500)-1
127	Iran	-0.03	(GDP1500/GDP1000)**(1/500)-1
128	Turkey	-0.03	(GDP1500/GDP1000)**(1/500)-1
129	UAE	-0.03	(GDP1500/GDP1000)**(1/500)-1
130	Qatar	-0.03	(GDP1500/GDP1000)**(1/500)-1
131	Tunisia	-0.04	(GDP1500/GDP1000)**(1/500)-1
132	Egypt	-0.05	(GDP1500/GDP1000)**(1/500)-1
133.5	Algeria	-0.06	(GDP1500/GDP1000)**(1/500)-1
133.5	Morocco	-0.06	(GDP1500/GDP1000)**(1/500)-1
135	Cyprus	-0.23	(GDP1500/GDP1000)**(1/500)-1

Table 6.3 GDP Growth Rates, 1500-1600			
Rank	Country	GRRL	Source
1	Netherlands	1.06	(GDP1600/GDP1500)**(1/100)-1
2	Taiwan	0.83	(GDP1600/GDP1500)**(1/100)-1
3	UK	0.76	(GDP1600/GDP1500)**(1/100)-1
4	Switzerland	0.60	(GDP1600/GDP1500)**(1/100)-1
5	Bulgaria	0.55	(GDP1600/GDP1500)**(1/100)-1
6	Cyprus	0.52	(GDP1600/GDP1500)**(1/100)-1
7	Greece	0.52	(GDP1600/GDP1500)**(1/100)-1
8	Czechia	0.51	(GDP1600/GDP1500)**(1/100)-1
9	Slovakia	0.51	(GDP1600/GDP1500)**(1/100)-1
10	Sweden	0.49	(GDP1600/GDP1500)**(1/100)-1
11	Philippines	0.48	(GDP1600/GDP1500)**(1/100)-1
12	Finland	0.46	(GDP1600/GDP1500)**(1/100)-1
13	Norway	0.46	(GDP1600/GDP1500)**(1/100)-1
14	Spain	0.45	(GDP1600/GDP1500)**(1/100)-1
15	China	0.44	(GDP1600/GDP1500)**(1/100)-1
16	Hong Kong	0.44	(GDP1600/GDP1500)**(1/100)-1
17	Germany	0.43	(GDP1600/GDP1500)**(1/100)-1
18.5	Algeria	0.41	(GDP1600/GDP1500)**(1/100)-1
18.5	Morocco	0.41	(GDP1600/GDP1500)**(1/100)-1
20	Austria	0.39	(GDP1600/GDP1500)**(1/100)-1
21	Ireland	0.38	(GDP1600/GDP1500)**(1/100)-1
22	France	0.36	(GDP1600/GDP1500)**(1/100)-1
23	Estonia	0.34	(GDP1600/GDP1500)**(1/100)-1
24	Slovenia	0.33	(GDP1600/GDP1500)**(1/100)-1
25	Belarus	0.32	(GDP1600/GDP1500)**(1/100)-1
26	Moldova	0.32	(GDP1600/GDP1500)**(1/100)-1
27	Lithuania	0.32	(GDP1600/GDP1500)**(1/100)-1
28	Ukraine	0.32	(GDP1600/GDP1500)**(1/100)-1
29	Latvia	0.32	(GDP1600/GDP1500)**(1/100)-1
30	Poland	0.32	(GDP1600/GDP1500)**(1/100)-1
31	Russia	0.32	(GDP1600/GDP1500)**(1/100)-1
32	Sierra Leone	0.30	(GDP1600/GDP1500)**(1/100)-1
33	Montenegro	0.30	(GDP1600/GDP1500)**(1/100)-1
34	Croatia	0.30	(GDP1600/GDP1500)**(1/100)-1
35	Serbia	0.30	(GDP1600/GDP1500)**(1/100)-1
36	Portugal	0.30	(GDP1600/GDP1500)**(1/100)-1
37	Ghana	0.29	(GDP1600/GDP1500)**(1/100)-1
38	Georgia	0.28	(GDP1600/GDP1500)**(1/100)-1
39	Armenia	0.28	(GDP1600/GDP1500)**(1/100)-1
40	Guinea	0.27	(GDP1600/GDP1500)**(1/100)-1
41	Mozambique	0.27	(GDP1600/GDP1500)**(1/100)-1
42	Guinea-Biss	0.27	(GDP1600/GDP1500)**(1/100)-1
43	Denmark	0.25	(GDP1600/GDP1500)**(1/100)-1
44	Iceland	0.25	(GDP1600/GDP1500)**(1/100)-1
45	Azerbaijan	0.25	(GDP1600/GDP1500)**(1/100)-1
46	Bosnia	0.25	(GDP1600/GDP1500)**(1/100)-1
47	Macedonia	0.24	(GDP1600/GDP1500)**(1/100)-1
48	Kosovo	0.24	(GDP1600/GDP1500)**(1/100)-1

Table 6.3 GDP Growth Rates, 1500-1600

Rank	Country	GRRL	Source
49	Belgium	0.24	(GDP1600/GDP1500)**(1/100)-1
50	Kazakhstan	0.23	(GDP1600/GDP1500)**(1/100)-1
51	Uzbekistan	0.23	(GDP1600/GDP1500)**(1/100)-1
52.5	Egypt	0.22	(GDP1600/GDP1500)**(1/100)-1
52.5	Tunisia	0.22	(GDP1600/GDP1500)**(1/100)-1
54	Japan	0.22	(GDP1600/GDP1500)**(1/100)-1
55	Italy	0.22	(GDP1600/GDP1500)**(1/100)-1
56	Korea, South	0.21	(GDP1600/GDP1500)**(1/100)-1
57	Korea, North	0.21	(GDP1600/GDP1500)**(1/100)-1
58	Pakistan	0.21	(GDP1600/GDP1500)**(1/100)-1
59	India	0.21	(GDP1600/GDP1500)**(1/100)-1
60	Bangladesh	0.21	(GDP1600/GDP1500)**(1/100)-1
61	Swaziland	0.20	(GDP1600/GDP1500)**(1/100)-1
62	South Africa	0.20	(GDP1600/GDP1500)**(1/100)-1
63	Nepal	0.19	(GDP1600/GDP1500)**(1/100)-1
64	Mongolia	0.19	(GDP1600/GDP1500)**(1/100)-1
65	Burundi	0.19	(GDP1600/GDP1500)**(1/100)-1
66	Lesotho	0.19	(GDP1600/GDP1500)**(1/100)-1
67	Turkmenistan	0.19	(GDP1600/GDP1500)**(1/100)-1
68	Madagascar	0.18	(GDP1600/GDP1500)**(1/100)-1
69	Tajikistan	0.18	(GDP1600/GDP1500)**(1/100)-1
70	Kyrgyzstan	0.18	(GDP1600/GDP1500)**(1/100)-1
71	Laos	0.17	(GDP1600/GDP1500)**(1/100)-1
72	Vietnam	0.17	(GDP1600/GDP1500)**(1/100)-1
73	Burma	0.17	(GDP1600/GDP1500)**(1/100)-1
74	Afghanistan	0.17	(GDP1600/GDP1500)**(1/100)-1
75	Cambodia	0.17	(GDP1600/GDP1500)**(1/100)-1
76	Malaysia	0.17	(GDP1600/GDP1500)**(1/100)-1
77	Singapore	0.17	(GDP1600/GDP1500)**(1/100)-1
78	Eritrea	0.15	(GDP1600/GDP1500)**(1/100)-1
79	Ethiopia	0.15	(GDP1600/GDP1500)**(1/100)-1
80	Zambia	0.15	(GDP1600/GDP1500)**(1/100)-1
81	Zimbabwe	0.15	(GDP1600/GDP1500)**(1/100)-1
82	Turkey	0.14	(GDP1600/GDP1500)**(1/100)-1
83	Malawi	0.13	(GDP1600/GDP1500)**(1/100)-1
84	Thailand	0.13	(GDP1600/GDP1500)**(1/100)-1
85	Hungary	0.12	(GDP1600/GDP1500)**(1/100)-1
86	Indonesia	0.11	(GDP1600/GDP1500)**(1/100)-1
87	Iran	0.11	(GDP1600/GDP1500)**(1/100)-1
88	Sri Lanka	0.11	(GDP1600/GDP1500)**(1/100)-1
89	Romania	0.10	(GDP1600/GDP1500)**(1/100)-1
90	South Sudan	0.09	(GDP1600/GDP1500)**(1/100)-1
91	Australia	0.06	(GDP1600/GDP1500)**(1/100)-1
92.5	Namibia	0.05	(GDP1600/GDP1500)**(1/100)-1
92.5	Somalia	0.05	(GDP1600/GDP1500)**(1/100)-1
94	Canada	0.05	(GDP1600/GDP1500)**(1/100)-1
95	Sudan	0.05	(GDP1600/GDP1500)**(1/100)-1
96	Albania	0.05	(GDP1600/GDP1500)**(1/100)-1

TABLE 6.3 GDP GROWTH RATES, 1500-1600

Rank	Country	GRRL	Source
97	New Zealand	0.04	(GDP1600/GDP1500)**(1/100)-1
98	Botswana	0.04	(GDP1600/GDP1500)**(1/100)-1
99	Uruguay	0.00	(GDP1600/GDP1500)**(1/100)-1
100	Iraq	0.00	(GDP1600/GDP1500)**(1/100)-1
104.5	Bahrain	0.00	(GDP1600/GDP1500)**(1/100)-1
104.5	Kuwait	0.00	(GDP1600/GDP1500)**(1/100)-1
104.5	Libya	0.00	(GDP1600/GDP1500)**(1/100)-1
104.5	Oman	0.00	(GDP1600/GDP1500)**(1/100)-1
104.5	Qatar	0.00	(GDP1600/GDP1500)**(1/100)-1
104.5	Saudi Arabia	0.00	(GDP1600/GDP1500)**(1/100)-1
104.5	UAE	0.00	(GDP1600/GDP1500)**(1/100)-1
104.5	Yemen	0.00	(GDP1600/GDP1500)**(1/100)-1
109	Lebanon	-0.03	(GDP1600/GDP1500)**(1/100)-1
110	Syria	-0.03	(GDP1600/GDP1500)**(1/100)-1
111	Jordan	-0.03	(GDP1600/GDP1500)**(1/100)-1
112	Israel	-0.03	(GDP1600/GDP1500)**(1/100)-1
113	Argentina	-0.16	(GDP1600/GDP1500)**(1/100)-1
114	Brazil	-0.17	(GDP1600/GDP1500)**(1/100)-1
115	US	-0.23	(GDP1600/GDP1500)**(1/100)-1
116	Chile	-0.34	(GDP1600/GDP1500)**(1/100)-1
117	Guatemala	-0.45	(GDP1600/GDP1500)**(1/100)-1
118	Costa Rica	-0.46	(GDP1600/GDP1500)**(1/100)-1
119	Bolivia	-0.46	(GDP1600/GDP1500)**(1/100)-1
120	Panama	-0.46	(GDP1600/GDP1500)**(1/100)-1
121	Ecuador	-0.46	(GDP1600/GDP1500)**(1/100)-1
122	Peru	-0.46	(GDP1600/GDP1500)**(1/100)-1
123	Venezuela	-0.46	(GDP1600/GDP1500)**(1/100)-1
124	El Salvador	-0.46	(GDP1600/GDP1500)**(1/100)-1
125	Colombia	-0.46	(GDP1600/GDP1500)**(1/100)-1
126	Nicaragua	-0.46	(GDP1600/GDP1500)**(1/100)-1
127	Paraguay	-0.46	(GDP1600/GDP1500)**(1/100)-1
128	Honduras	-0.47	(GDP1600/GDP1500)**(1/100)-1
129	Jamaica	-0.85	(GDP1600/GDP1500)**(1/100)-1
130	Puerto Rico	-0.85	(GDP1600/GDP1500)**(1/100)-1
131	Trinidad & T	-0.85	(GDP1600/GDP1500)**(1/100)-1
132	Cuba	-0.85	(GDP1600/GDP1500)**(1/100)-1
133	Haiti	-0.86	(GDP1600/GDP1500)**(1/100)-1
134	Dominican R	-0.86	(GDP1600/GDP1500)**(1/100)-1
135	Mexico	-1.03	(GDP1600/GDP1500)**(1/100)-1

Table 6.4 GDP Growth Rates, 1600-1700

Rank	Country	GRRL	Source
1	Jamaica	1.22	(GDP1700/GDP1600)**(1/100)-1
2	Trinidad & T	1.20	(GDP1700/GDP1600)**(1/100)-1
3	Puerto Rico	0.99	(GDP1700/GDP1600)**(1/100)-1
4	Cuba	0.99	(GDP1700/GDP1600)**(1/100)-1
5	Haiti	0.97	(GDP1700/GDP1600)**(1/100)-1
6	Dominican R	0.97	(GDP1700/GDP1600)**(1/100)-1
7	Mexico	0.82	(GDP1700/GDP1600)**(1/100)-1
8	Ireland	0.81	(GDP1700/GDP1600)**(1/100)-1
9	Taiwan	0.80	(GDP1700/GDP1600)**(1/100)-1
10	Portugal	0.70	(GDP1700/GDP1600)**(1/100)-1
11	Sweden	0.68	(GDP1700/GDP1600)**(1/100)-1
12	Netherlands	0.67	(GDP1700/GDP1600)**(1/100)-1
13	Uruguay	0.64	(GDP1700/GDP1600)**(1/100)-1
14	UK	0.58	(GDP1700/GDP1600)**(1/100)-1
15	Brazil	0.52	(GDP1700/GDP1600)**(1/100)-1
16	Argentina	0.48	(GDP1700/GDP1600)**(1/100)-1
17	Japan	0.47	(GDP1700/GDP1600)**(1/100)-1
18	Albania	0.46	(GDP1700/GDP1600)**(1/100)-1
19	Philippines	0.45	(GDP1700/GDP1600)**(1/100)-1
20	Estonia	0.40	(GDP1700/GDP1600)**(1/100)-1
21	Lesotho	0.40	(GDP1700/GDP1600)**(1/100)-1
22	Norway	0.39	(GDP1700/GDP1600)**(1/100)-1
23	Russia	0.39	(GDP1700/GDP1600)**(1/100)-1
24	Ukraine	0.39	(GDP1700/GDP1600)**(1/100)-1
25	Lithuania	0.39	(GDP1700/GDP1600)**(1/100)-1
26	Moldova	0.39	(GDP1700/GDP1600)**(1/100)-1
27	Latvia	0.39	(GDP1700/GDP1600)**(1/100)-1
28	Belarus	0.39	(GDP1700/GDP1600)**(1/100)-1
29	Belgium	0.38	(GDP1700/GDP1600)**(1/100)-1
30	South Africa	0.36	(GDP1700/GDP1600)**(1/100)-1
31	Swaziland	0.36	(GDP1700/GDP1600)**(1/100)-1
32	Switzerland	0.35	(GDP1700/GDP1600)**(1/100)-1
33	Romania	0.32	(GDP1700/GDP1600)**(1/100)-1
34	Sierra Leone	0.32	(GDP1700/GDP1600)**(1/100)-1
35	Ghana	0.30	(GDP1700/GDP1600)**(1/100)-1
36	Hungary	0.30	(GDP1700/GDP1600)**(1/100)-1
37	Chile	0.29	(GDP1700/GDP1600)**(1/100)-1
38	Guinea	0.29	(GDP1700/GDP1600)**(1/100)-1
39	Guinea-Biss	0.28	(GDP1700/GDP1600)**(1/100)-1
40	Poland	0.28	(GDP1700/GDP1600)**(1/100)-1
41	Armenia	0.25	(GDP1700/GDP1600)**(1/100)-1
42	Georgia	0.25	(GDP1700/GDP1600)**(1/100)-1
43	Iceland	0.25	(GDP1700/GDP1600)**(1/100)-1
44	Denmark	0.25	(GDP1700/GDP1600)**(1/100)-1
45	Azerbaijan	0.24	(GDP1700/GDP1600)**(1/100)-1
46	France	0.23	(GDP1700/GDP1600)**(1/100)-1
47	Madagascar	0.22	(GDP1700/GDP1600)**(1/100)-1

TABLE 6.4 GDP GROWTH RATES, 1600-1700			
Rank	Country	GRRL	Source
48	Uzbekistan	0.22	(GDP1700/GDP1600)**(1/100)-1
49	Turkmenistan	0.22	(GDP1700/GDP1600)**(1/100)-1
50	Kazakhstan	0.22	(GDP1700/GDP1600)**(1/100)-1
51	Korea, South	0.21	(GDP1700/GDP1600)**(1/100)-1
52	Korea, North	0.21	(GDP1700/GDP1600)**(1/100)-1
53	Bangladesh	0.20	(GDP1700/GDP1600)**(1/100)-1
54	India	0.20	(GDP1700/GDP1600)**(1/100)-1
55	Pakistan	0.20	(GDP1700/GDP1600)**(1/100)-1
56	Nepal	0.20	(GDP1700/GDP1600)**(1/100)-1
57	Mongolia	0.20	(GDP1700/GDP1600)**(1/100)-1
58	Guatemala	0.19	(GDP1700/GDP1600)**(1/100)-1
59	Costa Rica	0.19	(GDP1700/GDP1600)**(1/100)-1
60	Bolivia	0.19	(GDP1700/GDP1600)**(1/100)-1
61	Panama	0.19	(GDP1700/GDP1600)**(1/100)-1
62	Ecuador	0.18	(GDP1700/GDP1600)**(1/100)-1
63	Peru	0.18	(GDP1700/GDP1600)**(1/100)-1
64	Mozambique	0.18	(GDP1700/GDP1600)**(1/100)-1
65	Venezuela	0.18	(GDP1700/GDP1600)**(1/100)-1
66	El Salvador	0.18	(GDP1700/GDP1600)**(1/100)-1
67	Colombia	0.18	(GDP1700/GDP1600)**(1/100)-1
68	Nicaragua	0.18	(GDP1700/GDP1600)**(1/100)-1
69	Paraguay	0.18	(GDP1700/GDP1600)**(1/100)-1
70	Honduras	0.18	(GDP1700/GDP1600)**(1/100)-1
71	Burundi	0.17	(GDP1700/GDP1600)**(1/100)-1
72	Somalia	0.17	(GDP1700/GDP1600)**(1/100)-1
73	Austria	0.17	(GDP1700/GDP1600)**(1/100)-1
74	Finland	0.17	(GDP1700/GDP1600)**(1/100)-1
75	Tajikistan	0.17	(GDP1700/GDP1600)**(1/100)-1
76	Kyrgyzstan	0.17	(GDP1700/GDP1600)**(1/100)-1
77	Singapore	0.15	(GDP1700/GDP1600)**(1/100)-1
78	Malaysia	0.15	(GDP1700/GDP1600)**(1/100)-1
79	Laos	0.15	(GDP1700/GDP1600)**(1/100)-1
80	Vietnam	0.15	(GDP1700/GDP1600)**(1/100)-1
81	Burma	0.15	(GDP1700/GDP1600)**(1/100)-1
82	Afghanistan	0.15	(GDP1700/GDP1600)**(1/100)-1
83	Cambodia	0.15	(GDP1700/GDP1600)**(1/100)-1
84	Turkey	0.14	(GDP1700/GDP1600)**(1/100)-1
85	Eritrea	0.14	(GDP1700/GDP1600)**(1/100)-1
86	Ethiopia	0.14	(GDP1700/GDP1600)**(1/100)-1
87	Slovenia	0.12	(GDP1700/GDP1600)**(1/100)-1
88	Malawi	0.12	(GDP1700/GDP1600)**(1/100)-1
89	Indonesia	0.11	(GDP1700/GDP1600)**(1/100)-1
90	Iran	0.11	(GDP1700/GDP1600)**(1/100)-1
91	Thailand	0.11	(GDP1700/GDP1600)**(1/100)-1
92	Bulgaria	0.10	(GDP1700/GDP1600)**(1/100)-1
93	Slovakia	0.10	(GDP1700/GDP1600)**(1/100)-1
94	Serbia	0.10	(GDP1700/GDP1600)**(1/100)-1
95	Montenegro	0.10	(GDP1700/GDP1600)**(1/100)-1

Table 6.4 GDP Growth Rates, 1600-1700			
Rank	Country	GRRL	Source
96	Croatia	0.10	(GDP1700/GDP1600)**(1/100)-1
97	Czechia	0.10	(GDP1700/GDP1600)**(1/100)-1
98	Greece	0.09	(GDP1700/GDP1600)**(1/100)-1
99	Cyprus	0.09	(GDP1700/GDP1600)**(1/100)-1
100	South Sudan	0.09	(GDP1700/GDP1600)**(1/100)-1
101	Zambia	0.09	(GDP1700/GDP1600)**(1/100)-1
102	Zimbabwe	0.09	(GDP1700/GDP1600)**(1/100)-1
103	Sri Lanka	0.09	(GDP1700/GDP1600)**(1/100)-1
104	Germany	0.08	(GDP1700/GDP1600)**(1/100)-1
105	Spain	0.06	(GDP1700/GDP1600)**(1/100)-1
106	Australia	0.06	(GDP1700/GDP1600)**(1/100)-1
107	Bosnia	0.05	(GDP1700/GDP1600)**(1/100)-1
108	Sudan	0.05	(GDP1700/GDP1600)**(1/100)-1
109	New Zealand	0.05	(GDP1700/GDP1600)**(1/100)-1
110	Macedonia	0.05	(GDP1700/GDP1600)**(1/100)-1
111	Kosovo	0.05	(GDP1700/GDP1600)**(1/100)-1
112	Botswana	0.04	(GDP1700/GDP1600)**(1/100)-1
113	Italy	0.02	(GDP1700/GDP1600)**(1/100)-1
118.5	Bahrain	0.00	(GDP1700/GDP1600)**(1/100)-1
118.5	Iraq	0.00	(GDP1700/GDP1600)**(1/100)-1
118.5	Kuwait	0.00	(GDP1700/GDP1600)**(1/100)-1
118.5	Libya	0.00	(GDP1700/GDP1600)**(1/100)-1
118.5	Namibia	0.00	(GDP1700/GDP1600)**(1/100)-1
118.5	Oman	0.00	(GDP1700/GDP1600)**(1/100)-1
118.5	Qatar	0.00	(GDP1700/GDP1600)**(1/100)-1
118.5	Saudi Arabia	0.00	(GDP1700/GDP1600)**(1/100)-1
118.5	UAE	0.00	(GDP1700/GDP1600)**(1/100)-1
118.5	Yemen	0.00	(GDP1700/GDP1600)**(1/100)-1
124	Israel	-0.03	(GDP1700/GDP1600)**(1/100)-1
125	Jordan	-0.03	(GDP1700/GDP1600)**(1/100)-1
126	Syria	-0.03	(GDP1700/GDP1600)**(1/100)-1
127	Lebanon	-0.03	(GDP1700/GDP1600)**(1/100)-1
128	Egypt	-0.11	(GDP1700/GDP1600)**(1/100)-1
129	China	-0.15	(GDP1700/GDP1600)**(1/100)-1
130	Hong Kong	-0.15	(GDP1700/GDP1600)**(1/100)-1
131	Canada	-0.17	(GDP1700/GDP1600)**(1/100)-1
132	Tunisia	-0.22	(GDP1700/GDP1600)**(1/100)-1
133.5	Algeria	-0.25	(GDP1700/GDP1600)**(1/100)-1
133.5	Morocco	-0.25	(GDP1700/GDP1600)**(1/100)-1
135	US	-0.34	(GDP1700/GDP1600)**(1/100)-1

TABLE 6.5 GDP GROWTH RATES, 1700-1820			
Rank	Country	GRRL	Source
1	US	2.68	(GDP1820/GDP1700)**(1/120)-1
2	Canada	1.81	(GDP1820/GDP1700)**(1/120)-1
3	Trinidad & T	1.76	(GDP1820/GDP1700)**(1/120)-1
4	Haiti	1.54	(GDP1820/GDP1700)**(1/120)-1
5	Dominican R	1.54	(GDP1820/GDP1700)**(1/120)-1
6	Cuba	1.46	(GDP1820/GDP1700)**(1/120)-1
7	Jamaica	1.46	(GDP1820/GDP1700)**(1/120)-1
8	Puerto Rico	1.46	(GDP1820/GDP1700)**(1/120)-1
9	Brazil	1.36	(GDP1820/GDP1700)**(1/120)-1
10	Ireland	1.27	(GDP1820/GDP1700)**(1/120)-1
11	Finland	1.07	(GDP1820/GDP1700)**(1/120)-1
12	UK	1.02	(GDP1820/GDP1700)**(1/120)-1
13	Hungary	0.97	(GDP1820/GDP1700)**(1/120)-1
14	Romania	0.89	(GDP1820/GDP1700)**(1/120)-1
15	Hong Kong	0.85	(GDP1820/GDP1700)**(1/120)-1
16	China	0.85	(GDP1820/GDP1700)**(1/120)-1
17	Russia	0.78	(GDP1820/GDP1700)**(1/120)-1
18	Estonia	0.78	(GDP1820/GDP1700)**(1/120)-1
19	Sweden	0.77	(GDP1820/GDP1700)**(1/120)-1
20	Belarus	0.76	(GDP1820/GDP1700)**(1/120)-1
21	Lithuania	0.76	(GDP1820/GDP1700)**(1/120)-1
22	Ukraine	0.76	(GDP1820/GDP1700)**(1/120)-1
23	Moldova	0.76	(GDP1820/GDP1700)**(1/120)-1
24	Latvia	0.76	(GDP1820/GDP1700)**(1/120)-1
25	Uruguay	0.74	(GDP1820/GDP1700)**(1/120)-1
26	Norway	0.73	(GDP1820/GDP1700)**(1/120)-1
27	Slovenia	0.66	(GDP1820/GDP1700)**(1/120)-1
28	Serbia	0.63	(GDP1820/GDP1700)**(1/120)-1
29	Montenegro	0.63	(GDP1820/GDP1700)**(1/120)-1
30	Croatia	0.63	(GDP1820/GDP1700)**(1/120)-1
31	Switzerland	0.59	(GDP1820/GDP1700)**(1/120)-1
32	Taiwan	0.59	(GDP1820/GDP1700)**(1/120)-1
33	Denmark	0.59	(GDP1820/GDP1700)**(1/120)-1
34	Bosnia	0.59	(GDP1820/GDP1700)**(1/120)-1
35	Macedonia	0.58	(GDP1820/GDP1700)**(1/120)-1
36	Kosovo	0.58	(GDP1820/GDP1700)**(1/120)-1
37	Argentina	0.58	(GDP1820/GDP1700)**(1/120)-1
38	Belgium	0.57	(GDP1820/GDP1700)**(1/120)-1
39	Bulgaria	0.57	(GDP1820/GDP1700)**(1/120)-1
40	Germany	0.56	(GDP1820/GDP1700)**(1/120)-1
41	Poland	0.56	(GDP1820/GDP1700)**(1/120)-1
42	Mexico	0.56	(GDP1820/GDP1700)**(1/120)-1
43	Czechia	0.54	(GDP1820/GDP1700)**(1/120)-1
44	Slovakia	0.54	(GDP1820/GDP1700)**(1/120)-1
45	Thailand	0.53	(GDP1820/GDP1700)**(1/120)-1
46	Greece	0.52	(GDP1820/GDP1700)**(1/120)-1
47	Cyprus	0.52	(GDP1820/GDP1700)**(1/120)-1
48	Portugal	0.52	(GDP1820/GDP1700)**(1/120)-1

Table 6.5 GDP Growth Rates, 1700-1820

Rank	Country	GRRL	Source
49	France	0.50	(GDP1820/GDP1700)**(1/120)-1
50	Colombia	0.48	(GDP1820/GDP1700)**(1/120)-1
51	Philippines	0.47	(GDP1820/GDP1700)**(1/120)-1
52	Uzbekistan	0.44	(GDP1820/GDP1700)**(1/120)-1
53	Tajikistan	0.44	(GDP1820/GDP1700)**(1/120)-1
54	Kazakhstan	0.44	(GDP1820/GDP1700)**(1/120)-1
55	Turkmenistan	0.44	(GDP1820/GDP1700)**(1/120)-1
56	Madagascar	0.43	(GDP1820/GDP1700)**(1/120)-1
57	Austria	0.42	(GDP1820/GDP1700)**(1/120)-1
58	Spain	0.42	(GDP1820/GDP1700)**(1/120)-1
59	Lesotho	0.41	(GDP1820/GDP1700)**(1/120)-1
60	Kyrgyzstan	0.39	(GDP1820/GDP1700)**(1/120)-1
61	Chile	0.39	(GDP1820/GDP1700)**(1/120)-1
62	Armenia	0.37	(GDP1820/GDP1700)**(1/120)-1
63	Azerbaijan	0.37	(GDP1820/GDP1700)**(1/120)-1
64	Georgia	0.37	(GDP1820/GDP1700)**(1/120)-1
65	South Africa	0.37	(GDP1820/GDP1700)**(1/120)-1
66	Swaziland	0.37	(GDP1820/GDP1700)**(1/120)-1
67	Albania	0.37	(GDP1820/GDP1700)**(1/120)-1
68	Italy	0.36	(GDP1820/GDP1700)**(1/120)-1
69.5	Algeria	0.36	(GDP1820/GDP1700)**(1/120)-1
69.5	Morocco	0.36	(GDP1820/GDP1700)**(1/120)-1
71	Indonesia	0.31	(GDP1820/GDP1700)**(1/120)-1
72	Guatemala	0.29	(GDP1820/GDP1700)**(1/120)-1
73	Costa Rica	0.28	(GDP1820/GDP1700)**(1/120)-1
74	Bolivia	0.28	(GDP1820/GDP1700)**(1/120)-1
75	Panama	0.28	(GDP1820/GDP1700)**(1/120)-1
76	Ecuador	0.28	(GDP1820/GDP1700)**(1/120)-1
77	Peru	0.28	(GDP1820/GDP1700)**(1/120)-1
78	Mozambique	0.28	(GDP1820/GDP1700)**(1/120)-1
79	Venezuela	0.28	(GDP1820/GDP1700)**(1/120)-1
80	El Salvador	0.28	(GDP1820/GDP1700)**(1/120)-1
81	Nicaragua	0.27	(GDP1820/GDP1700)**(1/120)-1
82	Paraguay	0.27	(GDP1820/GDP1700)**(1/120)-1
83	Honduras	0.27	(GDP1820/GDP1700)**(1/120)-1
84	Burundi	0.26	(GDP1820/GDP1700)**(1/120)-1
85	Japan	0.25	(GDP1820/GDP1700)**(1/120)-1
86	Nepal	0.25	(GDP1820/GDP1700)**(1/120)-1
87	Mongolia	0.25	(GDP1820/GDP1700)**(1/120)-1
88	Eritrea	0.23	(GDP1820/GDP1700)**(1/120)-1
89	Ethiopia	0.23	(GDP1820/GDP1700)**(1/120)-1
90	Iran	0.21	(GDP1820/GDP1700)**(1/120)-1
91	Turkey	0.21	(GDP1820/GDP1700)**(1/120)-1
92	Cambodia	0.21	(GDP1820/GDP1700)**(1/120)-1
93	Afghanistan	0.21	(GDP1820/GDP1700)**(1/120)-1
94	Burma	0.21	(GDP1820/GDP1700)**(1/120)-1
95	Malaysia	0.21	(GDP1820/GDP1700)**(1/120)-1
96	Laos	0.21	(GDP1820/GDP1700)**(1/120)-1

Table 6.5 GDP Growth Rates, 1700-1820			
Rank	Country	GRRL	Source
97	Vietnam	0.21	(GDP1820/GDP1700)**(1/120)-1
98	Singapore	0.21	(GDP1820/GDP1700)**(1/120)-1
99	Sierra Leone	0.19	(GDP1820/GDP1700)**(1/120)-1
100	South Sudan	0.18	(GDP1820/GDP1700)**(1/120)-1
101	Ghana	0.17	(GDP1820/GDP1700)**(1/120)-1
102	Pakistan	0.17	(GDP1820/GDP1700)**(1/120)-1
103	India	0.17	(GDP1820/GDP1700)**(1/120)-1
104	Bangladesh	0.17	(GDP1820/GDP1700)**(1/120)-1
105	Guinea	0.16	(GDP1820/GDP1700)**(1/120)-1
106	Guinea-Biss	0.15	(GDP1820/GDP1700)**(1/120)-1
107	Malawi	0.13	(GDP1820/GDP1700)**(1/120)-1
108	Sudan	0.13	(GDP1820/GDP1700)**(1/120)-1
109	Iceland	0.13	(GDP1820/GDP1700)**(1/120)-1
110	Lebanon	0.13	(GDP1820/GDP1700)**(1/120)-1
111	Jordan	0.13	(GDP1820/GDP1700)**(1/120)-1
112	Syria	0.13	(GDP1820/GDP1700)**(1/120)-1
113	Israel	0.13	(GDP1820/GDP1700)**(1/120)-1
114	UAE	0.12	(GDP1820/GDP1700)**(1/120)-1
115	Qatar	0.12	(GDP1820/GDP1700)**(1/120)-1
116	Kuwait	0.12	(GDP1820/GDP1700)**(1/120)-1
117	Yemen	0.12	(GDP1820/GDP1700)**(1/120)-1
118	Saudi Arabia	0.12	(GDP1820/GDP1700)**(1/120)-1
119	Oman	0.12	(GDP1820/GDP1700)**(1/120)-1
120	Bahrain	0.12	(GDP1820/GDP1700)**(1/120)-1
121	Botswana	0.12	(GDP1820/GDP1700)**(1/120)-1
122	Korea, North	0.10	(GDP1820/GDP1700)**(1/120)-1
123	Korea, South	0.10	(GDP1820/GDP1700)**(1/120)-1
124	Iraq	0.10	(GDP1820/GDP1700)**(1/120)-1
125	Zimbabwe	0.10	(GDP1820/GDP1700)**(1/120)-1
126	Zambia	0.10	(GDP1820/GDP1700)**(1/120)-1
127	Namibia	0.08	(GDP1820/GDP1700)**(1/120)-1
128	Tunisia	0.07	(GDP1820/GDP1700)**(1/120)-1
129	Libya	0.06	(GDP1820/GDP1700)**(1/120)-1
130	New Zealand	0.05	(GDP1820/GDP1700)**(1/120)-1
131	Netherlands	0.05	(GDP1820/GDP1700)**(1/120)-1
132	Somalia	0.04	(GDP1820/GDP1700)**(1/120)-1
133	Sri Lanka	0.02	(GDP1820/GDP1700)**(1/120)-1
134	Egypt	-0.02	(GDP1820/GDP1700)**(1/120)-1
135	Australia	-0.19	(GDP1820/GDP1700)**(1/120)-1

TABLE 6.6 GDP GROWTH RATES, 1820-1870			
Rank	Country	GRRL	Source
1	Australia	7.28	(GDP1870/GDP1820)**(1/50)-1
2	Singapore	6.46	(GDP1870/GDP1820)**(1/50)-1
3	New Zealand	6.43	(GDP1870/GDP1820)**(1/50)-1
4	Canada	4.42	(GDP1870/GDP1820)**(1/50)-1
5	US	4.21	(GDP1870/GDP1820)**(1/50)-1
6	Hong Kong	3.97	(GDP1870/GDP1820)**(1/50)-1
7	Uruguay	3.78	(GDP1870/GDP1820)**(1/50)-1
8	Chile	3.14	(GDP1870/GDP1820)**(1/50)-1
9	South Africa	2.62	(GDP1870/GDP1820)**(1/50)-1
10	Sri Lanka	2.57	(GDP1870/GDP1820)**(1/50)-1
11	Argentina	2.50	(GDP1870/GDP1820)**(1/50)-1
12	Namibia	2.38	(GDP1870/GDP1820)**(1/50)-1
13	Honduras	2.27	(GDP1870/GDP1820)**(1/50)-1
14	Malaysia	2.27	(GDP1870/GDP1820)**(1/50)-1
15	Belgium	2.24	(GDP1870/GDP1820)**(1/50)-1
16	Swaziland	2.18	(GDP1870/GDP1820)**(1/50)-1
17	Venezuela	2.12	(GDP1870/GDP1820)**(1/50)-1
18	Dominican R	2.08	(GDP1870/GDP1820)**(1/50)-1
19	UK	2.05	(GDP1870/GDP1820)**(1/50)-1
20	Paraguay	2.04	(GDP1870/GDP1820)**(1/50)-1
21	Germany	2.00	(GDP1870/GDP1820)**(1/50)-1
22	Puerto Rico	1.98	(GDP1870/GDP1820)**(1/50)-1
23	Georgia	1.92	(GDP1870/GDP1820)**(1/50)-1
24	Azerbaijan	1.92	(GDP1870/GDP1820)**(1/50)-1
25	Armenia	1.92	(GDP1870/GDP1820)**(1/50)-1
26	Switzerland	1.91	(GDP1870/GDP1820)**(1/50)-1
27	Denmark	1.91	(GDP1870/GDP1820)**(1/50)-1
28	Philippines	1.84	(GDP1870/GDP1820)**(1/50)-1
29	Zimbabwe	1.81	(GDP1870/GDP1820)**(1/50)-1
30	Lesotho	1.79	(GDP1870/GDP1820)**(1/50)-1
31	Zambia	1.77	(GDP1870/GDP1820)**(1/50)-1
32	Brazil	1.77	(GDP1870/GDP1820)**(1/50)-1
33	Algeria	1.71	(GDP1870/GDP1820)**(1/50)-1
34	Netherlands	1.70	(GDP1870/GDP1820)**(1/50)-1
35	Norway	1.70	(GDP1870/GDP1820)**(1/50)-1
36	Iceland	1.66	(GDP1870/GDP1820)**(1/50)-1
37	Russia	1.64	(GDP1870/GDP1820)**(1/50)-1
38	Cuba	1.64	(GDP1870/GDP1820)**(1/50)-1
39	Mozambique	1.63	(GDP1870/GDP1820)**(1/50)-1
40	Sweden	1.62	(GDP1870/GDP1820)**(1/50)-1
41	Costa Rica	1.61	(GDP1870/GDP1820)**(1/50)-1
42	Moldova	1.61	(GDP1870/GDP1820)**(1/50)-1
43	Latvia	1.61	(GDP1870/GDP1820)**(1/50)-1
44	Estonia	1.61	(GDP1870/GDP1820)**(1/50)-1
45	Belarus	1.61	(GDP1870/GDP1820)**(1/50)-1
46	Lithuania	1.61	(GDP1870/GDP1820)**(1/50)-1
47	Ukraine	1.61	(GDP1870/GDP1820)**(1/50)-1

TABLE 6.6 GDP GROWTH RATES, 1820-1870			
Rank	Country	GRRL	Source
48	Finland	1.58	(GDP1870/GDP1820)**(1/50)-1
49	Cyprus	1.56	(GDP1870/GDP1820)**(1/50)-1
50	Greece	1.56	(GDP1870/GDP1820)**(1/50)-1
51	Eritrea	1.52	(GDP1870/GDP1820)**(1/50)-1
52	Ethiopia	1.52	(GDP1870/GDP1820)**(1/50)-1
53	Trinidad & T	1.51	(GDP1870/GDP1820)**(1/50)-1
54	Ecuador	1.47	(GDP1870/GDP1820)**(1/50)-1
55	Austria	1.45	(GDP1870/GDP1820)**(1/50)-1
56	Malawi	1.44	(GDP1870/GDP1820)**(1/50)-1
57	El Salvador	1.44	(GDP1870/GDP1820)**(1/50)-1
58	France	1.43	(GDP1870/GDP1820)**(1/50)-1
59	Colombia	1.43	(GDP1870/GDP1820)**(1/50)-1
60	Peru	1.42	(GDP1870/GDP1820)**(1/50)-1
61	Egypt	1.38	(GDP1870/GDP1820)**(1/50)-1
62	Tunisia	1.37	(GDP1870/GDP1820)**(1/50)-1
63	Somalia	1.36	(GDP1870/GDP1820)**(1/50)-1
64	Madagascar	1.36	(GDP1870/GDP1820)**(1/50)-1
65	Panama	1.30	(GDP1870/GDP1820)**(1/50)-1
66	Guatemala	1.25	(GDP1870/GDP1820)**(1/50)-1
67	Nicaragua	1.24	(GDP1870/GDP1820)**(1/50)-1
68	Italy	1.24	(GDP1870/GDP1820)**(1/50)-1
69	Kyrgyzstan	1.24	(GDP1870/GDP1820)**(1/50)-1
70	Kazakhstan	1.24	(GDP1870/GDP1820)**(1/50)-1
71	Turkmenistan	1.24	(GDP1870/GDP1820)**(1/50)-1
72	Tajikistan	1.24	(GDP1870/GDP1820)**(1/50)-1
73	Uzbekistan	1.23	(GDP1870/GDP1820)**(1/50)-1
74	Lebanon	1.23	(GDP1870/GDP1820)**(1/50)-1
75	Morocco	1.23	(GDP1870/GDP1820)**(1/50)-1
76	Czechia	1.20	(GDP1870/GDP1820)**(1/50)-1
77	Slovakia	1.20	(GDP1870/GDP1820)**(1/50)-1
78	Iraq	1.15	(GDP1870/GDP1820)**(1/50)-1
79	Botswana	1.14	(GDP1870/GDP1820)**(1/50)-1
80	Indonesia	1.10	(GDP1870/GDP1820)**(1/50)-1
81	Poland	1.07	(GDP1870/GDP1820)**(1/50)-1
82	Slovenia	1.05	(GDP1870/GDP1820)**(1/50)-1
83	Croatia	1.02	(GDP1870/GDP1820)**(1/50)-1
84	Montenegro	1.02	(GDP1870/GDP1820)**(1/50)-1
85	Serbia	1.02	(GDP1870/GDP1820)**(1/50)-1
86	Haiti	0.99	(GDP1870/GDP1820)**(1/50)-1
87	Bosnia	0.98	(GDP1870/GDP1820)**(1/50)-1
88	Macedonia	0.97	(GDP1870/GDP1820)**(1/50)-1
89	Kosovo	0.97	(GDP1870/GDP1820)**(1/50)-1
90	Libya	0.94	(GDP1870/GDP1820)**(1/50)-1
91	Spain	0.93	(GDP1870/GDP1820)**(1/50)-1
92	Israel	0.92	(GDP1870/GDP1820)**(1/50)-1
93	Iran	0.90	(GDP1870/GDP1820)**(1/50)-1
94	Laos	0.87	(GDP1870/GDP1820)**(1/50)-1
95	Ireland	0.87	(GDP1870/GDP1820)**(1/50)-1

Table 6.6 GDP Growth Rates, 1820-1870			
Rank	Country	GRRL	Source
96	Sierra Leone	0.87	(GDP1870/GDP1820)**(1/50)-1
97	Sudan	0.87	(GDP1870/GDP1820)**(1/50)-1
98	Vietnam	0.87	(GDP1870/GDP1820)**(1/50)-1
99	Syria	0.84	(GDP1870/GDP1820)**(1/50)-1
100	Guinea	0.83	(GDP1870/GDP1820)**(1/50)-1
101	Guinea-Biss	0.83	(GDP1870/GDP1820)**(1/50)-1
102	Hungary	0.83	(GDP1870/GDP1820)**(1/50)-1
103	Romania	0.83	(GDP1870/GDP1820)**(1/50)-1
104	Turkey	0.82	(GDP1870/GDP1820)**(1/50)-1
105	Jordan	0.81	(GDP1870/GDP1820)**(1/50)-1
106	Albania	0.75	(GDP1870/GDP1820)**(1/50)-1
107	Burundi	0.69	(GDP1870/GDP1820)**(1/50)-1
108	Bolivia	0.66	(GDP1870/GDP1820)**(1/50)-1
109	Portugal	0.66	(GDP1870/GDP1820)**(1/50)-1
110	Pakistan	0.65	(GDP1870/GDP1820)**(1/50)-1
111	Thailand	0.62	(GDP1870/GDP1820)**(1/50)-1
112	Bangladesh	0.54	(GDP1870/GDP1820)**(1/50)-1
113	India	0.48	(GDP1870/GDP1820)**(1/50)-1
114	Bulgaria	0.44	(GDP1870/GDP1820)**(1/50)-1
115	Mexico	0.44	(GDP1870/GDP1820)**(1/50)-1
116	Nepal	0.44	(GDP1870/GDP1820)**(1/50)-1
117	Afghanistan	0.42	(GDP1870/GDP1820)**(1/50)-1
118	Japan	0.40	(GDP1870/GDP1820)**(1/50)-1
119	South Sudan	0.39	(GDP1870/GDP1820)**(1/50)-1
120	Ghana	0.39	(GDP1870/GDP1820)**(1/50)-1
121	Burma	0.38	(GDP1870/GDP1820)**(1/50)-1
122	Oman	0.38	(GDP1870/GDP1820)**(1/50)-1
123	Taiwan	0.32	(GDP1870/GDP1820)**(1/50)-1
124	Saudi Arabia	0.31	(GDP1870/GDP1820)**(1/50)-1
125	Yemen	0.27	(GDP1870/GDP1820)**(1/50)-1
126	Mongolia	0.20	(GDP1870/GDP1820)**(1/50)-1
127	Cambodia	0.18	(GDP1870/GDP1820)**(1/50)-1
129.5	Bahrain	0.09	(GDP1870/GDP1820)**(1/50)-1
129.5	Kuwait	0.09	(GDP1870/GDP1820)**(1/50)-1
129.5	Qatar	0.09	(GDP1870/GDP1820)**(1/50)-1
129.5	UAE	0.09	(GDP1870/GDP1820)**(1/50)-1
132	Korea, North	0.09	(GDP1870/GDP1820)**(1/50)-1
133	Korea, South	0.09	(GDP1870/GDP1820)**(1/50)-1
134	Jamaica	-0.10	(GDP1870/GDP1820)**(1/50)-1
135	China	-0.37	(GDP1870/GDP1820)**(1/50)-1

Table 6.7 GDP Growth Rates, 1870-1880

Rank	Country	GRRL	Source
1	New Zealand	8.00	(GDP1880/GDP1870)**(1/10)-1
2	Argentina	5.80	(GDP1880/GDP1870)**(1/10)-1
3	Australia	4.95	(GDP1880/GDP1870)**(1/10)-1
4	Singapore	4.70	(GDP1880/GDP1870)**(1/10)-1
5	Costa Rica	4.43	(GDP1880/GDP1870)**(1/10)-1
6	Trinidad & T	4.42	(GDP1880/GDP1870)**(1/10)-1
7	Hong Kong	4.32	(GDP1880/GDP1870)**(1/10)-1
8	US	3.98	(GDP1880/GDP1870)**(1/10)-1
9	Malaysia	3.96	(GDP1880/GDP1870)**(1/10)-1
10	Burma	3.62	(GDP1880/GDP1870)**(1/10)-1
11	South Africa	3.57	(GDP1880/GDP1870)**(1/10)-1
12	Spain	3.56	(GDP1880/GDP1870)**(1/10)-1
13	Colombia	3.49	(GDP1880/GDP1870)**(1/10)-1
14	Chile	3.38	(GDP1880/GDP1870)**(1/10)-1
15	Mexico	3.28	(GDP1880/GDP1870)**(1/10)-1
16	Panama	3.14	(GDP1880/GDP1870)**(1/10)-1
17	Puerto Rico	3.12	(GDP1880/GDP1870)**(1/10)-1
18	Poland	3.09	(GDP1880/GDP1870)**(1/10)-1
19	Peru	3.01	(GDP1880/GDP1870)**(1/10)-1
20	Bulgaria	2.96	(GDP1880/GDP1870)**(1/10)-1
21	Nicaragua	2.96	(GDP1880/GDP1870)**(1/10)-1
22	Venezuela	2.93	(GDP1880/GDP1870)**(1/10)-1
23	Ecuador	2.87	(GDP1880/GDP1870)**(1/10)-1
24	Dominican R	2.61	(GDP1880/GDP1870)**(1/10)-1
25	Uruguay	2.59	(GDP1880/GDP1870)**(1/10)-1
26	Slovenia	2.54	(GDP1880/GDP1870)**(1/10)-1
27	Croatia	2.54	(GDP1880/GDP1870)**(1/10)-1
28	Serbia	2.54	(GDP1880/GDP1870)**(1/10)-1
29	Montenegro	2.54	(GDP1880/GDP1870)**(1/10)-1
30	Kosovo	2.54	(GDP1880/GDP1870)**(1/10)-1
31	Macedonia	2.54	(GDP1880/GDP1870)**(1/10)-1
32	Cuba	2.52	(GDP1880/GDP1870)**(1/10)-1
33	Greece	2.51	(GDP1880/GDP1870)**(1/10)-1
34	Cyprus	2.51	(GDP1880/GDP1870)**(1/10)-1
35	Albania	2.42	(GDP1880/GDP1870)**(1/10)-1
36	Brazil	2.42	(GDP1880/GDP1870)**(1/10)-1
37	Guatemala	2.40	(GDP1880/GDP1870)**(1/10)-1
38	Namibia	2.38	(GDP1880/GDP1870)**(1/10)-1
39	Israel	2.33	(GDP1880/GDP1870)**(1/10)-1
40	Egypt	2.33	(GDP1880/GDP1870)**(1/10)-1
41	Vietnam	2.29	(GDP1880/GDP1870)**(1/10)-1
42	Japan	2.27	(GDP1880/GDP1870)**(1/10)-1
43	Laos	2.23	(GDP1880/GDP1870)**(1/10)-1
44	Paraguay	2.23	(GDP1880/GDP1870)**(1/10)-1
45	Switzerland	2.23	(GDP1880/GDP1870)**(1/10)-1
46	Bolivia	2.20	(GDP1880/GDP1870)**(1/10)-1
47	Canada	2.19	(GDP1880/GDP1870)**(1/10)-1
48	Swaziland	2.18	(GDP1880/GDP1870)**(1/10)-1

Table 6.7 GDP Growth Rates, 1870-1880

Rank	Country	GRRL	Source
49	Belgium	2.16	(GDP1880/GDP1870)**(1/10)-1
50	Netherlands	2.15	(GDP1880/GDP1870)**(1/10)-1
51	Romania	2.09	(GDP1880/GDP1870)**(1/10)-1
52	Hungary	2.08	(GDP1880/GDP1870)**(1/10)-1
53	Algeria	2.07	(GDP1880/GDP1870)**(1/10)-1
54	Norway	2.06	(GDP1880/GDP1870)**(1/10)-1
55	Ukraine	2.03	(GDP1880/GDP1870)**(1/10)-1
56	Azerbaijan	2.03	(GDP1880/GDP1870)**(1/10)-1
57	Kyrgyzstan	2.03	(GDP1880/GDP1870)**(1/10)-1
58	Tajikistan	2.03	(GDP1880/GDP1870)**(1/10)-1
59	Russia	2.03	(GDP1880/GDP1870)**(1/10)-1
60	Latvia	2.03	(GDP1880/GDP1870)**(1/10)-1
61	Armenia	2.03	(GDP1880/GDP1870)**(1/10)-1
62	Turkmenistan	2.03	(GDP1880/GDP1870)**(1/10)-1
63	Lithuania	2.03	(GDP1880/GDP1870)**(1/10)-1
64	Moldova	2.03	(GDP1880/GDP1870)**(1/10)-1
65	Georgia	2.03	(GDP1880/GDP1870)**(1/10)-1
66	Uzbekistan	2.03	(GDP1880/GDP1870)**(1/10)-1
67	Estonia	2.03	(GDP1880/GDP1870)**(1/10)-1
68	Kazakhstan	2.03	(GDP1880/GDP1870)**(1/10)-1
69	Belarus	2.03	(GDP1880/GDP1870)**(1/10)-1
70	Austria	2.01	(GDP1880/GDP1870)**(1/10)-1
71	Sweden	1.99	(GDP1880/GDP1870)**(1/10)-1
72	Iraq	1.96	(GDP1880/GDP1870)**(1/10)-1
73	Tunisia	1.87	(GDP1880/GDP1870)**(1/10)-1
74	UK	1.86	(GDP1880/GDP1870)**(1/10)-1
75	Germany	1.84	(GDP1880/GDP1870)**(1/10)-1
76	Denmark	1.84	(GDP1880/GDP1870)**(1/10)-1
77	Lebanon	1.83	(GDP1880/GDP1870)**(1/10)-1
78	Czechia	1.81	(GDP1880/GDP1870)**(1/10)-1
79	Slovakia	1.81	(GDP1880/GDP1870)**(1/10)-1
80	Zimbabwe	1.81	(GDP1880/GDP1870)**(1/10)-1
81	Lesotho	1.79	(GDP1880/GDP1870)**(1/10)-1
82	Zambia	1.77	(GDP1880/GDP1870)**(1/10)-1
83	Finland	1.69	(GDP1880/GDP1870)**(1/10)-1
84	Syria	1.64	(GDP1880/GDP1870)**(1/10)-1
85	Mozambique	1.63	(GDP1880/GDP1870)**(1/10)-1
86	Philippines	1.60	(GDP1880/GDP1870)**(1/10)-1
87	Jamaica	1.58	(GDP1880/GDP1870)**(1/10)-1
88	El Salvador	1.55	(GDP1880/GDP1870)**(1/10)-1
89	Eritrea	1.52	(GDP1880/GDP1870)**(1/10)-1
90	Ethiopia	1.52	(GDP1880/GDP1870)**(1/10)-1
91	Afghanistan	1.52	(GDP1880/GDP1870)**(1/10)-1
92	Turkey	1.47	(GDP1880/GDP1870)**(1/10)-1
93	Malawi	1.44	(GDP1880/GDP1870)**(1/10)-1
94	Indonesia	1.41	(GDP1880/GDP1870)**(1/10)-1
95	Jordan	1.40	(GDP1880/GDP1870)**(1/10)-1
96	Iran	1.40	(GDP1880/GDP1870)**(1/10)-1

TABLE 6.7 GDP GROWTH RATES, 1870-1880			
Rank	Country	GRRL	Source
97	France	1.39	(GDP1880/GDP1870)**(1/10)-1
98	Somalia	1.36	(GDP1880/GDP1870)**(1/10)-1
99	Madagascar	1.36	(GDP1880/GDP1870)**(1/10)-1
100	Cambodia	1.30	(GDP1880/GDP1870)**(1/10)-1
101	Morocco	1.25	(GDP1880/GDP1870)**(1/10)-1
102	Iceland	1.22	(GDP1880/GDP1870)**(1/10)-1
103	Thailand	1.21	(GDP1880/GDP1870)**(1/10)-1
104	Botswana	1.14	(GDP1880/GDP1870)**(1/10)-1
105	Italy	1.11	(GDP1880/GDP1870)**(1/10)-1
106	Haiti	1.08	(GDP1880/GDP1870)**(1/10)-1
107	Taiwan	0.97	(GDP1880/GDP1870)**(1/10)-1
108	Libya	0.94	(GDP1880/GDP1870)**(1/10)-1
109	Korea, North	0.91	(GDP1880/GDP1870)**(1/10)-1
110	Sierra Leone	0.87	(GDP1880/GDP1870)**(1/10)-1
111	Sudan	0.87	(GDP1880/GDP1870)**(1/10)-1
112	Bosnia	0.86	(GDP1880/GDP1870)**(1/10)-1
113	Guinea	0.83	(GDP1880/GDP1870)**(1/10)-1
114	Guinea-Biss	0.83	(GDP1880/GDP1870)**(1/10)-1
115	Honduras	0.77	(GDP1880/GDP1870)**(1/10)-1
116	Korea, South	0.76	(GDP1880/GDP1870)**(1/10)-1
117	Burundi	0.70	(GDP1880/GDP1870)**(1/10)-1
118	Ghana	0.68	(GDP1880/GDP1870)**(1/10)-1
119	Qatar	0.66	(GDP1880/GDP1870)**(1/10)-1
120	Kuwait	0.66	(GDP1880/GDP1870)**(1/10)-1
121	Bahrain	0.66	(GDP1880/GDP1870)**(1/10)-1
122	UAE	0.66	(GDP1880/GDP1870)**(1/10)-1
123	Ireland	0.60	(GDP1880/GDP1870)**(1/10)-1
124	Sri Lanka	0.57	(GDP1880/GDP1870)**(1/10)-1
125	Pakistan	0.57	(GDP1880/GDP1870)**(1/10)-1
126	India	0.57	(GDP1880/GDP1870)**(1/10)-1
127	Nepal	0.55	(GDP1880/GDP1870)**(1/10)-1
128	Oman	0.54	(GDP1880/GDP1870)**(1/10)-1
129	Bangladesh	0.44	(GDP1880/GDP1870)**(1/10)-1
130	Yemen	0.44	(GDP1880/GDP1870)**(1/10)-1
131	Saudi Arabia	0.41	(GDP1880/GDP1870)**(1/10)-1
132	South Sudan	0.39	(GDP1880/GDP1870)**(1/10)-1
133	China	0.37	(GDP1880/GDP1870)**(1/10)-1
134	Portugal	0.34	(GDP1880/GDP1870)**(1/10)-1
135	Mongolia	0.24	(GDP1880/GDP1870)**(1/10)-1

Table 6.8 GDP Growth Rates, 1880-1890			
Rank	Country	GRRL	Source
1	Argentina	5.80	(GDP1890/GDP1880)**(1/10)-1
2	Singapore	4.70	(GDP1890/GDP1880)**(1/10)-1
3	Costa Rica	4.43	(GDP1890/GDP1880)**(1/10)-1
4	Trinidad & T	4.42	(GDP1890/GDP1880)**(1/10)-1
5	Hong Kong	4.32	(GDP1890/GDP1880)**(1/10)-1
6	Uruguay	4.31	(GDP1890/GDP1880)**(1/10)-1
7	US	3.98	(GDP1890/GDP1880)**(1/10)-1
8	Malaysia	3.96	(GDP1890/GDP1880)**(1/10)-1
9	Australia	3.94	(GDP1890/GDP1880)**(1/10)-1
10	Canada	3.92	(GDP1890/GDP1880)**(1/10)-1
11	Burma	3.62	(GDP1890/GDP1880)**(1/10)-1
12	South Africa	3.57	(GDP1890/GDP1880)**(1/10)-1
13	Colombia	3.49	(GDP1890/GDP1880)**(1/10)-1
14	Chile	3.38	(GDP1890/GDP1880)**(1/10)-1
15	Sri Lanka	3.36	(GDP1890/GDP1880)**(1/10)-1
16	Mexico	3.28	(GDP1890/GDP1880)**(1/10)-1
17	El Salvador	3.28	(GDP1890/GDP1880)**(1/10)-1
18	Finland	3.28	(GDP1890/GDP1880)**(1/10)-1
19	Panama	3.14	(GDP1890/GDP1880)**(1/10)-1
20	Puerto Rico	3.12	(GDP1890/GDP1880)**(1/10)-1
21	Poland	3.09	(GDP1890/GDP1880)**(1/10)-1
22	Switzerland	3.05	(GDP1890/GDP1880)**(1/10)-1
23	Peru	3.01	(GDP1890/GDP1880)**(1/10)-1
24	Bulgaria	2.96	(GDP1890/GDP1880)**(1/10)-1
25	Nicaragua	2.96	(GDP1890/GDP1880)**(1/10)-1
26	Germany	2.93	(GDP1890/GDP1880)**(1/10)-1
27	Ecuador	2.87	(GDP1890/GDP1880)**(1/10)-1
28	Portugal	2.65	(GDP1890/GDP1880)**(1/10)-1
29	Dominican R	2.61	(GDP1890/GDP1880)**(1/10)-1
30	Venezuela	2.56	(GDP1890/GDP1880)**(1/10)-1
31	Macedonia	2.54	(GDP1890/GDP1880)**(1/10)-1
32	Bosnia	2.54	(GDP1890/GDP1880)**(1/10)-1
33	Slovenia	2.54	(GDP1890/GDP1880)**(1/10)-1
34	Serbia	2.54	(GDP1890/GDP1880)**(1/10)-1
35	Croatia	2.54	(GDP1890/GDP1880)**(1/10)-1
36	Montenegro	2.54	(GDP1890/GDP1880)**(1/10)-1
37	Kosovo	2.54	(GDP1890/GDP1880)**(1/10)-1
38	Austria	2.52	(GDP1890/GDP1880)**(1/10)-1
39	Cuba	2.52	(GDP1890/GDP1880)**(1/10)-1
40	New Zealand	2.51	(GDP1890/GDP1880)**(1/10)-1
41	Greece	2.51	(GDP1890/GDP1880)**(1/10)-1
42	Cyprus	2.51	(GDP1890/GDP1880)**(1/10)-1
43	Honduras	2.49	(GDP1890/GDP1880)**(1/10)-1
44	Japan	2.47	(GDP1890/GDP1880)**(1/10)-1
45	Denmark	2.46	(GDP1890/GDP1880)**(1/10)-1
46	Brazil	2.43	(GDP1890/GDP1880)**(1/10)-1
47	Albania	2.42	(GDP1890/GDP1880)**(1/10)-1
48	Guatemala	2.40	(GDP1890/GDP1880)**(1/10)-1

TABLE 6.8 GDP GROWTH RATES, 1880-1890			
Rank	Country	GRRL	Source
49	Namibia	2.38	(GDP1890/GDP1880)**(1/10)-1
50	Israel	2.35	(GDP1890/GDP1880)**(1/10)-1
51	Vietnam	2.29	(GDP1890/GDP1880)**(1/10)-1
52	UK	2.24	(GDP1890/GDP1880)**(1/10)-1
53	Laos	2.23	(GDP1890/GDP1880)**(1/10)-1
54	Paraguay	2.23	(GDP1890/GDP1880)**(1/10)-1
55	Bolivia	2.20	(GDP1890/GDP1880)**(1/10)-1
56	Swaziland	2.18	(GDP1890/GDP1880)**(1/10)-1
57	Egypt	2.18	(GDP1890/GDP1880)**(1/10)-1
58	Belgium	2.10	(GDP1890/GDP1880)**(1/10)-1
59	Romania	2.09	(GDP1890/GDP1880)**(1/10)-1
60	Hungary	2.08	(GDP1890/GDP1880)**(1/10)-1
61	Netherlands	2.04	(GDP1890/GDP1880)**(1/10)-1
62	Belarus	2.03	(GDP1890/GDP1880)**(1/10)-1
63	Tajikistan	2.03	(GDP1890/GDP1880)**(1/10)-1
64	Lithuania	2.03	(GDP1890/GDP1880)**(1/10)-1
65	Turkmenistan	2.03	(GDP1890/GDP1880)**(1/10)-1
66	Kazakhstan	2.03	(GDP1890/GDP1880)**(1/10)-1
67	Russia	2.03	(GDP1890/GDP1880)**(1/10)-1
68	Latvia	2.03	(GDP1890/GDP1880)**(1/10)-1
69	Uzbekistan	2.03	(GDP1890/GDP1880)**(1/10)-1
70	Armenia	2.03	(GDP1890/GDP1880)**(1/10)-1
71	Kyrgyzstan	2.03	(GDP1890/GDP1880)**(1/10)-1
72	Georgia	2.03	(GDP1890/GDP1880)**(1/10)-1
73	Estonia	2.03	(GDP1890/GDP1880)**(1/10)-1
74	Moldova	2.03	(GDP1890/GDP1880)**(1/10)-1
75	Azerbaijan	2.03	(GDP1890/GDP1880)**(1/10)-1
76	Ukraine	2.03	(GDP1890/GDP1880)**(1/10)-1
77	Algeria	2.02	(GDP1890/GDP1880)**(1/10)-1
78	Iraq	1.96	(GDP1890/GDP1880)**(1/10)-1
79	Tunisia	1.87	(GDP1890/GDP1880)**(1/10)-1
80	Lebanon	1.83	(GDP1890/GDP1880)**(1/10)-1
81	Slovakia	1.81	(GDP1890/GDP1880)**(1/10)-1
82	Czechia	1.81	(GDP1890/GDP1880)**(1/10)-1
83	Zimbabwe	1.81	(GDP1890/GDP1880)**(1/10)-1
84	Lesotho	1.79	(GDP1890/GDP1880)**(1/10)-1
85	Zambia	1.77	(GDP1890/GDP1880)**(1/10)-1
86	Sweden	1.68	(GDP1890/GDP1880)**(1/10)-1
87	Syria	1.64	(GDP1890/GDP1880)**(1/10)-1
88	Mozambique	1.63	(GDP1890/GDP1880)**(1/10)-1
89	Philippines	1.60	(GDP1890/GDP1880)**(1/10)-1
90	Jamaica	1.58	(GDP1890/GDP1880)**(1/10)-1
91	Norway	1.53	(GDP1890/GDP1880)**(1/10)-1
92	Eritrea	1.52	(GDP1890/GDP1880)**(1/10)-1
93	Ethiopia	1.52	(GDP1890/GDP1880)**(1/10)-1
94	Afghanistan	1.52	(GDP1890/GDP1880)**(1/10)-1
95	Turkey	1.47	(GDP1890/GDP1880)**(1/10)-1
96	Malawi	1.44	(GDP1890/GDP1880)**(1/10)-1

Table 6.8 GDP Growth Rates, 1880-1890			
Rank	Country	GRRL	Source
97	Cambodia	1.43	(GDP1890/GDP1880)**(1/10)-1
98	Jordan	1.40	(GDP1890/GDP1880)**(1/10)-1
99	Iran	1.40	(GDP1890/GDP1880)**(1/10)-1
100	France	1.39	(GDP1890/GDP1880)**(1/10)-1
101	Somalia	1.36	(GDP1890/GDP1880)**(1/10)-1
102	Madagascar	1.36	(GDP1890/GDP1880)**(1/10)-1
103	Indonesia	1.32	(GDP1890/GDP1880)**(1/10)-1
104	Morocco	1.25	(GDP1890/GDP1880)**(1/10)-1
105	Pakistan	1.25	(GDP1890/GDP1880)**(1/10)-1
106	India	1.25	(GDP1890/GDP1880)**(1/10)-1
107	Italy	1.25	(GDP1890/GDP1880)**(1/10)-1
108	Iceland	1.22	(GDP1890/GDP1880)**(1/10)-1
109	Nepal	1.22	(GDP1890/GDP1880)**(1/10)-1
110	Thailand	1.21	(GDP1890/GDP1880)**(1/10)-1
111	Botswana	1.14	(GDP1890/GDP1880)**(1/10)-1
112	Bangladesh	1.11	(GDP1890/GDP1880)**(1/10)-1
113	Haiti	1.08	(GDP1890/GDP1880)**(1/10)-1
114	Taiwan	0.97	(GDP1890/GDP1880)**(1/10)-1
115	Libya	0.94	(GDP1890/GDP1880)**(1/10)-1
116	Korea, North	0.93	(GDP1890/GDP1880)**(1/10)-1
117	Sierra Leone	0.87	(GDP1890/GDP1880)**(1/10)-1
118	Sudan	0.87	(GDP1890/GDP1880)**(1/10)-1
119	Guinea	0.83	(GDP1890/GDP1880)**(1/10)-1
120	Guinea-Biss	0.83	(GDP1890/GDP1880)**(1/10)-1
121	Korea, South	0.76	(GDP1890/GDP1880)**(1/10)-1
122	Burundi	0.70	(GDP1890/GDP1880)**(1/10)-1
123	Ghana	0.68	(GDP1890/GDP1880)**(1/10)-1
124	UAE	0.66	(GDP1890/GDP1880)**(1/10)-1
125	Kuwait	0.66	(GDP1890/GDP1880)**(1/10)-1
126	Bahrain	0.66	(GDP1890/GDP1880)**(1/10)-1
127	Qatar	0.66	(GDP1890/GDP1880)**(1/10)-1
128	Oman	0.54	(GDP1890/GDP1880)**(1/10)-1
129	Yemen	0.44	(GDP1890/GDP1880)**(1/10)-1
130	China	0.42	(GDP1890/GDP1880)**(1/10)-1
131	Saudi Arabia	0.41	(GDP1890/GDP1880)**(1/10)-1
132	South Sudan	0.39	(GDP1890/GDP1880)**(1/10)-1
133	Spain	0.39	(GDP1890/GDP1880)**(1/10)-1
134	Mongolia	0.24	(GDP1890/GDP1880)**(1/10)-1
135	Ireland	0.03	(GDP1890/GDP1880)**(1/10)-1

TABLE 6.9 GDP GROWTH RATES, 1890-1900			
Rank	Country	GRRL	Source
1	Argentina	5.94	(GDP1900/GDP1890)**(1/10)-1
2	Hong Kong	5.16	(GDP1900/GDP1890)**(1/10)-1
3	Dominican R	4.80	(GDP1900/GDP1890)**(1/10)-1
4	Singapore	4.71	(GDP1900/GDP1890)**(1/10)-1
5	Mexico	4.60	(GDP1900/GDP1890)**(1/10)-1
6	Costa Rica	4.43	(GDP1900/GDP1890)**(1/10)-1
7	Trinidad & T	4.42	(GDP1900/GDP1890)**(1/10)-1
8	Malaysia	3.96	(GDP1900/GDP1890)**(1/10)-1
9	Burma	3.85	(GDP1900/GDP1890)**(1/10)-1
10	US	3.82	(GDP1900/GDP1890)**(1/10)-1
11	Sri Lanka	3.75	(GDP1900/GDP1890)**(1/10)-1
12	South Africa	3.57	(GDP1900/GDP1890)**(1/10)-1
13	Colombia	3.48	(GDP1900/GDP1890)**(1/10)-1
14	Germany	3.46	(GDP1900/GDP1890)**(1/10)-1
15	New Zealand	3.34	(GDP1900/GDP1890)**(1/10)-1
16	El Salvador	3.28	(GDP1900/GDP1890)**(1/10)-1
17	Uruguay	3.26	(GDP1900/GDP1890)**(1/10)-1
18	Panama	3.14	(GDP1900/GDP1890)**(1/10)-1
19	Puerto Rico	3.12	(GDP1900/GDP1890)**(1/10)-1
20	Canada	3.11	(GDP1900/GDP1890)**(1/10)-1
21	Finland	3.06	(GDP1900/GDP1890)**(1/10)-1
22	Switzerland	3.02	(GDP1900/GDP1890)**(1/10)-1
23	Peru	3.01	(GDP1900/GDP1890)**(1/10)-1
24	Chile	2.96	(GDP1900/GDP1890)**(1/10)-1
25	Nicaragua	2.96	(GDP1900/GDP1890)**(1/10)-1
26	Denmark	2.93	(GDP1900/GDP1890)**(1/10)-1
27	Ecuador	2.87	(GDP1900/GDP1890)**(1/10)-1
28	Iceland	2.82	(GDP1900/GDP1890)**(1/10)-1
29	Sweden	2.77	(GDP1900/GDP1890)**(1/10)-1
30	Austria	2.71	(GDP1900/GDP1890)**(1/10)-1
31	Poland	2.62	(GDP1900/GDP1890)**(1/10)-1
32	Venezuela	2.59	(GDP1900/GDP1890)**(1/10)-1
33	Japan	2.52	(GDP1900/GDP1890)**(1/10)-1
34	Cuba	2.52	(GDP1900/GDP1890)**(1/10)-1
35	Indonesia	2.50	(GDP1900/GDP1890)**(1/10)-1
36	Honduras	2.49	(GDP1900/GDP1890)**(1/10)-1
37	Cyprus	2.42	(GDP1900/GDP1890)**(1/10)-1
38	Greece	2.42	(GDP1900/GDP1890)**(1/10)-1
39	Guatemala	2.40	(GDP1900/GDP1890)**(1/10)-1
40	Egypt	2.39	(GDP1900/GDP1890)**(1/10)-1
41	Namibia	2.38	(GDP1900/GDP1890)**(1/10)-1
42	Albania	2.36	(GDP1900/GDP1890)**(1/10)-1
43	Israel	2.35	(GDP1900/GDP1890)**(1/10)-1
44	Bulgaria	2.30	(GDP1900/GDP1890)**(1/10)-1
45	Vietnam	2.29	(GDP1900/GDP1890)**(1/10)-1
46	Laos	2.23	(GDP1900/GDP1890)**(1/10)-1
47	Paraguay	2.23	(GDP1900/GDP1890)**(1/10)-1
48	Bolivia	2.20	(GDP1900/GDP1890)**(1/10)-1

Table 6.9 GDP Growth Rates, 1890-1900			
Rank	Country	GRRL	Source
49	Portugal	2.18	(GDP1900/GDP1890)**(1/10)-1
50	Swaziland	2.18	(GDP1900/GDP1890)**(1/10)-1
51	Czechia	2.17	(GDP1900/GDP1890)**(1/10)-1
52	Slovakia	2.17	(GDP1900/GDP1890)**(1/10)-1
53	Montenegro	2.12	(GDP1900/GDP1890)**(1/10)-1
54	Croatia	2.12	(GDP1900/GDP1890)**(1/10)-1
55	Serbia	2.12	(GDP1900/GDP1890)**(1/10)-1
56	Kosovo	2.12	(GDP1900/GDP1890)**(1/10)-1
57	Slovenia	2.12	(GDP1900/GDP1890)**(1/10)-1
58	Bosnia	2.12	(GDP1900/GDP1890)**(1/10)-1
59	Macedonia	2.12	(GDP1900/GDP1890)**(1/10)-1
60	Kyrgyzstan	2.10	(GDP1900/GDP1890)**(1/10)-1
61	Moldova	2.10	(GDP1900/GDP1890)**(1/10)-1
62	Armenia	2.10	(GDP1900/GDP1890)**(1/10)-1
63	Ukraine	2.10	(GDP1900/GDP1890)**(1/10)-1
64	Azerbaijan	2.10	(GDP1900/GDP1890)**(1/10)-1
65	Lithuania	2.10	(GDP1900/GDP1890)**(1/10)-1
66	Estonia	2.10	(GDP1900/GDP1890)**(1/10)-1
67	Latvia	2.10	(GDP1900/GDP1890)**(1/10)-1
68	Turkmenistan	2.10	(GDP1900/GDP1890)**(1/10)-1
69	Georgia	2.10	(GDP1900/GDP1890)**(1/10)-1
70	Russia	2.10	(GDP1900/GDP1890)**(1/10)-1
71	Uzbekistan	2.10	(GDP1900/GDP1890)**(1/10)-1
72	Tajikistan	2.10	(GDP1900/GDP1890)**(1/10)-1
73	Kazakhstan	2.10	(GDP1900/GDP1890)**(1/10)-1
74	Belarus	2.10	(GDP1900/GDP1890)**(1/10)-1
75	UK	2.09	(GDP1900/GDP1890)**(1/10)-1
76	Hungary	2.08	(GDP1900/GDP1890)**(1/10)-1
77	France	2.08	(GDP1900/GDP1890)**(1/10)-1
78	Taiwan	2.03	(GDP1900/GDP1890)**(1/10)-1
79	Algeria	2.02	(GDP1900/GDP1890)**(1/10)-1
80	Norway	1.99	(GDP1900/GDP1890)**(1/10)-1
81	Iraq	1.96	(GDP1900/GDP1890)**(1/10)-1
82	Romania	1.88	(GDP1900/GDP1890)**(1/10)-1
83	Tunisia	1.87	(GDP1900/GDP1890)**(1/10)-1
84	Belgium	1.84	(GDP1900/GDP1890)**(1/10)-1
85	Lebanon	1.83	(GDP1900/GDP1890)**(1/10)-1
86	Zimbabwe	1.81	(GDP1900/GDP1890)**(1/10)-1
87	Lesotho	1.79	(GDP1900/GDP1890)**(1/10)-1
88	Zambia	1.77	(GDP1900/GDP1890)**(1/10)-1
89	Ghana	1.73	(GDP1900/GDP1890)**(1/10)-1
90	Syria	1.64	(GDP1900/GDP1890)**(1/10)-1
91	Mozambique	1.63	(GDP1900/GDP1890)**(1/10)-1
92	Philippines	1.60	(GDP1900/GDP1890)**(1/10)-1
93	Jamaica	1.58	(GDP1900/GDP1890)**(1/10)-1
94	Netherlands	1.57	(GDP1900/GDP1890)**(1/10)-1
95	Eritrea	1.52	(GDP1900/GDP1890)**(1/10)-1
96	Ethiopia	1.52	(GDP1900/GDP1890)**(1/10)-1

Table 6.9 GDP Growth Rates, 1890-1900			
Rank	Country	GRRL	Source
97	Afghanistan	1.52	(GDP1900/GDP1890)**(1/10)-1
98	Turkey	1.47	(GDP1900/GDP1890)**(1/10)-1
99	Malawi	1.44	(GDP1900/GDP1890)**(1/10)-1
100	Cambodia	1.43	(GDP1900/GDP1890)**(1/10)-1
101	Spain	1.41	(GDP1900/GDP1890)**(1/10)-1
102	Jordan	1.40	(GDP1900/GDP1890)**(1/10)-1
103	Iran	1.40	(GDP1900/GDP1890)**(1/10)-1
104	Somalia	1.36	(GDP1900/GDP1890)**(1/10)-1
105	Madagascar	1.36	(GDP1900/GDP1890)**(1/10)-1
106	Italy	1.30	(GDP1900/GDP1890)**(1/10)-1
107	Morocco	1.25	(GDP1900/GDP1890)**(1/10)-1
108	Thailand	1.24	(GDP1900/GDP1890)**(1/10)-1
109	Botswana	1.14	(GDP1900/GDP1890)**(1/10)-1
110	Haiti	1.08	(GDP1900/GDP1890)**(1/10)-1
111	Libya	0.94	(GDP1900/GDP1890)**(1/10)-1
112	Nepal	0.89	(GDP1900/GDP1890)**(1/10)-1
113	Korea, North	0.88	(GDP1900/GDP1890)**(1/10)-1
114	Sierra Leone	0.87	(GDP1900/GDP1890)**(1/10)-1
115	Sudan	0.87	(GDP1900/GDP1890)**(1/10)-1
116	Guinea	0.83	(GDP1900/GDP1890)**(1/10)-1
117	Guinea-Biss	0.83	(GDP1900/GDP1890)**(1/10)-1
118	Australia	0.81	(GDP1900/GDP1890)**(1/10)-1
119	Brazil	0.79	(GDP1900/GDP1890)**(1/10)-1
120	Korea, South	0.76	(GDP1900/GDP1890)**(1/10)-1
121	Burundi	0.70	(GDP1900/GDP1890)**(1/10)-1
122	Bahrain	0.66	(GDP1900/GDP1890)**(1/10)-1
123	Kuwait	0.66	(GDP1900/GDP1890)**(1/10)-1
124	UAE	0.66	(GDP1900/GDP1890)**(1/10)-1
125	Qatar	0.66	(GDP1900/GDP1890)**(1/10)-1
126	China	0.61	(GDP1900/GDP1890)**(1/10)-1
127	Pakistan	0.58	(GDP1900/GDP1890)**(1/10)-1
128	Oman	0.54	(GDP1900/GDP1890)**(1/10)-1
129	Ireland	0.47	(GDP1900/GDP1890)**(1/10)-1
130	Bangladesh	0.45	(GDP1900/GDP1890)**(1/10)-1
131	Yemen	0.44	(GDP1900/GDP1890)**(1/10)-1
132	India	0.42	(GDP1900/GDP1890)**(1/10)-1
133	Saudi Arabia	0.41	(GDP1900/GDP1890)**(1/10)-1
134	South Sudan	0.39	(GDP1900/GDP1890)**(1/10)-1
135	Mongolia	0.24	(GDP1900/GDP1890)**(1/10)-1

TABLE 6.10 GDP GROWTH RATES, 1900-1913

Rank	Country	GRRL	Source
1	Argentina	6.42	(GDP1913/GDP1900)**(1/13)-1
2	Canada	6.25	(GDP1913/GDP1900)**(1/13)-1
3	Philippines	5.25	(GDP1913/GDP1900)**(1/13)-1
4	Hong Kong	5.16	(GDP1913/GDP1900)**(1/13)-1
5	Uruguay	5.14	(GDP1913/GDP1900)**(1/13)-1
6	Cuba	4.81	(GDP1913/GDP1900)**(1/13)-1
7	Singapore	4.70	(GDP1913/GDP1900)**(1/13)-1
8	Paraguay	4.14	(GDP1913/GDP1900)**(1/13)-1
9	Ghana	4.14	(GDP1913/GDP1900)**(1/13)-1
10	New Zealand	4.01	(GDP1913/GDP1900)**(1/13)-1
11	Panama	3.98	(GDP1913/GDP1900)**(1/13)-1
12	Honduras	3.96	(GDP1913/GDP1900)**(1/13)-1
13	Australia	3.96	(GDP1913/GDP1900)**(1/13)-1
14	US	3.95	(GDP1913/GDP1900)**(1/13)-1
15	El Salvador	3.94	(GDP1913/GDP1900)**(1/13)-1
16	Colombia	3.93	(GDP1913/GDP1900)**(1/13)-1
17	Trinidad & T	3.92	(GDP1913/GDP1900)**(1/13)-1
18	Malaysia	3.85	(GDP1913/GDP1900)**(1/13)-1
19	Italy	3.63	(GDP1913/GDP1900)**(1/13)-1
20	South Africa	3.57	(GDP1913/GDP1900)**(1/13)-1
21	Brazil	3.55	(GDP1913/GDP1900)**(1/13)-1
22	Costa Rica	3.55	(GDP1913/GDP1900)**(1/13)-1
23	Chile	3.53	(GDP1913/GDP1900)**(1/13)-1
24	Puerto Rico	3.41	(GDP1913/GDP1900)**(1/13)-1
25	Haiti	3.29	(GDP1913/GDP1900)**(1/13)-1
26	Venezuela	3.27	(GDP1913/GDP1900)**(1/13)-1
27	Nicaragua	3.27	(GDP1913/GDP1900)**(1/13)-1
28	Ecuador	3.25	(GDP1913/GDP1900)**(1/13)-1
29	Denmark	3.22	(GDP1913/GDP1900)**(1/13)-1
30	Turkmenistan	3.22	(GDP1913/GDP1900)**(1/13)-1
31	Belarus	3.22	(GDP1913/GDP1900)**(1/13)-1
32	Azerbaijan	3.22	(GDP1913/GDP1900)**(1/13)-1
33	Estonia	3.22	(GDP1913/GDP1900)**(1/13)-1
34	Georgia	3.22	(GDP1913/GDP1900)**(1/13)-1
35	Kazakhstan	3.22	(GDP1913/GDP1900)**(1/13)-1
36	Ukraine	3.22	(GDP1913/GDP1900)**(1/13)-1
37	Armenia	3.22	(GDP1913/GDP1900)**(1/13)-1
38	Latvia	3.22	(GDP1913/GDP1900)**(1/13)-1
39	Uzbekistan	3.22	(GDP1913/GDP1900)**(1/13)-1
40	Russia	3.22	(GDP1913/GDP1900)**(1/13)-1
41	Lithuania	3.22	(GDP1913/GDP1900)**(1/13)-1
42	Moldova	3.22	(GDP1913/GDP1900)**(1/13)-1
43	Tajikistan	3.22	(GDP1913/GDP1900)**(1/13)-1
44	Kyrgyzstan	3.22	(GDP1913/GDP1900)**(1/13)-1
45	Bulgaria	3.06	(GDP1913/GDP1900)**(1/13)-1
46	Dominican R	3.02	(GDP1913/GDP1900)**(1/13)-1
47	Germany	2.96	(GDP1913/GDP1900)**(1/13)-1
48	Peru	2.91	(GDP1913/GDP1900)**(1/13)-1

Table 6.10 GDP Growth Rates, 1900-1913

Rank	Country	GRRL	Source
49	Finland	2.89	(GDP1913/GDP1900)**(1/13)-1
50	Iceland	2.88	(GDP1913/GDP1900)**(1/13)-1
51	Guatemala	2.82	(GDP1913/GDP1900)**(1/13)-1
52	Bosnia	2.76	(GDP1913/GDP1900)**(1/13)-1
53	Kosovo	2.76	(GDP1913/GDP1900)**(1/13)-1
54	Slovenia	2.76	(GDP1913/GDP1900)**(1/13)-1
55	Croatia	2.76	(GDP1913/GDP1900)**(1/13)-1
56	Macedonia	2.76	(GDP1913/GDP1900)**(1/13)-1
57	Serbia	2.76	(GDP1913/GDP1900)**(1/13)-1
58	Montenegro	2.76	(GDP1913/GDP1900)**(1/13)-1
59	Indonesia	2.74	(GDP1913/GDP1900)**(1/13)-1
60	Netherlands	2.72	(GDP1913/GDP1900)**(1/13)-1
61	Norway	2.72	(GDP1913/GDP1900)**(1/13)-1
62	Romania	2.63	(GDP1913/GDP1900)**(1/13)-1
63	Mexico	2.59	(GDP1913/GDP1900)**(1/13)-1
64	Bolivia	2.58	(GDP1913/GDP1900)**(1/13)-1
65	Japan	2.49	(GDP1913/GDP1900)**(1/13)-1
66	Hungary	2.46	(GDP1913/GDP1900)**(1/13)-1
67	Austria	2.41	(GDP1913/GDP1900)**(1/13)-1
68	Namibia	2.38	(GDP1913/GDP1900)**(1/13)-1
69	Taiwan	2.36	(GDP1913/GDP1900)**(1/13)-1
70	Israel	2.35	(GDP1913/GDP1900)**(1/13)-1
71	Vietnam	2.29	(GDP1913/GDP1900)**(1/13)-1
72	Egypt	2.28	(GDP1913/GDP1900)**(1/13)-1
73	Laos	2.23	(GDP1913/GDP1900)**(1/13)-1
74	Burma	2.21	(GDP1913/GDP1900)**(1/13)-1
75	Albania	2.21	(GDP1913/GDP1900)**(1/13)-1
76	Sweden	2.21	(GDP1913/GDP1900)**(1/13)-1
77	Swaziland	2.18	(GDP1913/GDP1900)**(1/13)-1
78	Slovakia	2.17	(GDP1913/GDP1900)**(1/13)-1
79	Czechia	2.17	(GDP1913/GDP1900)**(1/13)-1
80	Switzerland	2.06	(GDP1913/GDP1900)**(1/13)-1
81	Algeria	2.00	(GDP1913/GDP1900)**(1/13)-1
82	Belgium	1.98	(GDP1913/GDP1900)**(1/13)-1
83	Cyprus	1.97	(GDP1913/GDP1900)**(1/13)-1
84	Greece	1.97	(GDP1913/GDP1900)**(1/13)-1
85	Iraq	1.96	(GDP1913/GDP1900)**(1/13)-1
86	Tunisia	1.87	(GDP1913/GDP1900)**(1/13)-1
87	Lebanon	1.83	(GDP1913/GDP1900)**(1/13)-1
88	Zimbabwe	1.81	(GDP1913/GDP1900)**(1/13)-1
89	Lesotho	1.79	(GDP1913/GDP1900)**(1/13)-1
90	Spain	1.77	(GDP1913/GDP1900)**(1/13)-1
91	Zambia	1.77	(GDP1913/GDP1900)**(1/13)-1
92	France	1.65	(GDP1913/GDP1900)**(1/13)-1
93	Syria	1.64	(GDP1913/GDP1900)**(1/13)-1
94	Thailand	1.64	(GDP1913/GDP1900)**(1/13)-1
95	Mozambique	1.63	(GDP1913/GDP1900)**(1/13)-1
96	Poland	1.55	(GDP1913/GDP1900)**(1/13)-1

Table 6.10 GDP Growth Rates, 1900-1913			
Rank	Country	GRRL	Source
97	Eritrea	1.52	(GDP1913/GDP1900)**(1/13)-1
98	Ethiopia	1.52	(GDP1913/GDP1900)**(1/13)-1
99	Afghanistan	1.52	(GDP1913/GDP1900)**(1/13)-1
100	Jamaica	1.51	(GDP1913/GDP1900)**(1/13)-1
101	UK	1.51	(GDP1913/GDP1900)**(1/13)-1
102	Turkey	1.47	(GDP1913/GDP1900)**(1/13)-1
103	Malawi	1.44	(GDP1913/GDP1900)**(1/13)-1
104	Cambodia	1.43	(GDP1913/GDP1900)**(1/13)-1
105	Jordan	1.40	(GDP1913/GDP1900)**(1/13)-1
106	Iran	1.40	(GDP1913/GDP1900)**(1/13)-1
107	Somalia	1.36	(GDP1913/GDP1900)**(1/13)-1
108	Madagascar	1.36	(GDP1913/GDP1900)**(1/13)-1
109	Sri Lanka	1.26	(GDP1913/GDP1900)**(1/13)-1
110	Morocco	1.25	(GDP1913/GDP1900)**(1/13)-1
111	Korea, South	1.24	(GDP1913/GDP1900)**(1/13)-1
112	Nepal	1.22	(GDP1913/GDP1900)**(1/13)-1
113	Botswana	1.14	(GDP1913/GDP1900)**(1/13)-1
114	Bangladesh	1.13	(GDP1913/GDP1900)**(1/13)-1
115	Pakistan	1.05	(GDP1913/GDP1900)**(1/13)-1
116	Mongolia	0.99	(GDP1913/GDP1900)**(1/13)-1
117	Libya	0.94	(GDP1913/GDP1900)**(1/13)-1
118	India	0.93	(GDP1913/GDP1900)**(1/13)-1
119	Korea, North	0.91	(GDP1913/GDP1900)**(1/13)-1
120	Sierra Leone	0.88	(GDP1913/GDP1900)**(1/13)-1
121	Sudan	0.87	(GDP1913/GDP1900)**(1/13)-1
122	Guinea	0.83	(GDP1913/GDP1900)**(1/13)-1
123	Guinea-Biss	0.83	(GDP1913/GDP1900)**(1/13)-1
124	Ireland	0.79	(GDP1913/GDP1900)**(1/13)-1
125	China	0.78	(GDP1913/GDP1900)**(1/13)-1
126	Burundi	0.70	(GDP1913/GDP1900)**(1/13)-1
127	Qatar	0.66	(GDP1913/GDP1900)**(1/13)-1
128	UAE	0.66	(GDP1913/GDP1900)**(1/13)-1
129	Kuwait	0.66	(GDP1913/GDP1900)**(1/13)-1
130	Bahrain	0.66	(GDP1913/GDP1900)**(1/13)-1
131	Oman	0.54	(GDP1913/GDP1900)**(1/13)-1
132	Portugal	0.46	(GDP1913/GDP1900)**(1/13)-1
133	Yemen	0.44	(GDP1913/GDP1900)**(1/13)-1
134	Saudi Arabia	0.41	(GDP1913/GDP1900)**(1/13)-1
135	South Sudan	0.39	(GDP1913/GDP1900)**(1/13)-1

TABLE 6.11 GDP GROWTH RATES, 1913-1920			
Rank	Country	GRRL	Source
1	Qatar	12.18	(GDP1920/GDP1913)**(1/7)-1
2	Kuwait	12.02	(GDP1920/GDP1913)**(1/7)-1
3	UAE	10.21	(GDP1920/GDP1913)**(1/7)-1
4	Honduras	9.30	(GDP1920/GDP1913)**(1/7)-1
5	Costa Rica	7.36	(GDP1920/GDP1913)**(1/7)-1
6	Panama	6.53	(GDP1920/GDP1913)**(1/7)-1
7	Nicaragua	6.21	(GDP1920/GDP1913)**(1/7)-1
8	Hong Kong	5.73	(GDP1920/GDP1913)**(1/7)-1
9	Israel	5.59	(GDP1920/GDP1913)**(1/7)-1
10	Malaysia	5.11	(GDP1920/GDP1913)**(1/7)-1
11	Korea, North	4.94	(GDP1920/GDP1913)**(1/7)-1
12	Philippines	4.91	(GDP1920/GDP1913)**(1/7)-1
13	Taiwan	4.74	(GDP1920/GDP1913)**(1/7)-1
14	Peru	4.71	(GDP1920/GDP1913)**(1/7)-1
15	Brazil	4.66	(GDP1920/GDP1913)**(1/7)-1
16	Cuba	4.62	(GDP1920/GDP1913)**(1/7)-1
17	Korea, South	4.62	(GDP1920/GDP1913)**(1/7)-1
18	Bahrain	4.37	(GDP1920/GDP1913)**(1/7)-1
19	Singapore	4.31	(GDP1920/GDP1913)**(1/7)-1
20	Saudi Arabia	4.12	(GDP1920/GDP1913)**(1/7)-1
21	Japan	4.06	(GDP1920/GDP1913)**(1/7)-1
22	Paraguay	3.93	(GDP1920/GDP1913)**(1/7)-1
23	Dominican R	3.87	(GDP1920/GDP1913)**(1/7)-1
24	Lebanon	3.82	(GDP1920/GDP1913)**(1/7)-1
25	Ghana	3.62	(GDP1920/GDP1913)**(1/7)-1
26	El Salvador	3.57	(GDP1920/GDP1913)**(1/7)-1
27	Morocco	3.51	(GDP1920/GDP1913)**(1/7)-1
28	South Africa	3.46	(GDP1920/GDP1913)**(1/7)-1
29	Bolivia	3.40	(GDP1920/GDP1913)**(1/7)-1
30	Haiti	3.24	(GDP1920/GDP1913)**(1/7)-1
31	Syria	3.13	(GDP1920/GDP1913)**(1/7)-1
32	Greece	3.08	(GDP1920/GDP1913)**(1/7)-1
33	Cyprus	3.08	(GDP1920/GDP1913)**(1/7)-1
34	Puerto Rico	3.08	(GDP1920/GDP1913)**(1/7)-1
35	Trinidad & T	3.00	(GDP1920/GDP1913)**(1/7)-1
36	Colombia	2.81	(GDP1920/GDP1913)**(1/7)-1
37	Iraq	2.81	(GDP1920/GDP1913)**(1/7)-1
38	New Zealand	2.77	(GDP1920/GDP1913)**(1/7)-1
39	Iran	2.66	(GDP1920/GDP1913)**(1/7)-1
40	Norway	2.55	(GDP1920/GDP1913)**(1/7)-1
41	Ecuador	2.39	(GDP1920/GDP1913)**(1/7)-1
42	Namibia	2.39	(GDP1920/GDP1913)**(1/7)-1
43	Tunisia	2.37	(GDP1920/GDP1913)**(1/7)-1
44	Jordan	2.22	(GDP1920/GDP1913)**(1/7)-1
45	Swaziland	2.18	(GDP1920/GDP1913)**(1/7)-1
46	Yemen	2.16	(GDP1920/GDP1913)**(1/7)-1
47	Jamaica	2.12	(GDP1920/GDP1913)**(1/7)-1
48	Netherlands	2.12	(GDP1920/GDP1913)**(1/7)-1

Table 6.11 GDP Growth Rates, 1913-1920

Rank	Country	GRRL	Source
49	Guatemala	2.07	(GDP1920/GDP1913)**(1/7)-1
50	US	1.98	(GDP1920/GDP1913)**(1/7)-1
51	Algeria	1.93	(GDP1920/GDP1913)**(1/7)-1
52	Burma	1.83	(GDP1920/GDP1913)**(1/7)-1
53	Zimbabwe	1.81	(GDP1920/GDP1913)**(1/7)-1
54	Lesotho	1.79	(GDP1920/GDP1913)**(1/7)-1
55	Zambia	1.77	(GDP1920/GDP1913)**(1/7)-1
56	Indonesia	1.69	(GDP1920/GDP1913)**(1/7)-1
57	Mozambique	1.63	(GDP1920/GDP1913)**(1/7)-1
58	Eritrea	1.52	(GDP1920/GDP1913)**(1/7)-1
59	Ethiopia	1.52	(GDP1920/GDP1913)**(1/7)-1
60	Spain	1.50	(GDP1920/GDP1913)**(1/7)-1
61	Denmark	1.49	(GDP1920/GDP1913)**(1/7)-1
62	Venezuela	1.45	(GDP1920/GDP1913)**(1/7)-1
63	Malawi	1.44	(GDP1920/GDP1913)**(1/7)-1
64	Iceland	1.40	(GDP1920/GDP1913)**(1/7)-1
65	Albania	1.37	(GDP1920/GDP1913)**(1/7)-1
66	Thailand	1.36	(GDP1920/GDP1913)**(1/7)-1
67	Somalia	1.36	(GDP1920/GDP1913)**(1/7)-1
68	Madagascar	1.36	(GDP1920/GDP1913)**(1/7)-1
69	China	1.22	(GDP1920/GDP1913)**(1/7)-1
70	Botswana	1.14	(GDP1920/GDP1913)**(1/7)-1
71	Egypt	0.97	(GDP1920/GDP1913)**(1/7)-1
72	Libya	0.94	(GDP1920/GDP1913)**(1/7)-1
73	Nepal	0.94	(GDP1920/GDP1913)**(1/7)-1
74	Sierra Leone	0.88	(GDP1920/GDP1913)**(1/7)-1
75	Sudan	0.87	(GDP1920/GDP1913)**(1/7)-1
76	Cambodia	0.83	(GDP1920/GDP1913)**(1/7)-1
77	Guinea	0.83	(GDP1920/GDP1913)**(1/7)-1
78	Guinea-Biss	0.83	(GDP1920/GDP1913)**(1/7)-1
79	Argentina	0.82	(GDP1920/GDP1913)**(1/7)-1
80	Afghanistan	0.77	(GDP1920/GDP1913)**(1/7)-1
81	Burundi	0.70	(GDP1920/GDP1913)**(1/7)-1
82	Vietnam	0.67	(GDP1920/GDP1913)**(1/7)-1
83	Mexico	0.67	(GDP1920/GDP1913)**(1/7)-1
84	South Sudan	0.40	(GDP1920/GDP1913)**(1/7)-1
85	Pakistan	0.38	(GDP1920/GDP1913)**(1/7)-1
86	Australia	0.38	(GDP1920/GDP1913)**(1/7)-1
87	Chile	0.31	(GDP1920/GDP1913)**(1/7)-1
88	Switzerland	0.21	(GDP1920/GDP1913)**(1/7)-1
89	Bangladesh	0.19	(GDP1920/GDP1913)**(1/7)-1
90	Italy	0.19	(GDP1920/GDP1913)**(1/7)-1
91	Oman	0.17	(GDP1920/GDP1913)**(1/7)-1
92	Laos	0.07	(GDP1920/GDP1913)**(1/7)-1
93	Mongolia	-0.11	(GDP1920/GDP1913)**(1/7)-1
94	Portugal	-0.11	(GDP1920/GDP1913)**(1/7)-1
95	Poland	-0.32	(GDP1920/GDP1913)**(1/7)-1
96	Canada	-0.39	(GDP1920/GDP1913)**(1/7)-1

Table 6.11 GDP Growth Rates, 1913-1920

Rank	Country	GRRL	Source
97	Sri Lanka	-0.50	(GDP1920/GDP1913)**(1/7)-1
98	India	-0.67	(GDP1920/GDP1913)**(1/7)-1
99	UK	-0.76	(GDP1920/GDP1913)**(1/7)-1
100	Sweden	-0.79	(GDP1920/GDP1913)**(1/7)-1
101	Uruguay	-0.86	(GDP1920/GDP1913)**(1/7)-1
102	Ireland	-0.91	(GDP1920/GDP1913)**(1/7)-1
103	Belgium	-1.11	(GDP1920/GDP1913)**(1/7)-1
104	Finland	-1.41	(GDP1920/GDP1913)**(1/7)-1
105	Czechia	-1.44	(GDP1920/GDP1913)**(1/7)-1
106	Slovakia	-1.44	(GDP1920/GDP1913)**(1/7)-1
107	Kosovo	-1.63	(GDP1920/GDP1913)**(1/7)-1
108	Serbia	-1.63	(GDP1920/GDP1913)**(1/7)-1
109	Slovenia	-1.63	(GDP1920/GDP1913)**(1/7)-1
110	Macedonia	-1.63	(GDP1920/GDP1913)**(1/7)-1
111	Montenegro	-1.63	(GDP1920/GDP1913)**(1/7)-1
112	Croatia	-1.63	(GDP1920/GDP1913)**(1/7)-1
113	Bosnia	-1.63	(GDP1920/GDP1913)**(1/7)-1
114	France	-1.95	(GDP1920/GDP1913)**(1/7)-1
115	Estonia	-2.04	(GDP1920/GDP1913)**(1/7)-1
116	Latvia	-2.04	(GDP1920/GDP1913)**(1/7)-1
117	Lithuania	-2.04	(GDP1920/GDP1913)**(1/7)-1
118	Hungary	-2.69	(GDP1920/GDP1913)**(1/7)-1
119	Germany	-4.63	(GDP1920/GDP1913)**(1/7)-1
120	Austria	-5.68	(GDP1920/GDP1913)**(1/7)-1
121	Bulgaria	-6.24	(GDP1920/GDP1913)**(1/7)-1
122	Georgia	-7.34	(GDP1920/GDP1913)**(1/7)-1
123	Moldova	-7.34	(GDP1920/GDP1913)**(1/7)-1
124	Romania	-7.40	(GDP1920/GDP1913)**(1/7)-1
125	Turkey	-8.35	(GDP1920/GDP1913)**(1/7)-1
126	Ukraine	-12.79	(GDP1920/GDP1913)**(1/7)-1
127	Uzbekistan	-12.79	(GDP1920/GDP1913)**(1/7)-1
128	Kazakhstan	-12.79	(GDP1920/GDP1913)**(1/7)-1
129	Armenia	-12.79	(GDP1920/GDP1913)**(1/7)-1
130	Turkmenistan	-12.79	(GDP1920/GDP1913)**(1/7)-1
131	Tajikistan	-12.79	(GDP1920/GDP1913)**(1/7)-1
132	Russia	-12.79	(GDP1920/GDP1913)**(1/7)-1
133	Belarus	-12.79	(GDP1920/GDP1913)**(1/7)-1
134	Azerbaijan	-12.79	(GDP1920/GDP1913)**(1/7)-1
135	Kyrgyzstan	-12.79	(GDP1920/GDP1913)**(1/7)-1

Table 6.12 GDP Growth Rates, 1920-1929			
Rank	Country	GRRL	Source
1	Venezuela	13.72	(GDP1929/GDP1920)**(1/9)-1
2	Qatar	12.18	(GDP1929/GDP1920)**(1/9)-1
3	Kuwait	12.02	(GDP1929/GDP1920)**(1/9)-1
4	Kyrgyzstan	11.88	(GDP1929/GDP1920)**(1/9)-1
5	Tajikistan	11.88	(GDP1929/GDP1920)**(1/9)-1
6	Azerbaijan	11.88	(GDP1929/GDP1920)**(1/9)-1
7	Belarus	11.88	(GDP1929/GDP1920)**(1/9)-1
8	Russia	11.88	(GDP1929/GDP1920)**(1/9)-1
9	Armenia	11.88	(GDP1929/GDP1920)**(1/9)-1
10	Kazakhstan	11.88	(GDP1929/GDP1920)**(1/9)-1
11	Uzbekistan	11.88	(GDP1929/GDP1920)**(1/9)-1
12	Turkmenistan	11.88	(GDP1929/GDP1920)**(1/9)-1
13	Ukraine	11.88	(GDP1929/GDP1920)**(1/9)-1
14	UAE	10.21	(GDP1929/GDP1920)**(1/9)-1
15	Malaysia	7.04	(GDP1929/GDP1920)**(1/9)-1
16	Turkey	6.78	(GDP1929/GDP1920)**(1/9)-1
17	Georgia	6.72	(GDP1929/GDP1920)**(1/9)-1
18	Uruguay	6.54	(GDP1929/GDP1920)**(1/9)-1
19	Slovakia	5.96	(GDP1929/GDP1920)**(1/9)-1
20	Czechia	5.96	(GDP1929/GDP1920)**(1/9)-1
21	Singapore	5.94	(GDP1929/GDP1920)**(1/9)-1
22	Argentina	5.69	(GDP1929/GDP1920)**(1/9)-1
23	Lithuania	5.63	(GDP1929/GDP1920)**(1/9)-1
24	Latvia	5.63	(GDP1929/GDP1920)**(1/9)-1
25	Estonia	5.63	(GDP1929/GDP1920)**(1/9)-1
26	Israel	5.59	(GDP1929/GDP1920)**(1/9)-1
27	Finland	5.42	(GDP1929/GDP1920)**(1/9)-1
28	Dominican R	5.24	(GDP1929/GDP1920)**(1/9)-1
29	Austria	5.24	(GDP1929/GDP1920)**(1/9)-1
30	Cuba	5.23	(GDP1929/GDP1920)**(1/9)-1
31	Chile	5.16	(GDP1929/GDP1920)**(1/9)-1
32	Hungary	5.10	(GDP1929/GDP1920)**(1/9)-1
33	France	4.94	(GDP1929/GDP1920)**(1/9)-1
34	Germany	4.92	(GDP1929/GDP1920)**(1/9)-1
35	Canada	4.89	(GDP1929/GDP1920)**(1/9)-1
36	Netherlands	4.85	(GDP1929/GDP1920)**(1/9)-1
37	Bulgaria	4.78	(GDP1929/GDP1920)**(1/9)-1
38	Switzerland	4.78	(GDP1929/GDP1920)**(1/9)-1
39	Honduras	4.76	(GDP1929/GDP1920)**(1/9)-1
40	Macedonia	4.70	(GDP1929/GDP1920)**(1/9)-1
41	Montenegro	4.70	(GDP1929/GDP1920)**(1/9)-1
42	Croatia	4.70	(GDP1929/GDP1920)**(1/9)-1
43	Slovenia	4.70	(GDP1929/GDP1920)**(1/9)-1
44	Serbia	4.70	(GDP1929/GDP1920)**(1/9)-1
45	Bosnia	4.70	(GDP1929/GDP1920)**(1/9)-1
46	Kosovo	4.70	(GDP1929/GDP1920)**(1/9)-1
47	Colombia	4.68	(GDP1929/GDP1920)**(1/9)-1
48	Guatemala	4.49	(GDP1929/GDP1920)**(1/9)-1

TABLE 6.12 GDP GROWTH RATES, 1920-1929

Rank	Country	GRRL	Source
49	Nicaragua	4.38	(GDP1929/GDP1920)**(1/9)-1
50	Bahrain	4.37	(GDP1929/GDP1920)**(1/9)-1
51	Portugal	4.26	(GDP1929/GDP1920)**(1/9)-1
52	Saudi Arabia	4.12	(GDP1929/GDP1920)**(1/9)-1
53	Taiwan	4.11	(GDP1929/GDP1920)**(1/9)-1
54	Sweden	4.11	(GDP1929/GDP1920)**(1/9)-1
55	Iceland	4.08	(GDP1929/GDP1920)**(1/9)-1
56	US	3.98	(GDP1929/GDP1920)**(1/9)-1
57	Brazil	3.95	(GDP1929/GDP1920)**(1/9)-1
58	Paraguay	3.91	(GDP1929/GDP1920)**(1/9)-1
59	Lebanon	3.82	(GDP1929/GDP1920)**(1/9)-1
60	Philippines	3.81	(GDP1929/GDP1920)**(1/9)-1
61	Hong Kong	3.69	(GDP1929/GDP1920)**(1/9)-1
62	Peru	3.64	(GDP1929/GDP1920)**(1/9)-1
63	Indonesia	3.64	(GDP1929/GDP1920)**(1/9)-1
64	Denmark	3.64	(GDP1929/GDP1920)**(1/9)-1
65	Ghana	3.62	(GDP1929/GDP1920)**(1/9)-1
66	Greece	3.61	(GDP1929/GDP1920)**(1/9)-1
67	Cyprus	3.61	(GDP1929/GDP1920)**(1/9)-1
68	Spain	3.60	(GDP1929/GDP1920)**(1/9)-1
69	Morocco	3.51	(GDP1929/GDP1920)**(1/9)-1
70	South Africa	3.46	(GDP1929/GDP1920)**(1/9)-1
71	Belgium	3.45	(GDP1929/GDP1920)**(1/9)-1
72	Jamaica	3.43	(GDP1929/GDP1920)**(1/9)-1
73	Japan	3.42	(GDP1929/GDP1920)**(1/9)-1
74	El Salvador	3.36	(GDP1929/GDP1920)**(1/9)-1
75	Puerto Rico	3.26	(GDP1929/GDP1920)**(1/9)-1
76	Norway	3.22	(GDP1929/GDP1920)**(1/9)-1
77	Sri Lanka	3.14	(GDP1929/GDP1920)**(1/9)-1
78	Syria	3.13	(GDP1929/GDP1920)**(1/9)-1
79	Australia	3.12	(GDP1929/GDP1920)**(1/9)-1
80	Poland	2.94	(GDP1929/GDP1920)**(1/9)-1
81	Burma	2.93	(GDP1929/GDP1920)**(1/9)-1
82	Italy	2.90	(GDP1929/GDP1920)**(1/9)-1
83	Haiti	2.88	(GDP1929/GDP1920)**(1/9)-1
84	Iraq	2.81	(GDP1929/GDP1920)**(1/9)-1
85	Bolivia	2.72	(GDP1929/GDP1920)**(1/9)-1
86	Iran	2.66	(GDP1929/GDP1920)**(1/9)-1
87	UK	2.64	(GDP1929/GDP1920)**(1/9)-1
88	Romania	2.62	(GDP1929/GDP1920)**(1/9)-1
89	Moldova	2.44	(GDP1929/GDP1920)**(1/9)-1
90	Namibia	2.38	(GDP1929/GDP1920)**(1/9)-1
91	Ecuador	2.38	(GDP1929/GDP1920)**(1/9)-1
92	Tunisia	2.37	(GDP1929/GDP1920)**(1/9)-1
93	Jordan	2.22	(GDP1929/GDP1920)**(1/9)-1
94	Swaziland	2.18	(GDP1929/GDP1920)**(1/9)-1
95	Yemen	2.16	(GDP1929/GDP1920)**(1/9)-1
96	Algeria	2.06	(GDP1929/GDP1920)**(1/9)-1

Table 6.12 GDP Growth Rates, 1920-1929

Rank	Country	GRRL	Source
97	Panama	1.97	(GDP1929/GDP1920)**(1/9)-1
98	Thailand	1.95	(GDP1929/GDP1920)**(1/9)-1
99	Korea, North	1.93	(GDP1929/GDP1920)**(1/9)-1
100	Zimbabwe	1.81	(GDP1929/GDP1920)**(1/9)-1
101	Trinidad & T	1.80	(GDP1929/GDP1920)**(1/9)-1
102	Lesotho	1.79	(GDP1929/GDP1920)**(1/9)-1
103	Zambia	1.77	(GDP1929/GDP1920)**(1/9)-1
104	Korea, South	1.74	(GDP1929/GDP1920)**(1/9)-1
105	Mozambique	1.63	(GDP1929/GDP1920)**(1/9)-1
106	India	1.58	(GDP1929/GDP1920)**(1/9)-1
107	Eritrea	1.52	(GDP1929/GDP1920)**(1/9)-1
108	Ethiopia	1.52	(GDP1929/GDP1920)**(1/9)-1
109	Malawi	1.44	(GDP1929/GDP1920)**(1/9)-1
110	Costa Rica	1.43	(GDP1929/GDP1920)**(1/9)-1
111	Albania	1.36	(GDP1929/GDP1920)**(1/9)-1
112	Somalia	1.36	(GDP1929/GDP1920)**(1/9)-1
113	Madagascar	1.36	(GDP1929/GDP1920)**(1/9)-1
114	Pakistan	1.26	(GDP1929/GDP1920)**(1/9)-1
115	Botswana	1.14	(GDP1929/GDP1920)**(1/9)-1
116	New Zealand	1.12	(GDP1929/GDP1920)**(1/9)-1
117	Mexico	0.98	(GDP1929/GDP1920)**(1/9)-1
118	Libya	0.94	(GDP1929/GDP1920)**(1/9)-1
119	Nepal	0.93	(GDP1929/GDP1920)**(1/9)-1
120	Egypt	0.90	(GDP1929/GDP1920)**(1/9)-1
121	Sierra Leone	0.88	(GDP1929/GDP1920)**(1/9)-1
122	Sudan	0.87	(GDP1929/GDP1920)**(1/9)-1
123	Cambodia	0.83	(GDP1929/GDP1920)**(1/9)-1
124	Guinea	0.83	(GDP1929/GDP1920)**(1/9)-1
125	Guinea-Biss	0.83	(GDP1929/GDP1920)**(1/9)-1
126	Bangladesh	0.78	(GDP1929/GDP1920)**(1/9)-1
127	Afghanistan	0.77	(GDP1929/GDP1920)**(1/9)-1
128	Burundi	0.70	(GDP1929/GDP1920)**(1/9)-1
129	Vietnam	0.67	(GDP1929/GDP1920)**(1/9)-1
130	Ireland	0.49	(GDP1929/GDP1920)**(1/9)-1
131	China	0.47	(GDP1929/GDP1920)**(1/9)-1
132	South Sudan	0.40	(GDP1929/GDP1920)**(1/9)-1
133	Oman	0.17	(GDP1929/GDP1920)**(1/9)-1
134	Laos	0.07	(GDP1929/GDP1920)**(1/9)-1
135	Mongolia	-0.11	(GDP1929/GDP1920)**(1/9)-1

Table 6.13 GDP Growth Rates, 1929-1938

Rank	Country	GRRL	Source
1	Qatar	12.18	(GDP1938/GDP1929)**(1/9)-1
2	Kuwait	12.02	(GDP1938/GDP1929)**(1/9)-1
3	UAE	10.21	(GDP1938/GDP1929)**(1/9)-1
4	Hong Kong	8.90	(GDP1938/GDP1929)**(1/9)-1
5	Korea, North	6.08	(GDP1938/GDP1929)**(1/9)-1
6	Ukraine	6.07	(GDP1938/GDP1929)**(1/9)-1
7	Russia	6.07	(GDP1938/GDP1929)**(1/9)-1
8	Uzbekistan	6.07	(GDP1938/GDP1929)**(1/9)-1
9	Belarus	6.07	(GDP1938/GDP1929)**(1/9)-1
10	Georgia	6.07	(GDP1938/GDP1929)**(1/9)-1
11	Kazakhstan	6.07	(GDP1938/GDP1929)**(1/9)-1
12	Azerbaijan	6.07	(GDP1938/GDP1929)**(1/9)-1
13	Turkmenistan	6.07	(GDP1938/GDP1929)**(1/9)-1
14	Kyrgyzstan	6.07	(GDP1938/GDP1929)**(1/9)-1
15	Tajikistan	6.07	(GDP1938/GDP1929)**(1/9)-1
16	Armenia	6.07	(GDP1938/GDP1929)**(1/9)-1
17	Turkey	5.68	(GDP1938/GDP1929)**(1/9)-1
18	Israel	5.59	(GDP1938/GDP1929)**(1/9)-1
19	Korea, South	5.46	(GDP1938/GDP1929)**(1/9)-1
20	Guatemala	5.04	(GDP1938/GDP1929)**(1/9)-1
21	Dominican R	4.68	(GDP1938/GDP1929)**(1/9)-1
22	Bulgaria	4.54	(GDP1938/GDP1929)**(1/9)-1
23	Bahrain	4.37	(GDP1938/GDP1929)**(1/9)-1
24	Panama	4.23	(GDP1938/GDP1929)**(1/9)-1
25	Lithuania	4.19	(GDP1938/GDP1929)**(1/9)-1
26	Estonia	4.19	(GDP1938/GDP1929)**(1/9)-1
27	Latvia	4.19	(GDP1938/GDP1929)**(1/9)-1
28	Saudi Arabia	4.12	(GDP1938/GDP1929)**(1/9)-1
29	Taiwan	4.10	(GDP1938/GDP1929)**(1/9)-1
30	Costa Rica	4.04	(GDP1938/GDP1929)**(1/9)-1
31	Paraguay	3.94	(GDP1938/GDP1929)**(1/9)-1
32	Singapore	3.91	(GDP1938/GDP1929)**(1/9)-1
33	Finland	3.90	(GDP1938/GDP1929)**(1/9)-1
34	Ecuador	3.82	(GDP1938/GDP1929)**(1/9)-1
35	Lebanon	3.82	(GDP1938/GDP1929)**(1/9)-1
36	Jamaica	3.71	(GDP1938/GDP1929)**(1/9)-1
37	Ghana	3.62	(GDP1938/GDP1929)**(1/9)-1
38	Japan	3.59	(GDP1938/GDP1929)**(1/9)-1
39	Morocco	3.51	(GDP1938/GDP1929)**(1/9)-1
40	Colombia	3.50	(GDP1938/GDP1929)**(1/9)-1
41	Puerto Rico	3.48	(GDP1938/GDP1929)**(1/9)-1
42	South Africa	3.46	(GDP1938/GDP1929)**(1/9)-1
43	Brazil	3.36	(GDP1938/GDP1929)**(1/9)-1
44	Venezuela	3.35	(GDP1938/GDP1929)**(1/9)-1
45	New Zealand	3.30	(GDP1938/GDP1929)**(1/9)-1
46	Trinidad & T	3.14	(GDP1938/GDP1929)**(1/9)-1
47	Syria	3.13	(GDP1938/GDP1929)**(1/9)-1
48	Norway	3.06	(GDP1938/GDP1929)**(1/9)-1

Table 6.13 GDP Growth Rates, 1929-1938

Rank	Country	GRRL	Source
49	Germany	3.01	(GDP1938/GDP1929)**(1/9)-1
50	Thailand	2.91	(GDP1938/GDP1929)**(1/9)-1
51	Haiti	2.85	(GDP1938/GDP1929)**(1/9)-1
52	Greece	2.84	(GDP1938/GDP1929)**(1/9)-1
53	Cyprus	2.84	(GDP1938/GDP1929)**(1/9)-1
54	Iraq	2.81	(GDP1938/GDP1929)**(1/9)-1
55	Bolivia	2.72	(GDP1938/GDP1929)**(1/9)-1
56	Iran	2.66	(GDP1938/GDP1929)**(1/9)-1
57	Iceland	2.64	(GDP1938/GDP1929)**(1/9)-1
58	Sweden	2.58	(GDP1938/GDP1929)**(1/9)-1
59	Philippines	2.53	(GDP1938/GDP1929)**(1/9)-1
60	Peru	2.50	(GDP1938/GDP1929)**(1/9)-1
61	Namibia	2.38	(GDP1938/GDP1929)**(1/9)-1
62	Tunisia	2.37	(GDP1938/GDP1929)**(1/9)-1
63	Denmark	2.22	(GDP1938/GDP1929)**(1/9)-1
64	Jordan	2.22	(GDP1938/GDP1929)**(1/9)-1
65	Swaziland	2.18	(GDP1938/GDP1929)**(1/9)-1
66	Yemen	2.16	(GDP1938/GDP1929)**(1/9)-1
67	Portugal	2.16	(GDP1938/GDP1929)**(1/9)-1
68	Australia	2.11	(GDP1938/GDP1929)**(1/9)-1
69	Romania	2.10	(GDP1938/GDP1929)**(1/9)-1
70	Mexico	1.97	(GDP1938/GDP1929)**(1/9)-1
71	UK	1.90	(GDP1938/GDP1929)**(1/9)-1
72	Moldova	1.87	(GDP1938/GDP1929)**(1/9)-1
73	Zimbabwe	1.81	(GDP1938/GDP1929)**(1/9)-1
74	Lesotho	1.79	(GDP1938/GDP1929)**(1/9)-1
75	Zambia	1.77	(GDP1938/GDP1929)**(1/9)-1
76	Mozambique	1.63	(GDP1938/GDP1929)**(1/9)-1
77	Italy	1.57	(GDP1938/GDP1929)**(1/9)-1
78	Poland	1.56	(GDP1938/GDP1929)**(1/9)-1
79	Eritrea	1.52	(GDP1938/GDP1929)**(1/9)-1
80	Ethiopia	1.52	(GDP1938/GDP1929)**(1/9)-1
81	Hungary	1.52	(GDP1938/GDP1929)**(1/9)-1
82	Algeria	1.52	(GDP1938/GDP1929)**(1/9)-1
83	Indonesia	1.50	(GDP1938/GDP1929)**(1/9)-1
84	Egypt	1.44	(GDP1938/GDP1929)**(1/9)-1
85	Malawi	1.44	(GDP1938/GDP1929)**(1/9)-1
86	Somalia	1.36	(GDP1938/GDP1929)**(1/9)-1
87	Madagascar	1.36	(GDP1938/GDP1929)**(1/9)-1
88	Bosnia	1.33	(GDP1938/GDP1929)**(1/9)-1
89	Croatia	1.33	(GDP1938/GDP1929)**(1/9)-1
90	Montenegro	1.33	(GDP1938/GDP1929)**(1/9)-1
91	Slovenia	1.33	(GDP1938/GDP1929)**(1/9)-1
92	Serbia	1.33	(GDP1938/GDP1929)**(1/9)-1
93	Macedonia	1.33	(GDP1938/GDP1929)**(1/9)-1
94	Kosovo	1.33	(GDP1938/GDP1929)**(1/9)-1
95	Botswana	1.14	(GDP1938/GDP1929)**(1/9)-1
96	Uruguay	1.14	(GDP1938/GDP1929)**(1/9)-1

Table 6.13 GDP Growth Rates, 1929-1938

Rank	Country	GRRL	Source
97	Argentina	1.10	(GDP1938/GDP1929)**(1/9)-1
98	Albania	1.07	(GDP1938/GDP1929)**(1/9)-1
99	Libya	0.94	(GDP1938/GDP1929)**(1/9)-1
100	Nepal	0.93	(GDP1938/GDP1929)**(1/9)-1
101	Pakistan	0.90	(GDP1938/GDP1929)**(1/9)-1
102	Sierra Leone	0.88	(GDP1938/GDP1929)**(1/9)-1
103	Sudan	0.87	(GDP1938/GDP1929)**(1/9)-1
104	Ireland	0.87	(GDP1938/GDP1929)**(1/9)-1
105	Guinea	0.83	(GDP1938/GDP1929)**(1/9)-1
106	Cambodia	0.83	(GDP1938/GDP1929)**(1/9)-1
107	Guinea-Biss	0.83	(GDP1938/GDP1929)**(1/9)-1
108	Bangladesh	0.77	(GDP1938/GDP1929)**(1/9)-1
109	Afghanistan	0.77	(GDP1938/GDP1929)**(1/9)-1
110	Burundi	0.70	(GDP1938/GDP1929)**(1/9)-1
111	Vietnam	0.67	(GDP1938/GDP1929)**(1/9)-1
112	El Salvador	0.63	(GDP1938/GDP1929)**(1/9)-1
113	Chile	0.60	(GDP1938/GDP1929)**(1/9)-1
114	China	0.58	(GDP1938/GDP1929)**(1/9)-1
115	Switzerland	0.56	(GDP1938/GDP1929)**(1/9)-1
116	India	0.48	(GDP1938/GDP1929)**(1/9)-1
117	South Sudan	0.40	(GDP1938/GDP1929)**(1/9)-1
118	Netherlands	0.33	(GDP1938/GDP1929)**(1/9)-1
119	Oman	0.17	(GDP1938/GDP1929)**(1/9)-1
120	Laos	0.07	(GDP1938/GDP1929)**(1/9)-1
121	Canada	-0.03	(GDP1938/GDP1929)**(1/9)-1
122	Belgium	-0.04	(GDP1938/GDP1929)**(1/9)-1
123	Czechia	-0.04	(GDP1938/GDP1929)**(1/9)-1
124	Slovakia	-0.04	(GDP1938/GDP1929)**(1/9)-1
125	Mongolia	-0.11	(GDP1938/GDP1929)**(1/9)-1
126	Cuba	-0.22	(GDP1938/GDP1929)**(1/9)-1
127	Sri Lanka	-0.25	(GDP1938/GDP1929)**(1/9)-1
128	Malaysia	-0.27	(GDP1938/GDP1929)**(1/9)-1
129	Austria	-0.28	(GDP1938/GDP1929)**(1/9)-1
130	France	-0.40	(GDP1938/GDP1929)**(1/9)-1
131	Burma	-0.44	(GDP1938/GDP1929)**(1/9)-1
132	US	-0.59	(GDP1938/GDP1929)**(1/9)-1
133	Honduras	-1.51	(GDP1938/GDP1929)**(1/9)-1
134	Spain	-3.71	(GDP1938/GDP1929)**(1/9)-1
135	Nicaragua	-3.81	(GDP1938/GDP1929)**(1/9)-1

Table 6.14 GDP Growth Rates, 1938-1950			
Rank	Country	GRRL	Source
1	Qatar	12.18	(GDP1950/GDP1938)**(1/12)-1
2	Kuwait	12.02	(GDP1950/GDP1938)**(1/12)-1
3	UAE	10.21	(GDP1950/GDP1938)**(1/12)-1
4	Moldova	8.34	(GDP1950/GDP1938)**(1/12)-1
5	Venezuela	8.05	(GDP1950/GDP1938)**(1/12)-1
6	Nicaragua	7.91	(GDP1950/GDP1938)**(1/12)-1
7	Cuba	6.01	(GDP1950/GDP1938)**(1/12)-1
8	Canada	5.78	(GDP1950/GDP1938)**(1/12)-1
9	Israel	5.40	(GDP1950/GDP1938)**(1/12)-1
10	El Salvador	5.35	(GDP1950/GDP1938)**(1/12)-1
11	Mexico	5.29	(GDP1950/GDP1938)**(1/12)-1
12	US	5.12	(GDP1950/GDP1938)**(1/12)-1
13	Hong Kong	5.06	(GDP1950/GDP1938)**(1/12)-1
14	Brazil	4.98	(GDP1950/GDP1938)**(1/12)-1
15	Dominican R	4.88	(GDP1950/GDP1938)**(1/12)-1
16	Trinidad & T	4.78	(GDP1950/GDP1938)**(1/12)-1
17	Ecuador	4.66	(GDP1950/GDP1938)**(1/12)-1
18	Singapore	4.63	(GDP1950/GDP1938)**(1/12)-1
19	Colombia	4.46	(GDP1950/GDP1938)**(1/12)-1
20	Panama	4.40	(GDP1950/GDP1938)**(1/12)-1
21	Bahrain	4.37	(GDP1950/GDP1938)**(1/12)-1
22	Paraguay	4.35	(GDP1950/GDP1938)**(1/12)-1
23	Jamaica	4.25	(GDP1950/GDP1938)**(1/12)-1
24	Saudi Arabia	4.12	(GDP1950/GDP1938)**(1/12)-1
25	Peru	4.07	(GDP1950/GDP1938)**(1/12)-1
26	Sweden	3.93	(GDP1950/GDP1938)**(1/12)-1
27	Switzerland	3.93	(GDP1950/GDP1938)**(1/12)-1
28	Lebanon	3.82	(GDP1950/GDP1938)**(1/12)-1
29	New Zealand	3.76	(GDP1950/GDP1938)**(1/12)-1
30	Honduras	3.70	(GDP1950/GDP1938)**(1/12)-1
31	Ghana	3.62	(GDP1950/GDP1938)**(1/12)-1
32	Argentina	3.61	(GDP1950/GDP1938)**(1/12)-1
33	Costa Rica	3.60	(GDP1950/GDP1938)**(1/12)-1
34	Morocco	3.51	(GDP1950/GDP1938)**(1/12)-1
35	Kyrgyzstan	3.49	(GDP1950/GDP1938)**(1/12)-1
36	Australia	3.43	(GDP1950/GDP1938)**(1/12)-1
37	South Africa	3.40	(GDP1950/GDP1938)**(1/12)-1
38	Puerto Rico	3.27	(GDP1950/GDP1938)**(1/12)-1
39	Iceland	3.21	(GDP1950/GDP1938)**(1/12)-1
40	Uruguay	3.17	(GDP1950/GDP1938)**(1/12)-1
41	Syria	3.13	(GDP1950/GDP1938)**(1/12)-1
42	Haiti	3.10	(GDP1950/GDP1938)**(1/12)-1
43	Kazakhstan	3.10	(GDP1950/GDP1938)**(1/12)-1
44	Norway	2.85	(GDP1950/GDP1938)**(1/12)-1
45	Pakistan	2.82	(GDP1950/GDP1938)**(1/12)-1
46	Iraq	2.81	(GDP1950/GDP1938)**(1/12)-1
47	Iran	2.66	(GDP1950/GDP1938)**(1/12)-1
48	Denmark	2.61	(GDP1950/GDP1938)**(1/12)-1

Table 6.14 GDP Growth Rates, 1938-1950

Rank	Country	GRRL	Source
49	Thailand	2.60	(GDP1950/GDP1938)**(1/12)-1
50	Armenia	2.59	(GDP1950/GDP1938)**(1/12)-1
51	Spain	2.52	(GDP1950/GDP1938)**(1/12)-1
52	Portugal	2.51	(GDP1950/GDP1938)**(1/12)-1
53	Malaysia	2.50	(GDP1950/GDP1938)**(1/12)-1
54	Chile	2.47	(GDP1950/GDP1938)**(1/12)-1
55	Tajikistan	2.41	(GDP1950/GDP1938)**(1/12)-1
56	Netherlands	2.38	(GDP1950/GDP1938)**(1/12)-1
57	Tunisia	2.37	(GDP1950/GDP1938)**(1/12)-1
58	Guatemala	2.34	(GDP1950/GDP1938)**(1/12)-1
59	Jordan	2.22	(GDP1950/GDP1938)**(1/12)-1
60	Finland	2.21	(GDP1950/GDP1938)**(1/12)-1
61	Swaziland	2.18	(GDP1950/GDP1938)**(1/12)-1
62	Georgia	2.17	(GDP1950/GDP1938)**(1/12)-1
63	Yemen	2.16	(GDP1950/GDP1938)**(1/12)-1
64	Egypt	2.10	(GDP1950/GDP1938)**(1/12)-1
65	Uzbekistan	2.03	(GDP1950/GDP1938)**(1/12)-1
66	Namibia	2.01	(GDP1950/GDP1938)**(1/12)-1
67	Sudan	1.99	(GDP1950/GDP1938)**(1/12)-1
68	Libya	1.92	(GDP1950/GDP1938)**(1/12)-1
69	Sri Lanka	1.82	(GDP1950/GDP1938)**(1/12)-1
70	Zimbabwe	1.81	(GDP1950/GDP1938)**(1/12)-1
71	Bolivia	1.81	(GDP1950/GDP1938)**(1/12)-1
72	Lesotho	1.79	(GDP1950/GDP1938)**(1/12)-1
73	Zambia	1.77	(GDP1950/GDP1938)**(1/12)-1
74	Russia	1.72	(GDP1950/GDP1938)**(1/12)-1
75	Turkmenistan	1.71	(GDP1950/GDP1938)**(1/12)-1
76	Albania	1.68	(GDP1950/GDP1938)**(1/12)-1
77	Mozambique	1.63	(GDP1950/GDP1938)**(1/12)-1
78	Estonia	1.55	(GDP1950/GDP1938)**(1/12)-1
79	Eritrea	1.52	(GDP1950/GDP1938)**(1/12)-1
80	Ethiopia	1.52	(GDP1950/GDP1938)**(1/12)-1
81	South Sudan	1.51	(GDP1950/GDP1938)**(1/12)-1
82	India	1.50	(GDP1950/GDP1938)**(1/12)-1
83	Latvia	1.49	(GDP1950/GDP1938)**(1/12)-1
84	Turkey	1.45	(GDP1950/GDP1938)**(1/12)-1
85	Algeria	1.45	(GDP1950/GDP1938)**(1/12)-1
86	Malawi	1.44	(GDP1950/GDP1938)**(1/12)-1
87	Botswana	1.42	(GDP1950/GDP1938)**(1/12)-1
88	Ukraine	1.41	(GDP1950/GDP1938)**(1/12)-1
89	Somalia	1.36	(GDP1950/GDP1938)**(1/12)-1
90	Madagascar	1.36	(GDP1950/GDP1938)**(1/12)-1
91	France	1.35	(GDP1950/GDP1938)**(1/12)-1
92	UK	1.34	(GDP1950/GDP1938)**(1/12)-1
93	Azerbaijan	1.30	(GDP1950/GDP1938)**(1/12)-1
94	Belgium	1.29	(GDP1950/GDP1938)**(1/12)-1
95	Kosovo	1.24	(GDP1950/GDP1938)**(1/12)-1
96	Macedonia	1.24	(GDP1950/GDP1938)**(1/12)-1

Table 6.14 GDP Growth Rates, 1938-1950			
Rank	Country	GRRL	Source
97	Bosnia	1.24	(GDP1950/GDP1938)**(1/12)-1
98	Serbia	1.24	(GDP1950/GDP1938)**(1/12)-1
99	Montenegro	1.24	(GDP1950/GDP1938)**(1/12)-1
100	Slovenia	1.24	(GDP1950/GDP1938)**(1/12)-1
101	Croatia	1.24	(GDP1950/GDP1938)**(1/12)-1
102	Italy	1.14	(GDP1950/GDP1938)**(1/12)-1
103	Ireland	1.13	(GDP1950/GDP1938)**(1/12)-1
104	Bulgaria	1.12	(GDP1950/GDP1938)**(1/12)-1
105	Belarus	1.06	(GDP1950/GDP1938)**(1/12)-1
106	Nepal	0.93	(GDP1950/GDP1938)**(1/12)-1
107	Sierra Leone	0.88	(GDP1950/GDP1938)**(1/12)-1
108	Guinea	0.83	(GDP1950/GDP1938)**(1/12)-1
109	Cambodia	0.83	(GDP1950/GDP1938)**(1/12)-1
110	Guinea-Biss	0.83	(GDP1950/GDP1938)**(1/12)-1
111	Afghanistan	0.77	(GDP1950/GDP1938)**(1/12)-1
112	Burundi	0.70	(GDP1950/GDP1938)**(1/12)-1
113	Vietnam	0.67	(GDP1950/GDP1938)**(1/12)-1
114	Bangladesh	0.64	(GDP1950/GDP1938)**(1/12)-1
115	Austria	0.56	(GDP1950/GDP1938)**(1/12)-1
116	Slovakia	0.25	(GDP1950/GDP1938)**(1/12)-1
117	Czechia	0.25	(GDP1950/GDP1938)**(1/12)-1
118	Oman	0.17	(GDP1950/GDP1938)**(1/12)-1
119	Lithuania	0.08	(GDP1950/GDP1938)**(1/12)-1
120	Laos	0.07	(GDP1950/GDP1938)**(1/12)-1
121	Romania	-0.04	(GDP1950/GDP1938)**(1/12)-1
122	Mongolia	-0.10	(GDP1950/GDP1938)**(1/12)-1
123	Taiwan	-0.41	(GDP1950/GDP1938)**(1/12)-1
124	Hungary	-0.41	(GDP1950/GDP1938)**(1/12)-1
125	Japan	-0.76	(GDP1950/GDP1938)**(1/12)-1 .
126	Poland	-0.91	(GDP1950/GDP1938)**(1/12)-1
127	Philippines	-1.04	(GDP1950/GDP1938)**(1/12)-1
128	China	-1.29	(GDP1950/GDP1938)**(1/12)-1
129	Indonesia	-1.50	(GDP1950/GDP1938)**(1/12)-1
130	Germany	-2.10	(GDP1950/GDP1938)**(1/12)-1
131	Cyprus	-2.19	(GDP1950/GDP1938)**(1/12)-1
132	Greece	-2.19	(GDP1950/GDP1938)**(1/12)-1
133	Korea, South	-2.75	(GDP1950/GDP1938)**(1/12)-1
134	Korea, North	-3.41	(GDP1950/GDP1938)**(1/12)-1
135	Burma	-3.58	(GDP1950/GDP1938)**(1/12)-1

TABLE 6.15 GDP GROWTH RATES, 1950-1960			
Rank	Country	GRRL	Source
1	Brunei	12.66	(GDP1960/GDP1950)**(1/10)-1
2	W Sahara	11.82	(GDP1960/GDP1950)**(1/10)-1
3	Iraq	11.45	(GDP1960/GDP1950)**(1/10)-1
4	Libya	11.35	(GDP1960/GDP1950)**(1/10)-1
5	Saudi Arabia	11.03	(GDP1960/GDP1950)**(1/10)-1
6	Bahrain	10.95	(GDP1960/GDP1950)**(1/10)-1
7	UAE	10.74	(GDP1960/GDP1950)**(1/10)-1
8	Israel	10.66	(GDP1960/GDP1950)**(1/10)-1
9	Mauritania	9.12	(GDP1960/GDP1950)**(1/10)-1
10	Malta	8.95	(GDP1960/GDP1950)**(1/10)-1
11	Jordan	8.86	(GDP1960/GDP1950)**(1/10)-1
12	Martinique	8.68	(GDP1960/GDP1950)**(1/10)-1
13	Oman	8.66	(GDP1960/GDP1950)**(1/10)-1
14	Japan	8.63	(GDP1960/GDP1950)**(1/10)-1
15	Jamaica	8.41	(GDP1960/GDP1950)**(1/10)-1
16	Taiwan	8.38	(GDP1960/GDP1950)**(1/10)-1
17	Germany	8.37	(GDP1960/GDP1950)**(1/10)-1
18	Barbados	7.94	(GDP1960/GDP1950)**(1/10)-1
19	Kosovo	7.79	(GDP1960/GDP1950)**(1/10)-1
20	Greenland	7.68	(GDP1960/GDP1950)**(1/10)-1
21	Romania	7.67	(GDP1960/GDP1950)**(1/10)-1
22	Algeria	7.67	(GDP1960/GDP1950)**(1/10)-1
23	Guadeloupe	7.51	(GDP1960/GDP1950)**(1/10)-1
24	Montenegro	7.43	(GDP1960/GDP1950)**(1/10)-1
25	St Kitts & N	7.39	(GDP1960/GDP1950)**(1/10)-1
26	Trinidad & T	7.32	(GDP1960/GDP1950)**(1/10)-1
27	Costa Rica	7.28	(GDP1960/GDP1950)**(1/10)-1
28	Kuwait	7.25	(GDP1960/GDP1950)**(1/10)-1
29	Albania	7.25	(GDP1960/GDP1950)**(1/10)-1
30	Bosnia	7.24	(GDP1960/GDP1950)**(1/10)-1
31	Macedonia	7.23	(GDP1960/GDP1950)**(1/10)-1
32	Qatar	7.21	(GDP1960/GDP1950)**(1/10)-1
33	Cyprus	7.20	(GDP1960/GDP1950)**(1/10)-1
34	Zambia	7.19	(GDP1960/GDP1950)**(1/10)-1
35	Greece	7.17	(GDP1960/GDP1950)**(1/10)-1
36	Suriname	6.91	(GDP1960/GDP1950)**(1/10)-1
37	Mayotte	6.91	(GDP1960/GDP1950)**(1/10)-1
38	Bermuda	6.89	(GDP1960/GDP1950)**(1/10)-1
39	Andorra	6.89	(GDP1960/GDP1950)**(1/10)-1
40	Comoros	6.85	(GDP1960/GDP1950)**(1/10)-1
41	Hong Kong	6.84	(GDP1960/GDP1950)**(1/10)-1
42	Turkmenistan	6.77	(GDP1960/GDP1950)**(1/10)-1
43	Serbia	6.74	(GDP1960/GDP1950)**(1/10)-1
44	Mexico	6.72	(GDP1960/GDP1950)**(1/10)-1
45	Iceland	6.70	(GDP1960/GDP1950)**(1/10)-1
46	Brazil	6.70	(GDP1960/GDP1950)**(1/10)-1
47	Bahamas	6.68	(GDP1960/GDP1950)**(1/10)-1
48	Kazakhstan	6.62	(GDP1960/GDP1950)**(1/10)-1

TABLE 6.15 GDP GROWTH RATES, 1950-1960			
Rank	Country	GRRL	Source
49	Gabon	6.62	(GDP1960/GDP1950)**(1/10)-1
50	Bulgaria	6.55	(GDP1960/GDP1950)**(1/10)-1
51	Austria	6.52	(GDP1960/GDP1950)**(1/10)-1
52	Italy	6.52	(GDP1960/GDP1950)**(1/10)-1
53	St Lucia	6.45	(GDP1960/GDP1950)**(1/10)-1
54	Dominican R	6.25	(GDP1960/GDP1950)**(1/10)-1
55	Russia	6.22	(GDP1960/GDP1950)**(1/10)-1
56	Guinea	6.20	(GDP1960/GDP1950)**(1/10)-1
57	Angola	6.15	(GDP1960/GDP1950)**(1/10)-1
58	Slovakia	6.13	(GDP1960/GDP1950)**(1/10)-1
59	Mongolia	6.06	(GDP1960/GDP1950)**(1/10)-1
60	Djibouti	6.02	(GDP1960/GDP1950)**(1/10)-1
61	Seychelles	6.02	(GDP1960/GDP1950)**(1/10)-1
62	Croatia	6.01	(GDP1960/GDP1950)**(1/10)-1
63	Hungary	5.97	(GDP1960/GDP1950)**(1/10)-1
64	Nicaragua	5.96	(GDP1960/GDP1950)**(1/10)-1
65	Philippines	5.93	(GDP1960/GDP1950)**(1/10)-1
66	Peru	5.90	(GDP1960/GDP1950)**(1/10)-1
67	Venezuela	5.88	(GDP1960/GDP1950)**(1/10)-1
68	Singapore	5.87	(GDP1960/GDP1950)**(1/10)-1
69	Turkey	5.84	(GDP1960/GDP1950)**(1/10)-1
70	Grenada	5.80	(GDP1960/GDP1950)**(1/10)-1
71	Cayman Is	5.80	(GDP1960/GDP1950)**(1/10)-1
72	San Marino	5.79	(GDP1960/GDP1950)**(1/10)-1
73	Tajikistan	5.72	(GDP1960/GDP1950)**(1/10)-1
74	Iran	5.71	(GDP1960/GDP1950)**(1/10)-1
75	Azerbaijan	5.71	(GDP1960/GDP1950)**(1/10)-1
76	Guinea-Biss	5.70	(GDP1960/GDP1950)**(1/10)-1
77	Zimbabwe	5.66	(GDP1960/GDP1950)**(1/10)-1
78	Monaco	5.57	(GDP1960/GDP1950)**(1/10)-1
79	Switzerland	5.55	(GDP1960/GDP1950)**(1/10)-1
80	Slovenia	5.54	(GDP1960/GDP1950)**(1/10)-1
81	Kiribati	5.53	(GDP1960/GDP1950)**(1/10)-1
82	South Africa	5.51	(GDP1960/GDP1950)**(1/10)-1
83	Somalia	5.50	(GDP1960/GDP1950)**(1/10)-1
84	Niger	5.48	(GDP1960/GDP1950)**(1/10)-1
85	Curacao	5.44	(GDP1960/GDP1950)**(1/10)-1
86	Sint Maarten	5.42	(GDP1960/GDP1950)**(1/10)-1
87	Cambodia	5.39	(GDP1960/GDP1950)**(1/10)-1
88	Saint Martin	5.38	(GDP1960/GDP1950)**(1/10)-1
89	Moldova	5.38	(GDP1960/GDP1950)**(1/10)-1
90	Czechia	5.37	(GDP1960/GDP1950)**(1/10)-1
91	Gibraltar	5.35	(GDP1960/GDP1950)**(1/10)-1
92	El Salvador	5.35	(GDP1960/GDP1950)**(1/10)-1
93	Korea, South	5.34	(GDP1960/GDP1950)**(1/10)-1
94	Macao	5.34	(GDP1960/GDP1950)**(1/10)-1
95	Uzbekistan	5.32	(GDP1960/GDP1950)**(1/10)-1
96	Ivory Coast	5.27	(GDP1960/GDP1950)**(1/10)-1

Table 6.15 GDP Growth Rates, 1950-1960

Rank	Country	GRRL	Source
97	Ecuador	5.26	(GDP1960/GDP1950)**(1/10)-1
98	Solomon Is	5.24	(GDP1960/GDP1950)**(1/10)-1
99	Turks & C Is	5.22	(GDP1960/GDP1950)**(1/10)-1
100	Finland	5.21	(GDP1960/GDP1950)**(1/10)-1
101	Virgin I, Br	5.17	(GDP1960/GDP1950)**(1/10)-1
102	N Mariana Is	5.16	(GDP1960/GDP1950)**(1/10)-1
103	Swaziland	5.16	(GDP1960/GDP1950)**(1/10)-1
104	Poland	5.15	(GDP1960/GDP1950)**(1/10)-1
105	Liechtenstn	5.15	(GDP1960/GDP1950)**(1/10)-1
106	Antigua & B	5.12	(GDP1960/GDP1950)**(1/10)-1
107	St Pierre&M	5.08	(GDP1960/GDP1950)**(1/10)-1
108	Botswana	5.03	(GDP1960/GDP1950)**(1/10)-1
109	Anguilla	5.02	(GDP1960/GDP1950)**(1/10)-1
110	Equatorial G	4.94	(GDP1960/GDP1950)**(1/10)-1
111	Spain	4.94	(GDP1960/GDP1950)**(1/10)-1
112	Korea, North	4.93	(GDP1960/GDP1950)**(1/10)-1
113	Netherlands	4.89	(GDP1960/GDP1950)**(1/10)-1
114	Burma	4.89	(GDP1960/GDP1950)**(1/10)-1
115	Micronesia	4.89	(GDP1960/GDP1950)**(1/10)-1
116	Faroe Is	4.87	(GDP1960/GDP1950)**(1/10)-1
117	Papua New G	4.87	(GDP1960/GDP1950)**(1/10)-1
118	Jersey	4.82	(GDP1960/GDP1950)**(1/10)-1
119	Chad	4.82	(GDP1960/GDP1950)**(1/10)-1
120	Ukraine	4.82	(GDP1960/GDP1950)**(1/10)-1
121	Tonga	4.76	(GDP1960/GDP1950)**(1/10)-1
122	Nigeria	4.76	(GDP1960/GDP1950)**(1/10)-1
123	Puerto Rico	4.73	(GDP1960/GDP1950)**(1/10)-1
124	Niue	4.73	(GDP1960/GDP1950)**(1/10)-1
125	Benin	4.70	(GDP1960/GDP1950)**(1/10)-1
126	Armenia	4.69	(GDP1960/GDP1950)**(1/10)-1
127	Luxembourg	4.69	(GDP1960/GDP1950)**(1/10)-1
128	France	4.68	(GDP1960/GDP1950)**(1/10)-1
129	Virgin I, US	4.68	(GDP1960/GDP1950)**(1/10)-1
130	Lithuania	4.67	(GDP1960/GDP1950)**(1/10)-1
131	Panama	4.59	(GDP1960/GDP1950)**(1/10)-1
132	Marshall Is	4.58	(GDP1960/GDP1950)**(1/10)-1
133	Thailand	4.54	(GDP1960/GDP1950)**(1/10)-1
134	Vanuatu	4.52	(GDP1960/GDP1950)**(1/10)-1
135	Reunion	4.51	(GDP1960/GDP1950)**(1/10)-1
136	Portugal	4.51	(GDP1960/GDP1950)**(1/10)-1
137	Afghanistan	4.50	(GDP1960/GDP1950)**(1/10)-1
138	Canada	4.48	(GDP1960/GDP1950)**(1/10)-1
139	Cook Is	4.48	(GDP1960/GDP1950)**(1/10)-1
140	Samoa	4.48	(GDP1960/GDP1950)**(1/10)-1
141	Dominica	4.44	(GDP1960/GDP1950)**(1/10)-1
142	St Vincent	4.40	(GDP1960/GDP1950)**(1/10)-1
143	Nauru	4.37	(GDP1960/GDP1950)**(1/10)-1
144	Estonia	4.37	(GDP1960/GDP1950)**(1/10)-1

Table 6.15 GDP Growth Rates, 1950-1960

Rank	Country	GRRL	Source
145	Belize	4.36	(GDP1960/GDP1950)**(1/10)-1
146	Montserrat	4.35	(GDP1960/GDP1950)**(1/10)-1
147	Tokelau	4.35	(GDP1960/GDP1950)**(1/10)-1
148	Gambia	4.30	(GDP1960/GDP1950)**(1/10)-1
149	Namibia	4.28	(GDP1960/GDP1950)**(1/10)-1
150	Saint Helena	4.26	(GDP1960/GDP1950)**(1/10)-1
151	Maldives	4.25	(GDP1960/GDP1950)**(1/10)-1
152	Norway	4.22	(GDP1960/GDP1950)**(1/10)-1
153	Svalbard	4.22	(GDP1960/GDP1950)**(1/10)-1
154	Georgia	4.21	(GDP1960/GDP1950)**(1/10)-1
155	Australia	4.21	(GDP1960/GDP1950)**(1/10)-1
156	Lebanon	4.20	(GDP1960/GDP1950)**(1/10)-1
157	Fr Polynesia	4.20	(GDP1960/GDP1950)**(1/10)-1
158	Honduras	4.15	(GDP1960/GDP1950)**(1/10)-1
159	Aruba	4.12	(GDP1960/GDP1950)**(1/10)-1
160	Wallis & Fut	4.12	(GDP1960/GDP1950)**(1/10)-1
161	Guernsey	4.05	(GDP1960/GDP1950)**(1/10)-1
162	Congo, Rep	4.03	(GDP1960/GDP1950)**(1/10)-1
163	Palau	3.97	(GDP1960/GDP1950)**(1/10)-1
164	Guyana	3.97	(GDP1960/GDP1950)**(1/10)-1
165	Kenya	3.92	(GDP1960/GDP1950)**(1/10)-1
166	Latvia	3.89	(GDP1960/GDP1950)**(1/10)-1
167	Cameroon	3.88	(GDP1960/GDP1950)**(1/10)-1
168	Congo, Dem R	3.87	(GDP1960/GDP1950)**(1/10)-1
169	Kyrgyzstan	3.87	(GDP1960/GDP1950)**(1/10)-1
170	Egypt	3.85	(GDP1960/GDP1950)**(1/10)-1
171	Tunisia	3.69	(GDP1960/GDP1950)**(1/10)-1
172	Cape Verde	3.69	(GDP1960/GDP1950)**(1/10)-1
173	Guatemala	3.69	(GDP1960/GDP1950)**(1/10)-1
174	Colombia	3.69	(GDP1960/GDP1950)**(1/10)-1
175	New Zealand	3.65	(GDP1960/GDP1950)**(1/10)-1
176	China	3.65	(GDP1960/GDP1950)**(1/10)-1
177	Laos	3.64	(GDP1960/GDP1950)**(1/10)-1
178	Tanzania	3.61	(GDP1960/GDP1950)**(1/10)-1
179	Sweden	3.56	(GDP1960/GDP1950)**(1/10)-1
180	US	3.55	(GDP1960/GDP1950)**(1/10)-1
181	Madagascar	3.53	(GDP1960/GDP1950)**(1/10)-1
182	Mozambique	3.51	(GDP1960/GDP1950)**(1/10)-1
183	New Caledon	3.50	(GDP1960/GDP1950)**(1/10)-1
184	Malawi	3.48	(GDP1960/GDP1950)**(1/10)-1
185	Denmark	3.44	(GDP1960/GDP1950)**(1/10)-1
186	Ghana	3.42	(GDP1960/GDP1950)**(1/10)-1
187	Belgium	3.39	(GDP1960/GDP1950)**(1/10)-1
188	Gaza Strip	3.30	(GDP1960/GDP1950)**(1/10)-1
189	South Sudan	3.30	(GDP1960/GDP1950)**(1/10)-1
190	Sudan	3.30	(GDP1960/GDP1950)**(1/10)-1
191	Mauritius	3.19	(GDP1960/GDP1950)**(1/10)-1
192	East Timor	3.16	(GDP1960/GDP1950)**(1/10)-1

Table 6.15 GDP Growth Rates, 1950-1960

Rank	Country	GRRL	Source
193	Fiji	3.10	(GDP1960/GDP1950)**(1/10)-1
194	Senegal	3.05	(GDP1960/GDP1950)**(1/10)-1
195	Malaysia	3.00	(GDP1960/GDP1950)**(1/10)-1
196	Bhutan	3.00	(GDP1960/GDP1950)**(1/10)-1
197	Rwanda	2.96	(GDP1960/GDP1950)**(1/10)-1
198	Togo	2.93	(GDP1960/GDP1950)**(1/10)-1
199	Uganda	2.93	(GDP1960/GDP1950)**(1/10)-1
200	Sierra Leone	2.91	(GDP1960/GDP1950)**(1/10)-1
201	India	2.90	(GDP1960/GDP1950)**(1/10)-1
202	Belarus	2.81	(GDP1960/GDP1950)**(1/10)-1
203	Samoa, Amer	2.80	(GDP1960/GDP1950)**(1/10)-1
204	Isle of Man	2.79	(GDP1960/GDP1950)**(1/10)-1
205	Mali	2.78	(GDP1960/GDP1950)**(1/10)-1
206	Falkland Is	2.73	(GDP1960/GDP1950)**(1/10)-1
207	Guam	2.68	(GDP1960/GDP1950)**(1/10)-1
208	Lesotho	2.66	(GDP1960/GDP1950)**(1/10)-1
209	Burkina Faso	2.65	(GDP1960/GDP1950)**(1/10)-1
210	Chile	2.64	(GDP1960/GDP1950)**(1/10)-1
211	Syria	2.59	(GDP1960/GDP1950)**(1/10)-1
212	Argentina	2.57	(GDP1960/GDP1950)**(1/10)-1
213	Vietnam	2.57	(GDP1960/GDP1950)**(1/10)-1
214	UK	2.51	(GDP1960/GDP1950)**(1/10)-1
215	Nepal	2.48	(GDP1960/GDP1950)**(1/10)-1
216	Paraguay	2.46	(GDP1960/GDP1950)**(1/10)-1
217	Ethiopia	2.31	(GDP1960/GDP1950)**(1/10)-1
218	CAR	2.31	(GDP1960/GDP1950)**(1/10)-1
219	Sri Lanka	2.28	(GDP1960/GDP1950)**(1/10)-1
220	Indonesia	2.07	(GDP1960/GDP1950)**(1/10)-1
221	Pakistan	2.06	(GDP1960/GDP1950)**(1/10)-1
222	Ireland	2.04	(GDP1960/GDP1950)**(1/10)-1
223	West Bank	2.00	(GDP1960/GDP1950)**(1/10)-1
224	Burundi	1.92	(GDP1960/GDP1950)**(1/10)-1
225	Cuba	1.83	(GDP1960/GDP1950)**(1/10)-1
226	Morocco	1.77	(GDP1960/GDP1950)**(1/10)-1
227	Liberia	1.74	(GDP1960/GDP1950)**(1/10)-1
228	Tuvalu	1.52	(GDP1960/GDP1950)**(1/10)-1
229	Haiti	1.42	(GDP1960/GDP1950)**(1/10)-1
230	Bangladesh	1.41	(GDP1960/GDP1950)**(1/10)-1
231	Uruguay	1.39	(GDP1960/GDP1950)**(1/10)-1
232	Eritrea	1.34	(GDP1960/GDP1950)**(1/10)-1
233	Yemen	1.31	(GDP1960/GDP1950)**(1/10)-1
234	Guiana, Fr	1.13	(GDP1960/GDP1950)**(1/10)-1
235	Sao Tome & P	1.01	(GDP1960/GDP1950)**(1/10)-1
236	Bolivia	0.21	(GDP1960/GDP1950)**(1/10)-1

Table 6.16 GDP Growth Rates, 1960-1970			
Rank	Country	GRRL	Source
1	Libya	23.29	(GDP1970/GDP1960)**(1/10)-1
2	Oman	20.26	(GDP1970/GDP1960)**(1/10)-1
3	UAE	15.59	(GDP1970/GDP1960)**(1/10)-1
4	Andorra	13.82	(GDP1970/GDP1960)**(1/10)-1
5	Sint Maarten	12.83	(GDP1970/GDP1960)**(1/10)-1
6	W Sahara	12.72	(GDP1970/GDP1960)**(1/10)-1
7	Saudi Arabia	12.06	(GDP1970/GDP1960)**(1/10)-1
8	Macao	11.34	(GDP1970/GDP1960)**(1/10)-1
9	Bahrain	11.21	(GDP1970/GDP1960)**(1/10)-1
10	Brunei	11.11	(GDP1970/GDP1960)**(1/10)-1
11	Iran	10.62	(GDP1970/GDP1960)**(1/10)-1
12	Japan	10.51	(GDP1970/GDP1960)**(1/10)-1
13	Taiwan	10.39	(GDP1970/GDP1960)**(1/10)-1
14	Singapore	10.01	(GDP1970/GDP1960)**(1/10)-1
15	Swaziland	9.99	(GDP1970/GDP1960)**(1/10)-1
16	Kuwait	9.81	(GDP1970/GDP1960)**(1/10)-1
17	Qatar	9.47	(GDP1970/GDP1960)**(1/10)-1
18	Botswana	9.46	(GDP1970/GDP1960)**(1/10)-1
19	Virgin I, US	9.45	(GDP1970/GDP1960)**(1/10)-1
20	Spain	9.36	(GDP1970/GDP1960)**(1/10)-1
21	Djibouti	9.10	(GDP1970/GDP1960)**(1/10)-1
22	Israel	9.01	(GDP1970/GDP1960)**(1/10)-1
23	Hong Kong	8.83	(GDP1970/GDP1960)**(1/10)-1
24	Greece	8.83	(GDP1970/GDP1960)**(1/10)-1
25	Korea, North	8.74	(GDP1970/GDP1960)**(1/10)-1
26	Malta	8.59	(GDP1970/GDP1960)**(1/10)-1
27	Mauritania	8.08	(GDP1970/GDP1960)**(1/10)-1
28	Korea, South	7.99	(GDP1970/GDP1960)**(1/10)-1
29	Kosovo	7.95	(GDP1970/GDP1960)**(1/10)-1
30	Angola	7.94	(GDP1970/GDP1960)**(1/10)-1
31	Ivory Coast	7.81	(GDP1970/GDP1960)**(1/10)-1
32	Bahamas	7.80	(GDP1970/GDP1960)**(1/10)-1
33	Panama	7.72	(GDP1970/GDP1960)**(1/10)-1
34	Comoros	7.71	(GDP1970/GDP1960)**(1/10)-1
35	Martinique	7.63	(GDP1970/GDP1960)**(1/10)-1
36	Bermuda	7.60	(GDP1970/GDP1960)**(1/10)-1
37	Nicaragua	7.44	(GDP1970/GDP1960)**(1/10)-1
38	Turkmenistan	7.43	(GDP1970/GDP1960)**(1/10)-1
39	Greenland	7.37	(GDP1970/GDP1960)**(1/10)-1
40	Reunion	7.31	(GDP1970/GDP1960)**(1/10)-1
41	Romania	7.30	(GDP1970/GDP1960)**(1/10)-1
42	Lebanon	7.25	(GDP1970/GDP1960)**(1/10)-1
43	Nauru	7.25	(GDP1970/GDP1960)**(1/10)-1
44	Barbados	7.24	(GDP1970/GDP1960)**(1/10)-1
45	St Lucia	7.12	(GDP1970/GDP1960)**(1/10)-1
46	Equatorial G	7.12	(GDP1970/GDP1960)**(1/10)-1
47	Puerto Rico	6.98	(GDP1970/GDP1960)**(1/10)-1
48	Macedonia	6.95	(GDP1970/GDP1960)**(1/10)-1

Table 6.16 GDP Growth Rates, 1960-1970

Rank	Country	GRRL	Source
49	Mongolia	6.84	(GDP1970/GDP1960)**(1/10)-1
50	Portugal	6.79	(GDP1970/GDP1960)**(1/10)-1
51	San Marino	6.78	(GDP1970/GDP1960)**(1/10)-1
52	South Africa	6.77	(GDP1970/GDP1960)**(1/10)-1
53	Mexico	6.77	(GDP1970/GDP1960)**(1/10)-1
54	Albania	6.70	(GDP1970/GDP1960)**(1/10)-1
55	Costa Rica	6.63	(GDP1970/GDP1960)**(1/10)-1
56	Liechtenstn	6.62	(GDP1970/GDP1960)**(1/10)-1
57	Montenegro	6.57	(GDP1970/GDP1960)**(1/10)-1
58	Guadeloupe	6.52	(GDP1970/GDP1960)**(1/10)-1
59	Italy	6.46	(GDP1970/GDP1960)**(1/10)-1
60	Thailand	6.44	(GDP1970/GDP1960)**(1/10)-1
61	El Salvador	6.43	(GDP1970/GDP1960)**(1/10)-1
62	Suriname	6.37	(GDP1970/GDP1960)**(1/10)-1
63	Cyprus	6.35	(GDP1970/GDP1960)**(1/10)-1
64	Tajikistan	6.32	(GDP1970/GDP1960)**(1/10)-1
65	Bosnia	6.31	(GDP1970/GDP1960)**(1/10)-1
66	Gabon	6.31	(GDP1970/GDP1960)**(1/10)-1
67	Iceland	6.06	(GDP1970/GDP1960)**(1/10)-1
68	Serbia	6.05	(GDP1970/GDP1960)**(1/10)-1
69	Gambia	6.01	(GDP1970/GDP1960)**(1/10)-1
70	Papua New G	6.01	(GDP1970/GDP1960)**(1/10)-1
71	Pakistan	5.90	(GDP1970/GDP1960)**(1/10)-1
72	Saint Martin	5.89	(GDP1970/GDP1960)**(1/10)-1
73	St Kitts & N	5.87	(GDP1970/GDP1960)**(1/10)-1
74	Iraq	5.84	(GDP1970/GDP1960)**(1/10)-1
75	Togo	5.82	(GDP1970/GDP1960)**(1/10)-1
76	Uzbekistan	5.79	(GDP1970/GDP1960)**(1/10)-1
77	Brazil	5.79	(GDP1970/GDP1960)**(1/10)-1
78	Malaysia	5.76	(GDP1970/GDP1960)**(1/10)-1
79	Gibraltar	5.75	(GDP1970/GDP1960)**(1/10)-1
80	Azerbaijan	5.72	(GDP1970/GDP1960)**(1/10)-1
81	Bulgaria	5.72	(GDP1970/GDP1960)**(1/10)-1
82	Turkey	5.71	(GDP1970/GDP1960)**(1/10)-1
83	Eritrea	5.70	(GDP1970/GDP1960)**(1/10)-1
84	France	5.69	(GDP1970/GDP1960)**(1/10)-1
85	Bolivia	5.67	(GDP1970/GDP1960)**(1/10)-1
86	Croatia	5.66	(GDP1970/GDP1960)**(1/10)-1
87	Ecuador	5.65	(GDP1970/GDP1960)**(1/10)-1
88	Tanzania	5.64	(GDP1970/GDP1960)**(1/10)-1
89	Russia	5.63	(GDP1970/GDP1960)**(1/10)-1
90	Switzerland	5.63	(GDP1970/GDP1960)**(1/10)-1
91	Ethiopia	5.62	(GDP1970/GDP1960)**(1/10)-1
92	Solomon Is	5.59	(GDP1970/GDP1960)**(1/10)-1
93	Zimbabwe	5.58	(GDP1970/GDP1960)**(1/10)-1
94	Guinea-Biss	5.55	(GDP1970/GDP1960)**(1/10)-1
95	Kenya	5.55	(GDP1970/GDP1960)**(1/10)-1
96	Jordan	5.54	(GDP1970/GDP1960)**(1/10)-1

Table 6.16 GDP Growth Rates, 1960-1970

Rank	Country	GRRL	Source
97	Peru	5.50	(GDP1970/GDP1960)**(1/10)-1
98	Australia	5.46	(GDP1970/GDP1960)**(1/10)-1
99	Kazakhstan	5.45	(GDP1970/GDP1960)**(1/10)-1
100	Samoa, Amer	5.39	(GDP1970/GDP1960)**(1/10)-1
101	Dominican R	5.39	(GDP1970/GDP1960)**(1/10)-1
102	Canada	5.38	(GDP1970/GDP1960)**(1/10)-1
103	Belgium	5.38	(GDP1970/GDP1960)**(1/10)-1
104	Lithuania	5.36	(GDP1970/GDP1960)**(1/10)-1
105	Monaco	5.35	(GDP1970/GDP1960)**(1/10)-1
106	Marshall Is	5.35	(GDP1970/GDP1960)**(1/10)-1
107	Faroe Is	5.35	(GDP1970/GDP1960)**(1/10)-1
108	Nigeria	5.32	(GDP1970/GDP1960)**(1/10)-1
109	Netherlands	5.32	(GDP1970/GDP1960)**(1/10)-1
110	Isle of Man	5.24	(GDP1970/GDP1960)**(1/10)-1
111	Fr Polynesia	5.22	(GDP1970/GDP1960)**(1/10)-1
112	Austria	5.20	(GDP1970/GDP1960)**(1/10)-1
113	Virgin I, Br	5.17	(GDP1970/GDP1960)**(1/10)-1
114	Antigua & B	5.16	(GDP1970/GDP1960)**(1/10)-1
115	Seychelles	5.14	(GDP1970/GDP1960)**(1/10)-1
116	Slovenia	5.13	(GDP1970/GDP1960)**(1/10)-1
117	Mozambique	5.13	(GDP1970/GDP1960)**(1/10)-1
118	Guernsey	5.13	(GDP1970/GDP1960)**(1/10)-1
119	Kiribati	5.12	(GDP1970/GDP1960)**(1/10)-1
120	Cayman Is	5.12	(GDP1970/GDP1960)**(1/10)-1
121	New Caledon	5.11	(GDP1970/GDP1960)**(1/10)-1
122	Finland	5.10	(GDP1970/GDP1960)**(1/10)-1
123	Tunisia	5.09	(GDP1970/GDP1960)**(1/10)-1
124	St Pierre&M	5.07	(GDP1970/GDP1960)**(1/10)-1
125	Curacao	5.04	(GDP1970/GDP1960)**(1/10)-1
126	Jamaica	5.02	(GDP1970/GDP1960)**(1/10)-1
127	Anguilla	5.02	(GDP1970/GDP1960)**(1/10)-1
128	Kyrgyzstan	4.98	(GDP1970/GDP1960)**(1/10)-1
129	Colombia	4.96	(GDP1970/GDP1960)**(1/10)-1
130	Sweden	4.96	(GDP1970/GDP1960)**(1/10)-1
131	Denmark	4.94	(GDP1970/GDP1960)**(1/10)-1
132	Hungary	4.88	(GDP1970/GDP1960)**(1/10)-1
133	Luxembourg	4.87	(GDP1970/GDP1960)**(1/10)-1
134	Poland	4.84	(GDP1970/GDP1960)**(1/10)-1
135	Sao Tome & P	4.82	(GDP1970/GDP1960)**(1/10)-1
136	Moldova	4.80	(GDP1970/GDP1960)**(1/10)-1
137	Cameroon	4.74	(GDP1970/GDP1960)**(1/10)-1
138	Svalbard	4.74	(GDP1970/GDP1960)**(1/10)-1
139	Norway	4.74	(GDP1970/GDP1960)**(1/10)-1
140	Niue	4.73	(GDP1970/GDP1960)**(1/10)-1
141	Jersey	4.73	(GDP1970/GDP1960)**(1/10)-1
142	Namibia	4.71	(GDP1970/GDP1960)**(1/10)-1
143	Estonia	4.68	(GDP1970/GDP1960)**(1/10)-1
144	Congo, Rep	4.66	(GDP1970/GDP1960)**(1/10)-1

Table 6.16 GDP Growth Rates, 1960-1970

Rank	Country	GRRL	Source
145	Egypt	4.65	(GDP1970/GDP1960)**(1/10)-1
146	Germany	4.61	(GDP1970/GDP1960)**(1/10)-1
147	Vanuatu	4.60	(GDP1970/GDP1960)**(1/10)-1
148	Ireland	4.60	(GDP1970/GDP1960)**(1/10)-1
149	Grenada	4.59	(GDP1970/GDP1960)**(1/10)-1
150	Guatemala	4.56	(GDP1970/GDP1960)**(1/10)-1
151	Armenia	4.54	(GDP1970/GDP1960)**(1/10)-1
152	Honduras	4.53	(GDP1970/GDP1960)**(1/10)-1
153	Micronesia	4.51	(GDP1970/GDP1960)**(1/10)-1
154	Ukraine	4.50	(GDP1970/GDP1960)**(1/10)-1
155	Bhutan	4.49	(GDP1970/GDP1960)**(1/10)-1
156	Cook Is	4.48	(GDP1970/GDP1960)**(1/10)-1
157	Paraguay	4.44	(GDP1970/GDP1960)**(1/10)-1
158	Belize	4.44	(GDP1970/GDP1960)**(1/10)-1
159	Philippines	4.42	(GDP1970/GDP1960)**(1/10)-1
160	Palau	4.35	(GDP1970/GDP1960)**(1/10)-1
161	Montserrat	4.35	(GDP1970/GDP1960)**(1/10)-1
162	Dominica	4.35	(GDP1970/GDP1960)**(1/10)-1
163	Tokelau	4.33	(GDP1970/GDP1960)**(1/10)-1
164	Zambia	4.32	(GDP1970/GDP1960)**(1/10)-1
165	US	4.25	(GDP1970/GDP1960)**(1/10)-1
166	Latvia	4.23	(GDP1970/GDP1960)**(1/10)-1
167	Algeria	4.22	(GDP1970/GDP1960)**(1/10)-1
168	Tonga	4.19	(GDP1970/GDP1960)**(1/10)-1
169	Wallis & Fut	4.12	(GDP1970/GDP1960)**(1/10)-1
170	Uganda	4.08	(GDP1970/GDP1960)**(1/10)-1
171	Samoa	4.08	(GDP1970/GDP1960)**(1/10)-1
172	Georgia	4.02	(GDP1970/GDP1960)**(1/10)-1
173	Guam	4.00	(GDP1970/GDP1960)**(1/10)-1
174	Venezuela	4.00	(GDP1970/GDP1960)**(1/10)-1
175	Maldives	3.99	(GDP1970/GDP1960)**(1/10)-1
176	N Mariana Is	3.93	(GDP1970/GDP1960)**(1/10)-1
177	Argentina	3.89	(GDP1970/GDP1960)**(1/10)-1
178	New Zealand	3.76	(GDP1970/GDP1960)**(1/10)-1
179	Guiana, Fr	3.75	(GDP1970/GDP1960)**(1/10)-1
180	Guinea	3.75	(GDP1970/GDP1960)**(1/10)-1
181	Morocco	3.73	(GDP1970/GDP1960)**(1/10)-1
182	Mayotte	3.71	(GDP1970/GDP1960)**(1/10)-1
183	Trinidad & T	3.70	(GDP1970/GDP1960)**(1/10)-1
184	Guyana	3.68	(GDP1970/GDP1960)**(1/10)-1
185	Aruba	3.67	(GDP1970/GDP1960)**(1/10)-1
186	Sierra Leone	3.56	(GDP1970/GDP1960)**(1/10)-1
187	Chile	3.53	(GDP1970/GDP1960)**(1/10)-1
188	Slovakia	3.53	(GDP1970/GDP1960)**(1/10)-1
189	Czechia	3.52	(GDP1970/GDP1960)**(1/10)-1
190	Lesotho	3.49	(GDP1970/GDP1960)**(1/10)-1
191	Belarus	3.43	(GDP1970/GDP1960)**(1/10)-1
192	Tuvalu	3.39	(GDP1970/GDP1960)**(1/10)-1

Table 6.16 GDP Growth Rates, 1960-1970

Rank	Country	GRRL	Source
193	Cape Verde	3.35	(GDP1970/GDP1960)**(1/10)-1
194	St Vincent	3.29	(GDP1970/GDP1960)**(1/10)-1
195	Madagascar	3.26	(GDP1970/GDP1960)**(1/10)-1
196	East Timor	3.20	(GDP1970/GDP1960)**(1/10)-1
197	Bangladesh	3.14	(GDP1970/GDP1960)**(1/10)-1
198	Niger	3.13	(GDP1970/GDP1960)**(1/10)-1
199	Malawi	3.10	(GDP1970/GDP1960)**(1/10)-1
200	Yemen	3.05	(GDP1970/GDP1960)**(1/10)-1
201	Burma	3.03	(GDP1970/GDP1960)**(1/10)-1
202	Congo, Dem R	2.93	(GDP1970/GDP1960)**(1/10)-1
203	Indonesia	2.84	(GDP1970/GDP1960)**(1/10)-1
204	Fiji	2.83	(GDP1970/GDP1960)**(1/10)-1
205	Syria	2.80	(GDP1970/GDP1960)**(1/10)-1
206	Falkland Is	2.73	(GDP1970/GDP1960)**(1/10)-1
207	UK	2.71	(GDP1970/GDP1960)**(1/10)-1
208	Turks & C Is	2.69	(GDP1970/GDP1960)**(1/10)-1
209	Rwanda	2.64	(GDP1970/GDP1960)**(1/10)-1
210	Chad	2.62	(GDP1970/GDP1960)**(1/10)-1
211	India	2.58	(GDP1970/GDP1960)**(1/10)-1
212	Laos	2.54	(GDP1970/GDP1960)**(1/10)-1
213	Sri Lanka	2.50	(GDP1970/GDP1960)**(1/10)-1
214	Senegal	2.27	(GDP1970/GDP1960)**(1/10)-1
215	Burkina Faso	2.25	(GDP1970/GDP1960)**(1/10)-1
216	Mali	2.24	(GDP1970/GDP1960)**(1/10)-1
217	Cambodia	2.09	(GDP1970/GDP1960)**(1/10)-1
218	Gaza Strip	2.03	(GDP1970/GDP1960)**(1/10)-1
219	Ghana	1.75	(GDP1970/GDP1960)**(1/10)-1
220	Mauritius	1.69	(GDP1970/GDP1960)**(1/10)-1
221	China	1.59	(GDP1970/GDP1960)**(1/10)-1
222	Afghanistan	1.59	(GDP1970/GDP1960)**(1/10)-1
223	Liberia	1.53	(GDP1970/GDP1960)**(1/10)-1
224	Burundi	1.52	(GDP1970/GDP1960)**(1/10)-1
225	Nepal	1.49	(GDP1970/GDP1960)**(1/10)-1
226	Cuba	1.41	(GDP1970/GDP1960)**(1/10)-1
227	South Sudan	1.37	(GDP1970/GDP1960)**(1/10)-1
228	Sudan	1.37	(GDP1970/GDP1960)**(1/10)-1
229	CAR	1.31	(GDP1970/GDP1960)**(1/10)-1
230	Vietnam	1.27	(GDP1970/GDP1960)**(1/10)-1
231	Benin	1.22	(GDP1970/GDP1960)**(1/10)-1
232	Uruguay	0.96	(GDP1970/GDP1960)**(1/10)-1
233	Haiti	0.61	(GDP1970/GDP1960)**(1/10)-1
234	Somalia	0.52	(GDP1970/GDP1960)**(1/10)-1
235	Saint Helena	0.41	(GDP1970/GDP1960)**(1/10)-1
236	West Bank	-1.28	(GDP1970/GDP1960)**(1/10)-1

Table 6.17 GDP Growth Rates, 1970-1980

Rank	Country	GRRL	Source
1	UAE	22.30	(GDP1980/GDP1970)**(1/10)-1
2	Botswana	16.25	(GDP1980/GDP1970)**(1/10)-1
3	Saudi Arabia	12.76	(GDP1980/GDP1970)**(1/10)-1
4	Brunei	12.11	(GDP1980/GDP1970)**(1/10)-1
5	Macao	11.11	(GDP1980/GDP1970)**(1/10)-1
6	Bahrain	10.77	(GDP1980/GDP1970)**(1/10)-1
7	Iraq	10.30	(GDP1980/GDP1970)**(1/10)-1
8	Singapore	9.73	(GDP1980/GDP1970)**(1/10)-1
9	Korea, South	9.30	(GDP1980/GDP1970)**(1/10)-1
10	Seychelles	9.29	(GDP1980/GDP1970)**(1/10)-1
11	Hong Kong	8.91	(GDP1980/GDP1970)**(1/10)-1
12	Taiwan	8.90	(GDP1980/GDP1970)**(1/10)-1
13	Jordan	8.37	(GDP1980/GDP1970)**(1/10)-1
14	Kosovo	8.21	(GDP1980/GDP1970)**(1/10)-1
15	Paraguay	8.12	(GDP1980/GDP1970)**(1/10)-1
16	Andorra	8.10	(GDP1980/GDP1970)**(1/10)-1
17	Malaysia	8.03	(GDP1980/GDP1970)**(1/10)-1
18	Brazil	7.89	(GDP1980/GDP1970)**(1/10)-1
19	Algeria	7.80	(GDP1980/GDP1970)**(1/10)-1
20	Yemen	7.71	(GDP1980/GDP1970)**(1/10)-1
21	Macedonia	7.68	(GDP1980/GDP1970)**(1/10)-1
22	Maldives	7.58	(GDP1980/GDP1970)**(1/10)-1
23	Dominican R	7.34	(GDP1980/GDP1970)**(1/10)-1
24	Mexico	7.32	(GDP1980/GDP1970)**(1/10)-1
25	Tunisia	7.28	(GDP1980/GDP1970)**(1/10)-1
26	Egypt	7.26	(GDP1980/GDP1970)**(1/10)-1
27	Cayman Is	7.26	(GDP1980/GDP1970)**(1/10)-1
28	Ecuador	7.19	(GDP1980/GDP1970)**(1/10)-1
29	Montenegro	7.17	(GDP1980/GDP1970)**(1/10)-1
30	Kuwait	6.87	(GDP1980/GDP1970)**(1/10)-1
31	Mongolia	6.77	(GDP1980/GDP1970)**(1/10)-1
32	Bosnia	6.67	(GDP1980/GDP1970)**(1/10)-1
33	Sint Maarten	6.50	(GDP1980/GDP1970)**(1/10)-1
34	Romania	6.46	(GDP1980/GDP1970)**(1/10)-1
35	Oman	6.42	(GDP1980/GDP1970)**(1/10)-1
36	Croatia	6.25	(GDP1980/GDP1970)**(1/10)-1
37	Serbia	6.22	(GDP1980/GDP1970)**(1/10)-1
38	Lebanon	6.18	(GDP1980/GDP1970)**(1/10)-1
39	Malawi	6.17	(GDP1980/GDP1970)**(1/10)-1
40	Gabon	6.07	(GDP1980/GDP1970)**(1/10)-1
41	Virgin I, US	6.07	(GDP1980/GDP1970)**(1/10)-1
42	Lesotho	6.07	(GDP1980/GDP1970)**(1/10)-1
43	Djibouti	6.04	(GDP1980/GDP1970)**(1/10)-1
44	Slovenia	6.02	(GDP1980/GDP1970)**(1/10)-1
45	Cyprus	6.02	(GDP1980/GDP1970)**(1/10)-1
46	Israel	5.99	(GDP1980/GDP1970)**(1/10)-1
47	Qatar	5.96	(GDP1980/GDP1970)**(1/10)-1
48	Syria	5.86	(GDP1980/GDP1970)**(1/10)-1

Table 6.17 GDP Growth Rates, 1970-1980			
Rank	Country	GRRL	Source
49	Korea, North	5.84	(GDP1980/GDP1970)**(1/10)-1
50	Congo, Rep	5.74	(GDP1980/GDP1970)**(1/10)-1
51	Ivory Coast	5.73	(GDP1980/GDP1970)**(1/10)-1
52	Greece	5.65	(GDP1980/GDP1970)**(1/10)-1
53	Cameroon	5.61	(GDP1980/GDP1970)**(1/10)-1
54	W Sahara	5.56	(GDP1980/GDP1970)**(1/10)-1
55	Haiti	5.54	(GDP1980/GDP1970)**(1/10)-1
56	Panama	5.52	(GDP1980/GDP1970)**(1/10)-1
57	Indonesia	5.50	(GDP1980/GDP1970)**(1/10)-1
58	Mayotte	5.50	(GDP1980/GDP1970)**(1/10)-1
59	Norway	5.46	(GDP1980/GDP1970)**(1/10)-1
60	Svalbard	5.46	(GDP1980/GDP1970)**(1/10)-1
61	Gambia	5.45	(GDP1980/GDP1970)**(1/10)-1
62	Spain	5.42	(GDP1980/GDP1970)**(1/10)-1
63	Philippines	5.38	(GDP1980/GDP1970)**(1/10)-1
64	Thailand	5.37	(GDP1980/GDP1970)**(1/10)-1
65	Costa Rica	5.32	(GDP1980/GDP1970)**(1/10)-1
66	Bhutan	5.31	(GDP1980/GDP1970)**(1/10)-1
67	Colombia	5.24	(GDP1980/GDP1970)**(1/10)-1
68	Malta	5.23	(GDP1980/GDP1970)**(1/10)-1
69	Solomon Is	5.21	(GDP1980/GDP1970)**(1/10)-1
70	Trinidad & T	5.19	(GDP1980/GDP1970)**(1/10)-1
71	Ireland	5.13	(GDP1980/GDP1970)**(1/10)-1
72	Honduras	5.12	(GDP1980/GDP1970)**(1/10)-1
73	Portugal	5.02	(GDP1980/GDP1970)**(1/10)-1
74	Turkey	4.95	(GDP1980/GDP1970)**(1/10)-1
75	Kenya	4.91	(GDP1980/GDP1970)**(1/10)-1
76	Swaziland	4.87	(GDP1980/GDP1970)**(1/10)-1
77	Sao Tome & P	4.74	(GDP1980/GDP1970)**(1/10)-1
78	Turks & C Is	4.74	(GDP1980/GDP1970)**(1/10)-1
79	Rwanda	4.72	(GDP1980/GDP1970)**(1/10)-1
80	Morocco	4.70	(GDP1980/GDP1970)**(1/10)-1
81	Isle of Man	4.69	(GDP1980/GDP1970)**(1/10)-1
82	Gibraltar	4.68	(GDP1980/GDP1970)**(1/10)-1
83	Barbados	4.55	(GDP1980/GDP1970)**(1/10)-1
84	South Africa	4.51	(GDP1980/GDP1970)**(1/10)-1
85	Japan	4.47	(GDP1980/GDP1970)**(1/10)-1
86	Namibia	4.44	(GDP1980/GDP1970)**(1/10)-1
87	St Lucia	4.38	(GDP1980/GDP1970)**(1/10)-1
88	Canada	4.36	(GDP1980/GDP1970)**(1/10)-1
89	Burma	4.29	(GDP1980/GDP1970)**(1/10)-1
90	Guatemala	4.29	(GDP1980/GDP1970)**(1/10)-1
91	Mauritius	4.26	(GDP1980/GDP1970)**(1/10)-1
92	Liechtenstn	4.25	(GDP1980/GDP1970)**(1/10)-1
93	Bolivia	4.25	(GDP1980/GDP1970)**(1/10)-1
94	Albania	4.23	(GDP1980/GDP1970)**(1/10)-1
95	Nigeria	4.18	(GDP1980/GDP1970)**(1/10)-1
96	Poland	4.12	(GDP1980/GDP1970)**(1/10)-1

Table 6.17 GDP Growth Rates, 1970-1980

Rank	Country	GRRL	Source
97	Austria	4.08	(GDP1980/GDP1970)**(1/10)-1
98	Tanzania	4.06	(GDP1980/GDP1970)**(1/10)-1
99	Italy	4.05	(GDP1980/GDP1970)**(1/10)-1
100	Marshall Is	4.05	(GDP1980/GDP1970)**(1/10)-1
101	Suriname	4.00	(GDP1980/GDP1970)**(1/10)-1
102	Peru	4.00	(GDP1980/GDP1970)**(1/10)-1
103	Kiribati	3.98	(GDP1980/GDP1970)**(1/10)-1
104	Iceland	3.97	(GDP1980/GDP1970)**(1/10)-1
105	N Mariana Is	3.94	(GDP1980/GDP1970)**(1/10)-1
106	Puerto Rico	3.90	(GDP1980/GDP1970)**(1/10)-1
107	Cuba	3.89	(GDP1980/GDP1970)**(1/10)-1
108	Sudan	3.87	(GDP1980/GDP1970)**(1/10)-1
109	South Sudan	3.87	(GDP1980/GDP1970)**(1/10)-1
110	Hungary	3.85	(GDP1980/GDP1970)**(1/10)-1
111	El Salvador	3.84	(GDP1980/GDP1970)**(1/10)-1
112	San Marino	3.83	(GDP1980/GDP1970)**(1/10)-1
113	Fr Polynesia	3.81	(GDP1980/GDP1970)**(1/10)-1
114	Monaco	3.79	(GDP1980/GDP1970)**(1/10)-1
115	Eritrea	3.79	(GDP1980/GDP1970)**(1/10)-1
116	Vanuatu	3.79	(GDP1980/GDP1970)**(1/10)-1
117	Gaza Strip	3.76	(GDP1980/GDP1970)**(1/10)-1
118	Finland	3.73	(GDP1980/GDP1970)**(1/10)-1
119	Antigua & B	3.72	(GDP1980/GDP1970)**(1/10)-1
120	Belgium	3.72	(GDP1980/GDP1970)**(1/10)-1
121	Belize	3.72	(GDP1980/GDP1970)**(1/10)-1
122	Pakistan	3.62	(GDP1980/GDP1970)**(1/10)-1
123	Mali	3.58	(GDP1980/GDP1970)**(1/10)-1
124	Faroe Is	3.56	(GDP1980/GDP1970)**(1/10)-1
125	Tuvalu	3.53	(GDP1980/GDP1970)**(1/10)-1
126	Czechia	3.49	(GDP1980/GDP1970)**(1/10)-1
127	Jersey	3.46	(GDP1980/GDP1970)**(1/10)-1
128	Australia	3.44	(GDP1980/GDP1970)**(1/10)-1
129	Virgin I, Br	3.43	(GDP1980/GDP1970)**(1/10)-1
130	Greenland	3.38	(GDP1980/GDP1970)**(1/10)-1
131	St Pierre&M	3.37	(GDP1980/GDP1970)**(1/10)-1
132	Anguilla	3.34	(GDP1980/GDP1970)**(1/10)-1
133	US	3.31	(GDP1980/GDP1970)**(1/10)-1
134	Somalia	3.31	(GDP1980/GDP1970)**(1/10)-1
135	Slovakia	3.30	(GDP1980/GDP1970)**(1/10)-1
136	West Bank	3.29	(GDP1980/GDP1970)**(1/10)-1
137	France	3.25	(GDP1980/GDP1970)**(1/10)-1
138	Niue	3.21	(GDP1980/GDP1970)**(1/10)-1
139	Bahamas	3.17	(GDP1980/GDP1970)**(1/10)-1
140	St Vincent	3.17	(GDP1980/GDP1970)**(1/10)-1
141	Germany	3.16	(GDP1980/GDP1970)**(1/10)-1
142	Saint Martin	3.15	(GDP1980/GDP1970)**(1/10)-1
143	Guiana, Fr	3.11	(GDP1980/GDP1970)**(1/10)-1
144	Cook Is	3.11	(GDP1980/GDP1970)**(1/10)-1

Table 6.17 GDP Growth Rates, 1970-1980

Rank	Country	GRRL	Source
145	Netherlands	3.11	(GDP1980/GDP1970)**(1/10)-1
146	Iran	3.07	(GDP1980/GDP1970)**(1/10)-1
147	Tokelau	3.06	(GDP1980/GDP1970)**(1/10)-1
148	Uzbekistan	3.00	(GDP1980/GDP1970)**(1/10)-1
149	Wallis & Fut	2.97	(GDP1980/GDP1970)**(1/10)-1
150	Turkmenistan	2.97	(GDP1980/GDP1970)**(1/10)-1
151	Guam	2.95	(GDP1980/GDP1970)**(1/10)-1
152	Montserrat	2.93	(GDP1980/GDP1970)**(1/10)-1
153	Guernsey	2.89	(GDP1980/GDP1970)**(1/10)-1
154	Ethiopia	2.87	(GDP1980/GDP1970)**(1/10)-1
155	Bermuda	2.87	(GDP1980/GDP1970)**(1/10)-1
156	China	2.84	(GDP1980/GDP1970)**(1/10)-1
157	Guinea	2.79	(GDP1980/GDP1970)**(1/10)-1
158	New Caledon	2.78	(GDP1980/GDP1970)**(1/10)-1
159	Russia	2.75	(GDP1980/GDP1970)**(1/10)-1
160	Zimbabwe	2.73	(GDP1980/GDP1970)**(1/10)-1
161	Bulgaria	2.71	(GDP1980/GDP1970)**(1/10)-1
162	Cape Verde	2.69	(GDP1980/GDP1970)**(1/10)-1
163	Venezuela	2.66	(GDP1980/GDP1970)**(1/10)-1
164	Laos	2.66	(GDP1980/GDP1970)**(1/10)-1
165	Lithuania	2.63	(GDP1980/GDP1970)**(1/10)-1
166	Samoa, Amer	2.62	(GDP1980/GDP1970)**(1/10)-1
167	Sri Lanka	2.60	(GDP1980/GDP1970)**(1/10)-1
168	Guyana	2.55	(GDP1980/GDP1970)**(1/10)-1
169	Estonia	2.51	(GDP1980/GDP1970)**(1/10)-1
170	Armenia	2.42	(GDP1980/GDP1970)**(1/10)-1
171	Denmark	2.41	(GDP1980/GDP1970)**(1/10)-1
172	Papua New G	2.37	(GDP1980/GDP1970)**(1/10)-1
173	Argentina	2.37	(GDP1980/GDP1970)**(1/10)-1
174	New Zealand	2.35	(GDP1980/GDP1970)**(1/10)-1
175	Moldova	2.30	(GDP1980/GDP1970)**(1/10)-1
176	Uruguay	2.28	(GDP1980/GDP1970)**(1/10)-1
177	Micronesia	2.28	(GDP1980/GDP1970)**(1/10)-1
178	Sweden	2.23	(GDP1980/GDP1970)**(1/10)-1
179	Martinique	2.22	(GDP1980/GDP1970)**(1/10)-1
180	Guadeloupe	2.19	(GDP1980/GDP1970)**(1/10)-1
181	Ukraine	2.18	(GDP1980/GDP1970)**(1/10)-1
182	Guinea-Biss	2.18	(GDP1980/GDP1970)**(1/10)-1
183	India	2.17	(GDP1980/GDP1970)**(1/10)-1
184	Mauritania	2.12	(GDP1980/GDP1970)**(1/10)-1
185	Saint Helena	2.09	(GDP1980/GDP1970)**(1/10)-1
186	Togo	2.06	(GDP1980/GDP1970)**(1/10)-1
187	Azerbaijan	2.05	(GDP1980/GDP1970)**(1/10)-1
188	Grenada	1.93	(GDP1980/GDP1970)**(1/10)-1
189	Switzerland	1.92	(GDP1980/GDP1970)**(1/10)-1
190	Latvia	1.91	(GDP1980/GDP1970)**(1/10)-1
191	Libya	1.91	(GDP1980/GDP1970)**(1/10)-1
192	Nauru	1.90	(GDP1980/GDP1970)**(1/10)-1

Table 6.17 GDP Growth Rates, 1970-1980			
Rank	Country	GRRL	Source
193	Reunion	1.89	(GDP1980/GDP1970)**(1/10)-1
194	UK	1.86	(GDP1980/GDP1970)**(1/10)-1
195	Vietnam	1.79	(GDP1980/GDP1970)**(1/10)-1
196	Belarus	1.73	(GDP1980/GDP1970)**(1/10)-1
197	Tajikistan	1.72	(GDP1980/GDP1970)**(1/10)-1
198	Falkland Is	1.67	(GDP1980/GDP1970)**(1/10)-1
199	Aruba	1.65	(GDP1980/GDP1970)**(1/10)-1
200	Fiji	1.62	(GDP1980/GDP1970)**(1/10)-1
201	Luxembourg	1.58	(GDP1980/GDP1970)**(1/10)-1
202	Afghanistan	1.58	(GDP1980/GDP1970)**(1/10)-1
203	Benin	1.52	(GDP1980/GDP1970)**(1/10)-1
204	Niger	1.45	(GDP1980/GDP1970)**(1/10)-1
205	Senegal	1.45	(GDP1980/GDP1970)**(1/10)-1
206	Burundi	1.43	(GDP1980/GDP1970)**(1/10)-1
207	Georgia	1.41	(GDP1980/GDP1970)**(1/10)-1
208	Chile	1.40	(GDP1980/GDP1970)**(1/10)-1
209	Cambodia	1.36	(GDP1980/GDP1970)**(1/10)-1
210	Palau	1.35	(GDP1980/GDP1970)**(1/10)-1
211	Zambia	1.30	(GDP1980/GDP1970)**(1/10)-1
212	Kazakhstan	1.14	(GDP1980/GDP1970)**(1/10)-1
213	Samoa	1.05	(GDP1980/GDP1970)**(1/10)-1
214	Kyrgyzstan	1.04	(GDP1980/GDP1970)**(1/10)-1
215	Sierra Leone	1.04	(GDP1980/GDP1970)**(1/10)-1
216	Dominica	1.03	(GDP1980/GDP1970)**(1/10)-1
217	Nepal	0.92	(GDP1980/GDP1970)**(1/10)-1
218	Madagascar	0.88	(GDP1980/GDP1970)**(1/10)-1
219	Bangladesh	0.82	(GDP1980/GDP1970)**(1/10)-1
220	Burkina Faso	0.79	(GDP1980/GDP1970)**(1/10)-1
221	Tonga	0.78	(GDP1980/GDP1970)**(1/10)-1
222	Nicaragua	0.76	(GDP1980/GDP1970)**(1/10)-1
223	CAR	0.29	(GDP1980/GDP1970)**(1/10)-1
224	Congo, Dem R	0.29	(GDP1980/GDP1970)**(1/10)-1
225	Curacao	0.00	(GDP1980/GDP1970)**(1/10)-1
226	Ghana	-0.08	(GDP1980/GDP1970)**(1/10)-1
227	East Timor	-0.10	(GDP1980/GDP1970)**(1/10)-1
228	Chad	-0.67	(GDP1980/GDP1970)**(1/10)-1
229	Jamaica	-0.67	(GDP1980/GDP1970)**(1/10)-1
230	Angola	-1.28	(GDP1980/GDP1970)**(1/10)-1
231	Liberia	-1.37	(GDP1980/GDP1970)**(1/10)-1
232	Comoros	-1.44	(GDP1980/GDP1970)**(1/10)-1
233	Equatorial G	-1.71	(GDP1980/GDP1970)**(1/10)-1
234	St Kitts & N	-1.97	(GDP1980/GDP1970)**(1/10)-1
235	Uganda	-2.87	(GDP1980/GDP1970)**(1/10)-1
236	Mozambique	-13.56	(GDP1980/GDP1970)**(1/10)-1

Table 6.18 GDP Growth Rates, 1980-1990

Rank	Country	GRRL	Source
1	Saint Martin	12.83	(GDP1990/GDP1980)**(1/10)-1
2	Botswana	10.94	(GDP1990/GDP1980)**(1/10)-1
3	Bhutan	10.56	(GDP1990/GDP1980)**(1/10)-1
4	N Mariana Is	10.12	(GDP1990/GDP1980)**(1/10)-1
5	Maldives	9.35	(GDP1990/GDP1980)**(1/10)-1
6	Korea, South	8.85	(GDP1990/GDP1980)**(1/10)-1
7	China	8.79	(GDP1990/GDP1980)**(1/10)-1
8	Oman	8.72	(GDP1990/GDP1980)**(1/10)-1
9	Swaziland	8.49	(GDP1990/GDP1980)**(1/10)-1
10	Singapore	7.64	(GDP1990/GDP1980)**(1/10)-1
11	Thailand	7.51	(GDP1990/GDP1980)**(1/10)-1
12	Solomon Is	7.48	(GDP1990/GDP1980)**(1/10)-1
13	W Sahara	7.44	(GDP1990/GDP1980)**(1/10)-1
14	St Lucia	7.24	(GDP1990/GDP1980)**(1/10)-1
15	Sint Maarten	7.11	(GDP1990/GDP1980)**(1/10)-1
16	Antigua & B	6.95	(GDP1990/GDP1980)**(1/10)-1
17	Hong Kong	6.89	(GDP1990/GDP1980)**(1/10)-1
18	Macao	6.75	(GDP1990/GDP1980)**(1/10)-1
19	Taiwan	6.70	(GDP1990/GDP1980)**(1/10)-1
20	Mayotte	6.64	(GDP1990/GDP1980)**(1/10)-1
21	Andorra	6.57	(GDP1990/GDP1980)**(1/10)-1
22	Cyprus	6.50	(GDP1990/GDP1980)**(1/10)-1
23	Pakistan	6.28	(GDP1990/GDP1980)**(1/10)-1
24	St Vincent	6.26	(GDP1990/GDP1980)**(1/10)-1
25	Malaysia	6.10	(GDP1990/GDP1980)**(1/10)-1
26	Indonesia	5.96	(GDP1990/GDP1980)**(1/10)-1
27	Turkey	5.87	(GDP1990/GDP1980)**(1/10)-1
28	Equatorial G	5.81	(GDP1990/GDP1980)**(1/10)-1
29	Mauritius	5.80	(GDP1990/GDP1980)**(1/10)-1
30	Turks & C Is	5.71	(GDP1990/GDP1980)**(1/10)-1
31	Cayman Is	5.65	(GDP1990/GDP1980)**(1/10)-1
32	St Kitts & N	5.58	(GDP1990/GDP1980)**(1/10)-1
33	Luxembourg	5.53	(GDP1990/GDP1980)**(1/10)-1
34	Guiana, Fr	5.52	(GDP1990/GDP1980)**(1/10)-1
35	India	5.50	(GDP1990/GDP1980)**(1/10)-1
36	Dominica	5.45	(GDP1990/GDP1980)**(1/10)-1
37	Mongolia	5.44	(GDP1990/GDP1980)**(1/10)-1
38	Egypt	5.44	(GDP1990/GDP1980)**(1/10)-1
39	Chad	5.39	(GDP1990/GDP1980)**(1/10)-1
40	Grenada	5.32	(GDP1990/GDP1980)**(1/10)-1
41	Kuwait	5.09	(GDP1990/GDP1980)**(1/10)-1
42	Cape Verde	5.09	(GDP1990/GDP1980)**(1/10)-1
43	Belize	4.84	(GDP1990/GDP1980)**(1/10)-1
44	Nepal	4.82	(GDP1990/GDP1980)**(1/10)-1
45	Angola	4.69	(GDP1990/GDP1980)**(1/10)-1
46	West Bank	4.69	(GDP1990/GDP1980)**(1/10)-1
47	Vanuatu	4.67	(GDP1990/GDP1980)**(1/10)-1
48	Vietnam	4.66	(GDP1990/GDP1980)**(1/10)-1

TABLE 6.18 GDP GROWTH RATES, 1980-1990

Rank	Country	GRRL	Source
49	Congo, Rep	4.65	(GDP1990/GDP1980)**(1/10)-1
50	Japan	4.55	(GDP1990/GDP1980)**(1/10)-1
51	Guinea-Biss	4.50	(GDP1990/GDP1980)**(1/10)-1
52	Gaza Strip	4.42	(GDP1990/GDP1980)**(1/10)-1
53	Djibouti	4.41	(GDP1990/GDP1980)**(1/10)-1
54	Samoa, Amer	4.23	(GDP1990/GDP1980)**(1/10)-1
55	Malta	4.10	(GDP1990/GDP1980)**(1/10)-1
56	Chile	4.03	(GDP1990/GDP1980)**(1/10)-1
57	Sri Lanka	4.02	(GDP1990/GDP1980)**(1/10)-1
58	Kenya	3.99	(GDP1990/GDP1980)**(1/10)-1
59	Paraguay	3.98	(GDP1990/GDP1980)**(1/10)-1
60	Seychelles	3.97	(GDP1990/GDP1980)**(1/10)-1
61	Lesotho	3.97	(GDP1990/GDP1980)**(1/10)-1
62	Zimbabwe	3.89	(GDP1990/GDP1980)**(1/10)-1
63	Marshall Is	3.75	(GDP1990/GDP1980)**(1/10)-1
64	Cambodia	3.75	(GDP1990/GDP1980)**(1/10)-1
65	Ireland	3.74	(GDP1990/GDP1980)**(1/10)-1
66	Reunion	3.74	(GDP1990/GDP1980)**(1/10)-1
67	Australia	3.69	(GDP1990/GDP1980)**(1/10)-1
68	Morocco	3.63	(GDP1990/GDP1980)**(1/10)-1
69	Colombia	3.63	(GDP1990/GDP1980)**(1/10)-1
70	Israel	3.60	(GDP1990/GDP1980)**(1/10)-1
71	San Marino	3.53	(GDP1990/GDP1980)**(1/10)-1
72	Tunisia	3.53	(GDP1990/GDP1980)**(1/10)-1
73	Burkina Faso	3.49	(GDP1990/GDP1980)**(1/10)-1
74	Bangladesh	3.45	(GDP1990/GDP1980)**(1/10)-1
75	Liechtenstn	3.42	(GDP1990/GDP1980)**(1/10)-1
76	Guernsey	3.37	(GDP1990/GDP1980)**(1/10)-1
77	Portugal	3.35	(GDP1990/GDP1980)**(1/10)-1
78	US	3.32	(GDP1990/GDP1980)**(1/10)-1
79	Gambia	3.23	(GDP1990/GDP1980)**(1/10)-1
80	Cameroon	3.23	(GDP1990/GDP1980)**(1/10)-1
81	Spain	3.22	(GDP1990/GDP1980)**(1/10)-1
82	Puerto Rico	3.19	(GDP1990/GDP1980)**(1/10)-1
83	East Timor	3.17	(GDP1990/GDP1980)**(1/10)-1
84	Finland	3.13	(GDP1990/GDP1980)**(1/10)-1
85	Greenland	3.11	(GDP1990/GDP1980)**(1/10)-1
86	Faroe Is	3.10	(GDP1990/GDP1980)**(1/10)-1
87	Comoros	3.08	(GDP1990/GDP1980)**(1/10)-1
88	Monaco	3.08	(GDP1990/GDP1980)**(1/10)-1
89	Bahamas	3.02	(GDP1990/GDP1980)**(1/10)-1
90	Jersey	2.93	(GDP1990/GDP1980)**(1/10)-1
91	Norway	2.93	(GDP1990/GDP1980)**(1/10)-1
92	Svalbard	2.93	(GDP1990/GDP1980)**(1/10)-1
93	Burundi	2.92	(GDP1990/GDP1980)**(1/10)-1
94	Isle of Man	2.89	(GDP1990/GDP1980)**(1/10)-1
95	Micronesia	2.85	(GDP1990/GDP1980)**(1/10)-1
96	Canada	2.82	(GDP1990/GDP1980)**(1/10)-1

Table 6.18 GDP Growth Rates, 1980-1990

Rank	Country	GRRL	Source
97	Fr Polynesia	2.82	(GDP1990/GDP1980)**(1/10)-1
98	Gibraltar	2.80	(GDP1990/GDP1980)**(1/10)-1
99	Latvia	2.79	(GDP1990/GDP1980)**(1/10)-1
100	Ghana	2.75	(GDP1990/GDP1980)**(1/10)-1
101	Algeria	2.74	(GDP1990/GDP1980)**(1/10)-1
102	Iceland	2.72	(GDP1990/GDP1980)**(1/10)-1
103	Virgin I, Br	2.69	(GDP1990/GDP1980)**(1/10)-1
104	Ecuador	2.68	(GDP1990/GDP1980)**(1/10)-1
105	Guinea	2.66	(GDP1990/GDP1980)**(1/10)-1
106	St Pierre&M	2.64	(GDP1990/GDP1980)**(1/10)-1
107	Benin	2.63	(GDP1990/GDP1980)**(1/10)-1
108	UK	2.63	(GDP1990/GDP1980)**(1/10)-1
109	Italy	2.62	(GDP1990/GDP1980)**(1/10)-1
110	Anguilla	2.62	(GDP1990/GDP1980)**(1/10)-1
111	Costa Rica	2.58	(GDP1990/GDP1980)**(1/10)-1
112	Uganda	2.58	(GDP1990/GDP1980)**(1/10)-1
113	Niue	2.56	(GDP1990/GDP1980)**(1/10)-1
114	Tanzania	2.56	(GDP1990/GDP1980)**(1/10)-1
115	Syria	2.55	(GDP1990/GDP1980)**(1/10)-1
116	Cook Is	2.53	(GDP1990/GDP1980)**(1/10)-1
117	Tokelau	2.51	(GDP1990/GDP1980)**(1/10)-1
118	Guam	2.48	(GDP1990/GDP1980)**(1/10)-1
119	Wallis & Fut	2.48	(GDP1990/GDP1980)**(1/10)-1
120	Switzerland	2.46	(GDP1990/GDP1980)**(1/10)-1
121	Laos	2.45	(GDP1990/GDP1980)**(1/10)-1
122	Jamaica	2.45	(GDP1990/GDP1980)**(1/10)-1
123	France	2.44	(GDP1990/GDP1980)**(1/10)-1
124	South Sudan	2.42	(GDP1990/GDP1980)**(1/10)-1
125	Sudan	2.42	(GDP1990/GDP1980)**(1/10)-1
126	Senegal	2.41	(GDP1990/GDP1980)**(1/10)-1
127	Honduras	2.40	(GDP1990/GDP1980)**(1/10)-1
128	Germany	2.40	(GDP1990/GDP1980)**(1/10)-1
129	Bulgaria	2.39	(GDP1990/GDP1980)**(1/10)-1
130	Denmark	2.34	(GDP1990/GDP1980)**(1/10)-1
131	New Zealand	2.34	(GDP1990/GDP1980)**(1/10)-1
132	Netherlands	2.33	(GDP1990/GDP1980)**(1/10)-1
133	Montserrat	2.33	(GDP1990/GDP1980)**(1/10)-1
134	Jordan	2.31	(GDP1990/GDP1980)**(1/10)-1
135	Austria	2.31	(GDP1990/GDP1980)**(1/10)-1
136	Dominican R	2.31	(GDP1990/GDP1980)**(1/10)-1
137	Gabon	2.26	(GDP1990/GDP1980)**(1/10)-1
138	Sweden	2.25	(GDP1990/GDP1980)**(1/10)-1
139	Bahrain	2.21	(GDP1990/GDP1980)**(1/10)-1
140	New Caledon	2.17	(GDP1990/GDP1980)**(1/10)-1
141	Malawi	2.17	(GDP1990/GDP1980)**(1/10)-1
142	Ethiopia	2.11	(GDP1990/GDP1980)**(1/10)-1
143	Belgium	2.11	(GDP1990/GDP1980)**(1/10)-1
144	Somalia	2.08	(GDP1990/GDP1980)**(1/10)-1

TABLE 6.18 GDP GROWTH RATES, 1980-1990

Rank	Country	GRRL	Source
145	Russia	2.07	(GDP1990/GDP1980)**(1/10)-1
146	Tonga	1.95	(GDP1990/GDP1980)**(1/10)-1
147	Rwanda	1.91	(GDP1990/GDP1980)**(1/10)-1
148	Cuba	1.86	(GDP1990/GDP1980)**(1/10)-1
149	Aruba	1.82	(GDP1990/GDP1980)**(1/10)-1
150	Iran	1.82	(GDP1990/GDP1980)**(1/10)-1
151	Uzbekistan	1.81	(GDP1990/GDP1980)**(1/10)-1
152	Mexico	1.79	(GDP1990/GDP1980)**(1/10)-1
153	Lithuania	1.76	(GDP1990/GDP1980)**(1/10)-1
154	Bermuda	1.72	(GDP1990/GDP1980)**(1/10)-1
155	Burma	1.70	(GDP1990/GDP1980)**(1/10)-1
156	Estonia	1.69	(GDP1990/GDP1980)**(1/10)-1
157	Yemen	1.67	(GDP1990/GDP1980)**(1/10)-1
158	Virgin I, US	1.67	(GDP1990/GDP1980)**(1/10)-1
159	Palau	1.63	(GDP1990/GDP1980)**(1/10)-1
160	Togo	1.62	(GDP1990/GDP1980)**(1/10)-1
161	Brazil	1.60	(GDP1990/GDP1980)**(1/10)-1
162	Korea, North	1.57	(GDP1990/GDP1980)**(1/10)-1
163	Saint Helena	1.57	(GDP1990/GDP1980)**(1/10)-1
164	Martinique	1.56	(GDP1990/GDP1980)**(1/10)-1
165	Moldova	1.54	(GDP1990/GDP1980)**(1/10)-1
166	Czechia	1.50	(GDP1990/GDP1980)**(1/10)-1
167	Ukraine	1.49	(GDP1990/GDP1980)**(1/10)-1
168	Eritrea	1.48	(GDP1990/GDP1980)**(1/10)-1
169	Kosovo	1.46	(GDP1990/GDP1980)**(1/10)-1
170	Tuvalu	1.39	(GDP1990/GDP1980)**(1/10)-1
171	Fiji	1.37	(GDP1990/GDP1980)**(1/10)-1
172	Nauru	1.37	(GDP1990/GDP1980)**(1/10)-1
173	Philippines	1.37	(GDP1990/GDP1980)**(1/10)-1
174	Panama	1.37	(GDP1990/GDP1980)**(1/10)-1
175	South Africa	1.36	(GDP1990/GDP1980)**(1/10)-1
176	Armenia	1.35	(GDP1990/GDP1980)**(1/10)-1
177	Belarus	1.34	(GDP1990/GDP1980)**(1/10)-1
178	Guadeloupe	1.31	(GDP1990/GDP1980)**(1/10)-1
179	Hungary	1.29	(GDP1990/GDP1980)**(1/10)-1
180	Papua New G	1.29	(GDP1990/GDP1980)**(1/10)-1
181	Ivory Coast	1.29	(GDP1990/GDP1980)**(1/10)-1
182	CAR	1.27	(GDP1990/GDP1980)**(1/10)-1
183	Namibia	1.27	(GDP1990/GDP1980)**(1/10)-1
184	Turkmenistan	1.24	(GDP1990/GDP1980)**(1/10)-1
185	Slovakia	1.24	(GDP1990/GDP1980)**(1/10)-1
186	Barbados	1.22	(GDP1990/GDP1980)**(1/10)-1
187	Falkland Is	1.22	(GDP1990/GDP1980)**(1/10)-1
188	Zambia	1.17	(GDP1990/GDP1980)**(1/10)-1
189	Venezuela	1.15	(GDP1990/GDP1980)**(1/10)-1
190	Azerbaijan	1.11	(GDP1990/GDP1980)**(1/10)-1
191	Nigeria	1.07	(GDP1990/GDP1980)**(1/10)-1
192	Congo, Dem R	1.07	(GDP1990/GDP1980)**(1/10)-1

Table 6.18 GDP Growth Rates, 1980-1990

Rank	Country	GRRL	Source
193	Mauritania	1.02	(GDP1990/GDP1980)**(1/10)-1
194	Guatemala	1.02	(GDP1990/GDP1980)**(1/10)-1
195	Albania	0.97	(GDP1990/GDP1980)**(1/10)-1
196	Samoa	0.95	(GDP1990/GDP1980)**(1/10)-1
197	Macedonia	0.92	(GDP1990/GDP1980)**(1/10)-1
198	Mali	0.89	(GDP1990/GDP1980)**(1/10)-1
199	Sierra Leone	0.85	(GDP1990/GDP1980)**(1/10)-1
200	Romania	0.78	(GDP1990/GDP1980)**(1/10)-1
201	Greece	0.70	(GDP1990/GDP1980)**(1/10)-1
202	Kiribati	0.65	(GDP1990/GDP1980)**(1/10)-1
203	Bosnia	0.41	(GDP1990/GDP1980)**(1/10)-1
204	Tajikistan	0.31	(GDP1990/GDP1980)**(1/10)-1
205	Madagascar	0.26	(GDP1990/GDP1980)**(1/10)-1
206	Slovenia	0.04	(GDP1990/GDP1980)**(1/10)-1
207	Kyrgyzstan	0.03	(GDP1990/GDP1980)**(1/10)-1
208	Uruguay	-0.03	(GDP1990/GDP1980)**(1/10)-1
209	Montenegro	-0.03	(GDP1990/GDP1980)**(1/10)-1
210	Haiti	-0.04	(GDP1990/GDP1980)**(1/10)-1
211	UAE	-0.10	(GDP1990/GDP1980)**(1/10)-1
212	Poland	-0.14	(GDP1990/GDP1980)**(1/10)-1
213	Kazakhstan	-0.19	(GDP1990/GDP1980)**(1/10)-1
214	Bolivia	-0.20	(GDP1990/GDP1980)**(1/10)-1
215	Mozambique	-0.25	(GDP1990/GDP1980)**(1/10)-1
216	Croatia	-0.28	(GDP1990/GDP1980)**(1/10)-1
217	Serbia	-0.30	(GDP1990/GDP1980)**(1/10)-1
218	Sao Tome & P	-0.36	(GDP1990/GDP1980)**(1/10)-1
219	Georgia	-0.71	(GDP1990/GDP1980)**(1/10)-1
220	Niger	-0.72	(GDP1990/GDP1980)**(1/10)-1
221	El Salvador	-0.75	(GDP1990/GDP1980)**(1/10)-1
222	Peru	-0.85	(GDP1990/GDP1980)**(1/10)-1
223	Suriname	-1.19	(GDP1990/GDP1980)**(1/10)-1
224	Saudi Arabia	-1.31	(GDP1990/GDP1980)**(1/10)-1
225	Qatar	-1.42	(GDP1990/GDP1980)**(1/10)-1
226	Nicaragua	-1.53	(GDP1990/GDP1980)**(1/10)-1
227	Argentina	-1.59	(GDP1990/GDP1980)**(1/10)-1
228	Curacao	-1.91	(GDP1990/GDP1980)**(1/10)-1
229	Lebanon	-2.12	(GDP1990/GDP1980)**(1/10)-1
230	Trinidad & T	-2.13	(GDP1990/GDP1980)**(1/10)-1
231	Iraq	-3.15	(GDP1990/GDP1980)**(1/10)-1
232	Guyana	-3.19	(GDP1990/GDP1980)**(1/10)-1
233	Brunei	-3.68	(GDP1990/GDP1980)**(1/10)-1
234	Afghanistan	-3.72	(GDP1990/GDP1980)**(1/10)-1
235	Libya	-5.46	(GDP1990/GDP1980)**(1/10)-1
236	Liberia	-7.54	(GDP1990/GDP1980)**(1/10)-1

Table 6.19 GDP Growth Rates, 1990-2000

Rank	Country	GRRL	Source
1	Mayotte	21.61	(GDP2000/GDP1990)**(1/10)-1
2	Equatorial G	19.67	(GDP2000/GDP1990)**(1/10)-1
3	Qatar	17.83	(GDP2000/GDP1990)**(1/10)-1
4	W Sahara	15.77	(GDP2000/GDP1990)**(1/10)-1
5	Bermuda	12.74	(GDP2000/GDP1990)**(1/10)-1
6	Libya	12.58	(GDP2000/GDP1990)**(1/10)-1
7	Samoa, Amer	10.82	(GDP2000/GDP1990)**(1/10)-1
8	Cape Verde	10.57	(GDP2000/GDP1990)**(1/10)-1
9	New Caledon	9.96	(GDP2000/GDP1990)**(1/10)-1
10	Brunei	9.68	(GDP2000/GDP1990)**(1/10)-1
11	Gibraltar	8.64	(GDP2000/GDP1990)**(1/10)-1
12	Niue	8.19	(GDP2000/GDP1990)**(1/10)-1
13	Saint Helena	8.14	(GDP2000/GDP1990)**(1/10)-1
14	St Pierre&M	7.76	(GDP2000/GDP1990)**(1/10)-1
15	Ireland	7.70	(GDP2000/GDP1990)**(1/10)-1
16	China	7.65	(GDP2000/GDP1990)**(1/10)-1
17	West Bank	7.58	(GDP2000/GDP1990)**(1/10)-1
18	Vietnam	7.41	(GDP2000/GDP1990)**(1/10)-1
19	Singapore	7.33	(GDP2000/GDP1990)**(1/10)-1
20	Bahrain	7.20	(GDP2000/GDP1990)**(1/10)-1
21	Malaysia	6.93	(GDP2000/GDP1990)**(1/10)-1
22	Turks & C Is	6.81	(GDP2000/GDP1990)**(1/10)-1
23	Chile	6.74	(GDP2000/GDP1990)**(1/10)-1
24	Uganda	6.57	(GDP2000/GDP1990)**(1/10)-1
25	Aruba	6.37	(GDP2000/GDP1990)**(1/10)-1
26	Oman	6.17	(GDP2000/GDP1990)**(1/10)-1
27	Virgin I, Br	6.14	(GDP2000/GDP1990)**(1/10)-1
28	Maldives	6.14	(GDP2000/GDP1990)**(1/10)-1
29	Dominican R	6.13	(GDP2000/GDP1990)**(1/10)-1
30	Luxembourg	6.09	(GDP2000/GDP1990)**(1/10)-1
31	Laos	6.05	(GDP2000/GDP1990)**(1/10)-1
32	Korea, South	6.02	(GDP2000/GDP1990)**(1/10)-1
33	Norway	5.93	(GDP2000/GDP1990)**(1/10)-1
34	Malta	5.92	(GDP2000/GDP1990)**(1/10)-1
35	Anguilla	5.90	(GDP2000/GDP1990)**(1/10)-1
36	El Salvador	5.85	(GDP2000/GDP1990)**(1/10)-1
37	Lebanon	5.83	(GDP2000/GDP1990)**(1/10)-1
38	Fr Polynesia	5.75	(GDP2000/GDP1990)**(1/10)-1
39	Mozambique	5.75	(GDP2000/GDP1990)**(1/10)-1
40	Israel	5.64	(GDP2000/GDP1990)**(1/10)-1
41	Afghanistan	5.61	(GDP2000/GDP1990)**(1/10)-1
42	Belize	5.60	(GDP2000/GDP1990)**(1/10)-1
43	Burma	5.54	(GDP2000/GDP1990)**(1/10)-1
44	Liberia	5.54	(GDP2000/GDP1990)**(1/10)-1
45	Turkey	5.39	(GDP2000/GDP1990)**(1/10)-1
46	Kiribati	5.39	(GDP2000/GDP1990)**(1/10)-1
47	Guiana, Fr	5.37	(GDP2000/GDP1990)**(1/10)-1
48	Taiwan	5.37	(GDP2000/GDP1990)**(1/10)-1

Table 6.19 GDP Growth Rates, 1990-2000			
Rank	Country	GRRL	Source
49	Cayman Is	5.36	(GDP2000/GDP1990)**(1/10)-1
50	UAE	5.30	(GDP2000/GDP1990)**(1/10)-1
51	Yemen	5.27	(GDP2000/GDP1990)**(1/10)-1
52	Botswana	5.19	(GDP2000/GDP1990)**(1/10)-1
53	Gaza Strip	5.17	(GDP2000/GDP1990)**(1/10)-1
54	India	5.09	(GDP2000/GDP1990)**(1/10)-1
55	Saudi Arabia	5.07	(GDP2000/GDP1990)**(1/10)-1
56	N Mariana Is	4.96	(GDP2000/GDP1990)**(1/10)-1
57	South Sudan	4.94	(GDP2000/GDP1990)**(1/10)-1
58	Burkina Faso	4.86	(GDP2000/GDP1990)**(1/10)-1
59	Costa Rica	4.86	(GDP2000/GDP1990)**(1/10)-1
60	San Marino	4.83	(GDP2000/GDP1990)**(1/10)-1
61	Papua New G	4.80	(GDP2000/GDP1990)**(1/10)-1
62	Panama	4.77	(GDP2000/GDP1990)**(1/10)-1
63	Tunisia	4.76	(GDP2000/GDP1990)**(1/10)-1
64	Cook Is	4.74	(GDP2000/GDP1990)**(1/10)-1
65	Sint Maarten	4.67	(GDP2000/GDP1990)**(1/10)-1
66	Seychelles	4.64	(GDP2000/GDP1990)**(1/10)-1
67	Nepal	4.64	(GDP2000/GDP1990)**(1/10)-1
68	Mexico	4.62	(GDP2000/GDP1990)**(1/10)-1
69	Guadeloupe	4.60	(GDP2000/GDP1990)**(1/10)-1
70	Iran	4.52	(GDP2000/GDP1990)**(1/10)-1
71	Argentina	4.50	(GDP2000/GDP1990)**(1/10)-1
72	Mauritius	4.49	(GDP2000/GDP1990)**(1/10)-1
73	Isle of Man	4.48	(GDP2000/GDP1990)**(1/10)-1
74	Grenada	4.35	(GDP2000/GDP1990)**(1/10)-1
75	Mali	4.28	(GDP2000/GDP1990)**(1/10)-1
76	Bangladesh	4.27	(GDP2000/GDP1990)**(1/10)-1
77	Bolivia	4.23	(GDP2000/GDP1990)**(1/10)-1
78	Martinique	4.23	(GDP2000/GDP1990)**(1/10)-1
79	Falkland Is	4.20	(GDP2000/GDP1990)**(1/10)-1
80	St Kitts & N	4.20	(GDP2000/GDP1990)**(1/10)-1
81	Sri Lanka	4.09	(GDP2000/GDP1990)**(1/10)-1
82	St Lucia	4.04	(GDP2000/GDP1990)**(1/10)-1
83	Cyprus	4.02	(GDP2000/GDP1990)**(1/10)-1
84	Namibia	3.98	(GDP2000/GDP1990)**(1/10)-1
85	Poland	3.93	(GDP2000/GDP1990)**(1/10)-1
86	Thailand	3.91	(GDP2000/GDP1990)**(1/10)-1
87	Guinea	3.90	(GDP2000/GDP1990)**(1/10)-1
88	Peru	3.88	(GDP2000/GDP1990)**(1/10)-1
89	Guyana	3.86	(GDP2000/GDP1990)**(1/10)-1
90	Antigua & B	3.83	(GDP2000/GDP1990)**(1/10)-1
91	Sudan	3.83	(GDP2000/GDP1990)**(1/10)-1
92	Jordan	3.81	(GDP2000/GDP1990)**(1/10)-1
93	Benin	3.80	(GDP2000/GDP1990)**(1/10)-1
94	Netherlands	3.77	(GDP2000/GDP1990)**(1/10)-1
95	Gambia	3.71	(GDP2000/GDP1990)**(1/10)-1
96	Hong Kong	3.70	(GDP2000/GDP1990)**(1/10)-1

Table 6.19 GDP Growth Rates, 1990-2000

Rank	Country	GRRL	Source
97	Bhutan	3.68	(GDP2000/GDP1990)**(1/10)-1
98	Pakistan	3.66	(GDP2000/GDP1990)**(1/10)-1
99	Nicaragua	3.63	(GDP2000/GDP1990)**(1/10)-1
100	Palau	3.62	(GDP2000/GDP1990)**(1/10)-1
101	Saint Martin	3.61	(GDP2000/GDP1990)**(1/10)-1
102	Spain	3.59	(GDP2000/GDP1990)**(1/10)-1
103	Honduras	3.52	(GDP2000/GDP1990)**(1/10)-1
104	Portugal	3.52	(GDP2000/GDP1990)**(1/10)-1
105	Guam	3.51	(GDP2000/GDP1990)**(1/10)-1
106	Monaco	3.49	(GDP2000/GDP1990)**(1/10)-1
107	Tonga	3.49	(GDP2000/GDP1990)**(1/10)-1
108	Vanuatu	3.48	(GDP2000/GDP1990)**(1/10)-1
109	Guatemala	3.46	(GDP2000/GDP1990)**(1/10)-1
110	US	3.46	(GDP2000/GDP1990)**(1/10)-1
111	Curacao	3.44	(GDP2000/GDP1990)**(1/10)-1
112	Andorra	3.38	(GDP2000/GDP1990)**(1/10)-1
113	Greece	3.33	(GDP2000/GDP1990)**(1/10)-1
114	Malawi	3.30	(GDP2000/GDP1990)**(1/10)-1
115	Syria	3.25	(GDP2000/GDP1990)**(1/10)-1
116	St Vincent	3.20	(GDP2000/GDP1990)**(1/10)-1
117	Mauritania	3.17	(GDP2000/GDP1990)**(1/10)-1
118	Egypt	3.16	(GDP2000/GDP1990)**(1/10)-1
119	Trinidad & T	3.12	(GDP2000/GDP1990)**(1/10)-1
120	Uruguay	3.12	(GDP2000/GDP1990)**(1/10)-1
121	Tanzania	3.08	(GDP2000/GDP1990)**(1/10)-1
122	Cambodia	3.07	(GDP2000/GDP1990)**(1/10)-1
123	Australia	3.07	(GDP2000/GDP1990)**(1/10)-1
124	Canada	3.00	(GDP2000/GDP1990)**(1/10)-1
125	Ghana	2.99	(GDP2000/GDP1990)**(1/10)-1
126	UK	2.97	(GDP2000/GDP1990)**(1/10)-1
127	Austria	2.94	(GDP2000/GDP1990)**(1/10)-1
128	Senegal	2.90	(GDP2000/GDP1990)**(1/10)-1
129	Philippines	2.87	(GDP2000/GDP1990)**(1/10)-1
130	Denmark	2.84	(GDP2000/GDP1990)**(1/10)-1
131	Zimbabwe	2.83	(GDP2000/GDP1990)**(1/10)-1
132	Chad	2.74	(GDP2000/GDP1990)**(1/10)-1
133	Lesotho	2.72	(GDP2000/GDP1990)**(1/10)-1
134	Solomon Is	2.62	(GDP2000/GDP1990)**(1/10)-1
135	Samoa	2.62	(GDP2000/GDP1990)**(1/10)-1
136	Macao	2.61	(GDP2000/GDP1990)**(1/10)-1
137	New Zealand	2.56	(GDP2000/GDP1990)**(1/10)-1
138	Brazil	2.54	(GDP2000/GDP1990)**(1/10)-1
139	Barbados	2.52	(GDP2000/GDP1990)**(1/10)-1
140	Micronesia	2.51	(GDP2000/GDP1990)**(1/10)-1
141	Slovenia	2.41	(GDP2000/GDP1990)**(1/10)-1
142	Indonesia	2.40	(GDP2000/GDP1990)**(1/10)-1
143	Nigeria	2.39	(GDP2000/GDP1990)**(1/10)-1
144	East Timor	2.35	(GDP2000/GDP1990)**(1/10)-1

Table 6.19 GDP Growth Rates, 1990-2000			
Rank	Country	GRRL	Source
145	Iraq	2.29	(GDP2000/GDP1990)**(1/10)-1
146	Colombia	2.28	(GDP2000/GDP1990)**(1/10)-1
147	Belgium	2.24	(GDP2000/GDP1990)**(1/10)-1
148	Albania	2.23	(GDP2000/GDP1990)**(1/10)-1
149	Eritrea	2.20	(GDP2000/GDP1990)**(1/10)-1
150	France	2.14	(GDP2000/GDP1990)**(1/10)-1
151	Ivory Coast	2.14	(GDP2000/GDP1990)**(1/10)-1
152	Paraguay	2.09	(GDP2000/GDP1990)**(1/10)-1
153	Iceland	2.06	(GDP2000/GDP1990)**(1/10)-1
154	South Africa	2.05	(GDP2000/GDP1990)**(1/10)-1
155	Burundi	2.04	(GDP2000/GDP1990)**(1/10)-1
156	Ethiopia	2.04	(GDP2000/GDP1990)**(1/10)-1
157	Finland	1.99	(GDP2000/GDP1990)**(1/10)-1
158	Morocco	1.94	(GDP2000/GDP1990)**(1/10)-1
159	Tuvalu	1.92	(GDP2000/GDP1990)**(1/10)-1
160	Liechtenstn	1.90	(GDP2000/GDP1990)**(1/10)-1
161	Bahamas	1.89	(GDP2000/GDP1990)**(1/10)-1
162	Venezuela	1.87	(GDP2000/GDP1990)**(1/10)-1
163	Algeria	1.78	(GDP2000/GDP1990)**(1/10)-1
164	Marshall Is	1.78	(GDP2000/GDP1990)**(1/10)-1
165	Sweden	1.77	(GDP2000/GDP1990)**(1/10)-1
166	Kenya	1.75	(GDP2000/GDP1990)**(1/10)-1
167	Italy	1.73	(GDP2000/GDP1990)**(1/10)-1
168	Germany	1.73	(GDP2000/GDP1990)**(1/10)-1
169	Togo	1.68	(GDP2000/GDP1990)**(1/10)-1
170	Gabon	1.67	(GDP2000/GDP1990)**(1/10)-1
171	Ecuador	1.61	(GDP2000/GDP1990)**(1/10)-1
172	Dominica	1.57	(GDP2000/GDP1990)**(1/10)-1
173	Fiji	1.56	(GDP2000/GDP1990)**(1/10)-1
174	Reunion	1.53	(GDP2000/GDP1990)**(1/10)-1
175	CAR	1.48	(GDP2000/GDP1990)**(1/10)-1
176	Madagascar	1.44	(GDP2000/GDP1990)**(1/10)-1
177	Cameroon	1.39	(GDP2000/GDP1990)**(1/10)-1
178	Slovakia	1.35	(GDP2000/GDP1990)**(1/10)-1
179	Greenland	1.32	(GDP2000/GDP1990)**(1/10)-1
180	Comoros	1.29	(GDP2000/GDP1990)**(1/10)-1
181	Guernsey	1.22	(GDP2000/GDP1990)**(1/10)-1
182	Switzerland	1.21	(GDP2000/GDP1990)**(1/10)-1
183	Jersey	1.20	(GDP2000/GDP1990)**(1/10)-1
184	Faroe Is	1.11	(GDP2000/GDP1990)**(1/10)-1
185	Suriname	1.09	(GDP2000/GDP1990)**(1/10)-1
186	Japan	0.97	(GDP2000/GDP1990)**(1/10)-1
187	Zambia	0.93	(GDP2000/GDP1990)**(1/10)-1
188	Puerto Rico	0.92	(GDP2000/GDP1990)**(1/10)-1
189	Congo, Rep	0.83	(GDP2000/GDP1990)**(1/10)-1
190	Swaziland	0.77	(GDP2000/GDP1990)**(1/10)-1
191	Wallis & Fut	0.71	(GDP2000/GDP1990)**(1/10)-1
192	Virgin I, US	0.51	(GDP2000/GDP1990)**(1/10)-1

TABLE 6.19 GDP GROWTH RATES, 1990-2000			
Rank	Country	GRRL	Source
193	Croatia	0.48	(GDP2000/GDP1990)**(1/10)-1
194	Hungary	0.46	(GDP2000/GDP1990)**(1/10)-1
195	Tokelau	0.41	(GDP2000/GDP1990)**(1/10)-1
196	Mongolia	0.40	(GDP2000/GDP1990)**(1/10)-1
197	Niger	0.30	(GDP2000/GDP1990)**(1/10)-1
198	Svalbard	0.29	(GDP2000/GDP1990)**(1/10)-1
199	Czechia	0.28	(GDP2000/GDP1990)**(1/10)-1
200	Jamaica	-0.03	(GDP2000/GDP1990)**(1/10)-1
201	Rwanda	-0.08	(GDP2000/GDP1990)**(1/10)-1
202	Haiti	-0.11	(GDP2000/GDP1990)**(1/10)-1
203	Sao Tome & P	-0.11	(GDP2000/GDP1990)**(1/10)-1
204	Macedonia	-0.11	(GDP2000/GDP1990)**(1/10)-1
205	Kuwait	-0.33	(GDP2000/GDP1990)**(1/10)-1
206	Guinea-Biss	-0.47	(GDP2000/GDP1990)**(1/10)-1
207	Angola	-0.47	(GDP2000/GDP1990)**(1/10)-1
208	Belarus	-1.21	(GDP2000/GDP1990)**(1/10)-1
209	Djibouti	-1.22	(GDP2000/GDP1990)**(1/10)-1
210	Romania	-1.90	(GDP2000/GDP1990)**(1/10)-1
211	Sierra Leone	-2.39	(GDP2000/GDP1990)**(1/10)-1
212	Estonia	-2.57	(GDP2000/GDP1990)**(1/10)-1
213	Turkmenistan	-2.60	(GDP2000/GDP1990)**(1/10)-1
214	Bulgaria	-3.01	(GDP2000/GDP1990)**(1/10)-1
215	Bosnia	-3.18	(GDP2000/GDP1990)**(1/10)-1
216	Montenegro	-3.19	(GDP2000/GDP1990)**(1/10)-1
217	Cuba	-3.38	(GDP2000/GDP1990)**(1/10)-1
218	Lithuania	-3.56	(GDP2000/GDP1990)**(1/10)-1
219	Kazakhstan	-3.82	(GDP2000/GDP1990)**(1/10)-1
220	Latvia	-3.90	(GDP2000/GDP1990)**(1/10)-1
221	Kyrgyzstan	-3.94	(GDP2000/GDP1990)**(1/10)-1
222	Russia	-4.13	(GDP2000/GDP1990)**(1/10)-1
223	Korea, North	-4.34	(GDP2000/GDP1990)**(1/10)-1
224	Armenia	-4.53	(GDP2000/GDP1990)**(1/10)-1
225	Azerbaijan	-5.19	(GDP2000/GDP1990)**(1/10)-1
226	Serbia	-5.28	(GDP2000/GDP1990)**(1/10)-1
227	Congo, Dem R	-5.35	(GDP2000/GDP1990)**(1/10)-1
228	Somalia	-5.91	(GDP2000/GDP1990)**(1/10)-1
229	Uzbekistan	-6.51	(GDP2000/GDP1990)**(1/10)-1
230	Nauru	-6.58	(GDP2000/GDP1990)**(1/10)-1
231	Kosovo	-7.30	(GDP2000/GDP1990)**(1/10)-1
232	Ukraine	-8.00	(GDP2000/GDP1990)**(1/10)-1
233	Montserrat	-8.80	(GDP2000/GDP1990)**(1/10)-1
234	Tajikistan	-9.14	(GDP2000/GDP1990)**(1/10)-1
235	Georgia	-11.90	(GDP2000/GDP1990)**(1/10)-1
236	Moldova	-13.26	(GDP2000/GDP1990)**(1/10)-1

TABLE 6.20 GDP GROWTH RATES, 2000-2010			
Rank	Country	GRRL	Source
1	Reunion	17.77	(GDP2010/GDP2000)**(1/10)-1
2	Mayotte	17.45	(GDP2010/GDP2000)**(1/10)-1
3	Monaco	17.20	(GDP2010/GDP2000)**(1/10)-1
4	Guiana, Fr	15.90	(GDP2010/GDP2000)**(1/10)-1
5	Turks & C Is	15.62	(GDP2010/GDP2000)**(1/10)-1
6	Azerbaijan	14.93	(GDP2010/GDP2000)**(1/10)-1
7	Equatorial G	14.85	(GDP2010/GDP2000)**(1/10)-1
8	Marshall Is	14.71	(GDP2010/GDP2000)**(1/10)-1
9	Cuba	13.75	(GDP2010/GDP2000)**(1/10)-1
10	Qatar	12.17	(GDP2010/GDP2000)**(1/10)-1
11	Macao	12.02	(GDP2010/GDP2000)**(1/10)-1
12	Tuvalu	11.98	(GDP2010/GDP2000)**(1/10)-1
13	Liechtenstn	11.46	(GDP2010/GDP2000)**(1/10)-1
14	Chad	11.29	(GDP2010/GDP2000)**(1/10)-1
15	Virgin I, Br	10.88	(GDP2010/GDP2000)**(1/10)-1
16	Angola	10.84	(GDP2010/GDP2000)**(1/10)-1
17	Martinique	10.13	(GDP2010/GDP2000)**(1/10)-1
18	Guadeloupe	10.04	(GDP2010/GDP2000)**(1/10)-1
19	Bermuda	9.84	(GDP2010/GDP2000)**(1/10)-1
20	China	9.75	(GDP2010/GDP2000)**(1/10)-1
21	Isle of Man	9.53	(GDP2010/GDP2000)**(1/10)-1
22	New Caledon	9.15	(GDP2010/GDP2000)**(1/10)-1
23	Bhutan	8.70	(GDP2010/GDP2000)**(1/10)-1
24	Kazakhstan	8.28	(GDP2010/GDP2000)**(1/10)-1
25	Ethiopia	8.10	(GDP2010/GDP2000)**(1/10)-1
26	Tajikistan	8.01	(GDP2010/GDP2000)**(1/10)-1
27	Georgia	7.93	(GDP2010/GDP2000)**(1/10)-1
28	Virgin I, US	7.92	(GDP2010/GDP2000)**(1/10)-1
29	Turkmenistan	7.78	(GDP2010/GDP2000)**(1/10)-1
30	Jersey	7.71	(GDP2010/GDP2000)**(1/10)-1
31	Sint Maarten	7.68	(GDP2010/GDP2000)**(1/10)-1
32	Andorra	7.63	(GDP2010/GDP2000)**(1/10)-1
33	Falkland Is	7.57	(GDP2010/GDP2000)**(1/10)-1
34	Belarus	7.45	(GDP2010/GDP2000)**(1/10)-1
35	Uganda	7.29	(GDP2010/GDP2000)**(1/10)-1
36	South Sudan	7.26	(GDP2010/GDP2000)**(1/10)-1
37	Mozambique	7.24	(GDP2010/GDP2000)**(1/10)-1
38	Laos	7.18	(GDP2010/GDP2000)**(1/10)-1
39	India	7.12	(GDP2010/GDP2000)**(1/10)-1
40	Rwanda	7.08	(GDP2010/GDP2000)**(1/10)-1
41	Jamaica	6.97	(GDP2010/GDP2000)**(1/10)-1
42	Saint Martin	6.90	(GDP2010/GDP2000)**(1/10)-1
43	Guernsey	6.80	(GDP2010/GDP2000)**(1/10)-1
44	Cambodia	6.80	(GDP2010/GDP2000)**(1/10)-1
45	Maldives	6.80	(GDP2010/GDP2000)**(1/10)-1
46	Vietnam	6.61	(GDP2010/GDP2000)**(1/10)-1
47	Cape Verde	6.52	(GDP2010/GDP2000)**(1/10)-1
48	Sierra Leone	6.51	(GDP2010/GDP2000)**(1/10)-1

Table 6.20 GDP Growth Rates, 2000-2010

Rank	Country	GRRL	Source
49	Russia	6.49	(GDP2010/GDP2000)**(1/10)-1
50	East Timor	6.40	(GDP2010/GDP2000)**(1/10)-1
51	Nigeria	6.36	(GDP2010/GDP2000)**(1/10)-1
52	Tanzania	6.35	(GDP2010/GDP2000)**(1/10)-1
53	Panama	6.26	(GDP2010/GDP2000)**(1/10)-1
54	Mongolia	6.24	(GDP2010/GDP2000)**(1/10)-1
55	Jordan	6.08	(GDP2010/GDP2000)**(1/10)-1
56	Mali	5.96	(GDP2010/GDP2000)**(1/10)-1
57	Zambia	5.93	(GDP2010/GDP2000)**(1/10)-1
58	Curacao	5.92	(GDP2010/GDP2000)**(1/10)-1
59	Bangladesh	5.90	(GDP2010/GDP2000)**(1/10)-1
60	Fr Polynesia	5.85	(GDP2010/GDP2000)**(1/10)-1
61	Burkina Faso	5.82	(GDP2010/GDP2000)**(1/10)-1
62	Kosovo	5.77	(GDP2010/GDP2000)**(1/10)-1
63	Liberia	5.71	(GDP2010/GDP2000)**(1/10)-1
64	Montserrat	5.70	(GDP2010/GDP2000)**(1/10)-1
65	Taiwan	5.69	(GDP2010/GDP2000)**(1/10)-1
66	Singapore	5.66	(GDP2010/GDP2000)**(1/10)-1
67	Trinidad & T	5.64	(GDP2010/GDP2000)**(1/10)-1
68	Bahrain	5.60	(GDP2010/GDP2000)**(1/10)-1
69	Peru	5.60	(GDP2010/GDP2000)**(1/10)-1
70	Albania	5.55	(GDP2010/GDP2000)**(1/10)-1
71	Cayman Is	5.42	(GDP2010/GDP2000)**(1/10)-1
72	Iran	5.32	(GDP2010/GDP2000)**(1/10)-1
73	Wallis & Fut	5.28	(GDP2010/GDP2000)**(1/10)-1
74	Slovakia	5.25	(GDP2010/GDP2000)**(1/10)-1
75	Malaysia	5.21	(GDP2010/GDP2000)**(1/10)-1
76	Egypt	5.16	(GDP2010/GDP2000)**(1/10)-1
77	Romania	5.15	(GDP2010/GDP2000)**(1/10)-1
78	Suriname	5.12	(GDP2010/GDP2000)**(1/10)-1
79	Dominican R	5.10	(GDP2010/GDP2000)**(1/10)-1
80	Ghana	5.03	(GDP2010/GDP2000)**(1/10)-1
81	W Sahara	4.99	(GDP2010/GDP2000)**(1/10)-1
82	Saudi Arabia	4.95	(GDP2010/GDP2000)**(1/10)-1
83	Congo, Dem R	4.94	(GDP2010/GDP2000)**(1/10)-1
84	Indonesia	4.92	(GDP2010/GDP2000)**(1/10)-1
85	Sudan	4.91	(GDP2010/GDP2000)**(1/10)-1
86	Morocco	4.88	(GDP2010/GDP2000)**(1/10)-1
87	Uzbekistan	4.87	(GDP2010/GDP2000)**(1/10)-1
88	Lithuania	4.87	(GDP2010/GDP2000)**(1/10)-1
89	Sri Lanka	4.84	(GDP2010/GDP2000)**(1/10)-1
90	Bosnia	4.83	(GDP2010/GDP2000)**(1/10)-1
91	Philippines	4.78	(GDP2010/GDP2000)**(1/10)-1
92	Kuwait	4.78	(GDP2010/GDP2000)**(1/10)-1
93	Argentina	4.74	(GDP2010/GDP2000)**(1/10)-1
94	Yemen	4.68	(GDP2010/GDP2000)**(1/10)-1
95	Mauritania	4.67	(GDP2010/GDP2000)**(1/10)-1
96	CAR	4.60	(GDP2010/GDP2000)**(1/10)-1

Table 6.20 GDP Growth Rates, 2000-2010			
Rank	Country	GRRL	Source
97	Niger	4.55	(GDP2010/GDP2000)**(1/10)-1
98	Tunisia	4.49	(GDP2010/GDP2000)**(1/10)-1
99	Oman	4.41	(GDP2010/GDP2000)**(1/10)-1
100	Sao Tome & P	4.40	(GDP2010/GDP2000)**(1/10)-1
101	Kenya	4.37	(GDP2010/GDP2000)**(1/10)-1
102	Korea, South	4.32	(GDP2010/GDP2000)**(1/10)-1
103	Thailand	4.31	(GDP2010/GDP2000)**(1/10)-1
104	Ukraine	4.30	(GDP2010/GDP2000)**(1/10)-1
105	Bulgaria	4.28	(GDP2010/GDP2000)**(1/10)-1
106	Turkey	4.27	(GDP2010/GDP2000)**(1/10)-1
107	Congo, Rep	4.26	(GDP2010/GDP2000)**(1/10)-1
108	Algeria	4.26	(GDP2010/GDP2000)**(1/10)-1
109	Poland	4.25	(GDP2010/GDP2000)**(1/10)-1
110	Serbia	4.23	(GDP2010/GDP2000)**(1/10)-1
111	Pakistan	4.21	(GDP2010/GDP2000)**(1/10)-1
112	Afghanistan	4.20	(GDP2010/GDP2000)**(1/10)-1
113	Honduras	4.19	(GDP2010/GDP2000)**(1/10)-1
114	Djibouti	4.15	(GDP2010/GDP2000)**(1/10)-1
115	Papua New G	4.13	(GDP2010/GDP2000)**(1/10)-1
116	Belize	4.12	(GDP2010/GDP2000)**(1/10)-1
117	Kyrgyzstan	4.10	(GDP2010/GDP2000)**(1/10)-1
118	Hong Kong	4.07	(GDP2010/GDP2000)**(1/10)-1
119	Latvia	4.06	(GDP2010/GDP2000)**(1/10)-1
120	Montenegro	4.06	(GDP2010/GDP2000)**(1/10)-1
121	Namibia	3.96	(GDP2010/GDP2000)**(1/10)-1
122	Bolivia	3.95	(GDP2010/GDP2000)**(1/10)-1
123	Botswana	3.91	(GDP2010/GDP2000)**(1/10)-1
124	Anguilla	3.88	(GDP2010/GDP2000)**(1/10)-1
125	Greenland	3.87	(GDP2010/GDP2000)**(1/10)-1
126	Syria	3.83	(GDP2010/GDP2000)**(1/10)-1
127	Libya	3.80	(GDP2010/GDP2000)**(1/10)-1
128	Colombia	3.79	(GDP2010/GDP2000)**(1/10)-1
129	Ecuador	3.75	(GDP2010/GDP2000)**(1/10)-1
130	Moldova	3.74	(GDP2010/GDP2000)**(1/10)-1
131	Chile	3.70	(GDP2010/GDP2000)**(1/10)-1
132	Costa Rica	3.69	(GDP2010/GDP2000)**(1/10)-1
133	Brazil	3.69	(GDP2010/GDP2000)**(1/10)-1
134	Senegal	3.62	(GDP2010/GDP2000)**(1/10)-1
135	Iraq	3.55	(GDP2010/GDP2000)**(1/10)-1
136	Solomon Is	3.53	(GDP2010/GDP2000)**(1/10)-1
137	South Africa	3.41	(GDP2010/GDP2000)**(1/10)-1
138	Czechia	3.37	(GDP2010/GDP2000)**(1/10)-1
139	Mauritius	3.31	(GDP2010/GDP2000)**(1/10)-1
140	Gibraltar	3.30	(GDP2010/GDP2000)**(1/10)-1
141	Estonia	3.29	(GDP2010/GDP2000)**(1/10)-1
142	Israel	3.26	(GDP2010/GDP2000)**(1/10)-1
143	Guatemala	3.26	(GDP2010/GDP2000)**(1/10)-1
144	Gambia	3.24	(GDP2010/GDP2000)**(1/10)-1

TABLE 6.20 GDP GROWTH RATES, 2000-2010

Rank	Country	GRRL	Source
145	Cyprus	3.14	(GDP2010/GDP2000)**(1/10)-1
146	Dominica	3.12	(GDP2010/GDP2000)**(1/10)-1
147	Nicaragua	3.09	(GDP2010/GDP2000)**(1/10)-1
148	Lesotho	3.09	(GDP2010/GDP2000)**(1/10)-1
149	Paraguay	3.08	(GDP2010/GDP2000)**(1/10)-1
150	Cameroon	3.04	(GDP2010/GDP2000)**(1/10)-1
151	Australia	3.04	(GDP2010/GDP2000)**(1/10)-1
152	Uruguay	2.98	(GDP2010/GDP2000)**(1/10)-1
153	Lebanon	2.97	(GDP2010/GDP2000)**(1/10)-1
154	Vanuatu	2.91	(GDP2010/GDP2000)**(1/10)-1
155	Samoa	2.78	(GDP2010/GDP2000)**(1/10)-1
156	Slovenia	2.78	(GDP2010/GDP2000)**(1/10)-1
157	Nepal	2.78	(GDP2010/GDP2000)**(1/10)-1
158	Burundi	2.77	(GDP2010/GDP2000)**(1/10)-1
159	Malawi	2.77	(GDP2010/GDP2000)**(1/10)-1
160	Macedonia	2.77	(GDP2010/GDP2000)**(1/10)-1
161	Armenia	2.76	(GDP2010/GDP2000)**(1/10)-1
162	Luxembourg	2.74	(GDP2010/GDP2000)**(1/10)-1
163	Venezuela	2.69	(GDP2010/GDP2000)**(1/10)-1
164	Croatia	2.65	(GDP2010/GDP2000)**(1/10)-1
165	Guinea-Biss	2.61	(GDP2010/GDP2000)**(1/10)-1
166	Faroe Is	2.61	(GDP2010/GDP2000)**(1/10)-1
167	New Zealand	2.57	(GDP2010/GDP2000)**(1/10)-1
168	Togo	2.51	(GDP2010/GDP2000)**(1/10)-1
169	Benin	2.48	(GDP2010/GDP2000)**(1/10)-1
170	Madagascar	2.45	(GDP2010/GDP2000)**(1/10)-1
171	Ireland	2.43	(GDP2010/GDP2000)**(1/10)-1
172	Seychelles	2.32	(GDP2010/GDP2000)**(1/10)-1
173	Guinea	2.22	(GDP2010/GDP2000)**(1/10)-1
174	Sweden	2.20	(GDP2010/GDP2000)**(1/10)-1
175	Hungary	2.19	(GDP2010/GDP2000)**(1/10)-1
176	Iceland	2.16	(GDP2010/GDP2000)**(1/10)-1
177	Puerto Rico	2.16	(GDP2010/GDP2000)**(1/10)-1
178	Swaziland	2.07	(GDP2010/GDP2000)**(1/10)-1
179	Comoros	1.92	(GDP2010/GDP2000)**(1/10)-1
180	Mexico	1.92	(GDP2010/GDP2000)**(1/10)-1
181	St Vincent	1.90	(GDP2010/GDP2000)**(1/10)-1
182	El Salvador	1.89	(GDP2010/GDP2000)**(1/10)-1
183	Spain	1.87	(GDP2010/GDP2000)**(1/10)-1
184	Switzerland	1.86	(GDP2010/GDP2000)**(1/10)-1
185	UAE	1.82	(GDP2010/GDP2000)**(1/10)-1
186	Ivory Coast	1.79	(GDP2010/GDP2000)**(1/10)-1
187	Finland	1.79	(GDP2010/GDP2000)**(1/10)-1
188	Antigua & B	1.75	(GDP2010/GDP2000)**(1/10)-1
189	Gaza Strip	1.74	(GDP2010/GDP2000)**(1/10)-1
190	Canada	1.65	(GDP2010/GDP2000)**(1/10)-1
191	Norway	1.65	(GDP2010/GDP2000)**(1/10)-1
192	US	1.64	(GDP2010/GDP2000)**(1/10)-1

Table 6.20 GDP Growth Rates, 2000-2010			
Rank	Country	GRRL	Source
193	UK	1.62	(GDP2010/GDP2000)**(1/10)-1
194	St Kitts & N	1.62	(GDP2010/GDP2000)**(1/10)-1
195	Greece	1.61	(GDP2010/GDP2000)**(1/10)-1
196	Grenada	1.59	(GDP2010/GDP2000)**(1/10)-1
197	Gabon	1.58	(GDP2010/GDP2000)**(1/10)-1
198	St Lucia	1.55	(GDP2010/GDP2000)**(1/10)-1
199	Niue	1.51	(GDP2010/GDP2000)**(1/10)-1
200	Belgium	1.45	(GDP2010/GDP2000)**(1/10)-1
201	Netherlands	1.39	(GDP2010/GDP2000)**(1/10)-1
202	Kiribati	1.36	(GDP2010/GDP2000)**(1/10)-1
203	Guam	1.31	(GDP2010/GDP2000)**(1/10)-1
204	Austria	1.29	(GDP2010/GDP2000)**(1/10)-1
205	Malta	1.29	(GDP2010/GDP2000)**(1/10)-1
206	Tonga	1.22	(GDP2010/GDP2000)**(1/10)-1
207	France	1.12	(GDP2010/GDP2000)**(1/10)-1
208	Guyana	1.11	(GDP2010/GDP2000)**(1/10)-1
209	Brunei	1.02	(GDP2010/GDP2000)**(1/10)-1
210	Germany	0.98	(GDP2010/GDP2000)**(1/10)-1
211	Fiji	0.83	(GDP2010/GDP2000)**(1/10)-1
212	Japan	0.80	(GDP2010/GDP2000)**(1/10)-1
213	Portugal	0.74	(GDP2010/GDP2000)**(1/10)-1
214	Eritrea	0.73	(GDP2010/GDP2000)**(1/10)-1
215	St Pierre&M	0.73	(GDP2010/GDP2000)**(1/10)-1
216	Barbados	0.69	(GDP2010/GDP2000)**(1/10)-1
217	Denmark	0.63	(GDP2010/GDP2000)**(1/10)-1
218	San Marino	0.43	(GDP2010/GDP2000)**(1/10)-1
219	Tokelau	0.32	(GDP2010/GDP2000)**(1/10)-1
220	Bahamas	0.28	(GDP2010/GDP2000)**(1/10)-1
221	West Bank	0.16	(GDP2010/GDP2000)**(1/10)-1
222	Micronesia	0.14	(GDP2010/GDP2000)**(1/10)-1
223	Haiti	0.09	(GDP2010/GDP2000)**(1/10)-1
224	Burma	0.07	(GDP2010/GDP2000)**(1/10)-1
225	Palau	0.02	(GDP2010/GDP2000)**(1/10)-1
226	Italy	-0.01	(GDP2010/GDP2000)**(1/10)-1
227	Korea, North	-0.03	(GDP2010/GDP2000)**(1/10)-1
228	Somalia	-0.37	(GDP2010/GDP2000)**(1/10)-1
229	Saint Helena	-0.74	(GDP2010/GDP2000)**(1/10)-1
230	Svalbard	-0.82	(GDP2010/GDP2000)**(1/10)-1
231	Cook Is	-0.97	(GDP2010/GDP2000)**(1/10)-1
232	Nauru	-1.17	(GDP2010/GDP2000)**(1/10)-1
233	N Mariana Is	-3.24	(GDP2010/GDP2000)**(1/10)-1
234	Samoa, Amer	-3.42	(GDP2010/GDP2000)**(1/10)-1
235	Aruba	-3.53	(GDP2010/GDP2000)**(1/10)-1
236	Zimbabwe	-13.08	(GDP2010/GDP2000)**(1/10)-1

Table 6.21 GDP Growth Rates, 2010-2012

Rank	Country	GRRL	Source
1	San Marino	25.79	(GDP2012/GDP2010)**(1/2)-1
2	Macao	17.04	(GDP2012/GDP2010)**(1/2)-1
3	Afghanistan	16.13	(GDP2012/GDP2010)**(1/2)-1
4	Zimbabwe	15.44	(GDP2012/GDP2010)**(1/2)-1
5	Mongolia	14.31	(GDP2012/GDP2010)**(1/2)-1
6	Virgin I, Br	13.58	(GDP2012/GDP2010)**(1/2)-1
7	Turkmenistan	12.75	(GDP2012/GDP2010)**(1/2)-1
8	Monaco	10.98	(GDP2012/GDP2010)**(1/2)-1
9	Iraq	10.72	(GDP2012/GDP2010)**(1/2)-1
10	Panama	10.65	(GDP2012/GDP2010)**(1/2)-1
11	Sierra Leone	10.40	(GDP2012/GDP2010)**(1/2)-1
12	Ghana	9.22	(GDP2012/GDP2010)**(1/2)-1
13	Bhutan	8.88	(GDP2012/GDP2010)**(1/2)-1
14	Solomon Is	8.80	(GDP2012/GDP2010)**(1/2)-1
15	Saudi Arabia	8.65	(GDP2012/GDP2010)**(1/2)-1
16	Sri Lanka	8.56	(GDP2012/GDP2010)**(1/2)-1
17	Laos	8.26	(GDP2012/GDP2010)**(1/2)-1
18	Georgia	8.24	(GDP2012/GDP2010)**(1/2)-1
19	Zambia	8.20	(GDP2012/GDP2010)**(1/2)-1
20	Ethiopia	8.19	(GDP2012/GDP2010)**(1/2)-1
21	Kosovo	8.13	(GDP2012/GDP2010)**(1/2)-1
22	Papua New G	8.13	(GDP2012/GDP2010)**(1/2)-1
23	China	7.95	(GDP2012/GDP2010)**(1/2)-1
24	South Sudan	7.88	(GDP2012/GDP2010)**(1/2)-1
25	Ecuador	7.56	(GDP2012/GDP2010)**(1/2)-1
26	Qatar	7.55	(GDP2012/GDP2010)**(1/2)-1
27	Rwanda	7.50	(GDP2012/GDP2010)**(1/2)-1
28	Eritrea	7.49	(GDP2012/GDP2010)**(1/2)-1
29	Liberia	7.46	(GDP2012/GDP2010)**(1/2)-1
30	Mozambique	7.25	(GDP2012/GDP2010)**(1/2)-1
31	Tajikistan	6.92	(GDP2012/GDP2010)**(1/2)-1
32	Congo, Dem R	6.87	(GDP2012/GDP2010)**(1/2)-1
33	Burkina Faso	6.77	(GDP2012/GDP2010)**(1/2)-1
34	Bangladesh	6.70	(GDP2012/GDP2010)**(1/2)-1
35	Niger	6.69	(GDP2012/GDP2010)**(1/2)-1
36	Chile	6.40	(GDP2012/GDP2010)**(1/2)-1
37	Estonia	6.40	(GDP2012/GDP2010)**(1/2)-1
38	Peru	6.36	(GDP2012/GDP2010)**(1/2)-1
39	Kazakhstan	6.34	(GDP2012/GDP2010)**(1/2)-1
40	CAR	6.32	(GDP2012/GDP2010)**(1/2)-1
41	Uzbekistan	6.30	(GDP2012/GDP2010)**(1/2)-1
42	Nigeria	6.30	(GDP2012/GDP2010)**(1/2)-1
43	Turkey	6.30	(GDP2012/GDP2010)**(1/2)-1
44	Tanzania	6.25	(GDP2012/GDP2010)**(1/2)-1
45	Botswana	6.22	(GDP2012/GDP2010)**(1/2)-1
46	Malaysia	6.22	(GDP2012/GDP2010)**(1/2)-1
47	Cambodia	6.16	(GDP2012/GDP2010)**(1/2)-1
48	Indonesia	6.09	(GDP2012/GDP2010)**(1/2)-1

TABLE 6.21 GDP GROWTH RATES, 2010-2012

Rank	Country	GRRL	Source
49	Latvia	6.02	(GDP2012/GDP2010)**(1/2)-1
50	India	5.92	(GDP2012/GDP2010)**(1/2)-1
51	East Timor	5.86	(GDP2012/GDP2010)**(1/2)-1
52	Bolivia	5.79	(GDP2012/GDP2010)**(1/2)-1
53	Lithuania	5.76	(GDP2012/GDP2010)**(1/2)-1
54	Vietnam	5.76	(GDP2012/GDP2010)**(1/2)-1
55	Gabon	5.74	(GDP2012/GDP2010)**(1/2)-1
56	Mauritania	5.70	(GDP2012/GDP2010)**(1/2)-1
57	W Sahara	5.52	(GDP2012/GDP2010)**(1/2)-1
58	Nicaragua	5.49	(GDP2012/GDP2010)**(1/2)-1
59	Palau	5.48	(GDP2012/GDP2010)**(1/2)-1
60	Suriname	5.30	(GDP2012/GDP2010)**(1/2)-1
61	Argentina	5.29	(GDP2012/GDP2010)**(1/2)-1
62	Colombia	5.16	(GDP2012/GDP2010)**(1/2)-1
63	Uruguay	5.08	(GDP2012/GDP2010)**(1/2)-1
64	Angola	5.05	(GDP2012/GDP2010)**(1/2)-1
65	Uganda	4.93	(GDP2012/GDP2010)**(1/2)-1
66	Mexico	4.87	(GDP2012/GDP2010)**(1/2)-1
67	Maldives	4.86	(GDP2012/GDP2010)**(1/2)-1
68	Namibia	4.84	(GDP2012/GDP2010)**(1/2)-1
69	Venezuela	4.81	(GDP2012/GDP2010)**(1/2)-1
70	Aruba	4.74	(GDP2012/GDP2010)**(1/2)-1
71	Seychelles	4.68	(GDP2012/GDP2010)**(1/2)-1
72	Sudan	4.64	(GDP2012/GDP2010)**(1/2)-1
73	Russia	4.64	(GDP2012/GDP2010)**(1/2)-1
74	Togo	4.63	(GDP2012/GDP2010)**(1/2)-1
75	Morocco	4.43	(GDP2012/GDP2010)**(1/2)-1
76	Costa Rica	4.42	(GDP2012/GDP2010)**(1/2)-1
77	Guyana	4.40	(GDP2012/GDP2010)**(1/2)-1
78	Australia	4.36	(GDP2012/GDP2010)**(1/2)-1
79	Cameroon	4.33	(GDP2012/GDP2010)**(1/2)-1
80	Kenya	4.32	(GDP2012/GDP2010)**(1/2)-1
81	Philippines	4.28	(GDP2012/GDP2010)**(1/2)-1
82	Dominican R	4.15	(GDP2012/GDP2010)**(1/2)-1
83	Nepal	4.13	(GDP2012/GDP2010)**(1/2)-1
84	St Kitts & N	4.12	(GDP2012/GDP2010)**(1/2)-1
85	Chad	4.07	(GDP2012/GDP2010)**(1/2)-1
86	Sao Tome & P	4.02	(GDP2012/GDP2010)**(1/2)-1
87	Cape Verde	4.01	(GDP2012/GDP2010)**(1/2)-1
88	Belize	3.99	(GDP2012/GDP2010)**(1/2)-1
89	Turks & C Is	3.98	(GDP2012/GDP2010)**(1/2)-1
90	Somalia	3.89	(GDP2012/GDP2010)**(1/2)-1
91	Honduras	3.88	(GDP2012/GDP2010)**(1/2)-1
92	Guinea	3.83	(GDP2012/GDP2010)**(1/2)-1
93	Anguilla	3.78	(GDP2012/GDP2010)**(1/2)-1
94	Israel	3.77	(GDP2012/GDP2010)**(1/2)-1
95	Equatorial G	3.70	(GDP2012/GDP2010)**(1/2)-1
96	Kiribati	3.60	(GDP2012/GDP2010)**(1/2)-1

Table 6.21 GDP Growth Rates, 2010-2012

Rank	Country	GRRL	Source
97	Thailand	3.58	(GDP2012/GDP2010)**(1/2)-1
98	Guatemala	3.51	(GDP2012/GDP2010)**(1/2)-1
99	Haiti	3.49	(GDP2012/GDP2010)**(1/2)-1
100	Malawi	3.44	(GDP2012/GDP2010)**(1/2)-1
101	Mauritius	3.43	(GDP2012/GDP2010)**(1/2)-1
102	Belarus	3.42	(GDP2012/GDP2010)**(1/2)-1
103	Burma	3.40	(GDP2012/GDP2010)**(1/2)-1
104	Singapore	3.28	(GDP2012/GDP2010)**(1/2)-1
105	Pakistan	3.22	(GDP2012/GDP2010)**(1/2)-1
106	South Africa	3.19	(GDP2012/GDP2010)**(1/2)-1
107	Kuwait	3.18	(GDP2012/GDP2010)**(1/2)-1
108	Congo, Rep	3.08	(GDP2012/GDP2010)**(1/2)-1
109	Saint Martin	3.07	(GDP2012/GDP2010)**(1/2)-1
110	Algeria	3.05	(GDP2012/GDP2010)**(1/2)-1
111	New Caledon	3.04	(GDP2012/GDP2010)**(1/2)-1
112	Fr Polynesia	3.03	(GDP2012/GDP2010)**(1/2)-1
113	Falkland Is	2.93	(GDP2012/GDP2010)**(1/2)-1
114	Egypt	2.91	(GDP2012/GDP2010)**(1/2)-1
115	Lesotho	2.91	(GDP2012/GDP2010)**(1/2)-1
116	Poland	2.87	(GDP2012/GDP2010)**(1/2)-1
117	Hong Kong	2.82	(GDP2012/GDP2010)**(1/2)-1
118	New Zealand	2.82	(GDP2012/GDP2010)**(1/2)-1
119	Curacao	2.79	(GDP2012/GDP2010)**(1/2)-1
120	Canada	2.77	(GDP2012/GDP2010)**(1/2)-1
121	Slovakia	2.76	(GDP2012/GDP2010)**(1/2)-1
122	Vanuatu	2.76	(GDP2012/GDP2010)**(1/2)-1
123	Ukraine	2.74	(GDP2012/GDP2010)**(1/2)-1
124	Korea, South	2.73	(GDP2012/GDP2010)**(1/2)-1
125	Brunei	2.71	(GDP2012/GDP2010)**(1/2)-1
126	Isle of Man	2.71	(GDP2012/GDP2010)**(1/2)-1
127	Saint Helena	2.71	(GDP2012/GDP2010)**(1/2)-1
128	Gaza Strip	2.71	(GDP2012/GDP2010)**(1/2)-1
129	UAE	2.66	(GDP2012/GDP2010)**(1/2)-1
130	Sint Maarten	2.59	(GDP2012/GDP2010)**(1/2)-1
131	Jordan	2.59	(GDP2012/GDP2010)**(1/2)-1
132	Bermuda	2.51	(GDP2012/GDP2010)**(1/2)-1
133	Germany	2.44	(GDP2012/GDP2010)**(1/2)-1
134	Senegal	2.44	(GDP2012/GDP2010)**(1/2)-1
135	Liechtenstn	2.43	(GDP2012/GDP2010)**(1/2)-1
136	Jersey	2.34	(GDP2012/GDP2010)**(1/2)-1
137	Madagascar	2.34	(GDP2012/GDP2010)**(1/2)-1
138	US	2.29	(GDP2012/GDP2010)**(1/2)-1
139	Comoros	2.26	(GDP2012/GDP2010)**(1/2)-1
140	Gibraltar	2.23	(GDP2012/GDP2010)**(1/2)-1
141	Samoa, Amer	2.19	(GDP2012/GDP2010)**(1/2)-1
142	St Vincent	2.18	(GDP2012/GDP2010)**(1/2)-1
143	Austria	2.12	(GDP2012/GDP2010)**(1/2)-1
144	Iceland	2.11	(GDP2012/GDP2010)**(1/2)-1

TABLE 6.21 GDP GROWTH RATES, 2010-2012

Rank	Country	GRRL	Source
145	Moldova	2.11	(GDP2012/GDP2010)**(1/2)-1
146	Samoa	2.10	(GDP2012/GDP2010)**(1/2)-1
147	Norway	2.09	(GDP2012/GDP2010)**(1/2)-1
148	Kyrgyzstan	2.09	(GDP2012/GDP2010)**(1/2)-1
149	Guam	2.05	(GDP2012/GDP2010)**(1/2)-1
150	Guernsey	2.04	(GDP2012/GDP2010)**(1/2)-1
151	Ivory Coast	1.99	(GDP2012/GDP2010)**(1/2)-1
152	Sweden	1.96	(GDP2012/GDP2010)**(1/2)-1
153	Burundi	1.95	(GDP2012/GDP2010)**(1/2)-1
154	Armenia	1.95	(GDP2012/GDP2010)**(1/2)-1
155	Taiwan	1.92	(GDP2012/GDP2010)**(1/2)-1
156	Brazil	1.86	(GDP2012/GDP2010)**(1/2)-1
157	El Salvador	1.84	(GDP2012/GDP2010)**(1/2)-1
158	Marshall Is	1.83	(GDP2012/GDP2010)**(1/2)-1
159	Wallis & Fut	1.75	(GDP2012/GDP2010)**(1/2)-1
160	Virgin I, US	1.74	(GDP2012/GDP2010)**(1/2)-1
161	Bahamas	1.65	(GDP2012/GDP2010)**(1/2)-1
162	Djibouti	1.64	(GDP2012/GDP2010)**(1/2)-1
163	Cayman Is	1.62	(GDP2012/GDP2010)**(1/2)-1
164	Montserrat	1.62	(GDP2012/GDP2010)**(1/2)-1
165	West Bank	1.60	(GDP2012/GDP2010)**(1/2)-1
166	Montenegro	1.53	(GDP2012/GDP2010)**(1/2)-1
167	Tonga	1.52	(GDP2012/GDP2010)**(1/2)-1
168	Cuba	1.51	(GDP2012/GDP2010)**(1/2)-1
169	Switzerland	1.45	(GDP2012/GDP2010)**(1/2)-1
170	Macedonia	1.45	(GDP2012/GDP2010)**(1/2)-1
171	Benin	1.35	(GDP2012/GDP2010)**(1/2)-1
172	Ireland	1.31	(GDP2012/GDP2010)**(1/2)-1
173	Bulgaria	1.30	(GDP2012/GDP2010)**(1/2)-1
174	Lebanon	1.28	(GDP2012/GDP2010)**(1/2)-1
175	Fiji	1.18	(GDP2012/GDP2010)**(1/2)-1
176	Azerbaijan	1.15	(GDP2012/GDP2010)**(1/2)-1
177	Nauru	1.13	(GDP2012/GDP2010)**(1/2)-1
178	Mali	1.12	(GDP2012/GDP2010)**(1/2)-1
179	Malta	1.08	(GDP2012/GDP2010)**(1/2)-1
180	Paraguay	1.07	(GDP2012/GDP2010)**(1/2)-1
181	Korea, North	1.05	(GDP2012/GDP2010)**(1/2)-1
182	France	1.03	(GDP2012/GDP2010)**(1/2)-1
183	Greenland	1.03	(GDP2012/GDP2010)**(1/2)-1
184	Micronesia	1.02	(GDP2012/GDP2010)**(1/2)-1
185	Finland	0.96	(GDP2012/GDP2010)**(1/2)-1
186	Romania	0.95	(GDP2012/GDP2010)**(1/2)-1
187	Faroe Is	0.94	(GDP2012/GDP2010)**(1/2)-1
188	Puerto Rico	0.90	(GDP2012/GDP2010)**(1/2)-1
189	St Lucia	0.89	(GDP2012/GDP2010)**(1/2)-1
190	Luxembourg	0.83	(GDP2012/GDP2010)**(1/2)-1
191	Tunisia	0.73	(GDP2012/GDP2010)**(1/2)-1
192	UK	0.73	(GDP2012/GDP2010)**(1/2)-1

TABLE 6.21 GDP GROWTH RATES, 2010-2012			
Rank	Country	GRRL	Source
193	Belgium	0.70	(GDP2012/GDP2010)**(1/2)-1
194	Albania	0.67	(GDP2012/GDP2010)**(1/2)-1
195	Bosnia	0.52	(GDP2012/GDP2010)**(1/2)-1
196	Denmark	0.52	(GDP2012/GDP2010)**(1/2)-1
197	Tuvalu	0.50	(GDP2012/GDP2010)**(1/2)-1
198	Iran	0.47	(GDP2012/GDP2010)**(1/2)-1
199	Tokelau	0.45	(GDP2012/GDP2010)**(1/2)-1
200	Japan	0.42	(GDP2012/GDP2010)**(1/2)-1
201	Grenada	0.42	(GDP2012/GDP2010)**(1/2)-1
202	Czechia	0.41	(GDP2012/GDP2010)**(1/2)-1
203	Spain	0.30	(GDP2012/GDP2010)**(1/2)-1
204	Trinidad & T	0.25	(GDP2012/GDP2010)**(1/2)-1
205	Mayotte	0.22	(GDP2012/GDP2010)**(1/2)-1
206	Italy	0.14	(GDP2012/GDP2010)**(1/2)-1
207	Barbados	0.12	(GDP2012/GDP2010)**(1/2)-1
208	Antigua & B	0.10	(GDP2012/GDP2010)**(1/2)-1
209	St Pierre&M	0.05	(GDP2012/GDP2010)**(1/2)-1
210	Serbia	0.04	(GDP2012/GDP2010)**(1/2)-1
211	Croatia	-0.04	(GDP2012/GDP2010)**(1/2)-1
212	Netherlands	-0.22	(GDP2012/GDP2010)**(1/2)-1
213	Hungary	-0.27	(GDP2012/GDP2010)**(1/2)-1
214	Bahrain	-0.32	(GDP2012/GDP2010)**(1/2)-1
215	Gambia	-0.38	(GDP2012/GDP2010)**(1/2)-1
216	Swaziland	-0.47	(GDP2012/GDP2010)**(1/2)-1
217	Syria	-0.67	(GDP2012/GDP2010)**(1/2)-1
218	Guinea-Biss	-0.82	(GDP2012/GDP2010)**(1/2)-1
219	Jamaica	-0.85	(GDP2012/GDP2010)**(1/2)-1
220	Slovenia	-0.97	(GDP2012/GDP2010)**(1/2)-1
221	Dominica	-1.06	(GDP2012/GDP2010)**(1/2)-1
222	Niue	-1.24	(GDP2012/GDP2010)**(1/2)-1
223	Cyprus	-1.32	(GDP2012/GDP2010)**(1/2)-1
224	Oman	-1.41	(GDP2012/GDP2010)**(1/2)-1
225	Cook Is	-1.44	(GDP2012/GDP2010)**(1/2)-1
226	Svalbard	-1.45	(GDP2012/GDP2010)**(1/2)-1
227	Guadeloupe	-1.68	(GDP2012/GDP2010)**(1/2)-1
228	N Mariana Is	-1.73	(GDP2012/GDP2010)**(1/2)-1
229	Portugal	-1.89	(GDP2012/GDP2010)**(1/2)-1
230	Martinique	-1.98	(GDP2012/GDP2010)**(1/2)-1
231	Guiana, Fr	-3.60	(GDP2012/GDP2010)**(1/2)-1
232	Yemen	-4.52	(GDP2012/GDP2010)**(1/2)-1
233	Reunion	-5.28	(GDP2012/GDP2010)**(1/2)-1
234	Greece	-5.92	(GDP2012/GDP2010)**(1/2)-1
235	Andorra	-6.33	(GDP2012/GDP2010)**(1/2)-1
236	Libya	-17.55	(GDP2012/GDP2010)**(1/2)-1

Table 6.22 GDP Growth Rates, 2012-2020, Forecast

Rank	Country	GRRL	Source
1	Mayotte	13.22	(GDP2020/GDP2012)**(1/8)-1
2	Equatorial G	12.37	(GDP2020/GDP2012)**(1/8)-1
3	Monaco	10.85	(GDP2020/GDP2012)**(1/8)-1
4	Turks & C Is	10.62	(GDP2020/GDP2012)**(1/8)-1
5	Macao	10.25	(GDP2020/GDP2012)**(1/8)-1
6	Reunion	9.12	(GDP2020/GDP2012)**(1/8)-1
7	Guiana, Fr	9.08	(GDP2020/GDP2012)**(1/8)-1
8	Virgin I, Br	8.91	(GDP2020/GDP2012)**(1/8)-1
9	Marshall Is	8.47	(GDP2020/GDP2012)**(1/8)-1
10	Bermuda	8.40	(GDP2020/GDP2012)**(1/8)-1
11	China	8.17	(GDP2020/GDP2012)**(1/8)-1
12	Azerbaijan	7.74	(GDP2020/GDP2012)**(1/8)-1
13	Bhutan	7.24	(GDP2020/GDP2012)**(1/8)-1
14	Angola	7.21	(GDP2020/GDP2012)**(1/8)-1
15	Cuba	6.91	(GDP2020/GDP2012)**(1/8)-1
16	New Caledon	6.87	(GDP2020/GDP2012)**(1/8)-1
17	Chad	6.71	(GDP2020/GDP2012)**(1/8)-1
18	W Sahara	6.68	(GDP2020/GDP2012)**(1/8)-1
19	Liechtenstn	6.65	(GDP2020/GDP2012)**(1/8)-1
20	Mongolia	6.60	(GDP2020/GDP2012)**(1/8)-1
21	Qatar	6.46	(GDP2020/GDP2012)**(1/8)-1
22	Isle of Man	6.43	(GDP2020/GDP2012)**(1/8)-1
23	South Sudan	6.30	(GDP2020/GDP2012)**(1/8)-1
24	Cape Verde	6.28	(GDP2020/GDP2012)**(1/8)-1
25	Mozambique	6.21	(GDP2020/GDP2012)**(1/8)-1
26	Uganda	6.21	(GDP2020/GDP2012)**(1/8)-1
27	Guadeloupe	6.10	(GDP2020/GDP2012)**(1/8)-1
28	Tuvalu	6.09	(GDP2020/GDP2012)**(1/8)-1
29	Turkmenistan	6.07	(GDP2020/GDP2012)**(1/8)-1
30	Maldives	6.07	(GDP2020/GDP2012)**(1/8)-1
31	Martinique	6.06	(GDP2020/GDP2012)**(1/8)-1
32	Singapore	5.99	(GDP2020/GDP2012)**(1/8)-1
33	Vietnam	5.97	(GDP2020/GDP2012)**(1/8)-1
34	Libya	5.93	(GDP2020/GDP2012)**(1/8)-1
35	Rwanda	5.89	(GDP2020/GDP2012)**(1/8)-1
36	Panama	5.84	(GDP2020/GDP2012)**(1/8)-1
37	India	5.78	(GDP2020/GDP2012)**(1/8)-1
38	Laos	5.74	(GDP2020/GDP2012)**(1/8)-1
39	Botswana	5.71	(GDP2020/GDP2012)**(1/8)-1
40	Ethiopia	5.58	(GDP2020/GDP2012)**(1/8)-1
41	Afghanistan	5.52	(GDP2020/GDP2012)**(1/8)-1
42	Burkina Faso	5.51	(GDP2020/GDP2012)**(1/8)-1
43	Tanzania	5.43	(GDP2020/GDP2012)**(1/8)-1
44	Kazakhstan	5.42	(GDP2020/GDP2012)**(1/8)-1
45	Zambia	5.34	(GDP2020/GDP2012)**(1/8)-1
46	San Marino	5.28	(GDP2020/GDP2012)**(1/8)-1
47	Taiwan	5.22	(GDP2020/GDP2012)**(1/8)-1
48	Korea, South	5.18	(GDP2020/GDP2012)**(1/8)-1

TABLE 6.22 GDP GROWTH RATES, 2012-2020, FORECAST

Rank	Country	GRRL	Source
49	Liberia	5.11	(GDP2020/GDP2012)**(1/8)-1
50	Saint Martin	5.10	(GDP2020/GDP2012)**(1/8)-1
51	Sri Lanka	5.06	(GDP2020/GDP2012)**(1/8)-1
52	Tajikistan	5.05	(GDP2020/GDP2012)**(1/8)-1
53	Falkland Is	5.03	(GDP2020/GDP2012)**(1/8)-1
54	Iraq	5.01	(GDP2020/GDP2012)**(1/8)-1
55	Malaysia	5.00	(GDP2020/GDP2012)**(1/8)-1
56	Nigeria	4.99	(GDP2020/GDP2012)**(1/8)-1
57	Cambodia	4.96	(GDP2020/GDP2012)**(1/8)-1
58	Dominican R	4.88	(GDP2020/GDP2012)**(1/8)-1
59	Bangladesh	4.87	(GDP2020/GDP2012)**(1/8)-1
60	Oman	4.87	(GDP2020/GDP2012)**(1/8)-1
61	Mali	4.86	(GDP2020/GDP2012)**(1/8)-1
62	Jersey	4.86	(GDP2020/GDP2012)**(1/8)-1
63	East Timor	4.85	(GDP2020/GDP2012)**(1/8)-1
64	Turkey	4.76	(GDP2020/GDP2012)**(1/8)-1
65	Kosovo	4.71	(GDP2020/GDP2012)**(1/8)-1
66	Saudi Arabia	4.70	(GDP2020/GDP2012)**(1/8)-1
67	Hong Kong	4.69	(GDP2020/GDP2012)**(1/8)-1
68	Sint Maarten	4.68	(GDP2020/GDP2012)**(1/8)-1
69	Gibraltar	4.66	(GDP2020/GDP2012)**(1/8)-1
70	Sierra Leone	4.64	(GDP2020/GDP2012)**(1/8)-1
71	Guernsey	4.63	(GDP2020/GDP2012)**(1/8)-1
72	Zimbabwe	4.60	(GDP2020/GDP2012)**(1/8)-1
73	Chile	4.60	(GDP2020/GDP2012)**(1/8)-1
74	Niger	4.52	(GDP2020/GDP2012)**(1/8)-1
75	Peru	4.50	(GDP2020/GDP2012)**(1/8)-1
76	Ghana	4.50	(GDP2020/GDP2012)**(1/8)-1
77	Yemen	4.45	(GDP2020/GDP2012)**(1/8)-1
78	Georgia	4.43	(GDP2020/GDP2012)**(1/8)-1
79	Fr Polynesia	4.40	(GDP2020/GDP2012)**(1/8)-1
80	Egypt	4.31	(GDP2020/GDP2012)**(1/8)-1
81	Papua New G	4.29	(GDP2020/GDP2012)**(1/8)-1
82	Curacao	4.23	(GDP2020/GDP2012)**(1/8)-1
83	Thailand	4.22	(GDP2020/GDP2012)**(1/8)-1
84	Belarus	4.21	(GDP2020/GDP2012)**(1/8)-1
85	Russia	4.21	(GDP2020/GDP2012)**(1/8)-1
86	Indonesia	4.20	(GDP2020/GDP2012)**(1/8)-1
87	Seychelles	4.15	(GDP2020/GDP2012)**(1/8)-1
88	Congo, Dem R	4.15	(GDP2020/GDP2012)**(1/8)-1
89	Mauritania	4.11	(GDP2020/GDP2012)**(1/8)-1
90	Argentina	4.10	(GDP2020/GDP2012)**(1/8)-1
91	Brunei	4.09	(GDP2020/GDP2012)**(1/8)-1
92	Jordan	4.03	(GDP2020/GDP2012)**(1/8)-1
93	CAR	3.99	(GDP2020/GDP2012)**(1/8)-1
94	Solomon Is	3.96	(GDP2020/GDP2012)**(1/8)-1
95	Namibia	3.96	(GDP2020/GDP2012)**(1/8)-1
96	Albania	3.95	(GDP2020/GDP2012)**(1/8)-1

Table 6.22 GDP Growth Rates, 2012-2020, Forecast

Rank	Country	GRRL	Source
97	Malawi	3.94	(GDP2020/GDP2012)**(1/8)-1
98	Belize	3.93	(GDP2020/GDP2012)**(1/8)-1
99	Luxembourg	3.89	(GDP2020/GDP2012)**(1/8)-1
100	Ireland	3.86	(GDP2020/GDP2012)**(1/8)-1
101	Sudan	3.86	(GDP2020/GDP2012)**(1/8)-1
102	Costa Rica	3.84	(GDP2020/GDP2012)**(1/8)-1
103	Virgin I, US	3.84	(GDP2020/GDP2012)**(1/8)-1
104	Bolivia	3.84	(GDP2020/GDP2012)**(1/8)-1
105	Svalbard	3.83	(GDP2020/GDP2012)**(1/8)-1
106	Tunisia	3.81	(GDP2020/GDP2012)**(1/8)-1
107	Mauritius	3.78	(GDP2020/GDP2012)**(1/8)-1
108	Lithuania	3.77	(GDP2020/GDP2012)**(1/8)-1
109	Norway	3.76	(GDP2020/GDP2012)**(1/8)-1
110	Trinidad & T	3.75	(GDP2020/GDP2012)**(1/8)-1
111	Jamaica	3.75	(GDP2020/GDP2012)**(1/8)-1
112	Iran	3.75	(GDP2020/GDP2012)**(1/8)-1
113	Nepal	3.73	(GDP2020/GDP2012)**(1/8)-1
114	Israel	3.71	(GDP2020/GDP2012)**(1/8)-1
115	Philippines	3.71	(GDP2020/GDP2012)**(1/8)-1
116	Slovakia	3.71	(GDP2020/GDP2012)**(1/8)-1
117	Poland	3.70	(GDP2020/GDP2012)**(1/8)-1
118	Anguilla	3.69	(GDP2020/GDP2012)**(1/8)-1
119	Morocco	3.66	(GDP2020/GDP2012)**(1/8)-1
120	Uzbekistan	3.63	(GDP2020/GDP2012)**(1/8)-1
121	Honduras	3.59	(GDP2020/GDP2012)**(1/8)-1
122	Romania	3.58	(GDP2020/GDP2012)**(1/8)-1
123	Suriname	3.58	(GDP2020/GDP2012)**(1/8)-1
124	Eritrea	3.55	(GDP2020/GDP2012)**(1/8)-1
125	Latvia	3.55	(GDP2020/GDP2012)**(1/8)-1
126	Pakistan	3.54	(GDP2020/GDP2012)**(1/8)-1
127	Djibouti	3.51	(GDP2020/GDP2012)**(1/8)-1
128	Congo, Rep	3.48	(GDP2020/GDP2012)**(1/8)-1
129	Australia	3.45	(GDP2020/GDP2012)**(1/8)-1
130	St Kitts & N	3.44	(GDP2020/GDP2012)**(1/8)-1
131	St Lucia	3.40	(GDP2020/GDP2012)**(1/8)-1
132	Guatemala	3.37	(GDP2020/GDP2012)**(1/8)-1
133	Cyprus	3.36	(GDP2020/GDP2012)**(1/8)-1
134	Sao Tome & P	3.36	(GDP2020/GDP2012)**(1/8)-1
135	Colombia	3.35	(GDP2020/GDP2012)**(1/8)-1
136	Bahrain	3.34	(GDP2020/GDP2012)**(1/8)-1
137	St Vincent	3.27	(GDP2020/GDP2012)**(1/8)-1
138	Nicaragua	3.23	(GDP2020/GDP2012)**(1/8)-1
139	Vanuatu	3.18	(GDP2020/GDP2012)**(1/8)-1
140	Guinea	3.14	(GDP2020/GDP2012)**(1/8)-1
141	Ecuador	3.12	(GDP2020/GDP2012)**(1/8)-1
142	Dominica	3.08	(GDP2020/GDP2012)**(1/8)-1
143	Uruguay	3.05	(GDP2020/GDP2012)**(1/8)-1
144	Lebanon	3.05	(GDP2020/GDP2012)**(1/8)-1

Table 6.22 GDP Growth Rates, 2012-2020, Forecast

Rank	Country	GRRL	Source
145	Malta	3.04	(GDP2020/GDP2012)**(1/8)-1
146	Saint Helena	3.02	(GDP2020/GDP2012)**(1/8)-1
147	Cameroon	3.02	(GDP2020/GDP2012)**(1/8)-1
148	Grenada	3.00	(GDP2020/GDP2012)**(1/8)-1
149	Estonia	3.00	(GDP2020/GDP2012)**(1/8)-1
150	Kenya	3.00	(GDP2020/GDP2012)**(1/8)-1
151	Wallis & Fut	2.98	(GDP2020/GDP2012)**(1/8)-1
152	Antigua & B	2.98	(GDP2020/GDP2012)**(1/8)-1
153	Senegal	2.98	(GDP2020/GDP2012)**(1/8)-1
154	Algeria	2.98	(GDP2020/GDP2012)**(1/8)-1
155	Gaza Strip	2.98	(GDP2020/GDP2012)**(1/8)-1
156	Montenegro	2.92	(GDP2020/GDP2012)**(1/8)-1
157	Kiribati	2.91	(GDP2020/GDP2012)**(1/8)-1
158	Gabon	2.89	(GDP2020/GDP2012)**(1/8)-1
159	Lesotho	2.89	(GDP2020/GDP2012)**(1/8)-1
160	Kyrgyzstan	2.84	(GDP2020/GDP2012)**(1/8)-1
161	Benin	2.81	(GDP2020/GDP2012)**(1/8)-1
162	Brazil	2.80	(GDP2020/GDP2012)**(1/8)-1
163	Mexico	2.79	(GDP2020/GDP2012)**(1/8)-1
164	Greenland	2.79	(GDP2020/GDP2012)**(1/8)-1
165	Bulgaria	2.72	(GDP2020/GDP2012)**(1/8)-1
166	Andorra	2.71	(GDP2020/GDP2012)**(1/8)-1
167	Guinea-Biss	2.70	(GDP2020/GDP2012)**(1/8)-1
168	Gambia	2.69	(GDP2020/GDP2012)**(1/8)-1
169	Ukraine	2.66	(GDP2020/GDP2012)**(1/8)-1
170	UK	2.63	(GDP2020/GDP2012)**(1/8)-1
171	Madagascar	2.62	(GDP2020/GDP2012)**(1/8)-1
172	Sweden	2.58	(GDP2020/GDP2012)**(1/8)-1
173	Syria	2.58	(GDP2020/GDP2012)**(1/8)-1
174	Swaziland	2.57	(GDP2020/GDP2012)**(1/8)-1
175	Spain	2.50	(GDP2020/GDP2012)**(1/8)-1
176	US	2.50	(GDP2020/GDP2012)**(1/8)-1
177	Bosnia	2.49	(GDP2020/GDP2012)**(1/8)-1
178	Slovenia	2.48	(GDP2020/GDP2012)**(1/8)-1
179	Burma	2.48	(GDP2020/GDP2012)**(1/8)-1
180	El Salvador	2.46	(GDP2020/GDP2012)**(1/8)-1
181	Faroe Is	2.46	(GDP2020/GDP2012)**(1/8)-1
182	New Zealand	2.44	(GDP2020/GDP2012)**(1/8)-1
183	Czechia	2.42	(GDP2020/GDP2012)**(1/8)-1
184	Iceland	2.40	(GDP2020/GDP2012)**(1/8)-1
185	Cayman Is	2.40	(GDP2020/GDP2012)**(1/8)-1
186	Austria	2.40	(GDP2020/GDP2012)**(1/8)-1
187	Montserrat	2.40	(GDP2020/GDP2012)**(1/8)-1
188	Samoa, Amer	2.39	(GDP2020/GDP2012)**(1/8)-1
189	UAE	2.39	(GDP2020/GDP2012)**(1/8)-1
190	Paraguay	2.38	(GDP2020/GDP2012)**(1/8)-1
191	Somalia	2.37	(GDP2020/GDP2012)**(1/8)-1
192	Serbia	2.36	(GDP2020/GDP2012)**(1/8)-1

Table 6.22 GDP Growth Rates, 2012-2020, Forecast

Rank	Country	GRRL	Source
193	West Bank	2.36	(GDP2020/GDP2012)**(1/8)-1
194	Togo	2.35	(GDP2020/GDP2012)**(1/8)-1
195	Finland	2.31	(GDP2020/GDP2012)**(1/8)-1
196	Greece	2.29	(GDP2020/GDP2012)**(1/8)-1
197	Guyana	2.28	(GDP2020/GDP2012)**(1/8)-1
198	Kuwait	2.25	(GDP2020/GDP2012)**(1/8)-1
199	Canada	2.23	(GDP2020/GDP2012)**(1/8)-1
200	Venezuela	2.22	(GDP2020/GDP2012)**(1/8)-1
201	Samoa	2.13	(GDP2020/GDP2012)**(1/8)-1
202	South Africa	2.11	(GDP2020/GDP2012)**(1/8)-1
203	Armenia	2.09	(GDP2020/GDP2012)**(1/8)-1
204	Ivory Coast	2.09	(GDP2020/GDP2012)**(1/8)-1
205	Macedonia	2.08	(GDP2020/GDP2012)**(1/8)-1
206	Belgium	2.04	(GDP2020/GDP2012)**(1/8)-1
207	Moldova	2.03	(GDP2020/GDP2012)**(1/8)-1
208	Netherlands	2.02	(GDP2020/GDP2012)**(1/8)-1
209	Comoros	2.01	(GDP2020/GDP2012)**(1/8)-1
210	Guam	2.00	(GDP2020/GDP2012)**(1/8)-1
211	Tonga	1.99	(GDP2020/GDP2012)**(1/8)-1
212	Burundi	1.96	(GDP2020/GDP2012)**(1/8)-1
213	Croatia	1.94	(GDP2020/GDP2012)**(1/8)-1
214	Portugal	1.94	(GDP2020/GDP2012)**(1/8)-1
215	Switzerland	1.87	(GDP2020/GDP2012)**(1/8)-1
216	Palau	1.82	(GDP2020/GDP2012)**(1/8)-1
217	Germany	1.79	(GDP2020/GDP2012)**(1/8)-1
218	St Pierre&M	1.77	(GDP2020/GDP2012)**(1/8)-1
219	France	1.71	(GDP2020/GDP2012)**(1/8)-1
220	Haiti	1.67	(GDP2020/GDP2012)**(1/8)-1
221	Hungary	1.64	(GDP2020/GDP2012)**(1/8)-1
222	Aruba	1.63	(GDP2020/GDP2012)**(1/8)-1
223	Barbados	1.59	(GDP2020/GDP2012)**(1/8)-1
224	Denmark	1.59	(GDP2020/GDP2012)**(1/8)-1
225	Bahamas	1.52	(GDP2020/GDP2012)**(1/8)-1
226	N Mariana Is	1.46	(GDP2020/GDP2012)**(1/8)-1
227	Japan	1.43	(GDP2020/GDP2012)**(1/8)-1
228	Italy	1.41	(GDP2020/GDP2012)**(1/8)-1
229	Puerto Rico	1.41	(GDP2020/GDP2012)**(1/8)-1
230	Korea, North	1.06	(GDP2020/GDP2012)**(1/8)-1
231	Fiji	0.88	(GDP2020/GDP2012)**(1/8)-1
232	Niue	0.78	(GDP2020/GDP2012)**(1/8)-1
233	Tokelau	0.63	(GDP2020/GDP2012)**(1/8)-1
234	Micronesia	0.58	(GDP2020/GDP2012)**(1/8)-1
235	Nauru	0.41	(GDP2020/GDP2012)**(1/8)-1
236	Cook Is	-1.83	(GDP2020/GDP2012)**(1/8)-1

Table 6.23 GDP Growth Rates, 2020-2030, Forecast			
Rank	Country	GRRL	Source
1	Turks & C Is	7.43	(GDP2030/GDP2020)**(1/10)-1
2	Virgin I, Br	6.68	(GDP2030/GDP2020)**(1/10)-1
3	Uganda	5.31	(GDP2030/GDP2020)**(1/10)-1
4	Angola	5.28	(GDP2030/GDP2020)**(1/10)-1
5	Chad	5.06	(GDP2030/GDP2020)**(1/10)-1
6	Mozambique	5.03	(GDP2030/GDP2020)**(1/10)-1
7	Zambia	4.93	(GDP2030/GDP2020)**(1/10)-1
8	Burkina Faso	4.92	(GDP2030/GDP2020)**(1/10)-1
9	Guiana, Fr	4.92	(GDP2030/GDP2020)**(1/10)-1
10	W Sahara	4.88	(GDP2030/GDP2020)**(1/10)-1
11	Tanzania	4.85	(GDP2030/GDP2020)**(1/10)-1
12	Niger	4.67	(GDP2030/GDP2020)**(1/10)-1
13	Rwanda	4.64	(GDP2030/GDP2020)**(1/10)-1
14	Afghanistan	4.61	(GDP2030/GDP2020)**(1/10)-1
15	Mali	4.55	(GDP2030/GDP2020)**(1/10)-1
16	Iraq	4.54	(GDP2030/GDP2020)**(1/10)-1
17	Nigeria	4.54	(GDP2030/GDP2020)**(1/10)-1
18	Liberia	4.54	(GDP2030/GDP2020)**(1/10)-1
19	South Sudan	4.53	(GDP2030/GDP2020)**(1/10)-1
20	Equatorial G	4.47	(GDP2030/GDP2020)**(1/10)-1
21	Mayotte	4.41	(GDP2030/GDP2020)**(1/10)-1
22	Yemen	4.16	(GDP2030/GDP2020)**(1/10)-1
23	Malawi	4.14	(GDP2030/GDP2020)**(1/10)-1
24	Ghana	4.13	(GDP2030/GDP2020)**(1/10)-1
25	East Timor	4.12	(GDP2030/GDP2020)**(1/10)-1
26	Singapore	4.10	(GDP2030/GDP2020)**(1/10)-1
27	Ethiopia	4.06	(GDP2030/GDP2020)**(1/10)-1
28	Solomon Is	3.96	(GDP2030/GDP2020)**(1/10)-1
29	Sierra Leone	3.93	(GDP2030/GDP2020)**(1/10)-1
30	Congo, Dem R	3.93	(GDP2030/GDP2020)**(1/10)-1
31	Botswana	3.89	(GDP2030/GDP2020)**(1/10)-1
32	CAR	3.87	(GDP2030/GDP2020)**(1/10)-1
33	Anguilla	3.86	(GDP2030/GDP2020)**(1/10)-1
34	Panama	3.84	(GDP2030/GDP2020)**(1/10)-1
35	Falkland Is	3.82	(GDP2030/GDP2020)**(1/10)-1
36	Mauritania	3.79	(GDP2030/GDP2020)**(1/10)-1
37	Papua New G	3.75	(GDP2030/GDP2020)**(1/10)-1
38	Tajikistan	3.73	(GDP2030/GDP2020)**(1/10)-1
39	Malaysia	3.73	(GDP2030/GDP2020)**(1/10)-1
40	Libya	3.72	(GDP2030/GDP2020)**(1/10)-1
41	Mongolia	3.71	(GDP2030/GDP2020)**(1/10)-1
42	New Caledon	3.70	(GDP2030/GDP2020)**(1/10)-1
43	Sudan	3.68	(GDP2030/GDP2020)**(1/10)-1
44	Congo, Rep	3.67	(GDP2030/GDP2020)**(1/10)-1
45	Saudi Arabia	3.65	(GDP2030/GDP2020)**(1/10)-1
46	Cambodia	3.60	(GDP2030/GDP2020)**(1/10)-1
47	India	3.58	(GDP2030/GDP2020)**(1/10)-1
48	Laos	3.57	(GDP2030/GDP2020)**(1/10)-1

Table 6.23 GDP Growth Rates, 2020-2030, Forecast			
Rank	Country	GRRL	Source
49	Macao	3.55	(GDP2030/GDP2020)**(1/10)-1
50	Turkmenistan	3.54	(GDP2030/GDP2020)**(1/10)-1
51	Bhutan	3.53	(GDP2030/GDP2020)**(1/10)-1
52	Marshall Is	3.51	(GDP2030/GDP2020)**(1/10)-1
53	Cape Verde	3.48	(GDP2030/GDP2020)**(1/10)-1
54	Bolivia	3.47	(GDP2030/GDP2020)**(1/10)-1
55	Liechtenstn	3.46	(GDP2030/GDP2020)**(1/10)-1
56	Belize	3.45	(GDP2030/GDP2020)**(1/10)-1
57	Philippines	3.42	(GDP2030/GDP2020)**(1/10)-1
58	Zimbabwe	3.40	(GDP2030/GDP2020)**(1/10)-1
59	Guatemala	3.39	(GDP2030/GDP2020)**(1/10)-1
60	Namibia	3.38	(GDP2030/GDP2020)**(1/10)-1
61	Maldives	3.38	(GDP2030/GDP2020)**(1/10)-1
62	Djibouti	3.37	(GDP2030/GDP2020)**(1/10)-1
63	Vietnam	3.37	(GDP2030/GDP2020)**(1/10)-1
64	Somalia	3.37	(GDP2030/GDP2020)**(1/10)-1
65	Egypt	3.36	(GDP2030/GDP2020)**(1/10)-1
66	Qatar	3.36	(GDP2030/GDP2020)**(1/10)-1
67	Jordan	3.35	(GDP2030/GDP2020)**(1/10)-1
68	Hong Kong	3.34	(GDP2030/GDP2020)**(1/10)-1
69	Reunion	3.34	(GDP2030/GDP2020)**(1/10)-1
70	Eritrea	3.34	(GDP2030/GDP2020)**(1/10)-1
71	Saint Martin	3.33	(GDP2030/GDP2020)**(1/10)-1
72	Bangladesh	3.33	(GDP2030/GDP2020)**(1/10)-1
73	Brunei	3.32	(GDP2030/GDP2020)**(1/10)-1
74	Dominican R	3.31	(GDP2030/GDP2020)**(1/10)-1
75	Oman	3.30	(GDP2030/GDP2020)**(1/10)-1
76	Guinea	3.30	(GDP2030/GDP2020)**(1/10)-1
77	Nepal	3.28	(GDP2030/GDP2020)**(1/10)-1
78	Honduras	3.26	(GDP2030/GDP2020)**(1/10)-1
79	Israel	3.26	(GDP2030/GDP2020)**(1/10)-1
80	Azerbaijan	3.26	(GDP2030/GDP2020)**(1/10)-1
81	Kazakhstan	3.24	(GDP2030/GDP2020)**(1/10)-1
82	Pakistan	3.23	(GDP2030/GDP2020)**(1/10)-1
83	Kosovo	3.23	(GDP2030/GDP2020)**(1/10)-1
84	Peru	3.21	(GDP2030/GDP2020)**(1/10)-1
85	Turkey	3.20	(GDP2030/GDP2020)**(1/10)-1
86	Sao Tome & P	3.18	(GDP2030/GDP2020)**(1/10)-1
87	Luxembourg	3.15	(GDP2030/GDP2020)**(1/10)-1
88	Senegal	3.11	(GDP2030/GDP2020)**(1/10)-1
89	Sri Lanka	3.11	(GDP2030/GDP2020)**(1/10)-1
90	Fr Polynesia	3.09	(GDP2030/GDP2020)**(1/10)-1
91	Svalbard	3.05	(GDP2030/GDP2020)**(1/10)-1
92	Chile	3.05	(GDP2030/GDP2020)**(1/10)-1
93	Norway	3.05	(GDP2030/GDP2020)**(1/10)-1
94	Cameroon	3.04	(GDP2030/GDP2020)**(1/10)-1
95	Benin	3.03	(GDP2030/GDP2020)**(1/10)-1
96	Indonesia	3.03	(GDP2030/GDP2020)**(1/10)-1

TABLE 6.23 GDP GROWTH RATES, 2020-2030, FORECAST

Rank	Country	GRRL	Source
97	Isle of Man	3.03	(GDP2030/GDP2020)**(1/10)-1
98	Argentina	3.03	(GDP2030/GDP2020)**(1/10)-1
99	Jersey	3.02	(GDP2030/GDP2020)**(1/10)-1
100	Guinea-Biss	3.01	(GDP2030/GDP2020)**(1/10)-1
101	Vanuatu	3.00	(GDP2030/GDP2020)**(1/10)-1
102	Morocco	3.00	(GDP2030/GDP2020)**(1/10)-1
103	Ireland	3.00	(GDP2030/GDP2020)**(1/10)-1
104	Gabon	2.97	(GDP2030/GDP2020)**(1/10)-1
105	San Marino	2.97	(GDP2030/GDP2020)**(1/10)-1
106	Guernsey	2.97	(GDP2030/GDP2020)**(1/10)-1
107	Sint Maarten	2.96	(GDP2030/GDP2020)**(1/10)-1
108	Guadeloupe	2.94	(GDP2030/GDP2020)**(1/10)-1
109	Costa Rica	2.93	(GDP2030/GDP2020)**(1/10)-1
110	Australia	2.88	(GDP2030/GDP2020)**(1/10)-1
111	Uzbekistan	2.86	(GDP2030/GDP2020)**(1/10)-1
112	Ecuador	2.85	(GDP2030/GDP2020)**(1/10)-1
113	Kiribati	2.84	(GDP2030/GDP2020)**(1/10)-1
114	Cyprus	2.83	(GDP2030/GDP2020)**(1/10)-1
115	Colombia	2.81	(GDP2030/GDP2020)**(1/10)-1
116	Nicaragua	2.79	(GDP2030/GDP2020)**(1/10)-1
117	Korea, South	2.79	(GDP2030/GDP2020)**(1/10)-1
118	Suriname	2.78	(GDP2030/GDP2020)**(1/10)-1
119	Tunisia	2.78	(GDP2030/GDP2020)**(1/10)-1
120	Kyrgyzstan	2.75	(GDP2030/GDP2020)**(1/10)-1
121	Bermuda	2.75	(GDP2030/GDP2020)**(1/10)-1
122	Antigua & B	2.75	(GDP2030/GDP2020)**(1/10)-1
123	Thailand	2.74	(GDP2030/GDP2020)**(1/10)-1
124	Bahrain	2.74	(GDP2030/GDP2020)**(1/10)-1
125	St Kitts & N	2.72	(GDP2030/GDP2020)**(1/10)-1
126	Syria	2.72	(GDP2030/GDP2020)**(1/10)-1
127	Martinique	2.70	(GDP2030/GDP2020)**(1/10)-1
128	Saint Helena	2.68	(GDP2030/GDP2020)**(1/10)-1
129	Madagascar	2.68	(GDP2030/GDP2020)**(1/10)-1
130	Tuvalu	2.67	(GDP2030/GDP2020)**(1/10)-1
131	Curacao	2.67	(GDP2030/GDP2020)**(1/10)-1
132	Albania	2.66	(GDP2030/GDP2020)**(1/10)-1
133	China	2.66	(GDP2030/GDP2020)**(1/10)-1
134	Iran	2.65	(GDP2030/GDP2020)**(1/10)-1
135	Kenya	2.65	(GDP2030/GDP2020)**(1/10)-1
136	Taiwan	2.64	(GDP2030/GDP2020)**(1/10)-1
137	Mauritius	2.62	(GDP2030/GDP2020)**(1/10)-1
138	Gambia	2.61	(GDP2030/GDP2020)**(1/10)-1
139	Monaco	2.60	(GDP2030/GDP2020)**(1/10)-1
140	Dominica	2.57	(GDP2030/GDP2020)**(1/10)-1
141	Cuba	2.57	(GDP2030/GDP2020)**(1/10)-1
142	Gaza Strip	2.56	(GDP2030/GDP2020)**(1/10)-1
143	Mexico	2.55	(GDP2030/GDP2020)**(1/10)-1
144	Algeria	2.54	(GDP2030/GDP2020)**(1/10)-1

Table 6.23 GDP Growth Rates, 2020-2030, Forecast

Rank	Country	GRRL	Source
145	Seychelles	2.52	(GDP2030/GDP2020)**(1/10)-1
146	US	2.52	(GDP2030/GDP2020)**(1/10)-1
147	St Lucia	2.52	(GDP2030/GDP2020)**(1/10)-1
148	Gibraltar	2.51	(GDP2030/GDP2020)**(1/10)-1
149	New Zealand	2.50	(GDP2030/GDP2020)**(1/10)-1
150	Togo	2.49	(GDP2030/GDP2020)**(1/10)-1
151	Brazil	2.48	(GDP2030/GDP2020)**(1/10)-1
152	Paraguay	2.47	(GDP2030/GDP2020)**(1/10)-1
153	Jamaica	2.47	(GDP2030/GDP2020)**(1/10)-1
154	Uruguay	2.46	(GDP2030/GDP2020)**(1/10)-1
155	Iceland	2.45	(GDP2030/GDP2020)**(1/10)-1
156	Guam	2.45	(GDP2030/GDP2020)**(1/10)-1
157	Slovakia	2.43	(GDP2030/GDP2020)**(1/10)-1
158	Burma	2.43	(GDP2030/GDP2020)**(1/10)-1
159	Swaziland	2.43	(GDP2030/GDP2020)**(1/10)-1
160	Lebanon	2.41	(GDP2030/GDP2020)**(1/10)-1
161	St Vincent	2.40	(GDP2030/GDP2020)**(1/10)-1
162	West Bank	2.37	(GDP2030/GDP2020)**(1/10)-1
163	UAE	2.36	(GDP2030/GDP2020)**(1/10)-1
164	Wallis & Fut	2.35	(GDP2030/GDP2020)**(1/10)-1
165	Canada	2.35	(GDP2030/GDP2020)**(1/10)-1
166	Venezuela	2.34	(GDP2030/GDP2020)**(1/10)-1
167	Faroe Is	2.33	(GDP2030/GDP2020)**(1/10)-1
168	Samoa	2.29	(GDP2030/GDP2020)**(1/10)-1
169	UK	2.29	(GDP2030/GDP2020)**(1/10)-1
170	Trinidad & T	2.29	(GDP2030/GDP2020)**(1/10)-1
171	Spain	2.28	(GDP2030/GDP2020)**(1/10)-1
172	Cayman Is	2.27	(GDP2030/GDP2020)**(1/10)-1
173	Malta	2.27	(GDP2030/GDP2020)**(1/10)-1
174	Russia	2.25	(GDP2030/GDP2020)**(1/10)-1
175	Kuwait	2.24	(GDP2030/GDP2020)**(1/10)-1
176	Poland	2.24	(GDP2030/GDP2020)**(1/10)-1
177	Sweden	2.23	(GDP2030/GDP2020)**(1/10)-1
178	Greenland	2.23	(GDP2030/GDP2020)**(1/10)-1
179	Montenegro	2.21	(GDP2030/GDP2020)**(1/10)-1
180	Austria	2.21	(GDP2030/GDP2020)**(1/10)-1
181	Finland	2.20	(GDP2030/GDP2020)**(1/10)-1
182	Guyana	2.19	(GDP2030/GDP2020)**(1/10)-1
183	Lithuania	2.19	(GDP2030/GDP2020)**(1/10)-1
184	El Salvador	2.19	(GDP2030/GDP2020)**(1/10)-1
185	Ivory Coast	2.19	(GDP2030/GDP2020)**(1/10)-1
186	Tonga	2.17	(GDP2030/GDP2020)**(1/10)-1
187	Belarus	2.17	(GDP2030/GDP2020)**(1/10)-1
188	Belgium	2.13	(GDP2030/GDP2020)**(1/10)-1
189	Grenada	2.12	(GDP2030/GDP2020)**(1/10)-1
190	N Mariana Is	2.10	(GDP2030/GDP2020)**(1/10)-1
191	Latvia	2.08	(GDP2030/GDP2020)**(1/10)-1
192	Lesotho	2.08	(GDP2030/GDP2020)**(1/10)-1

TABLE 6.23 GDP GROWTH RATES, 2020-2030, FORECAST

Rank	Country	GRRL	Source
193	Estonia	2.08	(GDP2030/GDP2020)**(1/10)-1
194	Andorra	2.05	(GDP2030/GDP2020)**(1/10)-1
195	South Africa	2.05	(GDP2030/GDP2020)**(1/10)-1
196	Slovenia	2.03	(GDP2030/GDP2020)**(1/10)-1
197	Comoros	2.02	(GDP2030/GDP2020)**(1/10)-1
198	Romania	2.02	(GDP2030/GDP2020)**(1/10)-1
199	Netherlands	2.01	(GDP2030/GDP2020)**(1/10)-1
200	Czechia	1.98	(GDP2030/GDP2020)**(1/10)-1
201	Greece	1.98	(GDP2030/GDP2020)**(1/10)-1
202	Haiti	1.97	(GDP2030/GDP2020)**(1/10)-1
203	Burundi	1.92	(GDP2030/GDP2020)**(1/10)-1
204	Portugal	1.87	(GDP2030/GDP2020)**(1/10)-1
205	Georgia	1.82	(GDP2030/GDP2020)**(1/10)-1
206	Palau	1.81	(GDP2030/GDP2020)**(1/10)-1
207	Denmark	1.81	(GDP2030/GDP2020)**(1/10)-1
208	Switzerland	1.80	(GDP2030/GDP2020)**(1/10)-1
209	Armenia	1.78	(GDP2030/GDP2020)**(1/10)-1
210	Macedonia	1.77	(GDP2030/GDP2020)**(1/10)-1
211	Samoa, Amer	1.76	(GDP2030/GDP2020)**(1/10)-1
212	France	1.75	(GDP2030/GDP2020)**(1/10)-1
213	Bosnia	1.74	(GDP2030/GDP2020)**(1/10)-1
214	Bulgaria	1.73	(GDP2030/GDP2020)**(1/10)-1
215	Serbia	1.73	(GDP2030/GDP2020)**(1/10)-1
216	Ukraine	1.73	(GDP2030/GDP2020)**(1/10)-1
217	Nauru	1.73	(GDP2030/GDP2020)**(1/10)-1
218	Croatia	1.68	(GDP2030/GDP2020)**(1/10)-1
219	Virgin I, US	1.65	(GDP2030/GDP2020)**(1/10)-1
220	Aruba	1.63	(GDP2030/GDP2020)**(1/10)-1
221	Barbados	1.63	(GDP2030/GDP2020)**(1/10)-1
222	Bahamas	1.61	(GDP2030/GDP2020)**(1/10)-1
223	Italy	1.57	(GDP2030/GDP2020)**(1/10)-1
224	Germany	1.57	(GDP2030/GDP2020)**(1/10)-1
225	Moldova	1.54	(GDP2030/GDP2020)**(1/10)-1
226	Micronesia	1.50	(GDP2030/GDP2020)**(1/10)-1
227	Hungary	1.50	(GDP2030/GDP2020)**(1/10)-1
228	Fiji	1.44	(GDP2030/GDP2020)**(1/10)-1
229	Korea, North	1.34	(GDP2030/GDP2020)**(1/10)-1
230	Japan	1.31	(GDP2030/GDP2020)**(1/10)-1
231	Puerto Rico	0.96	(GDP2030/GDP2020)**(1/10)-1
232	St Pierre&M	0.93	(GDP2030/GDP2020)**(1/10)-1
233	Tokelau	0.88	(GDP2030/GDP2020)**(1/10)-1
234	Montserrat	0.75	(GDP2030/GDP2020)**(1/10)-1
235	Niue	-1.59	(GDP2030/GDP2020)**(1/10)-1
236	Cook Is	-2.87	(GDP2030/GDP2020)**(1/10)-1

Appendix: Methodology and Definitions

Definition of Gross Domestic Product at Purchasing Power Parities

Typically, GDP is translated into U.S. dollars. The market foreign currency exchange rate, however, does not necessarily reflect differences in the actual purchasing power of different countries. The use of purchasing power parities (PPPs) is intended to eliminate this distortion. Purchasing power parities indicate how many currency units are needed in one country to buy the amount of goods and services that can be purchased for a currency unit in another country.

Definition of Population

The population of a country includes all residents regardless of legal status or citizenship — except for refugees not permanently settled in the country of asylum, who are generally considered part of the population of their country of origin. The values shown are midyear estimates.[1]

My principal source for Population for the latest years is the Encyclopedia Britannica. This population data is changed from year to year; I assume that the data from the latest edition of the *Encyclopedia Britannica Book of the Year* is the most correct. However, their population data is one year ahead of the year of their current yearbook. For example, the 2012 yearbook provides population data for 1960, 1970, 1980, 1990, 2000, 2010, 2013, 2020 (forecast), and 2030 (forecast). I could have taken the population data for 2012 from the previous year's *Britannica Book of the Year*, but the whole population time series from 1960 through 2030 is somewhat shifted in the previous year edition of the *Britannica Book of the Year* compared with their latest edition. I also use the Britannica population data for all these years in the annual companion to this handbook, *Quality of Life, Balance of Powers, and Nuclear Weapons*. So, in order for *Two Thousand Years* to by in sync with *Quality of Life, Balance of Powers, and Nuclear Weapons*, and to use general population time series from the latest edition of the *Britannica Book of the Year*, I use in this handbook population data for the current year (2012) calculated from the current edition of the *Britannica Book of the Year* according to the formula:

1 Economics: The World Bank.

POP2012 = POP2010 * (POP2013 / POP2010)2/3

where

POP2010 is population in 2010 according to the current edition of the Britannica Book of the Year;

POP2012 is calculated population in 2012;

POP2013 is population in 2013 according to the current edition of the Britannica Book of the Year.

Definition of the GDP Historical Data Since AD 1

I used information about GDP Per Capita in purchasing power parities for 1950 and the latest (current) year as the basis points. I also appropriated Angus Maddison's[2] hypothesis that GDP Per Capita in purchasing power parities cannot be less than 400 USD in 1990 prices, and utilized a logarithmic interpolation technique to slightly adjust Maddison's statistical curves for years other than basis years.

It is customary in historical comparisons of the countries of the world to use Gross Domestic Product (GDP) in purchasing power parities. If GDP in market exchange rates is used, then the historical picture becomes distorted in favor of the countries that have strong currencies in the last year of observations. In effect, many less developed countries would appear too weak in the past, having GDP per capita less than the minimum level of 400 dollars in 1990 prices.

The data is given for countries within their current (latest year) boundaries.

I interpolated per capita GDP at purchasing power parities. The reason I interpolated per capita as opposed to gross data is that per capita growth rates are more invariant than the gross growth rates (the latter to some degree depend on the growth rates of the population, which vary by time and country).

For years prior to 1950, the principal source of per capita GDP at purchasing power parities (GDP at PPP) is Angus Maddison.

For years after 1950, there are two main sources of per capita GDP at PPP: Angus Maddison for 1950 through 2000 and World Bank for 1980 through the current year. There is a small discrepancy between these two main sources. In order to harmonize these two sources, a four-step iteration was used:

The Angus Maddison data is in 1990 prices. There is also data from the World Bank for 1990 in current (that is 1990) prices. I assumed that the World Bank data, where available, is more correct. The Angus Maddison data was adjusted accordingly:

```
If G1990-WB exists then
Do;
     G1960-Maddison = G1960-Maddison * (G1990-WB / G1990-Maddison)1/4;
     G1970-Maddison = G1970-Maddison * (G1990-WB / G1990-Maddison)2/4;
     G1980-Maddison = G1980-Maddison * (G1990-WB / G1990-Maddison)3/4;
     G2000-Maddison = G2000-Maddison * (G1990-WB / G1990-Maddison));
     G1990-Maddison = G1990-WB;
End;
```

where

G1990-WB	per capita GDP at PPP in 1990 (in 1990 prices [WB])
G1960-Maddison	per capita GDP at PPP in 1960 (in 1990 prices [Maddison])
G1970-Maddison	per capita GDP at PPP in 1970 (in 1990 prices [Maddison])
G1980-Maddison	per capita GDP at PPP in 1980 (in 1990 prices [Maddison])
G1990-Maddison	per capita GDP at PPP in 1990 (in 1990 prices [Maddison])
G2000-Maddison	per capita GDP at PPP in 2000 (in 1990 prices [Maddison])

2 Economics: Maddison (1995), (2001), (2003), (2007).

Generally, the historical data available from the World Bank is in 2005 prices. Where this data existed for years prior to 2000, I assumed it to be more correct than Angus Maddison's data and made the following adjustment to results of the first step:

```
If G1980-WB exists then
Do;
        G1990-Maddison = G1980-Maddison * (G1990-WB / G1980-WB);
        G2000-Maddison = G1980-Maddison * (G2000-WB / G1980-WB);
End;
Else
If G1990-WB exists then
        G2000-Maddison = G1990-Maddison * (G2000-WB / G1990-WB);
```

where

G1980-WB	per capita GDP at PPP in 1980 (in 2005 prices [World Bank])
G1990-WB	per capita GDP at PPP in 1990 (in 2005 prices [World Bank])
G2000-WB	per capita GDP at PPP in 2000 (in 2005 prices [World Bank])
G1980-Maddison	per capita GDP at PPP in 1980 (in 2005 prices [Maddison])
G1990-Maddison	per capita GDP at PPP in 1990 (in 2005 prices [Maddison])
G2000-Maddison	per capita GDP at PPP in 2000 (in 1990 prices [Maddison])

For the year 2000 (the year of the change between 1990 and 2005 series) I computed per capita GDP at PPP in 1990 prices as a geometric average of the number according to Maddison and the number in 2005 prices weighted as per the U.S. ratio according to the following formula:

G2000-Maddison = (G2000-Maddison * (G2000-WB * (G-US-2000-Maddison / G-US-2000-WB))1/2;

where

G2000-Maddison	per capita GDP at PPP in 2000 (in 1990 prices [Maddison])
G2000-WB	per capita GDP at PPP in 2000 (in 2005 prices [World Bank])
G-US-2000-Maddison	U.S. per capita GDP at PPP(in 1990 prices [Maddison])
G-US-2000-WB	U.S. per capita GDP at PPP (in 2005 prices [World Bank])

After the first three adjustments, there are still general problems which I would call a "cross-country statistical parallax." These problems manifest themselves in the fact that, for any country, if we take per capita GDP at PPP for 1950 (in whatever year's constant prices), and multiply it by the index of per capita GDP at PPP for the current year (in the same year's constant prices), the result will, generally speaking, be somewhat (and sometimes substantially) different from the direct estimate of per capita GDP at PPP for the current year (in the same year's constant prices). For example, it can be noted that data for per capita GDP at PPP in constant prices for Switzerland would overestimate the GDP deflator of that country in comparison with the United States. So, if we take the ratio of the per capita GDP at PPP of Switzerland to that of the United States in 1950, and multiply it by the index per capita GDP at PPP of Switzeralnd for 1990 (or any other current year), the result would be consistently lower than the ratio of the per capita GDP at PPP of Swizerland to that of the United States when measured directly in 1990 (or any other current year). Conversely, for some countries we would underestimate the inflation in comparison with the United States. Usually, however, for a given country, there is consistently either underestimation or overestimation of inflation in comparison with the United States. I have assumed that the degree of such overestimation or underestimation of inflation for a given country would be constant for the entire period after 1950.

To adjust for the cross-country statistical parallax I have been using logarithmic interpolation.

The reason I use logarithmic interpolation, as opposed to exponential interpolation, is that exponential interpolation may often result in negative growth rates of per capita GDP, which seems unlikely. Logarithmic interpolation does not change the nature of the growth over an observed period: positive growth rates remain positive, negative ones remain negative. Moreover, periods of faster growth remain periods of faster growth and periods of slower growth remain periods of slower growth. The economic rationale for such an interpolation is that its most common use is when there is unaccounted inflation in the statistics of real growth. As a rule, such inflation is higher when economic growth is faster. So it makes sense to assume that the unaccounted deflator should be proportionally higher with higher growth rates. To achieve an interpolation with such qualities, I had to assume that over the period of 1950 to the current year there existed a constant degree to which the reported national growth rates should be raised in order to achieve the observed growth rates between 1950 and the current year. I weighted the growth rates of every country relative to the growth rates of the United States. Such a hypothesis produces a more credible growth curve than the one which would have been acquired if exponential interpolation were used.

The corresponding formulas for the interpolation of per capita GDP are:

$$Gyear_{corrected} = Gyear_{current} * (Gyear_{current} / Gcurrent_{current})$$
$$** (\log((Gcurrent_{current} * G - UScurrent_{1990}) /$$
$$(G19501990 * G - UScurrentcurrent)) / \log(Gcurrent1990 / G19501990))$$

where

$$Gyear_{current} = Gyear_{1990} * (Gcurrent_{current} / Gcurrent_{1990})$$
$$G1950_{current} = (G19501990 / G - US19501990) * G - US1950_{current}$$
$$G - US1950_{current} = G - US19501990 * (G - UScurrent_{current} / G - UScurrent_{1990})$$
$$Gcurrent_{1990} = G2000_{1990} * (Gcurrent_{2005} / G2000_{2005})$$
$$G - UScurrent_{1990} = G - US2000_{1990} * (G - UScurrent_{2005} / G\text{-}US2000_{2005})$$

The notations are identified below:

GPCPPP	per capita GDP at purchasing power parities
$Gyear_{corrected}$	GPCPPP for a particular year after the interpolation
$Gyear_{current}$	GPCPPP for a particular year in current-year prices
$Gyear_{1990}$	GPCPPP for a particular year in 1990 prices
$G1950_{1990}$	GPCPPP for the year 1950 in 1990 prices
$G\text{-}US1950_{1990}$	GPCPPP of the U.S. for the year 1950 in 1990 prices
$Gcurrent_{current}$	GPCPPP for the current year in current-year prices

$G\text{-}UScurrent_{current}$	GPCPPP of the U.S. for the current year in current-year prices
$G1950_{current}$	GPCPPP for the year 1950 in current-year prices
$G\text{-}US1950_{current}$	GPCPPP of the U.S. for the year 1950 in current-year prices
$Gcurrent_{1990}$	GPCPPP for the current year in 1990 prices
$G\text{-}UScurrent_{1990}$	GPCPPP of the U.S. for the current year in 1990 prices
$G2000_{1990}$	GPCPPP for the year 2000 in 1990 prices
$G\text{-}US2000_{1990}$	GPCPPP of the U.S. for the year 2000 in 1990 prices
$Gcurrent_{2005}$	GPCPPP for the current year in 2005 prices
$G\text{-}UScurrent_{2005}$	GPCPPP of the U.S. for the current year in 2005 prices
$G2000_{2005}$	GPCPPP for the year 2000 in 2005 prices
$G\text{-}US2000_{2005}$	GPCPPP of the U.S. for the year 2000 in 2005 prices

For the years prior to 1950, I used the formula:

$$Gyear_{current} = Gyear1990 * (G1950_{current} / G19501990)$$

Exceptions

My general rule was to take all available data from Angus Maddison and the World Bank (the emphasis here is on "all": I did not skip any applicable data from Angus Maddison and the World Bank for any year where it existed). When the data was unavailable from these sources, I took the CIA data. This rule, with application of the above described four-step algorithm, worked very well for about 230 countries for years after 1950.

Benin, Burundi, Iraq, Moldova, Mozambique, Qatar, and Uzbekistan were exceptions. For the latter countries I had to consider their special historical circumstances and make some modifications to the general rule of selecting all the available sources (for these countries, that amounted to ignoring some available but unreliable data or data leading to illogical results). Here is a summary of ignored data:

CODE	YEAR	USED DATA	SOURCE	IGNORED DATA	SOURCE OF IGNORED DATA
Benin					
1	1950	1,084	50(Maddison)		
1	1960	978	60(Maddison)		
1	1970	1,027	70(Maddison)		
1	1980	1,133	80(Maddison)		
2	1980	1,076.29	80(WB)		
1	1990	1,147	90(Maddison)		
A	1990	.		799.34	90(WB)
2	1990	1,100.03	90(WB)		
1	2000	1,323	00(Maddison)		
2	2000	1,232.18	00(WB)		
2	2010	1,321.27	10(WB)		
2	2012	1,364.20	12(WB)		
3	2012	1,557.16	12(WB)		

CODE	YEAR	USED DATA	SOURCE	IGNORED DATA	SOURCE OF IGNORED DATA
			Burundi		
1	1950	360	50(Maddison)		
1	1960	444	60(Maddison)		
1	1970	542	70(Maddison)		
1	1980	627	80(Maddison)		
2	1980	604.81	80(WB)		
1	1990	484.61	90(WB) WEIGHT(US(WB))	734	90(Maddison)
A	1990	500.35	90(WB)		
2	1990	688.56	90(WB)		
1	2000	325.48	00(WB) WEIGHT(US(WB))	575	00(Maddison)
2	2000	474.00	00(WB)		
2	2010	475.38	10(WB)		
2	2012	482.95	12(WB)		
3	2012	551.27	12(WB)		
			Iraq		
1	1950	1,364	50(Maddison)		
1	1960	2,735	60(Maddison)		
1	1970	3,473	70(Maddison)		
1	1980	6,377	80(Maddison)		
2	1980	.			
1	1990	3,840.41	90(Maddison) WEIGHT(00(WB))	2,458	90(Maddison)
A	1990	.			
2	1990	.			
1	2000	3,175.51	00(WB) WEIGHT(US Maddison))	1,221	00(Maddison)
2	2000	5,392.28	00(WB)		
2	2010	5,724.27	10(WB)		
2	2012	6,531.51	12(WB)		
3	2012	7,434.83	12(WB)		
			Moldova		
1	1950	2,515.58	PROXY(USSR(Maddison))		
1	1960	3,493.13	PROXY(USSR(Maddison))		
1	1970	4,936.44	PROXY(USSR(Maddison))		
1	1980	5,681.00	INTERPOL(Moldova(Maddison))		
2	1980	.			
1	1990	6,165	90(Maddison)		
A	1990	.			
2	1990	.			

CODE	YEAR	USED DATA	SOURCE	IGNORED DATA	SOURCE OF IGNORED DATA
1	2000	1,137.97	00(WB) WEIGHT(US(WB))	2,128	00(Maddison)
2	2000	1,657.25	00(WB)		
2	2010	2,793.39	10(WB)		
2	2012	2,950.88	12(WB)		
3	2012	3,368.28	12(WB)		
			Mozambique		
1	1950	1,133	50(Maddison)		
1	1960	1,327	60(Maddison)		
1	1970	1,743	70(Maddison)		
1	1980	309.73	80(WB) WEIGHT(US(WB))	1,220	80(Maddison)
2	1980	434.92	80(WB)		
1	1990	278.03	90(WB) WEIGHT(US(WB))	1,115	90(Maddison)
A	1990	287.06	90(WB)		
2	1990	395.04	90(WB)		
1	2000	342.39	00(WB) WEIGHT(US(WB))	1,432	00(Maddison)
2	2000	498.63	00(WB)		
2	2010	805.05	10(WB)		
2	2012	882.42	12(WB)		
3	2012	1,007.23	12(WB)		
			Qatar		
1	1950	30,387	50(Maddison)		
1	1960	33,104	60(Maddison)		
1	1970	33,160	70(Maddison)		
1	1980	29,552	80(Maddison)		
2	1980	.			
1	1990	15,000	90(CIA)	6,804	90(Maddison)
A	1990	.			
2	1990	.			
1	2000	44,309.99	00(WB) WEIGHT(US(WB))	8,042	00(Maddison)
2	2000	64,529.85	00(WB)		
2	2010	70,239.31	10(WB)		
2	2012	71,931.40	12(WB)		
3	2012	91,189.11	12(WB)		
			Uzbekistan		
1	1950	2,389.92	PROXY(USSR(Maddison))		
1	1960	3,318.63	PROXY(USSR(Maddison))		
1	1970	4,698.86	PROXY(USSR(Maddison))		
1	1980	4,725.39	INTERPOL(Uzbekistan(Maddison))		

CODE	YEAR	USED DATA	SOURCE	IGNORED DATA	SOURCE OF IGNORED DATA
2	1980	.			
1	1990	4,241	90(Maddison)		
A	1990	.			
2	1990	.			
1	2000	1,120.83	00(WB) WEIGHT(US(WB))	3,408	00(Maddison)
2	2000	1,632.30	00(WB)		
2	2010	2,753.56	10(WB)		
2	2012	3,095.28	12(WB)		
3	2012	3,533.11	12(WB)		

where

CODE = 1 for per capita GDP at PPP in 1990 prices;

CODE= 2 for per capita GDP at PPP in 2005 prices;

CODE = A for alternative data of per capita GDP at PPP in 1990 in 1990 prices according to the World Bank;

CODE = 3 for per capita GDP at PPP in 2012 in 2012 prices.

Special care was taken for calculation of GDP of the former U.S.S.R. for the year of 1920. In order to calculate an index of GDP 1913-1920, I used partial data for two sectors of the economy: agriculture and industry. The production of grain in these years constituted (Davies(1994), p. 320):

Production of grain	
1913	79.7 million tons
1920	44.5 million tons

Gross industrial production constituted (ibid., p. 321):

Gross industrial production	
1913	8,431
1920	1,718

Agriculture accounted for 50.7 percent of national income in 1913. Assuming that non-agricultural sectors of the economy shrank by 1920 in the same proportion as the industrial production, I obtained the following putative index of GDP:

GDP Index	
1913	100
1920	38.354

Special care was also taken for calculating the GDP of North Korea for the years after 1990. The available CIA estimates are inexact and tend to underestimate North Korean GDP at PPP. Our calculations are as follows:

Year	GDP Growth Rate	Source of GDP Growth Rate	GDP Index	WB US GDP Deflator	GDP, Bil. Current USD	GDP, Bil. 1990 USD	Population, Thousands	GDP Per Capita, 1990 Prices	GDP Per Capita, Current Prices
2012	1.3	CIA	65.293	114.145	59.054	37.365	24,589	1519.58	2401.64
2011	0.8	CIA	64.455						
2010	-05.	CIA	63.943	110.023	55.743	36.592	24,326	1504.23	2309.50
2009	-0.9	CIA	64.264						
2008	3.7	CIA	64.848						
2007	-2.3	CIA	62.534						
2006	-1.1	CIA	64.006						
2005	1.0	CIA	64.718	100.000	51.280	37.036			
2004	1.0	CIA	64.077						
2003	1.0	CIA	63.443						
2002	1.0	CIA	62.815						
2001	-3.0	CIA	62.193						
2000	-3.0	CIA	64.117	88.714	45.069	36.692	22,785	1610.36	1978.01
1999	1.0	CIA	66.100						
1998	-5.0	CIA	65.446						
1997	-3.7	CIA	68.890						
1996	-5.0	CIA	71.537						
1995	-17.0	Maddison	75.302						
1994	0.0	CIA	90.725						
1993	0.3	CIA	90.725						
1992	-7.7	Maddison	90.454						
1991	-2.0	CIA	98.000						
1990			100.000					2841	

Angus Maddison postulated that GDP per capita in purchasing power parities cannot be less than $400 in 1990 prices. However, if you look at some African countries in recent decades, you will see that many countries appear to have had less than that level of GDP per capita in PPP for prolonged periods of time. So I decided to use a modification of Angus Maddison's postulate, by supposing that at a per capita GDP of around 400 (1990 US dollars), the growth rate of GDP per capita becomes very slow. I postulated that at the level of 400 (1990 dollars), the annual growth rate would be 0.05%. Moreover, I postulated that at a level around or below 400 (1990 dollars), the annual growth rate would be proportional to the ratio of the current year level of GDP per capita to 400 (1990 dollars).

The formula for calculating the previous benchmark year GDP per capita is:

```
Previous_GDP = Current_GDP;
DO I = 1 TO Number_of_years_in_period;
Previous_GDP = Previous_GDP
/ (1 + Base_growth_rate * (Previous_GDP / Base_GDP_level));
END;
```

where

Current_GDP	Current year GDP per capita in PPP (1990 prices)
Previous_GDP	Previous year GDP per capita in PPP (1990 prices)
I	Iteration counter
Number_of_years_in_period	Total number of years in period
Base_growth_rate	Assumed to be 0.05%
Base_GDP_level	GDP per capita in PPP equal to 400 (1990 dollars)

References

Central Intelligence Agency, *The World Factbook*, annual

Davies, R. W., Mark Harrison, S. G. Wheatcroft, Eds. (1994) *The Economic Transformation of the Soviet Union, 1913-1945*, Cambridge University Press, Cambridge

Encyclopedia Britannica, Book of the Year, annual

Maddison, Angus (1995) *Monitoring the World Economy, 1820-1992*, OECD, Paris

________ (2001) *The World Economy: A Millennial Perspective*, OECD, Paris

________ (2003) *The World Economy: Historical Statistics*, OECD, Paris

________ *(2007) Contours of the World Economy, 1–2030AD*, Oxford University Press, New York

Mitchell, B.R. *(2003)(1) International Historical Statistics: Africa, Asia and Oceania, 1750-2000*, Palgrave Macmillan, London

________ (2003)(2) *International Historical Statistics: Europe, 1750-2000*, Palgrave Macmillan, London

________ (2003)(3) *International Historical Statistics: The Americas, 1750-2000*, Palgrave Macmillan, London

The World Bank World Development Indicators Online

Wikipedia